Best American Plays

NINTH SERIES
1983–1992

Best American Plays

NINTH SERIES

1983–1992

Edited by

Clive Barnes

Introduction by
Clive Barnes

Biographical Introductions by
Lori Weinless

Crown Publishers, Inc.
New York

Acknowledgment is due to the following for their cooperation in the preparation of this volume: Applause Theatre Books; Dramatists Play Service, Inc.; Farrar, Straus & Giroux, Inc.; Grove Press; International Creative Management, Inc.; Lucy Kroll Agency; Penguin Books USA, Inc.; Flora Roberts, Inc.; Random House, Inc.; Rosenstone/Wender.

Note: All plays in this volume are fully protected under the copyright laws of the United States of America, the British Empire, including the Dominion of Canada, and all other countries of the Copyright Union. Permission to reproduce, wholly or in part, by any method, must be obtained from the copyright owners or their agents. (See notices at the beginning of each play.)

Published by Crown Publishers, Inc., 201 East 50th Street, New York, New York 10022. Member of the Crown Publishing Group.

Random House, Inc. New York, Toronto, London, Sydney, Auckland

CROWN is a trademark of Crown Publishers, Inc.

Manufactured in the United States of America

Library of Congress Catalog Card Number: 57-12830

ISBN 0-517-57452-7

10 9 8 7 6 5 4 3 2 1

First Edition

Contents

Introduction

by Clive Barnes

What constitutes a Best Play? Strictly speaking, a sour-minded grammarian could insist that the very term "Best Play" is a solecism, as "Best" permits no peers and should be singular. Forgive us. . . . A series called "Better Plays" might sound prissy and oddly snobbish—a better class of play for a better class of person, perhaps?—and in any event, "Best Plays" seems more definitive and has served us now for eight series, and should do well enough for this ninth. Let's face it, though, what we might call a "Best Play" at the beginning of the nineties might not be so considered in, say, 2060 or 2070, just as some plays thought devilish fine in the twenties and thirties (*our* twenties and thirties!) seem pretty small beer right now. Fashions change. Taste changes. So perhaps that expression "Best Play" is more comparative than the grammarian would allow.

This series, started by my illustrious predecessor John Gassner and still proudly bearing his name, has all along been an expression of personal opinions, first his and then mine, regarding the merit of the individual work; but also, I hope, it has and does represent an overall view of what is generally thought of as significant works of playwrighting—either on the grounds of our subjective perception of simple merit or, sometimes, for reasons of contemporary impact—at a particular moment in time. History and fashion will doubtless be kind to some selections and cruel to others. In 2060 someone looking at this list—providing there is still at that time someone in a position to look at lists and that a list of plays might still be regarded as worthy of perusal—will doubtless be amazed at the inclusion of this or that, and probably be equally puzzled at the omission of some other contemporary piece here overlooked but by then regarded as a modern classic woefully neglected in its own lifetime. So be it.

What we must never forget is that in the natural hurly-burly of any art form, almost all the works produced for immediate consumption—be they initially admired as masterpieces or dismissed as failures—have the shelf life of Kleenex during a flu epidemic. Very few plays are classics; very few hold within them those seeds of immortality that enable them to speak, probably with variations of tone and even meaning, to generation after generation. And it is virtually impossible to tell which are the classics and which are not. At the midpoint of our present declining century, had you asked people of reasonable if conventional theatrical views which English-speaking playwright among, say, Maxwell Anderson, Noël Coward, Lillian Hellman, J. B. Priestley, and Sidney

Kingsley would be most likely to see out the century with a reputation unblemished and perhaps enhanced, I suspect that few of them would have come up with the name that now seems clear from the nineties—Coward! Time, taste, and fashion play weird tricks.

The real point is that we in the arts see the past through the rose-colored spectacles provided by an almost Darwinian process of natural selection. We look at eighteenth-century music and we see Mozart, not Salieri—we recognize and cherish the survivors, we count the classic gold and ignore the daily dross. But as to our own time, we are all too inclined to say, "Give us this day our daily dross." We like new things in the arts, we like the arts to be topical, to be the passing mirror of our time, and we want the arts to address us and our concerns with an immediacy and urgency that usually can come only from contemporaneity.

Of course, in the American theatre we do carry this admiration of the contemporary rather too far—indeed to the exclusion of virtually everything else. Perhaps the most remarkable aspect of the American theatre has been the absence from our stages of a significant classic repertory. Our theatre subsists very largely on texts actually created within the past five years. It is quite extraordinary. (To get an idea of how extraordinary, just imagine what would be the rude conclusion if our concert halls and opera houses chose their repertory with the same regard for modernity! Verdi, Mozart, and Wagner pushed brusquely aside for Philip Glass and John Adams, Beethoven playing second fiddle to John Cage—the results would be surprising. Similarly in the fine arts: Imagine Leonardo, Vermeer, and Van Gogh banished to the basement, while the Julian Schnabels ride it out cock-a-hoop on the main floor.)

Personally, I cannot convince myself that our theatre's preoccupation with novelty at the sore expense of tradition is at all a good thing. We lack respect for the dramatic literature of the past, and our audiences need the benefit of seeing the glories of that past made manifest through the actors and directors of today. The comparison between the American theatre and almost any European theatre—including the British, with which ours shares a stepmother tongue and thus a literature—is rather sad: It is always a problem for any art to live in the present without a very shrewd awareness of the past, as our American theatre, sadly, does.

The situation of the American theatre has changed enormously during the course of the century—changed enormously even since the end of World War II. The changes have been partly economic yet also partly changes in the esthetic landscape. All this has happened quite slowly, yet any comparison between the American theatre at the beginning of the century and our theatre here and now comes up against circumstances so changed that we might as well be talking about two quite different civilizations. And perhaps we are.

Before World War I, the theatre, or at least the popular theatre, was fundamentally the prime entertainment of the people. Dozens of commercial theatres existed on Broadway—of all kinds, but few of them highbrow. The theatre was not then in any degree elitist. Whether it offered drama, comedy, musical comedy, vaudeville, or even burlesque, the American theatre very happily thought of money rather than art. And it made money by entertaining people. Lots of people. The more people, the more money. An admirable philosophy for a popular art form—one that, for example, many years before had done Shakespeare proud and made Molière as happy as his private circumstances would permit.

But as we moved farther and farther into the twentieth century, the supremacy of the theatre, in all its forms, as *the* major art for the man in the street was severely challenged. No one took them seriously at first—those flickering shadows of the early moving-picture shows. But the shadows acquired, first, dramatic substance—with the likes of

Charlie Chaplin and D. W. Griffith, not to mention all those Germans and Russians—and then, in 1927, they acquired a voice. Theatre had finally been knocked off its perch—it was no longer the People's Choice. The movies—the silents, then the talkies—had taken over. And, of course, later, with the coming of the networks, radio. Then color movies. Then black-and-white television. Then rock music. Then color television. Then sport—I mean spectator sport as a kind of art form. Then home video. The theatre moved down and down the totem pole of popular regard.

Today it is an elitist art form on much the same level as classical music, dance, and opera—a long-haired performing art with certain crew-cut aspects made commercially viable and intentionally popular. This is the background against which the present situation—both economic and artistic—of the Broadway theatre has to be evaluated. It is useless to ask in a sort of sociological vacuum what has happened to the Broadway theatre, without taking into account all the various changes that have taken place both in the general cultural landscape and in the condition of our cities—New York City, of course, in particular.

The case history of Broadway today can probably be most clearly examined not by looking at the position of the play itself—although on that sometimes sad and sore subject we will certainly have something to say later—but by analyzing that very special part of the New York theatre, the Broadway musical. Unquestionably, Broadway has during this century been primarily fueled by the musical, and the Broadway musical is an indigenous genre, generally regarded as Broadway's great gift to international theatre.

The real history of the Broadway musical starts with a strange hybrid entertainment—part ballet, part opera, part melodrama—called *The Black Crook,* which made its debut at Niblo's Garden soon after the Civil War, on September 12, 1866. Probably by the turn of the century, unquestionably by the end of World War I, everything was in place for the emergence of the Broadway musical more or less as we now know it—or, at least, knew it. For the musical is not what it was . . . is it? The days of magnificent assurance—will history place them from the premiere of the lusty *Oklahoma!* to the premiere of the lustrous *My Fair Lady,* or can the period be extended a little on each end?—are perhaps now over. Certainly they are threatened.

At first the strength of the true Broadway musical rested in its composers: Irving Berlin, Jerome Kern, Richard Rodgers, George Gershwin, Cole Porter, Frank Loesser, the list is almost endless. Music was king. The early musicals by Gershwin, for example, had very little in the way of story line or, at times, human interest, and when Gershwin comes to Broadway today, as in the hodgepodge *My One and Only* or the reworking of *Girl Crazy* called *Crazy for You,* enormous care and imagination has to be taken to package the music and lyrics in a manner acceptable to contemporary audiences. Later, with the work of Rodgers—with either Lorenz Hart or Oscar Hammerstein—Loesser, or Frederick Loewe with Alan Jay Lerner, a complete and satisfying fusion came between words and music, drama and song.

But unfortunately, Goethe and MGM were wrong in their famous dictum. It is art that is short, and life that is long. Yes, of course, art can survive, but its traditions tend to run out. A specific style in any art can last a season, a few years, a few decades, or a few centuries. The Viennese and the French operetta traditions died because they died. Their day had come; their time had run out. The creators and the audience lost touch with each other, and it was over and out. I suspect that it may be this way with the Broadway musical. The party's over. Theatre forms never last forever, any more than any other styles in art, and what we see in the Broadway musical now is, generally speaking, decadence, desperation, and decay.

The main reason is, indeed, musical. At one time show music (Broadway and Hollywood) was synonymous with pop music. Berlin, Porter, Gershwin, Kern, Rodgers, Loewe, even the great Kurt Weill—these men wrote the simple tunes we whistled in the street. Their songs were our folk music. No longer. Pop music since 1955 or so has been rock, or rock derivatives and reactions. The people in charge of pop music couldn't care less about Broadway. A new industry has arisen, with different standards of success and different accounting procedures.

The musical has fought back, sometimes in gallant rearguard actions such as those divergent forays conducted on the one ear by Stephen Sondheim and on the other by Andrew Lloyd Webber. Some attempts, such as in the successful pastiche *Hair,* have been made to embrace rock music into the Broadway fold—in a sense, the Who's *Tommy* attempted something along those lines, and it was a musical peak. But from Lennon and McCartney to Elton John and Elvis Costello, the people who might have contributed to the "new" musical were not interested, spurning the theatre for the concert hall and the recording industry.

But Broadway soldiered on. So we have had ethnic musicals that put fiddlers on roofs, we have had "concept" musicals that examine the way we live and love, we have had directors' musicals that are all mechanized scenery to the sound of dying Muzak, and we have had the high-tech extravaganza musical. But there are many who think that the hope for the future of the Broadway musical is to pursue the course of pop opera.

Opera itself is perhaps a dead art—it subsists, very nicely, thank you, on the gorgeous resuscitation of its past. No one—pace Philip Glass and all that fragile crew—is going to write a serious opera again until the (unlikely) return of the serious conventional composer, a strain that seems to have ended with Benjamin Britten and Dimitry Shostakovich, despite perhaps the occasional maverick success of a John Corigliano, composer of *The Ghosts of Versailles.*

But pop opera is another matter. Here, opera and the musical could fuse to create a new genre, more dramatic, more intense, than the old musical. The possibilities of such a form could perhaps have been seen first—had anyone been looking—in the early work of Gian Carlo Menotti, which, had it been regarded more in the context of Broadway than the opera house, might have avoided a lot of clobbering. More confident strides in this direction were made by Bernstein's *West Side Story* and his dazzling *Candide;* now, of course, by Sondheim's work, particularly his *A Little Night Music, Sweeney Todd,* and, one of the "Best Plays" in this present series, *Into the Woods;* and also by some of the English pop operas, especially, I would say, Andrew Lloyd Webber's *The Phantom of the Opera* and, most of all, his *Aspects of Love.*

Now, the shifting status of the musical on Broadway has had a profound impact on the entire theatrical scene in the United States. Just as—or so they said—what is good for General Motors is good for America, so, by the same kind of subway token, what is good for the Broadway musical is good for the American theatre. In so many ways, our commercial theatre—still the bedrock of our entire theatrical structure to a degree unknown anywhere else in the world—is dependent on the prestige, publicity, and income derived from the necessary success of our musical theatre. Even at the very moment I write, when there are nineteen shows on Broadway, thirteen are musicals. And generally speaking these musicals are the largest-grossing shows on Broadway. For some years now we have included the occasional musical in our "Best Plays" series—although for obvious enough reasons this has been a major exception rather than any general rule. But with the diversity of our total theatrical scene, the economic power of the musical enables it to exert a quite disproportionate influence over the rest of the theatre. As we said, what is good for the Broadway musical is good for the American theatre! And, as we say, not all that much nowadays is good for the Broadway musical. Indeed, in that respect, Broadway seems to resemble more closely a road of revivals than a street of dreams.

But now let's look closer at that total theatrical scene and its diversity. If music is not the food of love—and one normally *quotes* Shakespeare, not *contradicts* him—it certainly comes in the same wondrous variety of richness. We do not go to pop superstar Prince for what we can get from almost pop superstar Pavarotti. In the context of circumstances, a late-night chanson encountered in a smoky cabaret can be as moving as a late Beethoven quartet. It was Noël Coward who observed how potent cheap music is, and I have never found any reason to quarrel with him on the point. We all know that not all music is the same in purpose, function, or even basic quality. And neither is all theatre—yet we often behave as if it were.

I personally have often been criticized for my catholic appreciation of the theatrical delicatessen. Some piffling academic once characterized me in a dictionary as being "often considered the major newspaper critic easiest to please." In something of the same vein, a teacher of acting in an ill-tempered but soon forgotten book once took me to task for a review of a revival of Clifford Odets's *The Country Girl*, in which I said that it was "precisely the kind of good-bad play Broadway needed." On an earlier occasion, my ambiguity regarding the premiere production of Arthur Miller's *The Price*—another "good-bad play" if ever there was one—was twisted out of context and equally questioned, even giving the entirely defensible review a certain notoriety. Yet the concept of the "good-bad play" is surely essential to the theatre, particularly the mass-appeal theatre represented (one hopes) by Broadway. It is integral to the idea of pop theatre, and pop theatre is much the same—not quite—to the serious theatre as pop music is to classical music.

I am not, I trust, being an elitist snob about this. I have many artistic preferences that elitist snobs would have to find low—and I prefer good pop anything to inferior classical pretensions. A good-bad play is not *merely* entertainment, it is *simply* entertainment. It manipulates our feelings rather than provokes them, it massages our prejudices rather than challenges them, and it soothes our brain waves rather than stimulates them. It takes a shortcut to our pleasure center. Now a play such as *Hamlet* is immensely entertaining, intensely pleasurable. Yet it is something more. It tries to leave us—it *succeeds* in leaving us—different for having seen it. It adds to our storehouse of life experience.

Such plays, such art, are not the stuff that high Nielsen ratings are made of. But luckily, the stage can offer cakes and ale as well as ambrosia. And very often, the cakes and ale come in the form of the good-bad play. Faced with a play such as Herb Gardner's *I'm Not Rappaport*, which I admire and have included in this volume, it is possible for a critic to be very high-minded and to reject its simple popular appeal out of hand—which most of my colleagues ("harder to please," they would doubtless claim), I am sorry to say, did. Anyone can see that it is not a *Hamlet*, and that its virtues are at a more modest level, although as a vehicle for virtuoso acting it has a Rolls-Royce efficiency. (I note in passing that Paul Scofield played its leading role in London with much the same attack and avidity he once brought to Hamlet.) Yes, *I'm Not Rappaport* can be attacked as easily as praised—and almost as validly. But theatrically, it works like magic. And this is the hallmark of the good-bad play—it works.

Of course, plays like *I'm Not Rappaport*, *The Country Girl*, and *The Price* are not great works of art—neither, on the TV front, were *Dynasty* and *Dallas*, neither are dozens of the top-grossing movies, and neither, leaving the performing arts, are the best-selling novels. Neither, for that matter, are *The Front Page*, nowadays regarded as an American classic, and many others that earlier have featured fairly and gloriously in these "Best Plays" series. If the Broadway theatre, as opposed to the Broadway musical, is to survive—although I am, admittedly, getting less certain about how much this matters to the artistic health of the American theatre as a whole—it will only make it through the good-bad play. The unpretentious pop drama has a genuine place in our hearts, and caters to a real need in—surely, if we are honest—all of us. As Noël Coward might well have said: "Extraordinary how potent cheap theatre is!"

So much for the good-bad play. But there is another category of play essential to the American theatre but never originating and rarely even found on the commercially safe thoroughfare of Broadway. Joseph Papp used to call them "broken-backed plays," while John Houseman was apt to refer to them as "orphan plays." Now, there are clearly some plays that only a mother could love—a mother or a midwife—and these are the broken-backed, half-baked orphans. They are loved, and more particularly cherished, because they may turn out to be the runts in the litter of genius.

So just as vital to the American theatre as the good-bad play on Broadway is this tail-wagging lame-dog play essential to the institutional theatre Off Broadway. It takes no clairvoyant to perceive that Broadway itself is in a bad way. It is in a bad way because the Broadway musical has at least temporarily run out of steam, and because the moneymen, who have taken over from the creative producers, are treating Broadway as an industry producing an assembly-line product designed for mass appeal, mass marketing, and, of course, mass consumption—like a TV series or a Hollywood blockbuster. The long-term economic folly of this we can leave to future historians, but one significant short-term effect is that—on Broadway, at least—the major creative artist of the theatre, the dramatist, is being refused his fundamental artistic right to fail. The costs of production do not permit such experiments. This is where the institutional theatre comes in, with its lame-dog plays limping gallantly, barking plaintively, and answering to the name of Spot!

Now I would like to tell you that behind every bad play (and I mean bad-bad plays) lies the promise of a good one, but such a Panglossian attitude is just not viable. Instinctive public perception is largely right. Most bad plays are plain bad, and often they are awful. Nevertheless, the lame dogs among them represent the spirit of the adventurous theatre. They are the Saint Bernards bearing the brandy of artistic resuscitation; they are the theatrical Lassies coming home to the art's future. The institutional theatre is in the survival business, not the money-making business—although both businesses, in this area and at this time, can get confused. Yet the most vital function of the institutional, nonprofit theatre—the thing that makes it a true alternative—lies in its ability to take chances. It is funded primarily to give lame dogs a chance.

Our major institutional theatres, the New York Shakespeare Festival Public Theater, the Manhattan Theatre Club, the Circle in the Square, Playwrights Horizons, the Roundabout Theatre, the Second Stage, the Circle Repertory Company, the Negro Ensemble Company, the Classic Stage Company (CSC), the New York Theatre Workshop, and all the rest of the struggling crew, fighting for the hot playwright and the subsidized hot buck, are at their noblest in defeat. The late Joe Papp did not exist to produce *A Chorus Line*—although he earned our gratitude for that—but to produce David Rabe's *In the Boom Boom Room*. Our theatre needs a place where a man of genius can go to a man of taste and say: "Have I got an idea for me!" Now, in the event the first man is *not* a man of genius (but let him dream, such dreams create angels) and the second man has only a *little* taste (but let him nurture his palate), the transaction between the two *might* (although it probably *won't*) produce art. But what it will produce is a whole kennelful of lame dogs in varying need of foot therapy.

So who needs lame-dog plays? Sure, in theory, you have to sift through a lot of cabbages before you come across a diamond, but who wants to watch the process? I believe the theatregoer does. I think the excitement of the genuinely new (rather than the cautiously reheated old) has its own special interest. Foremost, there is the quest for discovery that audiences are invited to share with theatres. Our best theatre organizations (and they, at least, know who they are) can offer their audiences nothing but blood, sweat, and the hope of tears, either tears of compassion or tears of joy. There are many difficulties and even unexpected temptations encountered by the alternative Off Broadway institutional theatres—the hope of our art. But remember that they are offering the thrill of the living, risk-taking playwright doing trapeze acts in public without a net. Roll up! You are being given the glinting promise of danger, and perhaps the glittering blessing of surprise.

Any diagnostic survey of the contemporary New York theatre must take into account the role of the critic. We critics—and this, by the way, should be the prime source of our tempering compassion—must remember that no one ever sets out to write a *bad* play. And, for that matter, no one ever sets out to write a good-bad play or even a lame-dog play. Everyone out there is trying to do his best. Actually, when it comes down to it, what all playwrights are really trying to do, apart from acquiring incidental satisfaction and perhaps even a living along the way, is to please the public, just like William Shakespeare tried to.

So when we talk about plays, players, and playwrights, it is essential to talk also about the public, or publics, they are trying to please. The audience is the most essential part of the theatre—the audience is the reason for the theatre. And the theatre audience, particularly the Broadway audience, is rapidly changing. I suspect that part of Broadway's universally perceived current malaise is due to one of those circles generally termed vicious. The audience gets the theatre it deserves, and the theatre (or rather the theatrical-production industry) gets the audience it deserves.

One of the least discussed yet most significant changes to occur in the theatre these last ten years has been in the constitution of its audience. A few years ago, Broadway's theatre producers and theatre owners, disturbed about dwindling profits, resolved to do something about the downturn. The solution was obvious. Either they had to sell more tickets or they had to make the tickets they did sell more profitable. So the captains of the theatre industry applied themselves to the task of establishing more viable profitability with considerable enterprise. As a result, Broadway has become possibly more profitable than ever before. It is still a high-risk enterprise (a gamble that is more like punting than making a book), but the potential rewards for bringing home a winner are enormous. The profit margin of shows like *Cats* and *Miss Saigon*—not, let us carefully note, that there are many shows like *Cats* or *Miss Saigon*—is, I suspect, far greater than for most if not all of the Broadway hits of the past. It can be bonanza time back at the old gold mine.

Now, Broadway has never been much of cultural institution. Oddly enough—despite all reports to the contrary—its prime concern has always been with commercial entertainment rather than art. No matter. That commercial entertainment can be and—particularly with regard to the musical theatre that Broadway patented—once was absolutely marvelous of its kind.

No one could complain about lack of quality in musicals such as *Oklahoma!* or *My Fair Lady* or an enormous number of shows far less distinguished but as a group having distinction enough. And it was Broadway—and not any institutional theatres, which in those days scarcely existed—that cosseted and showcased the genius of Eugene O'Neill, Arthur Miller, and Tennessee Williams, playwrights who are now the glory of our theatre. The present difficulty is that the traditional very sophisticated and knowledgeable Broadway audience has been allowed to erode to the point of nonexistence. In fairness to the producers, the rising ticket prices that have led to a falling off in regular audiences have been largely determined by rising costs in a labor-intensive, union-dominated industry. The situation has only been exacerbated by the typically urban problems of Manhattan (crime, poverty, et cetera), which have, in turn, led to a middle-class exodus to the suburbs, sadly reducing the potential size of the local percentage of the audience.

Producers have, not at all unnaturally, therefore been unwilling to take chances, and artists have been denied their right to fail. The result is usually safe and carefully packaged dullness or, at best, adventure imported from outside the Broadway limits—our own institutional theatres, the resident theatres outside New York, or, quite often, the still-flourishing theatrical scene in London. Furthermore, and most damagingly, the theatre has become tourist dominated, while New Yorkers have been taught to become event-conscious, rather than habitual, in their theatregoing.

Vast sums of money—often disproportionate to the basic cost of a show or the possibilities for return—are lavished on TV advertising, to promote the idea that a particular show is likely to make a night out into an occasion to remember. If you sell the theatre like soap—and this is essentially the new strategy—you get audiences who buy the theatre like soap. Oddly enough in all of this event-packaging, the so-called boulevard play, which was once the mainstay of the popular theatre, has grievously suffered. Such plays—and their equivalent in musicals—have been steamrollered out of existence by an economic system that permits only smash hits, which may still take a year or more to repay their capital investment after the working profits have been—often legitimately—skimmed by real estate holders and the various levels of theatrical management.

What results does not innately make its appeal to a theatre audience as such. It is designed for an audience that takes in a Broadway play much as it might take in the Empire State Building, or that subsumes theatregoing into the celebration of some occasion, with probably dinner and a few drinks thrown in for luck and pleasure. And this audience does not want—indeed, has been conditioned not to accept—the engaging mediocrity that has always kept Broadway and the whole theatre healthy. This audience has been trained to demand the superhyped *Cats*. For Broadway, it's a Pavlovian dog's life. And not a lame dog at that.

Someone once asked Bernard Shaw how he got on with Gabriel Pascal, the producer/director of such Shavian movies as *Major Barbara* and *Caesar and Cleopatra*. Shaw is said to have replied (the line is possibly apocryphal, for I have heard a similar remark attributed to other writers apropos the anecdotally ubiquitous Sam Goldwyn; nonetheless, I favor my own version): "Not very well, because all Pascal wanted to talk about was art, and all I wanted to talk about was money." So far—to various degrees—all we have been talking about here is money. Now let's drop in a few words on the subject of art.

This is the fourth Introduction in this series that it has been my good fortune to pen—or, in truth, nowadays, word-process—and looking back at its predecessors I find that many things I once found significant as epochal trends (those imperceptible-to-the-naked-eye movements beloved of journalists and the editors who spur them) are now either accepted or vanished, unremarkably, with the past. For instance, in the Introduction to the Sixth Series (first published in 1971), I find that I was having to explain the theatre's new use of obscenity and nudity, and pointing out that the series was finally having to use its first "four-letter" word. (I also, at that time, pleaded for better understanding of the performing arts as a loss operation and asked for support for more and better public subsidy for our serious theatre. The need for the latter plea, at least, hasn't changed—quite to the contrary. The outlook for public subsidy in this country is even grimmer now than it was twenty years ago.)

By the time the Seventh Series came along in 1975, I was heralding the rise of the black theatre—represented in this volume by August Wilson's *Joe Turner's Come and Gone*—celebrating the continued rise of Off Broadway (no fewer than ten of this present selection of plays started Off Broadway, and no fewer than seven never moved to the Great Gray Way at all), and confirming the earlier "trend in permissiveness in language and, of course, in stage nudity." That blasé "of course" does indeed suggest that we had taken stage nudity in our stride—which certainly remains true today—but interestingly, if memory serves, it was featured in only one (or is it two?) play (or is it plays?) of our current Series.

For the Eighth Series (1983) I continued to stress: "Nine years ago—even twenty years ago, if you had good eyesight—it was apparent that the general trend of the American theatre was a movement away from the private toward the public sector. And, of course, this would have a marked, possibly profound, effect on the plays written and, even more, the plays produced." The situation has hardly changed.

But more significantly, nine years ago I was also talking about the move from the traditional realism (or naturalism) of the American theatre to what at the time I dubbed a new "symbolic realism," prompted, I suggested, largely by the rival medium of the cinema.

It occurred to me very strongly then that the cinema—and, naturally, television—could provide a degree of verisimiltude totally outside the range of the theatre's "fourth wall," and it seemed that the theatre was facing through the esthetic competition of video (I have already mentioned the economic effect) almost a crisis of function. What is the point of holding a mirror up to nature when someone else quite clearly possesses a better looking glass? I compared the effect of the other dramatic media on theatrical writing to the slow-moving effect of still-camera photography on the art of painting. "The painter," I suggested, "had to move into different areas if only to exist. The result? Cézanne and all who have followed him from every 'ism' in the book, each 'ism' defining a new territory for art."

Indeed, the American theatre, weighted down with realism and naturalism, did soon after World War II find itself still Waiting for Lefty while the rest of the world was Waiting for Godot. But things changed, and not only did the American theatre catch up with the likes of Pirandello, Beckett, Pinter, and even Ionesco, but interestingly—something rather similar happened in American painting—a new kind of realism, quite evident in this present volume, also began to assert itself.

Nor is the camera the only technological toy of the twentieth century that has made an effect on our drama. I feel that the use of the tape recorder, almost as much as the new reportage made possible by the hand-held camera, has introduced us to the way people really speak rather than the way playwrights suggested to us that we, or our stage equivalents, spoke. The recorded interview has made us fully aware of the actual rhythms, repetitions, and banalities of common speech, and has thus made us oddly suspicious of any utterance that is not either completely commonplace or, by designed contrast, deliberately poetic.

David Mamet was one of the first American playwrights to realize this, and if you examine the verbal texture of his *Glengarry Glen Ross* in this volume, you will see the commonplace and the poetic fascinatingly fused. Many of the other plays herein show the same kind of aural fidelity to the facts of speech—plays as varied as David Rabe's *Hurlyburly*, A. R. Gurney's *The Cocktail Hour*, and Terrence McNally's *Frankie and Johnny in the Clair de Lune* also seek to catch this newly true turn of phrase, admittedly edited for effect yet still sounding basically honest and, in a sense, nontheatrical.

Not every playwright subscribes to this kind of documentary-soundtrack approach to everyday speech—Neil Simon, the master serious comedian of our contemporary stage, gives his characters an artificial characterization of specific wit and sharpness that they wear like costumes, and although often his best dramatic moments have nothing to do with verbal felicity or, sometimes, even humor, realism rather than naturalism is his basic method, as it is for Alfred Uhry in his vivid Southern memoir *Driving Miss Daisy*, Herb Gardner in his crochety and appealing *I'm Not Rappaport*, and Horton Foote in his atmospheric evocation of small-town America, *The Widow Claire*.

Some of the plays in this collection are boulevard theatre intended for nothing much more than entertainment or diversion—as if that were not enough. Such as *Driving Miss Daisy* and Jerry Sterner's *Other People's Money* (both made into movies, incidentally) are part of a still-valid Broadway boulevard tradition—although, as a fascinating sign of the times, both were in fact produced Off Broadway and never made it theatrically to what is still, financially, the big time. (Remember, incidentally, that for all the prestige and acclaim Off Broadway and the institutional theatre can offer the playwright, director, and actor alike, real financial rewards can still come only from Broadway and, in the special case of playwrights, the sale of movie or TV rights, or wide-scale international production.)

Although a few of the plays in this collection have found further life as movies, others could not easily be envisaged as anything else than plays: They show their regard for the world we live in in specifically theatrical rather than cinematic terms. William M. Hoffman's *As Is*, for example, not only one of the very first plays to deal with AIDS but also one of the very best, and Arthur Kopit's virtually surrealistic *End of the World* use a freestyle structure to achieve their ends that while clearly influenced by the movies retains its own clear stage identity. Both Tina Howe's *Painting Churches* and Michael Weller's *Spoils of War* have a more formal shape to them, but they too have a design that is essentially theatrical rather than anything else, and characters that seem to have a special dramatic reality. Horton Foote—better known perhaps as a filmmaker than as dramatist—could surely make *The Widow Claire* into a movie, but I wonder whether it would have quite the same flavor and sense of nuance. For that matter, Gurney's *The Cocktail Hour*—another of his telling reports from the East Coast WASP middle class—could hardly find a commensurate feeling of regret and loss in any other medium, for presumably its very staginess adds to the effectiveness of its message.

Shakespeare memorably refers to plays as "the abstract and brief chronicles of the time," and the theatre has continuously provided a commentary to the life and times of its writers and audiences—even at its most apparently irrelevant, that very irrelevance and triviality give a special significance to the passing moment. These, whatever else their failings, are scarcely trivial times, and the plays in this collection reflect in many ways the concerns and troubles of the day.

Some of them are very personal documents—notably the Horton Foote and the A. R. Gurney, and also Tina Howe's *Painting Churches*, which has an air of actual memory to it. But of course, the avowed memory play of this particular group is Neil Simon's *Brighton Beach Memoirs*. Virtually all Simon's plays seem to be to some extent essays in autobiography, but this is the first of the playwright's so-called Brighton Beach trilogy (the other two are *Biloxi Blues* and *Broadway Bound*) and actually sets down—with heightened imagination and a free dramatic license—his life up until his first engagement as a comedy writer.

Other plays in the current series offer a wider though not necessarily deeper view—the aforementioned AIDS play, *As Is*, for example; *Hurlyburly*, Rabe's incisive picture of dogs eating dogs in the hills of Hollywood; and *Joe Turner's Come and Gone*, a play from that extraordinarily ambitious and so-far successful cycle—perhaps the most ambitious

American dramatic concept since O'Neill's abandoned, or at least unfinished, American cycle—August Wilson's grand design of a play per decade to illustrate and demonstrate the black experience in this century's America.

On the whole, I am fairly satisfied with the current selection of plays—one play I would very much have liked to include is John Guare's *Six Degrees of Separation,* but for various copyright reasons this was not possible—though I am perfectly well aware that there are, happily, many other plays out there that could, with virtually equal justification, have been included in the present volume.

I am very proud to have the James Lapine–Stephen Sondheim *Into the Woods* here, especially as an example of America's new way with musicals, and in the next volume we might well have another musical, such as George C. Wolfe's *Jelly's Last Jam.* Indeed, there are a number of young American playwrights yet to be included in these collections—I am thinking particularly of John Patrick Shanley, Donald Margulies, Scott McPherson, Richard Nelson, Jon Robin Baitz, Wendy Wasserstein, Craig Lucas, Ken Ludwig, and Marsha Norman—all of whom (and there are others) have already done sterling work.

People will often tell you the theatre is dead. Nonsense. The theatre—that plank and a passion—will never be dead as long as there are people to write for it, and people to listen to them. At the moment, or so it seems to me, the theatre in America is very probably healthier than it has ever been in its life—simply because it has never before had so many talented and aspiring playwrights. Most theatre producers groan dramatically, Where are the plays? Where is the product?, when what they really mean is Where is the material from which we can make an easy fortune? But real plays, ordinary, common, and garden-variety plays (some of them broken-backed, or orphan, or lame-dog plays, perhaps), exist in extraordinary quantity and, often, of fascinating quality.

Today, a man or a woman with a way with words and a wish to have them heard is conceivably more tempted by the theatre than at any time since Elizabethan England. After all, at least for the moment, poetry is scarcely a viable means of mass communication—certainly hardly a means of making a living—and while a few best-selling novelists do extremely well, unless you want to write mass-production thrillers or romances, your chances as a serious novelist (and I'm thinking of people like Updike, Vidal, Mailer, and Bellow) of being heard and being able to survive financially are fairly slim. There is, of course, screenwriting, but the screenwriter, apart from a Woody Allen or an Ingmar Bergman who elects to become the director/auteur of his own work, lacks artistic control over his creation and, in the outcome, receives remarkably little credit for labor expended. As for television writing, although in many ways it seems to be the most practicable way for the creative writer to acquire a comfortable living wage, in other ways it appears, nowadays at least, to be singularly unsatisfying.

As a result, people today with a message to offer, a song to sing, or perhaps a joke to tell are beginning to favor the theatre, and despite the costs and the difficulties of working in our living and still-just-breathing theatre, there is more opportunity here than ever before. New York alone has more than 250 theatres—some of them basements, some of the attics, some of them holes in the wall, but all of them spaces for that plank and that passion. And that audience. This is just New York. Possibly the most significant fact about the performing arts in the United States since World War II has been their decentralization—and this is nowhere more true than in the theatre. Fifty years ago, almost all our non–New York theatre, other than summer stock, was either on its way to Broadway on preproduction tryout or on its way from Broadway on tour. Now there are professional resident theatres from sea to shining sea, each one of them with a subscription series and each one of them almost certainly offering at least one new play a year. Few of these theatres' productions—unless they lead to further sales—will make the playwright rich, although all can give a writer a hearing and set a career on a properly professional path.

Strangely enough, what our theatre most lacks is not new plays but old plays, and I stress once more the absence of a serious classical theatre in New York to match London's Royal Shakespeare Company, the Royal National Theatre, and the Royal Court Theatre, all, despite their misleading air of royal patronage and long establishment, theatres created within the past forty years. These splendid institutions not only provide opportunities for playwrights, actors, and directors but also lay down the foundation for a solid theatrical culture from which an audience can develop and an artist can grow. We need such institutions in the United States. This apart—and it is a big "this" and a big "apart"—our American theatre and our playwrights, as we move into the final decade before the millennium, seem almost unexpectedly healthy.

Brighton Beach Memoirs

NEIL SIMON

TO MY PARENTS, GRANDPARENTS, BROTHER, COUSINS, AUNTS, UNCLES, AND ESPE-
CIALLY TO THOSE WHO ENDURED THE PAINS, INSECURITIES, FEARS, JOYS, LOVE AND
FRIENDSHIP OF NEW YORK CITY IN THE DEPRESSION YEARS

First presented on December 10, 1982, at the Ahmanson Theatre, Los Angeles, and on March 27, 1983, at the Alvin Theatre, New York City, with the
following cast:

EUGENE	Matthew Broderick
BLANCHE	Joyce Van Patten
KATE	Elizabeth Franz
LAURIE	Mandy Ingber
NORA	Jodi Thelen
STANLEY	Željko Ivanek
JACK	Peter Michael Goetz

Directed by Gene Saks
Setting by David Mitchell
Lighting by Tharon Musser
Costumes by Patricia Zipprodt

SYNOPSIS OF SCENES

ACT ONE: Brighton Beach, Brooklyn, New York, September 1937–6:30 P.M.

ACT TWO: Wednesday, a week later, about 6:30 in the evening

Neil Simon is perhaps the most prolific, popular, and universally loved playwright of the twentieth century. In a span of thirty years, he has written twenty-seven theatrical plays and musicals and eighthteen screenplays, winning more Academy Awards and Tony nominations than any other writer. His work has been translated into twenty-four languages and produced worldwide. He is the only playwright who has ever had four plays running on Broadway simultaneously. In addition to the "Best Author" Tony Award he won for *The Odd Couple* and an honorary 1975 Tony, Simon has won the Drama Critics Circle Award for *Brighton Beach Memoirs* in 1984, the Tony Award for *Biloxi Blues* in 1985, and the Tony Award and the 1991 Pulitzer Prize for *Lost in Yonkers*.

Brighton Beach Memoirs is the story of two families living together and struggling to stay alive during the last years of the Depression, on the brink of World War II. Forced to live together in a small house in Brooklyn, they are confronted with cramped quarters, financial troubles, adolescent angst, sexual awakenings, and the fear of separation by an uncertain future. All this is seen through the eyes of a fifteen-year-old aspiring writer who narrates the story of his own coming of age. Like Horton Foote's *The Widow Claire*, this play concerns the universal desire for family stability and security.

From inception to completion, Simon reports, the play took nine years to write. "I let it sit for six years, I would think about it, and six years later I wrote thirty-five pages. . . . I'd never written a play like that—sort of a tapestry where everybody's story is very important. . . . Another three years, and then I sat down and went right through. . . . But the unconscious is doing the work, it's typing away. . . . It doesn't mean you're thinking about it all that time. . . . Your mind is clearing the path for this journey you're about to take. . . ." Once actually begun, the play took only four months to complete.

Brighton Beach Memoirs is the first play of a trilogy; *Biloxi Blues* and *Broadway Bound* complete the story. Simon has stated that his own life can be traced through his plays, which are derived from his experiences with family and friends: "The plays are all about things that have happened to me, are happening to me, or will happen to me." Many of Simon's plays deal with people in conflict living together in confined spaces, a narrative device that mirrors Simon's own unhappy childhood, in which he was separated from his mother and brother and made to live with an aunt after his parents divorced. "My childhood was extremely painful, but my memories are not. . . . I would go to the basement and read books or make model airplanes. . . . I lived as much as I could in the movies because it was the only true escape. . . . It was forming my personality, which was to be alone, to work out in my mind the kind of life I wanted."

Simon's comic instincts formed at an early age and provided a vehicle through which he could work out his personal problems. Like Eugene, the playwright's *Brighton Beach Memoirs* stand-in, Simon has learned to distance himself from the convoluted feelings lying beneath the surface of a seemingly cohesive family. Here, Simon remembers the tortures of adolescence with love and compassionate humor, painting unforgettable character portraits.

"Humor," Simon explains, "is a way of expressing your protest and being able to laugh too. . . . I do my funniest writing when I'm in a predicament. . . . *Brighton* opened a part of my mind that dealt with how I became the person I am." Simon's brother, Danny, encouraged him to write. ". . . No one in the family ever cared about literature, writing, books, the theatre. But my brother was very self-motivated and was the instigator." In 1946, when Simon was nineteen, he and his brother applied to work for the noted humor writer Goodman Ace, of CBS, and were hired after Ace read their parodistic description of a Joan Crawford movie. The Simons went on during the next decade to write for Victor Borge, Buddy Hackett, *The Phil Silvers Show*, the *Tallulah Bankhead Show* on NBC, and the Jackie Gleason and Red Buttons shows on CBS.

When his brother left the team in 1956, Simon continued to write for *The Sid Caesar Show*, (NBC, 1956–58), receiving Emmy nominations in 1957 and 1959. While writing for *The Garry Moore Show*, Simon, encouraged by his first wife, began work on a play, *Come Blow Your Horn*. It opened on Broadway in 1961 and, despite mixed reviews, ran for two seasons. Deciding to focus his efforts on the theatre, Simon wrote the book of the Coleman-Leigh musical *Little Me* (1962), then *Barefoot in the Park* (1963), which firmly established his reputation as a playwright. *The Odd Couple* followed in 1965, and *Sweet Charity* and *The Star-Spangled Girl* were produced in 1966. Simon established himself as a more-or-less permanent resident of Broadway with *Plaza Suite* and *Promises, Promises* in 1968, and *The Last of the Red Hot Lovers* in 1969.

With *The Gingerbread Lady* (1970) and *The Prisoner of Second Avenue* (1971), Simon began to write more seriously, combining humor with pathos, and Broadway in the seventies and eighties also saw *The Sunshine Boys* (1972), *The Good Doctor* (1973), *God's Favorite* (1974), *California Suite* (1976), *Chapter Two* (1977), *They're Playing Our Song* (1978), *I Ought To Be In Pictures* (1980), *Fools* (1981), *Brighton Beach Memoirs* (1983), *Biloxi Blues* (1984), and *Broadway Bound* (1986). *Lost in Yonkers* opened on Broadway in 1990, followed by *Jake's Women*, revised after an unsuccessful 1988 West Coast engagement, in 1992. In addition to the many film versions of his plays, original Simon films include *After the Fox* (1966), *The Out-of-Towners* (1970), *The Heartbreak Kid* (1972), *Murder by Death* (1976), *The Goodbye Girl* (1977), *The Cheap Detective* (1978), *Seems Like Old Times* (1980), *Max Dugan Returns* (1983), *The Lonely Guy* (1984), and *The Slugger's Wife*.

Simon, who has lived in California since 1975, writes daily from 10:00 A.M. to 5:00 P.M. ("I really like being alone in a room, writing," he says), setting aside ten or more attempted plays for each one that he finishes. If a play does make it past thirty-five pages, Simon usually completes it and then begins a process of meticulous revision. "I've been able to write during the worst periods of my life. . . . From the moment I would sit down at the typewriter, I could block out what was going on. . . . Writing is like painting: Most great painters . . . reorder nature."

ACT ONE

Brighton Beach, New York. September 1937. A wooden frame house, not too far from the beach. It is a lower-middle-income area inhabited mostly by Jews, Irish and Germans.

The entrance to the house is to the right: a small porch and two steps up that lead to the front door. Inside we see the dining room and living-room area. Another door leads to the kitchen . . . A flight of stairs leads up to three small bedrooms. Unseen are two other bedrooms. A hallway leads to other rooms . . .

It's around six-thirty and the late-September sun is sinking fast. KATE JEROME, *about forty years old, is setting the table. Her sister,* BLANCHE MORTON, *thirty-eight, is working at a sewing machine.* LAURIE MORTON, *aged thirteen, is lying on the sofa reading a book.*

Outside on the grass stands EUGENE JEROME, *almost but not quite fifteen. He is wearing knickers, a shirt and tie, a faded and torn sweater, Keds sneakers and a blue baseball cap. He has a beaten and worn baseball glove on his left hand, and in his right hand he holds a softball that is so old and battered that it is ready to fall apart.*

On an imaginary pitcher's mound, facing left, he looks back over his shoulder to an imaginary runner on second, then back over to the "batter." Then he winds up and pitches, hitting an offstage wall.

EUGENE. One out, a man on second, bottom of the seventh, two balls, no strikes . . . Ruffing checks the runner on second, gets the sign from Dickey, Ruffing stretches, Ruffing pitches—*(He throws the ball)* Caught the inside corner, steerike one! Atta baby! No hitter up there. *(He retrieves the ball)* One out, a man on second, bottom of the seventh, two balls, one strike . . . Ruffing checks the runner on second, gets the sign from Dickey, Ruffing stretches, Ruffing pitches—*(He throws the ball)* Low and outside, ball three. Come on, Red! Make him a hitter! No batter up there. In there all the time, Red.

BLANCHE *(Stops sewing).* Kate, please. My head is splitting.

KATE. I told that boy a hundred and nine times. *(She yells out)* Eugene! Stop banging the wall!

EUGENE *(Calls out).* In a minute, Ma! This is for the World Series! *(Back to his game)* One out, a man on second, bottom of the seventh, three balls, one strike . . . Ruffing stretches,

Ruffing pitches—*(He throws the ball)* Oh, no! High and outside, JoJo Moore walks! First and second and Mel Ott lopes up to the plate . . .

BLANCHE *(Stops again).* Can't he do that someplace else?

KATE. I'll break his arm, that's where he'll do it. *(She calls out)* Eugene, I'm not going to tell you again. Do you hear me?

EUGENE. It's the last batter, Mom. Mel Ott is up. It's a crucial moment in World Series history.

KATE. Your Aunt Blanche has a splitting headache.

BLANCHE. I don't want him to stop playing. It's just the banging.

LAURIE *(Looks up from her book).* He always does it when I'm studying. I have a big test in history tomorrow.

EUGENE. One pitch, Mom? I think I can get him to pop up. I have my stuff today.

KATE. Your father will give you plenty of stuff when he comes home! You hear?

EUGENE. All right! All right!

KATE. I want you inside *now!* Put out the water glasses.

BLANCHE. I can do that.

KATE. Why? Is his arm broken? *(She yells out again)* And I don't want any back talk, you hear?

(She goes back to the kitchen)

EUGENE *(Slams the ball into his glove angrily. Then he cups his hand, making a megaphone out of it and announces to the grandstands).* "Attention, ladeees and gentlemen! Today's game will be delayed because of my Aunt Blanche's headache . . ."

KATE. Blanche, that's enough sewing today. That's all I need is for you to go blind.

BLANCHE. I just have this one edge to finish . . . Laurie, darling, help your Aunt Kate with the dishes.

LAURIE. Two more pages, all right, Ma? I have to finish the Macedonian Wars.

KATE. Always studying, that one. She's gonna have some head on her shoulders. *(She calls out from the kitchen)* Eugene!!

EUGENE. I'm coming.

KATE. And wash your hands.

EUGENE. They're clean. I'm wearing a glove. *(He throws the ball into his glove again . . . then he looks out front and addresses the audience)* I hate my name! Eugene Morris Jerome . . . It is the second worst name ever given to a male child. The first worst is Haskell Fleischmann . . . How am I ever going to play for the Yankees with a name like Eugene Morris Jerome? You have to be a Joe ... or a Tony ... or Frankie ... If only I was born Italian . . . All the best Yankees are Italian ... My mother makes spaghetti with ketchup, what chance do I have?

(He slams the ball into his glove again)

LAURIE. I'm almost through, Ma.

BLANCHE. All right, darling. Don't get up too quickly.

KATE *(To LAURIE)*. You have better color today, sweetheart. Did you get a little sun this morning?

LAURIE. I walked down to the beach.

BLANCHE. Very slowly, I hope?

LAURIE. Yes, Ma.

BLANCHE. That's good.

EUGENE *(Turns to the audience again)*. She gets all this special treatment because the doctors say she has kind of a flutter in her heart ... I got hit with a baseball right in the back of the skull, I saw two of everything for a week and I still had to carry a block of ice home every afternoon . . . Girls are treated like queens. Maybe that's what I should have been born—an Italian girl . . .

KATE *(Picks up a sweat sock from the floor)*. EUGENE!!

EUGENE. *What?*

KATE. How many times have I told you not to leave your things around the house?

EUGENE. A hundred and nine.

KATE. What?

EUGENE. You said yesterday, "I told you a hundred and nine times not to leave your things around the house."

BLANCHE. Don't be fresh to your mother, Gene!

EUGENE *(To the audience)*. Was I fresh? I swear to God, that's what she said to me yesterday ... One day I'm going to put all this in a book or a play. I'm going to be a writer like Ring Lardner or somebody— that's if things don't work out first with the Yankees, or the Cubs, or the Red Sox, or maybe possibly the Tigers ... If I get down to the St. Louis Browns, then I'll definitely be a writer.

LAURIE. Mom, can I have a glass of lemonade?

BLANCHE. It'll spoil your dinner, darling.

KATE. A small glass, it couldn't hurt her.

BLANCHE. All right. In a minute, angel.

KATE. I'll get it. I'm in the kitchen anyway.

EUGENE *(To the audience)*. Can you believe

that? She'd better have a bad heart or I'm going to kill her one day ... *(He gets up to walk into the house, then stops on the porch steps and turns to the audience again . . . confidentially)* Listen, I hope you don't repeat this to anybody ... What I'm telling you are my secret memoirs. It's called, "The Unbelievable, Fantastic and Completely Private Thoughts of I, Eugene Morris Jerome, in this, the fifteenth year of his life, in the year nineteen hundred and thirty-seven, in the community of Brighton Beach, Borough of Brooklyn, Kings County, City of New York, Empire State of the American Nation—"

KATE *(Comes out of the kitchen with a glass of lemonade and one roller skate)*. A roller skate? On my kitchen floor? Do you want me dead, is that what you want?

EUGENE *(Rushes into the house)*. I didn't leave it there.

KATE. No? Then who? Laurie? Aunt Blanche? Did you ever see them on skates? *(She holds out the skate)* Take this upstairs ... Come here!

EUGENE *(Approaches, holding the back of his head)*. Don't hit my skull, I have a concussion.

KATE *(Handing the glass to LAURIE)*. What would you tell your father if he came home and I was dead on the kitchen floor?

EUGENE. I'd say, "Don't go in the kitchen, Pa!"

KATE *(Swings at him, he ducks and she misses)*. Get upstairs! And don't come down with dirty hands.

EUGENE *(Goes up the stairs. He turns to the audience)*. You see why I want to write all this down? In case I grow up all twisted and warped, the world will know why.

BLANCHE *(Still sewing)*. He's a boy. He's young. You should be glad he's healthy and active. Before the doctors found out what Laurie had, she was the same way.

KATE. Never. Girls are different. When you and I were girls, we kept the house spotless. It was Ben and Ezra who drove Momma crazy. *(We see EUGENE, upstairs, enter his room and take out a notebook and pencil and lie down on his bed, making a new entry in his "memoirs")* ... I've always been like that. I have to have things clean. Just like Momma. The day they packed up and left the house in Russia, she cleaned the place from top to bottom. She said, "No matter what the Cossacks did to us, when they broke into our house, they would have respect for the Jews."

LAURIE. Who were the Cossacks?

KATE. The same filthy bunch as live across the street.

LAURIE. Across the street? You mean the Murphys?

KATE. *All* of them.

LAURIE. The Murphys are Russian?

BLANCHE. The mother is nice. She's been very sweet to me.

KATE. Her windows are so filthy, I thought she had black curtains hanging inside.

BLANCHE. I was in their house. It was very neat. *Nobody* could be as clean as you.

KATE. What business did you have in their house?

BLANCHE. She invited me for tea.

KATE. To meet that drunken son of hers?

BLANCHE. No. Just the two of us.

KATE. I'm living here seven years, she never invited *me* for tea. Because she knows your situation. I know their kind. Remember what Momma used to tell us. "Stay on your own side of the street. That's what they have gutters for."

(She goes back into the kitchen)

EUGENE *(Writing, says aloud)*. "That's-what-they-have-gutters-for" . . . *(To the audience)* If my mother knew I was writing all this down, she would stuff me like one of her chickens . . . I'd better explain what she meant by Aunt Blanche's "situation." You see, her husband, Uncle Dave, died six years ago from *(He looks around)* this thing . . . They never say the word. They always whisper it. It was *(He whispers)* —cancer! I think they're afraid if they said it out loud, God would say, "I HEARD THAT! YOU SAID THE DREAD DISEASE! *(He points his finger down)* JUST FOR THAT, I SMITE YOU DOWN WITH IT!!" . . . There are some things that grownups just won't discuss. For example, my grandfather. He died from *(He whispers)* —diphtheria! Anyway, after Uncle Dave died, he left Aunt Blanche with no money. Not even insurance. And she couldn't support herself because she has *(He whispers)* —asthma . . . So my big-hearted mother insisted we take her and her kids in to live with us. So they broke up our room into two small rooms, and me and my brother Stan live on this side, and Laurie and her sister Nora live on the other side. My father thought it would just be temporary, but it's been three and a half years so far and I think because of Aunt Blanche's situation, my father is developing *(He whispers)* —high blood pressure!

(He resumes his writing)

KATE *(Comes out of the kitchen with a pitcher and says to LAURIE)*. Have some more lemonade, dear.

LAURIE *(Sits up)*. Thank you, Aunt Kate.

BLANCHE. Drink it slowly.

LAURIE. I am.

KATE *(Looks at BLANCHE)*. Blanche, that's enough already. Since seven o'clock this morning.

BLANCHE. I was just stopping.

KATE. You'll sew your fingers together.

BLANCHE. It's getting dark anyway. *(She stops, sits back and rubs her eyes)* I think I need new glasses.

LAURIE. Our teacher said you should change them every two years.

KATE *(To BLANCHE)*. Would it kill you to put a light on?

BLANCHE. I don't have to run up electric bills. I owe you and Jack enough as it is.

KATE. Have I asked you for anything? You see anybody starving around here? If I go hungry, you'll give me something from your plate.

BLANCHE. Kate! I'm going to pay you and Jack back someday. I don't know when, but I keep my word.

KATE. From your lips to the Irish Sweepstakes . . . Go in and taste the soup. See if it needs salt.

(BLANCHE goes into the kitchen)

LAURIE. Should I put out the water glasses or is Eugene going to do it?

(EUGENE, having heard, slams his "memoirs" shut angrily)

KATE *(Yells up)*. EUGENE! It's the last time I'm going to tell you! *(To LAURIE)* Just do the napkins, darling.

(She goes into the kitchen. LAURIE gets up and starts to set out the napkins)

EUGENE *(Sits up on his bed and addresses the audience)*. Because of her "condition," I have to do twice as much work around here. Boy, if I could just make the Yankees, I'd be in St. Petersburg this winter . . . *(He starts out and down the stairs)* Her sister Nora isn't too bad. She's sixteen. I don't mind her much. *(He is downstairs by now)* At least she's not too bad to look at. *(He starts taking down some glasses from the open cupboard)* To be absolutely honest, this is the year I started noticing girls that weren't too bad to look at. Nora started developing about eight months ago . . . I have the exact date written in my diary.

(Suddenly we hear a voice. It is NORA)

NORA. Mom! Laurie! Aunt Kate! *(We see*

NORA, *an absolutely lovely sixteen-and-a-half-year-old girl, with a developed chest, bound across the front steps and into the house. She is bubbling over with enthusiasm)* I've got incredible news, everybody!!

EUGENE. Hi, Nora!

NORA. Eugene! My sweet adorable handsome cousin! Wait'll I tell you what's happened to me. *(She throws her arms around him, hugs him close and kisses his cheek. Then she rushes into the other room to LAURIE)* I'm fainting! I'm absolutely fainting!

EUGENE *(Still stunned from the hug, turns to the audience).* I felt her chest! When she grabbed me, I felt my first chest.

NORA. I can't believe this whole day!

LAURIE. What happened?

NORA. Where's Mom? Aunt Kate? I have to tell everyone. *(She rushes to the kitchen door)* Everybody inside for the big news!

(KATE and BLANCHE come out of the kitchen. KATE is mashing potatoes in a pot)

KATE. What's all the excitement?

BLANCHE. You're all red in the face.

NORA. Sit down, Mom, because I don't want you fainting on the floor.

KATE. Sit down, Blanche.

LAURIE. Mom, sit down.

(BLANCHE sits)

NORA. You too, Aunt Kate. Okay. Is everybody ready?

LAURIE. Stop dragging it out. The suspense is *killing* me.

BLANCHE. Don't say things like that, Laurie.

KATE *(To the others).* Can I hear what the girl has to say? *(To NORA)* Go ahead, darling.

NORA *(A little breathless).* Okay! Here goes! ... I'm going to be in a Broadway show! *(They look at her in a stunned silence)* It's a musical called *Abracadabra.* This man, Mr. Beckman, he's a producer, came to our dancing class this afternoon and he picked out three girls. We have to be at the Hudson Theater on Monday morning at ten o'clock to audition for the dance director. But on the way out he took me aside and said the job was as good as mine. I have to call him tomorrow. I may have to go into town to talk to him about it. They start rehearsing a week from Monday and then it goes to Philadelphia, Wilmington and Washington . . . and then it comes to New York the second week in December. There are nine big musical numbers and there's going to be a big tank on the stage that you can see through and the big finale all

takes place with the entire cast all under water . . . I mean, can you believe it? I'm going to be in a Broadway show, Momma!

(They are all still stunned)

BLANCHE *(To KATE).* What is she talking about?

KATE. Do I know? Am I her mother?

LAURIE. How can you be in a show? Don't you have to sing and act?

NORA. I can sing.

LAURIE. No, you can't.

NORA. A little.

LAURIE. No, you can't.

NORA. I can carry a *tune.*

LAURIE. No, you can't.

NORA. Well, I probably won't have to. They're just looking for dancers.

LAURIE. On Broadway you have to sing and act.

NORA. How do *you* know? You never saw a Broadway show.

BLANCHE. Did you tell him how old you were?

NORA. He didn't ask me.

BLANCHE. He didn't ask if you were sixteen?

NORA. He just asked me to audition. My God, isn't anybody excited?

EUGENE. I am. It's the most fantastic thing I ever heard.

NORA. Thanks, Eugene. I'm glad somebody's excited.

EUGENE *(Turns to the audience).* My God! I'll be sleeping right next door to a *show girl!*

BLANCHE. How can you go to Philadelphia? What about school?

NORA. School? Momma, this is a Broadway show. This is what I want to do with my life. Algebra and English isn't going to help me on the stage.

LAURIE. *Aren't?*

NORA. Will you stay out of this!

BLANCHE. You mean not finish school? Not get a diploma? Do you know how hard it is today for a girl to get a good job without a high school diploma?

NORA. But I've *got* a job. And I'll be making more money than *ten* girls with diplomas.

LAURIE. You don't have it yet. You still have to audition.

NORA. It's as good as mine. Mr. Beckman told me.

BLANCHE. And what if you, God forbid, broke a leg? Or got heavy . . . How long do you think they'll keep you? Dancing is just for a few years. A diploma is forever. I know.

I never had one. I know how hard it is to find a decent job. Aunt Kate knows. Tell her, Kate.

KATE. It's very hard.

NORA. Then why did you send me to dancing school for three years? Why do I spend two hours a day on a subway, four days a week after school, with money that you make going half blind over a broken sewing machine? Why, Momma?

BLANCHE. Because it's my pleasure . . . Because I know how you love it . . . Because you asked me.

NORA. Then I'm asking you something else, Momma. Let me do something for *you* now. I could be making almost sixty dollars a week. Maybe even more . . . In two years when I get out of high school, I wouldn't make that much with a *college* diploma.

BLANCHE *(Takes a deep breath)*. I can't think now. It's almost dinnertime. Uncle Jack will be home soon. We'll discuss it later.

(She gets up)

NORA. I have to know *now*, Momma. I have to call Mr. Beckman and let him know if I can go to the audition on Monday . . . At least let me audition. Let me find out first if they think I'm good enough. Please don't say no until Monday.

(They all look at BLANCHE. *She looks down at her hands)*

EUGENE *(Turns toward the audience)*. It was a tense moment for everybody . . . I love tense moments! Especially when I'm not the one they're all tense about.

(He turns back and looks at BLANCHE*)*

BLANCHE. Well, God knows we can use the money. We all owe Aunt Kate and Uncle Jack enough as it is . . . I think they have as much say in this as I do. How do you feel about it, Kate?

KATE *(Shrugs)*. Me? I never voted before in my life, why should I start with my own family? . . . I have to heat up the potatoes.

(She goes into the kitchen)

BLANCHE. Then we'll leave it up to Uncle Jack. We'll let him make the decision.

(She starts for the kitchen)

NORA. Why, Momma? I love him but he's not my father.

BLANCHE. Because I need help. Because I don't always know what the right thing to do is . . . Because I say so, that's why.

(She goes into the kitchen, leaving LAURIE *and* EUGENE *standing there staring at the forlorn* NORA*)*

EUGENE. Eugene M. Jerome of New York casts one vote for "yes." *(*NORA *looks up at him, breaks into tears and runs out of the room and up the stairs.* LAURIE *follows her up. He turns toward the audience)* What I'm about to tell you next is so secret and private that I've left instructions for my memoirs not to be opened until thirty years after my death . . . I, Eugene M. Jerome, have committed a mortal sin by lusting after my cousin Nora. I can tell you all this now because I'll be dead when you're reading it . . . If I had my choice between a tryout with the Yankees and actually seeing her bare breasts for two and a half seconds, I would have some serious thinking to do . . .

KATE *(Comes out of the kitchen)*. I need bread.

EUGENE *(Turns quickly)*. What?

KATE. I don't have enough bread. Run across the street to Greenblatt's and get a fresh rye bread.

EUGENE. Again? I went to the store this morning.

KATE. So you'll go again this afternoon.

EUGENE. I'm always going to the store. When I grow up, that's all I'll be trained to do, go to the store.

KATE. You don't want to go? . . . Never mind, I'll go.

EUGENE. *Don't* do that! Don't make me feel guilty. I'll go.

KATE. And get a quarter pound of butter.

EUGENE. I bought a quarter pound of butter this morning. Why don't you buy a half pound at a time?

KATE. And suppose the house burned down this afternoon? Why do I need an extra quarter pound of butter?

(She goes back into the kitchen)

EUGENE *(Turns toward the audience)*. If my mother taught logic in high school, this would be some weird country.

(He runs out of the house to Greenblatt's. Our attention goes to the two girls upstairs in their room. NORA *is crying.* LAURIE *sits on the twin bed opposite her, watching)*

LAURIE. So? What are you going to do?

NORA. I don't know. Leave me alone. Don't just sit there watching me.

LAURIE. It's my room as much as yours. I don't have to leave if I don't want to.

NORA. Do you have to stare at me? Can't I have any privacy?

LAURIE. I'm staring into space. I can't help it if your body interferes. *(There is a pause)* I bet you're worried?

NORA. How would you feel if your entire life depended on what your Uncle Jack decided? ... Oh, God, I wish Daddy were alive.

LAURIE. He would have said "No." He was really *strict.*

NORA. Not with me. I mean, he was strict but he was fair. If he said "No," he always gave you a good reason. He always talked things out ... I wish I could call him somewhere now and ask him what to do. One three-minute call to heaven is all I ask.

LAURIE. Ask Mom. She talks to him every night.

NORA. Who told you that?

LAURIE. She did. Every night before she goes to bed. She puts his picture on her pillow and talks to him. Then she pulls the blanket halfway up the picture and goes to sleep.

NORA. She does not.

LAURIE. She does too. Last year when I had the big fever, I slept in bed with the both of them. In the middle of the night, my face fell on his picture and cut my nose.

NORA. She never told me that ... That's weird.

LAURIE. I can't remember him much anymore. I used to remember him real good but now he disappears a little bit every day.

NORA. Oh, God, he was so handsome. Always dressed so dapper, his shoes always shined. I always thought he should have been a movie star ... like Gary Cooper ... only very short. Mostly I remember his pockets.

LAURIE. His pockets?

NORA. When I was six or seven he always brought me home a little surprise. Like a Hershey or a top. He'd tell me to go get it in his coat pocket. So I'd run to the closet and put my hand in and it felt as big as a tent. I wanted to crawl in there and go to sleep. And there were all these terrific things in there, like Juicy Fruit gum or Spearmint Life Savers and bits of cellophane and crumbled pieces of tobacco and movie stubs and nickels and pennies and rubber bands and paper clips and his gray suede gloves that he wore in the wintertime.

LAURIE. With the stitched lines down the fingers. I remember.

NORA. Then I found his coat in Mom's closet and I put my hand in the pocket. And everything was gone. It was emptied and dry-cleaned and it felt cold ... And that's when I knew he was really dead. *(She thinks for a moment)* Oh, God, I wish we had our own place to live. I hate being a boarder. Listen,

let's make a pact ... The first one who makes enough money promises not to spend any on herself, but saves it all to get a house for you and me and Mom. That means every penny we get from now on, we save for the house. We can't buy *anything.* No lipstick or magazines or nail polish or bubble gum. *Nothing* ... Is it a pact?

LAURIE *(Thinks).* What about movies?

NORA. Movies too.

LAURIE. Starting when?

NORA. Starting today. Starting right now.

LAURIE. Can we start Sunday? I wanted to see *The Thin Man.*

NORA. Who's in it?

LAURIE. William Powell and Myrna Loy.

NORA. Okay. Starting Sunday ... I'll go with you Saturday.

(They shake hands, sealing their "pact," then both lie down in their respective beds and stare up at the ceiling, contemplating their "future home."

EUGENE *returns with a paper bag containing the milk and butter under his arm. He stops, pretends to be a quarterback awaiting the pass from center. The bread is his football)*

EUGENE. Sid Luckman of Columbia waits for the snap from center, the snow is coming down in a near blizzard, he gets it, he fades back, he passes *(He acts all this out)* —AND LUCKMAN'S GOT IT! LUCKMAN CATCHES HIS OWN PASS! HE'S ON THE FIFTY, THE FORTY, THE THIRTY, THE TWENTY ... IT'S A TOUCHDOWN! Columbia wins! They defeat the mighty Crimson of Harvard, thirteen to twelve. Listen to that crowd!

(He roars like a crowd ...)

KATE *(Comes out of the kitchen. She yells out).* EUGENE! STOP THAT YELLING! I HAVE A CAKE IN THE OVEN!

(She goes back into the kitchen. STANLEY JEROME *appears.* STAN *is eighteen and a half. He wears slacks, a shirt and tie, a zip-up jacket and a cap)*

STAN *(In half whisper).* Hey! Eugie!

EUGENE. Hi, Stan! *(To the audience)* My brother Stan. He's okay. You'll like him. *(To* STAN*)* What are you doing home so early?

STAN *(Looks around, lowers his voice).* Is Pop home yet?

EUGENE. No ... Did you ask about the tickets?

STAN. What tickets?

EUGENE. For the Yankee game. You said your boss knew this guy who could get passes. You didn't ask him?

STAN. Me and my boss had other things to

talk about. *(He sits on the steps, his head down, almost in tears)* I'm in trouble, Eug. I mean, really big trouble.

EUGENE *(To the audience)*. This really shocked me. Because Stan is the kind of guy who could talk himself out of *any* kind of trouble. *(To* STAN*)* What kind of trouble?

STAN. I got fired today!

EUGENE *(Shocked)*. Fired? You mean for good?

STAN. You don't get fired temporarily. It's permanent. It's a lifetime firing.

EUGENE. Why? What happened?

STAN. It was on account of Andrew. The colored guy who sweeps up. Well, he was cleaning the floor in the stockroom and he lays his broom against the table to put some junk in the trash can and the broom slips, knocks a can of linseed oil over the table and ruins three brand-new hats right out of the box. Nine-dollar Stetsons. It wasn't his fault. He didn't put the linseed oil there, right?

EUGENE. Right.

STAN. So Mr. Stroheim sees the oily hats and he gets crazy. He says to Andrew the hats are going to have to come out of his salary. Twenty-seven dollars. So Andrew starts to cry.

EUGENE. He cried?

STAN. Forty-two years old, he's bawling all over the stockroom. I mean, the man hasn't got too much furniture upstairs anyway, but he's real sweet. He brings me coffee, always laughing, telling me jokes. I never understand them but I laugh anyway, make him feel good, you know?

EUGENE. Yeah?

STAN. Anyway, I said to Mr. Stroheim I didn't think that was fair. It wasn't Andrew's fault.

EUGENE *(Astounded)*. You said that to him?

STAN. Sure, why not? So Mr. Stroheim says, "You wanna pay for the hats, big mouth?" So I said, "No. I don't want to pay for the hats." So he says, "Then mind your own business, big mouth."

EUGENE. Holy mackerel.

STAN. So Mr. Stroheim looks at me like machine-gun bullets are coming out of his eyes. And then he calmly sends Andrew over to the factory to pick up three new hats. Which is usually my job. So guess what Mr. Stroheim tells *me* to do?

EUGENE. What?

STAN. He tells me to sweep up. He says, for this week I'm the cleaning man.

EUGENE. I can't believe it.

STAN. Everybody is watching me now, waiting to see what I'm going to do. *(EUGENE nods in agreement)* Even Andrew stopped crying and watched. I felt the dignity of everyone who worked in that store was in my hands. So I grit my teeth and I pick up the broom, and there's this big pile of dirt right in the middle of the floor . . .

EUGENE. Yeah?

STAN. . . . and I sweep it all over Mr. Stroheim's shoes. Andrew had just finished shining them this morning, if you want to talk about irony.

EUGENE. I'm dying. I'm actually dying.

STAN *(Enjoying himself)*. You could see everyone in the place is about to bust a gut. Mrs. Mulcahy, the bookkeeper, can hardly keep her false teeth in her mouth. Andrew's eyes are hanging five inches out of their sockets.

EUGENE. This is the greatest story in the history of the world.

STAN. So Mr. Stroheim grabs me and pulls me into his back office, closes the door and pulls down the shades. He gives me this whole story how he was brought up in Germany to respect his superiors. That if he ever—*(With an accent)* "did soch a ting like you do, dey would beat me in der kopf until dey carried me avay dead."

EUGENE. That's perfect. You got him down perfect.

STAN. And I say, "Yeah. But we're not in Germany, old buddy."

EUGENE. You said that to him?

STAN. No. To myself. I didn't want to go too far.

EUGENE. I was wondering.

STAN. Anyway, he says he's always liked me and always thought I was a good boy and that he was going to give me one more chance. He wants a letter of apology. And that if the letter of apology isn't on his desk by nine o'clock tomorrow morning, I can consider myself fired.

EUGENE. I would have had a heart attack . . . What did you say?

STAN. I said I was not going to apologize if Andrew still had to pay for the hats . . . He said that was between him and Andrew, and that he expected the letter from me in the morning . . . I said good night, walked out of his office, got my hat and went home . . . ten minutes early.

EUGENE. I'm sweating. I swear to God, I'm sweating all over.

STAN. I don't know why I did it. But I got

so mad. It just wasn't fair. I mean, if you give in when you're eighteen and a half, you'll give in for the rest of your life, don't you think?

EUGENE. I suppose so . . . So what's the decision? Are you going to write the letter?

STAN *(Thinks)*. . . . No!

EUGENE. Positively?

STAN. Positively. Except I'll have to discuss it with Pop. I know we need the money. But he told me once, you always have to do what you think is right in this world and stand up for your principles.

EUGENE. And what if he says he thinks you're wrong? That you should write the letter.

STAN. He won't. He's gonna leave it up to me, I know it.

EUGENE. But what if he says, "Write the letter"?

STAN. Well, that's something we won't know until after dinner, will we?

(He walks into the house)

EUGENE *(Looks after him, then turns to the audience)*. All in all, it was shaping up to be one heck of a dinner. I'll say this though—I always had this two-way thing about my brother. Either I worshiped the ground he walked on or I hated him so much I wanted to kill him . . . I guess you know how I feel about him today.

(He walks into the house as KATE *comes out of the kitchen carrying a water pitcher for the table.* STAN *has stopped to look at the small pile of mail)*

KATE *(To* EUGENE*)*. All day it takes to bring home bread? Give Aunt Blanche the butter, she's waiting for it.

EUGENE. I was home a half-hour ago. I was talking to Stan.

(He goes into the kitchen)

STAN. Hey, I got a letter from Rosalyn Weiner. Remember her? She moved to Manhattan. They live up on Central Park West.

KATE. Why not? Her father's a gangster, her mother is worse. I don't get a kiss "Hello"?

STAN. Nope. I was going to save it up and give you a giant one for Christmas.

KATE. We don't have Christmas. I'll take it now, thank you. *(He puts his arms around her and kisses her warmly, then embraces her)* A hug too? When do I ever get a hug from you? You must have done something wrong.

STAN. You're too smart for me, Mom. I robbed a barbershop today.

KATE. Is that why you look so tired? You don't get enough sleep. Running around all night with your two hundred girl friends.

STAN. A hundred and thirty. That's all I have, a hundred and thirty.

KATE. How do you get any work done?

STAN. I get it done.

KATE. And your boss doesn't say anything to you? About being tired?

STAN. About being tired? No. He doesn't. *(He starts toward the stairs)*

KATE. Did you ask him about Thursday?

STAN. What?

KATE. You were going to ask him about getting paid this Thursday so I can pay Greenblatt's on Friday. Saturday is a holiday.

STAN. Oh. No. I forgot . . . I'll ask him tomorrow.

KATE. If it's a problem, don't ask him. Greenblatt can wait. Your boss is more important.

STAN. That's not true, Mom. My boss isn't any more important than Mr. Greenblatt.

(He goes upstairs and on to his room, where he lies down, tries to read his letter, then puts it down and stares up at the ceiling wondering about his predicament.

EUGENE *bursts out of the kitchen and practically staggers out of the house. He sits on the steps, his head down, looking very disconsolate. He addresses the audience)*

EUGENE. Oh, God! As if things weren't bad enough . . . and now this! The ultimate tragedy . . . liver and cabbage for dinner! A Jewish medieval torture! . . . My friend Marty Gregorio, an A student in science, told me that cooked cabbage can be smelled farther than sound traveling for seven minutes. If these memoirs are never finished, you'll know it's because I gagged to death one night in the middle of supper. *(We suddenly hear a crash of broken dishes in the kitchen.* EUGENE *turns toward the sound, then to the audience)* You're all witnesses. I was sitting here, right? But I'll get blamed for that, anyway.

(The kitchen door opens and KATE *comes out helping* BLANCHE, *who is wheezing and gasping quite badly. She can't catch her breath)*

BLANCHE. I'm all right. Just let me sit a minute.

KATE. Didn't I tell you to get out of that hot kitchen? *I* can't breathe in there and *I* don't have asthma. *(She calls out)* NORA! LAURIE! Come help your mother!!

(NORA and LAURIE jump up from their beds)

BLANCHE. I'm sick about the plates. I'll replace them. Don't worry about the plates.

KATE. Plates I can always get. I only have one sister.

(The girls have come down the stairs)

NORA. What happened?

BLANCHE. I'm all right. Don't run, Laurie.

KATE. It's another asthma attack. It's the second one this week. Nora, maybe you'd better get the doctor.

BLANCHE. I don't need doctors . . .

KATE. This is no climate for you, near the beach. What you need is someplace dry.

LAURIE. Like Arizona, Momma.

NORA. Should I get the doctor?

BLANCHE. No. No doctors. It's better. It's going away.

LAURIE. I can still hear the whistle.

NORA. Will you shut up!

BLANCHE *(To NORA)*. Help Aunt Kate in the kitchen, Nora. I broke her good plates.

KATE. Never mind—Eugene will do it. You go up and get your mother's medicine . . . Laurie, you sit there quiet and watch your mother. You look pale as a ghost. Eugene!

EUGENE and KATE. Come in here and help me!

JACK *(Offstage)*. Hello, Mrs. Kresky, how are you?

EUGENE *(Gets up, looks off down the street)*. In a minute, Ma. Pop's home!

LAURIE *(Sits next to her mother. To the audience)*. I would now like to introduce my father, a real hard worker. He was born at the age of forty-two . . . Hi, Pop! How you doin', Pop?

(JACOB "JACK" JEROME appears, a man about forty, who could pass for older. He wears a wrinkled suit, brown felt hat and black shoes. The Brooklyn Eagle *sticks up out of his side coat pocket. He carries two large and very heavy cardboard boxes, tied around with hemp cord. He appears to be very tired)*

JACK. How am I doin'?

EUGENE. Let me carry these for you, Pop. *(He reaches for one of the boxes)*

JACK. They're too heavy, you'll hurt yourself.

EUGENE. No. I can do it easy. *(He takes one of the boxes, tries to lift it. It weighs a ton)* Ugh! I just have to get a good grip.

(JACK stops and sits. He wipes his forehead with a handkerchief and holds his chest)

JACK. I want to sit a few minutes.

EUGENE. Are you okay, Pop?

JACK. I'm resting, that's all . . . Get me a glass of cold water.

EUGENE *(Struggles with the first box toward the house)*. I'll be out for the other box in a minute, Pop. *(To the audience)* I don't know how he does it. King Kong couldn't lift these . . . You know what's in here? Noisemakers and party favors. Pop sells them to night clubs and hotels after he gets through every day with his regular work, which is cutting material for ladies' raincoats.

JACK. Did you do your homework today?

EUGENE. Not all of it. Mom sent me to the store fifteen times. *Amos 'n' Andy* is on tonight.

JACK. Do your homework, then we'll discuss *Amos 'n' Andy.*

(EUGENE continues into the house as NORA comes down the stairs with her mother's medicine)

NORA. Here's your medicine, Mom. Laurie, go get some water.

BLANCHE. Laurie shouldn't be running.

EUGENE *(The hero)*. I'll get it, Nora.

NORA. You sure you don't mind?

EUGENE. No. No trouble at all. *(To the audience)* Two and a half seconds, that's all I ask. *(He goes into the kitchen)*

NORA *(To BLANCHE)*. When are you going to speak to Uncle Jack, Mom?

BLANCHE. When I speak to him, that's when I'll speak to him.

NORA. Tonight? I have to know tonight.

BLANCHE. I'll see . . . If he's not too tired, I'll talk to him tonight.

KATE *(Comes out of the kitchen)*. Jack's home. We'll eat in ten minutes. Nora, darling, go get Stanley . . . How's your mother, Laurie?

LAURIE. Much better. The whistling's stopped.

(KATE walks to the front door and goes out. JACK is sitting on the stoop, wiping his neck. NORA goes upstairs)

KATE. What's wrong? Eugene said you were holding your chest.

JACK. I wasn't holding my chest.

KATE. You have to carry that box every day? Back and forth to the city. You don't work hard enough, Jack?

JACK. You want the box, it's yours. Keep it. I don't need it anymore.

KATE. What do you mean?

JACK. Del Mars Party Favors went out of business. They closed him out. The man is bankrupt.

KATE. Oh, my God!

JACK. He never even warned me it was coming.

KATE. You told me he lived up on Riverside Drive. With a view of the river. A three-hundred-dollar-a-month apartment he had. A man like that.

JACK. Who are the ones you think go bankrupt? You live in a cold-water flat on Delancey Street, bankruptcy is the one thing God spares you.

KATE. All right . . . You can always find good in something. You don't have to lug that box anymore. You don't have to get up at five-thirty in the morning. We can all eat dinner at a decent hour. You still have your job with Jacobson, we won't starve.

JACK. I can't make ends meet with what I make at Jacobson's. Not with seven people to feed.

KATE *(Looks back toward the house)*. They'll hear you. We'll talk later.

JACK. I can't get by without that extra twenty-five dollars a week. I can't pay rent and insurance and food and clothing for seven people. Christmas and New Year's alone I made a hundred and fifty dollars.

KATE *(Nervous about someone hearing)*. Stop it, Jack. You'll only get yourself sick.

JACK. He didn't even pay me for the week, the bastard. Five salesmen are laid off and he's going to a Broadway show tonight. I stuffed every hat and noisemaker I could carry in that box and walked out of there. At his funeral I'll put on a pointy hat and blow a horn, the bastard!

KATE. Don't talk like that. Something'll come up. You'll go to temple this weekend. You'll pray all day Saturday.

JACK *(Smiles ironically)*. There's men in that temple who've been praying for forty years. You know how many prayers have to get answered before my turn comes up?

KATE *(Rubs his back where it pains him)*. Your turn'll come up. God has time for everybody.

(EUGENE has come out of the kitchen with two glasses of water. He walks over to BLANCHE)

EUGENE. Here's your water, Aunt Blanche.

BLANCHE. Thank you, darling.

EUGENE. Where's Nora?

LAURIE. She went up to call Stanley for dinner.

EUGENE. Hey, Laurie—you want to take a walk on the beach tonight?

LAURIE. I have homework. What do you want to walk with me for?

EUGENE. You, me and Nora. I just felt like taking a walk.

LAURIE. I think Nora has a date with Larry Clurman.

EUGENE. *Larry Clurman?* She likes Larry Clurman?

LAURIE. I don't know. Ask her yourself.

EUGENE. Larry Clurman is my father's age.

LAURIE. He's twenty.

EUGENE. Same thing . . . You think he's good-looking?

LAURIE. I don't think *anybody's* good-looking.

EUGENE. Larry Clurman? He doesn't even have a chin. His tie comes all the way up to his teeth.

KATE *(Calls out)*. Eugene! Where's your father's water?

EUGENE. I'm coming! I'm coming. *(As he walks through the front door, he turns to the audience)* Now I've got Larry Clurman to contend with. *(He comes out)* Here's your water, Pop. I put ice in it.

(He hands a glass of water to his father, who drinks it all)

KATE. Don't drink so fast.

EUGENE. Do you have time to look at my sneakers, Pop?

KATE. What does he want to look at your sneakers for?

EUGENE. They have no soles. They're hanging on by a tiny piece of rubber. I have to clench my toes when I run out for a fly ball.

JACK. I bought you new sneakers last month.

EUGENE. Last year, Pa. Not last month. I can only wear them two hours a day because my toes can't grow in them.

KATE. This is no time to talk to your father about sneakers. He's got enough on his mind. Turn the light down on the liver. *(EUGENE goes inside and into the kitchen. To JACK)* We'll talk about this tonight. You'll eat a nice dinner, relax, and when everybody's asleep, we'll figure things out calmly. I don't like it when you get upset.

BLANCHE. I'm feeling better. Come, dear, help me with dinner.

JACK *(Looks at the house)*. You think she'll ever get married?

KATE. Blanche?

JACK. She's not unattractive. I see men look at her on the beach. What does she want to waste her life in this house for?

KATE. She's raising two children.

JACK. Why doesn't she ever go out? If she wants to meet people, I know plenty of single men.

KATE. Blanche isn't the type to get married.

JACK. She was married once, wasn't she? Those are the type that get married.

KATE. Dave was different. She's not interested in other men.

JACK. What about that Murphy fellow across the street? He's plenty interested, believe me.

KATE. That drunk! The man can't find his way into the house at night. He slept in the doorway once. In the rain. He was there when I went out to get the milk.

JACK. He's got a good-paying job, lives alone with his mother. So he takes a drink on a Saturday night. Maybe what he needs is a good woman.

KATE. Not my sister. Let him meet someone lying in the next doorway. I don't want to discuss this anymore.

(She goes inside and into the kitchen. JACK sighs, gets up slowly and follows her in. Our attention goes to STANLEY on his bed still reading the letter from Rosalyn Weiner. He suddenly sits up. NORA knocks on the door)

STANLEY. Come in.

NORA *(Entering)*. Are you busy? I wanted to talk to you.

STANLEY. That's funny, because I wanted to talk to *you*.

NORA. About what?

STANLEY. I need a favor. Real bad. You're the only one who can help me.

NORA. What is it?

STANLEY. Well, when Pop comes home tired, he doesn't usually pay too much attention to me and Eugene. He's different with you. He's always interested in what you have to say.

NORA. Really? I hope so.

STANLEY. Oh, sure. You never noticed that?

NORA. Not really. What's the favor?

STANLEY. This may sound dumb, but at dinner, do you think you could steer the conversation in a certain direction?

NORA. What direction?

STANLEY. Well, something like how much you "admire people who stand up for their principles."

NORA. *What* people?

STANLEY. *Any* people. "Principles" is the important word. If you could work it in three or four times, I'd be very grateful.

NORA. Three or four times??

STANLEY. It'll be easy. I'll mention someone like Abraham Lincoln and you look up and say, "Now there's a man who really stood up for his principles."

NORA. I have my *own* things to bring up at dinner. I don't want to get into a discussion about Abraham Lincoln.

STANLEY. Not his whole life. Just his principles.

NORA. Why would I do such a stupid thing?

STANLEY. Because as of tomorrow I'm unemployed ... unless someone besides me mentions "sticking up for your principles."

NORA. What happened? Did you get fired?

STANLEY. I will be unless I write Kaiser Wilhelm a letter of apology. It's really up to my old man. I've decided to do whatever he tells me ...

NORA. When are you going to ask him?

STANLEY. Tonight. Right after dinner.

NORA. *Tonight?* Does it have to be tonight?

STANLEY. That's the deadline. I have to give my answer to Mr. Stroheim in the morning. Why?

NORA. Couldn't you ask your father in the morning?

STANLEY. He gets up at five-thirty. My mother has to line up his shoes at night because he can't make decisions at five-thirty. *(She is about to break into tears)* What's wrong, Nora?

NORA *(Angrily)*. I don't know what *you* have to complain about. At least your father is alive and around the house to make decisions. You don't know when you're well off, Stanley. Sometimes you make me sick!

(She runs out of the room, slamming the door behind her. STANLEY sits there looking bewildered. EUGENE walks into the dining room facing the audience. He looks at them and speaks)

EUGENE. Chapter Seven—"The Infamous Dinner"! *(The others drift into the dining room, taking their seats. BLANCHE and KATE bring most of the dishes, passing them around. They are all seated as he continues his narrative)* It started out like a murder mystery in Blenheim Castle. No one said a word but everyone looked suspicious ... It was so quiet, you could hear Laurie's soup going down her esophagus. *(They sit silent, eating)* Everyone had one eye on their plate and the other eye on Pop. Except me. I sat opposite Nora. *(He sits opposite NORA)* I kept dropping my napkin a lot so I could bend down to get a good look at those virginal creamy-white legs. She was really deep in thought because she left herself unguarded a few times and I got to see halfway up her thighs that led to the Golden Palace of the Himalayas.

KATE. Eugene! Keep your napkin on your lap and stop daydreaming.

EUGENE *(To the audience)*. Stanley knew what I was doing because he's the one who taught it to me. But he was busy with his own problems, like everyone else. You could hear the clock ticking in the kitchen. The tension in the air was so thick, you could cut it with a knife. Which is more than I could say for the liver.

(He tries to cut his liver)

JACK. Ketchup . . . mustard . . . pickles . . .

EUGENE. I'm through. I'll help with the dessert.

KATE. Finish your liver.

EUGENE. I finished. Do you see liver on my plate?

KATE. You buried it under the mashed potatoes. I know your tricks. Look how Laurie ate hers.

EUGENE *(To the audience).* I had a major problem. One more bite and I would have thrown up on the table. That's a sight Nora would have remembered forever. A diversion was my only escape from humiliation. *(To STANLEY)* So how's things down at Stroheim's, Stanley? *(STANLEY, who is drinking water, slams down the glass, splashing it. He glares at EUGENE, who continues to address the audience)* I felt bad about that, but for the moment, attention had shifted away from my liver.

JACK *(To STANLEY).* How long have you been working there now?

STANLEY. Where?

JACK. At Stroheim's.

STANLEY. At Stroheim's? Let me see . . . part-time a year and a half before I graduated high school. And a year since then.

JACK. So what's that?

STANLEY. Two and a half years, counting part-time.

JACK. And he likes you?

STANLEY. Who?

JACK *(Impatiently).* Mr. Stroheim.

STANLEY. Yeah. Usually he likes me. Sometimes I'm not sure.

JACK. You come in on time?

STANLEY. Yeah.

JACK. You do your work?

STANLEY. Yeah.

JACK. You get along with the other people?

STANLEY. Yeah.

JACK. So why shouldn't he like you? How much are you making now?

STANLEY. Seventeen dollars a week.

JACK. It's time you moved up. Tomorrow you go in and ask him for a raise.

STANLEY. A RAISE???

JACK. If you don't speak up, people take advantage of you. Tomorrow morning you go into his office, you're polite, you're respectful, but you're firm. You tell him you

think you're worth another five dollars a week.

STANLEY. *FIVE DOLLARS????*

JACK. He'll offer you a dollar and a quarter, you settle for two-fifty. I know how these things work. You're a high school graduate, he's lucky he's got you.

STANLEY. I don't think this is the time to ask him for a raise, Pop. I think his wife is very sick.

JACK. You're afraid to ask him? You want me to take you by the hand and walk into his office and say, "My little boy wants a raise"?

STANLEY. I'm not afraid.

KATE. Your father wouldn't ask you if he didn't think it was the right thing. Believe me, Stanley, now is the time to ask for it.

EUGENE *(Choking).* Ma, I think I have a bone in my throat.

KATE. There are no bones in liver.

(He runs into the kitchen)

LAURIE. So what's new at dancing school, Nora?

NORA *(Glares at her). Nothing* is new. Mind your own business.

LAURIE. I'm just trying to introduce the subject.

NORA. I don't need your help. Will you tell her to be quiet, Mother.

BLANCHE. Laurie, you may be excused if you're finished.

JACK. What happened at dancing school?

BLANCHE. Nora received a very nice compliment from her teacher. She said Nora had professional potential.

LAURIE. He didn't say "potential." "Potential" is the future. Mr. Beckman is interested in Nora's "immediate present."

JACK *(Still eating).* Isn't that something! Mr. Beckman is your teacher?

NORA. No. He's one of the most widely known and respected producers on Broadway.

JACK. Broadway? Imagine that. That's wonderful. And how are you doing in school otherwise?

NORA *(Looks at her mother).* I'm doing fine.

BLANCHE. She's doing very well.

LAURIE. I wish *I* was as smart as she is.

EUGENE. Isn't that the same Mr. Beckman who's producing the great Broadway extravaganza *Abracadabra?* I hear if a girl gets hired for the chorus of a show like that, not only is her career practically guaranteed, but the experience she gains is equal to a four-year college education.

KATE. Eugene, that's enough.

JACK. Only a four-year college education is equal to a four-year college education.

STANLEY. I don't think Abraham Lincoln went to college.

(NORA *goes into the kitchen*)

JACK. What about you, Laurie? You're feeling all right?

LAURIE. Yes, Uncle Jack.

JACK. You getting plenty of fresh air?

(NORA *returns*)

LAURIE. As much as I can hold in my lungs. Nora, did you tell Uncle Jack about the big tank that's filled with water?

BLANCHE. Girls, why don't we just let Uncle Jack eat his dinner? If we have something to discuss, we can discuss it later.

JACK. Somebody has something to discuss? If there's a problem, this is the time to bring it up. This is the family hour.

EUGENE. What a great idea for a radio show. *The Family Hour.* Every Wednesday night you hear a different family eating dinner discussing their problems of the week. And you get to hear different recipes. (*As announcer*) "WEAF presents dinner at Brighton Beach starring the Jacob Jerome Family and featuring tonight's specialty, liver and cabbage, brought to you by Ex-Lax, the mild laxative."

KATE. The whole country's going to hear about a fifteen-year-old boy gagging on liver?

JACK. Nothing to discuss? Nobody has any problems? Otherwise I want to turn on the news.

STANLEY. Well, as a matter of fact . . .

JACK. What?

STANLEY. Nothing.

EUGENE. I'll help with the dishes.

KATE. You sit there and finish your liver.

EUGENE. I can't swallow it. It won't go down. Remember the lima-bean catastrophe last month? Does anybody want to see a repeat of that disgusting episode?

JACK. Why does he always talk like it's a Sherlock Holmes story?

STANLEY. He thinks he's a writer.

EUGENE. And what do you think *you* are?

KATE. Eat half of it.

EUGENE. Which half? They're both terrible.

KATE. A quarter of it. Two bites.

EUGENE. *One* bite.

KATE. *Two* bites.

EUGENE. I know you. If I eat one bite, you'll make me eat another bite . . . I'll take it to my room. I'll eat it tonight. I need time to chew it.

JACK. These are not times to waste food. If you didn't want it, Eugene, you shouldn't have taken it.

EUGENE. I didn't take it. They gave it to me. It comes attached to the plate.

NORA. If it's so important to everybody, I'll eat your liver, Eugene.

(*They all look at her*)

EUGENE. You *will*?

NORA. It seems to be the only thing this family is worried about. (*She takes his plate*) Give me your liver so we can get on with more important things in our lives.

JACK. Nora's right. Take the liver away. If nobody likes it, why do you make it?

KATE (*Angrily*). Because we can't afford a roast beef for seven people.

(*She heads for the kitchen*)

EUGENE (*To the audience*). I suddenly felt vulgar and cheap.

JACK. Stanley, turn on the news.

BLANCHE. Laurie, get off your feet. You look tired to me.

STANLEY. Can I talk to you a minute, Pop? It's something really important.

JACK. More important than what's going on in Europe?

(*He turns on the radio*)

STANLEY. It's not more important. It's just coming up sooner.

JACK (*Fiddles with the dial*). Hitler's already moved into Austria. In a couple of months the whole world will be in it . . . What's the matter with this radio?

(*It is barely audible*)

KATE (*Comes out of the kitchen*). Someone's been fooling around with it. Haven't they, Eugene?

EUGENE. Why "Eugene"? Pop had the news on last night.

KATE. You weren't listening to the ball game this afternoon?

JACK. He's talking about Poland . . . Dammit! I don't want anyone touching this radio anymore, you understand?

EUGENE (*To the audience*). Guess who's gonna get blamed for the war in Europe?

KATE. Eugene! Bring in the knives and forks.

(*He does.* JACK *turns off the radio*)

STANLEY. You really think there'll be war, Pop? I mean, America too?

JACK. We're already in it. Not us maybe. But friends, relatives. If you're Jewish, you've got a cousin suffering *somewhere* in the world.

KATE *(Wiping the table)*. Ida Kazinsky's family got out of Poland last month. The stories she tells about what's going on there, you don't even want to hear.

STANLEY. How many relatives do we have in Europe?

KATE. Enough. Uncles, cousins. I have a great-aunt. Your father has nephews.

JACK. I have a cousin, Sholem, in Poland. His whole family.

BLANCHE. Dave had relatives in Warsaw. That's where his mother was born.

STANLEY. What if they got to America? Where would they live?

JACK. Who?

STANLEY. Your nephews. Mom's cousins and uncles. Would we take them in?

JACK *(Looks at* KATE*)*. What God gives us to deal with, we deal with.

STANLEY. Where would we put them?

KATE. What are you worrying about things like that now for? Go upstairs and work on your speech.

STANLEY. What speech?

KATE. How you're going to ask Mr. Stroheim for a raise tomorrow.

STANLEY *(Looks apprehensively at* EUGENE*)*. Can I talk to you later, Pop? After you've rested and read your paper?

EUGENE *(Has taken part of his father's paper, opens it)*. Lou Gehrig got two hits today. Larrupin Lou is hitting three-oh-two!

KATE *(Grabs the paper away)*. Is that your paper? How many times have I told you you don't read it until your father is finished?

EUGENE. I didn't break it. The print doesn't come off if I take a quick look at it.

JACK. Don't be fresh to your mother. Upstairs.

STANLEY. Pop?

JACK. Everybody.

STANLEY. I'll come down later, okay, Pop?

EUGENE. C'mon, Stan. I have to talk to you anyway.

(They start toward the stairs)

STANLEY *(To* EUGENE*)*. You're a pest! Did anyone ever tell you you're a pest?

EUGENE. Yeah. I have a list upstairs. You wanna add your name to it?

(He taps STANLEY *on the forehead with his forefinger. It is annoying and* STAN *chases him up the stairs)*

KATE *(To* JACK*)*. Maybe you should lie down. There's nothing in that paper that's going to cheer you up.

JACK *(Thoughtfully)*. What *would* we do,

Kate? Where would we put them if they got off the boat and knocked on our door? How would we feed them?

KATE. The boat didn't get here yet. I can't deal with boats that haven't landed yet.

*(*NORA *bursts out of the kitchen, apparently having just argued with her mother. She is followed by* BLANCHE *and* LAURIE*)*

NORA *(Determined)*. Uncle Jack! I know you're tired and you have a lot of things on your mind, but the rest of my life may depend on your decision and I have to know tonight because I have to call Mr. Beckman and let him know if I can go or not.

JACK. Who's Mr. Beckman?

NORA. The Broadway producer we talked about at dinner.

LAURIE. *Abracadabra?* Remember?

(We see STANLEY *walk to the bathroom—*EUGENE *walks into the bedroom)*

BLANCHE. Laurie! Upstairs! This minute . . . Nora, not now. This isn't the time.

NORA *(Angrily)*. It's *never* the time. You won't make a decision and I don't have anyone else I can talk to. Well, I'll make my own decision if no one else is interested. I'm sixteen and a half years old and I'll do what I *want* to do.

(The tears begin to flow as she runs out the front door to the yard)

JACK. What is this all about?

KATE. Go on out, Jack. Talk to her.

BLANCHE. I'll take care of it. Nora's right. It's my decision.

KATE. What are you going to tell her? That she can leave school? That she can throw her future away? Is that what you want to do?

BLANCHE. What if I'm wrong? What if she's got talent? What is it I'm *supposed* to say?

JACK. She can't talk to me? It's all the same family, isn't it? I'm her uncle, for God's sake.

KATE. She doesn't need an uncle tonight. She needs a father . . . Go on. She'll tell you.

*(*JACK *looks at them both, then walks out to the front yard.* NORA *is sitting on the bench, tearfully)*

BLANCHE. I never learned . . .

JACK *(To* NORA*)*. You mind if I sit with you?

BLANCHE. I wrapped my life up in Dave so much, I never learned to be their mother.

JACK. If you want to talk, we'll talk; if not, not.

KATE. We have enough mothers here. This is a family. The world doesn't survive without families . . . Laurie, do your homework. Blanche, make me some tea. You're the only one here who makes decent tea.

(LAURIE *goes up to her room.* BLANCHE *and* KATE *have gone into the kitchen*)

JACK. Listen . . . I know what it's like, Nora. Not to be heard.

NORA. You do?

JACK. I grew up in a family of four children. My father, before he died, never could remember our names. My oldest brother was "the big one," I was "the little one." My brother Sol was "the rotten one," Eddie was "the skinny one."

NORA. Who am I?

JACK. The pretty one . . . What's the problem?

(STANLEY *walks from the bathroom, into the bedroom*)

NORA. I don't know. It doesn't seem very important now.

JACK. I've never seen you cry over something that wasn't important. I know I'm not your father. It's not my place to make decisions for you. But I can offer advice. Advice is free. If it doesn't fit, you can always return it.

NORA. Can we walk down the block?

JACK. Sure. We'll take a look at the ocean. My father always used to say, "Throw your problems out to sea and the answers will wash back up on the shore."

NORA. Did they?

JACK. Not in Brighton Beach. Orange peels and watermelon pits washed up. That's why it's good to take someone who knows how to give advice.

(*She gets up and they walk off toward the beach.* STANLEY *is lying on his bed, hands under his head, deep in thought.* EUGENE *sits on his bed, banging a baseball into his glove*)

STANLEY. Will you stop that? I'm trying to think.

EUGENE. I'm glad I don't have your problems.

STANLEY. How'd you like an official American League baseball in your mouth?

EUGENE. I've got to talk to you, Stanley. I mean a really serious, important talk.

STANLEY. Everybody in this house has to have a talk with somebody. Take a number off the wall and wait your turn.

EUGENE. I had a dream last night. It was about this girl. I can't tell you her name but she's gorgeous. We were really kissing hard and rubbing up against each other and I felt this tremendous build-up coming like at the end of *The Thirty-nine Steps.* And suddenly there was an explosion. Like a dam broke

and everything rushed and flowed out to sea. It was the greatest feeling I ever had in my life . . . and when I woke up, I was—I was—

STANLEY. All wet.

EUGENE (*Surprised*). Yeah! How'd you know?

STANLEY (*Unimpressed*). It was a wet dream. You had a wet dream. I have them all the time.

EUGENE. You do? You mean there's nothing wrong with you if it happens?

STANLEY. You never had one before?

EUGENE. Yeah, but I slept through it.

STANLEY. Didn't you ever try to do it by yourself?

EUGENE. What do you mean?

STANLEY. Didn't you ever diddle with yourself?

EUGENE. No. Never.

STANLEY. Baloney. I've heard you. You diddle three, four times a week.

EUGENE. You're crazy! What do you mean, diddle?

STANLEY. Whack off. Masturbate.

EUGENE. Will you be quiet! Laurie might hear you.

STANLEY. There's nothing wrong with it. Everybody does it. Especially at our age. It's natural.

EUGENE. What do you mean, everybody? You know guys who do it?

STANLEY. Every guy I know does it. Except Haskell Fleischmann, the fat kid. He does it to the other guys.

EUGENE. I can't believe I'm having this conversation.

STANLEY. You can't grow up without doing it. Your voice won't change.

EUGENE. Where do you get this stuff from? Is it in a medical book or something?

STANLEY. It's puberty.

EUGENE. It's what?

STANLEY. Puberty. You never heard that word before? You don't read books?

EUGENE. Yeah. *The Citadel* by A. J. Cronin. He never mentioned puberty.

STANLEY. Even Pop did it.

EUGENE. Pop? *Our* pop? You know what, Stanley? I think you're full of shit.

STANLEY (*Sits up*). Hey! Don't you use that language. Who do you think you are? You're just a kid. Never let me hear you say that word again.

EUGENE. I don't get you. You mean it's okay for you to say "puberty" but I can't say "shit"?

STANLEY. "Puberty" is a scientific word. "Shit" is for those guys who hang around the beach.

EUGENE. What do you expect me to say when you tell me that Pop whacks off?

STANLEY. I don't mean he still does it, because he's married now. But when he was a kid. Fourteen or fifteen. The whole world whacks off.

EUGENE. President Roosevelt too?

STANLEY. Rich kids are the worst. They whack off from morning till night. In college, they sit around in their dorms drinking beer and whacking off.

EUGENE. Stanley, this is the most useful information you ever taught me . . . What about girls?

STANLEY. Five times as much as boys.

EUGENE. *Five* times as much? Is that an actual figure? Where do you know all this from?

STANLEY. You pick it up. You learn it. It's handed down from generation to generation. That's how our culture spreads.

EUGENE. Five times as much as boys? Some of them don't even say hello to you and they're home all night whacking off.

STANLEY. They're human just like we are. They have the same needs and desires.

EUGENE. Then why is it so hard to touch their boobs?

STANLEY. If you were a girl, would you like some guy jumping at you and grabbing your boobs?

EUGENE. If I had boobs, I would love to touch them, wouldn't you?

STANLEY. I've got my own problems to think about.

EUGENE. How do girls do it?

STANLEY. I can't explain it.

EUGENE. Please, Stanley. I'll be your slave for a month. Tell me how they do it.

STANLEY. I need a pencil and paper. I'll do it later.

EUGENE *(Quickly hands him his notebook and a pencil).* Do you want crayons? Maybe you should do it in color?

STANLEY. Hey, Eugene. I have a major problem in my life. I haven't got time to draw girls masturbating for you.

EUGENE. I'll bet Nora doesn't do it.

STANLEY. Boy, could I win money from you. You think she's in the bathroom seven times a day just taking showers?

EUGENE. She does it in the bathroom?

STANLEY. I knew two girls who used to do it in English class. I saw a girl do it during a final exam and she got a ninety-eight on her paper . . . Is she the one you were thinking about last night?

EUGENE. No. It was somebody else. One of the beach girls.

STANLEY. It was Nora. I see what's going on. I knew why you dropped your napkin twelve times at dinner tonight.

EUGENE. She drives me crazy. I think I'm in love with her.

STANLEY. Yeah? Well, forget it. She's your cousin.

EUGENE. What's wrong with being in love with your cousin?

STANLEY. Because it's against the laws of nature. If she was your stepsister, it would be dirty, but it would be okay. But you can't love your own cousin. Let me give you a piece of advice: When you're going through puberty, don't start with anyone in your own house.

EUGENE. Who made up those rules? Franklin Roosevelt married his cousin.

STANLEY. Maybe she was his second or third cousin. But you can't marry your first cousin. You get babies with nine heads . . . I wish Pop would get back. I got to talk to him tonight.

EUGENE. I still would love to see her naked. Just once. There's nothing wrong with that, is there?

STANLEY. No. I do it all the time.

EUGENE. *You've seen Nora naked?*

STANLEY. Lots of times. I fixed the lock on the bathroom door, then opened it pretending I didn't know anyone was in there.

EUGENE. I can't believe it. What a pig! . . . What did she look like?

STANLEY. All I can tell you is I was pretty miserable she was my first cousin.

(He lies back on his bed. EUGENE *turns and looks out at the audience)*

EUGENE. That was the night I discovered lust and guilt were very closely related. *(To* STANLEY*)* I have to wash up.

STANLEY *(Teasingly).* Have a good time.

EUGENE. I don't do that.

*(*BLANCHE *and* KATE *come out of the kitchen. They each have a cup of tea. They sit at the dining table)*

KATE. I'm sorry. I forgot it was this Tuesday. I'll change my doctor appointment.

BLANCHE. You don't have to change anything. The girls will be with me.

KATE. Have I ever missed a year going to

the grave? Dave was my favorite in the whole family, you know that.

BLANCHE. You realize it'll be six years? Sometimes I forget his birthday, but the day he died I never forget.

KATE. There wasn't another one like him.

BLANCHE. Laurie asks me questions about him all the time. Was he funny? What was the funniest thing he ever said, she asked me. I couldn't remember. Isn't that awful, Kate?

KATE. Sometimes you talk like your life is over. You're still a young woman. You're still beautiful, if you'd ever stop squinting so much.

BLANCHE. I went with him for two years before we were married. What was I waiting for? That's two married years I didn't have with him.

KATE. Listen. Jack's company is having their annual affair in New York next Wednesday. At the Commodore Hotel. You should see how some of those women get dressed up. Jack wants you to come with us. He told me to ask you.

BLANCHE. Me? Who do I know in Jack's company?

KATE. You'll be with *us*. You'll meet people. Max Green'll be at our table. He's the one whose wife died last year from *(She whispers)* —tuberculosis . . . He's their number one salesman. He lives in a hotel on the Grand Concourse. He's a riot. You'll like him. Maybe you'll dance with him. What else are you going to do here every night?

BLANCHE. I don't have a dress to wear for a thing like that.

KATE. You'll make something. Jack'll get you some material. He knows everybody in the garment district.

BLANCHE. Thank you, Kate. I appreciate it. I can't go. Maybe next year.

KATE. Next year you won't have any eyes altogether. What are you afraid of, Blanche? Dave is dead. You're not. If God wanted the both of you, you'd be laying in the grave next to him.

BLANCHE. I've made plans for next Wednesday night.

KATE. More important than this? They have this affair once a year.

BLANCHE. I'm having dinner with someone.

KATE. You're having dinner? With a man? That's wonderful. Why didn't you tell me?

BLANCHE. With Mr. Murphy.

(This stops KATE *right in her tracks)*

KATE. Who's Mr. Murphy? . . . Oh, my God! I don't understand you. You're going to dinner with that man? Do you know where he'll take you? To a saloon. To a Bar and Grill, that's where he'll take you.

BLANCHE. We're going to Chardov's, the Hungarian restaurant. You never even met the man, why do you dislike him so much?

KATE. I don't have to meet that kind. I just have to smell his breath when he opens the window. What do you think a man like that is looking for? I grew up with that kind on Avenue A. How many times have Stanley and Gene come home from school black and blue from the beatings they took from those Irish hooligans? What have you got to talk to with a man like that?

BLANCHE. Is that why you don't like him? Because he's Irish? When have the Jews and the Irish ever fought a war? You know who George Bernard Shaw is?

KATE. I don't care who he is.

BLANCHE. One of the greatest Irish writers in the world? What would you say if *he* took me to Chardov's next Wednesday?

KATE. Is Mr. Murphy a writer? Tell him to bring me some of his books, I'll be glad to read them.

BLANCHE. Kate, when are you going to give up being an older sister?

KATE. I've heard stories about him. With women. They like their women, you know. Well, if that's what you want, it's your business.

EUGENE *(To the audience)*. I decided to go downstairs and quiet my passion with oatmeal cookies.

BLANCHE. We took a walk along the beach last Thursday. He hardly said a word. He's very shy. Very quiet. He told me where his parents came from in Ireland. Their life wasn't any easier than Momma and Poppa's in Russia.

KATE. *Nobody* had it like they had it in Russia.

BLANCHE. He holds down a decent job in a printers' office and he didn't smell of liquor and he behaved like a perfect gentleman.

*(*EUGENE *comes down the stairs. He had been listening)*

KATE *(Without turning)*. No cookies for you. Not until you eat that liver.

EUGENE. You're still saving it? You mean it's going to be in the icebox until I grow up?

KATE. No cookies, you hear me?

EUGENE. I just want a glass of water.

KATE. You have water in your bathroom.

EUGENE. There's toothpaste in the glass. It makes me nauseous.

(He goes into the kitchen)

KATE *(To* BLANCHE*)*. Listen, there's no point discussing this. I'm going to bed. Do what you want.

BLANCHE. Kate! . . . I don't want to do anything that's going to make you unhappy. Or Jack. I owe too much to you. I can't live off you the rest of my life. Every decent job I've tried to get, they turn me down because of my eyes. The thought of marrying Frank Murphy hasn't even occurred to me. Maybe not even to him. But I don't think one dinner at Chardov's is the end of the world.

KATE. I just don't want to see you get hurt. I never mean you harm. I can take anything except when someone in the family is mad at me.

BLANCHE *(Embraces her)*. I could never be mad at you, Kate. That I promise you to my dying day.

KATE. Go on. Have dinner with Frank Murphy. If Poppa ever heard me say those words, he'd get up from the cemetery and stand in front of our house with a big stick.

*(*BLANCHE *kisses her again)*

BLANCHE. I told him to pick me up here. Is that all right?

KATE. *Here?* In *my* house?

BLANCHE. For two minutes. I wanted you to meet him. At least see what he's like.

KATE. Tell his mother to wash her windows, maybe I'd know what he's like.

(We see NORA *hurriedly cross the front yard and open the front door. She looks upset.* NORA *walks over to her mother, determined)*

NORA. Can I see Mr. Beckman tomorrow? Yes or no?

*(*JACK *crosses the front yard)*

BLANCHE. Did you talk to Uncle Jack?

NORA. I talked to Uncle Jack. I want an answer from *you,* Mother. Yes or no?

*(*JACK *enters the house)*

BLANCHE. What did he say?

NORA. It doesn't matter what he said. It's your decision or mine. Who's going to make it, Mother?

JACK. I said if I were her father, I'd tell her to finish high school. If she's got talent, there'll be plenty of other shows. I never got past the eighth grade and that's why I spend half my life on the subway and the other half trying to make a few extra dollars to keep this family from being out on the street.

NORA *(To* BLANCHE*)*. I don't want this just for myself, Momma, but for you and for Laurie. In a few years we could have a house of our own, instead of all being cooped up here like animals. We could pay Uncle Jack for what he's given us all these years. I'm asking for a way out, Momma. Don't shut me in. Don't shut me in for the rest of my life.

(They all turn and look at BLANCHE*)*

BLANCHE. You promised you'd do what Uncle Jack said.

NORA. He doesn't make decisions—he offers advice. I want a decision, Momma. From you . . . Please!

BLANCHE. You finish high school. You tell Mr. Beckman you're too young. You tell him your mother said "No" . . . That's my decision.

NORA *(Looks at her, frustrated)*. I see. *(To* JACK*)* Thank you very much, Uncle Jack, for your advice. *(To* BLANCHE*)* I'll let you know in the morning what *my* decision is.

(She rushes upstairs to her room. BLANCHE *starts to go after her)*

KATE. Let her go, Blanche. Let her sleep on it. You'll only make it worse.

BLANCHE. It seems no matter *what* I do, I only make it worse.

(She turns, starts up the stairs.

NORA *has slammed the door of her room.* STANLEY *hears it and opens his door and starts down)*

JACK *(To* KATE*)*. What could I tell her? What could I say?

KATE *(Shrugs)*. You inherit a family, you inherit their problems.

EUGENE *(Comes out of the kitchen)*. Well, good night.

KATE. Put the cookie on the table.

EUGENE. What cookie?

KATE. The oatmeal cookie in your pocket. Put it on the table.

EUGENE. You can smell an oatmeal cookie from ten feet away?

KATE. I heard the jar moving in the kitchen. Suddenly everybody's doing what they want in this house. Your father's upset, Aunt Blanche is upset, *put the cookie on that table!*

*(*EUGENE *puts the cookie on the table and starts up the stairs to his room. He passes* STANLEY*)*

STANLEY *(To* EUGENE*)*. I heard a lot of yelling. What happened?

EUGENE. I don't know, but it's my fault.

(He goes on up and into the bathroom.

NORA *is on her bed, crying.* LAURIE *sits on her bed and watches her)*

LAURIE. What are you going to do? *(*NORA

shakes her head, indicating she doesn't know) Do you want *me* to speak to Mom? I could tell her I was getting flutters in my heart again.

NORA *(Turns, angrily).* Don't you ever say that! Don't you pretend to be sick to get favors from anyone.

LAURIE. I'm not pretending. They're just not *big* flutters.

(STANLEY has been sitting at the top of the stairs trying to work up courage to talk to his father. JACK is sitting in the living room, disconsolate. KATE is puffing up pillows)

JACK. Stop puffing up pillows. The house could be burning down and you'd run back in to puff up the pillows.

KATE. Let's go to bed. You're tired.

JACK. When does it get easier, Kate? When does our life get easier?

KATE. At night. When you get seven good hours of sleep. That's the easiest it ever gets.

(NORA has put on her robe, left her room and opens the bathroom door. We hear a scream from EUGENE)

EUGENE. *CLOSE THE DOOR!!!*

NORA. Oh. I'm sorry. I didn't know anyone was in there.

(She rushes out, back to her room.

STANLEY *moves into the living room)*

STANLEY. Dad? Do you think I could talk to you now? It'll just take five minutes.

KATE. He's tired, Stanley. He's practically asleep.

STANLEY. Two minutes. I'll tell it as fast as I can.

JACK. Go on, Kate. Go to bed. The boy wants to tell me something.

KATE. Turn out the lights when you're through. *(She kisses JACK's head)* Don't worry about things. We've always made them work out.

(She leaves the room just as EUGENE darts out of the bathroom, rushes into his own room and slams the door)

EUGENE. She saw me on the crapper! Nora saw me on the crapper! *(He falls on his bed)* I might as well be dead.

STANLEY. I have a problem, Pop.

JACK. If you didn't, you wouldn't live in this house.

STANLEY. It must be tough being a father. Everybody comes to you with their problems. You have to have all the answers. I don't know if *I* could handle it.

JACK. Stop trying to win me over. Just tell me the problem.

STANLEY. I got fired today!

JACK. *What?!?*

STANLEY. Don't get excited! Don't get crazy! Let me explain what happened.

JACK. What did you do? You came in late? You were fresh to somebody? Were you fresh to somebody?

STANLEY. I'm not fired yet. I can still get my job back. I just need you to help me make a decision.

JACK. Take the job back. I don't care what it is. This is *not* the time for anybody to be out of work in this family.

STANLEY. When I was twelve years old you gave me a talk about principles. Remember?

JACK. All night you waited to tell me this news?

STANLEY. This is about principles, Pop.

JACK. How long were you going to go without telling me?

STANLEY. Will you at least hear my principles?

JACK. All right, I'll hear your principles. Then you'll hear mine.

STANLEY. Just sit back and let me tell you what happened. Okay? Well, it was on account of Andrew, the colored guy who sweeps up.

(JACK sits back and listens. STANLEY sits with his back to the audience, talking, but we can't hear him. Our attention is drawn to EUGENE up in his room)

EUGENE *(To the audience).* . . . So Stanley began his sad story. Pop never said a word. He just sat there and listened. Stanley was terrific. It was like that movie, *Abe Lincoln in Illinois.* Stanley was not only defending his principles, he was defending democracy and the United States of America. Pop must have been bleary-eyed because not only did he have to deal with Stanley's principles, Nora's career, the loss of his noisemaker business, how to get Aunt Blanche married off and Laurie's fluttering heart, but at any minute there could be a knock on the door with thirty-seven relatives from Poland showing up looking for a place to live . . . Finally, Stanley finished his story.

STANLEY. So—either I bring in a letter of apology in the morning or I don't bother coming in . . . I know it's late. I know you're tired. But I didn't want to do anything without asking you first.

JACK *(After a few moments of silence).* Ohh, Stanley, Stanley, Stanley!

STANLEY. I'm sorry, Pop.

JACK. You shouldn't have swept the dirt on his shoes.

STANLEY. I know.

JACK. Especially in front of other people.

STANLEY. I know.

JACK. He's your boss. He pays your salary. His money helps put food on our dining table.

STANLEY. I know, Pop.

JACK. And we don't have money to waste. Believe me when I tell you that.

STANLEY. I believe you, Pop.

JACK. You were sick three days last year and he only docked you a day and a half's pay, remember that?

STANLEY. I know. I can see what you're getting at. I'll write the letter. I'll do it to-night.

JACK. On the other hand, you did a courageous thing. You defended a fellow worker. Nobody else stood up for him, did they?

STANLEY. I was the only one.

JACK. That's something to be proud of. It was what you believed in. That's standing up for your principles.

STANLEY. That's why I didn't want to write the letter. I knew you'd understand.

JACK. The question is, Can this family afford principles right now?

STANLEY. It would make it hard, I know.

JACK. Not just on you and me. But on your mother. On Aunt Blanche, Nora, Laurie.

STANLEY. Eugene.

JACK. Eugene. Eugene would have to get a part-time job. Time he should be using studying books to get himself somewhere.

STANLEY. He wants to be a writer. He wants to go to college.

JACK. I wish I could have sent *you*. I've always been sick about that, Stanley.

STANLEY. I like working, Pop. I really do . . . Listen, I made up my mind. I'm going to write the letter.

JACK. I'm not saying you should . . .

STANLEY. I know. It's *my* decision. I really want to write the letter.

JACK. And how will your principles feel in the morning?

STANLEY. My principles feel better already. You told me you were proud of what I did. That's all I really cared about.

JACK. You know something, Stanley—I don't think there's much in college they could teach you that you don't already know.

STANLEY. Guess who I learned it from? . . . Thanks for talking to me, Pop. See you in the morning. You coming to bed?

JACK. I think I'll sit here for a while. It's the only time of day I have a few minutes to myself.

(STANLEY *nods, then bounds up the stairs to his room.* JACK *sits back in his chair and closes his eyes.*

STANLEY *enters his room.* EUGENE *is writing in his book of memoirs)*

EUGENE. How'd it go? Do you have to write the letter?

STANLEY. Yeah.

(He gets out a pad and his fountain pen)

EUGENE. I *knew* that's what he'd make you do.

STANLEY. He didn't *make* me do it . . . Be quiet, will ya! I have to concentrate.

EUGENE. What are you going to say?

STANLEY. I don't know . . . You want to help me? You're good at those things.

EUGENE. People used to get paid for that in the old days. Professional letter writers.

STANLEY *(Indignant).* I'm not going to pay you money.

EUGENE. I don't want money.

STANLEY. Then what *do* you want?

EUGENE. Tell me what Nora looked like naked.

STANLEY. How horny can you get?

EUGENE. I don't know. What's the highest score?

STANLEY. All right. When we finish the letter.

EUGENE. I don't trust you. I want to get paid first.

STANLEY. You know, you're a real shit!

EUGENE. Don't talk like that in front of me, I'm just a kid.

STANLEY. What do you want to know?

EUGENE. Everything. From the time you opened the door.

STANLEY. It happened so fast.

EUGENE. That's okay. Tell it slow.

STANLEY. Jesus! All right . . . I heard the shower running. I waited for it to stop. I gave a few seconds for the water to run off her body, then I knew she'd be stepping out of the shower. Suddenly I just opened the door. She was standing there on the bath mat, a towel on her head and nothing else in the whole wide world.

EUGENE. Slower. Don't go so fast.

STANLEY. Her breasts were gorgeous. Like two peaches hanging on the vine waiting to be plucked . . . Maybe nectarines. Like two nectarines, all soft and pink and shining in the morning sun . . .

Curtain

ACT TWO

Wednesday, a week later. About six-thirty in the evening.

KATE *comes down the stairs carrying a tray of food. She looks a little haggard.*

LAURIE *is lying on the sofa in the living room with a book.*

EUGENE *is in the backyard, sitting on the beach chair, writing in his book of memoirs.*

KATE. Laurie! You should see your mother. She looks gorgeous.

LAURIE. I'm waiting for her grand entrance . . . How's Uncle Jack?

KATE. He's resting. He ate a nice dinner. You can go up and see him later. *(She yells)* Eugene! Your father's resting. I don't want to hear any ball playing against the wall.

EUGENE. I'm not playing. I'm writing.

KATE. Well, do it quietly.

(She goes into the kitchen)

EUGENE *(To the audience).* She wants me to write quietly. If that was the only sentence I published in my memoirs, it would be a best seller . . . Everybody's been in a rotten mood around here lately . . . Three days ago Pop had a *(He whispers)* —heart attack. It wasn't a major *(He whispers)* —heart attack. It was sort of a warning. He passed out in the subway and a policeman had to bring him home. He was trying to make extra money driving a cab at nights and he just plain wore out . . . The doctor says he has to stay home for two or three weeks, but Pop won't listen to him. Mr. Jacobson has a brother-in-law who needs a job. He's filling in for Pop temporarily, but Pop's afraid that three weeks in bed could turn into permanently.

(STANLEY appears, coming home from work. He looks distraught. He half whispers to EUGENE)

STANLEY. I have to talk to you.

EUGENE. What's up?

STANLEY. Not here. In our room. Don't tell anybody.

EUGENE. What's the big secret?

STANLEY. Will you shut up! Wait'll I get upstairs, then follow me.

(He goes into the house)

EUGENE. If it's about Nora, I'm not interested. *(To the audience)* I forgot to tell you, I hate my cousin Nora. She's been real snotty to everybody lately. She doesn't say hello in the morning and eats her dinner up in her room. And she's been seeing this guy Larry No Chin Clurman every night. And she's not as pretty as I thought she was . . .

KATE *(Walking out of the kitchen).* Eugene! Did you bring your father his paper?

EUGENE. I'm coming. My knee hurts. I fell down the stairs at school.

KATE. Well, bring it up. Your father's waiting for it.

(She goes back into the kitchen)

EUGENE *(To the audience).* If I told her I just lost both my hands in an accident she'd say, "Go upstairs and wash your face with your feet" . . . I guess she's sore because she and Pop can't go to the affair at the Commodore Hotel. They had Glen Gray and his orchestra . . . I feel sorry for her 'cause she doesn't get to go out much. *(He gets up, starts toward the house)* And she's nervous about Frank Murphy coming over to pick up Aunt Blanche. She's angry at the whole world. *(He enters the house)* That's why she's making lima beans for dinner.

KATE *(Walks into the living room with a dish of nuts).* Would you like a cashew, Laurie?

LAURIE. Oh, thanks. *(She takes one)* And a Brazil nut too? *(She takes one)* And one almond? *(She takes one)*

KATE. You must be starved. We're having dinner late tonight. We'll wait till your mother goes out.

EUGENE *(Limps into the living room).* Can I have some nuts, Mom?

KATE. Just one. It's for the company. *(He takes one, starts upstairs)* We're eating in the kitchen tonight. You and Stanley help with the dishes.

(He goes upstairs)

KATE *(To LAURIE).* You look all flushed. You don't have a fever, do you? *(She feels* LAURIE*'s head)* Let me see your tongue. *(LAURIE shows her her tongue)* It's all spotted.

LAURIE. That's the cashew nut.

KATE. Don't you get sick on me too. If you're tired, I want you in bed.

LAURIE. I have a little stomach cramp. Maybe I'm getting my "ladies."

KATE. Your what?

LAURIE. My "ladies." That thing that Nora gets when she can't go in the water.

KATE. I don't think so. Not at your age. But if your stomach hurts real bad, you come and tell me. I made a nice tuna fish salad tonight. Call me when your mother comes down.

(She starts toward the kitchen)

LAURIE. Aunt Kate! . . . Does Momma like Mr. Murphy?

KATE. I don't know, darling. I don't think she knows him very well yet.

LAURIE. Do you like him?

KATE. I never spoke to the man.

LAURIE. You called him a Cossack. Are those the kind who don't like Jewish people?

KATE. I'm sure Mr. Murphy likes your mother, otherwise he wouldn't be taking her out to dinner.

LAURIE. If Mom married him, would we have to live in that dark house across the street? With that creepy woman in the window?

KATE. We're not up to that yet. Let's just get through Chardov's Restaurant first.

(She goes into the kitchen.

EUGENE *rushes into his room.* STANLEY *is lying on his bed, hands under his head, staring at the ceiling)*

EUGENE. Pop's feeling better. He threw the newspaper at me because I didn't bring him the evening edition.

STANLEY *(Sits up)*. Lock the door.

EUGENE *(Locking the door)*. You look terrible. You were crying. Your eyes are all red.

STANLEY. I'm in trouble, Eug. I mean, real, *real* trouble.

(He takes a single cigarette out of his shirt pocket, puts it in his mouth and lights it with a match)

EUGENE. When did you take up smoking?

STANLEY. I smoke in the stockroom all the time. Don't let me see you do it. It's a bad habit.

EUGENE. So how come *you* do it?

STANLEY. I like it.

EUGENE. What brand do you smoke?

STANLEY. Lucky Strikes.

EUGENE. I knew you would. That's the best brand.

STANLEY. Swear to God, what I tell you, you'll never tell a living soul.

EUGENE *(Raises his hand)*. I take an oath on the life of the entire New York Yankees . . . What happened?

STANLEY *(He paces before he can speak)*. . . . I lost my salary.

EUGENE. *What?*

STANLEY. The entire seventeen dollars. It's gone. I lost it.

EUGENE. Where? In the subway?

STANLEY. In a poker game. I lost it gambling.

EUGENE. IN A POKER GAME?

STANLEY. *Will you shut up??* You want to kill Pop right in his bedroom?

EUGENE. You never told me you gambled.

STANLEY. We would just do it at lunch hour. For pennies. I always won. A dime. A quarter. It wasn't just luck. I was really good.

EUGENE. Seventeen dollars!!

STANLEY. When Pop got sick, I thought I could make some extra money. To help out. So I played in this game over in the stockroom at Florsheim Shoes . . . Boy, did I learn about poker. They cleaned me out in twenty minutes . . .

EUGENE. What are you going to tell them?

STANLEY. I don't know. If Pop wasn't sick, I would tell him the truth. Last week he tells me how proud he is of me. He's driving a cab at nights and I'm playing poker at Florsheim's.

(He puts his head down and starts to cry)

EUGENE. Yeah, but suppose you won? Suppose you won fifty dollars? You just had bad luck, that's all.

STANLEY. I had no chance against those guys. They were gamblers. They all wore black pointy shoes with clocks on their socks . . . If Pop dies, I'll hang myself, I swear.

EUGENE. Don't talk like that. Pop isn't going to die. He ate three lamb chops tonight . . . Why don't you just say you lost the money? You had a hole in your pocket. You can tear a hole in your pocket.

STANLEY. I already used that one.

EUGENE. When?

STANLEY. In November when I lost five dollars. He said to me, "From now on, check your pockets every morning."

EUGENE. What happened to the five dollars? Did you gamble that too?

STANLEY. No. I gave it to a girl . . . You know. A pro.

EUGENE. A pro what? . . . A PROSTI-TUTE??? You went to one of those places? Holy shit!

STANLEY. I'm not going to warn you about that word again.

EUGENE. Is that what it costs? Five dollars?

STANLEY. Two-fifty. I went with this guy I know. He still owes me.

EUGENE. And you never told me? What was she like? Was she pretty? How old was she?

STANLEY. Don't start in with me, Eugene.

EUGENE. Did she get completely naked or what?

STANLEY *(Furious)*. Every time I get in trouble, I have to tell you what a naked girl looks like? . . . Do me a favor, Eugene. Go in the bathroom, whack off and grow up by yourself.

EUGENE. Don't get sore. If you were me, you'd ask the same questions.

STANLEY. Well, I never had an older

brother to teach me those things. I had to do it all on my own. You don't know how lucky you are to be the younger one. You don't have the responsibilities I do. You're still in school looking up girls' dresses on the staircase.

EUGENE. I work plenty hard in school.

STANLEY. Yeah? Well, let me see your report card. Today's the first of the month, I know you got it. I want to see your report card.

EUGENE. I don't have to show you my report card. You're not my father.

STANLEY. Yes, I am. As long as Pop is sick, I am. I'm the only one in the family who's working, ain't I?

EUGENE. Really? Well, where's your salary this week, Pop?

STANLEY (*Grabs* EUGENE *in anger*). I hate you sometimes. You're nothing but a lousy shit. I help you all the time and you never help me without wanting something for it. I hate your disgusting guts.

EUGENE (*Screaming*). Not as much as I hate yours. You snore at night. You pick your toenails. You smell up the bathroom. When I go in there I have to puke.

STANLEY (*Screaming back*). Give me your report card. Give it to me, goddammit, or I'll beat your face in.

EUGENE (*Starts to cry*). You want it? Here! (*He grabs it out of a book*) Here's my lousy report card . . . you fuck!!

(*He falls on the bed crying, his face to the wall.* STANLEY *sits on his own bed and reads the report card. There is a long silence*)

STANLEY (*Softly*). Four A's and a B . . . That's good. That's real good, Eugene . . . You're smart . . . I want you to go to college . . . I want you to be somebody important someday . . . Because I'm not . . . I'm no damn good. (*He is crying*) I'm sorry I said those things to you.

EUGENE (*Still faces the wall. It's too hard to look at* STAN). Me too . . . I'm sorry too.

(JACK *appears at the top of the stairs. He is in his pajamas, robe and slippers. He seems very shaky. He holds on to the banister and slowly comes down the stairs.*

He looks around, then sees LAURIE *and walks into the living room. His breath does not come easy*)

LAURIE (*Sees him*). Hi, Uncle Jack. Are you feeling better?

JACK. A little, darling. Your mother's not down yet?

LAURIE. No.

JACK. I wanted to see her before she goes out.

(KATE *comes out of the kitchen with a bowl of fruit. She sees* JACK)

KATE. Oh, my God! Are you crazy? Are you out of your mind? You're walking down the stairs?

JACK. I'm all right. I was tired lying in that bed. I wanted to see Blanche.

(*He sits down slowly*)

KATE. How are you going to get upstairs? You think I'm going to carry you? The doctor said you're not even supposed to go to the bathroom, didn't he?

JACK. You trust doctors? My grandmother never saw one in her life, she lived to be eighty-seven.

KATE. She didn't have high blood pressure. She never fainted on the subway.

JACK. She used to faint three, four times a week. It's in our family. We're fainters. Laurie, darling, go get your Uncle Jack a glass of ice water, please.

LAURIE. Now?

JACK. Yes. Now, sweetheart. (LAURIE *gets up and goes into kitchen*) That child is pampered too much. You should let her do more work around the house. You don't get healthy lying on couches all day.

KATE. No. You get healthy driving cabs at night after you work nine hours cutting raincoats. You want to kill yourself, Jack? You want to leave me to take care of this family alone? Is that what you want?

JACK. You figure I'll get better faster if you make me feel guilty? . . . I was born with enough guilt, Katey. If I need more, I'll ask you.

KATE. I'm sorry. You know me. I'm not happy unless I can worry. *My* family were worriers. Worriers generally marry fainters.

JACK (*Takes her hand, holds it*). I'm not going to leave you. I promise. If I didn't leave you for another woman, I'm certainly not going to drop dead just to leave you.

KATE (*Lets go of his hand*). What other woman? That bookkeeper, Helene?

JACK. Again with Helene? You're never going to forget that I danced with her two years in a row at the Commodore Hotel?

KATE. Don't tell me she isn't attracted to you. I noticed that right off.

JACK. What does a woman like that want with a cutter? She likes the men up front. The salesmen. She's a widow. She's looking to get married.

KATE. You're an attractive man, Jack. Women like you.

JACK. Me? Attractive? You really must think I'm dying, don't you?

KATE. You don't know women like I do. Just promise me one thing. If anything ever happened with you and that Helene, let me go to my grave without hearing it.

JACK. I see. Now that you're worried about Helene, you've decided you're going to die first.

(LAURIE *comes back in with a glass of ice water*)

LAURIE. I had to chop the ice. I'm all out of breath.

JACK. It's good for you, darling. It's exercise.

(*He takes the ice water.*

NORA *comes out of her room and goes bounding down the stairs*)

NORA *(Coldly).* I'm going out. I won't be having dinner. I'll be home late. I have my key. Good night.

KATE. Nora! Don't you want to see how your mother looks?

NORA. I'm sure she looks beautiful. She doesn't need me to tell her.

KATE. What about Mr. Murphy? I know your mother wants him to meet you and Laurie. He'll be here any minute.

NORA. I have somebody waiting for me. I can meet Mr. Murphy some other time.

JACK. I think it would be nice if you waited, Nora. I think your mother would be very hurt if you didn't wait to say goodbye.

NORA. I'm sure that's very good advice, Uncle Jack. I know *just* how my mother feels. I'm not so sure she knows how *I* feel.

(*She turns and goes out the front door.* JACK *and* KATE *look at each other*)

KATE. Jack! What'll I do?

JACK. Leave it alone. It's between Nora and Blanche. It's something *they* have to work out.

KATE. Who is she going out with? Where does she go every night?

LAURIE. With Larry Clurman. He borrows his father's car and takes her to the cemetery.

KATE. What cemetery?

LAURIE. Where Daddy is buried. She goes to see Daddy.

(BLANCHE *has come out of her room and appears at the head of the stairs. She is all dressed up and looks quite lovely. She comes down the stairs*)

KATE. What'll I tell her? I don't want to spoil this evening for her.

(BLANCHE *appears in the room*)

BLANCHE. Jack? What are you doing down here?

JACK. We have company coming. Where else should I be?

BLANCHE. I looked in your room. I got scared to death.

JACK. Well, you don't look it. You look beautiful.

KATE. Ohh, Blanche. Oh, my God, Blanche, it's stunning. Like a movie star. Who's the movie star I like so much, Laurie?

LAURIE. Irene Dunne.

KATE. Like Irene Dunne.

LAURIE. I think she looks like Rosalind Russell. Maybe Carole Lombard.

JACK. I think she looks like Blanche. Blanche is prettier than all of them.

BLANCHE. I had such trouble with the make-up. I couldn't see my eyes to put on the mascara. So I had to put my glasses on. Then I couldn't get the mascara on under the glasses.

(STANLEY *gets up from his bed, goes out to the bathroom and closes the door*)

KATE. Where are your glasses? Have you got your glasses?

BLANCHE. In my purse. I thought I'd put them on in the restaurant, when I'm looking at the menu.

KATE. Make sure you do. I don't want you coming home telling me you don't know what he looks like.

BLANCHE. I'm so glad to see you up, Jack. Then you're feeling better?

JACK. It was nothing. I needed a rest, that's all. Besides, I wanted to meet this Murphy fella. A stranger comes in, he likes to meet another man. Makes him feel comfortable.

BLANCHE. Thank you, Jack. That's very thoughtful of you.

KATE (*Takes something out of her pocket*). Here. Wear this. Don't say no to me. Just put them on, Blanche. Please.

BLANCHE. Kate! Your pearls. Your good pearls.

KATE. What are they going to do? Sit in my drawer all year? Pearls are like people. They like to go out and be seen once in a while.

BLANCHE. You were going to wear them to the affair tonight. I'm so wrapped up in my-self, I forgot you're missing the affair this year.

KATE. I can afford to miss it. I don't see Jack there the whole night anyway.

JACK. Let's see how they look.

BLANCHE. I'm so nervous I'll lose them.

(*She puts them on. They all look*)

KATE. All right. Tell me I don't have a beautiful sister.

JACK. Now I feel good. Now I feel I got my money's worth.

LAURIE. Definitely Carole Lombard.

BLANCHE. Laurie, go up and get Nora. I want to show them to Nora.

LAURIE. . . . She's not here. She left.

BLANCHE *(Looks at* KATE *and* JACK*)*. What do you mean, she left? Without saying goodbye?

KATE. She had to meet somebody. She wanted to wait for you.

BLANCHE. She could have come into my room. She knew I wanted to see her.

JACK. She'll see you when you get home. You'll look just as good at twelve o'clock.

BLANCHE. What did she say? Did she say anything?

KATE. You're going out. You're going to have a good time tonight. We'll talk about it later.

BLANCHE. She's making me pay for it, isn't she? She knows she can get to me so easily . . . That's what I get for making decisions.

JACK. I feel like ice cream for dessert. Laurie, you feel like ice cream for dessert?

LAURIE. Butter pecan?

JACK. Butter pecan for you, maple walnut for me. Go up and tell Eugene I want him to go to the store.

LAURIE. I'll go with him.

KATE. Don't run, darling.

JACK. Let her run. If she gets tired, she'll tell you. Let's stop worrying about each other so much.

*(*LAURIE *knocks on* EUGENE*'s door)*

LAURIE. Eugene! Your father wants us to go to the store.

EUGENE. Tell him I'm sick. My stomach hurts.

LAURIE. You don't want any ice cream?

EUGENE *(Thinks)*. Ice cream? Wait a minute. *(He sits up, looks out at the audience)* It's amazing how quickly you recover from misery when someone offers you ice cream.

JACK. She's only sixteen, Blanche. At that age they're still wrapped up in themselves.

EUGENE. How am I going to become a writer if I don't know how to suffer? Actually, I'd give up writing if I could see a naked girl while I was eating ice cream.

(He comes out of his room and goes down the stairs with LAURIE. STANLEY *comes out of the bathroom and goes back into his own room)*

BLANCHE. What time is it?

KATE. Six-thirty. He'll be here any minute. Get your mind off Nora, Blanche. Don't wear my pearls out tonight for nothing.

JACK. Eugene! Go to Hanson's. Get a half pint of butter pecan, a half pint of maple walnut, a half pint of chocolate for yourself. Kate, what do you want?

KATE. I'm in no mood for ice cream.

JACK. Get her vanilla. She'll eat it. And whatever Stanley likes.

EUGENE. I need money.

JACK. I just paid the doctor fifteen dollars. Go up to Stanley. He got paid today. Ask him for his salary.

EUGENE *(In shock)*. *What???*

KATE. Here. Here's a dollar. *(She takes it out of her pocket)* Hurry back so Laurie can meet Mr. Murphy. But don't run.

(They take the money and leave by the front door)

BLANCHE. You know what I worry about at night? That she'll run off. That I'll wake up in the morning and she'll be gone. To Philadelphia. Or Boston. Or God knows where.

KATE. Look how the woman's going out on a date. Is that what you're going to talk about? He'll start drinking in five minutes.

BLANCHE. You think so? What'll I do if he gets drunk?

KATE. You'll come right home. Do you have money? Do you have carfare?

BLANCHE. No. I didn't take anything.

KATE. Wait here. I'll get five dollars from Stanley. Now I have something *else* to worry about.

(She starts up the stairs)

JACK. I could use a cup of hot tea.

(He gets up)

BLANCHE. Sit there. I'll make it.

JACK. We'll both make it. Keep me company. We can hear the bell from the kitchen.

(They go off to the kitchen. KATE *is at* STANLEY*'s door. She knocks on it)*

KATE. Stanley? Are you in there? *(She opens the door.* STANLEY *is lying on his bed)* Open the window. You never get any air in this room . . . (She extends her hand)* I need five dollars for Aunt Blanche. *(He stares at the floor)* . . . Stanley? Did you get paid today?

STANLEY. Yes. I got paid today.

KATE. Take out your money for the week, let me have the envelope.

STANLEY *(Still stares down)*. I don't have it.

KATE. You don't have the envelope?

STANLEY. I don't have the money.

KATE. What do you mean, you don't have the money?

STANLEY. I mean I don't have the money. It's gone.

KATE *(Nervously, sits on the bed)*. It's gone? . . . Gone where?

STANLEY. It's just gone. I don't have it. I can't get it back. I'm sorry. There's nothing I can do about it anymore. Just don't ask me any more questions.

KATE. What do you mean, don't ask any more questions? I want to know what happened to seventeen dollars, Stanley!

STANLEY. You'll tell Pop. If I tell you, you're going to tell Pop.

KATE. Why shouldn't I tell your father? Why, Stanley? I want to know what happened to that money.

STANLEY. I gambled it! I lost it playing poker! All right? You happy? You satisfied now?

(He starts to weep)

KATE *(Her breath goes out of her body. She sits there numb, then finally takes a breath)*. I'm not going to deal with this right now. I have to get Aunt Blanche out of the house first. I have your father's health to worry about. You're going to sit in this room and you're going to think up a story. You were robbed. Somebody stole the money. I don't care who, I don't care where. That's what you're going to tell your father, because if you tell him the truth, you'll kill that man as sure as I'm sitting here . . . Tonight, after he goes to sleep, you'll meet me in the kitchen and we'll deal with this alone.

(She gets up, moves to the door)

STANLEY *(Barely audible)*. . . . I'm sorry.

(She goes, closes the door. STANLEY sits there as if the life has gone out of him.

KATE *walks down the stairs and into the living room. She goes over to the window, looks out and breaks into sobs.*

BLANCHE *comes out of the kitchen. She looks around the living room)*

BLANCHE. I left my purse in here. Without my glasses, I'm afraid to pour the tea. *(She notices KATE wiping her eyes with her handkerchief)* Kate? . . . What is it? What's wrong?

KATE. Nothing. I'm just all nerves today.

BLANCHE. You're worried about Jack. He shouldn't have come down the stairs.

KATE. He knows he's not supposed to get out of bed. What did we need a doctor for? He doesn't listen to them.

BLANCHE. I shouldn't have asked Mr. Murphy to come over. That's the only reason he came down.

KATE. It's not just Mr. Murphy. It's Stanley, it's Eugene, it's everybody.

BLANCHE. I'm sorry about Nora. Jack told me what she said when she left.

KATE. Why don't you get your purse, Blanche. He'll be here any minute.

BLANCHE. Did Nora say anything to hurt you, Kate? I know she's been very difficult these last few days.

KATE *(Suddenly turns, angrily)*. Why is it always *Nora?* Why is it only *your* problems? Do you think you're the only one in this world who has troubles? We *all* have troubles. We *all* get our equal share. *(It hits* BLANCHE *like a slap in the face)*

BLANCHE. I'm sorry. Forgive me, Kate. I'm sorry.

KATE. Maybe you're stronger than I am, I don't know. You survived Dave's death. I don't know if I could handle it if anything happens to Jack.

BLANCHE. He'll be all right, Kate. Nothing's going to happen to him. He's still a young man. He's strong.

KATE. When Dave died, I cried for his loss. I was so angry. Angry at God for taking such a young man . . . I never realized until now what *you* must have gone through. How did you get through it, Blanche?

BLANCHE. I had you. I had Jack . . . But mostly, you live for your children. Your children keep you going.

KATE *(Almost smiles)*. My children.

BLANCHE. I wake up every morning for Nora and for Laurie.

KATE. Nora hurts you so much and you can still say that?

BLANCHE. Why? Don't you think we hurt our parents? You don't remember how Momma cried when Celia left home? Sure it hurts, but if you love someone, you forgive them.

KATE. Some things you forgive. Some things you never forgive.

(LAURIE comes back into the house. She has a letter in her hand)

LAURIE. Is the ice cream here yet?

BLANCHE. No, darling. Didn't you go with Eugene?

LAURIE. No. I was across the street in the creepy house. It's just as creepy inside.

BLANCHE. In Mr. Murphy's house? You were just in there? Why?

LAURIE. She called me from the window. The old lady. I think it's his mother. She told me she had a letter for you. I had to go inside to get it.

(She hands the letter to BLANCHE)

KATE. What did she say to you?

LAURIE. She offered me a cookie but it was all green. I said I wasn't hungry.

(EUGENE *appears outside the house. He carries a brown paper bag with four small cartons of ice cream.* BLANCHE *opens the letter*)

EUGENE *(To the audience).* "Dear Mrs. Morton, I send regrets for my son Frank. I tried to reach you earlier, then realized you had no phone. Frank will be unable to keep his dinner engagement with you this evening. Frank is in hospital as a result of an automobile accident last night, and although his injuries are not serious, the consequences are. As a devoted mother I would end this letter here and forward my apologies. Despite all my son's faults, honesty and sincerity have never been his failings. He wanted me to tell you the truth. That while driving a friend's motorcar, he was intoxicated and was the cause of the aforementioned accident. The truth would come out soon enough, but Frank has too much respect and fondness for you to have you hear it from some other source. I hope you will not think I am just a doting mother when I tell you my boy has a great many attributes. A great many. As soon as Frank can get out of his difficulties here we have decided to move to upstate New York where there is a clinic that can help Frank and where we have relatives with whom we can stay. Frank sends, along with his regrets, his regard for a warm, intelligent, friendly and most delightful neighbor across the way . . . Yours most respectfully, Mrs. Matthew Murphy."

KATE. What is it?

(BLANCHE *hands the letter to* KATE)

BLANCHE. He's not coming. He's . . . in the hospital.

(KATE *reads the letter*)

EUGENE *(To the audience).* It was a sad letter, all right, but it sure was well written. Maybe I should have been born in Ireland.

(He walks into the house)

KATE *(As she reads).* I knew it. I said it right from the beginning, didn't I?

LAURIE. Why is he in the hospital?

BLANCHE. He was in a car accident . . . Oh, God. That poor woman.

LAURIE. Does that mean you're not going out to dinner?

KATE *(Nods her head as she finishes).* It could have been you in that car with him. I warned you the first day about those people.

BLANCHE. Stop calling them "those people." They're not "those people." She's a mother, like you and me.

KATE. And what is he? Tell me what he is.

BLANCHE. He's somebody in trouble. He's somebody that needs help. For God's sakes, Kate, you don't even know the man.

KATE. I know the man. I know what they're *all* like.

BLANCHE. Who are you to talk? Are we any better? Are we something so special? We're *all* poor around here, the least we can be is charitable.

KATE. Why? What have *I* got I can afford to give away? Am I the one who got you all dressed up for nothing? Am I the one who got your hopes up? Am I the one they're going to lock up in a jail somewhere?

LAURIE. They're going to put him in jail?

KATE. Don't talk to me about charity. Anyone else, but not me.

BLANCHE. I never said you weren't charitable.

KATE. All I did was try to help you. All I *ever* did was try to help you.

BLANCHE. I know that. Nobody cares for their family more than you do. But at least you can be sympathetic to somebody else in trouble.

KATE. Who should I care about? Who's out there watching over *me?* I did enough in my life for people. You know what I'm talking about.

BLANCHE. No, I don't. Say what's on your mind, Kate. What people?

KATE. You! Celia! Poppa, when he was sick. Everybody! . . . Don't you ask *me* "What people"! How many beatings from Momma did I get for things that you did? How many dresses did I go without so you could look like someone when you went out? I was the workhorse and you were the pretty one. You have no right to talk to me like that. No right.

BLANCHE. This is all about Jack, isn't it? You're blaming me for what happened.

KATE. Why do you think that man is sick today? Why did a policeman have to carry him home at two o'clock in the morning? So your Nora could have dancing lessons? So that Laurie could see a doctor every three weeks? Go on! Worry about your friend across the street, not the ones who have to be dragged home to keep a roof over your head.

(She turns away. JACK *walks in from the kitchen)*

JACK. What is this? What's going on here?

BLANCHE *(To* KATE*).* Why didn't you ever tell me you felt that way?

KATE *(Turns her back to her).* I never had the time. I was too busy taking care of everyone.

JACK. What is it, Blanche? What happened? *(She hands* JACK *the letter. He starts to read it)*

BLANCHE. It took all these years? It took something like that letter for you to finally get your feelings out?

KATE. I didn't need a letter ... I just needed you to ask me.

*(*BLANCHE *is terribly hurt and extremely vulnerable standing there)*

BLANCHE. Laurie! Please go upstairs. This conversation isn't for you.

EUGENE. The ice cream is ready.

BLANCHE. Eugene, put the ice cream in the icebox. I have to talk to your mother.

*(*EUGENE *goes into the kitchen)*

JACK *(Finishes the letter)*. I never spoke to the woman. They've lived in that house for three years, and I never exchanged a word with her.

KATE *(To* JACK*)*. What are you walking around for? If you're out of bed, at least sit in a chair.

BLANCHE. If I could take Nora and Laurie and pack them out of this house tonight, I would do it. But I can't. I have no place to take them.

JACK. Blanche! What are you talking about? Don't say such things.

BLANCHE *(Looks straight at* KATE*)*. If I can leave the girls with you for another few weeks, I would appreciate it. Until I can find a place of my own, and then I'll send for them.

JACK. You're not sending for anybody and you're not leaving anywhere. I don't want to hear this kind of talk.

KATE. Stay out of this, Jack. Let her do what she wants.

BLANCHE. I know a woman in Manhattan Beach. I can stay with her for a few days. And then I'll find a job. I will do *anything* anybody asks me, but I will *never* be a burden to anyone again.

(She starts for the stairs)

JACK. Blanche, stop this! Stop it right now. What the hell is going on here, for God's sakes? Two sisters having a fight they should have had twenty-five years ago. You want to get it out, Blanche, get it out! Tell her what it's like to live in a house that isn't yours. To have to depend on somebody else to put the food on your plate every night. I know what it's like because I lived that way until I was twenty-one years old ... Tell her, Kate, what it is to be an older sister. To suddenly be the one who has to work and shoulder all the

responsibilities and not be the one who gets the affection and the hugs when you were the only one there. You think I don't see it with Stanley and Eugene? With Nora and Laurie? You think I don't hear the fights that go on up in those rooms night after night? Go on, Kate! Scream at her! Yell at her. Call her names, Blanche. Tell her to go to hell for the first time in your life ... And when you both got it out of your systems, give each other a hug and go have dinner. My lousy ice cream is melting, for God's sakes.

(There is a long silence)

BLANCHE. I love you both very much. No matter what Kate says to me, I will never stop loving her. But I have to get out. If I don't do it now, I will lose whatever self-respect I have left. For people like us, sometimes the only thing we really own is our dignity ... and when I grow old, I would like to have as much as Mrs. Matthew Murphy across the street.

(She turns and goes up the stairs, disappearing into her room)

JACK. What did it, Kate? Something terrible must have happened to you tonight for you to behave like this. It wasn't Blanche. It was something else. What was it, Kate?

KATE *(Stares out the window)*. Tell the kids to come down in five minutes. We're eating in the kitchen tonight.

(She walks into the kitchen. JACK *stands there, staring after her.* EUGENE, *coming out of the kitchen, passes his father)*

JACK. Get Stanley and Laurie. Dinner is in five minutes.

*(*JACK *goes into the kitchen.* EUGENE *walks to the stairs and up toward his bedroom)*

EUGENE *(To the audience)*. It was the first day in my life I didn't get blamed for what just happened. I felt real sorry for everybody, but as long as I wasn't to blame, I didn't feel all *that* bad about things. That's when I realized I had a selfish streak in me. I sure hope I grow out of it. *(He enters his bedroom and says to* STANLEY*)* Aunt Blanche is leaving.

STANLEY *(Sits up)*. For where?

EUGENE *(Sits on his own bed)*. To stay with some woman in Manhattan Beach. She and Mom just had a big fight. She's going to send for Laurie and Nora when she gets a job.

STANLEY. What did they fight about?

EUGENE. I couldn't hear it all. I think Mom sorta blames Aunt Blanche for Pop having to work so hard.

STANLEY *(Hits the pillow with his fist)*. Oh,

God! . . . Did Mom say anything about me? About how I lost my salary?

EUGENE. You told her? Why did you tell her? I came up with twelve terrific lies for you.

(STANLEY opens his drawer, puts on a sweater)

STANLEY. How much money do you have?

EUGENE. Me? I don't have any money.

STANLEY *(Puts another sweater over the first one).* The hell you don't. You've got money in your cigar box. How much do you have?

EUGENE. I got a dollar twelve. It's my life's savings.

STANLEY. Let me have it. I'll pay it back, don't worry.

(He puts a jacket over the sweaters, then gets a fedora from the closet and puts it on. EUGENE *takes the cigar box from under the bed, opens it)*

EUGENE. What are you putting on all those things for?

STANLEY. In case I have to sleep out tonight. I'm leaving, Gene. I don't know where I'm going yet, but I'll write to you when I get there.

EUGENE. You're leaving home?

STANLEY. When I'm gone, you tell Aunt Blanche what happened to my salary. Then she'll know why Mom was so angry. Tell her please not to leave, because it was all my fault, not Mom's. Will you do that?

(He takes the coins out of the cigar box)

EUGENE. I have eight cents' worth of stamps, if you want that too.

STANLEY. Thanks. *(He picks up a small medal)* What's this?

EUGENE. The medal you won for the hundred-yard dash two years ago.

STANLEY. From the Police Athletic League. I didn't know you still had this.

EUGENE. You gave it to me. You can have it back if you want it.

STANLEY. It's not worth anything.

EUGENE. It is to me.

STANLEY. Sure. You can keep it.

EUGENE. Thanks . . . Where will you go?

STANLEY. I don't know. I've been thinking about joining the Army. Pop says we'll be at war in a couple of years anyway. I could be a sergeant or something by the time it starts.

EUGENE. If it lasts long enough, I could join too. Maybe we can get in the same outfit. "The Fighting 69th." It's mostly Irish, but they had a few Jewish guys in the movie.

STANLEY. You don't go in the Army unless they come and get you. You go to college. You hear me? Promise me you'll go to college.

EUGENE. I'll probably have to stay home and work if you leave. We'll need the money.

STANLEY. I'll send home my paycheck every month. A sergeant in the Army makes real good dough . . . Well, I better get going.

EUGENE *(On the verge of tears).* What do you have to leave for?

STANLEY. Don't start crying. They'll hear you.

EUGENE. They'll get over it. They won't stay mad at you forever. I was mad at you and *I* got over it.

STANLEY. Because of me, the whole family is breaking up. Do you want Nora to end up like one of those cheap boardwalk girls?

EUGENE. I don't care. I'm not in love with Nora anymore.

STANLEY. Well, you *should* care. She's your cousin. Don't turn out to be like me.

EUGENE. I don't see what's so bad about you.

STANLEY *(Looks at him).* Take care of yourself, Eug. *(They embrace. He opens the door, looks around, then back to* EUGENE*)* If you ever write a story about me, call me Hank. I always liked the name Hank.

(He goes, closing the door behind him.

EUGENE *sits there in silence for a while, then turns to the audience)*

EUGENE. I guess there comes a time in everybody's life when you say, "This very moment is the end of my childhood." When Stanley closed the door, I knew that moment had come to me . . . I was scared. I was lonely. And I hated my mother and father for making him so unhappy. Even if they were right, I still hated them . . . I even hated Stanley a little because he left me there to grow up all by myself.

KATE *(Yelling).* Eugene! Laurie! It's dinner. I'm not waiting all night.

EUGENE *(To the audience).* And I hated her for leaving Stanley's name out when she called us for dinner. I don't think parents really know how cruel they can be sometimes . . . *(A beat)* At dinner I tried to tell them about Stanley, but I just couldn't get the words out . . . I left the table without even having my ice cream . . . If it was suffering I was after, I was beginning to learn about it.

(KATE and JACK come out of the kitchen, heading upstairs)

JACK. It's ten o'clock, where is Stanley so late?

KATE. Never mind Stanley. You should have been in bed an hour ago.

JACK. Why won't you tell me what happened between you and that boy?

KATE. I'm tired, Jack. I've had enough to deal with for one day.

JACK. I want him to go to temple with me on Saturday. They stop going for three or four weeks, they forget their religion altogether.

(They go into the bedroom)

EUGENE. The house became quieter than I ever heard it before. Aunt Blanche was in her room packing, Pop and Mom were in their bedroom, and I had to talk to somebody or else I'd go crazy. I didn't have much choice. *(He walks over to her room and knocks on the door)* Laurie? It's Eugene. Can I come in?

LAURIE. What do you want? I'm reading.

EUGENE *(Opens the door)*. I just want to talk to you.

LAURIE. I didn't say yes, did I?

EUGENE. Well, I'm already in, so it's too late ... What are you reading?

LAURIE. *The Citadel* by A. J. Cronin.

EUGENE. I read it. It's terrific ... I hear your mother's leaving in the morning.

LAURIE. We're going too as soon as she finds a job.

EUGENE. I can't believe it. I'm going to be the only one left here.

LAURIE. You mean you and Stanley.

EUGENE. Stanley's gone. He's not coming back. I think he's going to join the Army.

LAURIE. You mean he ran away?

EUGENE. No. Only kids run away. When you're Stanley's age, you just leave.

LAURIE. He didn't say goodbye?

EUGENE. My parents don't even know about it. I'm going to tell them now.

LAURIE. I wonder if I'll have to go to a different school.

EUGENE. You'll have to make all new friends.

LAURIE. I don't care. I don't have any friends here anyway.

EUGENE. Because you're always in the house. You never go out.

LAURIE. I can't because of my condition.

EUGENE. You don't look sick to me. Do you *feel* sick?

LAURIE. No. But my mother tells me I am.

EUGENE. I don't trust parents anymore.

LAURIE. Why would she lie to me?

EUGENE. To keep you around. Once they find out Stanley's gone, they're going to handcuff me to my bed.

LAURIE. I wouldn't leave my mother anyway. Even when I'm older. Even if I get married. I'll never leave my mother.

EUGENE. Yeah? Mr. Murphy across the street never left his mother. And he ended up going to jail.

LAURIE. None of this would have happened if my father was alive.

EUGENE. How did you feel when he died?

LAURIE. I don't remember. I cried a lot because I saw my mother crying.

EUGENE. I would hate it if my father died. Especially with Stanley gone. We'd probably have to move out of this house.

LAURIE. Well ... then you and your mother could come and live with us.

EUGENE. So if we all end up living together, what's the point in breaking up now?

LAURIE. I don't know. I have to finish reading.

(She goes back to her book. EUGENE *gets up and looks at the audience)*

EUGENE. You don't get too far talking to Laurie. Sometimes I think the flutter in her heart is really in her brain. *(He leaves the room, closes the door and heads down the stairs)* I went into their bedroom and broke the news about Stanley. The monumental news that their eldest son had run off, probably to get killed in France fighting for his country. My mother said, "Go to bed. He'll be home when it gets cold out." I couldn't believe it. Their own son. It was then that I suspected that Stanley and I were adopted ... They finally went to bed and I waited out on the front steps until it got cold, but Stanley never showed up.

(He goes out the front door.

It is later that night, after midnight. We see NORA *enter the front yard.* BLANCHE *comes down the stairs in a nightgown and a robe. She waits at the foot of the stairs as* NORA *comes into the house and sees her)*

BLANCHE. I wanted to talk to you.

NORA. Now? It's late.

BLANCHE. I know it's late. We could have talked earlier if you didn't come home at twelve o'clock at night.

*(*BLANCHE *walks into the living room.* NORA *follows her in and stands in the doorway)*

NORA. How was your dinner?

BLANCHE. I didn't go. Mr. Murphy was in an accident.

NORA. I'm sorry. Is he all right?

BLANCHE. He's got his problems, like the rest of us ... I was very hurt that you left tonight without saying goodbye.

NORA. I was late. Someone was waiting for me.

BLANCHE. So was I. You knew it was important to me.

NORA. I'm not feeling very well.

BLANCHE. You purposely left without seeing me. You've never done that before.

NORA. Can we talk about this in the morning?

BLANCHE. I won't be here in the morning.

NORA. Then tomorrow night.

BLANCHE. I'm leaving, Nora. I'm moving out in the morning.

NORA. What are you talking about?

BLANCHE. Aunt Kate and I had a fight tonight. We said some terrible things to each other. Things that have been bottled up since we were children. I'm going to stay with my friend Louise in Manhattan Beach until I can find a job. Then I'll send for you and Laurie.

NORA. I can't believe it. You mean it's all right for you to leave *us* but it wasn't all right for me to leave *you?*

BLANCHE. I was never concerned about your leaving *me.* It was your future I was worrying about.

NORA. It was *my* future. Why couldn't *I* have something to say about it?

BLANCHE. Maybe I was wrong, I don't know. I never made the decisions for the family. Your father did. Aunt Kate was right about one thing: everyone always took care of me. My mother, my sisters, your father, even you and Laurie. I've been a very dependent person all my life.

NORA. Maybe that's all I'm asking for. To be *in*dependent.

BLANCHE *(Sternly).* You *earn* your independence. You don't take it at the expense of others. Would that job even be offered to you if somebody in this family hadn't paid for those dancing lessons and kept a roof over your head and clothes on your back? If anyone's going to pay back Uncle Jack, it'll be me—doing God knows what, I don't know—but one thing I'm sure of. I'll *steal* before I let my daughter show that man one ounce of ingratitude or disrespect.

NORA. So I have to give up the one chance I may never get again, is that it? I'm the one who has to pay for what you couldn't do with your own life.

BLANCHE *(Angrily).* What right do you have to judge me like that?

NORA. *Judge* you? I can't even talk to you. I don't exist to you. I have tried so hard to get close to you but there was never any room. Whatever you had to give went to Daddy, and when he died, whatever was left you gave to—

(She turns away)

BLANCHE. What? Finish what you were going to say.

NORA. . . . I have been jealous my whole life of Laurie because she was lucky enough to be born sick. I could never turn a light on in my room at night or read in bed because Laurie always needed her precious sleep. I could never have a friend over on the weekends because Laurie was always resting. I used to pray I'd get some terrible disease or get hit by a car so I'd have a leg all twisted or crippled and then once, maybe just once, *I'd* get to crawl into bed next to you on a cold rainy night and talk to you and hold you until I fell asleep in your arms . . . just once . . .

(She is in tears)

BLANCHE. My God, Nora . . . is that what you think of me?

NORA. Is it any worse than what you think of me?

BLANCHE *(Hesitates, trying to recover).* I'm not going to let you hurt me, Nora. I'm not going to let you tell me that I don't love you or that I haven't tried to give you as much as I gave Laurie . . . God knows I'm not perfect, because enough angry people in this house told me so tonight. But I am *not* going to be a doormat for all the frustrations and unhappiness that you or Aunt Kate or anyone else wants to lay at my feet . . . I did *not* create this universe. I do *not* decide who lives and dies, or who's rich or poor or who feels loved and who feels deprived. If you feel cheated that Laurie gets more than you, then I feel cheated that I had a husband who died at thirty-six. And if you keep on feeling that way, you'll end up like me—with something much worse than loneliness or helplessness and that's self-pity. Believe me, there is no leg that's twisted or bent that is more crippling than a human being who thrives on his own misfortunes . . . I am sorry, Nora, that you feel unloved and I will do everything I can to change it except apologize for it. I am *tired* of apologizing. After a while it becomes your life's work and it doesn't bring any money into the house. If it's taken your pain and Aunt Kate's anger to get me to start living again, then God will give me the strength to make it up to you, but I will *not* go back to being that frightened, helpless woman that *I* created! I've already buried someone I love. Now it's time to bury someone I hate.

NORA. I didn't ask you to hate yourself. I just asked you to love me.

BLANCHE. I do, Nora. Oh, God, why can't I make that clear to you?

NORA. I feel so terrible.

BLANCHE. Why?

NORA. Because I think I hurt you and I still want that job with Mr. Beckman.

BLANCHE. I know you do.

NORA. But I can't have it, can I?

BLANCHE. How can I answer that without you thinking I'm still depriving you?

NORA. I don't know ... Maybe you just did.

BLANCHE. I hope so, Nora. I pray to God it's so.

(KATE is coming down the stairs)

KATE. I heard voices downstairs. I didn't know who it was.

BLANCHE. I'm sorry if we woke you ... Go on up to bed, Nora. We'll talk again in the morning.

NORA. All right . . . Good night, Aunt Kate.

(NORA goes upstairs)

KATE. Is she all right?

BLANCHE. Yes.

KATE. She's not angry anymore?

BLANCHE. No, Kate. No one's angry anymore. *(NORA goes into the bedroom)* I just explained everything to Nora. The girls will help you with all the housework while I'm gone. Laurie's strong enough to do her share. I've kept her being a baby long enough.

KATE. They've never been any trouble to me, those girls. Never.

BLANCHE. I'll try to take them on the weekends if I can ... It's late. We could both use a good night's sleep.

(She starts out of the room)

KATE. Blanche! Don't go! *(BLANCHE stops)* I feel badly enough for what I said. Don't make me feel any worse.

BLANCHE. Everything you said to me tonight was true, Kate. I wish to God you'd said it years ago.

KATE. What would I do without you? Who else do I have to talk to all day? What friends do I have in this neighborhood? Even the Murphys across the street are leaving.

BLANCHE. You and I never had any troubles before tonight, Kate. And as God is in heaven, there'll never be an angry word between us again ... It's the girls I'm thinking of now. We have to be together. The three of us. It's what they want as much as I do.

KATE. All right. I'm not saying you shouldn't have it. But you're not going to find a job overnight. Apartments are expensive. While you're looking, why do you have to live with strangers in Manhattan Beach?

BLANCHE. Louise isn't a stranger. She's a good friend.

KATE. To me good friends are strangers. But sisters are sisters.

BLANCHE. I'm afraid of becoming comfortable here. If I don't get out now, when will I ever do it?

KATE. The door is open. Go whenever you want. When you got the job, when you find the apartment, I'll help you move. I can look with you. I know how to bargain with these landlords.

BLANCHE *(Smiles)*. You wouldn't mind doing that?

KATE. They see a woman all alone, they take advantage of you ... I'll find out what they're asking for the Murphy place. It couldn't be expensive, she never cleaned it.

BLANCHE. How independent can I become if I live right across the street from you?

KATE. Far enough away for you to close your own door, and close enough for me not to feel so lonely.

(BLANCHE looks at her with great affection, walks over to KATE and embraces her. They hold on dearly)

BLANCHE. If I lived on the moon, you would still be close to me, Kate.

KATE. I'll tell Jack. He wouldn't go to sleep until I promised to come up with some good news.

BLANCHE. I suddenly feel so hungry.

KATE. Of course. You haven't had dinner. Come on. I'll fix you some scrambled eggs.

(She heads toward the kitchen)

BLANCHE. I'll make them. I'm an independent woman now.

KATE. With your eyes, you'll never get the eggs in the pan.

(They walk into the kitchen.

EUGENE *appears in the front yard. He is carrying two bags of groceries. It is late afternoon. He stops to talk to the audience)*

EUGENE. So Aunt Blanche decided to stay while she was looking for a job. Nora went back to school the next morning, gave me a big smile and her legs looked as creamy-white as ever. Laurie was asked to take out the garbage but she quickly got a "flutter" in her heart, so I had to do it. Life was back to normal.

(He goes into the house. KATE comes out of the kitchen)

KATE. Eugene! Go back to Greenblatt's. I need flour.

EUGENE. How much? A teaspoonful? *(She glares at him, takes the bags and goes back into the kitchen. He turns to the audience)* Stanley didn't come home that night, and even though Mom didn't say anything, I knew she was plenty worried. She told Pop how Stanley lost the money playing poker, and from the sounds coming out of their room, I figured Stanley should forget about the Army and try for the Foreign Legion. *(STANLEY appears down the street)* And then all of a sudden, the next night about dinnertime, he came back. I was never so happy to see anyone in my whole life.

STANLEY. Hi! *(He looks around)* Where's Mom and Pop?

EUGENE. Mom's in the kitchen cooking. Pop's upstairs with his prayer book. They figured if God didn't bring you home, maybe her potato pancakes would . . . What happened? Did you join up?

STANLEY. I came pretty close. I passed the physical one two three.

EUGENE. I knew you would.

STANLEY. They were giving me cigarettes, doughnuts, the whole sales pitch. I mean, they really wanted me.

EUGENE. I'll bet.

STANLEY. But then, just as I was about to sign my name, I stopped cold. I put down the pen and said, "I'm sorry. Maybe some other time"—and walked out.

EUGENE. How come?

STANLEY. I couldn't do it to Pop. Right now he needs me more than the Army does . . . I knew Mom didn't really mean it when she said she'd never forgive me for losing the money, but if I walked out on the family now, maybe she never would.

EUGENE. Gee, I thought you'd be halfway to training camp by now . . . but I'm real glad you're home, Stan.

(They stand there looking at each other for a moment as KATE walks out of the kitchen to the yard)

KATE. Eugene. I need a pint of sweet cream. And some more sugar.

EUGENE. Stanley's home.

STANLEY. Hello, Mom.

KATE *(Looks at him, then to EUGENE)*. Get a two-pound bag. I want to bake a chocolate cake.

EUGENE. A two-pound bag from Greenblatt's? I'll need identification.

(He looks at STANLEY, then goes)

KATE *(To STANLEY)*. Are you staying for dinner?

STANLEY. I'm staying as long as you'll let me stay.

KATE. Why wouldn't I let you stay?? This is your home. *(KATE walks into the house, STANLEY follows. JACK comes down the stairs and goes over to his favorite chair. He opens up his paper)* Your father's been very worried. I think you owe him some sort of explanation.

STANLEY. I was just about to do that. *(KATE looks at him, wants to reach out to touch him, but can't seem to do it. She goes back into the kitchen as STANLEY walks into the living room)* Hi, Pop. How you feeling? *(JACK doesn't turn. He keeps reading his newspaper)* I'm sorry about not coming home last night . . . I know it was wrong. I just didn't know how to tell you about the money. I know it doesn't help to say I'll never do it again, because I won't. I swear. Never . . . *(He takes money out of his pocket)* I've got three dollars. Last night I went over to Dominick's Bowling Alley and I set pins till midnight and I could make another six on the weekend, so that makes nine. I'll get the seventeen dollars back, Pop, I promise . . . I'm not afraid of hard work. That's the one thing you taught me. Hard work and principles. That's the code I'm going to live by for the rest of my life . . . So—if you have anything you want to say to me, I'd be very glad to listen.

(He stands there and waits)

JACK *(Still looking at the paper)*. Did you read the paper tonight, Stanley?

STANLEY. No, Pop.

JACK. There's going to be a war. A terrible war, Stanley.

STANLEY. I know, Pop.

(He moves into the room, faces his father)

JACK. The biggest war the world has ever seen. And it frightens me. We're still not over the last one yet, and already they're starting another one.

STANLEY. We don't talk about it much in the store because of Mr. Stroheim being German and all.

JACK. My brother, Michael, was killed in the last war. I've told you that.

STANLEY. You showed me his picture in uniform.

JACK. He was nineteen years old. The day he left, he didn't look any older than Eugene. He was killed the second week he was overseas . . .

STANLEY. I know.

JACK. They didn't take me because I was sixteen years old, both parents were dead, and I lived with my Aunt Rose and Uncle Maury. They had two sons in the Navy, both of them wounded, both of them decorated.

STANLEY. Uncle Leon and Uncle Paul, right?

JACK *(Nods)*. My brother would have been forty years old this month. He was a handsome boy. Good athlete, good dancer, good everything. I idolized him. Like Eugene idolizes you.

STANLEY. No, he doesn't.

JACK. He does, believe me. I hear him outside, talking to his friends. "My brother this, my brother that"... Brothers can talk to each other the way fathers and sons never do ... I never knew a thing about girls until my brother taught me. Isn't it like that with you and Eugene?

STANLEY. Yeah, I tell him a few things.

JACK. That's good. I'm glad you're so close ... I missed all that when Michael went away. That's why I'm glad you didn't do anything foolish last night. I was afraid maybe you'd run away. I hear you talking with Eugene sometimes about the Army. That day will come soon enough, I'm afraid.

STANLEY. I did think about it. It was on my mind.

JACK. Don't you know, Stanley, there's nothing you could ever do that was so terrible, I couldn't forgive you. I know why you gambled. I know how terrible you feel. It was foolish, you know that already. I've lost money gambling in my time, I know what it's like.

STANLEY. You did?

JACK. You're so surprised? You think your father's a perfect human being? Someday I'll tell you some other things I did that wasn't so perfect. Not even your mother knows. If you grow up thinking I was perfect, you'll hate yourself for every mistake you ever make. Don't be so hard on yourself. That's what you've got a mother and father to do.

STANLEY. You're not hard on me. You're always fair.

JACK. I try to be. You're a good son, Stanley. You don't even realize that. We have men in our cutting room who haven't spoken to their sons in five, six years. Boys who have no respect for anyone, including themselves; who haven't worked a day in their lives, or who've brought their parents a single day's pleasure. Thank God, I could never say that about you, Stanley.

STANLEY. I gambled away seventeen dollars and you're telling me how terrific I am.

JACK. Hey, wait a minute. Don't get the wrong idea. If you were home last night when your mother told me, I would have thrown you and your clothes out the window. Today I'm calmer. Today I read the newspaper. Today I'm afraid for all of us.

STANLEY. I understand.

JACK. After dinner tonight, you apologize to your mother and give her the three dollars.

STANLEY. I will.

JACK. And apologize to your Aunt Blanche because she was worried about you too.

STANLEY. I will.

JACK. And you can thank your brother as well. He came into my bedroom this afternoon and told me how badly you felt. He was almost in tears himself. The way he pleaded your case, I thought I had Clarence Darrow in the room.

STANLEY. Eugene's a terrific kid.

JACK. All right. Go wash up and get ready for dinner. And tonight, you and I are going to go out in the backyard and I'm going to teach you how to play poker.

STANLEY (Smiles). Terrific!

(He turns to go when KATE comes out of the kitchen)

KATE. Is Eugene back yet?

STANLEY. No, Mom.

KATE. You look tired. Did you get any sleep?

STANLEY. I got enough. I slept at a friend's house. Can I talk to you after dinner, Mom?

KATE. Where am I going? To a night club?

STANLEY. I'll wash up and be right down.

(He turns and starts up the stairs)

KATE. Stanley! You didn't join anything, did you?

STANLEY. No, Mom.

KATE. You've got time yet. The family's growing up fast enough.

STANLEY. Yes, Mom.

(He turns and rushes up the stairs. KATE turns and looks at JACK)

JACK. It's all right. Everything is all right.

KATE. Who said it wasn't? Didn't I say he'd be home? (She calls up) Laurie! Call your sister. Time to set the table.

(EUGENE comes running into the house with a small bag and some letters)

EUGENE (Out of breath). I just broke the world's record to Greenblatt's. Next year I'm entering the Grocery Store Olympics. Here's some mail for you, Pop.

KATE. Is that my sweet cream?

EUGENE. Never spilled a drop. The perfect run. (She takes the bag and goes into the kitchen) Where's Stanley?

JACK (Takes the mail). He's cleaning up. (He looks at the mail) Oh, my God, I've got jury duty next week.

(He sits and opens up a letter. EUGENE rushes up the stairs and runs into his room. STANLEY is taking off his two sweaters)

EUGENE *(Closing the door)*. Are you back in the family?

STANLEY. Yeah. Everything's great.

EUGENE. Terrific... You want to take a walk on the boardwalk tonight? See what's doing?

STANLEY. I can't tonight. I'm busy.

EUGENE. Doing what?

STANLEY. I'm playing poker.

EUGENE. Poker? Are you serious?

STANLEY. Yeah. Right after dinner.

EUGENE. I don't believe you.

STANLEY. I swear to God! I got a poker game tonight.

EUGENE. You're crazy! You're genuinely crazy, Stanley... If you lose, I'm not sticking up for you this time.

STANLEY. If you don't tell anybody, I'll give you a present.

EUGENE. What kind of present?

STANLEY. Are you going to tell?

EUGENE. No. What's my present?

(STANLEY takes something wrapped in a piece of paper out of his jacket and hands it to EUGENE)

STANLEY. Here. It's for you. Don't leave it lying around the room.

(EUGENE starts to open it. It's postcard size)

EUGENE. What is it?

STANLEY. Open it slowly. *(EUGENE does)* Slower than that... Close your eyes. *(EUGENE does. It is unwrapped)* Now look!

(EUGENE looks. His eyes almost pop out)

EUGENE. OH, MY GOD!! ... SHE'S NAKED! YOU CAN SEE *EVERYTHING!!*

STANLEY. Lower your voice. You want to get caught with a thing like that?

EUGENE. Where did you get it? Who is she?

STANLEY. She's French. That's how *all* the women are in Paris.

EUGENE. I can't believe I'm looking at this! You mean some girl actually *posed* for this? She just lay there and let some guy take a picture?

(BLANCHE comes out of the kitchen)

BLANCHE. Laurie! Nora! Time for dinner.

(The girls come out of their room)

STANLEY. It belongs to the guy who owes me two and a half bucks. I can keep it until he pays me back.

EUGENE. Don't take the money. Let him keep it for a while.

(He lies back on the bed, staring at the picture. NORA and LAURIE go down the stairs as KATE comes out of the kitchen with plates and starts to set up the table)

STANLEY. That's my appreciation for being a good buddy.

EUGENE. Anytime you need a favor, just let me know.

STANLEY. Put it in a safe spot... Come on. It's dinner.

EUGENE. In a minute. I'll be down in a minute.

(He lies there, eyes transfixed. STANLEY starts down the stairs. NORA and LAURIE set out napkins and utensils. BLANCHE starts to arrange the chairs.

JACK, with a letter in his hand, gets up, looking excited, walks into the dining room)

JACK. Kate? Where's Kate?

KATE. Don't run. You're always running.

JACK *(Holds up the letter)*. It's a letter from London. My cousin Sholem got out. They got out of Poland. They're free, Kate!

BLANCHE. Thank God!

JACK. His wife, his mother, all four children. They're sailing for New York tomorrow. They'll be here in a week.

KATE. In a week?

LAURIE. Do they speak English?

JACK. I don't think so. A few words, maybe. *(To KATE)* They had to sell everything. They took only what they could carry.

STANLEY. Where will they stay?

JACK. Well, I'll have to discuss it with the family. Some with Uncle Leon, Uncle Paul—

KATE. With us. We can put some beds in the dining room. It's easier to eat in the kitchen anyway.

BLANCHE. The little ones can stay with Laurie. Nora can sleep with me—can't you, dear?

NORA *(Pleased)*. Of course, Momma.

STANLEY. Don't worry about money, Pa. I'm going to hit Mr. Stroheim for that raise.

JACK. They got out. That's all that's important. They got out.

(JACK sits down at the table to reread the letter. NORA, STANLEY and LAURIE look over his shoulder. BLANCHE and KATE set the table)

KATE *(Yells up)*. Eugene! We're all waiting for you!

EUGENE *(Calls down)*. Be right there! I just have to write down soemthing. *(He looks at photo again, then picks up fountain pen and his memoir book and reads as he begins to write)* "October the second, six twenty-five P.M. A momentous moment in the life of I, Eugene Morris Jerome. I have seen the Golden Palace of the Himalayas ... Puberty is over. Onward and upwards!"

Curtain

Painting Churches

TINA HOWE

First presented in February 1983 at The Second Stage, New York City, with the following cast:

FANNY CHURCH	Marian Seldes
GARDNER CHURCH	Donald Moffat
MARGARET CHURCH	Frances Conroy

Directed by Carole Rothman
Set Design by Heidi Landesman
Lighting by Frances Aronson
Costumes by Nan Cibula

PLACE: Beacon Hill—Boston, Massachusetts

TIME: A few years ago.

ACT I: Scene 1: A bright spring morning. Scene 2: Two days later. Scene 3: Twenty-four hours later.

ACT II: Scene 1: Three days later. Scene 2: The last day. There will be one intermission.

"Artists are the closest thing we have to heroes. I see them as seekers. And I don't know who else as a group fills that role in society...." Thus speaks Tina Howe, a truly original American playwright. Her play *Painting Churches* concerns Mags Church, a young portraitist on the verge of her first major show in an uptown Manhattan gallery, who returns to her ancestral Boston home to paint her parents' (the eponymous Churches) portrait and help them relocate to Cape Cod. The play concerns Mags's conflicting sense of responsibility to both herself and her aging parents, and its bittersweet reunion reflects the universal familial needs for love and the mutual approval that can come only from a resolution of the past and an acceptance of the present.

Painting Churches' characters derive from Tina Howe's own experience. "We were to the manor born," says Howe, "but there wasn't any manor. I was always aware from my very earliest memories that we were imposters. . . . We didn't have that kind of money—we lived by our wits rather than by inheritance—and my parents had completely different values. My father was a Democrat and an intellectual. . . . My mother? Well, she was what they call an original—very funny, very dramatic, always dressing in extreme clothing . . . just like the mother in *Painting Churches*. . . . The wonderful thing about art is that you can reinvent. There was more fear and suffering in their lives than I've shown—in that sense, the play's romantic. . . . I so much wanted to write a happier ending for them . . . for everybody's parents.

"A lot of people have asked me, 'Why don't we get to see the picture at the end of the play?' The answer is, 'The play is the picture.' I wanted to make it clear that when you see Gardner and Fanny dancing, *that* is the portrait Mags has been painting the whole week. The daughter realizes that as her parents waltz gracefully into the past, they're disappearing in front of her eyes. . . . I think that what an artist wants to do is to create the illusion that for a moment everything is stopped, beautiful. But you know it is just an illusion."

Tina Howe was born in 1937. She lived for most of her childhood three blocks from the Metropolitan Museum of Art, which, she says, has greatly influenced her life and work. Her mother was a painter; her father was the well-known radio and television commentator Quincey Howe. Her paternal grandfather was the Pulitzer Prize–winning author and poet Mark Antony DeWolfe Howe; her uncle Mark was a dean of the Harvard Law School; Julia Ward Howe, author of the "Battle Hymn of the Republic," is another ancestor. "We were New England Brahmins. . . . I grew up in a very literary household, where the emphasis was on being a writer. . . ." Howe attended a series of East Coast private schools, in which she felt out of place, but after her father left broadcasting and accepted a teaching post at the University of Illinois in the 1950s, she entered a "wildly experimental laboratory" high school in Urbana that encouraged creativity and in which she found acceptance. "It was my salvation," she says. Two unhappy years at Bucknell University followed, after which Howe transferred to Sarah Lawrence College, "with all those wildly creative women," including the young actress Jane Alexander, with whom Howe collaborated on her first play. Upon graduation, she went to Paris, intending to study philosophy at the Sorbonne. Instead, she met other writers and decided to write a play. "I was all bottled up, coming from my background, so naturally I became a writer. It was my way of turning somersaults, of wreaking havoc. . . . For whatever reason, we playwrights don't feel we're adequate players in real life, so we dress up in all these costumes and have actors fulfill our fantasies. . . ."

Back in the United States, she married Norman Levy in 1961, and throughout the sixties, husband and wife took turns teaching while the other wrote. Howe's first teaching position was at a school in Bath, Maine, in which she ran the theatre group and performed in her own plays. Her first professionally produced play, *The Nest* (1969–70), was a success in Provincetown but a disaster Off Broadway. In 1973, the couple settled in New York; besides writing plays, Howe teaches at New York University.

Painting Churches was first presented in 1983 by the Second Stage. Partly recast, it moved to the Lamb's Theatre in 1984. Marion Seldes, who played the role of Fanny Church in both engagements, says of Howe's plays, "They're realistic plays full of fantasies. They have credible plots, but within them the most incredible things happen. . . ." Joseph Papp, who produced two of Howe's plays, *Museum* (1976–77) and *The Art of Dining* (1979), stated: "To me, her plays are like Irish coffee: On top it's all sweet and effervescent, but when you reach bottom, what a zinger!" A trademark of Howe's style is the contrapuntal technique, in which her characters speak in parallel lines, each seemingly lost in his own thoughts, until finally the lines swerve and intersect, and the characters begin to talk to each other.

"I write about five or six hours a day," Howe says. "I have a profoundly rich and boring life. . . . You have to be like an athlete to write; you really can't go out. I think the whole joy of writing a play is to play with your imagination. The more you stick to reality, the duller it is. The point of playwriting is to exercise your imagination to make things happen that never did happen."

In 1983, Tina Howe was the recipient of the Rosamund Gilder Award for Distinguished Playwriting, a Rockefeller Playwright in Residence Award (which she used at the Second Stage), the John Gassner Award for Outstanding New American Playwright, and an Obie Award for *Painting Churches*. In 1984, *Painting Churches* earned her the Outer Critics Circle Award for Outstanding Off Broadway Production. In 1987, she won a Tony nomination for her play *Coastal Disturbances*. Her other plays include *Birth and After Birth* (1973), *To Dress and Train a Concert Pianist* (1979), and *Approaching Zanzibar* (1989). *Birth and After Birth, Museum, The Art of Dining,* and *Painting Churches* were published by Avon Books in 1983.

CHARACTERS

FANNY SEDGWICK CHURCH, a Bostonian from a fine old family, in her 60's.

GARDNER CHURCH, her husband, an eminent New England poet from a finer family, in his 70's.

MARGARET CHURCH (MAGS), their daughter, a painter, in her early 30's.

ACT ONE

SCENE 1

The living room of the Church's townhouse on Beacon Hill one week before everything will be moved to Cape Cod. Empty packing cartons line the room and all the furniture has been tagged with brightly colored markers. At first glance it looks like any discreet Boston interior, but on closer scrutiny one notices a certain flamboyance. Oddities from second hand stores are mixed in with the fine old furniture and exotic hand made curios vie with tasteful family objets d'art. What makes the room remarkable though, is the play of light that pours through three soaring arched windows. At one hour it's hard-edged and brilliant, the next, it's dappled and yielding. It transforms whatever it touches giving the room a distinct feeling of unreality. It's several years ago, a bright spring morning.

FANNY is sitting on the sofa wrapping a valuable old silver coffee service. She's wearing a worn bathrobe and fashionable hat. As she works, she makes a list of everything on a yellow legal pad. GARDNER can be heard typing in his study down the hall.

FANNY *(She picks up a coffee pot)*. God, this is good looking! I'd forgotten how handsome Mama's old silver was! It's probably worth a fortune. It certainly weighs enough! *(calling out)* GARRRRRRRRRRRRRRRRRRD-NERRRRRRRRRRRR . . . ? Well, it should bring us a pretty penny, that's for sure. *(Wraps it, places it in a carton and then picks up the tray that goes with it. She holds it up like a mirror and adjusts her hat; louder in another register.)* OH GARRRRRRRRRRRRRRRRRRD-NERRRRR . . . ? *(He continues typing. She then reaches for a small box and opens it with reverence.)* Grandma's Paul Revere tea spoons . . . ! *(She takes several out and fondles them.)* I don't care how desperate things get, these will never go! One has to maintain some standards! *(She writes on her list.)* "Grandma's Paul Revere tea spoons, Cotuit!" . . .

WASN'T IT THE AMERICAN WING OF THE METROPOLITAN MUSEUM OF ART THAT WANTED GRANDMA'S PAUL REVERE TEA SPOONS SO BADLY . . . ? *(She looks at her reflection in the tray again.)* This is a very good looking hat, if I do say so. I was awfully smart to grab it up. *(silence)* DON'T YOU REMEMBER A DISTINGUISHED LOOKING MAN COMING TO THE HOUSE AND OFFERING US $50,000 FOR GRANDMA'S PAUL REVERE TEA SPOONS . . . ? HE HAD ON THESE MARVELOUS SHOES! THEY WERE SO POINTED AT THE ENDS WE COULDN'T IMAGINE HOW HE EVER GOT THEM ON AND THEY WERE SHINED TO WITHIN AN INCH OF THEIR LIVES AND I REMEMBER HIM SAYING HE CAME FROM THE . . . AMERICAN WING OF THE METROPOLITAN MUSEUM OF ART! . . . HELLO? . . . GARDNER . . . ? ARE YOU THERE! *(The typing stops.)* YOO HOOOOOOO . . . *(like a fog horn)* GARRRRRRRRRRRDNERRRRRRR . . . ?

GARDNER *(offstage; from his study).* YES DEAR . . . IS THAT YOU . . . ?

FANNY. OF COURSE IT'S ME! WHO ELSE COULD IT POSSIBLY BE . . . ? DARLING, PLEASE COME HERE FOR A MINUTE. *(The typing resumes.)* FOR GOD'S SAKE, WILL YOU STOP THAT DREADFUL TYPING BEFORE YOU SEND ME STRAIGHT TO THE NUT HOUSE . . . ? *(in a new register)* GARRRRRRRRRRRR-RRDNERRRRRR . . . ? *(He stops.)*

GARDNER *(offstage).* WHAT'S THAT? MAGS IS BACK FROM THE NUT HOUSE . . . ? *(brief silence)* I'LL BE WITH YOU IN A MOMENT, I DIDN'T HEAR HER RING. *(He starts singing the refrain of "Nothing Could Be Finer."*)*

FANNY *(simultaneously).* I SAID . . . Lord, I hate this yelling . . . PLEASE . . . COME . . . HERE! It's a wonder I'm not in a straight jacket already. Actually, it might be rather nice for a change . . . Peaceful. DARLING . . . I WANT TO SHOW YOU MY NEW HAT!

(Silence, GARDNER enters, still singing. He's wearing mis-matched tweeds and is holding a stack of papers which keep drifting to the floor.)

---

*Note: Permission to produce *Painting Churches* does not include permission to use this song, which ought to be procured from the copyright owner.

GARDNER. Oh, don't you look nice! Very attractive, very attractive!

FANNY. But I'm still in my bathrobe.

GARDNER *(looking around the room, leaking more papers)*. Well, where's Mags?

FANNY. Darling, you're dropping your papers all over the floor.

GARDNER *(spies the silver tray)*. I remember this! Aunt Alice gave it to us, didn't she? *(He picks it up.)* Good Lord, it's heavy. What's it made of? Lead?!

FANNY. No, Aunt Alice did *not* give it to us. It was Mama's.

GARDNER. Oh yes... *(He starts to exit with it.)*

FANNY. Could I have it back, please?

GARDNER *(hands it to her, dropping more papers)*. Oh, sure thing . . . Where's Mags? I thought you said she was here.

FANNY. I didn't say Mags was here, I asked *you* to come here.

GARDNER *(papers spilling)*. Damned papers keep falling . . .

FANNY. I wanted to show you my new hat. I bought it in honor of Mags' visit. Isn't it marvelous?

GARDNER *(picking up the papers as more drop)*. Yes, yes, very nice . . .

FANNY. Gardner, you're not even looking at it!

GARDNER. Very becoming . . .

FANNY. You don't think it's too bright, do you? I don't want to look like a traffic light. Guess how much it cost?

GARDNER *(A whole sheaf of papers slides to the floor, he dives for them)*. OH SHIT!

FANNY *(gets to them first)*. It's alright, I've got them, I've got them. *(She hands them to him.)*

GARDNER. You'd think they had wings on them . . .

FANNY. Here you go . . .

GARDNER *(simultaneously)*. . . . damned things won't hold still!

FANNY. Gar . . . ?

GARDNER *(has become engrossed in one of the pages and is lost reading it)*. Mmmmm?

FANNY. HELLO?

GARDNER *(startled)*. What's that?

FANNY *(in a whisper)*. My hat. Guess how much it cost.

GARDNER. Oh yes. Let's see . . . $10?

FANNY. $10? . . . IS THAT ALL . . . ?

GARDNER. 20?

FANNY. GARDNER, THIS HAPPENS TO BE A DESIGNER HAT! DESIGNER HATS START AT $50 . . . 75!

GARDNER *(jumps)*. Was that the door bell?

FANNY. No, it wasn't the door bell. Though it's high time Mags were here. She was probably in a train wreck!

GARDNER *(looking through his papers)*. I'm beginning to get fond of Wallace Stevens again.

FANNY. This damned move is going to kill me! Send me straight to my grave!

GARDNER *(reading from a page)*.
"The mules that angels ride come slowly down
The blazing passes, from beyond the sun.
Descensions of their tinkling bells arrive.
These muleteers are dainty of their way . . ."

(pause) Don't you love that! "These muleteers are *dainty* of their way . . . !?"

FANNY. Gar, the hat. How much? *(GARDNER sighs.)*

FANNY. Darling . . . ?

GARDNER. Oh yes. Let's see . . . $50? 75?

FANNY. It's French.

GARDNER. 300!

FANNY *(triumphant)*. No, 85¢.

GARDNER. 85¢! I thought you said . . .

FANNY. That's right . . . eighty . . . five . . . *cents!*

GARDNER. Well, you sure had me fooled!

FANNY. I found it at the Thrift Shop.

GARDNER. I thought it cost at least $50 or 75. You know, designer hats are very expensive!

FANNY. It was on the mark-down table. *(She takes it off and shows him the label.)* See that? Lily Daché! When I saw that label, I nearly keeled over right into the fur coats!

GARDNER *(handling it)*. Well, what do you know, that's the same label that's in my bathrobe.

FANNY. Darling, Lily Daché designed hats, not men's bathrobes!

GARDNER. Yup . . . "Lily Daché" . . . same name . . .

FANNY. If you look again, I'm sure you'll see . . .

GARDNER. . . . same script, same color, same size. I'll show you. *(He exits.)*

FANNY. Poor lamb can't keep anything straight anymore. *(looks at herself in the tray again)* God, this is a good looking hat!

GARDNER *(returns with a nondescript plaid bathrobe; he points to the label)*. See that . . . ? What does it say?

FANNY *(refusing to look at it)*. Lily Daché was a *hat* designer! She designed ladies' *hats!*

GARDNER. What . . . does . . . it . . . say?

FANNY. Gardner, you're being ridiculous.

GARDNER *(forcing it on her)*. Read . . . the label!

FANNY. Lily Daché did *not* design this bathrobe, I don't care what the label says!

GARDNER. READ! *(FANNY reads it.)* ALL RIGHT, NOW WHAT DOES IT SAY . . . ?

FANNY *(chagrined)*. Lily Daché.

GARDNER. I told you!

FANNY. Wait a minute, let me look at that again. *(She does, then throws the robe at him in disgust.)* Gar, Lily Daché never designed a bathrobe in her life! Someone obviously ripped the label off one of her hats and then sewed it into the robe.

GARDNER *(puts it on over his jacket)*. It's damned good looking. I've always loved this robe. I think you gave it to me . . . Well, I've got to get back to work. *(He abruptly exits.)*

FANNY. Where did you get that robe anyway? . . . I didn't give it to you, did I . . . ? *(Silence; he resumes typing. Holding the tray up again and admiring herself.)* You know, I think I *did* give it to him. I remember how excited I was when I found it at the Thrift Shop . . . 50¢ and never worn! *I* couldn't have sewn that label in to impress him, could I? . . . I can't be that far gone! . . . The poor lamb wouldn't even notice it, let alone understand its cachet . . . Uuuuuh, this damned tray is even heavier than the coffee pot. They must have been amazons in the old days! *(writes on her pad)* "Empire tray, Parke Bernet Galleries," and good riddance! *(She wraps it and drops it into the carton with the coffee pot.)* Where *is* that wretched Mags? It would be just like her to get into a train wreck! She was supposed to be here hours ago. Well, if she doesn't show up soon, I'm going to drop dead of exhaustion. God, wouldn't that be wonderful? . . . Then they could just cart me off into storage with all the old chandeliers and china . . . *(The door bell rings.)*

FANNY. IT'S MAGS, IT'S MAGS! *(a pause; dashing out of the room, colliding into GARDNER)* GOOD GOD, LOOK AT ME! I'M STILL IN MY BATHROBE!

GARDNER *(simultaneously, offstage)*. COMING, COMING . . . I'VE GOT IT . . . COMING! *(dash- into the room colliding into FANNY)* I'VE GOT IT . . . HOLD ON . . . COMING . . . COMING. . .

FANNY *(offstage)*. MAGS IS HERE! IT'S MAGS . . . SHE'S FINALLY HERE!

(GARDNER exits to open the front door. MAGS comes staggering in carrying a suitcase and enor-mous duffle bag. She wears wonderfully distinctive clothes and has very much her own look. She's extremely out of breath and too wrought up to drop her heavy bags.)

MAGS. I'm sorry . . . I'm sorry I'm so late . . . Everything went wrong! A passenger had a heart attack outside of New London and we had to stop . . . It was terrifying! All these medics and policemen came swarming onto the train and the conductor kept running up and down the aisles telling everyone not to leave their seats under any circumstances . . . Then the New London fire department came screeching down to the tracks, sirens blaring, lights whirling, and all these men in black rubber suits started pouring through the doors . . . *That* took two hours . . .

FANNY *(offstage)*. DARLING . . . DARLING . . . WHERE ARE YOU . . . ?

MAGS. *Then,* I couldn't get a cab at the station. There just weren't any! I must have circled the block 15 times. Finally I just stepped out into the traffic with my thumb out, but no one would pick me up . . . so I walked . . .

FANNY *(offstage)*. Damned zipper's stuck.

GARDNER. You walked all the way from the South Station?

MAGS. Well actually, I ran . . .

GARDNER. You had poor Mum scared to death.

MAGS *(finally puts the bags down with a deep sigh)*. I'm sorry . . . I'm really sorry. It was a nightmare.

FANNY *(Re-enters the room, her dress over her head. The zipper's stuck, she staggers around blindly)*. Damned zipper! Gar, will you please help me with this?

MAGS *(squeezing him tight)*. Oh Daddy . . . Daddy!

GARDNER. My Mags!

MAGS. I never thought I'd get here! . . . Oh, you look wonderful!

GARDNER. Well, you don't look so bad yourself!

MAGS. I love your hair. It's gotten so . . . white!

FANNY *(still lost in her dress, struggling with the zipper)*. This is *so* typical . . . just as Mags arrives, my zipper has to break! *(FANNY grunts and struggles.)*

MAGS *(waves at her)*. Hi, Mum . . .

FANNY. Just a minute, dear, my zipper's . . .

GARDNER *(picks up MAGS' bags)*. Well, sit down and take a load off your feet . . .

MAGS. I was so afraid I'd never make it . . .

GARDNER *(staggering under the weight of her bags).* What have you got in here? Lead weights?

MAGS. I can't believe you're finally letting me do you.

FANNY *(flings her arms around* MAGS, *practically knocking her over).* OH, DARLING . . . MY PRECIOUS MAGS, YOU'RE HERE AT LAST

GARDNER *(simultaneously, lurching around in circles).* Now let's see . . . where should I put these . . . ?

FANNY. I was sure your train had derailed and you were lying dead in some ditch!

MAGS *(pulls away from* FANNY *to come to* GARDNER'S *rescue).* Daddy, please, let me . . . these are much too heavy.

FANNY *(finally noticing* MAGS*).* GOOD LORD, WHAT HAVE YOU DONE TO YOUR HAIR?!

MAGS *(struggling to take the bags from* GARDNER*).* Come on, give them to me . . . please? *(She sets them down by the sofa.)*

FANNY *(as her dress starts to slide off one shoulder).* Oh, not again! . . . Gar, would you give me a hand and see what's wrong with this zipper. One minute it's stuck, the next it's falling to pieces. *(*GARDNER *goes to her and starts fussing with it.)*

MAGS *(pacing).* I don't know, it's been crazy all week. Monday, I forgot to keep an appointment I'd made with a new model . . . Tuesday, I overslept and stood up my advanced painting students . . . Wednesday, the day of my meeting with Max Zoll, I forgot to put on my underpants . . .

FANNY. GODDAMNIT, GAR, CAN'T YOU DO ANYTHING ABOUT THIS ZIPPER?!

MAGS. I mean, there I was, racing down Broome Street in this gauzy Tibetan skirt when I tripped and fell right at his feet . . . SPLATT! My skirt goes flying over my head and there I am . . . everything staring him in the face . . .

FANNY. COME ON, GAR, USE A LITTLE MUSCLE!

MAGS *(laughing).* Oh well, all that matters is that I finally got here . . . I mean . . . there you are . . .

GARDNER *(struggling with the zipper).* I can't see it, it's too small!

FANNY *(whirls away from* GARDNER, *pulling her dress off altogether).* OH FORGET IT!

JUST FORGET IT! . . . The trolly's probably missing half its teeth, just like someone else I know. *(to* MAGS*)* I grind my teeth in my sleep now, I've worn them all down to stubs. Look at that! *(She flings open her mouth and points.)* Nothing left but the gums!

GARDNER. I never hear you grind your teeth . . .

FANNY. That's because I'm snoring so loud. How could you hear anything through all that racket? It even wakes me up. It's no wonder poor Daddy has to sleep downstairs.

MAGS *(looking around).* Jeez, look at the place! So, you're finally doing it . . . selling the house and moving to Cotuit year round. I don't believe it. I just don't believe it!

GARDNER. Well, how about a drink to celebrate Mags' arrival?

MAGS. You've been here so long. Why move now?

FANNY. Gardner, what are you wearing that bathrobe for . . . ?

MAGS. You can't move. I won't let you!

FANNY *(softly to* GARDNER*).* Really darling, you ought to pay more attention to your appearance.

MAGS. You love this house. *I* love this house . . . This room . . . the light.

GARDNER. So, Mags, how about a little . . . *(He drinks from an imaginary glass.)* to wet your whistle?

FANNY. We can't start drinking now, it isn't even noon yet!

MAGS. I'm starving. I've got to get something to eat before I collapse! *(She exits towards the kitchen.)*

FANNY. What *have* you done to your hair, dear? The color's so queer and all your nice curl is gone.

GARDNER. It looks to me as if she dyed it.

FANNY. Yes, that's it. You're absolutely right! It's a completely different color. She dyed it bright red! *(*MAGS *can be heard thumping and thudding through the ice box.)* NOW MAGS, I DON'T WANT YOU FILLING UP ON SNACKS . . . I'VE MADE A PERFECTLY BEAUTIFUL LEG OF LAMB FOR LUNCH! . . . HELLO? . . . DO YOU HEAR ME . . . ? *(to* GARDNER*)* No one in our family has *ever* had red hair, it's so common looking.

GARDNER. I like it. It brings out her eyes.

FANNY. WHY ON EARTH DID YOU DYE YOUR HAIR *RED,* OF ALL COLORS . . . ?!

MAGS *(returns, eating saltines out of the box).* I

didn't dye my hair, I just added some high-light.

FANNY. I suppose that's what your arty friends in New York do ... dye their hair all the colors of the rainbow!

GARDNER. Well, it's damned attractive if you ask me ... damned attractive! *(MAGS unzips her duffle bag and rummages around in it while eating the saltines.)*

FANNY. Darling, I told you not to bring a lot of stuff with you. We're trying to get rid of things.

MAGS *(pulls out a folding easel and starts setting it up).* AAAAAHHHHHH, here it is. Isn't it a beauty? I bought it just for you!

FANNY. Please don't get crumbs all over the floor. Crystal was just here yesterday. It was her last time before we move.

MAGS *(at her easel).* God, I can hardly wait! I can't believe you're finally letting me do you.

FANNY. *"Do"* us? ... What *are* you talking about?

GARDNER *(reaching for the saltines).* Hey, Mags, could I have a couple of those?

MAGS *(tosses him the box).* Sure! *(to FANNY)* Your portrait.

GARDNER. Thanks. *(He starts munching on a handful.)*

FANNY. You're planning to paint our portrait now? While we're trying to move ... ?

GARDNER *(mouth full).* Mmmmm, I'd forgotten just how delicious saltines are!

MAGS. It's a perfect opportunity. There'll be no distractions, you'll be completely at my mercy. Also, you promised.

FANNY. I did?

MAGS. Yes, you did.

FANNY. Well, I must have been off my rocker.

MAGS. No, you said, "You can paint us, you can dip us in concrete, you can do anything you want with us, just so long as you help us get out of here!"

GARDNER *(offering the box of saltines to FANNY).* You really ought to try some of these, Fan, they're absolutely delicious!

FANNY *(taking a few).* Why, thank you.

MAGS. I figure we'll pack in the morning and you'll pose in the afternoons. It'll be a nice diversion.

FANNY. These *are* good!

GARDNER. Here, dig in ... take some more.

MAGS. I have some wonderful news ... amazing news! I wanted to wait til I got here to tell you. *(They eat their saltines, passing the box back and forth as MAGS speaks.)* You'll die! Just fall over into the packing cartons and

die! Are you ready ... ? BRACE YOUR-SELVES ... OK, HERE GOES ... I'm being given a one woman show at one of the most important galleries in New York this fall. Me, Margaret Church, exhibited at Castelli's, 420 West Broadway ... Can you believe it?! ... MY PORTRAITS HANGING IN THE SAME ROOMS THAT HAVE SHOWN RAUSCHENBURG, JOHNS, WARHOL, KELLY, LICHTENSTEIN, STELLA, SERRA, ALL THE HEAVIES ... It's incredible, beyond belief ... I mean, at my age ... Do you know how good you have to be to get in there? It's a miracle ... an honest-to-God, star spangled miracle! *(pause)*

FANNY *(mouth full).* Oh, darling, that's wonderful. We're so happy for you!

GARDNER *(likewise, simultaneously).* No one deserves it more, no one deserves it more!

MAGS. Through some fluke, some of Castelli's people showed up at our last faculty show at Pratt and were knocked out ...

FANNY *(reaching for the box of saltines).* More, more ...

MAGS. They said they hadn't seen anyone handle light like me since the French Impressionists. They said I was this weird blend of Pierre Bonnard, Mary Cassatt and David Hockney ...

GARDNER *(swallowing his own mouthful).* I told you they were good.

MAGS. Also, no one's doing portraits these days. They're considered passé. I'm so out of it, I'm in.

GARDNER. Well, you're loaded with talent and always have been.

FANNY. She gets it all from Mama, you know. Her miniature of Henry James is still one of the main attractions at the Atheneum. Of course no woman of breeding could be a professional artist in her day. It simply wasn't done. But talk about talent ... that woman had talent to burn!

MAGS. I want to do one of you for the show.

FANNY. Oh, do Daddy, he's the famous one.

MAGS. No, I want to do you both. I've always wanted to do you and now I've finally got a good excuse.

FANNY. It's high time somebody painted Daddy again! I'm sick to death of that dreadful portrait of him in the National Gallery they keep reproducing. He looks like an undertaker!

GARDNER. Well, I think you should just do Mum. She's never looked handsomer.

FANNY. Oh, come on, I'm a perfect fright and you know it.

MAGS. I want to do you both. Side by side. In this room. Something really classy. You look so great. Mum with her crazy hats and everything and you with that face. If I could just get you to hold still long enough and actually pose.

GARDNER *(walking around, distracted).* Where are those papers I just had? God damnit, Fanny . . .

MAGS. I have the feeling it's either now or never.

GARDNER. I can't hold on to anything around here. *(He exits to his study.)*

MAGS. I've always wanted to do you. It would be such a challenge.

FANNY *(pulling MAGS next to her onto the sofa).* I'm so glad you're finally here, Mags. I'm very worried about Daddy.

MAGS. Mummy, please. I just got here.

FANNY. He's getting quite gaga.

MAGS. Mummy . . . !

FANNY. You haven't seen him in almost a year. Two weeks ago he walked through the front door of the Codman's house, kissed Emily on the cheek and settled down in the maid's room, thinking he was home!

MAGS. Oh come on, you're exaggerating.

FANNY. He's as mad as a hatter and getting worse every day! It's this damned new book of his. He works on it around the clock. I've read some of it, and it doesn't make one word of sense, it's all at 6s and 7s . . .

GARDNER *(poking his head back in the room, spies some of his papers on a table and grabs them).* Ahhh, here they are. *(and exits)*

FANNY *(voice lowered).* Ever since this dry spell with his poetry, he's been frantic, absolutely . . . frantic!

MAGS. I hate it when you do this.

FANNY. I'm just trying to get you to face the facts around here.

MAGS. There's nothing wrong with him! He's just as sane as the next man. Even saner, if you ask me.

FANNY. You know what he's doing now? You couldn't guess in a million years! . . . He's writing criticism! Daddy! *(She laughs.)* Can you believe it? The man doesn't have one analytic bone in his body. His mind is a complete jumble and always has been! *(There's a loud crash from GARDNER's study.)*

GARDNER *(offstage).* SHIT!

MAGS. He's abstracted . . . That's the way he is.

FANNY. He doesn't spend any time with me anymore. He just holes up in that filthy study with Toots. God, I hate that bird! Though actually they're quite cunning together. Daddy's teaching him Grey's Elegy. You ought to see them in there, Toots perched on top of Daddy's head, spouting out verse after verse . . . Daddy, tap tap tapping away on his typewriter. They're quite a pair.

GARDNER *(pokes his head back in).* Have you seen that Stevens' poem I was reading before?

FANNY *(long suffering).* NO, I HAVEN'T SEEN THAT STEVENS' POEM YOU WERE READING BEFORE . . . ! Things are getting very tight around here, in case you haven't noticed. Daddy's last Pulitzer didn't even cover our real estate tax, and now that he's too doddery to give readings anymore, that income is gone . . . *(suddenly handing MAGS the sugarbowl she'd been wrapping)* Mags, *do* take this sugarbowl. You can use it to serve tea to your students at that wretched art school of yours . . .

MAGS. It's called Pratt! The Pratt Institute.

FANNY. Pratt, Platt, whatever . . .

MAGS. And I don't serve tea to my students, I teach them how to paint.

FANNY. Well, I'm sure none of them has ever seen a sugarbowl as handsome as this before.

GARDNER *(reappearing again).* You're sure you haven't seen it . . . ?

FANNY *(loud and angry).* YES, I'M SURE I HAVEN'T SEEN IT! I JUST TOLD YOU I HAVEN'T SEEN IT!

GARDNER *(retreating).* Right you are, right you are. *(He exits.)*

FANNY. God! *(silence)*

MAGS. What do you have to yell at him like that for?

FANNY. Because the poor thing's as deaf as an adder! *(MAGS sighs deeply; silence.)*

FANNY *(suddenly exuberant, leads her over to a lamp).* Come, I want to show you something?

MAGS *(looking at it).* What is it?

FANNY. Something I made. *(MAGS is about to turn it on.)* WAIT, DON'T TURN IT ON YET! It's got to be dark to get the full effect. *(She rushes to the windows and pulls down the shades.)*

MAGS. What *are* you doing . . . ?

FANNY. Hold your horses a minute. You'll see . . . *(as the room gets darker and darker)* Poor me, you wouldn't believe the lengths I go to to amuse myself these days . . .

MAGS *(touching the lamp shade).* What is this? It looks like a scene of some sort.

FANNY. It's an invention I made . . . a kind of magic lantern.

MAGS. Gee . . . it's amazing . . .

FANNY. What I did was buy an old engraving of the Grand Canal . . .

MAGS. You *made* this?

FANNY. . . . and then color it in with crayons. Next, I got out my sewing scissors and cut out all the street lamps and windows . . . anything that light would shine through. Then I pasted it over a plain lampshade, put the shade on this old horror of a lamp, turned on the switch and . . . *(She turns it on.)* . . . VOILA . . . VENICE TWINKLING AT DUSK! It's quite effective, don't you think . . . ?

MAGS *(walking around it)*. Jeeez . . .

FANNY. And see, I poked out all the little lights on the gondolas with a straight pin.

MAGS. Where on earth did you get the idea?

FANNY. Well you know, idle minds . . . *(FANNY spins the shade, making the lights whirl.)*

MAGS. It's really amazing. I mean, you you could sell this in a store!

GARDNER *(enters, simultaneously)*. HERE IT IS, IT WAS RIGHT ON TOP OF MY DESK THE WHOLE TIME *(He crashes into a table)*. OOOOOWWWWW!

FANNY. LOOK OUT, LOOK OUT!

MAGS *(rushes over to him)*. Oh, Daddy, are you all right!

FANNY *(simultaneously)*. WATCH WHERE YOU'RE GOING, WATCH WHERE YOU'RE GOING!

GARDNER *(hopping up and down on one leg)*. GODDAMNIT! . . . I HIT MY SHIN!

FANNY. I was just showing Mags my lamp . . .

GARDNER *(limping over to it)*. Oh yes, isn't that something? Mum is awfully clever with that kind of thing . . . It was all her idea, the whole thing. Buying the engraving, coloring it in, cutting out all those little dots.

FANNY. Not "dots" . . . lights and windows, lights and windows!

GARDNER. Right, right . . . lights and windows.

FANNY. Well, we'd better get some light back in here before someone breaks their neck. *(She zaps the shades back up.)*

GARDNER *(puts his arm around MAGS)*. Gee, it's good to have you back.

MAGS. It's good to be back.

GARDNER. And I like that new red hair of yours. It's very becoming.

MAGS. But I told you, I hardly touched it . . .

GARDNER. Well, something's different. You've got a glow. So . . . how do you want us to pose for this grand portrait of yours . . . ? *(He poses self-consciously.)*

MAGS. Oh Daddy, setting up a portrait takes alot of time and thought. You've got to figure out the background, the lighting, what to wear, the sort of mood you want to . . .

FANNY. OOOOH, LET'S DRESS UP, LET'S DRESS UP! *(She grabs a packing blanket, drapes it around herself and links arms with GARDNER, striking an elegant pose.)* This *is* going to be fun. She was absolutely right! Come on, Gar, look distinguished!

MAGS. Mummy please, it's not a game!

FANNY *(more and more excited)*. You still have your tuxedo, don't you? And I'll wear my marvelous long black dress that makes me look like that fascinating woman in the Sargent painting! *(She strikes the famous profile pose.)*

MAGS. MUMMY . . . ?!

FANNY. I'm sorry, we'll behave, just tell us what to do. *(They settle down next to each other.)*

GARDNER. That's right, you're the boss.

FANNY. Yes, you're the boss.

MAGS. But I'm not ready yet, I haven't set anything up.

FANNY. Relax, darling, we just want to get the hang of it . . .

(They stare straight ahead, trying to look like suitable subjects, but they can't hold still. They keep making faces; lifting an eyebrow, wriggling a nose, twitching a lip, nothing grotesque, just flickering little changes; a half smile here, a self-important frown there. They steal glances at each other every so often.)

GARDNER. How am I doing, Fan?

FANNY. Brilliantly, absolutely brilliantly!

MAGS. But you're making faces.

FANNY. *I'm* not making faces, *(turning to GARDNER and making a face)* are *you* making faces, Gar?

GARDNER *(instantly making one)*. Certainly not! I'm the picture of restraint!

(Without meaning to, they get sillier and sillier. They start giggling, then laughing.)

MAGS *(can't help but join in)*. You two are impossible . . . completely impossible! I was crazy to think I could ever pull this off! *(laughing away)* Look at you . . . just . . . look at you!

Blackout

SCENE 2

Two days later, around five in the afternoon. Half of the Church's household has been dragged into the living room for packing. Overflowing cartons are everywhere. They're filled with pots and pans, dishes and glasses, and the entire contents of two linen closets. MAGS *has placed a stepladder under one of the windows. A pile of table cloths and curtains is flung beneath it. Two side chairs are in readiness for the eventual pose.*

———

MAGS *(Has just pulled a large crimson table cloth out of a carton. She unfurls it with one shimmering toss).* PERFECT . . . PERFECT . . . !

FANNY *(seated on the sofa, clutches an old pair of galoshes to her chest).* Look at these old horrors, half the rubber is rotted away and the fasteners are falling to pieces . . . GARDNER . . . ? OH GARRRRRRRRRRDNERRRRR . . . ?

MAGS *(rippling out the table cloth with shorter snapping motions).* Have you ever seen such a color . . . ?

FANNY. I'VE FOUND YOUR OLD SLEDDING GALOSHES IN WITH THE POTS AND PANS. DO YOU STILL WANT THEM?

MAGS. It's like something out of a Rubens . . . ! *(She slings it over a chair and then sits on a foot stool to finish the Sara Lee banana cake she started. As she eats, she looks at the table cloth making happy grunting sounds.)*

FANNY *(lovingly puts the galoshes on over her shoes and wiggles her feet).* God, these bring back memories! There were real snow storms in the old days. Not these pathetic little two inch droppings we have now. After a particularly heavy one, Daddy and I used to go sledding on the Common. This was way before you were born . . . God, it was a hundred years ago . . . ! Daddy would stop writing early, put on these galoshes and come looking for me, jingling the fasteners like castanets. It was a kind of mating call, almost . . . *(She jingles them.)* The Common was always deserted after a storm, we had the whole place to ourselves. It was so romantic . . . We'd haul the sled up Beacon Street, stop under the State House, and aim it straight down to the Park Street Church, which was much further away in those days . . . Then Daddy would lie down on the sled, I'd lower myself on top of him, we'd rock back and forth a few times to gain momentum and then . . . WHOOOOOOOOOSSSSS-

SSHHHHH . . . down we'd plunge like a pair of eagles locked in a spasm of love making. God, it was wonderful! . . . The city whizzing past us at 90 miles an hour . . . the cold . . . the darkness . . . Daddy's hair in my mouth . . . GAR . . . REMEMBER HOW WE USED TO GO SLEDDING IN THE OLD DAYS . . . ? Sometimes he'd lie on top of me. That was fun. I liked that even more. *(in her fog horn voice)* GARRRRRRRRRDNERRRRR . . . ?

MAGS. Didn't he say he was going out this afternoon?

FANNY. Why, so he did! I completely forgot. *(She takes off the galoshes.)* I'm getting just as bad as him. *(She drops them into a different carton.)* Gar's galoshes, Cotuit. *(a pause)*

MAGS *(picks up the table cloth again, holds it high over her head).* Isn't this fabulous . . . ? *(She then wraps* FANNY *in it.)* It's the perfect backdrop. Look what it does to your skin.

FANNY. Mags, what *are* you doing?

MAGS. It makes you glow like a pomegranate . . . *(She whips it off her.)* Now all I need is a hammer and nails . . . *(She finds them.)* YES! *(She climbs up the stepladder and starts hammering a corner of the cloth into the moulding of one of the windows.)* This is going to look so great . . . ! I've never seen such a color!

FANNY. Darling, what is going on . . . ?

MAGS. Rembrandt, eat your heart out! You 17th Century Dutch hasbeen, you. *(She hammers more furiously.)*

FANNY. MARGARET, THIS IS NOT A CONSTRUCTION SITE . . . PLEASE . . . STOP IT . . . YOO HOOOOO . . . DO YOU HEAR ME . . . ?

*(*GARDNER *suddenly appears, dressed in a raincoat.)*

FANNY. MARGARET, WILL YOU PLEASE STOP THAT RACKET?!

GARDNER. YES, DEAR, HERE I AM. I JUST STEPPED OUT FOR A WALK DOWN CHESTNUT STREET. BEAUTIFUL AFTERNOON, ABSOLUTELY BEAUTIFUL.

FANNY *(simultaneously, to* MAGS*).*YOU'RE GOING TO RUIN THE WALLS TO SAY NOTHING OF MAMA'S BEST TABLE CLOTH . . . MAGS, DO YOU HEAR ME? . . . YOO HOO . . . !

MAGS *(Is done, she stops).* There!

GARDNER. WHY THAT LOOKS VERY NICE, MAGS, very nice indeed . . .

FANNY *(simultaneously).* DARLING, I MUST INSIST you stop that dreadful . . .

MAGS *(steps down, stands back and looks at it).* That's it. That's *IT!*

FANNY *(to GARDNER, worried).* Where have you been?

(MAGS kisses her fingers at the backdrop and settles back into her banana cake.)

GARDNER *(to FANNY).* You'll never guess who I ran into on Chestnut Street . . . Pate Baldwin! *(He takes his coat off and drops it on the floor. He then sits in one of the posing chairs MAGS has pulled over by the window.)*

MAGS *(mouth full of cake).* Oh Daddy, I'm nowhere near ready for you yet.

FANNY *(picks up his coat and hands it to him).* Darling, coats do *not* go on the floor.

GARDNER *(rises, but forgets where he's supposed to go).* He was in terrible shape. I hardly recognized him. Well, it's the Parkinson's disease . . .

FANNY. You mean, Hodgkin's disease . . .

GARDNER. Hodgkin's disease . . . ?

MAGS *(leaves her cake and returns to the table cloth).* Now to figure out exactly how to use this gorgeous light . . .

FANNY. Yes, Pate has Hodgkin's disease, not Parkinson's disease. Sammy Bishop has Parkinson's disease. In the closet . . . your coat goes . . . in the closet!

GARDNER. You're absolutely right! Pate has Hodgkin's disease. *(He stands motionless, the coat over his arm.)*

FANNY. . . . and Goat Davis has Addison's disease.

GARDNER. I always get them confused.

FANNY *(pointing towards the closet).* That way . . . *(GARDNER exits to the closet; FANNY, calling after him.)* GRACE PHELPS HAS IT TOO, I THINK. Or, it might be Hodgkin's, like Pate. I can't remember.

GARDNER *(returns with a hanger).* Doesn't the Goat have Parkinson's disease.

FANNY. No, that's Sammy Bishop.

GARDNER. God, I haven't seen the Goat in ages! *(The coat still over his arm, he hands FANNY the hanger.)* He hasn't been well.

FANNY. Didn't Heppy . . . *die?!*

FANNY. What are you giving me this for? . . . Oh, Heppy's been dead for years. She died on the same day as Luster Bright, don't you remember?

GARDNER. I always liked her.

FANNY *(gives him back the hanger).* Here, I don't want this.

GARDNER. She was awfully attractive.

FANNY. Who?

GARDNER. Heppy!

FANNY. Oh yes, Heppy had real charm.

MAGS *(keeps experimenting with draping the table cloth).* Better . . . better . . .

GARDNER. . . . which is something the Goat is short on, if you ask me. He has Hodgkin's disease, doesn't he? *(puts his raincoat back on and sits down)*

FANNY. Darling, what *are* you doing? I thought you wanted to hang up your coat!

GARDNER *(after a pause).* OH YES, THAT'S RIGHT! *(He goes back to the closet; a pause.)*

FANNY. Where were we?

GARDNER *(returns with yet another hanger).* Let's see . . .

FANNY *(takes both hangers from him).* FOR GOD'S SAKE, GAR, PAY ATTENTION!

GARDNER. It was something about the Goat . . .

FANNY *(takes the coat from GARDNER).* HERE, LET ME DO IT . . . ! *(under her breath to MAGS)* See what I mean about him? You don't know the half of it! *(She hangs it up in the closet.)* Not the half.

MAGS *(still tinkering with the backdrop).* Almost . . . almost . . .

GARDNER *(sitting back down on one of the posing chairs).* Oh Fan, did I tell you, I ran into Pate Baldwin just now. I'm afraid he's not long for this world.

FANNY *(returning).* Well, it's that Hodgkin's disease . . . *(She sits in the posing chair next to him.)*

GARDNER. God, I'd hate to see him go. He's one of the great editors of our times. I couldn't have done it without him. He gave me everything, everything!

MAGS *(makes a final adjustment).* Yes, that's it! *(She stands back and gazes at them.)* You look wonderful . . . !

FANNY. Isn't it getting to be . . . *(She taps at an imaginary watch on her wrist and drains an imaginary glass.)* . . . cocktail time?!

GARDNER *(looks at his watch).* On the button, on the button! *(He rises.)*

FANNY. I'll have the usual, please. Do join us, Mags! Daddy bought some Dubonnet especially for you!

MAGS. Hey. I was just getting some ideas.

GARDNER *(To MAGS, as he exits for the bar).* How about a little . . . *Dubonnet* to wet your whistle?

FANNY. Oh Mags, it's like old times having you back with us like this!

GARDNER *(offstage).* THE USUAL FOR YOU, FAN?

FANNY. I wish we saw more of you . . . PLEASE! . . . Isn't he darling? Have you ever known anyone more darling than Daddy . . . ?

GARDNER (offstage; singing from the bar). "You Made Me Love You,"* etc. MAGS, HOW ABOUT YOU? . . . A LITTLE . . . DUBONNET . . . ?

FANNY. Oh, do join us!

MAGS (simultaneously, to GARDNER). No, nothing, thanks!

FANNY. Well, what do you think of your aged parents picking up and moving to Cotuit year round? Pretty crazy, eh what? . . . Just the gulls, oysters and us!

GARDNER (returns with FANNY's drink). Here you go . . .

FANNY. Why thank you, Gar. (to MAGS) You sure you won't join us?

GARDNER (lifts his glass towards FANNY and MAGS). Cheers! (GARDNER and FANNY take that first life-saving gulp.)

FANNY. Aaaaahhhhh!

GARDNER (simultaneously). Hits the spot, hits the spot!

MAGS. Well, I certainly can't do you like that!

FANNY. Why not? I think we look very . . . comme il faut! (She slouches into a rummy pose, GARDNER joins her.) WAIT . . . I'VE GOT IT! I'VE GOT IT! (She whispers excitedly to GARDNER.)

MAGS. Come on, let's not start this again!

GARDNER. What's that? . . . Oh yes . . . yes, yes . . . I know the one you mean. Yes, right, right . . . of course. (a pause)

FANNY. How's . . . this . . . ?! (FANNY grabs a large serving fork and they fly into an imitation of Grant Wood's "American Gothic.")

MAGS. . . . and I wonder why it's taken me all these years to get you to pose for me. You just don't take me seriously! Poor old Mags and her ridiculous portraits . . .

FANNY. Oh darling, your portraits aren't ridiculous! They may not be all that one hopes for, but they're certainly not . . .

MAGS. Remember how you behaved at my first group show in Soho? . . . Oh, come on, you remember. It was a real circus! Think back . . . It was about six years ago . . . Daddy had just been awarded some presidential medal of achievement and you insisted he

*Note: This song is still under copyright protection. Permission to use it in productions of Painting Churches ought to be procured from the copyright owner.

wear it around his neck on a bright red ribbon, and you wore this . . . huge feathered hat to match! I'll never forget it! It was the size of a giant pizza with 20 inch red turkey feathers shooting straight up into the air . . . Oh come on, you remember, don't you . . . ?

FANNY (leaping to her feet). HOLD EVERYTHING! THIS IS IT! THIS IS REALLY IT! Forgive me for interrupting, Mags darling, it'll just take a minute. (She whispers excitedly to GARDNER.)

MAGS. I had about eight portraits in the show, mostly of friends of mine, except for this old one I'd done of Mrs. Crowninshield.

GARDNER. All right, all right . . . let's give it a whirl. (A pause, then they mime Michelangelo's "Pieta" with GARDNER lying across FANNY's lap as the dead Christ.)

MAGS (depressed). "The Pieta." Terrific!

FANNY (jabbing GARDNER in the ribs). Hey, we're getting good at this.

GARDNER. Of course it would help if we didn't have all these modern clothes on.

MAGS. AS I WAS SAYING . . .

FANNY. Sorry, Mags . . . sorry . . . (Huffing and creaking with the physical exertion of it all, they return to their seats.)

MAGS. . . . As soon as you stepped foot in the gallery you spotted it and cried out, "MY GOD, WHAT'S MILLICENT CROWNINSHIELD DOING HERE?" Everyone looked up what with Daddy's clanking medal and your amazing hat which I was sure would take off and start flying around the room. A crowd gathered . . . Through some utter fluke, you latched on to the most important critic in the city, I mean . . . Mr. Modern Art himself, and you hauled him over to the painting, trumpeting out for all to hear, "THAT'S MILLICENT CROWNINSHIELD! I GREW UP WITH HER. SHE LIVES RIGHT DOWN THE STREET FROM US IN BOSTON. BUT IT'S A VERY POOR LIKENESS, IF YOU ASK ME! HER NOSE ISN'T NEARLY THAT LARGE AND SHE DOESN'T HAVE SOMETHING QUEER GROWING OUT OF HER CHIN! THE CROWNINSHIELDS ARE REALLY QUITE GOOD LOOKING, STUFFY, BUT GOOD LOOKING NONETHELESS!"

GARDNER (suddenly jumps up, ablaze). WAIT, WAIT . . . IF IT'S MICHELANGELO YOU WANT . . . I'm sorry, Mags . . . One more . . . just one more . . . please?

MAGS. Sure, why not? Be my guest.

GARDNER. *Fanny, prepare yourself! (He whispers into her ear.)*

FANNY. THE BEST!... IT'S THE BEST! OH MY DEAREST, YOU'RE A GENIUS, AN ABSOLUTE GENIUS! *(more whispering)* But I think *you* should be God.

GARDNER. Me? ... Really?

FANNY. Yes, it's much more appropriate.

GARDNER. Well, if you say so ...

(FANNY and GARDNER ease down to the floor with some difficulty and lie on their sides, FANNY as Adam, GARDNER as God, their fingers inching closer and closer in the attitude of Michelangelo's "The Creation." Finally, they touch.)

MAGS *(cheers, whistles, applauds).* THREE CHEERS ... VERY GOOD ... NICELY DONE, NICELY DONE! *(They hold the pose a moment more, flushed with pleasure, then rise, dust themselves off and grope back to their chairs.)* So, there we were ...

FANNY. Yes, *do* go on ...!

MAGS. ... huddled around Millicent Crowninshield, when you whipped into your pocketbook and suddenly announced, "HOLD EVERYTHING! I'VE GOT A PHOTOGRAPH OF HER RIGHT HERE, THEN YOU CAN SEE WHAT SHE REALLY LOOKS LIKE!" ... You then proceeded to crouch down to the floor and dump everything out of your bag, and I mean ... *everything!* ... Leaking packets of sequins and gummed stars, sea shells, odd pieces of fur, crochet hooks, a Monarch butterfly embedded in plastic, dental floss, antique glass buttons, small jingling bells, lace ... I thought I'd die! Just sink to the floor and quietly die! ... You couldn't find it, you see. I mean, you spent the rest of the afternoon on your hands and knees crawling through this ocean of junk muttering, "It's *got* to be here somewhere, I know I had it with me!" ... Then Daddy pulled me into the thick of it all and said, "By the way, have you met our daughter Mags yet? She's the one who did all these pictures ... paintings ... portraits ... whatever you call them." *(She drops to her hands and knees and begins crawling out of the room.)* By this time, Mum had somehow crawled out of the gallery and was lost on another floor. She began calling for me ... "YOO HOO, MAGS ... WHERE ARE YOU? ... OH MAGS, DARLING ... HELLO ...? ARE YOU THERE ...?" *(She reenters and faces them.)* This was at my *first* show.

Blackout

SCENE 3

Twenty-four hours later. The impact of the impending move has struck with hurricane force. FANNY *has lugged all their clothing into the room and dumped it in various cartons. There are coats, jackets, shoes, skirts, suits, hats, sweaters, dresses, the works. She and* GARDNER *are seated on the sofa, going through it all.*

FANNY *(wearing a different hat and dress, holds up a ratty overcoat).* What about this gruesome old thing?

GARDNER *(Is wearing several sweaters and vests, a Hawaiian holiday shirt, and a variety of scarves and ties around his neck. He holds up a pair of shoes).* God ... remember these shoes? Pound gave them to me when he came back from Italy. I remember it vividly.

FANNY. *Do* let me give it to the Thrift Shop! *(She stuffs the coat into the appropriate carton.)*

GARDNER. He bought them for me in Rome. Said he couldn't resist, bought himself a pair too since we both wore the same size. God, I miss him! *(pause)* HEY, WHAT ARE YOU DOING WITH MY OVERCOAT?!

FANNY. Darling, it's threadbare!

GARDNER. But that's my overcoat! *(He grabs it out of the carton.)* I've been wearing it every day for the past 35 years!

FANNY. That's just my point: it's had it.

GARDNER *(puts it on over everything else).* There's nothing wrong with this coat!

FANNY. I trust you remember that the cottage is an eighth the size of this place and you simply won't have room for half this stuff! *(She holds up a sports jacket.)* This dreary old jacket, for instance. You've had it since Hector was a pup!

GARDNER *(grabs it and puts it on over his coat).* Oh no you don't ...

FANNY. ... and this God-awful hat ...

GARDNER. Let me see that. *(He stands next to her and they fall into a lovely frieze.)*

MAGS *(suddenly pops out from behind a wardrobe carton with a flash camera and takes a picture of them).* PERFECT!

FANNY *(hands flying to her face).* GOOD GOD, WHAT WAS THAT ...?

GARDNER *(simultaneously, hands flying to his heart).* JESUS CHRIST, I'VE BEEN SHOT!

MAGS *(walks to the c. of the room, advancing the film).* That was terrific. See if you can do it again.

FANNY. What *are* you doing ...?

GARDNER *(feeling his chest)*. Is there blood?

FANNY. I see lace everywhere . . .

MAGS. It's all right, I was just taking a picture of you. I often use a Polaroid at this stage.

FANNY *(rubbing her eyes)*. Really Mags, you might have given us some warning!

MAGS. But that's the whole point: to catch you unawares!

GARDNER *(rubbing his eyes)*. It's the damndest thing . . . I see lace everywhere.

FANNY. Yes, so do I . . .

GARDNER. It's rather nice, actually. It looks as if you're wearing a veil.

FANNY. I *am* wearing a veil! *(The camera spits out the photograph.)*

MAGS. OH GOODY, HERE COMES THE PICTURE!

FANNY *(grabs the partially developed print out of her hands)*. Let me see, let me see . . .

GARDNER. Yes, let's have a look. *(They have another quiet moment together looking at the photograph.)*

MAGS *(tip toes away from them and takes another picture)*. YES!

FANNY. NOT AGAIN! PLEASE, DARLING!

GARDNER *(simultaneously)*. WHAT WAS THAT . . . ? WHAT HAPPENED . . . ?

(They stagger towards each other.)

MAGS. I'm sorry, I just couldn't resist. You looked so . . .

FANNY. WHAT ARE YOU TRYING TO DO . . . *BLIND* US?!

GARDNER. Really, Mags, enough is enough . . . *(GARDNER and FANNY keep stumbling about, kiddingly.)*

FANNY. Are you still there, Gar?

GARDNER. Right as rain, right as rain!

MAGS. I'm sorry, I didn't mean to scare you. It's just a photograph can show you things you weren't aware of. Here, have a look. *(She gives them to FANNY.)* Well, I'm going out to the kitchen to get something to eat. Anybody want anything? *(She exits.)*

FANNY *(looking at the photos, half amused, half horrified)*. Oh, Gardner, have you ever . . . ?

GARDNER *(looks at them and laughs)*. Good grief . . .

MAGS *(offstage from the kitchen)*. IS IT ALL RIGHT IF I TAKE THE REST OF THIS TAPIOCA FROM LAST NIGHT?

FANNY. IT'S ALL RIGHT WITH ME. How about you, Gar?

GARDNER. Sure, go right ahead. I've never been that crazy about tapioca.

FANNY. What are you talking about, tapioca is one of your favorites.

MAGS *(enters, slurping from a large bowl)*. Mmmmmmmm . . .

FANNY. Really, Mags, I've never seen anyone eat as much as you.

MAGS *(takes the photos back)*. It's strange. I only do this when I come home.

FANNY. What's the matter, don't I feed you enough?

GARDNER. Gee, it's hot in here! *(starts taking off his coat)*

FANNY. God knows, you didn't eat anything as a child! I've never seen such a fussy eater. Gar, what *are* you doing?

GARDNER. Taking off some of these clothes. It's hotter than Tofit in here! *(shedding clothes to the floor)*

MAGS *(looking at her photos)*. Yes, I like you looking at each other like that . . .

FANNY *(to GARDNER)*. Please watch where you're dropping things, I'm trying to keep some order around here.

GARDNER *(picks up what he dropped, dropping even more in the process)*. Right, right . . .

MAGS. Now all I've got to do is figure out what you should wear.

FANNY. Well, I'm going to wear my long black dress, and you'd be a fool not to do Daddy in his tuxedo. He looks so distinguished in it, just like a banker!

MAGS. I haven't really decided yet.

FANNY. Just because you walk around looking like something the cat dragged in, doesn't mean Daddy and I want to, do we, Gar? *(GARDNER is making a worse and worse tangle of his clothes.)* HELLO . . . ?

GARDNER *(looks up at FANNY)*. Oh yes, awfully attractive, awfully attractive!

FANNY *(to MAGS)*. If you don't mind me saying so, I've never seen you looking so forlorn. You'll never catch a husband looking that way. Those peculiar clothes, that Godawful hair . . . Really, Mags, it's very distressing!

MAGS. I don't think my hair's so bad, not that it's terrific or anything . . .

FANNY. Well, I don't see other girls walking around like you. I mean, girls from your background. What would Lyman Wigglesworth think if he saw you in the street?

MAGS. Lyman Wigglesworth?! . . . Uuuuuughhhhhhh! *(She shudders.)*

FANNY. Alright then, that brilliant Cabot boy . . . what *is* his name?

GARDNER. Sammy.

FANNY. No, not Sammy . . .

GARDNER. Stephen.

FANNY. Oh, for God's sake, Gardner . . .

GARDNER. Stephen . . . Stanley . . . Stuart . . . Sheldon . . . Sherlock . . . Sherlock. It's Sherlock!

MAGS. Spence!

FANNY. SPENCE, THAT'S IT! HIS NAME IS SPENCE!

GARDNER (simultaneously). THAT'S IT . . . SPENCE! SPENCE CABOT.

FANNY. Spence Cabot was first in his class at Harvard.

MAGS. Mum, he has no facial hair.

FANNY. He has his own law firm on Arlington Street.

MAGS. Spence Cabot has six fingers on his right hand!

FANNY. So, he isn't the best looking thing in the world. Looks isn't everything. He can't help it if he has extra fingers. Have a little sympathy!

MAGS. But the extra one has this weird nail on it that looks like a talon . . . it's long and black and (She shudders.)

FANNY. No one's perfect, darling. He has lovely handwriting and an absolutely saintly mother. Also, he's as rich as Croesus! He's alot more promising than some of those creatures you've dragged home. What was the name of that dreadful Frenchman who smelled like sweaty socks? . . . Jean Duke of Scripto?

MAGS (laughing). Jean-Luc Zichot!

FANNY. . . . and that peculiar little Oriental fellow with all the teeth! Really, Mags, he could have been put on display at the circus!

MAGS. Oh yes, Tsu Chin. He was strange, but very sexy . . .

FANNY (shudders). He had such tiny . . . feet! Really, Mags, you've got to bear down. You're not getting any younger. Before you know it, all the nice young men will be taken and then where will you be? . . . All by yourself in that grim little apartment of yours with those peculiar clothes and that bright red hair . . .

MAGS. MY HAIR IS NOT BRIGHT RED!

FANNY. I only want what's best for you, you know that. You seem to go out of your way to look wanting. I don't understand it . . . Gar, what are you putting your coat on for? . . . You look like some derelict out on the street. We don't wear coats in the house. (She helps him out of it.) That's the way . . . I'll just put this in the carton along with everything else . . . (She drops it into the carton, then pauses.) Isn't it about time for . . . cocktails!

GARDNER. What's that? (FANNY taps her wrist and mimes drinking. GARDNER looks at his watch.) Right you are, right you are! (exits to the bar) THE USUAL . . . ?

FANNY. Please!

GARDNER (offstage). HOW ABOUT SOMETHING FOR YOU, MAGS?

MAGS. SURE WHY NOT . . . ? LET 'ER RIP!

GARDNER (offstage). WHAT'S THAT . . . ?

FANNY. SHE SAID YES. SHE SAID YES!

MAGS (simultaneously). I'LL HAVE SOME DUBONNET!

GARDNER (poking his head back in). How about a little Dubonnet?

FANNY. That's just what she said . . . she'd like some . . . Dubonnet!

GARDNER (goes back to the bar and sings a Jolson tune). GEE, IT'S GREAT HAVING YOU BACK LIKE THIS, MAGS . . . IT'S JUST GREAT! (more singing)

FANNY (leaning closer to MAGS). You have such potential, darling! It breaks my heart to see how you've let yourself go. If Lyman Wigglesworth . . .

MAGS. Amazing as it may seem, I don't care about Lyman Wigglesworth!

FANNY. From what I've heard, he's quite a lady killer!

MAGS. But with whom? . . . Don't think I haven't heard about his fling with . . . Hopie Stonewall!

FANNY (begins to laugh). Oh God, let's not get started on Hopie Stonewall again . . . ten feet tall with spots on her neck . . . (to GARDNER) OH DARLING, DO HURRY BACK! WE'RE TALKING ABOUT PATHETIC HOPIE STONEWALL!

MAGS. It's not so much her incredible height and spotted skin, it's those tiny pointed teeth and the size 11 shoes!

FANNY. I love it when you're like this!

(MAGS starts clomping around the room making tiny pointed teeth nibbling sounds.)

FANNY. GARDNER . . . YOU'RE MISSING EVERYTHING! (still laughing) Why is it Boston girls are always so . . . tall?

MAGS. Hopie Stonewall isn't a Boston girl, she's a giraffe. (She prances around the room with an imaginary dwarf-sized Lyman.) She's perfect for Lyman Wigglesworth!

GARDNER (returns with FANNY's drink which he hands her). Now, where were we . . . ?

FANNY (trying not to laugh). HOPIE STONEWALL! . . .

GARDNER. Oh yes, she's the very tall one, isn't she? (FANNY and MAGS burst out laughing.)

MAGS. The only hope for us . . . "Boston girls" is to get as far away from our kind as possible.

FANNY. She always asks after you, darling. She's very fond of you, you know.

MAGS. Please, I don't want to hear!

FANNY. Your old friends are *always* asking after you.

MAGS. It's not so much how creepy they all are, as how much they remind me of myself!

FANNY. But you're not "creepy," darling . . . just . . . shabby!

MAGS. I mean, give me a few more inches and some brown splotches here and there, and Hopie and I could be sisters!

FANNY *(in a whisper to* GARDNER*)*. Don't you love it when Mags is like this? I could listen to her forever!

MAGS. I mean . . . look at me!

FANNY *(gasping)*. Don't stop, don't stop!

MAGS. Awkward . . . plain . . . I don't know how to dress, I don't know how to talk. When people find out Daddy's my father, they're always amazed . . . "Gardner Church is YOUR father?! Aw come on, you're kidding?!"

FANNY *(in a whisper)*. Isn't she divine . . . ?

MAGS. Sometimes I don't even tell them. I pretend I grew up in the midwest somewhere . . . farming people . . . we work with our hands.

GARDNER *(to* MAGS*)*. Well, how about a little refill . . . ?

MAGS. No, no more thanks. *(pause)*

FANNY. What did you have to go and interrupt her for? She was just getting up a head of steam . . . ?

MAGS *(walking over to her easel)*. The great thing about being a portrait painter you see is, it's the *other* guy that's exposed, you're safely hidden behind the canvas and easel. *(standing behind it)* You can be as plain as a pitchfork, as inarticulate as mud, but it doesn't matter because you're completely concealed: your body, your face, your intentions. Just as you make your most intimate move, throw open your soul . . . they stretch and yawn, remembering the dog has to be let out at five . . . To be so invisible while so enthralled . . . it takes your breath away!

GARDNER. Well put, Mags. Awfully well put!

MAGS. That's why I've always wanted to paint you, to see if I'm up to it. It's quite a risk. Remember what I went through as a child with my great masterpiece . . . ?

FANNY. You painted a masterpiece when you were a child . . . ?

MAGS. Well, it was a masterpiece to me.

FANNY. I had no idea you were precocious as a child. Gardner, do you remember Mags painting a masterpiece as a child?

MAGS. I didn't paint it. It was something I made!

FANNY. Well, this is all news to me! Gar, *do* get me another drink! I haven't had this much fun in years! *(She hands him her glass and reaches for* MAGS'.*)* Come on, darling, join me . . .

MAGS. No, no more, thanks. I don't really like the taste.

FANNY. Oh come on, kick up your heels for once!

MAGS. No, nothing . . . really.

FANNY. Please? Pretty please . . . ? To keep me company?!

MAGS *(hands* GARDNER *her glass)*. Oh, all right, what the hell . . .

FANNY. That's a good girl!

GARDNER *(simultaneously, exiting)*. Coming right up, coming right up.

FANNY *(yelling after him)*. DON'T GIVE ME TOO MUCH NOW. THE LAST ONE WAS AWFULLY STRONG . . . AND HURRY BACK SO YOU DON'T MISS ANYTHING . . . ! Daddy's so cunning, I don't know what I'd do without him. If anything should happen to him, I'd just . . .

MAGS. Mummy, nothing's going to happen to him . . . !

FANNY. Well, wait 'til you're our age, it's no garden party. Now . . . where were we . . . ?

MAGS. My first masterpiece . . .

FANNY. Oh yes, but *do* wait til Daddy gets back so he can hear it too . . . YOO HOOOO . . . GARRRRRRDNERRRRRRR? . . . ARE YOU COMING . . . ? *(silence)* Go and check on him, will you?

GARDNER *(Enters with both drinks; he's shaken)*. I couldn't find the ice.

FANNY. Well, *finally!*

GARDNER. It just up and disappeared . . . *(hands* FANNY *her drink)* There you go. *(*FANNY *kisses her fingers and takes a hefty swig.)* Mags. *(hands her hers)*

MAGS. Thanks, Daddy.

GARDNER. Sorry about the ice.

MAGS. No problem, no problem. *(*GARDNER *sits down; silence.)*

FANNY *(to* MAGS*)*. Well, drink up, drink up! *(*MAGS *downs it in one gulp.)* GOOD GIRL! . . . Now, what's all this about a masterpiece . . . ?

MAGS. I did it during that winter you sent

me away from the dinner table. I was about nine years old.

FANNY. We sent you from the dinner table?

MAGS. I was banished for six months.

FANNY. You *were* . . . ? How extraordinary!

MAGS. Yes, it *was* rather extraordinary!

FANNY. But why?

MAGS. Because I played with my food.

FANNY. You did?

MAGS. I used to squirt it out between my front teeth.

FANNY. Oh, I remember that! God, it used to drive me crazy, absolutely . . . crazy! *(pause)* "MARGARET, STOP THAT OOZING RIGHT THIS MINUTE, YOU ARE *NOT* A TUBE OF TOOTHPASTE!"

GARDNER. Oh yes . . .

FANNY. It was perfectly disgusting!

GARDNER. I remember. She used to lean over her plate and squirt it out in long runny ribbons . . .

FANNY. That's enough, dear.

GARDNER. They were quite colorful, actually; decorative almost. She made the most intricate designs. They looked rather like small, moist Oriental rugs . . .

FANNY *(to MAGS)*. But why, darling? What on earth possessed you to do it?

MAGS. I couldn't swallow anything. My throat just closed up. I don't know, I must have been afraid of choking or something.

GARDNER. I remember one in particular. We'd had chicken fricassee and spinach . . . She made the most extraordinary . . .

FANNY *(to GARDNER)*. WILL YOU PLEASE SHUT UP?! *(pause)* Mags, what *are* you talking about? You never choked in your entire life! This is the most distressing conversation I've ever had. Don't you think it's distressing, Gar?

GARDNER. Well, that's not quite the word I'd use.

FANNY. What word *would* you use, then?

GARDNER. I don't know right off the bat, I'd have to think about it.

FANNY. THEN, THINK ABOUT IT! *(silence)*

MAGS. I guess I was afraid of making a mess. I don't know, you were awfully strict about table manners. I was always afraid of losing control. What if I started to choke and began spitting up over everything . . . ?

FANNY. Alright, dear, that's enough.

MAGS. No, I was really terrified about making a mess, you always got so mad whenever I spilled. If I just got rid of everything in neat little curly-cues beforehand, you see . . .

FANNY. I SAID: THAT'S ENOUGH! *(silence)*

MAGS. *I* thought it was quite ingenious, but you didn't see it that way. You finally sent me from the table with, "When you're ready to eat like a human being, you can come back and join us!" . . . So, it was off to my room with a tray. But I couldn't seem to eat there either. I mean, it was so strange settling down to dinner in my *bedroom* . . . So I just flushed everything down the toilet and sat on my bed listening to you: clinkity clink, clatter clatter, slurp slurp . . . but that got pretty boring after awhile, so I looked around for something to do. It was wintertime because I noticed I'd left some crayons on top of my radiator and they'd melted down into these beautiful shimmering globs, like spilled jello, trembling and pulsing . . .

GARDNER *(eyes closed)*. "This luscious and impeccable fruit of life
Falls, it appears, of its own weight to earth . . ."

MAGS. Naturally, I wanted to try it myself, so I grabbed a red one and pressed it down against the hissing lid. It oozed and bubbled like raspberry jam!

GARDNER. "When you were Eve, its acrid juice was sweet,
Untasted, in its heavenly, orchard air . . ."

MAGS. I mean, that radiator was really hot! It took incredible will power not to let go, but I held on, whispering, "Mags, if you let go of this crayon, you'll be run over by a truck on Newberry Street, so help you God!" . . . So I pressed down harder, my fingers steaming and blistering . . .

FANNY. I had no idea about any of this, did you, Gar?

MAGS. Once I'd melted one, I was hooked! I finished off my entire supply in one night, mixing color over color until my head swam . . . ! The heat, the smell, the brilliance that sank and rose . . . I'd never felt such exhilaration! . . . Every week I spent my allowance on crayons. I must have cleared out every box of Crayolas in the city!

GARDNER *(gazing at MAGS)*. You know, I don't think I've ever seen you looking prettier! You're awfully attractive when you get going!

FANNY. Why, what a lovely thing to say.

MAGS. AFTER THREE MONTHS THAT RADIATOR WAS . . . SPECTACULAR! I MEAN, IT LOOKED LIKE SOME COLOSSAL FRUIT CAKE, FIVE FEET TALL . . . !

FANNY. It sounds perfectly hideous.

MAGS. It was a knockout; shimmering with pinks and blues, lavenders and maroons, turquoise and golds, oranges and creams ... For every color, I imagined a taste ... YELLOW: lemon curls dipped in sugar ... RED: glazed cherries laced with rum ... GREEN: tiny peppermint leaves veined with chocolate ... PURPLE: ...

FANNY. That's quite enough!

MAGS. And then the frosting ... ahhhh, the frosting! A satiny mix of white and silver ... I kept it hidden under blankets during the day ... My huge ... *(She starts laughing.)* ... looming ... teetering sweet ...

FANNY. I ASKED YOU TO STOP! GARDNER, WILL YOU PLEASE GET HER TO STOP!

GARDNER. See here, Mags, Mum asked you to ...

MAGS. I was so ... *hungry* ... losing weight every week. I looked like a scarecrow what with the bags under my eyes and bits of crayon wrapper leaking out of my clothes. It's a wonder you didn't notice. But finally you came to my rescue ... If you could call what happened a rescue. It was more like a rout!

FANNY. Darling ... *please!*

GARDNER *(simultaneously)*. Now look, young lady ...

MAGS. The winter was almost over ... It was very late at night ... I must have been having a nightmare because suddenly you and Daddy were at my bed, shaking me ... I quickly glanced towards the radiator to see if it was covered ... *It wasn't!* It glittered and towered in the moonlight like some ... gigantic Viennese pastry! You followed my gaze and saw it. Mummy screamed ... "WHAT HAVE YOU GOT IN HERE? ... MAGS, WHAT HAVE YOU BEEN DOING?" ... She crept forward and touched it, and then jumped back. "IT'S FOOD!" she cried ... "IT'S ALL THE FOOD SHE'S BEEN SPITTING OUT! OH, GARDNER, IT'S A MOUNTAIN OF ROTTING GARBAGE!"

FANNY *(softly)*. Yes ... it's coming back ... it's coming back ...

MAGS. Daddy exited as usual, left the premises. He fainted, just keeled over onto the floor ...

GARDNER. Gosh, I don't remember any of this ...

MAGS. My heart stopped! I mean, I knew it was all over. My lovely creation didn't have a chance. Sure enough ... Out came the blow torch. Well, it couldn't have *really* been a blow torch, I mean, where would you have ever gotten a blow torch ...? I just have this very strong memory of you standing over my bed, your hair streaming around your face, aiming this ... flame thrower at my confection ... my cake ... my tart ... my strudel ... "IT'S GOT TO BE DESTROYED IMMEDIATELY! THE THING'S ALIVE WITH VERMIN! ... JUST LOOK AT IT! ... IT'S PRACTICALLY CRAWLING ACROSS THE ROOM!" ... Of course in a sense you were right. It *was* a monument of my cast-off dinners, only I hadn't built it with food ... I found my own materials. I was languishing with hunger, but oh, dear Mother ... I FOUND MY OWN MATERIALS ...!

FANNY. Darling ... *please?!*

MAGS. I tried to stop you, but you wouldn't listen ... OUT SHOT THE FLAME! ... I remember these waves of wax rolling across the room and Daddy coming to, wondering what on earth was going on ... Well, what did you know about my abilities ...? You see, I had ... I mean, I *have* abilities ... *(struggling to say it)* I have abilities. I have ... strong abilities. I have ... very strong abilities. They are very strong ... very very strong ... *(She rises and runs out of the room overcome as FANNY and GARDNER watch, speechless.)*

The Curtain Falls

ACT TWO

SCENE 1

Three days later. Miracles have been accomplished. Almost all of the Church's furniture has been moved out and the cartons of dishes and clothing are gone. All that remains are odds and ends. MAGS' tableau looms, impregnable. FANNY and GARDNER are dressed in their formal evening clothes, frozen in their pose. They hold absolutely still. MAGS stands at her easel, her hands covering her eyes.

———

FANNY. All right, you can look now.

MAGS *(removes her hands)*. Yes ...! I told you you could trust me on the pose.

FANNY. Well, thank God you let us dress up. It makes all the difference. Now we really look like something.

MAGS *(starts to sketch them)*. I'll say ... *(A silence as she sketches.)*

GARDNER *(Recites Yeats' "The Song of Wan-*

dering Aengus" in a wonderfully resonant voice as they pose).

"I went out to the hazel wood,
Because a fire was in my head,
And cut and peeled a hazel wand,
And hooked a berry to a thread,
And when white moths were on the wing,
And moth-like stars were flickering out,
I dropped the berry in a stream
And caught a little silver trout.

When I had laid it on the floor
I went to blow the fire a-flame,
But something rustled on the floor,
And someone called me by my name:
It had become a glimmering girl
With apple blossoms in her hair
Who called me by my name and ran
And faded through the brightening air.

Though I am old with wandering
Through hollow lands and hilly lands,
I will find out where she has gone,
And kiss her lips and take her hands;
And walk among long dappled grass,
And pluck till time and times are done,
The silver apples of the moon,
The golden apples of the sun."
(silence)

FANNY. That's lovely, dear. Just lovely. Is it one of yours?

GARDNER. No, no, it's Yeats. I'm using it in my book.

FANNY. Well, you recited it beautifully, but then you've always recited beautifully. That's how you wooed me, in case you've forgotten . . . You must have memorized every love poem in the English language! There was no stopping you when you got going . . . your Shakespeare, Byron, and Shelley . . . you were shameless . . . *shameless!*

GARDNER *(eyes closed).*

"I will find out where she has gone,
And kiss her lips and take her hands . . ."

FANNY. And then there was your own poetry to do battle with; your sonnets and quatrains. When you got going with them, there was nothing left of me! You could have had your pick of any girl in Boston! Why you chose me, I'll never understand. I had no looks to speak of and nothing much in the brains department . . . Well, what did you know about women and the world . . . ? What did any of us know . . . ? *(silence)* GOD, MAGS, HOW LONG ARE WE SUP- POSED TO SIT LIKE THIS . . . ? IT'S AGONY!

MAGS *(working away).* You're doing fine . . . just fine . . .

FANNY *(breaking her pose).* It's so . . . boring!

MAGS. Come on, don't move. You can have a break soon.

FANNY. I had no idea it would be so boring!

GARDNER. Gee, I'm enjoying it.

FANNY. You *would* . . . ! *(a pause)*

GARDNER *(begins reciting more Yeats, almost singing it).*

"He stood among a crowd at Drumahair;
His heart hung all upon a silken dress,
And he had known at last some tender- ness,
Before earth made of him her sleepy care;
But when a man poured fish into a pile,
It seemed they raised their little silver heads . . ."

FANNY. Gar . . . PLEASE! *(She lurches out of her seat.)* God, I can't take this anymore!

MAGS *(keeps sketching GARDNER).* I know it's tedious as first, but it gets easier . . .

FANNY. It's like a Chinese water torture! . . . *(crosses to MAGS and looks at GARDNER posing)* Oh darling, you look marvelous, absolutely marvelous! Why don't you just do Daddy!?

MAGS. Because you look marvelous too. I want to do you both!

FANNY. Please . . . ! I have one foot in the grave and you know it! Also, we're way be- hind in our packing. There's still one room left which everyone seems to have forgotten about!

GARDNER. Which one is that?

FANNY. You know perfectly well which one it is!

GARDNER. I do . . . ?

FANNY. Yes, you do!

GARDNER. Well, it's news to me.

FANNY. I'll give you a hint. It's in . . . *that* direction. *(She points.)*

GARDNER. The dining room.

FANNY. No.

GARDNER. The bedroom.

FANNY. No.

GARDNER. Mags' room.

FANNY. No.

GARDNER. The kitchen.

FANNY. *Gar . . . ?!*

GARDNER. The guest room?

FANNY. Your God awful study!

GARDNER. Oh, shit!

FANNY. That's right, "oh shit!" It's books and papers up to the ceiling! If you ask me, we should just forget it's there and quietly tip toe away . . .

GARDNER. My study . . . !

FANNY. Let the new owners dispose of everything ...

GARDNER (gets out of his posing chair). Now, just one minute ...

FANNY. You never look at half the stuff in there!

GARDNER. I don't want you touching those books! They're mine!

FANNY. Darling, we're moving to a cottage the size of a handkerchief! Where, pray tell, is there room for all your books?

GARDNER. I don't know. We'll just have to make room!

MAGS (sketching away). RATS!

FANNY. I don't know what we're doing fooling around with Mags like this when there's still so much to do ...

GARDNER (sits back down, overwhelmed). My study ... !

FANNY. You can stay with her if you'd like, but one of us has got to tackle those books! (She exits to his study.)

GARDNER. I'm not up to this.

MAGS. Oh good, you're staying!

GARDNER. There's a lifetime of work in there ...

MAGS. Don't worry, I'll help. Mum and I will be able to pack everything up in no time.

GARDNER. God ...

MAGS. It won't be so bad ...

GARDNER. I'm just not up to it.

MAGS. We'll all pitch in ...

(GARDNER sighs, speechless. A silence as MAGS keeps sketching him. FANNY comes staggering in with an armload of books which she drops to the floor with a crash.)

GARDNER. WHAT WAS THAT ... ?!

MAGS (simultaneously). GOOD GRIEF!

FANNY (sheepish). Sorry, sorry ... (She exits for more.)

GARDNER. I don't know if I can take this ...

MAGS. Moving is awful ... I know ...

GARDNER (settling back into his pose). Ever since Mum began tearing the house apart, I've been having these dreams ... I'm a child again back at 16 Louisberg Square ... and this stream of moving men is carrying furniture into our house ... van after van of tables and chairs, sofas and loveseats, desks and bureaus ... rugs, bathtubs, mirrors, chiming clocks, pianos, ice boxes, china cabinets ... but what's amazing is that all of it is familiar ... (FANNY comes in with another load which she drops on the floor. She exits for more.) No matter how many items appear, I've seen every one of them before. Since my mother is standing in the midst of it directing traffic, I ask her where it's all coming from, but she doesn't hear me because of the racket ... so finally I just scream out ... "WHERE IS ALL THIS FURNITURE COMING FROM?" ... Just as a moving man is carrying Toots into the room, she looks at me and says, "Why, from the land of Skye!" ... The next thing I know, people are being carried in along with it ... (FANNY enters with her next load, drops it and exits.) ... people I've never seen before are sitting around our dining room table. A group of foreigners is going through my books, chattering in a language I've never heard before. A man is playing a Chopin Polonaise on Aunt Alice's piano. Several children are taking baths in our tubs from Cotuit ...

MAGS. It sounds marvelous.

GARDNER. Well, it isn't marvelous at all because all of these perfect strangers have taken over our things ... (FANNY enters, hurls down another load and exits.)

MAGS. How odd ...

GARDNER. Well, it is odd, but then something even odder happens ...

MAGS (sketching away). Tell me, tell me!

GARDNER. Well, our beds are carried in. They're all made up with sheets and everything, but instead of all these strange people in them, we're in them ... !

MAGS. What's so odd about that ... ?

GARDNER. Well, you and Mum are brought in, both sleeping like angels ... Mum snoring away to beat the band ...

MAGS. Yes ... (FANNY enters with another load, lets it fall.)

GARDNER. But there's no one in mine. It's completely empty, never even been slept in! It's as if I were dead or had never even existed ... (FANNY exits.) "HEY ... WAIT UP!" I yell to the moving men ... "THAT'S MY BED YOU'VE GOT THERE!" but they don't stop, they don't even acknowledge me ... "HEY, COME BACK HERE ... I WANT TO GET INTO MY BED!" I cry again and I start running after them ... down the hall, through the dining room, past the library ... Finally I catch up to them and hurl myself right into the center of the pillow. Just as I'm about to land, the bed suddenly vanishes and I go crashing down to the floor like some insect that's been hit by a fly swatter!

FANNY (staggers in with her final load, drops it with a crash and then collapses in her posing chair). THAT'S IT FOR ME! I'M DEAD!

(silence) Come on, Mags, how about you doing a little work around here.

MAGS. That's all I've been doing! This is the first free moment you've given me!

FANNY. You should see all the books in there . . . and papers! There are enough loose papers to sink a ship!

GARDNER. Why is it we're moving, again . . . ?

FANNY. Because life is getting too complicated here.

GARDNER *(remembering)*. Oh yes . . .

FANNY. And we can't afford it anymore.

GARDNER. That's right, that's right . . .

FANNY. We don't have the . . . *income* we used to!

GARDNER. Oh yes . . . *income!*

FANNY *(assuming her pose again)*. Of course we have our savings and various trust funds, but I wouldn't dream of touching those!

GARDNER. No, no, you must never dip into capital!

FANNY. I told Daddy I'd be perfectly happy to buy a gun and put a bullet through our heads so we could avoid all this, but he wouldn't hear of it!

MAGS *(sketching away)*. No, I shouldn't think so. *(pause)*

FANNY. I've always admired people who kill themselves when they get to our stage of life. Well, no one can touch my Uncle Edmond in that department . . .

MAGS. I know, I know . . .

FANNY. The day before his 70th birthday he climbed to the top of the Old North Church and hurled himself face down into Salem Street! They had to scrape him up with a spatula! God, he was a remarkable man . . . state senator, President of Harvard . . .

GARDNER *(rises and wanders over to his books)*. Well, I guess I'm going to have to do something about all of these . . .

FANNY. . . . Come on, Mags, help Daddy! Why don't you start bringing in his papers . . .

(GARDNER sits on the floor, picks up a book and soon is engrossed in it. MAGS keeps sketching, oblivious. Silence.)

FANNY *(to MAGS)*. Darling . . . ? HELLO . . . ? *(They both ignore her.)* God, you two are impossible! Just look at you . . . heads in the clouds! No one would ever know we've got to be out of here in two days. If it weren't for me, nothing would get done around here . . . *(She starts stacking GARDNER's books into piles.)* There! That's all the maroon ones!

GARDNER *(looks up)*. What do you mean, *maroon* ones . . . ?!

FANNY. All your books that are maroon are in *this* pile . . . and your books that are green in *that* pile . . . ! I'm trying to bring some order into your life for once. This will make unpacking so much easier.

GARDNER. But my dear Fanny, it's not the color of a book that distinguishes it, but what's *inside* it!

FANNY. This will be a great help, you'll see. Now what about this awful striped thing? *(She picks up a slim, aged volume.)* Can't it go . . . ?

GARDNER. No!

FANNY. But it's as queer as Dick's hat band! There are no others like it.

GARDNER. Open it and read. Go on . . . open it!

FANNY. We'll get nowhere at this rate.

GARDNER. I said . . . READ!

FANNY. Really, Gar, I . . .

GARDNER. Read the dedication!

FANNY *(opens and reads)*. "To Gardner Church, you led the way. With gratitude and affection, Robert Frost." *(She closes it and hands it to him.)*

GARDNER. It was published the same year as my "Salem Gardens."

FANNY *(picking up a very dirty book)*. Well, what about this dreadful thing? It's filthy. *(She blows off a cloud of dust.)*

GARDNER. Please . . . *please?!*

FANNY *(looking through it)*. It's all in French.

GARDNER *(snatching it away from her)*. Andre Malraux gave me that . . . !

FANNY. I'm just trying to help.

GARDNER. It's a first edition of Baudelaire's "Fleurs du Mal."

FANNY *(giving it back)*. Well, pardon me for living!

GARDNER. Why do you have to drag everything in here in the first place . . . ?

FANNY. Because there's no room in your study. You ought to see the mess in there! . . . WAKE UP, MAGS, ARE YOU GOING TO PITCH IN OR NOT . . . ?!

GARDNER. I'm not up to this.

FANNY. Well, you'd better be unless you want to be left behind!

MAGS *(stops her sketching)*. Alright, alright . . . I just hope you'll give me some more time later this evening.

FANNY *(to MAGS)*. Since you're young and in the best shape, why don't you bring in the books and I'll cope with the papers. *(She exits to the study.)*

GARDNER. Now just a minute . . .

FANNY *(offstage)*. WE NEED A STEAM SHOVEL FOR THIS!

MAGS. O.K., what do you want me to do?

GARDNER. Look, I don't want you messing around with my . . . *(FANNY enters with an armful of papers which she drops into an empty carton.)* HEY, WHAT'S GOING ON HERE . . . ?

FANNY. I'm packing up your papers. COME ON, MAGS, LET'S GET CRACKING! *(She exits for more papers.)*

GARDNER *(plucks several papers out of the carton)*. What is this . . . ?

MAGS *(exits into his study)*. GOOD LORD, WHAT HAVE YOU DONE IN HERE . . . ?!

GARDNER *(reading)*. This is my manuscript. *(FANNY enters with another batch which she tosses on top of the others.)* What *are* you doing . . . ?!

FANNY. Packing, darling . . . PACKING! *(She exits for more.)*

GARDNER. SEE HERE, YOU CAN'T MANHANDLE MY THINGS THIS WAY! *(MAGS enters, staggering under a load of books which she sets down on the floor.)* I PACK MY MANUSCRIPT! I KNOW WHERE EVERYTHING IS!

FANNY *(offstage)*. IF IT WERE UP TO YOU, WE'D NEVER GET OUT OF HERE! WE'RE UNDER A TIME LIMIT, GARDNER. KITTY'S PICKING US UP IN TWO DAYS . . . TWO . . . DAYS! *(She enters with a larger batch of papers and heads for the carton.)*

GARDNER *(grabbing FANNY's wrist)*. NOW, HOLD IT . . . ! JUST . . . HOLD IT RIGHT THERE . . . !

FANNY. OOOOOWWWWWWWW!

GARDNER. *I* PACK MY THINGS . . . !

FANNY. LET GO, YOU'RE HURTING ME!

GARDNER. THAT'S MY MANUSCRIPT! GIVE IT TO ME!

FANNY *(lifting the papers high over her head)*. I'M IN CHARGE OF THIS MOVE, GARDNER! WE'VE GOT TO GET CRACKING!

GARDNER. I said . . . GIVE IT TO ME!

MAGS. Come on, Mum, let him have it. *(They struggle.)*

GARDNER *(finally wrenches the pages from her)*. LET . . . ME . . . HAVE IT . . . ! THAT'S MORE LIKE IT . . . !

FANNY *(soft and weepy)*. You see what he's like . . . ? I try and help with his packing and what does he do . . . ?

GARDNER *(rescues the rest of his papers from the carton)*. YOU DON'T JUST THROW EVERYTHING INTO A BOX LIKE A PILE OF GARBAGE! THIS IS A BOOK, FANNY. SOMETHING I'VE BEEN WORKING ON FOR TWO YEARS . . . ! *(trying to assemble his papers, but only making things worse, dropping them all over the place)* You show a little respect for my things . . . you don't just throw them around every which way . . . It's tricky trying to make sense of poetry, it's much easier to write the stuff . . . that is, if you've still got it in you . . .

MAGS. Here, let me help . . . *(taking some of the papers)*

GARDNER. Criticism is tough sledding. You can't just dash off a few images here, a few rhymes there . . .

MAGS. Do you have these pages numbered in any way?

FANNY *(returning to her posing chair)*. HA!

GARDNER. This is just the introduction.

MAGS. I don't see any numbers on these.

GARDNER *(exiting to his study)*. The important stuff is in my study . . .

FANNY *(to MAGS)*. You don't know the half of it . . . *Not the half . . . !*

GARDNER *(offstage; thumping around)*. HAVE YOU SEEN THOSE YEATS POEMS I JUST HAD . . . ?

MAGS *(reading over several pages)*. What is this . . . ? It doesn't make sense. It's just fragments . . . pieces of poems.

FANNY. That's it, honey! That's his book. His great critical study! Now that he can't write his own poetry, he's trying to explain other people's. The only problem is, he can't get beyond typing them out. The poor lamb doesn't have the stamina to get beyond the opening stanzas, let alone trying to make sense of them.

GARDNER *(thundering back with more papers which keep falling)*. GOD DAMNIT, FANNY, WHAT DID YOU DO IN THERE? I CAN'T FIND ANYTHING!

FANNY. I just took the papers that were on your desk.

GARDNER. Well, the entire beginning is gone. *(He exits.)*

FANNY. I'M TRYING TO HELP YOU, DARLING!

GARDNER *(returns with another armload)*. SEE THAT . . . ? NO SIGN OF CHAPTER

ONE OR TWO . . . *(He flings it all down to the floor.)*

FANNY. Gardner . . . PLEASE?!

GARDNER *(kicking through the mess).* I TURN MY BACK FOR ONE MINUTE AND WHAT HAPPENS . . . ? MY ENTIRE STUDY IS TORN APART! *(He exits.)*

MAGS. Oh Daddy . . . don't . . . please . . . Daddy . . . *please?!*

GARDNER *(returns with a new batch of papers which he tosses up into the air).* THROWN OUT . . . ! THE BEST PART IS THROWN OUT! . . . LOST . . . *(He starts to exit again.)*

MAGS *(reads one of the fragments to steady herself).*

"I have known the inexorable sadness of pencils,
Neat in their boxes, dolor of pad and paper-weight,
All the misery of manila folders and mucilage . . ."

They're beautiful . . . just beautiful.

GARDNER *(stops).* Hey, what's that you've got there?

FANNY. It's your manuscript, darling. You see, it's right where you left it.

GARDNER *(to MAGS).* Read that again.

MAGS.
"I have known the inexorable sadness of pencils,
Neat in their boxes, dolor of pad and paper-weight,
All the misery of manila folders and mucilage . . ."

GARDNER. Well, well, what do you know . . .

FANNY *(hands him several random papers).* You see . . . no one lost anything. Everything's here, still in tact.

GARDNER *(reads).*
"I knew a woman, lovely in her bones,
When small birds sighed, she would sigh back at them;
Ah, when she moved, she moved more ways than one:
The shapes a bright container can contain! . . ."

FANNY *(hands him another).* And . . .

GARDNER. Ah yes, Frost. . . . *(reads)*
"Some say the world will end in fire,
Some say ice.
From what I've tasted of desire
I hold with those who favor fire."

FANNY *(under her breath to MAGS).* He can't give up the words. It's the best he can do.

(handing him another) Here you go, here's more.

GARDNER.
"Farm boys wild to couple
With anything   with soft-wooded trees
With mounds of earth   mounds
Of pinestraw   will keep themselves off
Animals by legends of their own . . ."

MAGS *(eyes shut).* Oh Daddy, I can't bear it . . . I . . .

FANNY. Of course no one will ever publish this.

GARDNER. Oh, here's a marvelous one. Listen to this!

"There came a Wind like a Bugle—
It quivered through the Grass
And a Green Chill upon the Heat
So ominous did pass
We barred the Windows and the Doors
As from an Emerald Ghost—

The Doom's electric Moccasin . . ."

SHIT, WHERE DID THE REST OF IT GO . . . ?

FANNY. Well, don't ask *me.*

GARDNER. It just stopped in mid air!

FANNY. Then go look for the original.

GARDNER. Good idea, good idea! *(He exits to his study.)*

FANNY *(to MAGS).* He's incontinent now too. He wets his pants, in case you haven't noticed. *(She starts laughing.)* You're not laughing. Don't you think it's funny? Daddy needs diapers . . . I don't know about you, but I could use a drink! GAR . . . WILL YOU GET ME A SPLASH WHILE YOU'RE OUT THERE . . . ?

MAGS. STOP IT!

FANNY. It means we can't go out anymore. I mean, what would people say . . . ?

MAGS. Stop it. Just stop it.

FANNY. My poet laureate can't hold it in! *(She laughs harder.)*

MAGS. That's enough . . . STOP IT . . . Mummy . . . I beg of you . . . *please stop it!*

GARDNER *(Enters with a book and indeed a large stain has blossomed on his trousers. He plucks it away from his leg).* Here we go . . . I found it . . .

FANNY *(pointing at it).* See that? See . . . ? He just did it again! *(goes off into a shower of laughter)*

MAGS *(looks, turns away).* SHUT . . . UP . . . ! *(building to a howl)* WILL YOU PLEASE JUST . . . SHUT . . . UP!

FANNY *(to* GARDNER*).* Hey, what about that drink?

GARDNER. Oh yes . . . sorry, sorry . . . *(He heads towards the bar.)*

FANNY. Never mind, I'll get it, I'll get it. *(She exits, convulsed. Silence.)*

GARDNER. Well, where were we . . . ?

MAGS *(near tears).* Your poem.

GARDNER. Oh yes . . . the Dickinson. *(He shuts his eyes, reciting from memory, holding the book against his chest.)*
"There came a Wind like a Bugle—
It quivered through the Grass
And a Green Chill upon the Heat
So ominous did pass
We barred the Windows and the Doors
As from an Emerald Ghost—"
(opens the book and starts riffling through it) Let's see now, where's the rest . . . ? *(He finally finds it.)* Ahhh, here we go . . . !

FANNY *(re-enters, drink in hand).* I'm back! *(takes one look at* GARDNER *and bursts out laughing again)*

MAGS. I don't believe you! How you can laugh at him . . . ?!

FANNY. I'm sorry, I wish I could stop, but there's really nothing else to do. Look at him . . . just . . . look at him . . . !
(This is all simultaneous as MAGS *gets angrier and angrier.)*

MAGS. It's so cruel . . . you're so . . . incredibly cruel to him . . . I mean, YOUR DISDAIN REALLY TAKES MY BREATH AWAY! YOU'RE IN A CLASS BY YOURSELF WHEN IT COMES TO HUMILIATION . . . !

GARDNER *(reading).*
"The Doom's electric Moccasin
That very instant passed—
On a strange Mob of panting Trees
And Fences fled away
And Rivers where the Houses ran
Those looked that lived—that Day—
The Bell within the steeple wild
The flying tidings told—
How much can come
And much can go,
And yet abide the World!"
(He shuts the book with a bang, pauses and looks around the room, confused.) Now, where was I . . . ?

FANNY. Safe and sound in the middle of the living room with Mags and me.

GARDNER. But I was looking for something, wasn't I . . . ?

FANNY. Your manuscript.

GARDNER. THAT'S RIGHT! MY MANUSCRIPT! My manuscript!

FANNY. And here it is all over the floor. See, you're standing on it.

GARDNER *(picks up a few pages and looks at them).* Why, so I am . . .

FANNY. Now all we have to do is get it up off the floor and packed neatly into these cartons!

GARDNER. Yes, yes, that's right. Into the cartons.

FANNY *(kicks a carton over to him).* Here, you use this one and I'll start over here . . . *(She starts dropping papers into a carton nearby.)* . . . BOMBS AWAY . . . ! Hey . . . this is fun . . . !

GARDNER *(picks up his own pile, lifts it high over his head and flings it down into the carton).* BOMBS AWAY . . . This *is* fun . . . !

FANNY. I told you! The whole thing is to figure out a system!

GARDNER. I don't know what I'd do without you, Fan. I thought I'd lost everything.

FANNY *(makes dive bomber noises and machine gun explosions as she wheels more and more papers into the carton).* TAKE THAT AND THAT AND THAT . . . !

GARDNER *(joins in the fun, outdoing her with dips, dives and blastings of his own).* BLAM BLAM BLAM BLAM! . . . ZZZZZZZZRAAAAAA FOOM! . . . BLATTY DE BLATTY DE BLATTY DE KABOOOOOOOOM . . . ! WHAAAAAAA . . . DA DAT DAT DAT DAT . . . WHEEEEEEEEAAAAAAAAAAAAA . . . FOOOOOO . . . *(They get louder and louder as papers fly every which way.)*

FANNY *(mimes getting hit with a bomb).* AEEEEEEIIIIIIIIIIIII! YOU GOT ME RIGHT IN THE GIZZARD! *(She collapses on the floor and starts going through death throes, having an absolute ball.)*

GARDNER. TAKE THAT AND THAT AND THAT AND THAT . . . *(a series of explosions follow)*

MAGS *(furious).* This is how you help him . . . ? THIS IS HOW YOU PACK HIS THINGS . . . ?

FANNY. I keep him company. I get involved . . . which is a hell of a lot more than you do!

MAGS *(wild with rage).* BUT YOU'RE MAKING A MOCKERY OF HIM . . . YOU TREAT HIM LIKE A CHILD OR SOME DIM-WITTED SERVING BOY. HE'S JUST AN AMUSEMENT TO YOU . . . !

FANNY *(Fatigue has finally overtaken her. She's*

calm to the point of serenity). . . . and to you who see him once a year, if that . . . What is he to *you?* . . . I mean, what do you give him from yourself that costs you something . . . ? Hmmmmmm . . . ? *(imitating her)* "Oh, hi Daddy, it's great to see you again. How have you been? . . . Gee, I love your hair. It's gotten so . . . *white!*" . . . What color do you expect it to get when he's this age . . . ? I mean, if you care so much how he looks, why don't you come and see him once in a while? . . . But oh no . . . you have your paintings to do and your shows to put on. You just come and see us when the whim strikes. *(imitating her)* "Hey, you know what would be really great? . . . To do a portrait of you! I've always wanted to paint you, you're such great subjects!" . . . *Paint* us . . . ?! What about opening your eyes and really *seeing* us . . . ? Noticing what's going on around here for a change! It's all over Daddy and me. This is it! "Finita la commedia!" . . . All I'm trying to do is exit with a little flourish, have some fun . . . What's so terrible about that? . . . It can get pretty grim around here, in case you haven't noticed . . . Daddy, tap, tap tapping out his nonsense all day; me traipsing around to the thrift shops trying to amuse myself . . . He never keeps me company anymore, never takes me out anywhere . . . I'd put a bullet through my head in a minute, but then who'd look after him? . . . What do you think we're moving to the cottage for . . . ? So I can watch him like a hawk and make sure he doesn't get lost. Do you think that's anything to look forward to? . . . Being Daddy's nursemaid out in the middle of nowhere? I'd much rather stay here in Boston with the few friends I have left, but you can't always do what you want in this world! "L'homme propose, Dieu dispose!" . . . If you want to paint us so badly, you ought to paint us as we really are. There's your picture . . . ! *(She points to GARD-NER who's quietly playing with a paper glider.)* . . . Daddy spread out on the floor with all his toys and me hovering over him to make sure he doesn't hurt himself! *(She goes over to him.)* YOO HOO . . . GAR . . . ? . . . HELLO? . . .

GARDNER *(looks up at her).* Oh, hi there, Fan. What's up?

FANNY. How's the packing coming . . . ?

GARDNER. Packing . . . ?

FANNY. Yes, you were packing your manuscript, remember? *(She lifts up a page and lets it fall into a carton.)*

GARDNER. Oh yes . . .

FANNY. Here's your picture, Mags. Face over this way . . . turn your easel over here . . . *(She lets a few more papers fall.)* Up, up . . . and away . . .

Blackout

SCENE 2

The last day. All the books and boxes are gone. The room is completely empty except for MAG's backdrop. Late afternoon light dapples the walls; it changes from pale peach to deeper violet. The finished portrait sits on the easel covered with a cloth. MAGS is taking down the backdrop.

FANNY *(offstage to GARDNER).* DON'T FORGET TOOTS!

GARDNER *(offstage from another part of the house).* WHAT'S THAT . . . ?

FANNY *(offstage).* I SAID: DON'T FORGET TOOTS! HIS CAGE IS SITTING IN THE MIDDLE OF YOUR STUDY! *(silence)*

FANNY *(offstage).* HELLO . . . ? ARE YOU THERE . . . ?

GARDNER *(simultaneously, offstage).* I'LL BE RIGHT WITH YOU, I'M JUST GETTING TOOTS!

GARDNER *(offstage).* WHAT'S THAT? I CAN'T HEAR YOU?

FANNY *(offstage).* I'M GOING THROUGH THE ROOMS ONE MORE TIME TO MAKE SURE WE DIDN'T FORGET ANYTHING . . . KITTY'S PICKING US UP IN 15 MINUTES, SO PLEASE BE READY . . . SHE'S DROPPING MAGS OFF AT THE STATION AND THEN IT'S OUT TO ROUTE 3 AND THE CAPE HIGHWAY . . .

GARDNER *(enters, carrying TOOTS in his cage).* Well, this is it. The big moment has finally come, eh what, Toots? *(He sees MAGS.)* Oh hi there, Mags, I didn't see you . . .

MAGS. Hi, daddy. I'm just taking this down . . . *(She does and walks over to TOOTS.)* Oh Toots, I'll miss you. *(She makes little chattering noises into his cage.)*

GARDNER. Come on, recite a little Grey's Elegy for Mags before we go.

MAGS. Yes, Mum said he was really good at it now.

GARDNER. Well, the whole thing is to keep at it every day. *(slowly to TOOTS)*
"The curfew tolls the knell of parting day,
The lowing herd wind slowly o'er the lea . . ."

Come on, show Mags your stuff!
(slower)
"The curfew tolls the knell of parting day,
The lowing herd wind slowly o'er the lea."
(Silence; he makes little chattering sounds.)
Come on, Toots, old boy . . .
MAGS. How does it go?
GARDNER *(to MAGS)*.
"The curfew tolls the knell of parting day,
The lowing herd wind slowly o'er the
lea . . ."
MAGS *(slowly to TOOTS)*.
"The curfew tolls for you and me,
As quietly the herd winds down . . ."
GARDNER. No, no, it's: "The curfew tolls
the knell of parting *day* . . . !
MAGS *(repeating after him)*. "The curfew
tolls the knell of parting day . . ."
GARDNER. . . . "The lowing herd wind
slowly o'er the lea . . ."
MAGS *(with a deep breath)*.
"The curfew tolls at parting day,
The herd low slowly down the lea . . . no,
knell!
They come winding down the *knell* . . . !"
GARDNER. Listen, Mags . . . *listen! (a pause)*
TOOTS *(loud and clear with GARDNER's inflec-
tion)*.
"The curfew tolls the knell of parting day,
The lowing herd wind slowly o'er the lea,
The ploughman homeward plods his
weary way,
And leaves the world to darkness and to
me."
MAGS. HE SAID IT . . . HE SAID IT!
. . . AND IN YOUR VOICE! . . . OH
DADDY, THAT'S AMAZING!
GARDNER. Well, Toots is very smart, which
is more than I can say for alot of people I
know . . .
MAGS *(to TOOTS)*. "Polly want a cracker?
Polly want a cracker?"
GARDNER. You can teach a parakeet to say
anything, all you need is patience . . .
MAGS. But *poetry* . . . that's so hard . . .
FANNY *(Enters carrying a suitcase and GARD-
NER's typewriter in its case. She's dressed in her
traveling suit wearing a hat to match)*. WELL,
THERE YOU ARE! I THOUGHT YOU'D
DIED!
MAGS *(to FANNY)*. He said it! I finally heard
Toots recite Grey's Elegy. *(leaning close to the
cage)* "Polly want a cracker? Polly want a
cracker?"
FANNY. Isn't it uncanny how much he
sounds like Daddy? Sometimes when I'm
alone here with him, I've actually thought he

was Daddy and started talking to him. Oh
yes, Toots and I have had quite a few meaty
conversations together!
*(FANNY wolf whistles into the cage, then draws
back. GARDNER covers the cage with a traveling
cloth. Silence.)*
FANNY *(looking around the room)*. God, the
place looks so bare.
MAGS. I still can't believe it . . . Cotuit, year
round. I wonder if there'll be any phosphorus
when you get there?
FANNY. What on earth are you talking
about? *(spies the backdrop on the floor, carries it
out to the hall)*
MAGS. Remember that summer when the
ocean was full of phosphorus?
GARDNER *(carrying TOOTS out into the hall)*.
Oh yes . . .
MAGS. It was a great mystery where it came
from or why it settled in Cotuit. But one
evening when Daddy and I were taking a
swim, suddenly it was there!
GARDNER *(returns)*. I remember.
MAGS. I don't know where Mum was . . .
FANNY *(re-enters)*. Probably doing the
dishes!
MAGS *(to GARDNER)*. As you dove into the
water, this shower of silvery-green sparks
erupted all around you. It was incredible! I
thought you were turning into a saint or
something, but then you told me to jump
in too and the same thing happened to
me . . .
GARDNER. Oh yes, I remember that . . . the
water smelled all queer.
MAGS. What *is* phosphorus, anyway?
GARDNER. Chemicals, chemicals . . .
FANNY. No, it isn't. Phosphorus is a green
liquid inside insects. Fireflies have it. When
you see sparks in the water it means insects
are swimming around . . .
GARDNER. Where on earth did you get that
idea . . . ?
FANNY. If you're bitten by one of them, it's
fatal!
MAGS. . . . and the next morning it was still
there . . .
GARDNER. It was the damndest stuff to get
off! We'd have to stay in the shower a good
ten minutes. It comes from chemical waste,
you see . . .
MAGS. Our bodies looked like mercury as
we swam around . . .
GARDNER. It stained all the towels a strange
yellow-green.
MAGS. I was in heaven, and so were you for
that matter. You'd finished your day's poetry

and would turn somersaults like some happy dolphin . . .

FANNY. Damned dishes . . . why didn't I see any of this . . . ?!

MAGS. I remember one night in particular . . . We sensed the phosphorus was about to desert us, blow off to another town. We were chasing each other under water. At one point I lost you the brilliance was so intense . . . but finally your foot appeared . . . then your leg. I grabbed it! . . . I remember wishing the moment would hold forever, that we could just be fixed there, laughing and iridescent . . . Then I began to get panicky because I knew it would pass, it was passing already. You were slipping from my grasp. The summer was almost over. I'd be going back to art school, you'd be going back to Boston . . . Even as I was reaching for you, you were gone. We'd never be like that again. *(silence)*

FANNY *(spies MAGS' portrait covered on the easel)*. What's that over there? Don't tell me we forgot something!

MAGS. It's your portrait. I finished it.

FANNY. You finished it? How on earth did you manage that?

MAGS. I stayed up all night.

FANNY. You did? . . . *I* didn't hear you, did you hear her, Gar . . . ?

GARDNER. Not a peep, not a peep!

MAGS. Well, I wanted to get it done before you left. You know, see what you thought. It's not bad, considering . . . I mean, I did it almost completely from memory. The light was terrible and I was trying to be quiet so I wouldn't wake you. It was hardly an ideal situation . . . I mean, you weren't the most cooperative models . . . *(She suddenly panics and snatches the painting off the easel. She hugs it to her chest and starts dancing around the room with it.)* Oh God, you're going to hate it! You're going to hate it! How did I ever get into this? . . . Listen, you don't really want to see it . . . it's nothing . . . just a few dabs here and there . . . It was awfully late when I finished it. The light was really impossible and my eyes were hurting like crazy . . . Look, why don't we just go out to the sidewalk and wait for Kitty so she doesn't have to honk . . .

GARDNER *(snatches the painting out from under her)*. WOULD YOU JUST SHUT UP A MINUTE AND LET US SEE IT . . . ?

MAGS *(laughing and crying)*. But it's nothing, Daddy . . . *really!* . . . I've done better with my eyes closed! It was so late I could hardly see

anything and then I spilled a whole bottle of thinner into my palette . . .

GARDNER *(sets it down on the easel and stands back to look at it)*. THERE!

MAGS *(dancing around them in a panic)*. Listen, it's just a quick sketch . . . It's still wet . . . I didn't have enough time . . . It takes at least 40 hours to do a decent portrait . . .

(Suddenly it's very quiet as FANNY and GARDNER stand back to look at it.)

MAGS *(more and more beside herself, keeps leaping around the room wrapping her arms around herself, making little whimpering sounds)*. Please don't . . . no . . . don't . . . oh please! . . . Come on, don't look . . . Oh God, don't . . . please . . . *(An eternity passes as FANNY and GARDNER gaze at it.)*

GARDNER. Well . . .

FANNY. Well . . . *(more silence)*

FANNY. I think it's perfectly dreadful!

GARDNER *(simultanoeusly)*. Awfully clever, awfully clever!

FANNY. What on earth did you do to my face . . . ?

GARDNER. I particularly like Mum!

FANNY. Since when do I have purple skin . . . ?!

MAGS. I told you it was nothing, just a silly . . .

GARDNER. She looks like a million dollars!

FANNY. AND WILL YOU LOOK AT MY HAIR . . . IT'S BRIGHT ORANGE!

GARDNER *(views it from another angle)*. It's really very good!

FANNY *(pointing)*. That doesn't look anything like me!

GARDNER. . . . first rate!

FANNY. Since when do I have purple skin and bright orange hair . . . ?!

MAGS *(trying to snatch it off the easel)*. Listen, you don't have to worry about my feelings . . . really . . . I . . .

GARDNER *(blocking her way)*. NOT SO FAST . . .

FANNY. . . . and look at how I'm sitting! I've never sat like that in my life!

GARDNER *(moving closer to it)*. Yes, yes, it's awfully clever . . .

FANNY. I HAVE NO FEET!

GARDNER. The whole thing is quite remarkable!

FANNY. And what happened to my legs, pray tell? . . . They just vanish below the knees! . . . At least my dress is presentable. I've always loved that dress.

GARDNER. It sparkles somehow . . .

FANNY *(to* GARDNER*).* Don't you think it's becoming?

GARDNER. Yes, very becoming, awfully becoming . . .

FANNY *(examining it at closer range).* Yes, she got the dress very well, how it shows off what's left of my figure . . . My smile is nice too.

GARDNER. Good and wide . . .

FANNY. I love how the corners of my mouth turn up . . .

GARDNER. It's very clever . . .

FANNY. They're almost quivering . . .

GARDNER. Good lighting effects!

FANNY. Actually, I look quite . . . *young,* don't you think?

GARDNER *(to* MAGS*).* You're awfully good with those highlights.

FANNY *(looking at it from different angles).* And *you* look darling . . . !

GARDNER. Well, I don't know about that . . .

FANNY. No, you look absolutely darling. Good enough to eat!

MAGS *(in a whisper).* They like it . . . They like it! *(A silence as* FANNY *and* GARDNER *keep gazing at it!)*

FANNY. You know what it is? The wispy brush strokes make us look like a couple in a French Impressionist painting.

GARDNER. Yes, I see what you mean . . .

FANNY. . . . a Manet or Renoir . . .

GARDNER. It's very evocative.

FANNY. There's something about the light . . . *(They back up to survey it from a distance.)* You know those Renoir café scenes . . . ?

GARDNER. She doesn't lay on the paint with a trowel, it's just touches here and there . . .

MAGS. They *like* it . . . !

FANNY. You know the one with the couple dancing . . . ? Not that we're dancing. There's just something similar in the mood . . . a kind of gaity, almost . . . The man has his back to you and he's swinging the woman around . . . OH GAR, YOU'VE SEEN IT A MILLION TIMES! IT'S HANGING IN THE MUSEUM OF FINE ARTS! . . . They're dancing like this . . . *(She goes up to him and puts an arm on his shoulder.)*

MAGS. They like it . . . they like it!

FANNY. She's got on this wonderful flowered dress with ruffles at the neck and he's holding her like this . . . that's right . . . and she's got the most rhapsodic expression on her face . . .

GARDNER *(getting into the spirit of it, takes* FANNY *in his arms and slowly begins to dance around the room).* Oh yes . . . I know the one you mean . . . They're in a sort of haze . . . and isn't there a little band playing off to one side . . . ?

FANNY. Yes, that's it!

*(*KITTY*'s horn honks outside.)*

MAGS *(is the only one who hears it).* There's Kitty! *(She's torn and keeps looking towards the door, but finally can't take her eyes off their stolen dance.)*

FANNY. . . . and there's a man in a dark suit playing the violin and someone's conducting, I think . . . And aren't Japanese lanterns strung up . . . ? *(They pick up speed, dipping and whirling around the room. Strains of a far-away Chopin waltz are heard.)*

GARDNER. Oh yes! There are all these little lights twinkling in the trees . . .

FANNY. . . . and doesn't the woman have a hat on . . . ? A big red hat . . . ?

GARDNER. . . . and lights all over the dancers too. Everything shimmers with this marvelous glow. Yes, yes . . . I can see it perfectly! The whole thing is absolutely extraordinary! *(The lights become dreamy and dappled as they dance around the room.* MAGS *watches them, moved to tears and . . .)*

The Curtain Falls

MUSIC IN THE PLAY

During the scene changes the opening measures of the following Chopin waltzes are played:

* As the house lights dim, the Waltz in A minor, opus posthumous.
* Setting up Act I, Scene 2, the Waltz in E minor, opus posthumous.
* Setting up Act I, Scene 3, the Waltz in E major, opus posthumous.
* To close Act I, the final notes of the Waltz in B minor, opus 69, #2.
* As the house lights dim for Act II, the Waltz in A flat major, opus 64, #3.
* Setting up Act II, Scene 2, repeat the Waltz in A minor, opus posthumous.
* To accompany the final moments of GARDNER's and FANNY's dance, the Waltz in D flat major, opus 70, #3.

Glengarry Glen Ross

DAVID MAMET

THIS PLAY IS DEDICATED TO HAROLD PINTER

First presented at The Cottlesloe Theatre, London, England, on September 21, 1983, with the following cast:

SHELLY LEVENE	Derek Newark
JOHN WILLIAMSON	Karl Johnson
DAVE MOSS	Trevor Ray
GEORGE AARONOW	James Grant
RICHARD ROMA	Jack Shepherd
JAMES LINGK	Tony Haygarth
BAYLEN	John Tams

Directed by BILL BRYDEN

The U.S. premiere of the play took place at The Goodman Theatre of the Arts Institute of Chicago in a Chicago Theatre Groups, Inc., production on February 6, 1984, with the following cast:

SHELLY LEVENE	Robert Prosky
JOHN WILLIAMSON	J. T. Walsh
DAVE MOSS	James Tolkan
GEORGE AARONOW	Mike Nussbaum
RICHARD ROMA	Joe Mantegna
JAMES LINGK	William L. Petersen
BAYLEN	Jack Wallace

Directed by GREGORY MOSHER

THE CHARACTERS: Williamson, Baylen, Roma, Lingk—Men in their early forties. Levene, Moss, Aaronow—Men in their fifties.

THE SCENE: The three scenes of ACT ONE take place in a Chinese restaurant. ACT TWO takes place in a real estate office.

"Always be closing," a sales maxim, succinctly describes the theme of *Glengarry Glen Ross,* David Mamet's searing play depicting the ruthless, double-dealing world of American business. Unlike Mamet's film *House of Games,* inhabited by shadowy subterranean characters, *Glengarry Glen Ross* is peopled with men who are all too real in the desperation that drives some of them down the path of degradation and ruin. Raunchy expletives are contained in almost every sentence, heightening the tension and serving to conceal the fear and panic of the characters. In this play, Mamet's famous ear for language, finely tuned to the repetitive colloquial speech of the working class, heightens to a soaring new crescendo.

Glengarry Glen Ross depicts men who hunger for the "quick deal" and the "fast buck," which leads them to lie, cheat, and deceive one another, not only for money but to prove their manliness and self-worth. As in Mamet's play *American Buffalo,* "Business is—people taking care of themselves.... The business of America is business ... we're a nation of entrepreneurs." What interests the writer is "the shadowy, elusive frontiers between business, friendship, greed, and altruism ... evil and good.... No one has ever decided what is a crime and what is not...." Mamet insists that there is no difference between the crimes of the ordinary workingman and of those in more privileged positions. "Part of the American myth, he says, "is that a difference exists, that at a certain point, vicious behavior becomes laudable.... There is no significant difference between the stealing that goes on in a Madison Avenue ad agency and an Eighth Avenue stickup."

In this play, five middle-aged real estate salesman compete for "leads," the names of prospective clients likely to buy the worthless land that they are selling. Meanwhile, they stalk, threaten, and deceive one another in an attempt to win an office sales competition (the loser will be fired); those in power are feared, envied, and bribed. Mamet states that it is not his intention to indict these men but to "create a closed moral universe and to leave the evaluation to the audience." When Mamet finished writing the play, it was given a staged reading; dissatisfied, he sent a copy of the text to Harold Pinter for advice. Pinter's response was that the only thing the play needed was a production; he in turn gave it to the British National Theatre, whose premiere production of *Glengarry Glen Ross* won the Society of West End Theatre Critics' Award as the year's best play. Its subsequent American premiere took place at the Goodman Theatre in Chicago; it was then presented on Broadway. The play was awarded the Pulitzer Prize for drama and the New York Drama Critics Circle Award in 1984. It was filmed in 1992.

David Mamet was born in 1947 on Chicago's South Side. He traces his acute awareness of language to his father, from whom he inherited an intense interest in semantics. While he was in high school, Mamet apprenticed at Chicago's Hull House Theatre. This, combined with his exposure to Chicago's famous Second City (where he bused tables), helped shape the development of his style: the short scenes between two characters, the repetitive phrases, the truncated sentences and staccato rhythms. After his graduation from Goddard College in 1969, between periods of teaching, acting, writing, and running his own theatre company, Mamet took a series of odd jobs that introduced him to the speech and behavior of the working class: He was a taxi driver, short-order cook, trucker, factory worker, and merchant marine; he also put in time in a real estate office. Mamet states, "The first thing I learned is that the exigent speak poetry. They don't speak the language of newspapers. I heard rhythms and expressions that dealt with an experience not covered in anything I'd ever read.... Actually, my main emphasis is on the rhythm...."

Mamet's entire life has been devoted to the theatre. At college, he wrote his first play, *Camel* (1969), which was followed by *Lakeboat* (1970). Returning to Goddard as an acting teacher, he organized the St. Nicholas Theatre Company and wrote scenes and short plays for his acting students. *The Duck Variations* (1972), *Mackinac* and *Marranos*, (both 1973), and *Sexual Perversity in Chicago* (1974) were all premiered in Chicago; the latter won that city's Joseph Jefferson Award. In 1976 and 1977, Mamet's *American Buffalo* was produced both Off Broadway and on, winning the New York Drama Critics Circle Award and the Village Voice Obie Award. It has subsequently been presented all over America and in England. *The Woods, The Water Engine, An American Fable, Lone Canoe,* and *A Life in the Theatre,* all originally produced in Chicago, followed. *Reunion, Dark Pony,* and *The Sanctity of Marriage* were produced at the Circle Repertory Theatre in the fall of 1979.

Mamet now divides his time between playwriting and writing for the cinema. He feels that screenwriting has greatly influenced his later stage work. "I write a million episodic plays . . . who cares? . . . The imperative of structure and story was driven home to me when I began to write movies. What matters is keeping people in their seats." Among his screenplays for film and television: *The Postman Always Rings Twice* (1982), *The Verdict* (1982; Academy Award nomination), *House of Games* (1987; also directed), *Things Change* (1988; also directed), *Lip Service* (1988), *We're No Angels* (1989), *The Untouchables* (1989), *Homicide* (1990; also directed), and episodes of both *Twin Peaks* and *Hill Street Blues* (1990). Mamet, who often writes in a cabin with no electricity in Vermont, says that one of his basic creative methods is eavesdropping on conversations, which he then translates into pages of dialogue and keeps in a file cabinet.

Other works include: *Some Freaks, The Revenge of the Space Pandas* (1977), *All Men Are Whores* (1977), *A Wet Day at Clark and Diversey* (1978), *Prairie du Chien* (1979), *Shoeshine* (1979), *A Sermon* (1981), *Five Unrelated Pieces* (1983), *The Disappearance of the Jews* (1983), *Edmond* (1982; Obie Award winner), *Warm and Cold* (1984), *The Owl* (with Lindsay Crouse), *The Shawl* (1985), *The Spanish Prisoner* (1985), *Mr. Happiness, The Frog Prince, Cross Patch* (1985), *Goldberg Street* (1985), *Speed-the-Plow* (1988), *Oleanna* (1992), the introduction to the *Practical Handbook for the Actor* (1987), *Writing in Restaurants,* a volume of poetry, a collection of lectures on filmmaking, and a television pilot, *Bradford.*

ACT ONE

SCENE ONE

A booth at a Chinese restaurant, Williamson and Levene *are seated at the booth.*

LEVENE. John ... John ... John. Okay. John. John. Look: *(Pause.)* The Glengarry Highland's leads, you're sending Roma out. Fine. He's a good man. We know what he is. He's fine. All I'm saying, you look at the *board*, he's throwing ... wait, wait, wait, he's throwing them *away*, he's throwing the leads away. All that I'm saying, that you're wasting leads. I don't want to tell you your *job*. All that I'm saying, things get *set*, I know they do, you get a certain *mindset.* ... A guy gets a reputation. We know how this ... all I'm saying, put a *closer* on the job. There's more than one man for the ... Put a ... wait a second, put a *proven man out* ... and you watch, now *wait* a second—and you watch your *dollar* volumes. ... You start closing them for *fifty* 'stead of *twenty-five* ... you put a *closer* on the ...

WILLIAMSON. Shelly, you blew the last ...

LEVENE. No. John. No. Let's wait, let's back up here, I did ... will you please? Wait a second. Please. I didn't "blow" them. No. I didn't "blow" them. No. One kicked *out*, one I closed ...

WILLIAMSON. ... you didn't close ...

LEVENE. ... I, if you'd *listen* to me. Please. I *closed* the cocksucker. His *ex*, John, his *ex*, I didn't know he was married ... he, the *judge* invalidated the ...

WILLIAMSON. Shelly ...

LEVENE. ... and what is that, John? What? Bad *luck*. That's all it is. I pray in your *life* you will never find it runs in streaks. That's what it does, that's all it's doing. Streaks. I pray it misses you. That's all I want to say.

WILLIAMSON *(Pause)*. What about the other two?

LEVENE. What two?

WILLIAMSON. Four. You had four leads. One kicked out, one the *judge*, you say ...

LEVENE. ... you want to see the court records? John? Eh? You want to go down ...

WILLIAMSON. ... no ...

LEVENE. ... do you want to go downtown ... ?

WILLIAMSON. ... no ...

LEVENE. ... then ...

WILLIAMSON. ... I only ...

LEVENE. ... then what is this "you *say*" shit, what is that? *(Pause.)* What is that ... ?

WILLIAMSON. All that I'm saying ...

LEVENE. What is this "you *say*"? A deal kicks out ... I got to *eat. Shit*, Williamson, *shit*. You ... Moss ... Roma ... look at the *sheets* ... look at the *sheets*. Nineteen *eighty*, eighty-*one* ... eighty-*two* ... six months of eighty-two ... who's there? Who's up there?

WILLIAMSON. Roma.

LEVENE. Under him?

WILLIAMSON. Moss.

LEVENE. Bullshit. John. Bull*shit*. April, September 1981. It's *me*. It isn't *fucking* Moss. Due respect, he's an *order* taker, John. He *talks*, he talks a good game, look at the *board*, and it's *me*, John, it's me ...

WILLIAMSON. Not lately it isn't.

LEVENE. Lately kiss my ass lately. That isn't how you build an org ... talk, talk to Murray. Talk to Mitch. When we were on Peterson, who paid for his fucking *car*? You talk to him. The *Seville*...? He came in, "You bought that for me Shelly." Out of *what*? Cold *calling. Nothing.* Sixty-*five*, when we were there, with Glen *Ross* Farms? You call 'em downtown. What was that? *Luck?* That was "luck"? *Bull*shit, John. You're burning my ass, I can't get a fucking *lead* ... you think that was luck. My stats for those years? Bull*shit* ... over that period of time ... ? Bull*shit*. It wasn't luck. It was *skill*. You want to throw that away, John ... ? You want to throw that away?

WILLIAMSON. It isn't me ...

LEVENE. ... it isn't you ... ? Who *is* it? Who is this I'm talking to? I need the *leads* ...

WILLIAMSON. ... after the thirtieth ...

LEVENE. Bull*shit* the thirtieth, I don't get on the board the thirtieth, they're going to can my ass. I need the leads. I need them now. Or I'm gone, and you're going to miss me, John, I swear to you.

WILLIAMSON. Murray ...

LEVENE. ... you *talk* to Murray ...

WILLIAMSON. I have. And my job is to marshal those leads ...

LEVENE. Marshal the leads ... marshal the leads? What the fuck, what bus did *you* get off of, we're here to fucking *sell. Fuck* marshaling the leads. What the fuck talk is that? What the fuck talk is that? Where did you learn that? In school? *(Pause.)* That's "talk," my friend, that's "talk." Our job is to *sell*. I'm the *man* to sell. I'm getting garbage. *(Pause.)*

You're giving it to me, and what I'm saying is it's *fucked.*

WILLIAMSON. You're saying that I'm fucked.

LEVENE. Yes. *(Pause.)* I am. I'm sorry to antagonize you.

WILLIAMSON. Let me . . .

LEVENE. . . . and I'm going to get bounced and you're . . .

WILLIAMSON. . . . let me . . . are you listening to me . . . ?

LEVENE. Yes.

WILLIAMSON. Let me tell you something, Shelly. I do what I'm hired to do. I'm . . . wait a second. I'm *hired* to watch the leads. I'm given . . . hold on, I'm given a *policy. My* job is to *do that.* What I'm *told.* That's it. You, wait a second, *anybody* falls below a certain mark I'm not *permitted* to give them the premium leads.

LEVENE. Then how do they come up above that mark? With *dreck* . . . ? That's *nonsense.* Explain this to me. 'Cause it's a waste, and it's a stupid waste. I want to tell you something . . .

WILLIAMSON. You know what those leads cost?

LEVENE. The premium leads. Yes. I know what they cost. John. Because I, *I* generated the dollar revenue sufficient to *buy* them. Nineteen senny-*nine*, you know what I made? Senny-*nine?* Ninety-six thousand dollars. John? For *Murray* . . . For *Mitch* . . . look at the sheets . . .

WILLIAMSON. Murray said . . .

LEVENE. *Fuck* him. *Fuck* Murray. John? You know? You tell him I said so. What does *he* fucking know? He's going to have a "sales" contest . . . you know what our sales contest used to be? *Money.* A *fortune.* Money lying on the ground. Murray? When was the last time *he* went out on a sit? Sales contest? It's *laughable.* It's cold out there now, John. It's tight. Money is *tight.* This ain't sixty-five. It ain't. It just ain't. See? See? Now, I'm a good *man*—but I need a . . .

WILLIAMSON. Murray said . . .

LEVENE. John. John . . .

WILLIAMSON. Will you please wait a second. Shelly. Please. Murray told me: the hot leads . . .

LEVENE. . . . ah, *fuck* this . . .

WILLIAMSON. The . . . Shelly? *(Pause.)* The hot leads are assigned according to the board. During the contest. *Period.* Anyone who beats fifty per . . .

LEVENE. That's fucked. That's fucked. You don't look at the fucking *percentage.* You look at the *gross.*

WILLIAMSON. Either way. You're out.

LEVENE. I'm out.

WILLIMSON. Yes.

LEVENE. I'll tell you why I'm out. I'm *out,* you're giving me toilet paper. John. I've *seen* those leads. I saw them when I was at Homestead, we pitched those cocksuckers Rio Rancho nineteen sixty-*nine* they wouldn't buy. They couldn't buy a fucking *toaster.* They're *broke,* John. They're cold. They're deadbeats, you can't judge on that. Even so. Even so. Alright. Fine. Fine. Even so. I go in, FOUR FUCKING LEADS they got their money in a *sock.* They're fucking *Polacks,* John. Four leads. I close two. *Two.* Fifty per . . .

WILLIAMSON. . . . they kicked out.

LEVENE. They *all* kick out. You run in *streaks,* pal. *Streaks.* I'm . . . I'm . . . don't look at the *board,* look at *me.* Shelly Levene. *Anyone. Ask* them on Western. Ask Getz at Homestead. Go ask Jerry Graff. You know who I am . . . I NEED A SHOT. I got to get on the fucking board. Ask them. *Ask* them. Ask them who ever picked up a check I was flush. Moss, Jerry Graff, Mitch himself . . . Those guys *lived* on the business I brought in. They *lived* on it . . . and so did Murray, John. You were here you'd of benefited from it too. And now I'm saying this. Do I want charity? Do I want *pity?* I want *sits.* I want leads don't come right out of a *phone book.* Give me a lead hotter than that, I'll go in and close it. Give me a chance. That's all I want. I'm going to *get* up on that fucking board and all I want is a chance. It's a *streak* and I'm going to turn it around. *(Pause.)* I need your help. *(Pause.)*

WILLIAMSON. I can't do it, Shelly. *(Pause.)*

LEVENE. Why?

WILLIAMSON. The leads are assigned randomly . . .

LEVENE. *Bullshit, bullshit,* you assign them. . . . What are you *telling* me?

WILLIAMSON. . . . apart from the top men on the contest board.

LEVENE. Then put me on the board.

WILLIAMSON. You start closing again, you'll *be* on the board.

LEVENE. I can't close these leads, John. No one can. It's a joke. John, look, just give me a hot lead. Just give me two of the premium leads. As a "test," alright? As a "test" and I promise you . . .

WILLIAMSON. I can't do it, Shel. *(Pause.)*

LEVENE. I'll give you ten percent. *(Pause.)*

WILLIAMSON. Of what?

LEVENE. Of my end what I close.

WILLIAMSON. And what if you don't close.

LEVENE. I *will* close.

WILLIAMSON. What if you *don't* close . . . ?

LEVENE. I *will* close.

WILLIAMSON. What if you *don't?* Then I'm *fucked*. You see . . . ? Then it's *my* job. That's what I'm *telling* you.

LEVENE. I *will* close. John, John, ten percent. I can get hot. You *know* that . . .

WILLIAMSON. Not lately you can't . . .

LEVENE. Fuck that. That's defeatist. Fuck that. Fuck it. . . . Get on my side. *Go* with me. Let's *do* something. You want to run this office, *run* it.

WILLIAMSON. Twenty percent. *(Pause.)*

LEVENE. Alright.

WILLIAMSON. And fifty bucks a lead.

LEVENE. John. *(Pause.)* Listen. I want to talk to you. Permit me to do this a second. I'm older than you. A man acquires a reputation. On the street. What he does when he's *up*, what he does otherwise. . . . I said "ten," you said "no." You said "twenty." I said "fine," I'm not going to fuck with you, how can I beat that, you tell me? . . . Okay. Okay. We'll . . . Okay. Fine. We'll . . . Alright, twenty percent, and fifty bucks a lead. That's fine. For now. That's fine. A month or two we'll talk. A month from now. Next month. After the thirtieth. *(Pause.)* We'll talk.

WILLIAMSON. What are we going to say?

LEVENE. No. You're right. That's for later. We'll talk in a month. What have you got? I want two sits. Tonight.

WILLIAMSON. I'm not sure I have two.

LEVENE. I saw the board. You've got *four* . . .

WILLIAMSON *(Snaps)*. I've got *Roma*. Then I've got Moss . . .

LEVENE. *Bullshit*. They ain't been in the office yet. Give 'em some stiff. We have a deal or not? Eh? Two sits. The Des Plaines. Both of 'em, six and ten, you can do it . . . six and ten . . . eight and eleven, I don't give a shit, you set 'em up? Alright? The two sits in Des Plaines.

WILLIAMSON. Alright.

LEVENE. Good. Now we're talking. *(Pause.)*

WILLIAMSON. A hundred bucks. *(Pause.)*

LEVENE. Now? *(Pause.)* Now?

WILLIAMSON. Now. *(Pause.)* Yes . . . When?

LEVENE. Ah, *shit*, John. *(Pause.)*

WILLIAMSON. I wish I could.

LEVENE. You fucking asshole. *(Pause.)* I haven't got it. *(Pause.)* I haven't got it, John. *(Pause.)* I'll pay you tomorrow. *(Pause.)* I'm coming in here with the sales, I'll pay you *tomorrow*. *(Pause.)* I haven't *got* it, when I pay, the *gas* . . . I get back the hotel, I'll bring it in tomorrow.

WILLIAMSON. Can't do it.

LEVENE. I'll give you thirty on them now, I'll bring the rest tomorrow. I've got it at the hotel. *(Pause.)* John? *(Pause.)* We do that, for chrissake?

WILLIAMSON. No.

LEVENE. I'm asking you. As a favor to me? *(Pause.)* John. *(Long pause.)* John: my *daughter* . . .

WILLIAMSON. I can't do it, Shelly.

LEVENE. Well, I want to tell you something, fella, wasn't long I could pick up the phone, call *Murray* and I'd have your job. You know that? Not too *long* ago. For what? For *nothing*. "Mur, this new kid burns my ass." "Shelly, he's out." You're gone before I'm back from lunch. I bought him a trip to Bermuda once . . .

WILLIAMSON. I have to go . . . *(Gets up.)*

LEVENE. Wait. Alright. Fine. *(Starts going in pocket for money.)* The one. Give me the lead. Give me the one lead. The best one you have.

WILLIAMSON. I can't split them. *(Pause.)*

LEVENE. Why?

WILLIAMSON. Because I say so.

LEVENE *(Pause)*. Is that it? Is that *it*? You want to do business that way . . . ?

*(*WILLIAMSON *gets up, leaves money on the table.)*

LEVENE. You want to do business that way . . . ? Alright. Alright. Alright. Alright. What is there on the other list . . . ?

WILLIAMSON. You want something off the B list?

LEVENE. *Yeah.* Yeah.

WILLIAMSON. Is that what you're saying?

LEVENE. That's what I'm saying. Yeah. *(Pause.)* I'd like something off the other list. Which, very least, that I'm entitled to. If I'm still *working* here, which for the moment I guess that I am. *(Pause.)* What? I'm sorry I spoke harshly to you.

WILLIAMSON. That's alright.

LEVENE. The deal still stands, our other thing.

*(*WILLIAMSON *shrugs. Starts out of the booth.)*

LEVENE. Good. Mmm. I, you know, I left my wallet back at the hotel.

SCENE TWO

A booth at the restaurant. MOSS *and* AARONOW *seated. After the meal.*

—

MOSS. Polacks and deadbeats.

AARONOW. . . . Polacks . . .

MOSS. Deadbeats *all.*

AARONOW. . . . they hold on to their money . . .

MOSS. All of 'em. They, *hey:* it happens to us all.

AARONOW. Where am I going to work?

MOSS. You have to cheer up, George, you aren't out yet.

AARONOW. I'm not?

MOSS. You missed a fucking sale. Big deal. A deadbeat Polack. Big deal. How you going to sell 'em in the *first* place . . . ? Your mistake, you shoun'a took the lead.

AARONOW. I had to.

MOSS. You had to, yeah. Why?

AARONOW. To get on the . . .

MOSS. To get on the board. Yeah. How you goan'a get on the board sell'n a Polack? And I'll tell you, I'll tell you what *else.* You listening? I'll tell you what else: don't ever try to sell an Indian.

AARONOW. I'd never try to sell an Indian.

MOSS. You get those names come up, you ever get 'em, "Patel"?

AARONOW. Mmm . . .

MOSS. You ever get 'em?

AARONOW. Well, I think I had one once.

MOSS. You did?

AARONOW. I . . . I don't know.

MOSS. You had one you'd know it. *Patel.* They keep coming up. I don't know. They like to talk to salesmen. *(Pause.)* They're *lonely,* something. *(Pause.)* They like to feel *superior,* I don't know. Never bought a fucking thing. You're sitting down "The Rio Rancho *this,* the blah blah blah," "The Mountain View—" "Oh yes. My brother told me that. . . ." They got a grapevine. Fuckin' Indians, George. Not my cup of tea. Speaking of which I want to tell you something: *(Pause)* I never got a cup of tea with them. You see them in the restaurants. A supercilious race. What is this *look* on their face all the time? I don't know. *(Pause.)* I don't know. Their broads all look like they just got fucked with a dead *cat, I* don't know. *(Pause.)* I don't know. I don't like it. Christ . . .

AARONOW. What?

MOSS. The whole fuckin' thing . . . The

pressure's just too great. You're ab . . . you're absolu . . . they're too important. All of them. You go in the door. I . . . "I got to *close* this fucker, or I don't eat lunch," "or I don't win the *Cadillac.* . . ." We fuckin' work too hard. You work too hard. We all, I remember when we were at Platt . . . huh? Glen Ross Farms . . . *didn't* we sell a bunch of that . . . ?

AARONOW. They came in and they, you know . . .

MOSS. Well, they fucked it up.

AARONOW. They did.

MOSS. They killed the goose.

AARONOW. They did.

MOSS. And now . . .

AARONOW. We're stuck with *this* . . .

MOSS. We're stuck with *this* fucking shit . . .

AARONOW. . . . *this* shit . . .

MOSS. It's too . . .

AARONOW. It is.

MOSS. Eh?

AARONOW. It's too . . .

MOSS. You get a bad month, all of a . . .

AARONOW. You're on this . . .

MOSS. All of, they got you on this "board . . ."

AARONOW. I, I . . . I . . .

MOSS. Some *contest* board . . .

AARONOW. I . . .

MOSS. It's not right.

AARONOW. It's not.

MOSS. No. *(Pause.)*

AARONOW. And it's not right to the *customers.*

MOSS. I know it's not. I'll tell you, you got, you know, you got . . . what did I learn as a kid on Western? Don't sell a guy one car. Sell him *five* cars over fifteen years.

AARONOW. That's right?

MOSS. Eh . . . ?

AARONOW. That's right?

MOSS. Goddamn right, that's right. Guys come on: "Oh, the blah blah blah, *I* know what I'll do: I'll go in and rob everyone blind and go to Argentina 'cause nobody ever *thought* of this before."

AARONOW. . . . that's right . . .

MOSS. Eh?

AARONOW. No. That's absolutely right.

MOSS. And so they kill the goose. I, I, I'll . . . and a fuckin' *man,* worked all his *life* has got to . . .

AARONOW. . . . that's right . . .

MOSS. . . . cower in his boots . . .

AARONOW *(simultaneously with "boots").* Shoes, boots, yes . . .

MOSS. For some fuckin' "Sell ten thousand and you win the steak knives . . ."

AARONOW. For some *sales* pro . . .

MOSS. . . . sales promotion, "You *lose*, then we fire your . . ." No. It's *medieval* . . . it's wrong. "Or we're going to fire your ass." It's wrong.

AARONOW. Yes.

MOSS. Yes, it is. And you know who's responsible?

AARONOW. Who?

MOSS. You know who it is. It's Mitch. And Murray. 'Cause it doesn't have to be this way.

AARONOW. No.

MOSS. Look at Jerry Graff. He's *clean*, he's doing business for *himself*, he's got his, that *list* of his with the *nurses* . . . see? You see? That's *thinking*. Why take ten percent? A ten percent comm . . . why are we giving the rest away? What are we giving ninety per . . . for *nothing*. For some jerk sit in the office tell you "Get out there and close." "Go win the Cadillac." Graff. He goes out and *buys*. He pays top dollar for the . . . you see?

AARONOW. Yes.

MOSS. That's *thinking*. Now, he's got the leads, he goes in business for *himself*. He's . . . that's what I . . . that's *thinking!* "Who? Who's got a steady *job*, a couple bucks nobody's touched, who?"

AARONOW. Nurses.

MOSS. So Graff buys a fucking list of nurses, one grand—if he paid two I'll eat my hat—four, five thousand nurses, and he's going *wild* . . .

AARONOW. He is?

MOSS. He's doing *very* well.

AARONOW. I heard that they were running cold.

MOSS. The nurses?

AARONOW. Yes.

MOSS. You hear a *lot* of things. . . . He's doing very well. He's doing *very* well.

AARONOW. With River Oaks?

MOSS. River Oaks, Brook Farms. *All* of that shit. Somebody told me, you know what he's clearing *himself*? Fourteen, fifteen grand a *week*.

AARONOW. Himself?

MOSS. That's what I'm *saying*. Why? The *leads*. He's got the good leads . . . what are we, we're sitting in the shit here. Why? We have to go to *them* to *get* them. Huh. Ninety percent our sale, we're *paying* to the *office* for the *leads*.

AARONOW. The leads, the overhead, the telephones, there's *lots* of things.

MOSS. What do you need? A *telephone*, some broad to say "Good morning," nothing . . . nothing . . .

AARONOW. No, it's not that simple, Dave . . .

MOSS. *Yes*. It *is*. It *is* simple, and you know what the hard part is?

AARONOW. What?

MOSS. Starting up.

AARONOW. What hard part?

MOSS. Of doing the thing. The dif . . . the difference. Between me and Jerry Graff. Going to business for yourself. The hard part is . . . you know what it is?

AARONOW. What?

MOSS. Just the *act*.

AARONOW. What act?

MOSS. To say "I'm going on my own." 'Cause what you do, George, let me tell you what you do: you find yourself in *thrall* to someone else. And we *enslave* ourselves. To *please*. To win some fucking *toaster* . . . to . . . to . . . and the guy who got there first made *up* those . . .

AARONOW. That's right . . .

MOSS. He made *up* those rules, and we're working for *him*.

AARONOW. That's the truth . . .

MOSS. That's the *God's* truth. And it gets me depressed. I *swear* that it does. At MY AGE. To see a goddamn: "Somebody wins the Cadillac this month. P.S. Two guys get fucked."

AARONOW. *Huh*.

MOSS. You don't *ax* your sales force.

AARONOW. No.

MOSS. You . . .

AARONOW. You . . .

MOSS. You *build* it!

AARONOW. That's what I . . .

MOSS. You fucking *build* it! Men come . . .

AARONOW. Men come *work* for you . . .

MOSS. . . . you're absolutely right.

AARONOW. They . . .

MOSS. They have . . .

AARONOW. When they . . .

MOSS. Look look look look, when they *build* your business, then you can't fucking turn around, *enslave* them, treat them like *children*, fuck them up the ass, leave them to fend for themselves . . . no. *(Pause.)* No. *(Pause.)* You're absolutely right, and I want to tell you something.

AARONOW. What?

MOSS. I want to tell you what somebody should do.

AARONOW. What?

MOSS. Someone should stand up and strike *back*.

AARONOW. What do you mean?

MOSS. *Somebody* . . .

AARONOW. Yes . . . ?

MOSS. Should do something to *them*.

AARONOW. What?

MOSS. Something. To pay them back. *(Pause.)* Someone, someone should hurt them. Murray and Mitch.

AARONOW. Someone should hurt them.

MOSS. Yes.

AARONOW *(Pause)*. How?

MOSS. How? Do something to hurt them. Where they live.

AARONOW. What? *(Pause.)*

MOSS. Someone should rob the office.

AARONOW. Huh.

MOSS. That's what I'm *saying*. We were, if we were that kind of guys, to knock it off, and *trash* the joint, it looks like robbery, and *take* the fuckin' leads out of the files . . . go to Jerry Graff. *(Long pause.)*

AARONOW. What could somebody get for them?

MOSS. What could we *get* for them? I don't know. Buck a *throw* . . . buck-a-half a throw . . . I don't know. . . . Hey, who knows what they're worth, what do they *pay* for them? All told . . . must be, I'd . . . three bucks a throw . . . *I* don't know.

AARONOW. How many leads have we got?

MOSS. The *Glengarry* . . . the premium leads . . . ? I'd say we got five thousand. Five. Five thousand leads.

AARONOW. And you're saying a fella could take and sell these leads to Jerry Graff.

MOSS. Yes.

AARONOW. How do you know he'd buy them?

MOSS. Graff? Because I worked for him.

AARONOW. You haven't talked to him.

MOSS. No. What do you mean? Have I talked to him about *this*? *(Pause.)*

AARONOW. Yes. I mean are you actually *talking* about this, or are we just . . .

MOSS. No, we're just . . .

AARONOW. We're just *"talking"* about it.

MOSS. We're just *speaking* about it. *(Pause.)* As an *idea*.

AARONOW. As an idea.

MOSS. Yes.

AARONOW. We're not actually *talking* about it.

MOSS. No.

AARONOW. Talking about it as a . . .

MOSS. *No.*

AARONOW. As a *robbery*.

MOSS. As a "robbery"?! No.

AARONOW. *Well.* Well . . .

MOSS. *Hey. (Pause.)*

AARONOW. So all this, um, you didn't, actually, you didn't actually go talk to Graff.

MOSS. Not actually, no. *(Pause.)*

AARONOW. You didn't?

MOSS. No. Not actually.

AARONOW. Did you?

MOSS. What did I say?

AARONOW. What did you say?

MOSS. Yes. *(Pause.)* I said, "Not actually." The fuck *you* care, George? We're just *talking* . . .

AARONOW. We are?

MOSS. Yes. *(Pause.)*

AARONOW. Because, because, you know, it's a *crime*.

MOSS. That's right. It's a crime. It is a crime. It's also very safe.

AARONOW. You're actually *talking* about this?

MOSS. That's right. *(Pause.)*

AARONOW. You're going to steal the leads?

MOSS. Have I said that? *(Pause.)*

AARONOW. Are you? *(Pause.)*

MOSS. Did I say that?

AARONOW. Did you talk to Graff?

MOSS. Is that what I said?

AARONOW. What did he say?

MOSS. What did he say? He'd *buy* them. *(Pause.)*

AARONOW. You're going to steal the leads and sell the leads to him? *(Pause.)*

MOSS. Yes.

AARONOW. What will he pay?

MOSS. A buck a shot.

AARONOW. For five thousand?

MOSS. However they are, that's the deal. A buck a throw. Five thousand dollars. Split it half and half.

AARONOW. You're saying "me."

MOSS. Yes. *(Pause.)* Twenty-five hundred apiece. One night's work, and the job with Graff. Working the premium leads. *(Pause.)*

AARONOW. A job with Graff.

MOSS. Is that what I said?

AARONOW. He'd give me a job.

MOSS. He would take you on. Yes. *(Pause.)*

AARONOW. Is that the truth?

MOSS. Yes. It is, George. *(Pause.)* Yes. It's a big decision. *(Pause.)* And it's a big reward. *(Pause.)* It's a big reward. For one night's work. *(Pause.)* But it's got to be tonight.

AARONOW. What?

MOSS. What? What? The *leads.*

AARONOW. You have to steal the leads tonight?

MOSS. That's *right,* the guys are moving them downtown. After the thirtieth. Murray and Mitch. After the contest.

AARONOW. You're, you're saying so you have to go in there tonight and . . .

MOSS. *You* . . .

AARONOW. I'm sorry?

MOSS. *You. (Pause.)*

AARONOW. Me?

MOSS. *You* have to go in. *(Pause.) You* have to get the leads. *(Pause.)*

AARONOW. I do?

MOSS. Yes.

AARONOW. I . . .

MOSS. It's not something for nothing, George, I took you in on this, you have to go. That's your thing. I've made the deal with Graff. I can't go. I can't go in, I've spoken on this too much. I've got a big mouth. *(Pause.)* "The fucking leads" et cetera, blah blah blah ". . . the fucking tight ass company . . ."

AARONOW. They'll know when you go over to Graff . . .

MOSS. What will they know? That I stole the leads? I *didn't* steal the leads, I'm going to the *movies* tonight with a friend, and then I'm going to the Como Inn. Why did I go to Graff? I got a better deal. *Period.* Let 'em prove something. They can't prove anything that's not the case. *(Pause.)*

AARONOW. *Dave.*

MOSS. Yes.

AARONOW. You want me to break into the office tonight and steal the leads?

MOSS. Yes. *(Pause.)*

AARONOW. No.

MOSS. Oh, yes, George.

AARONOW. What does that mean?

MOSS. Listen to this. I have an alibi, I'm going to the Como Inn, why? Why? The place gets robbed, they're going to come looking for *me.* Why? Because I probably did it. Are you going to turn me in? *(Pause.)* George? Are you going to turn me in?

AARONOW. What if you don't get caught?

MOSS. They come to you, you going to turn me in?

AARONOW. Why would they come to me?

MOSS. They're going to come to *everyone.*

AARONOW. Why would I *do* it?

MOSS. You wouldn't, George, that's why I'm talking to you. Answer me. They come to you. You going to turn me in?

AARONOW. No.

MOSS. Are you sure?

AARONOW. Yes. I'm sure.

MOSS. Then listen to this: I have to get those leads tonight. That's something I have to do. If I'm not at the *movies* . . . if I'm not eating over at the inn . . . If you don't do this, then *I* have to come in here . . .

AARONOW. . . . you don't have to come in . . .

MOSS. . . . and *rob* the place . . .

AARONOW. . . . I thought that we were only talking . . .

MOSS. . . . they *take* me, then. They're going to ask me who were my accomplices.

AARONOW. *Me?*

MOSS. Absolutely.

AARONOW. That's ridiculous.

MOSS. Well, to the law, you're an accessory. Before the fact.

AARONOW. I didn't ask to be.

MOSS. Then tough luck, George, because you are.

AARONOW. Why? *Why,* because you only *told* me about it?

MOSS. That's right.

AARONOW. Why are you doing this to me, Dave. Why are you talking this way to me? I don't understand. Why are you doing this at *all* . . . ?

MOSS. That's none of your fucking business . . .

AARONOW. Well, well, well, *talk* to me, we sat down to eat *dinner,* and here I'm a *criminal* . . .

MOSS. You *went* for it.

AARONOW. In the abstract . . .

MOSS. So I'm making it concrete.

AARONOW. Why?

MOSS. Why? Why *you* going to give me five grand?

AARONOW. Do you need five grand?

MOSS. Is that what I just said?

AARONOW. You need money? Is that the . . .

MOSS. Hey, hey, let's just keep it simple, what I need is not the . . . what do *you* need . . . ?

AARONOW. What is the five grand? *(Pause.)* What is the, you said that we were going to *split* five . . .

MOSS. I lied. *(Pause.)* Alright? My end is *my* business. Your end's twenty-five. In or out. You tell me, you're out you take the consequences.

AARONOW. I do?

MOSS. Yes. *(Pause.)*

AARONOW. And why is that?

MOSS. Because you listened.

SCENE THREE

The restaurant. ROMA *is seated alone at the booth.* LINGK *is at the booth next to him.* ROMA *is talking to him.*

———

ROMA. . . . all train compartments smell vaguely of shit. It gets so you don't mind it. That's the worst thing that I can confess. You know how long it took me to get there? A long time. When you *die* you're going to regret the things you don't do. You think you're *queer* . . . ? I'm going to tell you something: we're *all* queer. You think that you're a *thief?* So *what?* You get befuddled by a middle-class morality . . . ? Get *shut* of it. Shut it out. You cheated on your wife . . . ? You *did* it, *live* with it. *(Pause.)* You fuck little girls, so *be* it. There's an absolute morality? May *be.* And *then* what? If you *think* there is, then *be* that thing. Bad people go to hell? I don't *think* so. If you think that, act that way. A hell exists on earth? Yes. I won't live in it. That's *me.* You ever take a dump made you feel you'd just slept for twelve hours . . . ?

LINGK. Did I . . . ?

ROMA. Yes.

LINGK. I don't know.

ROMA. Or a *piss* . . . ? A great meal fades in reflection. Everything else gains. You know why? 'Cause it's only food. This shit we eat, it keeps us going. But it's only food. The great fucks that you may have had. What do you remember about them?

LINGK. What do I . . . ?

ROMA. Yes.

LINGK. Mmmm . . .

ROMA. I don't know. For *me,* I'm saying, what it is, it's probably not the orgasm. Some broads, forearms on your neck, something her *eyes* did. There was a *sound* she made . . . or, me, lying, in the, I'll tell you: me lying in bed; the next day she brought me café au lait. She gives me a cigarette, my balls feel like concrete. Eh? What I'm saying, what is our life? *(Pause.)* It's looking forward or it's looking back. And that's our life. That's *it.*

Where is the *moment? (Pause.)* And what is it that we're afraid of? Loss. What else? *(Pause.)* The *bank* closes. We get *sick,* my wife died on a plane, the stock market collapsed . . . the house burnt down . . . what of these happen . . . ? None of 'em. We worry anyway. What does this mean? I'm not *secure.* How can I be secure? *(Pause.)* Through amassing wealth beyond all measure? No. And what's beyond all measure? That's a sickness. That's a trap. There is no measure. Only greed. How can we act? The right way, we would say, to deal with this: "There is a one-in-a-million chance that so and so will happen. . . . *Fuck* it, it won't happen to *me.* . . ." No. We know that's not the right way I think. *(Pause.)* We say the *correct* way to deal with this is "There is a one-in-so-and-so chance this will happen . . . God *protect* me. I am powerless, let it not happen to me. . . . " But no to *that.* I say. There's something else. What is it? "If it happens, AS IT MAY for that is not within our powers, I will *deal* with it, just as I do *today* with what draws my concern today." I say *this* is how we must act. I do those things which seem correct to me *today.* I trust myself. And if security concerns me, I do that which *today* I think will make me secure. And every day I *do* that, when that day *arrives* that I need a reserve, (a) odds are that I have it, and (b) the *true* reserve that I have is the strength that I have of *acting each day* without fear. *(Pause.)* According to the dictates of my mind. *(Pause.)* Stocks, bonds, objects of art, real estate. Now: what are they? *(Pause.)* An opportunity. To what? To make money? Perhaps. To *lose* money? Perhaps. To "indulge" and to "learn" about ourselves? Perhaps. *So fucking what?* What *isn't?* They're an *opportunity.* That's all. They're an *event.* A guy comes up to you, you make a call, you send in a brochure, it doesn't matter, "There're these *properties* I'd like for you to see." What does it mean? What you *want* it to mean. *(Pause.)* Money? *(Pause.)* If that's what it signifies to you. Security? *(Pause.)* Comfort? *(Pause.)* All it is is THINGS THAT HAPPEN TO YOU. *(Pause.)* That's all it is. How are they different? *(Pause.)* Some poor newly married guy gets run down by a cab. Some *busboy* wins the lottery. *(Pause.)* All it is, it's a carnival. What's special . . . what *draws* us? *(Pause.)* We're all different. *(Pause.)* We're not the same. *(Pause.)* We are not the same. *(Pause.)* Hmmm. *(Pause. Sighs.)* It's been a long day. *(Pause.)* What are you drinking?

LINGK. Gimlet.

ROMA. Well, let's have a couple more. My name is Richard Roma, what's yours?

LINGK. Lingk. James Lingk.

ROMA. James. I'm glad to meet you. *(They shake hands.)* I'm glad to meet you, James. *(Pause.)* I want to show you something. *(Pause.)* It might mean *nothing* to you ... and it might not. I don't know. I don't know anymore. *(Pause. He takes out a small map and spreads it on a table.)* What is that? Florida. Glengarry Highlands. Florida. "Florida. *Bullshit.*" And maybe that's true; and that's what *I* said: but look *here:* what is this? This is a piece of land. Listen to what I'm going to tell you now:

ACT TWO

The real estate office. Ransacked. A broken plate-glass window boarded up, glass all over the floor. AARONOW *and* WILLIAMSON *standing around, smoking.*

Pause.

———

AARONOW. People used to say that there are numbers of such magnitude that multiplying them by two made no difference. *(Pause.)*

WILLIAMSON. Who used to say that?

AARONOW. In school. *(Pause.)*

*(*BAYLEN, *a detective, comes out of the inner office.)*

BAYLEN. Alright ... ?

*(*ROMA *enters from the street.)*

ROMA. *Williamson ... Williamson,* they stole the *contracts* ... ?

BAYLEN. Excuse me, sir ...

ROMA. Did they get my contracts?

WILLIAMSON. They got ...

BAYLEN. Excuse me, fella.

ROMA. ... did they ...

BAYLEN. Would you excuse us, please?

ROMA. Don't *fuck* with me, fella. I'm talking about a fuckin' Cadillac car that you owe me ...

WILLIAMSON. They didn't get your contract. I filed it before I left.

ROMA. They didn't get my contracts?

WILLIAMSON. They—excuse me ... *(He goes back into inner room with the* DETECTIVE.)

ROMA. Oh, *fuck. Fuck. (He starts kicking the desk.)* FUCK FUCK FUCK! WILLIAMSON!!! WILLIAMSON!!! *(Goes to the door*

WILLIAMSON *went into, tries the door; it's locked.)* OPEN THE FUCKING ... WILLIAMSON ...

BAYLEN *(coming out)*. Who are you?

*(*WILLIAMSON *comes out.)*

WILLIAMSON. They didn't get the contracts.

ROMA. Did they ...

WILLIAMSON. They got, listen to me ...

ROMA. Th ...

WILLIAMSON. Listen to me: They got *some* of them.

ROMA. Some of them ...

BAYLEN. Who told you ... ?

ROMA. Who told me wh ... ? You've got a fuckin', you've ... a ... who is this ... ? You've got a board-up on the window. ... *Moss* told me.

BAYLEN *(Looking back toward the inner office). Moss* ... Who told him?

ROMA. How the fuck do *I* know? *(To* WILLIAMSON:*) What ... talk* to me.

WILLIAMSON. They took *some* of the con ...

ROMA. ... some of the contracts ... Lingk. James Lingk. I closed ...

WILLIAMSON. You closed him yesterday.

ROMA. *Yes.*

WILLIAMSON. It went down. I filed it.

ROMA. You did?

WILLIAMSON. Yes.

ROMA. Then I'm over the fucking top and you owe me a Cadillac.

WILLIAMSON. I ...

ROMA. And I don't want any fucking shit and I don't give a shit, Lingk puts me over the top, you filed it, that's fine, any other shit kicks out *you* go back. You ... *you* reclose it, 'cause I *closed* it and you ... you owe me the car.

BAYLEN. Would you excuse us, please.

AARONOW. I, um, and may ... maybe they're in ... they're in ... you should, John, if we're ins ...

WILLIAMSON. I'm sure that we're insured, George ... *(Going back inside.)*

ROMA. Fuck insured. You owe me a car.

BAYLEN *(Stepping back into the inner room).* Please don't leave. I'm going to talk to you. What's your name?

ROMA. Are you talking to me? *(Pause.)*

BAYLEN. Yes. *(Pause.)*

ROMA. My name is Richard Roma.

*(*BAYLEN *goes back into the inner room.)*

AARONOW. I, you know, they should be insured.

ROMA. What do *you* care ... ?

AARONOW. Then, you know, they wouldn't be so ups . . .

ROMA. Yeah. That's swell. Yes. You're right. *(Pause.)* How are you?

AARONOW. I'm fine. You mean the *board?* You mean the *board* . . . ?

ROMA. I don't . . . yes. Okay, the board.

AARONOW. I'm, I'm, I'm, I'm fucked on the board. *You.* You see how . . . I . . . *(Pause.)* I can't . . . my mind must be in other places. 'Cause I can't do any . . .

ROMA. *What?* You can't do any *what?* *(Pause.)*

AARONOW. I can't close 'em.

ROMA. Well, they're old. I saw the shit that they were giving you.

AARONOW. Yes.

ROMA. Huh?

AARONOW. Yes. They are old.

ROMA. They're ancient.

AARONOW. Clear . . .

ROMA. Clear Meadows. That shit's dead. *(Pause.)*

AARONOW. It *is* dead.

ROMA. It's a waste of time.

AARONOW. Yes. *(Long pause.)* I'm no fucking good.

ROMA. That's . . .

AARONOW. Everything I . . . *you* know.

ROMA. That's not . . . Fuck that shit, George. You're a, *hey,* you had a bad month. You're a good man, George.

AARONOW. I am?

ROMA. You hit a bad streak. We've all . . . look at this: fifteen units Mountain View, the fucking things get stole.

AARONOW. He said he filed . . .

ROMA. He filed half of them, he filed the *big* one. All the little ones, I have, I have to go back and . . . ah, *fuck,* I got to go out like a fucking schmuck hat in my hand and re-close the . . . *(Pause.)* I mean, talk about a bad streak. That would sap *anyone's* self confi . . . I got to go out and reclose all my . . . Where's the phones?

AARONOW. They stole . . .

ROMA. They stole the . . .

AARONOW. What. What kind of outfit are we running where . . . where anyone . . .

ROMA *(To himself).* They stole the phones.

AARONOW. Where criminals can come in here . . . they take the . . .

ROMA. They stole the phones. They stole the leads. They're . . . *Christ. (Pause.)* What am I going to do this month? Oh, *shit* . . . *(Starts for the door.)*

AARONOW. You think they're going to catch . . . where are you going?

ROMA. Down the street.

WILLIAMSON *(Sticking his head out of the door).* Where are you going?

ROMA. To the restaura . . . what do you fucking . . . ?

WILLIAMSON. Aren't you going out today?

ROMA. With what? *(Pause.)* With what, John, they took the leads . . .

WILLIAMSON. I have the stuff from last year's . . .

ROMA. Oh. Oh. Oh, your "nostalgia" file, that's fine. No. Swell. 'Cause I don't have to . . .

WILLIAMSON. . . . you want to go out to-day . . . ?

ROMA. 'Cause I don't have to *eat* this month. No. Okay. *Give* 'em to me . . . *(To himself:)* Fucking Mitch and Murray going to shit a br . . . what am I going to *do* all . . .

(WILLIAMSON starts back into the office. He is accosted by AARONOW.)

AARONOW. Were the leads . . .

ROMA. . . . what am I going to *do* all month . . . ?

AARONOW. Were the leads insured?

WILLIAMSON. I don't know, George, why?

AARONOW. 'Cause, you know, 'cause they weren't, I know that Mitch and Murray uh . . . *(Pause.)*

WILLIAMSON. What?

AARONOW. That they're going to be upset.

WILLIAMSON. That's right. *(Going back into his office. Pause. To* ROMA:*)* You want to go out today . . . ?

(Pause. WILLIAMSON *returns to his office.)*

AARONOW. He said we're all going to have to go talk to the guy.

ROMA. What?

AARONOW. He said we . . .

ROMA. To the cop?

AARONOW. Yeah.

ROMA. Yeah. That's swell. *Another* waste of time.

AARONOW. A waste of time? Why?

ROMA. *Why?* 'Cause they aren't going to find the guy.

AARONOW. The cops?

ROMA. Yes. The cops. No.

AARONOW. They aren't?

ROMA. No.

AARONOW. Why don't you think so?

ROMA. Why? Because they're *stupid.* "Where were you last night . . ."

AARONOW. Where were you?

ROMA. Where was *I*?

AARONOW. Yes.

ROMA. I was at home, where were *you*?

AARONOW. At home.

ROMA. *See* . . . ? Were you the guy who broke in?

AARONOW. Was I?

ROMA. Yes.

AARONOW. No.

ROMA. Then don't sweat it, George, you know why?

AARONOW. No.

ROMA. You have nothing to hide.

AARONOW *(Pause)*. When I talk to the police, I get nervous.

ROMA. Yeah. You know who doesn't?

AARONOW. No, who?

ROMA. Thieves.

AARONOW. Why?

ROMA. They're inured to it.

AARONOW. You think so?

ROMA. Yes. *(Pause.)*

AARONOW. But what should I *tell* them?

ROMA. The truth, George. Always tell the truth. It's the easiest thing to remember.

(WILLIAMSON comes out of the office with leads. ROMA takes one, reads it.)

ROMA. Patel? Ravidam *Patel*? How am I going to make a living on these deadbeat *wogs*? Where did you get this, from the *morgue*?

WILLIAMSON. If you don't want it, give it back.

ROMA. I don't "want" it, if you catch my drift.

WILLIAMSON. I'm giving you *three* leads. You . . .

ROMA. What's the fucking point in *any* case . . . ? What's the *point*. I got to argue with *you*, I got to knock heads with the *cops*, I'm busting my *balls*, sell you *dirt* to fucking *deadbeats* money in the *mattress*, I come back you can't even manage to keep the contracts safe, I have to go back and close them *again*. . . . What the fuck am I wasting my time, fuck this shit. I'm going out and reclose last week's . . .

WILLIAMSON. The word from Murray is: leave them alone. If we need a new signature he'll go out himself, he'll be the *president*, just come *in*, from out of *town* . . .

ROMA. Okay, okay, okay, gimme this shit. Fine. *(Takes the leads.)*

WILLIAMSON. Now, I'm giving you three.

ROMA. Three? I count *two*.

WILLIAMSON. Three.

ROMA. Patel? Fuck *you*. Fuckin' *Shiva* handed him a million dollars, told him "sign the deal," he wouldn't sign. And Vishnu, too. Into the bargain. Fuck *that*, John. You know your business, I know mine. Your business is being an *asshole*, and I find out whose fucking *cousin* you are, I'm going to go to him and figure out a way to have your *ass* . . . fuck you—I'll wait for the new leads.

(SHELLY LEVENE enters.)

LEVENE. Get the *chalk*. Get the *chalk* . . . get the *chalk!* I closed 'em! I *closed* the cocksucker. Get the chalk and put me on the *board*. I'm going to Hawaii! Put me on the Cadillac board, Williamson! Pick up the fuckin' chalk. Eight units. Mountain View . . .

ROMA. You sold eight Mountain View?

LEVENE. You bet your ass. Who wants to go to lunch? Who wants to go to lunch? I'm buying. *(Slaps contract down on Williamson's desk.)* Eighty-two fucking grand. And twelve grand in commission. John. *(Pause.)* On fucking deadbeat magazine subscription leads.

WILLIAMSON. Who?

LEVENE *(Pointing to contract)*. *Read* it. Bruce and Harriett Nyborg. *(Looking around.)* What happened here?

AARONOW. Fuck. I had them on River Glen.

(LEVENE looks around.)

LEVENE. What happened?

WILLIAMSON. Somebody broke in.

ROMA. Eight units?

LEVENE. That's right.

ROMA. *Shelly* . . . !

LEVENE. Hey, big fucking deal. Broke a bad streak . . .

AARONOW. Shelly, the Machine, Levene.

LEVENE. You . . .

AARONOW. That's great.

LEVENE. Thank you, George.

(BAYLEN sticks his head out of the room; calls in, "Aaronow." AARONOW goes into the side room.)

LEVENE. Williamson, get on the phone, call Mitch . . .

ROMA. They took the phones . . .

LEVENE. They . . .

BAYLEN. *Aaronow* . . .

ROMA. They took the typewriters, they took the leads, they took the *cash*, they took the *contracts* . . .

LEVENE. Wh . . . wh . . . Wha . . . ?

AARONOW. We had a robbery. *(Goes into the inner room.)*

LEVENE *(Pause)*. When?

ROMA. Last night, this morning. *(Pause.)*

LEVENE. They took the leads?

ROMA. Mmm.

(MOSS comes out of the interrogation.)

MOSS. Fuckin' asshole.

ROMA. What, they beat you with a rubber bat?

MOSS. Cop couldn't find his dick two hands and a map. Anyone talks to this guy's an *asshole* . . .

ROMA. You going to turn State's?

MOSS. Fuck you, Ricky. I ain't going out today. I'm going home. I'm going home because nothing's *accomplished* here. . . . Anyone *talks* to this guy is . . .

ROMA. Guess what the Machine did?

MOSS. Fuck the Machine.

ROMA. Mountain View. Eight units.

MOSS. Fuckin' cop's got no right talk to me that way. I didn't rob the place . . .

ROMA. You hear what I said?

MOSS. Yeah. He closed a deal.

ROMA. Eight units. Mountain View.

MOSS *(To LEVENE)*. You did that?

LEVENE. Yeah. *(Pause.)*

MOSS. Fuck you.

ROMA. Guess who?

MOSS. When . . .

LEVENE. Just now.

ROMA. Guess who?

MOSS. You just this morning . . .

ROMA. Harriett and blah blah Nyborg.

MOSS. You did that?

LEVENE. Eighty-two thousand dollars. *(Pause.)*

MOSS. Those fuckin' *deadbeats* . . .

LEVENE. My ass. I told 'em. *(To ROMA:)* Listen to this: I said . . .

MOSS. Hey, I don't want to hear your fucking war stories . . .

ROMA. Fuck *you,* Dave . . .

LEVENE. "You have to believe in your*self* . . . you"—look—"alright . . . ?"

MOSS *(To WILLIAMSON)*. Give me some leads. I'm going out . . . I'm getting out of . . .

LEVENE. ". . . you have to believe in your*self* . . ."

MOSS. Na, fuck the leads, I'm going home.

LEVENE. "Bruce, Harriett . . . Fuck *me,* believe in your*self* . . ."

ROMA. We haven't got a lead . . .

MOSS. Why not?

ROMA. They took 'em . . .

MOSS. Hey, they're fuckin' garbage any case. . . . This whole goddamn . . .

LEVENE. ". . . You look around, you say, 'This one has so-and-so, and I have nothing . . .'"

MOSS. *Shit.*

LEVENE. " *'Why?* Why don't I get the opportunities . . . ?' "

MOSS. And did they steal the contracts . . . ?

ROMA. Fuck *you* care . . . ?

LEVENE. "I want to tell you something, Harriett . . ."

MOSS. . . . the fuck is *that* supposed to mean . . . ?

LEVENE. Will you shut up, I'm telling you this . . .

(AARONOW sticks his head out.)

AARONOW. Can we get some coffee . . . ?

MOSS. How ya doing? *(Pause.)*

AARONOW. Fine.

MOSS. Uh-huh.

AARONOW. If anyone's going, I could use some coffee.

LEVENE. "You *do* get the . . ." *(To ROMA:)* Huh? Huh?

MOSS. *Fuck* is that supposed to mean?

LEVENE. "You *do* get the opportunity. . . . You *get* them. As *I* do, as *anyone* does . . ."

MOSS. Ricky? . . . That I don't care they stole the contracts? *(Pause.)*

LEVENE. I got 'em in the kitchen. I'm eating her crumb cake.

MOSS. What does that mean?

ROMA. It *means,* Dave, you haven't closed a good one in a month, none of my business, you want to push me to answer you. *(Pause.)* And so you haven't got a contract to get stolen or so forth.

MOSS. You have a mean streak in you, Ricky, you know that . . . ?

LEVENE. Rick. Let me tell you. Wait, we're in the . . .

MOSS. Shut the fuck up. *(Pause.)* Ricky. You have a mean streak in you. . . . *(To LEVENE:)* And what the fuck are *you* babbling about . . . ? *(To ROMA:)* Bring that shit up. Of my volume. You were on a bad one and I brought it up to *you* you'd harbor it. *(Pause.)* You'd harbor it a long long while. And you'd be right.

ROMA. Who said "Fuck the Machine"?

MOSS. *"Fuck the Machine"? "Fuck the Machine"?* What is this. *Courtesy* class . . . ? You're *fucked,* Rick—are you fucking *nuts?* You're hot, so you think you're the *ruler* of this place . . . ?! You want to . . .

LEVENE. Dave . . .

MOSS. . . . Shut up. Decide who should be dealt with how? Is that the thing? I come into the fuckin' office today, I get humiliated by some jagoff cop. I get accused of . . . I get this *shit* thrown in my face by you, you genuine shit, because you're top name on the board . . .

ROMA. Is that what I did? Dave? I humiliated you? My *God* . . . I'm *sorry* . . .

MOSS. Sittin' on top of the *world*, sittin' on top of the *world*, everything's fucking *peachfuzz* . . .

ROMA. Oh, and I don't get a moment to spare for a bust-out *humanitarian* down on his luck lately. Fuck *you*, Dave, you know you got a big *mouth*, and *you* make a close the whole *place* stinks with your *farts* for a week. "How much you just ingested," what a big *man* you are, "Hey, let me buy you a pack of gum. I'll show you how to *chew* it." Your *pal* closes, all that comes out of your mouth is *bile*, how fucked *up* you are . . .

MOSS. *Who's* my pal . . . ? And what are you, Ricky, huh, what are you, Bishop *Sheean?* Who the fuck are *you*, Mr. Slick . . . ? What are you, friend to the *workingman?* Big deal. Fuck *you*, you got the memory a fuckin' *fly*. I never liked you.

ROMA. What is this, your farewell speech?

MOSS. I'm going home.

ROMA. Your farewell to the troops?

MOSS. I'm not going home. I'm going to Wisconsin.

ROMA. Have a good trip.

MOSS *(Simultaneously with "trip")*. And fuck *you*. Fuck the *lot* of you. Fuck you *all*.

(MOSS exits. Pause.)

ROMA *(To LEVENE)*. You were saying? *(Pause.)* Come on. Come on, you got them in the kitchen, you got the stats spread out, you're in your shirtsleeves, you can *smell* it. Huh? Snap out of it, you're eating her *crumb* cake. *(Pause.)*

LEVENE. I'm eating her *crumb* cake . . .

ROMA. How was it . . . ?

LEVENE. From the store.

ROMA. Fuck *her* . . .

LEVENE. "What we have to do is *admit* to ourself that we see that opportunity . . . and *take* it. *(Pause.)* And that's it." And we *sit* there. *(Pause.)* I got the pen out . . .

ROMA. "Always be closing . . ."

LEVENE. That's what I'm *saying*. The *old* ways. The *old* ways . . . convert the motherfucker . . . *sell* him . . . *sell* him . . . *make him sign the check. (Pause.)* The . . . Bruce, Harriett

. . . the kitchen, blah: they got their money in *government* bonds. . . . I say *fuck* it, we're going to go the whole route. I plat it out eight units. Eighty-two grand. I tell them. "This is now. This is that *thing* that you've been dreaming of, you're going to find that suitcase on the train, the guy comes in the door, the bag that's full of money. This is it, *Harriett* . . ."

ROMA *(Reflectively)*. Harriett . . .

LEVENE. *Bruce* . . . "I don't want to fuck *around* with you. I don't want to go *round* this, and *pussyfoot* around the thing, you have to look back on this. I do, too. I came here to do good for you and me. For *both* of us. Why take an interim position? *The only arrangement I'll accept* is full investment. Period. The whole eight units. I know that you're saying 'be safe,' I know what you're saying. I know if I left you to yourselves, you'd say 'come back tomorrow,' and when I walked out that door, you'd make a cup of *coffee* . . . you'd sit *down* . . . and you'd think 'let's be safe . . .' and not to disappoint me you'd go *one* unit or maybe two, because you'd become scared because you'd met possi*bi*/ity. But this won't do, and that's not the subject. . . ." Listen to this, I actually said this. "That's not the subject of our *evening* together." Now I handed them the pen. I held it in my hand. I turned the contract, eight units eighty-two grand. "Now I want you to sign." *(Pause.)* I sat there. Five minutes. Then, I sat there, Ricky, *twenty-two minutes* by the kitchen *clock. (Pause.)* Twenty-two minutes by the kitchen clock. Not a *word*, not a *motion*. What am I thinking? "My arm's getting tired?" *No*. I *did* it. I *did* it. Like in the *old* days, Ricky. Like I was taught . . . Like, like, like I *used* to do . . . I did it.

ROMA. Like you taught me . . .

LEVENE. Bullshit, you're . . . No. That's raw . . . well, if I *did*, then I'm *glad* I did. I, *well*. I locked on them. All on them, nothing on me. All my thoughts are on them. I'm holding the last thought that I spoke: "Now is the time." *(Pause.)* They signed, Ricky. It was *great*. It was fucking great. It was like they wilted all at once. No *gesture* . . . nothing. Like together. They, I swear to God, they both kind of *imperceptibly slumped*. And he reaches and takes the pen and signs, he passes it to her, she signs. It was so fucking solemn. I just let it sit. I nod like this. I nod again. I grasp his hands. I shake his hands. I grasp *her* hands. I nod at her like this. "Bruce . . . Harriett . . ." I'm beaming at them. I'm nodding like this. I point back in the living room, back to the sideboard. *(Pause.) I didn't fucking know there was a sideboard there!!* He goes back, he brings us a drink. Little shot glasses. A pattern in 'em. And we toast. In silence. *(Pause.)*

ROMA. That was a great sale, Shelly. *(Pause.)*

LEVENE. Ah, fuck. Leads! Leads! Williamson! *(WILLIAMSON sticks his head out of the office.)* Send me *out!* Send me *out!*

WILLIAMSON. The leads are coming.

LEVENE. *Get* 'em to me!

WILLIAMSON. I talked to Murray and Mitch an hour ago. They're coming in, you understand they're a bit *upset* over this morning's ...

LEVENE. Did you tell 'em my sale?

WILLIAMSON. How could I tell 'em your sale? Eh? I don't have a tel ... I'll tell 'em your sale when they bring in the leads. Alright? Shelly. Alright? We had a little ... You closed a deal. You made a good sale. Fine.

LEVENE. It's better than a good sale. It's a ...

WILLIAMSON. Look: I have a lot of things on my mind, they're coming in, alright, they're very upset, I'm trying to make some *sense* ...

LEVENE. All that I'm *telling* you: that one thing you can tell them it's a remarkable sale.

WILLIAMSON. The only thing remarkable is who you made it to.

LEVENE. What does *that* fucking mean?

WILLIAMSON. That if the sale sticks, it will be a miracle.

LEVENE. Why should the sale not stick? Hey, *fuck* you. That's what I'm saying. You have no idea of your job. A man's his job and you're *fucked* at yours. You hear what I'm saying to you? Your "end of month board ..." You can't run an office. I don't care. You don't know what it *is*, you don't have the *sense*, you don't have the *balls*. You ever been on a sit? *Ever?* Has this cocksucker ever been ... you ever sit down with a cust ...

WILLIAMSON. I were you, I'd calm down, Shelly.

LEVENE. *Would* you? *Would* you ... ? Or you're gonna *what*, fire me?

WILLIAMSON. It's not impossible.

LEVENE. On an eighty-thousand dollar *day?* And it ain't even *noon.*

ROMA. You closed 'em today?

LEVENE. Yes. I did. This *morning.* *(To WILLIAMSON:)* What I'm *saying* to you: things can

change. You *see?* This is where you fuck *up*, because this is something you don't *know.* You can't look down the *road.* And see what's *coming.* Might be someone *else*, John. It might be someone *new*, eh? Someone *new.* And you can't look *back.* 'Cause you don't know *history.* You ask them. When we were at Rio Rancho, who was top man? A month ... ? Two months ... ? Eight months in twelve for three years in a row. You know what that means? You know what that means? Is that *luck?* Is that some, some, some purloined leads? That's *skill.* That's *talent*, that's, that's ...

ROMA. ... *yes* ...

LEVENE. ... and you don't *remember.* 'Cause you weren't *around.* That's cold *calling.* Walk up to the door. I don't even know their *name.* I'm selling something they don't even *want.* You talk about soft sell ... before we had a name for it ... before we called it anything, we did it.

ROMA. That's right, Shel.

LEVENE. And, and, and, I *did* it. And I put a kid through *school.* She ... and ... Cold *calling*, fella. Door to door. But you don't know. You don't know. You never heard of a *streak.* You never heard of "marshaling your sales force...." What are you, you're a *secretary*, John. Fuck *you.* That's my message to you. Fuck you and kiss my ass. You don't like it, I'll go talk to Jerry Graff. Period. Fuck you. Put me on the board. And I want three worthwhile leads today and I don't want any bullshit about them and I want 'em close together 'cause I'm going to hit them all today. That's all I have to say to you.

ROMA. He's right, Williamson.

(WILLIAMSON goes into a side office. Pause.)

LEVENE. It's not right. I'm sorry, and I'll tell you who's to blame is Mitch and Murray.

(ROMA sees something outside the window.)

ROMA *(Sotto).* Oh, Christ.

LEVENE. The hell with him. We'll go to lunch, the leads won't be up for ...

ROMA. You're a client. I just sold you five waterfront Glengarry Farms. I rub my head, throw me the cue "Kenilworth."

LEVENE. What is it?

ROMA. Kenilw ...

(LINGK enters the office.)

ROMA *(To LEVENE).* *I* own the property, my *mother* owns the property, I put her *into* it. I'm going to show you on the plats. You look when you get home A-3 through A-14 and 26 through 30. You take your time and if you still feel.

LEVENE. No, Mr. Roma. I don't need the time, I've made a lot of *investments* in the last . . .

LINGK. I've got to talk to you.

ROMA *(Looking up).* Jim! What are you doing here? Jim Lingk, D. Ray Morton . . .

LEVENE. Glad to meet you.

ROMA. I just put Jim into Black Creek . . . are you acquainted with . . .

LEVENE. No . . . Black *Creek.* Yes. In *Florida?*

ROMA. Yes.

LEVENE. I wanted to *speak* with you about . . .

ROMA. Well, we'll do that this weekend.

LEVENE. My *wife* told me to look into . . .

ROMA. *Beautiful.* Beautiful rolling land. I was telling Jim and Jinny, Ray, I want to tell you something. *(To* LEVENE:*)* You, Ray, you eat in a lot of restaurants. I know you do. . . . *(To* LINGK:*)* Mr. Morton's with American Express . . . he's . . . *(To* LEVENE:*)* I can tell Jim what you do . . . ?

LEVENE. Sure.

ROMA. Ray is director of all European sales and services for American Ex . . . *(To* LEVENE:*)* But I'm saying you haven't had a *meal* until you've tasted . . . I was at the Lingks' last . . . as a matter of fact, what was that service feature you were talking about . . . ?

LEVENE. Which . . .

ROMA. "Home Cooking" . . . what did you call it, you said it . . . it was a tag phrase that you had . . .

LEVENE. Uh . . .

ROMA. Home . . .

LEVENE. Home cooking . . .

ROMA. The monthly interview . . . ?

LEVENE. Oh! For the *magazine* . . .

ROMA. Yes. Is this something that I can talk ab . . .

LEVENE. Well, it isn't coming *out* until the February iss . . . *sure.* Sure, go ahead, Ricky.

ROMA. You're sure?

LEVENE *(nods).* Go ahead.

ROMA. Well, Ray was eating at one of his company's men's home in France . . . the man's French, isn't he?

LEVENE. No, his *wife* is.

ROMA. Ah. Ah, his wife is. Ray: what *time* do you have . . . ?

LEVENE. Twelve-fifteen.

ROMA. Oh! My God . . . I've got to get you on the *plane!*

LEVENE. Didn't I say I was taking the two o' . . .

ROMA. No. You said the one. That's why you said we couldn't talk till Kenilworth.

LEVENE. Oh, my God, you're right! I'm on the one. . . . *(Getting up.)* Well, let's *scoot* . . .

LINGK. I've got to talk to you . . .

ROMA. I've got to get Ray to O'Hare . . . *(To* LEVENE:*)* Come on, let's hustle. . . . *(Over his shoulder:)* John! Call American Express in *Pittsburgh* for Mr. Morton, will you, tell them he's on the one o'clock. *(To* LINGK:*)* I'll see you. . . . Christ, I'm sorry you came all the way in. . . . I'm running Ray over to O'Hare. . . . You wait here, I'll . . . no. *(To* LEVENE:*)* I'm meeting your man at the bank. . . . *(To* LINGK:*)* I wish you'd phoned. . . . I'll tell you, wait: are you and Jinny going to be home tonight? *(Rubs forehead.)*

LINGK. I . . .

LEVENE. Rick.

ROMA. What?

LEVENE. *Kenilworth* . . . ?

ROMA. I'm sorry . . . ?

LEVENE. *Kenilworth.*

ROMA. Oh, God . . . Oh, God . . . *(*ROMA *takes* LINGK *aside, sotto)* Jim, excuse me. . . . Ray, I told you, who he is is *the* senior vice-president American Express. His family owns 32 per. . . . Over the past years I've sold him . . . I can't tell you the dollar amount, but *quite* a lot of land. I promised five *weeks* ago that I'd go to the wife's birthday party in Kenilworth tonight. *(Sighs.)* I *have* to go. You understand. They treat me like a member of the family, so I have to go. It's funny, you know, you get a picture of the Corporation-Type Company Man, all business . . . this man, *no.* We'll go out to his home sometime. Let's see. *(He checks his datebook.)* Tomorrow. No. Tomorrow, I'm in L.A. . . . *Monday* . . . I'll take you to lunch, where would you like to go?

LINGK. My wife . . . *(*ROMA *rubs his head.)*

LEVENE *(Standing in the door).* Rick . . . ?

ROMA. I'm sorry, Jim. I can't talk now. I'll call you tonight . . . I'm sorry. I'm coming, Ray. *(Starts for the door.)*

LINGK. My wife said I have to cancel the deal.

ROMA. It's a common reaction, Jim. I'll tell you what it is, and I know that that's why you married her. One of the reasons is *prudence.* It's a sizable investment. One thinks *twice* . . . it's also something *women* have. It's just a reaction to the size of the investment. *Monday,* if you'd invite me for dinner again . . . *(To* LEVENE:*)* This woman can *cook* . . .

LEVENE *(Simultaneously)*. I'm sure she can . . .

ROMA *(To* LINGK*)*. We're going to talk. I'm going to *tell* you something. Because *(Sotto:)* there's something about your acreage I want you to know. I can't talk about it now. I really shouldn't. And, in fact, by *law*, I . . . *(Shrugs, resigned.)* The man next to you, he bought his lot at forty-*two*, he phoned to say that he'd *already* had an offer . . . *(*ROMA *rubs his head.)*

LEVENE. Rick . . . ?

ROMA. I'm coming, Ray . . . what a day! I'll call you this evening, Jim. I'm sorry you had to come in . . . Monday, lunch.

LINGK. My wife . . .

LEVENE. Rick, we really have to go.

LINGK. My wife . . .

ROMA. Monday.

LINGK. She called the consumer . . . the attorney, I don't know. The attorney gen . . . they said we have three days . . .

ROMA. *Who* did she call?

LINGK. I don't know, the attorney gen . . . the . . . some consumer office, umm . . .

ROMA. Why did she do *that*, Jim?

LINGK. I don't know. *(Pause.)* They said we have three days. *(Pause.)* They said we have three days.

ROMA. Three days.

LINGK. To . . . you know. *(Pause.)*

ROMA. No, I don't know. *Tell* me.

LINGK. To change our minds.

ROMA. Of *course* you have three days. *(Pause.)*

LINGK. So we can't talk *Monday. (Pause.)*

ROMA. Jim, Jim, you saw my book . . . I *can't, you* saw my book . . .

LINGK. But we have to *before* Monday. To get our money ba . . .

ROMA. Three *business* days. They mean three *business* days.

LINGK. Wednesday, Thursday, Friday.

ROMA. I don't understand.

LINGK. That's what they are. Three business . . . if I wait till Monday, my time limit runs out.

ROMA. You don't count Saturday.

LINGK. I'm not.

ROMA. No, I'm saying you don't include Saturday . . . in your three days. It's not a *business* day.

LINGK. But I'm not *counting* it. *(Pause.)* Wednesday. Thursday. Friday. So it would have elapsed.

ROMA. What would have elapsed?

LINGK. If we wait till Mon . . .

ROMA. When did you write the check?

LINGK. Yest . . .

ROMA. What was yesterday?

LINGK. Tuesday.

ROMA. And when was that check cashed?

LINGK. I don't know.

ROMA. What was the *earliest* it could have been cashed? *(Pause.)*

LINGK. I don't know.

ROMA. *Today. (Pause.) Today.* Which, in any case, it was not, as there were a couple of points on the agreement I wanted to go over with you in any case.

LINGK. The check wasn't cashed?

ROMA. I just called downtown, and it's on their desk.

LEVENE. Rick . . .

ROMA. One moment, I'll be right with you. *(To* LINGK*:)* In fact, a . . . *one* point, which I spoke to you of which *(Looks around.)* I can't talk to you about here.

*(*DETECTIVE *puts his head out of the doorway.)*

BAYLEN. Levene!!!

LINGK. I, I . . .

ROMA. Listen to me, the *statute*, it's for your protection. I have no complaints with that, in fact, I was a member of the board when we *drafted* it, so quite the *opposite*. It *says* that you can change your mind three working days from the time the deal is closed.

BAYLEN. Levene!

ROMA. Which, wait a second, which is not until the check is cashed.

BAYLEN. Levene!!

*(*AARONOW *comes out of the* DETECTIVE*'s office.)*

AARONOW. I'm *through*, with *this* fucking meshugaas. No one should talk to a man that way. How are you *talking* to me that . . . ?

BAYLEN. Levene! *(*WILLIAMSON *puts his head out of the office.)*

AARONOW. . . . . how can you *talk* to me that . . . that . . .

LEVENE *(To* ROMA*)*. Rick, I'm going to flag a cab.

AARONOW. *I* didn't rob . . .

*(*WILLIAMSON *sees* LEVENE*.)*

WILLIAMSON. Shelly: get in the office.

AARONOW. *I* didn't . . . why should *I* . . . "Where were you last . . ." Is anybody listening to me . . . ? Where's Moss . . . ? Where . . . ?

BAYLEN. Levene? *(To* WILLIAMSON*:)* Is this Lev . . . *(*BAYLEN *accosts* LINGK*.)*

LEVENE *(Taking* BAYLEN *into the office)*. Ah.

Ah. Perhaps I can advise you on that.... *(To* ROMA *and* LINGK, *as he exits:) Excuse* us, will you ... ?

AARONOW *(Simultaneous with* LEVENE's *speech above)....* Come in here ... I *work* here, I don't come in here to be *mistreated* ...

WILLIAMSON. Go to *lunch,* will you ...

AARONOW. I want to *work* today, that's why I came ...

WILLIAMSON. The leads come in, I'll let ...

AARONOW. . . . that's why I came in. I thought I . . .

WILLIAMSON. Just go to lunch.

AARONOW. I don't *want* to go to lunch.

WILLIAMSON. Go to lunch, George.

AARONOW. Where does he get off to talk that way to a working man? It's not . . .

WILLIAMSON *(Buttonholes him).* Will you take it outside, we have people trying to do *business* here . . .

AARONOW. That's what, that's what, that's what *I* was trying to do. *(Pause.)* That's why I came *in* . . . I meet *gestapo* tac . . .

WILLIAMSON *(Going back into his office).* Excuse me . . .

AARONOW. I meet *gestapo* tactics . . . I meet *gestapo* tactics.... That's not right.... No man has the right to . . . "Call an attorney," that means you're guilt . . . you're under sus . . . "Co . . . ," he says, "cooperate" or we'll go downtown. *That's* not . . . as long as I've . . .

WILLIAMSON *(Bursting out of his office).* Will you get out of here. Will you get *out* of here. Will you. I'm trying to run an *office* here. Will you go to lunch? Go to lunch. Will you go to lunch? *(Retreats into office.)*

ROMA *(To* AARONOW). Will you excuse . . .

AARONOW. Where did Moss . . . ? I . . .

ROMA. Will you excuse us please?

AARONOW. Uh, uh, did he go to the restaurant? *(Pause.)* I . . . I . . . *(Exits.)*

ROMA. I'm *very* sorry, Jimmy. I apologize to you.

LINGK. It's not me, it's my wife.

ROMA *(Pause).* What is?

LINGK. I told you.

ROMA. Tell me again.

LINGK. What's going on here?

ROMA. Tell me again. Your wife.

LINGK. I told you.

ROMA. You tell me again.

LINGK. She wants her money back.

ROMA. We're going to speak to her.

LINGK. No. She told me "right now."

ROMA. We'll speak to her, Jim . . .

LINGK. She won't listen.

*(*DETECTIVE *sticks his head out.)*

BAYLEN. *Roma.*

LINGK. She told me if not, I have to call the State's attorney.

ROMA. No, no. That's just something she "said." We don't have to do that.

LINGK. She told me I *have* to.

ROMA. No, Jim.

LINGK. I *do.* If I don't get my *money* back . . .

*(*WILLIAMSON *points out* ROMA *to* BAYLEN.)

BAYLEN. Roma! *(To* ROMA:) I'm talking to you . . .

ROMA. I've . . . look. *(Generally:)* Will someone get this guy off my back.

BAYLEN. You have a problem?

ROMA. Yes, I have a problem. Yes, I *do,* my fr . . . It's not me that ripped the joint off, I'm doing *business.* I'll be with you in a *while.* You got it . . . ? *(Looks back.* LINGK *is heading for the door.)* Where are you going?

LINGK. I'm . . .

ROMA. Where are you going . . . ? This is *me.* . . . This is Ricky, Jim. Jim, anything you *want,* you *want* it, you *have* it. You understand? This is *me.* Something *upset* you. Sit down, now sit down. You tell me what it is. *(Pause.)* Am I going to help you fix it? You're goddamned right I am. Sit down. Tell you something . . . ? *Sometimes* we need someone from *outside.* It's . . . no, sit down. . . . Now *talk* to me.

LINGK. I can't negotiate.

ROMA. What does that mean?

LINGK. That . . .

ROMA. . . . what, what, *say* it. Say it to me . . .

LINGK. I . . .

ROMA. What . . . ?

LINGK. I . . .

ROMA. What . . . ? Say the words.

LINGK. I don't have the *power. (Pause.)* I said it.

ROMA. What power?

LINGK. The power to negotiate.

ROMA. To negotiate what? *(Pause.)* To negotiate what?

LINGK. *This.*

ROMA. What, "this"? *(Pause.)*

LINGK. The deal.

ROMA. The "deal," *forget* the deal. *Forget* the deal, you've got something on your mind, Jim, what is it?

LINGK *(rising).* I can't talk to you, *you* met my wife, I . . . *(Pause.)*

ROMA. What? *(Pause.)* What? *(Pause.)* What, Jim: I tell you what, let's get out of here . . . let's go get a drink.

LINGK. She told me not to talk to you.

ROMA. Let's . . . no one's going to know, let's go around the *corner* and we'll get a drink.

LINGK. She told me I had to get back the check or call the State's att . . .

ROMA. *Forget* the deal, Jimmy. *(Pause.)* Forget the deal . . . you know me. The deal's *dead.* Am I talking about the *deal?* That's *over.* Please. Let's talk about *you.* Come on. *(Pause. ROMA rises and starts walking toward the front door.)* Come on. *(Pause.)* Come on, Jim. *(Pause.)* I want to tell you something. Your life is your own. You have a contract with your wife. You have certain things you do *jointly,* you have a *bond* there . . . and there are *other* things. Those things are yours. You needn't feel *ashamed,* you needn't feel that you're being *untrue* . . . or that she would abandon you if she knew. This is your life. *(Pause.)* Yes. Now I want to *talk* to you because you're obviously upset and that *concerns* me. Now let's go. Right now.

(LINGK gets up and they start for the door.)

BAYLEN *(Sticks his head out of the door).* Roma . . .

LINGK. . . . and . . . and . . . *(Pause.)*

ROMA. What?

LINGK. And the check is . . .

ROMA. What did I *tell* you? *(Pause.)* What did I say about the three days . . . ?

BAYLEN. Roma, would you, I'd like to get some lunch . . .

ROMA. I'm talking with Mr. Lingk. If you please, I'll be back in. *(Checks watch.)* I'll be back in a while. . . . I told you, check with Mr. Williamson.

BAYLEN. The people downtown said . . .

ROMA. You call them again. Mr. Williamson . . . !

WILLIAMSON. Yes.

ROMA. Mr. Lingk and I are going to . . .

WILLIAMSON. Yes. Please. Please. *(To* LINGK:*)* The police *(Shrugs.)* can be . . .

LINGK. What are the police doing?

ROMA. It's nothing.

LINGK. What are the *police* doing here?

WILLIAMSON. Wē had a slight burglary last night.

ROMA. It was nothing . . . I was assuring Mr. Lingk . . .

WILLIAMSON. Mr. Lingk. James Lingk. Your contract went out. Nothing to . . .

ROMA. John . . .

WILLIAMSON. Your contract went out to the bank.

LINGK. You cashed the check?

WILLIAMSON. We . . .

ROMA. . . . Mr. Williamson . . .

WILLIAMSON. Your check was cashed yesterday afternoon. And we're completely insured, as you know, in *any* case. *(Pause.)*

LINGK *(To* ROMA*).* You cashed the check?

ROMA. Not to my knowledge, no . . .

WILLIAMSON. I'm sure we can . . .

LINGK. Oh, Christ . . . *(Starts out the door.)* Don't follow me. . . . Oh, Christ. *(Pause. To* ROMA:*)* I know I've let you down. I'm sorry. For . . . Forgive . . . for . . . I don't know anymore. *(Pause.)* Forgive me. *(*LINGK *exits. Pause.)*

ROMA *(To* WILLIAMSON*).* You stupid fucking cunt. *You,* Williamson . . . I'm talking to *you,* shithead. . . . You just cost me *six thousand dollars. (Pause.)* Six thousand dollars. And one Cadillac. That's right. What are you going to do about it? What are you going to do about it, asshole. You fucking *shit.* Where did you learn your *trade.* You stupid fucking *cunt.* You *idiot.* Whoever told you you could work with *men?*

BAYLEN. Could I . . .

ROMA. I'm going to have your *job,* shithead. I'm going *downtown* and talk to Mitch and Murray, and I'm going to Lemkin. I don't care *whose* nephew you are, who you know, whose dick you're sucking on. You're going *out,* I swear to you, you're going . . .

BAYLEN. Hey, fella, let's get this done . . .

ROMA. Anyone in this office lives on their *wits.* . . . *(To* BAYLEN:*)* I'm going to be with you in a second. *(To* WILLIAMSON:*)* What you're hired for is to *help* us—does that seem clear to you? To *help* us. *Not* to fuck us up . . . to help *men* who are going *out* there to try to earn a *living.* You *fairy.* You company man . . . I'll tell you something else. I hope you knocked the joint off, I can tell our friend here something might help him catch you. *(Starts into the room.)* You want to learn the first rule you'd know if you ever spent a day in your life . . . you never open your mouth till you know what the shot is. *(Pause.)* You fucking *child* . . . *(*ROMA *goes to the inner room.)*

LEVENE. You *are* a shithead, Williamsom . . . *(Pause.)*

WILLIAMSON. Mmm.

LEVENE. You can't think on your feet you should keep your mouth closed. *(Pause.)* You hear me? I'm *talking* to you. Do you hear me . . . ?

WILLIAMSON. Yes. *(Pause.)* I hear you.

LEVENE. You can't learn that in an office. Eh? He's right. You have to learn it on the streets. You can't *buy* that. You have to *live* it. Mmm.

WILLIAMSON. Mmm.

LEVENE. *Yes.* Mmm. *Yes. Precisely. Precisely.* 'Cause your partner *depends* on it. *(Pause.)* I'm *talking* to you, I'm trying to tell you something.

WILLIAMSON. You are?

LEVENE. Yes, I am.

WILLIAMSON. What are you trying to tell me?

LEVENE. What Roma's trying to tell you. What I told you yesterday. Why you don't belong in this business.

WILLIAMSON. Why I don't . . .

LEVENE. You listen to me, someday you might say, "Hey . . ." No, fuck that, you just listen what I'm going to say: your partner *depends* on you. Your partner . . . a man who's your "partner" *depends* on you . . . you have to go *with* him and *for* him . . . or you're shit, you're *shit,* you can't exist alone . . .

WILLIAMSON *(Brushing past him).* Excuse me . . .

LEVENE. . . . excuse you, *nothing,* you be as cold as you want, but you just fucked a good man out of six thousand dollars and his goddamn bonus 'cause you didn't know the *shot,* if you can do that and you aren't man enough that it gets you, then I don't know what, if you can't take *some thing* from that . . . *(Blocking his way.)* you're *scum,* you're fucking white-bread. You be as cold as you want. A *child* would know it, he's right. *(Pause.)* You're going to make something up, be sure it will *help* or keep your mouth closed. *(Pause.)*

WILLIAMSON. Mmm. (LEVENE *lifts up his arm.)*

LEVENE. Now I'm done with you. *(Pause.)*

WILLIAMSON. How do you know I made it up?

LEVENE *(Pause).* What?

WILLIAMSON. How do you know I made it up?

LEVENE. What are you talking about?

WILLIAMSON. You said, "You don't make something up unless it's sure to help." *(Pause.)* How did you know that I made it up?

LEVENE. What are you talking about?

WILLIAMSON. I told the customer that his contracts had gone to the bank.

LEVENE. Well, hadn't it?

WILLIAMSON. No. *(Pause.)* It hadn't.

LEVENE. Don't *fuck* with me, John, don't *fuck* with me . . . what are you saying?

WILLIAMSON. Well, I'm saying this, Shel: usually I take the contracts to the bank. Last night I didn't. How did you know that? One night in a year I left a contract on my desk. Nobody knew that but *you.* Now how did you know that? *(Pause.)* You want to talk to me, you want to talk to someone *else* . . . because this is *my* job. This is my job on the line, and you are going to *talk* to me. Now how did you know that contract was on my desk?

LEVENE. You're so full of shit.

WILLIAMSON. You robbed the office.

LEVENE *(Laughs).* Sure! I robbed the office. Sure.

WILLIAMSON. What'd you do with the leads? *(Pause. Points to the* DETECTIVE'*s room.)* You want to go in there? I tell him what I know, he's going to dig up *something.* . . . You got an alibi last night? You better have one. What did you do with the leads? If you tell me what you did with the leads, we can talk.

LEVENE. I don't know what you are saying.

WILLIAMSON. If you tell me where the leads are, I won't turn you in. If you *don't,* I am going to tell the cop you stole them, Mitch and Murray will see that you go to jail. Believe me they will. Now, what did you do with the leads? I'm walking in that door—you have five seconds to tell me: or you are going to jail.

LEVENE. I . . .

WILLIAMSON. I don't care. You understand? *Where are the leads? (Pause.)* Alright. (WILLIAMSON *goes to open the office door.)*

LEVENE. I sold them to Jerry Graff.

WILLIAMSON. How much did you get for them? *(Pause.)* How much did you get for them?

LEVENE. Five thousand. I kept half.

WILLIAMSON. Who kept the other half? *(Pause.)*

LEVENE. Do I have to tell you? *(Pause.* WILLIAMSON *starts to open the door.)* Moss.

WILLIAMSON. *That* was easy, *wasn't* it? *(Pause.)*

LEVENE. It was his idea.

WILLIAMSON. *Was* it?

LEVENE. I . . . I'm sure he got more than the five, actually.

WILLIAMSON. Uh-huh?

LEVENE. He told me my share was twenty-five.

WILLIAMSON. Mmm.

LEVENE. Okay: I ... look: I'm going to make it worth your while. I am. I turned this thing around. I closed the *old* stuff, I can do it again. *I'm* the one's going to close 'em. *I* am! *I* am! 'Cause I turned this thing a ... I can do *that*, I can do *anyth* ... last night. I'm going to tell you, I was ready to Do the Dutch. Moss gets me, "Do this, we'll get well...." Why not. Big fuckin' deal. I'm halfway hoping to get caught. To put me out of my ... *(Pause.)* But it *taught* me something. What it taught me, that you've got to get *out* there. Big deal. So I wasn't cut out to be a thief. I was cut out to be a salesman. And now I'm back, and I got my *balls* back ... and, you know, John, you have the *advantage* on me now. Whatever it takes to make it right, we'll make it right. We're going to make it right.

WILLIAMSON. I want to tell you something, Shelly. You have a big mouth. *(Pause.)*

LEVENE. What?

WILLIAMSON. You've got a big mouth, and now I'm going to show you an even bigger one. *(Starts toward the* DETECTIVE'*s door.)*

LEVENE. Where are you going, John? ... you can't do that, you don't want to do that ... hold, hold on ... hold on ... wait ... wait ... wait ... *(Pulls money out of his pockets.)* Wait ... uh, look ... *(Starts splitting money.)* Look, twelve, twenty, two, twen ... twenty-five hundred, it's ... take it. *(Pause.)* Take it all. ... *(Pause.)* Take it!

WILLIAMSON. No, I don't think so, Shel.

LEVENE. I ...

WILLIAMSON. No, I think I don't want your money. I think you fucked up my office. And I think you're going away.

LEVENE. I ... what? Are you, are you, that's why ... ? Are you nuts? I'm ... I'm going to *close* for you, I'm going to ... *(Thrusting money at him.)* Here, here, I'm going to *make* this office ... I'm going to be back there Number One.... Hey, hey, hey! This is only the beginning.... List ... list ... listen. Listen. Just one moment. List ... here's what ... here's what we're going to do. Twenty percent. I'm going to give you twenty percent of my sales.... *(Pause.)* Twenty percent. *(Pause.)* For as long as I am with the firm. *(Pause.)* Fifty percent. *(Pause.)* You're going to be my partner. *(Pause.)* Fifty percent. Of all my sales.

WILLIAMSON. What sales?

LEVENE. What sales ... ? I just *closed* eighty-two *grand*. ... Are you fuckin' ... I'm *back* ... I'm *back*, this is only the beginning.

WILLIAMSON. Only the beginning ...

LEVENE. Abso ...

WILLIAMSON. Where have you been, Shelly? Bruce and Harriett Nyborg. Do you want to see the *memos* ... ? They're nuts ... they used to call in every week. When I was with Webb. And we were selling Arizona ... they're nuts ... did you see how they were *living?* How can you delude yours ...

LEVENE. I've got the check ...

WILLIAMSON. Forget it. Frame it. It's worthless. *(Pause.)*

LEVENE. The check's no good?

WILLIAMSON. You stick around I'll pull the memo for you. *(Starts for the door.)* I'm busy now ...

LEVENE. Their check's no good? They're nuts ... ?

WILLIAMSON. Call up the bank. *I* called them.

LEVENE. You did?

WILLIAMSON. I called them when we had the lead ... four months ago. *(Pause.)* The people are insane. They just like talking to salesmen. *(*WILLIAMSON *starts for door.)*

LEVENE. Don't.

WILLIAMSON. I'm sorry.

LEVENE. *Why?*

WILLIAMSON. Because I don't like you.

LEVENE. John: John: ... my *daughter* ...

WILLIAMSON. Fuck you. *(*ROMA *comes out of the* DETECTIVE'*s door.* WILLIAMSON *goes in.)*

ROMA *(To* BAYLEN*)*. Asshole ... *(To* LEVENE*:)* Guy couldn't find his fuckin' couch the *living room* ... Ah, Christ ... what a day, what a day ... I haven't even had a cup of *coffee*. ... Jagoff John opens his mouth he blows my Cadillac.... *(Sighs.)* I swear ... it's not a world of men ... it's not a world of men, Machine ... it's a world of clock watchers, bureaucrats, officeholders ... what it is, it's a fucked-up world ... there's no adventure *to* it. *(Pause.)* Dying breed. Yes it is. *(Pause.)* We are the members of a dying breed. That's ... that's ... that's why we have to stick together. Shel: I want to talk to you. I've wanted to talk to you for some time. For a long time, actually. I said, "The Machine, there's a man I would work with. There's a man...." You know? I never said a thing. I should have, don't know why I didn't. And that shit you were slinging on my guy today was *so* good . . . it . . . it was, and, excuse me, 'cause it isn't even my place to say it. It was admirable . . . it was the old stuff. Hey, I've been on a hot streak, so *what?* There's things that I could learn from you. You eat today?

LEVENE. Me.

ROMA. Yeah.

LEVENE. Mm.

ROMA. Well, you want to swing by the Chinks, watch me eat, we'll talk?

LEVENE. I think I'd better stay here for a while.

(BAYLEN *sticks his head out of the room:*)

BAYLEN. Mr. *Levene* . . . ?

ROMA. You're done, come down and let's . . .

BAYLEN. Would you come in here, please?

ROMA. And let's put this together. Okay? Shel? Say okay. *(Pause.)*

LEVENE *(Softly, to himself)*. Huh.

BAYLEN. Mr. Levene, I think we have to talk.

ROMA. I'm going to the Chinks. You're done, come down, we're going to smoke a cigarette.

LEVENE. I . . .

BAYLEN *(Comes over)*. . . . Get in the room.

ROMA. Hey, hey, hey, *easy* friend, That's the "Machine." That is Shelly "The Machine" Lev . . .

BAYLEN. Get in the goddamn room. *(BAYLEN starts manhandling SHELLY into the room.)*

LEVENE. Ricky, I . . .

ROMA. Okay, okay, I'll be at the resta . . .

LEVENE. Ricky . . .

BAYLEN. "Ricky" can't help you, pal.

LEVENE. . . . I only want to . . .

BAYLEN. Yeah. What do you want? You want to *what?* (He pushes LEVENE *into the room, closes the door behind him. Pause.*)

ROMA. Williamson: listen to me: when the *leads* come in . . . listen to me: when the *leads* come in I want my top two off the list. For *me.* My usual two. Anything you give *Levene* . . .

WILLIAMSON. . . . I wouldn't worry about it.

ROMA. Well I'm *going* to worry about it, and so are you, so shut up and *listen.* (Pause.) I GET HIS ACTION. My stuff is *mine,* whatever *he* gets for himself, I'm talking half. You put me in with him.

(AARONOW enters.)

AARONOW. Did they . . . ?

ROMA. You understand?

AARONOW. Did they catch . . . ?

ROMA. Do you understand? My stuff is mine, his stuff is ours. I'm taking half of his commissions—now, *you* work it out.

WILLIAMSON. Mmm.

AARONOW. Did they find the guy who broke into the office yet?

ROMA. No. *I* don't know. *(Pause.)*

AARONOW. Did the leads come in yet?

ROMA. No.

AARONOW *(Settling into a desk chair)*. Oh, God, I hate this job.

ROMA *(Simultaneous with "job," exiting the office)*. I'll be at the restaurant.

End of the World

ARTHUR KOPIT

FOR AUDREY WOOD

First performed at the Kennedy Center in Washington, D.C., on March 28, 1984, and subsequently opened in New York at the Music Box Theater on May 6, with the following cast:

MICHAEL TRENT	John Shea
PHILIP STONE	Barnard Hughes
AUDREY WOOD	Linda Hunt
PAUL COWAN	Richard Seff
MERV ROSENBLATT	David O'Brien
STELLA	Elaine Petricoff
GENERAL WILMER	David O'Brien
STANLEY BERENT	Jaroslav Stremien
PETE	Peter Zapp
JIM	Nathaniel Ritch
ANN	Elaine Petricoff
TRENT'S SON	Wade Raley
STRANGERS, CHARLES, WAITERS	Larry Pine, Elaine Petricoff,
WAITRESSES, ATTACHÉ,	Nathaniel Ritch, Peter Zapp,
CUSTOMERS	Frank Hankey

Produced by the Kennedy Center and Michael Frazier
Directed by Harold Prince
Scenery by Clarke Dunham
Costumes by William Ivey Long
Lighting by Ken Billington
Sound by Rob Gorton
Music by Larry Grossman

End of the World was inspired by an idea initiated by Leonard Davis.

"Okay, so I sometimes think, now it's all over, and we're all up there in the big debriefing space in the sky, and the Good Lord decides to hold a symposium 'cause he's curious: how did this happen? And everybody says, 'Hey, don't look at me, I didn't wanna do it!' The end result being that everyone realizes *no* one wanted to do it! But there was suddenly no choice. Or no choice they could *see" (End of the World,* Act Two).

End of the World was first performed at the Kennedy Center in March 1984, and then opened at the Music Box Theatre in New York that May. Its inception occurred in 1981, when Leonard Davis, a wealthy insurance executive, commissioned Arthur Kopit to write a play about the dangers of impending nuclear holocaust that would serve as a warning to the world. Kopit interviewed political decision makers, generals, and nuclear experts in Washington, but "after doing a great deal of research on a subject I didn't know much about," he admitted, "I was stumped. I didn't know why anyone would go to see a play on this subject. . . . [It] was very depressing." Then Kopit's wife suggested that he write a play about a playwright who cannot write a play. The result is an odd mixture of parody, satire, discourse, and character study that is funny, frightening, and moving.

End of the World is structured as a surrealistic comic mystery. Its central character, a playwright named Michael Trent, is portrayed on stage, as a private investigator of the Philip Marlowe school. John Shea, who originated the role, states, "A dramatist is like a detective, always searching for clues." Kopit agrees, adding, "What I began to see was that I was a detective uncovering something that I hadn't read about or perceived, having to do with the darkness within. It was the conflicting sensation between life positive and life negative. . . . We are here to propagate and yet there is a part of us that wishes to destroy ourselves. . . ." Gaynor Bradish, with whom Kopit studied playwriting at Harvard's Dunster House Drama Workshop, has suggested that modern man has seen too much tragedy to view pain with detachment, and that "the modern tragicomic play has become the contemporary dramatist's final solution, with the comic framework providing the necessary perspective for the darker insights. . . ."

Prior to his research for the play, Kopit was a committed advocate of nuclear freeze. His experiences in Washington have made him see the issue differently. "I am not saying I turned against a nuclear freeze," he says, "but the hard-liners who say a freeze would be dangerous altered my thinking radically. . . ." In Washington, Kopit entered a nuclear world of inside-out logic that is reflected in the structure of *End of the World.* Nuclear-war theory is like game-playing theory, albeit with the highest stakes imaginable, Kopit learned. And as no game can be played perfectly forever, sooner or later someone will lose the nuclear-arms standoff. Even if it were possible for the game to be played endlessly, Kopit hypothesizes, this may lead to an impatience on the part of the players that will encourage, according to Russell Baker in *The New York Times,* "a crazy impulse to see what would happen if, just once, they made the wrong move." In *End of the World,* Kopit asserts the probability of nuclear annihilation and offers no way out. Instead, he paints a sobering portrait of deterrent strategy and provides, as well, insight into his own troubled psyche. He states, "The intention was never to promote a certain political position . . . but to move people emotionally . . . to bring them to some fresh understanding which I was also . . . to feel through the course of writing the play."

Meanwhile, Kopit's playwright cum detective offers us clues to the mysteries of the creative process and, perhaps, to Kopit's own career choice. Trent states, "But you don't go into it, as a profession, because that's where you figure the big bucks lie. You do it . . . and you spend your life doing it, because it *matters.* And you have a kind of pact with yourself. And it says you don't screw around with what matters or else it's gone."

Arthur Kopit was born in New York in 1937. He demonstrated an early interest in the theatre when he entertained his friends with improvised puppet shows. Like many playwrights of his generation, his literary development was influenced by radio, which he feels helped to develop his imagination. Although he entered Harvard University to study electrical engineering, after taking some creative-writing courses, he decided to become a playwright.

His first play, *The Questioning of Nick,* was awarded first prize in the Leverett House Contest in 1959. Among his other Harvard productions were *On the Runway of Life You Never Know What's Coming Off Next, Gemini, Don Juan in Texas, Across the River and into the Jungle, Sing to Me Through Open Windows,* and *To Dwell in a Palace of Strangers.* Graduating with a B.A. in 1959, he received a Shaw Traveling Fellowship and went to Europe to study theatre and to complete his play *Oh Dad, Poor Dad, Mamma's Hung You in the Closet and I'm Feelin' So Sad.* Subsidized by a Ford Foundation grant, the play was produced at the Agassiz Theatre in Cambridge, where it caused a minor scandal. Staged by Jerome Robbins, it opened at New York's Phoenix Theatre in 1962, and won both the Outer Critics Circle Award and the Vernon Rice Award. Several years elapsed before Kopit's next play, *Indians,* was produced. Its combination of social commentary and dark humor won it the 1969 Tony Award.

Arthur Kopit has also written *Asylum, or What the Gentlemen Are Up To, Not to Mention the Ladies* (1963), *Christmas with the Cannibals, Florida Preserved—Or the Last Resort* (1963), *Mhil'daiim* (1963), *The Day the Whores Came Out to Play Tennis* (1964), *Cody's Will, Chamber Music* (1965), *A Call On Kuprin, Good Help Is Hard to Find, Fame, What Happened to the Thorne's Place?* (1972), *Conquest of Everest* (1973), *The Hero* (1973), *Secrets of the Rich* (1976), *Discovery of America* (1979), *Eureka!* (with Maury Yeston), *Ropongo* (1982), *Bone-the-Fish* (1989), *Wings,* and *Road to Nirvana* (1990). His works for film and television include: *Buffalo Bill and the Indians* (1976), *The Sensuous Woman, Starstruck* (1979), *Legacy of a Mother's Murder, Hands of a Murderer* (1987), and *The Phantom of the Opera.* He wrote the libretto for the musical *Nine* (1982) and a musical version of *The Scarlet Pimpernel.* He has also translated and adapted Ibsen's *Ghosts* (1982).

AUTHOR'S NOTE

This play derives from real events. In the spring of 1981 I was approached by Leonard Davis, who wished to commission me to write a play about nuclear proliferation, based on a scenario he had written. Between that day and August 1983 I worked on the project—although not on his scenario—which turned out to be very different from his scenario. The events that unfold in my play mirror, almost exactly, the experiences I had when I embarked on the commission.

Much of the play—in particular the section entitled "The Investigation"—is based on personal interviews. Though some of those interviewed asked that they not be named, those who can be named include Walter Slocum, Fritz Ermath, Joel Resnick, Douglas Olin, Ambassador Edward Rowny, and Kurt Guthe. I would like to thank all of them for their patience, time, and generosity.

Those whose written work proved especially valuable in the creation of this play and in my understanding of the issues involved include Herman Kahn, Freeman Dyson, Colin Gray, Keith Payne, Jack Geiger, Jonathan Schell, George Kennan, Richard Pipes, and Edward Teller.

In particular I wish to thank Roger Molander for his extraordinary help and encouragement during the writing of this play, and Robert Scheer for allowing me to use an extensive section of his book *With Enough Shovels,* published by Random House, as the basis for Philip Stone's final speech. I would also like to thank Physicians for Social Responsibility for their continued support.

A word about Audrey Wood. Audrey Wood was my agent from 1960, when my play *Oh Dad, Poor Dad, Mamma's Hung You in the Closet and I'm Feelin' So Sad* was produced at Harvard, until 1981, when she suffered a devastating massive stroke. She was a crucial, integral, and loving part of my life. When I came to the writing of this play and found I needed to write in an agent for Michael Trent, my playwright/detective, I instinctively used Audrey's name, never intending to keep her name in the play. But I have done so.

I kept it in while writing it in the belief that her presence, as I went along, would force me to delve into the material and into myself as deeply as I could—for to do any less would be to belittle her.

And I kept it in in the hope that what I wrote might, in some small way, measure up to the measure of her.

A.K.

ACT ONE

The Commission

MUSIC: *lazy, bluesy music for a hard-boiled detective. It is "Trent's Theme." Curtain up.*

SPOTLIGHT *up on* MICHAEL TRENT, *downstage, in a trench coat. Stage dark around him. He puffs on a cigarette. The music continues under.*

TRENT. I have now, at most, two hours left—two hours to solve a mystery which so far seems to yield no solution. If I fail, it is highly possible that I and all of you will die sooner than we'd hoped. Do I exaggerate? Of course. That is my method. I am a playwright. My name is Trent, Michael Trent. I work out of Stamford, Connecticut—that's where my office is, that's where this case began, when Philip Stone came to see me with a notion for a play. Generally I don't take commissions. This time I did.

(Lights up on PHILIP STONE, *a man in his sixties, large, elegant, powerful.)*

STONE. I can only tell you it is a matter of great urgency, and I would be most appreciative if I could see you tonight!

(Blackout on STONE.*)*

TRENT. I'd never met the man, though I knew of course who he was—who didn't? He told me what he wanted, which was a play, but gave no details. He assured me he'd pay well—a man as rich as Stone ought to pay well; I told him to come right out. To put it mildly, I was in great need of money at the time. Most playwrights need money *all* the time. It's not one of your top-paying professions. Besides, I had a wife, a kid, and two golden retrievers to support. As things now stand, you won't see any one of them. I want to keep them out of this!

(Lights up on TRENT's *office in Stamford, Connecticut. It looks like the sort of office Philip Marlowe might use. On the glass door, reversed, are the following words:)*

MICHAEL TRENT, PLAYWRIGHT
—No Domestic Comedies—

This is my office. At least, as it looked ten months ago, on the night Stone came by and changed my life irrevocably. Actually, in *real* life, where these events occurred, it doesn't look like this at all. Neither do the characters who were, and still are, involved. I have altered these details, not so much to protect the innocent, as to heighten interest. That's how playwrights work. We've got limited time. You don't want to stay here all night any more than I do. *(A buzzer sounds on* TRENT's *cluttered desk)* Yah!

STELLA *(Voice only)*. Mike, there's a guy out here says his name is, get this—Philip Stone! *(Sound of* STELLA *giggling)*

TRENT. Hey, dollface, this guy *is* Philip Stone. Tell him I'll be with him in a minute. *(To audience)* It was important that Stone think I was in the middle of a project. If he didn't, he might figure he could get me cheap. My pulse was going wild; I'd been hoping to sell out for years. This could be it. *(Into the intercom)* Send Stone in. *(Back to audience)* Actually, I didn't even have a secretary. And that's all I'm going to tell you. From here on, you're going to have to figure out what I'm making up, and what I'm not, on your own. Be warned: the roads are very slippery, the ones we're going on tonight.

*(*TRENT *starts typing. The office door opens and* PHILIP STONE *walks in. Black greatcoat. Sense of mystery and menace.)*

STONE. Trent?

TRENT *(Typing wildly)*. Just a second, be right with you, finishing touches here. Yes ... Yes-yes, good, hah-hah, amazing, what a scene, never *seen* a scene like this!

STONE. Perhaps the moment is inopportune.

TRENT. NO! No-no, almost finished! Last few lines. Real bitch, this play; been working on it for a year—commission from the RSC. There! Yes! Got it! Beginning to think I'd *never* get it right! *(Rips the page from the typewriter, rises, and goes over to* STONE, *hand extended)* Mr. Stone, Michael Trent. Great honor to meet you. *(Into the intercom)* Stella, hold my calls. *(To* STONE*)* Can I offer you a drink?

STONE. Thank you. Yes. A Scotch would be welcome, most welcome indeed.

TRENT. All I've got is beer.

STONE. I'll stay like this ... Mr. Trent, I am not a man who wastes words or time; words take time to say, time is precious. I have conceived an outline for a play. I wish to see this play produced, and quickly. I will provide the capital, you will write it. How much do you want, when can you begin?

(Stunned pause. Then TRENT *rushes to the door.)*

TRENT. Stella!

(Enter STELLA, *a real dish.)*

STELLA. Yes, boss!

TRENT. Be an angel. Run down to B.J.'s and get a bottle of Scotch.

STELLA. Right, boss!

(Exit STELLA.)

TRENT *(To audience)*. If you're going to invent a secretary, might as well go with it all the way! *(To STONE, trying to control his euphoria)* Well, this is just very . . . very flattering. Let me check my appointment book here, see what sort of commissions I've got lined up. *(Rummages through the mess on his desk; he finds the appointment book)* Here it is. Let's see now . . . *(Flips the pages)* And you say you want this play written . . . ?

STONE. Right away!

TRENT. Right away, I see . . . Well, I could shuffle this, I guess. Delay this commission here . . . Might have to give up some work over here, that's something I really wanted too, *damn!* What, uh, kind of dollars exactly are we, uh, talking about?

STONE. As I said before, sir, tell me what you want.

TRENT. (So I *did* hear him right!) *What I WANT!* Well, that's not so . . . easy to say. It depends very much on how long this will take to *write*. Then to *rewrite!* . . . Then to rewrite *that* revision! I do very careful work, I'm sure you've heard. Then of course we have to factor in the research. If this project, I don't know it yet, takes research of some sort—

STONE. It will.

TRENT. There you are! So *that* must be factored in. Plus of course transportation, limousine, mind you now I don't absolutely *need* a limousine—

STONE. I use a limousine. No reason you should not.

TRENT. My God, the theater needs men like you!

STONE. Don't you want to hear the idea?

TRENT. No. No-no, I'll just begin. Obviously, if it matters all this much to you, it's got to be worth *something!* I'll need a day or two to figure out the terms, of course. Where can you be reached? You seem to have appeared a bit out of thin air.

STONE *(Handing him a card)*. My business card.

TRENT. Good. Thank you. Well! I don't see that we need to discuss this any further— you've got yourself a playwright! I've got myself a producer! *(STONE holds out a manila envelope)* This the idea?

STONE. Yes.

TRENT. Well, I can't wait to read it!

STONE. Why not read it now?

TRENT. Well, because right now I just can't give it my complete attention. We'll talk tomorrow. Sir, a great, *great* pleasure meeting you! *(TRENT ushers him out)* Till tomorrow.

STONE. Till tomorrow.

(Exit STONE.)

TRENT *(To audience)*. I didn't want to look at his idea while he was here in case I hated it.

(The door opens. STONE pops back in.)

STONE. Sir. Forgive me. But in my excitement I forgot to give you this . . . *(Hands TRENT an envelope)* . . . retainer. As a token of good faith. *(Leaves)*

(TRENT tears open the envelope. He pulls out five bills.)

TRENT. *Five thousand dollars! (Opens the door)* SIR, YOU ARE TOO GENEROUS!

STONE *(Offstage)*. What?

TRENT. *That* was the wrong thing to say. I meant to say, MAYBE WE CAN DO SOME *MORE* PLAYS! YOU KNOW—AFTER THIS! *(To the audience)* Five thousand dollars! . . . Well, it may not seem like a lot to you. But to a playwright, as an advance, it's enough to save his life. It really is.

(Enter STONE, somber-faced.)

STONE. Sir, you do not understand. I have no interest in producing plays. I am interested in producing one play only. *This is it!*

(Exit STONE.)

(TRENT clearly taken aback by this. Nervously, he opens the manila envelope and peeks inside. Cautiously, he slides the pages out. He stares down at the title page. Then he stares out with a look of alarm.)

(Blackout.)

(Lights up on AUDREY WOOD, TRENT's agent. She is a woman in her sixties. Very short. She wears a tiny pillbox hat. She is hardly visible above her desk. At the moment, she is talking on the phone with TRENT.)

AUDREY. Dear, I checked him out. He's legitimate, he has the money. So I'd say you've got a deal.

TRENT. Audrey, his idea is terrible!

AUDREY. Then don't take it.

TRENT. How can I not take a deal like this? This is a definitional sweetheart deal, this is the deal of a lifetime!

AUDREY. Dear, what do you want me to do?

TRENT. ADVISE me!

AUDREY. Take the deal.

TRENT. Audrey, you don't understand. You haven't read this man's scenario. There is no way anyone, ANYONE! can write a play based on this. Do you know why? Because the characters are completely cardboard, and the plot preposterous.

AUDREY. Dear, listen, calm down, brush your hair, make yourself presentable, come in and show me this notorious scenario. I'm sure it's not half as bad as you think. Really, dear, you're still young, you've got a lovely wife, a lovely child, this is no time to panic.

TRENT. I've used up the advance.

(Pause.)

AUDREY. *What?*

TRENT. *I've used up the advance.*

AUDREY. Darling, I'm sorry, I must have misunderstood. I thought you got this advance last night.

TRENT. I did.

(She checks her watch.)

AUDREY. Dear, it is ten-thirty in the morning. What do you *do* up there in Connecticut?

TRENT. Audrey, I used it to pay our mortgage. We owed three months—I'm sorry, that's the way it is—we're going through a rough time here.

AUDREY. Maybe you should go out to the Coast.

TRENT. I DON'T WANT TO GO TO THE COAST! I'LL START TAKING MORE DRUGS THAN I'M TAKING NOW!

AUDREY. Darling, you mustn't take drugs. It's bad for your health.

TRENT. I'll see you this afternoon.

AUDREY. Dear, I'm afraid you may have to take this deal.

TRENT. I'll see you this after—*(But AUDREY has already clicked off)* —noon. *(Lights off on AUDREY. TRENT turns to the audience)* Okay, I know exactly what you're thinking: Where is the problem? You take the money, you write what you can, the play's no good, no one does the play, you've got your money, basta! end of deal. If I could actually count on that, you're right, no problem. Here's the hitch: this guy is so rich he's liable to produce this play no matter *how* bad it is! Why should this matter?

AUDREY'S ASSISTANT *(Voice only)*. Miss Wood will see you now.

TRENT. One second! I'll be right with her. *(To audience)* People who write plays are a little crazy, okay? For one thing, no one writes plays to make money. I mean you *do*, of course. But you don't go into it, as a profession, because that's where you figure the big bucks lie. You do it . . . and you spend your life doing it, because it *matters*. And you have a kind of pact with yourself. And it says you don't screw around with what matters or else it's gone.

AUDREY'S ASSISTANT *(Voice only)*. Miss Wood will see you now!

TRENT. Yes, yes. Coming!

(Lights back up on AUDREY. TRENT walks over, manila envelope in hand.)

AUDREY. Dear, if you want to get out of this, I'll loan you the money.

TRENT. No, I can't do that.

AUDREY. Of course you can, don't be a fool.

TRENT. Look, here's his scenario. Four pages. Actually, only three. The first page is taken by the title.

AUDREY. What's the title?

TRENT. *The End of the World.*

AUDREY. Ohhhh, dear.

TRENT. You know what it deals with?

AUDREY. I was afraid to ask.

TRENT. Nuclear proliferation.

AUDREY. Oh dear, oh dear, oh dear.

TRENT. I mean, is that an exciting subject or isn't it?

AUDREY. Why does he want to *do* this play?

TRENT. No idea.

AUDREY. Well, let's call him up! *(Buzzing her intercom)* Get me Philip Stone. Bob Montgomery has his number. *(Back to TRENT)* Montgomery's his lawyer. He called after you did. Stone will agree to whatever terms you want.

TRENT. The man is mad!

AUDREY. That's no reason not to work with him. *(The intercom buzzes)* Yes?

AUDREY'S ASSISTANT *(Voice only)*. Philip Stone on the line.

AUDREY *(Into phone)*. Philip Stone? Audrey Wood—I am Michael Trent's agent. I gather you met with my client last night. Mr. Trent is sitting here with me in my office now. *(To TRENT)* Say hello, dear.

TRENT *(Picking up a second phone)*. Hello!

(Lights up on STONE, on the phone.)

STONE. Hello!

AUDREY *(Into phone)*. Dear, we would like to know why you're so anxious to produce this particular play.

STONE. I want to produce it because I believe the earth is doomed.

AUDREY. I'm sorry . . . *What?*

STONE. Doomed! I believe the earth is doomed!

(AUDREY stares at TRENT.)

AUDREY. He *is* mad! *(Into phone)* Mr. Stone, I'm sorry, are you suggesting that a production of your play could prevent this doom?

STONE. Yes, I think perhaps it could.

TRENT *(Sotto voce)*. Ask him if he's planning on road companies.

(She waves him off.)

AUDREY. Well, dear, I must say this is certainly one of the *worthiest* projects I've come across in a very long time.

STONE. Possibly ever.

AUDREY. . . . Yes. Possibly ever. *(To TRENT, sotto voce)* You've got to get out of this! *(Back to STONE)* Darling, you still there?

STONE. Still here!

AUDREY. How long would you say we have till doom strikes?

STONE. My statistics suggest it could be almost any time.

AUDREY. So then you'll be anxious to get it on this season.

STONE. I was hoping for this spring.

AUDREY *(To TRENT)*. I've never heard of anything like this. *(Back into phone)* I take it you've never produced before.

STONE. No.

AUDREY. Well, you have to be prepared for this play closing. Rapidly.

STONE. Why?

AUDREY. Well, I think there's a good chance audiences may not like it. Just by definition. Frankly, unless I'm missing some essential elements, it sounds rather *downbeat* to me.

STONE. I'm sorry, I don't understand. If audiences don't like it, do I *have* to close the play?

AUDREY *(Stunned)*. Well . . . no, of course not.

STONE. Then I won't.

AUDREY. But what if no one comes?

STONE. No one at *all?*

AUDREY. Dear, it's been known to happen!

STONE. I find it hard to believe someone would not come in *eventually.* *(AUDREY and TRENT stare at each other in astonishment)* In the winter, for example. It's *warm* inside a theater. People are bound to come in . . . No, I'm going to keep this thing running. The earth's future is at stake! One doesn't close a play when the earth's future is at stake.

AUDREY *(To TRENT, sotto voce)*. We've got to

keep this man to ourselves! (Back to STONE*)* Dear, I think this is one of the most unusual and worthwhile projects I've ever come across. Hold on a sec. *(Cups her hand over the mouthpiece)* What if he really *knows* something here?

TRENT. What do you mean?

AUDREY. About the earth! About its doom!

TRENT. Oh, my God.

AUDREY. Dear, listen, why take a chance? *Talk* with the man. If a play of yours could in some way help prevent global doom, well!

TRENT. Oh, my God!

AUDREY *(Into the phone)*. If you like, my client will meet with you this afternoon.

(Blackout on AUDREY and STONE.)

TRENT *(To audience)*. I was, of course, an innocent . . . As I soon found out.

(Lights up on STONE.)

STONE. To put it mildly, sir, I am thrilled by your stopping by. Already I feel hope rising in my breast. Charles! Some drinks! Scotch, if you like; we have it.

TRENT *(To audience)*. I told him I wanted nothing.

STONE. Good. All business. For me, then, nothing either.

TRENT *(To audience)*. Stone had requested that the meeting be at his place. Now I was in his apartment. *(STONE's sumptuous Fifth Avenue apartment glides into view)* If I'd ever wanted booze this was it, but something warned me. I sensed a need for clearheadedness: the height had already made me dizzy enough. As a rule, I dislike elevators. For some reason, I cannot rid my mind of the image of what lies underneath as I ascend. Because of this, whenever possible, I walk upstairs. Stone lived in a penthouse forty floors up. There is a limit to any neurosis; forty floors was mine. Now the world was reeling. Looking down through the half-opened window of Stone's library, which I desperately did not *want* to do but felt myself *compelled* to do, I saw the people on the streets below wobbling like rubber. Like dolls made of rubber. The buildings were also like rubber. And, in the hot summer sun, seemed to be *melting!*

STONE *(Coming up behind him)*. Extraordinary perspective from up here.

TRENT. . . . Yes.

STONE. Why don't you sit down?

TRENT. Thank you. *(STONE leads him to a seat. To audience)* And I missed the seat!

(TRENT, in sitting, indeed misses the seat. He

lands on the floor like a clown. Stunned expression. Beat.)

(Blackout.)

(Lights up on AUDREY.)

AUDREY *(To audience). What does an agent do?* *(Pause)* This is a question I am asked all the time ... In *theory*, an agent is supposed to find her client *work* ... Now, while this has certainly been *known* to happen, fortunately, for all concerned, we do much, much more. Take this instance here. Michael Trent had been my client now for nearly fifteen years, and, relatively speaking, we'd done well together; though he wasn't rich, neither was he starving. Comfortable, I would say, is what he was—till recently ... Now, all writers go through down periods; this was something more. What worried me about Michael was his growing eccentricity. He imagined himself as a kind of *detective!* Even on the hottest, brightest summer day he would wear a trench coat, collar up; slouch hat, brim down! Frankly, he looked ridiculous. Well, I'm very fond of him. And consider it my job to protect him from harm ... Anyway, when this Stone project came along, though financially the deal was incredible, unprecedented, something just said to me, *Audrey, watch out!* I decided I needed help ... So I called a meeting: Merv Rosenblatt—he's the president of our agency, and Paul Cowan, Agent to the Stars! Paul refused to come downstairs to *my* office, I refused to go up to *his*, so we agreed to meet for lunch at the Russian Tea Room. *(A booth from the Russian Tea Room glides on)* Paul was the first to arrive—*(Enter* PAUL COWAN, *in sweat suit)* —dressed in his normal dapper style.

PAUL *(Sullenly).* Hi, Audrey. *(Slides in next to her and starts chewing on a napkin)*

AUDREY. Merv Rosenblatt came next. *(Enter* MERV ROSENBLATT, *in sharp, pinstriped suit with carnation in lapel. He is suntanned)* He'd canceled a lunch with Frank Purdue, that's how important this meeting was!

MERV. Okay, what's this about global doom?

PAUL. I'm sure it's an exaggeration.

MERV. Hi, Paul. Hope that's not a contract you're chewing on.

PAUL. No-no. Napkin. Listen, why don't we get started. I've got a screening in twenty minutes. *(To someone unseen by us)* Hey! I'll be in till seven, gimme a call! *(To someone else)* Hi! *(Back to* AUDREY) Sorry, Audrey. Go ahead.

AUDREY. Gentlemen. At this very instant, not ten blocks from here, my client is meeting with Philip Stone.

PAUL. Who's he?

AUDREY. Paul, I sent you a memo on *all* of this!

PAUL. Well, I can't remember! What are we, playing games?

AUDREY. Philip Stone is the man who's vowed to keep my client's play running no matter what.

PAUL. Right. Now I remember! This is the kind of producer our theater NEEDS! Mervin, what would you like?

MERV. Campari and soda.

PAUL. CAMPARI AND SODA AND A BLOODY MARY! Now, when can I meet this guy?

AUDREY. Well—

HEADWAITER. PHONE CALL FOR MR. COWAN!

PAUL. Bring it here!

MERV. Isn't Stone the guy who says we're doomed?

AUDREY. He's the one.

MERV. Well, that's *not* the kind of producer our theater needs! What the hell's Paul talking about?

HEADWAITER *(Arriving with plug-in phone).* Here you are, Mr. Cowan.

PAUL. You think I'm gonna plug it in? Plug it in.

(The WAITER *climbs over* MERV.)

MERV *(From beneath the* WAITER). Paul, is this really necessary?

PAUL. How do I know? *(The* WAITER *climbs back out.* PAUL *picks up the phone. To the others)* Keep talking; I can listen. *(Starts scribbling on the tablecloth)*

AUDREY. Stone says he's willing to pay anything my client wants.

PAUL *(Still on phone).* Maybe it's a project Paramount would like.

AUDREY. I've read Stone's scenario and it's terrible.

PAUL. Why don't we let Paramount decide.

AUDREY. It's about nuclear war.

PAUL *(Into phone).* Hold on. *(To* AUDREY) Paramount will only consider projects about nuclear war if there's an upbeat ending.

AUDREY. This has no ending whatsoever.

PAUL. Well, that, I would say, is a problem. *(Back into phone)* Yeah. Go ahead. *(Continues scribbling on the tablecloth)*

AUDREY. My instinct is to turn the project down.

PAUL. Are you mad?

AUDREY. Paul, I will not stand for rudeness! I am seeking advice, all right? *Seeking.* And I've brought you in on this as a courtesy.

PAUL. Mervin, talk to her.

MERV. Audrey, if your client turns this project down, how will we find out if the earth is doomed?

PAUL. Right! At least have him stay with this till we find out *that.* I've got deals pending here.

AUDREY. My client feels it is unethical to—

MERV. *What?*

AUDREY. *Unethical—*

PAUL *(Into phone).* Hold on. *(To* AUDREY*)* WHAT?

AUDREY. My client feels it is unethical to accept a deal knowing from the outset that there's no way it can be done.

PAUL *(Into phone).* Did you hear that? Can you believe what you're hearing here? *(To* AUDREY*)* So you're advising him to turn this *down?*

AUDREY. I'm not advising him to do *anything.*

PAUL. WELL, WHAT KIND OF GODDAMN ADVICE IS *THAT?*

MERV. Paul!

PAUL. Where the hell are our drinks? WOULD YOU PLEASE BRING OUR GODDAMN DRINKS! *(Into phone)* I better call you back. *(Hangs up. To* AUDREY*)* Audrey, look, far be it for me to butt into your affairs, but how much did your client earn last year?

AUDREY. Not a lot.

PAUL. I will personally guarantee him twice what he made just to keep this project alive. Mervin, are you in on this?

MERV. Well—

PAUL. Mervin's in. Audrey, all your client has to do is string this guy along. Meanwhile, we interest him in *other* worthy projects— I've got I'd say ten—and, simultaneously, find out if the earth is doomed. If it is, we make plans.

AUDREY. What sort of plans?

PAUL. How do I know? You just gave me this today!

MERV. When he says doomed, does he mean the West Coast, too?

AUDREY. I believe that's included, yes.

PAUL. You know I have to tell you, from the little I am gleaning here, this doesn't sound like what I'd call a box-office smash.

MERV. Well now, *Earthquake* did quite well.

PAUL. As a FILM? Hey, this could be sensational. But I understand he's talking drama, right?

AUDREY. Drama.

PAUL *(To* MERV*).* We could take the Winter Garden after *Cats* is gone, blow the whole place up. I mean, it's halfway there already, right? *(To* AUDREY*)* What about this as a musical?

MERV. Paul!

PAUL. Don't reject things out of hand. *(To* AUDREY*)* Who are the main characters?

AUDREY. Well, the main one I would say is the President.

PAUL *(To* MERV*).* Who could we get?

*(*MERV *ponders.* PAUL *ponders. The same inspired casting idea hits them simultaneously.)*

AUDREY. Gentlemen, Ron is President, right now!

PAUL. Well, when he LEAVES!

AUDREY. The man wants to do the play this spring.

MERV. Name the other characters, we can always cast the President.

AUDREY. There's only one other major character: the Soviet premier.

*(*MERV *ponders.* PAUL *ponders.)*

PAUL. Ann-Margret's looking for something.

AUDREY. Paul, the premier is a *man!*

PAUL. It's written that it cannot be a woman? Where? In what Russian document? I don't speak Russian; do you speak Russian? The British have a woman; why can't the Russians?

MERV. Audrey, Ann-Margret's a good idea.

PAUL. No, great idea, *great* idea! Look, the important thing is this: cast it right, I don't care what the thing's about, it runs! You want my advice? Your client *doesn't* take this deal. He *grabs* this deal! GRABS this deal!

MERV. And, meanwhile, finds out if the earth is doomed.

PAUL. Right. CHECK!

(Blackout.)

(Lights up on TRENT, *still on the floor.* CHARLES *helps him to a chair.*

TRENT *(To* STONE*).* I don't know why . . . I suddenly felt quite dizzy.

STONE *(Warm and helpful).* Perhaps it was the open window . . . Many people—perfectly *normal* people, people of a *sunny disposition—*confronted suddenly by an open window, all at once find themselves wondering if they shouldn't jump. The notion takes their breath away. And they faint. Charles, bring our guest some water. *(Exit* CHARLES*)*

Now obviously I'm not saying this was you.

TRENT. It certainly sounds that way.

STONE. Well, I'm only speculating. Anyway, I don't think you were literally about to jump. I think you were just *thinking* about jumping!

TRENT. I'm the most self-protective person you have ever *met!*

STONE. That's why you fainted. Trent, look, why shilly-shally? You're a man of imagination. How can you *look* at a window and NOT think about jumping?

TRENT. I didn't realize that's what imagination led to.

STONE. For God's sake, man, the window was *open!* What do you want, a written invitation?

TRENT. I think I'd like something stronger than water.

STONE. CHARLES!

CHARLES *(Reentering instantly).* You shouted?

STONE. Our guest would like something stronger than water.

CHARLES. I'm not surprised.

(Exit CHARLES.)

STONE. Now listen, Trent. If you're not going to be honest with me, *or* yourself, what's the point of our going on? In front of you is an open window; beyond, forty exhilarating floors below, *oblivion!* Now. How can you, as a normal human being, not at least *contemplate* jumping out?

TRENT. I don't contemplate jumping out because I'm not in *despair.*

STONE. What's despair got to do with this?

TRENT. I'd have thought everything.

STONE. I'm beginning to think you're some kind of ninny. Trent, listen to me. We are on the verge of beating a dead horse. I did *not* expect you to jump out the window, all right? In fact, to be perfectly fair, I'd have been astounded had you even stood on the LEDGE! The point is this. *(Enter CHARLES, rolling a cart filled with booze)* Ah, thank you, Charles. The point is this. *(TRENT hurries toward the cart)* Trent, are you listening?

TRENT *(Grabbing a bottle).* Avidly.

STONE. THE POINT IS THIS! *(TRENT starts to open it)* The urge to leap out of windows does not derive from despair. It derives from *curiosity.*

TRENT. . . . Curiosity?

STONE. Yes sir, curiosity, rampant curiosity! I myself feel the urge *all the time.* Fortunately, I resist . . . Fortunate for me.

Fortunate for those down below. *(Grins)* Enough! On to business. Your agent informs me you have certain reservations about my scenario. If you'd be so kind, I'd like to hear what these reservations are; please speak freely, our relationship will founder if it isn't based on absolute, unwavering trust.

TRENT. Right. Uhhh, thank you. Well! I would say, offhand, that the single biggest problem with your scenario is that it's basically *implausible.*

STONE. It's *supposed* to be implausible.

TRENT. I see . . . Well, I didn't catch that.

STONE. Do you honestly think the next world war is going to start in some *plausible* way?

TRENT. No, I see what you mean.

STONE. In fact, *I* think this basic implausibility is the most plausible thing *in* my scenario . . . And I worked very hard to achieve it.

TRENT. Yes, well, you've succeeded.

STONE. So when can I expect a script? *(TRENT looks about as if for a way to escape)* You understand, I don't mean to rush you now, but time is clearly of the essence here, I'm sure you can see why.

TRENT. Doom, you mean.

STONE. Yes, sir, doom. Could be any moment now.

TRENT. Look, Stone, I've got to tell you something. The truth is, I just don't see doom in your scenario. I mean, I see *theatrical* doom. That's written all over the place. But historic doom? global doom? Can't seem to catch sight of it.

STONE. That's because it's not in.

TRENT. Not *in?*

STONE. My scenario.

TRENT. The global doom you are so concerned about is not IN your scenario?

STONE. That's correct.

TRENT. Well, don't you want to *put* it in?

STONE. No, sir!

TRENT. Why?

STONE. Because if I put in everything I know, no one will BELIEVE me, sir!

TRENT. But NO ONE WILL BELIEVE WHAT YOU'VE *GOT!*

STONE. By gad, we're at an impasse here!

TRENT. Maybe what we need is a new approach.

STONE. Good idea! What do you suggest?

TRENT. That you tell me what you know. And let *me* figure out how to dramatize it— how's that sound?

STONE. No, sir, I cannot.

TRENT. I thought our relationship was based on TRUST!

STONE. And so it is. And you're just going to have to trust me when I tell you doom approaches.

TRENT. Stone, listen. Let me explain something about basic dramatic construction: I cannot go out on the stage during my play and say to my audience, "Hey! Trust me! Doom approaches!" I have got to *convince* them that doom approaches. And how'm I going to do that if you can't convince ME?

STONE. It's a stickler.

TRENT. It's a stickler, absolutely right. Now, what I'm going to do—*(Downs his drink)*—is go home. *(Puts down his glass)* And let you think this whole thing over. It's been a fascinating afternoon. No need to show me to the door.

STONE. Trent! For God's sake, don't you understand? If I could just TELL you how I *know* doom is approaching, why, what's to stop me from telling *everyone?* You see? And then why would I need a play? I wouldn't!

TRENT. Stone. As I see it, there are only two possibilities here. Either you are certifiable. Or you're certifiable. In the first instance, you are certifiable because you've made all this up; in the second, you are certifiable because you *haven't* made it up but won't TALK! To this, I have but two possible responses. Out the door. And out the door. Farewell. Farewell.

STONE. No! Please, sir, you mustn't! Look, sir, I am on my knees! Future generations are on their knees!

TRENT. All I see is you.

STONE. That's because you are shortsighted, sir. You see only the immediate!

TRENT. No. I see a door, that's what I see. And I'm going through it!

STONE. Trent! *(Grabs* TRENT's *legs)* The fate of the world lies in your hands.

TRENT. Really? You know what? Fuck it! Let it blow!

STONE. It's attitudes like this, sir, that will do us in, attitudes like this!

TRENT. Hey! Hold on ... I've just figured out the problem. You know the problem? I'm the wrong writer for this project! With the right writer, this project could just go ZOOM! What you must do, right away, is call my agent: she will send you another writer!

STONE. But you, sir, are the writer that I want.

TRENT. Wonderful! Why?

STONE. I can't tell you that.

TRENT. Stone, listen to me: if you don't let me out this door this instant, I am going to create, before your eyes, in this room, a doom such as you have never dreamed! *(STONE takes out a gun)* Oh, my God.

STONE. Now I suggest you sit down over there.

TRENT. HELP!

STONE. I am the only tenant on this floor.

TRENT. CHARLES!

STONE. Charles works for me; he's used to my behavior. Sir, please sit down. This is no frivolous enterprise! My life is in jeopardy. And, like it or not, so is yours. *(TRENT decides to sit)* Now, when I am done, if you still wish to leave my employ, you may do so. Furthermore, you may keep the money I have paid so far. How does that strike you, sir? Is that fairness or not?

TRENT. That . . . seems quite fair. Yes.

STONE. Good. So, with your permission, then, I will put this morbid instrument away.

TRENT. Oh. Yes. Please.

STONE. I find guns tend to have a will of their own! Fascinating creatures. I call this particular gun Fred.

TRENT. Fred! That's a *nice* name for a gun.

STONE. Yes, it is. It's strong. Guns *need* good strong names. You can get into all *kinds* of trouble if your gun doesn't have a good strong name. Donald, for example. That's a dreadful name for a gun!

TRENT. Yes. Yes, I can see that. Gun wouldn't *respect* you if you called it Donald.

STONE. Exactly! Gun like that could turn on you and *kill* you! Any moment! Have *you* ever had a gun?

TRENT. No. *(Pause)* Well. Actually, I once had a BB gun.

STONE. And what did you call it?

TRENT. Uhhhhhhh, Jim.

STONE. Jim! Yes, that's a *good* name for a gun.

TRENT *(Heading for the phone)*. You know, I wonder, would you mind very much if I asked my agent to come over here?

STONE. No need, sir! We'll be through in a trice!

TRENT. Good.

STONE. Next time, though. Now, on to doom.

TRENT. Global doom!

STONE. Clear this whole thing up!

TRENT. Good.

STONE. Tell me, sir, what these ten countries have in common: India, Egypt, Iraq, Argentina, Israel, Japan, Korea, South Africa, Libya, Brazil.

TRENT. No idea.

STONE. Within ten years, sir, each of these countries will possess the bomb.

TRENT. Really!

STONE. Yes, sir.

TRENT. And to you this means we're doomed.

STONE. No, sir! No, not in and of itself. This is but the *clay* from which our doom will be shaped! Sculpted! Formed!

TRENT. You see doom as a work of *art?*

STONE. Yes sir. Exactly! And, to me, this is part of its *horror* . . . and *allure.* (STONE *smiles at* TRENT. TRENT *leans back and studies* STONE *with a new intensity. Sotto voce)* Now, the reason I believe doom approaches rapidly has to do with certain . . . *information* I stumbled upon quite by accident about a year ago, I shan't tell you how, not now at least . . . This information is at first blush so incredible that were I to simply tell you what it is, you would be bound not to believe it, just as I at first did not and in some ways still do not, *cannot!* though I know full well all of it is true. You see my dilemma here. If I tell you what I know, you will say Stone is mad, and leave. End of project, end of hope. On the other hand, if somehow you believe what I reveal, then I can only conclude that you are the one who's mad. So what am I to do? The answer's obvious. What I have come to know, on my own, you must somehow come to know on your own, as well . . . How? . . . By proceeding systematically . . . and *following your nose.*

TRENT. My nose tells me to get out of here.

STONE. Of course! To save yourself from a terror such as you have never known! Why do your eyes dart toward the window, sir? That's no way out.

TRENT. *Why a play?*

STONE. Why, indeed! . . . Because the theater, sir, alone among the arts, engages, in equal measure, the emotion and the intellect. And both must be touched here, if we are to survive.

(Silence.)

TRENT. Why me?

STONE. As I said, sir: I cannot tell you that.

TRENT. *Why?*

STONE. Because at this moment, sir, your greatest strength is your innocence.

(Pause.)

TRENT. Well, I can't work like that, I'm sorry. (STONE *turns away)* All right. Look. I *will* work on this, okay? . . . BUT *only* if you tell me what it is about *my* plays that makes you think I am right for this job.

STONE. Well, sir, the truth is, and I hope you take this in the proper spirit—I've never actually *seen* a play of yours.

TRENT. WHAT?

STONE. But I've been assured they're very good.

TRENT. Stone, you are out of your goddamn mind!

STONE. No sir. Would that I were.

TRENT. Well, something's cuckoo here. And I think I'll leave before it's me! *(Starts out)*

STONE *(Drawing his gun).* Sorry, sir, I object. *(*TRENT *sees the gun and stops)* Sir, I am a desperate man! . . . But I am also a *gambling* man. I will gamble. I will tell you this: . . . *we have met before.*

TRENT *(Amazed). Where?*

STONE. I cannot tell you that.

TRENT. STONE, I CANNOT TAKE THESE GAMES ANYMORE! NOW, IF YOU WANT TO SHOOT ME, SHOOT ME, BUT THAT'S IT, GOODBYE!

STONE. SIR!

TRENT. *I don't recall meeting you, all right?*

STONE. I am aware.

TRENT. So how important could this meeting have been?

STONE. To me, crucial.

TRENT. When did this meeting take place?

STONE. I can't tell you that.

TRENT. How many were there?

STONE. I can't tell you that, either!

TRENT. I see! And yet, at this meeting, something happened which has convinced you I could save the world from doom!

STONE. Yes, sir. Absolutely!

TRENT. Aren't you a bit surprised I don't remember?

STONE. No, sir. I *thought* you might blot it out.

TRENT. BLOT IT *OUT?*

STONE. Yes, sir.

TRENT. If the incident was anything like this, of COURSE I've blotted it out! People must be blotting you from their lives all the time! I AM LEAVING!

STONE. All right, sir! All right! *(*TRENT *stops and turns back)* I will tell you this . . . but *only* this . . . More than this and my cause is lost. *(Pause)* This . . . particular incident . . . *con-*

vinced me . . . that you, sir, had a thorough understanding of *evil.*

TRENT. . . . *I?*

STONE. Yes, sir. You. *(TRENT stares at him in astonishment)* And now, sir, it is *my* turn to leave. I hope you take this job. *(Warm smile)* Good day.

(TRENT turns to the audience. As he does, the light in the room fades almost to black. However, the sky beyond the open window does not dim at all. In this darkened room, STONE, *unmoving, is a shadowy presence.)*

TRENT. I had, of course, no idea what he meant. *(Pause)* I would say I took the job . . . because of *two* factors . . . *(Music: "Trent's Theme")* One, of course, was the money. How could I turn down a deal like that? *(Takes out a cigarette)* And the other, of course, was curiosity.

(Lights the cigarette. Puffs.)

(The light through the window has been growing brighter. Now, blazing white, it seems to beckon.)

Curtain

ACT TWO

THE INVESTIGATION

MUSIC: *"Trent's Theme." It continues as lights come up on a seedy hotel room. It is night. Through the one window in this room, a red neon hotel sign is visible across the street; the sign says "Sunset Motel." Except for this light, the only other light in the room comes from a lamp.* TRENT, *in his trench coat, looks out at the audience.*

TRENT. To be precise, ten months, five days, twelve hours, and . . . *(Checks his watch)* . . . twenty-three minutes have passed now since Philip Stone came into my life wielding a four-page scenario of dubious merit. Frankly, I've still no idea what he meant when he said I understood evil. As far as I know, I'm a pussycat, a sweetheart, aces—what the hell was he talking about? *(Puffs on a cigarette)* Not that I haven't uncovered some rather peculiar goings-on, you understand! No-no, quite the contrary, this case has been a real eye-opener! There's funny business going on out there, and I had no idea of it. Can't remember when I've been so depressed by a case. *(Pours a shot of bourbon)* And I've never made so much money, either.

Tells you something about money, doesn't it. You know what it tells you? Tells you, without all this money I'd be even *more* depressed. By the way, this is Washington. The Pentagon's back that way. I was there early this morning. *(There is a soft rap on the door. He tenses)* I know it isn't Stella; Stella has a key. *(Sets his glass down quietly)* She came down on the six o'clock shuttle. About an hour ago, I sent her across the street to case the lobby of a two-bit fleabag called the Sunset Motel— *(Starts moving cautiously toward the window)* —where I'm supposed to meet with a man who claims he can clear up everything. A man who calls himself The Shadow—really, I'm not kidding, that's what the message said. Is Stone behind all this? If so, I've been set up. Why? *(Another rap.* TRENT *peers out through the half-opened slats of the Venetian blinds)* I can see the lobby from here. No sign of Stella.

MUFFLED VOICE *(Softly, from other side of door).* Mr. Trent? *(TRENT turns off the lamp. The room is now dark except for the flickering neon sign of the Sunset Motel. Another knock)* Mr. Trent?

TRENT. The door's open.

(The door opens. A MAN *stands silhouetted in the bright hallway.)*

MAN IN HALLWAY. Mr. Trent?

TRENT. Stay where you are.

MAN IN HALLWAY. Mr. Trent! Apparently, you have not understood the conditions of this meeting . . . The man you are about to see is not supposed to talk to outsiders. By agreeing to do just this for *you,* he places into jeopardy not only his job but his life. For this reason, you were specifically instructed to come alone. Instead, you sent an emissary to check out our hotel. Naturally, the meeting place must now be changed. One more violation and the meeting will be off. We will come for you when we're ready. Your friend has been sent back to New York. *(Leaves)*

(TRENT visible only in the eerie red glow of the neon light.)

TRENT. Poor Stella. And she hates flying, too! *(MUSIC: "Trent's Theme")* I'll tell you, this whole thing, it's not been easy on her . . . Right from the start.

(Lights up on STELLA. *The hotel room disappears.)*

STELLA *(To audience).* Mike's instructions were simple. He said, "Dollface, I want you to get me every book and article published last year that deals with nuclear weapons." Wow, I thought! Within a week, his desktop looked like the Adirondacks.

TRENT. That's when the trouble began.

(Lights up on AUDREY.*)*

AUDREY *(To audience).* About a month after he'd started his research, Stella gave me a call at home. She asked if she could come by. She said it was urgent. I told her to come right over. *(To* STELLA*)* And he's been working?

STELLA. 'Round the clock!

AUDREY. So what's the problem, dear?

STELLA. Well, it's his . . . moaning.

AUDREY. . . . *Moaning?*

*(*STELLA *nods. She holds out a small cassette player. She pushes the Play button. A terrible loud moan is heard.* AUDREY *is aghast.)*

TRENT *(To audience).* Actually, I was not aware I was *making* this dreadful noise. I thought I was just reading quietly to myself. I did *hear* the noise, and thought it came from next door. I was in fact about to complain to the landlord, telling him it was hurting my concentration.

AUDREY. Well, this is not right, dear, not right at all. I'll call him in the morning.

TRENT *(To audience).* Which she did. Gave me a real chewing out!

AUDREY. I told him that, in my book, professionals, real professionals, do not sit around moaning. They knuckle down and DO THEIR JOB! No one had *asked* him to be a writer. He agreed.

TRENT. I told her not to worry, I'd figure out the problem. I asked her to arrange a meeting with Stone, and asked if she could be there, too. Frankly, I didn't want to be alone with this guy when I gave him the bad news.

(Lights up on STONE *in* AUDREY's *office. He is staring at* TRENT *in cold fury.)*

STONE. Well, sir, all I can say is, obviously I've misjudged you! A grave mistake, indeed.

AUDREY *(To* STONE*).* Now, let's not panic. I'm sure we can work this out. *(To* TRENT*)* Dear, Mr. Stone has been very generous to you. Don't you think you owe him a little more *time?*

TRENT. I cannot write a play from this material. NO one can write a play from this material! This stuff is INDESCRIBABLE!

AUDREY. Dear, we know the project's difficult. *(To* STONE*)* I think the research may be getting him down. *(Taking her client aside)* Dear, if you don't deliver a draft to this nice gentleman—doesn't have to be a *good* draft, you understand, just a *draft*—I think this man may not only destroy you financially but possibly have you killed, that's just a feeling I have. Now, what exactly is the problem, please spell it out; perhaps in the *talking,* things will seem easier. *(To* STONE*)* We're getting there!

TRENT *(With obvious pain).* I have been finding things . . . I did not *expect!*

AUDREY. Dear, that's what research is *about!*

STONE. This is a waste of time. Clearly, Mr. Trent does not have the temperament for serious material.

TRENT. Look, there are certain things playwrights *know!* One of those is what makes a play. This material does not!

AUDREY. Dear, that is the silliest thing you've ever said—*anything* can make a play. You just have to figure out how to *handle* it! I've never seen you like this, really! *(To* STONE*)* And yet something tells me we're not that far apart.

STONE. If this is not far apart, I am a rabbit!

TRENT *(To* STONE*).* Look! In every play there is a central character and this central character does not just *want* something; he NEEDS something, needs it so badly if he doesn't *get this thing* he will die . . . not necessarily physically, could be emotionally, spiritually, all right? In fact, dramatically, the worse his potential fate, the better. But! BUT! only up to a point. And that's the problem in this instance. Here, the consequences of failure are so far beyond our imagination, so far beyond anything we have ever experienced, or even *DREAMED,* an audience could not believe, fully believe, what it was watching . . . It will all seem like a lie.

AUDREY. Dear, maybe if you just gave it more *time.*

TRENT. I cannot READ this stuff anymore! I DON'T WANT TO *READ* ABOUT THIS STUFF ANYMORE! "The Prompt and Delayed Effects of Thermonuclear Explosions" is not what I wish to read at night! I am scaring the shit out of my family! My son runs from me in HORROR when he sees me coming. You know why? Because I have become a sentimental goddamn dishrag! I see him walking toward me and I start to weep. I see him playing on the lawn with his dogs and I start to weep. I DON'T WANT TO HAVE TO THINK ABOUT THIS STUFF EVERY DAY! WHAT SORT OF PEOPLE CAN *THINK ABOUT THIS STUFF EVERY DAY?* *(A sudden look of amazement comes over* TRENT's *face)* . . . I'll work on it.

AUDREY. *What?*

TRENT. I know what to do . . . I'll work on it, I can work on it! I KNOW WHAT TO DO! *(AUDREY stares at him in astonishment, then looks at STONE triumphantly. Lights to black on everyone but TRENT. To audience)* Through Stone, I arranged to meet with some of the people who think about this stuff every day . . . The ones I asked to meet held opinions that seemed to me to go against all common sense. Anyhow, it was a way in. When there's a mystery, there's at least the possibility of a play. Whatever—it was all I had to go on. Stone said he thought I was doing the right thing. *(Pause)* The first man I talked to, I will call . . . General Wilmer. *(The library of GENERAL WILMER's sumptuous Virginia estate starts to glide in)* He was one of the President's chief advisers on nuclear policy. He had a Ph.D. in physics. *(The GENERAL is seated behind an elegant Empire desk. There is an intercom on the desk. He wears casual country-squire clothes)* His house was in Virginia, about an hour's drive from Washington. Usually, he worked at the Pentagon. But this was a Saturday afternoon . . . *(The GENERAL lights a pipe)* A lovely autumn day.

GENERAL WILMER. So you want to make a play out of this.

TRENT. Well, that's what I'm hoping.

GENERAL WILMER. Some kind of Strangelove thing?

TRENT. No, I wouldn't think so.

GENERAL WILMER. Good. Because the Strangelove scenario only works if you postulate a Doomsday weapon, and no one contemplates that. To save ourselves by threatening to annihilate ourselves is surely the height of preposterousness!

TRENT. I would think so, yes.

(Silence.)

GENERAL WILMER. So have you got a plot?

TRENT. Well, no, I'm afraid I don't.

GENERAL WILMER. Don't plays *need* plots?

TRENT. Well, I'm hoping to find one. That's one of the reasons I've come down to Washington.

GENERAL WILMER *(Merrily)*. Not plot in the sense of conspiracy, I trust!

TRENT *(Laughing)*. No-no! Plot in the sense of narrative thrust. The thing that makes you ask what happens next. That kind of thing. *(The GENERAL smiles and tamps down the tobacco)* So how long have you known Philip Stone?

GENERAL WILMER. I've never met the man. *(Relights the pipe)*

TRENT. Well, then how did he arrange this meeting?

GENERAL WILMER. Someone else set it up. *(Puffs as an AIDE-DE-CAMP in military uniform enters. He carries a folder. The GENERAL gestures to his desk. The AIDE puts the folder on the desk and leaves)* So. You don't understand why we need more nuclear weapons.

TRENT. Right. It's probably 'cause I'm new at this.

(Pause.)

GENERAL WILMER. I gave a talk last month at Princeton, and it was on this very issue. And a number of the students started shouting, "Why don't we just *stop* this madness?" And I said, "You know, it's easy to avoid a nuclear war. All you have to do is surrender." *(Grins)* The problem is to find a way to *avoid* nuclear war while preserving the values that we cherish . . . Okay. Don't we have enough to accomplish this right now? Of course we do. Right *now*. But we don't need to deter the Russians now; why would they attack? They'd gain nothing . . . Deterrence comes into play during *crisis*. During crisis, people tend to think in peculiar ways. A successful deterrent says to the Russians, "No matter what, your best case scenario is just no good."

TRENT. But that's where we are right now.

GENERAL WILMER. Of course! But what makes you think we're going to stay where we are? . . . And things may turn better for us, or for them. Either way, it's dangerous. That's because any imbalance at all is dangerous, even if the imbalance is only *imagined*. In this business, it's how you're *perceived* that counts! *(The AIDE enters with a note, which he gives to the GENERAL, then leaves. The GENERAL glances at the note. Crumples it. Puts it in a pocket)* For example, the weaker side starts thinking: Maybe we'd better hit these guys before they get even *stronger*. The stronger side, knowing what the weaker side's thinking, says: Maybe we'd better do what they *think* we're gonna do, even though we don't want to, 'cause otherwise they *might*. In which case, we're done for. So they do. You see? And all this comes about because of one simple, fundamental truth, and it governs everything we do: the guy who goes first goes best.

TRENT. You want more so you can go *first*?

GENERAL WILMER. In a crisis? Absolutely.

TRENT. Well, that is a piece of encouraging news!

GENERAL WILMER. Well, what's the alternative? We say we'd never, under any conditions, go first. And the Russians actually believe us. So *they* go first.

TRENT. Why would they go first if they believe us? I thought you just said they'd go first because they're afraid *we'd* go first!

GENERAL WILMER. Either way.

TRENT. EITHER WAY?

GENERAL WILMER. Well, you certainly can't expect them to believe us *completely.*

TRENT.... So it doesn't matter *what* we say.

GENERAL WILMER. In a way, that's true.

TRENT. Maybe we should back up a bit. I think I may have started at too high a level! Why do we need nuclear weapons in the first place?

GENERAL WILMER. To prevent their use.

TRENT. Good. Just what I thought. YET if we suddenly realize we *can't* prevent their use, we'd better hurry up and use them.

GENERAL WILMER. Right.

TRENT. Isn't there some kind of basic contradiction here?

GENERAL WILMER. Absolutely! It's what makes the problem so difficult to solve.

TRENT. Do you enjoy this job?

GENERAL WILMER. Someone's got to do it. *(The intercom buzzes)* Yes?

MAN'S VOICE. The turtle is in Zurich.

GENERAL WILMER *(Stunned).* . . . Zurich? What's it doing in Zurich?

MAN'S VOICE. No one knows. *Should we feed it?*

GENERAL WILMER. . . . Not till we find out what it's doing there. *(Clicks off)*

TRENT. So the turtle is in Zurich! *(WILMER relights his pipe)* Well, I'm GLAD the turtle is in Zurich.

(WILMER smiles at him).

GENERAL WILMER. No, you're not. *(Pause)* Look. The sole purpose of possessing nuclear weapons . . .

TRENT.... is not to win wars but to *prevent* them. I've *got* that. Solid.

GENERAL WILMER. Good. Now. In order to *prevent* a nuclear war, you have to be able to *fight* a nuclear war at *all levels,* even though they're probably unwinnable and unfightable. You understand, this doesn't mean you want to. Doesn't even mean you *will.* That's because, for the purpose of deterrence, a bluff taken seriously is far more helpful than a serious threat taken as a bluff. What we're talking about now is credibility. Okay? ... To this end, what your opponent *thinks* you'll do is much more important than what you *actu-*

ally will do. *(Buzzer sounds. He flicks the intercom)* I'm sorry, not now. *(Clicks off)* For example, for the purpose of deterrence, it's a good idea to tell the Russians that if they move into Western Europe—*(Buzzer sounds. He flicks the intercom)* What?

LITTLE BOY'S VOICE. Dad?

GENERAL WILMER. Dear. Not now. All right? *(Clicks off)* —that if they move into Western Europe we will use nuclear weapons to stop their advance. No ambiguity there: you make *this* move, we make *this* move. However! Should deterrence fail, it would seem wiser not to use our nuclear weapons at all, the reason being that once we've gone nuclear, the likelihood of Soviet nuclear retaliation is overwhelming. *(Enter* AIDE *with note. He hands it to* WILMER. WILMER *keeps talking)* What's more, the probability is that it would escalate. What this means is that instead of Western Europe being overrun by the Soviets—*(He glances at the note)* —a thing we certainly don't want! *(To the* AIDE*)* Have his mother take care of it. *(Exit the* AIDE*)* —Western Europe, *and* the United States, AND the Soviet Union would quickly and effectively cease to exist. In fact, according to our latest figures, so probably would the entire world. *(Buzzer sounds. He flicks it. With annoyance)* Yes?

WOMAN'S VOICE. This is for *you* to handle, dear.

GENERAL WILMER. I'll take care of it later. *(Clicks off)* Okay, so here we are, then, with two policies, one overt—you move here and we will strike; the second, *covert*—we may choose not to do any such thing. The Soviets, who know it makes no *sense* for us to strike with nuclear weapons if they move in, nonetheless are deterred from moving in because it's *just possible* we might be *crazy* enough to do it. *Now.* What this means is that, for every level of engagement, we must possess a credible response, even if this response is quite incredible on its surface. This is one of the reasons it's important for our President, whoever he is, to every so often say something that sounds a bit insane. *(Pause)* Fear, you see. That's the great deterrent . . . Don't want to do too much to reduce the fear. By the way, that's the problem with a nuclear freeze: to the extent that it makes people feel safer, it raises the chances of war. You look shocked. I'll tell you something shocking—I think things are going just fine. And you should relax. We really *do* know what we're doing. Take a look. In the past forty years, have we had a nuclear war? No. Why? . . . Nuclear weapons. The fact is, nuclear weapons not only prevent *nuclear* war, they prevent *all* war . . . And I think they just may be the best damned thing that's ever happened to us. Really do!

(Beat. Blackout on everything but TRENT.*)*

MUSIC *("Trent's Theme."* TRENT *walks downstage to the audience).*

TRENT *(To audience).* My conversation with General Wilmer had left me in a quandary: I didn't know whether to laugh or cry. I was on the verge of doing both when the general gave me a call.

(Lights up on WILMER.*)*

GENERAL WILMER. I've been thinking. Maybe you should meet a man named Stanley Berent. If you like, I can set it up.

(Lights off on WILMER.*)*

TRENT *(To audience).* I'd come across Berent's name in my research. He was a Russian scholar, connected to Georgetown University, and a real hard-liner, particularly where the Soviet Union was concerned. *(Japanese koto music heard)* We met at a small Japanese restaurant I assume he frequented out of war guilt. We sat on tatami mats, cross-legged, which made the experience even more excruciating. An inescapable feeling of unreality began to hang over all of this.

(The restaurant has slid into view during the above.)

BERENT *(Eastern European accent).* No, I agree with you completely—our present nuclear policy does not make sense, not at all!

TRENT *(To audience).* Why had the general sent me to *this* man?

BERENT. What we must do—very simple: we must stop regarding nuclear war as some kind of goddamn inevitable holocaust . . . and start looking at it as a goddamn WAR!

TRENT. . . . What?

BERENT. We have to learn how to wage nuclear war *rationally.*

TRENT. *What?*

BERENT. Rationally. We have got to learn how to wage nuclear war *rationally.* I'm sorry—*sake?*

TRENT. Uhhhhh, thank you.

BERENT. You see, even though a strong case can be made for the fact that nuclear war is essentially an act of insane desperation, and therefore fundamentally irrational, this doesn't mean that once you're in the thing you shouldn't do it *right!*

TRENT. I see. *(Pause)* Of course, this would seem to suggest you think it's possible to *win* a nuclear war.

BERENT. No-no! *Limited* nuclear war. No one can win an all-out nuclear war. Unless, of course, the other side decides not to hit back, and one could never count on that, ALTHOUGH, I must say—*(Gives a brief, sharp command to a* WAITRESS *in fluent Japanese)* —although, I must say, in all the scenarios I've seen, the side that hits first definitely comes out best. So if push comes to shove, you do go first, no question of it, particularly if you employ what we call a controlled counterforce strike with restraint. In effect, you hit everything but your opponent's cities.

TRENT. That's the restraint part.

BERENT. Right. His cities are held hostage. And what you—I'm sorry! Chopsticks?

TRENT. Yes, chopsticks.

BERENT. And what you do is, you tell him you'll demolish them if he doesn't capitulate. Now, this is actually quite reasonable *if,* big if, *big* if, IF you have an adequate civil-defense system. That way, even if the Russians strike back, you should be able to absorb the blow and still have enough left to strike back at *them.* And this time just wipe them out. This is what I mean when I talk about credibility. What I have just described to you is a CREDIBLE offensive and defensive nuclear strategy. What we have now, forgive my French, is diddly-shit. *(To the* WAITRESS, *a short command in Japanese, at which she nods and leaves. To* TRENT*)* You don't speak Japanese, I take it.

TRENT. No. Why? Are you passing secrets?

BERENT *(Laughing).* Secrets? I'm not privy to any secrets. Ah, thank you. *(A* WAITER *delivers a noodle dish)* Now. Do I *really* know how to fight a limited nuclear war? Not at all. No one does. No one's *fought* one. And yet if we're not prepared, we're in the soup. Okay. What do I propose?

TRENT. You're not eating.

BERENT. I'm not hungry. What do I propose. I propose we send a clear signal to the Russians, and this signal says: You fuck around with us, we're gonna fuck around with you! This is the sort of talk the Russians understand. How do we do this? First, we build the MX, the Trident 2, the Pershing II, and the Cruise. Why do I want these things? Because they have the ability to take out hardened targets. If we get into a major crisis with these people, I want the ability to disarm them to the greatest extent possible.

TRENT. *Disarm?*

BERENT. Remove. Surgically remove. As much of their military capability as is possible.

TRENT. That's called a first strike, I believe.

BERENT. Oh, no.

TRENT. It's *not?*

BERENT. No.

(Pause.)

TRENT. Why?

BERENT. Because the connotation is *aggressive.* This is a *defensive* act.

TRENT. I see . . . Out of curiosity, what do you call it?

BERENT. Anticipatory retaliation.

TRENT. Ah!

BERENT. Some prefer "preemptive strike," but that can get cumbersome. Because, if you sense they're about to preempt *you,* then what you have to do is *pre*-preempt them.

TRENT *(Getting into the spirit now).* And of course if they should somehow become *aware* that you've discovered their *plans* to preempt, and are about to *pre*-preempt, they'll have to start discussing a *pre*-pre-preemptive strike. And one can obviously just get lost in this kind of talk.

BERENT. That's right. Anticipatory retaliation simply covers everything! Unfortunately, we can't even begin to consider this if we don't have the proper weapons.

TRENT. And we don't have them now?

BERENT. No, sir, we do not.

TRENT. I realize you're going to lose all respect for me. But isn't it possible we'd be better off *not* getting these things?

BERENT. Of course! . . . If the Russians didn't have them.

TRENT. They *have* them?

BERENT. They're *getting* them.

TRENT. WHERE DOES THIS ALL END?

BERENT. When each of us is secure.

TRENT. Well, that's fair enough.

BERENT. Unfortunately, we're not even close . . . To be secure, the United States must possess a credible nuclear-war fighting policy. Now, what might such a policy be?

TRENT. Got me.

BERENT. In a war, what do you think the Russian command would least like to lose?

TRENT. I would say, offhand, Russia.

BERENT. Short of that.

TRENT. Half of Russia?

BERENT. Short of *that.*

TRENT. A third of Russia.

BERENT. Wrong approach. The point is to avoid killing civilians needlessly. Now, come on, think. In a war, outside of its population, what can the Soviet leaders least afford to lose?

TRENT. . . . I don't know.

BERENT. Oh, come on!

TRENT. No, really, I don't know.

BERENT. ThemSELVES!

TRENT. Themselves?

BERENT. Of course! Without a Kremlin, without leadership—you know what Russia's got? It's got shit, that's what it's got!

TRENT. So how do we get rid of their leaders?

BERENT. Well, we know where they are. And we bomb them.

TRENT. . . . Surely they're not just going to sit there and *wait!*

BERENT. No-no! They're going to hide. That's expected.

TRENT. I would think Russia has a lot of hiding places.

BERENT. Of course. And we know where they are. And we target them.

TRENT. Sounds to me like you're about to wipe out all of Russia.

BERENT. Well, that's certainly not what we *intend.*

TRENT. It's just a side effect, you mean.

BERENT. Correct.

TRENT. And this wouldn't piss them off?

BERENT. Piss *who* off?

TRENT. The Russians who are left. I see! They're all *gone.*

BERENT. That's right.

TRENT. Listen. Question. Let's say we've successfully wiped out their leaders, somehow some of their population still exist, and we decide we want to stop this thing. With *whom* do we negotiate?

BERENT. Well, that is a genuine problem.

TRENT. Listen, this is just off the top of my head. Don't you think it might be a good idea to try really very seriously to *negotiate* something with these fellas *now?*

BERENT. Of course! That would be *wonderful!* And yet, if history shows anything, it shows that the Soviet Union cannot be trusted to keep the terms of a treaty!

TRENT. Hold it! Hold it, hold it! Are you trying to tell me we shouldn't enter into treaties with these guys till we're convinced they can be TRUSTED?

BERENT. That's correct.

TRENT. If we knew they could be trusted, why would we need TREATIES? *SAYONARA! (*BERENT *stares at him in astonishment. To audience)* I could barely contain my excitement! *(Rises as* BERENT *and the restaurant fade from view)* I called Stone at the first pay phone I could find. *(Lights up on* STONE. *He is in a room next to a wing chair, its back to us)* Okay, I've got it!

STONE *(Trace of nervousness in his voice).* Got what, sir?

TRENT. The answer. The mystery is solved. I've discovered why we're doomed.

STONE. Really. And why is that?

TRENT. We're in the hands of assholes! *(Silence)* . . . Hello?

STONE *(Sotto voce).* I'm afraid I cannot speak right now.

TRENT. Why?

(The lights have come up enough to reveal that there is a man sitting in the wing chair—we see only his legs. The man appears to be smoking, for smoke curls upward from the chair.)

STONE. Sir, I can only tell you, if you persist in believing these men you've met are not smart, or not . . . *(In a whisper) dangerous* . . . *(Back to his normal voice)* . . . you are gravely mistaken. I can say no more, not now.

*(*STONE *hangs up. Turns back to his mysterious companion. Lights to black on them both.)*

TRENT *(To audience).* There are times you want to chuck it all. This wasn't one. I was on to something here, no question. I decided to check out the guys they call war-gamers, the guys who *play* with these war scenarios. I called General Wilmer and asked if he could arrange it—things had gone so well with the last meeting he'd set up! He said he would. Gladly. And he did. *(Lights up on* JIM *and* PETE*)* I will call them Jim and Pete. *(We are in* JIM*'s kitchen)* Both were connected with the Harley Corporation, a government think tank in nearby Virginia. *(*PETE *and* JIM *are preparing a meal—tiny birds stuffed, seasoned, wrapped in gauze, to be cooked in a microwave)* But the place was off-limits to plain ol' folk like me, so they very graciously invited me to Jim's house, though perhaps it was Pete's, I was never altogether sure—*one* of theirs. For a meal in my honor. Why had they gone to all this trouble for me? Something was very odd.

JIM *(While working at the meal).* So you talked with Stanley Berent!

PETE *(Also while working at the meal).* Bet *that* was fun!

TRENT. He poked a lot of holes in our deterrence strategy.

JIM. I'm sure he was right, it's not hard to do.

(They work in tandem on the meal; lots of coordinated teamwork.)

PETE. There's a curious paradox built into deterrence strategy, and no one has a *clue* how to get around it. The paradox is this: Deterrence is dependent upon strength— well, that's obvious; the stronger your nuclear arsenal, the more the other side's deterred. *However,* should deterrence *fail* for any reason, your strength *instantly* becomes your greatest liability, *inviting* attack *instead* of preventing it.

JIM. HOIST on your own petard!

PETE. And *that* is where all these crazy scenarios come in in which war breaks out PRECISELY because *no one* WANTS it to! Really! I'm not kidding. This business is *filled* with paradox! Here, I'll run one by you.

JIM. I think, before you do, we should point out it isn't *easy* starting a nuclear war.

PETE. Right! Sorry. Getting carried away.

JIM. In fact, we can run scenario after scenario—the Persian Gulf is the most popular.

PETE. That's the hot spot!

JIM. People just will not go nuclear.

PETE. Right! And at first it absolutely drove us up the wall! Here we had all these tests designed to see what happens when people go nuclear?

JIM. And no one would do it!

PETE. To the man, they just refused to believe there wasn't some other way to resolve the crisis!

JIM. Well, the military started freaking out. They figured all those guys down in the silos?—maybe they won't push the button when they're told.

PETE. Real freak-out scene.

JIM. The whole Pentagon—

PETE. They just went bananas! *Total* banana scene.

JIM. Some general called me up. He said, "You incompetent jackass, what the hell kind of scenario are you *giving* these guys?" I said, "We're giving 'em every scenario we can think of, SIR! No one'll push the button, SIR!" You know what he said?

PETE. Get this!—"Don't tell 'em it's the button!"

JIM. "Really!" we said. "Then what good's the test?"

PETE. Anyway, happy ending.

JIM. Finally we solved it.

PETE. *You* solved it.

JIM. *I* solved it, *you* solved it, what's it matter? We *solved* the thing!

PETE. What a bitch!

JIM. People think it's *easy* starting a nuclear war?

PETE. Hey! Let 'em try!

TRENT. Okay, I'll bite: how *do* you start a nuclear war?

JIM. Well, *first* you have to assume that a nuclear war is the *last* thing either side wants.

PETE. Right! That's the key! Who would've thought it! Jim?

JIM. Okay. Let's say we're in a confrontation situation where we and the Soviets are facing down in the Middle East: let's say, Iran. Big Soviet pour-down. Let's further say we're losing conventionally on the ground—

PETE. Not hard to believe—

JIM. —and the President decides he wants the option of using nuclear weapons in the area, so he moves them in.

PETE. Mind you, he doesn't want to *use* them now.

JIM. Right! Absolutely not! Last thing he wants!

PETE. He's just hoping, by showing strength, the Soviets will rethink their position and pull back.

JIM. In other words, it's a *bluff.*

PETE. Right, good ol' poker bluff!

JIM. And, by the way, probably the proper move to make.

PETE. Now, at the *same* time we ask our NATO allies to join us in raising the military alert level in Europe. Why? We want to tie the Soviet forces down that are in Eastern Europe.

JIM. Again, absolutely the right move.

PETE. So far, the President's batting a thousand. No appeasement here. Yet not too strong, nothing precipitous.

JIM. Okay. The Soviets now go to a higher level of readiness themselves. Why? They want to tie *our* forces down so *we* don't shift 'em to the Middle East.

PETE. Now we start to move nuclear weapons out of storage! *(Mimics the sound of a trumpet)*

JIM. Okay, now let's suppose the Soviets, in the heat of this crisis, *misinterpret* the moves we've made, and believe that in fact we're about to *launch* these weapons! Not a far-fetched supposition!

PETE. Particularly, given their tendency to paranoia!

JIM. Right!

PETE. Okay. Now, at *this* point the issue for them is *not* do they want to be *in* a war.

JIM. They're already *in* a war in the Middle East!

PETE. Right. The issue isn't even do they want to launch a nuclear attack against the West.

JIM. That's because they know they'll HAVE to if the West attacks *them!*

PETE. You see?

JIM. *The only issue—*

PETE. Absolutely ONLY issue—

JIM. —is do they want to go *first* and preempt this attack?

PETE. Or wait it out—

JIM. —and go second.

PETE. Now, they recognize, just as much as we . . .

JIM. . . . that going *first*—

PETE. —is going *best.*

JIM. Right!

PETE. And by a shocking margin, too. No scenario *ever* shows ANYTHING else! I mean, these notions of our riding out a nuclear attack and then launching again, without substantial loss of capability—well, it's nonsense.

JIM. By the way, you have to posit here that events are moving rapidly. A short time frame is crucial to this scenario. No time to sit back and say, "Hey! wait, why would he want to shoot at me? I know he's in trouble, but he isn't crazy!" No. He doesn't have *time* to think things out. He's got to make a move! Okay, What's he do? *(PETE makes the gesture and sound of a missile taking off)* He shoots. Now, are we saying it's a *likely* thing? No. But, from the Soviet perspective, they HAVE to shoot. Under these conditions, holding back is clearly wrong, politically and militarily.

PETE. And *that*—

JIM. —is how a nuclear war begins.

PETE. Not out of anger.

JIM. Or greed.

PETE. But *fear!*

JIM. With neither side *wanting* to.

PETE. Yet each side *having* to.

JIM. 'Cause the other guy thinks they're *going* to.

PETE. So they'd better.

PETE and JIM *(Together, à la W. C. Fields).* HOIST ON OUR OWN PETARD!

JIM. By the way, where *is* the petard?

PETE *(Tossing a jar of mustard)*. Petard!

JIM *(Catching it)*. Petard!

PETE and JIM *(Together, à la W. C. Fields)*. Ahhhh, yes!

TRENT. You guys are a scream.

JIM. Actually—should we tell him?

PETE. Sure.

JIM. Actually, over at the center, we all try to scream at least once a day.

PETE. Usually it happens in the cafeteria.

JIM. Someone on the staff will stand up and shout "SCREAMIN' TIME!" And everyone just, you know . . . *(Gives a choked comic scream)*

PETE. It's a ritual we only do when no one from the Pentagon's around.

JIM. We did it once when some honcho military brass were there.

PETE. *Freaked them out!*

JIM. Within minutes we had lost I don't know *how* many grants! *(Laughs)*

PETE. So, anyway, now we're pretty choosy 'bout who we scream in front of.

JIM. I'll tell you . . . I sometimes think, if it really happens, and we all, you know . . . *(Makes the sound and gesture of a giant explosion)* . . . and by the way, the whole thing *could* be over! No matter what anybody says, no one knows *what* happens to the ozone layer in a nuclear war. Really! No idea! *(Laughs)* Okay, so I sometimes think, now it's all over, and we're all up there in the big debriefing space in the sky, and the Good Lord decides to hold a symposium 'cause he's curious: how did this thing happen? And everybody says, "Hey, don't look at me, I didn't wanna do it!" The end result being that everyone realizes *no* one wanted to do it! But there was suddenly no choice. Or no choice they could *see*. And the symposium gets nowhere.

TRENT. How do we get out of this?

PETE. Well, you try like hell to not get *into* these kinds of conflicts!

JIM. Obviously, sometimes it can't be helped.

TRENT. This is not pleasant news.

PETE *(Putting the birds into the microwave)*. On the other hand, let's not exaggerate. Things are not that bad, maybe we *shouldn't* get out of it. *(With a laugh, to JIM)* Would you not love to have a snapshot of this man's expression?

(JIM mimes taking a snapshot of TRENT.)

TRENT. So you mean we're just supposed to sit around, twiddle our thumbs, and WAIT?

PETE. Well . . .

JIM. Sometimes . . . there's really not an awful lot you *can* do.

PETE. Except *hold on*.

JIM. And hope for some kind of discontinuity.

PETE. Right.

TRENT. Ah! Discontinuity! What the hell is that?

PETE. It's an event . . . by definition unpredictable, which causes a sudden and radical shift in the general mode of thinking.

JIM. Sadat's going to Jerusalem is the prime example.

PETE. Sadat looked down the road and saw nuclear weapons in Cairo and Alexandria in maybe five, ten years, and he just didn't like what he saw.

JIM. So he decided he was gonna do something about it.

PETE. And what he decided to do no one, I mean *no* one, anticipated.

JIM. And it changed the whole ball game.

PETE. *Just like that!*

JIM. And THAT—

PETE. —is a discontinuity.

TRENT. Okay! all right! . . . any candidates?

PETE. Well, I'd say the best we've come up with so *far* is . . . *(Looks to JIM for help)*

JIM *(To PETE)*. Extraterrestrial?

PETE. Yah. *(To TRENT)* Extraterrestrial.

TRENT *(Stunned)*. You mean, like E.T. comes down?

PETE. You got it!

TRENT. Jesus Christ!

JIM. That's another!

TRENT. You guys are a riot!

JIM. Hey! Is this business? Important to keep smiling.

TRENT. No, I can see that. Listen, have you guys given any real thought to, you know, touring the country? Nightclubs, things like that?

PETE. Oh, sure, it's occurred to us.

TRENT. I'm sure it has.

JIM. People are very interested in this nuclear issue.

PETE. And we're right there at the dirty heart of it!

TRENT. Good. Listen, while we're on the subject of humor, what's your attitude toward doom?

PETE. . . . Doom?

(PETE looks at JIM. JIM looks at PETE.)

JIM. It's just no solution.

PETE. No. No solution.

TRENT. I'm being serious!

PETE and JIM *(Together).* So are we! *(They smile at* TRENT*)*

(Blackout on JIM *and* PETE. TRENT *turns to the audience.)*

MUSIC: *"Trent's Theme."*

TRENT. Okay. Even with *my* lousy sinuses, I could tell something wasn't smelling right. I figured it was *my* fault. What've I missed? I decided to retrace my steps. *(*TRENT*'s office has begun to reappear)* The next day I was back in my office in Stamford, going through all my notes, when Stella came in with a rather large package.

(Enter STELLA *pushing a huge flat object wrapped in plain brown paper.)*

STELLA. Boy, is this big!

(On the wrapper, crayoned in enormous black letters, are these words:)

MICHAEL TRENT—PLAYWRIGHT
and
DETECTIVE

TRENT. Hey, dollface, what gives?

STELLA. I dunno. I found it in the hallway. Someone left it outside your door. I had t' bring it in, 'cause otherwise I couldn't get out. *(Starts to unwrap it)*

TRENT *(To audience).* It had no return address.

(Inside the package is an oversized, framed photograph of a crazy crate.)

*(*TRENT *and* STELLA *stare at it in silence.)*

STELLA. Hey, Mike, how do ya *build* a box like that?

TRENT. I dunno.

STELLA. Hey! Maybe there's instructions in the back. *(Checks in back)* Mikey! Look! . . . A card.

*(*STELLA *hands the small white card to* TRENT. TRENT, *not needing to read, moves toward the audience. As he does,* STELLA, *the box, and the office disappear into the dark.)*

TRENT *(To audience).* The card said, "If you want help with your quest, be in Washington tomorrow night, ten o'clock." And it was signed "The Shadow." *(There is the sound of a knock from the darkness behind him.* TRENT *turns toward the sound)* It's open!

(The door of his hotel room has appeared. It opens. The MAN *who appeared earlier is seen, silhouetted against a dazzlingly bright white hallway light.)*

MAN IN HALLWAY. We're ready, Mr. Trent.

TRENT. Right! *(Blackout except for a pin-spot of light on* TRENT*)* I am led down the backstairs to a car—an old Ford wagon. In the rear seat are two men. I get in. No one says a word to me. And the car pulls out . . . Fog moves in off the Potomac . . . We are heading toward the center of the capital, that much I can tell. We move at a crawl. Even the road is scarcely visible. *(Pause)* And then . . . the sky begins to *glow.* A dazzling milky phosphorescence! I have never seen anything like this in my life! And then I hear *music. (Music dimly heard) . . . Band* music. *(So it is)* And then I see the *source* of this strange light! *(Music louder)* We approach the Jefferson Memorial. On the grounds surrounding it are rows upon rows of giant klieg lights! The lawn—what I can see of it—is packed. Obviously, it's a concert of some sort. We pass near a clearing in the fog, and I see that in the crowd are many men in military uniforms! . . . The car stops. I can see a sign but can't make out what it says. The people who have brought me here tell me to get out. "But how will I recognize The Shadow?" I say. "Don't worry," they say. "But where should I walk?" "Wherever you wish." So I get out and the car drives off. *(Pause)* I head for the sign. The sign says: U.S. Marine Corps Band. *(Music louder)* Well, I don't like crowds in the best of times, and this is terrible! So I decide to go toward the Memorial, which looms through the fog like a spectral white mushroom. *(The interior of the Jefferson Memorial begins to form around him)* The rotunda is empty. I look down through the fog and can see . . . almost no one. *(Jefferson's statue can be discerned only in shape. The same for the surrounding columns)* And then I hear . . .

(Footsteps suddenly moving toward him. Then they stop on the far side of a shimmering shaft of light caused by the klieg lights' piercing the fog. All we can see of this MAN *are the bottoms of his legs.)*

MAN'S VOICE. Mr. Trent?

TRENT. And I recognize the voice!

(The MAN *walks toward* TRENT, *through the eerie light. The first feature we see is that he is in uniform. But we can't yet make out his face. And then he moves forward, into a better light. It is* GENERAL WILMER. *He smiles.)*

GENERAL WILMER *(Warmly).* Shall we talk? *(Beat. Blackout.)*

Curtain

ACT THREE

THE DISCOVERY

Lights up on TRENT *in his trench coat.*

TRENT. Okay. I have proceeded systematically, I have followed my nose and have found the piece of the puzzle I was looking for. Unfortunately, instead of the puzzle being solved, the puzzle has expanded . . . I am a man who knows too much . . . and not enough. *Why me? Why has Stone picked me? (The cozy living room of* TRENT's *house in Connecticut slides into view. Through rear windows, open, with curtains fluttering in a gentle spring breeze, we can see trees and a meadow)* By the way, this is my house in Connecticut—my beloved retreat to which I have retreated. Fat chance! About an hour ago, Stone called to say he was coming out to see how I'm doing. *How I'm doing!* . . . All right, the truth: I have told him the meeting with The Shadow was canceled. Actually, I didn't have the nerve to tell him this directly, I left a message. I've told the same thing to my agent and my wife. I need time to think things through! It's not an easy racket, writing plays; stay out of it!

ALEX *(Offstage)*. DAD!

TRENT. That's my son. He's eleven.

BOY'S VOICE. I think your producer's here!

TRENT. Great. Here it goes.

BOY'S VOICE. Should I tell Mom to let him in?

TRENT. No-no! Let him find his own way in! *(To audience)* My wife is on the patio, in a chaise, reading Yeats. That's what life's like here in the country. Now, if things go well today—and at this point I've no idea just how that's possible—you won't be meeting either my wife *or* my son; as I said earlier, I don't want them involved in this!

STONE. TRENT!

TRENT. The Call of the Wild! *(To* STONE) I'M IN THE LIVING ROOM, PHIL! *(To audience)* What you are about to see is scrambling of the highest order! *(*TRENT *removes his trench coat. Enter* STONE) Phil! *(*STONE *stops and turns his gaze on* TRENT. *He stares at* TRENT *closely. Then, after a moment,* STONE *grins)* Well, I'm glad to see you're happy!

*(*STONE *walks slowly over to* TRENT *and rests his hands on* TRENT's *shoulders.* TRENT *stares back, terrified.* STONE *continues to grin.)*

STONE. I haven't seen you in such a long time!

TRENT. That's right! About . . . a month, I guess—maybe . . . more.

STONE. Why was the meeting canceled?

TRENT. Oh! With, uhh, The Shadow? I don't know, they didn't say. Security, I suspect. I'm waiting now to see when it will be rescheduled.

STONE. What makes you think it will be rescheduled?

TRENT. Well, that's what they said.

STONE. And yet, for some reason, they neglected to tell you why it was canceled.

TRENT. No-no, uh, *security!* . . . I mean they, you know, *said* that. Said it. "Too risky for him to meet with you tonight"—that's what they said.

(Enter ANN, TRENT's *wife. She is in her sixth month of pregnancy.)*

ANN. Dear, Audrey has arrived.

TRENT. What?

ANN *(Going toward* STONE). Hi! I'm Ann Trent.

TRENT. Ann! Out! Get out!

ANN. *What?*

(He rushes toward her.)

TRENT *(Sotto voce)*. Get out of here! Go! I'll tell you about it later. I don't want you involved in this! Out, get out! *(Leads/pushes/coaxes her out of the room as* AUDREY *enters)* Audrey!

STONE. I was not aware you were joining us today!

AUDREY. No. Nor was my client. Dear, I need to speak to you alone.

TRENT *(Startled)*. Of course.

AUDREY. Mr. Stone, would you mind very much if my client and I went into—

STONE. No, please, dear lady, you stay here, I can use the time to look around the house. I *love* country houses! And this is such a charming one. *(Exits)*

*(*TRENT *stares after him, perplexed.)*

TRENT. Well, he's the weirdest man I've ever met!

AUDREY. Dear, I'm afraid I have some extremely bad news for you.

TRENT. Oh!

AUDREY. Could I have a drink?

TRENT. Uhhhh, right. Ummmm—

AUDREY. *Martini.*

TRENT. With an *olive!*

AUDREY. No, dear. Lemon twist.

TRENT. Right, of course. *(Heading for the bar)* So what's the, uh, bad news?

AUDREY. Well. It seems, dear, that your producer has instituted legal action against you.

TRENT. *What?*

AUDREY. He is bringing suit against you, dear. For fraud and breach of contract.

TRENT. WHAT?

AUDREY. Sssh. Dear. Please.

TRENT. *Why?*

AUDREY. I'm not sure.

TRENT. Well, how much is he suing me for? I mean, is it the retainer, the advance?

AUDREY. I'm afraid it's a bit more than that.

TRENT. How can it be for more, that's all I made!

AUDREY. The suit is for fifteen million dollars.

TRENT. Fifteen million DOLLARS?

AUDREY. Yes, dear, dollars.

TRENT. But that makes no SENSE!

AUDREY. I know.

TRENT. Maybe it's not dollars! Maybe it's zlotys!

AUDREY. No, dear, dollars, Yankee dollars.

TRENT. WHAT'S HE THINK I'VE *GOT?*

AUDREY. Well ... it's not worth a *great* deal ... but you've got this house.

TRENT *(Staring in direction that* STONE *went).* Oh, my God!

AUDREY. Perhaps if you turned in your *script!*

TRENT. Oh, come on, Audrey! No one sues a playwright for fifteen million dollars because he's a few weeks late delivering a script! I mean, what's he hope to gain? A house? He doesn't need another house!

STONE *(Who has entered, unnoticed).* It's not the house that interests me . . . It's your *ruination. (They turn to him, astonished)* And I expect your legal fees alone should accomplish that. You look surprised; that surprises me. Did you really think I'd allow your treachery to go unchallenged?

TRENT. What are you talking about?

STONE. Sir, please, the time for innocence is past.

AUDREY. *What* treachery?

STONE. Evidence suggests, madam, that your client has in fact found what he set *out* to find.

TRENT. That's not TRUE!

STONE. And I believe otherwise.

AUDREY. Michael, have you lied to Mr. Stone?

TRENT. Not at all.

AUDREY. You owe my client an apology.

STONE. Tell this lady what you've done.

TRENT. *I don't know WHAT you are TALKING about.*

STONE. Does the name "The Shadow" ring a bell?

TRENT. The meeting was called OFF!

STONE. AND THAT, SIR, IS A LIE!

AUDREY. Mr. Stone, forgive me. If my client says the meeting was called off, the meeting was called off.

STONE. I disagree.

AUDREY. Michael?

TRENT. It was called off.

AUDREY. The matter's closed.

STONE. THIS MAN HAS VIOLATED THE TERMS OF OUR AGREEMENT!

AUDREY. Mr. Stone!

TRENT. Audrey.

AUDREY. Dear, let me handle this! *(To* STONE*)* I believe the time has come, sir, for you to leave.

STONE *(To* TRENT*).* Tell her what you've done.

AUDREY. Is there something wrong, sir, with your ears?

TRENT. Audrey.

AUDREY. I SAID STAY OUT OF THIS! I CAN HANDLE THIS! *(To* STONE*)* Mr. Stone, if my client says the meeting was called off, it was called off. My clients do not lie to me.

TRENT *(Weakly).* Audrey, please.

AUDREY. DEAR, STAY OUT OF THIS! *(To* STONE*)* The matter's therefore closed. Except, sir, for your appalling lack of manners. Where, may I ask, were you brought up?

TRENT. I LIED!!!! *(She turns to him as if struck)* I lied, I lied! I'm sorry! *(He holds his head in his hands and fights tears. She does not know what to do, where to turn. She turns to* STONE*)*

AUDREY *(To* STONE*).* Would you ... be so kind ...

STONE. A drink?

AUDREY. Yes, please, some ... water would be nice, I think. *(To* TRENT*)* Why? Don't you trust me?

TRENT. Of course I trust you! This has nothing to do with trust! I just had no idea what to say. I haven't even told Ann! I've told no one!

AUDREY *(Taking the glass from* STONE*).* I owe you an apology.

STONE. Not at all.

AUDREY *(To* TRENT*).* I don't understand what's happening.

TRENT *(To* STONE, *angrily).* Did you set the meeting up? *(*STONE *shakes his head no)* Then how do you know it happened?

STONE. I've had you followed, sir. Ever since you accepted this job.

TRENT. Great!

STONE. I should add, in all this time my emissaries have never actually seen you *writing.*

TRENT. What do you think, I write in the *street?* I write in my OFFICE!

STONE. Good! Then you can show me some pages.

TRENT. *Pages?*

STONE. Sir, doom approaches, I need pages.

TRENT. ANYONE CAN WRITE PAGES!

STONE. I ask only to see yours.

TRENT. Well, I never show pages till I'm done. Audrey can confirm this. Audrey, are you all right? *(She nods)* Anyhow, the important thing isn't pages, the important thing is *concept!* CONCEPT is what we should be talking about! Without a concept, a play is nothing.

STONE. Sir, a play may be nothing without a concept—without pages, it is even less.

TRENT. Who said that? Aristotle, I believe.

AUDREY *(Sotto voce).* Dear, this man is *suing* you!

TRENT. Okay, fine, you want pages? I'll give you pages! I've got pages *here— (Runs to a drawer, opens it)* —and in here—*(Opens another drawer)* —pages everywhere! You want pages? Here! Pages! *(Starts flinging the pages into the air.* STONE *looks down at them)*

STONE. These are not pages from a play!

TRENT. Right! For that, you need a CONCEPT!

AUDREY. *Michael.*

TRENT *(To* AUDREY, *sotto voce).* I'm okay, I know what I'm doing. Really. *(To* STONE*)* Now, do you want to hear what my concept is? Because I will tell you. Gladly. Because this is a concept I am wild about! And it took a long time finding. In fact, I only found it today. But well worth the waiting, because this concept means this play will be *fun.*

STONE. *What?*

TRENT. Fun! Fun to write, fun to look at.

AUDREY. Dear, are we talking about the same play?

TRENT. Of course! The play that deals with doom! Going to be fun! So you want to hear what this concept is? Okay, here it is . . . *(Very long pause, during which time he takes out a cigarette and hopes that a concept will come. The lighting of the cigarette, in a kind of Philip Marlowe way, seems to do the trick. A look of astonishment comes over his face, which he masks from the oth-ers)* The playwright . . . is conceived . . . as being very much like a *detective. (To* AUDREY*)* Wha'd'ya think?

STONE. *What* playwright?

TRENT. The playwright who's at the CENTER of this play!

STONE. What's a playwright doing in this play?

TRENT. He's in this play because he is the only reality I can hang on to here! And this playwright is sent on a *strannnnge* mission by a man, I would say quite like *you,* a kindly man, a man who would surely never, for example, sue anyone. And this playwright *respects* this man because this playwright is without doubt the very salt of the earth! Though possibly with some knowledge of evil—I still haven't figured that one out, I may have to come back to you for that, I'm nowhere on that so far, that's the truth, I just can't remember where we met. *(Silence)* Okay, so this playwright, down he goes to Washington, figuring if this mystery can be solved anywhere, there's the spot.

AUDREY. Dear, what happened down in Washington?

TRENT. The case took a turn for the worse, all right? I didn't think it possible.

AUDREY. Michael, *please!*

TRENT. I DO NOT BELIEVE WHAT THE SHADOW TOLD ME, OKAY? And there you are. Now, what am I to do with that?

(Enter ANN TRENT, *carrying a tea tray.)*

ANN. Tea time!

TRENT *(Angry, sotto voce).* Ann, I asked you specifically—

ANN. Dear, I am not coming to sit in on your meeting, this is *your* meeting, not mine. *(To* AUDREY *and* STONE*)* I just thought you might all like some iced tea. The mint is from the garden. *(To* TRENT, *sotto voce)* I was being *nice.* You might try the same. *(She sets the tray down and leaves. Silence)*

STONE. When is your wife due?

TRENT. Uh, due where? . . . Oh! Uhhh, she's, let's see, in her sixth month, so in four, I mean three. Unless doom strikes first, of course. I'm sorry, I'm just very edgy today.

*(*ANN *comes back in, holding the sugar bowl. She comes face to face with a glowering* TRENT. *She puts the bowl down on the floor.)*

ANN. The sugar.

(She tiptoes back out.)

STONE. She's very graceful, your wife.

TRENT. Yes. *(Silence)* Look, you want to

know what happened down in Washington? You show me what to do with it, I'll tell you what happened. Is that fair? Fair enough? Terrific. This guy, The Shadow, he says, "Okay, tell me what you *think* you know." So I started in. I told him I thought the notion of using nuclear weapons to prevent the use of nuclear weapons—*(To* AUDREY*)*—which is the system we depend upon—*(To them both)*—simply doesn't work, not in the *long* run, too many places where the system just plain breaks down! Breakdown, in fact, I said, seems built in. What we've got, I said, is a fail-safe built-in breakdown machine. He said: "So how can I help you?" I said I want to know where I've gone wrong. He said: "You're not wrong. You've *got it!*" *(*AUDREY *stares at him, stunned. To* STONE, *with a gesture toward* AUDREY*)* I would think my expression probably looked a bit like that! *(To them both)* I said, "Wait, hold on, you're telling me the system doesn't work?" He said: "Why are you surprised? That's what you told me." I said: "But I didn't think I was right!" He said: "Well, you are." I said: "Well then, how come you and I are the only two who seem to know it?" You know what he said? Hold on to your seats, folks. He said actually *everybody* knew. It was common knowledge.

AUDREY. . . . Dear, that makes no sense.

TRENT *(Excitedly)*. That's right! Of COURSE it makes no sense! But WHY does it make no sense?

AUDREY. Well . . . *(Pause)* Well, because if everyone knows . . . that what they're working on doesn't *work* . . .

TRENT. . . . Yes?

AUDREY. . . . Why would they keep working?

TRENT. EXACTLY!

AUDREY. I assume these are people who can find other jobs.

ALEX *(Offstage)*. DAD, CAN I ASK YOU A QUESTION?

TRENT. No! And stay out of here. Go to your room. *(Back to* AUDREY *and* STONE*)* All right. So I asked what you asked: If they know it doesn't work, why do they keep working? . . . *"Because they don't believe what they know!"* *(*AUDREY *stares at him blankly)* Look, look, they know it doesn't work, okay? I mean, they've run the charts, the projections, intellectually they are fine, they understand, *but* they just can't BELIEVE it! Why? Because it SEEEEEEMS as if it should work. It's worked so far, right? So why not forever?

You see? Logic! Worst thing that's ever *happened* to man! Oh, my God!

AUDREY. What?

TRENT. Down in Washington? Where I went to interview all these guys? There was something on their walls. I mean, each one had it. And I remember thinking: I wonder if these guys belong to some kind of club. Anyway, I didn't give it too much thought . . . Other guys, they put up posters of Bo Derek. These guys—they had Escher prints! *(Pause)* The Shadow! Let me show you how he got in touch with me! *(Looks up)* DOWN!

(The photograph of the "crazy crate" descends on wires.)

AUDREY *(To audience)*. Aren't playwrights' houses *wonderful!*

TRENT. Look. You see? It doesn't work! And yet it *does*. It's not possible! And yet it *is*.

AUDREY. How does one *construct* an object like this?

TRENT. Not quite sure.

AUDREY. I'd love one in my office.

TRENT. So would I. Here's the Escher print they all had. DOWN!

(Another hugely oversized print descends on wires, this one larger even than the first. AUDREY *stares up, puzzled.)*

AUDREY. Dear, what's happened to your second floor? *(Now she sees the picture)* . . . Well, there's something very wrong with this.

(They stare at the picture.)

AUDREY. I'm afraid I'm quite confused. How does one get the water to flow both up and down?

TRENT. It's a puzzler. *(Snaps his fingers, and the Escher print disappears)*

AUDREY. Thank you, dear.

TRENT. Okay, what he said so far, that the system doesn't work, that I can accept. But I said, "Surely, not *everyone* is like this. *Some* must believe what they know. You, for instance." "Absolutely," he said. "So, then, why are *you* working on it?" And he grinned . . . and said, *"Guess."* *(Silence)* Well, I was stumped. So I went back to the very first question I'd asked him, weeks before: "If the system doesn't work, why do we need more weapons?" His answer remained the same: we need more so we can strike first.

AUDREY. What!

TRENT. It's a defensive act.

AUDREY. Hitting someone first is a *defensive* act?

TRENT. If you know he's planning to hit you.

AUDREY. Why would he be planning to hit you?

TRENT. Because he thinks you're planning to hit him.

AUDREY. Well . . . he's *right.*

TRENT. There you are.

AUDREY. Dear, by this scheme, nobody does anything *offensive.*

TRENT. Exactly. Every act of aggression is defensive here. It's a completely moral system!

AUDREY. Well, something's wrong with it!

TRENT. I know.

AUDREY. Not quite sure what.

TRENT. It's a puzzler! *(To* STONE*)* So I said to him, "This is crazy, this is suicidal! If we strike first, they'll just retaliate, and wipe us out in return!"

AUDREY. THAT'S what's wrong with it!

TRENT. That's just one of them.

AUDREY. With one like that, you don't *need* any more.

TRENT. Exactly! And he agreed! *"That's why we've abandoned deterrence." (Looks to* AUDREY *for her response)*

AUDREY. . . . What?

TRENT. Exactly! WHAT? I mean, even if deterrence *doesn't* work, it works a *bit.* You don't just chuck it out, not without a substitute! Not a substitute, he said. An *improvement!* . . . And he grinned and said: "It seems, at least in theory, that a better mousetrap has been designed!" . . . Look, he said, an attack by us right now is suicidal because the enemy can always retaliate and wipe us out. However—what if we could *prevent* retaliation? "Well, in the future," he said, "which is what we're working toward, we think it may be possible, technologically, to do just this. And if we *can,* even if for the briefest time, a week, a month, create some kind of invulnerable window shade allowing our missiles out but nothing in, a kind of 'ion curtain'—incoming missiles hit it, bam! they disintegrate; then, in that brief moment of invulnerability, we can just . . . *take care of things."*

AUDREY. That's barbaric!

TRENT. Ahhhh! Watch! No! Not at all! It's *defensive!* It's defensive because the Russians are working on the very same plan!

AUDREY. How do we know?

TRENT. Well, if *we* are, they *have* to be. Just in case *we* are. Which means *they* are—you see? Defensive! Again, a completely moral system. *(To* STONE*)* I *told* you this was fun! *(To* AUDREY*)* BUT! *(To* STONE*)* Here's the

best part. *(To* AUDREY*)* Here's the *twist!* Even *this* doesn't work. *(To them both)* Watch! Let's say this ion curtain has been built and Sears has it, we call up and order one. Two weeks for delivery, they say. Well, that's not so bad, so we say send it on. PROBLEM: Surely the Soviets know somebody who works for Sears. "Psst! Guess what the Americans have just ordered!" Well! The Soviets know what's in store for them if we get this thing. Which means they have got to preempt. Which means we must PRE-preempt! We're right back where we started! You cannot beat the system, not from within; it simply doesn't work, *cannot* work, not in ANY permutation! It's that goddamn Escher print. "Right!" he said. And I could see his eyes—they were on FIRE! I mean, this man was *excited!* I thought, Am I dreaming this? This makes no sense! *(Pause)* And a moment later he was gone, in the fog, by the bandstand.

(Long silence.)

AUDREY. Dear, there's something very *wrong* here, something . . . you have *missed,* I think, I couldn't . . . say, of course, just *what,* I'm not an expert, dear, but clearly somewhere in your research you've gone wrong, that's just obvious, because this just makes no sense, as you yourself have even pointed out. *(Pause)* I mean, the world you are describing, dear, this is not a world I know. Furthermore, it's not a world I *care* to know, that's the truth, dear, I don't want to know any more. I think I need some air . . . Perhaps a stroll across the field! It's such a lovely day. Not the sort of day one wants to spend inside! *(She smiles and goes to get her purse. She stops near* STONE. *Pause)* Mr. Stone, if you would be so kind as to help him. Show him where he's wrong. I don't think I can be much more help to him on this . . . Not right now. I need to think this through. *(She stares at* TRENT. *Pause)* Keep with it, dear. *(She walks out. Long pause)*

TRENT. Is this what you mean by doom? That no one will believe?

STONE. Not quite. *(He smiles ever so faintly. Then he rises and pours himself a glass of iced tea)*

TRENT. Look, Stone, I am stumped, all right? I am at the end! What the hell was The Shadow up to? And why have you picked me for this?

*(*STONE *stares at him. Pause.)*

STONE. Have you ever been to the South Pacific?

TRENT *(Puzzled).* No.

STONE. Remarkable place! Beautiful

beyond imagining! The imagination belittles its beauty. *(Pause)* Anyway, I was there in the early fifties. A close friend of mine was involved in our nuclear tests and asked if I'd like to go along on the viewing ship. It was not inappropriate for me to be there, for among my many financial interests at that time was a laboratory and development center. It was in Utah.

TRENT. . . . You make weapons?

STONE *(Slight smile)*. I used to. *(Pause)* In any event, there we were on this ship, this battleship, not too far from where the detonation was to take place, which was near an island known, interestingly enough, as Christmas Island. *(Smiles. Pause)* We'd been told the bomb was to be a small one, and so none of us was particularly worried. Even though I'd never seen one go off, I figured, well, these people must know what they are doing! *(Pause)* Actually, the truth is I was in a kind of funk! That's because I hadn't come all this way just to see a *little* bomb! This one was ten kilotons, smaller even than the bomb at Hiroshima! These bombs were classified as *tactical* weapons. These are weapons you would use in combat. And, quite frankly, I was disappointed. I wanted some BIG-time stuff, and I'm not ashamed to say it, either. There's a glitter to nuclear weapons. I had sensed it in others and *felt it in myself.* If you come to these things as a scientist, it is irresistible, to feel it's there in your hands, so to speak, the ability to release this energy that fuels the stars! . . . to make it do your bidding! to make it perform these miracles! to lift a million tons of rock into the sky. And all from a thimbleful of stuff. *Irresistible! (Pause)* Well, we were standing by the railing when the countdown came on, we could hear it over the P-A. We'd all been adequately briefed, and we were in suits, some kind of lead, tinted visors on our helmets. And then I saw these . . . *birds.* Albatrosses! Phenomenal creatures, truly! They'd been flying beside the ship for days, accompanying us to the site, so to speak. Watching them was a wonder! *(Pause. Then in a tone of great amazement)* And suddenly I could see that they were smoking. Their feathers were on fire! And they were doing cartwheels . . . The light persisted for some time. It was instantaneously bright, and lingered, long enough for me to see the birds crash into the water. *(ALEX has come in unobserved by the others, and stands to the side, listening)* They were sizzling.

Smoking! They were not vaporized, it's just that they were absorbing such intense radiation that they were being consumed by the heat! And so far there'd been no shock, none of the blast damage we talk about when we discuss the effects of these bombs. Instead, there were just these smoking, twisting, fantastically contorted birds crashing into things . . . And I could see vapor rising from the inner lagoon as the surface of the water was heated by the intense flash. *(Pause)* Well, I'd never seen anything like this in my life! . . . And I thought: *This is what it will be like at the end of time. (Pause)* And we all felt . . . the *thrill* of that idea. *(Long pause.* STONE *stares at* TRENT, *who stares back at him in horror)* This is your son, I believe. *(*TRENT *turns toward his son in horror.* ALEX *looks frightened)* I've never met the lad, though of course I heard you speak of him many years ago. I guess he must be . . . eleven now. *(*TRENT *turns toward* STONE. TRENT *seems stunned by this last remark. To* ALEX*)* I met your father shortly after you were born.

*(*TRENT *is reeling now. He stares from one to the other.)*

ALEX. Was that a movie you saw?

STONE. Just now? Describing? *(*ALEX *nods)* Yes. A movie. *(*ALEX *nods and leaves.* TRENT *stares out, stunned. The lights start to fade on everything but* TRENT*)* I think I'm going to have some more iced tea! *(He crosses to the pitcher and pours himself a glass of tea. Soon* STONE *is but a shape in the dark)*

(Light on TRENT.*)*

TRENT. Now I know where we met! . . . It was at *our* place, our apartment! We were living in the city then, and some friends came by to see our child, he'd just been born; obviously, one of them brought Stone— who? doesn't matter, Stone was there, I can see him, in a corner, *listening,* as I . . . tell. *(Pause)* But evil? *(Long pause)* Our son had just been born. We'd brought him home. He was what, five days old, I guess. *(Pause)* And then one day my wife went out . . . And I was left alone with him. And I was very excited. Because it was the first time I was alone with him. And I picked him up, this tiny thing, and started walking around the living room. We lived on a high floor, overlooking the river, the Hudson. Light was streaming in; it was a lovely, lilting autumn day, cool, beautiful. And I looked down at this tiny creature, this tiny thing, and I realized . . . *(Pause)* I realized I had never had anyone completely in my power before! ... And I'd never known what that *meant!* Never felt anything remotely like that before! And I saw I was standing near a window. And it was open. It was but a few feet away. And I thought: I could ... *drop him out!* And I went *toward* the window, because I couldn't believe this thought had come into my head—*where had it come from?* Not one part of me felt anything for this boy but love, not one part! My wife and I had planned, we were both in love, there was no anger, no resentment, nothing dark in me toward him at all, no one could ever have been more in love with his child than I, as much yes, but not more, not more, and I was thinking: I can throw him out of here! ... and then he will be falling ten, twelve, fifteen, twenty stories down, and as he's falling, I will be *unable to get him back!* ... And I felt a *thrill!* I FELT A THRILL! IT WAS THERE! ... And, of course, I resisted this. It wasn't hard to do, resisting wasn't hard ... BUT I DIDN'T STAY BY THE WINDOW! ... AND I CLOSED IT! I resisted by moving away, back into the room ... And I sat down with him. *(Pause)* Well, there's not a chance I would have done it, not a chance! *(Pause)* But I couldn't *take* a chance, it was very, very ... seductive. *(Pause. He looks at* STONE. *The lights come back a bit.* STONE *is sipping his tea, eyes on* TRENT*)* If doom comes ... it will come in *that* way.

STONE. I would think.

(Pause.)

TRENT. You want it to come, don't you!

STONE. What?

TRENT. Doom. You'd like to see it come!

STONE. No-no, of course not, that's ridiculous. *(He sips)* I just know that if it did, it would not be altogether without interest. I mean, it has its appeal, that's all I mean. It arouses my *curiosity. (Smiles)* But then, many things arouse my curiosity. Mustn't make too much of it. This is really good iced tea! My compliments to your wife. I think the secret is fresh mint, nothing like fresh mint; if you don't mind, I shall pick some from your garden when I leave. *(Pause)* I'm glad you've taken this job.

TRENT. Don't you understand, I can't write this play! Really, that's the truth, it is totally beyond me!

*(*STONE *puts his hands on* TRENT*'s shoulders.)*

STONE *(Warmly).* Work on it.

(He turns and starts out. At the rear of the room, by the window, he stops and looks out. Then he looks back at TRENT*.)*

(The lights go nearly to black on everything but TRENT *and the field outside the house. In this darkened room,* STONE *is but a shadowy presence. The curtains on the rear window flutter.* TRENT *stares out, lost in thought. Through the rear window,* ANN *can be seen strolling out across the bright field, hand in hand with* ALEX*.)*

Curtain

Hurlyburly

DAVID RABE

FOR ELLEN NEUWALD

Originally produced at the Goodman Theatre, Chicago, Gregory Mosher, Artistic Director, on April 2, 1984, with the following cast:

EDDIE	William Hurt
PHIL	Harvey Keitel
MICKEY	Christopher Walken
ARTIE	Jerry Stiller
DONNA	Cynthia Nixon
DARLENE	Sigourney Weaver
BONNIE	Judith Ivey

Directed by Mike Nichols
Scenery by Tony Walton
Costumes by Ann Roth
Lighting by Jennifer Tipton
Sound by Michael Schweppe
Production Stage Manager: Peter Lawrence.

The New York premiere of the play took place on June 21, 1984 at the Promenade Theatre presented by Icarus Productions and Frederick M. Zollo, with Ivan Bloch and ERB Productions and William P. Suter as Associate Producer. It opened with the same cast and designers as in Chicago and under the direction of Mike Nichols.

Hurlyburly premiered on Broadway in New York at the Ethel Barrymore Theatre on August 7, 1984, again presented by Icarus Productions and Frederick M. Zollo, with Ivan Bloch and ERB Productions and William P. Suter as Associate Producer. The cast and designers were the same as in the two previous presentations, except that the part of Mickey was played by Ron Silver instead of Christopher Walken, and the sound was by Otts Munderloh. The direction was again by Mike Nichols.

"The fact that I write a play with only the slightest premeditation regarding the intentions and implications, and then come ... with the process or rehearsal and study to an intense and extensive understanding of the completed play's subterranean nature and needs, and ... am then devoted to the expression of these themes with a fanatical ardor, is a continual experience of amazement for me" (David Rabe).

The word "hurlyburly" is defined as turbulence, commotion, and disorder. Rabe's original title for this play was *The Guys' Play*, but, the writer says, "One day while the play was in rehearsal, I was looking at a piece of prose ... in which the word 'hurlyburly' occurred. ... Then one morning, looking for justification for the title, I found it in the beginning of Shakespeare's *Macbeth*: 'When shall we three meet again? In thunder, lightning, or in rain? When the hurlyburly's done, when the battle's lost and won." Here, the word turns up in one of the protagonist's speeches, in a reference to "this vague hurlyburly, this spin-off of what was once prime-time life."

Hurlyburly is set in a house on the outskirts of Hollywood, shared by two divorced casting agents. Along with two other friends, they are caught up in a whirlwind of cocaine and liquor, abusing one another and the three women in their lives. In trying to control these women, the men resort to cruelty, vicious verbal games, and phony compassion. Unable to establish any real intimacy, they are desperate to anesthetize their pain with sex and drugs. *Hurlyburly* shows us the "Hollywood dream" turned into a nightmare world of failed male bonding, betrayal, and violence, themes also explored in Rabe's Vietnam trilogy, *The Basic Training of Pavlo Hummel, Sticks and Bones,* and *Streamers.*

Hurlyburly was originally produced at Chicago's Goodman Theatre in April 1984. Its New York premiere took place two months later at the Promenade Theatre, from which the play moved to Broadway's Ethel Barrymore Theatre in August 1984. It was also staged in Australia in 1986 and in Sweden in 1987. The play was inspired by Rabe's own experience as a Hollywood screenwriter. "I set it there because it was my last spasm in the bachelor world. ... It's about guys being thrown back in a second adolescence. ... You're frozen in a certain way and it starts to take a particular toll. It's like suspended animation ... a kind of rigidity that takes over and that will ultimately be lifeless. ..."

David Rabe was born in 1940 in Dubuque, Iowa. His father taught high school history until he found that he could earn more money as a meat packer, and his mother worked at a JCPenney department store. In his youth, Rabe's father had written a novel, *The Killing Time*, which Rabe later revised. Rabe's early ambition was to become a professional football player (he is still an avid sports fan and plays rugby). After attending Roman Catholic parochial schools, Rabe went to Loras College, a Catholic institution in Dubuque, where he began to write short stories and plays.

Upon graduation, Rabe went to Villanova University for a master's degree in theatre, but he eventually dropped out of the program, working at odd jobs while trying to establish himself as a writer. In 1965, he was drafted and served two years in the army, eleven months of that time in South Vietnam, as a hospital support worker. When he returned home, he found himself estranged from his family and friends, who, he felt, did not understand what he had lived through. Rabe tried to return to Vietnam as a war correspondent, but when his efforts proved unsuccessful he returned to Villanova to complete his master's. A former professor arranged to have the balance of an uncompleted Rockefeller Grant given to Rabe, and with it he wrote, almost simultaneously, *The Basic Training of Pavlo Hummel* and *Sticks and Bones,* in which he poured out his bitter memories of the war and its aftermath. He also took a job in 1969 with the *New Haven Register* in Connecticut, where a series of his articles earned him an Associated Press Award in 1970.

Joseph Papp produced *Pavlo Hummel* at the New York Shakespeare Festival's Public Theater in May 1971; it won an Obie Award, a Drama Guild Award, and a Drama Desk Award. Six months later, Papp produced *Sticks and Bones,* making Rabe the first playwright to have two plays running simultaneously at the Public. *Sticks and Bones* transferred to Broadway's Golden Theatre in March 1972; it won the Tony Award, a Drama Critics Circle Special Citation, and the Hull-Warriner Award. *The Orphan* (1973) and *Streamers* (1976) followed, the latter winning the New York Drama Critics Circle Award.

"If I'd never gone to war, I might be playing football. The war was the triggering device that forced me to write. . . . I go through a thing in [my] plays where the play shocks me. I don't think I've ever written anything where there wasn't a moment when I said, 'Oh, I don't want to write this' or 'Is that me? Where's it coming from?' *Hurlyburly* was like that—I had a note for about six years. It was literally three or four lines. Then I got kicked into starting and . . . stayed on it for three or four months to write the first draft. . . ."

David Rabe has also written the following plays: *In the Boom Boom Room* (1973), *Frankie* (1973), *Burning* (1974), *Goose and Tomtom* (1982), and *Those the River Keeps* (1990). His screenplays include *In the Boom Boom Room, The Basic Training of Pavlo Hummel, Prince of the City* (adaptation), *I'm Dancing As Fast As I Can* (adaptation), *First Blood* (adaptation), *Just Married, Streamers, It Gave Somebody Something to Do* (adaptation), *Casualties of War,* and *Sticks and Bones.*

CHARACTERS

EDDIE   DARLENE
PHIL   BONNIE
MICKEY   DONNA
ARTIE

ACT ONE

SCENE ONE

TIME: A little while ago.

PLACE: A two-story house crowded into one of the canyons between Sunset Boulevard and Mulholland Drive in the Hollywood Hills.

A spacious living room leading into an open kitchen make up the entire first floor of the house. Steps lead upstairs to an exposed balcony which overlooks the living room. A rail runs along the balcony and stairway. Three doors feed onto the balcony—Eddie's bedroom and Mickey's bedroom, which are separated by a bathroom. Stage right there is a couch and a low coffee table with a portable television on top of it and piles of newspapers and magazines on the couch and the floor around it. Directly upstage and yet slightly off center is the door to the outside. Along this wall there is perhaps a closet door with a mirror inside of it. Slightly right of center stage is an armchair angled toward the couch. A hassock sits beside it. Upstage of the couch is a window seat, the outdoor foliage visible beyond it; books, photos, résumés are scattered on the window seat. At the far stage left is a pile of throw pillows; and if the closet door and mirror are inappropriate along the back wall, perhaps they are in this wall. The kitchen area is a nook, with a counter running out downstage and swivel chairs on either side. Upstage are the stove, refrigerator, cabinets. The nook itself has shelves in which there are liquor bottles, magazines, scripts.
The house is completely surrounded by wild vegetation, which is visible through greenhouse-like windows in the living room and kitchen. At the far right is an old rocking chair. It is worth noting that in the characters' speeches phrases such as "whatchamacallit," "thingamajig," "blah-blah-blah" and "rapateta" abound. These are phrases used by the characters to keep themselves talking and should be said unhesitatingly with the authority and conviction with which one would have in fact said the missing word.
As the curtain rises, Eddie is asleep on the couch.

The TV on the coffee table in front of the couch is droning out the early morning news. Eddie is a mess, his shirt out, wrinkled, unbuttoned, his trousers remaining on him only because one leg is yet tangled around one ankle. He lies with his head downstage, and as the door opens and Phil, a muscular, anxious man in a hurry comes rushing in, Eddie instantly sits straight up and appears to be looking right at Phil. ———

PHIL. Eddie.

EDDIE. What? *(EDDIE flops back onto the couch as if he has just been hit on the head.)*

PHIL. Eddie, you awake or not?

EDDIE. I don't know. How about you?

PHIL. Eddie, I'm standin' here. How you doin'?

EDDIE. I don't know. Did I leave the door open?

PHIL. It was open.

EDDIE *(Sitting up, a man in command, and talking, almost bragging, as he turns off the TV).* I come home last night, I was feelin' depressed. I sat around, I watched some TV. Somebody called and hung up when I answered. I smoked some dope, took a couple of ludes. The TV got to look very good. It was a bunch of shit, but it looked very good due to the dope and due to the ludes. So I musta fell asleep at some point. *(As nodding a little, it appears he might sleep again.)*

PHIL *(Heading for the kitchen).* Maybe I'll make us some coffee. Where is everything? By the stove and stuff?

EDDIE. What time is it?

PHIL *(Holding up his left wrist and watch, he yells).* I can't tell you what time it is: my watch was broken by the blow.

EDDIE. There's a clock on the stove.

PHIL. It's over.

EDDIE. What?

PHIL. Everything.

EDDIE *(Rising, staggering toward the kitchen, his trousers dragging along by the ankle).* What EVERYTHING?

PHIL. Me and Susie.

EDDIE. Whata you mean, "everything"?

PHIL. Everything. The whole thing. You know. Our relationship. I really fucked up this time. I really did. *(Sitting on a swivel chair,* EDDIE *reaches around the counter to soak a towel in the sink.* PHIL *is filling the coffee pot.)*

EDDIE. You had a fight. So what? Give her a little time and call her up, you know that. Don't be so goddamn negative.

PHIL. This was a big one.

EDDIE. Bigger than the last one?

PHIL. Yeah.

EDDIE. So what'd you do, shoot her? *(He covers his face with the wet towel. Silence, as PHIL is putting the coffee into the filter for the coffee machine. EDDIE peeks out from behind the towel.)* You didn't shoot her, Phil. You got a gun?

PHIL. On me?

EDDIE. You didn't shoot her, Phil.

PHIL. No.

EDDIE *(He puts the towel back over his face, pressing it against his eyes).* So, she'll take you back. She always takes you back.

PHIL. Not this time.

EDDIE *(Bursting out from behind the towel, he begins rummaging around the counter for aspirin, which he finds).* What happened?

PHIL. I went too far. She ain't going to take me back.

EDDIE. You want me to call her?

PHIL. She'll give you the fucking business. She hates you.

EDDIE. Whata you mean, she hates me?

PHIL. She hates you.

EDDIE. What are you talking about, she hates me? Susie don't hate me. She likes me.

PHIL. She hates you; she told me.

EDDIE. She hates me? How can she hate me?

PHIL. She hates you. She tol' me. In the middle of the fight.

EDDIE *(His head killing him, takes some aspirin).* What are you talking about: you two are in the middle of this bloodbath—the goddamn climactic go-round of your seven-year career in, you know what I mean, marital carnage and somewhere in the peak of this motherfucker she takes time out to tell you she hates good ol' Eddie. Am I supposed to believe that?

PHIL. I was surprised too. I thought she liked you.

EDDIE. You're serious.

PHIL. Yeah.

EDDIE. So fuck her. What a whore. She hates me. Are you serious? This is unacceptable goddamn behavior.

PHIL. She's unbelievable.

EDDIE *(Rising, he is kicking at his slacks, stepping on them to get them off, and starting toward the stairs and the bathroom).* This is unbelievable. I mean, what is she, a goddamn schizophrenic, here? Is this a goddamn psychotic we've been dealing with here? I mean, isn't she always friendly with me? You have seen this, right? I mean, I'm not a goddamn imbe-

cile to have thought she liked me. She acted like she liked me.

PHIL *(Following after EDDIE).* I thought she liked me.

EDDIE *(As they climb the stairs together).* I thought she liked you, too. I mean, she don't like anybody, is that the situation, the pathetic bitch?

PHIL. I knew she hated Artie.

EDDIE. I knew she hated Artie, too. *(He goes into the bathroom.)* But Artie's an obnoxious, anal obsessive pain in the ass who could make his best friend hire crazed, unhappy people with criminal tendencies to cut off his legs, which we have both personally threatened to do. So she hates a guy who, though we both love him, we both personally know it is somewhat in spite of him that we love him. So that proves nothing. *(There is the sound of the toilet flushing and then EDDIE, carrying a pair of jogging shorts, steps back into the hallway.)* I mean, what the hell does she think gives her justification to hate me?

PHIL. She didn't say.

EDDIE. She didn't say?

PHIL. No. *(He goes into the bathroom.)*

EDDIE *(Pulling on the jogging shorts).* She gave no rhyme nor reason? She just—you gotta help me picture this—she what? In the middle of some goddamn retort, or was it out of the blue?

PHIL. Whata you mean?

EDDIE. I mean, did she have a point of reference, some sort of reference from within your blowup out of which she made some goddamn association which was for her justification that she come veering off to dump all this unbelievable vituperative horseshit over me—whatever it was. I wanna get it straight. *(Toilet is flushed, and PHIL comes out of the bathroom.)*

PHIL. You got some weed? I need some weed. *(Followed by PHIL, EDDIE heads down the stairs to the kitchen counter where he pulls from a shelf his drug box and, opening it, takes out a rolled joint.)*

EDDIE. I got great weed. You wanna toke up?

PHIL. I need somethin'.

EDDIE *(Handing a joint to PHIL).* You just help me out, all right; I got to get this straight.

PHIL. I'm tryin', Eddie. You know that.

EDDIE *(As PHIL inhales, trying to remember, EDDIE sits PHIL down on the swivel chair outside the counter).* So what'd she say about me? You know, think back. So the two of you are hurling insults and she's a bitch, blah, blah, blah, you're a bastard, rapateta. *(Moving to serve coffee to* PHIL.*)* So in the midst of this TUMULT where do I come in?

PHIL *(Remembering suddenly)*. You're just like me, she says.

EDDIE. What? *(At the coffee, he freezes midgesture.)* We're alike? She said that?

PHIL. Yeah—we were both whatever it was she was calling me at the time.

EDDIE. I mean, that's sad. She's sad. They're all sad. They're all fucking crazy. What is she thinking about?

PHIL. I don't know.

EDDIE. What do you think she's thinking about?

PHIL. We're friends. You know. So she thinks we got somethin' in common. It's logical.

EDDIE. But we're friends on the basis of what, Phil? On the basis of opposites, right? We're totally dissimilar is the basis of our friendship, right?

PHIL. Of course.

EDDIE. I mean, I been her friend longer than I been yours. What does she think, that I've been—what? More sympathetic to you than her in these goddamn disputes you two have? If that's what she thought she should have had the guts to tell me, confront me!

PHIL. I don't think that's what she thought.

EDDIE. SO WHAT WAS IT?

PHIL. I don't know. I don't think she thinks.

EDDIE *(Settling onto the swivel chair opposite* PHIL*)*. None of them think. I don't know what they do.

PHIL. They don't think.

EDDIE. They calculate. They manipulate. So what's she up to? They express their feelings. I mean, my feelings are hurt, too.

PHIL *(Growing frenzied)*. Mine, too.

EDDIE. They're all nuts.

PHIL *(And more frenzied)*. I pity them, I fuckin' pity them. She makes me crazy. I ain't gonna see her any more.

EDDIE. This is terrible on a certain level. I mean, I liked you two together.

PHIL *(Agitated, starting to pace away from* EDDIE*)*. I know. Me, too. A lot of people did. I'm very upset. Let me have some more weed. *(Reaching back he grabs the joint from* EDDIE, *then immediately paces on, roaming the living room.)* It was terrible. It was somethin'. Blah-blah-blah!

EDDIE. Rapateta. Hey, absolutely.

PHIL. Blah-blah-blah! You know, I come home in the middle 'a the night—she was out initially with her girlfriends, so naturally I was alone and went out too. So I come home, I'm ripped, I was on a tear, but I'm harmless, except I'm on a talking jag, you know, who cares? She could have some sympathy for the fact that I'm ripped, she could take that into consideration, let me run my mouth a little, I'll fall asleep, where's the problem? That's what you would do for me, right?

EDDIE. Yeah.

PHIL *(Rushing to* EDDIE *to hand him the joint)*. She can't do that.

EDDIE. What's she do? What the hell's the matter with her, she can't do that?

PHIL. I'm on a tear, see, I got a theory how to take Las Vegas and turn it upside down like it's a little rich kid and shake all the money out of its pockets, right?

EDDIE. Yeah. So what was it?

PHIL. It was bullshit, Eddie. *(Sitting back down opposite* EDDIE.*)* I was demented and totally ranting, so to that extent she was right to pay me no attention, seriously, but she should of faked it. But she not only sleeps, she snores. So I gotta wake her up, because, you know, the most important thing to me is that, in addition to this Las Vegas scam, I have this theory on the Far East, you know; it's a kind of vision of Global Politics, how to effect a real actual balance of power. She keeps interrupting me. You know, I'm losing my train of thought everytime she interrupts me. It's a complex fucking idea, so I'm asking her to just have some consideration until I get the whole thing expressed, then she wants to have a counterattack, I couldn't be more ready.

EDDIE. She won't do that?

PHIL. No.

EDDIE. That's totally uncalled for, Phil. All you're asking for is civilization, right? You talk and she talks. That's civilization, right? You take turns!

PHIL. I don't think I'm asking for anything unusual, but I don't get it.

EDDIE. Perverse.

PHIL. Perverse is what she wrote the book on it. I am finally going totally crazy. *(Jumping back up on his feet.)* I've totally lost track of my ideas. I'm like lookin' into this hole in which was my ideas. I arrive thinkin' I can take Vegas and save the world. Forty-five seconds with her and I don't know what I'm talking about. So I tell her—"LISTEN!—

lemme think a second, I gotta pick up the threads." She says some totally irrelevant but degrading shit about my idea and starts some nitpicking with which she obviously intends to undermine my whole fucking Far Eastern theory on the balance of powers, and I'm sayin', "Wait a minute," but she won't. So WHACK! I whack her one in the face. Down she goes.

EDDIE. You whacked her.

PHIL. I whacked her good. You see my hand. *(Moving to* EDDIE, PHIL *holds out his hand.)*

EDDIE *(Rising to look at* PHIL*'s hand).* You did that to your hand?

PHIL. Her fuckin' tooth, see.

EDDIE *(Teasing* PHIL *a little).* You were having this political discussion with which she disagreed, so you whacked her out, is that right?

PHIL. It wasn't the politics. I didn't say it was the politics.

EDDIE. What was it? You were ripped?

PHIL. Yeah. But it wasn't that. I don't know what it was. *(*PHIL *sits down on the couch, starts to play with a toy, a magic cube sitting on the table.)*

EDDIE. What was it? *(Moving to sit beside* PHIL*.)*

PHIL. I don't know. I had this idea and then it was gone.

EDDIE *(Eager).* Yeah.

PHIL. It was just this disgusting cloud like fucking with me and I went crazy.

EDDIE *(Delighted).* Right. Whata you mean?

PHIL. You know this fog, and I was in it and it was talking to me with her face on it. Right in front of me was like this cloud with her face on it, but it wasn't just her, but this cloud saying all these mean things about my ideas and everything about me, so I was like shit and this cloud knew it. There was no way out. I couldn't get my thoughts together. They were all over the place. And once they were all over the place they weren't anything any more. That was when it happened.

EDDIE. You whacked her.

PHIL. Yeah.

EDDIE. Was she all right?

PHIL. She was scared, and I was scared. I don't know if I was yelling I would kill her or she was yelling she was going to kill me.

EDDIE. Somebody was threatening somebody, though.

PHIL. Definitely.

EDDIE *(Rising, he paces in a meditative, investigative manner across the room for more coffee).* So

try and remember how was it before you whacked her or after you whacked her that she made her reference to me?

PHIL. You mean that she hated you?

EDDIE. Yeah.

PHIL. Before. It was in the vicinity of Vegas, I think, but it gets blurry.

EDDIE. So what musta happened is she decided I had some connection to your Vegas scam and this was for her justification to dump all this back-stabbing hostility all over me.

PHIL. She didn't say that. She just says we're both assholes.

EDDIE. But it would be logical that if this petty, cheap-shot animosity was in the vicinity of Vegas, it would have to do with Vegas. THAT WOULD ONLY BE LOGICAL.

PHIL. EXCEPT SHE AIN'T LOGICAL.

EDDIE. True.

PHIL. SHE'S JUST A NASTY BITCH AND I MARRIED HER.

EDDIE. You know what I think?

PHIL. What?

EDDIE. She hates men.

PHIL *(Crossing toward* EDDIE, *very interested).* Whata you mean?

EDDIE. She hates you, she hates me. She hates men. I don't know what else to think. It's a goddamn syllogism. Susie hates Phil, Susie hates Eddie. She hates men.

PHIL. And Artie, too.

EDDIE. Artie, Eddie, Phil are men, she hates men. The fucker's irrefutable, except that's not how it works, GODDAMNIT.

PHIL. What?

EDDIE. You go from the general to the particular. I'm talking about a syllogism, here.

PHIL. Yeah.

EDDIE *(Irritated, storming off, he slumps into the big armchair, the better to think).* Damnit! What the hell goes the other way?

PHIL. Which way?

EDDIE. Something goes the other goddamn way!

PHIL. What?

EDDIE. You start from the particular in something. Susie hates Eddie, Susie hates Phil. Phil and Eddie are men, therefore, blah, blah, blah.... Oh, my god, do you know what it is?

PHIL. What?

EDDIE. Science! What goes the other way is science, in which you see all the shit like data and go from it to the law. This is even better. We have just verified, and I mean scientifically, the bitch has been proven to basically hate all men. She doesn't need a reason to hate me in particular—she already hates me in the fucking abstract.

PHIL. You gonna call her?

EDDIE. You want me to?

PHIL. You said you were gonna!

EDDIE. That was before I understood the situation. Now that I understand the situation, the hell with her. The bitch wants to go around hating me in the fucking abstract! Are you nuts? Call her? I wouldn't piss on her if the flames were about to engulf her goddamn, you know, central nervous system! *(As* MICKEY *staggers out of his bedroom onto the balcony,* PHIL *grabs up a bottle of bourbon from the counter.)*

PHIL. I am going to hole up here and ossify myself.

EDDIE. I MEAN, WHERE THE HELL DOES SHE GET OFF? *(It is important to note that there is an element of play in this whole scene between* PHIL *and* EDDIE*: on some level it is a game, a riff and that* EDDIE *tends to adopt* PHIL*'s mannerisms when alone with him.)*

MICKEY. Didn't I beg you to let me have some goddamn quiet this morning? Eddie, I begged you!

EDDIE *(Runs to the base of the stairs, yelling up).* Phil has left Susie again, only this time it's final!

MICKEY. So what are YOU screaming about?

PHIL *(Following after* EDDIE*).* The deceitful bitch has been badmouthing Eddie. That's been part of the problem from the beginning.

EDDIE. Her attitude has been deceitful and degrading!

MICKEY. So when did this happen?

PHIL. It's been goin' on.

MICKEY. It'll blow over. *(*MICKEY *goes reeling into the bathroom.)*

EDDIE. No!

PHIL. I don't think so.

EDDIE *(Having a fit at the base of the stairs, yet there is a note of sheer delight in it).* I mean, she thinks she can do this shit and get away with it? He goes back, he's nuts. He deserves her. You go back this time, Phil, I'm never gonna speak to you again.

PHIL. I know that. I agree with you.

MICKEY *(Coming out of the bathroom).* He's not serious, Phil.

EDDIE. Whata you know about it?

MICKEY. You're serious, if Phil goes back to his wife, you don't ever want to speak to him

again? *(Descending the stairs,* MICKEY *is all but attacked by* EDDIE*.)*

EDDIE. I'm serious. *(As* MICKEY *moves to the kitchen,* EDDIE *and* PHIL *follow him, both yelling at* MICKEY *and one another, an element of fun between them that they are tormenting* MICKEY *with their noise and craziness when he has just awoken.)*

MICKEY. That's not serious.

EDDIE. Says you! I know when I'm serious and I'm serious, and Phil knows it even if you don't.

PHIL. I hate her anyway!

EDDIE. See! And you'd know it, too, if you were my goddamn friend like you think you are.

PHIL. I'm done with her!

EDDIE *(Grabbing his box of cocaine and other drugs from its shelf under the breakfast nook counter).* See!

MICKEY. You guys are in a fucking frenzy here. Have some breakfast, why don't you? Eat an orange, why don't you? Calm you down. We need some fruit in this house. Where's the fruit? *(As* MICKEY *looks in the refrigerator,* EDDIE *has handed a vial of coke to* PHIL *and has spread a line for himself on the countertop.* PHIL *hovers beside* EDDIE*.)* Where's the food? We need some food in this house. Eddie, where's all the food? *(Seeing* EDDIE *preparing to snort some cocaine.)* What are you doing?

EDDIE. What's it look like I'm doin'?

MICKEY. It looks like—What does it look like? It looks like you are doin' a line of coke on the kitchen counter here at eight forty-five in the morning.

EDDIE. Very good. *(*EDDIE *and* PHIL *snort coke and exchange glances and pokes throughout this, clearly a conspiracy against* MICKEY*; almost like two bad little boys with a baby-sitter they don't much respect.)*

MICKEY. What are you becoming, a coke fiend, Eddie?

EDDIE. How'm I gonna wake up? I gotta wake up!

MICKEY. Some people have coffee.

EDDIE. The caffeine is fucking poison, don't you know that?

MICKEY. Right. So what is this, Bolivian health food? Some people risk it with coffee to wake up in the morning, rather than this shit which can make you totally chemically insane. Don't you watch the six o'clock news?

EDDIE. I watch all the news.

MICKEY *(Looking under the counter, he finds a package of English muffins containing two muffins which he waves with a flourish).* Bread. I found some fucking bread. All right, we can have some muffins for breakfast. We can have some mouldy muffins along with our Bolivian Blow for breakfast. How long have I slept? Last time I saw you, you were a relatively standard everyday alcoholic Yahoo, Eddie. Now the bread's mouldy and you're sniffin' around the goddamn breakfast nook like a wart hog.

EDDIE. I had a rough night. Whata you want from me?

MICKEY. You should go to bed. (MICKEY *is cutting a muffin, putting butter and jelly on it.*)

EDDIE. How'm I going to get to bed?

MICKEY. I don't know. Most people manage it. I don't know. Is this an outrageous suggestion, that he should get to bed? He's down here half the night, Phil, crashing around and talking to the TV like a goddamn maniac. Want half a dead English muffin, Phil? (*Offering jellied muffins on a plate to* PHIL, *who looks at* EDDIE, *and* MICKEY *shifts the plate toward* EDDIE.) Eddie?

EDDIE (*Clearly snubbing* MICKEY, EDDIE *turns to* PHIL, *who is spooning coke from the vial*). I gotta wake up. (*As* PHIL *puts the coke to one of* EDDIE's *nostrils.*) I got a lot of work today. (PHIL *puts coke to* EDDIE's *other nostril and* EDDIE *snorts, then grabs* PHIL's *face between his hands.*) The shit that went down here last night was conspiratorial. It was unbelievable. (EDDIE *walks toward the front door,* PHIL *following along.*) I mean, first of all the eleven o'clock news has just devastated me with this shitload of horror in which it sounds like not only are we headed for nuclear devastation if not by the Russians then by some goddamn primitive bunch of middle-eastern motherfuckers— (*Opening the front door, he reaches out and picks up several newspapers, glancing at them as he talks to* PHIL. MICKEY, *abandoned in the kitchen nook, eats the muffins.*) —and I don't mean that racially but just culturally, because they are so far back in the forest in some part of their goddamn mental sophistication, they are likely to drop the bomb just to see the light and hear the big noise. I mean, I am talking not innate ability, but sophistication here. They have got to get off the camels and wake up! (*Handing the newspapers to* PHIL, EDDIE *starts up the stairs.*) So on top of this, there's this accidental electrical fire in which an entire family is incinerated, the father trying to save everybody by hurling them out the window, but he's on the sixth floor, so he's, you know—they're like eggs on the sidewalk. So

much for heroics. (*Having paused partway up the stairs, he now pivots to hasten up the remainder.*) So then my wife calls! You wanna have some absurdity?

PHIL. I thought you was divorced.

EDDIE. I am.

PHIL. You said, "wife."

EDDIE (*Pausing on the balcony to look down*). Why would I do that? I hate my ex-wife. I might have said "mother" instead of "ex-wife," but not "wife."

PHIL. Why would you do THAT?

EDDIE (*Playfully exasperated*). Because I could have made a Freudian slip!

PHIL. You don't believe in that shit, do you?

EDDIE. Whata you know about it?

PHIL. Somethin'. I know somethin'. I was in prison.

EDDIE (*Going into his room*). Mickey, what'd I say?

MICKEY. I wasn't listening.

PHIL (*With all the newspapers, he sits on the arm of the couch and yells up at* EDDIE's *door*). I mean, how would that shit work? You'd have WHAT?—all that stuff from your neighborhood like chasing you?

MICKEY. You mean like from your background.

PHIL. You believe in that Freudian shit, Mickey?

MICKEY. What Freudian shit?

PHIL. You know. All those books!

MICKEY. No.

PHIL. Me neither. (*Crossing to join* MICKEY.) I mean, how would that work? What? Ghosts?

MICKEY. It wouldn't.

PHIL. So assholes pay all this money, right. (*As* EDDIE, *having come out of his room, buttoning a clean shirt but still wearing the jogging shorts, is descending the stairs.*) It's unbelievable; and it don't work.

MICKEY. Eddie's done it.

PHIL. You done it, Eddie?

EDDIE (*Taking a newspaper from* PHIL). What?

PHIL. What we're talkin' about here. You were just talkin' about it, too!

MICKEY. Freud.

EDDIE (*As he settles in the armchair to read*). Right. One of the real prestige guys of blow. A pioneer. (*And opening the paper, he closes the conversation.*)

MICKEY. So, Phil, you left your wife. I liked your wife.

PHIL. You can have her. *(Rising, he moves off to the couch carrying what's left of the newspapers.)*

MICKEY. Don't kid yourself. You find anybody whatsoever with her when you go back, let alone me, of whom your affection is borderline to say the least, you'll kill them.

PHIL. I ain't going back.

MICKEY. So your personal life's a shambles, how's your career?

PHIL. I'm up for some very interesting parts at the moment, and on several of them—my agent says on this new cop show for NBC, my agent says I'm a lock, that's how close I am. I been back six times; the director and I have hit it off. It's very exciting.

MICKEY. Who's the director?

PHIL. He's this terrific Thomas Leighton.

EDDIE *(Quite exasperated)*. This is the Thomas Leighton thing? *(It is clearly a topic he put time and energy in trying to make clear for* PHIL.*)* He's a scumbag, I tol' you, Phil. He's a scumbag faggot who likes to jerk tough guys like you around. He'll bring you back a hundred times, you'll get nothing.

PHIL *(A little distressed that* EDDIE *is saying these things in front of* MICKEY*)*. My agent says he likes me, and it's between me and this other guy who is taller, and that the only problem is when they cast the lead, if he's a different physical type than me, then I'll have a very good shot.

EDDIE. The leads are always a different physical type than you, Phil. This is America. This is TV.

PHIL *(Leaping to his feet, he bolts for the door)*. What are you tryin' to discourage me for?

EDDIE *(Rushing to stop* PHIL *from leaving)*. I'm not trying to discourage you.

MICKEY *(Easing toward the stairs)*. This is Eddie's particular talent—to effortlessly discourage people.

EDDIE *(His hand on* PHIL, *he almost follows* MICKEY *up the stairs so urgent is his point)*. If Phil wants to obliquely pick my brain about our area of expertise here, Mickey, am I supposed to pretend that you and I are not casting directors or I haven't noticed the whys and wherefores of how the thing happens in this town? I mean, right, Phil?

PHIL *(A little like a kid on a street corner, he hangs around one of the balcony support beams)*. I mean, Eddie, I trust that you are not deliberately trying to discourage me, but in all honesty, I gotta tell you, I'm feelin' very discouraged.

EDDIE *(Genuinely wanting to impart sincere and friendly wisdom to* PHIL*)*. No, no. Look, you have to exploit your marketable human qualities, that's all. You have certain qualities and you have to exploit them. I mean, basically we all know the M.O. out here is they take an interesting story, right? They distort it, right? Cut whatever little truth there might be in it out on the basis of it's unappealing, but leave the surface so it looks familiar—cars, hats, trucks, trees. So, they got their scam, but to push it they have to flesh it out, so this is where you come in, because then they need a lot of authentic sounding and looking people—high-quality people such as yourself, who need a buck. So like every other whore in this town, myself included, you have to learn to lend your little dab of whatever truth you can scrounge up in yourself to this total, this systematic sham—so that the fucking viewer will be exonerated from ever having to confront directly the fact that he is spending his life face to face with total shit. So that's all I'm sayin'. "Check with me," is all I'm sayin'. Forget about this Leighton thing. *(Together, they have ended up back by the couch and TV.)*

PHIL. Forget about it? I got nothin' else to do. What about the things you're currently working on? Anything for me?

MICKEY *(Descending the steps, dressed for work, and carrying a handful of résumés and photographs)*. Nothing.

PHIL. Who asked you? *(MICKEY settles down on the window seat to sort the résumés.)*

EDDIE. There's a thing down the road a month or so, it might be a good thing for you. *(He crosses to the breakfast nook counter where scripts are piled on shelves.)*

PHIL. What is it?

EDDIE. It's a special or a pilot, they haven't decided. *(Picking a joint from an ashtray on the counter, he prepares to light up.)*

PHIL. But there might be somethin' in it for me. You got a script? *(He strides over and takes the script that* EDDIE *is pulling from the pile.)*

EDDIE. This is shit, though. I don't wanna hear about the quality, because this is total shit. *(He inhales the joint.)*

MICKEY. Don't get fucked up, Eddie. We got that meeting with the guy.

EDDIE. So maybe you could handle things alone this morning? Whataya think?

MICKEY. I think they're expecting both of us, that's what I think.

PHIL *(Leaning against the wall, he has been leafing through the script)*. This is shit, huh?

EDDIE. Total.

PHIL. But there might be somethin' in it for me?

EDDIE. Yeah. *(PHIL, grabbing his coat, starts off. EDDIE jumps after him, fearful PHIL's feelings have been hurt again.)* Where you goin'?

PHIL *(Indicating the stairs).* I'm going to read it. And also, I'm beat. I'm really beat. It's been one exhausting thing I went through. I'm gonna pass out in your room, Eddie, okay?

EDDIE *(As PHIL is going up the stairs).* We'll do something later. *(EDDIE takes a huge toke on the joint.)*

MICKEY. Do you realize, Eddie, that you are now toking up at eight fifty-eight in the morning on top of the shit you already put up your nose? You're going to show up at work looking like you got a radish for a nose. You're going to show up talking like a fish.

EDDIE. Don't worry about it, okay?

MICKEY. Is that supposed to fuck me up? *(MICKEY moves from the window seat to the couch where he sits.)*

EDDIE. You don't have to worry about me, Mickey.

MICKEY. What kind of tone is that?

EDDIE. What do you mean, what kind of tone is that? That's my tone.

MICKEY. So what does it mean?

EDDIE. My tone? What does my tone mean? I don't have to interpret my fucking tone to you, Mickey. I don't know what it means. What do you think it means?

MICKEY. Just don't get clandestine on me, Eddie; that's all I'm saying.

EDDIE. But there are not a lot of dynamite ladies around anywhere you look, Mickey, as we both know, and I am the one who met Darlene first. I am the one who brought her by, and it was obvious right from the get-go that Darlene was a dynamite lady, this was a very special lady.

MICKEY. We hit it off, Eddie, you know. I asked you.

EDDIE *(All ease and smiles, he seems to be only after clarity).* Absolutely. Look, I'm not claiming any reprehensible behavior on anybody's part, but don't ask me not to have my feelings hurt, okay. I'm not saying anything went on behind my back or I was deceived or anything. Nevertheless, the situation has had an effect on me. I mean, we are all sophisticated people, and Darlene and I most certainly had no exclusive commitment of any kind whatsoever to each other, blah-blah-blah.

MICKEY *(Moving to the kitchen to get some coffee, he is relieved at their agreement).* That's exactly what I'm saying. Rapateta.

EDDIE. There's no confusion here, Mickey, but have a little empathy for crissake. *(MICKEY nods, for "empathy" is certainly something he can afford to give.)* I bring this very special lady to my house to meet my roommate, my best friend, and I haven't been interested in a woman for years, seriously, I have this horror show of a marriage in my background, and everybody knows it, so blah-blah-blah, they have THIS ATTRACTION to each other. *(Seeing now that EDDIE is after more than "empathy," MICKEY pretends exasperation and bows his head to the counter in mock self-abasement.)* My roommate and my new girl—I'm just trying to tell the story here, Mickey; nobody's to blame. *(Patting MICKEY on the back.)* Certainly not you. I mean, you came to me, you had experienced these vibes between yourself and Darlene— isn't that what you said?—I mean, you correct me if I'm wrong—but would I mind, you wondered, if you and Darlene had dinner in order to, you know, determine the nature of these vibes, or would that bother me? That's a fair—I mean, reasonable representation of what you asked.

MICKEY *(Moving out with his coffee toward the armchair, he addresses invisible masses—his voice, of course, slightly self-mocking, not totally, by any means, serious).* I just—I mean, from my point of view, the point is—the main point is, I asked.

EDDIE. I know this.

MICKEY. That—in my opinion—is the paramount issue, the crucial issue. And I don't want it forgotten.

EDDIE *(Though charming, he is not without an ominous note in his tone and smile).* Nothing from yesterday is forgotten, Mickey. You don't have to worry about that.

MICKEY. Why do we have to go through this? I just wanna have some breakfast. I mean, couldn't you have said, "no"? Couldn't you have categorically, definitively said "no" when I asked? But you said—"Everybody's free, Mickey." That's what you said.

EDDIE. Everybody is free.

MICKEY. So what's this then?

EDDIE. This? You mean this? This conversation?

MICKEY. Yeah.

EDDIE. This is JUST ME trying to maintain a, you know, viable relationship with reality. I'm just trying to make certain I haven't drifted off into some, you know, solitary paranoid fantasy system of my own, totally unfounded and idiosyncratic invention. I'm just trying to stay in reality, Mickey, that's all. Don't you want me to be in reality? I personally want us both to be in reality.

MICKEY. Absolutely. That's what I want. *(And* MICKEY *almost rushes to the chair opposite* EDDIE *at the counter, as if with this move he will end the conversation on this note.)* I mean, I want us both to be in reality. Absolutely.

EDDIE *(Very reassuring).* So that's what's going on here, you know, blah-blah-blah. Don't take it personally.

MICKEY *(Very affirmative).* Blah-blah-blah!

EDDIE. So I was just wondering. You came in this morning at something like six-oh-two, so your dinner must have been quite successful. These vibes must have been serious. I mean, sustaining, right?

MICKEY. Right. Yeah. You know.

EDDIE. Or does it mean—and I'm just trying to get the facts straight here, Mickey—does it mean you fucked her?

MICKEY. Darlene?

EDDIE. Right.

MICKEY. Darlene? Did I fuck Darlene? Last night? Eddie, hey, I asked you. I thought we were clear on this thing.

EDDIE. We're almost clear.

MICKEY *(With a take-charge manner, as if he has at last figured out what it is that* EDDIE *wants).* What I mean, Eddie is, THINGS HAPPEN, but if this bothers you, I mean, if this bothers you, I don't have to see her again. This is not worth our friendship, Eddie; you know that.

EDDIE *(Recoiling in a mockery of shock, yet not without a real threat).* Wait a minute. You're not saying that you took my new girl, my very special dynamite girl out and fucked her on a whim, I mean, a fling and it meant nothing!? You're not saying that?

MICKEY. No, no, no.

EDDIE. I mean, these vibes were serious, right? These vibes were the beginnings of something very serious, right? They were the first, faint, you know, things of a serious relationship, right?

MICKEY. Hey, whatever.

EDDIE *(Munching the remnants of one of the muffins, he is quite happy).* I mean, I don't want to interfere with any possibilities for happiness in your life, Mickey.

MICKEY. Believe me, this is not a possibility for happiness in my life.

EDDIE. Well, it was in mine. It was such a possibility in mine.

MICKEY. I think you just have it maybe all out of proportion here, Eddie.

EDDIE. Yeah? So do me a breakdown.

MICKEY. I just think maybe she's not as dynamite as you might think. *(*MICKEY*'s remark nearly catapults* EDDIE *across the room.)*

EDDIE. Fuck you!

MICKEY. You always go a little crazy about women, Eddie.

EDDIE. You wanna let it alone, Mickey.

MICKEY. It's not a totally, you know, eccentric thing to happen to a guy, so don't get fucking defensive.

EDDIE. I mean, there's nothing here that necessitates any sort of underground smear campaign against Darlene.

MICKEY. No, no, no. I just want you to think about the possibility that things have gotten a little distorted, that's all.

EDDIE. No.

MICKEY. You won't think about it?

EDDIE. I mean, bad-mouthing her just to get yourself off the hook—don't think you can do that.

MICKEY. Never.

EDDIE. It's not that I DON'T understand—it's that I DO understand. It's just that I'm not so fucking sophisticated as to be totally beyond this entire thing, you see what I'm saying, Mickey. Blah-blah-blah—my heart is broken—blah-blah-blah. *(He flops down on the couch, as if he might go back to sleep.)*

MICKEY. Blah—blah—blah. Absolutely. So you want me to toast you what's left of the muffin? We can put some raisins on it—be a sort of Danish. Somebody's got to go shopping.

EDDIE. You think we couldn't handle a dog around here?

MICKEY. I wouldn't want to be a fucking dog around here. Dogs need stability.

EDDIE. I like dogs.

MICKEY *(As he goes into the kitchen to start cleaning up the mess there).* You could borrow Artie's dog.

EDDIE. I hate Artie's dog. It looks like a rat; it doesn't look like a dog. I like big dogs.

MICKEY. So did you get any sleep at all?

EDDIE. Fucking Agnes had to call. Why does she have to call?

MICKEY. Why do you talk to her is the real question?

EDDIE. I have to talk to her. We have a kid.

MICKEY. That's a thought to turn the

mind to pure jello—you or any man daring to get that close to Agnes. Are you sure you did it?

EDDIE. Only with a borrowed cock.

MICKEY. I mean, you might as well put your balls in her teeth as pick up the phone.

EDDIE. Because she thinks she's smarter than me; she thinks I'm afraid of her and that I agree with her assessment of what went wrong between us.

MICKEY *(Quite superior)*. But every time you talk to her, you end up in this total, this absolute nonproductive shit-fit over what she said, or meant, or might have been implying, and in the process deliver her conclusive proof of what for her is already irrefutable—namely that you're a mess. *(As ARTIE and DONNA come in the front door.)* And then you go crazy for days!

EDDIE. What do you want me to do, abandon my kid in her hands and with no other hope? Forget about it! *(He is turning over as if to hide his head or go to sleep, so he doesn't see ARTIE or DONNA.)*

(ARTIE is about ten years older than EDDIE and MICKEY. He is slick in appearance, dressed very California; a mix of toughness and arrogance, a cunning desperation; he carries a shoulder satchel or briefcase. With him is DONNA; blonde, about fifteen. Carrying a Walkman Tape Player, she has earphones on. Under her arm she has a record album which she will carry everywhere. She wears tattered shorts, a T-shirt, a buckskin jacket, and beat-up cowboy boots. Seeing ARTIE, MICKEY addresses him as if he's been standing there for years.)

MICKEY. Artie, so what's the haps, here?

ARTIE. You guys in the middle of something, or what?

MICKEY. You didn't tell us you got married.

ARTIE. Her? I found her on the elevator.

DONNA. Where's the bathroom?

EDDIE. What kind of accent is that? What kind of accent you got?

DONNA. I'm from the Midwest, so that's it.

ARTIE *(To MICKEY)*. You want her?

MICKEY. Whata you mean?

ARTIE. It's too crowded, see?

DONNA. Artie, they got a bathroom?

ARTIE. Sure they got a bathroom.

EDDIE *(From the couch)*. What's she want with our bathroom, Artie? Is this a goddamn coke fiend you brought with you here?

DONNA. I gotta go.

EDDIE. Where?

DONNA. I gotta go to the bathroom.

ARTIE. This is Eddie.

DONNA. Hi, you got a bathroom?

EDDIE. It's upstairs.

DONNA. Great.

MICKEY *(As DONNA hurries up the stairs)*. I'm Mickey. It's the first door.

DONNA. Great, Mickey. I'm Donna. *(She goes into the bathroom, shutting the door.)*

MICKEY. Cute, Artie, very cute.

ARTIE *(To MICKEY)*. You want her?

EDDIE. You keep sayin' that, Artie.

ARTIE *(As if irritated at her)*. She was on the goddamn elevator. In the hotel. I'm going out for coffee in the morning, I take the elevator, there she is.

MICKEY *(Moving to get ARTIE some coffee)*. You want coffee. We got coffee, muffins, coke and raisins.

ARTIE *(Glancing at his watch, he settles into the swivel chair in front of the counter)*. It's too early for breakfast, but I'll have some coffee. This was yesterday. So I come back from coffee, she's in the elevator. It's an hour. So that's a coincidence. Then I'm going out for dinner. Right? This is seven—eight hours later. She's in the elevator.

MICKEY. She's livin' in the elevator.

ARTIE. Yeah, so after dinner, there she is. So I ask her: Is she livin' in the elevator? She says her boyfriend tried to kill her, so she's stayin' off the street.

MICKEY *(Handing ARTIE the coffee, MICKEY stands behind the counter, leaning on it toward ARTIE)*. Why'd he want to kill her?

ARTIE. She says he was moody. So, I took her in. But I figured, I don't need her, you know, like you guys need her. You guys are a bunch of desperate guys. You're very desperate guys, right? You can use her. So I figured on my way to the studio, I'd drop her by, you can keep her. Like a CARE package, you know. So you can't say I never gave you nothing.

EDDIE *(From the couch)*. You're giving her to us?

ARTIE. Yeah.

EDDIE. What are we going to do with her?

ARTIE. What do you want to do with her?

EDDIE. Where's she from?

MICKEY *(As if EDDIE is an imbecile)*. What has that got to do with anything?

EDDIE. I wanna know.

MICKEY. Somewhere in the Middle West. I heard her.

EDDIE. That could be anywhere.

MICKEY. So what?

EDDIE *(Crossing toward them to get coffee)*. I'm

just trying to figure out what we're going to do with her. You wanna pay attention.

ARTIE *(Intervening on* MICKEY*'s behalf)*. What do you want, Eddie, an instruction manual? This is a perfectly viable piece of ass I have brought you, and you're acting totally like WHAT? What's going on here? Are we in sync or not?

EDDIE. Like she'll be a pet, is that what you're saying, Artie?

ARTIE. Right.

MICKEY *(Patting* ARTIE, *his arm ending up around* ARTIE*)*. Right.

ARTIE. You can keep her around. *(*ARTIE *and* MICKEY *exchange a look with which to patronize* EDDIE*.)*

EDDIE. She'll be like this pet we can keep and fuck her if we want to?

ARTIE. Sure. Just to stay in practice. In case you run into a woman.

EDDIE. I guess he hasn't heard about Darlene. *(It is as if the name, "*DARLENE*" is a punch from which* MICKEY *reels.)* I guess you haven't heard about Darlene, Artie.

ARTIE. No. Is this important?

EDDIE. Mickey has gotten involved with this truly dynamite bitch in a very serious relationship.

MICKEY. Bullshit. *(Rising,* MICKEY *escapes across the room to the window seat where he sits down, picking up a* Variety*.)*

ARTIE. Is this true, Mickey? Is this the same Darlene, Eddie? You had a Darlene.

EDDIE *(Leaning across the counter to* ARTIE*)*. What I'm inferring here, Artie, is that Mickey is unlikely to be interested in this bimbo you have brought by for fear of, you know, contaminating his feelings and catching some vile disease in addition.

ARTIE. So when did this happen, Mickey? You guys switched, or what? I miss everything. So you're in a serious relationship, Mickey. That's terrific.

MICKEY. Except I ain't serious about anything, Artie, you know that. *(As* DONNA *comes out of the bathroom and down the stairs, her shoes clumping loudly.)*

EDDIE. You wanna live with us for a while, Donna?

DONNA *(Pausing at the base of the stairs to look at* EDDIE*)*. Hmmmmmmmmmmmmmm?

ARTIE *(He crosses toward her, as* MICKEY *comes up behind her)*. Okay, I gotta go. All she has to do for me is go down to the hotel twice a day and walk my dog.

MICKEY *(Arm around her)*. Right. *(As he blows*

the word in her ear, DONNA *yelps and scurries several steps away.)*

EDDIE. What if she runs away?

ARTIE. What do you want from me, Eddie, a guarantee? *(Draping an arm over her shoulder,* ARTIE *slides a hand under her shirt and fiddles with her breast.)* I can't guarantee her. She worked last time I used her. You want a guarantee, talk to the manufacturer. I'm not the manufacturer.

EDDIE *(Settling down on the swivel chair and picking up the phone)*. You're the retailer.

ARTIE. Frankly, from the look of you, what I am is a goddamn charity organization having some compassion on some pathetic fuck who is you, that's what I am. *(After all,* EDDIE *sits there still in his jogging shorts, and his partially buttoned shirt.)* I'm having some generosity toward the heartbreaking desperation I encounter here every time I come by and have to look at you. You don't mind if I have a little mercy.

EDDIE. So where you goin'? You goin' to the studio?

ARTIE. I said that.

EDDIE. You didn't say what for.

ARTIE. You didn't ask what for. I got a meeting.

EDDIE. You know what happens to you doesn't happen to normal people.

ARTIE. I did good deeds in an earlier lifetime. How do I know?

EDDIE. Yeah, but being a highly developed bullshit artist does not normally translate into this kind of situation.

ARTIE. He's a blocked writer, and my stories about my life unblock him. You know, it was his idea, and secretly, I always dreamed of it.

EDDIE. Dreamed of what?

ARTIE *(Advancing on* EDDIE, *he leaves* DONNA*)*. Having an interesting life and a capacity to relate some of it does not constitute a criminal offense against you personally, Eddie.

EDDIE. Hey, you're misinterpreting my whole slant here; forget about it.

ARTIE. I intend to forget about it.

EDDIE. You're an ungrateful prick, Artie.

ARTIE *(In a state of total delight, he pats* EDDIE*'s cheek)*. I'm desperate. *(And he starts for the door.)*

EDDIE. Just keep me informed. I want to be of help. You got a deal, right?

ARTIE *(The door open, his hand on the knob, he stops, and, looking back, he is very happy, very confident, almost grand: He will, it seems, soon own the entire town of Hollywood).* Things look VERY good. They look VERY good. You know, who can tell in this town?

EDDIE. Did they write the check? If they wrote the check, you got a deal.

ARTIE. So they didn't.

EDDIE. Then you don't.

ARTIE. YET. They didn't YET.

EDDIE. Then you don't YET. If they didn't YET, you don't YET.

ARTIE. But we're close. We're very close.

EDDIE. The game in this town is not horseshoes, Artie.

ARTIE *(Rushing back to EDDIE to make his point).* How come you're being such a prick to me?

EDDIE. Envy!

ARTIE. I didn't think you knew.

EDDIE. Of course I know. What do you think, I don't know what I'm feeling?

ARTIE. It happens.

EDDIE. Everything happens. *(Standing up, the phone still in his hand.)* But what I'm after here, I mean ultimately, is for your own good, for your clarity. You lose your clarity in this town next thing you know you're waking up in the middle of the night on the beach with dogs pissing on you, you think you're on vacation. You panic in this town, Artie, they can smell it in your sweat.

ARTIE. Who's gonna panic? I been learning these incredible, fantastic relaxation techniques.

EDDIE *(Sitting back down, he begins dialing the phone).* Who's the producer you're most often in the room with?

ARTIE. Simon! He's got a distribution deal now with Universal.

MICKEY. What relaxation techniques?

ARTIE. They are these ones that are fantastic, Mickey, in as much as you can do them under the table, you're in some goddamn meeting, you just tense your feet and—

EDDIE. HERB Simon? HERB Simon? Is this who we're talking about? *(He slams down the phone.)*

ARTIE. What about him?

EDDIE *(Standing, EDDIE leans toward ARTIE like a fighter in his corner).* This is the guy you're dealing with? This guy's a known snake. I got the right guy, Artie. Herb Simon.

ARTIE. Yeh. Universal.

EDDIE. THIS GUY'S AN ANACONDA. HE'S A KNOWN ANACONDA.

ARTIE *(Shrugging, he's heard everything).* I heard that.

EDDIE. I mean, you gotta make this guy pay you if you say "Hello" to him, right? You're not crossing the street free for this guy, are you?

ARTIE. We gotta do a treatment.

EDDIE. No!

ARTIE. It's nothin'. He's a major guy. I don't want to piss him off.

EDDIE. These fucking snakes are sharks out here, Artie, you know that.

MICKEY. He's right, Artie.

ARTIE. We have hit it off, Mickey. He likes me.

MICKEY. Good.

EDDIE. If it's true, it's good.

ARTIE. Fuck you. The guy is at this juncture where he's sick of himself; he's looking for some kind of fucking turnaround into decency.

EDDIE. You base this opinion on what, Artie, your desperate desire to succeed?

ARTIE. Something happened and I saw it, goddamnit.

MICKEY. So what happened?

ARTIE. It was the other day after lunch.

EDDIE. Who paid?

ARTIE *(Snapping at EDDIE, snarling).* He did. He paid. *(And then back to MICKEY, developing a manner of high confidence, his story that of an amazing and rare intimacy with a creature of almost royal importance.)* So we're crossing the street. You know, he gets this terrible pain in his stomach. I mean, his stomach made a noise and he doubles over like this. It's a noise like a gorilla could have made it. And he's over like this and he's paralyzed. We're all paralyzed in the middle of the street. So we get across the street. I'm asking him, is he okay. Maybe the food was bad. "No," he says. "Maybe," I says. "No. It's all the lies I tell," he says. He looks me in the eye and says, "It's this town and all the lies it makes me tell," See? He tol' me that.

MICKEY. Herb Simon said that?

ARTIE. Yeah!

EDDIE. So?

ARTIE *(Moving in righteous anger at EDDIE).* So, he was straight with me, you cynical prick.

EDDIE. So, what's the point? This fucking snake tells you he lies a lot, so you figure you can trust him? That's not clear, Artie. Wake up! This guy is legendary among snakes. He is permanently enshrined in the reptilian hall of Hollywood fucking fame, this guy. You don't wake up, they are going to eat you alive. As an appetizer! You won't even be the main course. They're just going to whet their appetites on what is to you your entire motherfucking existence.

ARTIE *(Caught, his words are light little chunks of fury).* You're making me nervous.

EDDIE. I'm trying to make you nervous. Don't you know a ploy when you see one?

ARTIE. I considered whether it was a ploy, and I come down on the side of I would trust him a little.

EDDIE. Why trust him at all?

ARTIE. I gotta work with him.

EDDIE. You're not telling me you can't work with somebody you don't trust.

ARTIE. No.

EDDIE. I'm not saying, "Don't work with him!" I'm saying, "Don't trust him!"

ARTIE. I'll talk to him! *(Looking at his watch,* ARTIE *panics and starts scurrying around, gathering his things.)*

EDDIE. Get some money! Get some bucks!

ARTIE. For crissake, I'm gonna be late with this bullshit you put me through, Eddie. What do you do this to me for? He's gonna be pissed at me, goddamnit! *(He rushes out the door.)*

DONNA. Bye, Artie.

EDDIE. You think I was too hard on him?

MICKEY. No.

EDDIE. You gotta be hard on him, right?— he's a hard-head himself.

MICKEY *(On the move toward* DONNA*).* So how is Goldilocks doing here? You had any breakfast? *(His fingers are in her hair.)*

EDDIE *(Heading for the refrigerator).* You want a beer?

DONNA *(Rising, she moves toward the counter).* Sure.

EDDIE *(At the refrigerator).* Where'd you say you were from?

MICKEY *(Lighting a joint, he follows along after her).* She said Midwest. I remember. Isn't that what you said?

DONNA. Yeah.

MICKEY. See

EDDIE *(Handing her a beer).* So you came out here to get into the movies?

DONNA. We were hitchhiking.

MICKEY. Where to?

DONNA. The Grand Canyon.

EDDIE. It's not in L.A.

DONNA. I just kept going.

MICKEY. So you were in Artie's elevator? *(Having drawn the smoke in, he puts his mouth on* DONNA*'s and blows the smoke into her.)*

DONNA. It wasn't his. Can I turn on the TV?

EDDIE *(Imitating her accent).* Sure. *(DONNA goes scurrying to the TV, which she turns on and sits in front of.)* So if Artie hadn't invited you off the elevator, would you still be on it?!

DONNA. I saw some interesting things I was on it!

MICKEY *(Yelling over the loud volume of the TV).* Like what?! *(He crosses to sit beside her on the couch.)*

DONNA *(Yelling).* Different people!

EDDIE *(Yelling).* This was interesting! *(EDDIE crosses to stand leaning against the side of the armchair facing the couch.)*

DONNA *(Yelling).* You could hear their conversation! Some were about their rooms and the hotel carpeting, or the pictures in the hall! There was sometimes desperation you couldn't get a handle on it! They talked about their clothes! *(MICKEY, reaching forward, turns off the volume of the TV.)*

MICKEY. So you evidently would have starved to death mesmerized by the spellbinding panorama on this elevator, it wasn't for Artie.

DONNA. I'da got off to eat. That's crazy. It was nice of Artie nevertheless to take a chance on me and everything. He's been just, you know, fantastic. *(Again* MICKEY *puts his mouth to* DONNA*'s and blows the smoke into her, and then he pulls back.)* Except it is boring how he sits sometimes at the table, he's got these pencils, and he doesn't say anything to you. *(Moving to the floor,* MICKEY *pulls her boot off, and her sock. She quickly grabs up her boot, clutching it.)* And he's got this paper, and I couldn't watch any TV except with the sound off because the noises would bother his train of thought. It was interesting for a while to watch TV in silence like old-time movies, except you didn't have a clue. *(When* MICKEY *goes to work on her second boot, pulling it off, she grabs it from him, trying to interest him in her points about TV.)* You know, how they would put those words up every now and then in old-time movies so you could sort of hang on to the direction things were taking. And they acted like deaf people talking. Well, on TV there was none of these advantages, so I had to work up my own story a lot. *(As* MICKEY *is reaching up to unbuckle the waist of her shorts, she leaps to her feet.)* Did he say what time I should walk his dog? *(MICKEY grabs her arm to tug her back onto the couch while* EDDIE *moves to take from her the record she carries.)*

EDDIE. What's this?

DONNA. It's just my favorite record for very particular reasons.

EDDIE. Willie Nelson sings "Stardust," "Unchained Melody," "All of Me"?

DONNA. Nobody ever agrees with me, people just scream at me.

MICKEY. What?

DONNA *(As she talks,* MICKEY, *his arm around her, nuzzles her).* My friends, when I argue with them, they just scream at me, but it's these really terrific old songs sung by this new guy, right, Willie Nelson, only he's an old guy, and they're all like these big-city songs like Chicago or New York, right, Sinatra kind of songs, only Willie, who they are sung by, is this cowboy, so it's like this cowboy on the plains singing to his cows, and the mountains are there but it's still the deep, dark city streets, so it's like the mountains and the big sky are this nightclub in the night and this old cowboy, this old, old cowboy under a street light in the middle of the mountains is singing something old and modern, and it's everything, see. You wanna hear it?

EDDIE. No.

MICKEY. Sure. *(He kisses* DONNA, *his hand moving to unbuckle her shorts as* EDDIE'*s bedroom door opens and* PHIL *steps out, hair tousled, shirt off.)*

PHIL. Anybody got any valium around here, Eddie?

EDDIE. Look at this. Artie brought her by.

PHIL. Where's Artie?

MICKEY. He's gone.

PHIL. Artie was here?

EDDIE. Yeah.

PHIL. Who's this?

EDDIE. He brought her by for us. Like a CARE package. *(Reaching,* EDDIE *takes* DONNA *by the arm and lifts her from* MICKEY.)

PHIL. Yeah? Whata you mean?

EDDIE. Not for Mickey, though.

MICKEY *(Certain it's a joke).* Get off my back, you—

EDDIE *(Arms around* DONNA*).* This is for Phil and me because we don't have any serious relationships. This is a CARE package. Didn't you hear him? This is a CARE package for people without serious relationships.

MICKEY. You prick.

DONNA. What're you guys talking about?

EDDIE. Fucking you.

DONNA. Oh.

EDDIE. Phil and me, but not Mickey because he has a serious relationship. He has to preserve it.

DONNA. You gotta work at it, Mickey.

PHIL. You're sayin' seriously this is includin' me?

EDDIE. So we'll go upstairs, okay, Donna?

DONNA *(A little stoned and scared).* Okay. *(She carries her boots and record as she and* EDDIE *head for the stairs.)*

PHIL. He can't, but I can?

EDDIE. Yeah.

MICKEY. You sonofabitch. *(MICKEY is about to follow* EDDIE *and* DONNA *up the stairs.)*

EDDIE *(Whirling at the base of the stairs to face* MICKEY*).* Don't you even think about it. Right, Phil?

MICKEY. I'll—*(Looking up,* MICKEY *meets* PHIL*'s eyes.)* You jerk-off, Eddie! You jerk-off! I'll get her sometime you're not around.

EDDIE *(Bounding up the stairs).* I can only do so much for you, Mickey. That'll be on your conscience.

MICKEY. Give me a break.

EDDIE *(Looking down on* MICKEY*).* This is for your own good.

PHIL *(Joining* EDDIE*).* I got here just in time.

EDDIE *(To* MICKEY*).* You'll thank me later! *(And whirling,* EDDIE *follows* DONNA *into his room.)*

MICKEY. You're nuts, Eddie; you're fucking nuts!

PHIL. So this is the bachelor life!

(PHIL goes into the bedroom, slamming the door, and the MUSIC STARTS: Willie Nelson singing "All of Me" as MICKEY *stands, looking up for a beat, and the music plays.)*

Blackout
The music continues.

SCENE TWO

TIME: Evening of the same day.

The music, Willie Nelson, singing "All of Me" continues. DARLENE, *beautiful and fashionable, is seated on one of the swivel chairs at the breakfast nook counter. Photography equipment is on the floor beside the chair. She is examining a contact sheet of photographs as the lights come up, and then the door opens and* EDDIE *comes in dressed for work, carrying several scripts and a* New York Times, *which he is reading as he walks, so he doesn't see* DARLENE.. *The music goes out.*

DARLENE. Hi.

EDDIE *(Though he is startled, we would never know it).* Hi, Darlene. Mickey around?

DARLENE. I'm supposed to meet him. Is it okay?

EDDIE. Sure. What?

DARLENE. I was going to wait outside.

EDDIE *(Heading for the refrigerator for a beer, he is all smiles).* What? Are you crazy? No, no, no. Sit down. How you doing? You look good.

DARLENE. It's a facade.

EDDIE. What isn't? That's what I meant, you know. I wasn't saying anything more. That's what I was saying. It's a terrifically successful facade. *(He sits in the swivel chair opposite her.)* So, how's life in the world of photojournalism, Darlene?

DARLENE. Can I have a beer, too? I just feel . . . wow . . . you know?

EDDIE. What?

DARLENE. Weird, weird, weird.

EDDIE. I mean, you're not giving this whole situation a second thought, are you?

DARLENE. I certainly am. I . . .

EDDIE. No, no, no.

DARLENE. What situation? What do you mean? Do you—

EDDIE. Us. Mickey, you, me. Us.

DARLENE. Of course I am. That's what I thought you meant.

EDDIE. Don't be crazy.

DARLENE. Well, I have my mad side, you know. I have my feelings.

EDDIE. I don't mean "mad" by "crazy." I mean, "mad" has a kind of grandeur about it. I mean more like "silly." Is that what I mean?

DARLENE. Well, if you don't know, maybe you should stop talking till you figure it out and not go around just spewing out all this incomprehensible whatever it is you're saying and you know, hurting a person's feelings. That might have some value.

EDDIE. I opted for spontaneity, you know.

DARLENE. Well, sure. I'm just saying, "strike a balance."

EDDIE. Is that what you were saying?

DARLENE. Yes. That's right. What did you think I was saying?

EDDIE. I mean, we've all had our feelings hurt. That's the one thing this situation has given us all in common, I would say. I would hope you're not trying to construct some unique, you know, strictly personal interpretation of things on that basis.

DARLENE. What are you getting at?

EDDIE. I'm not exactly certain.

DARLENE. Well . . . are you exactly uncertain?

EDDIE. Possibly.

DARLENE. Where's Mickey?

EDDIE. I haven't checked. Is he late?

DARLENE. This is a perfect example of what could drive a person right off the wall about you. I mean, you are totally off the wall sometimes.

EDDIE. In what way? Everybody has their flaws, Darlene.

DARLENE *(Rising, she roots around in her camera case).* This total way you exaggerate this enchantment you have with uncertainty— the way you just prolong it and expect us all to think we ought to try and live in it and it's meaningful. It's shit.

EDDIE. This bothers you.

DARLENE. It bothers everyone.

EDDIE. No, it bothers you. And don't think this is a surprise. I am well aware of how what might to another person appear as honesty, but to you, it's—

DARLENE. Some other person such as who?

EDDIE. You want a list?

DARLENE. I want an answer. And a beer.

EDDIE. The beer is in the refrigerator. *(She storms past* EDDIE *who lifts his knees up to his chest to make room for her as she rushes to the refrigerator.)* And the answer, if you want it from me, is coming along the lines I am speaking it, which is the only way it can come, since it's my answer, and if it is to come at all, it—

DARLENE *(Charging past him with her beer).* I don't have time. I mean, your thoughts are a goddamn caravan trekking the desert, and then they finally arrive and they are these senseless, you know, beasts, you know, of burden. Okay? So just forget about it.

EDDIE. You asked me a question.

DARLENE *(Pacing away from him).* I also asked you to forget about it.

EDDIE. But I don't want to forget about it.

DARLENE. I made a mistake.

EDDIE *(Rising).* But you don't deny you asked it.

DARLENE. Eddie, you look like a man with a hammer in his hand.

EDDIE. So what? And I don't. Or are you a liar on top of everything else? You asked me a question!

DARLENE. All right!

EDDIE. Some sensitivity is the quality a person might have. Sure, I can come up with all the bullshit anytime—some clearcut diagnosis totally without a solid, actual leg to stand on but presented with all the necessary postures and tones of voice full of conviction and all the necessary accessories and back-up systems of control and sincerity to lend total credibility to what is total bullshit; but I chose instead, and choose quite frequently, to admit it if I don't know what I'm talking about; or if I'm confused about what I'm feeling, I admit it. But this is too much of SOMETHING for you—I don't know what—so at least we found out in time. That's some good luck.

DARLENE. Liar on top of WHAT ELSE?

EDDIE. Whata you mean?

DARLENE. You said, "liar on top of everything else."

EDDIE. I did?

DARLENE. Just a minute ago.

EDDIE. What was I talking about?

DARLENE. Me.

EDDIE. I did? No. What'd I say? *(The front door opens, and* MICKEY, *carrying a bag of groceries, comes in directly behind* DARLENE.*)*

DARLENE. "LIAR ON TOP OF EVERYTHING ELSE!"

MICKEY. Hi.

DARLENE. Hi.

MICKEY. How you doing?

EDDIE *(Heading for the armchair, where he sits, picking up the newspaper)*. Great. You?

MICKEY *(Moving to the kitchen, he sets the bag down on the counter, taking out beers)*. Terrific. Anybody need a beer?

EDDIE. No.

DARLENE. Sure. *(*MICKEY *pops open a beer for her and then moves to start up the stairs where he abruptly halts.)*

MICKEY. You know what I'm going to do? I'm going to venture a thought that I might regret down the road. And anticipating that regret makes me, you know, hesitate. In the second of hesitation, I get a good look at the real feeling that it is, this regret—a kind of inner blackmail that shows me even further down the road where I would end up having to live with myself as a smaller person, a man less generous to his friends than I would care to be. *(Slowly, carefully, he descends the stairs.)* So, you know, we'll have to put this through a multiprocessing here, but I was outside, I mean, for a while; and what I heard in here was—I mean, it really was passion. Sure, it was a squabble, and anybody could have heard that, but what I heard was more. We all know—everybody knows I'm basically on a goof right now. I'm going back to my wife

and kids sooner or later—I don't hide that fact from anybody. And what I really think is that fact was crucial to the development of this whole thing because it made me WHAT? Safe. A viable diversion from what might have actually been a genuine, meaningful, and to that same extent and maybe even more so—threatening—connection between you two. I'm not going to pretend I wasn't up for it, too—but I was never anything but above board. You know—a couple jokes, nice dinner, that's my style. Good wine, we gotta spend the night—and I don't mean to be crass—because the point is maybe we have been made fools of here by our own sophistication, and what am I protecting by not saying something about it, my vanity? Ego? Who needs it? So, I'm out in the yard and I'm thinking, "Here is this terrific guy, this dynamite lady, and they are obviously, definitely hooked up on some powerful, idiosyncratic channel, so what am I doing in the middle?" Am I totally off base here, Eddie, or what? *(He ends huddling with* EDDIE, *who is in the armchair, while* DARLENE *is seated on the swivel chair behind* MICKEY.*)*

EDDIE. You're—I mean, obviously you're not TOTALLY. You know that.

MICKEY. That's exactly what I'm saying.

EDDIE. I mean, from my end of it.

MICKEY. For my own well-being, I don't want to serve as the instrument of some neurotic, triangular bullshit being created here between you two. That's the main issue for me. I mean, from my point of view.

EDDIE. Right.

DARLENE *(Leaning forward, trying to insert herself into their attention)*. I mean, I certainly haven't felt right—I mean, good about it, that's—

MICKEY *(Whirling toward her)*. Everything went so fast.

DARLENE. Everything just happened.

MICKEY. You met him, you met me.

DARLENE. I met Eddie, and then Eddie, you know, introduces me to you.

EDDIE. It's too fast.

DARLENE. It was fast.

MICKEY *(He strides about between them)*. Just—What is this, the electronic age? Sure. But we're people, not computers; the whole program cannot be just reprogrammed without some resolution of the initial, you know, thing that started everything. So I'm going to—I don't know what—but go. Somewhere. Out. And you two can just see where it takes you. Go with the flow. I mean, you guys should see yourselves.

DARLENE. I'm just—I mean, I don't—weird, weird, weird.

MICKEY *(Patting* DARLENE*'s hand).* In all honesty, Darlene, you told me this is what you wanted in more ways than I cared to pay attention to. *(Backing for the door, he looks at* EDDIE.*)* And you, you prick, you were obviously madly in love. *(To* DARLENE.*)* Go easy on him. I'll catch you all later.

EDDIE. Down the road.

DARLENE. Bye.

MICKEY. Just remember, Darlene, you made the wrong choice. *(*MICKEY *goes.)*

EDDIE *(Pacing toward the door as if in awe of* MICKEY*).* Where the hell did he come up with the . . . I mean, clarity to do that?

DARLENE. That wasn't clarity.

EDDIE *(Turning toward* DARLENE, *he perches on the couch arm).* No, no, I mean, it wasn't clarity. But he had to HAVE clarity.

DARLENE. I don't know what it was. Generosity?

EDDIE. Whatever it was, you don't see it very often. I don't expect that from Mickey, I mean, that kind of thing.

DARLENE. Who expects that from anybody? We're all so all over the place.

EDDIE. Self-absorbed.

DARLENE. And distracted. I'm distracted by everything. I mean, I'm almost always distracted, aren't you?

EDDIE. Absolutely.

DARLENE. Everything is always distracting me from everything else.

EDDIE. Everything is very distracting, but what I've really noticed is that mainly, the thing I'm most distracted by is myself. I mean, I'm my own major distraction, trying to get it together, to get my head together, my act together.

DARLENE. Our little minds just buzzzzzzzz! What do they think they're doing?

EDDIE. However Mickey managed to get through it, though, I know one thing—I'm glad he did.

DARLENE. Are you really?

EDDIE. I really missed you. It was amazing. That was probably it—he got his clue from the fact that I never shut up about you. I think I was driving him crazy. How do you feel?

DARLENE. Great. I think I was, you know, into some form of obsession about you, too, some form of mental loop. I feel scared is what I feel. Good, too. I feel good, but mainly scared.

EDDIE. I'm scared.

DARLENE. I mean, a year ago, I was a basket case. If we had met a year ago, I wouldn't have had a prayer.

EDDIE. Me, too. A year ago, I was nuts. And I still have all kinds of things to think through. Stuff coming up, I have to think it through.

DARLENE. Me, too.

EDDIE. And by thinking, I don't mean just some ethereal mental thing either, but being with people is part of it, being with you is part of the thinking, that's how I'm doing the thinking, but I just have to go slow, there's a lot of scar tissue.

DARLENE. There's no rush, Eddie.

EDDIE. I don't want to rush.

DARLENE. I don't want to rush.

EDDIE. I can't rush. I'll panic. If I rush, I'll panic.

DARLENE. We'll just have to keep our hearts open, as best we can.

EDDIE. No pressure.

DARLENE. And no guilt, okay?

EDDIE. No guilt.

DARLENE. We don't want any guilt. I mean, I'm going to be out of town a lot. We both have our lives.

EDDIE. We just have to keep our options open.

DARLENE. And our hearts, okay?

EDDIE. I mean, the right attitude. . . .

DARLENE. Exactly. If we have the right attitude. . . .

EDDIE. Attitude is so important. And by attitude I don't mean just attitude either, but I mean real emotional space.

DARLENE. We both need space.

EDDIE. And time. We have to have time.

DARLENE. Right. So we can just take the time to allow the emotional space for things to grow and work themselves out.

EDDIE. So you wanna go fuck?

(They kiss and the MUSIC STARTS: Willie Nelson singing "Someone to Watch Over Me.")

Blackout

Note: It might be that as the scene progresses, they end up on the couch, undressing each other as they conduct their negotiations; or perhaps it is more strictly a negotiation with distance between them. Or perhaps it is a combination so that each time there is a sense of the negotiations being completed so that physical contact can begin—an embrace, a kiss—some bit of outstanding business is then remembered, and one or the other moves away.

SCENE THREE

TIME: Late Afternoon of the next day.

The music, Willie Nelson singing "Someone to Watch Over Me" continues. DONNA, *moving to the music, crosses, carrying a beer, and turns on the TV, the volume loud. She flops down on the couch, picking up a magazine, while the music and TV are both playing. The door opens and* PHIL *comes in looking disheveled, in a hurry. He starts talking almost immediately, clearly thinking* EDDIE *is around. He carries two six-packs of beer and a grocery bag containing meat and bread for sandwiches and two huge bags of popcorn. In his pocket is a pint of bourbon in a paper bag from which he sips every now and then.*

PHIL. So this broad is always here, you know what I mean? What is she, a chair? What are you, a goddamn chair? You sit around here and you would let anybody do anything to you, wouldn't you? Whatsamatter with you? Don't you have any self-respect? You're all alike. She is!

DONNA. Who you talkin' to?

PHIL *(Yelling up the stairs towards* EDDIE'*s room).* She's got the goddamn TV on and the record player on! Who you workin' for, the electric company? *(He turns off the record player.)*

DONNA. Who you talkin' to, Phil?

PHIL. Don't call me Phil, okay. Just don't. I'm talkin' to you. Who asked you anyway?

DONNA. You ain't talkin' to me, I could tell by your tone. Who you talkin' to?

PHIL. You're very observant. You're very smart. Who was I talkin' to?

DONNA. I don't know. I'm the only one here.

PHIL. I was talkin' to Eddie.

DONNA. Eddie ain't here.

PHIL. He's up in his room.

DONNA. He ain't.

PHIL *(Running up the stairs to look into the bathroom and then* EDDIE'*s room).* EDDIE! EDDIE! Where the hell are you? *(Stepping out of* EDDIE'*s room.)* I was just talkin' to him.

DONNA. That's what I been trying to explain to you.

PHIL *(Leaning over the railing to yell down to her).* Get off my back, will you? You dumb bitch. Get off it. You're on me all the time.

DONNA. I ain't.

PHIL *(Heading toward* MICKEY'*s room, he opens the door and looks in).* The fuck you ain't.

DONNA. I'm sorry. I'm just sittin' here.

PHIL. Like hell you are.

DONNA. I'm sorry.

PHIL *(Coming down the stairs).* You oughta be sorry. You're a sorry goddamn piece of just whatever the hell you are.

DONNA. Am I botherin' you? I am just sitting here.

PHIL. With your head up your ass.

DONNA. I was readin' a magazine.

PHIL. With your head up your ass.

DONNA. Boy, you are really an insulting form of person. Honest to god. Let a person have some rest. *(On his way to the kitchen,* PHIL *freezes and then whirls to face her.)*

PHIL. Meaning me?

DONNA. Whata you mean?

PHIL. I mean, "meanin' me?" Who's SOMETHIN'?

DONNA. I didn't mean nothin'. I never mean nothin'.

PHIL. You said it though, didn't you?

DONNA. What?

PHIL. What you said? You fuckin' said it.

DONNA. I don't know what you're talkin' about. Exactly.

PHIL *(Heading into the kitchen where he starts to pour the popcorn in a bowl and tries to make sandwiches).* What I'm talkin' about is how you are and what you said. You see a guy has undergone certain difficulties so his whole appearance thing is a mood thing of how he is obviously in a discouraged state, he's full of turmoil, does it occur to you to say a kindly thing or to cut his fuckin' heart out? You got your tongue out to sharpen your knife is what you're up to, or do you want to give me some other explanation?

DONNA. Sure, because—

PHIL. So what is it?

DONNA. What?

PHIL. Your so-called explanation! Let's hear it.

DONNA. I'm just—

PHIL. Bullshit. Bull Shit!

DONNA. No.

PHIL *(As* EDDIE *comes in the front door with a bag of pretzels and clothes from the cleaners).* Would you listen to this air head?

EDDIE. How's everything?

PHIL. Terrific. It's all totally fucked up, which I wouldn't have it any other way. I thought you was here.

EDDIE. I hadda go out.

PHIL *(Moving toward* EDDIE*)*. Your car was here. What the fuck is going on?

EDDIE. It wasn't far, so I walked. Donna, hey, I thought you were on your way to—

PHIL. Listen, Eddie! I saw the car, I thought you were here, you know, I was talkin' to you, you wasn't here, so I sounded like this asshole, so the ditz here has got to get on me about it.

EDDIE. Don't fuck with Phil, Donna.

DONNA. I wasn't, Eddie.

EDDIE. I mean, did you bring her, Phil?

PHIL. Who?

DONNA. No, no, no.

EDDIE. She's here ain't she!

DONNA. I was hitchhiking, Eddie, and it was like he come outa nowhere and it was, wow, Mickey. Whata hot car. So I set out for San Francisco like we talked about but I ended up here.

PHIL. I mean, what is it with this goddamn broad that makes her tick? I wanna know what makes her fuckin' tick. You answer me that goddamn question, will you?

DONNA. What?

PHIL. What makes you tick? I come here to see Eddie, you gotta be here. I wanna watch the football game and talk over some very important issues which pertain to my life, you gotta be here. What the fuck makes you tick?

DONNA. What's he talkin' about?

EDDIE. I don't know.

PHIL. What I'm talkin' about is—

EDDIE. Listen, Phil, if Darlene comes by, you just introduce Donna as your ditz, okay? *(He starts up the stairs for his room.)*

PHIL. What?

EDDIE. You found her, you know. Darlene's gonna be by at any second, we're goin' to the desert for the weekend. Can you do that? *(As he goes running into his room.)*

DONNA. Who's Darlene, Phil?

PHIL *(Crossing to get some of his food)*. I'm beggin' you. I'm beggin' you. I don't wanna see you, okay? I don't wanna see you.

DONNA. Okay.

PHIL. I mean, I come in here and you gotta be here; I'm thinkin' about football, and you gotta be here with your tits and your ass and this tight shrunken clothes and these shriveled jeans, so that's all I'm thinking about from the minute I see you is tits and ass. Football doesn't have a chance against it. It's like this invasion of tits and ass overwhelm-ing my own measly individuality so I don't have a prayer to have my own thoughts about my own things except you and tits and ass and sucking and fucking and that's all I can think about. My privacy has been demolished. You think a person wants to have that kind of thing happen to their heads—they are trying to give their own problems some serious thought, the next thing they know there's nothing in their brains as far as they can see but your tits and ass? You think a person likes that?

DONNA. Who's playin'?

PHIL. You think a person likes that?

DONNA. No.

PHIL. Who's playin' what?

DONNA. Football.

PHIL. None of your fuckin' business.

DONNA. I like it.

PHIL. What are you talkin' about? I don't know what you're talkin' about.

DONNA. Football.

PHIL. You're nuts.

DONNA. I wanna watch it with you.

PHIL. You're nuts! You wanna watch the game? You're talkin' about you wanna watch the football game? Are you nuts? Are you crazy?

DONNA. What?

PHIL. How you gonna watch it? You don't know about it. You don't know nothing about it.

DONNA. I do. I know the points, and the insignias, and the—

PHIL. That's not the game.

DONNA. And when they go through the air and they catch it.

PHIL. Get outta here. I don't want you here.

DONNA. I know about the mascots.

PHIL. You wanna know about the game? You wanna know about it? *(He has moved to grab her head between his two hands.)* You don't know about the fucking game. Hut, hut, hut—

DONNA. What are you doin'? What are you—*(He butts his head into hers.)*

PHIL. That's the game. That's the game.

DONNA. Ohh, ouch ouch, awwwww owwwwww. *(*EDDIE *comes out of his bedroom, a bunch of clothes in his hands.)*

EDDIE. What's this now?

PHIL. She's cryin'. What the fuck is the matter with her?

DONNA. He hit me, he hit me.

PHIL. She says she wants to know about the game.

EDDIE. What game?

DONNA. Football—

PHIL. —football!

DONNA. That's all.

PHIL. She's nuts.

DONNA. He hurt me. Am I bleedin'? Eddie, Eddie, Eddie.

EDDIE. No.

DONNA *(Running to the record player, grabbing the record)*. This is shit, this is shit. This is shit.

EDDIE. What happened?

PHIL. I don't know. It was over too fast.

EDDIE. What? *(DONNA is running up the stairs now.)*

PHIL. This thing here, whatever it was that happened here. She wanted to know about football, you know, the crazy bitch. She can't know about football. It's impossible. It's totally one hundred percent impossible. So this is what happens. *(Going into the bathroom, DONNA slams the door.)* So how you doin'?

EDDIE. Great. Me and Darlene are goin' to the desert.

PHIL. So guess what?

EDDIE *(He disappears back into his room)*. What?

PHIL *(Heading up the stairs)*. It's almost decided. I'm almost decided about going back to Susie.

EDDIE *(From off)*. What?

PHIL *(Hovering outside EDDIE's room)*. I can't stand it. The loneliness. And some form of totally unusual and unpredictable insanity is creeping up on me about to do I don't know WHAT—God forbid I find out. So I been thinkin' maybe if we had the kid, everything, or at least the main things, might be okay.

EDDIE *(Coming out of his bedroom)*. What kid?

PHIL. We were tryin' to have a kid. That's what we been doin'.

EDDIE. You and Susie?

PHIL. Eddie, wake up here! Who you think? Yeah, me and Susie. She wants a kid. All her friends have been havin' 'em.

EDDIE *(As he backs along the balcony toward the bathroom door)*. It's that goddamn age where it hits 'em like a truck, this maternal urge; they gotta have a kid—they don't know what hit 'em. *(EDDIE knocks on the bathroom door.)*

PHIL. So it hit Susie; but maybe it's what I need, you know.

EDDIE. Were you doin' that insanity with the thermometer and, you know, you gotta fuck on schedule?

PHIL. Unbelievable!

EDDIE. Because that stuff is insanity. *(And again EDDIE knocks on the bathroom door, which opens, and DONNA comes out, walking straight to MICKEY's room.)*

PHIL. The trouble is though, what if it doesn't work out the way I planned it?

EDDIE. Nothin' does, Phil. *(He steps into the bathroom, and PHIL comes around to stand looking in at EDDIE.)*

PHIL. I mean, I wanna have a kid sometimes, and sometimes I'm scared to death, and mostly though, I mean, for the last month or so it was like in my thoughts in my mind sometimes this little baby had this big gun to my head and she would shoot me sooner or later.

EDDIE *(As EDDIE comes out of the bathroom, zipping up a shaving kit, and heading for his room)*. So you don't want a kid.

PHIL. I do and I don't. I do and I don't.

EDDIE *(Pausing on the balcony, he faces PHIL)*. I think this might be the thing here, you know, about which you two have been fighting so much lately. You shouldn't probably have one now. Just go back and get some, you know, clarity, so you both know what the issues are. This is the relationship I'm talkin' about. Straighten that out.

PHIL. Right. And then see. That makes sense.

EDDIE. Sure. *(EDDIE steps into his room.)*

PHIL. Except she has to have one.

EDDIE *(Coming out of his room, carrying a small suitcase, the shaving kit, and a garment bag)*. She don't have to have one.

PHIL *(Following EDDIE as they descend the stairs)*. I tried tellin' her that, because you know I got three kids, two little boys and a girl who are now, you know, I don't know how old, in Toledo, I haven't seen 'em since I went to prison. I don't want any more kids out there, you know, rollin' around their beds at night with this sick fucking hatred of me. I can't stand it.

EDDIE. Who could stand it?

PHIL. Right.

EDDIE. So don't have the kid now.

PHIL. Right. *(As EDDIE, at the kitchen counter grabs his dope box in order to pack it.)* Except she's desperate. I can't stand it when she cries.

EDDIE. You can't stand it when she cries is no reason to have a kid, Phil. I mean, a kid is a big fuckin' gamble.

PHIL. Hey, as we both well know, Eddie, what isn't a gamble? You're alive, you gamble!

EDDIE. Yeh, but the collateral here is, you know, this other person you can't even ask what they think of the odds. There is involved here an innocent helpless person totally dependent on your good will.

PHIL. It's fuckin' depressing. How about some weed? I want some weed.

EDDIE. What I'm sayin', Phil, is first things first.

PHIL. Like what?

EDDIE. The marriage; the marriage. (Giving a joint to PHIL, EDDIE lights it for him and gives PHIL complete attention now at the kitchen counter.) I mean, no kid and a divorce is who-gives-a-fuck, but you have a kid and it's seismic. A big ten on the Richter scale. Carnage, man, that's what I'm sayin', gore on the highway. Add in the kid and it's a major disaster.

PHIL (Passing the lit joint to EDDIE, PHIL sits on the swivel chair outside the counter). Right. Sure. Except, see, the trouble is, Susie has wanted to be a mother since she was twelve, you know. She had dolls and teddy bears and she dressed them up in diapers—you know—she still does it, sometimes. It was all she ever dreamed about.

EDDIE. Still does what?

PHIL. I wanna make her happy, Eddie. I mean, if she's happy, maybe I'll be happy. So she's got teddy bears, so what.

EDDIE (Sitting opposite PHIL). I mean, you're not thinkin' of going back and just, you know, hoping for the best; I mean, just trusting it to luck that she won't get pregnant. You're not thinkin' that.

PHIL. No, fuck, no.

EDDIE. Because you won't have a chance if you're sayin' that, and you go back.

PHIL. I got it covered, Eddie.

EDDIE. She'll eat you alive.

PHIL. I got it covered, Eddie, is what I'm sayin'. I got the situation totally covered. There's nothin' to worry about on that score. I been takin' this stuff and messing the whole thing up, which is why we ain't pregnant at this very minute.

EDDIE. Whata you mean?

PHIL. You know, my sperm count is monstrous on its own.

EDDIE. Whata you mean?

PHIL. I have a very high sperm count. It's record setting.

EDDIE. What stuff?

PHIL. Stuff. You know, it's harmful to the sperm and I'm messing myself up.

EDDIE. You're taking some kind of—Wait

a minute! You're telling me you're taking some kind of poison?

PHIL. That's why I hadda talk to you, Eddie.

EDDIE. Do you know what the hell you're saying to me?

PHIL. What?

EDDIE (Leaping to his feet, EDDIE marches to the clothes from the cleaners). This is insane! You're taking some kind of goddamn poison because—This is crazy, Phil! This is nuts! It's fucking nuts!

PHIL. It's not poison.

EDDIE (Ripping open the paper wrapped around the box containing the shirts). Listen to me. Do me a favor. Tell her what's been going on. You can tell her, can't you?

PHIL. Sure.

EDDIE (Putting shirts into the suitcase). So do it. If you're going back, you gotta do it. She's your wife, for god's sake, you can talk to her.

PHIL. Sure.

EDDIE. So explain the situation to her. (Grabbing the dope box, he starts to go with it to put it in the suitcase.) I mean, don't you think maybe this is why the hell you two been fighting?

PHIL. Are you mad at me?

EDDIE. No.

PHIL. You're sure.

EDDIE. I'm just excited. Sometimes I get like I'm angry when I get excited. (He is putting the sport jacket and trousers from the cleaners in the clothing bag.)

PHIL. Right. Because you are absolutely without a doubt one hundred percent right in everything you're saying, but if I don't do it, what's gonna happen?

EDDIE. You gotta do it.

PHIL. She gets so sad. Eddie, she gets so goddamn sad, I can't stand it.

EDDIE. But it'll be worse if you have the kid—it'll just all be a million zillion times worse. You know that. That's what we've been talking about here.

PHIL. Without a doubt. And I'm going to do it, I just want to know what kind of latitude I have regarding our friendship if my mind gets changed.

EDDIE. Listen to me—are you a deaf man? Am I only under the delusion that I'm speaking? What you're telling me is a horror story—one part of you is begging another part to stop, but you don't hear you. But I do, I hear—you have got to stop, Phil.

PHIL. I know this, Eddie. But what if I

can't? Give me some sort of hint regarding your reaction, so I know.

EDDIE. What'd she do, hypnotize you? Is this voodoo? You're a grown man. You have asked me to tell you. I'm telling you: "Tell her!"

PHIL. You're not answering my question. I'm talking about our friendship here!

EDDIE. You're switching the goddamn subject is what you're doing.

PHIL. What the hell are you talking about? Why are you avoiding my question?

EDDIE. Our friendship doesn't matter here. Our friendship is totally, categorically, one hundred percent irrelevant here.

PHIL. Eddie, listen to yourself! This is our friendship—this conversation—these very exchanges. We are in our friendship. What could be more important?

EDDIE. I mean, I don't feel . . . What?

PHIL. Scorn. You feel scorn for me.

EDDIE. No.

PHIL. It's in your eyes.

EDDIE. No. What? *(He unzips the shaving kit to get out a container of Alka Seltzer.)*

PHIL. These dark thoughts, Eddie, I see them reflected in your eyes, they pertain to something other than me, or what?

EDDIE. I'm not having dark thoughts.

PHIL. Beyond the thoughts you're thinking, Eddie.

EDDIE *(Crossing to the sink for water)*. No!

PHIL. Then what the hell are you thinking about? I come for advice and you're off on some other totally unrelated tangent, is that the thing here, the goddamn bottom line? I need your attention, and you're off in some fucking daydream? I'm desperate and you are, for crissake, distracted? Is this friendship, Eddie? Tell me!

EDDIE. Wait a minute.

PHIL. You want a fucking minute?

EDDIE. I don't know what you're talking about. *(He drops the tablets in a glass of water.)*

PHIL *(Trying to be helpful, to explain)*. Dark thoughts. Your dark thoughts, Eddie. This is not uncommon for people to have them. You were provoked; think nothing of it. But please—this, now—dark thoughts and everything included, this is our friendship. Pay attention to it, it's slipping by.

EDDIE. Right! Yeh! I wanna!

PHIL *(Patiently explaining)*. I mean, if I do something you consider foolhardy, you won't just dismiss my feelings and my effort and the fact that I came to you.

EDDIE. I feel like you're drillin' little fuckin' chunks of cottage cheese into my brain. I'm gettin' confused here, Phil, I tol' you, I don't feel good. *(He is moving, almost staggering toward the couch.)*

PHIL *(Following along, puffing a joint)*. It's chaotic is why you're confused, Eddie. That's why you're confused. Think nothin' of it. I'm confused. The goddamn situation is like this masked fucking robber come to steal the goods, but we don't even know is he, or isn't he. I mean, we got these dark thoughts, I see 'em in you, you don't think you're thinkin' 'em, so we can't even nail that down, how we going to get beyond it? They are the results of your unnoticed inner goings-on or my gigantic paranoia, both of which exist, so the goddamn thing in its entirety is on the basis of what has got to be called a coin toss.

EDDIE. I can figure it, I can—It's not a goddamn coin toss!

PHIL. You think I'm being cynical when I say that? Nothing is necessary, Eddie. Not a fucking thing! We're in the hands of something, it could kill us now or later, it don't care. Who is this guy that makes us just— you know—WHAT? THERE'S A NAME FOR THIS—IT HAPPENS—THERE'S A WORD FOR IT—EVERYBODY KNOWS IT, I CAN'T THINK OF IT. IT'S LIKE A LAW. IT IS A LAW. WHAT'S A LAW? WHAT THE FUCK IS A LAW? Cynicism has nothing to do with it, Eddie, I've done my best. The fucking thing is without a clue, except the mess it leaves behind it, the guts and gore. What I'm sayin' is, if my conclusion is contrary to your wishes, at least give me the fucking consideration and respect that you know that at least from my point of view it is based on solid thought and rock hard evidence that has led me to I have no other choice, so you got no right to fuck with me about it. I want your respect, Eddie. *(He ends leaning intently toward Eddie on the couch.)*

EDDIE. You got that, Phil.

PHIL. I do?

EDDIE. Don't you know that? I'm just sayin'—all I'm sayin' is, "Don't have the baby thoughtlessly."

PHIL. Eddie, for god sake, don't terrify me that you have paid no attention! If I was thoughtless would I be here? I feel like I have pushed thought to the brink where it is just noise and of no more use than a headful of car horns, because the bottom line here that I'm getting at is just this—I got to go back to her. I got to go back to Susie, and if it means havin' a kid, I got to do it. I mean, I have hit a point where I am going round the bend several times a day now, and so far I been on the other side to meet me, but one a these days it might be one time too many, and who knows who might be there waitin'? If not me, who? I'm a person, Eddie, and I have realized it, who needs like a big-dot-thing, you know—this big-dot-thing around which I can just hang and blab my thoughts and more or less formulate everything as I go, myself included. I mean, I used to spend my days in my car; I didn't know what the fuck I was doin' but it kept me out of trouble until nothin' but blind luck led me to I-am-married, and I could go home. She was my big-dot-thing. Now I'm startin' in my car again, I'm spendin' days on the freeways and rain or no rain I like the wipers clickin', and all around me the other cars got people in 'em the way I see them when they are in cars. These heads, these faces. These boxes of steel with glass and faces inside. I been the last three days without seeing another form of human being in his entirety except gas station attendants. The family men in the day with their regular food and regular hours in their eyes. And then in the night, these moonlighters; they could be anything. In the wee hours of the morning, it's derelicts, and these weird spooky kids like they have recently arrived from outer space, but not to stay. The cloverleafs, they got a thing in them, it spins me off. There's little back roads and little towns sometimes I never heard of them. I start to expect the gas station attendants to know me when I arrive. I get excited that I've been there before. I want them to welcome me. I'm disappointed when they don't. Something that I don't want to be true starts lookin' like it's all that's true only I don't know what it is. No. No. I need my marriage. I come here to tell you. I got to stay married. I'm lost without her.

(The door to MICKEY's *room slams loudly as out comes* DONNA. *She is dressed in shorts far too snug for her, and a tight T-shirt shortened above her belly button, and she carries her record and other belongings.)*

DONNA *(At the top of the stairs)*. You guys have cooked your goose. You can just walk your own dog, and fuck yourselves. These particular tits and ass are taking a hike. *(She stomps down the stairs and struts to the door, opens it, turns, looks at* EDDIE *who is staring at her, quite*

ill.) So this is goodbye. *(She goes out, slamming the door.)*

Curtain

ACT TWO

SCENE ONE

TIME: Night. A year later.

PLACE: The same.

EDDIE *lies on the floor, nestled on pillows, while* MICKEY *is seated, legs dangling through the spokes of the second floor railing. Each has a drink.* PHIL *and* ARTIE *are a twosome, a kind of team, standing and drinking, both involved with one another and their memory of the event in which they recently participated and which they are trying to communicate to* MICKEY *and* EDDIE. PHIL *has ice wrapped in a towel around his right hand.* ARTIE *is so proud of* PHIL *you would think he had himself performed the deed they are excitedly relating. At the breakfast nook, he pours drinks for himself and* PHIL.

PHIL. This guy, what a fuckin' guy.

ARTIE. You shoulda seen him. He was unbelievable.

EDDIE. So what happened?

PHIL. I decked him; he deserved it.

EDDIE. So what happened?

PHIL. He made me mad.

ARTIE. He was a jerk.

EDDIE. So you decked this guy.

ARTIE *(Rushing near to* PHIL, *hugging him, patting him)*. You shoulda seen it. The guy went across the room. He looked like he was on wheels.

EDDIE. So what'd he do?

PHIL. He got up.

ARTIE. The dumb fuck.

EDDIE. I mean, why'd you hit him?

PHIL. He got up!

EDDIE *(Sitting up, trying to make his point)*. I mean, before he got knocked down—the first time you hit him, why'd you hit him?

ARTIE. You wouldn't believe this guy. He was genuinely irritating.

PHIL. This is the pitiful part. I don't think he could help himself.

ARTIE. I mean, this is the way this pathetic jerk-off must go through his life. IRRITATING!

PHIL. It's a curse to be this guy! I shoulda had some consideration.

EDDIE *(Going to the kitchen)*. BUT WHAT HAPPENED?

ARTIE. He was sayin' this unbelievable dumb stuff to this broad.

EDDIE *(In the kitchen* EDDIE *pours another drink)*. Some broad you knew?

ARTIE. Noooo! *(As if this is the dumbest question anybody ever could have asked.)* Just this genuinely repulsive broad.

PHIL. And he's talkin' to her like she's somethin' gorgeous. THIS DOG! It was offensive. Who'd he think he was with, you know? This was nobody of any even remotely dynamite qualities, you know what I mean? You don't talk to some dog in the manner he's talking. It's disgusting!

ARTIE. Very irritating guy.

EDDIE. I can see that.

PHIL. You shoulda been there. I ask him to shut up, and he says he isn't botherin' anybody. I says he is botherin' me; he looks at me like I'm an asshole; I can see he's askin' for it, so I warn him one more time.

EDDIE. What'd you say?

PHIL. I don't SAY nothing. I look at him very seriously, you know, bullets and razors and bloodshed in my eyes, but all under control, so he can have the option of knowing nothing need happen if he don't push me. But he's gotta push me.

MICKEY. So what happened?

PHIL. It all went very quickly—

ARTIE. —the guy goes right off the stool!

EDDIE *(With his drink,* EDDIE *leans intently in toward* PHIL, *exasperated, yet playing at the exasperation, enjoying the fact that they cannot seem to make any sense to one another)*. But what happened?

ARTIE. He got up.

EDDIE. He got up?

MICKEY. He got up? This is unbelievable. You knock him down, he gets up?

ARTIE. Phil don't just knock him down. He knocks him across the room. *(And now* ARTIE *in order to demonstrate, runs crashing backwards into a wall.)* It's like this goddamn vortex just snarfs him up and fucking magnetizes him to the wall for a full second before he slides to the floor. SO THEN HE GETS UP! Do you believe this guy?

PHIL. Personally, this is where the guy gets a raw deal, though, 'cause the second time I was wired into some other frequency, and the whack I put on him was beyond the

realm of normal human punches. That he didn't disintegrate was both his and my good fortune.

MICKEY. This is some tough guy, huh?

ARTIE and PHIL. NOOOOO! NOOOO! *(As if this is an insanely stupid question.)*

PHIL. Absolutely not. This is a weak link on the chain of humanity other than in his particular capacities of irritating; and this is where the real irony comes in. Because I don't think, looking back, that when he got up on his feet again he any longer had a clue to where he was or what he was doin'.

ARTIE. He was totally fuckin' unconscious.

PHIL. Exactly. Looking back, I can see he was no longer from his point of view in the bar even. From his point of view he was on his way to catch a bus or something.

ARTIE. It was his reflexes.

PHIL. Exactly, but I don't see he's harmless in time to take charge of my own reflexes, which see nothing at all except that he's comin' toward me. So I gotta let him have it. It's him or me.

ARTIE. But as far as attacking Phil, it's the farthest thing from his mind.

PHIL. No, he's like going shopping or something. He don't know what he's doing. It's just his reflexes.

ARTIE. His reflexes got the best of him.

PHIL. So we are both victims of our reflexes.

MICKEY *(Pronouncing from where he sits on high)*. So, this is a tragedy here.

PHIL. I don't know about that, but it was a mess, and I coulda got into real trouble, because the force with which I hit him is even in my memory of it nerve-wracking.

ARTIE. Don't get morose, Phil, huh? *(Patting* PHIL, *trying to cheer him up.)* Pay attention to the upside.

PHIL. You pay attention to the upside— you're the big deal—I'm the fuck-up. *(Pulling away from* ARTIE, PHIL *moves over to the TV where he has spied a vial of coke.)*

EDDIE *(Following after* PHIL*)*. You let off some steam, Phil. This is the purpose of this kind of, you know, out and out bullshit.

PHIL *(Picking up the coke)*. You wanna tell me how come I have all the necessary realizations that any normal human being might have—only I have them too late, so that I understand he's a pathetic, unconscious jerk-off who can't help irritating people and is oblivious to the fact that he is on his feet— only by the time I understand it, he's unconscious and nothing but luck has kept me from doing a lifetime in the can; so the realizations can serve no possible useful purpose on earth but to torment me with the thought that I am a merciless, totally out of control prick. Whata you wanna call that? I call it horseshit.

ARTIE. Phil has got violent karma, that's all; it's in the cards. *(Behind the breakfast nook counter he has a notebook in which he starts to scribble.)*

PHIL. Yeh, well, I am running out of patience with being good for nothing but whacking people in the face they do some irrelevant thing that drives me nuts. If this is my karma, to be an asshole and have such a thing as this, fuck it.

MICKEY *(Rising languidly to his feet)*. Absolutely, right; fuck destiny, fate and all metaphysical stuff.

PHIL *(Bolting to the base of the stairway where he glares up at Mickey)*. You, you cynical bastard, watch the fine line you are walking between my self-awareness and my habitual trend to violence. 'Cause on the one hand I might appear worried, but on the other I could give a fuck, you know, and my urge to annihilate anyone might just fixate on you.

MICKEY *(Descending the stairs toward a bottle of Scotch by the TV)*. And the vortex get me—fling me, you might say, wallward, magnetically.

PHIL. Exactly. So you can help us both out by watching your goddamn, you know—right? Am I making myself clear?

MICKEY *(Slipping by PHIL)*. Step.

PHIL. Yeah. P's and Q's. *(Moving after Mickey, but yelling to ARTIE who is busy scribbling at the breakfast nook.)* So, Artie, you got any inside dope on this karma thing, or you just ranting?

ARTIE. Everybody knows something, it's a popular topic.

PHIL *(Turning to ARTIE)*. But what I'm asking you is, "You said it, do you know it?"

EDDIE *(Moving near Phil)*. I mean, Phil, isn't the fact of the matter here that you signed your divorce papers today?

PHIL. Who said anything about that? One thing does not lead to another.

EDDIE. I mean, I think that's what you're wired up about.

PHIL. Eddie, you're jumpin' around on me, here, what's your point?

EDDIE. The baby, the baby. The divorce. This is the ambush you been worried about. They got you. They blew you the fuck right

out of orbit, and if you see maybe that's what's cooking under the whole thing, you might just get a hold of yourself.

MICKEY. And pull yourself back into orbit.

PHIL. But what orbit? I'm in an orbit.

MICKEY. It's just it's a useless fucking orbit.

PHIL *(Crossing slowly to MICKEY)*. Do you know, Mickey, I could kick your eyes out and never think about it a second time, that's the depths to which my animosity runs?!

MICKEY. I know that.

PHIL. So why do you take these chances and risk ruining both our lives?

MICKEY. This is the very point Artie was, I think, making.

PHIL. Artie, is this your point? *(Turning, looking for ARTIE.)*

ARTIE. What? *(Unnoticed by the others, ARTIE has settled down in the corner on a pile of pillows and he does not even look up from his scribbling, as PHIL comes rushing toward him.)*

PHIL. Is this your point?

ARTIE. What?

EDDIE *(Moving in on MICKEY)*. Mickey! Will you just cut the goofy shit for a second? This is a serious point I'm trying to make here.

MICKEY. He knows his life is a mess.

EDDIE. He doesn't know it enough.

MICKEY. He knows it so goddamn well he's trying to avoid it.

EDDIE. That's my point! I mean, Phil, if you see the goddamn issue here. PHIL!

PHIL *(Looking up from ARTIE's endeavor)*. YEAH. What's Artie doin'?

ARTIE. I had a thought.

PHIL. So you wrote it down? Everybody has a thought, Artie, this is no justification they go around writing them down.

EDDIE *(Approaching PHIL, trying to force his attention)*. You're just on a goddamn wild roll here because of the state of your life being a shambles! The baby's born and you sign the divorce papers all in the same month, so you're under stress.

PHIL. I'm aware of that.

EDDIE. So that's what I'm sayin'. See the connection.

PHIL. But why are you trying to torment me, Eddie? I thought I could count on you.

EDDIE. But lighten up is what I'm saying. Give yourself a break. I mean, the real issues are not you hitting people or not hitting people, but are these other issues of your divorce and baby. You enjoy hitting people and you know it.

PHIL. My point is not that I don't enjoy it

but that it is dangerous, and mostly dangerous that I do enjoy it, so what's the point in that? And my point is that I am wired beyond my reasons. I know my reasons, but I am wired beyond them.

MICKEY *(Moving near, his manner a seeming friendliness).* You're right on schedule, Phil, that's all. You're a perfectly, rapateta, blah-blah-blah, modern statistic; you have the baby, you get the divorce. You're very "now" is all, but not up to it. You're the definitive representative of the modern male in this year, but you're not willing to accept it.

PHIL *(Undergoing an impulse to throw MICKEY through a wall).* This is what I gotta talk to Artie about. *(He turns and finds ARTIE at the breakfast nook, picking up the phone.)* Artie, what the fuck are you doing?

ARTIE. I'm checking my messages.

PHIL *(Hurrying to ARTIE).* You got a minute, this is a disaster here. I'm on the brink and you're checking your fucking messages. Have some compassion. *(He is trying to get ARTIE to hang up.)*

ARTIE. Just a second. *(He beeps his beeper into the phone.)*

EDDIE. So who'd you hear from, huh? You got studio executives lined up on your goddamn machine beep after beep. *(Mimicking different voices.)* "Great project, Arthur." "Terrific treatment." "Must have lunch."

ARTIE. I have a career. I am not ashamed, I have a career. You want me to be ashamed?

EDDIE. What I want you to understand, Artie, is the absurdity of this business, and the fact that you're a success in it is a measure of the goddamn absurdity of this business to which we are all desperate to belong as a bunch of dogs.

ARTIE. You're a small-minded prick, Eddie; I hope you know that.

MICKEY *(Having settled down on the window seat).* He does.

EDDIE. I am familiar with the opinion. However, I do not myself hold it.

PHIL *(Unable to wait any longer, he grabs at the phone, but ARTIE eludes him, determined to get his messages).* But what I need, Artie, is a little more, you know what I mean, Artie. What I'm wondering here is, you got any particularly useful, I mean, hard data on this karma stuff, you know, the procedures by which this cosmic shit comes down. That's what I'm asking: Do you know what you're talking about?

MICKEY. He's a Jew.

PHIL. I know he's a Jew. I'm talking to him, ain't I? Destiny is a thing you have to be somewhat educated to have a hint about it, so he might know somebody, right, Artie? You know anybody?

EDDIE. But it's another tradition, Phil.

PHIL. Who gives a fuck!? Of course I know that. But I'm not talking about tradition here—I'm asking him about the cosmos and has he come upon anything in all the fucking books he reads that might tell me more than I pick up off the TV which is, strictly speaking, dip-shit.

ARTIE *(Behind PHIL, hanging up the phone).* Sure.

PHIL. See. So what is it?

ARTIE. Hey, you know, past lives, you have past lives and the karmic stuff accrues to it. You have debts and credits and you have to work your way out from under the whole thing, so you—

MICKEY. Artie! This is not your investment counselor we're talking about here.

EDDIE. This is not cosmic Visa, Artie.

(MICKEY and EDDIE are both laughing now—MICKEY, wanting fun and to keep PHIL from being taken seriously by anyone, and EDDIE because he is irritated that PHIL seems more interested in ARTIE's opinions than in the advice EDDIE himself has tried to give.)

ARTIE. We could be in the process of working out the debits and credits of our past lives with the very way we relate to each other at this very instant. It could be that Phil owes some affection to me, I owe him some guidance, and—

EDDIE *(Laughing even more now. MICKEY and EDDIE both breaking up).* Guidance?

MICKEY. The fact that you're talking, Artie, does not necessarily make it destiny speaking, I hope you know this.

ARTIE. And you two pricks owe some negative shit to everybody.

PHIL. Artie, he's right. You make it sound like the cosmos is in your opinion this loan shark. This is disappointing.

ARTIE. You asked me.

PHIL. Because I thought you might know.

MICKEY. That's the TV fucking version, and don't you pretend you learned that anywhere but on the evening news.

EDDIE. Some goddamn Special Project.

PHIL. I was hoping, you know, he's a Jew. He's got this insane religious history running out behind him, he might have picked up something, you know. That's what I was hoping. There might be some crazed Hasidic motherfucker in his family; you know, he came to dinner, he had his pigtail, nobody could shut him up about karma, destiny, the way of the stars; it might have rubbed off on Artie.

MICKEY. You disappointed him, Artie. You built him up, you disappointed him.

ARTIE. It happens.

MICKEY. He's at a critical juncture in his life, here.

ARTIE. Who isn't?

EDDIE. You guys need to get laid.

MICKEY. You, however, don't, huh?

EDDIE. I am, in fact, sustaining a meaningful relationship.

ARTIE *(Irritated that* EDDIE *and* MICKEY *have teased him, he thinks he will tease back, snapping out his real feelings).* The only thing sustaining that relationship is the fact that she's out of town two out of every three weeks.

EDDIE *(Glaring at* ARTIE*).* Well, she's in town tomorrow.

MICKEY *(After an uneasy second).* I wouldn't mind getting laid. What are we thinking about?

EDDIE. We could call somebody.

PHIL. Do it.

ARTIE. Do it now!

EDDIE. I was thinking primarily of setting Phil up, that's what I meant, primarily.

ARTIE. What about me?

EDDIE. Give me a break, Artie. Phil is in a totally unique situation, here, back out in the single life.

PHIL. I'm in a totally fucked-up state of mind, too.

ARTIE. I mean, that little blonde might still be around, you hadn't decided to beat the shit out of her.

PHIL. Is everything my fault, Artie? I mean, relent, I beg you, I am feeling suicidal. Haven't I explained myself?

ARTIE. She liked us. She would have stayed a long time.

PHIL. I was teaching her football. It was an accident. I went too far.

EDDIE. So I could call Bonnie.

ARTIE. You're not going to get Bonnie for Phil?

PHIL. I don't believe this treachery. Artie, have some mercy.

*(*PHIL *and* ARTIE *spin off into their own little squabble,* PHIL *pushing at* ARTIE*, trying to shut him up, while* EDDIE *goes to the phone to start dialing and* MICKEY *watches them all.)*

ARTIE. This is sex we're talking about now, Phil. Competitive sex.

PHIL. That's what I'm saying. I need help.

ARTIE. You're such a jerk-off, you're such a goof-off. I don't believe for a second you were seriously desperate about trying to pick that bitch up.

PHIL. That's exactly how out of touch I am, Artie—I have methods so out-dated they appear to you a goof.

ARTIE *(*ARTIE *runs toward* MICKEY, PHIL *chasing playfully after him).* Fuck you. He's got this thing.

PHIL. Styles have changed. Did you see the look of disgust on that bimbo's excuse for a face? It was humiliating.

ARTIE *(Trying to tell* MICKEY*).* He's got this thing!

PHIL. It used to work. *(Pulling* ARTIE *away from* MICKEY, PHIL *throws him toward the couch, where the two of them collapse, giggling.)*

MICKEY. What thing? *(*EDDIE *is at the phone, dialing.)*

PHIL. It's a vibrator that I carry around, see.

MICKEY. You carry around a vibrator with you?

PHIL. As a form of come-on, so they see I'm up for anything right from the get-go. It's very logical if you think about it. But tonight there were extenuating circumstances.

ARTIE. It's a logic apparent to you alone, Phil.

EDDIE *(Slamming down the phone).* Bonnie, get off the fucking phone!

MICKEY. He had a vibrator.

PHIL. I had a vibrator. So what?

EDDIE. It's logical.

PHIL. Right. Eddie understands me, thank god for it. So when I'm coming on to the broad, see, I sort of pull it out, and have it there. It's like some other guy might have a nail file or something only I got a vibrator— so this Bonnie's a terrific broad, huh?

EDDIE. Terrific.

ARTIE. So you got your thing.

PHIL. So I'm delivering my pitch, you know, and we can have a good time if we get an opportunity to be alone, and as a kind of mood-setter, I turn it on, you know. Except I forgot about the goddamn weights.

EDDIE. What?

MICKEY. THE WEIGHTS? YOU FORGOT ABOUT THE WEIGHTS?

PHIL. I forgot about 'em. Unbelievable!

MICKEY. UNBELIEVABLE! YOU FORGOT ABOUT THE WEIGHTS! *(To* EDDIE *across the room.)* HE FORGOT ABOUT THE GODDAMN WEIGHTS!

ARTIE. Do you know what he's talking about?

MICKEY. No, I don't know what he's talking about!

PHIL. You prick. You disgust me. I'm talking about the weights.

ARTIE. See, he has been transporting his barbells and weights in the back of the car, with all his inability to know where he lived.

PHIL. So the weights were in the back of the car.

MICKEY. Right.

PHIL. The train of events in this thing is perfectly logical to anybody with half a heart to see them, unless that person is a nasty prick. So what had to happen, happened, and I threw the weights into the trunk of the car carelessly and hit the vibrator without thinking about it.

EDDIE. So you pulled out a broken vibrator on this broad.

PHIL. Exactly.

EDDIE. This is an emergency. I think this is an emergency situation here. *(Whirling back to the phone he begins furiously dialing.)*

PHIL. This is what I'm trying to tell you.

EDDIE. You're a desperate human being, Phil.

PHIL. I'm begging. Get Bonnie! I got this broken vibrator, and so when I turn it on, it goes round sort of all weird like, you know, and the motor's demented sounding, it's going around all crooked and weird, changing speeds. She's looking at me.

EDDIE *(Dialing again and again)*. This really happened to you?

PHIL. What can I do, Eddie? Help me.

EDDIE. I'm trying.

PHIL. So this broad is looking at me. She's givin' me this look. This thing's in my hand, arrrggghhh, like I'm offering to put this goddamn model airplane inside her. It's liable to come apart and throw her across the room.

EDDIE. Bonnie, please. *(He slams down the phone.)*

ARTIE. This thing's goin', arrrggghhh, arrrghhh. Phil's sayin', "Want to come home with me?"

PHIL. Arrghhhhh, arghhh, want to come home with me? *(EDDIE, on the stool by the phone, stares at PHIL.)*

EDDIE. You really did this, Phil?

PHIL. Yeah.

EDDIE. Listen to me. You're a rare human being.

PHIL *(Very pleased)*. So how come everything turns to shit?

EDDIE. I don't know, but we're going to find out. You're a rare, precious human being.

PHIL. I suspected as much.

EDDIE. Underneath all this bullshit, you have a real instinctive thing, you know what I mean. It's like this wide open intuition.

PHIL *(Rising now, he glides across the room to stand beside EDDIE)*. This is what I think sometimes about myself.

EDDIE. I mean, it's unique; this goddamn imagination—you could channel it.

PHIL. I have thoughts sometimes they could break my head open.

EDDIE. Whata you mean?

PHIL. I mean, these big thoughts. These big goddamn thoughts. I don't know what to do with them.

EDDIE. This is what I'm saying: if you could channel them into your talent. I mean, under all this crazed bullshit you've been forced to develop—

PHIL. I get desperate. I feel like my thoughts are all just going to burst out of my head and leave me; they're going to pick me up and throw me around the room. I fight with them. It's a bloodbath this monster I have with my thoughts. Maybe if I channeled them.

EDDIE. I never took you so seriously before. I mean, quite so seriously.

PHIL. Me neither.

EDDIE. I'm calling Bonnie, Phil. I'm calling her for you.

PHIL. So call her.

MICKEY *(Leaning from his window seat toward ARTIE on the couch)*. Could this be it, Artie?

ARTIE. What? *(Though busy with the phone, EDDIE and PHIL are clearly eavesdropping on MICKEY and ARTIE.)*

MICKEY. Could this be destiny in fact at work, Artie, and we are witnessing it?—the pattern in the randomness, so that we see it: man without a home, careless weights; broken vibrator, disappointed broad. And from this apparent mess, two guys fall in love.

EDDIE. He's jealous, Phil. Don't worry about his petty jealousy.

PHIL. He could choke on his own spit, I would feel nothing. No. I would feel glee. I would be a kid at an amusement park. *(As EDDIE disgustedly hangs up the phone.)* She's still busy?

EDDIE. I'm gonna get her for you, Phil, don't worry.

PHIL. So who is this bitch she's on the phone forever, some goddamn agent?

EDDIE. No, no, she's terrific, you're gonna love her. This is a bitch who dances naked artistically in this club. That's her trip.

MICKEY. With a balloon.

EDDIE. That's what makes it artistic. Without the balloon, what is she?

ARTIE. A naked bitch.

EDDIE. You would wanna fuck her, though.

ARTIE. Anybody would.

EDDIE. She's a good bitch, though, you know what I mean? She's got a heart of gold.

MICKEY. What's artistic about her is her blow jobs.

PHIL *(Grabbing* EDDIE, *turning him back to the phone).* Get her, Eddie; get her.

MICKEY. She's critically acclaimed.

EDDIE. And the best part about her is that she's up for anything.

MICKEY. Like the airport.

EDDIE. What airport? *(Then he screams into the phone.)* Bonnie, please!

MICKEY. So we ask her to go to the airport.

EDDIE *(Remembering, he puts down the phone).* Oh Jesus, the airport!

*(*EDDIE *moves to* MICKEY *as the story, the claims of old times, the competitiveness of memory and telling the story draw* MICKEY *and* EDDIE *into a teamlike intimacy, leaving* PHIL *to flop down in the big armchair.)*

MICKEY. This was amazing. Robbie Rattigan was coming in.

EDDIE. He was coming in, see, he was up for this major part in this pilot for an ABC series. Right? He's flying in, we wanna make him feel welcome.

MICKEY. He's gonna be all screwed up from the flight, he's got this big meeting.

EDDIE. Bonnie jumps at the chance. She's seen him as a featured killer on several cop shows which he was on almost every one of them as a killer. "Meet him at the airport," we tell her.

MICKEY. "He's a friend of ours," we tell her. We want you to relax him on the drive back to town.

EDDIE. She says to us that she has been very impressed by his work when she saw it.

MICKEY. She's a fuckin' critic.

EDDIE. So we meet the plane. Robbie gets off, you know; we meet him, we get in the car. Hey, hey, blah-blah, blah-blah-blah.

We're on the freeway, she's in the back seat with Robbie.

MICKEY. She's just there.

EDDIE. We made a point of just introducing her like she's somebody's girlfriend, you know, or just some bitch we know, she happens to be in the back seat when we pick him up.

MICKEY. An accident.

EDDIE. No big deal.

MICKEY. So Robbie's talkin' about the part he's up for, and getting very serious, "rapateta." So Bonnie reaches over and unzips his fly. He looks at her like she just fell out of a tree. "Don't mind me," she says. *(Having drifted together to the kitchen,* EDDIE *is again on the chair by the phone;* MICKEY, *behind the counter.)*

EDDIE. I'm tellin' him to keep on talkin'.

MICKEY. We're acting like we don't know what's goin' on.

EDDIE. She just had this impulse. He's irresistible.

MICKEY. That's the impression.

EDDIE. That he's this irresistible guy. That's the impression we want to make.

MICKEY. So she's gone down on him.

EDDIE. You can tell by his face.

MICKEY. She's very energetic.

EDDIE *(Dialing one more time).* So he starts to curse us out. You would not believe the cursing he does.

MICKEY. "Robbie," I tell him, "Welcome to L.A.!"

EDDIE *(Into the phone).* Bonnie! Hello! *(Everybody freezes.)* Hello. Hey. Bonnie. Eddie. Yeah. C'mon over. Yeah. C'mon over. *(He hangs up.)* She's comin' over.

PHIL. She's comin' over? She's really comin'?

EDDIE. Yeah. Oh, the look on Robbie's face, and the look on the kid's face. Remember that?

MICKEY. No. What?

EDDIE. The kid. Oh, yeah. Christ, the kid. She's got a six-year-old daughter, and she was there.

MICKEY. She was with us?

EDDIE. In the front seat. I forgot about the kid. Wasn't she there?

MICKEY. Yeah. Remember?

EDDIE. Yeah.

MICKEY. So Robbie's wong comes out, and he's got one. I mean, this guy is epic.

EDDIE. Monstrous. The kid is petrified.

MICKEY. I mean, there's her mother goin' into combat with this horse.

EDDIE. It's a goddamn snake.

MICKEY. This is sick, isn't it? I'm gettin' a little sick.

EDDIE. We were ripped though, weren't we? We were ripped.

MICKEY. Maybe we were blotto.

EDDIE. Then we woulda forgot the whole thing. Which we didn't.

MICKEY. We nearly did. I mean, about the kid, right?

EDDIE. I don't think the mitigating circumstances are sufficient! I ended up takin' care of her. She started to cry, remember?

MICKEY. No.

EDDIE. Sure. I mean, she didn't start to cry, but she looked like somebody whacked her in the back of the head with a rock. So I hadda take care of her. You remember, Mickey!

MICKEY. Almost. I was drivin'. So then what happened? I was personally blotto.

EDDIE. Bullshit! We ended up, I'm holdin' her, we're tellin' her these goddamn stories, remember? She was there. We were makin' up this story about elves and shit, and this kingdom full of wild rabbits, and the elves were getting stomped to death by gangs of wild rabbits.

MICKEY. Jungle Bunnies, I think, is what we called them.

EDDIE. Fuck. Everywhere I turn I gotta face my own depravity. Jungle Bunnies are stomping elves to death so the elves start to hang them. Is that the story?

MICKEY. Yeah. And we were doin' the voices. (Now they are moaning and pounding their heads on the counter in a mix of mock and real remorse.)

EDDIE. I don't wanna think about it. High-pitched, right?

MICKEY. Yeah, high-pitched . . .

MICKEY and EDDIE. And rural!

EDDIE. The kid was catatonic. I think maybe that was it, Mickey; we turned the corner in this venture.

MICKEY. Right. What venture?

EDDIE. Life. That was the nose dive. I mean, where it began. We veered at that moment into utter irredeemable depravity. (As they collapse upon the counter.)

MICKEY. I feel sick to my stomach about myself. A little. That I could do that. How could I do that?

PHIL (Leaping to his feet). Hey! You guys! Don't get crazy! You had a WHIM. This is what happens to people. THEY HAVE WHIMS. So you're sittin' around, Robbie's

comin'. You want him to like you, you want him to think well of you. So you have this whim. Did she have to do it? Did anybody twist her arm? (MICKEY and EDDIE have straightened slowly.)

MICKEY. Phil's right, Eddie. What'd we do? I mean, objectively. Did anybody say, "Bring your kid."

EDDIE. It's the airwaves.

MICKEY. Exactly. (MICKEY heads up the stairs.)

EDDIE. TV. TV. Once it was a guy from TV, what chance did she have? (PHIL lounges in the armchair while ARTIE is flopped on the couch. MICKEY goes upstairs and emerges from the bathroom with a huge hashish pipe and a Variety with which he flops down on the floor of the balcony.) She couldn't help herself. And I think subconsciously we knew this. Didn't we know it? I mean, what does she watch? About a million hours of TV a week, so the airwaves are all mixed with the TV waves and then the whole thing is scrambled in her brain waves so, you know, her head is just full of this static, this fog of TV thoughts, to which she refers for everything. I mean, this is an opportunity to mix with the gods we're offering her in the back seat of our car.

(As EDDIE finishes, he is reclining on top of the kitchen counter, his back against the wall. MICKEY has given up reading and is flat on the floor, his arm dangling through the rails. The door opens and in comes BONNIE.)

BONNIE. Hi!

EDDIE. Bonnie.

ARTIE. Hi!

BONNIE. Hi, Artie, hi, Mickey. Your call was a miracle, Eddie.

MICKEY. Hi.

EDDIE. This is Phil.

BONNIE. Hi.

PHIL. Hi.

EDDIE. He's recently divorced.

BONNIE. Everybody I know is either recently married or recently divorced, some of them the same people. It's a social epidemic.

PHIL. I'm recently divorced.

BONNIE. I've got to have some blow, Eddie, can you spare it?

EDDIE. Sure, hey.

BONNIE. Doom and gloom have come to sit in my household like some permanent kind of domestic appliance. My brain has been invaded with glop. If you could spare some blow to vacuum the lobes, I would be eternally grateful.

PHIL. We could go buy some.

EDDIE. I got plenty. (BONNIE *has moved to* EDDIE, *who is digging out some coke for her as* PHIL *drifts toward them.*)

PHIL. She and me could go. I know where to buy it like it grows on trees.

BONNIE. I was in mortal longing for someone to call me. I was totally without hope of ever having worthwhile companionship tonight, a decent fucking conversation. (PHIL, *sidling up to* BONNIE, *puts his arm around her as* EDDIE *spoons her some coke.*)

PHIL. Eddie's got some stuff here to really round off your—you know, rough spots.

BONNIE. I couldn't be happier.

PHIL. We been having a good time, too.

BONNIE. Is this particular guy just being ceremonial here with me, Eddie, or does he want to dick me?

EDDIE. I thought we'd get around to that later.

BONNIE (*To* PHIL). Eddie thought we'd get around to that later.

PHIL (*Hands off, backing away*). Hey, if I have overstepped some invisible boundary here, you notify me fast because I respond quickly to clear-cut information while, you know, murk and innuendo make me totally demented.

ARTIE. We couldn't have less of any idea what we're doing here, Bonnie.

BONNIE. I'm sure he has his saving graces.

MICKEY. Why don't you list them? I bet he'd like you to list them! (*With this* MICKEY *breaks himself up;* ARTIE *erupts in a fit of giggles as* PHIL *tries awkwardly to join in.*)

PHIL. You could make a list of what you think might be my saving graces based on some past savings account in the sky.

BONNIE. Is everybody ripped here?

MICKEY. We're involved in a wide variety of pharmaceutical experiments. (*This, of course, keeps them laughing.*)

EDDIE. Testing the perimeters of the American Dream of oblivion.

BONNIE (*Giving* EDDIE *a little kiss on the forehead*). Well, I can't express the gratitude for your generosity that led you to including me.

PHIL. You want people to call, you might spend less time on the phone.

BONNIE (*Turning to look for* PHIL, *who is sitting on the arm of the couch with a bottle*). This is exactly my point. This bozo would not get off the phone.

MICKEY. You could hang up.

BONNIE (*Moving toward* MICKEY). His reaction was to call me back so quickly I considered whether he had magical powers or not.

PHIL. You could leave the phone off the hook.

BONNIE. Which I did. (*As she moves to* PHIL *for the bottle.*)

PHIL. This explains the infinite length of your busy signal.

BONNIE (*To* PHIL). See! This is what I was afraid of: Friends might call. You see the dilemma I was in.

PHIL (*Almost scolding her*). Eddie called and called.

EDDIE. We called as if it was a religious duty.

BONNIE. Thank god you persisted. (*She crosses to* EDDIE.) This guy was pushing me beyond my own rational limits so I was into hallucinatory kinds of, you know, considerations, like would I invite him over and then hack him to death with a cleaver.

PHIL. Who is this guy? (*Moving after her, he drops into the armchair, kneeling in the seat looking over the back toward her and* EDDIE.) I know ways to make guys stop anything. They might think they couldn't live without it until I talk to them. They might think they have the courage of cowboys, but I can change their minds. Who is this guy?

BONNIE. This is what I'm getting at, Eddie, a person like this guy can only be found in your household. What's your name again?

PHIL. Phil.

ARTIE. He's dangerous, Bonnie.

BONNIE. Who isn't?

ARTIE. I mean, in ways you can't imagine.

BONNIE. That's very unlikely, Artie. (EDDIE *hands her a lighted joint.*) Drugs. I mean, I'm telling this guy on the phone that drugs are and just have been as far as I can remember, an everpresent component of my personality. I am a drug-person. And I would not, if I were him, consider that anything unusual, unless he is compelled to reveal to the entire world his ignorance of the current situation in which most people find themselves—so that's what I'm telling this guy.

PHIL. Who is this guy? He's drivin' me nuts, this guy.

BONNIE. Some guy. Don't worry about it. (*Crossing to* PHIL *to give him a joint and almost to console him with her explanation, as she sits on the hassock beside the armchair.*) I mean, my life in certain of its segments has just moved into some form of automation on which it runs as if my input is no longer required. So my girlfriend Sarah gets involved with this guy who is totally freaked out on EST, so she gets proportionally freaked out on EST, this is what love can do to you, so then they are both attempting to freak me out on EST, as if my certainty that they are utterly full of shit is some non-negotiable threat to them rather than just my opinion and so they must—out of their insecurity, assault me with this goddamn EST ATTACK so that everywhere I turn I am confronted with their booklets and god knows what else, these pictures of this Werner Shmerner and the key to them that I must get rid of is my drug-desires, which is the subject of their unending, unvaried, you know, whatchamacallit.

EDDIE. Proselytizing.

BONNIE *(Looking to* EDDIE*).* They will not shut up about it. So I am trying to make to this guy what is for me an obvious point, which is that unlike those who have lost their minds to EST, I am a normal person: I need my drugs! *(*PHIL *has coke which he gives her. They have booze to share, grass.)* Has he been in the hospital lately? I am asking him. Because you go in the hospital, where I have recently had reason to go, and along with everything else you can get there, the anesthesiologist, the minute I am strong enough, he is offering to sell me coke of which he says he is himself deeply fond along with twenty or thirty percent of the nurses and a sprinkling of the interns, as he reported it. I am scoffed at for this remark, so, being civilized, I attempt to support my point with what Sarah and I both know from our mutual girlfriend Denise. "Does Denise not work as a legal secretary in this building full of lawyers?" I tell him. Well, she says these lawyers are totally blow oriented, and you go in there in the after-hours where some of them are still working, it sounds like a goddamn hog farm, she says. Well, Sarah and this guy react to this with two absolutely unaltered onslaughts, and while they're yelling at me, I'm yelling at them, that since I am a drug-person, I must give them a drug-person's answer: *(Sliding off the hassock to the pillows on the floor.)* "Thbgggggggggghhhhhhhgggggghhhhh!" I go, and slam down the phone and hang it up. *(Ending up lying on her back on the floor at* PHIL*'s feet.)*

PHIL. So that's when we called.

BONNIE. When I picked it up, you were there. Eddie was there.

PHIL. And now you're here.

MICKEY *(Gazing down on* PHIL *and* BONNIE*).* Is this the hand of destiny again, Eddie, look at it.

EDDIE *(Still lying on the counter).* I'm looking.

MICKEY. The hand of destiny again emerging just enough from, you know, all the normal muck and shit, so that, you know, we get a glimpse of it.

BONNIE. Whata you mean, Mickey? What's he mean?

EDDIE. It's a blind date.

BONNIE. Ohh, you invited me over for this guy, Eddie?

EDDIE. Yeah. Why?

BONNIE. Oh, you know, I thought. . . .

PHIL. She don't have to, Eddie. *(*PHIL *storms away toward the kitchen.)*

BONNIE. No, no, I just didn't know it was a setup.

PHIL *(Behind the counter getting a beer).* I mean, she should know it could be the final straw for me to justify some sort of butchery, but that's just a fact of life and not in any way meant to influence the thing here.

EDDIE *(Dropping off the counter,* EDDIE *moves to join* BONNIE *on the floor).* You disappointed in Phil?

BONNIE. I wasn't thinking about it.

EDDIE. What were you thinking about?

BONNIE. Eddie, look, it doesn't matter.

EDDIE. He's nervous.

PHIL *(At the counter with his drink).* I'm very nervous.

BONNIE *(Standing up).* Right. So what's the agenda?

EDDIE *(Giving her some coke).* Hey, I figured I'd just sort of rough in the outline, you'd have the rest at your fingertips; you know, operating at an instinctual level.

BONNIE *(Walking to* PHIL*, she spoons coke to his nose, and he snorts).* So you wanna go upstairs? *(*PHIL *shakes his head no.)* No?

PHIL. Out. Eddie, can I borrow your car? I don't have a car.

BONNIE. So we'll go over to my place. *(Picking up a joint.)* Can I take this, Eddie?

EDDIE. What happened to your car?

PHIL. My wife got all the keys. She put one a those locks on it so it fuckin' screams at you.

BONNIE. I got a car.

PHIL. You got a car? *(*BONNIE *is running around, collecting supplies, picking up her shoes.)*

BONNIE. So we'll be back in a little, you guys'll be here?

EDDIE. Where else?

BONNIE. Bye.

MICKEY *(As* BONNIE *and* PHIL *go out the door).* Have a nice time, kids.

EDDIE. Bye.

MICKEY. She's some bitch.

EDDIE *(Settling back on the pillows on the floor).* Balloons. Balloons.

ARTIE *(Lounging, staring at the ceiling).* Eddie, can I ask you something? I wanna ask you something.

EDDIE. Sure.

ARTIE. You don't mind?

EDDIE. What?

ARTIE. I'm just very curious about the nature of certain patterns of bullshit by which people pull the wool over their own eyes.

EDDIE. Yeah?

ARTIE. So could you give me a hint as to the precise nature of the delusion with which you hype yourself about this guy, that you treat him the way you do?

EDDIE. Artie, hey, you know, I have a kind of intuitive thing with Phil. Don't get in a fuckin' snit about it.

ARTIE. Because you desert me for this fucking guy all the time. What is it about you, you gotta desert me?

EDDIE. I don't desert you.

ARTIE *(Rising now, he moves toward* EDDIE*).* But what is it you really think about me, so that in your estimation you can dump on me, and treat Phil like he's some—I don't know what—but you lost a paternity suit and he was the result.

EDDIE. Artie, you're the only one old enough around here to be everybody's father, so what are you talking about?

ARTIE. Age don't mean shit in a situation like this.

EDDIE. First of all, I don't consider your statement that I dump on you accurate, so why should I defend against it? *(Slowly now,* EDDIE *is getting to his feet, his back to* ARTIE*.)*

ARTIE. It's subtle. Hey, you think that means I'm gonna miss it? It's an ongoing, totally pervasive attitude with which you dump on me subtly so that it colors almost every remark, every gesture. And I'm sick of it.

EDDIE *(Turning, he faces* ARTIE*).* I'm sorry your deal fell through. *(And walks away, looking for something, heading toward* MICKEY, *who lies on the balcony as he has been, arm dangling, watching everything.)*

ARTIE. You lie to yourself, Eddie.

EDDIE. Yeah?

ARTIE *(Pursuing* EDDIE*).* That's right. You lie to yourself.

EDDIE *(As* MICKEY *hands* EDDIE *the big hashish pipe).* Just because you're Jewish doesn't make you Freud, you prick.

ARTIE. And just because you're whatever the fuck you are doesn't make you whatever the hell you think you are. The goddamn embodiment of apple pie here is full of shit.

EDDIE *(Sitting down on the stairs to light the pipe).* So I lie, huh? Who better? I'm a very good liar, and I'm very gullible. This makes for an accomplishment in the field never before imagined.

ARTIE. And my deal didn't fall through, anyway. That's just stunningly diversionary on your part even if it did. Which it didn't. You're a deceptive sonofabitch, Eddie. Is everything a ploy to you?

EDDIE. What are you talking about?

ARTIE. You know what I mean.

EDDIE. I don't.

ARTIE. The hell you don't. Doesn't he Mickey? He knows.

EDDIE. I don't. I swear it.

ARTIE. You're just avoiding the goddamn confrontation here.

EDDIE. What confrontation?

ARTIE. We're having a confrontation here.

EDDIE. We are?

ARTIE. Yeah! I am! I'm gettin' out of here. Mickey, you wanna get out of here?

MICKEY. Sure. *(*ARTIE *starts up the stairs, but* EDDIE *blocks the way.)*

EDDIE. Where you goin'?

ARTIE. I'm goin' to the can, and then I'm getting out of here. *(He squeezes past* EDDIE*.)* And you, you sonofabitch, I'm going to tell you the goddamn bottom line because if you don't know it, you are—I mean, a thousandfold—just utterly—and you fucking know it!

EDDIE. What?

ARTIE *(Retreating toward the door of the bathroom).* Hey, you don't have to deal any further with my attempts at breathing life into this corpse of our friendship. Forget about it. *(He bolts into the bathroom, slamming the door.)*

EDDIE. You're a schmuck, Artie! You're a schmendrick! Go check your messages! *(Flopping down on the stairs, he turns to* MICKEY, *lying on the balcony floor just above* EDDIE*'s head.)* What was that?

MICKEY *(Unmoving).* I think what he was trying to get at is that he, you know, considers your investment in Phil, which is in his mind sort of disproportionate and maybe even—and mind you, this is Artie's thought, not mine—but maybe even fraudulent and secretly self-serving on your part. So you know, blah-blah-blah, rapateta—that this investment is based on the fact that Phil is very safe because no matter how far you manage to fall, Phil will be lower. You end up crawling along the sidewalk, Phil's gonna be on his belly in the gutter looking up in wide-eyed admiration. *(Bolting upright,* EDDIE *heads for the couch, where he grabs up a bottle.)*

EDDIE. This is what Artie thinks.

MICKEY *(Getting slowly to his feet now,* MICKEY *starts dressing to go out with* ARTIE: *putting on a belt, tucking in a shirt, putting on his shoes).* Yeah. And it hurts his feelings, because, you know, he'd like to think he might be capable of an eyeball-to-eyeball relationship with you based not necessarily on equality, but on, nevertheless, some real affinity—and if not the actuality, at least the possibility of respect. So your, you know, decision, or whatever—compulsion—to shortchange yourself, in his estimation, and hang out with Phil is for him a genuine disappointment, which you just saw the manifestation of.

EDDIE *(Has been drinking quite a bit throughout the evening and is now taking in great quantities, throwing his head back to drink from the bottle).* That was his hurt feelings.

MICKEY. Yeah.

EDDIE. What's everybody on my case for all of a sudden?

MICKEY. Nobody's on your case.

EDDIE. What do you think you're doing, then, huh? What is this? What was Artie doing?

MICKEY *(Having descended the stairs,* MICKEY *is now sitting down in the armchair, putting on his shoes).* You have maybe some misconceptions is all, first of all about how smart you are. And then maybe even if you are as smart as you think you are, you have some misconception about what that entitles you to regarding your behavior to other human beings. Such facts being pointed out is what's going on here, that's all. Don't take it personally.

EDDIE. What would make you mad, Mickey?

MICKEY. Hey, I'm sure it's possible. *(*MICKEY *moves now into the kitchen, looking for something to eat in the refrigerator.)*

EDDIE. What would it be? I'm trying to imagine.

MICKEY. The truth is, Artie isn't really that pissed at you anyway.

EDDIE. He got close enough.

MICKEY. You know, his feelings got hurt.

EDDIE. That's what I'm talking about. Don't I have feelings, too?

MICKEY *(Standing at the breakfast nook, eating ice cream).* Except it makes him feel good to have his feelings hurt, that's why he likes you. You're a practicing prick. You berate him with the concoction of moral superiority which no doubt reassures him everything is as it should be, sort of reminding him in a cozy way of his family in whose eyes he basked most of his life as a glowing disappointment.

EDDIE. You're just too laid back for human tolerance sometimes, Mickey. A person wonders if you really care.

MICKEY. I get excited.

EDDIE. You have it figured somehow. What's it according to—some schematic arrangement—grids of sophistication—what's the arrangement by which you assess what's what so you are left utterly off the hook?

MICKEY. It's a totally unconscious process.

EDDIE. Fuck you, Mickey.

MICKEY. Ask Darlene if she won't let you go back to coke, why don't you? Booze seems to bring out some foul-spirited streak in you.

EDDIE. That's the fucking bottom line, though, huh, nobody's going to take substantial losses in order to align and endure with what are totally peripheral—I mean, transient elements in their life. I mean, we all know we don't mean shit in one another's eyes, finally.

MICKEY. Do you realize you're turning nasty right before my eyes?

EDDIE. I'm feeling a little grim, if you don't mind. *(He takes a drink.)*

MICKEY. Just so you're aware of it.

EDDIE. Hey, if I wasn't, there's plenty of judgmental jerks around here to remind me. *(He takes another drink.)*

MICKEY. You gonna remember any of this tomorrow, or is this one of your, you know, biodegradable moments?

EDDIE. Lemme in on your point of view, Mickey, we can have a dialectic.

MICKEY. Hey. Just in case you notice me walk out of the room, you can reflect back on this, all right?

EDDIE. All right. On what?

MICKEY *(Now backing toward the door).* That, you know, this foul mood of yours might have been sufficient provocation to motivate my departure, see. You know, lock that in so you can minimize the paranoia.

EDDIE. You sound like my goddamn mother.

ARTIE *(As coming out of the bathroom, he starts down the stairs)*. Father.

EDDIE. Mother.

ARTIE. So you coming with us, Eddie, or not?

EDDIE *(Slumped on the couch, drinking)*. Where you going?

ARTIE. I don't know. Where we going, Mickey?

MICKEY. It was your idea.

EDDIE. No.

MICKEY *(To EDDIE)*. We'll go somewhere. We'll think of somewhere; change the mood.

EDDIE. No. Fuck no. I'm gonna get ripped and rant at the tube.

MICKEY. What's a matter with you?

EDDIE. Nothing.

ARTIE. You don't wanna.

EDDIE. No. *(As MICKEY, shrugging, goes strolling out the door.)*

ARTIE. You gonna be all right?

EDDIE. Who cares?

ARTIE. This is not caring I'm expressing here. This is curiosity. Don't misconstrue the behavior here and confuse yourself that anybody cares!

MICKEY *(From off)*. Artie, let's go.

EDDIE. Artie, relax. You're starting to sound like an imitation of yourself, and you're hardly tolerable the first time.

ARTIE. Eddie, don't worry about a thing. This is just some sort of irreversible chemical pollution of your soul. Your body has just gone into shock from all the shit you've taken in, so you're suffering some form of virulent terminal toxic nastiness. Nothing to worry about.

(ARTIE, with his last word, is out the door, and the phone is ringing. EDDIE looks at the phone and starts toward it.)

EDDIE. Who's worried? The only thing worrying me, Artie, was that you might decide to stay. *(Grabbing up the phone.)* Yeah. Agnes. Whata you want? *(As he talks, he arranges a nest of pillows onto which he flops with the phone and his bottle of vodka.)* I said, were you worried I might be having a pleasant evening, you didn't want to take any chances that I might not be miserable enough without hearing from you? No, I did not make an obscene call to you. What'd he say? It can't

be too dirty to say, Agnes, HE said it. Every call you make to me is obscene. Everything you say to me is obscene. Of course I'm drunk. If you don't want to talk to me when I'm drunk, call me in the daytime. I'm sober in the daytime, but of course we both know you do want to talk to me when I'm drunk. You get off on it, don't you. Reminds you of the good old days. If you hurt my little girl, I'll kill you . . . I said, "If you hurt my little girl, I'll kill you!"

(BONNIE enters through the front door, her clothing ripped and dirty, her knee scraped. Limping, she carries one of her shoes in her hand. Seeing her, EDDIE gets to his feet.)

BONNIE. Eddie . . . !

EDDIE *(Into the phone)*. I have to go. I'll call you tomorrow. Goodbye. *(He hurries toward BONNIE who, leaning against one of the balcony support beams, starts hobbling toward him.)* Where's Phil?

BONNIE. You know, Eddie, how come you gotta put me at the mercy of such a creep for? Can I ask you that?

EDDIE. Where is he? *(He is helping her toward the armchair.)*

BONNIE. He threw me out of my own car, Eddie.

EDDIE. What'd you do?

BONNIE *(Pulling away from him, slapping at his arms in a little fit)*. Whata you mean, what'd I do? He's a fucking guy, he should be in a ward somewhere! You could have at least warned me!

EDDIE *(Struggling to help her)*. Nobody listens to me.

BONNIE *(Still pushing or hitting at him)*. I listen to you and you damn well know it.

EDDIE. You're all right. *(Patting her, as she sits in the armchair, he heads for the bar to make her a drink and wet a washcloth in the sink with which to wash off her knee.)*

BONNIE. I'm alive, if that's what you mean, but I am haunted by the suspicion that it is strictly a matter of luck. Nor is it enough that I have my various limbs, you know, operational. I wouldn't mind having a little, you know—LIKE A GODDAMN, YOU KNOW, A SLEEPING CAT HAS IT!

EDDIE. Contentment.

BONNIE. I'm a nervous wreck! This guy is a debilitating experience. I mean, you should reconsider your entire evaluation of this guy, Eddie. *(Hobbling toward him, as if with urgent news.)* This is a guy, he is totally without redeeming social value!

EDDIE *(Handing her the drink, he guides her back to the chair).* Where is he?

BONNIE. I mean, I came down here in good faith, Eddie, I hope you are not going to miss that point.

EDDIE *(As he kneels down to tend her knee with the washcloth).* Will you get off your high horse about Phil, all right? So he took your car, so what. He'll bring it back.

BONNIE. He didn't just take my car, Eddie; HE THREW ME OUT OF IT.

EDDIE *(Trying to shrug the whole thing off).* So what?

BONNIE *(Ripping the washcloth from his hands).* Whata you mean, "so what?"

EDDIE. So what? *(Reaching to get the washcloth back.)*

BONNIE. Eddie, it was moving!

EDDIE. He slowed it down. *(Still he tries to get the washcloth, but she will not let him have it.)*

BONNIE. Right. He slowed it down. But he didn't slow it down enough. I mean, he didn't stop the fucking car. He slowed it down. Whata you mean, "he slowed it down?" As if that was enough to make a person feel, you know, appropriately handled. He threw me out of my own slowly moving car and nearly killed me.

EDDIE *(Indicating her knee which is right in front of him).* You scraped your knee!

BONNIE. I just missed cracking open my head on a boulder that was beside the road.

EDDIE. What boulder?

BONNIE. Whata you mean, what boulder? This boulder beside the road. THAT boulder.

EDDIE. Will you please get to the fucking point?

BONNIE. No.

EDDIE. Then shut up! *(Whirling, he flops furiously back on his pillows. Grabbing up his bottle, he drinks.)*

BONNIE. No! *(Rising now, she starts to angrily pull off her skirt and then her pantyhose in order to tend to her knee and other wounds.)* Because what I wanna know about maybe is you, and why you would put a friend of yours like me in that kind of jeopardy. Why you would let me go with this creep, if I was begging, let alone instigate it, that's what I'm wondering when I get right down to it, though I hadn't even thought about it. But maybe it's having a goddamn friendship with you is the source of jeopardy for a person. *(Swinging her skirt at him, she storms over to the bar for more to drink, for water and ice for her wounds.)*

EDDIE *(His feelings have been hurt: as far as he's concerned, he's been trying to help).* You want to take that position.

BONNIE. It could be.

EDDIE. You wanna—you take it if you want to.

BONNIE. I'm not sayin' I want to. I'm saying maybe I should want to, and if I think about it, maybe that's what I'll do and you ought to know I am going to think about it.

Due to his drinking, EDDIE, *from the instant* BONNIE *first hurled the shoe or hit at him, has been reacting increasingly as a little boy. Scolded by* ARTIE *and scolded by* MICKEY, *he tries to hold his ground against* BONNIE, *yet to placate her. When she yells at him, he winces, as if her words are physical. Behind her back he sometimes mimics her as she talks. When she, out of her own frustration, swings at him with a shoe, a blouse, her pantyhose, he recoils as a child might. Though he is attempting to contend with* BONNIE, *he is far away and with someone from long ago.*

EDDIE. Don't, you know, strain yourself.

BONNIE. I hurt my foot, too, and my hip and my elbow along with my knee.

EDDIE. I'm sorry about that.

BONNIE. Maybe you might show something more along the lines of your feelings and how you might explain yourself so that I might have them to think about when I'm thinking about it all, so I give you a fair shot. I mean, this guy, Eddie, is not just, you know, semi-weird; he is working on genuine berserk. Haven't you noticed some clue to this?

EDDIE. You must have done SOMETHING.

BONNIE. I SAT THERE. *(Behind the bar, she drinks, puts ice on her wounds.)* He drove; I listened to the music on the tape deck like he wanted, and I tol' him the sky was pretty, just trying, you know, to put some sort of fucking humanity into the night, some sort of spirit so we might, you know, appear to one another as having had at one time or another a thought in our heads and were not just these totally fuck-oriented, you know, things with clothes on.

EDDIE. What are you getting at?

BONNIE. What I'm getting at is I did nothing, and in addition, I am normally a person who allots a certain degree of my energy to being on the alert for creeps, Eddie. I am not so dumb as to be ignorant of the vast hordes of creeps running loose in California as if every creep with half his screws loose has slid here like the continent is tilted. But because this guy was on your recommendation, I am caught unawares and nearly maimed. That's what I'm getting at. I mean, this guy is driving, so I tell him we can go to my house. He says he's hungry, so I say, "Great, how about a Jack-In-The-Box?" He asks me if that's code for something. So I tell him, "No, it's California-talk, we have a million of 'em, is he new in town?" His answer is, do I have a water bed? "No," I tell him, but we could go to a sex motel, they got water beds. They got porn on the in-house video. Be great! So then I detect he's lookin' at me, so I smile, and he says, "Whata you smilin' about?" I say, "Whata you mean?" He says, like he's talkin' to the steering wheel, "Whata you thinkin'?" or some shit. I mean, but it's like to the steering wheel; he's all bent out of shape.

EDDIE. See. You did something.

BONNIE. What?

EDDIE. I don't know.

BONNIE. I smiled.

EDDIE. Then what?

BONNIE *(Hitting at him with her pantyhose)*. I smiled, Eddie, for chrissake, I smiled is what I did. It's a friendly thing in most instances, but for him it promotes all this paranoid shit he claims he can read in it my secret opinions of him, which he is now saying. The worst things anybody could think about anybody, but I ain't saying nothing. He's sayin' it. Then he screams he knew this venture was a one-man operation and the next thing I know he's trying to push me out of the car. He's trying to drive it, and slow it down, and push me out all at once, so we're swervin' all over the road. So that's what happened. You get it now?

EDDIE. He's been having a rough time.

BONNIE. Eddie, it's a rough century all the way around—you say so yourself, Eddie. Who does anybody know who is doing okay? So this is some sort of justification for us all to start pushing each other out of cars?— things aren't working out personally the way we planned?

EDDIE. Aren't you paying any fucking attention to my point here? I'm talking about a form of desperation you are maybe not familiar with it.

BONNIE. Oh.

EDDIE. I'm talking about a man here, a guy he's had his entire thing collapse. Phil has been driven to the brink.

BONNIE. Oh. Okay. *(Now, angrily,* BONNIE

begins to dress.) You consider desperation you and your friend's own, private, so-called— thingamajig. Who would have thought other? I mean, I can even understand that due to the attitude I know you hold me in, which is of course mainly down. Because deep down, a person does not live in an aura of—you know, which we all have them, auras—and they spray right out of us and they are just as depressing and pushy on the people in our company as anything we might, you know, knowingly and overtly badmouth them with. But at the same time, you certainly should be told that in my opinion you are totally, one hundred percent, you know, with your head up your ass about me.

EDDIE. Yeah.

BONNIE. That's what I'm saying. "Wrong," is what I'm saying. See, because I am a form of human being just like any other, get it! And you wanna try holding onto things on the basis of your fingernails, give me a call. So desperation, believe it or not, is within my areas of expertise, you understand? I am a person whose entire life with a child to support depends on her tits and this balloon and the capabilities of her physical grace and imaginary inventiveness with which I can appear to express something of interest in the air by my movement and places in the air I put the balloon along with my body, which some other dumb bitch would be unable to imagine or would fall down in the process of attempting to perform in front of crowds of totally incomprehensible and terrifying bunch of audience members. And without my work what am I but an unemployed scrunt on the meat market of these streets? Because this town is nothin' but mean in spite of the palm trees. So that's my point about desperation, and I can give you references, just in case you never thought of it, you know; and just thought I was over here—some mindless twat over here with blonde hair and big eyes.

EDDIE. I hadn't noticed your hair or eyes.

BONNIE. I'm gonna level with you, Eddie, I came here for a ride home and an apology. *(Finished dressing, she pivots furiously and starts for the door.)*

EDDIE *(Rising up on his knees)*. Don't you fuck everybody you meet?

BONNIE. Whata you mean? WHAT?

EDDIE. You know what I'm talking about.

BONNIE *(Coming back at him)*. I fuck who I want. What does one thing have to do with—I mean, what's the correlation, huh?

EDDIE *(He is headed toward her on his knees).* You fuck everybody.

BONNIE. I fuck a lot of different guys: That's just what I do. It's interesting. You know that. You learn a lot about 'em. That's no reason to assume I can be thrown out of a car as random recreation, however. If I want to jump, I'll jump. Not that that's the point, I hope.

EDDIE. It's not far from it.

BONNIE. I mean, I fuck different guys so I know the difference. That's what I'm saying. There's a lot of little subtleties go right by you don't have nothing to compare them to.

EDDIE. But you're getting these airs is what I'm getting at. I mean you're assuming some sort of posture, like some attitude of I pushed you into some terrible, unfamiliar circumstances and normally you're very discreet about who you ball and who you don't, when normally you—

BONNIE. He coulda hurt me, Eddie.

EDDIE *(Trying to stand up).* I don't care!

BONNIE. Don't tell me that.

EDDIE (EDDIE *careens backward against the stairway and bounces forward onto the floor on his hands and knees).* You're just some bitch who thinks it matters that you run around with balloons and your tits out. Nobody's going to take substantial losses over what are totally peripheral, totally transient elements. You know, we're all just background in one another's life. Cardboard cutouts bumping around in this vague, you know, hurlyburly, this spin-off of what was once prime time life; so don't hassle me about this interpersonal fuck-up on the highway, okay? *(Having struggled to the sink, he is putting water on his face.)*

BONNIE. You oughta have some pity.

EDDIE. I'm savin' it.

BONNIE. For your buddies.

EDDIE. For myself. *(The front door opens and* PHIL *bursts in, sweating, looking worried, clutching a handkerchief.)*

BONNIE. Oh, no. (BONNIE *flees away from* PHIL *toward* EDDIE *behind the counter.)*

PHIL. I'm perfectly, you know, back to earth now. I can understand if you don't believe me, but there's nothing to be concerned about.

BONNIE. I oughta call the cops, you prick.

PHIL. Your car's just outside; it's okay.

BONNIE. I'm talking about murder almost.

PHIL *(Grabbing the phone as if he will present it to her).* You want me to dial it for you, Bonnie; you have every right.

EDDIE. Shut up. Can you do that? Can you just SHUT UP? *(Grabbing the phone from* PHIL, *he storms away from both of them.)*

PHIL. I'm sorry, Eddie.

EDDIE. I mean, I'm disgusted with the both of you.

PHIL. I don't blame you, Eddie.

EDDIE *(Trying to get away, to be alone, he goes to the far corner, the couch. Done with them, he grabs up a newspaper, yet he is too angry).* I did my best for the both of you. I did everything I could to set you up nicely, but you gotta fuck it up. Why is that?

PHIL. I'm some kind of very, very unusual jerk, is what I figure.

BONNIE. You had no rhyme nor reason for what you did to me.

PHIL *(Following after* EDDIE, *perhaps sitting down next to* EDDIE, *as in an odd way he's giving an explanation for* EDDIE's *sake).* It's broads, Eddie. I got all this hubbub for a personality with which I try to make do, but they see right through it to where I am invisible. I see 'em see through; it makes me crazy, but it ain't their fault.

EDDIE. I go out of my way for you, Phil; I don't know what more I can do. Now I have Artie pissed at me, I have Bonnie pissed.

PHIL. She has every right; you have every right. Artie's pissed, too?

EDDIE. You know that.

PHIL. I didn't know it.

EDDIE. In your heart I'm talkin' about, Phil; that's what I'm talking about.

PHIL. It's—you know, my imaginary side, Eddie—like we were sayin', I get lost in it. I gotta channel it into my work more.

EDDIE. Fuck your work. What work? *(Getting up, backing away, yet towering over* PHIL.) You don't have any work, Phil, you're background, don't you know that? They just take you on for background. They got all these bullshit stories they want to fill the air with, they want to give them some sense of reality, some fucking air of authenticity, don't they? So they take some guy like you and stick him around the set to make the whole load of shit look real. Don't you know that? *You're a prop.* The more guys like you they got looking like the truth, the more bullshit they can spread all around you. You're like a tree, Phil. (PHIL *is standing.)* You're like the location! They just use you to make the bullshit look legitimate! *(Grabbing up a vodka bottle from the coffee table.)*

PHIL. What about my, you know, talent; you said I ought to . . . you know. . . . Remember?

EDDIE *(Moving to slump down in the rocking chair).* That was hype. I don't know what I was doin'.

PHIL. Oh.

EDDIE. Hype. You know.

PHIL. You were what—puttin' me on?

EDDIE. This is the real goods.

PHIL. You mean, all that you said about how I oughta, you know, have some faith in myself, it wasn't true.

EDDIE. Whata you think? Did you ever really believe it?

PHIL. Yeah. Sorta.

EDDIE. Not really. No.

PHIL. Well, you know. No.

EDDIE. So who we been kiddin'?

PHIL. Me. We been kiddin' me. *(Moving nearer to* EDDIE *now.)* But this is the real goods . . . now, right? I mean, we're gettin' down to the real goods now.

EDDIE. Yeah.

PHIL. So you musta decided it would be best for me to hear the truth.

EDDIE. Naw.

PHIL. So I could try and straighten myself out. *(By this eerie, unrelenting positiveness,* PHIL *seems to be almost demanding an escalation from* EDDIE.*)*

EDDIE. I'm just sick of you, Phil.

PHIL. Oh. How long you been sick of me? It's probably recent.

EDDIE. No.

PHIL. So it's been a long time. . . . So what caused it?

EDDIE. I'm gonna let you off the hook now, Phil. I'm not gonna say any more. *(Clutching his newspaper and bottle,* EDDIE *bolts away, heading for the stairs.)*

PHIL. You gotta.

EDDIE. I'm gonna lighten up. I'm gonna give you a break.

PHIL *(Grabbing* EDDIE *partway up the stairs).* Eddie, you gotta give me the entire thing now. I don't need a break. I want it all. I can take it. It's for my own good, right? I can take it. I gotta have it. I got a tendency to kid myself everything is okay. So, you know, you tell me what are the things about me that are for you, you know, disgusting. I want to know. Tell me what they are.

EDDIE. Everything. Everything about you.

PHIL. Everything? Everything? You really had me fooled, Eddie.

EDDIE. That was the point. *(Nodding, he slumps head bowed, on the stairs.)*

BONNIE. You guys are crazy.

EDDIE. Whata you mean? *(Looking drunkenly up at* PHIL.*)* What does she mean? You . . . look terrible, Phil. *(As trying to stand, he slips and bumps down several steps.)*

BONNIE. You ain't lookin' so good yourself, Eddie.

EDDIE. I feel awful.

BONNIE. Whatsamatter?

EDDIE. I dunno. I'm depressed.

PHIL. What about?

EDDIE. Everything. *(Gesturing, the newspaper still in his hand, he notices it.)* You read this shit. Look at this shit.

PHIL. You depressed about the news, Eddie?

EDDIE. Yeh.

PHIL. You depressed about the newspaper?

EDDIE. It's depressing. You read about this fucking neutron bomb? Look at this. *(Hands a part of the paper to* PHIL, *as* BONNIE *is inching nearer.* PHIL *sits on the arm of the couch, looking at the paper.* EDDIE, *clutching a part of the paper, is trying to stand.)*

PHIL. It's depressing. You depressed about the neutron bomb, Eddie?

EDDIE. Yeah.

There is an element here of hope in both BONNIE *and* PHIL *that* EDDIE *may tell them something to explain, in fact, what's been going on.*

BONNIE. It's depressing. *(Kneeling on the armchair, she looks over the back at* EDDIE *and* PHIL *with their newspapers.)* The newspaper is very depressing. I get depressed every time I read it.

EDDIE. I mean, not that I would suggest that, you know, the anxiety of this age is an unprecedented anxiety, but I'm fucking worried about it, you know. *(Taking a big drink, which empties the bottle he has.)*

PHIL. So it's the newspaper and all the news got you down, huh, Eddie?

EDDIE *(Crossing with his tattered newspaper to the coffee table for another bottle sitting there).* I mean, the aborigine had a lot of problems—nobody is going to say he didn't—tigers in the trees, dogs after his food; and in the Middle Ages, there was goblins and witches in the woods. But this neutron bomb has come along and this sonofabitch has got this AT-TITUDE. I mean, inherent in the conception of it is this fucking ATTITUDE about what is worthwhile in the world and what is worth preserving. And do you know what this fastidious prick has at the top of its hierarchy—what sits at the pinnacle? THINGS! *(He takes a huge drink of vodka.)* Put one down in the vicinity of this room and we're out. The three of us—out, out, out! "Well, I think I'll go downtown tomorrow and buy some new shoe—" WHACK! You're out! *(He goes reeling toward the kitchen.)* "Well, I thought I'd apologize for my reprehensible—" You're out! No shoes, no apologize. But guess what? The glasses don't even crack. *(He has a glass.)* The magazine's fine. The chairs, the table— *(He knocks a chair over.)* The phone'll ring if there's anybody to call. The things are un-fucking-disturbed. It annihilates people and saves THINGS. It loves things. It is a thing that loves things. Technology has found a way to save its own ass! And whether we know it or not, we KNOW it—that's eating at us. *(Lurching now, he grabs up a wastebasket, appears about to vomit in it, clutches it.)* And where other, older, earlier people—the Ancients might have had some consolation from a view of the heavens as inhabited by this thoughtful, you know, meditative, maybe a trifle unpredictable and wrathful, but nevertheless UP THERE—this divine onlooker— *(Staggering about with his bottle and basket.)* —we have bureaucrats devoted to the accumulation of incomprehensible data—we have connoisseurs of graft and the filibuster—virtuosos of the three-martini lunch for whom we vote on the basis of their personal appearance. The air's bad, the water's got poison in it, and into whose eyes do we find ourselves staring when we look for providence? We have emptied out the heavens and put oblivion in the hands of a bunch of aging insurance salesmen whose jobs are insecure. *(He ends up leaning against the counter, the basket under his arm, the bottle in his hand.)*

BONNIE. Yeah, well, Eddie, it's no reason to be mean to your friends.

EDDIE. Says you.

BONNIE. Exactly.

EDDIE. You want me to have reasons? I got to have fucking reasons? *(Suddenly woozy,* EDDIE *is trying to move away, collapsing onto his hands and knees and crawling.)* And you probably want me to say them, don't you. And you probably want them to be the right reasons, and I say them. They're whores, don't you know that? Logic is a slut. Be consoled that inasmuch as you are indiscreet you are logical.

PHIL *(Jumping to his feet, heading for the door).* I gotta get something from the car.

EDDIE. What?

PHIL. I'll be right back. *(He goes out the door.)*

EDDIE. No. I say no. You want me "nice." You want me "polite." "Good." *(Crawling as he talks, dragging along his bottle and basket.)* "Kinder." "More considerate." But I say no. I will be a thing. I will be a thing and loved; a thing and live. *(At his nest of pillows, he drops.)* Be harder, colder, a rock or polyurethane, that's my advice. Be a thing and live ... that's my advice. . . . *(He is on his back now, clutching his garbage can and his bottle. He turns onto his side as if to sleep.* BONNIE *walks to him and stands looking down.)*

BONNIE. Boy, Eddie, you are just transforming right before my eyes, and I used to have an entirely optimistic opinion of you. What is going on with you? *(She pokes him with her foot.)*

EDDIE *(He tries to look up).* Pardon me?

BONNIE. You know what I'm saying. I mean, you were once upon a time a totally admirable person, but it's reached the point I feel like a goddamn magnifying glass couldn't find what's left of your good points.

EDDIE. Suck my dick.

BONNIE. I'm being serious here, Eddie, I thought you had this girlfriend and it was a significant, you know, mutually fulfilling relationship, but you're hardly a viable social entity at the moment, that's what I think.

EDDIE. Things have taken a turn for the worse, that's all. Suck my dick, Bonnie.

BONNIE. Like what?

EDDIE. Everything has gotten relatively unconventional within me, but who'm I going to complain to? *(Turning away as if to hide or sleep.)* Who's listenin'? And even if they are, what can they do about it?

BONNIE. I'm listenin'.

EDDIE. She doesn't love me.

BONNIE. Who?

EDDIE. My girlfriend.

BONNIE. Whata you mean?

EDDIE. Whata you mean, whata I mean? She doesn't love me. *(Trying to get away, crawling, and dragging with him his bottle, his garbage can, his pillow. He doesn't get far, but has a new nest of sorts.)* Is that some sort of arcane, totally off-the-wall, otherworldly sentiment that I am some oddity to find distressing so that nobody to whom I mention it has any personal reference by which they can understand me? What is going on here? My girl-friend doesn't love me.

BONNIE. Sure she does.

EDDIE. No.

BONNIE. Why?

EDDIE. I don't know, but she doesn't.

BONNIE. Are you sure?

EDDIE *(Angry, pounding on the pillow in petulance, having a little fit)*. She's out of town all the time. She's always out of town. She takes every job that comes across her desk, you know, as long as it takes her out of town.

BONNIE. So you miss her.

EDDIE. She's a photographer, you know. Fuck her. There's pictures here. It's Hollywood.

BONNIE. Sure. You should tell her.

EDDIE. Talking about love makes you feel like you're watching TV, Bonnie, that why you're so interested? *(Suddenly sitting up, startled, focusing on her.)* I'm real, Bonnie. I'm real. I'm not a goddamn TV image in front of you, here; this is real. I'm a real person, Bonnie, you know that, right? Suck my dick.

BONNIE. You know, if your manner of speech is in any way a reflection of what goes on in your head, Eddie, it's a wonder you can tie your shoes.

EDDIE. You're right. You ever have that experience where your thoughts are like these totally separate, totally self-sustaining phone booths in this vast uninhabited shopping mall in your head? You ever have that experience? My inner monologue has taken on certain disquieting characteristics, I mean, I don't feel loved. Even if she loves me, I don't feel it. I don't feel loved, and I'm sick of it, you know what I mean?

BONNIE. I'm gonna go.

EDDIE. What for?

BONNIE. Home. I'm going home. Maybe you been doin' too much shit, Eddie. Even outlaws have to take precautionary measures.

EDDIE. Says who?

ARTIE *and* MICKEY *come in the door.* MICKEY *heads up to his room, while* ARTIE *goes to the kitchen for a drink.*

MICKEY. Hi.

ARTIE. Hey.

BONNIE. I'm going home. *(EDDIE is scrambling to his feet, trying to appear okay.)*

MICKEY. How was your date?

ARTIE. We saw your date out in the bushes there like a madman. What's the haps, here, huh?

BONNIE. The hell with the bunch of you.

EDDIE. He threw her out of her car. *(Staggering to the couch where he flops down.)*

BONNIE. Can't you just keep your mouth shut, Eddie? Does everybody have to know?

EDDIE. Suck my dick.

BONNIE *(Heading for the door)*. Goodbye.

ARTIE. Whata you doin' tomorrow, Bonnie?

BONNIE. Why?

ARTIE. I wanna know.

BONNIE. I don't wanna tell you, it's none of your business, I'm taking my kid to Disneyland. We're goin' for the day, so I won't be home.

EDDIE. You haven't been to Disneyland yet?

BONNIE. Of course we been. We been a hundred times. We like it.

ARTIE. I'll go with you.

BONNIE. You wanna?

ARTIE. Sure.

BONNIE. Great. Come by about eleven.

ARTIE. Okay.

BONNIE. Bye. *(As she goes out the door,* MICKEY *comes down the stairs and crosses into the kitchen to join* ARTIE.*)*

MICKEY. Bye.

ARTIE. Bye.

EDDIE. You guys see Phil outside?

ARTIE. So she likes to be thrown out of cars. I threw a bitch out of bed once.

EDDIE. It ain't the same thing.

ARTIE. Did I say it was?

MICKEY. What happened?

EDDIE. You implied it.

ARTIE. She was harassing me. We were ballin' away, she's tellin' me, "Faster, faster, slower, higher, do this, do that. Faster. Higher." So I says to her, "Hey, listen, am I in your way here, or what?" *(The front door opens, and* PHIL *comes in carrying a baby wrapped in a blanket.)*

PHIL. I got my baby.

ARTIE. What?

MICKEY. Phil.

PHIL. I got my baby.

MICKEY. Whata you mean?

PHIL. I went and took her.

ARTIE. He got his kid. You got your kid, Phil.

MICKEY. Where's your wife?

PHIL. Sleepin'.

MICKEY. She doesn't know? *(Tentatively,* ARTIE *and* MICKEY *move to gather around* PHIL *and peek at the baby.)*

PHIL. I snuck. I coulda been anybody. I coulda done anything. You like her?

ARTIE. You kidnapped her.

PHIL. You want me to kill you, Artie? This is my baby here. She's mine.

MICKEY. She looks like you, Phil.

ARTIE. Around the eyes.

MICKEY. And the mouth. Look at the mouth. That's Phil's mouth.

PHIL. I don't see it.

ARTIE. It's unmistakable.

MICKEY. You don't see it in the eyes?

PHIL. No, I look real hard, and I try like to think I'm looking into my own eyes, but I don't see anything of my own at all. I wish I did. Nothing familiar. Just this baby. Cute. But like I found her.

ARTIE. Look how she's looking at you.

PHIL. They can't see. It's the sound vibrations and this big blur far away like a cloud, that's all. Wanna hold her, Eddie?

EDDIE. My hands are dirty.

PHIL. 'At's okay. You want her, Mickey?

MICKEY. Sure.

PHIL *(Carefully he passes the baby to* MICKEY*).* She's light as a little feather, huh? You can hold her in one hand.

ARTIE. Does she cry?

PHIL. She's very good-natured.

MICKEY. What if she cries? *(*MICKEY, *eager to get rid of the baby passes her to* EDDIE.*)*

ARTIE. Tell her a joke.

EDDIE *(Taking the baby).* Ohh, she's real cute. What's happenin', little baby? Makes me miss my kid, huh?

ARTIE. Makes me miss my kid.

MICKEY. I got two of 'em.

EDDIE. This really makes me hate my ex-wife. *(*EDDIE *laughs a little, and looks at* MICKEY, *who laughs.)* I mean, I really hate my ex-wife. *(Now they start to make jokes, trying to break each other up, and top each other, all except, of course,* PHIL.*)*

ARTIE. And this little innocent thing here, this sweet little innocent thing is a broad of the future.

MICKEY. Hard to believe, huh?

EDDIE. Awesome.

ARTIE. Depressing.

EDDIE. Maybe if we kept her and raised her, she could grow up and be a decent human being.

MICKEY. Unless it's just biologically and genetically inevitable that at a certain age they go nasty.

PHIL. Except for the great ones.

MICKEY. The great ones come along once in a lifetime.

ARTIE. Not in my lifetime.

PHIL. Like the terrific athletes of any given generation, there's only a few.

MICKEY. You think it might be wise or unwise to pay attention to the implications of what we're saying here?

EDDIE. Who has time?

MICKEY. Right. Who has time?

EDDIE. It's hard enough to say what you're sayin', let alone to consider the goddamn implications.

ARTIE. Lemme see her, okay? *(As the baby is briefly in* PHIL*'s hands while on her way from* EDDIE *to* ARTIE, PHIL *stares at the child.)*

PHIL. We was all that little: each one of us. I'm gonna ask Susie to give me one more try. Just one more. I'm gonna beg her.

MICKEY. You oughta call her, Phil; tell her you got the kid, anyway.

PHIL. I'll take the kid back. I'll beg her. I can beg.

EDDIE. Phil, listen to me; you're a rare fuckin' human being. Underneath it all, you got this goddamn potential, this unbelievable potential. You really do; you could channel it.

PHIL *(Unable to look at* EDDIE, *he pulls away).* I mean, I'm startin' in my car again, Eddie. I was three days on the highway last week. Three whole days with nothing but gas station attendants. You know what I'm sayin', Eddie? I'll beg her. I'll follow her around on my hands and knees throughout the house. I won't let her out of my sight. *(*ARTIE *yelps and and stares down at the baby.)* What happened?

ARTIE *(Hurrying to pass the baby back to her father).* She shit herself.

MICKEY. Look at that smile. Ohhh, she shit herself, and look at that big smile.

PHIL *(Cradling the baby).* They're very honest.

ARTIE. Yeah, well, she's a broad already, Phil. Just like every other broad I ever met, she hadda dump on me.

Curtain

ACT THREE

SCENE ONE

TIME: Several days later, early evening.

PLACE: The same.

MICKEY *and* DARLENE *are laughing. They are at the breakfast nook counter,* MICKEY *behind it, pouring wine, while* DARLENE *is seated in front of it.*

────────

MICKEY. All I said was "Has anybody seen him levitate?" So she says to me, "Well, he's an honest person and he has been working at it for years, so if he says he levitates, I see no reason for you to doubt it."

DARLENE. Yeah, Mickey, what are you, a cynic?

MICKEY. I mean, not only is she miffed at me, but the entire room is in sympathy. This is the group consensus: the guy has worked at it, so for asking a question such as, "Has anybody seen him levitate?" I'm crude. Or I don't know what.

DARLENE *(Tapping his nose with her forefinger).* Bad, bad, bad. Bad, bad.

As MICKEY *imitates the moans of a guilty dog,* EDDIE *comes in through the front door and stands for a beat, looking at them.*

EDDIE. Bad what?

MICKEY. Dog.

DARLENE. Hi, honey.

Everyone, a little embarrassed, is avoiding one another's eyes.

MICKEY. We were talking about that levitation guy, right?

DARLENE. Which led to bad dog. Somehow.

EDDIE. It would have to.

MICKEY. I think it was a logical but almost untraceable sequence of associations.

EDDIE. Been waiting long?

MICKEY *and* DARLENE *speak almost simultaneously.*

DARLENE. No.

MICKEY. Yeah. *(Pause.)* I have, she hasn't. I gotta go.

EDDIE. Phil call?

MICKEY *(Rushing about now, preparing to leave).* Not that I know of. How's he doin'?

EDDIE. I got a lot of frantic messages at work, and when I tried his house, Susie called me an "asshole" and hung up, and from then on the phone was off the hook. So much for reconciliation.

MICKEY. It would appear they've found a pattern to their liking.

DARLENE. I mean, Phil's a lot of fun, but on a day-to-day basis, I would have to have a lot of sympathy for Susie.

EDDIE *(Heading to the kitchen and the refrigerator).* She's a very sympathetic bitch. That's her staple attribute.

MICKEY *(Near the door).* You want me to try and hook up with you later, or you up for privacy?

EDDIE. Depends on do I locate Phil or not.

DARLENE. You could call, or we could leave a message.

MICKEY. I'll check my service. See you. *(*MICKEY *goes out the door.)*

EDDIE. Let's just hang around a little in case he calls.

DARLENE. I'm tired anyway.

EDDIE. It's the kid thing, you know, that's the thing. He could walk in a second it wasn't for the kid.

DARLENE. He should have then.

EDDIE. Exactly. But he couldn't. *(Heading for the stairs, beginning to take off his jacket.)* So what am I talking about? It's just a guy like Phil, for all his appearances, this is what can make him nuts. You don't ever forget about 'em if you're a guy like Phil. I mean, my little girl is a factor in every calculation I make—big or small—she's a constant. You can imagine, right?

DARLENE. Sure. I had a, you know—and that was—well, rough, so I have some sense of it, really, in a very funny way.

EDDIE *(As he goes into his bedroom).* What?

DARLENE. My abortion. I got pregnant. I wasn't sure exactly which guy—I wasn't going crazy or anything with a different guy every night or anything, and I knew them both very well, but I was just not emotionally involved with either one of them, seriously. *(Emerging from the bedroom, he freezes, staring down at her, his shirt half off.)* Though I liked them both. A lot. Which in a way made the whole thing even more confusing on a personal level, and you know, in terms of trying to figure out the morality of the whole thing, so I finally had this abortion completely on my own without telling anybody, not even my girlfriends. I kept thinking in my mind that it wasn't a complete baby, which it wasn't, not a fully developed person, but a fetus which it was, and that I would have what I would term a real child later, but nevertheless, I had these nightmares and totally unexpected feelings in which in my dreams I imagined the baby as this teenager, a handsome boy of real spiritual consequences, which now the world would have to do without, and he was always like a refugee, full of regret, like this treasure that had been lost in some uncalled-for way, like when a person of great potential is hit by a car. I felt

I had no one to blame but myself, and I went sort of out of my mind for a while, so my parents sent me to Puerto Rico for a vacation, and I got myself back together there enough to come home with my head on my shoulders at least semi-straight. I was functional, anyway. Semi-functional, anyway. But then I told everybody what had happened. I went from telling nobody to everybody.

EDDIE. This was . . .

DARLENE. What?

EDDIE. When?

DARLENE. Seven and a half years ago.

EDDIE. That's what I mean, though; those feelings.

DARLENE. I know. I understood, see, that was what you meant, which was my reason for trying to make the effort to bring it up, because I don't talk about it all that much at all anymore, but I wanted you to know that when you said that about your daughter, I, in fact, in a visceral sense, knew what you were talking about.

EDDIE *(Moving down the stairs toward her, as it seems they agree on everything).* I mean, everybody has this baggage, and you can't ignore it or what are you doing?

DARLENE. You're just ignoring it.

EDDIE. You're just ignoring the person then, that's all. But at the same time your own feelings are—it's overwhelming or at least it can be. You can't take it all on.

DARLENE. No.

EDDIE *(Holding her hand, he pats her in consolation).* There's nothing I can do about all that, you know, that happened to you.

DARLENE. No.

EDDIE. It really messed you up, though.

DARLENE. For a while. But I learned certain things from it, too, you know.

EDDIE *(Still holding her hand).* Sure.

DARLENE. It was painful, but I learned these things that have been a help ever since, so something came out of it good.

EDDIE. So . . . these two guys. . . . Where are they?

DARLENE. Oh, I have no idea. This was in Cincinnati.

EDDIE. Right. *(Now he rises and begins mixing drinks for them both.)*

DARLENE. I don't know what happened to them. I think one got married and I have this vague sense that—I don't know what EXACTLY—but . . . No. I can't remember. But I have this sense that SOMETHING happened to him. I don't know what. Anyway, I rarely think about it anymore. I'm a very different person.

EDDIE. Did . . . they know each other?

DARLENE. The two guys?

EDDIE. Yeah.

DARLENE. No. I mean, not that I know of. Why?

EDDIE. Just wondering.

DARLENE. What?

EDDIE. Nothing. Just . . . you know.

DARLENE. You must have been wondering something. People don't just wonder nothing.

EDDIE. No, no. I was just wondering, you know, was it a pattern? That's all.

DARLENE. No.

EDDIE. I mean, don't get irritated. You asked me.

DARLENE. You asked me. I mean, I was trying to tell you something else entirely.

EDDIE. I know that.

DARLENE. So what's the point?

EDDIE. I'm aware absolutely of what you were trying to tell me. And I heard it. But am I just supposed to totally narrow down my whole set of perceptions, just filter out everything, just censor everything that doesn't support your intention? I made an association. And it was not an unreasonable association.

DARLENE. It was totally off the wall, and hostile.

EDDIE. Hostile?

DARLENE. And you know it.

EDDIE. Give me a break! What? I'm supposed to sit still for the most arcane association I ever heard in my life, that levitation leads to dogs? But should I come up with an equally—I mean, equally, shit—when I come up with a hundred percent more logical association, I'm supposed to accept your opinion that it isn't?

DARLENE. No, no, no.

EDDIE. Well, that's all it was. An association. That's all it was.

DARLENE. Okay.

EDDIE. I mean, for everybody's good, it appeared to me a thought worth some exploration, and if I was wrong, and I misjudged, then I'm sorry.

DARLENE. It's just something I'm very, sometimes, sensitive about.

EDDIE. Sure. What? The abortion.

DARLENE. Yeah.

EDDIE *(Handing her the drink, he pats her*

hand). Sure. Okay, though? You okay now? You feel okay?

DARLENE. I'm hungry. You hungry?

EDDIE. I mean, if we don't talk these things out, we'll just end up with all this, you know, unspoken shit, following us around. You wanna go out and eat? Let's go out. What are you hungry for? How about Chinese?

DARLENE. Sure.

EDDIE *(Grabbing up the phone and starting to dial)*. We could go to Mr. Chou's. Treat ourselves right.

DARLENE. That's great. I love the seaweed.

EDDIE. I mean, you want Chinese?

DARLENE. I love Mr. Chou's.

EDDIE. We could go some other place. How about Ma Maison?

DARLENE. Sure.

EDDIE *(Hanging up the phone)*. You like that better than Mr. Chou's?

DARLENE. I don't like it better, but it's great. Which one is your preference?

EDDIE. Well, I want—you know—this should be—I'd like this to be your choice.

DARLENE. It doesn't matter to me.

EDDIE. Which one should I call?

DARLENE. Surprise me.

EDDIE. I don't want to surprise you. I want to, you know, do whatever you say.

DARLENE. Then just pick one. Call one. Either.

EDDIE. I mean, why should I have to guess? I don't want to guess. Just tell me. I mean, what if I pick the wrong one?

DARLENE. You can't pick the wrong one. Honestly, Eddie, I like them both the same. I like them both exactly the same.

EDDIE. Exactly?

DARLENE. Yes. I like them both.

EDDIE. I mean, how can you possibly think you like them both the same? One is French and one is Chinese. They're different. They're as different as—I mean, what is the world, one big blur to you out there in which everything that bears some resemblance to something else is just automatically put at the same level in your hierarchy, for chrissake, Darlene, the only thing they have in common is that they're both restaurants!

DARLENE. Are you aware that you're yelling?

EDDIE. My voice is raised for emphasis, which is a perfectly legitimate use of volume. Particularly when, in addition, I evidently have to break through this goddamn cloud in which you are obviously enveloped in which everything is just this blur totally void of the most rudimentary sort of distinction.

DARLENE. Just call the restaurant, why don't you.

EDDIE. Why are you doing this?

DARLENE. I'm hungry. I'm just trying to get something to eat before I faint.

EDDIE. The fuck you are. You're up to something.

DARLENE. What do you mean, what am I up to? You're telling me I don't know if I'm hungry or not? I'm hungry!

EDDIE. Bullshit!

DARLENE *(Leaping up from her chair, she strides across the room)*. "Up to?" Paranoia, Eddie. Para-fucking-noia. Be alert. Your tendencies are coming out all over the place.

EDDIE. I'm fine.

DARLENE *(Pacing near the base of the stairs)*. I mean, to stand there screeching at me about what-am-I-up-to is paranoid.

EDDIE. Not if you're up to something, it's not.

DARLENE. I'm not. Take my word for it, you're acting a little nuts.

EDDIE. I'm supposed to trust your judgment of my mental stability? I'm supposed to trust your evaluation of the nuances of my sanity? You can't even tell the difference between a French and a Chinese restaurant!

DARLENE. I like them both.

EDDIE. But they're different. One is French, and the other is Chinese. They are totally fucking different.

DARLENE. Not in my inner, subjective, emotional experience of them.

EDDIE. The tastes, the decors, the waiters, the accents. The fucking accents. The little phrases the waiters say. And they yell at each other in these whole totally different languages, does none of this make an impression on you?

DARLENE. It impresses me that I like them both.

EDDIE. Your total inner emotional subjective experience must be THIS EPIC FUCKING FOG! I mean, what are you on, some sort of dualistic trip and everything is in twos and you just can't tell which is which so you're just pulled taut between them on this goddamn high wire between people who might like to have some kind of definitive reaction from you in order to know!

DARLENE. Fuck you!

EDDIE. What's wrong with that?

DARLENE. Is that what this is all about?

Those two guys. I happened to mention two guys!

EDDIE. I just want to know if this is a pattern. Chinese restaurants and you can't tell the difference between people. *(They stand, staring at each other.)*

DARLENE. Oh, Eddie. Oh, Eddie, Eddie.

EDDIE. What?

DARLENE. Oh, Eddie, Eddie. *(Moving to the couch, she slumps down, sits there.)*

EDDIE. What?

DARLENE. I just really feel awful. This is really depressing. I really like you. I really do.

EDDIE. I mean . . .

DARLENE. What?

EDDIE. Well, don't feel too bad, okay?

DARLENE. I do, I feel bad. I feel bad.

EDDIE *(Moving now, he sits down on the edge of the armchair, and leans toward her).* But, I mean, just—we have to talk about these things, right? That's all. This is okay.

DARLENE. No, no.

EDDIE. Just don't—you know, on the basis of this, make any sort of grand, kind of over-whelming, comprehensive, kind of, you know, totally conclusive assessment here. That would be absurd, you know. I mean, this is an isolated, individual thing here, and—

DARLENE. No.

EDDIE *(Moving to the couch, he tries to get close to her, settles on his knees on the floor beside the couch).* Sure. I mean, sometimes what is it? It's stuff, other stuff; stuff under stuff, you're doing one thing you think it's something else. I mean, it's always there, the family thing, the childhood thing, it's—sometimes it comes up. I go off. I'm not even where I seem any-more. I'm not there.

DARLENE. Eddie, I think I should go.

EDDIE. I'm trying to explain.

DARLENE *(Sliding away from him).* I know all about it.

EDDIE. Whata you know all about?

DARLENE. Your fucking childhood, Eddie. You tol' me.

EDDIE. Whata you know?

DARLENE. I know all I—what is this, a test? I mean, I know: Your parents were these religious lunatics, these pious frauds, who periodically beat the shit out of you.

EDDIE. They weren't just religious, and they didn't just—

DARLENE. Your father was a minister, I know.

EDDIE. What denomination?

DARLENE. Fuck you. *(She bolts away, starts gathering up her things: She's going to leave.)*

EDDIE. You said you knew.

DARLENE. I don't think there's a lot more we ought to, with any, you know, honesty, allow ourselves in the way of bullshit about our backgrounds to exonerate what is our just plain mean behavior to one another.

EDDIE. That's not what I'm doing.

DARLENE. So, what are you doing?

EDDIE *(Following her).* They took me in the woods; they prayed and then they beat the shit out of me; they prayed and beat me with sticks. He talked in tongues.

DARLENE. She broke your nose and blacked your eyes, I know.

EDDIE. Because I wanted to watch *Range Rider* on TV, and she considered it a violent program. *(Phone rings.)* So she broke my nose. That's insane.

DARLENE. But I don't care, Eddie. I don't care. *(She's really ready to go now.)*

EDDIE. Whata you mean?

DARLENE. I mean, it doesn't matter. *(She steps for the door.)*

EDDIE. It doesn't matter? What are you talking about? *(Grabbing her by the arm to detain her.)*

DARLENE. It doesn't.

EDDIE. No, no, no. *(As he grabs up the phone and yells into it.)* Hold on. *(Clutching* DARLENE *in one hand and the phone in the other, he turns to her.)* No, no; it matters, and you care. What you mean is, it doesn't make any differ-ence. *(Releasing her, he speaks into the phone.)* Hello.

DARLENE. I can't stand this goddamn se-mantic insanity anymore, Eddie—I can't be that specific about my feelings—I can't. Will you get off the phone!

EDDIE *(Into the phone).* What? Oh, no. No, no. Oh, no.

DARLENE. What?

EDDIE *(Into phone).* Wait there. There. I'll come over. *(He hangs up and stands.)*

DARLENE. Eddie, what? You look terrible. What? *(He starts toward the front door.)* Eddie, who was that? What happened? Eddie!

EDDIE. Phil's dead.

DARLENE. What?

EDDIE. Car. Car.

DARLENE. Oh, Eddie, Eddie.

EDDIE. What?

DARLENE. I'm so sorry.

*(*EDDIE *gives her a look and goes, and as he*

leaves her alone in the room, "Someone to Watch Over Me" sung by Willie Nelson starts to play.)

Blackout
(The music continues.)

SCENE TWO

TIME: Several days later. Evening.

PLACE: The same.
(In the dark "Someone to Watch Over Me" continues. MICKEY, ARTIE *and* EDDIE *come in through the front door. They wear dark suits.* EDDIE *is carrying a stack of mail. As* MICKEY *turns on the lights, the music goes out.)*

———

ARTIE. So now what? *(*EDDIE *walks to the kitchen, where he stands sorting the mail, while* MICKEY, *oddly buoyant, straightens up the room a little.)*
MICKEY. I'm beat. What's his name, his agent, wasn't there. You see him?
ARTIE. He's an asshole. *(Settling into the swivel stool at the counter.)* He probably would have gone berserk to be at Phil's funeral. I was almost berserk.
MICKEY. So it was just as well he didn't come.
ARTIE. Fuck him. There's no excuse.
MICKEY. Funerals aren't for everybody, Artie. You know. Life . . . isn't for everybody. As Phil demonstrated. Life wasn't for him. *(Moving behind the counter, he empties an ashtray in the waste can.)*
ARTIE. You think he meant it?
MICKEY. As much as he meant anything. How you doin'?
ARTIE. I'm okay. Except I feel, though, somewhat like at any moment I could turn into a hysterical like, you know, rabbit.
MICKEY. Yeah. What would that be like?
ARTIE. I think I'm gonna go home. I think I'm gonna go home, Eddie. What time is it? I'm whipped.
MICKEY. Ten twenty . . . two.
ARTIE. Ten? Ten? It feels like goddamn four in the morning. I feel like I been awake for years.
MICKEY. It's ten twenty-two.
ARTIE. It is, isn't it. My watch is stopped. What happened to my watch? I'm whipped. It takes it out of you, huh, Eddie, a day like this.
MICKEY. Death . . . takes it out of you?
ARTIE. Yeah.

EDDIE. What you gonna do tomorrow?
ARTIE. I got a bunch of meetings. We got a development deal.
EDDIE. Yeah?
ARTIE. Set, too. On paper. Good terms; very good terms. Terms I'm totally overjoyed about. *(There is an echo in this of their first act scene:* ARTIE *is aggressive and positive here; he is not going to let* EDDIE *get at him again.)*
EDDIE *(Smiling).* Come by, okay?
ARTIE. Sure. Late. *(Starting for the door.)*
EDDIE. Whatever.
ARTIE. Take care, you guys.
MICKEY. You, too, Artie. Fuck him, huh?. *(At the door,* ARTIE *hesitates, glances back.)*
ARTIE. The jerk-off. *(He goes.)*
*(*MICKEY, *crossing behind* EDDIE, *pats him lightly on the back.)*
MICKEY. How you doin', Edward?
EDDIE. I don't know. You?
MICKEY. Okay. *(Starting for the stairs.)*
EDDIE. Oh, I'm okay. I mean, I'm okay. Is that what you're askin'?
MICKEY. Yeah.
EDDIE. Yeah, shit. I'm okay.
MICKEY. Good.
(As MICKEY *climbs the stairs,* EDDIE *freezes and stands staring at a letter.)*
EDDIE. Holy Jesus holy Christ, I got a letter. Phil. Phil.
MICKEY. What?
EDDIE *(Tearing open the letter).* Yeah.
MICKEY. What's it say? *(Coming to the stairway rail to stare down at* EDDIE.*)*
EDDIE. What? WHAT? *(Reads.)* "The guy who dies in an accident understands the nature of destiny. Phil."
MICKEY. What?
EDDIE. That's what it says. *(Handing the letter up through the rails to* MICKEY, EDDIE *is examining the envelope.)* It's postmarked—the—this is the day. He mailed it on the day.
MICKEY *(Staring at the letter).* "The guy who dies in an accident understands the nature of destiny."
EDDIE. To die in—what the fuck? I mean, Mickey, what, what, what?
MICKEY *(With a shrug).* It's a fucking fortune cookie. *(He hands the letter back down to* EDDIE *who takes it.)*
EDDIE. I mean, if he killed himself, this is the note.
MICKEY. Whata you mean "if"?
EDDIE. I'm giving him the benefit of the doubt. *(Sitting back against the swivel chair to intently study the letter.)*

MICKEY. Eddie, c'mon, you wanna look this thing in the eye. You don't do a hundred down that narrow crease in the high ground because you're anxious to get home. A hundred MPH down Mulholland on a star-filled night is not the way to longevity. The guy behaved often, and finally, like some, you know, soulful jerk-off. Fuck him and forget him. What more can I say. *(He starts for his room.)*

EDDIE. I'm gonna look up the words. *(Standing up, he heads for the stairway.)*

MICKEY. What?

EDDIE. On the thing here, I'm gonna see if the dictionary might help.

MICKEY *(As* EDDIE *comes running up the stairs).* Look up the words? Are you out of your mind? Don't get involved in this thing. Don't waste your time.

EDDIE. But this is it—this is what he wanted to tell us. *(*EDDIE *goes into his bedroom.)*

MICKEY. He had somethin' to say he could a give us a phone call; he could have stopped by; our door was open. He wants to get some information to me now, he's going to have to bridge the gap directly; he's going to have to make an appearance, difficult as it might be. *(*EDDIE, *carrying a dictionary, comes out of the bedroom.)* Listen to me: Stay away from this shit. He's dead: He didn't want to discuss it before, I don't want to discuss it after. *(He grabs the dictionary from* EDDIE'S *hands.)* He had enough to keep him goin', Eddie—the wife, the kid, the career was decent—blah, blah, blah—but he had some secrets and he kept 'em, they ate a hole in his brain where his self-restraint might have been, his sense of proportion might have lingered, and without that—

EDDIE *(Grabbing the dictionary back).* But that's exactly what I'm talking about—this is the clue. To something. Maybe why. I want to know why. *(And* EDDIE *heads down the stairs with* MICKEY *rushing after him.)*

MICKEY. What why? There's no why in a disaster like this. You know, the earth moved. He was in the wrong place; this big hole opens up, what's he gonna do?

EDDIE. Your attitude, Mickey—will you please examine your fucking attitude?

MICKEY. This is a dead end is all I'm saying. There's no traffic with this thing. You go in, you don't come out. The guy made a decision beyond communication.

EDDIE *(Waving the note at* MICKEY, *who grabs it).* He left a note.

MICKEY. The note is tangential. It's part of his goof, you know, that he was a rational human being, when he wasn't. *(Balling up the note, he throws it on the floor.)* I want no part of this fucking, beyond-the-grave extension of his jerk-off sensibility.

EDDIE *(Grabbing the note up protectively, he smooths it out on the kitchen counter in preparation to study it).* The note is what he wanted us to think.

MICKEY. Bullshit.

EDDIE. He left it.

MICKEY. To drive us nuts from long distance. Lemme see that—what is this?

*(*MICKEY *grabs the note and paces around while* EDDIE, *sitting on the the the swivel chair on the living room side of the counter, focuses on the dictionary.)*

EDDIE. I'm gonna look up the words.

MICKEY. It's a fucking fortune cookie. What's to look up? "A guy who." That's him. "Dies." In case we didn't know, he gave us a demonstration. "Accident" is to propel yourself into a brief but unsustainable orbit, and then attempt to land in a tree on the side of a cliff-like incline. "Understand" is what he had no part of. "Nature" is the tree, and "destiny" is, if you're him, you're an asshole.

EDDIE *(He is busily turning pages in the dictionary).* Look. Count the letters.

MICKEY. What?

EDDIE. Count the words and the letters, I want to know how many letters.

MICKEY. Eddie, this is dementia, here. You've flipped a circuit. Grief has put you out of order.

EDDIE. You never heard of an anagram?

MICKEY. Sure.

EDDIE. So maybe it's an anagram.

MICKEY. You think this is an anagram?

EDDIE. I'd like to find out.

MICKEY. You think this is an anagram?

EDDIE *(Leaping up,* EDDIE *grabs* MICKEY *by the arm and marches him to the armchair where he sits* MICKEY *down, handing him a pencil).* You don't have to have any faith in the fucking thought, but just as a favor, you know, participate, okay. Help me move it along. That's all I'm asking. And keep your sarcasm to yourself.

MICKEY. What sarcasm?

EDDIE *(Getting back to the counter, the dictionary).* Can you do that?

MICKEY. What sarcasm? I'm—you know—this is—What sarcasm? This is insulting.

EDDIE. You're getting sidetracked.

MICKEY. I'll do this goddamn lunacy. I'll count the letters here, but get one thing straight, all right? There's no sarcasm here.

(He is so irritated, he cannot stay seated. He's up, he's down, dropping the pencil, picking it up, he steps toward EDDIE, then back to the armchair.) I've indulged in nothing even remotely sarcastic here, and I want that understood because you have obviously not understood it. So I'll make allowances, but if I've been flip, it's to put some humor into what could be totally and utterly morbid—and there have been times in the goddamn history of mankind where a little humor won a person some affection for the effort, you know, not to go under; anybody can go under. I mean, we're all goin' fuckin' under, so how about a little laugh along the way? So I'm flip. So what!

EDDIE. I don't feel like being flip.

MICKEY. Right. But you wanna do a goddamn anagram, right? On his death note. Whata you expect to uncover, the buried treasure of his mid-life crisis, and how it might hope to be viewed retrospectively? Fine. I'll give you a hand, but if you think there's blood in this stone, man, just forget about it.

EDDIE. "Flip" IS "sarcastic," Mickey.

MICKEY *(Rising, starting to cross toward EDDIE).* It is not. It's—"flip." On a whole other level, a whole other lower level and just lighter.

EDDIE. To me, it's "sarcastic." *(EDDIE is bowed over the dictionary, his fingers marking pages as MICKEY, carrying the note comes up behind him.)*

MICKEY. But that's crazy! Sarcastic is "heavy." It's mean. Funny, sure, but mean. I do both, but this was flip.

EDDIE. You shoulda heard yourself.

MICKEY. I did.

EDDIE. You shoulda listened closer.

MICKEY. You wanna get on with this. *(He crosses around to the kitchen side of the counter and flops into the other swivel chair, starting to pour himself a drink.)* So whata you got there?

EDDIE *(Reading from the dictionary).* So I have "accident" here, and "destiny." "Accident: a happening that is not expected, foreseen or intended. Two, an unfortunate occurrence or mishap, sudden fall, collision, usually resulting in physical injury." Blahblah, just repeats basically. And "destiny," we have, "The inevitable or necessary succession of events. What will necessarily happen to any person or thing." So, if you die in a happening that is not expected, foreseen or intended, you understand the inevitable or necessary succession of events.

MICKEY. Fuck him. *(He tosses the note into the trash can.)*

EDDIE. It makes sense.

MICKEY *(Moving off toward the couch and TV).* It makes no sense.

EDDIE *(Following MICKEY).* I mean, we owe him to understand as best we can what he wanted. Nobody has to believe it.

MICKEY. Anyway, he did it on purpose, so it was no goddamn accident. *(Sitting down on the couch, MICKEY grabs the TV Guide):* And if it was no accident, then his note is categorically, definitively irrelevant.

EDDIE *(Sinking onto the edge of the armchair, squeezing the dictionary, looking at MICKEY).* But how did he get there? Exactly how did he get to that point where in his own mind he could do it on purpose? That's what—

MICKEY. It's not that big a deal—that's the fucking truth, you know, you make an adjustment, that's all—you shift your point a view a little and what was horrible looks okay. All the necessary information that might deter you gets locked away. Little gremlins divert the good thoughts so you don't hear them. You just hear the bad thoughts, which at this point are convincing you they're a good idea. *(Rising, loosening his tie, taking off his jacket, MICKEY moves toward the kitchen.)* You get an idea, that's all. You don't understand the scope of it; you just lose the scope of it. So there you are, foot's on the gas, you're flying. So far so good. No big deal. Road, trees, radio. What's a little flick of the steering wheel? Maybe an inch's rotation. Nothing to it. An inch, what's that? So you do it. *(From the cabinets he grabs a bowl and a box of Cheerios.)* But with that, what? You've gone beyond what you can come back from. You've handed control over now, it's gravity and this big machine, which is a car, who are in charge now. Only it's not a car anymore. It's this hunk of metal rearranging itself according to the laws of physics, force and reaction, stress and resistance; heat, friction, collapse, and then you're gone, who knows where. *(With a shrug, he heads triumphantly for the refrigerator to get some milk.)*

EDDIE. So how many letters?

MICKEY. Right. The fucking anagram. This is exciting, Eddie; I've never been involved with a being from another planet before. *(Picking the crumpled note from the trash can, he tosses it toward EDDIE.)* Twelve and fifty-four. *(The note lands on the floor, and MICKEY pours milk on his cereal.)*

EDDIE. Twelve words and fifty-four letters. That's interesting. *(Picking up the note.)*

MICKEY. It's interesting, huh?

EDDIE *(With the note and dictionary, he settles on the floor, making a little desk of the coffee table).* Don't you see?

MICKEY *(Standing behind the counter, he eats).* You're in charge here, Eddie.

EDDIE. But don't you see?

MICKEY. Yes. I almost see.

EDDIE. I mean, they're both even. For one thing. There's lots of relationships.

MICKEY. Can I ask you something?

EDDIE. Sure. No!

MICKEY. I can't?

EDDIE. No.

MICKEY. How ripped are you?

EDDIE. I don't have time for your question. *(Furious, EDDIE rises up on his knees.)* You can make a worthwhile contribution to this project here, or you can forget about it, but your animosity, or whatever it is—resistance—it's nothing but static. I need some goddamn support and you're delivering all this—whatever it is. I mean, give me a break.

MICKEY. Common sense.

EDDIE *(Advancing on MICKEY, carrying the dictionary and note).* Is that what you think you're going to talk me into? Like what, for example, based on your vast experience with common sense is the take on this?

MICKEY. It happens.

EDDIE *(Something wild is entering into EDDIE as he faces MICKEY across the counter).* "It happens?" On a friend's death, you absolutely ransack the archives of your whole thing and come up with "It happens." *(As it appears EDDIE is now going to work on the counter, MICKEY grabs a* Daily Variety *and starts away.)* You need some help, Mickey. Common sense needs some help.

MICKEY *(Moving with his* Daily Variety *to the couch, he flops down to read).* You need some sleep.

EDDIE *(Working at the counter).* I mean, I think if he did it this way, if it is an anagram, it wouldn't be cryptic. The cryptic element would have been, you know, more than handled by the fact that it was in a fucking anagram to begin with, right?

MICKEY *(Reading).* Sure.

EDDIE. I mean, that makes sense, right?

MICKEY *(Turning a page).* Absolutely.

EDDIE. Mickey, for crissake, have all the goddamn private disdain you want in re-

serve, but follow the logic of what I'm saying. It's logical.

MICKEY *(Glancing up).* I'm in total fucking agreement. Anagram would more than handle cryptic.

EDDIE. I tried to warn him, you know. She was a snake. And I tried to tell him, you know, she was out to absolutely undermine the little faith he had in himself. I saw it coming; she hadda see it coming. I mean, for all his toughness, he was made out of thin air, he was a pane of glass, and if you went near him, you knew it. I'm gonna call her. *(Whirling, EDDIE reaches for the phone.)*

MICKEY. Who? Susie? *(Rushing to the phone to stop EDDIE.)* Eddie, you don't know what you're doing. You can't call her up in the middle of the night; she's a widow. She just put her husband in the ground.

EDDIE. I want her to have some fucking cognizance of this event.

MICKEY. She knows.

EDDIE. She killed him? You ain't sayin' she's looking at it from the context she killed him?

MICKEY. What?

EDDIE. You bet you're not because what she knows is he's dead and that's how much better than him she is. No more teddy bears—she's takin' care of business, so she's a together bitch, and he's weak, he punked out. A person cannot keep up their self-respect they know they look like some goddamn crazed insensitive prick who goes around dropping kids out of his life like they're trash to him. I saw it in him. She should have. What the hell was she thinking about?

MICKEY. Herself. I don't know. What do people think about?

EDDIE. Fuck her. What's she got to think about?

MICKEY. She wanted things. I don't know. So she thought about the things she wanted. You want to kill her for what she was doing—to get things she wanted. You can't kill people for that.

EDDIE *(Grabbing his box of dope and coke from its shelf under the counter).* She killed him.

MICKEY. You're gonna die a this shit, Eddie. Does it not cross your mind?

EDDIE. Hey, don't get serious here, Mickey. You know, don't get morbid here and ruin a nice evening. *(Spreading his vials out on the counter.)* Die of it is a little extreme. You have to admit that. And even if it isn't, take care of myself for what? For some state-of-the-art bitch to get her hooks into me. They're fucking ghouls, Mickey. They eat our hearts.

MICKEY. You don't know what you're saying. You don't. *(Pouring a large glass of vodka.)*

EDDIE. I do.

MICKEY *(Moving restlessly with his vodka and* Variety, *not quite knowing where to go, he ends up perched then on the edge of the big armchair).* I know what you think you're saying, but you're not saying it.

EDDIE. I do. I do. I know what I'm saying. I don't know what I mean, but I know what I'm saying. Is that what you mean?

MICKEY. Yeah.

EDDIE *(Snorting a line of coke off the kitchen counter).* Right. But who knows what anything means, though, huh? It's not like anybody knows that, so at least I know I don't know, which is more than most people. They probably think they know what they mean, not just what they think they mean. You feel that, Mickey, huh? *(He starts to move around behind* MICKEY, *coming up on his right side.)* About death, that when it comes, you're just going along in this goddamn ongoing inner rapateta, rapateta, blah-blah-blah, in which you understand this or that, and tell yourself about it, and then you ricochet on, and then it just cuts out—mid-something. Mid-realization. "Oh, now I under—" Blam! You're gone. Wham! Comatose. Dead. You think that's how it is? *(Ending up close to* MICKEY'S *head, stretched around the armchair, whispering into* MICKEY'S *right ear.)*

MICKEY. I'm going to bed. *(He stands and takes a gulp of vodka.)* And you should, too. Go to bed. You're a mess. Phil would want you to get your rest.

EDDIE. Fuck you about him, Mickey. *(Getting to his feet.)* I mean, where do you get the goddamn cynicism, the goddamn scorn to speak his name, let alone—

MICKEY. Eddie, Eddie, is everything my fault?

EDDIE. What'd you ever do but mock him and put him down?

MICKEY. Relent, I beg you.

EDDIE *(Advancing on* MICKEY*).* You ain't saying you ever did one good thing for him, are you, not one helpful thing!?

MICKEY. No, Eddie, what I'm saying is that unlike you, I never lied to him.

EDDIE *(Trapping* MICKEY *against the counter).* And you never loved him either.

MICKEY. Right, Eddie. Good taste has no doubt deprived me of a great many things. *(Slipping free now,* MICKEY *glides behind the counter to get a drink.)*

EDDIE. You lie to yourself, Mickey.

MICKEY. Who better?

EDDIE. No guts. No originality; no guts. *(He moves toward the couch, as* MICKEY, *behind the counter is furiously pouring himself some vodka in a water glass.)*

MICKEY. You want this goddamn ultra-modern, post-hip, comprehensive, totally fucking cost-efficient explanation of everything by which you uncover the preceding events which determined the following events, but you're not gonna find it. *(And* MICKEY *takes a drink.)*

EDDIE. Says you.

MICKEY. You wanna believe that if you do or don't do certain things now, certain other things will or won't happen down the road, accordingly. You think you're gonna parlay this finely tuned circuitry you have for a brain into some form of major participation in the divine conglomerate, man, but all you're gonna really do is make yourself and everyone around you, nuts. *(And* MICKEY *drinks again.)*

EDDIE. Hey, I'm just tryin' to level out here, Mick—the lobes are humming, you know—I got sonar bouncing off the moon; I got—

MICKEY. I mean, to whatever extent THIS FUCKING TORMENT OF YOURS is over whatshername, Darlene, believe me, she isn't worth it.

EDDIE. Ohhh, that move you made when you gave her up for her own good, that was genius. Whatever prayer I might have had was gone. She had you down as some form of totally unique, altruistic phenomenon, instead of the fact that you had a low opinion of her and what you really wanted was to fuck the bubble-brain Artie had brought us.

MICKEY. So what?

EDDIE. You're no better off than me.

MICKEY. Just slightly.

EDDIE. You don't have any feelings at all.

MICKEY. I don't have your feelings, Eddie; that's all. I have my own. They get me by.

EDDIE. So what kind of friendship is this?

MICKEY. Adequate. Goodnight. *(Turning, he starts for the stairs.)*

EDDIE. Somethin' terrible is goin' on, Mickey. It's a dark time.

MICKEY. People been sayin' that since the

beginning of time, Eddie. Don't feel particularly put upon, okay. Forget about it.

EDDIE. That doesn't mean forget about it. That just means it's been going on a long time.

MICKEY *(At the top of the stairs, he turns to look down).* I mean, Eddie, it's not the time that's dark, it's just you. You know? It's just you.

EDDIE *(A mix of fury and scorn).* C'mon, scumbag, where you goin'? We'll rant at the tube.

MICKEY. No.

EDDIE. The tube, the tube—it's the asshole of our times. You'll love it.

MICKEY. Wait up for Phil, why don't you? Wouldn't that be great if Phil came by? To keep you company. I'm sure he will. He always did.

EDDIE *(Turning on the TV and getting, instantly* The Tonight Show, *the intro music loud).* I can't hear you, Mickey. I got the tube. The tube and twenty-seven cable channels. I'm set for life.

MICKEY. Goodnight. *(MICKEY goes toward his bedroom door.)*

EDDIE. The tube. The tube. The best and brightest predigested. The dream devoured and turned to incandescent shit. *(MICKEY's door slams.)* Fuck you, Mickey. All right. All right. I'm on my own. *(He starts talking to* Johnny Carson *on the TV.)* How you doin', huh, John? *(Rushes to the counter, his coke vial in his hand. Behind the counter, he pulls out booze bottles, several joints and then a bunch of vials of pills.)* Hey, Carson! Hey, you motherfucker, huh? It's you and me, that's right. Head to head. Eyeball to eyeball, John. And I am fortified. *(Holding up his various drugs and vials.)* Here's for my left lobe. Here's for my right lobe. And here's to keep the spark plugs blasting. *(From the TV, the audience is shouting* "Yo" to Johnny.*)* Yo! Yo! *(Johnny announces that this is* The Tonight Show's *19th anniversary.)* Your anniversary! Oh, my god. Your anniversary! No, you didn't get my card because I didn't send you a fucking card, John! *(Johnny says that Ed looks like a "large penguin," as* EDDIE *at the counter begins sorting pills from vials; he drops pills into a large water glass.)* Penguins? You think that's funny? Bullshit! Funny is your friends disappearing down roads and hallways. Out of cars and behind closed doors. We got a skull in our skin, John, and we got ghosts. That's funny. *(John talks about "foreplay.")* Foreplay? Foreplay? Grow up! They're talking about quarks. They want us to think about quarks. They're going to

teach our children about quarks. And Black Holes. Imagine that. Black holes, John. The heavens. Astronauts. Men in—OH! *(Suddenly remembering.)* This morning, John, there was this guy—*(Running to the TV, carrying his glass of pills and a bottle of booze, which he sets down)* —Oh, you want funny? This one'll put you away, John—*(Grabbing up the newspaper.)* We got this guy on the obit page—he WAS an astronaut, who went round the moon and ended up in Congress and had surgery for a malignancy in his nose, then passed away six months later. *(Having rummaged in the paper, he now finds the page.)* I know, I know, it's touchy material, John, but it's rich, it's ripe, you'll love it. His campaign slogan was, "I was privileged to be one of the few who viewed our earth from the moon, and that vision taught me that technology and commitment can overcome any challenge." Here's a guy who went into orbit; he rendezvoused with the moon, and from that vantage what most impressed him was HIS OWN ABILITY TO GET THERE! Hovering in the heavens, what he saw was the MAGNIFICENCE OF MEN AND MACHINES! HE MIGHT AS WELL HAVE BEEN IN DETROIT. Right? And if technology and commitment are the instruments to overcome any challenge, I want to ask him, what about his nose?! *(Laughter from the TV. The front door is slowly opened, as* DONNA *comes in, fearfully, quite slowly. She stares at* EDDIE, *ranting at the TV. She looks around and sneaks closer, moving along behind the couch to see what he's looking at. She is heavily made up, her clothing in disarray, and tattered, her makeup old and smeared in some places.)* I know, I know, I could have crossed the boundary here of discretion. It's possible: my own sense of discrimination has taken quite a blast. I've been humbled, John. I been blasted. And I mean, I'm not tryin' to make a finished thing here, just rough in a couple of ideas. You could refine 'em, put your stable on 'em. Right? *(He takes a huge drink of vodka.)* Right, John?? You're not listening to me. You never listen to me. *(He is hitting the TV with a newspaper.* DONNA *has been reaching to touch him, to get his attention.)* You never listen to me! *(And now her hand hits his shoulder. He jumps. She jumps back, moving backwards so she ends up in front of him.)*

DONNA. Hey, Eddie! I ain't mad anymore. You mad? See my, ah, you know, outfit? I got a little bit from everywhere I been so I'm like my own, you know, whatchamacallit. Right?

Bits and pieces. So you can look at me and get the whole picture. See—here's Florida. *(She points to a patch on her clothes.)* And here's Vermont. *(Another patch.)* Which is a New England state. So if you put it together with a little thought, you can see I hitchhiked up and down the entire East Coast.

EDDIE. Unless you took a plane.

DONNA. Oh, no. I didn't. Airplane? Where would I get the money? How you been?

EDDIE. I'm a wreck.

DONNA *(Hobbling a little, she leans against the armchair to pull off one shoe. She is weary; her sock is torn, her foot sore).* You look a wreck, actually, but I didn't want to be impolite and mention it.

EDDIE. I don't know what I'm doing, you know what I mean?

DONNA. You're watchin' TV.

EDDIE. Right.

DONNA *(Tentatively, she is looking about for something to eat and drink; she is edging for the kitchen).* I'm gonna eat something, okay?

EDDIE. I don't know when I thought of you last, and in you walk. I don't get it.

DONNA. I'm a surprise is all.

EDDIE *(Rising, EDDIE moves after her).* But I mean, I don't know what pertains to me and what doesn't.

DONNA *(A little startled by his sudden movement, she falters).* Whata you mean?

EDDIE. I mean, everything. Right? I don't know what of everything going on pertains to me and what is of no account at all.

DONNA. Everything pertains to you, Eddie.

EDDIE. Yeah?

DONNA. Sure. *(Finding a plate with leftover bread on it.)* It's all part of the flow of which we are a part, too, and everything pertains to everything one way or another, see what I mean?

EDDIE. But I don't know, see, I don't KNOW.

DONNA. It doesn't matter.

EDDIE. So I'm just in this flow, right, like you in your elevator.

DONNA *(Finding an open bottle of water).* It wasn't mine.

EDDIE. So how'm I supposed to feel about it? See that's what I don't know.

DONNA *(Moving to the armchair to eat).* You have total, utter, complete freedom on that score, Eddie, because it doesn't make a bit of difference.

EDDIE *(Following her).* What I feel, it doesn't matter? This flow don't care!

DONNA. I don't think so.

EDDIE. So fuck it then! What good is it?

DONNA. I don't know.

EDDIE. Wait a minute, wait a minute—I don't think you know what I'm talking about. And I'm trying to grasp and, you know, incorporate as good advice what is your basic and total misunderstanding. I mean, is it pertinent, for example, that you came by?

DONNA. It doesn't matter.

EDDIE. I know that's what you think, but that's only because you have totally missed my point.

DONNA. Oh, no. So what is it?

EDDIE. I'm trying to say.

DONNA. Great!

EDDIE. I HAVE SO MUCH TO FIGURE OUT. *(Pacing near the TV, EDDIE grabs up the newspaper.)* I mean, there's you there, and then there's other items like this and this, and does it pertain to me, FOR EXAMPLE, that I read that - my - government - is - selling - baby - milk - formula - to - foreign - countries - in - order - that - the - mothers' - milk - will - dry - up - from - lack - of - use - and - the - formula - supply—you following me so far?—the - formula - supply - is - cut - off - and - the - babies - starve. I mean, how am I supposed to feel about that? First of all, I can't even be certain that it's even true. All I can be sure of is that it's printed in this goddamn newspaper. And I can't find out. How'm I supposed to find out? Write my congressman? Hire a goddamn private detective? Bring my private life to a screeching halt and look into it? I couldn't even if I wanted to. And should I ever figure it out, how the hell do I influence the course of these things? I mean, what am I supposed to do about all these things?

DONNA. I don't know.

EDDIE. That's my point, that's what I'm saying.

DONNA. So I do know your point.

EDDIE. But do they pertain to me?

DONNA. You're certainly worried about them.

EDDIE. I'm aware that I'm worried about them.

DONNA. I mean, I was saying to you that they all pertain to you as much as they're part of everything, right? That's what I was saying.

EDDIE. But as real things or as rumors?

DONNA. Whichever they are.

EDDIE. Which we don't know.

DONNA. Right. So this would qualify as a mystery, Eddie, right?

EDDIE. Yeah.

DONNA. So you can't straighten out a mystery, right? That's all I'm saying.

EDDIE. Did you know Phil is dead?

DONNA. Wow. What happened?

EDDIE. He drove his car off Mulholland.

DONNA. What happened?

EDDIE. The car crashed.

DONNA. No shit. I read about that. I read about that in the paper, but I didn't recognize his name, even though it was the same name.

EDDIE. Funeral was today.

DONNA. Wow. So that's why you're such a wreck, Eddie. No wonder. You were at the funeral.

EDDIE. Yeah.

DONNA. That'd wreck anybody.

EDDIE. Yeah.

DONNA. Was it sad?

EDDIE *(With a shrug, EDDIE gets through it quickly, not seeming to care at all).* You know, everybody wears the suits, you do the things. Everybody's there; you hang around, you know. The cars. Everybody gets to the church. So the priest is there, he blah-blah, blah-blah-blah, some guy is singing, mmmmmmmmmmmmnnnnnnnnn, mmmmm, you drive to the cemetery, right. Everybody's in a line, cars all in a line. Brrrmmmm, brrrrrrmmmm. Everybody's in the cars; blah-blah, blah-blah-blah. So we get to the cemetery, the priest's got some more to say, rapateta, rapateta. So there's the hole, put him in. Blah-blah, blah-blah-blah.

DONNA. Was it sad?

EDDIE *(Somewhere, here it hits him, a grief that, though there are tears, is beyond them: It is in his body, which heaves, and wracks him).* There was in the church we were all like a bunch of dogs. This guy would sing with his beautiful voice. He had this beautiful high voice. All alone. No organ or anything. Just his voice. And we would all start to cry. The priest could say anything, a lot a nice things; sad things. Nothin'. But then this guy from way in the back of the church would sing, and you couldn't hear the words even, just this high, beautiful, sad sound, this human sound, and we would all start to cry along with him. *(He gasps, tries to breathe.)*

DONNA. You know somethin', Eddie. I didn't really go to all these actual places on my clothes.

EDDIE. No.

DONNA. No. *(Moving closer to him.)* I thought about them all though, and bought the souvenirs at a local souvenir place, and I dreamed these big elaborate dreams about these places. First, I would buy this book all about these places like Lauderdale, and Miami and Boston, and then I knew what I was dreaming about, and I could dream with accurate and convincing details, but actually I went out of here north toward San Francisco, but I got no further than Oxnard.

EDDIE *(Sitting up, trying to get himself under control).* I know where Oxnard is.

DONNA *(With immense enthusiasm).* Great!

EDDIE *(Laughing a little).* What's so great about me knowing where Oxnard is?

DONNA. It's great when people know what each other are talking about, right, isn't that what we been talking about? I fell in love with a Mexican there. But after a while it wasn't love.

EDDIE. What was it?

DONNA. A mess. So I'm gonna sleep here if you don't mind. You got room?

EDDIE. I'm gonna be up for a while.

DONNA *(Standing up, looking around).* Oh, I don't care. I'm just happy to get off the streets at the moment. The desperation out there is paranormal.

EDDIE. I don't know if I'm going to sleep ever again. I might stay awake forever.

DONNA. That's okay; should I lay down on the floor?

EDDIE. No, there's room here.

(EDDIE slides to one end of the couch, while DONNA, carrying her coat, settles in against him, covering herself with her coat, then she looks up at him.)

DONNA. You wanna fuck me or anything, Eddie, before I go to sleep?

EDDIE. No.

DONNA. Great. Not that I don't want to, I'm just sleepy.

EDDIE. You want a lude, or anything?

DONNA. No. *(Turning back to go to sleep.)*

EDDIE. Valium?

DONNA. No. 'Night.

EDDIE. Goodnight.

DONNA. Pleasant dreams.

(He holds her.)

Black Out

Curtain

As Is

WILLIAM M. HOFFMAN

IN MEMORY OF: R.A., S.A., FORTUNATO ARICO, M.B., MICHAEL BASELEON, KENNETH BURGESS, FRANCIS BRADY, STEPHEN BUKER, PHIL CAREY, GREGORY Y. CONNELL, DANIEL CORCORAN, WILFREDO DAVILLA, ARTHUR ELLENBOGEN, BILL ELLIOT, TOM ELLIS, TIMOTHY FARRELL, CHRISTIAN FINCKE, NEIL FLANAGAN, GEORGE HARRIS, ANTHONY HOLLAND, MARK JOHNSON, CHARLES LOUBIER, CHARLES LUDLAM, J.J. MITCHELL, PIERRE MURVE, ARTHUR NAFTAL, STEPHEN PENDER, GLENN PERSON, RUSSELL REDMOND, L.S., TONY SERCHIO, GIULIO SORRENTINO, LARRY STANTON, DAVID SUMMERS, RICK WADSORTH, LARRY WAURIN, STUART WHITE

Developed in the playwrights' and directors' workshops at the Circle Repertory Company, New York City, under the leadership of Daniel Irvine. It was directed by George Boyd. It was first presented by the Circle Repertory Company and The Glines, at the Circle Repertory Company, March 10, 1985. Produced by John Glines/Lawrence Lane, Lucille Lortel, and The Shubert Organization (associate producer Paul A. Kaplan), the play opened at the Lyceum Theatre, May 1, 1985. It was directed by Marshall W. Mason; the settings were by David Potts; the lighting was by Dennis Parichy; the costumes were by Michael Warren Powell; the sound was by Chuck London Media/Stewart Warner; the production stage manager was Fred Reinglas. The cast, for both productions, was as follows:

HOSPICE WORKER	Claris Erickson
RICH	Jonathan Hogan
SAUL	Jonathan Hadary
CHET	Steven Gregan
LILY	Lily Knight
BROTHER	Ken Kliban
BUSINESS PARTNER	Claris Erickson
PICKUP 1	Ken Kliban
PICKUP 2	Lou Liberatore
CLONE 1	Mark Myers
CLONE 2	Lou Liberatore
CLONE 3	Steven Gregan
BARTENDER	Ken Kliban
MARTY	Mark Myers
VINNIE	Steven Gregan
PWA 1	Mark Myers
PWA 2	Lily Knight
PWA 3	Ken Kliban
PWA 4	Lou Liberatore
PAT	Lou Liberatore
BARNEY	Ken Kliban

NURSE   Claris Erickson
HOSPITAL WORKER   Lou Liberatore

Special Thanks: Jerry Vezzuso, Beth Allen, Nestor Almendros, John Bishop, George Boyd, Victor Bumbalo, John Corigliano, David Courier, Penny Dashinger, Barry Davidson, East End Gay Organization, Gay Men's Health Crisis, Barbara Grande-LeVine, Jay Harris, Stephen Harvey, Joel Honig, Reed Jones, Daniel Irvine, David Kapihe, Robert Kubera, Rodger McFarland, Terrence McNally, Barbara Myers, Claris Nelson, Constance Mary O'Toole, Kent Paul, Candida Scott Piel, David Richardson, Luis Sanjurjo, Mary Scarborough, June Stein, Paul Theobald, Dr. Kenneth Unger, Tobin Wheeler, Lanford Wilson, the New York Foundation for the Arts, for their support, with gratitude and love to Albert Poland, and Marshall W. Mason.

As Is was developed by William M. Hoffman in collaboration with director Marshall W. Mason as part of the Playwrights and Directors Workshops of the Circle Repertory Company in New York. It was presented by Circle Rep in March 1985 and moved to the Lyceum Theatre on Broadway two months later. It was nominated for several Tony awards and earned both the Drama Desk Award as Outstanding Play and a 1985 Obie Award. It has subsequently been produced all over the United States and around the world. A television version was made for Showtime Cable in 1986, and in 1987, Circle Rep revived the play at its Sheridan Square theatre. The theatre's managers asserted their obligation to remount the play because societal responses to the AIDS crisis had not changed enough to warrant its dismissal. In fact, the play had become more timely than ever.

Tanya Berezin, one of Circle Rep's founders, notes, "This was the first major play to deal with AIDS, and it was praised for the depth of anger, grief, and love it created."

As Is takes the form of a collage of events in the lives of two gay men, a poet who contracts AIDS, and his former lover, who devotes himself to caring for his stricken friend. Comprised of a series of moving monologues and dialogues, at times humorous and sentimental, at other times biting and graphic, *As Is* is, foremost, a love story. Hoffman chose, he said, to concentrate on one person with AIDS rather than on several case studies so as to focus on the unique humanity of his protagonist and the circumstances surrounding his often trying relationships with his family and friends. The intent is to make the viewer see the disease not from a distance but from the protagonist's point of view.

The play was nurtured through Circle Rep's development program before it reached a final version. Jonathan Hogan, who originated the role of the poet, Rich, states, "This is one of the . . . plays I've seen improved by the workshop process." In the original version, there were no female characters; women were added at the urging of a workshop participant. Hogan says, "One of the most chilling moments is when [one of the women characters] says, 'My husband has AIDS, and I have AIDS, and I'm eight months' pregnant.' "

As Is was born of tragic circumstances in Hoffman's own life. His father had had a stroke, and an uncle was stricken with cancer. Both were dying, and AIDS was killing close friends of Hoffman's. "My friends were dying, and I was feeling bad, but my feelings were not being reflected in the media, so I was feeling alone and scared. . . . I fell into a depression. . . . Sometime in 1982, as a sort of a therapy, I started to express my feelings on paper. I decided to write a play about a man named Rich—a writer and a runner—who comes down with AIDS, his former lover, Saul, and their friends and families. . . . On a deep, irrational level, I was terrified of catching [AIDS] by identifying with those who had it. Consequently, for a long period, my central characters, Rich and Saul, were shadowy and underdeveloped, compared with the background figures. But one day I realized the depth of my fear [and] permitted the play to be funny. I found that the audiences . . . responded to the humor. It enabled them to accept the pain of the sadder material. . . ."

William M. Hoffman was born in 1939 in New York City. "When I was a kid we were too poor to buy books, so I practically moved into the Inwood branch of the New York Public Library . . . and read books like Freud's *The Interpretation of Dreams* and *Introduction to Psychoanalysis*. . . . I loved reading about neurotics, psychotics, and perverts—all of whom I identified with. I also had a taste for poetry . . . the more incomprehensible the poetry, the more I revered the book. My favorites were Ezra Pound's *Cantos* and Gertrude Stein's *Four Saints in Three Acts*. . . ."

Upon graduation from the City College of New York, Hoffman supported himself as a copy editor for Hill and Wang, a fact checker for Scribner's Publishing Company, and in numerous other editorial jobs. Now, after the success of *As Is*, he earns his living from his writing. His work has been produced by Showtime and Disney Productions, and *The Ghosts of Versailles*, his collaboration with composer John Corigliano, was recently produced, with enormous success, at the Metropolitan Opera.

Hoffman's career as a playwright began at New York's Caffe Cino, where he met Marshall W. Mason, who has since directed many of his plays at Caffe Cino, La Mama, and at Circle Rep. Of his early playwrighting days Hoffman has said, "Suddenly my world changed from book publishing . . . to plays . . . a gay play. For its time, it was outrageous." Now Hoffman tries to write every day. "I don't always do this, but my ideal day begins at six o'clock in the morning. I like to run and exercise and meditate. Then by nine I like to be at work. I'll work four or five hours and then I have the rest of the day [free]. . . . I use a word processor. My cats tell me what to write." In between writing stints, the playwright likes to read about politics, history, and science. "My education was scientific for a long time. If I had another lifetime, I'd probably be an archeologist. Also, I read a lot of mysteries. I like P. D. James, Agatha Christie . . . my new favorite is Lawrence Block."

Hoffman confides his most "positive fantasy" about *As Is*: "I want to reach lots of people . . . to know that I had a part in demystifying the whole thing, making the subject more talkable, so that people with AIDS would be treated better. I want people to see that my characters are just like them; they are not creatures of the night. They are you and I."

Hoffman's other work includes *Saturday Night at the Movies* and *Goodnight, I Love You* (both for Caffe Cino), *Spring Play, Gilles de Rais, Cornbury: The Queen's Governor* (written with Anthony Holland), *Gulliver's Travels* and *A Book of Etiquette*, (both written with John Braden), and *Thank You, Miss Victoria*. Hoffman edited *Gay Plays: The First Collection* (Avon, 1979) and four other play anthologies, and his poetry has appeared in numerous magazines. His song cycle *The Cloisters* premiered at Town Hall in New York City.

CHARACTERS

SAUL
RICH

Depending on the budget and the skills and aptitudes of the performers, at least four other men and two women play the following:

HOSPICE WORKER
CHET
BROTHER
BUSINESS PARTNER
LILY
TV ANNOUNCER (PRERECORDED)
DOCTORS (5)
BARTENDER
PICKUPS (2)
MARTY
VINNIE
CLONES (3)
PEOPLE WITH AIDS (4)
AVERAGE PEOPLE (6)
HOTLINE COUNSELORS (2)
NURSE
HOSPITAL WORKER
DRUG DEALERS AND CUSTOMERS (5)

The play is set in New York City in the present. Stage right is Saul's fashionable loft space, suggested by a sofa, Barcelona chair, bench, and area rug. Upstage Center is a bar, Stage Left, a bench. Except for short exits, the actors remain onstage for the whole play. There is no intermission.

"The 'Red Death' had long devastated the country. No pestilence had ever been so fatal, or so hideous. . . . The scarlet stains upon the body . . . were the pest ban which shut the victim out from the sympathy of his fellow-men. . . . But the Prince Prospero was happy and dauntless and sagacious. When his dominions were half depopulated, he summoned to his presence a thousand hale and light-hearted friends . . . and with these retired to the deep seclusion of one of his castellated abbeys. . . . A strong and lofty wall girdled it in. The wall had grates of iron. The courtiers brought furnaces and massy hammers and welded the bolts. . . . With such precautions the courtiers might bid defiance to contagion. In the meantime it was folly to grieve, or to think. The Prince had provided all the appliances of pleasure. There were buffoons, there were improvisatori, there were ballet-dancers, there were musicians, there was Beauty, there was wine. All these and security were within. Without was the 'Red Death.' "

—Edgar Allan Poe, *The Masque of the Red Death*

My tale was heard, and yet it was not told;
My fruit is fallen, and yet my leaves are green;
My youth is spent, and yet I am not old;
I saw the world, and yet I was not seen;
My thread is cut, and yet it is not spun;
And now I live, and now my life is done.
Chidiock Tichborne, *Elegy*

The hospice worker, a dowdy middle-aged woman walks downstage center and addresses the audience.

HOSPICE WORKER. Mother Superior always used to say, "Watch out for the religious cranks, Sister Veronica." When I started working for the hospice I had a touch of the crank about me. I think maybe that's why they gave me the old heave-ho from the convent. But I've kept my vow of chastity and I've made a pilgrimage to Lourdes.

My job is to ease the way for those who are dying. I've done this for the last couple of years. I work mainly here at St. Vincent's. During the day I have a boring secretarial job, which is how I support my career as a saint.

I was much more idealistic when I started. I had just left the convent. I guess I thought working with the dying would give me spiritual gold stars. I thought I'd be able to impart my great wisdom to those in need of improvement. I wanted to bear witness to dramatic deathbed conversions, see shafts of light emanating from heaven, multicolored auras hovering above the heads of those in the process of expiring. I always imagined they would go out expressing their gratitude for all I had done.

A quick joke: Did you hear about the man who lost his left side? . . . He's all *right* now. All right now. *(She laughs.)* We tell a lot of jokes in my line of work. *(She takes her seat. Lights come up on two casually dressed men in their thirties seated in the living area.)*

RICH. You take Henry.
SAUL. Cut him in half.

RICH. You can keep him.

SAUL. What are we going to do about him?

RICH. I said he's yours.

SAUL. You found him.

RICH. I don't want him.

SAUL. Chet doesn't like cats?

RICH. I knew this would happen. Don't start in.

SAUL. We gotta get things settled.

RICH. Then let's. How 'bout if we simplify things: sell everything and split the cash.

SAUL. Even the cobalt glass?

RICH. Yes.

SAUL. And Aunt Billie's hooked rug? Say, how's she doing?

RICH. She's on medication. Sell the rug.

SAUL. I will not sell the manikin heads. I don't care what you say.

RICH. Then take them.

SAUL. And the chromium lamp? I love that lamp.

RICH. Take it.

SAUL. And the Barcelona chair?

RICH. The Barcelona chair is *mine! (Beat.)* Fuck it. Take it. Take everything. I won't be Jewish about it. *(He rises to go.)*

SAUL. Why didn't you warn me we were going to play Christians and Jews today? I would have worn my yellow star.

RICH. I've gotta go. *(RICH is leaving.)*

SAUL. Where're you going?

RICH. I'm not feeling so hot. Let's make it another day.

SAUL. *(Blocking his way).* Sit down.

RICH *(Pushing his hand away).* Don't push me.

SAUL. Sorry. I don't like this any more than you, but we gotta do it. It's been six months. *(Lightening things up.)* A divorce is not final until the property settlement.

RICH. Saul . . . ? *(He's about to say something important.)*

SAUL. What, Rich? *(He waits expectantly.)* What?

RICH. Never mind.

SAUL. What? . . . What? . . . You always do that!

RICH. I want the chair.

SAUL. You can have the fucking Barcelona chair if Chet wants it so bad! . . . What about the paintings? Do you want to sell the Paul Cadmus?

RICH. Yes.

SAUL. You love the Cadmus. *(Silence.)* And who's going to buy the Burgess drawings? Did you hear that Kenny died?

RICH. We'll donate them to the Metropolitan.

SAUL. Just what they always wanted: the world's largest collection of Magic Marker hustler portraits. *(RICH nods.)*

RICH. They're yours.

SAUL. But you commissioned them. We'll split them up: I get the blonds and you get the blacks—or vice versa.

RICH. All yours.

SAUL. Then you get the Mickey Mouse collection.

RICH. Sell it.

SAUL. You don't sell collectibles. Not right now. What's with this money mania? Between the book and the catering, I thought you were doing well.

RICH. I want to build a swimming pool.

SAUL. You don't swim.

RICH. I want a Mercedes.

SAUL. You don't drive. It's Chet—he'll bankrupt you! *(Beat.)* I don't believe I said that . . . *(Sincerely.)* Your book is beautiful.

RICH. I never thanked you for the cover photograph.

SAUL *(Shrugging off the compliment).* How's it selling?

RICH. Not bad—for short stories. Everyone mentions your photo. Ed White said—

SAUL. Your book is terrific. Really.

RICH. I'm glad you like it.

SAUL. One minor thing.

RICH. What's that?

SAUL. I thought the dedication was a bit much.

RICH. Why are you doing this?

SAUL. Don't you think quoting Cavafy in Greek is a little coy?

RICH. Please!

SAUL. Why didn't you just say, "To Chet, whose beautiful buns inspired these tales"?

RICH. Jesus Christ!

SAUL. I'm sorry! *(Silence.)*

RICH. I sold the IBM stock. You were right about it. You have always been right about money. *(He hands SAUL a check.)* This includes the thousand I borrowed for the periodontist.

SAUL. You sure?

RICH. Take it.

SAUL. I'm not desperate for it.

RICH. It's yours.

SAUL. I don't want it.

RICH. Damn it!

SAUL *(Taking the check).* Okay.

RICH. That makes us even now.

SAUL *(Examining the check).* Clouds and trees.

RICH. Let's get on with this.

SAUL. Is he waiting for you downstairs? You could have told him to come up.

RICH. Shit. No! Can it. *(Beat.)* I won't be wanting the copper pots.

SAUL. Why not? When you and Chet move to your space you'll want to cook again.

RICH. I just don't want them! People change. *(Silence.)* I'm eating out a lot.

SAUL. Chet can't cook?

RICH *(Deciding not to respond with a bitchy comment).* You keep the rowing machine.

SAUL. Have you lost weight?

RICH. And the trampoline.

SAUL. There's some Black Forest cake in the fridge. *(SAUL goes toward the kitchen to get the cake.)*

RICH. Stop it.

SAUL. Stop what?

RICH. Just stop.

SAUL. I can't.

RICH. We're almost through.

SAUL. I have feelings.

RICH. You have only one feeling.

SAUL. He won't make you happy.

RICH. Here we go again. *(RICH gets up to go.)*

SAUL. Don't!

RICH. Keep everything.

SAUL. I'm not myself.

RICH. Nothing is worth this.

SAUL. I've been upset.

RICH. I mean it.

SAUL. Don't go. Please. *(RICH sits. Long pause.)* I visited Teddy today at St. Vincent's. It's very depressing . . . He's lying there in bed, out of it. He's been out of it since the time we saw him. He's not in any pain, snorting his imaginary cocaine, doing his poppers. Sometimes he's washing his mother's floor, and he's speaking to her in Spanish. Sometimes he's having sex. You can see him having sex right in front of you. He doesn't even know you're there. *(Pause. Both men look down at their feet.)* Jimmy died, as you must have heard. I went out to San Francisco to be with him the last few weeks. You must have heard that, too. He was in a coma for a month. Everybody wanted to pull the plug, but they were afraid of legal complications. I held his hand. He couldn't talk, but I could see his eyelids flutter. I swear he knew I was with him. *(Pause.)* Harry has K.S., and Matt has trouble breathing. He went for tests today . . . I haven't slept well for weeks. Every morning I examine my body for swellings, marks. I'm terrified of every pimple, every rash, even though I've tested negative. If I cough I think of Teddy. I wish he would die. He *is* dead. He might as well be. Why can't he die? I feel the disease closing in on me. All my activities are life and death. Keep up my Blue Cross. Up my reps. Eat my vegetables.

Sometimes I'm so scared I go back on my resolutions: I drink too much, and I smoke a joint, and I find myself at the bars and clubs, where I stand around and watch. They remind me of accounts of Europe during the Black Plague: groping in the dark, dancing till you drop. The New Wave is the corpse look. I'm very frightened and I miss you. Say something, damn it. *(Beat.)*

RICH. I have it. *(Immediately the lights come up on the L. side of the stage.)*

CHET *(A handsome, boyish man in his early twenties).* You what?

LILY *(A beautiful woman, thirtyish).* You have what?

BROTHER *(To his wife, whom we don't see).* He has AIDS.

SAUL. I don't think that's funny.

PARTNER. Don't be ridiculous.

RICH. That's the bad news.

PARTNER. You ran the goddamned marathon.

LILY *(Overlapping).* Darling!

RICH. The good news is that I have only the swollen glands. *(Two doctors appear in white gowns.)*

DOCTOR 1. We call it a "Pre-AIDS Condition."

DOCTOR 2 *(Overlapping).* "AIDS-related Complex."

RICH. I've lost some weight.

SAUL. I'm in a state of shock.

LILY. Move in with me. Chet doesn't know how to take care of you.

RICH *(Overlapping).* I tire easily. My temperature goes up and down.

DOCTOR 1. Your suppressor cells outnumber your helper cells.

BROTHER. I don't care what he has, Betty, he's my brother.

CHET. You're my lover.

LILY. You're my buddy.

PARTNER. Rich and I started the business about a year ago. But now word got out that Rich is ill. I tried to explain: he doesn't touch the food; I do all the cooking. But they won't listen.

BROTHER *(Overlapping).* I'm not in the habit

of kissing my brother. I touched him on the back when I arrived and when I left.

PARTNER. Why would they? I wonder if I'd use a caterer who had AIDS.

SAUL. Doctors make mistakes all the time.

DOCTOR 2. I can put you on AZT.

DOCTOR 1 (Simultaneously). And Pentamadine Mist.

LILY. I got this job.

CHET. If you don't mind, I'll sleep on the couch tonight. You've been sweating a lot.

LILY. I can't turn it down. The work is pure dreck, and who wants to tour Canada in January, but they're paying a fortune. I'll be back in four weeks.

BROTHER (Overlapping). When he offered me a cup of coffee I told him I'd have a can of beer.

PARTNER (Overlapping). I can understand what he's going through. Myself, I've been wrestling with cancer for a while.

SAUL. Remember when they told my niece she had skin cancer? It turned out to be dry skin.

PARTNER (Overlapping). I'm winning.

CHET. I hope you don't mind, but I'll use the red soap dish and you'll use the blue.

RICH. Christ! I've been putting the blocks to you nightly for months and now you're worried about sharing the fucking soap dish?

BROTHER (Overlapping). Christ, I didn't even use the bathroom, even though I had to take a leak so bad I could taste it. Now, that's paranoid.

PARTNER. I wonder if it's safe to use the same telephone, or whether I'm being paranoid.

CHET. I know I'm being paranoid.

LILY. They're flying me out to the Coast. I hate that place.

RICH (Simultaneously). Chet, you've been out every night this week. Do you have to go out again?

BROTHER. I know you're scared, Betty, but I will not tell my own brother he's not welcome in my house.

CHET. Need something from outside?

BROTHER. He's spent every Christmas with us since we got married, and this year will be no exception.

RICH. Forget I said anything: just don't wake me up when you get in.

BROTHER. You're forcing me to choose between you and my brother.

CHET. See you later.

LILY. I've been dating this guy, Mick—can you imagine me dating? Well, he's very nice, and he's got a lot of money, and he's not impressed with my life in the theater, and he's straight—and that's why I haven't been up to see you. Rich?

CHET (Simultaneously). You know I'd do anything for you.

RICH. You're walking out on me.

BROTHER. We're going to Betty's mother for Christmas.

CHET. I need more space to get my head together.

SAUL. What did you expect?

RICH. Chet, please, I need you! (RICH tries to put his arms around CHET. Everyone except SAUL pulls back terrified.)

CHET, BROTHER, LILY, PARTNER, DOCTORS. Don't touch me! (Beat.)

LILY. Please forgive me!

CHET. This thing has me blown away.

BROTHER. If it weren't for the kids.

PARTNER. I don't know what the hell we're going to do.

SAUL. Bastards! (CHET, the brother, the partner, and LILY put on white gowns and become doctors.)

RICH (To DOCTOR 1). Doctor, tell me the truth. What are my chances?

DOCTORS 1 and 2. We have some highly effective treatments.

RICH (To DOCTOR 2). Doctor, tell me the truth. What are my chances?

DOCTOR 2. The medical advances are astounding.

RICH (To DOCTOR 3). What are my chances?

DOCTOR 3. We're optimistic.

RICH (To DOCTORS 4 and 6). Am I going to make it, doctors, yes or no?!

DOCTOR 4. Just hang in there.

TV ANOUNCER (Prerecored, simultanoeus to RICH's questions). Scientists tell us that millions of people worldwide are infected. So far, a vast majority of the cases in this country have been homosexual or bisexual men or intravenous drug users of both sexes, but the disease is beginning to make inroads into the general population. When will science conquer this dreaded plague? We don't know. We don't know. We simply don't know. Don't know. (Etc.)

SAUL. Rich?

DOCTORS. We don't know.

SAUL. And for three months you kept this from me. (The doctors exit. We're back in SAUL's apartment.)

RICH. I don't want your pity.

SAUL. You're my friend. You'll stay with me till you feel better.

RICH. Aren't you afraid I'll infect you?

SAUL. We'll take reasonable precautions.

RICH. Paper plates, plastic cups, face masks—

SAUL. You have HIV, you're not radioactive.

RICH. I'd prefer to live alone, thank you.

SAUL. You need me.

RICH. Besides, if I live with you, where am I going to bring my tricks?

SAUL. You pick up people?

RICH *(Standing at the bar)*. I go to bars . . . I pick up guys . . . but I give them a medical report before we leave . . . *(Without a pause, we're in a bar.* RICH *is talking to a stranger.)* I should tell you something.

PICKUP 1. You like something kinky. Whips? Golden showers? Fist?

RICH. It's not like that.

PICKUP 1. I once picked up a guy liked to be yelled at in German. The only German I know is the "Ode to Joy" from Beethoven's Ninth. *(Yelling like an enraged Nazi.)* "O Freude, schöner Götterfunken, Schweinehund, Tochter aus Elysium, Dummkopf!"

RICH. I have a very mild case of lymphadenopathy.

PICKUP 1. What's that?

RICH. An AIDS-related condition.

PICKUP 1. Oh, shit.

RICH. Just the swollen glands—

PICKUP 1. No way. Uh-uh . . . Good luck . . . Oh, man . . . *(*PICKUP 1 *exits. We're back with* RICH *and* SAUL.*)*

RICH. So I stopped telling them.

SAUL. You mean you take them home and don't tell them?

RICH. We do it there in the bar.

SAUL. How can you?

RICH. I lurk in dark corners where they can't see my lumps. I'm like a shark or a barracuda, and I snap them up and infect them.

SAUL. How can you joke about this?

RICH. I don't care. I'm going to die! I'll take as many as I can with me. And I've pissed in the Croton Reservoir. I'm going to infect the whole fucking city! Wheeeee!

SAUL. No fucking around, give me a straight answer. Do you still pick up people?

RICH. Maybe I ought to wear a sign around my neck and ring a bell: "AIDS, I've got AIDS, stand clear!" Would that make you

happy? Or maybe I should dig a hole in the ground, douse myself with kerosene, and have a final cigarette. No muss, no fuss. Is that what you want?

SAUL. Forgive me for not trusting you. It's just that I'm frightened of it. I don't know what I'm saying half the time.

RICH. How the fuck do you think I feel? My lover leaves me; my family won't let me near them; I lose my business; I can't pay my rent. How the fuck do you think I feel?

SAUL. You'll stay here with me.

RICH. Till death do us part.

SAUL. I love you.

RICH. I don't want your love!

SAUL. Take what you can . . . [get]! I didn't mean that. I love you. I always have. You have nowhere to go. You've got to stay with me.

RICH. Shit shit shit.

SAUL. You were kidding about picking up people.

RICH. What do you think? What would you do in my place?

SAUL. I wouldn't . . . I'd . . . Therapy! . . . I don't know what I'd do. *(We're back in the bar.)*

PICKUP 2. Jesus, I've told you all about myself. I've really spilled my guts to you. I *needed* to do that. Maybe I shouldn't say this, but, Christ, you know something? I like you very much. Even though you *are* a writer . . . Would you like to come home with me?

RICH. I'd like to very much . . . *(He checks his watch.)* but I have an appointment.

PICKUP 2. Then tomorrow, how about tomorrow? I don't want to lose track of you. I don't know when I've had such a good time. I can *talk* to you.

RICH. I've enjoyed myself, too.

PICKUP 2. Then maybe we'll have dinner, maybe go to the movies. Do you like movies? There's a Mapplethorpe retrospective at MOMA. Or maybe we could see the new Everett Quinton—

RICH. Thanks, but I have to tell you something. I have—

PICKUP 2. You have a lover. I knew it. You're too nice to be unattached.

RICH. I have . . . I have . . . I have a lover. *(We're back with* SAUL.*)*

SAUL. You have a lover.

RICH. I don't even know where he is.

SAUL. I don't mean Chet. I mean me. *(*RICH *turns away. He's back in the bar with another stranger,* CLONE 1, *who is wearing a leather jacket* *and reflecting aviator glasses.* SAUL *continues to plead to* RICH*'s back.)* What about me? *(*RICH *tries in vain to get* CLONE 1*'s attention.)*

RICH. Pardon me.

SAUL. What about me?

RICH. Yo. Yoo-hoo. Hello.

SAUL. What about *me?!*

RICH *(To* CLONE 1*).* What about me?!

CLONE 1. What about you?

RICH. I'm a very interesting guy. You look like a very interesting guy. Let's talk. And if you don't want to talk, let's go back there and let's . . . *(*RICH *stares* CLONE 1 *straight in the face.)* I'll do anything you want. Anything.

CLONE 1. I want you to get the fuck out of my face. Can't you see I'm cruising that dude over there? *(We notice for the first time an identically dressed man standing across the room.)*

RICH. Well, fuck you.

CLONE 1. What's that, buddy? *(*RICH *turns his back on* CLONE 1 *and starts talking loudly to the bartender.)*

RICH. Gimme a Jack Daniels straight up— *no* ice—make it a double, and a Heinekens chaser.

BARTENDER. Double Jack up, Heinie back. *(*CLONE 2 *has moseyed on over to* CLONE 1*. They stand side by side, facing the audience, feigning indifference to each other.)*

CLONE 2. Your name Chip?

RICH. No ice!

BARTENDER. No ice.

CLONE 1. Chuck.

RICH. Hate ice.

CLONE 2 *(Extending his hand).* Chad. *(The clones shake hands.)*

RICH *(To the bartender).* Put 'er there, Chet—I mean Chump. You come here often? *(He downs the shot and beer as quickly as he can.)*

CLONE 2. Thought you were this guy Chip I met here on Jockstrap Night.

CLONE 1. Haven't been here since the Slave Auction.

CLONE 2. Look familiar. *(With synchronized actions the clones turn to look at each other, then turn away.)*

CLONE 1. Go to the Spike?

CLONE 2. Been there.

RICH *(To the bartender).* Quiet for a Friday . . .

CLONE 1. I know where.

RICH. Not much action.

CLONE 2. Limelight?

RICH *(Offering his glass).* Same . . .

CLONE 1. Nah.

RICH. They're home watching pornos.

CLONE 1. Bookstore on Christopher. Ever go there?

CLONE 2. Not in years.

CLONE 1. Gotta be real careful.

RICH. Or having sex on the phone.

CLONE 2. Right. Me, I'm HIV negative.

CLONE 1. Can you prove it? *(He punches* CLONE 2 *on the arm.)* Kidding.

CLONE 2. Gotta be real careful. Run six miles a day.

RICH. My philosophy is: you've got it, you've got it. Nothing you can do about it. *(He offers his glass.)* Same.

CLONE 1 *(Tweaking* CLONE 2*'s nipple).* So what're you up for?

CLONE 2. Come right to the point, don't you? *(The clones perform a macho mating ritual of arm wrestling, punching, and ass grabbing to determine who is the "top man.")*

RICH. Poor bastards that got it: cancer, pneumonia, herpes all over. I mean, I'd kill myself if I had to go through all that shit. Get a gun and perform fellatio on it . . .

CLONE 2. What're you up for, Daddy?

RICH. Slash my wrists *with* the grain . . .

CLONE 1. Me top.

RICH. Subway tracks?

CLONE 1. Got some beautiful . . . *(He snorts deeply to indicate cocaine.)*

CLONE 2. Ever do opium?

CLONE 1. I have a water pipe. We'll smoke it through some Southern Comfort.

RICH. Or maybe I'd mix myself a Judy Garland: forty reds and a quart of vodka. *(He hands his glass to the bartender.)* Fuck the beer!

CLONE 1. We're roommates now. What about you?

RICH *(The ecstatic drunken poet).* "Glory be to God for dappled things . . ."

CLONE 2. I'm free, white, and twenty-four.

RICH. "For skies of couple-colour as a brinded cow . . ."

SAUL. I know it sounds stupid, but take care of your health.

RICH. "For rose-moles all in stipple upon trout that swim . . ."

CLONE 2. In bed, I mean.

RICH. I don't care what anybody says, I believe that somewhere, you know, deep down. *(He holds out his glass.)*

CLONE 1. I'll do anything you want.

RICH. Beyond all this incredible pain and confusion, anxiety, fear, terror . . . *(He holds out his glass.)*

BARTENDER. No ice.

CLONE 2. Anything?

RICH. I believe that there might be . . . *(Searching for words to describe the Supreme Being.)* that there could be . . . that there is—

CLONE 1. Safe sex!

SAUL. You're drinking too much.

RICH. I believe in a perfect . . . *(He is having a booze-fueled vision of the Godhead.)*

CLONE 2. Mirrors . . .

RICH. Shining . . .

CLONE 1. Chains . . .

RICH. Powerful . . .

SAUL. Vitamins . . .

RICH. Pure . . . *(A third clone appears.)*

CLONE 3. Condoms . . .

CLONE 1. Dildo . . .

SAUL. Diet . . .

RICH. Free . . .

CLONE 2. Dungeon . . .

SAUL. Acupuncture . . .

RICH. Truthful . . .

CLONE 3. Ten inches . . .

SAUL. Interferon . . .

RICH. Beautiful . . .

CLONE 3 *(Approaching the bar, to the bartender).* Beer! *(He accidentally spills beer on RICH.)*

CLONE 2. Watersports.

RICH *(Raging drunkenly).* Asshole!

CLONE 1. Hey!

RICH. I'll kill ya, faggot!

SAUL *(Intervening).* Hey! . . . He's been drinking.

BARTENDER. Get that jerk outta here!

RICH. What's a matter, can't you fight like a man?

SAUL *(Gently but firmly).* Rich.

RICH. Fuck all that shit!

SAUL. Rich.

RICH. Let Him cure me!

SAUL *(Trying to distract him).* Did you hear the one about Irving Berlin? What's he doing now?

RICH *(To God in the sky, shaking his fist).* You hear me, motherfucker?

SAUL. He's decomposing.

RICH. Cure me! *(They are out on the street by now.)*

SAUL. C'mon, keep moving.

RICH. I'm a very bad person.

SAUL. You're an asshole.

RICH. I wanted to go to bed with that guy.

SAUL. I practically beg you to move in—

RICH. I wasn't going to tell him about me or anything.

SAUL. And what do you do?

RICH. But you want to know something?

SAUL. You disappear for two weeks.

RICH. I wouldn't do that. I would *never* do that.

SAUL. I almost called the cops.

RICH. You believe me?

SAUL. Believe what?

RICH. I never never never would ever do that.

SAUL. Do you remember the one about the Polish Lesbian?

RICH. Never.

SAUL. She liked men. *(The joke pretty much sobers RICH up.)*

RICH. You asshole.

SAUL. You schmuck.

RICH. You prick.

SAUL. God, I miss talking dirty.

RICH. Talking dirty makes it feel like spring. *(He is the superstud.)* Suck my dick, faggot.

SAUL *(Superstud).* Kiss my ass, cocksucker.

RICH. Sit on it, punk.

SAUL. Lick boot, fruit.

RICH. God, how I used to love sleaze: the whining self-pity of a rainy Monday night in a leather bar in early spring; five o'clock in the morning in the Mineshaft, with the bathtubs full of men dying to get pissed on and whipped; a subway john full of horny high school students; Morocco—getting raped on a tombstone in Marrakesh. God, how I miss it.

SAUL. I miss my filthy old ripped-up, patched button-fly jeans that I sun-bleached on myself our first weekend on the Island. Remember? It was Labor Day—

RICH. Memorial Day.

SAUL. And we did blotter acid. Remember acid before they put the speed in it? And we drank muscadet when we got thirsty.

RICH. Which we did a lot.

SAUL. Remember?

RICH. Remember Sunday afternoons blitzed on beer?

SAUL. And suddenly it's Sunday night and you're getting fucked in the second-floor window of the Hotel Christopher and you're being cheered on by a mob of hundreds of men.

RICH. And suddenly it's Friday a week later, and he's moved in, sleeping next to you, and you want him to go because you've met his brother Rod or Lance—

SAUL *(Practically sighing).* Miles.

RICH. —late of the merchant marines, who's even humpier.

SAUL. Orgies at the baths—

RICH. Afternoons at the Columbus Avenue bookstore. *(They are in the back room of a gay porno shop, or "bookstore." They play their favorite bookstore habitués.)* More! *Give* it to me!

SAUL. Give it to *you?* Give it to *me!* Get out of my way, he's mine!

RICH. No, he's mine! Keep your hands off my wallet!

SAUL *(A black queen).* Sistuhs, theyuh's plenty heah fo' ivry-body.

RICH *(A tough New York queen).* Hey, Mary, the line forms at the rear.

SAUL. And whose rear might that be, sugar? *(Two other men appear in the bookstore.)*

MARTY. Hey, Vinnie?

VINNIE. Marty?

MARTY. What are you doing here? You said you were gonna buy the papers.

VINNIE. You said you were gonna walk the dogs.

MARTY. You trash! *(They exit, bickering.)*

SAUL. I always knew when you were fucking around.

RICH. You did your share.

SAUL. *Moi?*

RICH. I knew why Grand Union wouldn't deliver to our house. *(They have returned to the loft.)*

SAUL. God, I used to love promiscuous sex.

RICH. Not "promiscuous," Saul, nondirective, noncommitted, nonauthoritarian—

SAUL. Free, wild, rampant—

RICH. Hot, sweaty, steamy, smelly—

SAUL. Juicy, funky, hunky—

RICH. Sex.

SAUL. Sex. God, I miss it. *(RICH lowers his eyes. SAUL nods and goes to RICH. He takes RICH's face in both hands and tries to kiss him square on the mouth. RICH pulls away frantically.)*

RICH. NO!

SAUL. It's safe!

RICH. You don't know what you're doing!

SAUL. It's my decision!

RICH *(Shaking his head).* No. Uh-uh. NO! *(SAUL sits on the sofa. RICH tries to take SAUL's hand, but SAUL pulls it away. Beat.)* The best times for me were going out with you on shoots.

SAUL. I thought you found them boring.

RICH. I enjoyed them.

SAUL. I was always afraid of boring you.

RICH. Remember staying up all night shooting the harvest moon at Jake's place?

SAUL. My fingers got so cold I could barely change film.

RICH. It was almost as bright as daylight. Remember the apple tree stuck out in the middle of the pasture, how the moonlight drained it of color?

SAUL. I remember the smell of the blanket we took from the barn.

RICH. Remember, I bet you I could find five constellations?

SAUL. You found six . . . I never wanted us to break up.

RICH. Passive aggression.

SAUL. I wanted things to always remain the same. I'm still like that. I even like eating the same things day after day.

RICH. Pork chops, French fries—

SAUL. No change. I used to love our routine together. I'd go to work and then you'd be there when I got home, writing—

RICH. Drinking.

SAUL. I'd do this and you'd do that, and then we'd . . . *(He makes a graceful gesture to indicate making love.)* for a while—while *Mission Impossible*'d be on low in the background.

RICH. And then *Star Trek.*

SAUL. I never got tired of the same—

RICH. We were stagnating.

SAUL. —day after day the same, so we'd have a structure to fall back on when life dealt us its wild cards or curve balls. I want to be just half awake, like at the seashore, watching the waves roll in late in the afternoon, hypnotized by the glare of the sun, smelling the sea breeze and suntan lotion. *(Beat.)*

Mom is what? She's lying there next to Dad on the Navaho blanket, with white gunk on her nose, and my baby sister has finally stopped screaming and is sucking on the ear of her dollie. And Aunt Ellie—the one who said she thought I had good taste when she met you—is snoring next to husband number three. Her bazooms are going up and down, up and down, almost popping out of her bathing suit. It's so peaceful. *(Long pause.)*

I was at the gym soaking in the hot tub when I first heard about AIDS. It was how many years ago? My friend Brian—remember him?—was soaking, too, and he told me about a mutual friend who had died the week before. It was "bizarre," he said . . . *(A group enters, quietly talking.)*

1ST MAN. The first person I knew who had AIDS was George. I had just seen him at the movies—*Mommie Dearest*—and we had a big laugh together. I remember he had a little cough. I ran into his mother it couldn't have been a week later and she told me he had died. It was absurd. I had just seen George.

1ST WOMAN *(Overlapping).* The first time it really hit me was when my boss got ill. When Roger got out of the hospital I didn't know what to say. I said, "You look so much taller." He said, "Well, I lost about forty-five pounds."

2ND WOMAN. The first time I heard about it I was standing in my kitchen.

1ST MAN. It hit home after that.

2ND WOMAN. I was about to go out shopping for my youngest's birthday party. The phone rang. It was this doctor calling me about my son Bernard. He used all these words I can't pronounce. And then he said, "Do you understand what I've told you?" I said yes. Right before he hung up he said, "So you know he has AIDS." That's the first time I heard the word.

1ST MAN *(Simultaneously).* Do you understand what I've told you?

1ST WOMAN. So you know he has AIDS.

JOHN *(Overlapping).* The first time I heard about AIDS was in 1981. I was on the seven A.M. shuttle to Boston, trying to make a nine o'clock appointment in Cambridge. I was looking over the shoulder of the man next to me, at his newspaper, and I caught the words "cancer," "Promiscuous," "homosexual." I turned white.

COP. The word never really registered in my mind until they transferred this guy with AIDS to our unit. The guys on the job were up in arms that they were going to expose us to it. I didn't know what to think. I got used to Kenny though. He wanted to keep working very badly. I think he had a lot of courage.

1ST WOMAN & JOHN. *(Overlapping).* I think he had a lot of courage.

2ND MAN. The first memorial service I went to was on the set of *Oh Calcutta!* It was for Bill. He was in the theatre. They filled the house. He had hidden the fact that he was ill for a year. A while before he asked me if I wanted his dog—a beautiful Huskie. I couldn't figure it out. He loved that dog . . . Since that time I've been to how many memorial services? Seth . . . Robby . . .

2ND WOMAN *(Simultaneously).* He was in the theatre.

COP *(Simultaneously).* I couldn't figure it out.

1ST WOMAN. . . . Fortunato

2ND WOMAN. . . . Francis . . .

COP . . . Steve . . .

JOHN. . . . Greg . . .

2ND MAN. . . . Phil . . .

2ND WOMAN. . . . Freddy . . .

1ST WOMAN. . . .Arthur . . .

1ST MAN. . . . Tom . . .

JOHN & COP. . . . Tim . . .

1ST MAN. . . . Christian . . .

2ND WOMAN. . . . Neil . . .

JOHN. . . . Pierre . . .

2ND WOMAN. . . . Glenn . . .

COP. . . . Stephen . . .

2ND WOMAN. . . . Julie . . .

1ST & 2ND MAN & 1ST WOMAN. . . . Russell . . . Luis . . . Larry & his lover Danny . . . David . . . Stuart . . . J.J. . . . Maria . . . Jamal . . .

COP. . . . Luis . . . Larry & his lover Danny . . . Stuart . . . J.J. . . . Maria . . . Jamal . . .

JOHN. . . . Larry . . . David . . . Stuart . . . J.J. . . . Maria . . . Jamal . . . Charles . . . Tony

2ND WOMAN. David . . . Stuart . . . J.J. . . . Maria . . . Jamal . . . Tony . . .

(The group exits)

SAUL. . . . and he told me about a mutual friend who had died the week before. It was "bizarre," he said. Brian died last week of the same thing. And he and I once soaked in the same hot tub, making a kind of human soup . . . That's all I ever wanted to do was relax. *(Long pause.)* You'll stay with me. I won't bother you.

RICH. Just until I feel better.

SAUL. I understand: you're not coming back to be my lover.

RICH. Right. Is that okay?

SAUL. Schmuck. *(Mimicking him.)* Is that okay? Is that okay? It's *okay!* Asshole. Who the fuck wants you anyhow? And when I have guests stay the night, you disappear into your room. Right?

RICH. Right. Understood. *(Offhand.)* You seeing somebody?

SAUL. I said when I have guests.

RICH. You planning an orgy?

SAUL. Just so we understand each other.

RICH. I should mention one thing.

SAUL. No, you do not have to spend Passover with the tribe.

RICH. I miss your father.

SAUL. Then go live with him. He *likes* you. The two of you could be very happy together.

RICH. One thing.

SAUL. He's never really liked me.

RICH. Saul.

SAUL. He's always been polite but—

RICH. Are you finished?

SAUL. No, I will not bring you coffee in bed. I only do that for lovers. Besides, I broke your blue mug.

RICH. Saul, please.

SAUL. On purpose.

RICH. One thing. I'm embarrassed. I'm just about broke. The doctors. Tests.

SAUL. I thought you were insured.

RICH. They're pulling a fast one.

SAUL. We'll sue. I'll call Craig. He'll know what—

RICH. Craig told me not to have high hopes.

SAUL. We'll get by. You'll see.

RICH. I'll keep track of every cent you spend on me. You'll get it all back when I can work. I swear.

SAUL. Not to worry, I'll take it out in trade.

RICH. Saul, I'm frightened! *(SAUL takes him in his arms.)*

SAUL. We'll be okay, we'll be okay . . . *(They hold each other.* LILY *walks into the scene with* CHET. *She's dressed in evening wear and is carrying a number of accessories, including a mirror and a shawl.* CHET *is dressed in cutoffs and a sweatshirt. We are in a flashback.)*

LILY. Rich, congratulations! It's fantastic that they're going to publish your book. *(SAUL tries to break from the clinch, but* RICH *holds him back.)*

RICH. No autographs, please.

LILY. It's wonderful, it really is, but can you guys celebrate later?

SAUL *(To* RICH*)*. Let me go. *(To* CHET.*)* How do you do? I'm Saul.

LILY. Shit. Saul, Rich—my cousin Chet.

SAUL *(Trying to shake hands)*. Hi, Chet. *(To* RICH.*)* You're strangling me.

CHET. Hi.

RICH *(To* SAUL*)*. It's your last chance to kiss the author before he becomes famous and goes straight.

SAUL. Straight to the bars. *(To* CHET.*)* So how do you like New York?

CHET. I only got here yesterday. Lily's taking me to a show tonight.

RICH. Do you think success will change me?

SAUL. God, I hope so.

LILY. I know I'm being a pig, but I need head shots by six o'clock. *(She lowers a roller of colored background paper.)* It's a dazzling role for me and *(To* SAUL.*)* you're such an artist.

SAUL. Rich is the "artiste" in the family.

LILY. Chet, be an angel and bring Saul his camera. It's by the bar. *(CHET looks for the camera.)*

SAUL *(To* CHET.*)*. Don't let your cousin push you around the way she does me.

LILY. Come on, Saul, make click-click.

SAUL. Unless you like that sort of thing.

RICH. That's all I get?

LILY *(To* RICH, *about* SAUL*)*. Leave the boy alone.

RICH. A hug and a bitchy remark?

SAUL *(To* RICH*)*. That and a subway token.

RICH *(To* SAUL*)*. No "Gee, Rich, I'm so proud of you"?

SAUL *(Smiling falsely)*. Gee, Rich, I'm so proud of you.

RICH. I finally have some good news and he's annoyed.

CHET *(To* LILY, *holding the camera)*. What should I do with this?

SAUL. Well, your brother called, while you were out guzzling lunch with your agent, Dr. Mengele. Call him back.

RICH. What'd he have to say?

SAUL. Call him and ask him. I'm not your secretary.

RICH *(Imitating him)*. I'm not your—

SAUL. He forgot my fucking name again. How long we been together?

RICH. Too long. Forget my brother. It's my first fucking book. Let's celebrate.

SAUL. You celebrate.

LILY. I'll throw a party.

RICH. What'll you serve, organic cabbage juice?

SAUL *(To* LILY*)*. His brother's a scumbag.

RICH. He likes you, too.

CHET *(To* SAUL, *still holding the camera)*. Do you want this?

SAUL *(To* CHET*)*. Thanks, Chuck.

CHET. Chet. *(SAUL accepts the camera from* CHET, *but ignores the correction.)*

LILY *(Fondly, to* RICH*)*. You're such a lush.

RICH. Whatever happened to my old drinking buddy?

LILY. Did you know they have gay A.A. meetings? *(RICH makes a face.)*

SAUL *(To* RICH, *trying to be nice)*. It's great news, babes, really.

RICH. You really don't give a fuck.

SAUL. Just how many copies you think a book of "fairy tales" will sell?

LILY. I picked a fine day to have my picture taken.

SAUL. If you only knew how much I love doing head shots.

RICH (To SAUL). Ah, fuck it, I guess I'm being childish.

SAUL. I shouldn't have said that. I'm thoughtless. (RICH shrugs.)

LILY. And I'm Sneezy. No, really, I'm selfish. But I want that role so bad. I play the ghost of Marie Antoinette. (To SAUL, throwing the scarf around her neck and taking a tits-and-ass pose.) How do you like this, hon? "Let them eat . . ." (She drops the pose immediately as SAUL starts to photograph her.)

SAUL. Move your head a little to the . . . (She moves her head.) Good. (SAUL snaps her.)

RICH (Going to the living area, followed by CHET). I'm going running. (RICH changes into jogging clothes.)

CHET. How far do you run?

RICH. Depends. I'm in training for the marathon.

CHET. The marathon! Hey, that's great. I run, too.

RICH. Oh, yeah? (LILY and SAUL are busy taking pictures in the other side of the loft. They can see RICH and CHET, but they can't easily hear them.)

LILY. How's this?

CHET. Congratulations on the book.

RICH. Thanks.

SAUL. That's right.

LILY. I forget the director's name. He's Lithuanian.

CHET. That poem of yours that Lily has hung up in her kitchen, I read it. I think it's great.

SAUL. Great.

RICH. You don't much look like the poetry type.

LILY. Latvian.

CHET. I'm not. I just love your poem.

RICH. Are you a student?

CHET. Just graduated from San Francisco State.

LILY. Everybody in the play is dead.

SAUL. Your cousin's hot. Is he gay?

LILY. I don't know. I'll ask him. (Yelling to CHET.) Chet, are you gay?

SAUL. Christ.

RICH. That's what I call tact.

LILY. Well?

CHET (Loud, to LILY). Yes.

LILY. Thanks, hon.

SAUL. Give us a little more cheek . . .

CHET. There's a line of your poem I don't understand.

RICH. Only one? I have no idea what any of it means.

CHET. "The final waning moon . . ."

SAUL. Don't smile.

RICH. "And the coming of the light."

CHET. I love the way it sounds.

SAUL. Smile.

CHET. "The final waning moon / And the coming of the light."

SAUL (Indicating to LILY that he wants a sexy pose). He loves you.

CHET. Oh, I get it.

RICH. Lily tells me you're looking for a place to stay.

CHET. New York is so expensive.

SAUL. He lusts for you.

RICH. A friend of mine wants someone to take care of his loft while he's in L.A.

SAUL. He wants to ravage you.

CHET. I'll do it.

RICH. He has eight cats.

CHET. Eight tigers, I don't care.

LILY. I love that play.

RICH. It's in Tribeca.

SAUL (Yelling to RICH). I apologize about the book. (RICH and CHET ignore SAUL.)

CHET. Where's Tribeca?

SAUL. Did you hear me?

RICH. On the isle of Manhattan.

CHET. We're on the isle of Manhattan.

RICH. We are.

LILY. The main characters are all ghosts.

CHET. I know that.

SAUL. I'll throw him a party.

RICH. That's about all you have to know.

SAUL. A big bash.

CHET. Is it?

LILY. We'll do it together.

RICH. I'll tell you a few more things.

CHET. Will you?

SAUL. I'll even invite his brother.

RICH. You bet your ass I will.

SAUL (Snapping up the roller of background paper). Finished. (LILY, RICH, and CHET leave. SAUL goes to the sofa. The hospice worker comes forward.)

HOSPICE WORKER. A woman is told by her doctor that she has cancer and has only a month to live. "Now wait just one minute," she tells the doctor. "I'll be wanting a second opinion." To which the doctor replies, "Okay, you're ugly, too."

David told me that one. He was an old Jewish man who had survived the Lodz ghetto in World War II. He'd seen everything in his life, and when the time came for him to go, he accepted it. The doctors wanted to go to obscene lengths to keep his body alive, but he refused. I loved him.

But most of my people are more like Margaret. She was in her nineties. She half accepted the fact that she was dying. One moment she'd be talking to you about which nephew she was definitely going to cross out of her will, and the next she'd be telling you about the summer vacation she was planning in Skibbereen. She had terminal cancer! But I always go along with what they have to say. My job is not to bring enlightenment, only comfort.

Which reminds me: Margaret's family saw her as some kind of prophet. The whole clan was in the room waiting to hear her last words. She had developed a distinct dislike for her family, so I was sitting closest to her when she went, and therefore I could hear what the poor soul was whispering. After it was all over, they asked me what prayer she had been uttering. I told them the Lord's Prayer. I didn't have the heart to tell them that what she was saying was "Oh, shit, oh, shit, oh, shit."

I've worked with thirty-five people altogether. About a third of them had AIDS. It *is* the Village. (*She exits. Lights come up on* L. *area. An AIDS support group is in session.*)

PERSON WITH AIDS 1. Funny thing is, I wasn't at all promiscuous.

PWA 4. Oh, please.

PWA 1. I swear. And I never drank much— once in a while a beer with Mexican food— and I don't smoke, and drugs, forget ... I met Jerry in my sophomore year—we shared the same dorm room at Hofstra—and we fell in love, and that was it for me. When the sex revolution thing happened, I remember I felt retarded. Everybody was doing all those wild things. Me, I was going to the opera a lot. As far as I know, Jerry didn't screw around. He swore he didn't. But then ... he's not around for me to cross-examine. He left me.

RICH. Well, I ...

PWA 3. What?

RICH. No.

PWA 2 (*A young housewife, eight months pregnant*). At least when I come here I don't have to lie. Like "Bernie's doing better. I'm fine." I can even crack up if I want to. Don't worry, I won't do it two weeks in a row. I mean, who's there to talk to in Brewster? These things don't happen in Brewster. Police officers don't shoot up heroin, cops don't come down with the "gay plague"—that's what they call it in Brewster. I can't talk to Bernie.

I'll never forgive him. Have a chat with the minister? "Well, Reverend Miller, I have this little problem. My husband has AIDS, and I have AIDS, and I'm eight months pregnant, and I ..." You guys know what I mean. You're the only people in this world who know what I mean.

PWA 5. I know what you guys are going to tell me: I'm suffering from the homophobia that an oppressive society blah blah blah. I never felt good about being gay.

PWA 4. Oh, Mary.

PWA 5. Gay was grim. It was something I did because I had to. Like a dope fiend needs his fix. It always left me feeling like shit afterward. And that's the truth. I felt guilty. I still feel that way.

(PWA 2 *leans over to put a consoling hand on him. He pulls away.*)

PWA 4. I was part of a team trying to teach robots how to use language. (*He moves and talks like a robot.*) "I'm Harris, your android model 3135X. I can vacuum the floors, cook cheeseburgers, play the piano." It's much harder to teach robots to understand. (*Instructing a backward robot.*) "Joke." (*The robot responds dutifully.*) "Noun: a clash of values or levels of reality, producing laughter. Example: Have you heard about the disease attacking Jewish American princesses? It's called MAIDS. You die if you *don't* get it. Ha. Ha." My co-workers asked me to leave. They were afraid of contracting AIDS through the air, or by my looking at them. You see, they are scientists. My last act before I left was programming one final robot. (*He behaves like a robot again.*) "Good morning. This is Jack—(*He suddenly becomes a flamboyantly gay robot.*) but you can call me Jackie—your *fabulous* new android model 1069. If you wish to use me—and I *love* being used—press one of those cunning little buttons on my pecs. Go on, press one—(*He switches from a campy tone to an almost angry, accusatory one.*) or are you afraid of me, too?" That was my stab at immortality.

RICH. I'm not sure I have it anymore. I feel guilty saying this, like somehow I'm being disloyal to the group. I'm getting better, I know it. I just have these lumps, which for some reason won't go away, and a loss of weight, which has made me lighter than I've been for years."

PWA 3 (*Like a TV commercial*). Ladies, see those ugly pounds just melt away.

RICH. But anyway, I feel great. I feel the

disease disappearing in me. Only a tiny percentage of those with the swollen glands come down with the rest. I'm going to *not* come here next week. I'm sorry.

PWA 3. Rich?

SAUL *(Calling to* RICH *as if he were in the next room, while feeling the glands in his neck and armpits).* Rich?

RICH *(Still to group).* Why do I keep on apologizing?

SAUL. Rich?

RICH. If I *really* thought that I was coming down with it . . . We all have *options.*

PWA 4. Rich?

SAUL. Rich.

RICH *(Entering* SAUL*'s area).* What?

SAUL. Here, feel my glands.

RICH. You are such a hypochondriac.

SAUL. Do you think they're swollen?

RICH *(Placing his hands around* SAUL*'s neck).* They feel okay to me. *(Transylvanian accent.)* But your neck—eet is grotesquely meesshapen. *(Suddenly mock-strangling* SAUL*.)* Here, let me feex it. *(They start wrestling on sofa.)*

SAUL. Not fair!

RICH. You're such a hypochondriac.

SAUL. Ow! *I'm* such a hypochondriac. You and your vitamins!

RICH. You and your yoga!

SAUL. You and your wheat grass!

RICH. It's working. My ratio's up.

SAUL. All right! *(To the tune of "New York, New York."*)*

T-cells up,
The suppressors are down.
New York, New York.

RICH. Hey, I love you! You know that?

SAUL. If you love me, get off my chest!

RICH. I don't dare. You'd try and get even. You're that way.

SAUL. We'll call a truce. One, two, three . . .

RICH & SAUL. Truce. *(As* RICH *climbs off* SAUL*'s chest,* SAUL *pulls him down, lifting his shirt, and gets him in a hammerlock.)*

SAUL. You were right. You never should have trusted me.

RICH. Unfair . . . foul . . . most unfair!

SAUL. Fuck fair. The winner gets his way with the loser. *(They tussle until* RICH *gives up.)* Having vanquished the good ship *Socrates,* the savage pirate chief Bigmeat takes the first mate as his captive.

RICH *(In falsetto).* No, Captain Bigmeat, no!

*See Special Note on copyright page.

SAUL. I've had me eye on ye since that time we met in Bangalore. Ye can't escape me now, matey. I shall ravish ye fer sure. *(SAUL tickles* RICH*.)*

RICH. No! . . . I'm pure of blood and noble born! *(Gradually their play turns more and more sexual, which* RICH *resists at first.)* No! . . . No! . . . *(Relents.)* Perhaps . . . Please!

SAUL. Now I got ye, boy-o . . . boy-o . . . boy-o . . . Oh, boy! *(Finally* RICH *stops struggling.* RICH *and* SAUL *are close together, panting, exhausted.* SAUL *is about to make love to* RICH *when he notices a mark on his back.)*

RICH. What? *(SAUL ignores him and looks at the mark carefully.)* What? You seduce me, you finally succeed in getting me hot and bothered, and what do you do as I lie here panting? You look at my birthmark. *(SAUL looks at* RICH*'s back. He touches some marks.)* What is it?

SAUL. Nothing.

RICH. What is it? Tell me!

SAUL. I'm sure it's nothing!

RICH. What! WHAT! *WHAT!* . . . *(Immediately, the hospice worker draws a curtain that surrounds the entire living area of* SAUL*'s loft, hiding it from view. Overlapping the closing of the curtain, we hear the ringing of two telephones. Lights up on two men sitting side by side, answering multiline telephones.)*

PAT. Hotline, Pat speaking.

BARNEY. Hotline. This is Barney. *(To* PAT, *covering the phone.)* Oh, no, it's her again.

PAT. Are you a gay man?

BARNEY. Didn't we speak a few days ago? *(To* PAT, *covering the phone.)* She doesn't stop.

PAT. We're all worried.

BARNEY. Is he bisexual?

PAT. Calm down, first of all. *(The third line rings.)*

BARNEY. Is he an IV drug user?

PAT. It's not all that easy to get it—*if* you take a few precautions. *(To* BARNEY, *covering the phone.)* Okay, I'll get it. *(He speaks into the phone.)* Please hold on. *(He presses a button.)*

BARNEY. It wasn't my intention to insult you.

PAT. Hotline . . . Shit. *(To* BARNEY, *pressing a button.)* Lost him. Fucking phone.

BARNEY. So what makes you think he has AIDS?

PAT *(To phone).* Hello.

BARNEY. He is what?

PAT. The disease is spread through the blood and the semen.

BARNEY. Samoans are *not* a risk group. *(To* PAT, *covering the phone.)* Samoans?

PAT. So wear a condom.

BARNEY. There's half a zillion diseases he has symptoms of.

PAT. Make *him* wear a condom. *(The phone rings.)*

BARNEY. Please hold. *(He presses a button.)*

PAT. Kissing is acceptable.

BARNEY. Hotline . . . *(In response to a hate call.)* And your mother eats turds in hell! . . . Thank you. *(He presses a button.)*

PAT. Myself, I don't do it on the first date.

BARNEY. I would definitely check it out with a physician.

BARNEY. Spots? I'm not a doctor . . . Go to a doctor.

PAT *(Simultaneously).* Stroking, holding, rubbing, mirrors, whips, chains, jacking off, porno—use your imagination.

BARNEY. I'm sorry you're lonely.

PAT. Our motto is: "On me, not in me."

BARNEY. Madam, we're busy here. I can't stay on the line with you all day.

PAT. You have a nice voice, too, but I'm seeing someone.

BARNEY. Hello?

PAT. Thanks.

BARNEY *(To PAT).* Thank God.

PAT. Good luck. *(They hang up at the same time.)*

BARNEY. Spots. I love it.

PAT *(To himself).* I am not seeing anyone.

BARNEY. What are you talking about?

PAT. I was saying how much I love being celibate. *(He kisses his palm.)* So how the fuck are you?

BARNEY. Tired, broke, depressed, and Tim is moving out this afternoon. Well, you asked. I hear you have a new PWA.*

PAT. Sorry about Tim. Yes, I have a new baby, a writer. Why do I get all the tough customers?

BARNEY. Because you're so tough.

PAT. So butch.

BARNEY. So mean.

PAT. Weathered by life like the saddle under a cowboy's ass.

BARNEY. Ooooh. I could never be a CMP.** Where do you get your energy?

PAT. Drugs. I don't do that anymore either. What *do* I do? I wait tables, answer phones, and work with ingrates like Rich. Boy, is he pissed. He calls me Miss Nightingale or Florence and throws dishes and curses his

*Person With Aids.
**Crisis Management Partner.

roommate and won't cooperate with the doctor and won't see his shrink and isn't interested in support groups *and he shit in the fucking bathtub!* He shit—

BARNEY. Is he incontinent?

PAT. Fuck, no. He ain't that sick yet. He said it was "convenient." I don't know why he shit in the tub.

BARNEY. A real sweetheart.

PAT. I'm going out of my mind. Thank God they put him in the hospital.

BARNEY. First time?

PAT. Yep.

BARNEY. I'd probably be a real bastard.

PAT. I wouldn't take it lying down.

BARNEY. You'd take it any way you can get it.

PAT. Go on, girlfriend.

BARNEY. Me, if I got sick I'd shove a time bomb up my tush and drop in on Timmy for tea and meet his new lover: Jimmy.

PAT. Jimmy?

BARNEY. I swear: Jimmy. *(Visiting* TIMMY *and* JIMMY *for high tea.)* "Timmy has told me so much about you. I've been *dying* to meet you." And kaboom! There goes Timmy and Jimmy.

PAT. Timmy and Jimmy? *(The telephone rings.)*

BARNEY. Ain't it a gas?

PAT. Gag me, for sure.

BARNEY. For sure.

PAT *(Answering the phone).* Hotline. Pat speaking.

BARNEY *(Raging).* When are we going to get some more help around here??!! I'm going out of my mind! *(Suddenly, sweet and sultry as he answers the phone.)* Hotline, Barney speaking.

PAT. Are you a gay man?

BARNEY. Are you a gay man? *(The lights quickly fade on the two men. The curtain opens, revealing a hospital room, with bed, chair, and bed table. The loft space and bar have disappeared.* RICH *is in bed.* LILY, SAUL, *and a* NURSE *are standing nearby.)*

NURSE. Temperature and blood pressure, Mr. Farrell.

LILY. Can you come back later?

SAUL. He's had some bad news.

NURSE. He's last on my rounds.

RICH *(To SAUL).* You lied to me.

SAUL. I didn't know.

LILY. He didn't know. I swear.

NURSE. It'll just take a minute.

RICH. What other little details are you keeping from me? They let him lie there like a dog. What else? *(A Hispanic hospital worker comes in to empty the waste basket.)* You! *Váyase!* Get the wetback out of here! *Váyase!*

HOSPITAL WORKER. I not do nothing! He crazy.

RICH. You, get out of here before I breathe on you! *Ahora! Ahora! Váyase!*

NURSE. Mr. Farrell, please.

SAUL. Come back later. *Más tarde, por favor.*

RICH. Go back to your picket line. *(To* SAUL.*)* They want a wage hike, no less. He tried to get me to bribe him to clean my room—

HOSPITAL WORKER. *Qué coño estás diciendo?* [What the fuck are you saying?]

NURSE. Please cooperate.

LILY. He didn't say anything.

RICH. He won't go near my bed, but he's not afraid to touch my money.

SAUL. You misunderstood him.

RICH. *El dinero está limpio, ah? Tu madre.* [Money is clean, huh, motherfucker?]

HOSPITAL WORKER. *Maricón.* [Faggot.]

RICH *(To* SAUL*).* They're unionizing primates now.

LILY *(To* RICH*).* Sh!

HOSPITAL WORKER. *No entiendo.* [I don't understand.] I going. *(He exits.)*

LILY *(Aside to* SAUL*).* I shouldn't have told him about Chet.

SAUL *(Aside to* LILY*).* Better you than someone else.

RICH *(Imitating* LILY *and* SAUL*).* Bzzz bzzz bzzz.

NURSE *(Trying to put a blood pressure cuff on* RICH*'s arm).* Will you be still a moment so I can check your blood pressure?

RICH. Are you a union member, too?

NURSE *(To* SAUL*).* What shall I do?

LILY. A good friend of his just passed away.

NURSE. AIDS? *(She resumes struggling with the cuff.)*

RICH. The undertakers' union. Go away, I'm on strike, too; I refuse to participate in the documentation of my own demise.

SAUL. She's only trying to help you.

RICH *(To the* NURSE, *ripping off the cuff).* Go find another statistic for the Center for Disease Control.

NURSE *(To* SAUL*).* I'm a patient woman, but he wants me to lose it. I swear that's what he's after.

RICH. Lady, fuck off!

SAUL *(To the* NURSE*).* Please. Can't you see he's upset?

NURSE *(To* RICH*).* Okay, you win. I'm losing

it. Are you happy? I'm *angry,* angry, Mr. Farrell.

LILY. Will you please go!

NURSE. A person can take only so much. I give up. I don't have to put up with this shit. I'm gonna speak to my supervisor. *(The* NURSE *exits.)*

RICH *(Applauding).* Three gold stars for self-assertion!

LILY *(To* SAUL*).* I should have kept my mouth shut.

RICH. Having brought Romeo the news that Juliet is dead, Balthasar makes a tearful exit.

LILY. I don't know what to say. *(*LILY *looks at* RICH, *then* SAUL.*)*

RICH. I said: Balthasar makes a tearful exit.

LILY. I know how you're feeling.

RICH. No matter. Get thee gone and hire those horses.

LILY. I loved Chet, too.

RICH. Tush, thou art deceived.

LILY. He told me he was sorry for the way he treated you.

RICH. Do the thing I bid thee.

LILY. He didn't belong in New York. He thought he was so sophisticated, but he was just a kid from Mendocino. I'm sorry I let him go home.

RICH. The messenger must go. The hero wishes to be alone with his confidant. *(*RICH *turns his back on* SAUL *and* LILY*)*

LILY. I'll be back tomorrow. *(Aside to* SAUL.*)* I've got half a crown roast from Margo. She went vegetarian. I'll be up. I have to have a talk with Mick. He's irrational on the subject of AIDS. He can go to hell. If he's so afraid, let him move out. *(To* RICH.*)* I won't let him come between us. You're my buddy. *(*SAUL *indicates that* LILY *should leave. She gathers up her belongings, mimes dialing a telephone, and blows* SAUL *a kiss.)* Rich? *(*SAUL *shakes his head no. She leaves.* SAUL *tries to think of something to say to* RICH. *He abandons the effort and picks up the Sunday* New York Times *crossword puzzle.)*

SAUL. "African quadruped." *(Writing.)* G-n-u . . . "Hitler's father." *(Counting on his fingers.)* One, two . . . five letters. Let's see: Herman? Herman Hitler? *(Counting.)* That's six . . . Otto? . . . Werner? . . . Rudi? . . . Putzi? *(He shrugs.)* Fuck. *(He reads on.)* Thank God: "Jewish rolls." Starts with a *b,* six letters: bagels. *(He starts to write it in.)* Shit, that won't work. I need a *y.*

RICH *(Without turning).* Bialys.

SAUL. *B-i-a-l-y-s.*

RICH. Short for Bialystok, a large industrial city in eastern Poland . . . *(Turning to* SAUL.*)* hometown of Ludwig Zamenhof, inventor of Esperanto, an artificial international lan-. guage. Alois Hitler! *A-l-o—*

SAUL *(Putting down the puzzle).* Outclassed again. Why do I bother? He knows everything.

RICH. When I was a kid I used to spend all my time in libraries. My childhood was—

SAUL. If I had a father like yours I would have done the same thing.

RICH. But thanks to that son of a bitch I could tell you how many metric tons of coal the Benelux countries produced per annum, and the capital city of the Grand Duchy of Liechtenstein.

SAUL. I give up.

RICH. Vaduz.

SAUL. Miss Trivial Pursuit.

RICH. I knew to which great linguistic family the Telegu language of South India belongs.

SAUL. Telegu? Isn't that the national dish of Botswana?

RICH *(Ignoring him).* The Dravidian. *(*SAUL *straightens up the bed table.)* I've always loved words . . . I wrote poetry when I was a kid. My brother used to make fun of me . . . Winter, winter, How you glinter, With holidays' array. And the snow We all know Is here all day. *(*SAUL *smiles.)* I was eight, nine when I wrote that. I had just come in from sledding down Indian Hill—a steep road that connects Jefferson Heights to the valley.

SAUL. You showed it to me on our grand tour of West Jersey.

RICH. It was a late afternoon just before sundown and the sky was intensely blue and intensely cold and you could see the stars already. For some reason nobody was home when I came back, so I stood there at the stamped enamel-top kitchen table dripping in my frozen corduroys and wrote that poem.

SAUL. Are you comfortable? *(*RICH *shrugs.* SAUL *fixes his pillows.)*

RICH. I was a good kid, but I was lonely and scared all the time. I was so desperate to find people like myself that I looked for them in the indexes of books—under *H.* I eventually found them—

SAUL. But not in books.

RICH. The next thing you know I moved to the city and was your typical office-worker-slash-writer. I hated my job, so I grew a beard and wore sandals, hoping they would

fire me and give me permanent unemployment. I wanted to stay at home in my rent-controlled apartment and drink bourbon and write poems. I did that for a period. I loved it. The apartment got filthy and I did, too, and I'd go out only at night—to pick up guys. And then I found you—in a porno theater— *(He takes* SAUL*'s hand.)* and we semi-settled down and you took my picture and I started to jog. We bought a loft—

SAUL. and raised a cat—

RICH. and loved each other. But that wasn't enough for me. I don't think you ever understood this: you weren't my muse, you were . . . *(He searches for the word.)* Saul. *(*SAUL *rises and looks out the window.)* I loved you but I wanted someone to write poems to. During our marriage I had almost stopped writing and felt stifled even though our loft had appeared in *New York* magazine. And then I met Chet and left you in the lurch and lived with him at the Chelsea Hotel. He was shallow, callow, and selfish, and I loved him, too.

We did a lot of coke and I wrote a lot of poetry and the catering was booming and *The New Yorker* published a story of mine and I ran in the marathon. I was on a roll. *(With mounting excitement as he relives the experience.)* I remember training on the East River Drive for the first time. I didn't realize how narrow and dark the city streets were until I got to the river and all of a sudden there was the fucking river. The sky was the same color as that twilight when I was a kid. I came from the darkness into the light. I'm running downtown and I make this bend and out of nowhere straight up ahead is the Manhattan Bridge and then the Brooklyn Bridge, one after another, and my earphones are playing Handel's *Royal Fireworks Music.* It can't get better than this, I know it. I'm running and crying from gratitude. I came from the darkness into the light. I'm running and telling God I didn't know He was *that* good or *that* big, thank you, Jesus, thanks, thanks . . . *(He slumps back, exhausted from the effort.)*

The next morning I woke up with the flu and stayed in bed for a couple of days and felt much better. But my throat stayed a little sore and my glands were a little swollen . . . *(Long silence. Casually.)* Saul, I want you to do something for me. Will you do something for me, baby?

SAUL. Sure, babe.

RICH. Now listen. I want you to go out of

here and go to the doctor and tell him you aren't sleeping so hot—

SAUL. I'm sleeping okay.

RICH. Sh! Now listen: you tell him you want something to make you sleep and Valium doesn't work on you, but a friend once gave you some Seconal—

SAUL. *No!* I won't do it!

RICH *(Pressuring SAUL relentlessly)*. I tried hoarding the pills here, but every night the nurse stays to watch me swallow them down.

SAUL. I can't do that.

RICH. I don't want to end up like Chet.

SAUL. I won't listen.

RICH. If you love me, you'll help me. I have something that's eating me up. I don't want to go on. I'm scared to go on.

SAUL. Don't do this to me! I can't handle it. I'll go out the window, I swear, don't do this—

RICH. Don't you see, it's the only way. Just get the pills.

SAUL. No!

RICH. Just have them around. You'll get used to the idea. And when the lesions spread above my neck so that I don't look the same, you'll want me to have them.

SAUL. Help me, help me!

RICH. It's all right. Not now.

SAUL. No.

RICH. Tomorrow.

SAUL. No.

RICH. The day after.

SAUL. No.

RICH. We'll see. *(RICH's brother, wearing a surgical mask, gown, and gloves and carrying a small shopping bag, tiptoes in, stopping when he notices RICH and SAUL.)*

SAUL. Oh, my God. I think it's your brother.

BROTHER. I'll come back later.

SAUL *(Pulling himself together)*. No, I was just going.

BROTHER. It's all right, really.

SAUL. I've been here for a while.

BROTHER. I'm interrupting.

SAUL. Really.

RICH *(To his brother)*. Unless you're planning to come into intimate contact with me or my body fluids, none of that shit you have on is necessary.

BROTHER. The sign says—

RICH. But please restrain your brotherly affection for my sake; who knows what diseases you might have brought in with you? *(The brother removes the mask, gown, and gloves.)*

SAUL. You two haven't seen each other for a while, so why don't I just—

RICH. By all means. You need a break, kid. Think about what I said.

SAUL. It stopped raining. I'll take a walk.

RICH. Have a nice walk.

BROTHER. Good seeing ya . . . ? *(He has forgotten SAUL's name.)*

SAUL. Saul. Yeah. *(SAUL exits. Beat.)*

BROTHER. I owe you an apology . . . *(RICH won't help him.)* I was very frightened . . . I'm afraid I panicked . . . Please forgive me.

RICH. Nothing to forgive.

BROTHER *(Brightly)*. Betty sends her love. She sent along a tin of butter crunch. *(He offers RICH a tin, which RICH ignores.)* You're not on any special diet? I told Betty I thought maybe you'd be on one of those macrobiotic diets. I read in the papers that it's helped some people with . . .

RICH. AIDS.

BROTHER. Yes. I keep a file of clippings on all the latest medical developments. *(He takes a clipping out of his wallet.)* Looks like they're going to have a vaccine soon. The French—

RICH. That's to *prevent* AIDS. I already *have* AIDS.

BROTHER. They have this new drug, AZT.

RICH. I'm on it.

BROTHER. Right . . . So how are you doing?

RICH *(Smiling cheerfully)*. I have Kaposi's sarcoma, a hitherto rare form of skin cancer. It's spreading. I have just begun chemotherapy. It nauseates me. I expect my hair will fall out. I also have a fungal infection of the throat called candidiasis, or thrush. My life expectancy is . . . I have a greater chance of winning the lottery. Otherwise I'm fine. How are you?

BROTHER. I'm sorry . . . *(Brightly again, after a long pause.)* Mary Pat sends her love. She won her school swimming competition and I registered her for the South Jersey championship. Oh, I forgot, she made this for you . . . *(He takes a large handmade fold-out card from the shopping bag. It opens downward a full two feet.)*

RICH. Say, have you heard about the miracle of AIDS?

BROTHER. What?

RICH. It can turn a fruit into a vegetable. What's the worst thing about getting AIDS? *(The brother lets the card fall to the floor.)*

BROTHER. Stop it!

RICH. Trying to convince your parents that you're Haitian. Get it?

BROTHER. I came here to see if I could help you.

RICH. Skip it. So what do you want?

BROTHER. I don't want anything.

RICH. Everything I own is going to Saul—

BROTHER. I don't want anything.

RICH. Except for the stuff Mom left us. I told Saul that it's to go to you. Except for the Barcelona chair—

BROTHER. I don't care about—

RICH. I'm leaving Saul the copyright to my book—

BROTHER. Why are you doing this to me?

RICH. So you don't want my worldly possessions, such as they are; you want me to relieve your guilt.

BROTHER. Stop it.

RICH *(Making the sign of the cross over his brother, chanting).* I hereby exonerate you of the sin of being ashamed of your queer brother and being a coward in the face of—

BROTHER. Stop! Don't! *(The brother grabs* RICH*'s hand.)*

RICH. No!

BROTHER. Richard, don't! . . . *(He attempts to hug* RICH, *who resists with all his strength.)* I don't care . . . I don't care! . . . Rich! . . . Richie . . . Richie . . . *(*RICH *relents. They hug.)*

RICH. I'm so . . . [frightened]

BROTHER. Forgive me. Forgive me.

RICH. I don't want to . . . [die]

BROTHER. It's all right. I'm here . . . I'm here . . . *(They hold each other close for a beat. The hospital worker rushes into the room.)*

HOSPITAL WORKER. Psst. Oye. Psst. *(*RICH *and his brother notice the worker.)*

RICH. What do you want now?

HOSPITAL WORKER *(Shakes his head no). Viene. Viene.* He come. He come. *(He pulls the brother from* RICH.)

RICH. Who come?

HOSPITAL WORKER. *Su amigo.* Your freng. He no like.

BROTHER. What's he saying? *(*RICH *starts to laugh. Enter* SAUL. *The worker starts sweeping and whistling with an air of exuberant nonchalance. The following is overlapping.)*

RICH *(Laughing).* He . . . he . . .

SAUL. What's going on?

BROTHER. Richie, what's so damned funny?

RICH. He thought we . . . *(He breaks up.)* that he and I were cheating on you.

BROTHER. He thought that you and I were . . . *(He laughs.)*

RICH. He came in to warn me that you

were coming! *(He laughs. To the worker.) Gracias! Muchas gracias!*

SAUL. He thought you two were . . . *(He laughs.)*

HOSPITAL WORKER *(To* RICH*). De nada.* [You're welcome.] Why you laugh? *(The worker laughs.) Como hay maricones.* [What a bunch of faggots.]

RICH. *Es mi hermano.*

HOSPITAL WORKER. *Coño.*

RICH. *Perdona por lo que dije antes. Yo (Pointing to himself.) era mucho estupido.* [He's my brother. Forgive me for what I said to you before. I was being very stupid.]

HOSPITAL WORKER. *De nada. Somos todos estúpidos, chico.* [We're all stupid, my friend.] *(He exits. The giggles subside.)*

BROTHER *(Checking watch, stiffening his spine).* I've got to be going now.

RICH. I'm glad you came by.

BROTHER. I'll be back tomorrow with Mary Pat. She's been dying—wanting to come by. She's been writing poetry and—

RICH. I'd love to see her. And tell Betty thanks for the . . . ?

BROTHER. Butter crunch. *(Exiting, shaking hands with* SAUL*.)* Good seeing ya . . . ? *(He has forgotten* SAUL*'s name again.)*

SAUL. Saul.

BROTHER. Sorry. Bye. *(He exits.)*

SAUL. I won't get upset. I won't get upset.

RICH. What's the matter?

SAUL. It's *my* problem.

RICH. What?

SAUL. Rich, I've thought about things.

RICH. What?

SAUL *(Suddenly exploding).* Goddamn it! That prick doesn't know my name after— how many years are we together?

RICH. *Were* together.

SAUL. Pardon me, I forgot we got an annulment from the pope. Fuck it, I won't get upset.

RICH *(Overlapping).* My brother finds it hard to deal with the fact that—

SAUL. I said fuck it.

RICH. Don't you see, it was a big step for him—

SAUL. Your brother hates my fucking guts. Haven't you ever told him I didn't turn you queer?

RICH. My brother—

SAUL. I didn't give you AIDS either.

RICH. My brother—

SAUL. Why're you always defending him? What about me?

RICH. My brother's got a few feelings, too, even if he isn't a card-carrying member of the lavender elite.

SAUL. Let's hear it for our working-class hero.

RICH. You've never tried talking to him. You're so self-centered that it never occurred to you—

SAUL. I'm self—Now wait one minute! I'm so self-centered that I was willing to buy the pills for you.

RICH. You have the pills? *(The other actors create the sleazy atmosphere of Christopher Street near the Hudson River.)*

DEALER 1. Yo, my man.

SAUL. I was willing to go down to Christopher Street, where all the drug dealers hang out.

DEALER 2. What's 'attenin', what's 'attenin'? *(SAUL turns his back to RICH and immediately he is on Christopher Street.)*

SAUL *(To DEALER 2)*. Nice night.

RICH. I told you to go to the doctor's.

DEALER 1. Smoke 'n' acid, MDA 'n' speed. Smoke 'n' acid, MDA 'n' speed . . .

DEALER 2 *(Simultaneously)*. Crack . . . crack . . . crack . . .

SAUL *(To DEALER 1)*. I said, "Nice night."

DEALER 1. Real nice. What's shakin', babe?

RICH. All you would've had to say to the doctor was "My roommate has AIDS and I'm not sleeping well."

SAUL *(To DEALER 1)*. I'm not sleeping well.

DEALER 1. I have just the thing. Step right into my office.

DEALER 3. Speed, acid, mesc, ups, downs . . .

SAUL. I'll take one hundred.

DEALER 1. Two dollars a cap.

RICH. Forty's enough.

SAUL. I wanted enough for both of us.

DEALER 1. You got the cash, I got the stash.

RICH. Tristan and Isolde.

DEALER. Hey, man, you want them or not?

SAUL. You don't understand anything!

DEALER 1. Look, man, I can't handle all that emotiating.

SAUL *(Near the breaking point)*. You've never understood anything!

DEALER 1. Gimme the greens, I'll give you the reds.

RICH. The widow throws herself on her husband's funeral pyre.

SAUL *(Hitting the bed with his fists. If RICH were the bed he'd be dead)*. SHIT! SHIT! SHIT! You selfish bastard!

RICH. What stopped you?

SAUL. From hitting you?

RICH. From buying the pills.

SAUL. The pills? Nothing stopped me. I bought them.

RICH. Thank you. Where are they?

SAUL. I threw them away.

RICH. Why?

SAUL. Let me help you live!

RICH. What's so hot about living when you're covered with lesions and you're coming down with a new infection every day? . . . If it gets too bad, I want to be able to quietly disappear.

SAUL. I won't argue the logic of it. I can't do what you want me to do.

RICH. I just want them around. You keep them for me—just in case.

SAUL. I won't.

RICH. Then I'll get them myself. I'll go out of here and get them. *(He climbs out of bed. He's shaky.)*

SAUL. You're crazy.

RICH. I don't need you to do my dirty work. *(He takes a few steps.)* Where're my clothes? Where'd they put them?

SAUL. Get back in bed!

RICH. I want to get out of here! *(He puts on his robe.)* This place is a death machine! *(He starts to leave but collapses on the floor.)*

SAUL *(Rushing to his aid)*. You idiot.

RICH *(Catching his breath)*. Well, here we are again. *(SAUL tries to help him back to bed.)* No. Let me sit . . . Fuck . . . *(He sits in chair.)* "Dependent": from the Late Latin "to hang from."

SAUL. I tried to do what you asked me to do. Just like always.

RICH. You don't have to apologize.

SAUL. I want you to understand something.

RICH. I understand.

SAUL. It's important. Listen. I had made up my mind to give you half of the pills and keep the other half for myself. I was walking past Sheridan Square. It was starting to drizzle again. You've never seen Sheridan Square look grungier: a drunk was pissing on the pathetic little flowers. And that crazy lady—you know the one that sings off-key at the top of her lungs—she was there, too. And my favorite, the guy with his stomach out to here—

RICH. I get the picture.

SAUL. There I was walking with the pills in my pocket, contemplating our suicides. And I was getting wet and cold. As I passed the square, Seconal seemed too slow to me. You don't have a monopoly on pain.

RICH. I never thought—

SAUL. Shut up. Anyway, I had stopped in front of the Pleasure Chest. I looked up and there in the window were sex toys and multi-colored jockstraps, lit by a red neon sign. I said, "Help me, God." Which is funny coming from an atheist, let me tell you . . . I said it out loud.

RICH. And you could walk again.

SAUL. Well, it wasn't exactly a miracle.

RICH. Thank God.

SAUL. Anyway, there I was in front of a sex shop, and I looked down and there was a puddle. Now this'll sound stupid.

RICH. Couldn't sound stupider than the rest.

SAUL. In this dirty little puddle was a reflection of the red neon sign. It was beautiful. And the whole street was shining with the incredible colors. They kept changing as the different signs blinked on and off . . . I don't know how long I stood there. A phrase came to my head: "The Lord taketh and the Lord giveth."

RICH. You blew your punch line.

SAUL. It's the other way around. Anyway, there went two hundred bucks down the sewer.

RICH. Take it off your taxes.

SAUL. Don't you see, I just don't have the right to take your life or mine.

RICH. The Miracle of the Pleasure Chest.

SAUL. Hang in there, Rich.

RICH. Our Lady of Christopher Street.

SAUL. Maybe I'm being selfish, but I want you here. I need you.

RICH. My future isn't exactly promising.

SAUL. I'll take you as is.

RICH. But what happens when it gets worse? It's gonna get worse.

SAUL. I'll be here for you no matter what happens.

RICH. Will you?

SAUL. I promise.

RICH. Shit.

SAUL. What do you want me to say?

RICH. You're so goddamned noble.

SAUL. How do you want me to be?

RICH. I can't afford to be noble. The only thing holding me together is rage. It's not fair! Why me?

SAUL. Why *not* you? Maybe I'm next. No one knows.

RICH. I reserve the right to put an end to all this shit.

SAUL. All right, but if you kill yourself they won't bury you in hallowed ground and you'll go to hell with all us Jews.

RICH. I bet they have a separate AIDS section in the cemetery so I don't infect the other corpses. *(Beat, then suddenly he speaks fiercely.)* Do you promise to stick with me no matter what happens?

SAUL. I do.

RICH. Prodigies and signs, why not? It's the end of an era.

SAUL. What do you think'll come next?

RICH. *Do you? (He searches* SAUL*'s face for the answer.)* I need you. *(Long silence. He releases* SAUL.*)* Paradise in a puddle.

SAUL. You couldn't resist that, could you?

RICH. Next? After I'm gone?

SAUL. Don't be maudlin. You know I didn't mean that.

RICH. I know you didn't . . . I've been wondering what happens after I die . . . Do you think things go on and on? I don't know. Is this all the time I have? I hope not . . . Do you think anywhere out there is a place as sweet as this one? I like it here—even though right now I am going through a lot of . . . *(Searching for the word.)* difficulty . . . *(He goes back to bed.)* And if we get to come back, where do we get to come back to? I don't feature leaving here and going to a god-damned naphtha swamp in the Z sector of some provincial galaxy to live as some kind of weird insect . . . But if life is a kind of educational process in which each piece of the universe eventually gets to discover its own true divine nature, if it is, then a methane bog on Jupiter might serve just as well as a meadow in the Berkshires . . . I want to be cremated and I want my ashes to fertilize the apple tree in the middle of Jake's pasture. When you take a bite of an apple from that tree think of me.

SAUL. You'd be the worm in it.

RICH. Saul?

SAUL. What, Rich?

RICH. There's a cafe way over by Tompkins Square Park, off of B. It holds maybe ten tables and has the scuzziest art on the walls.

SAUL. What about it?

RICH. I want to read my work there.

SAUL. You turned down the Y.

RICH. People go there, gay, straight, with their weird hair and their ears pierced ninety-nine different ways, they go there late in the evening, and there's a guitarist, and they sit there politely and listen. They look newborn, but slightly depraved. I want to read there when I get out of here. And you'll take pictures. Okay?

SAUL. Sounds okay. Sounds good to me.

RICH. Forgive me for being such a fuck.

RICH. You're a faggot.

SAUL. You're a fruit.

RICH. You know, if we took precautions . . .

SAUL. If what? What? You always do that.

RICH. I don't know.

SAUL. Would you like to?

RICH. If we're careful. Do you want to?

SAUL. I'd love to. What do you think?

RICH. I think it'd be okay.

SAUL. What'll we do?

RICH. I don't know. Something safe.

SAUL. We'll think of something.

RICH. Close the curtain.

SAUL. Do you think we should?

RICH. Well, we can't do it like this.

SAUL. Right.

RICH. Right.

SAUL. What if someone comes in?

RICH. So what?

SAUL. Right. *(SAUL doesn't move.)*

RICH. So what are you waiting for?

SAUL. I'm scared.

RICH. So am I. Do you think we should?

SAUL. God, I want to.

RICH. Well, close the fucking curtain! *(The hospice worker ends the impasse by closing the curtain.)* Thanks.

SAUL. Thanks. *(When the curtain is completely shut, the hospice worker walks D.C.)*

HOSPICE WORKER. I have a new AIDS patient, Richard. He still has a lot of denial about his condition. Which is normal. I think most of us would go crazy if we had to face our own deaths squarely. He's a wonderful man. He writes extraordinarily funny poems about the ward. His lover's there all the time, and he's got a lot of friends visiting, and both families. I only hope it keeps up. It's only his second time in the hospital. They get a lot of support at first, but as the illness goes on, the visitors stop coming—and they're left with only me.

But something tells me it's not going to happen in his case. You should see how his lover takes care of him. God forbid they treat Rich badly, Saul swoops down and lets them have it. He's making a real pain in the ass of himself, which is sometimes how you have to be in this situation.

Rich should be out of the hospital again in a week or so. For a while. He's a fighter . . . The angry phase is just about over and the bargaining phase is beginning. If he behaves like a good little boy, God will do what Rich tells Him to do . . . I certainly hope that God does.

I don't know anymore. Sometimes I think I'm an atheist. No. Not really. It's more that I'm angry at God: how can He do this? *(Pause.)* I have a lot of denial, I am angry, and I bargain with God. I have a long way to go towards acceptance. Maybe it's time for me to resign. Maybe I'm suffering from burnout.

But what would I do if I didn't go to St. Vincent's? And it's a privilege to be with people when they are dying. Sometimes they tell you the most amazing things. The other night Jean-Jacques—he's this real queen, there's no other word for it—he told me what he misses most in the hospital is his corset and high heels. I mean he weighs all of ninety pounds and he's half dead. But I admire his spirit. The way they treat him. Sometimes they won't even bring the food to his bed. And I'm afraid to complain for fear they take it out on him! Damn them! . . . I've lost some of my idealism, as I said. Last night I painted his nails for him. *(She shows the audience her vividly painted fingernails.)* Flaming red. He loved it.

End of Play

I'm Not Rappaport

HERB GARDNER

FOR SHEL

Originally presented by the Seattle Repertory Theatre in December 1984.

The play was subsequently presented by James Walsh, Lewis Allen, and Martin Heinfling at the American Place Theater in New York City on June 6, 1985. The cast was as follows:

NAT	Judd Hirsch
MIDGE	Cleavon Little
DANFORTH	Michael Tucker
LAURIE	Liann Pattison
GILLEY	Jace Alexander
CLARA	Cheryl Giannini
THE COWBOY	Ray Baker

Directed by Daniel Sullivan
Setting by Tony Walton
Costumes by Robert Morgan
Lighting by Pat Collins.

This production was transferred to the Booth Theatre in New York City on November 19, 1985, with the following cast:

NAT	Judd Hirsch
MIDGE	Cleavon Little
DANFORTH	Gregg Almquist
LAURIE	Liann Pattison
GILLEY	Jace Alexander
CLARA	Mercedes Ruehl
THE COWBOY	Steve Ryan

Scene:

Early October 1982. A bench near a path at the edge of the lake in Central Park, New York City.

Act I: Three in the afternoon.

Act II: Scene 1: Three in the afternoon, the next day. Scene 2: Six in the evening, the next day. Scene 3: Twelve days later, eleven in the morning.

Note: All stage directions and set descriptions are given from the audience's left and right.

I'm Not Rappaport was originally presented in informal readings at the Manhattan Theatre Club and at the Circle Repertory Theatre in New York in 1983. It was then presented, with Judd Hirsch and Cleavon Little in the leading roles, at New York's American Place Theatre in 1985. This production transferred to the Booth Theatre on Broadway, opening to an oddly mixed response of wildly enthusiastic audiences and lukewarm reviews. It subsequently won three Tony Awards: Best Play of 1986, Best Actor (Judd Hirsch), and Best Lighting (Pat Collins).

I'm Not Rappaport is an urban comedy of male bonding. Two feisty men, both in their eighties, are a study in contrasts. Nat is an old-time Jewish radical who weaves incredible fantasies to make his daily life bearable. Midge is a pragmatic black man who just wants to stay out of trouble. As Nat cannot stop telling stories and as Midge cannot stop listening to them, the two ultimately find themselves facing their problems together, with courage and humor, and without self-pity. Playwright Herb Gardner says: "I endow my characters with all the courage I don't have, the conviction . . . the integrity that's willing to be tested. . . ."

The play, in two acts, also includes an interesting cast of supporting characters: a street punk, a cowboy drug dealer, a jogger, the yuppie president of a tenants association, an art student drug addict, and Nat's concerned, albeit self-righteous, daughter. Cleavon Little says, "[The play] is about friendship, courage, and the human spirit."

Gardner reveals the play's real-life origin: "There was an old white guy and an old black guy. . . . They were obviously friends and getting a big kick out of hollering at each other. I was writing something else entirely, but I started imagining what these two old guys were yelling, and why they were friends, and it just took over. . . . I go around haunted by something until I write it down. . . . I grew up with these people who lived at the tops of their voices . . . against all evidence to the contrary, they had not given up an image of a better world. If they didn't argue about Lenin, they argued about the egg salad."

Gardner has always considered himself primarily a writer, although he is also an accomplished sculptor, doll inventor, and cartoonist. While attending the High School of Performing Arts in New York City, he worked as an orange-juice salesman and coat checker at various Broadway theatres. "That way," he says, "I could see the same show as often as 150 times and really get to know what was good and what was bad. . . ."

Gardner attended Carnegie-Mellon University and Antioch University, studying writing, theatre, and art. It was during this period that he had the idea for the Nebbish (Yiddish for "poor thing"). Made in rubber, Gardner's figurines did not take off at first, but after appearing in a comic strip, they became a national craze, appearing on ashtrays, sweatshirts, greeting cards, and in seventy-four newspapers. The financial success of this enterprise enabled Gardner to devote himself full time to his writing. His novel *A Piece of the Action* was published by Simon and Schuster, one of his short stories was included in *Best Short Stories of 1968*, and a television play won first prize in a contest sponsored by David Susskind's Talent Associates. Perhaps most important, his celebrated play *A Thousand Clowns* (1962) established him at age twenty-seven as a respected playwright. Gardner's screenplay for *A Thousand Clowns* won the Screenwriters Guild Award for Best Screenplay in 1965.

"For a number of years," Gardner says, "I wrote only in loose-leaf notebooks, because I wanted to think it was just my homework. If I actually thought it was my profession, I'd be paralyzed. . . . How do I explain that I write plays, that I speak in the voices of other people, because I don't know my own? . . . I cannot offer an explanation of why I write plays because there is none. Playwriting is an irrational act . . . your days are spent making up things that no one ever said to be spoken by people who do not exist for an audience that may not come. . . . The most difficult problem is . . . that I love it. Because it's alive, exactly what is terrible is wonderful: the gamble, the odds. . . . In a theatre, the ones in the dark and the ones under the lights need each other. For a few hours, all of us, the audience, the actors, the writers, we are all a little more real together than we ever were apart. That's the ticket and that's what the ticket's for." Other work by Herb Gardner includes *Who Is Harry Kellerman and Why Is He Saying Those Terrible Things About Me?* (Screenplay, 1971); *Thieves* (1974); the dialogue for Bob Fosse's 1978 musical *Dancin'* (in collaboration with Paddy Chayevsky); the playlet *Word of Mouth*, (for *Love, Liberty, and Lunch*, ABC-TV, 1976); *Love and/or Death*; three one-act plays: *I'm with Ya, Duke, How I Crossed the Street for the First Time All by Myself*, and *The Forever Game* (1979); *One Night Stand* (1980); and *Conversations with My Father* (1991).

ACT ONE

SCENE: *A battered bench on an isolated path at the edge of Central Park Lake, early October, 1982, about three in the afternoon. To the left of this center bench is a smaller even more battered one with several of its slats missing. Behind these benches is the Gothic arch of an old stone tunnel, framed above by an ornate Romanesque bridge which spans the width of the stage.*

Before the curtain rises we hear the sound of a Carousel Band-Organ playing "The Queen City March."

AT RISE: *Two men,* MIDGE *and* NAT, *both about eighty years old, are seated at either end of the center bench; they sit several feet apart, an old briefcase between them.* MIDGE *is black and* NAT *is white.* MIDGE *wears very thick bifocals and an old soft hat; he is reading* The Sporting News. NAT *wears a beret and has a finely trimmed beard, a cane with an elegant ivory handle rests next to him against the bench. The two men do not look at each other. A Jogger runs by on the bridge above, exists at right. An autumn leaf or two drifts down through the late afternoon light. Silence for a few moments; only the now distant sound of the Carousel Music.*

NAT. O.K., where was I? *(No response. He smacks himself on the forehead.)* Where the hell was I? What were we talking about? I was just about to make a very important point here. *(To* MIDGE:*)* What were we talking about?

MIDGE *(No response. He continues to read his newspaper for a moment).* We wasn't talking. *You* was talking. *(Turns page.)* I wasn't talking.

NAT. O.K., so what was I saying?

MIDGE. I wasn't listening either. You was doing the whole thing by yourself.

NAT. Why weren't you listening?

MIDGE. Because you're a goddamn liar. I'm not listening to you anymore. Two days now I ain't been listening.

NAT. Stop pretending to read. You can't see anything.

MIDGE. Hey, how 'bout you go sit with them old dudes in fronta the Welfare Hotel, them old butter brains—*(pointing about the lake)* the babies at the Carousel, them kids in the boat—or some o' them junkie-folk yon-der, whyn't you go mess with them? 'Cause I'm not talking to you anymore, Mister. Put-tin' you on notice of that. You may's well be talking to that tree over there.

NAT. It's a lamppost.

MIDGE. Sittin' here a week now, ain't heard a worda truth outa you. Shuckin' me every which way till the sun go down.

NAT *(slapping the bench).* I demand an explanation of that statement!

MIDGE. O.K., wise-ass; for example, are you or are you not an escaped Cuban terror-ist?

NAT *(slapping the bench).* I am not!

MIDGE. O.K., and your name ain't Her-nando—

NAT. Absolutely not!

MIDGE. So it's a lie—

NAT. It's a cover-story! *(Pause.)* My line of work, they give you a cover-story.

MIDGE. Are you sayin'—?

NAT. All I'm saying, and that's *all* I'm say-ing, is that in my particular field you gotta have a cover-story. More than that I can't divulge at the present time.

MIDGE. Honey bun, you sayin' you're a spy?

NAT. I'm saying my name is Hernando and I'm an escaped Cuban terrorist.

MIDGE. But what kinda weirdo, bullshit cover-story is—?

NAT. You don't think I *said* that to them? That's what *I* said to them. I said to them, an eighty-one-year-old Lithuanian is a Cuban Hernando? That's right, they said, tough luck, sweetheart; yours is not to reason why. That's how they talk. Of *course* you don't believe it! You think *I* believe it? Such dopes. But it's a living. I beg you not to inquire further.

MIDGE. But why'd they pick an old—

NAT. Do *I* know? You tell *me.* A year ago I'm standing in line at the Medicaid, a fellah comes up to me—boom, I'm an undercover.

MIDGE *(impressed).* Lord . . .

NAT. Who knows, maybe they got some-thing. They figure an old man, nobody'll pay attention. Could wander through the world like a ghost, pick up some tidbits.

MIDGE *(nodding thoughtfully).* Yeah . . .

NAT. So maybe they got something, even though, I grant you, they screwed up on the cover-story. All I know is every month a thousand bingos is added to my Social Secu-rity check.

MIDGE. Bingos?

NAT. Bingos. Dollars. Cash. It's a word we use in the business. Please don't inquire further. *(Silence.)* Please, I'm not at liberty. *(Longer silence.)* O.K.; they also gave me a code name, "Harry."

MIDGE. "Harry"?

NAT. Harry Schwartzman.

MIDGE. What's your real name?

NAT. Sam Schwartzman. *(Outraged.)* Can you believe it? Can you *believe* it? That's some imaginative *group* they got up there, right? That's some bunch of geniuses! *(Then, shrugging.)* What the hell, a thousand bananas on your Social Security every month you don't ask fancy questions.

MIDGE. Best not, best not. *(Leaning closer.)* So, do ya … do ya ever pick up any information for them?

NAT. Are you kidding? Sitting on a bench all day with a man who can't tell a tree from a lamppost? Not a shred. *(Glances about, leans closer.)* Fact is, I think they got me in what they call "deep cover." See, they keep you in this "deep cover" for years; like five, maybe ten years they keep you there, till you're just like this regular person in the neighborhood … and then, boom, they pick you out for the big one. Considering my age and general health, they're not too bright. *(Reaches into briefcase.)* O.K., snack time.

MIDGE *(nodding).* Yeah. Deep cover. I hearda that …

NAT *(taking foil-wrapped sandwich from briefcase).* Here. Tuna salad with lettuce and tomato on whole wheat toast. Take half.

MIDGE *(accepting sandwich).* Thank ya, Sam; thank ya.

NAT. Yeah, comes three o'clock, there's nothing like a nice, fresh tuna salad sandwich.

MIDGE *(chewing).* Uh-huh.

NAT *(chewing).* Crisp.

(Silence for several moments as their old jaws work on the sandwiches.)

MIDGE *(suddenly).* Bullshit! *(Sits upright.)* Bullshit! Lord, you done it to me *again!* You done it! *(Throws the sandwich fiercely to the ground.)* Promised myself I wouldn't let ya, and ya done it again! Deep cover! Harry Schwartzman! Bingos! You done it again!

NAT *(smiling to himself as he continues eating).* That was nice … a nice long story, lasted a long time …

MIDGE *(shouting, poking Nat sharply).* That's it! That's it, no more conversin'! Conversin' is over now, Mister! No more, ain't riffin' *me* no more!

NAT. Please control yourself—

MIDGE. *Move* it, boy; *away* with ya! This here's *my* spot!

NAT. Sir, I was—

MIDGE. This is *my* spot. I come here first!

NAT. I was merely—

MIDGE. Get offa my spot 'fore I lay you out!

NAT. *Your* spot? Who made it *your* spot? Show me the plaque. Where does it say that?

MIDGE. Says right here … *(Remains seated, slowly circling his fists in the air like a boxer.)* You read them hands? Study them hands, boy. Them hands wore Golden Gloves, summer of Nineteen and Twenty-Four. This here's *my* spot, *been* my spot six months now, my good and peaceful spot till you show up a week ago start playin' Three Card Monte with my head. Want you *gone*, Sonny! *(Continues circling his fists.)* Givin' ya three t'make dust; comin' out on the count o'three. One—

(MIDGE rises, moving to his corner of the "ring.")

NAT. Wait, a brief discussion—

MIDGE. Sound of the bell, I'm comin' out. *You* won't hear it but I *will.* Two—

NAT. How you gonna hit me if you can't *see* me?

MIDGE. Dropped Billy D'Amato in the sixth round with both eyes swole shut. I just keep punchin' till I hear crunchin'. *Three!*

NAT *(rising, with dignity).* Please, sir—this is an embarrassing demonstration—

MIDGE *(moving in NAT's general direction, a bit of remembered footwork, jabbing).* O.K., comin' out, comin' out; comin' at ya, boy, comin' at ya—

NAT *(moving behind bench for protection).* Sir, you … you have a depressing personality and a terrible attitude!

MIDGE. *Prepare* yourself, Mister, prepare yourself, get your—

(MIDGE suddenly lunges, bumping against the bench, stumbling—he struggles to keep his balance, grabbing desperately at the air—then falls flat on his back in the path. He lies there silently for several moments.)

MIDGE *(quietly, frightened).* Oh, shit …

NAT *(aware that MIDGE is in danger, whispering).* Mister … ? *(No response. He leans forward urgently.)* Mister, Mister … ? *(Silence. He moves towards MIDGE as quickly as possible.)* Don't move, don't move …

MIDGE *(trembling).* I know …

NAT. Could be you broke something …

MIDGE *(softly)*. I know. Oh, shit. Never fall down, *never* fall down . . .

NAT *(kneeling next to him, trying to calm him)*. It's nothing; I fall down every morning. I get up, I have a cup of coffee, I fall down. That's the system; two years old you stand up and then, boom, seventy years later you fall down again. *(Gently, firmly:)* O.K., first thing; can you lift your head? *(MIDGE hesitates, frightened, then raises his head a bit.)* Good sign. Put your head back. *(As MIDGE carefully rests his head back.)* Good, good, good . . . *(Carefully, knowledgeably, touching MIDGE, checking for damage.)* O.K., feeling for breaks, checking the pelvic area . . . feeling the hip now . . . If you like this we're engaged. *(MIDGE moans softly, frightened.)* Don't worry; breaks is also nothing. Everybody breaks. Me, I got a hip like a teacup. Twice last year; I just got rid of my walker. *(Continues checking MIDGE's left leg; MIDGE winces.)* I was also dead once for a while. Six minutes. Also nothing; don't worry. They're doing a bypass, everything stops; they had to jump-start me like a Chevrolet. *(Starts checking MIDGE's right leg; MIDGE apprehensive.)* Six minutes dead, the doctor said. You know what it's like? Boring. First thing you float up and stick to the ceiling like a kid's balloon, you look around. Down below on the bed there's a body you wouldn't give a nickel for. It's you. Meanwhile you're up on the ceiling; nobody sees you. Not bad for a while, nice; you meet some other dead guys, everybody smiles, you hear a little music; but mostly boring. *(He has finished checking MIDGE's legs.)* O.K.; can you move your arms? *(MIDGE demonstrates a few, short boxing jabs.)* Excellent. O.K., good news: each item functional. Now, from experience, lie there and relax five minutes before you get up. *(MIDGE murmurs obediently.)* O.K., best thing for relaxing is jokes—*(Rising to center bench near him.)* Willy Howard, you heardof him? The best. O.K., years ago he had this great routine, see—

MIDGE. That was another lie, wasn't it?

NAT. What?

MIDGE. 'Bout you bein' dead.

NAT. A *fact*, that was an absolute—

MIDGE. Man, you ain't even *friendly* with the truth! *Lies.* Goddamn *lies!* *(Slaps the ground.)* It's your goddamn lies put me on the canvas here! Got me fightin', fallin' down—

NAT. *Not* lies—*(Sits upright on bench.)* Alterations! I make certain alterations. Sometimes the truth don't fit; I take in here, I let out there, till it fits. The *truth?* What's true is a triple bypass last year at Lenox Hill, what's true is Grade Z cuts of meat from the A and P, a Social Security check that wouldn't pay the rent for a chipmunk; what's true is going to the back door of the Plaza Hotel every morning for yesterday's club-rolls. I tell them it's for the pigeons. I'm the pigeon. Six minutes dead is *true*— *(takes bunch of pages from briefcase)* here, Dr. Reissman's bills; here's the phone number, call him. A fact. And that was my *last* fact. Since then, alterations. Since I died, a new policy! This morning I tell the counterman at the Farm Fresh Deli I'm an American Indian. An Iroquois. He listens; next thing I know I'm remembering the old days on the plains, the broken treaties, my Grandpa fighting the cavalry. Not important *he's* convinced; *I* am, and I love it. I was one person for eighty-one years, why not a hundred for the next five?!

MIDGE *(after a moment, resting on his elbows, thoughtfully)*. Them club-rolls; how early you figure a fellah oughta show up down there to—

NAT. *Rolls, rolls;* you missed the whole *point*—

MIDGE *(rising carefully to small bench)*. The *point?* I *got* the point; the point is you're crazy, the point is you ain't never seein' your marbles again!

NAT. Ah, how fortunate, an expert on mental health. My daughter Clara, she's another expert—*(holds up one of the pages)* here, wants to put me in a home for the ridiculous. "No sense of reality," she writes, "in need of supervision," she writes. This she writes to my therapist, Dr. Engels. Trouble is I don't have a therapist and I'm Dr. Engels. I give her the address of the Young Socialists' Club on Eighty-Sixth; I'm listed there as Doctor Friedrich Engels. *(Leans closer to him.)* Crazy, you say? Listen to me, listen to Dr. Engels. You're a wreck. Look at you; is this who you want to be? Is this what you had in mind for old, this guy here? A man who obviously passed away some time ago? Whatta you got left, five minutes, five months? Is this how you want to spend it? Sitting and staring, once in a while for a thrill falling down? *(Urgently:)* No, *wrong;* you gotta shake things up, fellah; you gotta make things *happen*—

MIDGE *(truly outraged)*. Hold it now! Hold that mouth right there! You tellin' *me* how to live? *You* tellin' *me?* You talkin' to an *em*ployed person here, Mister! *(Retrieving his* *newspaper from* NAT*'s bench, returning with great dignity to his own.)* Midge Carter; you talkin' to Midge Carter here, boy—Super-in-tendent in charge of Three Twenty-One Central Park West; *run* the place, *been* runnin' it forty-two years, July. They got a furnace been there long as *I* have—an ol' Erie City Special, fourteen *tonner,* known to *kill* a man don't show he's boss. Buildin' don't move without that bull and that bull don't move without *me.* Don't have to make up nobody to be when I *am* somebody! *(Settling himself proudly on small bench.)* Shake things up, huh? Don't shake *nothin'* up. How you figure I keep my job? Near fifteen years past retirement, how you figure I'm still super there? I ain't mentioned a raise in fifteen years, and they ain't neither. Moved to the night-shift three years ago, outa the public eye. Daytime a buncha A-rab Supers has come and gone, not Midge. Dozen Spic Doormen dressed up like five-star generals, come and gone, not Midge. Mister, you lookin' at the wise old invisible man.

NAT. No, I'm looking at a dead man! *(Points cane at him.)* Fifteen years, no raise; it's a dead person, a ghost! You let them rob you!

MIDGE. They don't rob me; *nobody* robs me, got a system. You see that boy come every day, five o'clock? That's Gilley; give him three bucks, nobody robs me. Ten blocks from here to my place, walks me there, protects me.

NAT. From who?

MIDGE. Him, for one. Fifteen a week, he don't rob me—but nobody *else* neither, see; now *that's* Social Security—

NAT *(laughing).* Oh, God—

MIDGE. Keep chucklin', sugar; ain't nobody dyin' of old age in *this* neighborhood.

NAT. Job! I see what your *job* is. Groveling! You're a licensed groveler!

MIDGE *(rises from bench, shouting).* Super at Three Twenty-One, still got a *callin'*—only thing people got to call *you* is, "hey, old man!"

NAT. What do *you* know? What does a *ghost* know? *(Rising proudly.)* People *see* me; they *see* me! I *make* them see me! *(His cane in the air.)* The night they rushed me to Lenox Hill for the bypass, as they carried me out on the *stretcher,* six tenants called the Landlord to see if my apartment was available. Now, every *day,* every day at dawn I ring their bells, all six of them—the door opens, I holler "Good morning, Vulture; Four B is still

unavailable!" I hum the first two bars of "The Internationale" and walk away.

MIDGE *(moving towards him).* Old *fool,* crazy old fool; they can't see *you.* They can hear ya, but they sure can't *see* ya. Don't want to *look* at your old face; mine neither—I just help 'em out. Don't you get it, baby?—*both* of us ghosts only *you* ain't noticed. We old and not rich and done the sin of leavin' slow. No use to fight it, you go with it or you break, boy; 'specially bones like *we* got.

NAT *(shouting).* Traitor! Traitor in the ranks! It's people like you give old a bad name—

DANFORTH'S VOICE *(shouting).* Carter—

NAT. It's *your* type that—

DANFORTH'S VOICE. Carter—(PETER DANFORTH *enters on the bridge, Up Left, jogging; he is the same man who ran by earlier.* DANFORTH *is in his early forties and wears a newly purchased jogging outfit.)* Carter . . . ah, good, *there* you are, Carter . . .

MIDGE *(glancing about, not sure who it is or where the voice is coming from).* Midge Carter, here I am.

DANFORTH *(slowing his pace).* Here, up here . . . on the bridge . . . *(jogging in place, cordially:)* Danforth . . . Peter Danforth, Twelve H . . .

MIDGE *(squinting up).* Danforth, right . . .

DANFORTH *(breathlessly).* Been looking for you—several days now—they told me you might be in this area—our meeting, remember?

MIDGE. Our meetin', yeah . . .

DANFORTH. How about right here, soon as I finish my run?

MIDGE. Right here, you got it.

DANFORTH. Be right with you . . . *(Quickening his pace again.)* Three more miles, be right with you, Carter; looking forward to it . . .

MIDGE *(shouting up, as* DANFORTH *exits right).* Lookin' forward to the meetin', yessir; been on my schedule . . . *(Suddenly whispering, terrified.)* Oh shit, the Man, the Man, he found me—

NAT. What man?

MIDGE. *The* Man, *the* Man, been duckin' him, he *found* me.

NAT. *What* man? What is it, Carter?

MIDGE *(sits on center bench, trembling, brushing off clothes, adjusting hat, trying to pull himself together).* Mr. Danforth, Twelve H, Head o' the Tenants' Committee. Place is goin' Co-op, he says they got some reorganizin' to do, says he wants to see me private . . .

NAT *(softly, nodding)*. Ah, yes . . .

MIDGE. Last fellah wanted to see me private was when they found my wife Daisy under the Seventy-Ninth Street Crosstown. *(Buttoning sweater, trying for a bit of dignity.)* See, problem is, it's been gettin' around the buildin' that I'm kinda nearsighted—

NAT *(sitting next to him)*. Nearsighted? Helen *Keller* was *near*sighted.

MIDGE. Got the place memorized, see. But last week I'm in the basement, lady from Two A sees me walk right smack into the elevator door. Mrs. Carsten, Two A, she's standin' in the laundry room watchin' me. Figured I'd fake her out, so I do it *again*, like I was *meanin'* to do it, like it's this *plan* I got to walk into the elevator door—dumb, dumb, *knowed* it was a dumb move while I was *doin'* it. Just kept slammin' into that elevator door till she went away. I'm shoutin', "gonna have this thing fixed in a jiffy, Mrs. Carsten!" Next thing I know Danforth wants to see me private. *(Hits himself on the head.)* Panicked on the *ropes* is what I did; that's what blew it for me in the ring too . . .

(Silence for a moment.)

NAT *(quietly)*. Are the cataracts in both eyes?

MIDGE *(after a moment; quietly)*. Yeah.

NAT. How many times removed?

MIDGE. Left twice, the right once. But they come back.

NAT. That's what they do. They're dependable. And how bad is the glaucoma?

MIDGE. Drops an' pills keep it down. 'Cept night-times. Night-times—

NAT. Night-times it's like you're trying to close your lid over a basketball.

MIDGE. No lie. No *lie*. When'd it start with you? Start with me four, five years back; nothin' on the sides. No p'ripheral vision, doc says. Five years back—*(he waves)* so long, p'ripheral vision. Then one mornin' there's this spot in the middle . . .

NAT. Ah, the spot, the spot . . .

MIDGE. Like the moon, this dead pearly spot . . .

NAT. The moon exactly . . .

MIDGE. And it gets to growin' . . .

NAT. Oh, yes . . .

MIDGE. Then, thank the Lord, it stops. Then what you got is the pearly moon spot, no p'ripherals, and this ring between 'em where folks come in and out.

NAT. Exactly; like birds. *(Leans close to him.)* You get color or black and white?

MIDGE. Mostly blue. Blue shadows like. Weird thing is, all my dreams is still in full color, see everything real sharp and clear like when I was young—then I wake up and it's real life looks like a dream.

NAT. Exactly! Same with me *exactly!* I hadn't thought about it till this minute! *(His arm around MIDGE.)* Carter, we're connected. Why? Because we both got vision. Who needs sight when we got vision! Connected! Yes, even with your cowardly personality and your chicken-shit attitude. Yes, I'm sure now. Our meeting with Danforth will go well, I'm convinced.

MIDGE. *Our* meetin'? What—

NAT. Yes, I have decided to handle this Danforth matter for you. Don't worry, the Exploiters, the Land Owners, the Capitalist Fat Cats, I eat them for lunch.

MIDGE *(alarmed)*. Hold on now, boy, I never asked—

NAT. Don't thank me. I ask for nothing in return, only to see justice. Don't thank *me;* thank Karl Marx, thank Lenin, thank Gorky, thank Olgin—

MIDGE. Hey, don't need *none* o' you guys—

NAT. But mostly thank Ben Gold; in Nineteen-Nineteen I join the Communist Party and the human race and meet Ben Gold. *He's* the one, *that* was vision—*(as MIDGE starts to edge away from him on the bench)* Ben Gold, who organized the Fur Workers and gave them a heart and a center and a voice! What a voice, you thought it was yours. I'm matching skins at Supreme Furs, he makes me Assistant Shop Chairman; I'm at his side when we win. A ten percent wage increase and the first forty-hour week in the city! We win! *(Bangs his cane on the ground.)* Where is he? Where is Danforth? Bring him to me. Bring me the Fascist four-flusher!

MIDGE *(softly, covering his face)*. Oh my God . . .

NAT *(turns to answer MIDGE)*. O.K., O.K., the Soviet Union, throw it up to me; everybody does. They screwed up, I'm the first one to admit it. I promise you, Carter, they lost me, *finished*. I gave up on them . . . but I never gave up on the ideas. The triumph of the proletariat, a workers' democracy, the ideas are still fine and beautiful, the ideas go on, they are better than the people who had them. Ben Gold, they hit him with the Taft-Hartley and the fire goes out, but the voice goes on; the conflict goes on like the turning of the stars and we will crush Danforth before suppertime.

(NAT taps his cane with finality; sits back, crosses his legs, waiting for his adversary. MIDGE is silent for a moment. Then he turns to NAT, quietly, calmly.)

MIDGE. You done now? You finished talkin'? *(NAT nods, not looking at him.)* O.K., listen to me; Danforth comes, don't want you speakin'. Not a word. Not one word. Don't even want you here. Got it? You open your face once I'm gonna give Gilley ten bucks to nail you permanent. Got that? Am I comin' through clear?

NAT *(turns to MIDGE, smiling graciously).* Too late. I have no choice. I'm obligated. The conflict between me and Danforth is inevitable. I am obligated to get you off your knees and into the sunlight.

MIDGE. No you ain't. Lettin' you outa that obligation right now. *(Leans towards NAT, urgently:)* Please, it's O.K., I got it all worked out what to say to him. Just gotta hang in till I get my Christmas tips, see—they only got to keep me three more months till Christmas and I'll be—

NAT. Christmas! Compromises! How do you think we lost Poland? Danforth has no right! The man has no right to dismiss you before your time—

MIDGE. Man, I'm eighty-*one*—

NAT. And when we finish with *him,* at five o'clock we'll take care of the hoodlum, Gilley. Together we'll teach *that* punk a lesson!

MIDGE *(looks up at the sky, desperately).* Why, Lord? Why are you doing this to me? Lord, I asked you for help and you sent me a weird Commie blind man . . .

NAT. What Lord? Who is this Lord you're talking to? Oh *boy,* I can see I've got a lot of work to do here . . .

MIDGE *(turning sharply up right).* Shit, here he comes, the Man comin' now . . .

NAT *(turning up right).* Ah, good, I'm ready . . .

MIDGE *(grips NAT's arm).* Please, baby; I'm askin' ya, please be quiet—

NAT. Calm down, Carter—

MIDGE. Never done you no harm—

NAT. It's not him anyway. *(Leans to right, peering up at bridge.)* No, definitely not him. It's a pretty girl.

MIDGE. How do you know?

NAT. Because of the glow. When I could see, all pretty girls had a glow. Now what's left is the glow. That's how you can tell.

(LAURIE enters Up Right on the bridge, and she is a pretty girl—soft, delicate, innocent, about twenty-five, wearing a dress to match the gentle October day. Carrying a large sketchpad and a box of charcoals, she crosses to an old stone ledge beneath a lamppost at the far left side of the bridge, unaware of MIDGE and NAT, who are some distance below her. Once at the ledge she closes her eyes and breathes deeply, inhaling the view of the lake; then she settles herself on the ledge and proceeds briskly, studiously, to sketch the view—all this as MIDGE and NAT continue their dialogue.)

NAT. Yes, definitely; a pretty girl . . .

MIDGE *(rising urgently from bench).* Maybe so, but the Man comin' *soon*— *(pulling NAT to his feet)* time for the *Man,* time for you to *go*—

NAT. Calm down, Carter, you're hysterical—

MIDGE *(moving NAT away from bench).* Ain't you got an appointment someplace? Whyn't you go tell somebody you're an Apache—

NAT *(with genuine concern).* All right, all right, *you* will handle Danforth; I will permit it.

MIDGE *(warily).* You mean that?

NAT. Of course, but first you must calm yourself—

MIDGE. I'll calm myself—

NAT. This is essential. In your present state the Land Baron will walk all over you; I cannot allow that. Here, this will do the trick—*(Reaches quickly into his jacket pocket, withdrawing small brown business envelope.)* Here, some Government Grass to relax you. Official, legal; dope from Uncle Sam. The doctor prescribes, the government pays; two ounces a month for the glaucoma. Dilates the capillaries, relieves the pressure; everywhere. *(Takes a joint from the envelope.)* Here. All rolled. Be my guest. Medicaid is paying.

MIDGE *(peering anxiously off right).* Better not; makes me foolish sometimes. Ain't no time to get foolish—

NAT. Not foolish. Happy. I promise, you'll laugh at the Six O'Clock News. Even your children become amusing. *(Lights joint, inhales, hands it out to MIDGE.)* Please, calm yourself. Here, take a hit, Danforth will be a piece of cake; one puff, the man is a Danish.

MIDGE *(still very much on guard).* You swear you'll keep your mouth shut when the Man comes, shut *tight*—I'll take a puff.

NAT. Here, direct from the White House. *(MIDGE hesitates a moment; then takes a deep drag.)* Good; now hold it in as long as you—

MIDGE. I know, I know; I was smokin' dope

while you was eatin' matzoh-balls, baby. *(Another deep drag, hands it back to* NAT.*)* Fair stuff. Just fair.

(The distant sound of the Carousel Band-Organ begins off left as though carried on the autumn breeze. LAURIE *looks up from her sketching for a moment, smiles, hearing the gently drifting melody of "That Old Gang of Mine."* MIDGE *and* NAT *will pass the joint back and forth between them as their dialogue continues, the grass gradually starting to reach them.)*

MIDGE *(glancing anxiously up right).* Man say three miles, he sure takin' it slow.

NAT. Maybe he dropped dead. *(On the inhale, handing joint to* MIDGE.*)* A lot of these running people; boom.

MIDGE *(on the inhale).* Young fellah like him?

NAT. They're the first ones; the young ones. Boom. They're running, they're smilin'; boom. You should be here in the evening, they drop like flies . . . *(Chuckling, taking joint from* MIDGE.*)* Boom, boom, boom . . . *(*MIDGE *chuckles along with him,* NAT *studies the joint fondly for a moment.)* All my life I fought for Socialized Medicine . . .

MIDGE. Stopped smoking dope when I turned seventy . . .

NAT *(peering up at* LAURIE*).* That girl just went from very pretty to beautiful . . .

MIDGE. Scared of goin' foolish. My Daddy went foolish five years before he died, didn't know his own name. Sad to see. Hope I ain't the only one hearin' that music.

NAT *(moving towards bench, squinting up at* LAURIE*).* Now she's Hannah Pearlman . . .

MIDGE. Who?

NAT *(sits on bench; softly).* Hannah Pearlman. She worked as a Finisher, stitched linings for yachting caps, Shiffman's Chapeaux on West Broadway. Nineteen Twenty-One.

MIDGE *(joins* NAT *at bench; squints up at* LAURIE *for a moment).* No, ain't her. Tell you who you got there; that's Ella Mae Tilden . . .

(Both looking up at LAURIE *as they talk, getting more and more stoned; the gentle Carousel Music continuing, bringing the past with it on the breeze. Now, in this delicate, dappled, late-afternoon light,* LAURIE *truly seems to have the glow that* NAT *described.)*

NAT. Very shy, shyer even than me. She would sit on her stoop in the early evening, a fine, fine face like an artist would paint . . .

MIDGE. Ella Mae; best wife I had, number three. Five all told. It's Ella Mae give me

John, it's John give me Billy, and it's Billy give me these teeth . . .

NAT. I passed that stoop a million times; I couldn't say hello. Funny-looking fingers from the stitching, she sat on the stoop with her hands hidden, like so . . .

MIDGE. Eight grandchildren professionals and Billy's the dentist. Billy give me this smile. *(He demonstrates.)* Put the teeth in, smiled, and left Ella Mae. Smile needed a new hat, and the hat made me walk a new way, which was out . . .

NAT. Also she was married. Yeah, went to work so her greenhorn husband could go to law school, become an American Somebody. Comes June, Arnold Pearlman graduates, suddenly finds out he's an attorney with a Yiddish-speaking wife who finishes yachting caps; boom; he leaves her for a smooth-fingered Yankee Doodle he met at school. Four months later Hannah took the gas; a popular expression at that time for putting your head in an oven . . .

MIDGE. Poor Ella Mae cryin', me hearin' my new mouth say goodbye. She was near seventy then, but when my mind moves to her she is fresh peach prime . . .

NAT. September, a month before she took the gas, I see her in the Grand Street Library, second floor reading-room. A special place, quiet, not even a clock; I'm at the main table with *Macbeth*. I look up, there's Hannah Pearlman. She doesn't see me; her head is buried in a grammar book for a ten-year-old. She looks up, she knows me, she smiles. My heart goes directly into my ears, bang, bang, bang, I'm deaf. I don't speak. I can't speak. I'm there in the house of words, I can't speak. She puts her hands under the table, goes back to her book. After a while she leaves. I didn't *speak* . . .

MIDGE *(bangs his fist on the bench).* Goddamn smile got me two more wives and nothin' but trouble! Damn these teeth and damn my wanderin' ways . . . *(Takes out huge handkerchief; the Carousel Music fades.)*

NAT. I didn't *speak,* I didn't *speak* . . .

MIDGE *(blowing his nose).* There's dope makes you laugh and dope makes you cry. I think this here's cryin' dope.

NAT *(bangs his cane on the ground).* Stop, stop! Nostalgia, I hate it! The dread disease of old people! Kills more of us than heart failure!

MIDGE *(drying his eyes).* When's the last time you made love to a woman?

NAT. Listen to him, more nostalgia! My poor shmeckle, talk about nostalgia! It comes up once a year, like Ground Hog Day. The last time I made love was July Tenth, Nineteen Seventy-One.

MIDGE. Was your wife still alive?

NAT. I certainly hope so.

MIDGE. No, I meant—

NAT. I know what you meant. With Ethel it wasn't always easy to tell. *(Smacks his forehead.) Shame* on me! A good woman, a fine woman, was it *her* fault I would always be in love with Hannah Pearlman?

MIDGE. See, last time for me I was bein' unfaithful. Damn my fickle soul, I cheated on them all. Daisy, I was seventy-six, still had somethin' on the side; somethin' new.

NAT. Carter, this is the most courageous thing I ever heard about you.

MIDGE. No courage to it, it's a curse. "Don't do it, Midge; don't *do* it," I kept sayin' while I did it. *Damn* my cheatin' soul.

NAT. No, no, you were *right!* You dared and did, I yearned and regretted. I *envy* you. You were always what I have only recently become.

MIDGE. A dirty old man.

NAT. A *romanticist!* A man of hope! Listen to me, I was dead once so I know things—it's not the sex, it's the romance. It's all in the head. Now, finally, I know this. The shmeckle is out of business, but still the romance remains, the adventure. That's all there *ever* was. The body came along for the ride. Do you understand me, Carter?

MIDGE. I'm thinkin' about it . . .

NAT. Because, frankly, right now I'm in love with this girl here.

MIDGE *(after a moment).* Well, fact is, so am I. I got to admit. *(Peers up at* LAURIE *for a few seconds.)* Son of a gun . . . First time I ever fell in love with a white woman.

NAT. The first? Why the first?

MIDGE. Worked out that way.

NAT. All the others were black? Only black women?

MIDGE. Listen, you ran with a wild, Commie crowd; where *I* come from you stuck with your own. Bein' a black man, I—

NAT. A what?

MIDGE. A black man. Y'see, in *my* day—

NAT. Wait. Stop. Excuse me . . . *(A beat; then* NAT *takes his bifocals out of his jacket pocket, puts them on, leans very close to* MIDGE. *He studies him for a few moments; then, quietly:)* My God, you're right. You *are* a black man.

(Silence for a moment. Then NAT *bursts into laughter, pointing at* MIDGE.*)*

MIDGE *(after a moment, catching on to the joke, a burst of laughter).* Sly devil, you sly ol' devil . . .

NAT *(laughing happily, pointing at* MIDGE*).* Hey, had ya goin', had ya *goin'* there for a minute, didn't I . . . ?

MIDGE *(claps his hands, delighted laughter building).* Had me goin', had me *goin',* yeah . . . Lord, Lord . . .

NAT *(hitting his knees, roaring).* I love it, I love it, I love it—

(Fresh gales of stoned laughter; they rock on the bench.)

MIDGE. Stop, stop, I'm gonna die . . .

NAT. I'm gonna drop dead right here . . . *(Suddenly stops laughing.)* Wait a minute, Carter; is it *this* funny?

MIDGE *(Stops laughing. Considers it. Bursts into laughter again).* Yes, it is. It is, definitely . . .

(They point at each other, laughing at each other's laughter, laughing now at the fact that they are laughing; they fall on each other, shaking with mirth, threatening to roll off the bench. MIDGE *suddenly leans back on the bench and abruptly falls asleep, snoring loudly.)*

NAT. Carter, what are you doing? We're right in the middle . . . *(*MIDGE *keeps snoring.)* How do you like that? One joint, look at this.

*(*MIDGE *suddenly wakes up and, as if by request, bursts into song.)*

MIDGE *(singing).*
"I'm Alabamy bound,
there'll be no heebie-jeebies hangin' 'round . . .

(Rises to his feet, singing, strutting, gradually working in a small soft-shoe.)

Just gave the meanest ticket-man on earth all I'm worth
to put my tootsies in an upper berth.
Just hear that choo-choo sound,
I know that soon we're gonna cover ground . . ."

*(*NAT *rises to his feet, inspired, joining in the soft-shoe, finishing the song with him.)*

MIDGE *and* NAT *(harmonizing).*
"And then I'll holler so the world will know, here I go,
I'm Alabamy booooouuuund!"

*(*LAURIE, *who has been listening to* MIDGE *and* NAT *sing their song from her ledge on the bridge, far above them, smiles at them now, nods her approval, holds her hands up in a brief moment of applause, then returns to her sketching.)*

MIDGE. I think the woman's crazy about us.

NAT. Please, I knew it when she first showed up.

MIDGE. You got any more of that dope?

NAT. Now we're gonna do a Willy Howard routine. You think you were laughing *before*, wait'll you hear—

MIDGE. How about I do a Joe Turner song first, and *then* we do Willy Howard?

NAT. You just sang.

MIDGE *(sitting NAT on bench)*. That was half an hour ago.

NAT. Really?

MIDGE *(looking up, announcing this for LAURIE)*. "So Long, Goodbye Blues," by Big Joe Turner, Boss of the Blues—

(Singing soulfully; a slow steady rhythm, snapping his fingers, performing for LAURIE.)

"Well now, so long, good-bye, baby

Yeah, well, soon now I'm gonna be gone

And that's why I'm sayin', baby—"

NAT *(a burst of applause, rising)*. That was exquisite. Now here's Willy Howard—

(Glancing up at LAURIE, performing this for her.) O.K., Carter, I'm Willy Howard, you're the Straight Man. Whatever I say to you, you say to me, "I'm not Rappaport." You got that?

MIDGE. Yeah.

NAT. O.K., picture we just met.

MIDGE. O.K.

NAT. Hello, Rappaport!

MIDGE. I'm not Rappaport.

NAT. Hey, Rappaport, what happened to you? You used to be a tall, fat guy; now you're a short, skinny guy.

MIDGE. I'm not Rappaport.

NAT. You used to be a young fellah with a beard; now you're an old guy without a beard! What happened to you?

MIDGE. I'm not Rappaport.

NAT. What happened, Rappaport? You used to dress up nice; now you got old dirty clothes!

MIDGE. I'm not Rappaport.

NAT. And you changed your *name* too!

(A beat—then NAT bursts into laughter; even if he wasn't stoned, this routine would leave him helpless. MIDGE regards him solemnly, thinking it over—then suddenly gets it, joining NAT's laughter, pounding NAT's shoulder.)

MIDGE *(through his laughter)*. "And you changed your *name* too . . ." Lord, Lord . . . *(Shouting up at LAURIE to make sure she got the punch-line.)* "And you changed your *name too!*"

DANFORTH'S VOICE *(shouting)*. Right with you, Carter . . .

(DANFORTH enters on bridge, at left, jogging.)

MIDGE *(still laughing)*. Oh, shit; he's here . . .

DANFORTH. Right with you . . .

NAT *(laughing)*. He's here! Good!

MIDGE *(trying to control his laughter)*. He's here, gotta shape up, boy . . . *(Scurries to bench to get NAT's briefcase.)*

NAT *(delighted)*. Don't worry, we'll take care of him—

MIDGE. No, no, there's no *"we"*; there's no "we" here—*(Grips NAT's arm urgently, tries to stop himself from laughing.)* You don't say *nothin'*, Mister, you don't open your *mouth* . . . *(A fresh burst of laughter.)* You'll ruin me, boy; I'll be out on the street *tomorrow* . . .

(DANFORTH stops on bridge, winding down from his run, jogging in place, controlling his breaths, stretching himself against the bridge lamppost at right.)

NAT. A piece of cake. The little I can see, the man is a wreck.

MIDGE *(still chuckling softly)*. Please, *please*, baby . . . are you my friend?

NAT. Of course.

MIDGE. Then go over there, friend. *(Points to stone ledge, far left, at edge of lake.)* Sit over there and don't open your mouth. Not a word.

NAT *(after a moment)*. You'll call me when you need me?

MIDGE *(hands NAT his briefcase)*. Soon's I need you. Please, move it.

NAT *(he has stopped chuckling)*. O.K., O.K. . . . *(Reluctantly, he starts down left.)* Remember, I'm ready.

MIDGE. I know that.

(DANFORTH, having completed his winding-down ritual on the bridge, starts down towards MIDGE at the bench, entering through the Tunnel Archway, mopping himself with a towel. NAT settles himself with some dignity on the far left ledge, some distance from them, crossing his legs, his briefcase and his cane at his side. LAURIE has stretched out on the bridge ledge above, her eyes closed, a Walkman plugged into her ears, her shoulder-bag under her head.)

DANFORTH. Carter, hi.

MIDGE. Hi.

DANFORTH. Don't think we've ever really been formally introduced. I'm Pete Danforth.

(They shake hands.)

MIDGE. Hi, Pete. They call me "Midge."

DANFORTH. Hi, Midge. Glad we decided to

meet here. Chance to stay outside, y'know, after my run. Truth is, I hate running. Being immortal takes too much time. *(He chuckles.)*

MIDGE *(sitting on bench)*. "Midge" for Midget. My third wife give me the name; near two and three-quarter inches taller'n me, so she called me "Midge." Name stuck with me fifty years.

DANFORTH. Tell ya one thing, it's good to be reminded of what a great park this is. Goddamn oasis in the middle of the jungle.

MIDGE. Next two wives was normal-sized women, so it didn't make much sense. Name stuck with me anyway.

DANFORTH. Luckily my teaching schedule gives me two free afternoons this semester. Chance to really use this park. It's been years. I teach Communication Arts over at the Manhattan Institute on Sixtieth. No air in the place. Dreary. Been thinking about holding one of my classes out here in the—

MIDGE. What kinda arts?

DANFORTH. Communication. Communications of all kinds. Personal, interpersonal, and public; pretty much the whole range of—

MIDGE. You teach talkin'.

DANFORTH *(smiles)*. More or less; yes.

MIDGE. So you must know we 'bout at the end of the chit-chat section now; right?

DANFORTH. Right, right . . . *(Sits next to* MIDGE *on bench, carefully folding his towel.)* Funny thing, by the way, I really didn't know—that is, I wasn't aware until just a few days ago—that you actually worked in the building; that you were employed there.

MIDGE. Keep to myself. Do my job.

DANFORTH. Of course. I just wanted you to know that the problem we've got here had not come to my attention sooner simply because you, personally, had not come to my attention. Frankly, I've been living there three years and I've never run into you.

MIDGE. I'm mostly down in the boiler room; don't get a lot of drop-ins.

DANFORTH. Of course.

(Silence for a moment.)

MIDGE. Keep movin', boy, you on a roll now.

DANFORTH. Yes, well, as you know, Three Twenty-One will be going Co-op in November. We'll be closing on that in November. We've got Brachman and Rader as our managing agent; I think they're doing an excellent job. As President of the Tenants' Committee I'm pretty much dependent, the whole Committee is really, on their advice; we've basically got to place our faith in the

recommendations of our Managing Agency.

MIDGE. And they're recommendin' you dump me.

DANFORTH. Midge, we've got some real problems about your remaining with the building staff.

MIDGE. Ain't that the same as dumpin' me?

DANFORTH *(after a moment)*. Midge, it's not for four weeks, it's not till November, but, yes, we will have to let you go. There are various benefits, Union Pension Plan, six weeks Severance pay; that's a check for six weeks salary the day you leave, that's . . . Midge, I'm sorry . . . *(sadly; shaking his head)* God, I hate this; I really hate this, Midge . . .

MIDGE. How 'bout *I* hate it first, then you get your turn.

DANFORTH *(quietly)*. Midge, think about it, isn't this the best thing for *every*body? The pressure on you, tenants' complaints, trying to keep up. *(His hand on* MIDGE'*s arm.)* Time, Midge—we're not dealing with an evil Tenants' Committee or a heartless Managing Agent—the only villain here is time. We're *all* fighting it. Jesus, man, have you seen me *run?* It's a joke. I can't do what *I* did a few years ago either.

MIDGE. Hey, don't sweat it, son. See, Brachman and Rader, all due respect, is full of shit. Fact is, you need me. *(Leans back calmly.)* Got an ol' Erie City boiler down there; heart of the buildin'. Things about that weird machine no livin' man knows, 'cept Midge Carter. Christmas. Take me till Christmas to train a new man how to handle that devil. *(Pats* DANFORTH'*s knee.)* You got it, have the new man set up for ya by Christmas.

DANFORTH. Midge, we're replacing the Erie City. We're installing a fully automatic Rockmill Five Hundred; it requires no maintenance. *(Silence for a moment;* MIDGE *does not respond.)* You see, the Rockmill's just one of many steps in an extensive modernization plan; new electrical system, plumbing arteries, lobby renovation—

MIDGE. Well, *now* you're *really* gonna need me. Pipes, wires, you got forty years of temporary stuff in there, no blueprints gonna tell you where. Got it all in my head; know what's behind every wall, every stretch of tar. *(Clamps his hand on* DANFORTH'*s shoulder.)* O.K., here's the deal. My place in the basement, *I* stay on there free like I been, *you* get all my consultin' free. No *salary*, beauty deal for ya—

DANFORTH. Midge, to begin with, your unit in the basement is being placed on the co-op market as a garden apartment—

MIDGE. Don't you get it, baby? Blueprints, blueprints, I'm a walkin' treasure-map—

DANFORTH. Please understand, we've had a highly qualified team of building engineers doing a survey for months now—

MIDGE (suddenly). Hey, forget it.

DANFORTH. You see, they—

MIDGE. I said forget it. Ain't interested in the job no more. Don't want the job. Withdrawin' my offer. (Turns away; opens his newspaper.)

DANFORTH (moving closer). Midge, listen to me . . .

MIDGE. Shit, all these years I been livin' in a garden apartment. Wished I knew sooner, woulda had a lot more parties.

DANFORTH. I have some news that I think will please you . . . (His hand on MIDGE's arm.) Two of the older tenants on the Committee, Mrs. Carpenter, Mr. Lehman, have solved your relocation problem. Midge, there's an apartment for you at the Amsterdam. No waiting list for you, Mr. Lehman seems to know the right people. Caters especially to low-income senior adults and it's right here in the neighborhood you've grown used to—

MIDGE. Amsterdam's ninety percent foolish people. Ever been in the lobby there? Ever seen them sittin' there? Only way you can tell the live ones from the dead ones is how old their newspapers are.

DANFORTH. As I understand it from Mr. Lehman—

MIDGE. Amsterdam's the end of the line, boy.

DANFORTH. I'm sorry, I thought—

MIDGE. You ask Mr. Lehman he wants to go sit in that lobby; you ask Mrs. Carpenter she ready to leave the world. You tell 'em both "no thanks" from Midge, he's lookin' for a garden apartment.

DANFORTH. See, the problem is—

MIDGE. Problem is you givin' me bad guy news, tryin' to look like a good guy doin' it.

DANFORTH (after a moment). You're right, Midge. You're right. You're dead right. (Bows his head, genuinely upset.) I've handled this whole thing badly, stupidly, stupidly. I'm sorry, this whole thing . . . this is terrible . . .

MIDGE (patting DANFORTH's hand). Don't worry, Pete, you're gonna get through it.

DANFORTH (rises, pacing in front of bench).

Damn it, I tell you what I can do—what I will do—I'm getting you ten weeks Severance, Midge. Forget six, a check for ten weeks salary the day you go, I'm gonna hand it to you personally. And if the Committee doesn't agree, the hell with them; I'll shove it through, that's all. Least I can do. Ten weeks Severance—how does that sound to ya?

MIDGE. Well, better than six, I guess . . . (Nods thoughtfully.) Sounds better, but I—

DANFORTH (shaking MIDGE's hand with both of his). That's a promise, Midge. Shove it down their throats if I have to. (Moving briskly towards the stone steps at right to exit.) I'm sure we'll have no problem with—

NAT. Unacceptable. (Calmly, rising from ledge at far left.) We find that unacceptable. (DANFORTH stops, NAT moves slowly towards him.) Mr. Danforth . . . Mr. Danforth, I'll speak frankly, you're in a lot of trouble (Brisk handshake.) Ben Reissman; Reissman, Rothman, Rifkin and Grady. Forgive me for not announcing myself sooner, but I couldn't resist listening to you bury yourself. Our firm represents Mr. Carter, but, more to the point, we act as legal advisors to the HURTSFOE unit of Mr. Carter's union. HURTSFOE; I refer to the Human Rights Strike Force, a newly formed automatic-action unit who, I'm sorry to say, you're going to be hearing a lot from in the next few weeks. (Sits next to MIDGE on bench, DANFORTH standing before them.) Personally, I find their methods too extreme; but I report and advise, that's all I can do. The ball is rolling here, Mr. Danforth.

MIDGE. Go away.

NAT. Mr. Carter keeps saying to us "go away"; we were arguing this very point as you ran by earlier. But, of course, as he knows, we are an automatic function of his union for the protection of all members. I have no choice.

MIDGE (grips NAT's arm). Man wants to give me ten weeks Severance—

NAT. A joke. The fellow is obviously a jokester.

DANFORTH. Mr. Reissman—

NAT. Speak to me.

DANFORTH. I'm not sure that I understand the—

NAT. Of course not. How could you? (Crosses his legs, continuing calmly.) I will educate you. The situation is simple, I will make it simpler. We don't accept ten weeks Severance, we don't accept twenty. What we accept is that Mr. Carter be retained in the

capacity of advisor during your reconstruc-
tion period, which I assume will take a year,
maybe two. At this point, we'll talk further.

MIDGE *(to* DANFORTH*)*. I don't know him; I
don't *know* this man.

NAT. Quite so; Mr. Carter is more familiar
with Rifkin and Grady, the gentler gentlemen in our firm. It was thought best to send
"The Cobra" in on this one. An affectionate
term for me at the office.

DANFORTH *(sharply)*. Look, Reissman—

NAT. Speak to me.

DANFORTH *(steps towards him, firmly)*. I don't
know what your game is, fellah, and I don't
know your organization; but I *do* know Local
Thirty-Two of the Service Employees
Union—

NAT. And do *they* know you're planning to
fire Mr. Carter?

DANFORTH. Not yet, but we—

NAT. And do *you* know that there's no man-
datory retirement age in Mr. Carter's union?
And do *you* know, further, that this means
Carter has the right to call an arbitration
hearing where he can defend his competence? And that you will have to get a minimum of four tenants to *testify* against him?
Oh, that will be interesting. *Find* them. I want
to *see* this, Danforth. Four tenants who want
to be responsible—*publicly* responsible—for
putting this old man out of his home and
profession of forty-two years. *(His hand on*
MIDGE*'s shoulder.)* A man who was named
"Super of the Year" by the New York Post in
Nineteen Sixty-Eight: a man who fought in
World War Two, a man who served with the
now legendary Black Battalion of Bastogne
at the Battle of the Bulge. The clippings will
be Xeroxed and circulated, the worms you
find to testify will be informed. *(Rises from
bench, pointing cane at* DANFORTH*.)* And—and
are you aware that for as long as you insist on
pursuing this matter, for as long as this hearing lasts—and I promise you we will make it
a *long* one—you can *make* no contract with
Local Thirty-Two? That without a union
contract you can *have* no co-op sale, no
building corporation? Time, my friend, the
will be *your* villain now. My firm will go
beyond this hearing if justice fails us there. I'm
talking *months,* cookie; I'm talking litigation,
appeals, the full weight and guile of Rothman, Rifkin, Grady, and The Cobra. *(He lowers his cane to his side, moves slowly towards*
DANFORTH; *quietly:)* Sir, I urge you to consider, win or lose, the massive and draining

legal fees you will incur in pursuing this
matter. I urge you to compare this time, cost,
and embarrassment to the tiny sum it will
take to keep Mr. Carter on salary. I urge you
for *all* our sakes.

*(*DANFORTH *stands there in silence for a few
moments, clearly confused.* MIDGE *has remained on
the bench, listening with fascination.)*

DANFORTH. Reissman . . .

NAT. Speak to me.

DANFORTH. I'm, frankly, a little thrown by
this. I . . . I mean, you're asking me to just
accept—

NAT. Accept or don't accept; I'm obligated
to report this to HURTSFOE immediately.

DANFORTH. I knew about the right to arbitration—Midge, I just didn't think you'd really want—

NAT. He wants. Meanwhile HURTSFOE
goes after you tomorrow anyway. They'll
make an example of you, you're perfect for
them—

DANFORTH. But what have I—?

NAT. Idiot, you've hit every Human Rights
nerve there is. I'm talking old, I'm talking
black, I'm talking racial imbalance—

DANFORTH. Racial *imbalance?* The man was
walking into *walls.* For God's sake, the man's
an easy *eighty.*

NAT. There's nothing, I promise you, easy
about eighty. Damn it, why am I even bothering to *warn* you? *(Picks up his briefcase.)* Tomorrow you'll see it all. Time to let
HURTSFOE out of its cage—*(Turns sharply,
starts walking towards stone steps at right, to exit.)*

DANFORTH *(moves towards him, angrily)*.
Now look, Reissman, I find it hard to believe
that I would be held personally responsible
for—

NAT *(starting briskly up steps)*. You'll believe
it tomorrow when they picket in front of
your school. What was the name of that
place, the Manhattan Institute? They'll believe it too. And then the demonstrations in
front of your apartment building—*(Stops
halfway up steps, pointing cane down at* DAN-
FORTH*.)* The name Danforth will start to
mean something—you'll become an *adjective,*
my friend, a symbol, a new word for the
persecution of the old and disabled, the black
and the blind!

DANFORTH. Wait a minute—

NAT. *Do it, Danforth, fire him, it's your one
shot at immortality! Do it . . . (*MIDGE *holds his
hand up in alarm.)* Yes, Carter, forgive me, I
want it to happen . . . I want to see

HURTSFOE in action again . . . *(Tenderly, looking away.)* Those crazy wildcats, it's hard not to love them. Those mad, inspired men. I want to hear the old words, alive again and pure . . . "Strike for a humane existence" . . . "Strike for universal justice"—*(His cane in the air, shouting:)* Strike, strike—

DANFORTH *(shouting)*. Hold it! Wait a minute! This . . . this whole goddamn mess has gotten out of *hand* . . . *(Continuing firmly:)* Reissman, believe me, this was never my own, personal thing; I represent a *Committee,* the joint wishes of a—

NAT. I'm sorry, the spotlight falls on you because it must. Because you are so extraordinarily ordinary, because there are so many of you now. *(Starts down steps towards him.)* You collect old furniture, old cars, old pictures, everything old but old people. Bad souvenirs, they talk too much. Even quiet, they tell you too much; they look like the future and you don't want to know. Who *are* these people, these oldies, this strange race? They're not my type, put them with their own *kind,* a building, a town, *put* them someplace. *(Leans towards him.)* You idiots, don't you know? One day you *too* will join this weird tribe. Yes, Mr. Chairman, you *will* get old; I hate to break the news. And if you're frightened now, you'll be terrified then. The problem's *not* that life is short but that it's very long; so you better have a policy. Here we are. Look at us. We're the coming attractions. And as long as you're afraid of *it,* you'll be afraid of *us,* you will want to hide us or make us hide from you. You're dangerous. *(Grips his arm urgently.)* You foolish bastards, don't you under*stand?* The old people, they're the *survivors,* they *know* something, they haven't just stayed late to ruin your party. The very old, they are miracles like the just-born; close to the end is precious like close to the beginning. What you'd like is for Carter to be nice and cute and quiet and go away. But he won't. I won't let him. Tell him he's slow or stupid—O.K.—but you tell him that he is unnecessary and that is a sin, that is a sin against life, that is abortion at the other end. *(Silence;* NAT *studies him for a moment.)* HURTSFOE waits. The arena is booked, the lions are hungry . . .

DANFORTH *(quietly, earnestly)*. Ben, I'm glad you shared these thoughts with me. I'd never really—

NAT. I'm through communicating with you, I'm communicating with Carter now.

(Sits next to MIDGE *on bench.)* Carter, what shall we do with him? I leave it to you.

MIDGE. I think . . . I think we should give him a break.

DANFORTH. Ben, I'm sure that I can persuade the members of the Committee to reevaluate Midge's—

NAT. Carter, what are you *saying?* What happens to the Cause? Are you saying you just want to keep your job and forget about the Cause?

MIDGE. Frankly, yes; that's what I'm sayin'. Forget the Cause, keep the job.

DANFORTH *(perches opposite them on small bench)*. I think it's essential that we avoid any extreme—

NAT. Carter, are you asking The Cobra *not* to strike?

MIDGE. Don't want that Cobra to strike, no.

DANFORTH. Next Committee meeting's in two weeks. I'll explain the—

NAT. Mr. Danforth, my client has instructed me to save your ass. Quickly, the bomb is ticking . . . *(*DANFORTH *leans towards him intently.)* Two weeks is too late. Tonight. Jog home to your phone, call the members of your committee. Don't persuade, don't explain; announce. Tell them there's a job for Carter. Guide. Counselor. How about Superintendent Emeritus? Has a nice sound to it. Meanwhile, speak to *no* one—the union, your managing agent, *no* one. HURTSFOE gets wind of this, we're *all* in trouble. *(Hands him business-card from briefcase.)* When you're finished with the Committee, call here. Before ten tomorrow if you want to stop HURTSFOE. Speak only to the lady on the card, Mrs. Clara Gelber; tell her to reach a man called "Pop"—he's one of HURTSFOE's top people—tell her to inform him that the Carter matter has been resolved, this "Pop" fellow will take it from there.

DANFORTH *(reading from card)*. "Park East Real Estate Agency . . ."

NAT. HURTSFOE's advisory group; smart people, good hearts, they negotiate with management. *(Hands him another card.)* Here; if there's trouble tonight, call me—*(They both rise.)* That's my club on Eighty-Sixth, ask for Dr. Engels, he'll contact me. *(Pats* DANFORTH*'s cheek.)* Goodbye and good luck.

*(*DANFORTH *moves quickly towards the stone steps; stops, turns to them.)*

DANFORTH *(quietly)*. Midge . . . Ben . . . I want you to know that this has been a very important conversation for me, for *many* reasons . . . a lot of primary thoughts . . .

NAT. I think it's been an important conversation for all of us. Goodbye.

DANFORTH. An important exchange of ideas, a . . . a sudden awareness of certain generational values that I—

NAT. I warn you, one more word and there'll be a citizen's arrest for crimes against the language.

DANFORTH *(he smiles, shakes his head).* Fact is, certain areas, I *do* have trouble talking . . .

NAT. Also leaving. Go now, the phone! *(DANFORTH races briskly up the steps.)* Quickly. Let me see those sneakers flash!

(DANFORTH exits. NAT turns triumphantly towards MIDGE, his cane held high in the air like a sword of victory.)

MIDGE *(he slumps on the bench).* Never; we ain't never gettin' away with this . . .

NAT *(to himself, smiling).* Truth is, I always *did* want to be a lawyer . . . but years ago there were so many choices . . .

MIDGE. Black Battalion of *Bastogne?* . . . We ain't never gettin' away with this . . . Gonna catch *on* to us, only a matter of *time* now; find out you ain't no lawyer, find out there ain't no HURTSFOE—

NAT. You're better off than you were twenty minutes ago, right? You still have your job, don't you? A week, a month, by then I'll have a *better* idea, *another* plan. What's wrong with you? Why aren't you awed by this triumph? Why aren't you embracing me?

MIDGE *(rising, angrily).* Was playin' that boy just *right* 'fore you opened your mouth. Had him goin' for extra Severance—catches on now, I lose it *all.* What I do to deserve you? What I *do*, Reissman—

NAT. I'm not Reissman. Reissman is the name of my pickpocket surgeon.

MIDGE. O.K., *Schwartz*man, you're Sam Schwartzman—

NAT. Not him either.

MIDGE. Then who the hell *are* you, Mister? Shit, if you ain't Hernando and you ain't Schwartzman, and you ain't Rappaport, then—

NAT *(softly, looking away).* Just now I was Ben Gold. I was Ben for a while . . . You use who you need for the occasion. An occasion arises and one chooses a suitable person to—

(During these last few lines GILLEY has stepped forward from the shadows on the bridge above, at left, near the ledge where LAURIE has drifted off to sleep—a sudden sense of his presence has awakened her; frightened, she has swept up her bag and art supplies, raced across the bridge and exited at right. GILLEY is an Irish kid, about sixteen; an impassive, experienced, and almost unreadable face. The faded color of his jeans and jean-jacket and his careful, economical movements make him inconspicuous and, in a sense, part of the park; for all we know he may have been standing there in the shadows for an hour. He has a constant awareness of everything around him, the precision of a pro and the instincts of a street creature. We hear the distant sound of the Carousel Band-Organ playing "Queen City March," the last melody of the fading day. During the last fifteen minutes or so the pretty colors of the autumn afternoon have gradually given way to the dark shadows of early evening, the faint chatter of crickets and the lonely lights of the two lampposts on the bridge, reminding us of the isolated and near-empty section of the park we are in. GILLEY stands quite still now on the bridge, a silhouette beneath the lamplight, looking off at what must be the other benches along the lakeside, studying the few remaining people on them and their possessions, considering the possibilities. NAT has suddenly interrupted his last speech to look up at the Bridge.)

NAT. Who's that? There's no glow, the girl is gone.

(MIDGE knows the all too familiar figure on the bridge and that it is the appointed "collection" time; he turns away, trying to look unconcerned.)

MIDGE. Nobody. That's nobody.

NAT. That's *him*, right? The punk.

MIDGE. Ain't *the* punk, just some punk.

NAT. That's our punk, isn't it?

MIDGE. Not *our* punk, not *our* punk; just *my* punk.

NAT. Excuse me, I have something to discuss with him—

(He starts towards the Bridge—MIDGE grabs both of NAT's arms and quite forcefully pulls him back—GILLEY starts slowly, casually down the back stairs to the Tunnel, towards MIDGE and NAT.)

MIDGE *(a strong grip on NAT, whispering urgently).* Now you listen here to *me*, No-Name. This kid, you run your mouth on *him* he finish you, then finish me sure. Sit down— *(Shoves NAT down on bench, sits next to him.)* These kids is crazy; beat up old folks for *exercise*, boy. Sass this kid, he stomp us *good*— *(pointing to the offstage benches)* and these folks here, while he's doin' it they gonna keep *score*, gonna watch like it's happenin' on the TV.

(GILLEY *appears in the darkened Tunnel, some distance behind them. He remains quite still, deep in the Tunnel, waiting.*)

MIDGE. Toll on this bridge is three dollars and that bridge gonna take me home. *(Rises, taking his newspaper.)* Call it a *day*, boy. See you sometime.

(MIDGE *starts into the Tunnel towards the waiting* GILLEY. *Silence for a moment.*)

GILLEY *(flatly).* Who's that?

MIDGE. Friend of mine.

GILLEY. Where's he live?

MIDGE. Dunno. Hangs out here; he—

GILLEY *(moves down behind* NAT's *bench, leans towards him; quietly).* Where you live?

NAT. First I'll tell you where I work. I work at the Nineteenth Precinct—*(Turns, holds out his hand.)* Danforth; Captain Pete Danforth, Special Projects, I—

GILLEY *(takes his hand; not shaking it, just holding it tightly).* Where you live?

NAT. Not far, but I'm—

GILLEY. Walk you home, y'know.

NAT. That won't be necessary, it's—

GILLEY. Cost you three.

NAT. Listen, son, I don't need—

GILLEY. Cost you four. Just went up to four, y'know. *(To both:)* Saw this lady this morning. Dog-walker, y'know. Five, six dogs at a time. Give me an idea. Walk you both home. Terrific idea, huh? *(To* NAT:*)* Terrific idea, right? *(Silence for a moment.* GILLEY *tightens his grip on* NAT's *hand.* NAT *nods in agreement.* GILLEY *lets go of his hand; pats* NAT *gently on the head.)* Right. Walk you both; four each.

MIDGE. But our deal was—

GILLEY. Four.

MIDGE. O.K.

GILLEY. Right. *(Starts into Tunnel.)* O.K., boys; everybody walkin'; convoy movin' out. *(*MIDGE *walks dutifully behind* GILLEY. NAT *remains seated. A moment;* GILLEY *moves slowly back to* NAT's *bench, stands behind him.)* Hey, that's everybody, right? *(Silence for a moment.* NAT *hesitates; then picks up his briefcase and slowly, obediently rises, his head bowed.* GILLEY *nods his approval, turns, starts walking into the Tunnel;* MIDGE *following.)* O.K.; nice and slow; movin' out, headin' home, boys . . .

(NAT *remains standing at the bench. This immobility is not a conscious decision on* NAT's *part; he just finds himself, quite simply, unable to move.*)

MIDGE *(stops, turns to* NAT; *a frightened whisper).* Come on, *please*, move . . . *move*, Mister . . .

(GILLEY *stops in the Tunnel, aware that he is not being followed. He turns to* NAT; *starts quickly to the bench, shoving* MIDGE *out of his way as he moves towards* NAT. NAT *holds his hand up urgently,* GILLEY *stops just in front of him.)*

NAT *(quickly).* Take it easy, I don't fight with Irish kids. I know the same thing now that I knew sixty-five years ago: don't fight with an Irish kid. *(Points to him.)* How did I know Irish? I hear; I know all the sounds. But better, I know the feelings. This is because sixty-five years ago I was you. Irish kids, Italian, Russian, we *all* stole. Then, like now, the city lives by Darwin; this means everybody's on somebody's menu—*(Passionately, moving closer to him:)* Trouble is, you got the wrong supper here. Me and Midge, you're noshing on your own. We live in the streets and the parks, we're dead if we stay home; just like you, Gilley. You're angry. You should be. So am I. But the trouble's at the top, like always—the Big Boys, the Fat Cats, the String-Pullers, the *top*—we're down here with you, kid. You, me, Midge, we have the same enemy, we have to stick together or we're finished. It's the only chance we got.

(Silence for a moment.)

GILLEY. Five. Went up to five. Y'mouth just cost ya a dollar. *(*NAT *does not respond.* GILLEY *holds out his hand.)* O.K., that's five; in advance, y'know.

NAT *(softly).* No. I can't do that. I won't do that. Gilley, please understand; we mustn't do this. *(Touching his jacket pocket.)* I have twenty-two dollars; I would share it with you, gladly share. But not like *this;* not us . . .

GILLEY. Great. Gimme the twenty-two. *(Shaking his head:)* Y'mouth, I'm tellin' ya. It's costin', y'know.

NAT *(quietly, sadly).* I'm . . . I'm very disappointed . . .

MIDGE *(whispering).* Give it to him.

NAT. I can't do that, kid; not *all;* that's unreasonable. (GILLEY *reaches for* NAT's *pocket,* NAT *shoves his hand sharply away.)* I have limited funds. I can't do that.

GILLEY *(calmly takes hunting knife in fancy leather sheath from his belt; unsheathes the knife, holding it down at his side).* Ask you once more.

MIDGE *(from Tunnel, trembling).* Please, *give* it to him, Mister . . . please . . .

NAT. Gilley, this is a mistake. Don't do this. (GILLEY *glances quickly about the area to see if he is being observed, then holds up his knife; a demonstration.)* No, no knives, not for us. Not between us. We're together—

(NAT makes a sharp underhand move with his cane, hitting GILLEY's wrist; GILLEY drops the knife, holding his wrist in pain and surprise; GILLEY looks at MIDGE as though to ask for aid with a misbehaving child, then kneels down quickly to pick up his knife. NAT, more in fear and frustration than courage, raises his cane in the air with both hands, shouting—an angry, guttural, old battle cry—and strikes a sharp blow on the back of the kneeling GILLEY. GILLEY cries out in pain, rising, outraged, leaving his knife, slapping the cane out of NAT's hand—NAT steps back, helpless now; GILLEY grabs him by both shoulders and swings him around fiercely, flinging him backward with a powerful throw, NAT falling back against the stone ledge at the edge of the lake, hitting the ledge sharply and then rolling off onto the path where he lies quite still, face down, away from us. GILLEY glances about, grabs up the wallet from NAT's coat, then moves quickly towards the Tunnel, shouting over his shoulder at MIDGE.)

GILLEY. Tell your friend the rules! You better tell your friend the rules, man—

(GILLEY stops—looks back at the very still form of NAT—then races quickly off into the darkened Tunnel, forgetting his knife, disappearing into the shadows of the park.

MIDGE *moves down towards* NAT *as quickly as possible, kneels next to him.)*

MIDGE *(quietly).* Hey . . . hey, Mister . . . ? *(Silence. He touches NAT, gently.)* Come on now, wake up . . . wake up . . .

(NAT remains quite still. Silence again. MIDGE rises to his feet, shouting out at the lake.)

MIDGE. Help! . . . Over here! . . . *(No response.* MIDGE *looks out across the lake, a near-blind old man staring into the darkness around him.)* Look what we got here . . .

(Silence again; only the sound of the early evening crickets. The park grows darker, MIDGE's face barely visible now in the lamplight as . . .

The Curtain Falls.

ACT TWO

SCENE: *The same; three in the afternoon, the next day. Before the curtain rises we hear the Carousel Band-Organ playing "We All Scream For Ice Cream."*

AT RISE: *Midge is alone on the path; he is seated at the far left end of the center bench, his*

newspaper unopened on his lap, looking straight ahead, unable to relax in the pleasant sunlight that shines on the bench. The Carousel Music continues distantly now; the melody drifts in and out with the gentle autumn breeze. Laurie is in her usual position on the bridge, far above Midge, sketching dreamily. Midge continues looking solemnly out at the lake. A full minute passes.

We begin to hear Nat's voice, off left, singing "Puttin' on the Ritz," approaching slowly. Midge looks left, then immediately opens his newspaper, holds it up to his bifocals, "reading." Nat enters Up Left, moving slowly down the path within an aluminum walker. The walker is a three-sided, four-legged device with three metal braces holding the sides together; his briefcase and cane are hooked over two of the braces; there is a three-inch gauze bandage above his right eye. Although Nat moves very slowly he manages to incorporate the walker into his natural elegance, using the walker rhythmically rather than haltingly, a steady ambulatory tempo to the bouncy beat of his song, as he approaches the bench. Midge is turned away with his newspaper, ignoring him completely.

Nat continues towards the bench, singing the song with great gusto, pausing momentarily to tap his walker on the path for rhythmic emphasis, then continuing to the bench, parking the walker next to it as he finishes the last line of the song. Nat sits carefully on the bench. Midge continues to read his newspaper, making no acknowledgment of Nat's arrival.

NAT *(rubbing his hands together).* Well, that punk, we got him on the run now. *(He leans back comfortably.)* Yessir, got him where we want him now. *(Jabbing the air.)* Boom, on the arm I got him; boom on the back. Boom, boom, boom—

MIDGE *(not looking up from paper).* Tell me somethin', Rocky; you plannin' to sit here on this bench? 'Cause if you *are*, I got to move to another spot.

NAT. I'm sure you were about to inquire about my health. *(Taps his hip.)* Only a slight sprain, no breaks, no dislocations. I am an expert at falling down. I have a gift for it. The emergency room at Roosevelt was twenty dollars. Not a bad price for keeping the bandit at bay.

MIDGE *(folding newspaper)*. *You* movin' or am *I* movin'? Answer me.

NAT. I guarantee he will not return today. He wants the easy money, he doesn't want trouble—

MIDGE *(puts on his hat)*. O.K., leavin' now.

NAT. And if by some odd chance he *does* return, I feel we were close to an understanding. We must realize, you and I, that this boy is caught like us in the same dog eat dog trap—

MIDGE *(he rises)*. Goodbye; gonna leave you two dogs to talk it over. Movin' on now.

NAT. Wait, Carter—

MIDGE *(leans close to him)*. Can't see your face too good; what I *can* see got Cemetery written all over it. So long for *good,* baby.

NAT. Sir, a friendship like ours is a rare—

MIDGE. Ain't no friendship. Never *was* no friendship. Don't even know your goddamn *name.*

NAT. Yesterday you helped a fallen comrade—

MIDGE. You was out *cold,* Mister. Waited for the ambulance to come, done my duty same's I would for *any* lame dog. Said to myself, that ain't gonna be *me* lyin' there. *(Takes* GILLEY'S *leather sheathed hunting knife from pocket.)* See this item here? Kid run off without his weapon, see. He comin' back for it today sure. I come here to give it back to him, stay on that boy's *good* side. *(Starts down path towards stone ledge at far left.)* O.K., waitin' over here so he sees you and me is no longer *associated;* which we *ain't,* got that? He comes, don't want you *talkin'* to me, *lookin'* at me, contactin' me any way whatever.

NAT. So; the Cossack leaves his sword and you return it.

MIDGE. You bet. *(Settles down on the ledge.)*

NAT *(leans towards him)*. You have had a taste of revolution and will not be able to return to subjection, to living in an occupied country!

MIDGE. Watch me.

*(*MIDGE *closes his eyes, puts his huge handkerchief over his face, curls up on ledge.*

CLARA *enters on the stone steps at right; attractive, early forties, stylishly bohemian clothes; she is walking quickly, purposefully down the steps towards* NAT'S *bench.* NAT *rises, using the bench for support, unaware of the approaching* CLARA, *pointing his cane at* MIDGE.)*

NAT. No, *no,* you must not pay this punk for your existence, to live in your own land!

MIDGE *(from under the handkerchief)*. Nap time now. You're talkin' to nobody.

NAT. Exactly! No one! Surrender to the oppressors and you are no one! *(*MIDGE *begins to snore quietly.)* Sure, sleep! Sleep then, like any bum in the park—

CLARA *(stopping on steps)*. Excuse me . . .

NAT *(still to* MIDGE*)*. A *napper* . . .

CLARA. Excuse me, I hate to interrupt you when you're driving somebody crazy . . .

NAT. A napper and a groveler! Why did I waste my time?!

CLARA *(seeing the walker, the bandage; concerned, frightened, moving towards bench)*. God, what happened? . . . Are you all right?

NAT. Everything's fine; don't worry, don't worry . . .

CLARA. Stitches this time?

NAT. A scratch.

CLARA. Your hip?

NAT. A sprain, a sprain . . .

CLARA. Dad, what happened? Why didn't you *call* me? Another fight, right? You got into another fight, didn't you?

NAT *(sits on small bench)*. *What* fights? I don't fight.

CLARA. How about four weeks ago? How about attacking that poor butcher at Gristede's? What was that?

NAT. I didn't attack the butcher. I attacked the meat. That was because of the prices.

CLARA. He said you shoved all the meat off his display counter with your cane—

NAT. It was a demonstration—there were thirty people in the store, I was trying to rally them, the meat-shoving was an illustration—

CLARA. The meat hit the butcher and you threw out your hip. Also the chances of starting a commune on Seventy-Second and Broadway are very slim. What happened this time, Dad?

NAT. Well, a young boy—confused, disadvantaged, a victim of society—

CLARA. A mugger. *(She nods.)* You fought with a mugger. *(Pacing anxiously behind center bench.)* Of course, of course, it was the next step; my God . . .

NAT. We were talking, we reached an impasse—

CLARA. That's it. No more. I can't let this happen anymore. I let it go, I've been irresponsible. You have to be watched. I'm not letting you out of my sight, Dad.

NAT. Stop this, you're frightening me.

CLARA. Oh, *I'm* frightening *you*, huh? I live in terror—the phone will ring, the police, the hospital. My God. It was quiet for a month, but I should have known. This guy Danforth calls this morning and I know you're on the loose again—

NAT. Ah, good, he called—

CLARA. Oh, he *called* all right—*(Takes out message; reads:)* "Tell HURTSFOE that the Carter matter is settled; I reached the Committee; Reissman said to call." . . . Jesus, *HURTSFOE* again; HURTSFOE's on the march again. I take it you're Reissman.

NAT. That was yesterday—

CLARA. And tomorrow who? And tomorrow *what?* I came to tell you it's the last *time!* No more calls—

NAT. You *covered,* didn't you?

CLARA. Yes, yes. Once again, once again. Christ, in one year I've been the headquarters for the Eighth Congressional District, CBS News, the Institute for Freudian Studies, and the United Consumers Protection Agency . . .

NAT *(fondly).* Ah, yes, *UCPA* . . .

CLARA *(sighs, nodding).* UCPA, UCPA . . . Look, Dad—

NAT. What's *happened* to you? My own daughter has forgotten what a principle is!

CLARA. *What* principle? There's no *principle* here. It's fraud. Personal, daily fraud. A one-man reign of terror and I'm the one who gets terrorized. Never knowing who the hell I'm supposed to be every time some poor sucker calls my office. A *principle?* You mean when that panic-stricken Manager of the Fine Arts Theatre called thinking there was going to be a Congressional Investigation because he showed German movies? I *still* don't understand how you convinced him you were a congressman—

NAT. What, you never saw an elder statesman before?

CLARA. But there's no such *thing* as a Floating Congressional District—

NAT. It's *because* he didn't know that he deserved it! That and showing movies by ex-Nazis. These people think that nobody *notices,* Clara—

CLARA. No *more!* It's over! Today was my last cover, that's what I came to tell you. Little did I know you were also back in combat again. *(Sits on center bench, opposite him.)* Searched this damn park for two hours— *(Pointing up right.)* What happened? You're not giving speeches at the Bethesda Fountain anymore?

NAT. Why should I? So you can find me there? shut me up, embarrass me?

CLARA. It's *me,* huh? It's me who embarrasses *you*—

NAT. Exactly; hushing me like I was a babbling child, a—

CLARA. Embarrassment, let's talk about embarrassment, O.K.? Three weeks ago I come back to my office after lunch, they tell me my Parole Officer was looking for me.

NAT *(bangs his cane on the ground).* Necessary retaliation! It was important that you see what it's like to be pursued, watched, guarded . . . *(Turns to her, quietly:)* You *do* frighten me, Mrs. Gelber. You do frighten me, you know. I'm afraid of what you'll do out of what you think is love. Coming to the Fountain once a week—it's not stopping me from talking; that's not so bad. It's the test questions.

CLARA. I don't—

NAT. The test questions to see if I'm too old. *(Taps his head.)* Checking on the arteries. "Do you remember what you did yesterday, Dad?" "Tell me what you had for lunch today, Dad?" *One wrong answer you'll wrap me in a deckchair and mail me to Florida; two mistakes you'll put me in a home for the forgettable.* I know this. My greatest fear is that someday soon I will wake up silly, that time will take my brain and *you* will take me. That you will put me in a place, a home—or worse, *your* house. Siberia in Great Neck. Very little frightens me, as you know; just that. Only what you will do.

CLARA. Dad . . .

NAT. I don't answer the door when you come. That's why. I watch through the hole in the door and wait for you to go away. That's why I moved from the Fountain, Clara. And why next week you won't find me *here* either.

CLARA *(after a moment).* You don't understand; I . . . I care . . . Someone has to watch out for you. Jack doesn't care, or Ben or Carole. They don't even speak to you anymore.

NAT. Good; God bless them; lovely children. Lovely, distant children.

CLARA. This isn't fair, Dad; I don't deserve this . . .

NAT. Dad. Who is this "Dad" you refer to? When did *that* start? I'm a "Pop," a Pop or a Papa, like I always was. You say "Dad" I keep looking around for a gentleman with a pipe.

CLARA. O.K., why don't I just call you "Dr. Engels" then? *(Silence for a moment. NAT turns to her.)* Did you really think you fooled me? Dr. Engels the therapist? Dr. Fred Engels from the Socialists' Club? Really now.

NAT. But why did you keep writing all those letters to him—?

CLARA. Normal conversation with you is hopeless. Seemed like the best way to reach you. I sent "Dr. Engels" twelve letters in two months, I said everything I felt.

NAT. Smart. Smart girl. Well, at least you're still smart . . . even though the passions are gone, even though the ideals have evaporated . . .

CLARA. Stop . . .

NAT. I remember when you believed that the world did *not* belong to the highest bidder . . .

CLARA. The old song, stop . . .

NAT. This, of course, was before you went into Park East Real Estate, before you gave up Marx and Lenin for Bergdorf and Goodman . . .

CLARA. Jesus, at least get a new set of words—

NAT. Look at you! Look what you've become! Queen of the Condominiums, peasant skirts for two hundred dollars, betrayer of your namesake—

CLARA. Goddamn *name*—

NAT. Clara Lemlich, who stood for something—

CLARA. You *gave* me the name; I had no *choice*—

NAT. Clara Lemlich, who stood for something and stood up for it . . .

CLARA *(leans back on bench)*. Ah, you're rolling now . . .

NAT. Cooper Union; November, Nineteen-Nine . . .

CLARA. You're only eight . . .

NAT *(looking away)*. I'm only eight, the Shirtwaist Makers are there, thousands of them . . .

CLARA *(whispering)*. You're standing in back with your father . . .

NAT. I'm standing in the back with my father; he holds me up so I can see. A meeting has been called to protest conditions. Gompers speaks, and Mary Drier, Panken, and Myer London. All speak well and with passion, but none with the courage to call a general strike. All speak of the bosses who

value property above life and profits above people, but all speak with caution . . .

CLARA *(whispering)*. Until suddenly . . .

NAT. Until suddenly from the back of the hall, just near us, rises a skinny girl, a teenager; she runs up onto the platform, this little girl, she runs up unafraid among the great ones; she shouts in Yiddish to the thousands, this girl, with the power of inspiration . . . this girl is Clara Lemlich. "I am a working girl, one of those striking against intolerable conditions. I am *tired* of listening to speakers! I offer a resolution that a general strike be called—*now!*" *(Softly:)* A moment of shock . . . and then the crowd screams, feet pound the floor! The chairman, Feigenbaum, calls for a second; the thousands cry "second!" in one voice. Feigenbaum trembles, he shouts to the hall, "Do you mean this in good faith? Will you take the Jewish oath?" Three thousand hands are raised—my father is holding me up, his hands are not free. "Raise your hand, boy, raise your hand for us and I will say the oath"—my hand goes up; I feel his heart beating at my back as my father with the thousands chants the solemn oath: "If I turn traitor to the cause I now pledge, may this hand wither from the arm I raise!" Again there is silence in the hall . . .

CLARA *(softly; caught up in the story again, as always)*. And then Feigenbaum shouts . . .

NAT. And Feigenbaum shouts—*(he raises his fist in the air)* a general strike has been called! *(A moment; then he lowers his fist.)* Thirty-two years later, December, Forty-One, Roosevelt vows vengeance upon the Fascists, and the next day *you* are born with a powerful scream at Kings County Hospital—I say to your mother, "Ethel, sounds to me like Clara Lemlich." This is the name . . .

CLARA and NAT *(together)*. And this is the passion you were born with . . .

CLARA. *Finish.*

NAT *(turns to her)*. And only forty-one years later you have turned into my own, personal K.G.B.

CLARA. Go to hell.

NAT. I can't; you'll follow me.

(She turns to him, sharply.)

CLARA. Clara, Clara—it's not a name, it's a curse. The Cause, the goddamn *Cause*—everybody else gets a two-wheeler when they're ten, I got "Das Kapital" in paperback. Sundays you sent me out for bagels and lox and the Weekend Daily Worker; I hide it in the bag so half of Flatbush Avenue doesn't point at me. Fights at school, kids avoiding me, daughter of the Reds. My friend Sally— my *only* friend—we're down in the street on a Saturday morning; she tells me she believes in God. I'm confused, I run upstairs to the Central Committee; "Pop, Sally Marcus says she believes in God. What should I tell her?" "Tell her she'll get over it," you say. I tell her, she tells her mother, and the next day I got *nobody* on the block to play with; *alone* again, *alone*—

NAT *(leans towards her)*. Unfair! This isn't *fair*. Later you believed in your *own* things and I loved you for it. You gave up on the Party, I respected you. The Civil Rights, the Anti-War; you marched, you demonstrated, you *spoke*—that was *you*, nobody *made* you, you loved it—

CLARA. I *did* love it—

NAT. You *changed*—

CLARA. No, I just noticed that the world didn't.

NAT. Ah, first it was me, then it was the world. It's nice to know who to blame. Ten *years*, what have you done?

CLARA. *What have I done? I got married and had two children and lived a life. I got smarter and fought in battles I figured I could win. That's what I've done.*

NAT. Lovely. And now, at last, everybody on the block plays with you, don't they? Yes, all the kids play with you now. You married Ricky the smiling Radiologist; he overcharged his way into a house in Great Neck where your children, as far as I can see, believe firmly in Cable Television. They'll fight to the death for it! And all the kids play with *them* too. It's the new utopia: everybody plays with everybody! My enemies, I keep up! My enemies, I don't forget; I cherish them like my friends, so I know what to *do*—

CLARA. And what's that? What the hell do you do? Lead raids on lambchops at Gristede's? Oh, God, it's all so easy for you, I almost envy you. You always know what side to be on because you fight old wars; old, old wars . . . *(At bench, leaning towards him.)* The battle is *over*, Comrade; didn't you notice? Nothing's *happened*, nothing's changed! And the Masses, have you checked out your beloved Masses lately? They don't *give* a crap. *(He turns away.)* Are you listening? *(Grips his arm urgently.)* Are you *listening* to me? I have received your invitation to the Revolution

and I send regrets. I'm busy. I've given up on the Twentieth Century in favor of getting through the week. I have decided to feel things where I can get to feel something *back*; got it?

NAT. I was wrong; you're not even smart anymore. So not much changed. So what? You think I don't know this? The proper response to the outrages is still to be out-raged. To be out*raged!*

CLARA *(her arms outstretched in mock supplication)*. Forgive me, Father; I'm not on the bar-ricades anymore! I haven't been arrested for ten years, I'm obviously worthless! If you were talking to me in *jail* right now, you'd be overjoyed—

NAT. Not overjoyed. *Pleased* maybe . . .

CLARA. Christ, I was the only kid at the Columbia riots whose father showed up to coach! I *still* don't believe it! There you are on the steps of the Administration Building, shouting at the cops, pointing at me—*(Imitating NAT:)* Hey Cossacks, look at this one! You can't stop her! *Four* of you—it'll take *four* of you to put her in the wagon!

NAT. It took *six!*

CLARA *(she suddenly starts to laugh)*. My fa-ther, my riot manager; God, I still don't be-lieve it . . . a night in the slammer, and you waiting for me in the street when I got out . . . champagne, you had *champagne* . . .

NAT *(laughing with her)*. It was a graduation. What parent doesn't show up for a gradua-tion?

CLARA. Why the hell am I laughing?

NAT. Because it was funny.

CLARA *(shaking her head)*. Jesus, what am I going to do with you?

NAT *(quietly)*. Hello, Rappaport . . . *(No response; he raises his voice.)* Hello, Rappaport!

CLARA. I'm not playing.

NAT. Come on, we'll do the "don't slap me on the back" one. You remember.

CLARA *(turns away)*. I don't.

NAT. Hello, Rappaport!

CLARA. Stop . . .

NAT. Hello, Rappaport; how's the family?

CLARA *(after a moment, softly)*. I'm not Rap-paport.

NAT. Hello, Rappaport; how's the shoe business?

CLARA *(smiling)*. I'm not Rappaport.

NAT *(leans towards her, slaps her on the back)*. Hello, Rappaport; how the hell are ya?

CLARA *(doing the routine)*. I'm not Rap-paport, and don't slap me on the back!

NAT. Who are *you* to tell me how to say hello to Rappaport?

(They both laugh. Silence for a moment.)

CLARA *(turns to him; quietly)*. Pop, I have to do something about you.

NAT. No, you don't.

CLARA. Pop—

NAT. At least I'm "Pop" again—

CLARA. You'll get killed. The next time you'll get killed. I dream about it.

NAT. In general, you need better dreams—

CLARA. I want you out of this neighborhood, I want you off the street. I want you safe. I'm determined.

NAT *(reaching for walker)*. I have an appointment—

CLARA *(holds his arm, firmly)*. O.K., we have three possibilities, three solutions. You'll have to accept one of them. First, there's living with me in Great Neck; you'll have your own room, your own separate—

NAT. Rejected.

CLARA. Second; Ricky has found a place, not far from us, Maple Hills Senior Residence. I've checked it out; it's the *best* of them—*(taking Maple Hills book from handbag, showing pages)* really attractive grounds, Pop; this open, sunny, recreation area—

NAT. Rejected.

CLARA. O.K. . . . O.K., there's one more possibility; I'm not crazy about it, but I'm willing to try it for one month. You stay at your place, you do not hide from me, you make yourself available for visits by me or some member of the family once a week. You don't wander the streets, you don't hang around the park; you go out every afternoon to *this* place . . . *(More gently, taking brochure from handbag:)* West End Senior Center; I was there this morning, Pop; this is a great place. Hot lunch at noon and then a full afternoon of activities . . .

NAT *(puts on bifocals, holds brochure up to his eyes, reading)*. "One o'clock: Dr. Gerald Spitzer will present a slide presentation and informative program on home health services; refreshments will be served. Two o'clock: Beginners Bridge with Rose Hagler. Three-fifteen: Arts and Crafts Corner supervised by Ginger Friedman . . ." *(He studies the brochure for a moment.)* O.K. . . . we got three possibilities; we got exile in Great Neck, we got Devil's Island, and we got kindergarten. All rejected. *(Hands her back the brochure; rises from bench, opening the walker.)* And now, if you'll excuse me . . .

(He starts moving down the path to the right with the walker. We begin to hear the distant sound of the Carousel as he continues down the path.)

CLARA. All right, here it is: I'm taking legal action, Pop, I'm going to court. *(NAT stops on the path, his back to her. She remains on the bench.)* I saw a lawyer a month ago after the Gristede Uprising; I'm prepared. Article Seventy-Eight of the Mental Hygiene Law, judicial declaration of incompetency, I'll get Ricky and me authorized as custodians. According to the lawyer I've got more than enough evidence to prove that you are both mentally and physically incapable of managing yourself or your affairs. In addition to a proven history of harrassment, impersonation, and assault. *(She turns away; quietly, firmly:)* I look at that bandage, I . . . You can hardly see, and with that walker you're a sitting duck. I don't want you hurt, I don't want you dead. Please, don't force me to go to court. If you fight me, you'll lose. If you run away, I'll find you. I'm prepared to let you hate me for this.

(Silence for a moment.)

NAT. You're not kidding.

CLARA. I'm not.

(Silence again; only the sound of the distant, gentle, Carousel Music. He moves back to the bench, sits next to her.)

NAT *(quietly)*. Clara, I've got to tell you something. I put it in my papers, a letter for you when I died, you would have known then . . . *(Hesitates a moment, then proceeds gently:)* Your mother and I, it was not the liveliest association, but there was great fondness between us. Whatever I tell you now, you must know that. August, Nineteen Thirty-Nine, I'm at the Young Workers' Club on Houston Street; you talked about dialectical materialism and you met girls. It's a Friday night, the day of the Hitler-Stalin Pact; Ribbentrop shakes hands with Molotov on the front page of the Journal-American and this woman bursts into tears. Everyone's arguing, discussing, but this woman sits there with her tears falling on the newspaper. This was Ethel, your mother. My heart was hers. Soon we are married; two years later you are born—and during the next ten years those other people. Fine. All is well. Then . . . then comes October, Fifty-Six . . . October Third. . .

(He lapses into silence, turns away.)

CLARA. Tell me. What is it?

NAT. I met a girl. I fell in love.

CLARA. You're human, Pop, it happens. There's no need to feel—

NAT. I mean in *love,* Clara. For the first and only time in my life; boom.

CLARA. Don't worry, it's not—

NAT. Clara, she was a *girl.* Twenty-four; I was fifty-five.

CLARA *(riveted).* What happened? Where did you meet her?

NAT. It was in the Grand Street Library, second floor reading-room. I'm at the main table, I look up, I see this lovely girl, Hannah, Hannah Pearlman; she's studying a grammar book. She looks up; she *smiles* at me. I can't speak. She goes back to her book. She has a sad look, someone alone. I see a girl, troubled, lost, marks on her hands from the needle-trades. She rises to leave. Someone should speak to her. Can it be me? Can I have the courage . . . ? *(Softly, with love:)* I speak. I *speak* to her; and for hours our words come out, and for hours and days after that in her little room on Ludlow Street. It was the most perfect time. She tells me I have saved her from killing herself . . . I saved her just in time . . . just in time, Clara . . . she did not die, she did not die . . . *(Silence for a moment. Then he speaks briskly, as though awakening from a dream.)* Well, I'm married to Ethel, nothing can come of it. Four months, it's over. She goes to live in Israel, a new life. Six months later, a letter . . . there is a child . . .

CLARA. My God . . .

NAT. A girl . . . And then, every year or two a letter. Time goes by; I think often of the library and Ludlow Street. Then silence; there are no letters, never another. Three months ago there's a message for me at the Socialists' Club: Sergeant Pearlman will be here at five. Five o'clock, at the door, Sergeant Pearlman is a girl. In Israel, women, everybody's in the Army for two years. Well, Sergeant Pearlman . . .

CLARA. Yes . . .

NAT. Sergeant Pearlman is my daughter. Twenty-six, a face like her mother; a fine face, like a painting. She herself is an artist; she comes to this country to study at the Art Students' League and to find me. *(Silence for a moment.)* Here's the point. She has decided to take care of me; to live with me. That's why I've told you all this, so you'll know. In December, we leave for Israel. This is where I will end my days. You see, there is nothing for you to worry about.

(Silence for a few moments.)

CLARA *(quietly).* This is . . . this is a lot

for me to take in, all at once. A lot of information . . .

NAT. Not easy, but I'm glad I told you. Better you know now.

CLARA. I want to meet her.

NAT. You shall.

CLARA. When?

NAT. In two days. Friday. At the Socialists' Club, in the dining room, Friday at lunchtime. I'll bring sandwiches.

CLARA. Good. *(After a moment; softly:)* She'll . . . she'll take care of you.

NAT. That's the point.

CLARA *(letting it all sink in).* Israel . . .

NAT. Yes, Clara. *(She turns away, trying to cover her emotion. He touches her arm; gently:)* Clara, don't be upset. I'll be fine. It's for the best, Clara . . .

(She rises briskly from the bench.)

CLARA. Well, at last you've got a daughter who's a soldier.

NAT. Sit. Where are you going?

CLARA *(checks watch).* My train. You know, the Siberian Express.

NAT *(holds out his hand to her).* They got them every half-hour. Sit a minute.

CLARA. Got to go. See you Friday. *(She moves quickly towards the stone steps at right; near tears.)*

NAT. Wait a minute—*(She goes quickly up the steps.)* Hey, Rappaport! Hello, Rappaport! *(She exits.)* Rappaport, what happened to you? You used to be a tall, fat guy; now you're a—*(She is gone. He shouts.)* Rappaport! *(Silence for a moment. He speaks quietly.)* Hey, Rappaport . . .

(Silence again. NAT *remains quite still on the bench; he strokes his beard nervously, sadly. He suddenly winces, as though aware for the first time of the pain in his hip; shifts position on the bench.* MIDGE, *still lying on the stone ledge at far left, lifts the handkerchief off his face.)*

MIDGE. You made it up.

NAT *(softly).* Of course.

MIDGE. You made it all up . . .

NAT. Go back to sleep.

MIDGE. Conned your own kid, that's a sin.

NAT. I did it to save a life. Mine.

MIDGE *(sitting up on ledge).* You ain't a nice guy. 'Shamed I even sung a song with you.

NAT. You don't understand. Nursing homes danced in her head; desperate measures were required. *(Grips walker, rising forcefully from bench.) You;* you would just go toddling off to Maple Hills.

MIDGE. Wouldn't hustle my own child to save my ass.

NAT. She's not mine anymore. She has become unfamiliar. *(Starts moving Up Left on path, in walker, as though to exit past MIDGE at ledge.)*

MIDGE. Won't get away with it anyway. In two days, she'll—

NAT *(continuing forcefully up path)*. In two days I'll be in Seattle . . . Hong Kong, Vladivostok, Newark; I'll be where she can't get me.

MIDGE. Seattle, shit, you can't get dow*town*, boy.

NAT. I'll be *gone, some*where. When she comes to the Club, I'll be *gone*—

MIDGE *(angrily, blocking his path)*. And what *she* do? Wait there all day, thinkin' you're dead? *(NAT stops, MIDGE pointing at him.)* What kinda man *are* you? Smart talk and fancy notions, you don't *give* a damn!

NAT. A *letter*, I'll . . . I'll leave a letter for her . . . *(Silence for a moment; he sits on the small bench, upset, confused.)* I'll send her a letter; I'll explain the necessity for . . . my behavior . . .

(He trails off into silence, exhausted, at a loss for words; he stares thoughtfully out at the lake.)

MIDGE *(suddenly looks up at bridge, whispering)*. Gilley—

(We have seen THE COWBOY enter Up Right on the bridge several moments earlier, strolling halfway across the bridge before MIDGE notices him; a tall, genial-looking tourist, about thirty-five, he wears an immaculate white Stetson, finely tailored buckskin jacket, and polished boots. He moves politely towards LAURIE, stopping a respectful distance from her, peering at the sketch she's been working on; LAURIE apparently unaware of him. NAT, lost in his own thoughts, continues to look out at the lake, unaware of MIDGE and the scene above him.)

MIDGE *(softly, squinting up at them)*. Ain't Gilley; too big . . .

THE COWBOY *(smiling, pleasantly, a well-mannered western voice)*. Well now, M'am, you sure got that lake just right. Fine work, I'd say. Looks just like—

LAURIE *(not looking at him)*. Fuck off, Cowboy.

THE COWBOY *(cordially, tipping his Stetson as though returning her greeting)*. Afternoon, M'am.

LAURIE. How did you find me?

THE COWBOY. Natural-born hunter, Miss Laurie. 'Specially rabbits.

LAURIE. Ever tell you how much I hate that bullshit drawl? *(Turns to him.)* What is this, Halloween? You haven't been west of Jersey City.

THE COWBOY. Pure accident of birth, M'am. My soul's in Montana where the air is better.

LAURIE *(abruptly hands him bank-envelope)*. See ya later, Cowboy.

(She starts briskly, calmly, across bridge to right.)

THE COWBOY. Well, thank you, M'am.

(Opens envelope, starts counting bills inside.)

MIDGE. Sure don't *sound* like Ella Mae . . .

THE COWBOY *(quietly)*. Three hundred and twenty . . . ? *(LAURIE quickens her pace across the bridge, almost running.)* Three hundred and twenty outa two *thousand*—

(LAURIE races towards the stone steps at right, THE COWBOY darts up left, disappearing. MIDGE quickly grabs NAT, breaking into his reverie, pulling him to his feet.)

MIDGE. Come on now—*(Moving NAT into the safety of the shadows at the left of the bridge, whispering:)* Bad business . . . bad park business here.

(LAURIE races breathlessly down the stone steps towards the Tunnel, an escape—but THE COWBOY suddenly emerges from the Tunnel, blocking her path.)

THE COWBOY *(calmly, evenly)*. See the rabbit run. Dirty little rabbit. *(Grips her arms, thrusts her forward towards the bench; she bumps against the bench, dropping her sketchpad. He remains a few steps away; continuing quietly, evenly:)* I live in a bad city. What's *happenin'* to this city? City fulla dirty little rabbits. Park fulla junkies, *un*reliable, *dis*honorable junkies . . .

LAURIE. That's all I could—

THE COWBOY *(holding up the envelope)*. Kept your nose filled and your head happy for a year and a half, and look what you do. Look what you do.

LAURIE *(moving towards him)*. Sorry, right now that's the best I—

(He slaps her hard across the face with the bank-envelope, jerking her head back; then he throws the envelope full of bills to the ground.)

NAT *(from shadows at far left)*. What? What happened . . . ?

MIDGE *(holding NAT's arm, whispering)*. Shhhh . . . stay now.

THE COWBOY *(calmly again)*. You . . . you got to take me serious. 'Cause you don't take me serious, I don't get my money and you don't get older. *(A moment passes; then he moves past her at the bench, starting towards the Tunnel.)* My cash. Tomorrow. Here. Six o'clock.

LAURIE *(moving towards him)*. Need more time . . . not enough time, I can't—

(In one quick, almost mechanical movement, he turns and hits her sharply in the face, as though correcting an error. She blinks, dizzy from the blow, sits down on the bench, trembling; there is blood on her lip. NAT *takes a step forward in his walker, but* MIDGE *holds him firmly in the shadows.)*

THE COWBOY *(kneels next to her at the bench; quietly)*. Mustn't say "can't," Miss Laurie. Don't say that. You are the little engine that can. I believe in you. *(Takes out his handkerchief, starts quite delicately, carefully, to dab the blood off her mouth.)* This gets around, folks'll start thinkin' The Cowboy's got no teeth. Law and order ain't reached these parts; fellah like me got to protect himself, right? *(She nods.)* My cash. Tomorrow. Here. Six o'clock. And don't try to hide from me, little rabbit. Don't do that. That would be a mistake. *(She nods. He rises, puts his handkerchief back in his pocket; shakes his head sadly.)* Damn town. Damn town's turnin' us all to shit, ain't it? *(Turns, walks briskly into the darkened Tunnel, tipping his hat cordially as he exits.)* Afternoon, M'am.

*(*LAURIE *kneels down on the ground, sobbing, retrieving the envelope and the scattered bills.* MIDGE *moves out of the shadows and quickly towards her,* NAT *moves slowly towards her in his walker.* MIDGE *reaches his hand out tentatively, tenderly touches her shoulder.)*

MIDGE. You O.K., lady?

LAURIE *(tears streaming down her face)*. Great. Just great. *(She looks up at them.)* Fellahs . . . how ya doin', fellahs?

MIDGE. Here . . . take this. *(Gently hands her his handkerchief; she accepts it, rising to sit on bench.* MIDGE *points in the direction of* THE COWBOY*'s exit.)* That boy; he a dealer, or a shark?

LAURIE. Dealer. But he gave me credit.

MIDGE. Can you get the money? *(She shakes her head hopelessly. He nods.)* Uh-huh. What I heard, lady, you best get outa town; fast and far.

LAURIE. I was just gettin' it together . . . straightening out, Mister . . . *(Shaking with sobs, opening sketchpad, showing him the pages.)* Art school, I started art school, see . . .

MIDGE *(softly, touching her shoulder)*. Outa town, chil'; fast and far.

LAURIE. These guys, you don't get away; they got branch offices, man, they got chain stores . . .

NAT. She's right. *(Parks his walker next to the bench.)* Other measures are called for. *(He sits next to her.)* Tell me, Miss; two days from now, Friday, what are you doing for lunch on Friday?

LAURIE *(quietly, trembling)*. Friday . . . ? Jesus, looks like Friday I'll be in the hospital. Or dead maybe . . . or dead . . .

NAT *(his arm around her; gently, firmly)*. No, you won't be in the hospital. I promise you. And you will not die . . . you will not die.

(Blackout. In the darkness we hear the sound of the Carousel Band-Organ playing "The Sidewalks of New York"; the music building gradually louder in the darkness, reaching a peak and then slowly fading as the lights come up.

It is six o'clock, the evening of the next day. MIDGE *and* NAT *are alone on the path, seated on the center bench.* NAT *wears dark sunglasses, a white silk scarf, and an old but stylish Homburg, his cane at his side, his walker folded and hidden behind the bench. He looks serious and elegant.* MIDGE *wears an old suit-jacket instead of his usual sweater, and a hat that he had once considered fashionable. The bridge lampposts are lit above; the dark shadows of early evening gather in the Tunnel and along the path.* MIDGE *glances anxiously up and down the path. He lights a cigarette, inhales, coughs. Silence for a few moments.)*

————

NAT. Time, please.

MIDGE *(takes out pocket-watch, holds it up against his bifocals)*. Ten to six.

NAT. Good. Say my name again.

MIDGE. I got it, I got it; you keep—

NAT. Say the name.

MIDGE. Donatto.

NAT. The whole name.

MIDGE. Anthony Donatto.

NAT. Better known as?

MIDGE *(impatiently)*. Tony the Cane. O.K.? Now will ya—

NAT. Tony the Cane Donatto. Good. O.K., *your* name.

MIDGE. I—

NAT. Your name.

MIDGE *(with a sigh of resignation)*. Kansas City Jack.

NAT. *Missouri* Jack, *Missouri* Jack. *See,* it's lucky I asked.

MIDGE. Missouri Jack, Kansas City Jack, what the hell's the *difference?* He ain't even gonna ask me.

NAT. It could come *up.* In these matters

details are very important. Details is the whole game, believe me. What time is it?

MIDGE. I just told—

NAT. Missouri Jack is better than Kansas City Jack. Has a sound to it. Music. I know these things. Details is everything. You should introduce yourself to him.

MIDGE. Nossir, *nossir;* do what I *said* I'd do and that's *it.* Don't even like doin' *that* much. Dicey deal here, say the least—*(Starts to cough, indicates cigarette.)* Looka me, ain't had a cigarette thirty-two years, July; you got me smokin' again. *(Pointing at him.)* O.K., promised that po' girl I'd help her out, but I ain't hangin' around here a second longer'n I have to. You a time-bomb, Mister, I hear you tickin'.

NAT. I ask you to look at the record, sir! I ask you to look at the *harm* I've done you! Gilley did not return yesterday as I predicted and he did not come today. No more payoffs; correct?

MIDGE. O.K., so far he—

NAT. And your job—has anybody there *mentioned* firing you since I dealt with Danforth? Do you still have your home?

MIDGE. Yeah, well, O.K., so far they—

NAT. And today a few minutes of your time to help the victim of Gene Autry; the woman requires our aid. He comes here, you go up to him, you say "excuse me, my boss wants to see you," you send him over to me and you're *done;* finished.

MIDGE. You bet; then I *split,* that's *it.* Go home, hear about it on the TV. *(Shaking his head mournfully.)* Still don't see why you even need me to—

NAT. *Details, details;* gives him the feeling I've got a staff, an organization. It fills in the picture. Details are crucial. I know my business. What time is it? *(MIDGE sighs, takes out his pocket-watch. NAT turns, squinting into the Tunnel.)* Never mind; he's here. On the button.

(MIDGE turns sharply as THE COWBOY emerges from the darkened Tunnel. NAT adjusts his Homburg, crosses his legs, leans back on the bench. THE COWBOY walks down to the ledge at far left, glances about, then looks solemnly up at the bridge. After a few moments he sits down at the edge of the ledge, takes off his Stetson, starts cleaning it carefully with a small brush, waiting. MIDGE remains quite still on the bench, looking out at the lake. Silence for a few moments.)

NAT *(whispering).* Now. *(MIDGE continues to look out at the lake. NAT whispers again.)* Now, Carter.

(MIDGE rises, buttons his jacket, straightens his hat, preparing himself; then crosses to within six feet of THE COWBOY. THE COWBOY is looking away from him, watching the path at left.)

MIDGE *(barely audible).* Excuse me, my boss wants to see you. *(No response. He speaks a bit louder.)* Excuse me, Mister . . . my boss wants to see you.

THE COWBOY *(turns to MIDGE).* You talkin' to *me,* partner?

MIDGE. Yeah. *(Points behind him.)* My boss over there, he wants to see you.

THE COWBOY. Your boss?

MIDGE. Yeah, I'm on his staff. He wants to see you.

THE COWBOY. Who the hell're you?

MIDGE. Me? I'm nobody. I'm on the staff.

THE COWBOY *(leans towards him).* What do you want with me? Who are you?

MIDGE. I'm . . . I'm Missouri Jack.

THE COWBOY. Missouri Jack. Sounds familiar. You ever—

MIDGE. You don't know me. I'm nobody.

THE COWBOY. Nobody?

MIDGE. Yeah, definitely. Nobody at all; believe me. *(THE COWBOY shrugs, turns away.)* Him, over there, he's somebody. He wants to see you.

THE COWBOY. I'm busy.

MIDGE. He's the boss. Donatto. Tony Donatto.

THE COWBOY *(sharply).* Great. I'm *busy.*

(He leans back on the ledge, looking the other way, ignoring MIDGE, watching the path.)

MIDGE. O.K. then, guess I'll be on my way. *(He turns, starts walking briskly towards the stone steps at far right.)* Yeah, gotta be gettin' along now. Nice meetin' you, pleasure talkin' to you . . .

NAT *(to COWBOY, loudly).* Hey, Tom Mix. *(THE COWBOY turns; NAT pats the bench.)* You, Roy Rogers, over here.

THE COWBOY. What do *you* want?

NAT. I want not to shout. Come here. *(No response. MIDGE quickens his pace up the steps.)* Laurie Douglas, two thousand dollars.

THE COWBOY. What—

NAT. You know the name? You know the sum? *(Pats bench.)* Here. We'll talk.

(THE COWBOY starts towards him. MIDGE stops in the shadows halfway up the steps, turns, curious, watching them at a safe distance. NAT will remain aloof behind his sunglasses, seldom facing THE COWBOY, never raising his voice.)

THE COWBOY *(approaching bench).* What *about* Laurie Douglas? Who are you?

NAT. I am Donatto. Sit.

THE COWBOY. Look, if that junkie bimbo thinks she can—

NAT. The junkie bimbo is my daughter. Sit.

THE COWBOY. She's got a father, huh? *(Sits.)* Thought things like her just accumulated.

NAT *(taking old silver case from jacket, removing small cigar).* Not that kind of father. Another kind of father. I have many daughters, many sons. In my family there are many children. I am Donatto.

(He lights the cigar. THE COWBOY *studies him.)*

THE COWBOY. I never heard of—

NAT. On your level, probably not. *(Patting* THE COWBOY*'s knee.)* A lot of you new boys don't know. I fill you in. My people, we work out of Phoenix. We take commands from Nazzaro, Los Angeles; Capetti, New Orleans . . . *(No response;* NAT *leans towards him.) Capetti, New Orleans . . . (turns to* MIDGE:*)* Jack, he doesn't know Capetti, New Orleans . . . *(*NAT *chuckles heartily,* MIDGE *stares blankly back at him;* NAT *turns to* THE COWBOY *again.)* Capetti will be amused by you. I am not. Capetti, many years ago, he gives us our name—I talk of the old days now, the good days—he calls us, me and Jack, "The Travel Agents." This is because we arrange for trips to the place of no return. You understand?

THE COWBOY *(sharply, snapping his fingers).* Let's get *to* it, pal, there's some *bucks* owed me—

NAT *(covers* THE COWBOY*'s snapping fingers with his hand, gently).* Please don't do that, it upsets me. We will speak of your problem now. The girl, Laurie; I am not pleased with her. A two-grand marker for drugs, she brings shame on my house. She says she is slapped, threatened. I am unhappy with this. It is not for you to deal with her. She is of my family. Forget the girl; you never met her. Forget, Cowboy, or you yourself become a memory.

THE COWBOY *(smiles, leans back on bench).* You tryin' t'tell me that two old guys like you—

NAT. Of course not. We don't touch people like you; we have *people* who touch people like you. I pick up a phone, you disappear. I make a call, they find you floating. Yes, we are old now, the Travel Agents; many years since we did our own work. In Fifty-Four, our last active year . . . *(turns to* MIDGE:*)* How many floating, Jack? *(Silence,* MIDGE *stares blankly back at him.)* He doesn't remember either. I think if we count Schwartzman, it was fourteen—

THE COWBOY *(leaning very close to him).* Don't like the sound of this, hoss; it does not ring right in the ear.

NAT. Don't you understand? Missouri and me, we fly here personally from Phoenix last night to speak to you—

THE COWBOY. If you just came in from Phoenix, what were you doing here yesterday?

NAT. Yesterday? What're you—

THE COWBOY. And the day before that. Seen you here two days runnin'.

NAT. You . . . you are mistaken—

*(*MIDGE *starts to retreat up the steps towards the exit.)*

THE COWBOY *(lifts walker up from behind bench).* Had this with you yesterday. I got an antenna picks up all channels, Dad; helps me not to wake up dead.

NAT. I advise you to call your people, check the name—

THE COWBOY. Game's over, stop it—

NAT. Call them now—

THE COWBOY. Please don't continue this. I'm gettin' depressed—

NAT. You are making a serious mistake, a very serious—

THE COWBOY. *Please* don't do this—*(He throws the walker clattering to the ground.)* Hate bein' played foolish; *hate* it. First she cons me, then she gets two old creeps to front for her. Don't *like* it. *(Pacing behind bench.)* City gone rotten, shills like you, this Big Apple's just rottin' away . . . *(*NAT *starts to rise;* THE COWBOY *pulls him sharply back down onto the bench.)* This is hurtin' me. Makin' me *feel* bad. *(Pulls off* NAT*'s sunglasses.)* Who *are* you, man? *(Yanks off his Homburg.)* What's the deal? Where is she?

NAT *(quietly).* A . . . a note was left with my attorney this morning. If I do not return by Seven, they will send people here. His card—*(Hands him business card.)*

THE COWBOY *(crushing the card in his hand).* You're out of aces, friend. Where's she hidin'? Where's she at?

NAT. I am not at liberty to—

THE COWBOY *(grips* NAT*'s scarf, pulls him close).* Run a street business. Lookin' bad on the street, girl's makin' me look like shit on the street. Got folks *laughin'* at me. *(Gives him one fierce shake.)* You got to take me *serious* now. You got to tell me where she's *at.*

NAT *(quietly, unable to make his mind work).* Allow me to introduce myself; I . . . I'm . . .

(THE COWBOY *pulls the scarf tighter around* NAT'*s neck, like a kind of noose, shaking him violently now, shouting.*)

THE COWBOY. You in harm's way, Dad, you in harm's *way* now! Got to *tell* me, got to *tell* me! Gonna rock you till the *words* come out—(*Shaking him fiercely, continuously, rhythmically,* NAT *halfway off the bench now, almost falling to the ground.*) Rock you, *rock* you, *rock* you—

MIDGE (*taking a step down the stairs*). Leave him be! Leave him *be* now!

THE COWBOY (*continues shaking* NAT). Rock you, *rock* you—

MIDGE. Leave the man be! Leave him go else I get a cop!

THE COWBOY (*turns, still holding* NAT). Well now, it's Mr. Nobody . . .

MIDGE (*retreating a step*). You . . . you go away, you leave him be else I get a cop. (*Pointing Up Right, trembling.*) Cop right near—cop-car at the boathouse this hour, right near.

THE COWBOY. That case you don't *move,* little man, you stay right *there . . .*

(MIDGE *hesitates; then starts up the stairs.*)

THE COWBOY. I ask you not to go, little man . . .

(MIDGE *continues up the stairs as quickly as he can;* THE COWBOY *lets go of* NAT, *letting him fall to the ground, starts towards the stairs.*)

THE COWBOY. Askin' you to *stop,* buddy; stop right *there—*

(MIDGE *stops on the stairs, his back to* THE COWBOY. THE COWBOY *continues towards the base of the stairs;* MIDGE *turns, holding* GILLEY'*s unsheathed hunting knife high in the air; the large blade glistens.* THE COWBOY *stops; backs up a bit towards the Tunnel. The knife is shaking;* MIDGE *grips the handle with both hands to steady it.*)

THE COWBOY (*tips back his Stetson*). Well now, well now . . . what do we got here?

MIDGE. We got a crazy old man with a knife.

THE COWBOY. Crazy ol' man, you can't even see me.

MIDGE (*still trembling*). See a blue shadow with a hat on it. Come close enough, I stick you. (*A step forward, thrusting knife.*) I swear I stick you, boy.

(THE COWBOY *starts retreating back towards the Tunnel; smiles, tips his hat, as though gracefully admitting defeat.*)

THE COWBOY. Afternoon, Jack.

(*He turns as though exiting into the Tunnel; it* would appear to MIDGE *that* THE COWBOY *is leaving, but we can see that he has merely ducked into the shadows within the Tunnel, at right, where he waits for* MIDGE. MIDGE *continues towards the Tunnel, his courage and pride building, his knife raised high.*)

NAT (*from the ground, whispering*). Get away, Carter . . . get away . . .

MIDGE (*moving into Tunnel, shouting*). Now *you* the one goes away, *you* the one does the leavin', Cowboy; this here's *my* spot . . . (*Continuing into Tunnel, unaware that* THE COWBOY *is hidden just behind him in the shadows of the Tunnel Archway.*) Mess with me, I peel you like an apple! Sliced Cowboy comin' up! Cowboy Salad to go—

(THE COWBOY *moves suddenly out of the shadows behind* MIDGE—*we see the sharp, violent thrust of* THE COWBOY'*s hand as he grabs* MIDGE'*s shoulder—*

Blackout; the sudden loud, pulsing rhythm of the Carousel Band-Organ playing "Springtime in the Rockies." The powerful sound of the Band-Organ continues in the darkness for a few moments, and then the red-orange colors of autumn gradually light up the sky behind the bridge, leaving the downstage area in darkness and the bridge and the Archway in stark silhouette. Leaves fall against the red-orange sky; the Carousel Music continuing powerfully for several moments and then slowly fading into the distant, more delicate melody of "The Queen City March" as the rest of the lights come up.

It is twelve days later, a cloudy autumn morning, eleven o'clock. NAT *is alone on the path, seated at the far left end of the bench. He wears his bifocals, a thick woolen scarf, and a faded winter coat; his walker is folded at his side, his briefcase nowhere in sight. He remains quite still, staring rather listlessly out at the lake; from time to time he shivers slightly in the October breeze, holds the scarf up closer about his neck. He seems fragile, older—or rather he seems to be his own age, very much like any old man whiling away his morning on a park bench. Several moments pass. A few autumn leaves drift lazily down onto the path. Silence except for the now quite distant and gentle sound of the Carousel Music. After a while* NAT *reaches into his jacket pocket, takes out the West End Senior Center brochure, holds it up to his bifocals, studying it. Several more moments pass.*

We see MIDGE *appear in the darkened Tunnel; he is moving slowly and carefully through the Tunnel with the aid of a "quad-cane"—a cane with four aluminum rubber-tipped legs at its base. It takes him several moments to reach the bench; he crosses in front of* NAT, *ignoring him, sits at the far right end of the bench, opens his copy of* The Sporting News, *starts to read. The Carousel Music fades out. Silence for a few moments.* NAT *turns, leans towards* MIDGE.)

MIDGE *(quietly).* Don't say a word.

NAT *(after a moment).* I was only—

MIDGE. Not a word, please.

(Silence again. MIDGE *continues to read his newspaper.)*

NAT. I was only going to say that, quite frankly, I have missed you, Carter.

MIDGE. O.K., now you said it.

NAT *(after a moment).* I would also like to express my delight at your safe return from the hospital. I only regret that you did not allow me into your room to visit you.

MIDGE. Ain't lettin' *you* in there—shit, tell 'em you're a doctor, start loppin' off pieces of my foot. Had twelve beautiful days an' nights without you.

NAT. Quite right. I don't blame you.

MIDGE. Told 'em, don't let him in what*ever* he says—he tell you he the head of the hospital, tell you he invented *novocaine,* you don't let him in.

NAT. I certainly don't blame you. The fact is I've stopped doing that.

MIDGE. Yeah, *sure*—

NAT. It's true. Since the Cowboy—an episode during which, may I say, you behaved magnificently; not since General Custer has there been such behavior—since that time I have been only myself. That Friday, Clara comes lunchtime to the Socialists' Club; I tell her the truth. She comes, there are tears in her eyes, I decide to tell her the truth. I will admit I was helped in this decision by the fact that the girl, Laurie, did not show up. *(He turns away, quietly.)* I could have covered, another story, my heart wasn't in it. My mouth, a dangerous mouth; it makes you Missouri Jack and almost kills you; makes an Israeli family and breaks my daughter's heart. I have retired my mouth.

MIDGE *(still looking away, bitterly).* Yeah, well, long's we talkin' *mouth* damage, boy— lawyer for the Tenants' Committee found out there ain't no HURTSFOE; I'm outa my *job* now. Yeah, movin' me and the Erie City out in four weeks. No extra Severance neither. Danforth come to the hospital to tell me personal; bring me a basket of fruit. Now

'stead of my Christmas cash I got six fancy pears wrapped in silver paper.

NAT. I . . . I deeply regret—

MIDGE. 'Sides which, look what you done to Laurie. How you expect her to show up? Said you'd help her with that Cowboy; now she's in worse trouble than ever. *(Bangs his quad-cane on the ground.)* 'Sides which, there ain't one good hip left on this bench now. And long's we keepin' score here, what happened to Gilley? Tell me the truth; Gilley's *back,* ain't he?

NAT *(after a moment).* Yes. *(Quietly.)* He charges six dollars now.

MIDGE. So seems to me you pretty much come up O for Five on the whole series here.

NAT. Please, I assure you, my wounds require no further salt . . .

MIDGE. 'Nother thing—I ain't no General Custer. Way I heard it, the General got wiped out. Well, not *this* boy. Shit, wasn't for a lucky left jab I near blew that Cowboy away. *(Takes a small piece of buckskin fringe from his pocket.)* See this? Small piece of that Cowboy is what it is. His jacket, anyways. Near took a good slice outa that boy, 'fore he dropped me. *(Leans back on bench, smiling.)* Know what I seen in the hospital every night, fronta my bed? I seen that Cowboy's eyes, them scared eyes, them big chicken eyes when my weapon come out. That was one, surprised, frozen-solid, near-shitless Cowboy. Dude didn't know *what* happened. Dude figured he had me on the ropes, out come my weapon and he turn *stone.* Lord, even eyes like mine I seen *his* eyes, they got *that* big lookin' at me. Yeah, yeah, he seen *me,* all right, he *seen* me; gonna be a while 'fore he mess with *this* alley cat again. *(Studying the piece of buckskin.)* Must be a way to frame a thing like this . . .

(Silence; then the distant Carousel Band-Organ starts playing its first song of the day, "Sidewalks of New York"; NAT *looks up, realizing what time it must be.)*

NAT *(starts to rise, using bench for support).* Unfortunately, I must leave now . . .

MIDGE *(turns to him, smiles).* Best news I heard all day.

NAT. I am expected at the Senior Center at noon. The day begins at noon there. I must be prompt; Clara checks up. *(Unfolding the walker.)* Also weekends in Great Neck. I am seldom in the park anymore.

MIDGE *(returns to his newspaper).* News is gettin' better and better . . .

NAT *(steps inside of walker, his hands on the rails).* The hospital said you just got out, I came today on the chance of seeing you. I felt I owed you an apology; also the truth. My name is Nat Moyer; this is my actual name. I was a few years with the Fur Workers' Union, this was true, but when Ben Gold lost power they let me go. I was then for forty-one years a waiter at Deitz's Dairy Restaurant on Houston Street; that's all, a waiter. I was retired at age seventy-three; they said they would have kept me on except I talked too much, annoyed the customers. I presently reside, and have for some time, at the Amsterdam Hotel; here my main occupation is learning more things about tuna fish than God ever intended. In other words, whatever has been said previously, I was, and am now, no one. No one at all. This is the truth. Goodbye and good luck to you and your knife. *(He starts moving slowly down the path with his walker towards the exit at left.)* Better get going to the Center. At Twelve guest speaker Jerome Cooper will lecture on "Timely Issues for the Aging"; refreshments will be served to anyone who's alive at the end . . .

MIDGE *(quietly, shaking his head).* Shit, man, you *still* can't tell the truth.

NAT *(continues moving away).* That was the truth.

MIDGE. Damn it, tell me the truth.

NAT. I *told* you the truth. That's what I was, that's *all*—

MIDGE *(angrily, slapping the bench).* No, you wasn't a waiter. What was you really?

NAT. I was a waiter . . .

MIDGE *(shouting angrily).* You wasn't just a waiter, you was *more* than that! Tell me the truth, damn it—

NAT *(he stops on the path; shouts).* I was a waiter, that's *it!* *(Silence for a moment; then he continues down the path on his walker. He stops after a few steps; silence for several moments. Then, quietly:)* Except, of course, for a brief time in the motion picture industry.

MIDGE. You mean the movies?

NAT. Well, *you* call it the movies; *we* call it the motion picture industry.

MIDGE. What kinda job you have there?

NAT. A job? What I did you couldn't call a job. You see, I was, briefly, a mogul.

MIDGE. Mogul; yeah, I hearda that. Ain't that some kinda Rabbi or somethin'?

NAT. In a manner of speaking, yes. *(Moving towards MIDGE at bench.)* A sort of motion picture rabbi, you might say. One who leads, instructs, inspires; that's a mogul. It's the early Fifties, Blacklisting, the Red Scare, terror reigns, the industry is frozen. Nobody can make a move. It's colleague against colleague, brother against brother. I had written a few articles for the papers, some theories on the subject. Suddenly, they call me, they fly me there—boom, I'm a mogul. *(Sitting on bench.)* The industry needs answers. What should I do?

MIDGE *(leans towards him, intently).* What *did* you do?

NAT. Well, that's a long story . . . a long and complicated story . . .

He crosses his legs, leans back on the bench, about to launch into his story, the Carousel Music building loudly as . . .

The Curtain Falls

The Widow Claire

HORTON FOOTE

First presented by the Circle In The Square, Inc., at the Circle In The Square Downtown, in New York City, on December 17, 1986. The cast, in order of appearance, was as follows:

SPENCE	Spartan McClure
ED CORDRAY	William Youmans
FELIX	Victor Slezak
ARCHIE	Anthony Weaver
HORACE ROBEDAUX	Matthew Broderick
WIDOW CLAIRE	Hallie Foote
MOLLY	Sarah Michelle Gellar
BUDDY	John Damon
VAL	Patrick James Clark
ROGER	Dan Butler

PLACE: Harrison, Texas—1911

The play was performed without an intermission.

Directed by Michael Lindsay-Hogg
Setting by Eugene Lee
Costumes by Van Broughton Bamsey
Lighting by Natasha Katz
Hair and Makeup by Hiram Ortiz
Dance sequences by Margie Castleman
Fight sequences by B. H. Barry
Production Stage Manager: Carol Klein

In a distinguished fifty-year career, Horton Foote has created enduring pieces for both stage and screen. Almost all his work is set in the imaginary town of Harrison, Texas, closely modeled on Foote's native town of Wharton, a small community southwest of Houston. Foote depicts life in Main Street America in the early part of this century, evoking a nominally gentler, more innocent world that often conceals, as in *The Widow Claire*, inner turbulence.

"These stories," Foote explains, "have haunted me all my life. . . . I did not choose this task, this place, or these people to write about so much as they chose me. . . ." *The Widow Claire* is one of nine plays in *The Orphans' Home Cycle*, a series of interwoven narratives that are loosely based on incidents in the lives of Foote's parents and maternal grandparents between 1902 and 1928 (the others in the cycle are *1918, On Valentine's Day, Courtship, Roots in a Parched Ground, Lily Dale, Cousins, Convicts*, and *The Death of the Pope*). These narratives chronicle the transformation of the aristocratic preindustrial Old South into a mercantile region. They also celebrate the family and community relationships through which people are able to endure hardship and surmount defeat. "I believe very deeply in the human spirit," Foote avers. "I have an awe about it. . . ."

The Widow Claire, like all Foote's work evoking mood rather than plot, presents the playwright's recurring theme of the universal desire for family security and stability through the eyes of Horace Robedaux, who comes of age in a small Texas town during the course of an evening and early morning in 1911. In an interview with David Mamet, Foote stated that Horace Robedaux's characterization was inspired by his own father, who "[thought] of himself as an orphan who [needed] to establish a home. . . . I wrote against the Texas myth, the cowboy and the trails. . . ."

The Widow Claire is populated with an unforgettable cast of impeccably drawn characters. "I was born in a family of talkers and I adored them," Foote says. "I'm a born listener and I was totally absorbed by my family's stories." In this play, we see typical Foote elements: the thwarted lives ending in futility and the characteristic strong, independent, yet gentle women, "these women who have very little in possessions but have a great dignity. . . ." The yearnings of innocent children, often depicted in Foote's plays, are rendered here tenderly and with great passion.

Horton Foote was born in 1916. At the extreme of the Great Depression, when he was sixteen years old, he decided to become an actor; his father gave him a small amount of money and told him to make the most of it. Foote traveled to California and became an apprentice at the Pasadena Playhouse. A year later, he traveled to New York to study Method acting. Foote credits his writing technique and his continued emphasis on characterization and mood to this early study.

Foote's early stage work included acting stints at the 1939 New York World's Fair and in a tour of *Yankee Doodle Comes to Town* in 1940. Then he joined the American Actors Theatre, whose founder, Mary Hunter, encouraged him to write a play after viewing some of his improvisations based on people he remembered from childhood. His first plays, a one-act called *Wharton Dance* and the three-act *Texas Town*, were staged by the American Actors Theatre in 1940. An encouraging review by *New York Times* critic Brooks Atkinson launched Foote's career. *Out of My House* and *Only the Heart* were staged in 1942. In 1943, *Miss Lou, The Girls, The Lonely, Goodbye*, and *Daisy Lee* were all staged at the Neighborhood Playhouse by Sanford Meisner.

In 1944, Foote moved to Washington, D.C., where *Homecoming, In My Beginning, People in the Show*, and *The Return* were staged at the King-Smith School of the Creative Arts. He was then hired by NBC to write for the *Gabby Hayes Show* and for the dramatic anthology series *Television Playhouse*, cosponsored by Philco and Goodyear. Foote's television plays include *The Chase, The Trip to Bountiful* (later produced on Broadway and, in the eighties, for the cinema), *A Young Lady of Property, Expectant Relations, The Old Beginning, The Midnight Caller, The Death of the Old Man, The Tears of My Sister,* and *The Oil Well.* As the golden age of television was drawing to a close, Foote adapted Faulkner's short stories "Old Man," for which he won an Emmy Award, "Tomorrow," and "The Shape of the River." During this time, Foote also wrote *Roots in a Parched Ground,* the first play in *The Orphans' Home Cycle.*

Beginning in 1955, Foote spent twelve years adapting both his work and others' for Hollywood. Foote's screenplays include *Storm Fear, To Kill a Mockingbird* (for which he won an Academy Award in 1962), *Baby the Rain Must Fall, The Chase,* and *Hurry Sundown.*

Horton Foote says that he felt out of tune with the sixties, alienated from both the new experimental theatre and the materialism of the cinema. He retired with his family to a farm in New Hampshire and continued *The Orphans' Home Cycle.* Foote did take time off to write a screenplay for Robert Duvall—*Tender Mercies,* which earned Foote and Duvall 1983 Academy Awards for Best Original Screenplay and Best Actor respectively. Also during this period, Herbert Berghof, founder of the HB Studio Playhouse in New York, began producing some of the plays in *The Orphans' Home Cycle.* Foote and members of his family then formed an independent movie company, which began to film the cycle. *Courtship, 1918,* and *On Valentine's Day* have been shown on PBS's *American Playhouse.* The entire cycle has also been published by Grove Press.

Foote writes his early drafts in longhand, and then laboriously edits and reedits. "You have to give yourself time to think things through," he says. "I just ask a lot of questions: Why did she do that, and where was she going, and why do you want to use him? . . . Then something evolves and I begin to shape it. . . . If nothing of mine was ever read again or produced again, I would still write. I mean it's some kind of a compulsion. . . ."

NOTES ON THE CIRCLE IN THE SQUARE DOWNTOWN PRODUCTION

This first production of *The Widow Claire* was done at the Circle in the Square Downtown, which is a theatre in the round. The stage directions of the published play are based on that production.

The action of the play progresses from a room in a boarding house to the living room, porch and yard of Claire's house, back to boarding house and back to Claire's house and yard a number of times.

It was Eugene Lee's idea (and I think a fine one for this space) to use the room in the boarding house and Claire's living room as one—defined by the entrance of the characters inhabiting their respective rooms. Far Upstage, always present, he had the realistic front of Claire's house, with windows and a porch running Front and Stage Left of the house. Upstage Left was a fence with a gate.

We entered Claire's house and yard in different ways—sometimes from Downstage Right, sometimes through the audience Down Center and sometimes from the front door of the house or from the fence gate. The boarding house was always entered through the audience Down Center, except by Horace who exits and enters once Up Left Center.

The space to be occupied by both the men of the boarding house and Claire, her children and suitors is furnished simply with furniture and props that can be used by both Claire and the male boarders.

In this theatre space Lee's production scheme allowed great fluidity of performance.

Some of the audience (very few) actually took a few moments to adjust to this use of space for both boarding house and living room but soon accepted it on its own terms. In a more conventional space, of course, the scenic solutions may be quite different. But I urge all who do the play to think carefully of Eugene Lee's solution, no matter what the space is, because I feel it serves the play admirably.

HORTON FOOTE

Harrison, Texas 1911.

The house lights start to fade. We see a room with a table with four chairs around it. Also in the room are a hat rack, a Victrola, a small dresser and, far Down Left, a day bed.

Far Upstage is the front of CLAIRE's *house. There is a porch across the front, continuing around the Left side of the house. Up Left of the house is a fence with a gate. The shades in the windows of the house are up at the beginning of the play.*

ARCHIE, 22, FELIX, 24, SPENCE, 20, ED COR-DRAY, 24, *and* HORACE ROBEDAUX, 21, *enter through auditorium.* HORACE *crosses to dresser, finishes dressing for a date. The four men are in the middle of a poker game as the lights come up.*

————

SPENCE. When I get some money ahead I'm going into Houston and get into some big games. *(A pause.)* They have some big games in Houston. *(A pause.)* They have a game going day and night at the Milby Hotel. They say you don't need to know nobody. You just go into the lobby of the Milby and ask the desk clerk the room where the game is being held, and he tells you, and you go up to the room . . .

ED *(Interrupting).* Shut up and play cards. *(There is a silence.* HORACE *finishes tying his tie. He whistles "Waltz Me Around Again,* Willie.")* Shut up, Horace. *(*HORACE *stops whistling. He puts his coat on.)*

FELIX. Archie is the ladies' man to beat all ladies' men. When a girl calls up and he answers the phone, they ask him what he's doing and he says "Thinking of you."

ED. Will you shut up, Felix. Get out of the game if you're going to talk. *(*HORACE *gets a clothes brush and brushes his coat.* ED *throws his cards down.* ARCHIE *begins to take money from the pot.* ED *walks away from the table.)* I'm through. I'm cleaned out.

SPENCE. Don't you have any more money?

ED. No.

ARCHIE. Come on and play, Horace.

HORACE. I can't. I have a date.

ED. Loan me a little money until Saturday, Horace.

HORACE. I can't, Ed.

ED. Come on, be a friend.

HORACE. I can't. I leave for business school tomorrow. I need all my money for that.

SPENCE. I'll loan you some money until Friday, Ed. *(He gives him five dollars.)*

*See Special Note on Copyright Page.

ARCHIE. You better get in the game, Horace, you could double your money.

HORACE. No, thank you. I tried that before.

FELIX. Horace has worse luck at poker than his Uncle Albert.

ARCHIE. Let's shoot some craps. Maybe you'll have some luck with that.

HORACE. Not me. *(*HORACE *looks again at his watch and looks at himself again in the mirror.)*

ARCHIE. Who is your date with?

HORACE. Claire.

ARCHIE. The Widow Claire?

HORACE. Yes.

FELIX. I had a date with her a month ago, but her kids wouldn't leave us alone.

HORACE. No?

FELIX. No. *(*HORACE *glances at himself again in the mirror; he whistles "Waltz Me Around Again, Willie".)* How do you get away from them kids? My God, how can you ever feel romantic with kids every place?

ED. I'd keep away from her. Who wants those kids around your neck? Whoever gets her is gonna get it.

ARCHIE. Do you think she's good-looking?

ED. Kind of . . .

FELIX. She used to be. I think she's losing her looks. She used to be a beauty. *(*HORACE *looks at his watch.)* Are we keeping you, boy? Don't let your old pals keep you from your date.

HORACE. No, it's still early. I want to give her time to put the kids to bed.

ED. How many dates have you had with her, Horace?

HORACE. Two.

SPENCE. Were those kids always there?

HORACE. In the house. Sometimes they are in bed.

FELIX. They weren't in bed the night I was there. They were crawling all over me the whole time, asking me every five minutes if I'd brought them a present. Finally, I had to give them both a nickel to shut them up.

ED. I never went out with a widow.

ARCHIE. Hell, you never go out with anybody.

ED. I've had a date.

FELIX. Who with Cow Pen Annie?

ED. You're kind of funny, aren't you?

SPENCE. They tell me widows can be dangerous. You be careful over there, Horace.

HORACE. I can take care of myself.

SPENCE. Famous last words. *(*HORACE *looks again at his watch.)*

HORACE. I've got to go.

FELIX. Give me five dollars and I'll come over and entertain the children while you're courting the Mama.

ED. I'll do it for three. I'll even take them for a nice long walk and I'll whistle loud to let you know when I'm bringing them home.

HORACE. Thank you. I may take you up on that one of these nights.

FELIX. She's seeing a lot of other fellows, too, you know.

ED. She's seeing Val and she's seeing . . .

HORACE. I know who all she's seeing. She makes no secret about it. (HORACE *exits through audience.*)

SPENCE. Maybe old Horace is turning into a ladies' man like Archie. What does Archie say when those gals call up, Felix?

FELIX. Thinking of you. (*He tries to whistle a tune.*) What was the name of the song Horace was whistling?

SPENCE. "Waltz Me Around Again, Willie."

FELIX. That's right. I can't get the damn thing out of my head. What are the words?

SPENCE. Search me.

FELIX. Do you know the words, Archie?

ARCHIE. Maybe. (*A pause. He tries to think of them.*) Waltz me around again, Willie..Da..-Da..Da..Da.. That's all I know.

FELIX. Claire has that song on her Victrola. That's where I heard it last. (ED *starts out.*) Where are you going?

ED. Just going to wander downtown. See what's up. (ED *exits auditorium.*)

FELIX. How does that song go again?

ARCHIE. Waltz me around again, Willie. Da..Da..Da..Da..Da..

FELIX. That's right. (*"Waltz Me Around Again, Willie" plays—The men gather money and cards and exit through audience. As the music begins to play we see* CLAIRE *pulling down the shades inside the house. As the men exit she comes out of the front door and walks into the room. She lights a cigarette and begins to dance around the room. She is not a very experienced smoker and this should be obvious from how she smokes a cigarette.* HORACE *enters through the gate and crosses to the front door of house and knocks.* CLAIRE *turns off the Victrola, puts out cigarette, waving away the smoke accumulating in the room and calls out.*)

CLAIRE. Who is it?

HORACE. It's me. It's Horace.

CLAIRE. Oh, Horace. Come in.

HORACE. These are for you. (*He comes inside. He hands her a small box of candy.*)

CLAIRE. Oh, thank you. Sit down. I just finished putting the children to bed. I pulled down the shades so I could smoke a cigarette. The neighbors watch everything I do over here.

HORACE. Do they?

CLAIRE. They sure do. And I'm sick and tired of it. I'm going to sell my house and move.

HORACE. Where will you move to?

CLAIRE. Some place where I can have some privacy and not be spied on all the time. (HORACE *draws her to him. They embrace. They kiss. They hear a noise and separate as* MOLLY, *9, comes into the room from D.SR.*) Molly, what are you doing out of bed?

MOLLY. Buddy won't let me sleep, He's made a tent out of his bed and he's playing soldier.

CLAIRE. Go tell him I said to stop it and get to sleep.

MOLLY. I did, but he won't listen to me. He says he's the Major and nobody can give orders but him.

CLAIRE. Well, you go on back to bed and I'll be in in a minute and tell him he has to go to sleep right away.

MOLLY. I want you to tell me a story first.

CLAIRE. I told you two stories.

MOLLY. I want another one.

CLAIRE. Not now, Molly. (MOLLY *cries.*) My God, Molly, won't you ever give me any peace?

HORACE. I'll tell her a story. Come here to me, Molly. (MOLLY *goes to him.*)

CLAIRE. I'll go straighten Buddy out. (*She leaves* D.R.)

HORACE. What story do you want me to tell you?

MOLLY. What story do you tell your little girl?

HORACE. I don't have a little girl.

MOLLY. Do you have a little boy?

HORACE. No.

MOLLY. What stories did your Mama and Daddy tell you when you were a little boy?

HORACE. They didn't tell me any.

MOLLY. Didn't you have a Mama and a Daddy?

HORACE. Yes, but they didn't tell me any stories.

MOLLY. How did they get you to go to sleep?

HORACE. My Daddy used to sing to me when I was real little. He would rock me and sing.

MOLLY. Do you know the story about Goldilocks?

HORACE. Yes, I do.

MOLLY. Tell me that one.

HORACE. All right. Once upon a time . . . there was a little girl with long golden curls. They called her Goldilocks . . .

MOLLY *(Interrupting)*. Don't tell me that one. Tell me about Red Riding Hood.

HORACE. All right. Red Riding Hood was going to see her Grandmother one day and . . .

MOLLY *(Interrupting again)*. What was the song your Daddy used to sing to you?

HORACE. He sang a lot.

MOLLY. Do you live with your Mama and Daddy?

HORACE. No, my Daddy is dead.

MOLLY. Is your Mama dead, too?

HORACE. No, she lives in Houston.

MOLLY. Did your Daddy have a pretty voice?

HORACE. Yes, he did.

MOLLY. Sing me one of the songs. *(HORACE sings "Lily Dale."* MOLLY interrupting.)* I like you.

HORACE. Thank you. I like you.

MOLLY. I like you better than the other men that come to see my Mama. Do you know old Val?

HORACE. Yes, I do.

MOLLY. Do you like him?

HORACE. Well . . . I . . . *(CLAIRE comes in. MOLLY doesn't see her.)*

MOLLY. I don't like Val at all.

CLAIRE. Why don't you like Val?

MOLLY. Because Buddy said he hit you and made you cry.

CLAIRE. Buddy has a big mouth.

MOLLY. I'm going to tell him you said that.

CLAIRE. I'll tell him myself. Come on, let's go to bed. Buddy promises to behave himself.

MOLLY. I haven't heard my story.

HORACE. Come on, I'll tell it to you in bed.

CLAIRE. Are you sure you don't mind?

HORACE. No.

CLAIRE. And will you promise to go to sleep then?

MOLLY. Yes, Ma'am. *(HORACE and MOLLY exit D.R. CLAIRE puts chairs back, gets water, whiskey, pitcher, and two glasses. HORACE comes back in.)*

HORACE. I don't want Val pushing you around. I'm going to speak to Val.

CLAIRE. He was drunk, Horace. You know how he gets when he's drunk. He was sorry the next day. Would you like a drink?

*See Special Note on copyright page.

HORACE. Thanks. *(She pours him some whiskey.)*

CLAIRE. Are you jealous of Val?

HORACE. No, why should I be?

CLAIRE. Well, don't be. I don't like him at all.

HORACE. What do you see him for then?

CLAIRE. I see lots of fellows. You know that. I see him to pass the time. *(She pours a drink for herself. They embrace. BUDDY, 10, comes in D.R.)*

BUDDY. Mama, Molly's crying.

CLAIRE. Oh, Jesus! You didn't do anything to make her cry, did you?

BUDDY. No, Ma'am.

CLAIRE. You're sure?

BUDDY. I swear to you, Mama.

CLAIRE. Well, you better not have. *(She exits D.R.)*

BUDDY *(To HORACE)*. Hi . . .

HORACE. Hi, Buddy.

BUDDY. You got a nickel for me?

HORACE. I think so. Here's one for Molly, too. *(He gives it to him.)*

BUDDY. Thanks. Molly is crying because she says she misses our Daddy. Did you know our Daddy?

HORACE. I sure did.

BUDDY. Our Daddy is dead.

HORACE. I know.

BUDDY. He had the typhoid. He died in that room in there. Did you ever see the room he died in?

HORACE. No.

BUDDY. You want to see it?

HORACE. No, thank you.

BUDDY. I was scared to go in there for a long time. I was afraid his ghost would be in there. There is nothing in there, though. Mama used to keep his clothes in there but she gave them all away last month. *(A pause.)* Did she give any to you?

HORACE. No.

BUDDY. I think they would have fit you. There was a winter suit and a summer suit. He's been dead a year. He worked at the wholesale grocery. Another man has his job now. Molly says your Daddy is dead. *(HORACE and BUDDY sit at table.)*

HORACE. He is.

BUDDY. Did he die with the typhoid?

HORACE. No.

BUDDY. What did he die of?

HORACE. He just died.

BUDDY. How old were you when your Daddy died?

HORACE. Twelve.

BUDDY. I was ten when my Daddy died.

HORACE. I know.

BUDDY. Were you sad when your Daddy died?

HORACE. Yes, I was.

BUDDY. Did you cry?

HORACE. Yes, I did.

BUDDY. I cried too. Do you have a picture of your Daddy?

HORACE. Yes, somewhere.

BUDDY. We don't have a picture of my Daddy. He died before he even had his picture taken. I remember him, though. Do you remember him?

HORACE. Sure I do.

BUDDY. Tell me what he looked like.

HORACE. Well, he was good-looking and he had a real nice personality and he was certainly well liked by everybody.

BUDDY. Mama says he had good character. Do you think he did?

HORACE. Oh, yes, I do. And he was smart, Buddy. He was a very smart man and a good business man. I expect in time he would have been rich.

BUDDY. Are you rich?

HORACE. No, I'm just starting out in life. (BUDDY *opens his hand. He is holding a pocket knife.*)

BUDDY. Look here.

HORACE. Where did you get that?

BUDDY. Uncle Ned. He's a drummer that comes to see us every time he gets to town. He brought Molly a doll. He got them in New Orleans, he said. I like him better than Uncle Val. He never brings us anything. He just tells us to get out and leave him and Mama alone. Where do you work?

HORACE. I've been working in Mr. Jackson's store. I'm going to school, day after tomorrow.

BUDDY. High school?

HORACE. No, business school. Mr. Jackson has been very nice to me. (CLAIRE *comes back in with* MOLLY. MOLLY *carries a doll.*)

CLAIRE. Molly is scared. I told her she could sit with us for awhile.

BUDDY. Can I, too?

CLAIRE. All right.

BUDDY. He gave us a nickel. Here's yours.

CLAIRE. Did you ask him for that nickel, Buddy?

BUDDY. No.

CLAIRE. Are you sure?

BUDDY. Yes.

CLAIRE. I don't like you asking my friends for things, Buddy.

BUDDY. I know that.

CLAIRE. If you want a nickel you ask me for it. I can afford to give you a nickel.

BUDDY. That's the doll Uncle Ned gave Molly.

MOLLY. I call it Eunice Anne.

BUDDY. Uncle Ned is always giving us presents. Isn't he, Mama?

CLAIRE. Uncle Horace brought us some candy.

BUDDY. Who is Uncle Horace?

CLAIRE (*Pointing to* HORACE). He is.

MOLLY (*Looking at the box and reading*). Assorted chocolates. What does that mean?

CLAIRE. It means all kinds. (HORACE *takes the candy and opens it.*)

HORACE. Have a piece.

BUDDY. How many pieces can I have?

CLAIRE. One.

BUDDY. Two?

CLAIRE. All right, two.

MOLLY. Can I have two, too?

CLAIRE. Yes.

BUDDY. If she's going to have two, I should have three.

MOLLY. Why?

BUDDY. Because I'm older than you are.

CLAIRE. Now, be quiet or you won't have any at all.

MOLLY. I want the ones with pecans in them. I got vents on them, Buddy. What kind do you want?

BUDDY. I want the ones with pecans, too.

MOLLY. Well, you can't have them because I want them.

CLAIRE. Be quiet both of you. And be polite. Offer Uncle Horace a piece first. (MOLLY *goes to* HORACE *with box of candy.*)

HORACE. No, thank you.

MOLLY. Don't you like candy?

HORACE. Not too much.

MOLLY. I love it. Mama, do you like candy?

CLAIRE. Oh, yes, I do.

MOLLY. Uncle Ned brings us candy, too.

CLAIRE. Yes, he does. Ned just spoils the children to death.

BUDDY. He brought me a knife and a mouth organ and a BB gun and a slingshot.

MOLLY. He almost killed me with the BB gun.

BUDDY. I did not.

MOLLY. You did, too. You pointed it right at me and said: "I think I'll kill you."

BUDDY. I was only joking.

CLAIRE. That's no way to joke, Buddy. If you joke that way again, I'll get Uncle Ned to take the BB gun back to New Orleans.

BUDDY. I know where you live. Over behind the courthouse.

HORACE. That's right.

BUDDY. Can I come over and see you sometime?

HORACE. Sure. When I get back from Houston.

BUDDY. When will that be?

HORACE. In about six weeks.

MOLLY. Mama's wearing a new dress tonight.

BUDDY. It cost a lot of money.

CLAIRE. It didn't cost that much, Buddy. I bought the material and picked out the pattern myself and Sissy made it for me. Do you think it's becoming?

HORACE. Oh, yes, I do. I think it's very becoming.

MOLLY. My Mama smokes cigarettes, but don't tell anybody.

CLAIRE. He knows I smoke cigarettes.

BUDDY. Do you smoke cigarettes, Horace?

CLAIRE. Uncle Horace, Buddy . . .

BUDDY. Do I have to call him Uncle Horace?

HORACE. No, you don't.

BUDDY. Do you smoke cigarettes?

HORACE. Cigars.

BUDDY. Give me one.

HORACE. Wait until you're older, Buddy.

BUDDY. How old were you when you started smoking?

HORACE. About twelve.

BUDDY. Cigars?

HORACE. No. I started on a pipe.

BUDDY. Do you chew tobacco?

HORACE. Sometimes.

BUDDY. Mama says that's a filthy habit.

CLAIRE. Buddy!!

MOLLY. Buddy smokes.

BUDDY. I do not.

MOLLY. You do too. You smoke Mama's cigarettes. I seen you.

CLAIRE. Be quiet, Molly.

MOLLY. Can I smoke one of your cigarettes, Mama?

CLAIRE. No.

MOLLY. Can I have some of your whiskey?

CLAIRE. No. And stop being fresh or you'll go right back to bed.

BUDDY. Mama, let me see you and Horace dance.

CLAIRE. Maybe he don't want to dance, Buddy.

BUDDY. Do you want to dance, Horace?

HORACE. Sure.

CLAIRE. Are you sure?

HORACE. Sure, I'd love to.

CLAIRE. All right. (HORACE *turns on Victrola. He extends his hand to* CLAIRE. *She takes it. They begin to dance around the room.* BUDDY *and* MOLLY *watch in delight.*)

BUDDY. He's a good dancer, Mama.

CLAIRE. Of course, he is. He's kin to Miss Virgie. He has to be. (HORACE *twirls and dips with* CLAIRE. *It is obvious he enjoys dancing.*)

BUDDY. Look there, Mama. He's a fancy dancer.

MOLLY. Val can't dance.

BUDDY. He sure can't.

MOLLY. Val is mean. I don't like Val.

CLAIRE. Sh, Molly. Don't talk that way.

MOLLY. Can Uncle Ned dance, Mama?

CLAIRE. He sure can.

BUDDY. Uncle Ned is an old man. He's too old to dance.

CLAIRE. He is not old, Buddy.

BUDDY. He is, too.

CLAIRE. Well, don't ever tell him that. He would die. (*To* HORACE.) He's a lonely fellow. He travels with the J.C. Taylor Tailoring Company. They have their headquarters in Chicago. He has the southern territory.

HORACE. I know him. He sold tailoring to my Uncle.

BUDDY. He asked Mama to marry him.

CLAIRE. Buddy!!

BUDDY. Didn't he?

CLAIRE. Yes, but you're not supposed to tell the whole world.

MOLLY. Are you going to marry him?

CLAIRE. I don't know. One day I think I might and the next day I decide that nothing can ever get me to marry again.

BUDDY. Show Horace the ring he gave you.

CLAIRE. I don't have it on.

BUDDY. Why don't you have it on?

CLAIRE. Because I haven't decided to keep it.

BUDDY. Why won't you keep it?

CLAIRE. Because it's an engagement ring.

MOLLY. It's a diamond ring. (*Music ends.* BUDDY *goes over to a table and gets some pictures and a stereoscope. He goes to* HORACE.)

BUDDY. Uncle Ned brought us these pictures of the Wonders of the World. We got pictures of the Leaning Tower of Pisa and the Eiffel Tower and Niagara Falls. You want to see them?

CLAIRE. Not now, Buddy. Some other time.

MOLLY. Have you ever been out of Texas?

HORACE. No.

MOLLY. Uncle Ned has. He travels all over the South. (CLAIRE *turns on Victrola.*)

HORACE. I hope to travel, too, when I finish business school.

CLAIRE. Wouldn't I love that.

BUDDY. Uncle Ned has a house in Galveston. We're going to visit him there sometime.

MOLLY. I'm going to marry and have twelve children.

CLAIRE. God help you then! (HORACE and CLAIRE dance.) When do you leave?

HORACE. Tomorrow.

CLAIRE. How long will you be gone?

HORACE. Six weeks.

CLAIRE. I'll miss you.

HORACE. I'll miss you, too.

CLAIRE. I bet there are a lot of pretty girls in Houston.

HORACE. I expect so. I won't have time for girls. I'll have to study a lot to keep up with the courses.

CLAIRE. I bet you will. I know it will be hard. I'd be scared to go to school in Houston.

HORACE. My Cousin Minnie is going to help me.

CLAIRE. I remember her. Where has she been all this time?

HORACE. Living in Houston. She's a school teacher now.

CLAIRE. Oh, everything has changed so much around here. Why, half the people lived on this street when I was growing up have moved away. (A pause.) There's to be a dance at the Courthouse next week. You better postpone your trip until after then.

HORACE. I wish I could, but the term starts day after tomorrow.

BUDDY. How old are you, Horace?

CLAIRE. He's twenty-one.

BUDDY. You're twenty-seven. You're six years older than he is.

CLAIRE. Buddy . . .

HORACE. That don't make any difference, Buddy. My Aunt Virgie is six years older than my Uncle Doc.

CLAIRE. What are your plans when you finish business school?

HORACE. I don't have any, except to find a job.

CLAIRE. Will you go back to work for Mr. Jackson?

HORACE. No. I want to do better than that if I can. That's why I'm going to business school, to help me get a better job. Do you remember Barsoty? He used to live here and . . .

CLAIRE. Why, yes, I do.

HORACE. He's a traveling man now, too. He wrote me a letter and he said to get in touch with him when I finished business school and he would see if he could help me get a traveling line.

CLAIRE. Would you like that?

HORACE. Yes, I would. As long as it's in the South some place. I wouldn't care to travel up North, because of the cold.

CLAIRE. It can be plenty cold here let me tell you.

HORACE. It sure can. (Music ends. HORACE turns Victrola off.) If it gets so cold here, imagine what it will be like in the North.

MOLLY. Uncle Ned is a traveling man. He travels in the South.

CLAIRE. He knows that, Molly.

MOLLY. Do you know Uncle Ned, Horace?

HORACE. Yes, I do.

BUDDY. And he knows Val, too.

CLAIRE. Laura Lee is going with Mr. Barsoty, still?

HORACE. Yes.

CLAIRE. I wonder if they'll ever marry? Have you heard who's taking her to the dance?

HORACE. No.

CLAIRE. Have you heard who's going with who?

HORACE. Archie is taking a girl from out of town who is here visiting the Pridgen girls.

CLAIRE. I heard that. Who are the Pridgen girls going with?

HORACE. I don't know.

CLAIRE. Didn't you used to take out Gladys?

HORACE. I had two or three dates with her.

CLAIRE. Do you think they are attractive?

HORACE. Who?

CLAIRE. The Pridgen girls.

HORACE. Yes. I think they are. In a way..

CLAIRE. Which do you think is the prettiest—Gladys or Lovella?

HORACE. I hadn't thought about it one way or the other.

CLAIRE. I hear they are both very cold. Vernon Dale went with them both and he said they were very cold.

HORACE. He did?

CLAIRE. Yes. Frigid. Do you think they have good personalities?

HORACE. Well . . .

CLAIRE. Vernon said they never would talk when he took them out. He said he had to do all the talking.

BUDDY. What happened to him, Mama?

CLAIRE. Who?

BUDDY. Uncle Vernon. He never comes around anymore.

CLAIRE. No. He likes to own people. Nobody likes to be owned, you know.

HORACE. Ed and Felix don't have dates yet.

CLAIRE. They don't?

HORACE. No.

CLAIRE. Well, they better hurry. All the gals in town will be asked.

HORACE. I know.

CLAIRE. Well, I don't think I've known Ed to have a date. Have you?

HORACE. No, I don't think I have. He said tonight he had, but I don't remember it.

CLAIRE. I think he's very shy.

HORACE. I guess.

CLAIRE. Sissy said she would watch the children for me if I wanted to go, but I don't think I will. Even if anybody asks me, which they haven't. Sissy said "You've mourned a year. No one can criticize your going to the dance now." "I'm not worrying about that," I said, "but no one has asked me. I can't go by myself." No one wants to take an old married woman with two half-grown children to a dance. "You were a child when you were married." Sissy said, "all of sixteen." "I can't help that," I said, "I'm not a child now." (HORACE turns on Victrola. He then crosses to CLAIRE. They walk onto the porch.)

HORACE. I wish I were going to be here. I would take you.

CLAIRE. You're just saying that to be nice.

HORACE. No. I would love to take you.

CLAIRE. You're not just saying that?

HORACE. No.

CLAIRE. I haven't been to a dance in so long I wouldn't know how to act.

HORACE. You know, I don't think I've ever seen you at a dance.

CLAIRE. I guess you haven't. When I went, you were still in knee breeches.

HORACE. Didn't you ever go after you were married?

CLAIRE. No. We went to the first Christmas dance after we were married and then we stopped going. (A pause.) Yesterday was the anniversary of my wedding.

HORACE. Was it? I remember the day you got married.

CLAIRE. Do you?

HORACE. Sure.

CLAIRE. Did you go to the wedding?

HORACE. No, but I remember my Aunt Inez coming home and telling about it.

CLAIRE. She was my Matron of Honor.

HORACE. I remember.

CLAIRE. I had a big church wedding. The church was full. I had a beautiful dress. (A pause.) I was a mother at seventeen. "Don't look back" is my motto . . . "Look ahead." None of my sisters are married except Sissy. The others say they are going to learn from my experience and marry them rich husbands. I thought I was so in love with my husband when I married him that I didn't worry if he was rich or not. He didn't leave me destitute, you know. He left me this house. It's got five bedrooms—four upstairs and one downstairs . . . and two rent houses. Both of my rent houses are rented. Thank God. Although you don't get rich renting houses here. Sissy nags me all the time to marry again, find someone who is fond of children. (A pause.) But not me. I'm twenty-seven. And I've been married for eleven of those twenty-seven years; a mother for ten of them. (A pause.) You're a very good dancer. I guess you know that.

HORACE. Thank you. You're very good, too. Very light on your feet.

CLAIRE. Thank you. I love to dance.

HORACE. So do I.

CLAIRE. I was nervous when you first asked me to dance. I was afraid I'd forgotten how.

HORACE. I don't think you ever forget something like that.

CLAIRE. I guess not.

HORACE. Do you think dancers are born or can it be taught?

CLAIRE. Oh, I don't know. What do you think?

HORACE. My Aunt Virgie says they are born. She says you can't really teach someone to dance who wasn't born with the gift. (Music ends. They re-enter and cross to the Victrola.)

CLAIRE. She should know. I expect she's taught more people to dance than anyone in this town.

HORACE. I guess she has.

CLAIRE. What's your favorite song?

HORACE. I have a number of them. I like "Hello, Central, Give Me Heaven." I was at the opera house the night Chauncey Olcott sang that song. When he finished, there wasn't a dry eye in the house.

CLAIRE. Wasn't there?

HORACE. Not a one. But I like "Goodnight, Mr. Elephant" and "Mighty Lak A Rose," "I Love You Truly," and "Waltz Me Around Again, Willie" .. I like a lot of them.

CLAIRE. Sometimes I think I'll sell the house and go into Houston with the children. I've never lived in a city. *(HORACE turns on music. They dance slowly, staying D.C.)*

HORACE. Neither have I.

CLAIRE. Sissy and her husband leave in the winter for Houston. Your mother still lives there?

HORACE. Yes.

CLAIRE. And your sister?

HORACE. Yes.

CLAIRE. Will you live with them?

HORACE. No. At the boarding house where my Cousin Minnie stays.

CLAIRE. Oh, yes, you told me. Why don't you live with your mother in Houston?

HORACE. She's no room. She has a very small house. If I can, I'll try to come down and see you one weekend before my school is finished.

CLAIRE. That would be nice.

HORACE. I'll write you and tell you what weekend.

CLAIRE. I look forward to that.

HORACE. Maybe, you can get someone to stay with the children and we could go to a picture show.

CLAIRE. All right. *(He glances over at the children. They are both asleep.)*

HORACE. Look there. They're sound asleep. *(She glances over at them.)*

CLAIRE. They're worn out. They go so hard all day. *(He tries to kiss her.)* Be careful. They might wake up and see us. They tell everything they see, you know. *(He persists. She lets him kiss her. They dance a while longer. He kisses her again.)* Your Aunt Inez has stopped speaking to me. Do you know why? We used to be best friends even though she is a lot older than I am. Do you know why she is angry with me?

HORACE. No.

CLAIRE. She was so attentive all the time my husband was sick and afterwards she used to come to see me almost every day. But then she stopped coming and she's given a tea and a bridge party since then and didn't invite me to either one. Sissy says it's because I'm receiving company again, she says she doesn't approve of that. "Sissy, what does she want me to do?," I said.. *(He kisses her—they embrace.)* We better take them to bed. *(She picks up MOLLY. He takes up BUDDY. They exit D.R. The Victrola keeps playing. A man's voice is heard from the auditorium calling:* "CLAIRE . . . CLAIRE . . . CLAIRE." CLAIRE *re-enters and crosses*

D.C. VAL *and* ROGER *are discovered in the auditorium.)* Oh..I thought I heard someone.

VAL. What are you doing?

CLAIRE. I have a date.

VAL. Who with?

CLAIRE. Horace Robedaux.

VAL. Can we come in and visit for a little?

CLAIRE. I guess so. *(VAL and ROGER come into the room.* HORACE *comes in.)* Are they still asleep?

HORACE. Yes.

CLAIRE. They didn't move a muscle when we were bringing them in.

HORACE. No.

CLAIRE. Horace and I had to carry the children to their beds. The fell asleep on the couch watching us dance. Horace is a grand dancer. Do you dance, Roger?

ROGER. A little. *(A pause.)* Val can't dance.

VAL. Who the hell wants to dance?

CLAIRE. Some people like to dance, Val.

VAL. Dancing is for sissies.

ROGER. I guess so, if you say so.

VAL. I know so. Mrs. Kieth has started a dancing school for young ladies and gentlemen, she says. My fool sister-in-law enrolled my brother's oldest boy in the dancing school without telling him. When he found out about it, he had a fit. "What are you trying to do—turn him into a sissie?" he said. He yanked him out of that damn dancing school, bought him a twenty-two and took him deer hunting.

ROGER. Did they get any deer?

VAL. They got all the law allowed. "I'm not gonna have any sissie for a son," my brother said.

HORACE. How do you think a dancing school will do here?

VAL. I think she's gonna starve to death. Would you let a son of yours go to dancing school?

CLAIRE. Sissy wants me to go to the dance next week. "How can I go, Sissy," I said, "unless someone asks me."

ROGER. Who's "Sissy"?

CLAIRE. My oldest sister, Bertie Lee. We all call her "Sissy."

ROGER. Oh, hasn't anybody asked you to go to the dance?

CLAIRE. No.

HORACE. I want to take you, but I'll be in Houston.

CLAIRE. Horace is going to Houston to business school for six weeks. *(A pause. An uncomfortable pause.)* Do you boys want a drink?

ROGER. I don't know. Do you, Val?

VAL. It doesn't make any difference to me one way or the other. What have you got to drink?

CLAIRE. Whiskey.

VAL. Is that the whiskey that old traveling salesman brought you?

CLAIRE. Yes, but he's not old.

VAL. He's forty-two.

CLAIRE. I don't consider that old. Do you Roger?

ROGER. I don't know. I don't have any opinion about it, one way or the other.

VAL. Don't you have any opinion about anything?

ROGER. Some things I do.

VAL. You don't call forty-two old?

ROGER. I don't know. I hadn't thought about it.

VAL. What the hell do you call old, Roger?

ROGER. I don't know what do you call old, Horace?

VAL. What are you bringing Horace into it for?

ROGER. I don't know. I guess I just wanted to hear what he had to say.

VAL. Where is the whiskey?

CLAIRE. I'll get two more glasses.

VAL. We don't need glasses. (VAL *takes a swig from the bottle and hands it to* ROGER.)

CLAIRE. Anyway, he is not forty-two. He is thirty-eight.

VAL. Who says?

CLAIRE. He did.

VAL. You'd believe anything. He looks more like fifty-two to me. He dyes his hair.

CLAIRE. He does not dye his hair. (ROGER *has a drink and hands the bottle back to* VAL.)

VAL. You want a drink, Horace?

HORACE. Thanks. (He takes the bottle and has a drink.)

CLAIRE. What makes you think he dyes his hair?

VAL. Because I know he does. (HORACE *hands the bottle back to* VAL. VAL *offers it to* CLAIRE.) Claire? . . .

CLAIRE. No, thank you. (She lights a cigarette.)

VAL. Give me one of your cigarettes. (She *hands him the package. He takes one.*) Roger, you want a cigarette?

ROGER. Thank you. (He takes it. He gives the package back to VAL.)

VAL. You want a cigarette, Horace?

HORACE. No, I smoke cigars.

VAL. What are you trying to do? Act the big man and show off? When did you start smoking cigars?

HORACE. I always have.

CLAIRE. Anybody feel like dancing? (A *pause. No one says anything.*) Horace? . . .

HORACE. Sure. (HORACE *turns on the Victrola.* HORACE *and* CLAIRE *dance.* MOLLY *comes in D.R.*)

MOLLY. Mama, I can't sleep with that music.

CLAIRE. All right, Honey. (She turns it off.) Go on back to bed now.

MOLLY. I want Horace to take me to bed.

CLAIRE. Oh, Molly!

HORACE. I don't mind. (He takes her up and *goes out with her D.R.*)

VAL. Get rid of him.

CLAIRE. You go on and then I will.

VAL. Come on, Roger. (VAL *and* ROGER *exit U.R.* HORACE *comes in from D.R.*)

CLAIRE. I'm sorry they came by that way. I didn't know what to say. (HORACE *goes over to her*) Horace, I'm going to have to excuse myself. I have a headache.

HORACE. I was going to have to go anyway. *(She kisses him.)*

CLAIRE. You're a very nice fellow. I'm going to miss you. (They walk onto porch.)

HORACE. Thank you. I'll miss you too.

CLAIRE. You'll write to me?

HORACE. I sure will. (She kisses him again.)

CLAIRE. Good night.

HORACE. Good night.

CLAIRE. You're very sweet . . .

HORACE. Oh, no, I'm not.

CLAIRE. Yes, you are and I'll miss you. Write me now.

HORACE. I will. (HORACE *exits through gate door.* CLAIRE *exits through front door.* ARCHIE *and* FELIX *enter from auditorium.*)

FELIX. I wonder where Ed got to.

ARCHIE. What time is it?

FELIX. Eleven.

ARCHIE. Then he's probably sitting around down at the drugstore. Let's walk over to Little Bobby's and watch the poker game.

FELIX. No, I don't enjoy watching.

ARCHIE. I think I'll walk over and see how they're doing. Sure you won't go with me?

FELIX. Nope. (ARCHIE *exits through audience.* FELIX *has a drink of whiskey. He tries to whistle* "Waltz Me Around, Again Willie." *He begins a game of solitaire.* HORACE *enters from auditorium.*) You're back early?

HORACE. She had a headache. (A pause.) Who are you taking to the dance?

FELIX. I don't know yet. Archie is taking an out of town girl. She's visiting the Pridgens'.

HORACE. I know that.

FELIX. They asked me to take her, but I said I wouldn't unless they showed me a picture first. "She might be homely," I told them. "She's not homely," they said. "Then let me see her picture," I said.

HORACE. Claire doesn't have a date. Her year of mourning is up. I think she would like to go if someone would ask her.

FELIX. Nobody has asked her?

HORACE. No.

FELIX. How do you know?

HORACE. She told me. Why don't you ask her?

FELIX. A date costs a lot of money. It's cheaper going stag. *(A pause.)* Did she tell you to ask me to take her?

HORACE. No.

FELIX. What made you ask me?

HORACE. Because I think she would like to go and she said her sister, Sissy, said she should go since her mourning was over, but no one had asked her. I said I would ask her if I were going to be here.

FELIX. Would you ask her?

HORACE. Sure.

FELIX. Do you like her?

HORACE. Yes, I do.

FELIX. Does she like you?

HORACE. She likes me. I don't know how much. She sees Val Stanton, too. And a traveling man and some others I guess. *(FELIX has a drink. He goes to HORACE and offers him a drink.)*

FELIX. I'm going to bed. Are you turning in now?

HORACE. In a little. I can stay up as late as I want tonight. I don't have to get up in the morning and go to work.

FELIX. You sure don't.

HORACE. Felix . . .

FELIX. Yes?

HORACE. Will you take her to the dance?

FELIX. Who?

HORACE. Claire.

FELIX. Let some of the fellows she's seeing take her.

HORACE. They haven't asked her. Will you take her as a favor to me?

FELIX. I can't afford to take a girl I like.

HORACE. I'll give you the money.

FELIX. I thought you had to be so careful with your money.

HORACE. I do, but I'll cut back on something else.

FELIX. All right.

HORACE. Don't tell her I asked you to do this.

FELIX. I won't.

HORACE. I changed my mind. I think I'll turn in, too.

FELIX. And I've changed my mind. I don't want to take Claire. If she's seeing Val, let him take her.

HORACE. He can't dance.

FELIX. Let him learn.

BUDDY *(Calling from audience)*. Horace . . . Horace.

HORACE. Buddy? What do you want, Buddy?

BUDDY. Val is beating up my Mama.

FELIX. You better stay out of that, boy.

HORACE. I can take care of myself. *(HORACE exits through audience. BUDDY goes to FELIX.)*

BUDDY. Give me a nickel.

FELIX. I don't have a nickel. *(BUDDY exits through audience. FELIX goes to dresser. ED enters through audience. He is very drunk.)* Where the hell have you been?

ED. I'm drunk.

FELIX. I know you're drunk.

ED. No, I mean I'm real drunk. I'm so drunk it took me an hour to find the damn house. I'm so drunk I got mixed up and I walked and I walked and I kept hollering where the hell is my boarding house but nobody heard me and so I kept on walking and you know where I ended up?

FELIX. No.

ED. Damn right you don't. Guess . . .

FELIX. No. I don't want to guess. I want to go to bed.

ED. The graveyard. I was in the middle of the damn graveyard and I said this sure as hell ain't the boarding house and I met old Matt Johnson.

FELIX. In the graveyard?

ED. I weren't in the graveyard then. I don't know where the hell I was and I said "Matt, where the hell is the boarding house I live in" and he brought me to the corner and he pointed and he said "There it is yonder." And so here I am. Where's the bed? I'm so drunk I can't find the bed.

FELIX. There's the bed over there.

ED. Where?

FELIX. Right there. Get your clothes off and get in it.

ED. I'm drunk. *(He falls over the bed.)*

FELIX. I thought you were broke. How did you buy whiskey if you were broke?

ED. I got friends. *(ED collapses over the bed as*

the lights fade. FELIX *exits through audience.* ED *stays on bed.* HORACE *and* BUDDY *enter* D.R.)

HORACE. Did your Mama tell you to come for me?

BUDDY. Yes, sir.

HORACE. You're sure?

BUDDY. Yes, sir. Give me another nickel, please.

HORACE. I gave you a nickel earlier.

BUDDY. I lost it on the way to get you. (HORACE *gives him a nickel. They start for the house as* CLAIRE *comes outside.)*

CLAIRE. Horace, you're going to think we're crazy. Val came over here after you left and Buddy and Molly heard him and asked me to tell him to go and I did and he began to get upset, and started talking loud and arguing . . .

BUDDY. He hit you.

CLAIRE. He didn't hit me, Buddy.

BUDDY. He did, too.

CLAIRE. He did not, now. He threatened to hit me. He's a bully, but I'm not afraid of him.

BUDDY. He hit you . . .

CLAIRE. Buddy, he didn't hit me.

BUDDY. He did, too, I saw him and Molly saw him.

CLAIRE. You thought you saw him hit me.

BUDDY. And he wouldn't leave when you asked him to go.

CLAIRE. Well, he's gone now, so let's all go to bed. You won't be able to keep your eyes open tomorrow in school. (BUDDY *goes into the house.)* Aren't you going to thank Horace for coming over here?

BUDDY. Thank you, Horace. *(He pauses.)* Can I have another piece of that candy before I go to bed?

CLAIRE. No.

BUDDY. Why?

CLAIRE. Because I don't want you eating candy this time of night.

BUDDY. I just want one piece.

CLAIRE. All right. Just one piece and then get right into bed. (BUDDY *goes into the house.)*

HORACE. How is your headache?

CLAIRE. It's a little better. I'm awfully sorry we bothered you.

HORACE. I can sleep in there on the couch the rest of the night if it would make you feel better.

CLAIRE. No. Val won't be back tonight. He wouldn't have come here in the first place if he hadn't been drinking. I made the mistake of offering him another drink, thinking that would get rid of him, but it didn't, of course,

it just set him off. And he began to act in a way he shouldn't and I had to ask him to behave and he began to argue and that woke the children up and they got frightened. (BUDDY *comes out.)*

BUDDY. Not but three pieces of candy left out of that whole box. What hog has been into that candy?

CLAIRE. I don't know, Buddy. I only had one piece.

BUDDY. I think the name of the hog is Val.

CLAIRE. Don't be fresh, Buddy, and go on to bed. You probably have been helping yourself to that candy all night behind my back.

BUDDY. I have not.

CLAIRE. Well, don't stand there and argue with me in the middle of the night. Go on to bed, please. (BUDDY *goes back into the house.)* Look, there's a new moon. Make a wish. *(She closes her eyes and makes a wish.* HORACE *closes his eyes and makes a wish. She opens her eyes. He opens his eyes.)* Did you make a wish?

HORACE. Yes, I did.

CLAIRE. Don't tell me what it was though, because then it won't come true. *(A pause.)* Did any of the wishes you ever made on a new moon come true?

HORACE. I don't think so.

CLAIRE. One of mine almost did. I wished last summer we could take the children to Colorado during the hottest part of the summer, but we ended up in Galveston instead, because it was cheaper to go there. Anyway, we got out of the heat here. I think if I hadn't gotten away some place after my husband died, I'd a gone crazy. *(A pause.* CLAIRE *sits on porch steps.)* This was the hottest summer of all, I think. I wished many a day this summer I was back in Galveston. My friend Ned has a house in Galveston and he keeps asking us there, but I don't like to feel obligated. His sister keeps the house for him. He says she would love to have us, too. She's never married. How did you feel when your Mother married again?

HORACE. Well . . .

CLAIRE. Did you want her to marry again?

HORACE. Yes, and no. Sometimes I did and sometimes I didn't.

CLAIRE. How long did she wait before she married again?

HORACE. Three or four years.

CLAIRE. Did your father leave her some money?

HORACE. No.

CLAIRE. How did she support you and your sister?

HORACE *(Sits on porch steps)*. Well, she kept a boarding house with her sister for a while, but they couldn't make a go of it. They couldn't even collect the money from the boarders. Then she went into Houston and got a job working as a seamstress in Munn's Department Store.

CLAIRE. Did you live with her in Houston?

HORACE. No. She left me back here with my grandparents. She took my sister with her. That's where she met Mr. Davenport.

CLAIRE. Who is that?

HORACE. The man she married.

CLAIRE. Why didn't you go and live with them then?

HORACE. Because Mr. Davenport didn't want me. He had to go to work when he was twelve and he thought that was good for a boy, so they left me here and I lived with my grandparents until they died and then I lived with my Aunt Virgie. She has been like a mother to me. I'm crazy about my Aunt Virgie.

CLAIRE. She's a lovely lady.

HORACE. I think so. *(A pause.)*

CLAIRE. Funny thing it's so quiet all of a sudden isn't it?

HORACE. Yes, it is.

CLAIRE. Everybody on this street has gone to bed but us.

HORACE. Not everybody. There is a gambling game over at Mr. Bobby's. That could go on all night.

CLAIRE. Do you like to gamble?

HORACE. Not a whole lot. I have an Uncle that gambles all the time. My Uncle Albert. He's had farms and he's lost them all by gambling. He gambles every night all night long. I'm a pretty serious person, I guess, Claire. I hope you don't think I'm too serious.

CLAIRE. No, I don't.

HORACE. But I sure want to amount to something. I'm ambitious. I don't really know what I'm ambitious about just yet. But I sure am ambitious. That's why I'm going to Houston to take a business course; I thought for a while of reading law in Mr. George Tyler's office, but his son is reading law there now, and anyway I'm not sure I want to be a lawyer, even though my father was. *(A pause.)* We were so poor when my father died we didn't have enough money to put a tombstone on his grave. The first money I get

ahead I'm going to put a tombstone on his grave.

CLAIRE. That was the first thing I did was put a tombstone on my husband's grave. A big one, too. As big as any they've got out there. Sissy said "Have you gone crazy? You can't afford a big tombstone like that. You'll go to the poor house in a month if you keep on spending money like that." "Well, I can't help it," I said. "I may be going to the poorhouse but he's going to have a fine, big tombstone." Do you have a picture of your father?

HORACE. Yes, we do.

CLAIRE. Well, that's a comfort. I don't have one of my husband. I wish I did for the children's sake.

HORACE. Do you have a picture of yourself?

CLAIRE. Yes, I do. I went down and had one taken a week after my husband died, so in case anything happened to me the children would at least have my picture to remember me by.

HORACE. May I have a picture of you to take with me to Houston?

CLAIRE. You certainly can. And may I have a picture of you to remember you by?

HORACE. Yes, you can. As soon as I have some taken.

CLAIRE. Molly says you have a beautiful voice.

HORACE. Oh, I don't know about that.

CLAIRE. Sing something for me. I love to hear people sing. I missed all of that by marrying so young. So many of the young men go around and serenade different girls at night. Have you ever done that?

HORACE. Once or twice. *(He sings, "Sweet Alice Ben Bolt."*)*

CLAIRE. That's a very sad song.

HORACE. Yes, I guess it is.

CLAIRE. I always feel like crying when I hear that song.

HORACE. I'm sorry. I didn't mean to make you feel sad.

CLAIRE. It doesn't take a lot to make me feel sad these days. That's why I like you to come over. I always feel better after talking to you. I'll miss you while you're away in Houston.

HORACE. And I'll miss you. *(He goes to her. He holds her.)*

CLAIRE. Are you going to forget all about me while you're in Houston?

*See Special Note on copyright page.

HORACE. No.

CLAIRE. You promise me?

HORACE. I promise. (MOLLY *comes out front door onto porch.*)

MOLLY. Buddy has his mouth so full of candy he almost choked to death.

CLAIRE. Is he all right now?

MOLLY. Yes. I wish he had choked. He's a hog.

CLAIRE. Now, you don't mean that.

MOLLY. I do, too. He ate every last piece of that candy.

CLAIRE. We'll get you some tomorrow. Now go on back to bed.

MOLLY. When are you going to bed?

CLAIRE. Pretty soon.

MOLLY. I'm going to wait for you.

CLAIRE. Buddy is in bed.

MOLLY. But he's not asleep. He's whistling.

CLAIRE. Tell him to stop.

MOLLY. He won't listen to me..Anyway, he says he's whistling to keep Val away. He says if Val comes back here and hears him whistling he'll think there is a man in the house and be scared and leave.

CLAIRE. Now, you go tell Buddy not to worry. He's not coming back tonight.

MOLLY. Is he ever coming back?

CLAIRE. Yes, when he can behave like a gentleman.

MOLLY. Buddy says he heard Val say Uncle Ned dyes his hair. Is that true?

CLAIRE. No.

MOLLY. Why did he say it if it wasn't true?

CLAIRE. Because he's jealous of your Uncle Ned.

MOLLY. Why?

CLAIRE. Because Uncle Ned asked me to marry him and he thinks I might.

MOLLY. Please come to bed now, Mama.

CLAIRE. All right, Darling. (*She takes* HORACE's *hand.*) Goodnight, Horace.

HORACE. Goodnight.

CLAIRE. Write to us.

HORACE. I will. Goodnight Molly. (HORACE *exits U.L. through gate.* CLAIRE *picks up* MOLLY *and kisses her.*)

MOLLY. Why are you doing that?

CLAIRE. Because I love you.

MOLLY. Do you love Buddy, too?

CLAIRE. Of course I love Buddy. (*She sings a snatch of "Sweet Alice Ben Bolt."*)

MOLLY. That's a sad song, Mama. Don't sing that song. I don't like it.

CLAIRE. I don't either.

MOLLY. Sing me a happy song. Sing me "Goodnight, Irene."

CLAIRE. All right. If I can remember it. (*She sings "Goodnight, Irene." She enters the house singing as* FELIX *and* ARCHIE *enter through audience.* ARCHIE *crosses to coat rack and takes off coat.* FELIX *crosses to dresser.*)

FELIX. I guess Spence is staying over at Little Bobby's until the game breaks up.

ARCHIE. I guess so.

FELIX. Maybe they'll even let him into the game.

ARCHIE. Oh, no. Not that game. That's a serious game with very high stakes.

FELIX. Spence says his ambition is to become a professional gambler. Do you think he'll ever get to be one?

ARCHIE. I don't know.

FELIX. What do you want to become Archie?

ARCHIE. Oh, hell. I don't know. Have a good time, I guess. (*A pause.*) What do you want to do?

FELIX. I don't know. Maybe we should go to business school in Houston like Horace.

ARCHIE. No. No.

FELIX. We have to do something.

ARCHIE. I've had jobs.

FELIX. Not many.

ARCHIE. And you've had jobs.

FELIX. Not many. I helped take the census one year.

ARCHIE. That was a job.

FELIX. I worked for two months over at the cotton gin during cotton season.

ARCHIE. And that was a job, too. (*They continue playing.*)

FELIX. I hope to be rich one day that's all I know.

ARCHIE. What are your plans for getting rich?

FELIX. Marry me a rich woman.

ARCHIE. Maybe you should set up to Claire.

FELIX. She's not rich.

ARCHIE. She has three houses. One she lives in and two she rents.

FELIX. You can't give houses away here.

ARCHIE. Three houses are better than nothing.

FELIX. Not for me. I'm talking about real rich. (*A pause.*) Do you think that's what old Horace has on his mind? Getting hold of those rent houses.

ARCHIE. I don't know. What the hell is Ed doing in my bed?

FELIX. He came home so drunk he didn't know what bed he was in. *(HORACE enters through audience crosses to dresser.)*

HORACE. I thought you would all be asleep.

FELIX. We were, but Ed came home drunk and woke us up.

ARCHIE. Want to play some cards?

HORACE. Nope.

ARCHIE. Come on . . .

HORACE. No. I'm scared to. I only have enough money to last me the six weeks in Houston. I won't even be able to afford cigars or a newspaper. If I even lost a dollar I would be in trouble.

ARCHIE. Felix said you were going to give him the money to take Claire to the dance. How were you going to do that if you have so little money?

HORACE. I don't know. It was crazy of me. I would have been in trouble if he'd taken me up on it.

FELIX. Maybe you'd win. Then you'd have a little extra.

HORACE. No.

ARCHIE. I'll loan you a dollar. If you lose it, you can pay me back when you get back from Houston and go back to work.

FELIX. Come on, Horace.

HORACE. All right, but if I lose this dollar, that's the end of it. *(They all sit down at table. ARCHIE gives HORACE a dollar in change.)*

FELIX. Dwight Lester came by here and wanted me to go serenading some of the gals in town this weekend. He wanted three fellows to go with him, and hire a guitar and a fiddle player to go around with us. I said no. No more serenading for me. It costs too much. Let the girls come here and serenade me. Last September we went serenading and when we got to Eloise Dockery's house, I started singing and Old Man Dockery came out with a shotgun and said if we didn't shut up, he'd blow our brains out.

ARCHIE. Do you think he meant it?

FELIX. We didn't wait to find out.

HORACE. How much does it cost to hire a guitar and a fiddle player?

FELIX. Plenty. More than I have. Why, are you thinking of serenading someone?

HORACE. Maybe.

FELIX. Who?

HORACE. Claire.

ARCHIE. Tonight?

HORACE. No, not tonight, when I get back from Houston. *(ARCHIE shuffles the cards.)*

FELIX. Did you straighten Val out?

HORACE. He was gone by the time I got there.

ARCHIE. I think he's after her money.

HORACE. Whose money?

ARCHIE. Claire's.

HORACE. She doesn't have any money.

ARCHIE. She owns her house and two rent houses. That's more than Val has.

HORACE. Did you ever know a man that dyed his hair?

ARCHIE. No.

FELIX. I knew a man once that did. The dye got stuck in his skin some way and turned his skin a blue-gray.

ARCHIE. Who was that?

FELIX. I forgot his name. Why did you ask that question, Horace?

HORACE. Because Val said the traveling man that calls on Claire dyes his hair. Claire says he doesn't.

FELIX. Val is a lot of hot air.

ARCHIE. What's the name of the traveling man?

HORACE. Ned.

ARCHIE. Ned what? *(HORACE shuffles cards.)*

HORACE. I don't know. I only know Ned. He sold to my uncle. He don't have any gray hairs come to think of it and I think he's older than my Uncle Albert. My uncle Albert already has some gray hairs.

ARCHIE. And he calls on Claire.

HORACE. Yep.

ARCHIE. I wonder why she lets an old man like that call on her.

HORACE. She gets lonely, she says.

ARCHIE. I talked to White Jenkins the other day. He said he was walking around the other night. He couldn't sleep, he said. He walked all over town trying to get sleepy.

FELIX. White is very nervous.

ARCHIE. He's taking medicine for it.

HORACE. For his nerves?

ARCHIE. Yes. He carries a little bottle of medicine around with him all the time and every time he gets nervous he takes a swig from the bottle.

FELIX. I bet it's just whiskey. *(HORACE deals cards.)*

ARCHIE. No. It's medicine. He got a prescription. He showed it to me. Anyway, he said the other night when he was walking around he seen Val come out of Claire's house at five o'clock just before daybreak. *(A pause.)* He said he's seen him come out of there at all hours.

HORACE. Let's play cards if we're going to play.

FELIX. I wonder if he's ever seen old Horace come out of there at daybreak? (ARCHIE *and* FELIX *laugh.*)

ARCHIE. Has he, Horace?

HORACE. Let's play cards.

FELIX. Old Horace is blushing. (ARCHIE *and* FELIX *laugh again. This time* HORACE *joins them and they begin to play cards.* ED *stirs in his sleep.*)

ED (*Muttering*). Roberta . . .

HORACE. Who's Roberta?

FELIX. I don't know. Who is Roberta, Archie?

ARCHIE. I never heard of her.

FELIX. Who is Roberta, Ed?

ED (*Muttering*). Roberta . . . Roberta . . .

FELIX. I never knew Ed to go with a girl . . . Did you? I thought he was too shy to go with a girl.

ARCHIE. He's too shy to go with a nice girl. I've known him to take out plenty of the other kind.

FELIX. I've heard a lot of nice girls say they wouldn't go out with him, because he didn't respect women.

ED (*Muttering*). Roberta . . . Roberta . . .

FELIX. Shut up, Ed. Roberta ain't here.

ARCHIE. I wonder if Roberta is a nice girl.

FELIX. And I wonder if he respects her. (BUDDY *calls from audience*)

BUDDY. Horace . . . (*A pause.*) Horace . . . (HORACE *puts the cards down and goes D.C.*)

HORACE. What do you want now, Buddy?

BUDDY. Val snuck back into the house. My Mama doesn't know me and Molly heard him. She thinks we're asleep. Come beat him up, Horace.

HORACE. It's none of my business, Buddy, if your Mama wants him there.

BUDDY. She don't want him there, but she's scared to tell him to leave.

HORACE. How do you know?

BUDDY. She told me that. She's afraid he'll hit her.

HORACE. Now he doesn't hit her, Buddy. That's just your imagination. She told me that. You had better go on home, Buddy. (ED *gives a wild, bloodcurdling scream.*)

BUDDY (*Terrified*). What's that?

HORACE. It's one of the fellows in there.

BUDDY. What's the matter with him? Is somebody trying to kill him?

HORACE. He's drunk.

BUDDY. My God! I thought they were trying to kill him.

HORACE. He'll be all right.

ED (*Calling*). Roberta . . . Roberta . . .

BUDDY. Who is he calling?

HORACE. Roberta.

BUDDY. Who is Roberta?

HORACE. We don't know. You better go on home, Buddy.

BUDDY. You walk with me. I'm scared.

HORACE. You weren't scared to come over here.

BUDDY. But now I heard that drunk man hollering like someone was trying to kill him. I'm scared.

HORACE. All right. Come on. (*The lights change.* ED *screams.* HORACE *and* BUDDY *cross U.R.*) This is as far as I'm going.

BUDDY. Give me a nickel.

HORACE. Now, I gave you two nickels tonight.

BUDDY. This is for Molly you only gave her one. It hurt her feelings when I told her you gave me two.

HORACE. All right. (*He gives him the nickel.*)

BUDDY. Do you think Uncle Ned dyes his hair?

HORACE. I don't know.

BUDDY. Val says he does. I think Val's a liar, don't you?

HORACE. I don't know. (VAL *comes out of the house.*)

BUDDY. Yonder comes Val. I told you he was in there. (*He calls.*) Val, Horace is going to beat you up. (BUDDY *crosses onto porch.*)

VAL. Yeah? I'm scared to death. (*He grabs* HORACE.) Look, I don't like being spied on.

HORACE. I'm not spying on you. (*He throws* VAL's *hands off.* VAL *pushes him. He pushes him back. They start to fight. It's a savage fight.* ARCHIE, FELIX *and* ED *exit through audience during fight.*)

BUDDY (*Yelling*). Mama . . . Molly . . . Come watch . . . They're having a fight! Horace is going to kill Val! Kill him, Horace! Kill him!

CLAIRE (*Offstage*). Buddy. Where are you? Buddy, is that you down there? Molly, why didn't you tell me he left his room?

MOLLY (*Offstage*). He made me swear not to.

CLAIRE (*Offstage*). What in the world is going on—Do you know?

MOLLY (*Offstage*). No, Ma'am.

CLAIRE (*Offstage*). Buddy, Buddy where are you? (CLAIRE *and* MOLLY *enter porch.*) Stop it! Stop it! Val, have you gone crazy? Buddy, be careful! (*Fight ends.*) Go on home, Val.

VAL. That damn sneak was spying on us.

CLAIRE. Go on home, Val. (VAL *exits through gate.*)

MOLLY. Is he dead, Mama?

CLAIRE. I don't think so. (CLAIRE *bends over*

him.) Horace . . . Horace . . . *(HORACE opens his eyes.)* Are you all right? *(HORACE sits up.)*

HORACE. Yes. Where did he go?

CLAIRE. He went home. Now you go home, too. And no more fighting. Do you promise me? *(HORACE sways.)* Are you all right?

HORACE. I'll be all right.

CLAIRE. Buddy, did you bring him back over here? Buddy?

BUDDY. Molly, he gave you a nickel too.

CLAIRE. Buddy, I don't want you changing the subject on me. Did you go and get Horace and bring him here?

BUDDY. Well . . .

HORACE. I wasn't spying, you know. I don't spy on people. Buddy came over to the house to tell me he had come back and I said it was none of my business, and for him to go on home, but he was afraid to walk back by himself.

BUDDY. Because of this drunk man. He hollered like he was being stabbed to death and he hollered this lady's name. What was her name, Horace?

HORACE. Roberta.

BUDDY. Do you know who that is, Mama?

CLAIRE. No.

HORACE. I'll come back next weekend from Houston and take you to the dance.

CLAIRE. Thank you, but I've already been asked.

HORACE. Who asked you?

CLAIRE. Val.

HORACE. I thought he couldn't dance.

CLAIRE. He can't, but he's coming over before then and I'm going to teach him. Thank you anyway. *(HORACE is on his feet now.)* And he asked me to marry him, too.

HORACE. He did?

CLAIRE. Yes. Now I have two offers of marriage and I'm real confused about what to do.

MOLLY. Don't marry Val, Mama.

CLAIRE. Sh, now you mind your own business. Val is rough and all, but to tell you the truth I like him better than Ned.

MOLLY. Why?

CLAIRE. Because he's nearer my own age, of course, but then he doesn't have a job. He says he's going to get one soon, but I've never known him to keep a job more than a week or two. What do you think I ought to do, Horace?

HORACE. I don't know. I swear, I don't.

BUDDY. Don't marry Val.

CLAIRE. I'm asking Horace not you.

BUDDY. I'll run away from home if you marry Val.

CLAIRE. Be quiet, Buddy, and go on back to bed. And you too, Molly.

MOLLY. I like Uncle Ned. We have a picture of Uncle Ned in there. Did you ever see what he looks like, Horace?

CLAIRE. Yes, Horace knows what he looks like, Molly. Now go on. Both of you. *(They cross onto porch.)* Say goodnight to Horace.

BUDDY. Goodnight.

MOLLY. Goodnight.

HORACE. Goodnight.

CLAIRE. Goodnight. *(They exit through front door.)* Sissy says Val is just after what I have. She says he'll marry me and get me to sell my houses, spend the money, and leave me flat. That's what Sissy says he'll do. Val says I'm the first girl he's ever asked to marry because I'm the first girl he's ever loved. Ned says he's determined to be married before he's forty and he'll be forty soon. I guess you're too young to think about marrying yet, aren't you?

HORACE. I think about it.

CLAIRE. Did you ever meet a girl you'd like to marry?

HORACE. I like you.

CLAIRE. You don't think I'm too old for you?

HORACE. No. My Aunt Virgie is six years older than my Uncle Doc.

CLAIRE. You told me that . . . And are they happily married?

HORACE. Oh, yes. I think so.

CLAIRE. They certainly seem congenial.

HORACE. But I couldn't consider marriage to anyone at present . . .

CLAIRE. You couldn't?

HORACE. No. I couldn't. I have no job. I have no money. I would want to have a job and a little money saved before I married.

CLAIRE. After my husband died I swore I would never marry again. Maybe I won't. Maybe I won't marry anybody. I mean why Should I? I have a nice life. I can take care of myself and the children. I can have all the company I want. Sissy said my husband wanted me to marry again. He never said that to me, but Sissy said just before he died he called her into the room and he said "I know I'm going to die and I want you to promise one thing before I die; I want you to promise me you'll see to it that Claire marries again. Because I want my children to have a father as they're growing up." Do you believe he said that?

HORACE. I don't know.

CLAIRE. Sometimes I think he did, but then

again I think he didn't. Sissy will tell you anything to get you to do what she wants and she wants me to marry again that's for sure. I said "Sissy, worry about the others. You have three other sisters that have never married and in my opinion if they wait much longer are in danger of becoming old maids. Nag them about marrying." "They're not twenty-five yet," Sissy says, "so I wouldn't worry about their becoming old maids." "You were married at fourteen," I said, "Mama was fifteen and I was sixteen. What's wrong with them?" "They're waiting for rich husbands," she said. "So am I," I said. "Well, then marry Ned," she said, "he's rich." "How do you know what he's worth?" I said. "Well, I got eyes," she said, "he has a good job and is always buying you and the children presents." And he is of course. He gave me the ring and a wristwatch and the next time he comes he says he wants me to go with him to the jewelry store and pick me out a diamond bar pin. *(MOLLY comes out of front door.)* Have you gone crazy? It's four in the morning. Get on back to bed.

MOLLY. I can't find Uncle Ned's picture.

CLAIRE. What do you want with his picture?

MOLLY. I want to look at it.

CLAIRE. At four in the morning?

MOLLY. Where did you put it?

CLAIRE. My God, Molly, I don't know where I put it. It was on my dresser the last I remember.

MOLLY. It's not there now.

CLAIRE. I bet it is. I just bet you didn't see it, is all. You never can find anything.

MOLLY. I bet Val took it.

CLAIRE. Why would he take it?

MOLLY. Buddy said he did.

CLAIRE. Buddy is crazy. He blames Val for everything.

MOLLY. Here's the ring and the wristwatch he gave Mama.

CLAIRE. Where did you get those?

MOLLY. In your dresser. *(She shows them to HORACE.)* They're real diamonds. Aren't they, Mama?

CLAIRE. Yes.

MOLLY. He said they cost a lot of money, didn't he, Mama?

CLAIRE. Yes.

MOLLY. How much?

CLAIRE. He didn't say exactly. Now, go put them back where you found them. If you lost them I would die. *(BUDDY comes out with the picture through front door.)*

BUDDY. I found Uncle Ned's picture.

MOLLY. Where was it?

BUDDY. On Mama's dresser.

CLAIRE. See . . . I told you. Now get back to bed . . . both of you! And take the picture and the jewelry and put them back on my dresser. And in the future, if you please, don't touch my things without permission.

BUDDY. Let me show his picture to Horace first.

CLAIRE. My God, Buddy, he doesn't want to see his picture. How many times do I have to tell you a thing?

BUDDY. Do you want to see it, Horace? *(HORACE glances at it.)* Do you think he's a nice-looking fellow?

HORACE. Yes, I do.

BUDDY. Do you think he dyes his hair like Val says?

HORACE. I don't know, Buddy.

MOLLY. Val is a liar.

CLAIRE. Sh.

MOLLY. Buddy says he is.

CLAIRE. Don't call people liars. It isn't nice.

HORACE. Now go on to bed, Buddy. Mind your Mama.

MOLLY. Uncle Ned never sends us away. He just begs Mama to let us stay with him at all times.

CLAIRE. Well, Horace isn't your Uncle Ned. So go on to bed now both of you, before I get mad. *(They go through front door.)* Sissy says they need a man's discipline and I guess they do. Their Daddy never could say "No" to them about a thing. He was always soft-hearted as far as they were concerned. *(HORACE reaches out to her. They embrace. They kiss. She touches his face.)* Horace, you have blood on your face.

HORACE. It doesn't matter. *(He reaches out to her again.)*

CLAIRE. I'll go and get some water and wash it off. *(She starts away. He pulls her back to him.)*

HORACE. No, don't go.

CLAIRE. Well, give me your handkerchief and I'll wipe it off. *(He takes out his handkerchief. She wipes the blood away.)*

HORACE. When I come back from Houston, I'm going to get together with some fellows and a guitar and a fiddle player and we'll come over here one night and serenade you.

CLAIRE. Oh, that would be nice. I would like that. I've never had anyone serenade me in my whole life. *(ROGER comes in through audience. He has a bottle of whiskey.)*

ROGER. Oh, excuse me. I was looking for Val.

CLAIRE. Val's not here.

ROGER. Oh, excuse me. He told me he was coming over here.

CLAIRE. Well, he's not here.

ROGER. Was he here?

CLAIRE. Yes. But he's gone.

ROGER. Has he been gone long?

CLAIRE. Not too long.

ROGER. He asked me to loan him the money to buy a bottle of whiskey and I said I would and then he asked if I would mind buying it and bringing it to him over here as he was coming back over here to see you and he wanted to give you a little present.

CLAIRE. He was here but he left.

ROGER. Oh, I'm sorry I was so late getting over here, but he told me to take my time and I got to talking to some friends where I went to get the whiskey. I had to get this fellow out of bed to sell me the whiskey and that made him mad as a hornet at first, being awakened out of a sound sleep and all. But then I told him the circumstances and all and he was real nice about it. *(He hands her the bottle.)* I guess this is for you.

CLAIRE. Thank you.

ROGER. It's not the best whiskey in the world, but it is the best I could do this time of night. I think it's as good as the whiskey that fellow from Galveston brought you, though.

CLAIRE. I appreciate it, thank you.

ROGER. I meant to say earlier I'm not much of a dancer myself, but if you could stand it, I would like to take you to the dance next week myself.

CLAIRE. Thank you, but I've already been asked.

ROGER. Who asked you?

CLAIRE. Val.

ROGER. He did?

CLAIRE. Yes.

ROGER. When?

CLAIRE. Just now.

ROGER. He can't dance.

CLAIRE. I'm going to teach him. *(ROGER reaches in his hip pocket and takes out a bottle.)*

ROGER. I bought myself a bottle the same time I bought yours. Can I offer anyone a drink?

CLAIRE. Not me. Thank you.

ROGER. Horace?

HORACE. No, thank you.

ROGER. Do you mind if I have one? I find it damp and cold out. *(He has a swig. MOLLY calls from inside the house.)*

MOLLY. Mama . . .

CLAIRE. What?

MOLLY. Buddy has Uncle Ned's picture in bed with him. *(CLAIRE goes inside the house. Lines are said from inside the house.)*

CLAIRE *(Offstage)*. Has he gone crazy? Why is he doing something foolish like that?

MOLLY *(Offstage)*. I had it under my pillow and as I was falling asleep, he snuck over and took it and put it in his bed.

CLAIRE *(Offstage)*. What do you want me to do about it?

MOLLY *(Offstage)*. I want it under my pillow.

CLAIRE *(Offstage)*. Oh, my God!

ROGER. Val says he stays over here sometimes. You know like a husband and wife. But Val is such a big liar I don't know if he's telling the truth or not. Do you think he does?

HORACE. I don't know.

ROGER. He says he tells her he's going to marry her, so she'll let him stay. But he says he don't have no intention of marrying nobody. I thought to myself, she'd be a fool to marry you, a man that can't even buy a bottle of whiskey as a present. I think she's right pretty. Don't you?

HORACE. Yes, I do.

ROGER. And she comes from a lovely family, you know.

HORACE. I know she does.

ROGER. She has four sisters. One is married and three aren't. The married one is called, "Sissy." The unmarried ones are called Nadine, Lily Belle and Clara Gertrude.

HORACE. Yes. I know them all.

ROGER. They are going to have a hard time getting married; they are all three plain. I understand they all went to live with an aunt in Nagadoches as no one here will ask them out . . . *(A pause.)* Claire is the beauty. She's as pretty as any girl in town. Do you think she would go out with me if I asked her?

HORACE. Who?

ROGER. Miss Claire.

HORACE. I don't know.

ROGER. Val says she wouldn't. He says I'm not refined enough for her. "I may not be refined," I says, "but I have a job and I work steady." I don't have to borrow money to buy anyone a bottle of whiskey. Do you always bring a present when you come to see her?

HORACE. Yes, I do.

ROGER. What did you bring tonight?

HORACE. Candy.

ROGER. Do you think any of it's handy? I have a sweet tooth. I'd like a piece of candy.

HORACE. It's all gone.

ROGER. That's all right. What kind of candy was it?

HORACE. Assorted chocolates.

ROGER. I love chocolates of all kinds. *(A pause.)* I like hot tamales, too. Do you like hot tamales?

HORACE. Yes, I do.

ROGER. That Mescan Eli sure makes good hot tamales. Don't you think so?

HORACE. Yes, I do.

ROGER. I think I heard you say you're going to business school?

HORACE. Yes, in Houston.

ROGER. I'd have a hard time in business school even if I could afford it. I only went to the second grade in school. How far did you go?

HORACE. Sixth.

ROGER. Why did you quit?

HORACE. I had to go to work.

ROGER. Where did you work?

HORACE. All over. At a plantation store, over in a store in Glen Flora, then for my Uncle here and Mr. Jackson.

ROGER. That's quite a record. *(A pause.)* Do you prefer the light or the dark meat of chicken?

HORACE. The light.

ROGER. I prefer the dark—drumsticks and second joints. *(A pause.)* My God, there's daylight beginning! You reckon she'll be back out?

HORACE. I don't know.

ROGER. I expect she'll be back to say good night to you at least. *(A pause.)* Well, I'll say good night to you. I have to work tomorrow. Say good night to Claire for me. Tell her I'm sorry I had to leave before I could tell her good night myself. *(ROGER exits U.R. CLAIRE comes out front door.)*

CLAIRE. It's come to me just as clear what to do. I'm not going to marry anybody.

HORACE. You're not?

CLAIRE. No. I'm going to sell these three houses and move to Houston with the children and get me a duplex. We can live downstairs and rent out the upstairs, that way I'll always have some income. So, don't be surprised if you get a call at your boarding house saying I'm here. *(A pause.)* Kiss me good night now and go home. I'm mortally tired and I know you must be. *(He kisses her.)* I'm so relieved now it's come to me what to do. The kids almost had a fit when I told them I wasn't going to marry Ned. But I said,

"Shoot, I'm not getting married just to please you. I have a right to lead my own life." Don't you think?

HORACE. Yes, I do. *(She kisses him again.)*

CLAIRE. Good night, Horace.

HORACE. Good night.

CLAIRE. Buddy and Molly say good night.

HORACE. Tell them good night for me.

CLAIRE. They sure like you.

HORACE. I like them.

CLAIRE. Next to Ned they say they like you best of all the men that come to see me.

HORACE. Thank you.

CLAIRE. Here's my picture I promised you.

HORACE. Thank you very much. *(A pause.)* Claire?

CLAIRE. Yes.

HORACE. I'm glad you're not marrying right away. I'm certainly glad about that.

CLAIRE. Are you? Well I'm glad about it, too. Good night.

HORACE. Good night. *(HORACE holds on porch steps. CLAIRE exits through front door. FELIX, ARCHIE and SPENCE enter through audience and sit at table. ED enters, crosses to bed and collapses.)*

SPENCE. Because you don't keep your mind on the damn game. Poker is a serious business. It's a science. I saw thousands of dollars pass hands tonight. Luck had nothing to do with it. Cool heads won. There were two gamblers there from Galveston. They never said a word to nobody all evening. Just kept their eyes on the cards. Of course, everybody says they won by cheating.

ARCHIE. Do you think they cheated?

SPENCE. If they did, no one caught them at it.

ARCHIE. One of those gamblers was red-headed and the other had black hair.

SPENCE. That's right. *(HORACE comes off steps crosses to dresser. He has the picture of CLAIRE.)*

ARCHIE. We found out who Roberta was.

HORACE. Who is she?

ARCHIE. She's a twin. She has a twin sister named Alberta. Alberta and Roberta. They travel in a medicine show. Spence and Ed met them over at a barbecue outside of Ganado.

HORACE. What were they doing in Ganado?

SPENCE. I don't know, I didn't ask them. *(A pause.)* I went over to that gambling game at Little Bobby's. Your Uncle Albert was in it. He lost his shirt.

HORACE. It's not the first time.

SPENCE. But it might be the last. This time they got him for fifteen thousand dollars. He put up his house and the stock of his store . . . everything just to stay in the game.

FELIX. Who took his money? Anyone from here?

SPENCE. No, those two gamblers from Galveston. Someone said they had been run out of Galveston for cheating. I don't know about that. But they've taken everything he has. *(A Pause.)* Someone asked him if he was going to quit gambling now that he's lost everything. "The day I quit gambling," he says, "is the day I die."

ED. *(Mutters).* Roberta . . . Roberta . . .

SPENCE. You never can tell about old Ed can you? I thought he was stuck on Alberta. Of course, it was hard to tell them apart. I thought Roberta was the one I had, but I could have been wrong. I told them they should wear signs so you could tell them apart. *(A pause.)* How was the widow?

HORACE. She was all right.

FELIX. Whose picture is that?

HORACE. Claire's. (FELIX *takes it.)*

FELIX *(Reading).* "For Horace lest he forget his friend, Claire."

SPENCE. Lest he forget?

ARCHIE. That's what it says.

SPENCE. Lest he forget?

ARCHIE. Yes.

SPENCE. What happened to your face?

HORACE. I got into a fight.

SPENCE. Who with?

HORACE. Val.

SPENCE. Leave him alone. He cut a man once you know fighting over a woman. Cut him from ear to ear.

FELIX. Did the man die?

SPENCE. I don't think so.

BUDDY *(Calling from audience).* Horace . . . Horace (HORACE *goes D.C.)*

HORACE. Yes, Buddy.

BUDDY. My Mama says to stop by on the way to the station. She has something to tell you.

HORACE. All right, Buddy. Tell her I'm packing now. I'll be by in about an hour.

BUDDY. Yes, sir. How is that man now?

HORACE. What man?

BUDDY. The one that was hollering so.

HORACE. He's asleep.

BUDDY. Did you ever find out who Roberta was?

HORACE. Yes. It was a girl he met over in Ganado.

BUDDY. Yes, Sir. *(He goes.* HORACE *gets a suitcase and he begins to pack.)*

SPENCE. I got someone to take your share of the rent while you're gone, Horace.

HORACE. Good.

FELIX. Do you think you're ever coming back, Horace?

HORACE. I don't know.

SPENCE. I have five dollars says he'll never come back . . . any takers?

FELIX. You'll bet on anything.

ARCHIE. I'll bet you'll meet plenty of pretty widows in Houston, Horace.

HORACE. Think so?

FELIX. Is Claire the first widow you've gone with?

HORACE. Yes.

ARCHIE. She's the first widow anyone's gone with. There is no other widow here, is there?

FELIX. Not under fifty.

ED *(Muttering).* Roberta . . . Roberta . . .

ARCHIE. Were those twins pretty?

SPENCE. Pretty enough.

FELIX. They all look alike in the dark. (HORACE *continues packing.)*

ARCHIE. Let's go across the track and get a woman.

FELIX. I'm broke.

SPENCE. Don't you even have fifty cents? You can have any woman over there for fifty cents.

FELIX. I don't have a dime.

ARCHIE. How are you going to eat to-day?

FELIX. I don't know. I'll go over to my Aunt's and see if she'll feed me.

SPENCE. Here, I'll loan you fifty cents. *(He hands it to him.)*

FELIX. Thanks. *(He takes it.)*

ARCHIE. We better wake up Ed. He'll be mad if he wakes up and finds we've gone without him.

SPENCE. He's drunk. He's not going to wake up.

ARCHIE. You want to come along, Horace?

HORACE. I don't have time. My train leaves at eight o'clock.

ARCHIE. Don't study too hard.

HORACE. I won't.

SPENCE. Good luck to you, Horace.

HORACE. Thanks.

FELIX. Send us a postcard.

HORACE. I will. *(They exit through audience.* HORACE *finishes packing, exits through audience.)*

ED *(As he exits through audience).* Roberta . . . Roberta . . . *(As* ED *exits,* CLAIRE, MOLLY, *and* BUDDY *enter D.R.)*

MOLLY. Mama, I can't find my spelling book.

CLAIRE. Did you leave it in your room?

MOLLY. No.

CLAIRE. Are you sure?

MOLLY. Yes.

BUDDY *(Starting to leave auditorium).* I'm going to school now.

CLAIRE. You wait for Molly, Buddy.

BUDDY. No, I'll be late. I don't want to be late.

MOLLY. Wait for me, Buddy.

BUDDY. Well, come on then.

MOLLY. I can't go without my spelling book. *(CLAIRE is looking around the room.)*

CLAIRE. Here it is. Now see. Kiss me goodbye. *(MOLLY does so.)* Buddy, kiss me goodbye. *(He does so. They exit through auditorium. CLAIRE puts on "Waltz Me Around Again, Willie." HORACE enters through gate, crosses onto porch with suitcase.)* Oh, hello, Horace. On your way?

HORACE. Yes.

CLAIRE. Thank you for coming by. I said to the children, "Horace is going to think I'm crazy asking him to stop by on his way to the train," but I wanted to tell you myself that I changed my mind after you left. I looked at the children asleep and I thought, "What if the duplex in Houston doesn't work out and I can't find a renter and all my money will be gone and what will become then of me and the children?" I have to think of what will become of them, you know, because if I don't who will? I woke them both up and we had a good long talk and I decided then and there to marry Ned for their sake, so I sent him a wire as to my decision to marry him and I asked him to come here next weekend. When I did that I said to Buddy, "You go tell Horace now, to come by here on the way to the train so I can tell him my decision . . . as I want him to hear it from nobody but me." Do you think I'm doing the right thing?

HORACE. I guess so.

CLAIRE. The children do. They couldn't wait to get to school and tell all their friends. They went over to Sissy's and woke her up to tell her. Anyway, right or wrong, we won't be here when you come home.

HORACE. You won't?

CLAIRE. No. Because Ned wants us to live in his house in Galveston. So we'll move there after we're married. I don't know what will happen to his sister.

HORACE. Maybe she'll live on with you.

CLAIRE. Maybe so. Ned says she's sweet and easy to get along with and likes children as much as he does. If you're ever in Galveston, come to see us and have a meal with us.

HORACE. Thank you. *(She hands him paper.)*

CLAIRE. I wrote out the address for you.

HORACE. Thank you.

CLAIRE. Ned says they have a lot of oleander in the front and back yard. I love them. Don't you?

HORACE. Yes. My father's people all lived in Galveston.

CLAIRE. Did they?

HORACE. Yes, his father was sent there by the Confederate government. He was in charge of shipping cotton for the Confederacy.

CLAIRE. If you're going to be a traveling man, you and Ned will have a lot in common.

HORACE. Well, I'm not sure, of course, that I'll be a traveling man. It's just that when I finish my business course, I hope to get a job traveling.

CLAIRE. Well, if you do, I hope you will have great success at it. Ned says it pays very well if you're good at it.

HORACE. I've heard that, too.

CLAIRE. And I'm sure you'll be good at it. You have a very nice personality.

HORACE. Thank you. I guess I'll have to go now, Claire.

CLAIRE. I know. I'd ask you to kiss me goodbye, but it's daylight and all the neighbors are watching.

HORACE. I understand.

CLAIRE. It's been very nice knowing you and the children and I wish you a lot of luck.

HORACE. Claire, if I come into the house could I kiss you goodbye?

CLAIRE. Sure. *(She goes inside. He follows her. He kisses her. A train whistle blows.)* There's your train. Hurry, or you'll miss it. *(They cross onto porch. He gets his suitcase.)*

HORACE. So long, Claire.

CLAIRE. So long.

HORACE. Good luck.

CLAIRE. Good luck to you. *(The train whistle blows again. He crosses the stage. When he reaches D. She calls out.)* Good luck.

HORACE. Thank you. Good luck to you. *(She waves a last farewell. After HORACE exits she has one final.)*

CLAIRE. Good luck. *(She turns and exits through front door. As the lights fade, "Waltz Me Around Again, Willie" is played.)*

Curtain

Burn This

LANFORD WILSON

The Circle Repertory production of *Burn This* was first presented by Gordon Davidson at the Mark Taper Forum in Los Angeles, California, on January 22, 1987. The cast was:

ANNA	Joan Allen
BURTON	Jonathan Hogan
LARRY	Lou Liberatore
PALE	John Malkovich

Directed by Marshall W. Mason
Settings by John Lee Beatty
Costumes by Laura Crow
Lighting by Dennis Parichy
Music by Peter Kater
Fight direction by Randy Kovitz
Dramaturg for the production was Jack Viertel
Production Stage Manager: Mary Michele Miner

The production played at the 890 Theatre in New York City, produced by the Circle Repertory Company for one month starting February 18, 1987; and at the Royal George Theatre in Chicago, produced by the Steppenwolf Theatre Company, beginning on September 13, 1987

Burn This opened in New York City at the Plymouth Theatre on October 14, 1987, produced by James B. Freydberg, Stephen Graham, Susan Quint Gallin, Max Weitzenhoffer, Harold Reed, and Maggie Lear

Burn This was written on commission from the Circle Repertory Company

Burn This was first presented in 1987 at the Mark Taper Forum in Los Angeles and subsequently moved to the Plymouth Theatre in New York. The play concerns the aftermath of the accidental death of a young gay man, and the encounter between his two roommates and his boorish brother. A love story that depicts the search for real attachments in a divisive world; *Burn This* is similar to Terrence McNally's *Frankie and Johnny in the Clair de Lune* in its portrayal of people who angrily challenge each other to embark on honest relationships.

The language of this play is undeniably vulgar, a departure for author Lanford Wilson, who states: "It is life as we know it, not tempered or censored for the stage. Everyone says what they're thinking. . . ." The title came from Wilson's instinctively scrawling across the bottom of every page as he worked on the play: "Burn this." Wilson says, "A writer isn't doing his job unless he feels he'd better destroy the work. A story should become a dangerous secret he can't risk telling."

Marshall W. Mason, who has assisted Wilson with the writing of his plays and has directed most of them since 1965, states, "Both Lanford and I are very interested in people seen in their social, political, and psychological context. His plays emphasize the choices a human being encounters and the values that influence those choices."

The play was inspired partly by David Rabe and partly by an anxiety attack. "I don't think I would have written *Burn This* if I hadn't seen *Hurlyburly* four times," Wilson says. "It's almost as if someone has thrown down a gauntlet and you decide to pick it up." He adds, "I had mentioned a very brief outline to a friend and he promptly said that it reminded him of a similar situation. . . . He told me about having to go to his roommate's funeral in Connecticut . . . and the dead boy's family having no idea he was gay. Then having to go out with his dead roommate's brother, a rough raw guy who drank only brandy." Nothing further happened with the story for four years, until Wilson, who hadn't written anything for three years, panicked. "I couldn't work here . . . at home . . . I couldn't work anywhere. . . . I said: 'Well, write an anxiety attack,' and before I knew it, I had one page and this character, Pale . . . very terrifying. It lasted about two days. . . . I wrote one page about some guy complaining about things, about his brother, about his life . . . I said, 'What the hell is that?' and suddenly I said, 'My God, that guy at the funeral!' "

Wilson flew through a first draft in four months. The dead man, Bobby, became a dancer, and the brother, Pale (named for his predilection for VSOP brandy), was modeled partly on a bartender, partly on the brother Wilson had heard about, and partly on a sound editor Wilson knew: "I took the circumstances of one, the sound of another, and the history of the third." The character of Anna, one of Bobby's two roommates, was based on a modern dancer Wilson had once shared an apartment with in Chicago. "That's where I got all the specifics of a dancer's life," he says.

Lanford Wilson is one of this country's few experimental playwrights to achieve commercial success. With Marshall W. Mason and Tanya Berezin, he founded the Circle Repertory Company, of which he is the resident playwright. Wilson was born in 1937 in Lebanon, Missouri. In 1955, he moved to San Diego to live with his estranged father, a reunion later depicted in the play *Lemon Sky*. For a year, Wilson attended San Diego State College, where he discovered an ability to create strong, naturalistic dialogue through writing short stories. He then left California for Chicago, where he worked as an apprentice artist for an advertising agency, continued to write short stories, and discovered the theatre. "I was completely enthralled. In *Brigadoon,* the stage was covered with a mist and out of nowhere this town appeared. . . . For me, at that time, it was magic."

Arriving in New York during the summer of 1962, Wilson gravitated toward Off Off Broadway theatre, where he met Joe Cino, whose Caffe Cino gave nine-performances runs of plays by aspiring playwrights. "We wrote furiously ... a play a week. I don't think we edited our plays or rewrote them. ..." *So Long at the Fair* was Wilson's first Caffe Cino play. In 1964, Cino mounted Wilson's *The Madness of Lady Bright*, immediately canceling all other plays and extending *Lady Bright*'s run for 168 performances. Wilson's other plays during this time included *Home Free, Ludlow Fair, This Is the Rill Speaking, Days Ahead,* and *Wandering. Sand Castle* premiered in 1965 at Cafe La Mama. The *Rimers of Eldritch,* produced in 1967, won the Drama Desk Award. That same year, Wilson also won a Rockefeller Grant for playwriting and an ABC fellowship for motion-picture writing at Yale.

The *Gingham Dog, Serenading Louie, Lemon Sky, The Family Continues, The Great Nebula in Orion,* and *Ikke, Ikke, Nye, Nye* followed between 1968 and 1972. *The Hot L Baltimore* (1973) was Wilson's first real commercial success; it won an Obie Award for Best Play. Later successes include *The Mound Builders* (1975; Obie Award winner), *Brontosaurus* (1977), and the celebrated Talley trilogy: *Fifth of July* (1978; Tony nomination, Best Play), *Talley's Folly* (1979; Pulitzer Prize for drama, Theatre Club Award, New York Critics Circle Award, Tony nomination, Best Play), and *Talley and Son* (1981). In 1990, Wilson won the John Steinbeck Award for Sustained Achievement.

Other plays written by Lanford Wilson include *Balm in Gilead* (1965), *Sextet* (1971), *The Migrants* (written with Tennessee Williams, 1972), *Angels Fall* (1982), *The Betrothal* (1988), and *A Poster of the Cosmos* (1988). He also wrote the libretto for Lee Hoiby's opera of Tennessee Williams's *Summer and Smoke* and *Taxi!,* a television play.

THE CHARACTERS

ANNA
BURTON
LARRY
PALE

ACT ONE

The setting is a huge loft in a converted cast-iron building in lower Manhattan, New York City. Factory windows, a very large sloping skylight, a kitchen area, a sleeping loft, a hall to the bathroom and LARRY'*s bedroom, and another door to* ANNA'*s bedroom. The place is sparsely furnished. There is an exercise barre on one mirrored wall and a dining area. There are pipes on the ceiling, and an old sprinkler system is still intact. There is new oak flooring; the walls are white; the only picture is a large framed dance poster. A fire escape runs across the entire upstage.*

It is the sort of place that you would kill for or wouldn't be caught dead in.

The time is the present. It is six o'clock in the evening, mid-October. The sky has the least color left, one lamp has been turned on.

ANNA *is huddled on a sofa, smoking. She has a drink. She is thirty-two, very beautiful, tall and strong. A dancer. A buzzer sounds. A moment later it sounds again. She hears it this time and jumps. She looks at the buzzer. It sounds again. She gets up and goes to it.*

———

ANNA. Hello?

BURTON'S VOICE. Hi, it's me. I just heard.

ANNA. Uh, Burton, could we make it another . . . *(Sighs, buzzes him in, opens the apartment door and leaves, going toward the bathroom. After a moment* BURTON *comes in. He is tall, athletic, and rather good-looking. He has big feet and big hands that he admires, cracking his knuckles, stretching his neck and shoulders. He is a writer and very interested in his process. He is in a sweat suit)*

BURTON. Oh, God, darlin', I heard twenty minutes ago.

ANNA. Yeah, it's not been fun. I didn't know if I wanted to let you in. I think if I have someone to cry on, I'll fall apart completely.

BURTON. Oh, God, how'd it happen?

ANNA. Oh, he and Dom rented a boat—you know, a little motorboat, and some yacht or something ran them down.

BURTON. Goddamn.

ANNA. They were in the middle of the bay—it was just getting dark. Freak accident. They were taking their things off the island. They could have ferried the damn car over, but I guess they thought a boat would be more of an adventure, I don't know. The assholes. I've just been so angry with him. I mean, if you don't swim, damnit! There was a huge picture of Robbie in the *Post.* I threw it out. BRILLIANT YOUNG DANCER DROWNS. That bit. They shipped Dom's body back to California.

BURTON. That's where his folks are? Oh, man. I was gonna run, I saw Kelly in the park, I just hopped in a cab. You went to the funeral?

ANNA. Go? God. Larry and I spent the best years of our lives at that funeral yesterday. And then I got shanghaied into spending the night with the family.

BURTON. Oh, God.

ANNA. Really. I've been smoking one of Robbie's cigarettes that he squirreled away. First cigarette I've had since college. I've forgot how to smoke. And drinking vodka. I feel like a piece of shit, I'm not very good company.

BURTON. No, come on. I just wish I'd been here for you.

ANNA. Who knew where to reach you?

BURTON. I called from the lodge Wednesday, that's the only phone we saw in a week.

ANNA. Yeah, I got the message. Thanks. The kid who took it is a major fan of yours.

BURTON. Of mine?

ANNA. He was impressed all to hell.

BURTON. Nobody knows who writes movies.

ANNA. Sure they do. He's a sci-fi freak. He thinks you and . . . somebody are the two best writers in the business.

BURTON. Exactly.

*(*LARRY *enters holding groceries. He is twenty-seven, medium everything, very bright, gay)*

LARRY. When the hell did you get home? I've been calling all day.

ANNA. I'm sorry, love, I turned the phone off.

LARRY *(To* BURTON*).* Now you show up.

BURTON. Great timing, huh?

LARRY. Where were you?

ANNA. You don't want to know, really.

BURTON. She got waylaid into spending the night with the family.

LARRY. Oh, God.

ANNA. Really. *(She refills her drink)*

LARRY. Vodka? Is that two?

ANNA. I think three.

LARRY. You're going to get sloppy. Not that it matters. What do you want? You want bright and cheery, nothing happened? You want quiet, leave me alone? Or maybe talk about it and cry? You know me. I'm always willing to drape the joint in crepe.

ANNA. How are you?

LARRY. Oh, who knows? Hi, beautiful. How was Canada?

BURTON. Great. Cold. Snowy. Exhausting. How's the advertising business?

LARRY. It sucks the big one.

ANNA. Poor baby, everything got dumped on Larry. You were in Canada, I was in Houston. He had to go out there and identify Dom and Robbie, notify their families, get Robbie's suit down for the funeral. Had to buy a dress shirt and tie; Robbie didn't own one.

LARRY. Yeah, it was a lot of laughs. She told you about the funeral?

BURTON. I just walked in.

LARRY. The single most depressing experience of my life.

ANNA. Really. There was this great baroque maroon-and-gold casket with these ormolu geegaws all over it—angels and swags. Robbie would have hated it.

LARRY. It looked like a giant Spode soup tureen.

ANNA. Everything was wrong. The whole company's in Sacramento, so only about six of his friends were there. The eulogy was— the priest hadn't seen him in six years. His folks hadn't seen him in five, did you know that?

LARRY. Jesus.

ANNA. Well, have you ever heard him talk about his family?

LARRY. One brother, I think.

ANNA. Now we know why. *(To* BURTON*)* There's brothers and sisters, aunts and uncles for days. And none of them had seen him dance!

BURTON. You gotta be kidding.

ANNA. Never. Can you believe it? We couldn't believe it. Oh, God, it was a total nightmare.

LARRY. They had no idea who he was at all.

ANNA. I was the *girlfriend,* can you stand it?

BURTON. Oh, good Lord.

ANNA. It hadn't even crossed my mind. Of course, living with a woman, what else is it going to be?

BURTON. Yeah, but he was hardly living in a closet. I mean, interviews in *The Advocate.*

ANNA. Well, they obviously don't subscribe. Oh, God. Okay. Larry and I take the bus out there.

LARRY. The whole town is a combat zone.

ANNA. I don't know what industry it was built on, but it's not there anymore.

LARRY. In its heyday it couldn't have been much more than a place to leave.

ANNA. At the station we're met by a rented black Cadillac and either the sister or sister-in-law. Did you hear?

LARRY. Not a word.

ANNA. She spoke so softly; we asked three times and finally just pretended to hear. We get to the church—

LARRY. Everyone descended on Anna like a plague of grasshoppers.

ANNA. No joke, they just thrashed me. I'm chaff.

LARRY. She's rushed off to the first five rows, with the family.

ANNA. I said, I'm the grieving—

BURTON. You're the bereaved widow, of course.

ANNA. Some aunt patting my arm, everyone sobbing and beating their breasts. Most of them had never seen him in their lives, you understand. We get to the cemetery. I got the distinct feeling I was expected to throw myself across that hideous casket.

LARRY. Absolutely.

ANNA. I'd have given fifty dollars for a veil. *(Pause)* I just kept thinking the three of us grew up in such different circumstances. I mean, what could I know about the world living in Highland Park? But, Lord, Robbie grew up in such—I looked for his teacher, I couldn't remember her name; I asked them, they'd never even heard of her.

BURTON. He probably had to sneak off to class.

ANNA. No, he did, literally, I knew that. I tried to tell them about the dance Robbie and I were working on and how important he was to me. With all that drive. Having a friend who was that good pushing you. They wouldn't let me talk about his dancing at all. I thought I could be truthful about something.

BURTON. I wanted to see it.

ANNA. Our dance?

LARRY. It was good.

ANNA. Yeah, even Larry liked it. No, it had no volume, it was too much like Charley's work, anyway. But even my mother keeps a scrapbook, and all she wants is grandchildren.

BURTON. Someone to take over the business.

ANNA. Listen, that's probably all I'm good for, anyway. And quick. Oh, Lord, tell us about Canada. Maybe it'll take my mind off myself.

LARRY. No joke, we've been like this for three days.

BURTON. Feel my thigh. Just her.

ANNA. Good Lord. It must have been beautiful, huh?

BURTON. Yeah, but more strange. Very strange things happen to you up there. Very disconcerting. Two days it's seventy something, we're skiing across this hilltop; we're stark naked, carrying our backpacks.

LARRY. That must have been scenic. *(He goes to his room)*

BURTON. Oh sure. Next day it was ten degrees and snowing. But amazing country. Incredible skies. Some of the land looks like the moon, all gouged out. Very heavy glacier activity. Very barren, very lonely. I missed you up there. I think I came up with an idea, though.

LARRY. God knows we need it.

ANNA. That's great.

BURTON. Whole new thing, not a space flick. Whole different venue. Takes place in maybe Jasper, way up in northern Alberta in ... with the aurora and ... I don't know, about ten different things. This one's weird. Amazing things happen to your mind, you feel like you're all alone, or you're one with the ... something, or ... well ... we don't have to talk about it now.

ANNA. No, what? Something should come from this week.

BURTON *(Getting juice from the fridge)*. It was like a vision I had while we were going along this ridge, like the top of the world—all this snow, this bright sun, you get into a kind of trance. And I saw this whole story, kind of a weird-ass love story—

ANNA. Burton, a love story?

BURTON. —or really more like a—what? The wives of the whalers or sailors, out to sea ...

ANNA. The wives out to sea?

BURTON. No, you know. Oh, great. The men, for years on end and the wives waiting on their widow's walk, waiting, walking back and forth, watching the water, the waves coming in, the sun going down, and the men

never coming home. Sort of their *heart,* or the men out there on the sea, their *heart.* Where's that love, or what is it, that power that allows those people to sustain that feeling? Through loss, through death. Is it less than the feelings we have? So they can humanly *cope?* Or is it more? I think they felt things in a much more profound way. There's some humongous mega-passion, something felt much deeper than we know. I don't know.

ANNA. I love it when you get an idea. You're so confused and enthusiastic.

BURTON. Am I?

ANNA. It's a good sign.

BURTON. It's there, it's just all fragmented. I had this book of Nordic tales, totally foreign from our stupid urban microcosm, all that crap.

ANNA. You never write urban microcosms, anyway.

BURTON. Well, I know, thank God. But out there ... or the prairies, hell, the seas of grass, those huge distances, sodbusters, no one within three thousand miles. What *sustains* those people? Out to sea, two or three years at a time, some of those whaling voyages; the fortitude of that kind of love. God ... But light. Subtle. Don't bang 'em over the head. I don't know. *(Pause)* I don't think I can use it.

ANNA. Why not? It sounds terrific.

BURTON. No, it's all been done. It's not right. I'd write it, in shooting it'd all be degenerated into some goddamned gothic horror. The handsome sailor away at sea, the evil brother usurps the estate. Seen it a thousand times. Write a sodbuster, they'd turn out *Little House on the Prairie.*

(LARRY reenters)

ANNA. No, do it. I want to see it.

BURTON. No, that's just a phantom that haunts you up there. Everything is so good it makes you want to do something good, too. Or I just haven't got that thing yet ... how that environment impinges on the personalities, what that does to the women, the men ... the ... what?

LARRY. Robots.

BURTON. No robots. I love the space stuff, but on this one I'm looking for passions, faith, myths, love, derring-do, for godsake. Heroes and heroines.

LARRY. Senta throwing herself into the sea.

BURTON. Who's Senta?

LARRY. After the Dutchman sails away.

BURTON. I don't know it.

LARRY. *The Flying Dutchman.*

BURTON. I don't know *The Flying* fuckin' *Dutchman.*

ANNA. It's probably in your book of Nordic myths.

LARRY. Really. The Dutchman's this sailor who is like condemned to perdition unless he finds a girl who'll really love him. But he can come ashore only about once every seven years to look for her.

BURTON. Why?

LARRY. You don't ask why in Wagner. So he goes to Norway and Senta falls in love with him, but she has this boyfriend hanging around and the Dutchman gets uptight and sails off again. And Senta throws herself into the . . . fjord.

BURTON. To prove she loved him.

LARRY. To save him from perdition, to break the spell. The sea starts boiling, the Dutchman's ship sinks, all hell breaks loose.

ANNA. Big finish.

BURTON. I like the sea boiling, but I'm not that much of an opera queen.

LARRY. I'm not an opera queen, Burton. I've seen opera queens, and believe me, I rank no higher than Lady-in-Waiting.

BURTON *(Looks at his watch)*. Oh, Christ, I have to call Signer. I was supposed to have dinner with him tonight.

ANNA. No, don't call it off, tell him the new idea.

BURTON. What do you want to do?

ANNA. I'm going to soak in a tub. Really. I've been in these clothes for two days. You go. Tell him about—

BURTON. No, I'm not ready for him. I shouldn't even be talking about it at this stage. It's the same song every time I see him. God knows what I'd say. Met him once after he'd read a first draft; he's got this crushed look, he hands me the script, says, "What happened to the tiny Australian Bushman?" I still don't know what the fuck he was talking about.

LARRY. Doesn't it just rip you to pieces what they do to your scripts? Did you see *Far Voyager?* After they got through with it?

BURTON. I saw my bank account when they bought it.

LARRY. You don't need money.

BURTON. Tell me what I need.

LARRY. You're rich as Croesus; you were born rich as Croesus.

BURTON. Even Croesus needed money.

LARRY. There was some beautiful writing in—

BURTON. Beautiful writing? It's anathema

to a movie. No, you can't get involved with it. You'd kill yourself. You can't worry what they're going to do to it. Start something else; take your two hundred thou and split.

LARRY. It could have been a good movie if you'd—

BURTON. It couldn't have been a good movie; there is no such thing as a good movie.

LARRY. *Far Voyager* was wonderful before—

BURTON. There are no good movies. Did you coach him? It can't happen. There cannot be a good movie. When a good movie happens, which it might, on a roll of the dice, once in five years, it's like this total aberration, a freak of nature like the Grand Canyon, they're ashamed of it. They can't wait to remake it in another ten years and fuck it up the way it's supposed to be. Movies are some banker's speculation about how the American adolescents want to see themselves that week. Period. They're produced by whores, written by whores, directed by—

LARRY. Burton, you don't have to tell me about whores, you're talking to someone who works in advertising. Besides, I don't want to hear it. I think movies are gorgeous: "Who are you? Where did you come from? What do you want? It's me, isn't it? You've always wanted me. You want to have your filthy way with me in the hot desert sun. Ravage me like I've never been ravaged before." *Lust in the Dust.*

BURTON. He memorized that?

LARRY. Burton, you don't memorize. There are some things so true that they enter your soul as you hear them. You should be producing your own stuff, anyway; at least you wouldn't have done that Pit and the Pendulum scene in *Far Voyager.* Saved by forty midgets.

BURTON. *Midgets?*

LARRY. I thought you saw it.

BURTON. No, I just wrote it; I couldn't sit through it. I heard what they did. The cave with the Vampire Queen—hanging upside down. No point in putting yourself through that kind of . . . Midgets?

LARRY. Munchkins. They did everything but sing "Ding Dong the Witch Is Dead."

BURTON. Oh, Jesus. Well, Signer's short, he gets off on little people. I'm not as intrepid as Anna: quitting dance, trying to break into choreography . . .

ANNA. Huh? Oh yeah, at this late date. By myself.

LARRY. What, doll?

ANNA. Nothing. What?

BURTON. We're being insensitive and stupid.

ANNA. No, I'm just out of it.

BURTON. Would it be better if I left?

ANNA. Actually, maybe so.

BURTON. Okay.

ANNA. Really. You should talk about Canada and I want to hear, but all I want to do right now is soak in a hot tub. What time's your dinner?

BURTON. I'll have to get some of this in the computer if I'm going to see him. I came over, I didn't know you'd still be here. You finished with Houston?

ANNA. You kidding? I've got to go back at noon for the reception tomorrow night. I didn't even pack, I just got on a plane. I don't suppose you have any desire to see Houston?

BURTON. Why not?

ANNA. No, I'm okay. I'm glad you're back.

BURTON. When we're not feeling so bad about this, we've got to get away. Go up to the Vineyard. Take a week off.

ANNA. Maybe it's time for us to just move up there permanently.

BURTON. I'd love it.

LARRY. Bye, beautiful.

BURTON. Yeah, sure. Take care of her. I gotta get gone. Call tomorrow.

ANNA. Bye-bye.

(BURTON *exits*)

LARRY. I don't know why you don't just marry him and buy things.

ANNA. I'm glad he's come up with something. I think he was beginning to panic.

LARRY. I didn't visibly blanch when he said he gets two hundred thousand dollars for a first draft, did I?

ANNA. Well, he's got a name. You know. He's good. God, I'm as stiff as a board. I haven't exercised in two days. I'm completely out of touch with my body.

LARRY. When's your plane tomorrow?

ANNA. Noon. But I'm back the day after. Here for a week, then go to Seattle for no more than six days, and then that's it. No more teaching other companies Charley's dance.

LARRY. Concentrate on your own work.

ANNA. Whatever that is. I've already signed up for a class just to get Charley's damn movements out of my muscles. No lie; I could walk down the street, it's Charley walking down the street, it isn't me.

LARRY. Should we have waited for you? After the funeral. Kelly had to work.

ANNA. No, I should have come with you. God. Just as I think I'm out of there, some relatives drive me back to the house. The place is mobbed. I'm dragged through everybody eating and drinking and talking, to some little back bedroom, with all the aunts and cousins, with the women, right? Squashed into this room. His mother's on the bed with a washcloth on her forehead. I'm trying to tell them how I've got to get a bus back to civilization.

LARRY. This is very moving, but I'm double-parked.

ANNA. Exactly.

LARRY. This is a *wake?*

ANNA. I couldn't tell you *what* it was, Larry, I guess. In about eight seconds I know they have no idea that Robbie's gay.

LARRY. I could have told you that.

ANNA. They've never heard of Dom. God, I'm making up stories, I'm racking my brain for every interesting thing anyone I know has done to tell them Robbie did it. Wonderful workaholic Robbie, and I couldn't tell them a thing about him. It was all just so massively sad.

LARRY. Oh, Lord.

ANNA. It gets worse, it gets much worse. And they *never saw him dance!* I couldn't believe it. All the men are gorgeous, of course. They all look exactly like Robbie except in that kind of blue-collar, working-at-the-steel-mill kind of way, and *drink?* God, could they knock it back. So then it's midnight and the last bus has left at ten, which they knew, I'm sure, damn them, and I hadn't checked, like an idiot. So I have to spend the night in Robbie's little nephew's room in the attic. The little redhead, did you see him?

LARRY. I didn't see him.

ANNA. He's been collecting butterflies all day, and they're pinned around the room to the walls—a pin in each wing, right?

LARRY. I'm not liking this little redheaded nephew.

ANNA. Darling, wait. So. I get to sleep by about two, I've got them to promise to get me up at six-thirty for the seven-something bus. I wake up, it's not quite light, really; you can't see in the room much—but there's something *in* there.

LARRY. Oh, God.

ANNA. There's this intermittent soft flutter sound. I think what the hell is—Larry, the—oh, Lord, the walls are just pulsating. All those butterflies are alive. They're all beating their bodies against the walls—all around me. The kid's put them in alcohol; he thought he'd killed them, they'd only passed out.

LARRY. Oh, God.

ANNA. I started screaming hysterically. I got the bedsheet around me, ran down to the kitchen; I've never felt so naked in my life. Of course I was naked—a sheet wrapped around me. This glowering older brother had to go get my clothes, unpinned the butterflies, who knows if they lived. I got the whispering sister—

LARRY. What a family!

ANNA. —to drop me off at the bus station; they were glad to get rid of me. I was an hour and a half early, I didn't care. I drank about twenty cups of that vending-machine coffee. Black; the cream and sugar buttons didn't work. The bus-station attendant is ogling me. I'm so wired from the caffeine, if he'd said anything I'd have kneecapped him. There's these two bag ladies yelling at each other, apparently they're rivals. I fit right in.

LARRY. Oh, God. To wake up to those—I can just see them.

ANNA. Oh, Lord, I shrieked like a madwoman. They were glad to get rid of me.

LARRY. I was going to ask if you wanted coffee.

ANNA. No, I don't think that's going to do it.

LARRY. Not one of your better nights.

ANNA. Not one of my better nights. Not one of my better mornings.

LARRY. Jesus. What are we going to do about Robbie's mail?

ANNA. I guess save it. We have to bring Robbie's things down from the loft. Someone's coming over for them.

LARRY. He only had about two pairs of jeans and three sweatshirts. A lot of shoes.

ANNA. Clothes didn't mean much to him.

LARRY. What did, except work and you and Dominic? In the room there's his futon, a candle, and a paperback of *Ancient Evenings*.

ANNA. *(Pause. She looks around).* I left this place, went down to Houston . . . I thought everything important to the future of dance was going to happen in this room. Oh, God. It's too early to go to bed.

LARRY. Go to bed now, you'd be wide awake at 2 A.M.

ANNA. Actually, you want to know the callous truth: if I were still dancing, I'd probably be brilliant tonight. *(Pause)* How was work? Did they buy the idea?

LARRY. You have no notion of the stupidity involved in designing a Christmas card for a national company. Especially if it's Chrysler. Just for starters, there are a hundred seventy religions in America and only one of them believes in Santa Claus. Nothing religious; that would offend the non-believers. Reindeer are out—Santa Claus again. No snow; that would offend California and Florida. No evergreens, holly, pines—out of the question—mistletoe, no bells. They said the only thing everyone believes in is the family and children. I said that was only going to offend homosexuals.

ANNA. Which didn't matter to them at all.

LARRY. No, I said it as a joke; they bought it.

ANNA. So what?

LARRY. They're still batting it around, but they're leaning toward a car. Which is tantamount to saying the only thing everyone believes in is the automobile.

ANNA. They're probably on to something there.

LARRY. Oh, I have no quarrel with that. A little plastic Chrysler that you can or not hang on your Christmas tree or Hanukkah bush that says *Season's Greetings from Chrysler Corp.* Made in Taiwan, appropriately. It's too complicated, production will get fucked completely, it's going to be late, and the cost is astronomical, but we won't have offended anyone. Except anyone with a modicum of taste. *(He looks at her, she stares off)* What are you going to do about food? *(A very long pause)* You wanta order in? Mexican? Pizza? Chinese? *(Pause)* I haven't stopped thinking about it since it happened.

ANNA. I'm just so annoyed with myself, because all I can feel is anger. I was angry with Robbie and Dom for doing something that stupid; now I'm angry with his family. They just had no goddamned right. He was my friend, damnit. I danced with him for three years. They didn't even know him.

LARRY. They didn't do anything; there's no reason to be angry with them.

ANNA. Well, I am. And there is. And they did. I mean, it's half sentimental horseshit, but damnit, they wouldn't leave me alone. I didn't even have a damn minute to say goodbye. I'll never forgive those bastards for that.

(Music up, the lights fade. After a moment of darkness there is a pounding on the apartment door)

PALE'S VOICE *(Offstage).* Annie, hey,

Annie— Just go fuck yourself, fella. Get laid, do you good. Annie. Hey. Come on.

(ANNA turns on a light; she has quickly thrown on a Hapi coat. She looks through the peephole)

PALE *(Offstage).* Come on. Come on. Jesus.

(She opens the door. PALE *comes in. He is thirty-six, shorter than* BURTON, *well built, and can be good-looking, but is certainly sexy. He wears a very good suit)*

PALE. Goddamn this fuckin' place, how can anybody live this shit city? I'm not doin' it, I'm not drivin' my car this goddamn sewer, every fuckin' time. Who are these assholes? Some bug-eyed, fat-lipped half nigger, all right; some of my best friends, thinks he owns this fuckin' *space.* The city's got this *space* specially reserved for his private use. Twenty-five fuckin' minutes I'm driving around this garbage street; I pull up this space, I look back, this fuckin' baby-shit green Trans Am's on my ass going *beep-beep.* I get out, this fucker says that's my *space.* I showed him the fuckin' tire iron; I told the fucker, You want this space, you're gonna wake up tomorrow, find you slept in your fuckin' car. This ain't your space, you treasure your pop-up headlights, Ho-Jo. Am I right? That shit? There's no talkin' to shit like that.

ANNA. I'm sorry, do I know you?

PALE. How's that?

ANNA. I mean, you're obviously some relation of Robbie's—you could be his double—but—

PALE. Double, shit, with that fuckin' nose of his? Sure you know me—"Do I know you"—we met. I'm the one who saved you from the ferocious butterflies.

ANNA. You have such a large family, I didn't really catch any *names.*

PALE. Jimmy. I was listening to all that molasses you was pouring over Mom and all the cousins and neighbor bitches, I had to go take a shot of insulin.

ANNA. I remember now, you're the older brother.

PALE. Twelve years, so what? What's older? Older than what?

ANNA. Older than Robbie.

PALE. I said, didn't I? Twelve years. You hear me say that? He lived in this joint? I mean no personal disparagement of the neighborhood in which you have your domicile, honey, but this street's dying of crotch rot. The only thing save this part of the city, they burn it down. They call that a street out

there? You could lose a Toyota some of those potholes. The people run your fuckin' city's got no respect for the property of the people livin' here. This is why people act the way they do, this shit. *(Beat)* This has made me not as, you know—whatever—as I usually am. But I'm trying to parallel-park in the only fuckin' space a twenty-block radius, you don't crawl up my butthole in your shit-green Trans Am and go *beep-beep,* you know? *(Looking around)* So'd you get the stuff together?

ANNA. The what?

PALE. The things, the things, the stuff, Robbie's shit.

ANNA. Wait a minute, you've come for Robbie's things?

PALE. Didn't I say?

ANNA. It's been over a month. I called your mother. She gave me some numbers where I could reach you, but . . .

PALE. Ya, sure. Listen, I don't want you bothering my family, okay? I don't like messages. The first one, you think, okay, fuck, I messed up. I'll take care of it, my fault, something came up, no problem. Then you get, you know, a couple of days, here's another fuckin' message. And it's like I heard you the first time, okay? Don't leave messages for me. I don't need the pool hall and the bar where I go and the auto-repair man on my back saying some bitch called and giving me a little piece of paper.

ANNA. Saying what? Some bitch called? You were the one who was—

PALE. That's the way he talks, what are we talkin'? A fuckin' bartender, what does he know? He's working some dark hole, listening to the dregs of the race vomit their life all over the bar six nights; he's got a low opinion of humanity, okay? I don't like little pieces of paper. You put them in your pocket, you got six or eight little pieces of paper stuffed all over you, it ruins your clothes, you know? I don't read 'em. They're nothin' you don't already know. Somebody *wants* me, big fuckin' deal, take a number. I said I'd come, I'm here. A man would like to think people are gonna believe him. There's a certain satisfaction in being thought of as a man of your—? There's something wrong with these shoes, my feet are in boiling water. *(He takes off one of his shoes)* Look at that, oh man, I never had that.

ANNA. Are they new?

PALE. Yeah, first time I put them on. Don't

worry about stinkin', I'm clean. They should invent a machine break in shoes—fuckin' killing the top of my foot. That's genuine lizard, two hundred forty-five bucks, fuckin' pinchin' everywhere. Jesus. *(He takes off the second shoe)* You'd think a lizard's got to be supple, right? They got to move quick. Feel that. Steel plating. *(Walking)* Oh man. *(Beat)* What a fuckin' neighborhood. What a place to live.

ANNA. Actually, we like it.

PALE. Yeah, yeah, yeah, yeah, it's supposed to be arty, I know. It's quaint. Look at it— you should make automobile parts here; it's a fuckin' factory. *(LARRY stands in the doorway in T-shirt and shorts)* So who are you?

LARRY. . . . "Where did you come from? What do you want? It's me, isn't it? You've always wanted me. You want to have your filthy way with me in the hot desert sun. Ravage me like I've never been ravaged before." *(To* ANNA*)* Are you all right?

ANNA. I'm fine. Larry, this is Jimmy, Robbie's brother.

LARRY. I could tell.

PALE. Your girlfriend is in very capable hands.

ANNA. Larry's my other roommate.

PALE. You're the replacement; that didn't take long—in one door, out the other.

LARRY. The three of us got the place together.

PALE. Didn't see you at the wake.

LARRY. I wasn't invited. I'm going to bed, then. *(He exits)*

ANNA. Good night.

PALE. "Good night," shit. Sleep tight. What am I gonna rip off the TV? He another dancer?

ANNA. No. Listen, Jimmy, Robbie's things are in the basement. No way could you get them tonight without waking up the building. I've already called the Salvation Army, I hadn't been able to reach you.

PALE. So what? What's this huge rush? They're on fire or something? Spontaneous combustion, something? *(There's a noise from the radiator)* What's that?

ANNA. The heat.

PALE. Heat, yet. The fuckin' room's a oven, bake pizza here, they turn on some heat. *(He takes his jacket and tie off, pulls his shirttail out)*

ANNA. It's cold. It's the middle of winter.

PALE. I got like a toaster oven I carry around with me in my belly someplace. I don't use heat. I sleep the windows open, no covers, I fuckin' hate things over me. Ray'll tell you: Here comes the dumb fuck Pale with the radiator up his ass. What time they turn it off?

ANNA. Midnight. It comes back on at five.

PALE. Five's ass, shit. It can't be no five. What'd I do with my watch?

ANNA. Actually, I've got to get back to—

PALE. Actually, would you just hold it a second, okay? *(Looking for his watch)* What'd I do with my—no, it's cool, I got it. *(He opens a window)* Jesus, it's a fuckin'—you could pass out. How long did he live here?

ANNA. About three years. He was a lot of fun.

PALE. Yeah . . . he was very light, a lotta guys are dark . . . he was very light.

ANNA. Yes he was. *(Pause)* You want some coffee?

PALE. Sure, whatta you got to drink?

ANNA. Coffee.

PALE. Sure. I'm not difficult.

ANNA. You're Pale.

PALE. V.S.O. Pale, that's me.

ANNA. Robbie mentioned you.

PALE. Yeah? He *mentioned* me? Well, I'm very mentionable.

ANNA. He didn't talk about his family much. You were the one he liked.

PALE *(Looking out the window)*. That's the bay, huh, the river? Jesus. What a thing to look at. Oh, look, darling, they got tugboats pushin', like, these flatcars; like, five flatcars piled about a mile high with all this city garbage and shit. Who the fuck wants to look at that? You pay for a view of that? Maybe there's people find that fascinating, that's not what I call a view.

ANNA. Are you high?

PALE. How's that?

ANNA. Are you high? I mean, I know you've been drinking; I wondered if you were high, too.

PALE. Yeah, I did maybe a couple lines with Ray, it don't affect me.

ANNA. No, it doesn't affect you. *(She carries the coffee to the living area)*

PALE. It don't affect me. This is the way I am, what you see, little girl. Straight or high. *(LARRY stands in the doorway, only in his shorts)* What is this, a slow strip act? *(LARRY leaves)* Jesus. Little girls your age don't have roommates, you know? This is not just me, this is prevailing opinion, here. *(He's looking out the window)*

ANNA. I have a problem with prevailing opinions.

PALE. I could tell.

ANNA. They're putting up that building; it's going to block about half our view.

PALE. No, I'm trying to see where I parked my car. That jerk-off. People aren't human, you ever notice that? This bar tonight, Ray, you know?

ANNA. No.

PALE. Ray, Ray, Ray.

ANNA. No, I don't know him.

PALE. You may not know him. That didn't stop you asking him to write out your number on a piece of paper, give it to me; it didn't stop—

ANNA. Fine; Ray, fine, what about him?

PALE. Boy. So what? You dance here?

ANNA. Robbie and I used it as a studio, yes.

PALE. That's why you got no furniture, no curtains; you'll fall down over 'em, somethin'.

ANNA. Actually, we've tried to keep it as spare as possible.

PALE. This ain't spare. This is a empty fuckin' warehouse. *(He has found a bottle of brandy and pours himself a drink)*

ANNA. That's not V.S.O.P.

PALE. I can tell. I got one area of expertise: food and drink.

ANNA. Very—Something—Old—Pale.

PALE. "Special." Most people don't even know what that means. Very Special Old Pale. This ain't bad, though, this ain't rotgut.

ANNA. Thank you.

PALE. What? You think it's hot shit? It's okay. It's no better than Rémy. I'd come in, I'd say Very Special Old Pale up, about the third time Ray says, Hey, Pale, on me.

ANNA. This was when?

PALE. When; shit, who knows? Ten, fifteen years. So you dance, too.

ANNA. I did, I've taken off for a while.

PALE. Couldn't stick it.

ANNA. I decided it might be interesting to have a personal life.

PALE. So. You got too good.

ANNA. No, Robbie thought he saw a choreographer in me.

PALE. So what do they do?

ANNA. Choreographers? They make the dance. You have bodies, space, sculptural mass, distance relationships; if they're lucky, they might even discover they have something to say—

PALE. So, you like it?

ANNA. It's an interesting challenge. Well, it's becoming kind of an obsession.

PALE. So you like it.

ANNA. Uh, possibly. Look, if you wanted to come back seven, seven-thirty, we could go down to the basement and get—

PALE. Seven-thirty I'm long outta here. No good. I'm a worker. Part of this country's great working force.

ANNA. What do you do?

PALE. Who me? Whatta I do?

ANNA. It doesn't matter.

PALE. I do anything. On call. Twenty-four hours a day and night. We never close. I deliver. Water. I'm a water deliverer. For fires. I put out fires. I'm a relief pitcher. Like Sparky Lyle.

ANNA. For whom?

PALE. Anybody needs relieving. I'm a roving fireman. Very healthy occupation. I'm puttin' out somebody else's fire, I'm puttin' out my own. *Quid pro*—something; symbiosis. Or sometimes you just let it burn. *(Pause)*

ANNA. What did you do to your hand?

PALE. No, this bar tonight, Ray, you know?

ANNA. Good ol' Ray, sure. I mean, we've only talked on the phone.

PALE. There was this character runnin' off at the mouth; I told him I'm gonna push his face in, he don't shut up. Now, this should be a fairly obvious statement, right? But this dipshit starts trying to explain to me what he's been saying *ad nauseam* all night, like there was some subtle gradation of thought that was gonna make it all right that he was mouthing this horseshit. So when I'm forced to bust the son of a bitch, he's down on the floor, he's dripping blood from a split lip, he's testing a loose tooth, and that fucker is *still talking.* Now, some people might think that this was the problem of this guy, he's got this motor going, he's not privy to where the shutoff valve is. But I gotta come to the conclusion that I'm weird. Cause I try to communicate with these jerkoffs in what is *essentially* the mother tongue, but no one is picking me up; they're not reading me. There's some mystery here. Okay, sometimes they're just on a rap. I respect rap. You're not supposed to be listening. You can read the paper, watch TV, eat pistachios, I'm not talking that. I'm talking these jerkoffs think you're listening. You said the choreographer organizes what? Sculptured space? What is that?

ANNA. Oh, God. I'm sorry—What did you say? I'm sorry.

PALE. Now, see, that I can't take. I can't stand that.

ANNA. I'm sorry, really, but—

PALE. Well, see, fine, you got these little social phrases and politenesses—all they show me is this—like—giganticness of unconcern with your "I'm sorrys," man. The fuckin' world is going down the fuckin' toilet on "I'm sorrys." I'm sorry is this roll of toilet paper—they're growing whole forests, for people to wipe their asses on with their "I'm sorrys." Be a tree. For one day. And know that that tree over there is gonna be maybe music paper, the Boss is gonna make forty million writin' some poor-slob-can't-get-work song on. This tree is gonna be ten-dollar bills, get passed around, buy things, *mean something,* hear stories; we got sketch pads and fuckin' "I don't love you anymore" letters pinned to some creep's pillow—something of *import.* Headlines, box scores, some great book or movie script—Jack Nicholson's gonna mark you all up, say whatever he wishes to, anyway, out in some fuckin' desert, you're supposed to be his *text,* he's gonna lay out this line of coke on you—Tree over there is gonna be in some four-star restaurant, they're gonna call him parchment, bake pompano in him. And you're stuck in the ground, you can't go nowhere, all you know is some fuckin' junkie's gonna wipe his ass and flush you down the East River. Go floating out past the Statue of Liberty all limp and covered with shit, get tangled up in some Saudi Arabian oil tanker's fuckin' propellers—you got maybe three hundred years before you drift down to Brazil somewhere and get a chance to be maybe a coffee bush. "I'm sorrys" are fuck, man. *(Pause)* How long did he live here?

ANNA. Three years. Did you know he was studying, Pale?

PALE. Robbie? Didn't do much better than me. I was popular, you know. I don't think he wasn't so popular.

ANNA. Dance, I mean. Did you know he wanted to be a dancer?

PALE. Shit. I don't know. Whatta I know? He was seven, I was outta there. Who knew him? I didn't know him.

ANNA. Actually, I was thinking that.

PALE. Oh, beautiful, I love that. You're gonna be a cunt like everybody else? "You didn't really know him, Pale." *Deeply,* you

gotta say. Did you know him deeply, honey? He know you deeply? You guys get deep together? 'Cause neither of you strikes me as the type.

ANNA. Fine.

PALE. What the fuck does that mean, "fine"?

ANNA. It means I'm tired, it's five-thirty in the morning; if you don't want to talk about him, I certainly don't. You're completely closed; you knew him, I didn't. You don't want to hear what I have to say, fine. It means fine.

PALE. What? I don't have feelings? I'm not capable of having a talk here?

ANNA. There's no doubt in my mind that you have completely mastered half the art of conversation. *(PALE whistles)* I'm tired. I'm sorry. I miss him. You remind me of him.

PALE. Shit.

ANNA. Completely aside from any familial resemblance, just having his brother here reminds me. At the—whatever that wake was after the funeral—it was obvious none of your family knew anything about him. Had you seen him dance? *(PALE shakes his head)* Well, see, that's impossible for me to understand.

PALE. Anybody good as he was, you said. He was good?

ANNA. Yes.

PALE. Well, see, that shows what the experts know. You saw him and say he was good. I didn't even see him, I know he was shit.

ANNA. Pale, I can't stay up till the people in the building wake up, I have a class at nine, I have to get some rest.

PALE. You teach?

ANNA. What? No, a class I'm taking. I teach too, but this is a class. Then I come back here and work till six, so I've got a long day . . . *(Pause)* What?

PALE. Awww, shit. *(Pause. He stifles a sob)* Fuckin' . . . drinkin' and thinkin', man, worse than drinkin' and drivin'. Drinkin' and thinkin'. Aw shit. He wasn't dark, you know, like . . .

ANNA *(Pause).* He worked really hard.

PALE. Aww, Jesus . . . feed the fish, man . . . Jesus. *(He sobs enormously and long, she goes to him, he moves away. She touches his shoulder)*

ANNA. I know.

PALE. Come on, don't mess with me. I don't like being messed with. My heart hurts, I think I'm dying. I think I'm havin'—like—a heart attack. I messed up my stomach, I think I ate somethin'. *(Sobs again)* I don't do this, this ain't me. *(He gets up, walks around)* Aww shit. I'm trying to imagine him here.

ANNA. His room was up in the loft.

PALE. Yeah? What'd you do, you guys eat here; you have—like—parties, that shit?

ANNA. Sometimes. When we were all home, which wasn't often enough, we'd trade around. We're all pretty good cooks. Robbie was really the best.

PALE. Robbie cook?

ANNA. He was working his way through *The Cuisine of Southern Italy.* Cookbook . . . Dom . . . someone gave him for Christmas.

PALE. Shit. Fuckin' Christmas parties. Presents and that shit. Look out! Ribbons! I fuckin' hate that crap.

ANNA. What do you like, Pale?

PALE. I like a lot of things. You want bullshit, you want to know what turns me on?

ANNA. Nothing. That's fine. I can imagine.

PALE. Yeah, well, I don't like being imagined. I like the ocean. That hurricane. I stayed on the pier—hanging on to this fuckin' pipe railing, wind blowin' so hard you couldn't breathe. Couldn't open my hands the next day. Try to get excited over some fuckin' roller coaster, some loop-the-loop after that. I like those gigantic, citywide fires—like Passaic, wherever; fuckin' Jersey's burnin' down three times a week. Good riddance. Avalanches! Whole villages wiped out. Somethin' that can—like—amaze you. People don't want to hear that shit, they want-like you should get turned on by some crap—you know, Häagen-Dazs ice cream, "I like everyone to be nice." That shit. Chicks or somethin'. Gettin' laid's okay. A really hot shower's good. Clean underwear, smells like Downy softener. *(Beat)* So you guys all cook for each other. Sittin' here, makin' polite conversation about the state of the world and shit.

ANNA. Dancers mainly talk about dance.

PALE. Man, I'm fuckin' up my pants all fucked up.

ANNA. That's a nice suit.

PALE. Yeah, I'm a dresser. I keep myself neat. I'm fuckin' up the back of my pants, gettin' all fucked up. Fuckin' linen. Half linen, half wool—fuckin' useless. I could've been the dancer. Who needs it? Our old man, when we was kids, music all over the place. You couldn't hear yourself think. Vivaldi, Puccini, we all knew all that crap, Shostakovich. I've done—like—whole symphonies, amazed people, natural talent, totally original shit, like in the shower. I don't sing Hall & Oates, I compose—like—these tone poems, concertos and shit—huge big orchestrations, use like two orchestras.

ANNA. Do you read music?

PALE. What for? Nobody does that shit. I get going some symphony, these like giant themes come to me, these like world-shaking changes in tempo and these great huge melodies, these incredible variations, man. Get like the whole fuckin' war in it. *(He stops, bends over)* My heart's killing me. My throat's hurtin', burnin', man. What a fuckin' night. Bust up my hand on that fucker's tooth. *(He looks out the window. Pause)* Half my fuckin' adult life, I swear to Christ, has been spent looking for a place to park. *(Beat. He looks at her)* What are you wearin' that thing?

ANNA. I keep hoping I'll have a chance to go back to bed and get my rest.

PALE. Sure. Don't worry about rest, we'll all get our rest. Whatta you call that thing?

ANNA. It's called a Hapi coat.

PALE. That's somethin' to wear, you do your Hapi? The Indians wear that, the Hopis?

ANNA. I got it in Japan.

PALE. Those Orientals are short, it might give them better cover.

ANNA. I just grabbed something.

(Pause. He looks at her, looks around the room. Back to her)

PALE. So the three of you lived here. You and the two faggots.

ANNA *(A long stunned pause)*. We were all very good friends.

PALE. Tellin' Mom and Aunt Ida and all the neighborhood bitches how you and Robbie did things, horseback, and the races and shit. Said everything except your little boy was a real hot fuck.

ANNA *(Pause)*. It was very humiliating. They didn't know; it wasn't my place to tell them.

PALE. They know, they just don't know.

ANNA. Well, whatever. I didn't feel it was my place.

PALE *(Banging on the sofa)*. Fuckin' fruit. Fuck! Fuck! Fuck! Fuck! Fuck! Bastard! Taking his fuckin' little Greek boyfriend out to the island, talking about him in the paper, on that TV thing. "You dance real good." "Well, I get a lot of help from my friend Dominic." Suckin' my dick for me, whatever the fuck they do.

ANNA. Don't you know? I thought you'd

know. They have anal intercourse, take turns
having oral—

PALE. HEY! HEY! People don't *see* those programs! On TV, Channel Q, whatever, don't
matter. People see that. People say, I saw
your queer brother on the TV with his boyfriend. People the family works for. That
crap. He live here, too? Dominic?

ANNA. He spent about half the time here.
We'd been trying to get him to move in,
there's plenty of room. Dom was great, you'd
have liked him. It's very different here without them.

PALE. I'm just trying to get a picture—

ANNA. Well, don't bother if you didn't give
a damn for him; it's a little late to cry now.

PALE. —Robbie cookin', Dominic serving
wine, you lighting candles. The fruit in there
running around without his clothes on. *What
do you know what I feel?* I got my hand bleeding
again. Fuckin' myself into little pieces here.
I got to wear this look like a fuckin' bum. *(He
bends over, starts to cry, stifles it)* Shit, man; shit,
man. Awww shit. *(Taking off his pants)* I can't
get fucked up; you go get your rest, you're
worried about rest. I can't fuckin' stand up; I
sit down, I'm gonna cry. Come undone. I got
to wear these tomorrow—*(Presses them on
table)* I can't fuck myself.

ANNA *(Overlapping).* Jimmy, for godsake.
Jimmy. If you're worried, I can press them in
the morning. Seven o'clock we can go down
to the basement. Listen, if you're very quiet,
we can sneak down now. We'll take the
stairs, 'cause the elevator—Jimmy. Jimmy.
*(He has crawled onto the sofa and completely cov-
ered himself with an afghan, head and all. His body
is racked with crying.* ANNA *looks at him for a
moment. She finishes the last of her coffee. What the
hell—finishes his brandy as well)* I know. I
miss him like hell. I go to the studio, I think
I see him ten times a day. Someone dressed
like him, or walking like him. Then I remember he's gone, and it's all that loss all
over again. I know.

PALE *(He has poked his head from the afghan).*
He was always . . . very . . . *(Gestures light)*

ANNA. I know. He worked harder than
anyone I've ever known.

PALE *(Looks around).* Where's my . . .

ANNA. I drank it.

PALE. I'm gonna have to have another. *(She
gets up)* I'll get it.

ANNA. That's okay, you got the last one.

PALE. I'll send you a fuckin' case.

ANNA. It's fine, Jimmy. Just—what? Cool it,
okay?

PALE. Jimmy you're callin' me. I like that.
Nobody calls me that. Fuckin' place, man.
Fuckin' haunted.

ANNA. Yes, it is. So's the studio. So's the
streets around the neighborhood. *(Sitting on
the sofa)* So's the whole island of Manhattan.

PALE. So's Jersey. *(Pause)* I'm gonna be sick
here.

ANNA. The brandy doesn't help.

PALE. No, it's good for it. You don't do
nothing to your hair? It's just like that?

ANNA. It costs a fortune. *(Pause)* Oh, God.

PALE. You're done in, huh?

ANNA. No, I'm up. I'm an early riser, anyway. Not usually this early, but . . . No, I'm
just . . . blue. Remember that? When people
used to feel blue? I'm feeling blue.

PALE. Me too. *(Not looking at her breasts or
touching them)* You almost got no tits at all,
you know?

ANNA. I know. Thanks.

PALE. No, that's beautiful. That's very provocative. Guy wants to look, see just how
much there is. Tits are very deceptive things.
*(Pause. Rubs his chin on the top of her head. Sings
very softly, very slowly)* "I'd . . . rather . . . be
. . . blue . . . thinking of you . . ."

ANNA. You're burning up.

PALE *(sings, same).* "Oh . . . oh . . . oh . . . I'm
on fire . . ." That's just the toaster oven.
Always like that.

ANNA. You're not sick, you don't have a
fever?

PALE. Normal temperature about a hundred and ten. Aww, man, I'm so fucked. My
gut aches, my balls are hurtin', they're gonna
take stitches on my heart; I'm fuckin' *grievin'*
here and you're givin' me a hard-on. Come
on, don't go away from me—everybody's
fuckin' flyin' South, man . . . like I was the
. . . aw shit, man. I'm gonna cry all over your
hair. *(He does cry in her hair)*

ANNA. What, Jimmy?

PALE. Come on, don't look at me.

ANNA. Jimmy, stop. Enough already, don't;
you're gonna hurt yourself or something.

PALE. Good. Good. Don't look.

ANNA. I was very angry at the funeral. I
thought I hadn't had a chance to have a moment, but Larry and I went back to the cemetery a couple of days after and we cried the
whole day; but don't break your heart. You
know? *(Kisses him lightly)* Jimmy?

PALE. You went back?

ANNA. Larry and I.

PALE. Come on. You make me upset.

ANNA. You're making yourself upset.

PALE. No, the other way. I'm getting all riled here. I got no place for it. I got like a traffic jam here. *(Kisses her lightly)* You okay?

ANNA. I'm fine.

PALE. I'm like fallin' outta the airplane here. *(Pause)* You always smell like that?

ANNA. Shampoo.

PALE. My shampoo don't make me smell like that. Let's just start up the engines real slow here . . . maybe go halfway to the city and stop for somethin' to eat . . . You talk to me, okay? . . . You're gonna find out there's times . . . I'm a real good listener.

(Music up, fade to black. After a few moments the lights come back up. Very early morning. Sunny. LARRY *enters from outside)*

LARRY *(Entering yelling)*. He might have told me I was going to have to load his car by myself. I adore manual labor at 6:50 A.M. God, I thought he was going to help.

ANNA *(Coming in from the bedroom)*. He's been on the phone.

LARRY. Where the hell is he?

ANNA. Taking a shower.

LARRY. Any great tone poems come out of there yet?

ANNA. Not a peep.

LARRY. He's probably going to be another big bruiser with a bad back.

ANNA. No, I don't think so.

LARRY. One is not allowed to be smug just because one got laid. *(At* PALE'*s jacket and pants, holds up a pistol)* Please note.

ANNA. Don't touch it. I saw.

LARRY. Robbie's address book just happened to fall out of one of the boxes and into my pocket. "Pale: 17 Oak Street, Montclair, New Jersey." Phone number at home, phone number at work.

ANNA. What would you say to an omelette?

LARRY. Uh . . . *Bonjour, omelette.* I'm exhausted, of course; my eyes did not close. I had one hand on the phone and the other with a finger poised to dial 911. Actually, that's not true. With all the music coming out of this room, I abused myself terribly. *(PALE enters, fresh shirt and tie, puts on pants, steps into shoes while dialing)* You always carry a spare shirt in the car?

PALE. What? Yeah. *(On phone)* Joe. Pale. Fifteen minutes. You just be damn sure you hold them. Just don't fuck me. Fifteen minutes. You got what? No, no, I can't use it. No. I'm leavin' now. *(Hangs up)* More fuckin' trouble than my old lady.

LARRY. Than your old what?

PALE. What, you think I'm weird or something? Sure I got an old lady. Two kids, perfect family. *(Hands* ANNA *his opened wallet.)* Boy and girl.

ANNA. Won't she be curious where you spent the night?

PALE. Naw, she trusts me; they're down in Coral Gables. She knows I'm cool. I never cheated on her once.

ANNA *(Handing him the wallet)*. They're beautiful.

PALE. You get that crap in the car?

LARRY. All loaded.

ANNA. You want coffee? Maybe an omelette?

PALE. Got no time. Don't use food in the morning. I can't drink coffee, burn your guts out. You got my keys? cigarette lighter?

LARRY. On the counter. That's a great-looking car.

PALE. Fuckin' pain in the ass, too. Okay, people, I'm out of here. *(He exits)*

LARRY. He's one of those people you know right away isn't going to say, "Have a nice day." So, is he utterly fantastic in the sack?

ANNA. Uh . . . quite interesting.

LARRY *(Sings)*. "I'd rather be blue, thinking of you—"

ANNA *(Glaring at him)*. How much did you hear?

LARRY. I'm trying to remember . . . No, I don't think I missed anything.

ANNA. Sorry. Very bad form. It was all very—oh, what the hell. The bird-with-the-broken-wing syndrome.

LARRY. You bring the poor little bird home, doll. You make a splint for its poor little wing. You feed the little bugger chicken soup if you must. You don't, however, fuck it. *(He has been dialing the phone)* Hello. Is Pale there?

ANNA. You're not.

LARRY. Eleven? What exactly is his position there? Manager. And this is the . . . Da Signate Ristorante.

ANNA. Oh no. Hang up.

LARRY. Thank you. No, no message, he hates them. *Grazie. (Hangs up)* Manages a restaurant. I love it.

ANNA. Oh, God. He's a relief pitcher. Yeah, of sangría.

LARRY. I've been there; it's celebrity city, two stars or something.

ANNA. Well, he said he worked hard.

LARRY. They do, too. Tom managed a restaurant in the Village for two years. He had to be down at the Fulton Fish Market at six in the morning or it was gone.

ANNA. That's probably who he was calling.

LARRY. "This is Pale, hold my fish." I love it. With a gun, though?

ANNA. If he makes the deposits at night.

LARRY. I think you're very wise. One of those people it'd be impossible to get rid of any other way. *(Phone rings)* That's Burton to tell you how many laps he made around the reservoir.

ANNA. Seven o'clock on the nose.

LARRY *(On the phone)*. Hello, beautiful. I get up early sometimes. Part of my charming unpredictability. Actually, I was up with Anna all night. No, nothing serious. Said she felt like she had a terrible weight on her stomach . . . *(Looking at her)* I just hope she doesn't come down with something. I'm sure she'd love to, only nothing too physical, she looks exhausted.

ANNA *(Taking the phone)*. Hi, Burt. No, I'm fine, never better.

LARRY. Rub it in.

ANNA. What's to see? Yeah, that'd be fun. Or the other one. No, I don't think so. I've just got no interest in it. The what? *(Covers the phone)* Would you shut up? That's good, then. Okay, sevenish. *(Hangs up the phone)*

LARRY *(Sings, simultaneously)*. "I'd rather be blue, thinking of you, I'd rather be blue over you. Than be happy with somebody called Burton."

LARRY. Slut.

ANNA. Oh, God. He wants to go out tonight.

LARRY. And of course, out of abject guilt, you said sure. You could always have said, I couldn't possibly, I was fucked blind last night.

ANNA. Go to hell.

LARRY. Please note how contact with your restaurateur has eroded our speech. We're just at the age where we pick that sort of thing up.

ANNA. I'm going back to bed.

LARRY. You'll miss class and you've got work to do.

ANNA. I'll take a shower and think about it.

LARRY. What would you say to a waffle?

ANNA. Get lost, waffle. Get thee behind me. Which is exactly where it would go. *(She starts for the bathroom. Sings)* "I'd rather be blue, thinking of you, I'd rather be blue over you . . . than be . . ."

(She stops with a shock, turns to look at LARRY.

Pause. LARRY *stands looking at her. He sings softly)*

LARRY. "Oh . . . oh . . . oh . . . I'm on fire . . ."

Music up, the lights fade

ACT TWO

Late New Year's Eve. 2 A.M. ANNA *is in a gown,* BURTON *in a tux.* ANNA *has a script in her hands. She finishes reading it.*

BURTON. That's as far as I've got.

ANNA. Oh, I like it. It's so sad. God.

BURTON. Sad? I thought they were having fun.

ANNA. Oh no, sure. But underneath all that, God, they're so lonely.

BURTON. Yeah, I know, but I don't want to think about that part or I won't be able to do it. Aw, to hell with it, anyway. I want something larger than life. Those people are smaller than life.

ANNA. They're very real, and I think it's exciting. And you have your space. Only it's distance between people rather than distance between places.

BURTON. No, give me kinky or quirky or sadistic— Where's the pain? Where's the joy? Where's the ebullience?

ANNA. It's there. Everything doesn't have to be epic.

BURTON. Yes! Yes! Not in treatment, but at least in feeling. Reach! Reach for something! God! Reach for the sun! Go for it! . . .

ANNA. I don't think I've been sober on New Year's Eve before in my life.

BURTON. Not necessarily recommended.

ANNA. You were doing all that coke.

BURTON. Not the same thing.

ANNA. I've missed you. How was your family?

BURTON. Rich, self-satisfied, alcoholically comatose, boring. *(Pause)* Before we get off the subject, you really did like it?

ANNA. I really do. That other character is Larry, isn't he?

BURTON. Larry? No. Well, you know. Some him, some—no more than ninety percent. How's it been going here?

ANNA. I'm working like a dog. I almost feel as if I've finally burst my chrysalis after thirty years of incubation. That's the wrong word.

BURTON. Metamorphosis.

ANNA. The day after you left, Fred asked me to do a piece with a company he's putting together.

BURTON. All right!

ANNA. It's kinda exciting, really. Guaranteed coverage, maybe a little more—what?—political than I'd like—three new woman choreographers. Twelve minutes or so each. The first half of a new program he's working on. God. He pays the rent, the advertising. Overall theme, very loosely, is love. Mother love, which God knows I know nothing about—yet. And then something else, and he wants me to do the *pas de deux*. Two couples, not one.

BURTON. *Pas de quatre.*

ANNA. He's got four great kids for me to work with. I try things out here and work with them at Fred's studio. I think it'd be fair to say it's not going well. I'm beginning to think that as an artist I have absolutely no life experience to draw from. Or else I'm just too chicken to let anyone see what I really am.

BURTON. What you need is to do a little research on this love stuff. Tonight.

ANNA. Well, if I'm going to pretend to know anything about it . . .

BURTON. It might get a little X-rated.

ANNA. A *pas de quatre* for Fred, that's absolutely *de rigueur*.

BURTON. What's your schedule tomorrow?

ANNA. Totally clean slate.

BURTON. Me too.

ANNA. Actually, I planned ahead. You've been ambushed. *(She takes a bottle of champagne from the fridge)* I even bought a new flute. Have you ever seen anything that beautiful in your life? Listen. *(She rings the glass lightly)* Do you believe that?

BURTON. What's the difference between a flute and a glass?

ANNA. About fifty bucks. Would it be unbearably provocative if I slipped into something less formal?

BURTON. Unbearably, without doubt. Do it.

ANNA. Undo.

BURTON. Whatever happened to zippers? There's nothing so beautiful as the sound of a long zipper down a woman's back.

ANNA. I'll remember.

BURTON. Also, I need the practice. It's been a while, you know.

ANNA. You have to give the story another week—I want to see where it goes. *(Exits into the bedroom)*

BURTON *(Raising his voice slightly)*. No, you were saying you were chicken; I think that's

what's happening. I don't want to know. I need to get out of the city or something—do something—shake things up. You sure you don't want to give up this loft and move in my place?

ANNA *(Offstage)*. Never. You want to live with me, you move in here.

BURTON. Maybe I should. Have kids or something.

ANNA *(Offstage)*. At least then I could do the piece on mother love. That's something I haven't thought about much. Or every time I did, I pushed it out of my mind. But now—I don't know. I think my body chemistry is changing, or maybe I just have time to think of things like that now. I can feel a kind of anxiety or panic creeping up on me. The sound of the biological clock or something. Which is probably only another way of avoiding work. Any excuse.

BURTON. I know the feeling. Every time I start to work on the love story I swiftly segue into droid-busting on Barsoom. I've been working on a kind of extension of the *Far Voyager* story—

ANNA. Do the other one.

BURTON. The space stuff's more fun. The other one isn't fun. I'm talking about myself again! I don't believe it. It's unconscious. *(ANNA comes back into the room in full dressing gown)* That's gorgeous. *(He holds her a moment. They sit and start to toast. There is a noise at the door)* What the hell?

ANNA. What time is it? It's Harrison across the hall, or maybe Larry coming home.

BURTON. Oh, God, let it be Harrison across the hall. I thought Larry wasn't due back till tomorrow.

ANNA. I think tonight.

BURTON. Well, fuck.

ANNA. Well, later at least.

LARRY *(Enters carrying three huge suitcases. He drops them and staggers across the room, collapsing on the sofa)*. I'm dying. Oh, God. Ask me where I was when we rang in the New Year. My arms are dead, they're falling off.

ANNA. Where were you when we rang in the New Year?

LARRY. Circling about ten thousand feet over Queens. And we had been for forty-five minutes. And we continued to for another hour. I was praying we would crash and burn. There was not a happy person on the plane. Everyone was going to a party. Nobody made it. Midnight came and went, nobody said a word. We just glared at each other. The last hour there wasn't a stewardess in sight, they were all up in the cabin with the pilot; we landed, one of them was visibly drunk.

BURTON. I thought you like to travel; you liked meeting people.

LARRY. The man next to me, I strongly suspect, was either Jerry Falwell himself or a member of the Supreme Court. Total Nazi. After half an hour of theories on the Sanctity of the Home and the American Family as the Last Bastion of Christian Liberty (whatever the hell that is) I said, "Well, being a cock-sucker, of course, I disagree with everything you've said." I was so angry I didn't even get off on it. That's what going home does to me—I lose my protective sense of humor. My arms are falling off.

ANNA. Happy New Year.

LARRY. Fuck you both. What are you doing here? Why aren't you out partying?

ANNA. It's two-thirty, we're back.

LARRY. From where?

ANNA. We went to a party. I liked it, didn't you?

BURTON. Yeah, it was fun. Up in SoHo.

ANNA. A bunch of the new young geniuses and starlets. I didn't know many of them. Burt can tell you.

BURTON. Nice group. So how's beautiful Detroit?

LARRY. Burton, "beautiful Detroit" is an oxymoron. Detroit is the South's revenge. You don't want to start your New Year with the story of the faggot's Christmas in Wales, believe me. *(He lights a cigarette)*

ANNA. When did you start smoking?

LARRY. How long have I been gone?

ANNA. You've got a dozen invitations to parties; hop in a cab, have some fun. They'll go on all night.

LARRY. Have you ever been to a gay New Year's Eve party? The suicide rate is higher than all of Scandinavia combined. My arms are falling off, my head hurts, I'm exhausted. For the first time in my life I have sympathy for Olga in *Three Sisters*.

ANNA. Go out. Meet someone.

LARRY. Anna, an Olympic gym team performing naked would not turn me on. The defensive front line of the Pittsburgh Steelers could rape me on the floor of the locker room, I'd bring them up on charges. If you're trying to ditch me, forget it. Go to Burton's. Oh, God. I have six nephews I'd never met before. And hope not to see again until they're sixteen. And two nieces. Both of my sisters *and* my brother's wife have turned

into baby machines. What is happening to women? Ten years ago they were exciting entities; they're all turning into cows.

BURTON. We were just talking about that.

ANNA. I get more of an image of a brood sow. Flat out in the mud, with about ten piglets squealing around you, trying to nurse. Have you ever seen that? Their eyes rolled back in their heads? Lying back in the sun, in some other world.

LARRY. I hope you don't think you're making it attractive. They all wrote down their kids' birthdays so I'd be sure to send something. There's a doomsday factor in our genes somewhere. Through the entire history of the species it's been the same story— the wrong people reproduce. *(Goes to ANNA)* Happy New Year. *(Kisses her lightly on the lips)*

ANNA. Happy New Year.

LARRY *(Goes to BURTON, kisses him lightly on the lips)*. Happy New Year.

BURTON. Happy New Year, Uncle Larry.

LARRY. Burton—you're a black belt in karate—

BURTON. Brown.

LARRY. You teach judo at the "Y"—

BURTON. Akido.

LARRY. I don't care. One more crack and I'll rip your eyes out. Oh, God, when did you last see a grown man cry?

ANNA. Uh . . . actually—when was it? The day after you left. I ran into an old friend of yours.

LARRY. I have no old friends. If I do have, I won't after this trip, because I'm going to be unbearable for a month.

ANNA. I think he was actually closer to Robbie than to you.

LARRY. Oh, please. I loved him dearly, but all Robbie's friends talked about dance with that fanatical glazed look across their eyes that always— Closer, how? You don't mean he was crying in his V.S.O. cognac . . . ?

ANNA. I think that's the only thing he drinks.

LARRY. And this was where . . . ?

ANNA. Midtown. Mid-morning. One drink. And I fled.

LARRY. Drinking in the mid-morning. You *have* gone downhill without me.

ANNA. I had coffee.

BURTON. Who was this?

LARRY. Just a Pale page from my checkered past. I don't think he came here more than once. Or I should say, I don't think he's *been* here more than once. Please note, my last cigarette. *(He stubs out the cigarette and puts the pack away)* Did Anna tell you she's working on a dance for Fred?

BURTON. Yeah, that's great.

ANNA. Oh sure—scares the hell out of me.

LARRY. I love it. I come home, she's dancing up a storm.

ANNA. I was flying around here the other day. I flop down, I think that's great; then I thought, I wonder if I could get arrested for that?

LARRY. In some states . . .

ANNA. I think it's all getting a little too personal.

BURTON. Good, it's supposed to be— Make it as personal as you can. Believe me, you can't imagine a feeling everyone hasn't had. Make it personal, tell the truth, and then write "Burn this" on it.

ANNA. Burton, at least, has made a giant leap into the unknown.

BURTON. Yeah, I've taken up skydiving.

ANNA. He's started working on something real.

BURTON. Naw, that's nothing, goes nowhere.

ANNA. It takes place in the city, and is some kind of love story with real people, so, of course, he doesn't trust it.

BURTON. I don't even know why I wrote it down. I was bored.

ANNA. I think it's very hot.

LARRY. So am I gonna hear it?

ANNA. Let him read it—it's only twenty pages.

BURTON. No, it's nothing. Come on.

LARRY. This is the Northern thing?

BURTON. The what? Oh no . . . I tried to do something on the Northern thing; it turned into this city thing.

ANNA. We were about to toast the New Year.

LARRY. Where did those come from? They're gorgeous.

ANNA. Baccarat. They were in the window.

LARRY. How many?

ANNA. Four. It did in my life savings.

LARRY. I'm in love. I'm going to sleep with them.

ANNA. Happy New Year. *(They all toast, say "Happy New Year," and drink)* Oh, Lord. That makes you understand what they mean by champagne.

LARRY. Home again, home again . . .

ANNA. Jiggity-jig.

(A distant bell sounds)

BURTON. Where the hell is there a bell at this hour?

LARRY. I didn't imagine there was such a thing as a real bell anymore. I thought they were all recordings blasted over loudspeakers.

BURTON. The first year I was in New York I had a job as a messenger. I took a package to this poet's loft—

ANNA. Messenger?

BURTON. I must have been eighteen.

ANNA. God knows you didn't need the money.

BURTON. I know, but I decided I should experience work—I forget why. Anyway, this poet was over on Fourth Avenue, across from the church there. And we got to talking. He asked me what I did and I said I was a writer; turned out he was a poet and I'd read some of his stuff, and he was impressed and I was impressed, and we had a drink and a joint and sat around—this is not a job that I kept for very long.

LARRY. I can see that. Actually, I imagine he was trying to think of a way to get in your pants.

BURTON. Oh, for godsake—why is it always that? Why does it always have to be that with you?

LARRY. Burton, you're talking about a poet. Why does it always have to be that? Ask your priest; I didn't invent people. It's just always that. Anyway.

BURTON. So anyway—the church bells started ringing. We were sitting in the open window, on a big window seat, right across the street from the bell tower, and he said, Poe, Edgar Allan Poe used to live in that apartment. And those bells were the bells, bells, bells, bells, bells, bells.

ANNA. Oh, God. The tintinnabulation. Where?

BURTON. Fourth Avenue and about East Tenth. He got the apartment because of them.

ANNA. Of course he did.

BURTON. Actually, Larry—this'll give you a thrill—he *was* gay and I knew it, and it never crossed my mind he was anything but sincere. I really don't think he was trying to make me.

LARRY. It's possible, Burton. In a different world. But who knows what world poets live in, so—

BURTON. You want to know something? One time—you should know this—when I was twenty—two years later—I'd been here

two years and a half. I was up around Columbia. I decided to walk down to the Village. I had to piss so bad—about Fifteenth
Street and Eighth or Ninth Avenue—middle
of the—say 1 A.M.—and I mean, it's cold. It'd
started to snow, so everything was white. I
pissed up alongside a doorway, I was feeling
very high—on the night, nothing chemical—and this guy sidles up to me from nowhere—there wasn't another person on the
street—and he says, "You live around here?"
Or some dumb thing.

LARRY. Have you got a match? Yeah.

BURTON. And I think, This is something I
should know about. I'm a writer, I'm supposed to know about these things.

LARRY. Always a dangerous supposition.

BURTON. I just shook it off and turned
around and leaned against the wall and
watched it snow while he went down on me.
I came, and he put it away and said thank
you, if you believe it, and I said, Have a good
life, and went on walking down to the Village. And I never thought about it again. So
I'm not completely unversed in your world.

LARRY. That is gorgeous. With the snow
falling. God. I mean it's not *Wuthering Heights,*
but . . . God.

BURTON. It was very nice, and I never
thought about it. And it didn't mean anything, but I've never been sorry it happened
or any of that crap.

LARRY. Lord, the innocence and freedom
of yesterday.

ANNA. I was just thinking that.

LARRY. Actually, I don't like those ships-
that-pass-in-the-night scenes. That doesn't
mean that the image of you getting blown in
the snow won't haunt me till I die. I think I'll
probably be a happier— Did you have your
shirt up?

BURTON. I had on a jacket, a scarf, a hat,
gloves, galoshes. I had my fly unzipped.

LARRY. You don't care if, in my mind, I sort
of push your shirt up to above your navel,
and let your pants fall to about mid-thigh, do
you?

BURTON. Be my guest. Larry, we're getting
ready to go to bed here— I'm just trying to
burn a little clock.

(There is a noise outside the door)

LARRY. What the hell's that?

ANNA. That's got to be Harrison.

LARRY. Happy New Year, Harrison. You
old queen.

ANNA. Oh, he is not.

LARRY. He just doesn't know it. He's going
to wake up on his fortieth birthday in a dress.

BURTON. Did he knock?

LARRY. No way, shy as a nun. Has anyone
ever really seen a shy nun? *(He opens the door,*
PALE *falls in)* Oh shit. Scare me to death. Are
you hurt?

BURTON. What the hell's happening?

LARRY. It's Pale. Not in the best shape. Are
you okay?

*(PALE staggers, half on his hands and knees, to
the bathroom)*

ANNA. Absolutely not, Jimmy. No way. I'm
sorry. Jimmy! Damnit all! Who the hell does
he think he is?

BURTON. Who the hell *is* he?

ANNA. Oh, God. He's a maître d' or . . .

LARRY. Manager.

ANNA. Manager.

LARRY. Of a restaurant.

ANNA. The Il Santalino or something.

LARRY. Da Signate.

ANNA. Over in Short Hills.

LARRY. Montclair.

ANNA *(Beat).* New Jersey.

LARRY. If after five attempts, you think you
get any points for New Jersey . . .

BURTON. He just walks in? What the fuck's
he doing here? He live in the building?

LARRY. He's Robbie's brother.

BURTON. Oh shit.

LARRY. Yeah, he's pretty crushed.

ANNA. Well, he can be crushed somewhere
else. Really. He can't just bulldoze his way in
here every time he hangs one on. Is he being
sick?

LARRY. I would say affirmative, except I try
not to talk like that.

ANNA. Oh, God.

BURTON. It's a little late, gang, for a neighborly visit, you know?

LARRY *(At the bathroom door).* Jimmy—are
you—yes, he's being sick. Jesus. Doll, are you
all right?

PALE *(Offstage).* What the fuck do you
know, fruit?

LARRY. I beg your pardon?

PALE. What the fuck do you know?

LARRY. What do I know?

PALE. What the fuck do you fuckin' know?
Fruit?

LARRY. Jimmy, that's one of those questions
one never knows whether to answer with
hubris or humility. Are you okay?

PALE. Get the fuck out! *(Slams the door in*
LARRY's *face)*

LARRY. In layout design I could whip his ass. I think this would be a good time to relax and finish the champagne.

BURTON. You want him out of here?

ANNA. Oh, for God's sake. *(Goes to bathroom door)* Jimmy. Jimmy. Are you—well, obviously he's not all right. Jimmy, what's up? *(*PALE *opens the door, his face wet, mopping it with a towel, hangs on to her, kisses her)* Come on. What the hell do you think this is?

BURTON. Hey, fella. What the hell do you think you're doing?

PALE *(Drops the towel, drops to one knee, holding the wall to steady himself)*. Who the fuck are you?

ANNA. Hey, Burt, come on. Burton, this is Jimmy, Robbie's brother—Jimmy, this is my friend Burton. I feel like an idiot. Larry, shut up. Jimmy, we're not entertaining tonight, so I don't think you can stay.

LARRY *(simultaneously)*. Where the fuck did you come from? What the fuck do you want? It's me, isn't it? You've always wanted to fuck me. You want to have your filthy fuckin' way with me in the hot desert sun . . . Ravage me like I've never been ravaged before.

PALE. You another dancer?

ANNA. Burton's a writer.

PALE. Same thing.

BURTON. Do you need something? Or is this just a friendly visit? Jimmy?

PALE. "Jimmy," shit. Nobody calls me Jimmy. They call me Pale.

BURTON. What?

ANNA. Pale.

BURTON. As in bucket?

ANNA. As in a bucket of brandy. Pale, it's 3 A.M. I know you don't get off work till late, but we're about to call it a . . . year here, you know?

BURTON. You need help getting down to the street or something?

*(*PALE *gets up, manages to stumble to a chair, almost turning over a table. Sits)*

ANNA. Oh, you are in great shape. You look like a bum.

BURTON. What do you mean? He is a bum.

ANNA. He's not a bum.

BURTON. Who the hell is he?

ANNA. I told you, Burton, damnit. He's the maître d'—

LARRY. God! Manager! Of the Da Signate Ristorante in Montclair, New Jersey. Jesus.

ANNA. He has a very demanding job.

BURTON. Don't we all. You need help, buddy? 'Cause you're not staying.

PALE. What the fuck do you know?

ANNA. Very little, I'm sure. About anything.

BURTON. I know you're leaving. You call tomorrow. Late, okay?

PALE. About Robbie? Huh? Fuckin' zip.

ANNA. Pale, it's been two months. More. I'm sorry, but you can't grieve forever. Not even you. *I* can't. He gets drunk, he thinks about him. Guilt and that number.

BURTON. He's gonna pass out. Unless you intend to put him up here, I'm gonna help him out into the street. I seem to remember we were having a party.

PALE. You're not "right," are you. You're a little funny.

BURTON. We'll see if you laugh.

PALE *(To* ANNA*)*. Tell your friend good night. Let's go.

BURTON. You're the one who's leaving, buddy.

*(*PALE *lunges at* BURTON. BURTON, *with a deft move, drives* PALE *straight into a wall headfirst.* PALE *sits on the floor, his back against the wall, staring at them)*

ANNA. Burt. Pale. Oh, for godsake.

BURTON. What the hell does he think he's doing?

ANNA *(To a blinking* PALE*)*. I should have mentioned, Burt teaches akido at the "Y."

BURTON. Six years, that's the first time I ever used it.

LARRY *(Lighting a cigarette)*. Please note, I'm smoking again. Also, that's not the smartest thing to do. He carries a gun.

BURTON. A what? And you let him in here?

LARRY. He fell in.

ANNA. He takes the deposits to the bank at night. I asked; we were right. I don't believe it.

PALE. What fuckin' accident? No fuckin' accident.

LARRY. What's that?

PALE. Robbie and Dominic out in the fuckin' bay—I said there wasn't any fuckin' accident.

ANNA. Not again, Jimmy—I think we've done that number.

PALE. What are you wearin' that thing?

LARRY. What about the accident, Pale?

PALE *(To* ANNA*)*. You ain't cold, that thing?

ANNA. No. *(To* LARRY*)* It's nothing, believe me.

BURTON. Then I'm sorry, fella, we can't serve you here . . . after hours, buddy.

PALE *(Looks at* BURTON*)*. Who's Bruce Lee?

You're cute. You think I can't break a candy
ass like him?

ANNA. When I saw him before, he was
saying the mob did it. They have some interest in the restaurant.

LARRY. Oh, please.

BURTON. When was this you saw him?

LARRY. There were definitely no mobster
types when I went to the restaurant.

PALE. What assholes. I thought you people
was supposed to be *with* it, you're supposed
to "swing," you "know what's coming down."
Show me a restaurant ain't connected, I'll
show you an establishment don't serve food
and drink, okay? I can't stay here *(Getting up)*
with you assholes. I got me a reputation to
uphold here. You're too stupid for me to stay
with.

BURTON. If you know something—

LARRY. Or think you do, you should—

(As BURTON *approaches* PALE, PALE *decks him;
tripping him, kicking him in the groin and again
in the back as soon as he hits the floor)*

ANNA. Pale—damnit. Burton, are you all
right?

PALE. Nobody does that shit, nobody pulls
that shit.

*(*BURTON *is up, winded and shocked; they
square off, circle)*

BURTON. All right, fella, I was being nice;
I'm gonna take you apart. I'm gonna enjoy
this.

ANNA. Burton, stop it, goddamnit. Both of
you. Come on.

PALE. Come on, come on—*(He makes a
lunge and* BURTON *sends him flying)*

ANNA. Burton! Goddamnit, for Christ's
sake, this is my apartment! What the fuck do
you two think you're doing? *(She steps between
them.* BURTON *shoves her aside very roughly; she
falls. He clips* PALE—PALE *sprawls)* Burton.
Goddamnit.

BURTON. No way, buddy, nobody blind-
sides me, no way.

ANNA. Okay, leave, then, go on. Burton,
damnit, I said leave. *(Pushes him away—*PALE
stands off)

BURTON. I'm not leaving you here with him.

ANNA. Yes, you are, and now.

BURTON. No way am I leaving you alone
with this fucker. *(*PALE *has sat down)* Go on,
buddy, out.

ANNA. You first, just go— Really, I'm not
going to have it. That's not the way I live.

BURTON. We were going to have a party—
that son-of-a-bitch comes over; no way.

ANNA. Leave, go on. I'll see you tomorrow.
I can't have it.

BURTON. Anna, what kind of a man is going
to leave you alone with him? Huh? What's he
going to do?

ANNA. Nothing.

BURTON. You don't know him.

ANNA. I know him, he's fine. I can't kick
him out, so I'm asking you to leave.

BURTON. I'll kick him out, no problem.

ANNA. Go. Damnit. You're the one I don't
know right now.

PALE. You fuckin' him, too?

(A stunned pause)

BURTON. What'd you say?

ANNA. Would you please not do this crap?

PALE. Good night.

ANNA. Burton, really, good night.

BURTON. What's he talking about?
You're . . .

ANNA. It's utterly beside the point. Good
night. Tomorrow.

BURTON. I'm gonna have to rethink everything here. I mean our whole relationship
here. This isn't it. This is nothing I want any
part of.

ANNA. Good night.

*(*BURTON *gets his coat, goes to the door without
looking back, and leaves)*

PALE. Good night, Bruce.

LARRY. Did you hurt your arm?

ANNA. Oh—no more than I've been hurt
every week since I was eight. Pale, you're
going to have to—*(*PALE *puts his arms around
her, his hands under her robe)* Stop it, damnit.
I'm not your whore, for you to come and
have every time you get drunk. Stop it. *(Pulls
away)* Goddamnit, both of you with that
macho bullshit. Okay, now you. Get it together and get it out of here. Up. Go on.

LARRY. Pale? It's not as butch as Burton,
but if you don't leave, I'll hit you over the
head with a skillet. I'm not joking.

ANNA. I should have had you and Burton
carry him out. I didn't want them breaking
each other's faces out on the street. *Gunfight
at the O.K. Corral.*

PALE. I ain't got it.

LARRY. You ain't got—don't have what?

PALE. The gun. I lost the fucker.

ANNA. When?

PALE. Last week. It's gone. I ain't got it.

ANNA. Where? Well, that's a stupid . . .
Pale, don't stretch out and—Pale? Oh,
God . . .

LARRY. You don't mean it.

ANNA. Sleeping like a baby.

LARRY. Oh, great. He could have broken Burton's back or something— Oh, Lordy. *(He pours them each a glass of champagne)* Is it too cold to drag him out?

ANNA. With the anti-freeze he's got in him, he should be good for a month. If he'd had the grace to pass out a minute sooner, Burton'd still be here. I had almost decided if he proposed again I was going to accept him.

LARRY. That's why you dressed like Lucia di Lammermoor. *(He hands her her glass)*

ANNA. Thank you. Happy New Year.

LARRY. A real auspicious beginning.

ANNA. I loathe violence. What is that? I could live my life very well, thank you, without ever seeing another straight man.

LARRY. Me too. Don't hold me to that. What was that about the accident?

ANNA. Oh, when I saw him last week, he was saying he and his dad and their cronies got to drinking, someone says I saw your fruit brother on the TV with his boyfriend. All the usual fag-baiting braggadocio. Someone ought to off the fucker, embarrassment to the family, that crap. And a couple of nights later, Robbie's dead, so he had no way of knowing if—

LARRY. Oh, give me a break.

ANNA.That's what I said. Massive guilt trip.

LARRY. Good. Serves you right, Pale. I have to carry those fuckin' bags down to my room.

ANNA. Get them tomorrow.

LARRY. Never put off till tomorrow what might kill you today. Also, my toothbrush is in there somewhere. God, how it's missed its own glass. Are you going to bed? *(He gets his bags)*

ANNA. Yes. Pale? Oh damn.

LARRY. Get a blanket down from Robbie's room, I guess.

ANNA. He doesn't like to be covered.

LARRY. That's right. He'll be sorry.

(ANNA turns off the lights. The living room is dark)

(They are both in their rooms)

LARRY. My own bed, my own sheets, my own pillow . . .

ANNA. Should I set an alarm or something for him, so he doesn't miss work again?

LARRY. They're probably closed tomorrow.

ANNA. Then to hell with it. *(She goes into the bathroom, turns on the light)* Good night, love.

LARRY *(Offstage)*. 'Night, doll. *(Sings)* "At night I wake up with the sheets soaking wet

There's a freight train runnin'

Through the middle of my head . . .

And you, you cool my desire.

Oh . . . oh . . . oh . . . I'm on fire . . ."

(PALE sits up on the sofa. He gets up, looks around, moves to the window, opens it, and steps out onto the fire escape. He walks the distance of the windows, lights a cigarette. ANNA comes from the bathroom to her room. After a moment PALE flicks his cigarette out into the night. He comes back into the apartment and walks to her room. The lights fade, music up)

(LARRY is in the kitchen. Coffee has been made. PALE, dressed in one of ANNA's robes, comes from her room)

LARRY. It does nothing for you. I couldn't wait to sleep the clock around in my own bed. I woke up at eight.

PALE *(Sleepy)*. What time is it?

LARRY. About nine. You off today?

PALE. Yeah.

LARRY. Sleep late, for godsake; once, anyway.

PALE. Can't do it.

LARRY. I made coffee, you don't use it. What about tea?

PALE. Whatta you got?

LARRY *(Looking through cabinet)*. We got: English Breakfast, Irish Breakfast, something that tastes exactly like I imagine burned rubber tires would taste . . .

PALE. Lapsang Souchong.

LARRY. You want it, you'd be doing us a favor.

PALE. You got no plain orange pekoe tea?

LARRY. —Jasmine, Sleepytime, Red Zinger, Camomile. And plain Red Rose orange pekoe tea. *(Puts the bag in a mug)* The water's still hot. I thought your familiarity with the finer foods of life—

PALE. Stop. Whattaya doin'? You gonna make a pot a tea, you gonna make one cup? It's not even economical.

LARRY. We actually have a teapot, but I've never seen it used for anything except to put flowers in. *(Takes it out of cabinet)*

PALE. Get out, go on, you're useless. I thought you clowns were supposed to be worthwhile in the kitchen at least.

LARRY. I never really claimed any expertise in the area. You cook?

PALE *(Turns up heat under water until it boils)*. I'd better cook. Cook ain't in, I'm it. What? Six—eight times cook don't show, snowstorm, somethin', I gotta cook. I'm okay. *(Pours water in pot, empties it)*

LARRY. There? Professionally? I've been to your place; twice, actually. It's very good.

PALE. Yeah, I told the cook people couldn't tell the difference. He didn't like it. Next time it snowed he slept inna kitchen. *Gourmet* magazine, they print recipes from like these famous restaurants; I take in the magazine, twice now. I say, So how come you left out the paprika in one; in the other, how come there ain't no lemon juice and no nutmeg? And the butter ain't clarified? He says, Okay, they'll make it at home, then they'll come here and think, Son-of-a-bitch, that man's just a better cook than I am. *(He puts the water and three tea bags in the pot, looks for a tea towel, covers the pot with it)*

LARRY. Whatever you're doing, I'm impressed.

PALE. What? Twenty years the restaurant business, I can't make a pot of tea, I'm in trouble.

LARRY. You know, it's very unlikely anyone did your family the favor of arranging Robbie's accident.

PALE. I don't wanta talk about it, okay?

LARRY. This would be the situation where the little boy says, "I hate Daddy and I want him to die," and two days later Daddy goes off to the hospital and doesn't come home again. And the little boy thinks it's his fault.

PALE. Yeah? That mighta been the night the angels decided to listen to the little boy.

LARRY. I don't think so.

PALE. That's the way Catholics think; we're fucked.

LARRY. It all sounds very unlikely.

PALE. Yeah, one side of my brain knows that—the other side drinks.

LARRY. Anna said she might be wrong, but she doesn't remember your wife at Robbie's funeral.

PALE. She wasn't there.

LARRY. So she's still in Coral Gables?

PALE. You remember everything everybody says, huh?

LARRY. It's a gift.

PALE. She couldn't take the heat, so she took the kids. Who the fuck cares? I'm home three hours a night, work seventeen hours some days; more'n sixty-five hours a week. I get off midnight, I gotta unwind; I get home at two, I'm up at five. Who can live with that?

LARRY. How can you?

PALE. I'm used to it.

LARRY. You'll burn yourself out, too. She should have taken a job as a waitress at the restaurant.

PALE. You got a real sense of humor there, that could be valuable to you. Her work? Not while I'm makin' nine hundred bucks a week. Six of it off the books, more like nineteen hundred.

LARRY. Jesus.

PALE. I bust my butt, don't worry.

LARRY. So you're divorced?

PALE. What's with questions, this hour the morning? I might want to experience the day here. Take inventory, somethin'. Her give me a divorce? She split, you should see how religious she got. The medals, the saints, the candles, never seen such crap. I coulda dragged her ass back. Who needs it? Sicka lookin' at her. Married a week outta school— what'd I know, I'm eighteen. It was good about six days. *(Pouring tea, adds milk)*

LARRY. Milk?

PALE. Yeah, it—like—ties up the tannic acid, it don't burn your guts.

LARRY. There's lemon in the fridge.

PALE. Lemon'll kill ya.

LARRY. Citric acid's vitamin C—cure anything.

PALE. Acid's acid.

(Phone rings; we hear LARRY's voice)

LARRY'S VOICE. Hello. Neither Anna nor I can come to the phone just now. Please leave a message when you hear the beep.

(Pause—beep)

BURTON'S VOICE. Uh, Anna? It's Burton. Listen, I think I had too much blow last night, I—

PALE. He hang up? *(Pause)* He hang up?

LARRY. She picked it up in the bedroom.

PALE *(To phone)*. You got somethin' talk about, Bruce, come over, we'll talk. *(Laughs)* He hung up.

LARRY *(Lighting a cigarette)*. You are hazardous to people's health, Pale.

ANNA *(Enters, in jeans and T-shirt)*. Goddamnit, Pale, what the hell do you think you're doing? That phone call happened to be—oh, real cute. Thanks. *(She slams down on the sofa. He goes to her. Sips his tea, offers her some)* That looks strong.

PALE. You want a cup?

ANNA. I guess.

PALE. You want some eggs? *(He pours her a cup of tea)*

LARRY. He cooks.

ANNA. No, I don't want to admit I'm still awake. Uh, Pale . . .

LARRY. I'm going to take a shower.

ANNA. In a minute, okay? Pale, would you do me a favor?

PALE. Sure.

ANNA. I don't want you to think that we've started something here.

PALE. . . . How come?

ANNA. I just don't. We're apples and oranges.

PALE. Yeah? Who's the apple and who's the orange?

ANNA. Pale.

PALE. You ever had that apple tart, glazed with marmalade?

ANNA. No, I haven't. I have to work; you have work to do.

PALE. Yeah? You get the job?

ANNA. What? Yes, I'm making a dance for a very important concert and it has me a little hysterical and it's occupying my time completely. This just isn't for me. I'm sorry if I led you on in any way. I don't feel well, and I'm not up for one of your scenes, but I'd like to not see you anymore.

PALE. How come?

ANNA. I don't know. I think you're dangerous.

PALE. Bullshit. You walk down the street, a brick falls on your head.

ANNA. But not in my apartment.

PALE. You gonna never leave your room, what?

ANNA. I might.

PALE. How come you don't feel good?

ANNA. I'm tired, my stomach's upset.

PALE. Who wouldn't be tired after what we did—?

ANNA. Pale.

PALE. I'm tired, too; I'm fuckin' hung out to dry here. That tea's no good for a bad stomach. You want some milk?

ANNA. No. Please, Pale.

PALE. You're a real different person in the sack than you are standin' up.

ANNA. I know.

PALE. Which one's the lie? Were you fakin' it?

ANNA. I'm not lying now. And no, it isn't possible for me to fake it in bed.

PALE. You kiddin' me? Easiest thing in the world. Done it all my life. Half the time I'd fake it, too fuckin' tired to have interest. My ol' lady'd run in and douche herself, come back feelin' fucked, cuddle up to me; I didn't know whether to hate the bitch for believin' me or for flushin' me out. Both of 'em lies. Lies happen like every ten seconds. Half the people you see on the street don't mean a thing they're doin'. Hug up some bitch, don't mean nothin' to them. Bitch smilin' up into his eyes, have more fun pushin' the bastard

through a sausage grinder. My brother Sammy, older'n me, kissed his bride, said he wanted to bite the lips off her. People ain't easy.

ANNA. I know.

PALE. You said last night in the sack you ain't been with nobody since a month ago when you was with me. I ain't either. I figger one more time, we got us a hat trick. I got a vacation comin' up. I thought we'd go someplace.

ANNA. I'm working.

PALE. Hawaii, Brazil. See places.

ANNA. Really, Pale. Really.

LARRY (After a long pause). I think I should go straighten my room.

PALE. Naw, you stay here, like she wanted. I'll split. I don't hurt people. (He goes into her room)

ANNA. No cracks, okay.

LARRY. Okay.

ANNA. No jokes.

LARRY. Even if it kills me.

ANNA. May I go to your room and lock the door? I don't want to see him.

LARRY. Of course you may.

PALE (He has put his pants on, but nothing else; comes from her room). No, I don't like it. You're gettin' me mad here. Lived with that bitch sixteen years, all we ever do is yell, never touched her once. Never felt nothin' for her.

ANNA. How would you be with someone you felt something for?

PALE. I never felt nothin' for nobody. How do I know? Whatta you want, a contract here? I'll write it out: I ever hit you, take my car or somethin'. What's causin' this crap?

ANNA. Pale, I don't even know how this nonsense started; it never should have.

PALE. It did.

ANNA. It didn't. Well, it did and it shouldn't have. I'm tired and sick, and I've got work to do.

PALE. Everybody's off today.

ANNA. Then I've got to sleep; you don't sleep, I sleep.

PALE. So we'll sleep.

ANNA. No . . . definitely not; I'm tired.

PALE. Me too. So what? My pants look like a pig's wearin' 'em, I got a hangover here, I'm puttin' on weight, I'm losin' my hair, and you're talkin' like that? I'm not dangerous. You don't think I'm dangerous; you think you're afraid of me is what you think.

ANNA. Okay, fine.

PALE. Why? (Pause) You're afraid you might get interested. Have to feel somethin'.

ANNA. I feel, Pale, all the time. I'm a crack-erjack feeler, thank you. *(Pause. To* LARRY*)* I'll go to your room.

LARRY. Sure. If he breaks the door in, somebody else pays for it.

PALE. I don't break in doors.

LARRY. I did once. Nearly killed myself. Cost three hundred dollars to replace.

PALE. Annie! Hey!

ANNA *(At* LARRY*'s door)*. Pale, don't do this.

PALE. Do what? What am I doin'? You're the one doin' here.

ANNA. Oh, God. I'll try to say this so you can understand where . . . my point of view. I almost said "where I'm coming from." I have a friend that I'm seeing, Pale, and—

PALE. Who's that, Bruce?

ANNA. Burton. And we see—

PALE. You like him so much, why ain't you makin' it with him?

ANNA. . . . and we see things very similarly, and share a great deal, and I like being with him. I, at least, would like to give us the time to see if we're as compatible as we seem to be.

PALE. No, I can tell you.

ANNA. And I'm at a time in my life when—well, I just don't feel like fucking around. Sleeping around.

PALE. So don't.

ANNA. Pale, I have never had a personal life. I wasn't scared of it, I just had no place for it, it wasn't important. And all that is different now and I'm very vulnerable, I'm not going to be prey to something I don't want. I'm too easy. Go somewhere else.

PALE. I come to you.

ANNA. No. I said no. I don't want this. I'm not strong enough to kick you out physically. Why are you being so damned truculent? I said I don't like you. I don't want to know you. I don't want to see you again. There is no reason for you to come here. I have nothing for you. I don't like you and I'm frightened of you.

*(*PALE *looks at her, goes into the bedroom, comes out with his clothes. Goes to his cup of tea, finishing it. He doesn't look at her; they both stare at him)*

PALE *(Not looking up from tying his shoes)*. What does that mean, "truculent"?

LARRY. Fierce, or actually, I think, uh, "like a truck."

PALE *(Mumbles)*. Like a truck. Great. *(He finishes and goes to her, kisses her and leaves.* ANNA *is on the brink of tears to the end of the scene)*

LARRY. I didn't think you'd get rid of him

by telling him to go. You say, "I'm desperately in love with you, never leave my side; I want to have your baby," and they'll leave.

ANNA. Could you go see if he actually is leaving?

LARRY. He actually is leaving.

ANNA. Go watch, I'm not kidding. Jesus, I reek of Jimmy.

LARRY. A little brandy-perspiration and cologne. Not that bad, really. As he said, he's clean.

ANNA. The whole bedroom reeks of him. God. I'm going to have a shower, make the bed with clean sheets, and sleep the entire day. *(Leaving)* Thanks for staying for that. *(She is gone)*

LARRY *(Half calling to her)*. Think nothing of it. It was a completely new experience for me. And that is something I've never enjoyed. I'm not really that improvisational. I like having a rough copy to work from, at least. Something to go by.

(She re-enters with an enormous wad of sheets)

ANNA. What?

LARRY. Nothing.

ANNA. I'm sick of the age I'm living in. I don't like feeling ripped off and scared.

LARRY *(Not campy)*. You'd rather be pillaged and raped?

ANNA. I'm *being* pillaged and raped. I'm being pillaged and I'm being raped. And I don't like it. *(Stands in the middle of the pile of sheets. All the wind goes out of her)*

LARRY. What? What is it, doll? Huh?

*(*ANNA *almost cries; her shoulders shake)*

ANNA. Ohhhhh! *I feel miserable!* Oh, damnit all. Did he leave?

LARRY. Yes.

ANNA. Aw, Jesus. Is he still out there, or did you see him drive off?

LARRY. I saw him drive off. If you didn't want him to go, you sure fooled me. It's okay, doll.

ANNA. It's not okay, doll; it fucking sucks.

LARRY. Okay, it sucks. You're absolutely right, it fucking sucks. Man, does it suck. It sucks so bad. God, does it suck.

ANNA. Don't. Come on.

LARRY. What?

ANNA. Goddamnit, I can't take it. *(She goes to the closet, gets her coat)* I'm gonna have to see some more kids tomorrow—I'm working with four, I think I need six. Three couples. If I can't have a life at least I can work.

LARRY. Where you going?

ANNA. To Fred's studio. No one will be there today; I can get something done.

LARRY. Work here.

ANNA. No, no offense, but I want to be by myself.

LARRY. I'll leave.

ANNA. No.

LARRY. Eat something first.

ANNA. No, I'm not hungry. I'll pick up something later. Happy New Year. Get some rest.

LARRY. Well, don't just whip out of here, take a shower first.

(She is at the door, coat on, bag in her hand, looking for her keys. She looks up at him steadily for a moment, studio keys in her hand. The music rises. She exits, closing the door behind her)

Blackout

(BURTON stands center, still, rather in a daze. He holds a script. LARRY comes from his room, putting on a sweatshirt. The door remains open; it's a gray day)

LARRY. Sorry—I had but nothing on. Foul day, huh? *(Beat)* You want to get the door? *(Pause)* Burt? You want to get the door? *(Pause. He goes to shut the door)*

BURTON. Is Anna here?

LARRY. No. She's been busting her butt, you know, on the piece. It's glorious, of course.

BURTON. I'm, uh, I want to see it.

LARRY. It starts tonight, so she's probably there. It's only on for four nights—which is a long run for that kind of thing, if you can believe it. It's wonderful. I saw a tech run-through last night—It's miles and away the best piece on the program.

BURTON. She hasn't answered any of my messages. I wrote; I've been calling for a month.

LARRY. Maybe our machine isn't working; I don't think we're getting our messages . . .

BURTON. No, that's okay, you don't have to do that.

LARRY. . . . . Good. You been working?

BURTON. Yeah, I did . . . the city thing. Most of it. I wanted to—I wanted her to read it.

LARRY. That's great. She'd love to. So would I.

BURTON. No, I don't think I'm ready for . . . well, okay. You're in it, sure. Don't pass it around.

LARRY. I'm in it?

BURTON. Nobody's safe around a writer. I thought you knew that.

LARRY. What do I do? Never mind, I'll find out. You want a drink?

BURTON. No, I haven't been drinking. Sure, what you got?

LARRY. Anything. Well, actually, vodka and Wild Turkey.

BURTON. Wild Turkey neat.

LARRY. Why not?

BURTON. Has she been seeing him?

LARRY. "Him"?

BURTON. Yeah.

LARRY *(Making two drinks, vodka on the rocks)*. I'm wondering what my procedure is here. We haven't talked about anything. She's not been out one night this month. But it kinda doesn't matter. I mean, except work. She comes home, I say, Hi, how was it, and she says, It's going well but it's difficult, and I say, You want something to eat, and she says, I stopped by some Chinese place on the way home, and she makes a drink and picks up a book and I go out to eat, and when I come home she's in her room with the light on and the door closed. Reading, I presume. She's working. But I *can* testify that the work she's doing is phenomenal. It's great.

BURTON. Then she's not seeing him?

LARRY. Burton, at least say, Good, she's working, or, Terrific, the work's good. Nothing else is important. She's already got a commission from it; no one's even seen it except a few bigwigs.

BURTON *(Drinking, second sip)*. What the hell is this?

LARRY. What?

BURTON. I asked for Turkey up; this is vodka rocks.

LARRY. I'm sorry.

BURTON. That's okay.

LARRY. No, that's just my mind. *(Pours BURTON's drink into his, makes another)*

BURTON. So, has she been seeing him?

LARRY. I thought I answered that.

BURTON. What'd you say?

LARRY. . . . . What'd I say? You tell me.

BURTON *(Thinking)*. You said—I was listening; I was just listening too closely. You said, "I'm wondering about my procedure. We haven't talked at all; she's not been out one night in a month, but it kinda doesn't matter, she comes home, I say, Hi—"

LARRY. Stop. That's phenomenal.

BURTON. What? She's not been out one night this month?

LARRY. I said it kinda doesn't matter.

BURTON. What does that mean?

LARRY. It doesn't matter if she's seen him. It doesn't matter. The dance she's done is

Pale and Anna. No, he hasn't been over. No, she hasn't seen him; it doesn't matter.

BURTON. Is that what it's called? Pale and Anna? Pale and me? What music are they using?

LARRY. You're not thinking. You've seen Fred's stuff; when have you ever heard music? It's a synthesized kind of city noise, with a foghorn and gulls and—it's here. This loft. Only more so. It's kind of epic. Well, for twelve minutes.

BURTON. How do you know it's supposed to be he?

LARRY. Well, for one thing, I've never seen a man on stage in a dance—it's a man and a— It's very startling. It just has to do with the center of gravity, I guess, but . . . or something. I mean it's a regular man—dancing like a man dances—in a bar or something, with his girl. You've never seen anything like it. I can't describe a dance; you might as well try to describe a piece of music.

BURTON. No, I know what you mean. I have this problem I'm trying to cope with here. I was a rich kid, you know.

LARRY. I know.

BURTON. And I've never really—I've always had pretty much my own—I've never lost anything before. Or, I've never lost. Before. *(Pause)* See, what gets to me is, I keep feeling angry. You know, I could tear the shithead apart.

LARRY. I know.

BURTON. I could. But, you know, that doesn't mean anything. What's bothering me is, I keep feeling "Fuck *her,*" you know?—and then I know that that's not really what I'm feeling—that's just a protective mechanism sort of thing that I've always used so I wouldn't lose. You know? 'Cause I've never lost. And I don't really feel "Fuck her" at all. That's just my immune system defending me.

LARRY. It's a handy thing to have.

BURTON *(Setting his glass on the table).* Hit me.

LARRY. I beg your pardon? Oh, another, sure. *(Pours, leaves the bottle)* It's perfectly natural you'd be pissed.

BURTON. Well, see . . . uh . . . I think you were supposed to say, "Hell, the race isn't over yet, kid, hang in there and fight."

LARRY. I'm sorry, Burton. "Win one for the Gipper" sticks in my craw.

BURTON. That's all right. So, I guess she

really is in love with someone. We ought to celebrate. How's he feel about her?

LARRY. His entire mechanism is beyond my pale, doll. Anyway, we've not seen him. He hasn't come around. I would say he feels pretty much the same, but she threw him out so . . .

BURTON. She what? She threw him out? Boy, she is a piece of work, isn't she? And then goes off and makes a dance about him, great.

LARRY. She's had a very protected life. I mean, she's never had to even carry her own passport or plane tickets—she's not had to make her own way much.

BURTON. Yeah, I know. So what's she planning to do with her life? Live here with you?

LARRY *(Pause).* I . . . uh . . . think I'll duck that one, if you don't mind.

BURTON. Sorry, I didn't intend that to sound like it did.

LARRY. No, actually that's very vivid. Put like that. *(Makes himself another drink)* And by extension, what the fuck am I doing?

BURTON. Well, listen, it's none of my business. Tell her, you know, what we said, if you want to. Or not.

LARRY *(Beat).* Huh? . . . Oh, uh . . . no, I definitely will.

BURTON. This isn't the way I was hoping . . .

LARRY. Tell me about it.

BURTON. Well . . . I got work. Read that, let me know what you think. I don't know. Give it to her. Tell her I'd like to hear—you know—what she thought about its—whatever.

LARRY. It's starting to snow, Burton, it's getting dark. Surely we could find a welcoming doorway somewhere on the block.

BURTON *(Smiles).* Are you going to make me sorry I told you that?

LARRY. No. Thought I should mention it.

BURTON. I just haven't felt that open to the world since those days. Have a good life.

(He leaves. LARRY stands in the middle of the room. Music up, lights fade)

(The apartment is dark; it is after midnight. ANNA unlocks the door and comes in. She is in a party dress and a coat. She goes immediately toward the back without turning on the light, taking off her coat)

PALE. I'm here. Don't be scared.

ANNA. Oh, God!

PALE. Don't be scared. I'm stone-cold sober.

ANNA. I'm half drunk. How the hell'd you get in?

PALE. Your friend gave me a key.

ANNA. Larry? Why?

PALE. He come by the bar, he left me a note and the key and shit. The ticket.

ANNA. What ticket?

PALE. I saw your dance tonight. *(Pause)* I looked for you, I didn't see you.

ANNA. I was hiding in the light booth.

PALE. You shoulda had Robbie for it. That guy didn't look right. He moved okay, he dances good, but he didn't look right.

ANNA. . . . I did it for Robbie, actually. In my mind Robbie did it.

PALE. I could tell. *(Pause)* It wasn't what I thought it'd be.

ANNA. . . . Me either.

PALE. The other stuff—those first two things was shit. That's why I never went to no modern dance. I knew that's what it was gonna be. I almost had to leave. I didn't stay for that piece after yours.

ANNA. You would have hated it.

PALE. Your thing was good.

ANNA. Thank you.

PALE *(Pause)*. It was real good. Everybody stood up and yelled.

ANNA. Eight or ten people stood up.

PALE. How'd that feel when they did that?

ANNA. I was very surprised. I was afraid everyone would hate it. It was a relief.

PALE. Made me feel good, too. *(Pause)* That was me and you up there. Only we ain't never danced. I could probably sue you for that.

ANNA. Probably.

PALE. I was kind—it's kinda embarrassing . . . to see somebody being you up there.

ANNA. Yes, it is.

PALE. He did okay. He moves good. She was good. She ain't as pretty as you.

ANNA. What are you doing going to a dance in the middle of the— Did you take off work?

PALE. Shit. Yeah, I quit. Bust my nuts twenty years, that guy. Been managing three years, not one day off. I'm tending bar at Danny's. You know . . . Ray? Fuckin' vacation. Work eight hours, like not workin'. *(Pause)* You didn't go to the party? I thought there was a party for you.

ANNA. . . . I went; it was too noisy. Larry said he'd be here. I came home.

PALE. You been set up. Me too. He said he'd be here.

(A long pause)

ANNA. Pale . . . I don't want this. *(She begins to cry softly)*

PALE. I know. I don't want it, too.

ANNA. What'd he say? The bastard. In the note?

PALE. I read it ten times already. I wasn't gonna come. I almost know it by heart. *(Fishes it out of his pocket, hands it to her)*

ANNA *(Trying to read it, gives up)*. That's okay. I can't . . .

PALE. . . . What?

ANNA. I can't read it.

PALE. . . . You cryin'? Somebody's always cryin' at your house.

ANNA. I know. I'm sorry. *(Hands it back to him)* I can't read it.

PALE. It says: "Pale, doll. Here's a ticket for the program tonight and my keys. We're going to the cast party and won't be home until three. I don't know how you're doing, but Anna is in pretty bad shape. This isn't opera, this is life, why should love always be tragic? Burn this." *(He hands it to her. She folds it into a tent, puts it in an ashtray)* I been in pretty bad shape here, too. I'm thirty-six years old, I got a wife, I got two kids, I never felt nothin' like this.

ANNA. . . . I . . . uh . . . I haven't either.

PALE. I don't know what to do with myself here.

ANNA. I know. *(She lights a match, puts it under LARRY's note; they watch it burn)*

PALE. I thought you didn't like me, so I got lost. You know? 'Cause I didn't want you to do something you didn't like.

ANNA. I know. I was having a pretty difficult time not calling you.

PALE. I didn't know. *(Pause)* I'm real scared here.

ANNA. I don't want this . . . Oh, Lord, I didn't want this . . .

PALE. I know. I don't want it, either. *(He stands beside one end of the sofa; she sits at the other. They look at each other)* I didn't expect nothin' like this. *(He reaches his hand toward her; she reaches toward him. They touch. He moves over the back of the sofa and sits at the other end. She lies down, her back against his chest)* I'm gonna cry all over your hair.

(The music rises as the lights fade)

Curtain

Into the Woods

STEPHEN SONDHEIM AND
JAMES LAPINE

FOR PHOEBE LAPINE

Workshopped at Playwrights Horizons in New York City, *Into the Woods* was first produced at the Old Globe Theatre in San Diego, California, in December 1986. The play opened on Broadway on November 5, 1987. Since its inception, the play has been directed by James Lapine. The settings were designed by Tony Straiges and the lighting by Richard Nelson. Original costume design work was by Ann Hould-Ward and Patricia Zipprodt; Hould-Ward went on to design the costumes for Broadway.

Into the Woods was first workshopped at Playwrights Horizons; its world-premiere staging occurred in 1986 at the Old Globe Theatre in San Diego, California. After a staged workshop at the 890 Studios in New York, it opened on Broadway at the Martin Beck Theatre in November 1987. *Into the Woods* won three Tony Awards in 1987, including Best Score and Best Book, and the Drama Desk Award for Best Musical. It was filmed for PBS, and staged in London in 1990.

Taking off from the fairy tales of the Brothers Grimm (its characters include Cinderella, Little Red Riding Hood, Jack of "Jack and the Beanstalk," Rapunzel, Snow White, and the Sleeping Beauty), *Into the Woods* is an entirely new and original work devised by James Lapine, who wrote the book, and Stephen Sondheim, who wrote the lyrics and music. Lapine introduced two new characters, a baker and his wife, through whom the traditional characters interact.

Prior to his work on *Into the Woods,* Sondheim had never read any fairy tales, his only acquaintance with the genre coming from viewing Disney movies. Initially, Sondheim wanted to base the musical on the Dungeons and Dragons games or the *Arabian Nights.* Neither appealed to Lapine, who states, "Eventually, Steve told me to write what I wanted to write. I knew he wanted to do something that involved a search or a quest." Lapine's first idea was to write an original fairy tale, a project he had once started but never finished. Eventually, he arrived at the hybrid idea that forms the basis of this musical. Lapine recognizes that fairy tales have their own dreamlike logic, and adds, "In many ways, *Into the Woods* is closer to the original folk sources than most adaptations, because it explores the symbolic and psychological aspects of these tales."

The play is divided into two acts, a lighter and more humorous opening, and a darker and more emotional conclusion. Sondheim's score is composed of interrelated themes and recurring motifs, witty lyrics and engaging tunes, internal rhymes and sly puns. The opening title song sets the storybook tone and creates a lively theme for the entire play; however, the emotional concerns of the very human characters are fully dramatized in musical numbers that are often quite moving: "I Know Things Now," "Giants in the Sky," "It Takes Two," "On the Steps of the Palace," "Moments in the Woods," "Last Midnight," "No More," and "No One Is Alone" merge classic fairy-tale imagery with contemporary concerns, resulting in an ingenious score.

The lyrics and libretto are spare and stylized, which the collaborators deemed necessary for this kind of material. Lapine says that "even though fairy tales use flowery language, they are essentially underwritten in terms of plot. So we thought it best to keep it sounding light and simple."

Stephen Joshua Sondheim was born in New York City in 1930. At the age of four, he could pick out tunes on the piano; at the age of six, he could read through *The New York Times.* When he was ten years old, his parents divorced, and he was sent to a military school. At this time, his mother moved to Pennsylvania to live near an old friend of the family, Oscar Hammerstein II, with whom Sondheim spent all his spare time. "Oscar was everything to me," Sondheim recalls. "I wanted to be exactly like him." When Sondheim was fifteen, he wrote his first musical, *By George,* which he asked Hammerstein to read objectively. While analyzing Sondheim's score, Hammerstein taught the young songwriter how to build numbers, introduce characters and tell a story, and showed him the relationship between lyrics, music, and characterization.

Sondheim attended Williams College; upon graduation, he won the Hutchinson Prize, a fellowship to study and compose music, and apprenticed with Milton Babbitt in 1950. In 1953, Sondheim wrote the music and lyrics for *Saturday Night,* which was never produced, and became a scriptwriter for the NBC television comedy series *Topper.* Two years later, playwright Arthur Laurents introduced Sondheim to Leonard Bernstein, with whom Laurents was collaborating on *West Side Story.* Bernstein brought Sondheim onto the team to write the lyrics.

West Side Story opened in 1957 to rave reviews. Sondheim was then hired to write the lyrics to Jule Styne's music for *Gypsy,* which opened on Broadway in 1959 and ran for two years. Sondheim's first solo score was for *A Funny Thing Happened on the Way to the Forum* (his most commercially successful work) in 1962. It was also his first collaboration with producer (later producer-director) Harold Prince; the two worked together for more than fifteen years. A brief bleak period ensued in which *Anyone Can Whistle* (solo score; 1964) and *Do I Hear A Waltz?* (Sondheim's last full lyricist-only score, 1965) proved unsuccessful. In 1970, Prince and Sondheim collaborated on *Company,* a brilliant departure from conventional musical theatre that won several Tony awards and the New York Drama Critics Circle award. This was followed by *Follies* (1971) for which the two again won Tony awards and the Drama Critics Circle Award, *A Little Night Music* (1973; six Tonys, including Best Musical and Best Score; Drama Critics Circle Award), *Pacific Overtures* (1975), *Sweeney Todd* (1979; eight Tonys, including Best Musical and Best Score; Drama Critics Circle Award), *Merrily We Roll Along* (1981), *Sunday in the Park with George* (1983; Pulitzer Prize for drama; Drama Critics Circle Award), *Into the Woods,* and *Assassins* (1990).

Sondheim is a constant pioneer, who creates each work as a new art form. He does not write music to propel the action of a scene, he writes music to propel the *idea* of the scene, and the music becomes the idea itself. Sondheim states that he "does not understand the kind of writer who keeps writing the same stuff over and over. . . . I have to go for something I haven't done before. . . . Not to change is death to me. . . ." Critic Jack Viertel says that "the best Sondheim melodies seem to emerge from the very deepest reaches of music, to be hammered out of an enormous personal anguish . . . his music does not buzz around in our heads . . . but haunts us in some dark place."

Sondheim's music and/or lyrics have also been heard in *The Girls of Summer* (1956), *Invitation to a March* (1960), *The Frogs, Marry Me a Little,* the 1974 revision of *Candide,* and *Side by Side by Sondheim* (1978).

He wrote songs for the television musical *Evening Primrose* (1966), the screenplay for *The Last of Sheila* (1973, with Anthony Perkins), and the scores for the films *Stavinsky* and *Reds* (1981). He recently contributed songs to the film *Dick Tracy,* one of which received the Academy Award for Best Song. He was the president of the Dramatists Guild from 1973 to 1981, and was elected to the American Academy and Institute of Arts and Letters in 1983.

CHARACTERS

NARRATOR
CINDERELLA
JACK
JACK'S MOTHER
BAKER
BAKER'S WIFE
CINDERELLA'S STEPMOTHER
FLORINDA
LUCINDA
CINDERELLA'S FATHER
LITTLE RED RIDINGHOOD
WITCH
CINDERELLA'S MOTHER
MYSTERIOUS MAN
WOLF
GRANNY
RAPUNZEL
RAPUNZEL'S PRINCE
CINDERELLA'S PRINCE
STEWARD
GIANT
SNOW WHITE
SLEEPING BEAUTY

MUSICAL NUMBERS

ACT ONE

PROLOGUE: INTO THE WOODS
  Company
HELLO, LITTLE GIRL
  Wolf, Little Red Ridinghood
I GUESS THIS IS GOODBYE
  Jack
MAYBE THEY'RE MAGIC
  Baker's Wife
I KNOW THINGS NOW
  Little Red Ridinghood
A VERY NICE PRINCE
  Cinderella, Baker's Wife
GIANTS IN THE SKY
  Jack
AGONY
  Cinderella's Prince, Rapunzel's Prince
IT TAKES TWO
  Baker, Baker's Wife
STAY WITH ME
  Witch
ON THE STEPS OF THE PALACE
  Cinderella
EVER AFTER
  Narrator, Company

ACT TWO

PROLOGUE: SO HAPPY
  Company
AGONY
  Cinderella's Prince, Rapunzel's Prince
LAMENT
  Witch
ANY MOMENT
  Cinderella's Prince, Baker's Wife
MOMENTS IN THE WOODS
  Baker's Wife
YOUR FAULT
  Jack, Baker, Witch, Cinderella, Little Red
Ridinghood
LAST MIDNIGHT
  Witch
NO MORE
  Baker, Mysterious Man
NO ONE IS ALONE
  Cinderella, Little Red Ridinghood, Baker,
Jack
FINALE: CHILDREN WILL LISTEN
  Witch, Company

ACT ONE

SCENE 1

Downstage, three structures:
Far left, the home of CINDERELLA. *She is in the kitchen, cleaning.*
Center, the cottage where JACK *lives. He is inside, milking his pathetic-looking cow, Milky-White.*
Far right, the home/workplace of the BAKER *and his* WIFE. *They are preparing tomorrow's bread.*
Behind these homes, a drop depicts a large forest which separates them from the rest of the kingdom.
A NARRATOR *steps forward.*

NARRATOR. Once upon a time—
(Music, sharp and steady. Light on CINDERELLA.*)*
CINDERELLA *(Singing to us)*. I wish . . .
NARRATOR. —in a far-off kingdom—
CINDERELLA. More than anything . . .
NARRATOR. —lived a young maiden—
CINDERELLA. More than life . . .
NARRATOR. —a sad young lad—
(Light on JACK *and the cow.)*
CINDERELLA. More than jewels . . .
JACK *(To us)*. I wish . . .
NARRATOR. —and a childless baker—
(Light on the BAKER *and his* WIFE.*)*

JACK. More than life . . .

CINDERELLA, BAKER. I wish . . .

NARRATOR. —with his wife.

JACK. More than anything . . .

CINDERELLA, BAKER, JACK. More than the moon . . .

WIFE. I wish . . .

CINDERELLA. The King is giving a Festival.

BAKER, WIFE. More than life . . .

JACK. I wish . . .

CINDERELLA. I wish to go to the Festival—

BAKER, WIFE. More than riches . . .

CINDERELLA. —and the Ball . . .

JACK. I wish my cow would give us some milk.

CINDERELLA, WIFE. More than anything . . .

BAKER. I wish we had a child.

JACK *(To cow)*. Please, pal—

WIFE. I want a child . . .

JACK. Squeeze, pal . . .

CINDERELLA. I wish to go to the Festival.

JACK *(Overlapping)*. I wish you'd give us some milk

Or even cheese . . .

BAKER, WIFE *(Overlapping)*. I wish we might have a child.

ALL FOUR. I wish . . .

(CINDERELLA's STEPMOTHER and stepsisters, FLORINDA and LUCINDA, enter.)

STEPMOTHER *(To CINDERELLA)*. *You* wish to go to the Festival?

NARRATOR. The poor girl's mother had died—

STEPMOTHER. You, Cinderella, the Festival?

You wish to go to the Festival?

FLORINDA *(Overlapping)*. What, *you,* Cinderella, the Festival?

The Festival?!

LUCINDA *(Overlapping)*. What, *you* wish to go to the Festival?!

ALL THREE. The Festival?!

The King's Festival!!!???

NARRATOR. —and her father had taken for his new wife—

STEPMOTHER. The *Festival!!!???*

NARRATOR. —a woman with two daughters of her own.

FLORINDA *(To CINDERELLA)*. Look at your nails!

LUCINDA. Look at your dress!

STEPMOTHER. People would laugh at you—

CINDERELLA. Nevertheless—I still wish to go

To the Festival.

STEPSISTERS *(Overlapping)*. You still wish to go

To the Festival—

STEPMOTHER *(Overlapping)*. She still wants to go

To the Festival—

STEPSISTERS, STEPMOTHER. —and dance before the Prince?!

(They chortle with laughter musically, then fall about out of control. Music stops.)

NARRATOR. All three were beautiful of face, but vile and black of heart.

(Music resumes.)

Jack, on the other hand, had no father, and his mother—

JACK'S MOTHER *(Entering)*. I wish . . .

NARRATOR. Well, she was not quite beautiful—

JACK'S MOTHER. I wish my son were not a fool.

I wish my house was not a mess.

I wish the cow was full of milk.

I wish the walls were full of gold—

I wish a lot of things . . .

(To JACK, music continuing under) You *foolish* child! What in heaven's name are you doing with the cow inside the house?

JACK. A warm environment might be just what Milky-White needs to produce his milk.

JACK'S MOTHER *(Beat; flabbergasted)*. It's a she! How many times must I tell you? Only "she"s can give milk.

(Two knocks on the BAKER's door; WIFE opens door; it is LITTLE RED RIDINGHOOD.)

WIFE. Why, come in, little girl.

LITTLE RED RIDINGHOOD. I wish . . .

It's not for me,

It's for my granny in the woods.

A loaf of bread, please—

To bring my poor old hungry

Granny in the woods . . .

(Insistent)

Just a loaf of bread, please . . .

(BAKER gives her a loaf of bread.)

NARRATOR. Cinderella's stepmother had a surprise for her.

(STEPMOTHER throws a pot of lentils into the fireplace.)

STEPMOTHER. I have emptied a pot of lentils into the ashes for you. If you have picked them out again in two hours' time, you shall go to the Ball with us.

(STEPMOTHER and STEPSISTERS exit.)

LITTLE RED RIDINGHOOD. And perhaps a sticky bun? . . .

Or four? . . .

(Smiles sheepishly)

CINDERELLA. Birds in the sky,
Birds in the eaves,
In the leaves,
In the fields,
In the castles and ponds . . .

LITTLE RED RIDINGHOOD. . . . and a few of those pies . . .

CINDERELLA *(Overlapping)*. Come, little birds,
Down from the eaves
And the leaves,
Over fields,
Out of castles and ponds . . .

JACK. No, *squeeze, pal* . . .

CINDERELLA *(Falling into a trance)*. Ahhh.

(Music continues as birds descend to the fireplace.)

Quick, little birds,
Flick through the ashes.
Pick and peck, but swiftly,
Sift through the ashes
Into the pot . . .

(Birds start picking at the lentils and dropping them into the pot, each one landing with a clang; music continues under.)

JACK'S MOTHER. Listen well, son. Milky-White must be taken to market.

(Clangs continue under as the birds work.)

JACK. But, Mother, no—he's the best cow—

JACK'S MOTHER. Was. Was! *She's* been dry for a week. We've no food nor money and no choice but to sell her while she can still command a price.

JACK. But Milky-White is my best friend in the whole world!

JACK'S MOTHER. Look at her!
There are bugs on her dugs.
There are flies in her eyes.
There's a lump on her rump
Big enough to be a hump—

JACK. But—

JACK'S MOTHER. Son,
We've no time to sit and dither,
While her withers wither with her—
(Two clangs.)
And no one keeps a cow for a friend!
Sometimes I fear you're touched.

(LITTLE RED RIDINGHOOD has been compulsively eating sweets at the BAKER's house; she now swallows, wiping her hands and mouth.)

LITTLE RED RIDINGHOOD. Into the woods,
It's time to go,
I hate to leave,

I have to, though.
Into the woods—
It's time, and so
I must begin my journey.
Into the woods
And through the trees
To where I am
Expected, ma'am,
Into the woods
to Grandmother's house—
(Mouth full)
Into the woods
To Grandmother's house—

WIFE. You're certain of your way?

LITTLE RED RIDINGHOOD. The way is clear,
The light is good,
I have no fear,
Nor no one should.
The woods are just trees,
The trees are just wood.
I sort of hate to ask it,
But do you have a basket?

BAKER. Don't stray and be late.

WIFE. And save some of those sweets for Granny!

LITTLE RED RIDINGHOOD. Into the woods
And down the dell,
The path is straight,
I know it well.
Into the woods,
And who can tell
What's waiting on the journey?

Into the woods
To bring some bread
To Granny who
Is sick in bed.
Never can tell
What lies ahead.
For all that I know,
She's already dead.

But into the woods,
Into the woods,
Into the woods
To Grandmother's house
And home before dark!

(The birds have helped CINDERELLA with her task and are flying off.)

CINDERELLA. Fly, birds,
Back to the sky,
Back to the eaves
And the leaves
And the fields
And the—

(FLORINDA and LUCINDA enter, dressed for the Ball.)

FLORINDA. Hurry up and do my hair, Cinderella!

(To LUCINDA, as CINDERELLA fusses with her hair)
Are you really wearing *that*?

LUCINDA *(Pointing to her sleeve)*. Here, I found a little tear, Cinderella!

(To FLORINDA, eyeing her hair)
Can't you hide it with a hat?

CINDERELLA. You look beautiful.

FLORINDA. I know.

LUCINDA. She means me.

FLORINDA *(To CINDERELLA)*. Put it in a twist.

LUCINDA. Who will be there? . . .

(She and FLORINDA continue babbling underneath.)

CINDERELLA *(To herself)*. Mother said be good,
Father said be nice,
That was always their advice.
So be nice, Cinderella,
Good, Cinderella,
Nice good good nice—

FLORINDA. Tighter!

CINDERELLA. What's the good of being good
If everyone is blind
Always leaving you behind?
Never mind, Cinderella,
Kind Cinderella—

(Accenting each word with a twist of a strand of hair)
Nice good nice kind good nice—

FLORINDA *(Screams and slaps CINDERELLA)*. Not *that* tight!

CINDERELLA *(Backing away)*. Sorry.

FLORINDA. Clod.

(A beat.)

LUCINDA. Hee hee hee—

(FLORINDA glares at her.)
Hee hee—

(She stops. Music continues under.)

NARRATOR. Because the baker had lost his mother and father in a baking accident— well, at least that is what he believed—he was eager to have a family of his own, and concerned that all efforts until now had failed.

(A knock on the BAKER's door.)

BAKER. Who might that be? *(He looks off to see)*

WIFE. We have sold our last loaf of bread . . .

BAKER. It's the witch from next door.

(The WITCH enters; music resumes.)

WIFE, BAKER. We have no bread.

WITCH. Of course you have no bread!

BAKER. What do you wish?

WITCH. It's not what I wish. It's what *you* wish. *(Points to WIFE's belly)* Nothing cooking in there now, is there?

NARRATOR. The old enchantress went on to tell the couple that she had placed a spell on their house.

BAKER. What spell?

WITCH. In the past, when you were no more than a babe, your father brought his young wife and you to this cottage. They were a handsome couple, but not handsome neighbors. You see, your mother was with child and she had developed an unusual appetite. She took one look at my beautiful garden and told your father that what she wanted more than anything in the world was

Greens, greens, and nothing but greens:
Parsley, peppers, cabbages and celery,
Asparagus and watercress and
Fiddleferns and lettuce—!
(Falling into "rap" style)
He said, "All right,"
But it wasn't, quite,
'Cause I caught him in the autumn
In my garden one night!
He was robbing me,
Raping me,
Rooting through my rutabaga,
Raiding my arugula and
Ripping up the rampion
(My champion! My favorite!)—
I should have laid a spell on him
("Spell" chord)
Right there,
Could have turned him into stone
Or a dog or a chair
Or a sn—
(Drifts off into a momentary trance)
But I let him have the rampion—
I'd lots to spare.
In return, however,
I said, "Fair is fair:
You can let me have the baby
That your wife will bear.

And we'll call it square."
(Music stops.)

BAKER. I had a brother?

WITCH. No. But you had a sister.

NARRATOR. But the witch refused to tell

him any more of his sister. Not even that her name was Rapunzel. She went on:

(Music resumes.)

WITCH. I thought I had been more than reasonable, and that we all might live happily ever after. But how was I to know what your father had also hid in his pocket?! You see, when I had inherited that garden, my mother had warned me I would be punished if I ever were to lose any of the

Beans.

BAKER, WIFE. Beans?

WITCH. The special beans.

(Getting worked up)

I let him go,
I didn't know
He'd stolen my beans!
I was watching him crawl
Back over the wall—!
("Rap")
And then bang! Crash!
And the lightning flash!
And—well, that's another story,
Never mind—
Anyway, at last
The big day came
And I made my claim.
"Oh, don't take away the baby,"
They shrieked and screeched,
But I did,
And I hid her
Where she'll never be reached.

And your father cried,
And your mother died
When for extra measure—
I admit it was a pleasure—
I said, "Sorry,
I'm still not mollified."

And I laid a little spell on them—
("Spell" chord)
You too, son—
That your family tree
Would always be
A barren one . . .
(WITCH levitates in her chair, laughing as she goes; BAKER and WIFE gasp in disbelief.)

So there's no more fuss
And there's no more scenes
And my garden thrives—
You should see my nectarines!
But I'm telling you the same
I tell Kings and Queens:

Don't ever never ever
Mess around with my greens!
Especially the beans.
(Her chair returns to the ground; music continues under; JACK has his cap and coat on.)

JACK'S MOTHER. Now listen to me, Jack. Lead Milky-White to market and fetch the best price you can. Take no less than five pounds. Are you listening to me?

JACK. Yes.

JACK'S MOTHER. Now how much are you to ask?

JACK. No more than five pounds.

(She pinches his ear hard.)

JACK'S MOTHER, JACK. Less! Than five.

(She lets go.)

JACK'S MOTHER. Jack Jack Jack,
Head in a sack,
The house is getting colder,
This is not a time for dreaming.

Chimney-stack
Starting to crack,
The mice are getting bolder,
The floor's gone slack.
Your mother's getting older,
Your father's not back,
And you can't just sit here dreaming pretty dreams.

To wish and wait
From day to day
Will never keep
The wolves away.

So into the woods,
The time is now.
We have to live,
I don't care how.
Into the woods
To sell the cow,
You must begin the journey.
Straight through the woods
And don't delay—
We have to face
The marketplace.
Into the woods to journey's end—

JACK. Into the woods to sell a friend—

(Music continues under.)

JACK'S MOTHER. Someday you'll have a real pet, Jack.

JACK. A piggy?

(MOTHER shakes her head in disbelief.)

NARRATOR. Meanwhile, the witch, for purposes of her own, explained how the baker might lift the spell:

WITCH. You wish to have
The curse reversed?
I'll need a certain
Potion first.

Go to the wood and bring me back
One: the cow as white as milk,
Two: the cape as red as blood,
Three: the hair as yellow as corn,
Four: the slipper as pure as gold.

Bring me these
Before the chime
Of midnight
In three days' time,
And you shall have,
I guarantee,
A child as perfect
As child can be.

Go to the wood!
(She disappears. Fanfare.)
STEPMOTHER. Ladies.
(Fanfare.)

Our carriage waits.
(CINDERELLA shows her the plate of lentils.)
CINDERELLA. Now may I go to the Festival?
STEPMOTHER. The *Festival*—!
Darling, those nails!
Darling, those clothes!
Lentils are one thing but
Darling, with those,
You'd make us the fools of the Festival
And mortify the Prince!
(CINDERELLA'S FATHER enters.)
CINDERELLA'S FATHER. The carriage is waiting.
STEPMOTHER. We must be gone.
(They exit with a flourish.)
CINDERELLA. Good night, Father.
(He grunts and exits.)

I wish . . .
(CINDERELLA sits dejected, crying. Music continues under. The BAKER, having gone off, returns in hunting gear.)
BAKER. Look what I found in Father's hunting jacket.
WIFE. Six beans.
BAKER. I wonder if they are the—
WIFE. Witch's beans? We'll take them with us.
BAKER. No! You are not coming.
WIFE. I know you are fearful of the woods at night.

BAKER. The spell is on *my* house.
Only I can lift the spell,
The spell is on *my* house.
WIFE *(Overlapping)*. No, no, the spell is on *our* house.
We must lift the spell together,
The spell is on *our* house.
BAKER *(Overlapping)*. No. You are not to come and that is final.
Now what am I to return with?
WIFE *(Annoyed)*. You don't remember?

The cow as white as milk,
The cape as red as blood,
The hair as yellow as corn,
The slipper as pure as gold—
BAKER *(Memorizing)*. The cow as white as milk,
The cape as red as blood,
The hair as yellow as corn,
The slipper as pure as gold . . .
NARRATOR *(Overlapping)*. And so the baker, reluctantly, set off to meet the enchantress's demands. As for Cinderella:
CINDERELLA. I still wish to go to the Festival,
But how am I ever to get to the Festival?
BAKER *(Simultaneously, muttering as he gets ready to leave)*. The cow as white as milk,
The cape as red as blood,
The hair as yellow as corn—
WIFE *(Prompting)*. The slipper—
BAKER. The slipper as pure as gold . . .
CINDERELLA *(Overlapping)*. I know!
I'll visit Mother's grave,
The grave at the hazel tree,
And tell her I just want to
Go to the King's Festival . . .
BAKER. The cow, the cape,
The slipper as pure as gold—
WIFE. The hair—!
BAKER, CINDERELLA. Into the woods,
It's time to go,
It may be all
In vain, you (I) know.
Into the woods—
But even so,
I have to take the journey.
BAKER, CINDERELLA, WIFE. Into the woods,
The path is straight,
You (I) know it well,
But who can tell—?
BAKER, WIFE. Into the woods to lift the spell—
CINDERELLA. Into the woods to visit Mother—

WIFE. Into the woods to fetch the things—
BAKER. To make the potion—
CINDERELLA. To go to the Festival—
BAKER, WIFE, CINDERELLA, JACK, JACK'S
MOTHER. Into the woods
Without regret,
The choice is made,
The task is set.
Into the woods,
But not forget-
Ting why I'm (you're) on the journey.

Into the woods
To get my (our) wish,
I don't care how,
The time is now.
JACK'S MOTHER. Into the woods to sell the
cow—
JACK. Into the woods to get the money—
(Leads Milky-White into the woods)
WIFE. Into the woods to lift the spell—
BAKER. To make the potion—
(He sets off for the woods)
CINDERELLA. To go to the Festival—
(She sets off for the woods)
LITTLE RED RIDINGHOOD *(Skipping by)*. Into
the woods to Grandmother's house . . .
Into the woods to Grandmother's
house . . .
ALL. The way is clear,
The light is good,
I have no fear,
Nor no one should.
The woods are just trees,
The trees are just wood.
No need to be afraid there—
BAKER, CINDERELLA *(Apprehensive)*. There's
something in the glade there . . .
*(CINDERELLA'S FATHER, STEPMOTHER and
STEPSISTERS are seen riding in their carriage.)*
ALL. Into the woods
Without delay,
But careful not
To lose the way.
Into the woods,
Who knows what may
Be lurking on the journey?

Into the woods
To get the thing
That makes it worth
The journeying.
Into the woods—
STEPMOTHER, STEPSISTERS. To see the
King—
JACK, JACK'S MOTHER. To sell the cow—

BAKER, WIFE. To make the potion—
ALL. To see—
To sell—
To get—
To bring—
To make—
To lift—
To go to the Festival—!

Into the woods!
Into the woods!
Into the woods,
Then out of the woods,
And home before dark!

SCENE 2

The woods. Late afternoon.
*The stage is filled by trees of all varieties, many
twisted and gnarled, others going straight forward
to the sky without a branch. Bright sunlight
streams through, creating a wonderful light-maze.
As the scene progresses, the sunlight is gradually
replaced by moonlight. The foliage rustles in the
breeze, with an occasional gust blowing about low-
lying fog.*
CINDERELLA *enters and kneels before a tree
filled with birds.*
_____

NARRATOR. Cinderella had planted a
branch at the grave of her mother and she
visited there so often, and wept so much, that
her tears watered it until it had become a
handsome tree.
CINDERELLA. I've been good and I've been
kind, Mother,
Doing only what I learned from you.
Why then am I left behind, Mother,
Is there something more that I should do?
What is wrong with me, Mother?
Something must be wrong.
I wish—
*(Suddenly, the ghost of CINDERELLA'S MOTHER
appears within the tree.)*
CINDERELLA'S MOTHER. What, child? Spec-
ify. Opportunity is not a lengthy visitor and
good fortune, like bad, can befall when least
expected.
CINDERELLA. I wish . . .
CINDERELLA'S MOTHER. Do you know what
you wish?
Are you certain what you wish
Is what you want?
If you know what you want,
Then make a wish.

Ask the tree,
And you shall have your wish.
CINDERELLA. Shiver and quiver, little tree.
Silver and gold throw down on me.
(A gold-and-silver dress and fancy slippers drop from the tree.)
I'm off to get my wish.
(CINDERELLA picks up the clothes and dashes off. JACK is walking through the woods. He leads Milky-White. He stops.)
JACK. Quiet. Silence everywhere, Milky-White. Not to my liking . . .
(Pause. Music fades out.)
MYSTERIOUS MAN *(Steps from behind a tree).* Hello, Jack.
JACK. How did you know my name?!
MYSTERIOUS MAN. When first I appear I seem mysterious. But when explained, I am nothing serious.
JACK. Say that again.
MYSTERIOUS MAN. On your way to market? You might have been there long ago. Taking your time, Jack?
JACK. No, sir.
MYSTERIOUS MAN. Is that the truth?
JACK. Well, you see, now I'm *resting*—
MYSTERIOUS MAN. How much are you asking for the animal?
JACK. No less than five pounds, sir.
MYSTERIOUS MAN. Oh now, Jack. Why such a sum?
JACK. My mother told me—
MYSTERIOUS MAN. Your mother? A boy your age? Why you'd be lucky to exchange her for a sack of beans.
JACK. Well, I—
(Before JACK can respond, the MYSTERIOUS MAN has disappeared.)
Come along, Milky-White. There are spirits here . . .
(He exits)
(Another part of the woods. LITTLE RED RIDINGHOOD, skipping to the accompaniment of "Into the Woods," is surprised by the WOLF. Music stops.)
WOLF. Good day, young lady.
LITTLE RED RIDINGHOOD. Good day, Mr. Wolf.
(Music resumes, LITTLE RED RIDINGHOOD continues. WOLF stops her again. Music stops.)
WOLF. Whither away so hurriedly?
LITTLE RED RIDINGHOOD. To my grandmother's.
(Music resumes; LITTLE RED RIDINGHOOD continues briefly. WOLF stops her once more.)
WOLF. And what might be in your basket?

LITTLE RED RIDINGHOOD. Bread and wine, so Grandmother will have something good to make her strong.
WOLF. And where might your grandmother live?
(BAKER appears behind a tree and eavesdrops.)
LITTLE RED RIDINGHOOD. A good quarter of a league further in the woods; her house stands under three large oak trees.
(WOLF grunts lasciviously, sings to himself as he watches her skip off.)
WOLF. Mmmh . . .
(Rubbing his thighs)
Unhh . . .

Look at that flesh,
Pink and plump.
(To himself)
Hello, little girl . . .

Tender and fresh,
Not one lump.
Hello, little girl . . .

This one's especially lush,
Delicious . . .
Mmmh . . .
(Smacks his lips, then runs over and pops up in front of LITTLE RED RIDINGHOOD)
Hello, little girl,
What's your rush?
You're missing all the flowers.
The sun won't set for hours,
Take your time.
LITTLE RED RIDINGHOOD. Mother said,
"Straight ahead,"
Not to delay
Or be misled.
WOLF. But slow, little girl,
Hark! And hush—
The birds are singing sweetly.
You'll miss the birds completely,
You're traveling so fleetly.
(LITTLE RED RIDINGHOOD stops to listen; the WOLF devours her with his eyes, mutters to himself.)
Grandmother first,
Then Miss Plump . . .
What a delectable couple:
Utter perfection
One brittle, one supple—
(Seeing LITTLE RED RIDINGHOOD start to move off again)
One moment, my dear—!
(LITTLE RED RIDINGHOOD stops again.)
LITTLE RED RIDINGHOOD. Mother said,

"Come what may,
Follow the path
And never stray."
WOLF. Just so, little girl—
Any path.
So many worth exploring.
Just one would be so boring.
And look what you're ignoring . . .
(He gestures to the trees and flowers; LITTLE
RED RIDINGHOOD *looks around.)*
(To himself)
Think of those crisp,
Aging bones,
Then something fresh on the palate.
Think of that scrumptious carnality
Twice in one day—!
There's no possible way
To describe what you feel
When you're talking to your meal!
(The BAKER *enters, but hides behind a tree at
the sight of the* WOLF.*)*
LITTLE RED RIDINGHOOD. Mother said
Not to stray.
Still, I suppose,
A small delay . . .
Granny might like
A fresh bouquet . . .

Goodbye, Mr. Wolf.
WOLF. Goodbye, little girl.
And hello . . .
*(He howls and exits in the direction of the
cottage.)*
BAKER *(Horrified).* Is harm to come to that
little girl . . . in the red cape!
*(*WITCH *surprises him as she hangs from a tree;
music under.)*
WITCH. Forget the little girl and get the
cape!
BAKER *(Clutching his chest).* You frigh-
tened me.
WITCH *(Nasty).* That's the cape. Get it. Get
it. Get it!
BAKER. How am I supposed to get it?
WITCH. You go up to the little thing, and
you take it.
BAKER. I can't just take a cloak from a little
girl. Why don't you take it!
WITCH. If I could, I would! But I—
(We suddenly hear RAPUNZEL *singing in the
distance.)*
(Sweetly) Ahh, my Rapunzel . . . listen to
her beautiful music . . . *(Yelling)* Get me what
I need. Get me what I need! *(She disappears
back up into the tree)*
BAKER *(Distraught).* This is ridiculous. I'll

never get that red cape, nor find a golden
cow, or a yellow slipper—or was it a golden
slipper and a yellow cow? Oh, no . . .
*(*WIFE *appears.)*
WIFE. The cow as white as milk,
The cape as red as blood,
The hair as yellow as corn,
The slipper as pure as—
BAKER *(Overlapping).* What are you doing
here?
WIFE *(Takes a scarf and tries to put it around
his neck).* You forgot your scarf—
BAKER *(Taking scarf off).* You have no busi-
ness being alone in the woods. And you have
no idea what I've come upon here. You
would be frightened for your life. Now go
home immediately!
WIFE. I wish to help.
BAKER. No!

The spell is on *my* house—
WIFE. *Our* house.
BAKER. Only I can lift the spell,
The spell is on *my* house—!
WIFE *(Overlapping).* We must lift the spell
together,
The spell is on—
*(She puts her hand across his mouth; we see
JACK at the other side of the stage.)*
A cow as white as—
(She takes her hand away; music stops.)
BAKER, WIFE. —milk.
*(*WIFE *pushes* BAKER *in* JACK'S *direction; she
follows.)*
BAKER. Hello there, young man.
JACK. Hello, sir.
BAKER. What might you be doing with a
cow in the middle of the forest?
JACK *(Nervous).* I was heading toward mar-
ket—but I seem to have lost my way.
WIFE *(Coaching* BAKER*).* What are you plan-
ning to do there—?
BAKER. And what are you planning to do
there?
JACK. Sell my cow, sir. No less than five
pounds.
BAKER. Five pounds! *(To* WIFE*)* Where am
I to get five pounds!
WIFE *(Taking over).* She must be generous
of milk to fetch five pounds?
JACK *(Hesitant).* Yes, ma'am.
WIFE. And if you can't fetch that sum?
Then what are you to do?
JACK. I hadn't thought of that. . . . I sup-
pose my mother and I will have no food to
eat.

(BAKER *has emptied his pocket; he has a few coins and the beans in hand.*)

BAKER *(To* WIFE*).* This is the sum total . . .

WIFE *(Loudly).* Beans—we mustn't give up our beans! Well . . . if you feel we must.

BAKER. Huh?

WIFE *(To* JACK*).* Beans *will* bring you food, son.

JACK. Beans in exchange for my cow?

WIFE. Oh, these are no ordinary beans, son. These beans carry magic.

JACK. Magic? What kind of magic?

WIFE *(To* BAKER*).* Tell him.

(MYSTERIOUS MAN *enters behind a tree.*)

BAKER *(Nervous).* Magic that defies description.

JACK. My mother would—

MYSTERIOUS MAN. You'd be lucky to exchange her for a sack of beans. *(He exits before anyone sees him)*

JACK. How many beans?

BAKER. Six.

WIFE. Five! We can't part with all of them. We must leave one for ourselves. Besides, I'd say they're worth a pound each, at the very least.

JACK. Could I buy my cow back someday?

BAKER *(Uneasy).* Well . . . possibly.

(*He hands* JACK *the beans, counting out five and keeping one for his pocket;* WIFE *then takes the cow; music.*)

Good luck there, young lad.

JACK *(Tearful; to the cow).* I guess this is goodbye, old pal.

You've been a perfect friend.
I hate to see us part, old pal,
Someday I'll buy you back.
I'll see you soon again.
I hope that when I do,
It won't be on a plate.

(*Overcome with emotion,* JACK *leaves; music continues under.*)

BAKER *(Angry).* Take the cow and go home!

WIFE. I was trying to be helpful.

BAKER. Magic beans! We've no reason to believe they're magic! Are we to dispel this curse through deceit?

WIFE. No one would have given him more for that creature. We did him a favor. At least they'll have some food.

BAKER. Five beans!

WIFE. If you know
What you want,
Then you go
And you find it

And you get it—

BAKER *(Pointing off).* Home.

WIFE. Do we want a child or not?

—and you give
And you take
And you bid
And you bargain,
Or you live
To regret it.

BAKER. Will you please go home.

WIFE. There are rights and wrongs
And in-betweens—
No one waits
When fortune intervenes.
And maybe they're really magic.
Who knows?

Why you do
What you do,
That's the point,
All the rest of it
Is chatter.

BAKER *(Gesturing toward Milky-White).* Look at her, she's crying.

WIFE. If the thing you do
Is pure in intent,
If it's meant,
And it's just a little bent,
Does it matter?

BAKER. Yes.

WIFE. No, what matters is that
Everyone tells tiny lies—
What's important, really, is the size.

(Pause; no response)

Only three more tries
And we'll have our prize.
When the end's in sight,
You'll realize:
If the end is right,
It justifies
The beans!

BAKER. Take the cow and go home. I will carry this out in my own fashion!

(WIFE *and* BAKER *exit in different directions.* RAPUNZEL *is heard singing off in the distance. Her tower appears; music continues.*)

NARRATOR. And so the baker continued his search for the cape as red as blood. As for Rapunzel, the witch was careful not to lose this beauty to the outside world, and so shut her within a doorless tower. And when the old enchantress paid a visit, she called forth:

WITCH. Rapunzel. Rapunzel. Let down your hair to me.

(RAPUNZEL *stops singing and her hair descends.*

The WITCH, *with great difficulty, and with great pain to* RAPUNZEL, *climbs up her hair;* RAPUNZEL'S PRINCE *comes from around a tree.)*

RAPUNZEL'S PRINCE *(To himself)*. Rapunzel, Rapunzel. What a strange name. Strange but beautiful . . . and fit for a Prince. Tomorrow, before that horrible witch arrives, I will stand before her window and ask her to let down her hair to *me*.

(Another part of the woods. The BAKER *steps into* LITTLE RED RIDINGHOOD's *path; the girl is eating a sweet.)*

BAKER. Hello there, little one.

LITTLE RED RIDINGHOOD. Hello.

BAKER. Have you saved some of those sweets for Granny?

LITTLE RED RIDINGHOOD *(Embarrassed)*. I ate all the sweets, *and* half the loaf of bread.

BAKER. Where did you get that beautiful cape? I so admire it.

LITTLE RED RIDINGHOOD. My granny made it for me.

BAKER. Is that right? I would love a red cloak like that.

LITTLE RED RIDINGHOOD *(Giggling)*. You'd look pretty foolish.

*(*BAKER *goes to her and grabs her cape.)*

BAKER. May I take a look at it?

LITTLE RED RIDINGHOOD *(In panic)*. I don't like to be without my cape. Please, give it back!

BAKER *(Frustrated)*. I want it badly.

LITTLE RED RIDINGHOOD. Give it back, please!

WITCH'S VOICE. Forget the little girl and get the cape!

*(*BAKER *suddenly dashes away with the cape under his arm.* LITTLE RED RIDINGHOOD *stands numb for a moment, then lets out a bloodcurdling scream, followed by hysterical weeping.)*

BAKER *(Sheepishly returning with cape, placing it on* LITTLE RED RIDINGHOOD's *shoulders)*. I just wanted to make certain that you *really* loved this cape. Now you go to your granny's— and you be careful that no wolf comes your way.

LITTLE RED RIDINGHOOD. I'd rather a wolf than you, any day.

(She stomps hard on the BAKER's *toe and exits.)*

BAKER *(In pain)*. If you know
What you need,
Then you go
And you find it
And you take it—
Do I want a child or not?
(Feeling stronger)

It's a cloak,
What's a cloak?
It's a joke,
It's a stupid little cloak.
And a cloak is what you make it.
(Nods, convincing himself)
So you take it.
(With resolve)
Things are only what you need them for,
What's important is who needs them more—
(Music continues under as he exits.)

NARRATOR. And so the baker, with new-found determination, went after the red cape. As for the little girl, she was surprised to find her grandmother's cottage door standing open.

(We see GRANNY's *cottage. The walls are made of scrim.* LITTLE RED RIDINGHOOD *enters. The* WOLF, *dressed as* GRANNY, *is in the bed.)*

LITTLE RED RIDINGHOOD *(To herself)*. Oh, dear. How uneasy I feel. Perhaps it's all the sweets. *(Towards the bed)* Good day, Grandmother. *(Moves to the bed)* My, Grandmother, you're looking *very* strange. What big ears you have!

WOLF *(In a* GRANNY *voice)*. The better to hear you with, my dear.

LITTLE RED RIDINGHOOD. But Grandmother, what big eyes you have!

WOLF. The better to see you with, my dear.

LITTLE RED RIDINGHOOD. But Grandmother, what large hands you have!

WOLF. The better to hug you with, my dear.

LITTLE RED RIDINGHOOD. Oh, Grandmother. What a terrible, big, wet mouth you have!

WOLF. The better to eat you with!

(Bloodcurdling scream from LITTLE RED RIDINGHOOD *as lights fade to black.)*

NARRATOR. And scarcely had the wolf said this, than with a single bound he was devouring the little girl. Well, it was a full day of eating for both. And with his appetite appeased, the wolf took to bed for a nice long nap.

*(*WOLF *snores;* BAKER *is outside cottage.)*

BAKER. That grandmother has a mighty snore. *(He goes up to the window and looks in)* Odd. Where is the little one? Eating, no doubt.

*(*BAKER *turns to walk away;* WOLF *belches;* BAKER *suddenly stops.)*

Or eaten!

*(*BAKER *enters the house and timidly goes over to*

316 ────────────────────────────────────── INTO THE WOODS

the bed, his knife stretched before him. He lets out a yelp when he sees the WOLF *with his swollen belly.)*

Grandmother, hah! *(He draws the knife back, then stops)* What is this red cloth in the corner of your mouth? Looks to me to be a piece of—ah-hah! I'll get the cape from within your stomach.

(He slits the WOLF's *stomach, then recoils in disgust.)*

LITTLE RED RIDINGHOOD *(Stepping out of the* WOLF, *bloodied)*. What a fright! How dark and dank it was inside that wolf.

*(*GRANNY *emerges from* WOLF.)*

GRANNY *(Wheezing)*. Kill the devil! Take that knife and cut his evil head off! Let's see the demon sliced into a thousand bits. Better yet, let the animal die a painful, agonizing, hideous death.

LITTLE RED RIDINGHOOD *(Shocked)*. Granny!

GRANNY. Quiet, child. This evil needs to be destroyed. Fetch me some great stones! We'll fill his belly with them, then we'll watch him try to run away!

BAKER *(Faint)*. Well, I will leave you to your task.

GRANNY. Don't you want the skins?

BAKER. No. No! You keep them.

GRANNY *(With disdain)*. What kind of a hunter are you?

BAKER. I'm a baker!

*(*GRANNY *pulls him into the house as* LITTLE RED RIDINGHOOD *walks downstage, as if to gather stones. Lights change; music.)*

LITTLE RED RIDINGHOOD. Mother said,
"Straight ahead,"
Not to delay
Or be misled.
I should have heeded
Her advice . . .

But he seemed so nice.
And he showed me things,
Many beautiful things,
That I hadn't thought to explore.
They were off my path,
So I never had dared.
I had been so careful
I never had cared.
And he made me feel excited—
Well, excited and scared.

When he said, "Come in!"
With that sickening grin,
How could I know what was in store?
Once his teeth were bared,

Though, I really got scared—
Well, excited and scared—

But he drew me close
And he swallowed me down,
Down a dark slimy path
Where lie secrets that I never want to know,
And when everything familiar
Seemed to disappear forever,
At the end of the path
Was Granny once again.

So we wait in the dark
Until someone sets us free,
And we're brought into the light,
And we're back at the start.

And I know things now,
Many valuable things,
That I hadn't known before:
Do not put your faith
In a cape and a hood—
They will not protect you
The way that they should—
And take extra care with strangers,
Even flowers have their dangers.
And though scary is exciting,
Nice is different than good.
Now I know:
Don't be scared.
Granny is right,
Just be prepared.

Isn't it nice to know a lot!

. . . and a little bit not . . .

*(*BAKER *crosses stage.* LITTLE RED RIDING-HOOD *crosses to him.)*

Mr. Baker, you saved our lives. Here. *(She hands him her cape)*

BAKER. Are you certain?

LITTLE RED RIDINGHOOD. Yes. Maybe Granny will make me another with the skins of that wolf.

BAKER. Thank you.

(They exit in different directions.)

NARRATOR. And so the baker, with the second article in hand, feeling braver and more satisfied than he had ever felt, ran back through the woods.

(A cutout of JACK's *house appears.)*

As for the lad Jack:

*(*JACK'S MOTHER *and* JACK *come from behind the cutout.)*

JACK'S MOTHER *(Livid)*. Only a dolt would

exchange a cow for beans! *(She throws the beans to the ground)*

JACK. Mother, no— *(He goes to pick them up)*

JACK'S MOTHER. To bed without supper for you!

(She grabs the boy and marches him into the house as it goes offstage.)

NARRATOR. Little did they know those beans would grow into an enormous stalk that would stretch into the heavens.

(Music; WIFE enters upstage tugging at Milky-White. Ball music in the distance, growing louder. CINDERELLA dashes onstage, looking over her shoulder. She falls; music stops.)

WIFE. Are you all right, miss?

CINDERELLA *(Breathless)*. Yes. I just need to catch my breath.

WIFE. What a beautiful gown you're wearing. Were you at the King's Festival?

CINDERELLA *(Preoccupied)*. Yes.

WIFE. Aren't you the lucky one. Why ever are you in the woods at this hour?

(Fanfares in the distance, growing louder. We hear men's voices offstage. CINDERELLA signals to WIFE to keep quiet, then ducks behind a tree. CINDERELLA'S PRINCE runs onstage, followed by his STEWARD. They look about for a moment, then notice WIFE.)

CINDERELLA'S PRINCE. Have you seen a beautiful young woman in a ball gown pass through?

(WIFE bows.)

WIFE *(Breathless)*. I don't think so, sir.

STEWARD. I think I see her over there.

(CINDERELLA'S PRINCE signals him off in that direction, then takes another look at WIFE before following. Music continues under.)

WIFE. I've never lied to royalty before. I've never *anything* to royalty before!

CINDERELLA. Thank you.

WIFE. If a Prince were looking for me, I certainly wouldn't hide.

CINDERELLA *(Defensive)*. Well, what brings *you* here—and with a cow?

WIFE. Oh, my husband's somewhere in the woods. *(Proud)* He's undoing a spell.

CINDERELLA *(Impressed)*. Oh?

WIFE. Oh, yes. Now, the Prince, what was he like?

CINDERELLA. He's a very nice Prince.

WIFE. And—?

CINDERELLA. And—

It's a very nice Ball.

WIFE. And—?

CINDERELLA. And—

When I entered, they trumpeted.

WIFE. And—?

The Prince—?

CINDERELLA. Oh, the Prince . . .

WIFE. Yes, the Prince!

CINDERELLA. Well, he's tall.

WIFE. Is that all?

Did you dance?

Is he charming? They say that he's charming.

CINDERELLA. We did nothing *but* dance.

WIFE. Yes—? And—?

CINDERELLA. And it made a nice change.

WIFE. No, the Prince!

CINDERELLA. Oh, the Prince . . .

WIFE. Yes, the Prince.

CINDERELLA. He has charm for a Prince, I guess . . .

WIFE. Guess?

CINDERELLA. I don't meet a wide range.

And it's all very strange.

WIFE. Are you to return to the Festival tomorrow eve?

CINDERELLA. Perhaps.

WIFE. Perhaps? Oh, to be pursued by a Prince. All that pursues me is tomorrow's bread.

(We hear the first chime of midnight.)

What I wouldn't give to be in your shoes.

(Second chime; chimes continue under.)

CINDERELLA. Will you look over there.

(Milky-White stands and looks.)

An enormous vine growing next to that little cottage.

WIFE *(Looking down at CINDERELLA's feet)*. . . . I mean slippers.

CINDERELLA. It looks like a giant beanstalk rising into the sky.

WIFE *(Excited)*. As pure as gold?

CINDERELLA. I must get home. *(Begins to leave)*

WIFE. Wait!

(CINDERELLA exits.)

I need your shoes!

(WIFE starts off after CINDERELLA; Milky-White lets out a "Moo!" and takes off in the other direction; WIFE stops, torn between Milky-White and CINDERELLA.)

WIFE *(To CINDERELLA)*. Hey! *(To Milky-White)* Come back here!

(WIFE takes off after Milky-White; final chime of midnight; music continues under; one by one, each of the characters appears moving through the woods, darting in and out of the trees and paths, pursuing their errands, mostly oblivious to one another.

The night turns gradually into dawn.

The following lines are spoken rhythmically as each character appears and disappears.)

BAKER. One midnight gone . . .

MYSTERIOUS MAN. No knot unties itself . . .

WITCH. Sometimes the things you most wish for

Are not to be touched . . .

PRINCES. The harder to get, the better to have . . .

CINDERELLA'S PRINCE. Agreed?

RAPUNZEL'S PRINCE. Agreed.

FLORINDA. Never wear mauve at a ball . . .

LUCINDA. Or pink . . .

STEPMOTHER *(To stepdaughters).* Or open your mouth . . .

JACK *(Looking up and off at the beanstalk).* The difference between a cow and a bean

Is a bean can begin an adventure . . .

JACK'S MOTHER *(Looking off in* JACK'*s direction).* Slotted spoons don't hold much soup . . .

LITTLE RED RIDINGHOOD. The prettier the flower, the farther from the path . . .

CINDERELLA'S FATHER. The closer to the family, the closer to the wine . . .

RAPUNZEL *(Offstage).* Ah-ah-ah-ah-ah . . .

WITCH *(Reappearing suddenly).* One midnight gone! . . .

GRANNY. The mouth of a wolf's not the end of the world . . .

STEWARD. A servant is not just a dog, to a Prince . . .

CINDERELLA. Opportunity is not a lengthy visitor . . .

WIFE. You may know what you need,

But to get what you want,

Better see that you keep what you have.

(All sing, overlapping.)

BAKER. One midnight gone . . .

WITCH. Sometimes the things you most wish for

Are not to be touched . . .

PRINCES. The harder to get the better to have . . .

CINDERELLA'S PRINCE. Agreed?

RAPUNZEL'S PRINCE. Agreed.

BAKER. One midnight gone . . . one midnight gone . . .

FLORINDA. Never wear mauve at a ball . . .

LUCINDA. Or pink . . .

JACK'S MOTHER. Slotted spoons don't hold much soup . . .

BAKER'S WIFE. To get what you want better keep what you . . .

LITTLE RED RIDINGHOOD. The prettier the flower . . .

ALL. One midnight one midnight one midnight gone . . .

Into the woods,

Into the woods,

Into the woods, then out of the woods

And home before—

SCENE 3

BAKER *sleeps beneath a tree.*

Music; JACK *appears suddenly from the trees, carrying an oversized money sack.*

———

JACK. There are giants in the sky!

There are big tall terrible giants in the sky!

When you're way up high

And you look below

At the world you've left

And the things you know,

Little more than a glance

Is enough to show

You just how small you are.

When you're way up high

And you're on your own

In a world like none

That you've ever known,

Where the sky is lead

And the earth is stone,

You're free to do

Whatever pleases you,

Exploring things you'd never dare

'Cause you don't care,

When suddenly there's

A big tall terrible giant at the door,

A big tall terrible lady giant sweeping the floor.

And she gives you food

And she gives you rest

And she draws you close

To her giant breast,

And you know things now that you never knew before,

Not till the sky.

Only just when you've made

A friend and all,

And you know she's big

But you don't feel small,

Someone bigger than her

Comes along the hall

To swallow you for lunch.

STEPHEN SONDHEIM AND JAMES LAPINE ——————————— 319

And your heart is lead
And your stomach stone
And you're really scared
Being all alone . . .

And it's then that you miss
All the things you've known
And the world you've left
And the little you own—

The fun is done.
You steal what you can and run!
And you scramble down
And you look below,
And the world you know
Begins to grow:

The roof, the house, and your mother at the door.
The roof, the house, and the world you never thought to explore.
And you think of all of the things you've seen,
And you wish that you could live in between,
And you're back again,
Only different than before,
After the sky.

There are giants in the sky!
There are big tall terrible awesome scary wonderful
Giants in the sky!

(BAKER *stirs;* JACK *bounds over to him.*)

JACK. Good fortune! Good fortune, sir! Look what I have! Here's five gold pieces.

BAKER (*Astounded*). Five gold pieces! (*He examines the gold*)

JACK. I had more, but my mother made me surrender them. She allowed me these five to do with as I pleased.

BAKER. Oh, my . . .

JACK. Where is Milky-White?

BAKER. Milky-White is back home with my wife.

JACK. Let's go find them! (*He grabs* BAKER *and starts to pull him away*)

BAKER. Wait! I don't know that I wish to sell.

JACK. But you said I might buy her back.

BAKER. I know, but I'm not certain that five gold pieces would—

JACK. Are you saying that you wish more money?

BAKER. More money is always—

JACK (*Hands him gold*). Keep this. I will go fetch more.

BAKER. Wait. I didn't say—

(JACK *exits;* BAKER *looks at money.*)

Five gold pieces! With this money I could buy baking supplies for a year. I could buy a new thatched roof *and* a new chimney.

(MYSTERIOUS MAN *appears from nowhere.*)

MYSTERIOUS MAN. But could you buy yourself a child?

BAKER (*Startled*). Who are you?

MYSTERIOUS MAN. When first I appear I seem delirious. But when explained, I am nothing serious. Could you buy yourself a child?

BAKER. I don't understand.

MYSTERIOUS MAN. How badly do you wish a child? Five gold pieces? Ten? Twenty?

BAKER. I've not thought to put a price on it.

MYSTERIOUS MAN. Exactly. (*He walks over and distracts the* BAKER *and takes the gold*) You've not thought about many things, have you, son?

BAKER. Give me back the money! It is not yours—

MYSTERIOUS MAN. Nor is it Jack's. The money is not what's important. What's important is that your wish be honored.

(MYSTERIOUS MAN *goes around a tree and disappears;* BAKER *begins darting around trees looking for him.*)

BAKER. Come back here! Damn! Give me back—

(*He sees* WIFE, *who comes from around another tree.*)

What are you doing here now?

WIFE (*Quickly switching gears*). I see you've the red cape.

BAKER. Yes. I've the cape. Only two items left to locate.

WIFE. Three.

BAKER. Two. I've the cape and the cow.

WIFE (*Faking enthusiasm*). You've the cape!

BAKER. WHAT HAVE YOU DONE WITH THE COW?!

WIFE. She ran away. I never reached home. I've been looking for her all night.

BAKER. I should have known better than to have entrusted her to you.

WIFE. She might just as easily have run from you!

BAKER. But she didn't!

WIFE. BUT SHE MIGHT HAVE!

BAKER. BUT SHE DIDN'T!!!

(WITCH *appears from nowhere.*)

WITCH. WHO CARES! THE COW IS GONE! GET IT BACK! *GET IT BACK!!!*

(*All three settle down.*)

BAKER (*Walks over to* WITCH). We were just going to do that. (*Offers cape*) Here. I can give you this—

WITCH. DON'T GIVE ME THAT, FOOL!! I don't want to touch that! Have you no sense?

(RAPUNZEL *is heard suddenly, singing in the background.*)

My sweetness calls. (*Tough*) By tomorrow's midnight—deliver the items or you'll wish you never thought to have a child!

(WITCH *zaps them with lightning and leaves.*)

BAKER. I don't like that woman.

WIFE (*Contrite*). I'm sorry I lost the cow.

BAKER. I shouldn't have yelled. (*Beat*) Now, please, go back to the village.

(WIFE, *annoyed, turns her back and begins to walk away.*)

I *will* make things right. And then we can just go about our life. No more hunting about in the woods for strange objects. No more witches and dimwitted boys and hungry little girls.

(WIFE *begins to move back towards him.*)

Go!

(*They exit in opposite directions.*

Two fanfares. Another part of the forest. CINDERELLA'S PRINCE, *somewhat bedraggled, crosses the stage. He is met by* RAPUNZEL'S PRINCE.)

RAPUNZEL'S PRINCE. Ah, there you are, good brother. Father and I had wondered where you had gone.

CINDERELLA'S PRINCE. I have been looking all night . . . for her.

RAPUNZEL'S PRINCE. Her?

CINDERELLA'S PRINCE. The beautiful one I danced the evening with.

RAPUNZEL'S PRINCE. Where did she go?

(WIFE *begins walking by; noticing the* PRINCES, *she hides behind a tree and eavesdrops.*)

CINDERELLA'S PRINCE. Disappeared, like the fine morning mist.

RAPUNZEL'S PRINCE. She was lovely.

CINDERELLA'S PRINCE. The loveliest.

RAPUNZEL'S PRINCE. I am not certain of that! I must confess, I too have found a lovely maiden. She lives here in the woods.

CINDERELLA'S PRINCE (*Incredulous*). The woods?

RAPUNZEL'S PRINCE. Yes! In the top of a tall tower that has no door or stairs.

CINDERELLA'S PRINCE. Where?

RAPUNZEL'S PRINCE. Two leagues from here, due east, just beyond the mossy knoll.

CINDERELLA'S PRINCE. And how do you manage a visit?

RAPUNZEL'S PRINCE. I stand beneath her tower and say, "Rapunzel, Rapunzel, let down your hair to me." And then she lowers the longest, most beautiful head of hair— yellow as corn—which I climb to her.

(WIFE *reacts.*)

CINDERELLA'S PRINCE (*Starts laughing hysterically*). Rapunzel, Rapunzel! What kind of name is that? You jest! I have never heard of such a thing.

RAPUNZEL'S PRINCE (*Defensive*). I speak the truth! She is as true as your maiden. A maiden running from a Prince? None would run from us.

CINDERELLA'S PRINCE (*Sober*). Yet one has. (*Music.*)

Did I abuse her
Or show her disdain?
Why does she run from me?
If I should lose her,
How shall I regain
The heart she has won from me?

Agony!
Beyond power of speech,
When the one thing you want
Is the only thing out of your reach.
RAPUNZEL'S PRINCE. High in her tower,
She sits by the hour,
Maintaining her hair.
Blithe and becoming,
And frequently humming
A lighthearted air:
(*Hums* RAPUNZEL's *theme*)
Ah-ah-ah-ah-ah-ah-ah—
Agony!
Far more painful than yours,
When you know she would go with you,
If there only were doors.
BOTH. Agony!
Oh the torture they teach!
RAPUNZEL'S PRINCE. What's as intriguing—
CINDERELLA'S PRINCE. Or half so fatiguing—
BOTH. As what's out of reach?
CINDERELLA'S PRINCE. Am I not sensitive, clever,
Well-mannered, considerate,
Passionate, charming,
As kind as I'm handsome,
And heir to a throne?
RAPUNZEL'S PRINCE. You are everything maidens could wish for!
CINDERELLA'S PRINCE. Then why no—?
RAPUNZEL'S PRINCE. Do I know?

CINDERELLA'S PRINCE. The girl must be mad!

RAPUNZEL'S PRINCE. You know nothing of madness
Till you're climbing her hair
And you see her up there
As you're nearing her,
All the while hearing her
"Ah-ah-ah-ah-ah-ah-ah-ah-ah-ah-ah-ah—"

BOTH. Agony!

CINDERELLA'S PRINCE. Misery!

RAPUNZEL'S PRINCE. Woe!

BOTH. Though it's different for each.

CINDERELLA'S PRINCE. Always ten steps behind—

RAPUNZEL'S PRINCE. Always ten feet below—

BOTH. And she's just out of reach.
Agony
That can cut like a knife!

I must have her to wife.

(They exit.)

WIFE. *Two* Princes, each more handsome than the other. *(She begins to follow the PRINCES; she stops)* No! Get the hair! *(She heads in the other direction)*

(JACK'S MOTHER enters frantically; music fades.)

JACK'S MOTHER. Excuse me, young woman. Have you encountered a boy with carrot-top hair and a sunny, though occasionally vague, disposition, answering to the name of Jack?

WIFE. Not the one partial to a white cow?

JACK'S MOTHER. He's the one.

WIFE. Have you seen the cow?

JACK'S MOTHER. No, and I don't care to ever again. *(Confidential)* Children can be very queer about their animals. You be careful with your children . . .

WIFE. I have no children.

(Beat.)

JACK'S MOTHER. That's okay, too.

WIFE. Yes . . . well, I've not seen your son today.

JACK'S MOTHER *(Annoyed)*. I hope he didn't go up that beanstalk again. Quit while you're ahead, *I* say. *(She begins to exit)* Jack . . . ! Jack . . . !

(WIFE, after a moment's pause, exits in the other direction; BAKER enters looking for the cow.)

BAKER *(Forlorn)*. Moo . . . . Moo . . .

(MYSTERIOUS MAN appears from nowhere.)

MYSTERIOUS MAN. Moo! Looking for your cow?

(MYSTERIOUS MAN signals offstage and Milky-White enters.)

BAKER. Where did you find her?

(MYSTERIOUS MAN ducks back behind a tree as BAKER goes to cow. He turns, and sees the old man is gone.)

Hello?

(BAKER takes cow and exits. MYSTERIOUS MAN reappears and watches after BAKER. WITCH surprises him.)

WITCH. What are you doing?

MYSTERIOUS MAN. I am here to make amends.

WITCH. I want you to stay out of this, old man!

MYSTERIOUS MAN. I am here to see your wish is granted.

WITCH. You've caused enough trouble! Keep out of my path!

(WITCH zaps MYSTERIOUS MAN; he runs off; she follows him; WIFE approaches RAPUNZEL's tower.)

WIFE *(To herself)*. I hope there are no witches to encounter. *(Calling up)* Rapunzel, Rapunzel? Let your hair down to me.

RAPUNZEL *(Dubious)*. Is that you, my Prince?

WIFE *(In a deep voice)*. Yes.

(RAPUNZEL lowers her hair.)

WIFE. Excuse me for this.

(WIFE yanks hair three times; each time RAPUNZEL lets out an increasingly loud scream. On the third yank, the hair falls into WIFE's hands; WIFE runs away to another part of the woods; CINDERELLA enters as if pursued; she falls at WIFE's feet.)

You do take plenty of spills, don't you?

CINDERELLA *(Recognizing WIFE)*. It's these slippers. They're not suited for these surroundings. Actually, they're not much suited for dancing, either. *(She sits, taking off shoes)*

WIFE. I'd say those slippers were as pure as gold.

CINDERELLA. Yes. They are all you could wish for in beauty.

WIFE. What I wouldn't give for just one.

CINDERELLA. One is not likely to do you much good. *(She giggles)*

WIFE. Was the Ball just as wonderful as last evening?

CINDERELLA. Oh, it's still a nice Ball.

WIFE. Yes—? And—?

CINDERELLA. And—
They have far too much food.

WIFE. No, the Prince—

CINDERELLA. Oh, the Prince . . .

WIFE. Yes, the Prince!

CINDERELLA. If he knew who I really was—
WIFE. Oh? Who?
CINDERELLA. I'm afraid I was rude.
WIFE. Oh? How?
CINDERELLA. Now I'm being pursued.
WIFE. Yes? And—?
CINDERELLA. And I'm not in the mood.

I have no experience with Princes and castles and gowns.
WIFE. Nonsense, every girl dreams—
(Fanfare in the distance; we hear voices advancing.)
STEWARD *(Off)*. Look, sir! Look!
CINDERELLA'S PRINCE *(Off)*. Yes, there she is! Move!
CINDERELLA. I must run.
(WIFE grabs a shoe.)
WIFE. And I must have your shoe.
CINDERELLA. Stop that!
(The two engage in a violent tug-of-war over the shoe. CINDERELLA wins the battle and desperately runs off; WIFE is embarrassed by her own behavior. She straightens herself up as CINDERELLA'S PRINCE and STEWARD bound onstage.)
CINDERELLA'S PRINCE. Where did she go?
WIFE *(Bows)*. Who?
STEWARD. Don't play the fool, woman!
WIFE. Oh! You mean the beautiful young maiden in the ball gown? She went in that direction. I was trying to hold her here for you . . .
CINDERELLA'S PRINCE. I can capture my own damsel, thank you. *(He begins to go off towards CINDERELLA)*
WIFE. Yes, sir.
(PRINCE and STEWARD dash offstage. We hear FLORINDA, LUCINDA and STEPMOTHER. They enter, first looking behind them, then looking towards the PRINCE.)
STEPMOTHER *(To WIFE)*. Where did he go?
WIFE. Who?
LUCINDA. The Prince, of course!
WIFE. That direction. But you'll never reach them!
FLORINDA. We would have if that mongrel with the cow hadn't molested us.
WIFE. Cow?
(The stepsisters giggle. BAKER runs onstage with Milky-White. They are both out of breath.)
BAKER *(Holding up ear of corn)*. Please, let me just compare this color with that of your own.
(LUCINDA and FLORINDA chortle.)
LUCINDA AND FLORINDA. He wants to compare our hair to corn!

(The threesome exits laughing hysterically. There is a long moment of silence. WIFE and BAKER stare at one another.)
BAKER *(Dejected)*. I thought you were returning home. *(Angry)* I've had no luck.
WIFE. You've the cow!
BAKER. Yes. I've the cow. We've only two of the four.
WIFE. Three.
BAKER. Two.
WIFE *(Pulls the hair from her pocket)*. Three! Compare this to your corn.
(BAKER does so and smiles.)
BAKER. Where did you find it?
WIFE *(False modesty)*. I pulled it from a maiden in a tower.
BAKER *(Looking at hair)*. Three!
WIFE. And I almost had the fourth, but she got away.
BAKER. We've one entire day left. Surely we can locate the slipper by then.
WIFE. *We?* You mean you'll allow me to stay?
BAKER *(Retreating)*. Well . . . perhaps it will take the two of us to get this child.
(Music.)
WIFE. You've changed.
You're daring.
You're different in the woods.
More sure.
More sharing.
You're getting us through the woods.

If you could see—
You're not the man who started,
And much more open-hearted
Than I knew
You to be.
BAKER. It takes two.
I thought one was enough,
It's not true:
It takes two of us.
You came through
When the journey was rough.
It took you.
It took two of us.

It takes care,
It takes patience and fear and despair
To change.
Though you swear
To change,
Who can tell if you do?
It takes two.
WIFE. You've changed.
You're thriving.

There's something about the woods.
Not just
Surviving,
You're blossoming in the woods.

At home I'd fear
We'd stay the same forever.
And then out here
You're passionate, charming, considerate,
clever—
BAKER. It takes one
To begin, but then once
You've begun,
It takes two of you.
It's no fun,
But what needs to be done
You can do
When there's two of you.

If I dare,
It's because I'm becoming
Aware of us
As a pair of us,
Each accepting a share
Of what's there.
BOTH. We've changed.
We're strangers.
I'm meeting you in the woods.
Who minds
What dangers?
I know we'll get past the woods.
And once we're past,
Let's hope the changes last

Beyond woods,
Beyond witches and slippers and hoods,
Just the two of us—
Beyond lies,
Safe at home with our beautiful prize,
Just the few of us.

It takes trust.
It takes just
A bit more
And we're done.
We want four,
We had none.
We've got three.
We need one.
It takes two.
(We hear the slow chimes of midnight begin; a hen dashes onstage, closely followed by JACK.*)*
JACK. STOP HER! STOP THAT HEN!
*(*BAKER *grabs hen.)*
Oh, Providence! My Milky-White. *(He gives cow a kiss)*

And the owners. *And* my hen!
BAKER *(Squeals).* Look what this hen has dropped in my hand!
WIFE *(Excited).* A golden egg! I've never seen a golden egg!
JACK. You see, I promised you more than the five gold pieces I gave you, sir.
WIFE. Five gold pieces?
JACK. Now I'm taking my cow.
WIFE. Five gold pieces?
BAKER *(To* JACK*).* Now, I never said I would sell.
JACK. But you took the five gold pieces.
WIFE. You took five gold pieces?!
BAKER. I didn't take, you gave.
WIFE. Where are the five gold pieces?
BAKER. An old man—
*(*JACK *goes to take Milky-White.* BAKER *holds her rope from him. Simultaneous dialogue:)*
JACK *(Getting upset).* You said I could have my cow!
BAKER. Now I never said you could. I said you might.
WIFE. You would take money before a child?!
(Milky-White lets out a terrible moan, and falls to the ground, dead. Silence. JACK *runs to her, puts his ear to her chest. Silence.)*
JACK. Milky-White is dead . . .
BAKER, WIFE *(Exasperated).* Two!
(Last chime of midnight; blackout.)

SCENE 4

Again, the characters appear one by one, as night changes into dawn.
———
WITCH. Two midnights gone!
CINDERELLA. Wanting a ball is not wanting a Prince . . .
CINDERELLA'S PRINCE. Near may be better than far,
But it still isn't *there* . . .
RAPUNZEL'S PRINCE. Near may be better than far,
But it still isn't *there* . . .
CINDERELLA. The ball . . .
CINDERELLA'S PRINCE. So near . . .
RAPUNZEL'S PRINCE. So far . . .
STEPMOTHER. You can never love somebody else's child—
FLORINDA, LUCINDA. Two midnights gone!
STEPMOTHER. —the way you love—
CINDERELLA'S PRINCE. So near . . .
STEPMOTHER. —your own.
CINDERELLA. The Prince . . .

RAPUNZEL'S PRINCE. So far . . .

GRANNY. The greatest prize can often lie
At the end of the thorniest path . . .

ALL. Two midnights gone!
Two midnights gone!

SCENE 5

As the lights come up, we see the WIFE *and the*
BAKER, *bedraggled and exhausted.*

NARRATOR. Two midnights gone. And the
exhausted baker and his wife buried the dead
Milky-White, believing that when the witch
said a cow as white as milk, she was referring
to a live one.

BAKER. You must go to the village in search
of another cow.

WIFE. And what do you propose I use to
purchase this cow?

BAKER *(Takes remaining bean from pocket)*.
Here. Tell them it's magic.

WIFE. No person with a brain larger than
this is going to exchange a cow for a bean.

BAKER *(Losing patience)*. Then steal it.

WIFE *(Angry)*. Steal it? Just two days ago *you*
were accusing *me* of exercising deceit in
securing the cow.

BAKER. Then don't steal it and resign yourself to a childless life.

WIFE *(Calm, but cold)*. I feel it best you go for
the cow, as I have met a maiden with a golden
slipper these previous eves, and I think I might
succeed in winning one of her shoes.

BAKER. Fine. That is simply fine.

*(*WIFE *gathers her things and begins to exit in
one direction, the* BAKER *in the other; we hear*
RAPUNZEL *scream; they run off in fear.*

NARRATOR. Unfortunately for Rapunzel—

RAPUNZEL *(Off)*. No!

NARRATOR. —the witch discovered her af-
fections for the Prince before he could spirit
her away.

*(*WITCH *drags* RAPUNZEL *on. Music.)*

WITCH. What did I clearly say?
Children must listen.

(Grabs RAPUNZEL'S *hair, takes out scissors)*

RAPUNZEL. No, no, please!

WITCH. What were you not to do?
Children must see—

RAPUNZEL. No!

WITCH. And learn.

*(*RAPUNZEL *screams in protest.)*

Why could you not obey?
Children should listen.

What have I been to you?
What would you have me be?
Handsome like a Prince?

*(*RAPUNZEL *whimpers.)*

Ah, but I am old.
I am ugly.
I embarrass you.

RAPUNZEL. No!

WITCH. You are ashamed of me.

RAPUNZEL. No!

WITCH. You are ashamed.
You don't understand.

(Music continues under.)

RAPUNZEL. It was lonely atop that tower.

WITCH. I was not company enough?

RAPUNZEL. I am no longer a child. I wish to
see the world.

WITCH *(Tender but intense)*. Don't you know
what's out there in the world?
Someone has to shield you from the world.
Stay with me.

Princes wait there in the world, it's true.
Princes, yes, but wolves and humans, too.
Stay at home.
I am home.

Who out there could love you more
than I?
What out there that I cannot supply?
Stay with me.

Stay with me,
The world is dark and wild.
Stay a child while you can be a child.
With me.

*(*RAPUNZEL *just whimpers; music continues
under.)*

I gave you protection and yet you dis-
obeyed me.

RAPUNZEL. No!

WITCH. Why didn't you tell me you had a
visitor?

*(*RAPUNZEL *keeps whimpering; music crescen-
dos.)*

I will not share you, but I *will* show you a
world you've never seen. *(She cuts* RAPUNZEL'S
hair)

RAPUNZEL. No! NO!

*(*WITCH *drags* RAPUNZEL *off.* BAKER *enters, followed by* MYSTERIOUS MAN.*)*

MYSTERIOUS MAN. When is a white cow not
a white cow?

BAKER. I don't know! Leave me alone!

MYSTERIOUS MAN. Haven't I left you alone long enough?

BAKER. Your questions make no sense, old man! Go away!

MYSTERIOUS MAN. In need of another cow?

(He drops sack of gold; BAKER turns around at the sound of the falling coins; MYSTERIOUS MAN exits as BAKER picks up money and exits. JACK comes upon LITTLE RED RIDINGHOOD, who wears a cape made of wolfskins. She walks with a certain bravado.)

JACK. What a beautiful cape!

(LITTLE RED RIDINGHOOD swerves around, brandishing a knife.)

LITTLE RED RIDINGHOOD. Stay away from my cape or I'll slice you into a thousand bits!

JACK *(Stepping back)*. I don't want it! I was just admiring it!

LITTLE RED RIDINGHOOD *(Proud)*. My granny made it for me from a wolf that attacked us. And I got to skin the animal—and best of all, she gave me this beautiful knife for protection.

JACK *(Competitive)*. Well, look what *I* have. A hen that lays golden eggs.

LITTLE RED RIDINGHOOD *(Suspicious)*. I don't believe that egg came from that hen. Where did you get that egg?

JACK. I stole this from the kingdom of the giant—up there. And if you think this is something, you should see the golden harp the giant has. It plays the most beautiful tunes without your even having to touch it.

LITTLE RED RIDINGHOOD *(Smirking)*. Of course it does. Why don't you go up to the kingdom right now and bring it back and show me?

JACK. I could.

LITTLE RED RIDINGHOOD. You could not!

JACK. I could!

LITTLE RED RIDINGHOOD. You could not, Mr. *Liar! (She makes a hasty exit)*

JACK. I am not a liar! I'll get that harp. You'll see! *(He exits)*

NARRATOR. After having cast out Rapunzel to a remote desert, the witch returned to take the Prince by surprise.

(RAPUNZEL's tower. RAPUNZEL'S PRINCE climbs RAPUNZEL's hair when suddenly the WITCH pops out from the tower.)

WITCH. You would fetch your dearest, but the bird no longer sits in her cage.

(The WITCH pushes RAPUNZEL'S PRINCE from the tower. He falls and screams, grabbing his eyes. The WITCH laughs with delight.)

NARRATOR. And unfortunately, the Prince fell into a patch of thorns which pierced his eyes and blinded him.

(RAPUNZEL'S PRINCE stumbles helplessly offstage.)

As for Cinderella, she returned from her final visit to the Festival.

(Lights dim. CINDERELLA hobbles onstage, wearing but one shoe.)

CINDERELLA. He's a very smart Prince,
He's a Prince who prepares,
Knowing this time I'd run from him,
He spread pitch on the stairs.
I was caught unawares.

And I thought: well, he cares—
This is more than just malice.
Better stop and take stock
While you're standing here stuck
On the steps of the palace.

You think, what do you want?
You think, make a decision.
Why not stay and be caught?
You think, well, it's a thought,
What would be his response?
But then what if he knew
Who you were when you know
That you're not what he thinks
That he wants?

And then what if you are
What a Prince would envision?
Although how can you know
Who you are till you know
What you want, which you don't?
So then which do you pick:
Where you're safe, out of sight,
And yourself, but where everything's wrong?
Or where everything's right
And you know that you'll never belong?

And whichever you pick,
Do it quick,
'Cause you're starting to stick
To the steps of the palace.

It's your first big decision,
The choice isn't easy to make.
To arrive at a Ball
Is exciting and all—
Once you're there, though, it's scary.
And it's fun to deceive
When you know you can leave,
But you have to be wary.

There's a lot that's at stake,
But you've stalled long enough
'Cause you're still standing stuck
In the stuff on the steps . . .

Better run along home
And avoid the collision.
Even though they don't care,
You'll be better off there
Where there's nothing to choose,
So there's nothing to lose.

So you pry up your shoes.

Then from out of the blue,
And without any guide,
You know what your decision is,
Which is not to decide.

You'll just leave him a clue:
For example, a shoe.
And then see what he'll do.

Now it's he and not you
Who is stuck with a shoe,
In a stew,
In the goo,
And you've learned something, too,
Something you never knew,
On the steps of the palace.
(WIFE races onstage.)
CINDERELLA. Don't come any closer to me!
WIFE *(Breathless)*. Please, just hear me out!
CINDERELLA. We have nothing to discuss.
You have attacked me once before—
WIFE. I did not attack *you!* I attacked your
shoe. I need it.
*(CINDERELLA begins to run away; WIFE reaches
into her pocket.)*
Here. Here is a magic bean in exchange
for it.
(CINDERELLA stops; WIFE hands her the bean.)
CINDERELLA. Magic bean? *(Takes bean, looks
at it)* Nonsense! *(Throws the bean away)*
WIFE. Don't do that! *(Drops to the ground and
searches for it)*
CINDERELLA. I've already given up one
shoe this evening. My feet cannot bear to
give up another. *(Begins to leave)*
WIFE *(Rising, desperate)*. I need that shoe to
have a child!
CINDERELLA. That makes no sense!
(We hear rumblings from the distance.)
WIFE. Does it make sense that you're run-
ning from a Prince?
STEWARD *(Off)*. Stop!

WIFE. Here. Take my shoes. You'll run
faster.
*(WIFE gives CINDERELLA her shoes, and takes
the golden slipper. CINDERELLA exits. STEWARD
bounds onstage; looks about.)*
STEWARD. Who was that woman?
WIFE. I do not know, sir.
STEWARD. Lying will cost you your life!
(BAKER enters with another cow.)
WIFE. I've done nothing . . .
BAKER. I've the cow.
WIFE *(Sees the cow; excitedly to BAKER)*. The
slipper! We've all four! *(She runs to the BAKER)*
STEWARD *(Goes to WIFE and takes the shoe)*. I
will give this to the Prince and we will search
the kingdom tomorrow for the maiden who
will fit this shoe.
WIFE *(Tries to grab the slipper back)*. It's mine!
*(They begin to struggle; MYSTERIOUS MAN
comes from around a tree.)*
I don't care if this costs me my life—
MYSTERIOUS MAN *(Simultaneously)*. Give her
the slipper and all will—
*(Suddenly there is a long sound of crackling
wood, followed by an enormous thud. This noise is
frighteningly loud: very bass, with the kind of re-
verberation that will shake the audience. All action
onstage stops. There is a moment of stunned silence.
CINDERELLA'S PRINCE races onstage.)*
CINDERELLA'S PRINCE. What was that noise?
STEWARD. Sir. Just a bolt of lightning in a
far-off kingdom.
CINDERELLA'S PRINCE *(To STEWARD)*. How
dare you go off in search without me!
STEWARD. My apologies, sir. I thought that
I might—
CINDERELLA'S PRINCE. Enough of what you
thought! I employed a ruse and had the en-
tire staircase smeared with pitch. And there,
when she ran down, remained the maiden's
slipper. *(He produces the slipper)*
STEWARD. Brilliant!
CINDERELLA'S PRINCE. I thought so. It did
create quite a mess when the other guests
left.
STEWARD. And sir, I have succeeded in ob-
taining the other slipper!
MYSTERIOUS MAN *(To STEWARD)*. Give them
the slipper, and all will come to a happy end.
STEWARD. Who are you, old man?
MYSTERIOUS MAN. When first I appear, I
seem deleterious—
STEWARD. Shut up!
CINDERELLA'S PRINCE. Do as he says. He's
obviously a spirit of some sort, and we only
need one.

STEWARD. Oh . . .

(He hands slipper back to WIFE. *Loud scream.* JACK'S MOTHER *comes running onstage, still screaming.)*

JACK'S MOTHER *(Hysterical; she bows).* There's a dead giant in my backyard!

*(*CINDERELLA'S PRINCE *shoots* STEWARD *a look.)*

(More hysterical) I heard Jack coming down the beanstalk, calling for his axe. And when he raced to the bottom he took it and began hacking down the stalk. Suddenly, with a crash, the beanstalk fell, but there was no Jack. For all I know, he's been crushed by the ogre.

(She cries; long pause; CINDERELLA'S PRINCE *goes to her.)*

CINDERELLA'S PRINCE. Worrying will do you no good. If he's safe, then he's safe. If he's been crushed, well, then, there's nothing any of us can do about that, now is there? *(To* STEWARD*)* We must be off. I need my rest before tomorrow's search is to commence.

*(*PRINCE *and* STEWARD *begin to exit.)*

JACK'S MOTHER. Doesn't anyone care a giant has fallen from the sky?

CINDERELLA'S PRINCE *(Stops)*. He is dead, isn't he?

JACK'S MOTHER. With such a thud, I would suppose.

*(*CINDERELLA'S PRINCE *nods, and exits with* STEWARD. WITCH *appears, frantic; looks up to the sky.)*

WITCH *(Unpleasant)*. The third midnight is near. I see a cow. I see a slipper.

BAKER *(Pulling items from his bag)*. And the cape as red as blood.

WIFE. And the hair as yellow as corn.

WITCH *(Amazed)*. You've all the objects?

WIFE. Yes. *(She brings the cow forth)*

WITCH. That cow doesn't look as white as milk to me.

WIFE *(Moving towards cow)*. Oh, she is. *(Patting cow)* She is!

(White powder flies about as WIFE *pats the cow.* BAKER *pulls her away as* WITCH *approaches.)*

WITCH. This cow has been covered with flour!

BAKER. We had a cow as white as milk. Honestly we did.

WITCH. Then where is she?

WIFE. She's dead.

BAKER. We thought you'd prefer a live cow.

WITCH. Of course I'd prefer a live cow! So bring me the dead cow and I'll bring her back to life!

BAKER. You could do that?

WITCH. Now!

*(*WITCH *zaps* BAKER *with lightning;* WITCH, WIFE *and* BAKER *scamper upstage towards Milky-White's grave and we see dirt flying into the air as they dig into the grave;* JACK *comes running onstage with a golden harp that sings.)*

JACK'S MOTHER *(Relieved)*. There you are! *(She hits him)* I've been worried sick.

JACK. Mother, look. The most beautiful harp. *(He hands harp to her)*

JACK'S MOTHER. You've stolen too much! You could have been killed coming down that plant.

BAKER *(Off)*. She's too heavy.

JACK. What's happening?

JACK'S MOTHER. Milky-White is dead, but don't worry. They're going to bring her back to life!

*(*WITCH *waves her hand, causing a puff of smoke. Milky-White suddenly stands, restored to life.* BAKER *and* WIFE *bring the cow forward.)*

JACK. Milky-White! Now I have two friends. A cow and a harp.

WITCH. Quiet! Feed the objects to the cow!

JACK, WIFE, BAKER. What?

WITCH. You heard me. Feed them to the cow.

(Music; the BAKER *begins to feed Milky-White the objects. With great effort, the cow chews them and with greater effort, swallows. We hear the first chime of midnight. The remaining eleven sound through the rest of the scene. All stare intently at the cow. The* WITCH *pulls a silver goblet from her cloak and gives it to the* BAKER.*)*

Fill this!

JACK *(Going to Milky-White)*. I'll do it. She'll milk only for me. Squeeze, pal.

*(*JACK *milks her feverishly. Nothing.* WITCH *goes and takes the goblet back; she turns it upside down.)*

WITCH. Wrong ingredients. Forget about a child.

WIFE. Wait! We followed your instructions. One, the cow is as white as milk, correct?

WITCH. Yes.

WIFE. And two, the cape was certainly as red as blood.

WITCH. Yes.

WIFE. And three, the slipper—

WITCH. Yes.

BAKER. And four, I compared the hair with this ear of corn.

WIFE. I pulled it from a maiden in a tower and—

WITCH. YOU WHAT?! What were *you* doing there?

WIFE. Well, I happened to be passing by—

WITCH. I touched that hair! Don't you understand? I cannot have touched the ingredients!

BAKER, WIFE *(Moaning)*. Nooooo . . .

(MYSTERIOUS MAN comes from around a tree.)

MYSTERIOUS MAN. The corn! The corn!

BAKER. What?

MYSTERIOUS MAN. The silky hair of the corn. Pull it from the ear and feed it to the cow. Quickly!

(BAKER does so, hurriedly.)

WITCH. This had better work, old man, before the last stroke of midnight, or your son will be the last of your flesh and blood.

BAKER. Son?

MYSTERIOUS MAN *(To witch)*. Please. Not now.

WITCH. Yes. Meet your father. *(She moves to cow)*

BAKER. FATHER? Could that be you? I thought you died in a baking accident.

MYSTERIOUS MAN. I didn't want to run away from you, son, but—

(Cow lets out a bloodcurdling moan and begins to shake feverishly.)

WIFE. It's working!

(Cow squeals.)

JACK. She's milking!

BAKER *(To MYSTERIOUS MAN)*. I don't understand.

MYSTERIOUS MAN. Not now! *(To WIFE)* Into the cup!

(WIFE holds goblet under cow's udder as JACK milks; all eyes are on the cow. WIFE hands the filled goblet to the WITCH; BAKER and WIFE dance with joy as WITCH drinks potion. They go to her.)

BAKER. We've given you what you wish.

WIFE. Now when can we expect a child?

(WITCH begins to shake and move away.)

BAKER. What's wrong? What's happening?

WIFE. Wait. Where are you going?

(The last stroke of midnight.)

MYSTERIOUS MAN *(Falling to the ground)*. Son! Son!

BAKER *(Going to MYSTERIOUS MAN's side)*. Father!

(MYSTERIOUS MAN lets out a groan.)

MYSTERIOUS MAN. All is repaired. *(He dies)*

BAKER. He's dead!

(The WITCH with a flourish turns around. She has been transformed into a beautiful woman. Blackout.)

SCENE 6

Music under; the MYSTERIOUS MAN *removes elements of his costume, revealing that he is also the* NARRATOR. *He tosses the* MYSTERIOUS MAN's *clothing away.*

_____

NARRATOR. And so the mysterious man died, having helped end the curse on his house. For the baker, there would be no reunion with his father, and he and his wife, bewildered, returned home. The witch, who had been punished with age and ugliness that night when her beans had been stolen and the lightning flashed, was now returned to her former state of youth and beauty. And Milky-White, after a night of severe indigestion, was reunited with the now wealthy Jack. As for the Prince, he began his search for the foot to fit the golden slipper.

(Fanfare; CINDERELLA'S PRINCE *and* STEWARD *enter on horseback.)*

When he came to Cinderella's house, Cinderella's stepmother took the slipper into Florinda's room.

(FLORINDA tries on shoe; STEPMOTHER *struggles to help her.)*

FLORINDA. Careful, my toe—!

STEPMOTHER. Darling, I know—

FLORINDA. What'll we do?

STEPMOTHER. It'll have to go—

(FLORINDA reacts as STEPMOTHER *suddenly brandishes a knife.)*

But when you're his bride
You can sit or ride.
You'll never need to walk!

(STEPMOTHER looks at her encouragingly and cuts off toe.)

NARRATOR. The girl obeyed, swallowing the pain, and joined the Prince on his horse, riding off to become his bride.

(PRINCE puts FLORINDA on the back of his horse; they arrive at the grave of CINDERELLA'S MOTHER; birds cry from the tree.)

CINDERELLA'S MOTHER. Look at the blood within the shoe;
This one is not the bride that's true.
Search for the foot that fits.

(PRINCE looks at FLORINDA's foot and sees blood trickling from the shoe. They return to CINDERELLA's home.)

NARRATOR. The Prince returned the false bride, and asked the other sister to put on the shoe.

(STEPMOTHER *tries forcing shoe onto* LUCINDA's *foot.*)

LUCINDA. Why won't it fit?

STEPMOTHER (*Holding the knife*). Darling, be still.

Cut off a bit
Of the heel and it will.
And when you're his wife

You'll have such a life,
You'll never need to walk!

(STEPMOTHER *looks at her encouragingly and cuts off heel.*)

NARRATOR. The girl obeyed and swallowed her pain. But as she was helped on the back of the horse by the Prince, he noticed blood trickling from the shoe.

(PRINCE *takes shoe off, pours blood from it and, ashen, returns it to* STEPMOTHER.)

CINDERELLA'S PRINCE. Have you no other daughters?

NARRATOR. To which the woman replied:

STEPMOTHER. No, only a little stunted kitchen wench which his late wife left behind, but she is much too dirty; she cannot present herself.

CINDERELLA'S PRINCE. I insist.

(CINDERELLA *appears.*)

NARRATOR. And when Cinderella presented herself and tried on the blood-soaked slipper, it fit like a glove.

CINDERELLA'S PRINCE. This is the true bride!

CINDERELLA'S FATHER. I always wanted a son!

(CINDERELLA'S FATHER *is admonished by* STEPMOTHER *and stepsisters; fanfare.*)

NARRATOR. And much to the dismay of the stepmother and her daughters, he took Cinderella on his horse and rode off.

(CINDERELLA'S PRINCE *and* CINDERELLA *ride up to the grave.*)

CINDERELLA'S MOTHER. No blood at all within the shoe;

This is the proper bride for you,
Fit to attend a Prince.

(RAPUNZEL, *with babies, enters.* RAPUNZEL'S PRINCE *falls into her arms; his sight is restored.*)

NARRATOR. And finally, as for Rapunzel, she bore twins, and lived impoverished in the desert until the day her Prince, wandering aimlessly, heard a voice so familiar that he went towards it. And when he approached, Rapunzel, overjoyed at seeing him, fell into his arms, weeping. Two of her tears wetted his eyes and their touch restored his vision.

(WITCH *enters.*)

WITCH (*To* RAPUNZEL). I was going to come fetch you as soon as you learned your lesson.

RAPUNZEL. Who are you?

WITCH. Surely you remember.

RAPUNZEL. Mother?

WITCH. This is who I truly am. Come with me, child. We can be happy as we once were. (*She offers* RAPUNZEL *her hand*)

RAPUNZEL'S PRINCE (*Pulling* RAPUNZEL *back*). She will not go with you!

WITCH. Let her speak for herself!

(RAPUNZEL *shakes her head "no."*)

You give me no choice!

(WITCH *goes to put a spell on them, but only a pathetic puff of smoke comes from her hand; she tries again. No success. The couple, bewildered, exit.*)

NARRATOR. As is often the way in these tales, in exchange for her youth and beauty, the witch lost her power.

(WITCH, *frustrated, breaks her cane and exits.*)

When the wedding with the Prince was celebrated, Lucinda and Florinda attended, wishing to win favor with Cinderella and share her good fortune.

(CINDERELLA, *in her wedding gown, and* CINDERELLA'S PRINCE *enter with* STEPMOTHER, CINDERELLA'S FATHER, LUCINDA *and* FLORINDA.)

But as the sisters stood by the blessed couple, pigeons swooped down upon them and poked out their eyes and punished them with blindness.

(FLORINDA *and* LUCINDA *are blinded by birds and stagger offstage, screaming;* WIFE, *very pregnant, enters.*)

WIFE. I see your Prince has found you.

CINDERELLA. Yes.

WIFE (*Patting her belly*). Thank you for the slipper.

(BAKER *enters.*)

CINDERELLA. I didn't think I'd wed a Prince.

CINDERELLA'S PRINCE. I didn't think I'd ever find you.

CINDERELLA, CINDERELLA'S PRINCE, BAKER, WIFE. I didn't think I could be so happy!

(*The company comes onstage; segue to Finale music.*)

NARRATOR. And it came to pass, all that seemed wrong was now right, the kingdoms were filled with joy, and those who deserved to were certain to live a long and happy life. Ever after . . .

COMPANY. Ever after!

NARRATOR. Journey over, all is mended,

And it's not just for today,
But tomorrow, and extended
Ever after!
COMPANY. Ever after!
NARRATOR. All the curses have been ended,
The reverses wiped away.
All is tenderness and laughter
For forever after!
COMPANY. Happy now and happy hence
And happy ever after!
NARRATOR. There were dangers—
COMPANY. We were frightened—
NARRATOR. And confusions—
COMPANY. But we hid it—
NARRATOR. And the paths would often swerve.
COMPANY. We did not.
NARRATOR. There were constant—
COMPANY. It's amazing—
NARRATOR. Disillusions—
COMPANY. That we did it.
NARRATOR. But they never lost their nerve.
COMPANY. Not a lot.
NARRATOR, COMPANY. And they (we) reached the right conclusions,
And they (we) got what they (we) deserve!
COMPANY. Not a sigh and not a sorrow,
Tenderness and laughter.
Joy today and bliss tomorrow,
And forever after!
FLORINDA. I was greedy.
LUCINDA. I was vain.
FLORINDA. I was haughty.
LUCINDA. I was smug.
BOTH. We were happy.
LUCINDA. It was fun.
FLORINDA. But we were blind.
BOTH. Then we went into the woods
To get our wish
And now we're really blind.
WITCH (Overlapping). I was perfect.
I had everything but beauty.
I had power,
And a daughter like a flower,
In a tower.
Then I went into the woods
To get my wish
And now I'm ordinary.
Lost my power, and my flower.
FLORINDA, LUCINDA. We're unworthy.
FLORINDA, LUCINDA, WITCH. We're (I'm) unhappy now, unhappy hence,
As well as ever after.
Had we used our common sense,
Been worthy of our discontents . . .
COMPANY. To be happy, and forever,

You must see your wish come true.
Don't be careful, don't be clever.
When you see your wish, pursue.
It's a dangerous endeavor,
But the only thing to do—
(In three groups)
Though it's fearful,
Though it's deep, though it's dark,
And though you may lose the path,
Though you may encounter wolves,
You mustn't stop,
You mustn't swerve,
You mustn't ponder,
You have to act!
When you know your wish,
If you want your wish,
You can have your wish,
But you can't just wish—
No, to get your wish
(In unison)
You go into the woods,
Where nothing's clear,
Where witches, ghosts
And wolves appear.
Into the woods
And through the fear,
You have to take the journey.

Into the woods
And down the dell,
In vain perhaps,
But who can tell?

Into the woods to lift the spell,
Into the woods to lose the longing.
Into the woods to have the child,
To wed the Prince,
To get the money,
To save the house,
To kill the wolf,
To find the father,
To conquer the kingdom,
To have, to wed,
To get, to save,
To kill, to keep,
To go to the Festival!

Into the woods,
Into the woods,
Into the woods,
Then out of the woods—
NARRATOR. To be continued . . .
(A giant beanstalk emerges from the ground and stretches to the heavens; the characters are oblivious to its presence.)
ALL. —and happy ever after!

(The parties head off to their respective homes, as the lights dim to black.)

ACT TWO

SCENE 1

Downstage, three structures:
Far left, the castle where CINDERELLA *now lives. She sits on her throne, as* FLORINDA *and* LUCINDA, *both still blind, attend to her. The* STEP-MOTHER *supervises.*

Center, the cottage where JACK *lives, now dramatically improved. He and his* MOTHER *are inside, along with Milky-White and the golden harp.*

Far right, the home/workplace of the BAKER *and his* WIFE. *It is very cluttered with both baking supplies and nursery items.* WIFE *holds their baby, who does not stop crying.*

Behind these homes the backdrop of the forest remains.

NARRATOR *steps forward.*

———

NARRATOR. Once upon a time—
(Music.)

—later—
(Light on CINDERELLA.*)*
CINDERELLA. I wish . . .
NARRATOR. —in the same far-off king-dom—
CINDERELLA. More than anything . . .
NARRATOR. —lived a young Princess—
CINDERELLA. More than life . . .
NARRATOR. —the lad Jack—
(Light on JACK.*)*
CINDERELLA. More than footmen . . .
JACK. I wish . . .
NARRATOR. —and the baker and his fam-ily—
(Light on the BAKER *and his* WIFE *with their baby.)*
BABY. Waaah!
JACK. No, I miss . . .
CINDERELLA, BAKER. I wish . . .
BABY. Waaah!
JACK. More than anything . . .
CINDERELLA, BAKER, JACK. More than the moon . . .
WIFE *(To the baby).* There, there . . .
CINDERELLA. I wish to sponsor a Festival.
BABY. Waaah!
BAKER. More than life . . .
JACK. I miss . . .

CINDERELLA. The time has come for a Fes-tival . . .
BABY. Waaah!
WIFE. Shh . . .
BAKER *(Overlapping).* More than riches . . .
CINDERELLA. And a Ball . . .
JACK. I miss my kingdom up in the sky.
CINDERELLA, BAKER. More than any-thing . . .
WIFE. I wish we had more room . . .
JACK *(To harp).* Play, harp . . .
BAKER. Another room . . .
*(*JACK *strums the harp, and it sings.)*
NARRATOR. But despite some minor incon-veniences, they were all content . . .
*(*CINDERELLA'S PRINCE *enters castle.)*
CINDERELLA. I never thought I'd wed a Prince . . .
CINDERELLA'S PRINCE. I never thought I'd find perfection . . .
BOTH. I never thought I could be so happy!
CINDERELLA. Not an unhappy moment since . . .
JACK, JACK'S MOTHER. I didn't think we'd be this rich . . .
CINDERELLA'S PRINCE. Not a conceivable objection . . .
BAKER, WIFE. I never thought we'd have a baby . . .
CINDERELLA, CINDERELLA'S PRINCE, JACK, JACK'S MOTHER. I never thought I could be so happy!
BAKER, WIFE *(Overlapping)* I'm so happy!
STEPMOTHER. Happy now,
Happy hence,
Happy ever after—
STEPMOTHER, STEPSISTERS *(To* CINDERELLA*).*
We're so happy you're so happy!
Just as long as you stay happy,
We'll stay happy! . . .
CINDERELLA, CINDERELLA'S PRINCE. Not one row . . .
JACK'S MOTHER. Pots of pence . . .
JACK. With my cow . . .
BAKER, WIFE. Little gurgles . . .
CINDERELLA'S PRINCE *(To* CINDERELLA*).*
Darling, I must go now . . . *(Exits)*
JACK'S MOTHER *(To* JACK*).* We should really sell it.
BAKER *(To* WIFE*).* Where's the cheesecloth?
ALL OTHERS. Wishes may bring problems,
Such that you regret them.
ALL. Better that, though,
Than to never get them . . .
CINDERELLA. I'm going to be a perfect wife!

JACK *(Overlapping)*. I'm going to be a perfect son!

WIFE, JACK'S MOTHER. I'm going to be a perfect mother!

BAKER. I'm going to be a perfect father! I'm so happy!

CINDERELLA, JACK, JACK'S MOTHER, WIFE. I'm going to see that he (she)
Is so happy!

ALL. I never thought I'd love my life! I would have settled for another!

CINDERELLA. Then to become a wife . . .

JACK, JACK'S MOTHER. Then to be set for life . . .

BAKER, WIFE. Then to beget a child . . .

ALL. That fortune smiled . . .
I'm so happy.

(Music continues under.)

WIFE *(Handing the baby to the BAKER, who is very awkward holding the child)*. If only this cottage were a little larger.

BAKER. I will expand our quarters in due time.

WIFE. Why expand when we could simply move to another cottage?

(Baby cries.)

BAKER. We will not move. This was my father's house, and now it will be my son's.

WIFE. You would raise your child alongside a witch?

BAKER *(Edgy)*. Why does he always cry when *I* hold him.

WIFE. Babies cry. He's fine. You needn't hold him as if he were so fragile.

BAKER. He wants his mother. Here.

(BAKER carefully passes baby back to his WIFE; baby stops crying.)

WIFE. I can't take care of him all of the time!

BAKER. I will care for him . . . when he's older.

BAKER, WIFE, JACK, JACK'S MOTHER. We had to go through thick and thin.

STEPMOTHER, LUCINDA, FLORINDA. We had to lose a lot to win.

CINDERELLA. I ventured out and saw within.

ALL. I never thought I'd be so much I hadn't been!
I'm so hap—

(The song is interrupted by a loud rumbling noise followed by an enormous crash. The BAKER's house caves in. He is caught underneath the rubble as the WIFE runs forward with their baby. Action stops onstage. JACK and his MOTHER look concerned. CINDERELLA sends her STEPMOTHER out

to investigate. We should be momentarily uncertain as to whether there has truly been an accident onstage.

BAKER *(Stunned)*. Are you all right?

WIFE. I think so.

BAKER. And the baby?

WIFE. Yes, he's fine. And you?

(He nods; WITCH races in; she is disheveled. Music under.)

BAKER. YOU! Have you done this to our house?

WITCH. Always thinking of yourself! Look at my garden.

WIFE. What of your garden?

WITCH. Look!

(BAKER and WIFE move to window.)

BAKER. Destroyed.

WIFE. What has happened?

WITCH. I was thrown to the ground. I saw nothing.

WIFE. What could do such a thing?

BAKER. An earthquake.

WITCH. No earthquake! My garden has been trampled. Those are footprints!

WIFE. Who could do such a thing?

WITCH. Anything that leaves a footprint that large is no "who."

BAKER. Do you think it was a bear?

WITCH. A bear? Bears are sweet. Besides, you ever see a bear with forty-foot feet?

WIFE. Dragon?

WITCH *(Shakes her head)*. No scorch marks—
Usually they're linked.

BAKER. Manticore?

WITCH. Imaginary.

WIFE, BAKER. Griffin?

WITCH. Extinct.

BAKER. Giant?

WITCH. Possible.
Very, very possible . . .

(Music fades under.)

BAKER. A giant . . .

WIFE. Maybe we should tell someone.

WITCH. Who are you going to tell?

BAKER. The royal family, of course.

WITCH *(Lets out a loud cackle)*. I wouldn't count on that family to snuff out a rat! With a giant, we'll all have to go to battle! *(Change of tone)* A giant's the worst! A giant has a brain. Hard to outwit a giant. A giant's just like us—only bigger! Much, much bigger! *(She sees a bug crawling across the floor)* So big that we are just an expendable bug beneath its foot. *(She steps on the bug)* BOOM CRUNCH!

(We hear the bug crunch as she grinds it into the floor; she then picks it up and eats it; she exits.)

WIFE. We are moving!

NARRATOR. And so, the baker proceeded to the castle, but not before visiting Jack and his mother.

(Music continues; knock on JACK's door; BAKER enters.)

JACK. Look, Milky-White. It's the butcher.

BAKER. The baker.

JACK. The baker . . .

JACK'S MOTHER *(Pushing JACK out of the way).* What can we do for you, sir?

BAKER. I'm here to investigate the destruction that was wrought upon our house today.

JACK'S MOTHER *(Defensive).* Jack has been home with me all day.

NARRATOR. The baker told Jack and his mother that he feared there was a giant in the land.

JACK. I can recognize a giant's footstep! I could go to your house—

JACK'S MOTHER. You'll do no such thing!

BAKER. Any help at all—

JACK'S MOTHER. I am sorry, but you'll get none from us. *(She opens the door for the BAKER)* No one cared when there was a giant in my backyard! I don't remember *you* volunteering to come to my aid.

BAKER. A giant in your backyard is one thing. A crushed home is quite another.

JACK'S MOTHER *(Change of tone).* Look, young man. Giants never strike the same house twice. I wouldn't worry.

BAKER. I am taking the news to the castle, nonetheless. *(He exits)*

NARRATOR. When the baker reached the castle, it was the Princess who greeted his news. The story unfolds.

(Fanfare; STEWARD enters.)

STEWARD. Excuse me, madame. This small man insists on seeing you.

(BAKER enters.)

BAKER. Princess, I've come to report the appearance of a giant in the land.

CINDERELLA. Where did you see a giant?

BAKER. Well, I didn't exactly see it.

STEWARD. Then how do you know there is a giant in the land?

BAKER. Our house was destroyed and there are footprints—

STEWARD. That could have been caused by any number of things. I will show you to the door.

CINDERELLA. Wait.

BAKER. A nearby household was visited by a giant not long ago . . . descending from a beanstalk—

CINDERELLA. Yes, I remember.

STEWARD. That giant was slain. Now come along—

BAKER *(Apologetic).* Wait, please. We have a young child! Princess, our child was very difficult to come by. His safety is of great importance to me.

STEWARD. Are we entirely through now?

BAKER. Yes.

CINDERELLA. I will take this news up with the Prince when he returns. Thank you.

(BAKER and STEWARD exit.)

JACK'S MOTHER *(With her coat on).* I'm going off to market, Jack.

JACK. Goodbye, Mother.

JACK'S MOTHER. Now, I want you to stay inside.

JACK. But I haven't been outside all day!

JACK'S MOTHER. Jack. Listen to me! I don't want you out when there might be a giant on the loose.

JACK. But I know how to kill a giant!

JACK'S MOTHER. Please! We've had our fill of giants.

JACK. But Mother, if I could help—

JACK'S MOTHER. Enough! Promise me, son, you won't leave your surroundings.

JACK. But Mother, I'm a man now.

JACK'S MOTHER. You're still a little boy in your mother's eyes. I want you to promise. *(Pause; she smacks him)* Promise!

JACK *(Humiliated).* I promise.

(JACK'S MOTHER gives him a peck on the cheek, exits. LITTLE RED RIDINGHOOD knocks on the BAKER's door and enters.)

LITTLE RED RIDINGHOOD. What happened to your house?

WIFE. We've had a baking accident.

BAKER. Baking accident?

WIFE *(Whispers to him).* No use frightening the young thing.

BAKER *(Whispers back).* You can't frighten her.

LITTLE RED RIDINGHOOD. Well, I guess Granny will have to do without the bread and sweets. Besides, I have all I can carry.

WIFE. Why such a load?

LITTLE RED RIDINGHOOD. Oh. I'm moving in with Granny. We had an accident, too. I came home to find our house collapsed. As if a big wind blew it in. I couldn't find my mother anywhere.

WIFE. Oh, no.

LITTLE RED RIDINGHOOD. So I salvaged what I could, and now I'm off.

(Music continues; birds descend; they chirp to CINDERELLA.*)*

CINDERELLA. Oh, good friends. What news have you?

(She listens.)

What of Mother's grave?

(She listens.)

What kind of trouble?!

(She listens.)

Oh, no. I can't investigate. A Princess is not supposed to go into the woods unescorted.

(She begins to cry; birds chirp.)

Good idea! I will disguise myself and go to see what's wrong. Thank you, birds.

(Birds ascend. CINDERELLA *exits.)*

WIFE. We'll take you to Granny's.

BAKER. What?!

WIFE *(Whispers)*. We're not going to let her go alone!

BAKER. All right. I will take you.

LITTLE RED RIDINGHOOD. I don't need anyone to take me. I've gone many times before.

BAKER. But not when there have been such winds blowing.

WIFE. That's right. We'll all take you.

BAKER. No!

WIFE. I'm not about to stay here with the baby when a "wind" might return to this house, too.

*(*CINDERELLA *returns, dressed in her dirty attire from Act One.)*

JACK. I know Mother made me promise, but I'm going to find that giant anyway!

*(*CINDERELLA, JACK, BAKER, WIFE *and* LITTLE RED RIDINGHOOD *make their way into the woods; music.)*

BAKER. Into the woods,
It's always when
You think at last
You're through, and then
Into the woods you go again
To take another journey.

WIFE. Into the woods,
The weather's clear,
We've been before,
We've nought to fear . . .
Into the woods, away from here—

JACK. Into the woods, to find a giant—!

LITTLE RED RIDINGHOOD. Into the woods to Grandmother's house . . .

BAKER. Into the woods,
The path is straight,

No reason then
To hesitate—

WIFE. Into the woods,
It's not so late,
It's just another journey . . .

CINDERELLA. Into the woods,
But not too long:
The skies are strange,
The winds are strong.
Into the woods to see what's wrong . . .

JACK *(Picking up a huge pair of broken eyeglasses)*. Into the woods to slay the giant!

WIFE. Into the woods to shield the child . . .

LITTLE RED RIDINGHOOD. To flee the winds . . .

BAKER. To find a future . . .

WIFE. To shield . . .

JACK. To slay . . .

LITTLE RED RIDINGHOOD. To flee . . .

BAKER. To find . . .

CINDERELLA. To fix . . .

WIFE. To hide . . .

LITTLE RED RIDINGHOOD. To move . . .

JACK. To battle . . .

CINDERELLA. To see what the trouble is . . .

(Music fades.)

SCENE 2

The woods. Something is wrong. The natural order has been broken. Trees have fallen. The birds no longer chirp.

RAPUNZEL *enters, screaming. The* BAKER, WIFE *and* LITTLE RED RIDINGHOOD, *frightened, run off in one direction,* JACK *in the other.* RAPUNZEL *sits weeping as the* WITCH *appears; music stops.*

WITCH *(Urgent)*. Rapunzel! What are you doing here?

*(*RAPUNZEL *whimpers.)*

What's the matter?

RAPUNZEL *(Suddenly laughs)*. Oh, nothing! You just locked me in a tower without company for fourteen years, then blinded my Prince and banished me to a desert where I had little to eat, and again no company, and then bore twins! Because of the way *you* treated me, I'll never, *never* be happy! *(She cries)*

WITCH *(Defensive, yet sincere)*. I was just trying to be a good mother.

*(*RAPUNZEL *screams and runs off.)*

Stay with me! There's a giant running about! *(She follows* RAPUNZEL*)*

(RAPUNZEL'S PRINCE *enters;* CINDERELLA'S PRINCE *enters from another direction.*)

RAPUNZEL'S PRINCE. Good brother! What a surprise.

CINDERELLA'S PRINCE. Brother. How good to see you.

RAPUNZEL'S PRINCE. What brings you into the wood today?

CINDERELLA'S PRINCE. I am investigating news of a giant.

RAPUNZEL'S PRINCE. You? Investigating news of a giant? Father would not even do that! That is business for your steward—or less.

CINDERELLA'S PRINCE *(Defensive)*. Well, what brings *you* into the wood?

RAPUNZEL'S PRINCE. My Rapunzel has run off.

CINDERELLA'S PRINCE. Run off?

RAPUNZEL'S PRINCE. She's a changed woman. She has been subject to hysterical fits of crying. Moods that no soul could predict. I know not what to do.

CINDERELLA'S PRINCE. What a pity.

RAPUNZEL'S PRINCE. And Cinderella?

CINDERELLA'S PRINCE. She remains well.

RAPUNZEL'S PRINCE *(Conspiratorial)*. Does she? Now, brother. Do tell what you're *really* doing here.

(Music.)

CINDERELLA'S PRINCE. High in a tower—
Like yours was, but higher—
A beauty asleep.
All 'round the tower
A thicket of briar
A hundred feet deep.

Agony!
No frustration more keen,
When the one thing you want
Is a thing that you've not even seen.

RAPUNZEL'S PRINCE. I've found a casket
Entirely of glass—
(As CINDERELLA'S PRINCE *starts to protest)*
No, it's unbreakable.
Inside—don't ask it—
A maiden, alas,
Just as unwakeable—

BOTH. What unmistakable agony!
Is the way always barred?

RAPUNZEL'S PRINCE. She has skin white as snow—

CINDERELLA'S PRINCE. Did you learn her name?

RAPUNZEL'S PRINCE. No,
There's a dwarf standing guard.

BOTH. Agony

Such that princes must weep!
Always in thrall most
To anything almost,
Or something asleep.

CINDERELLA'S PRINCE. If it were not for the thicket—

RAPUNZEL'S PRINCE. A thicket's no trick.
Is it thick?

CINDERELLA'S PRINCE. It's the thickest.

RAPUNZEL'S PRINCE. The quickest
Is pick it
Apart with a stick—

CINDERELLA'S PRINCE. Yes, but even one prick—
It's my thing about blood.

RAPUNZEL'S PRINCE. Well, it's sick!

CINDERELLA'S PRINCE. It's no sicker
Than your thing with dwarves.

RAPUNZEL'S PRINCE. Dwarfs.

CINDERELLA'S PRINCE. Dwarfs . . .

RAPUNZEL'S PRINCE. Dwarfs are very upsetting.

BOTH. Not forgetting
The tasks unachievable,
Mountains unscalable—
If it's conceivable
But unavailable,
Ah-ah-ah-ah-ah-ah-ah-ah-ah-ah-ah—

Agony!

CINDERELLA'S PRINCE. Misery!

RAPUNZEL'S PRINCE. Woe!

BOTH. Not to know what you miss.

CINDERELLA'S PRINCE. While they lie there for years—

RAPUNZEL'S PRINCE. And you cry on their biers—

BOTH. What unbearable bliss!
Agony
That can cut like a knife!

Ah, well, back to my wife . . .
(We hear a wail in the distance.)

RAPUNZEL'S PRINCE *(Disappointed)*. Rapunzel. I must be off. Godspeed to you, brother.

CINDERELLA'S PRINCE. Godspeed.

(They exit in different directions; BAKER, WIFE *and* LITTLE RED RIDINGHOOD *enter from another part of the woods; music.)*

BAKER. Are you certain this is the right direction?

LITTLE RED RIDINGHOOD. We went down the dell.

WIFE. Perhaps you forgot the way.

LITTLE RED RIDINGHOOD. The path is straight.

BAKER. Was straight. Now there is no path.

LITTLE RED RIDINGHOOD (Increasingly upset). Where's the stream? Where's the lily pond? Where's Granny?

WIFE. Calm down.

(The baby starts to cry.)

(To BAKER) Maybe we should turn back.

LITTLE RED RIDINGHOOD. NO!

BAKER. We will just have to find Granny's house without the path.

LITTLE RED RIDINGHOOD (Crying). But Mother warned me never to stray from the path!

BAKER. The path has strayed from you.

LITTLE RED RIDINGHOOD. Wait. That looks familiar. See, in the distance, three oak trees.

(We hear voices approaching.)

BAKER. Yes. I recognize—

WIFE. Who might that be?

(STEWARD, STEPMOTHER, CINDERELLA'S FATHER, LUCINDA and FLORINDA, bedraggled, make their way downstage.)

BAKER. It's the steward and the royal family.

(They bow.)

What brings you into the woods?

CINDERELLA'S FATHER. The castle has been set upon by a giant.

WIFE. Oh, no . . .

BAKER (To STEWARD). I warned you! Why didn't you do something?

STEWARD. I don't make policy. I just carry it out!

(WITCH appears.)

WITCH (To BAKER). And I warned you that you can't count on a royal family to solve your problems.

WIFE. I think it best we go back to the village.

WITCH (Bitter). I wouldn't be in such a rush if I were you. Guess which path the giant took to the castle.

WIFE. Oh, no . . .

BAKER. What?

WITCH (Displaying a small sack). All that's left of my garden is a sack of beans—and there's not much left of your house either.

BAKER. But I heard giants never strike the same house twice.

WITCH. You heard wrong.

LITTLE RED RIDINGHOOD. Well, maybe we should go back to—

(Suddenly the ground begins to shake. A frightening and increasingly loud crunching noise approaches. The huge shadow of a giant envelops the stage. The earth stops shaking as everyone looks up, astonished.)

WITCH (Total amazement). The giant's a woman!

BAKER. That size!

(We do not see the giant, but when she speaks, the sound is loud and comes downward, from the direction of the shadow.)

GIANT. Where is the lad who killed my husband?

STEWARD. There is no lad here!

BAKER. We haven't seen him.

GIANT. I want the lad who climbed the beanstalk.

WITCH. We'll get him for you right away. Don't move!

(LITTLE RED RIDINGHOOD pulls a knife from beneath her cape and runs towards the giant; BAKER restrains her, but she threatens the giant anyway.)

LITTLE RED RIDINGHOOD. It was you who destroyed our house—not a great wind! It's because of you I've no mother!

GIANT. And who destroyed my house? That boy asked for shelter, and then he stole our gold, our hen, and our harp. Then he killed my husband. I must avenge the wrongdoings.

WIFE. We are not responsible for him.

WITCH. You're wasting your breath.

STEWARD. She's right. You can't reason with a dumb giant!

(The ground gives a mighty shake; leaves and twigs fall from above.)

GIANT. Not all giants are dumb. Give me the boy!

LITTLE RED RIDINGHOOD. We told you, he's not here!

CINDERELLA'S FATHER. The girl is telling the truth!

GIANT. I know he's there. And I'm going to wait right here until he's delivered to me.

(Music.)

NARRATOR. The giant, who was nearsighted, remained convinced that she had found the lad. There was no consensus among them as to which course of action to take.

WIFE. Put a spell on her.

WITCH. I no longer have my powers. If I did, you think I'd be standing here with all of you? (Getting down to business) Now, we'll have to give her someone.

OTHERS. Who?

WITCH. The steward. (She grabs him and begins pulling him toward the giant) It's in his line of duty to sacrifice his life—

STEWARD (Struggling). Don't be ridiculous! I'm not giving up my life for anyone!

(He breaks loose; music stops.)

GIANT. I'm waiting.

(Music.)

NARRATOR. You must understand, these were not people familiar with making choices—their past experiences in the woods had in no way prepared them to deal with a force *this* great.

WITCH *(Approaches the giant; confidential).* Excuse me. Would you like a blind girl, instead?

*(*FLORINDA *and* LUCINDA *scream.)*

STEPMOTHER. How dare you!

WITCH. Put them out of their misery.

STEPSISTERS *(Bitter).* We're not *that* miserable!

BAKER. What are you talking about.

WIFE. She doesn't want a woman!

WITCH. Fine. Then what do *you* suggest we do?

(Music stops.)

GIANT. I'm still waiting.

(Music.)

NARRATOR. It is interesting to examine the moral issue at question here. The finality of stories such as these dictates—

*(*NARRATOR *turns upstage and notices everyone looking at him menacingly. They move towards him. Music stops.)*

(To the group) Sorry, I tell the story, I'm not part of it.

LITTLE RED RIDINGHOOD. That's right. *(Pulls out knife)*

WITCH. Not one of us.

BAKER. Always on the outside.

*(*BAKER *grabs the* NARRATOR *and the group begins to pull him slowly towards the giant.)*

NARRATOR *(Nervous).* That's my role. You must understand, there must always be someone on the outside.

STEWARD. You're going to be on the inside now.

NARRATOR *(Frantic).* You're making a big mistake.

STEPMOTHER. Nonsense.

NARRATOR. You need an objective observer to pass the story along.

WITCH. Some of us don't like the way you've been telling it.

(They pull him further.)

NARRATOR. If you drag me into this mess, you'll never know how your story ends. You'll be lost!

BAKER *(To group).* Wait! He's the only one who knows the story.

(They stop the struggle.)

NARRATOR. Do you think it will be fun when you have to tell it yourselves? *(To* WIFE*)* Think of your baby.

WIFE. Stop! He's right! Let him go!

(Slowly and reluctantly, they let go of him.)

(To LITTLE RED RIDINGHOOD*)* Put that knife away.

NARRATOR. Now, that's better. You don't want to live in a world of chaos. *(Calms down; begins to inch his way back to the apron)* There must always be an outside obser—

WITCH *(Screaming, racing towards the* NARRATOR*).* Here's the lad!

(She grabs the NARRATOR *and drags him across the stage and pushes him into the wing towards the giant; there is a sudden earth tremor; all eyes swoop upwards to suggest the* NARRATOR *has been picked up by the giant. We hear the* NARRATOR *yell from a distance.)*

NARRATOR *(Off).* I'm not the lad!

GIANT. This is not the lad.

BAKER. Don't drop—

(Their eyes swing from the giant to the ground, and we hear a thud. They recoil in horror as we hear the NARRATOR *splat; a beat.)*

BAKER *(To* WITCH*).* Why did you push him into her arms?

WITCH *(Uneasy).* You wanted to get rid of him, too.

WIFE. We might have thought of something else.

WITCH. If it was up to you, a decision would never be made.

LITTLE RED RIDINGHOOD *(Looking towards* NARRATOR*'s spot; panic).* Now that he's gone, we'll never know what will happen next.

WIFE. We'll manage.

GIANT. Must I search among you?!

*(*JACK'S MOTHER *enters.)*

GROUP. No!

JACK'S MOTHER *(Tough).* Jack is just a boy! We had no food to eat and he sold his beloved cow in exchange for magic beans. If anyone is to be punished, it's the man who made that exchange.

LITTLE RED RIDINGHOOD. That's right!

BAKER. Shhh.

WIFE *(Simultaneously).* Nonsense.

GIANT. He was your responsibility. Now I must punish him for his wrongs!

JACK'S MOTHER. We've suffered, too. Do you think it was a picnic disposing of your husband's remains?

GIANT. You are getting me angry!

JACK'S MOTHER *(More worked up).* What about *our* anger? What about *our* loss? Who has been flouncing through our kingdom?

STEWARD. Shhh. Be quiet.

JACK'S MOTHER *(More)*. I'll hide my son and you'll never find him!

BAKER *(Through clenched teeth)*. Don't upset the giant.

JACK'S MOTHER. You'll never, never find him!

GIANT. I'm warning you!

JACK'S MOTHER *(Out of control)*. And if you don't go back this instant, we'll get *you* for all that *you've* done! We'll—

(STEWARD comes behind her and slams her over the head with his staff. She staggers a moment, then stands motionless.)

GIANT. Where is your son?

(RAPUNZEL runs onstage screaming; she sees the giant.)

Is that him?

(WITCH restrains RAPUNZEL.)

WITCH *(To giant)*. No. No. This is not the boy. *(To RAPUNZEL)* Stay here!

(RAPUNZEL'S PRINCE enters.)

STEWARD *(To giant)*. The boy is hiding in the steeple tower. You can find him there.

STEPMOTHER. Yes, that's true.

FLORINDA, LUCINDA. Yes . . .

RAPUNZEL'S PRINCE. Rapunzel! *(Signals to her)* Rapunzel!

GIANT. If he is not, I will return and find *you!*

(We hear the giant beginning to depart. On the second footstep, RAPUNZEL runs toward the giant; RAPUNZEL'S PRINCE races after her in panic.)

STEWARD *(To giant)*. No! Don't step on the—

(We hear a loud squishing noise; the group recoils in horror; after a stunned moment RAPUNZEL'S PRINCE returns, shaking his head; JACK'S MOTHER moans and BAKER goes to her side. He touches her head and quickly pulls his hand back to discover it covered with blood.)

BAKER *(Panic-stricken)*. She's in poor condition.

WIFE. Wake up.

JACK'S MOTHER *(Fighting for breath)*. Don't let them get Jack.

WIFE. We won't.

JACK'S MOTHER. Promise me you won't let him be hurt. As I stand here at death's door.

BAKER. I'll do all I can.

JACK'S MOTHER *(Insistent)*. Promise!

BAKER *(Annoyed)*. All right. I promise!

(JACK'S MOTHER expires; LITTLE RED RIDINGHOOD sidles up to her and stares.)

WIFE. No, no. Come away from there.

(Pulls her away; to STEWARD) You killed her!

STEWARD. I was thinking of the greater good. That's my job.

(Music; BAKER, CINDERELLA'S FATHER and STEWARD drag JACK'S MOTHER offstage. The group, hushed, watches; the WITCH stands alone.)

WITCH *(Looking off after RAPUNZEL)*. This is the world I meant.

Couldn't you listen?
Couldn't you stay content,
Safe behind walls,
As I
Could not?
(Looks at the group, then at us)
No matter what you say,
Children won't listen.
No matter what you know,
Children refuse
To learn.

Guide them along the way,
Still they won't listen.
Children can only grow
From something you love
To something you lose . . .

(STEWARD and CINDERELLA'S FATHER return, followed by BAKER.)

STEPMOTHER *(To CINDERELLA'S FATHER)*. Life was so steady, and now this! When are things going to return to normal?

STEWARD. We must be gone if we're to arrive before nightfall.

BAKER. Where are you going?

LUCINDA. We're off to a hidden kingdom.

STEPMOTHER. Shhh! We can't take everyone.

WITCH. Fools! There is nowhere to hide!
(Music fades.)

BAKER. You'll never get there. We have to stay here and find our way out of this together.

STEPMOTHER *(Sincere)*. Some people are cut out to battle giants, and others are not. I don't have the constitution. And as long as I can be of no help, I'm going to hide. Everything will work out fine in the end.

BAKER. Not always.

(Stepfamily and STEWARD exit.)

LITTLE RED RIDINGHOOD. I hope the giant steps on them all.

WIFE. You shouldn't say that!

(WITCH, who has been quietly standing off to the side, turns around.)

WITCH. You were thinking the same thing.

LITTLE RED RIDINGHOOD. This is terrible. We just saw three people die!

WITCH *(Bitter)*. Since when are you so squeamish? How many wolves have *you* carved up?

LITTLE RED RIDINGHOOD. A wolf's not the same.

WITCH. Ask a wolf's mother!

BAKER. Stop it!

WITCH. I suggest we find that boy now and give her what she wants.

LITTLE RED RIDINGHOOD. If we give her the boy, she'll kill him, too.

WITCH. And if we don't, she'll kill half the kingdom!

WIFE. One step at a time. Maybe if he apologizes. Makes amends.

BAKER. Yes! He'll return the stolen goods.

LITTLE RED RIDINGHOOD. Yes!

WIFE. He's really a sweet boy at heart. She'll see that.

WITCH. You people are so blind. It's because of that boy there's a giant in our land. While you continue *talking* about this problem, *I'll* find that lad, and I'll serve him to the giant for lunch! *(She exits)*

LITTLE RED RIDINGHOOD. Are we going to let her feed the boy to the giant?

WIFE. No!

BAKER. I'll have to find him first.

WIFE. I'll go, too.

BAKER. No! Stay here with the baby.

WIFE. We'll fan out. It will increase our chances of finding him.

BAKER. What if one of us gets lost?

WIFE. We'll count our steps from right here.

(LITTLE RED RIDINGHOOD comes over.)

No. You stay here with the baby. I do not want you roaming about the woods.

BAKER. You would leave our child with her?

WIFE. Yes. The baby is asleep. He will be safe with the girl.

BAKER. But what if the giant were to return here—?

WIFE. The giant will not harm them. I know.

BAKER. How do you know?

WIFE. I know!

BAKER. But what if—

WIFE. But what if! BUT WHAT IF! Will only a giant's foot stop your arguing! One hundred paces—GO!

(Music; pause.)

BAKER. One . . . two . . . three . . . four . . .

(The BAKER and WIFE march off in opposite

directions, leaving LITTLE RED RIDINGHOOD *and the baby; we follow the* WIFE *as she crosses paths with* CINDERELLA'S PRINCE; *she is nervous and excited in his presence; music fades.)*

WIFE. Eighty-one . . . eighty-two . . . eighty-three . . . eighty-four . . . *(She sees* PRINCE *and bows)* Hello, sir.

CINDERELLA'S PRINCE *(Continuing to walk)*. Hello.

WIFE. You must be here to slay the giant.

CINDERELLA'S PRINCE. Yes.

WIFE. Have you come upon the giant yet?

CINDERELLA'S PRINCE. No.

WIFE. I have.

CINDERELLA'S PRINCE *(He stops)*. You have?

WIFE. Yes.

CINDERELLA'S PRINCE. And why are you alone in the woods?

WIFE. I came with my husband. We were . . . well, it's a long story.

CINDERELLA'S PRINCE. He would let you roam alone in the woods?

WIFE. No, actually, it was my choice. I'm looking for a lad.

(Music.)

CINDERELLA'S PRINCE *(Moves closer)*. Your choice? How brave.

WIFE. Brave?

CINDERELLA'S PRINCE *(Next to her)*. Yes.

Anything can happen in the woods.
May I kiss you?
(WIFE blinks.)

Any moment we could be crushed.

WIFE. Uh—

CINDERELLA'S PRINCE. Don't feel rushed.

(He kisses her. She is stunned, steps away and turns to us.)

WIFE. This is ridiculous,
What am I doing here?
I'm in the wrong story.
(She resumes the kiss, then pulls away; music stops.)

Wait one moment, please! We can't do this! You have a Princess.

CINDERELLA'S PRINCE. Well, yes, I do.

WIFE. And I have a . . . baker.

CINDERELLA'S PRINCE. Of course, you're right. How foolish.

(Music resumes.)

Foolishness can happen in the woods.
Once again, please—
Let your hesitations be hushed.
Any moment, big or small,

Is a moment, after all.
Seize the moment, skies may fall
Any moment.
(He kisses her again.)
WIFE. But this is not right!
CINDERELLA'S PRINCE. Right and wrong
don't matter in the woods,
Only feelings.
Let us meet the moment unblushed.
Life is often so unpleasant—
You must know that, as a peasant—
Best to take the moment present
As a present for the moment.
*(The PRINCE scoops up the WIFE and carries
her into a glade; elsewhere the BAKER enters and
encounters CINDERELLA at her Mother's grave; she
is weeping.)*
BAKER *(Offstage, then entering).* Jack! Jack!
Eighty-one . . . eighty-two . . . eighty-
three . . .
(He sees CINDERELLA; music fades.)
What's wrong, ma'am? May I be of some
service?
*(She turns away from him lest she be recog-
nized.)*
CINDERELLA. The tree has fallen. Mother's
grave, destroyed.
BAKER. Oh. I'm sorry.
CINDERELLA. My wishes have just been
crushed.
BAKER. Don't say that.
CINDERELLA. It's true. You wouldn't under-
stand.
BAKER. Well, you can't stay here. There's a
giant on the loose.
CINDERELLA. I'm certain the Prince will see
to it that the giant is rid from our land.
BAKER. There's been no sign of the Prince.
No doubt he's off seducing some young
maiden.
CINDERELLA *(Turning to him).* What?
BAKER. I understand that's what Princes do.
CINDERELLA *(Indignant).* Not every Prince!
BAKER. You look just like the Princess—
but dirty.
(She turns away.)
You *are* the Princess. *(He drops to his knees)*
CINDERELLA. Please. Get up. Get up! *(He
does)* I'm not a Princess here.
BAKER. What are you to do?
CINDERELLA. I must be on my way back to
the castle.
BAKER. You haven't heard? We came upon
the royal family. The castle has been set
upon by the giant.
CINDERELLA. And the Prince?

BAKER. He was not with them.
(Beat; music.)
You must come with me. You shall be safe
in our company.
*(Reluctantly, she joins him and they exit; we
return to WIFE and CINDERELLA'S PRINCE, who
are on the ground, kissing; he pulls away; music
stops.)*
CINDERELLA'S PRINCE. I must leave you.
WIFE *(Flustered).* Why?
CINDERELLA'S PRINCE. The giant.
(Music.)
WIFE. The giant. I had almost forgotten.
Will we find each other in the woods again?
CINDERELLA'S PRINCE. This was just a mo-
ment in the woods.
Our moment,
Shimmering and lovely and sad.
Leave the moment, just be glad
For the moment that we had.
Every moment is of moment
When you're in the woods . . .
(Music continues under.)

(Smooth) Now I must go off to slay a giant.
That is what the *next* moment holds for me.
(He gives her a quick kiss) I shall not forget you.
How brave you are to be alone in the woods.
And how alive you've made me feel. *(He
exits)*
(WIFE sits, stunned; music stops.)
WIFE. What was that?
(Music resumes.)

Was that me?
Was that him?
Did a Prince really kiss me?
And kiss me?
And kiss me?
And did I kiss him back?

Was it wrong?
Am I mad?
Is that all?
Does he miss me?
Was he suddenly
Getting bored with me?
(She stands)
Wake up! Stop dreaming.
Stop prancing about the woods.
It's not beseeming.
What is it about the woods?
(Firm)
Back to life, back to sense,
Back to child, back to husband,
No one lives in the woods.

There are vows, there are ties,
There are needs, there are standards,
There are shouldn'ts and shoulds.

Why not both instead?
There's the answer, if you're clever:
Have a child for warmth,
And a baker for bread,
And a Prince for whatever—

Never!
It's these woods.

Face the facts, find the boy,
Join the group, stop the giant—
Just get out of these woods.
Was that him? Yes, it was.
Was that me? No, it wasn't,
Just a trick of the woods.

Just a moment,
One peculiar passing moment.

Must it all be either less or more,
Either plain or grand?
Is it always "or"?
Is it never "and"?
That's what woods are for:
For those moments in the woods . . .

Oh, if life were made of moments,
Even now and then a bad one—!
But if life were only moments,
Then you'd never know you had one.

First a witch, then a child,
Then a Prince, then a moment—
Who can live in the woods?
And to get what you wish,
Only just for a moment—
These are dangerous woods . . .

Let the moment go . . .
Don't forget it for a moment, though.
Just remembering you've had an "and,"
When you're back to "or,"
Makes the "or" mean more
Than it did before.
Now I understand—
(Sighs, starts walking faster)
And it's time to leave the woods.
(WIFE begins counting her steps as she heads offstage. She stops and retraces her steps, uncertain of her direction. She begins to go in another direction when she stops, hearing the approach of the giant in the distance. The sound moves steadily

towards her. In panic she retreats. Loud noise and dramatic light and set changes as WIFE *falls backwards. Blackout. Music fades. Lights up on* BAKER, CINDERELLA *and* LITTLE RED RIDINGHOOD.*)*

BAKER *(Worried)*. She should be back by now.

LITTLE RED RIDINGHOOD. She wouldn't get lost.

CINDERELLA. I'm sure she'll return.

BAKER. No. I must go in search of her.

LITTLE RED RIDINGHOOD. We'll come, too.

BAKER. No. You stay here. I will count one hundred paces. I shall return soon.

(WITCH makes a noisy entrance with JACK *in tow; she keeps a firm grip on his ear.* JACK *drops* WIFE's *scarf as he enters.)*

WITCH. Look who I found!

JACK. Please don't let her give me to the giant!

WITCH. It's not our fault the giant wants you!

JACK. You're hurting me.

(BAKER notices scarf, goes over and picks it up.)

CINDERELLA. Let go of him!

LITTLE RED RIDINGHOOD. Leave him alone!

BAKER *(Quiet)*. Where did you find this?

(WITCH lets go of JACK, *who runs behind* BAKER *for protection.)*

Where is my wife?

(Beat.)

WITCH. She's dead.

BAKER *(Stunned)*. What?

JACK. I'm sorry, sir. I came upon her. She was under a tree . . .

WITCH. He was sobbing over her like she was his own mother.

CINDERELLA. How awful . . .

BAKER *(Beat; lost)*. How could this happen? I should never have let her wander off *alone*.

JACK. I buried her in a footprint.

BAKER. I should have insisted she stay home.

WITCH *(Impatient)*. Remorse will get you nowhere.

BAKER *(Angry)*. My wife is dead!

WITCH. Wake up! People are dying all around you. You're not the only one to suffer a loss. When you're dead, you're dead. *(Advancing towards* JACK*)* Now it's time to get this boy to the giant before we're all so much dead meat. Boom crunch!

(She goes toward JACK; *music.)*

CINDERELLA *(Protecting* JACK*)*. Keep away from him!

LITTLE RED RIDINGHOOD *(Joining* CINDERELLA*)*. No!

WITCH. This is no time to be soft-hearted! He's going to the giant and I'm taking him—

BAKER *(Advancing, distraught)*. Yes! He's the one to blame! *(To* JACK*)* It's because of you there's a giant in our midst and my wife is dead!

JACK. But it isn't my fault,
I was given those beans!
(To BAKER*)*
You persuaded me to trade away
My cow for beans!
And without those beans
There'd have been no stalk
To get up to the giants
In the first place!

BAKER. Wait a minute, *magic* beans
For a cow so old
That you had to tell
A lie to sell
It, which you told!
Were they worthless beans?
Were they oversold?
Oh, and tell us who
Persuaded you
To steal that gold!

LITTLE RED RIDINGHOOD *(To* JACK*)*. See, it's your fault.

JACK. No!

BAKER. So it's your fault . . .

JACK. No!

LITTLE RED RIDINGHOOD. Yes, it is!

JACK. It's not!

BAKER. It's true.

JACK. Wait a minute, though—
I only stole the gold
To get my cow back
From you!

LITTLE RED RIDINGHOOD *(To* BAKER*)*. So it's your fault!

JACK. Yes!

BAKER. No, it isn't!
I'd have kept those beans,
But our house was cursed.
(Referring to WITCH*)*
She made us get a cow to get
The curse reversed!

WITCH. It's his father's fault
That the curse got placed
And the place got cursed
In the first place!

LITTLE RED RIDINGHOOD. Oh.
Then it's his fault!

WITCH. So.

CINDERELLA. It was his fault . . .

JACK. No.

BAKER. Yes, it is,
It's his.

CINDERELLA. I guess . . .

JACK. Wait a minute, though—
I chopped down the beanstalk,
Right? That's clear.
But without any beanstalk,
Then what's queer
Is how did the second giant get down here
In the first place?
(Confused)
Second place . . .

CINDERELLA. Yes!

LITTLE RED RIDINGHOOD. How?

BAKER. Hmm . . .

JACK. Well,
Who had the other bean?

BAKER. The other bean?

CINDERELLA. The other bean?

JACK *(To* BAKER*)*. You pocketed the other bean.

BAKER. I didn't!
Yes, I did.

LITTLE RED RIDINGHOOD. So it's *your* f—!

BAKER. No, it isn't,
'Cause I gave it to my wife!

LITTLE RED RIDINGHOOD. So it's *her* f—!

BAKER. *No, it isn't!*

CINDERELLA. Then whose is it?

BAKER. Wait a minute!
(To CINDERELLA*)*
She exchanged that bean
To obtain your shoe,
So the one who knows what happened
To the bean is *you!*

CINDERELLA. You mean *that* old bean—
That your *wife*—? Oh, dear—
(As they all look at her)
But I never knew,
And so I threw—
Well, don't look here!

LITTLE RED RIDINGHOOD. So it's your fault!

CINDERELLA. But—

JACK. See, it's her fault—

CINDERELLA. But—

JACK. And it isn't mine at all!

BAKER *(To* CINDERELLA*)*. But what?

CINDERELLA *(To* JACK*)*. Well, if you hadn't gone
Back up again—

JACK. We were needy—

CINDERELLA. You were greedy!
Did you need that hen?

JACK. But I got it for my mother—!

LITTLE RED RIDINGHOOD. So it's *her* fault then!

CINDERELLA. Yes, and what about the harp
In the third place?
BAKER. The harp—yes!
JACK (*Referring to* LITTLE RED RIDINGHOOD).
She went and dared me to!
LITTLE RED RIDINGHOOD. *I* dared you to?
JACK. You dared me to!
(*To the others*)
She said that I was scared—
LITTLE RED RIDINGHOOD. *Me?*
JACK. —to.
She dared me!
LITTLE RED RIDINGHOOD. No, I didn't!
BAKER, CINDERELLA, JACK. So it's your fault!
LITTLE RED RIDINGHOOD. Wait a minute—!
CINDERELLA. If you hadn't dared him to—
BAKER (*To* JACK). And you had left the harp
alone,
We wouldn't be in trouble
In the first place!
LITTLE RED RIDINGHOOD (*To* CINDERELLA,
overlapping). Well, if you hadn't thrown away
the bean
In the first place—!
It was your fault!
CINDERELLA (*Looking at* WITCH). Well, if she
hadn't raised them in the first place—!
JACK (*Overlapping, to* WITCH). Yes, if you
hadn't raised them in the first place—!
LITTLE RED RIDINGHOOD, BAKER (*To*
WITCH). Right! It's you who raised them in
the first place—!
CINDERELLA (*Simultaneously*). You raised
the beans in the first place!
JACK. It's *your* fault!
CINDERELLA, JACK, LITTLE RED RIDINGHOOD,
BAKER. You're responsible!
You're the one to blame!
It's your fault!
WITCH. Shhhhhhhhhhh!
(*They stop in their tracks; beat.*)

It's the last midnight.
It's the last wish.
It's the last midnight,
Soon it will be boom—
(*Stamps her foot; drum.*)

Squish!
(*Squishes.*)

Told a little lie,
Stole a little gold,
Broke a little vow,
Did you?
Had to get your Prince,

Had to get your cow,
Have to get your wish,
Doesn't matter how—
Anyway, it doesn't matter now.

It's the last midnight,
It's the boom—
Splat!
Nothing but a vast midnight,
Everybody smashed flat!

Nothing we can do . . .
Not exactly true:
We can always give her the boy . . .
(*They protect* JACK *as she reaches for him.*)

No?
No, of course what really matters
Is the blame,
Someone you can blame.
Fine, if that's the thing you enjoy,
Placing the blame,
If that's the aim,
Give me the blame—
Just give me the boy.
LITTLE RED RIDINGHOOD, CINDERELLA. No!
WITCH (*To all*). No . . .
You're so nice.
You're not good,
You're not bad,
You're just nice.
I'm not good,
I'm not nice,
I'm just right.
I'm the witch.
You're the world.

I'm the hitch,
I'm what no one believes,
I'm the witch.
You're all liars and thieves,
Like his father,
Like his son will be, too—
Oh, why bother?
You'll just do what you do.

It's the last midnight,
So goodbye, all.
Coming at you fast, midnight—
Soon you'll see the sky fall.

Here, you want a bean?
(*She starts scattering her beans all around; the
others frantically try to pick them all up.*)

Have another bean.
Beans were made for making you rich!

Plant them and they soar—
Here, you want some more?
Listen to the roar:
Giants by the score—!
Oh well, you can blame another witch.

It's the last midnight,
It's the last verse.
Now, before it's past midnight,
I'm leaving you my last curse:

I'm leaving you alone.
You can tend the garden, it's yours.
Separate and alone,
Everybody down on all fours.
(Looking upward)
All right, Mother, when?
Lost the beans again!
Punish me the way you did then!
Give me claws and a hunch,
Just away from this bunch
And the gloom
And the doom
And the boom
Cruuunch!
(She disappears; long beat. Everybody slowly rises.)
JACK *(Quiet)*. Maybe I shouldn't have stolen from the giant . . .
LITTLE RED RIDINGHOOD *(Quiet)*. Maybe I shouldn't have strayed from the path . . .
CINDERELLA *(Quiet)*. Maybe I shouldn't have attended the Ball . . .
BAKER *(Bitter)*. Yes. Maybe you shouldn't have . . . *(He begins to exit)*
JACK. Where are you going?
BAKER. Away from here.
LITTLE RED RIDINGHOOD *(Frightened)*. But you said we had to find our way out of this together.
BAKER. It doesn't matter whether we're together or apart.
JACK. We need your help.
BAKER. You don't understand. My wife was the one who really helped. I depended on her for everything. *(Moves further away)*
CINDERELLA. You would leave your child?
BAKER *(Despondent)*. My child will be happier in the arms of a Princess . . . *(He exits)*
CINDERELLA. But wait . . .
(Music; another part of the woods. BAKER crosses stage and is startled by MYSTERIOUS MAN.)
BAKER. I thought you were dead.
MYSTERIOUS MAN *(Bright)*. Not completely. Are we ever?
BAKER *(Cold)*. As far as I'm concerned, you are.

MYSTERIOUS MAN. Is that true?
BAKER. It's because of you all of this happened.
MYSTERIOUS MAN. I strayed into the garden to give your mother a gift. And I foolishly took some of those beans for myself. How was I to know? How are we ever to know? And when she died, I ran from my guilt. And now, aren't you making the same mistake?
BAKER. No. *(He begins to exit)*
MYSTERIOUS MAN. Aren't you running away?
BAKER. No more questions.
Please.
No more tests.
Comes the day you say, "What for?"
Please—no more.
MYSTERIOUS MAN. We disappoint,
We disappear,
We die but we don't . . .
BAKER. What?
MYSTERIOUS MAN. They disappoint
In turn, I fear.
Forgive, though, they won't . . .
BAKER. No more riddles.
No more jests.
No more curses you can't undo,
Left by fathers you never knew.

No more quests.
No more feelings.
Time to shut the door.
Just—no more.
(He sits in despair)
MYSTERIOUS MAN. Running away—let's do it,
Free from the ties that bind.
No more despair
Or burdens to bear
Out there in the yonder.

Running away—go to it.
Where did you have in mind?
Have to take care:
Unless there's a "where,"
You'll only be wandering blind.
Just more questions,
Different kind.

Where are we to go?
Where are we ever to go?

Running away—we'll do it.
Why sit around, resigned?
Trouble is, son,
The farther you run,

The more you feel undefined
For what you have left undone
And, more, what you've left behind.

We disappoint,
We leave a mess,
We die but we don't . . .
BAKER. We disappoint
In turn, I guess.
Forget, though, we won't . . .
BOTH. Like father, like son.
(MYSTERIOUS MAN *disappears.*)
BAKER. No more giants,
Waging war.
Can't we just pursue our lives
With our children and our wives?
Till that happier day arrives,
How do you ignore
All the witches,
All the curses,
All the wolves, all the lies,
The false hopes, the goodbyes, the reverses,
All the wondering what even worse is
Still in store?

All the children . . .
All the giants . . .
(*After a moment's thought*)
No more.
(*With resolve,* BAKER *returns to the waiting group.*)
CINDERELLA. I knew you wouldn't give up.
JACK. He wouldn't leave his baby.
LITTLE RED RIDINGHOOD. It looked like he was going to.
(CINDERELLA *and* JACK *shoot her a look.*)
BAKER. Give me my son.
(*He takes baby in his arms; baby begins to cry.*)
He always cries when I—
(*He pulls baby close to him and baby stops crying; beat.*)
CINDERELLA. Now what are we to do?
BAKER. We must have a plan before the giant returns.
JACK. What?
BAKER. We all have to think!
JACK. If there were just some way we could surprise her.
LITTLE RED RIDINGHOOD. She's too tall to surprise.
(*Birds descend.*)
CINDERELLA. Oh, good friends. I need your help now more than ever.
(*She listens.*)
What of the Prince?

(*She listens with resolve.*)
I don't care! What's important now is that we find a way to fell the giant. How can you help?
(*She listens.*)
You could do that?
(*She listens.*)
How can I ever thank you?
(*Birds fly off.*)
LITTLE RED RIDINGHOOD. You can talk to birds?
CINDERELLA. The birds will help.
JACK. How?
CINDERELLA. When the giant returns, they'll attack her and peck out her eyes till she's blind.
BAKER. What good will that do?
CINDERELLA. Then you can surprise her. Strike her, or whatever you do to kill a giant.
BAKER. Once she's blinded, she'll stagger about.
JACK. She'll get angry.
LITTLE RED RIDINGHOOD. And she'll crush us all.
(*Beat.*)
BAKER. Smear the ground with pitch.
CINDERELLA. Yes!
BAKER. We'll lure her to an area smeared with pitch.
CINDERELLA. Her shoes will stick, and she won't be able to move.
JACK. And I will climb a tree and strike her from behind.
BAKER. I will climb the tree, too. It may take two mighty blows.
LITTLE RED RIDINGHOOD. I'm excited!
JACK. I'm going to kill another giant!
BAKER. Quick! It will be dark soon. We must find the pitch.
(*They begin to exit;* BAKER *stops and hands the baby to* CINDERELLA.)
The baby will be safest here with you. This will take no time.
(BAKER, LITTLE RED RIDINGHOOD *and* JACK *exit. Baby begins to cry.*)
CINDERELLA. Oh, no. Now, now. Don't cry, little one. I know. You want your mother.
(*Baby begins to calm down;* CINDERELLA'S PRINCE *bounds onstage; he doesn't recognize* CINDERELLA.)
CINDERELLA'S PRINCE. Hello. (*He begins to cross the stage*)
CINDERELLA. The giant went in that direction.
CINDERELLA'S PRINCE (*Realizing it is* CINDERELLA). My darling. I did not recognize

you. What are you doing in those old clothes? And with a child? You must go back to the castle at once. There's a giant on the loose.

CINDERELLA. The giant has been to the castle.

CINDERELLA'S PRINCE. No! Are you all right?

(He moves to her; she nods and walks away.)
My love. Why are you being so cold?

CINDERELLA. Maybe because I'm not your only love. Am I?

CINDERELLA'S PRINCE *(Beat)*. I love you. Truly I do. *(Pause)* But yes, it's true.

CINDERELLA. Why, if you love me, would you have strayed?

CINDERELLA'S PRINCE. I thought if you were mine, that I would never wish for more. And part of me is content and as happy as I've ever been. But there remains a part of me that continually needs more.

CINDERELLA. I have, on occasion, wanted more. But that doesn't mean I went in search of it. If this is how you behave as a Prince, what kind of King will you be?

CINDERELLA'S PRINCE. I was raised to be charming, not sincere. I didn't ask to be born a King, and I am not perfect. I am only human.

CINDERELLA. I think you should go.

CINDERELLA'S PRINCE. Leave? But I *do* love you.

CINDERELLA. Consider that I have been lost. A victim of the giant.

CINDERELLA'S PRINCE. Is that what you really wish?

CINDERELLA. My father's house was a nightmare. Your house was a dream. Now I want something in-between. Please go.

(He begins to exit.)

CINDERELLA'S PRINCE. I shall always love the maiden who ran away.

CINDERELLA. And I the faraway Prince.

(He exits. Another moment for CINDERELLA with the baby. LITTLE RED RIDINGHOOD enters.)

LITTLE RED RIDINGHOOD. They're almost finished. You see over there between those two trees? When the giant comes, we are to send her over there.

CINDERELLA. Good.

LITTLE RED RIDINGHOOD. I wanted to climb the tree, too.

CINDERELLA. I'm glad you're here to help me.

(LITTLE RED RIDINGHOOD begins to cry; music.)

What's wrong?

LITTLE RED RIDINGHOOD. My granny's gone.

CINDERELLA *(Moves to comfort her)*. Oh, no. I'm so sorry.

LITTLE RED RIDINGHOOD. I think my granny and my mother would be upset with me.

CINDERELLA. Why?

LITTLE RED RIDINGHOOD. They said to always make them proud. And here I am about to kill somebody.

CINDERELLA. Not somebody. A giant who has been doing harm.

LITTLE RED RIDINGHOOD. But the giant's a person. Aren't we to show forgiveness? Mother would be very unhappy with these circumstances.

CINDERELLA. Mother cannot guide you.
Now you're on your own.
Only me beside you.
Still, you're not alone.
No one is alone, truly.
No one is alone.

Sometimes people leave you,
Halfway through the wood.
Others may deceive you.
You decide what's good.
You decide alone.
But no one is alone.

LITTLE RED RIDINGHOOD. I wish . . .

CINDERELLA. I know . . .

(LITTLE RED RIDINGHOOD moves close to CINDERELLA, who comforts her; JACK and the BAKER, atop nearby trees.)

JACK. Wait until my mother hears I've slain the giant.

BAKER. Jack. Your mother is dead.

JACK *(Stunned)*. Dead? Was she killed by the giant?

BAKER. She was arguing with the giant—trying to protect you—and she was struck a deadly blow by the Prince's steward.

JACK. Oh no. Why would he do that?

BAKER. He was afraid she was provoking the giant.

JACK *(Upset)*. Can no one bring her back?

BAKER. No one.

JACK. The steward will pay for this. After we slay the giant, I will slay him.

BAKER. You'll do nothing of the kind!

JACK. But he shouldn't have killed my mother. Right?

BAKER. I guess not.

JACK *(Cold)*. Then he must die.

BAKER. Well, no.

JACK *(Getting worked up)*. Why not?

BAKER. Because that would be wrong.

JACK. What he did was wrong. He should be punished.

BAKER. He will be, somehow.

JACK. How?

BAKER. I don't know! *(Angry)* Stop asking me questions I can't answer.

JACK *(Cold)*. I'm going to kill him!

BAKER. Then kill him! *(Beat)* No, don't kill him.

(Music.)

CINDERELLA *(To* LITTLE RED RIDINGHOOD*)*. Mother isn't here now.

BAKER *(To* JACK*)*. Wrong things, right things . . .

CINDERELLA. Who knows what she'd say?

BAKER. Who can say what's true?

CINDERELLA. Nothing's quite so clear now—

BAKER. Do things, fight things . . .

CINDERELLA. Feel you've lost your way?

BAKER. You decide,

But you are not alone.

CINDERELLA *(Overlapping)*. You are not alone,

Believe me.

No one is alone.

BAKER. No one is alone,

Believe me.

CINDERELLA. Truly . . .

BAKER, CINDERELLA. You move just a finger,

Say the slightest word,

Something's bound to linger,

Be heard.

BAKER. No one acts alone.

Careful,

No one is alone.

BAKER, CINDERELLA. People make mistakes.

BAKER. Fathers,

CINDERELLA. Mothers,

BAKER, CINDERELLA. People make mistakes,

Holding to their own,

Thinking they're alone.

CINDERELLA. Honor their mistakes—

BAKER. Fight for their mistakes—

CINDERELLA. Everybody makes—

BAKER, CINDERELLA. —one another's

Terrible mistakes.

Witches can be right,

Giants can be good.

You decide what's right,

You decide what's good.

CINDERELLA. Just remember:

BAKER. Just remember:

BAKER, CINDERELLA. Someone is on your side.

JACK, LITTLE RED RIDINGHOOD. *Our* side.

BAKER, CINDERELLA. Our side—

Someone else is not.

While we're seeing our side—

JACK, LITTLE RED RIDINGHOOD. Our side . . .

BAKER, CINDERELLA. Our side—

BAKER, CINDERELLA, LITTLE RED RIDINGHOOD, JACK. Maybe we forgot:

They are not alone.

No one is alone.

CINDERELLA. Hard to see the light now.

BAKER. Just don't let it go.

BAKER, CINDERELLA. Things will come out right now.

We can make it so.

Someone is on your side—

(Song is interrupted by the sound of the giant approaching in the distance; music fades.)

LITTLE RED RIDINGHOOD. Here she comes.

CINDERELLA. Remember. Don't let her know our plan.

(Ground trembles; shadow is cast.)

GIANT. Where is the boy?

LITTLE RED RIDINGHOOD *(Yelling upwards)*. We don't know!

CINDERELLA. Yes we do! We can't go on hiding him any longer. He must pay the price for his wrongs.

GIANT. Quick! Tell me where he is.

LITTLE RED RIDINGHOOD *(Points)*. Over there.

CINDERELLA. See that tree where the birds are clustered? Jack is in that tree, hiding.

GIANT. Thank you. Now justice will be served and I shall leave your kingdom.

*(*GIANT *turns and heads away. We hear the sounds of birds attacking in the distance;* CINDERELLA *and* LITTLE RED RIDINGHOOD *watch eagerly. We barely hear them over the roar of the giant; music.)*

CINDERELLA. Good birds!

(Cry from the giant.)

LITTLE RED RIDINGHOOD. She doesn't look happy.

(We hear the giant pounded on the head; another cry.)

CINDERELLA *(Grimace)*. Ouch!

(Another cry.)

LITTLE RED RIDINGHOOD *(Disgusted)*. The club is stuck in her head!

CINDERELLA. They've done it! She's swaying.

LITTLE RED RIDINGHOOD. She's bleeding all over.

CINDERELLA. She's beginning to fall!

LITTLE RED RIDINGHOOD *(Panicked)*. She's beginning to fall this way!

(They back off the stage quickly, as the loudest noise of all resounds. The giant's forehead and mane of hair fall from the wing. LITTLE RED RIDINGHOOD *and* CINDERELLA *race off in the direction of* JACK *and the* BAKER. *Finale music begins. During the following sequence the characters enter, give their morals and remain onstage.*

JACK'S MOTHER. The slotted spoon *can* catch the potato . . .

MYSTERIOUS MAN. Every knot was once straight rope . . .

*(*PRINCES *enter with* SNOW WHITE *and* SLEEPING BEAUTY.)*

PRINCES. The harder to wake, the better to have . . .

SNOW WHITE, SLEEPING BEAUTY *(Yawn)*. Excuse me.

STEWARD. The greater the good, the harder the blow . . .

STEPMOTHER. When going to hide, know how to get there.

CINDERELLA'S FATHER. And how to get back . . .

FLORINDA, LUCINDA. And eat first . . .

GRANNY. The knife that is sharp today may be dull by tomorrow . . .

RAPUNZEL. Ah-ah-ah-ah-ah . . .

*(*JACK, BAKER, CINDERELLA *and* LITTLE RED RIDINGHOOD *enter from upstage of giant's head. Music continues under.)*

BAKER. Now we can all return home and let us hope there will be no more killing.

JACK. Where am I to go? I have no one to take care of me.

BAKER. You'll have to take care of yourself now, Jack. It's time.

LITTLE RED RIDINGHOOD. No it's not. I'll take care of him.

JACK. You will?

LITTLE RED RIDINGHOOD. Yes. I'll be your mother now.

JACK. I don't want another mother, I want a friend. And a pet.

LITTLE RED RIDINGHOOD *(To* BAKER*)*. Of course, we have nowhere to go, so we'll move in with you.

BAKER. Oh, no.

LITTLE RED RIDINGHOOD. It'll be fun!

BAKER. My house is a shambles and there is hardly room for—

LITTLE RED RIDINGHOOD. It'll be fun!

BAKER. No. You don't— *(Beat)* Of course you can come home with us.

JACK *(To* CINDERELLA*)*. And you shall join us, too.

BAKER. You'll not return to the castle?

CINDERELLA. I'll gladly help you with your house. There are times when I actually enjoy cleaning.

(Beat.)

BAKER *(Stepping away)*. How proud my wife would have been of us. And how sad it is that my son will never know her.

(Baby cries.)

Maybe I just wasn't meant to have children—

WIFE *(Enters behind him)*. Don't say that! Of course you were meant to have children . . .

BAKER. But how will I go about being a father
With no one to mother my child?

(Baby cries.)

WIFE. Just calm the child.

BAKER *(Attempting to do so)*. Yes, calm the child.

WIFE. Look, tell him the story
Of how it all happened.
Be father and mother,
You'll know what to do.

BAKER. Alone . . .

WIFE. Sometimes people leave you
Halfway through the wood.
Do not let it grieve you,
No one leaves for good.
You are not alone.
No one is alone.

Hold him to the light now,
Let him see the glow.
Things will be all right now.

(Baby whimpers.)

Tell him what you know . . .

(Baby cries.)

BAKER. Shhh. Once upon a time . . .

*(*WITCH *enters.)*

. . . in a far-off kingdom . . . lived a young maiden,
. . . a sad young lad . . . and a childless baker . . . with his wife.

WITCH *(Simultaneously with* BAKER*)*. Careful the things you say,
Children will listen.
Careful the things you do,

Children will see.
And learn.

Children may not obey,
But children will listen.
Children will look to you
For which way to turn,
To learn what to be.

Careful before you say,
"Listen to me."
Children will listen.
COMPANY. Careful the wish you make,
Wishes are children.
Careful the path they take—
Wishes come true,
Not free.

Careful the spell you cast,
Not just on children.
Sometimes the spell may last
Past what you can see
And turn against you . . .
WITCH. Careful the tale you tell.
That is the spell.
Children will listen . . .
COMPANY *(In three groups)*. Though it's fearful,
Though it's deep, though it's dark
And though you may lose the path,
Though you may encounter wolves,
You can't just act,
You have to listen.
You can't just act,
You have to think.

Though it's dark,
There are always wolves,
There are always spells,
There are always beans,
Or a giant dwells there.
(In unison)
So
Into the woods you go again,
You have to every now and then.
Into the woods, no telling when,
Be ready for the journey.

Into the woods, but not too fast
Or what you wish you lose at last.

Into the woods, but mind the past.
Into the woods, but mind the future.
Into the woods, but not to stray,
Or tempt the wolf or steal from the giant—

The way is dark,
The light is dim,
But now there's you,
Me, her and him.
The chances look small,
The choices look grim,
But everything you learn there
Will help when you return there.
BAKER, JACK, CINDERELLA, LITTLE RED RIDINGHOOD *(Softly)*. The light is getting dimmer . . .
BAKER. I think I see a glimmer—
ALL. Into the woods—you have to grope,
But that's the way you learn to cope.
Into the woods to find there's hope
Of getting through the journey.

Into the woods, each time you go,
There's more to learn of what you know.
Into the woods, but not too slow—
Into the woods, it's nearing midnight—

Into the woods
To mind the wolf,
To heed the witch,
To honor the giant,
To mind,
To heed,
To find,
To think,
To teach,
To join,
To go to the Festival!

Into the woods,
Into the woods,
Into the woods,
Then out of the woods—
And happy ever after!
CINDERELLA. I wish . . .
(Pause; chord; blackout.)

The End

Frankie and Johnny in the Clair de Lune

TERRENCE McNALLY

FOR MAURINE McELROY

First produced by Manhattan Theatre Club Stage II at City Center in New York City on June 2, 1987, with the following cast:

FRANKIE	Kathy Bates
JOHNNY	F. Murray Abraham
VOICE OF RADIO ANNOUNCER	Dominic Cuskern

It transferred to Manhattan Theatre Club Stage I at City Center on October 14, 1987, with the following cast:

FRANKIE	Kathy Bates
JOHNNY	Kenneth Welsh
VOICE OF RADIO ANNOUNCER	Dominic Cuskern

Both productions were directed by Paul Benedict
Sets by James Noone
Costumes by David Woolard
Lighting by David Noling
Sound by John Gromada
Production Stage Manager: Pamela Singer.

This production transferred to the Westside Arts Theatre in New York City on December 4, 1987. It was produced by Steven Baruch, Thomas Viertel, Richard Frankel and Jujamcyn Theatres/Margo Lion.

TIME: The present.

PLACE: New York City.

SETTING: Frankie's one-room apartment in a walk-up tenement in the west 50's. The fourth wall looks onto the backyard and the apartments behind. When the sofa bed is down, as it is for much of the play, the room is quite cramped.

CHARACTERS:

FRANKIE. Striking but not conventional good looks. She has a sense of humor and a fairly tough exterior. She is also frightened and can be very hard to reach.

JOHNNY. Johnny's best feature is his personality. He works at it. He is in good physical condition.

JOHNNY: This is the only chance we have to come together, I'm convinced of it. People are given one moment to connect. Not two, not three, one! They don't take it, it's gone forever. . . .

FRANKIE: Boy, are you barking up the wrong tree.

JOHNNY: We have to connect or we die. . . .

Frankie and Johnny in the Clair de Lune depicts two lonely, middle-aged people, a short-order cook and a waitress, in a romantic tug of war. While both desire closeness with another human being, one pursues it with agression and passion while the other backs off and runs away. Playwright Terrence McNally explains: "What drives Frankie crazy is that she's found someone who loves her. We all walk around saying we want someone to love us unconditionally and then when someone does, we make up new conditions. . . ."

Frankie and Johnny opened at the Manhattan Theatre Club in June 1987, transferring to the Off Broadway Westside Arts Theatre in December 1987. Kathy Bates, who won an Obie for creating the role of Frankie, states, "I think the play is really about miracles. . . . In accepting her relationship with Johnny, Frankie is finally allowed to see the possibilities of her life. . . . It's also a celebration of love. . . . Terrence never hides the fact that love is scary. It's a risk. . . ."

McNally wrote *Frankie and Johnny* in reaction to the alienation he saw around him—kids forever wearing headphones, adults buying videos for solitary Saturday nights. "We've created a society where it's easy to isolate yourself, talk to answering machines. . . . We rent movies—it's easy to keep your mind away from your feelings. Society entertains us. I think I wanted to write about people in a room with no entertainment. . . . I think [this play has] had a wide audience . . . because people have trouble breaking out of their shells of isolation. I usually get my idea for a play by starting out with an image of people, which is how I thought of *Frankie and Johnny*. . . . Maybe it has to do with my getting older, my feeling how fragile life is and how terribly important relationships are."

McNally often keeps a play in his head for a long time, sometimes as much as a year, before trying to put anything on paper. "To someone else, I might seem very idle, but actually it's sort of mulling in my head . . . and then you start writing it. Then I live like a hermit and become very compulsive . . . nothing can distract me. Your imagination starts taking off and you start hearing your characters in your head and you become like a stenographer. . . . What keeps me happiest is writing plays. . . . I've always written with actors in mind . . . it helps to have a voice while I'm writing. . . . When I write for specific actors, I'm asking them to embody my deepest secrets. I'm asking them to say things in public I couldn't or wouldn't. Actors I write for encourage me to expose my most private self."

Terrence McNally was born in 1939 in St. Petersburg, Florida, then moved with his family to Corpus Christi, Texas. A solitary boy, he listened to radio programs like *The Green Hornet, The Lone Ranger,* and *Let's Pretend.* "I had to make a theatre in my head for these shows," he recalls. "I made a little stage for the Metropolitan Opera broadcasts every Saturday. I had little figures of Rigoletto and Aïda. I'd move the scenery. To me that was more real than life." McNally was encouraged in his interest in the performing arts by his parents, who would return home from visits to New York with theatre programs and Broadway cast albums. He was also spurred by a high school English teacher who conducted afternoon seminars on Shakespeare. After high school graduation, McNally enrolled as a journalism major at Columbia University and worked during visits home for a Corpus Christi newspaper. In his senior year, he won a Columbia University Henry Evans Traveling Fellowship and wrote the university's varsity revue.

McNally used his fellowship to go to Puerto Vallarta, Mexico, where he concentrated on playwriting. In 1961, he sent some of his work to Molly Kazan, writer and cofounder of the Actors Studio in New York, who suggested that he join the studio as a stage manager. While in New York, he completed a one-act play, *This Side of the Door,* which won the Stanley Drama Award given by the Wagner College Department of Literature. In 1963, he completed *And Things That Go Bump in the Night,* which with a grant from the Rockefeller Foundation was produced at the Tyrone Guthrie Theatre.

While working as an assistant editor for *Columbia College Today,* McNally won a Guggenheim Fellowship in 1966. This inspired a prolific period of writing one-act plays: *Tour* (1966), *Botticelli* (1966), *Noon* (1967), *Witness* (1968), *Sweet Eros* (1968) and *Next* (1968). During this time, McNally also wrote the book for *Here's Where I Belong*, a failed musical version of John Steinbeck's *East of Eden*. In 1971, McNally wrote two full-length comedies, *Where Has Tommy Flowers Gone?* and *Whiskey*; these were not received with much critical enthusiasm. McNally returned to the one-act form with *Bad Habits* (1974), which won him an Obie Award and the Dramatists Guild's Hull-Warriner Award. Following this success, McNally revised an early play, *The Tubs*, into *The Ritz* (1974), a box-office hit for which Rita Moreno won the 1975 Tony Award as Best Supporting Actress in a Play.

Broadway, Broadway followed, unsuccessfully, in 1978. Six bleak years followed in which McNally worked on several ultimately abandoned plays and completed *The Five Forty-Eight*, a PBS television adaptation of a John Cheever story, and initial episodes of *Mama Malone*, a CBS comedy series. McNally returned to Broadway with his book for the musical *The Rink* (1984). Off Broadway saw *The Lisbon Traviata* (1985), a revision of *Broadway, Broadway* entitled *It's Only a Play* (1986), and then, in 1987, *Frankie and Johnny in the Clair de Lune*, which opened to universal acclaim.

McNally is a member of the American Academy of Arts and Letters and is vice president of the Dramatists Guild. His other works include *The Lady of the Camellia* (1963), *Cuba Sí* (1968), *Prelude to Liebestod* (1988), *Urban Blight, Up in Saratoga* (1988), *Andre's Mother* (PBS-TV, 1990), the book for the musical *Kiss of the Spider Woman* (1990), *A Perfect Ganesha* (1991), *Lips Together, Teeth Apart* (1991), the film version of *Frankie and Johnny*, *Apple Pie*, and *Last Gasps* (WNET-TV). *Five in Hand*, a collection of McNally plays, was published by Random House.

ACT ONE

AT RISE: Darkness. We hear the sounds of a man and woman making love. They are getting ready to climax. The sounds they are making are noisy, ecstatic and familiar. Above all, they must be graphic. The intention is a portrait in sound of a passionate man and woman making love and reaching climax together.

The real thing.

They came.

Silence. Heavy breathing. We become aware that the radio has been playing Bach's Goldberg Variations in the piano version.

By this point, the curtain has been up for at least two minutes. No light, no dialogue, just the sounds of lovemaking and now the Bach.

———

FRANKIE. God, I wish I still smoked. Life used to be so much more fun. *(JOHNNY laughs softly.)* What?

JOHNNY. Nothing. *(He laughs again, a little louder.)* Oh, God!

FRANKIE. Well it must be something!

JOHNNY. It's dumb, it's gross, it's stupid, it's . . . *(He howls with laughter.)* I'm sorry. Jesus, this is terrible. I don't know what's gotten into me. I'll be all right. *(He catches his breath. FRANKIE turns on a bedside lamp.)* Really, I'm sorry. It has nothing to do with you.

FRANKIE. Are you okay now?

JOHNNY. Yes. No! *(He bursts into laughter again. And now FRANKIE bursts into laughter: a wild, uncontrollable, infectious sound.)* What are you laughing at?

FRANKIE. I don't know! *(Now they are both laughing hilariously. It is the kind of laughter that gets out of control and people have trouble breathing. FRANKIE rolls off the bed and lands on the floor with a slight thud.)*

JOHNNY. Are you okay?

FRANKIE. No! *(Now it is FRANKIE who is laughing solo. It is a wonderfully joyful sound: a lot of stored-up feeling is being released.)*

JOHNNY. Should I get you something?

FRANKIE. Yes! My mother!

JOHNNY. A beer, a Coke, anything?

FRANKIE. A bag to put over my head!

JOHNNY. You really want your mother?

FRANKIE. Are you crazy?

JOHNNY. You have the most . . . the most wonderful breasts.

FRANKIE. Thank you. *(She bursts into new laughter. This time JOHNNY doesn't join in at all. Eventually they are both still. They listen to the*

Bach in silence and without moving.) That's nice music. Very . . . I want to say "chaste."

JOHNNY. I'll tell you why I was laughing. All of a sudden—just like that!—I remembered this time back in high school when I was making out with this really beautiful girl and was feeling incredibly suave and sophisticated and wondering if anybody would believe my good fortune and worrying if she was going to let me go all the way—I think it would have been her first time too—when all of a sudden I let out this incredibly loud fart. Like that. Only louder. It was awful. *(He laughs again.)* And there was no pretending it wasn't me. You couldn't say something like "Boy, did you hear that thunder?" or "Jesus, Peggy, was that you?" The best I could come up with was "May I use your bathroom?" which only made it worse. And there in the bathroom was her mother taking a bath at ten o'clock at night. She had one arm up, washing her armpit. I said something real cool like, "Hello, Mrs. Roberts." She screamed and I ran out of the house. I tripped over the garbage cans and tore my pants climbing over the backyard fence. I must've run twenty blocks, most of them with dogs chasing me. I thought my life was over. We never mentioned what happened and I never dated her again and I lost my virginity with someone else. But why that fart banged back into my consciousness just then . . . !

FRANKIE. Could we change the subject?

JOHNNY. What's the matter?

FRANKIE. I'm not a prude . . .

JOHNNY. I know that! Any woman who . . .

FRANKIE. I just . . . we all draw the line somewhere.

JOHNNY. And with you it's farts?

FRANKIE. Is that going to be a problem?

JOHNNY. You don't think any kind of farting is funny?

FRANKIE. Not off the top of my head I don't.

JOHNNY. Hunh! I always have. I don't know why I find a lot of things funny. Like Corgies.

FRANKIE. Corgies?

JOHNNY. You know the dogs the Queen of England has?

FRANKIE. No.

JOHNNY. Sure you do. They're about this big, tan and look like walking heads. Everytime I see one, I get hysterical. Show me a Corgie and I'm yours.

FRANKIE. I guess a farting Corgie would really lay you out!

JOHNNY. See? You do have a sense of humor about it! *(They both laugh. Then silence. The Bach plays on.)*

FRANKIE. You know what I mean? About the music? It's pure.

JOHNNY. Did you come?

FRANKIE. No one's that good at faking it.

JOHNNY. I thought so. Good. I'm glad.

FRANKIE. There! Hear that? It makes me think of . . . grace.

JOHNNY. You mean, the thing it's good to be in the state of?

FRANKIE. The movement kind. You know. . . . *(She moves her arm in a flowing gesture and sways her shoulders to the music.)* Flowing.

JOHNNY. So why were you laughing?

FRANKIE. I don't know. Because you were, I guess. You sounded so happy. Little did I know!

JOHNNY. I *was* happy. I'm still happy. Where are you going?

FRANKIE. Nowhere.

JOHNNY. You're going somewhere.

FRANKIE. The closet.

JOHNNY. Why?

FRANKIE. A robe.

JOHNNY. You don't need a——.

JOHNNY. I'm cold.

JOHNNY. I want to bask in your nakedness.

FRANKIE. Sure you do. *(FRANKIE turns on the overhead room light.)*

JOHNNY. Ow!

FRANKIE. I'm sorry, I'm sorry! *(She turns off the overhead light. The first quick impression we have of the room is that it is modest and not especially tidy.)*

JOHNNY. Warn somebody when you're going to do that! I hate bright lights but especially right after making love. Talk about a mood changer! Besides, I think you see the other person better in the light of the afterglow. *(Pause.)* Did you hear what I just said?

FRANKIE. Yes.

JOHNNY. Just checking. *(While FRANKIE gets robe out of the closet, JOHNNY goes through her purse on the bed table until he finds a pair of sunglasses.)*

FRANKIE. Remember when everybody used to light up the second it seemed they were through making love? "I'm coming, I'm coming, I came. You got a match?"

JOHNNY. I didn't smoke.

FRANKIE. Never?

JOHNNY. Ever.

FRANKIE. You've got a smoker's personality.

JOHNNY. That's what they tell me.

FRANKIE. I just made that up.

JOHNNY. So did I. And I didn't like women who did.

FRANKIE. Did what? Smoked? Then you would have hated me. Marla the Human Furnace.

JOHNNY. Marla? I thought your name was Francis.

FRANKIE. It is, it is! Don't panic. I just made that up, too. I don't know where it came from. From what Freudian depth it sprung.

JOHNNY. Marla! Ecchh!

FRANKIE. You put too much stock in this name business, John. *(She comes back to bed wearing a bathrobe. JOHNNY looks fairly ridiculous in her sunglasses.)*

JOHNNY. It's Johnny, please.

FRANKIE. Are those mine? I wish you'd stay out of my—

JOHNNY. I hate John.

FRANKIE. Did you hear me?

JOHNNY. I heard you.

FRANKIE. I wish you'd act like you heard me.

JOHNNY. May I wear your sunglasses?

FRANKIE. Yes.

JOHNNY. Thank you. God, you're beautiful. Are you coming back to bed?

FRANKIE. I don't know.

JOHNNY. John sounds like a toilet or a profession. And Jack only works if you're a Kennedy or a Nicholson.

FRANKIE. I read somewhere there are millions of young people, a whole generation, who don't have a clue who John Kennedy was. Do you believe it? To me, he was only yesterday. I love Jack Nicholson. Did you see *Prizzi's Honor?*

JOHNNY. Six times.

FRANKIE. Six times?

JOHNNY. The first time I popped for it, six bucks, the good old days, remember them? Seven bucks gets my goat, don't get me started! Then five on VCR, you know a rental, when I was getting over my hernia and I couldn't get out of bed so hot.

FRANKIE. You've got a VCR?

JOHNNY. Oh sure. Stereo TV, VCR. I'm working on a dish.

FRANKIE. And you've got a hernia?

JOHNNY. Had, had. Here, I'll show you.

FRANKIE. Wow. That's big. Did it hurt?

JOHNNY. Comme ci, comme ça. You got any scars?

FRANKIE. Everybody has scars.

JOHNNY. Where? I'll just look.

FRANKIE. No.

JOHNNY. Okay, okay. You know, they filmed it right near where I live.

FRANKIE. *Prizzi's Honor?*

JOHNNY. Oh sure.

FRANKIE. In Brooklyn?

JOHNNY. Brooklyn Heights. Please, don't get us confused with the rest of the borough. Would you like it if I referred to your neighborhood as Chinatown?

FRANKIE. Fifty-third and Tenth?

JOHNNY. Anyway! You know the house that guy lived in, the one with the funny voice? Hinley or something? He got nominated for an Oscar or something but I don't think he won. Or maybe he did.

FRANKIE. The one who played the Don?

JOHNNY. That's the one. Headley, Henkley, Hinley.

FRANKIE. You live in that house?

JOHNNY. No, but I can see their roof from my bathroom window.

FRANKIE. Oh.

JOHNNY. You know what those movie stars get when they're on location like that? Their own trailers with their name on the door. Big long trailers. Not like the kind you see in Montauk, those ugly little Airstream jobbies. At least I think they're ugly. No, these are the big long kind like you see sitting up on blocks in a trailer park that people live in full time, people who aren't going anywhere in 'em they're so big! I'm talking trailers with bedrooms and bathtubs. I'm talking major mobile homes.

FRANKIE. I hate trailers.

JOHNNY. So do I. That's not the point.

FRANKIE. I'd rather die than live in a trailer. The very words "mobile home" strike me with such terror.

JOHNNY. I believe I had the floor.

FRANKIE. Who the hell wants a living room that moves for Christ's sake? Ecch! Sorry.

JOHNNY. Anyway, they each have their own trailer. I mean, Jack Nicholson is on one side of the street in his block-long trailer and Kathleen Turner is on the other in hers.

FRANKIE. I'm sorry but I don't get her message.

JOHNNY. Will you let me finish?

FRANKIE. Do you?

JOHNNY. Yes, but that's not the point either. They also give these trailers to people you never even heard of, like this Hinley, Headley, Hinckley, what's-his-face character.

FRANKIE. Is that the point?

JOHNNY. I'm not saying he's not a good actor but his own trailer? I'm in the wrong business.

FRANKIE. We both are.

JOHNNY. Do you think I talk too much?

FRANKIE. I don't think you always give the other person a chance to—

JOHNNY. That's what my best friend says, "I talk because I got a lot to say, Ernie," I tell him but he doesn't seem to understand that. Talking to you comes real easy. I appreciate that. And I won't pretend I wasn't looking forward to this evening.

FRANKIE. Well, it's been very. . . .

JOHNNY. What do you mean, "been"? It still is. "The night is young, the stars are clear and if you care to go walking, dear." I admit I love the sound of my own voice. So shoot me, give me the electric chair, it ain't over till the fat lady sings. Can I have a beer?

FRANKIE. I'm sorry.

JOHNNY. You say that too much. *(He goes to refrigerator as FRANKIE crosses to floor lamp by easy chair and turns it on.)*

FRANKIE. Is this okay? I hate gloom.

JOHNNY. Light like this is fine. It's the harsh blinding kind I can't stand. Now where are you going?

FRANKIE. Just in here. *(She goes to bathroom door, opens it, turns on light, goes in, leaving door open so that more light spills into the room.)* Keep talking. I can hear you.

JOHNNY. You mean about the light? There are some delicatessens I just won't go into, they're so bright. There's one over on Madison Avenue and 28th Street that is so bright from the overhead fluorescents that you wouldn't believe it. I complained. I don't even shop there and I complained. "What are you trying to do? Get an airplane to land in here?" They just looked at me like I was an idiot. Of course, I doubt if they even spoke English. Most Koreans don't. It's getting to the point where you can count on one hand the number of people who speak English in this city. *(He goes to the bathroom door and stands watching FRANKIE within)* Look, I know I talk too much. It's just that certain things get my goat. Things like ninety-foot trailers for people I never heard of . . . *(FRANKIE comes out of the bathroom. She has changed into a brightly colored kimono. She has a hairbrush in her hand and will brush her hair during the following.)* Hi there.

FRANKIE. Hello.

JOHNNY. . . . . waste, especially water—you got a leaky faucet around here? Lady, I'm your plumber—and the fact this is supposed to be an English speaking nation only nobody speaks English anymore. Other than that, I'm cool and I'll shut up now and won't say another word. I'm locking my mouth and throwing away the key. *(He watches* FRANKIE *brush her hair.)*

FRANKIE. Did you get Easter off? *(*JOHNNY *shakes his head.)* Neither did I. And watch us twiddle our thumbs. Last Easter you could've shot moose in there. Forget tips. I've already decided, I'm gonna call in sick. Life's too short, you know? You want some juice? It's homemade. I mean, I squeezed it myself. That's right, you're working on a beer. I'd offer you a joint but I don't do that anymore. Not that I think other people shouldn't. It's just that I can't personally handle it anymore. I mean, I didn't like what it was doing to me. I mean, the bottom line is: it isn't good for you. For me, I mean. It isn't good for me. Hey, come on, don't!

JOHNNY. Can I say one more thing?

FRANKIE. I wish you would.

JOHNNY. I could watch you do that for maybe the rest of my life.

FRANKIE. Get real.

JOHNNY. I think a woman brushing and fixing her hair is one of the supremely great sights of life. I'd put it up there with the Grand Canyon and a mother nursing her child. Triumphant facts of nature. That's all. Now I'm locking my eyes shut and throwing away the key. *(He closes his eyes.)*

FRANKIE. What am I supposed to do?

JOHNNY. Sshh, pretend you can't hear. Next thing she'll want is your ears.

FRANKIE. Oh my God, it's three o'clock! Look, I'd ask you to stay over but . . . I don't know about you but I'm kind of drained, you know? I mean, that was pretty intense back there. Harrowing. No, not harrowing, that doesn't sound right. I'm too pooped to pop, all right? Oh come on, you know what I mean! *(*JOHNNY *inhales very slowly and very deeply.)*

JOHNNY. She's wearing something new. This part is called Scent Torture. I love it, I love it!

FRANKIE. You know, you're a very intense person. One minute you're making love like somebody just let you out of jail and the next you're telling me watching me brush my hair

is like the Grand Canyon. Very intense or very crazy. Look, I'm glad what happened happened. If we both play our cards right, maybe it will happen again. . . . Hello?

JOHNNY. I hear you.

FRANKIE. I wish you'd open your eyes. *(*JOHNNY *very slowly opens his eyes and turns to face* FRANKIE. *He reacts as if blinded.)*

JOHNNY. Aaaagggg! It's worse than the delicatessen! Such blinding beauty!

FRANKIE. I'm serious. *(*JOHNNY *stops screaming and looks at her again.)*

JOHNNY *(Quietly.)* So am I.

FRANKIE. That's exactly what I mean. One minute you're kidding and the next you're looking at me like that.

JOHNNY. Like what?

FRANKIE. Like that! People don't go around looking at one another like that. It's too intense. You don't look, you stare. It gives me the creeps. I suppose it's very flattering but it's not something I feel real comfortable with. It's like if you would send me a million roses, I'd be impressed but I wouldn't know where to put them. I don't need a million roses. One would be just fine. So if you just looked at me *occasionally* in the future like that. Look, obviously I like you. I like you a lot. What's the matter?

JOHNNY. I'm just drinking all this in.

FRANKIE. You're not the easiest person to talk to anybody ever met.

JOHNNY. I certainly hope not. How old are you?

FRANKIE. None of your business. How old are you?

JOHNNY. What do you think?

FRANKIE. Mid-forties.

JOHNNY. Ouch!

FRANKIE. Maybe late thirties.

JOHNNY. I can live with that.

FRANKIE. Come on, how old are you?

JOHNNY. I don't know.

FRANKIE. Everybody knows how old they are.

JOHNNY. I used to, then I forgot.

FRANKIE. That's a great answer. Can I borrow it?

JOHNNY. I did.

FRANKIE. Who from?

JOHNNY. Some old lady on the Carson show? I don't remember. Half the things I got up here, I don't remember where they came from. It doesn't seem fair. People ought to get credit for all the things they give and teach us. You're fabulous.

FRANKIE. I feel like I'm supposed to say "thank you."

JOHNNY. It's not necessary.

FRANKIE. Instead, I want to ask you to quit sneaking up on me like that. We're talking about one thing, people who teach, and wham! you slip in there with some kind of intimate, personal remark. I like being told I'm fabulous. Who wouldn't? I'd like some warning first, that's all. This is not a spontaneous person you have before you.

JOHNNY. You're telling me that wasn't spontaneous?

FRANKIE. That was different. I'm talking about the larger framework of things. What people are doing in your life. What they're doing in your bed is easy or at least it used to be back before we had to start checking each other out. I don't know about you but I get so sick and tired of living this way, that we're gonna die from one another, that every so often I just want to act like Saturday night really is a Saturday night, the way they used to be.

JOHNNY. I'm very glad we had this Saturday night.

FRANKIE. I never would have said that if I knew you better.

JOHNNY. How well do you want to know me?

FRANKIE. I'll let you know Monday between orders. "I got a BLT down working!" "Tell me about your childhood." "Take the moo out of two!" "Were you toilet trained?"

JOHNNY. Come here.

FRANKIE. Are you sure you don't want something before you go?

JOHNNY. Come here.

FRANKIE. I've got some meatloaf in the fridge.

JOHNNY. Come here. (FRANKIE *moves a few steps towards* JOHNNY *who is sitting on the edge of the bed*)

FRANKIE. What?

JOHNNY. Closer. (FRANKIE *moves closer to* JOHNNY *who pulls her all the way towards him and buries his face in her middle.*)

FRANKIE. I can toast some bread. Butter and catsup. A cold meat loaf sandwich. All the way back to Brooklyn . . .

JOHNNY. Heights.

FRANKIE. Heights! This time of night. Aren't you hungry?

JOHNNY. I'm starving.

FRANKIE. No!

JOHNNY. Why not?

FRANKIE. We just did.

JOHNNY. So?

FRANKIE. I can't.

JOHNNY. What do you mean, you can't?

FRANKIE. I don't want to. (JOHNNY *immediately stops nuzzling* FRANKIE. *Both hands fly up with palms outwards.*) You don't have to take it like that. I'm sorry. Just not right now. You know, you're right: I do say "I'm sorry" a lot around you. There's something about you that makes me feel like I'm letting you down all the time. Like you have all these expectations of me that I can't fulfill. I'm sorry—there I go again!—but what you see here is what you get. I am someone who likes to eat after making love and right now I feel like a cold meat loaf sandwich on white toast with butter and catsup with a large glass of very cold milk and I wish you would stop looking at me like that.

JOHNNY. Open your robe.

FRANKIE. No. Why?

JOHNNY. I want to look at your pussy.

FRANKIE. No. Why?

JOHNNY. It's beautiful.

FRANKIE. It is not. You're just saying that.

JOHNNY. I think it is. I'm telling you, you have a beautiful pussy—!

FRANKIE. I hate that word, Johnny!

JOHNNY. —alright, thing! and I'm asking you to open your robe so I can look at it. Just look. Fifteen seconds. You can time me. Then you can make *two* cold meat loaf sandwiches and *two* big glasses of milk. Just hold the catsup on one.

FRANKIE. I don't know if you're playing games or being serious.

JOHNNY. Both. Serious games. Do you have to name everything? If I had said "You have a beautiful parakeet" you'd have let me see it and we'd be eating those sandwiches already.

FRANKIE. I had a parakeet. I hated it. I was glad when it died. (*She opens her robe.*) Okay?

JOHNNY. Oh! Yes!

FRANKIE (*Continuing to hold her robe open as* JOHNNY *sits on edge of bed and looks*). I'm timing this! I told my cousin I didn't want a bird. I hate birds. She swore I'd love a parakeet. What's to love? (*She almost drops the robe.*) They don't do anything except not sing when you want them to, sing when you don't and make those awful scratching noises on that awful sandpaper on the floor of their cell. I mean cage! If I ever have another pet it'll be a dog. A Golden Lab. Something that shows a little enthusiasm when you walk through the door. Something you can hold. The only time I got my hands on that goddamn parakeet was the day it dropped dead and I had to pick it up to throw it in the garbage can. Hey, come on! This has gotta be fifteen seconds. *(FRANKIE closes her robe. JOHNNY takes her hand, kisses it, rubs his cheek against it. FRANKIE stands awkwardly.)* You really would like a sandwich?

JOHNNY. But no catsup.

FRANKIE. Catsup's what makes a cold meat loaf sandwich good.

JOHNNY. I'm allergic. Catsup and peaches.

FRANKIE. Ugh!

JOHNNY. Well not in the same dish! *(He is still nuzzling her fingers.)*

FRANKIE. Can I have my hand back?

JOHNNY. Do you want it back?

FRANKIE. Well you want a sandwich, don't you?

JOHNNY. I want you to notice how we're connecting. My hand is flowing into yours. My eyes are trying to see inside yours.

FRANKIE. That's not connecting. That's holding and staring. Connecting is when the other person isn't even around and you could die from just thinking of them.

JOHNNY. That's missing. This is connecting.

FRANKIE. Yeah, well it ain't how a sandwich gets made. *(She takes her hand from JOHNNY and goes to kitchen area of the apartment where she takes out all the makings of her meat loaf sandwich and begins to prepare them. JOHNNY will just watch her from his place on the bed.)* My father used to say a good meat loaf and gravy with mashed potatoes was food fit for the gods.

JOHNNY. You're kidding! That's exactly what my old man used to say.

FRANKIE. Of course, considering our family budget we didn't have too many other options. Guess what, pop? I still don't. *(She laughs. JOHNNY laughs with her)* You want to turn on the television?

JOHNNY. Why?

FRANKIE. We don't have to watch it. You know, just sound. I do it all the time. Company. It beats a parakeet.

JOHNNY. I'd rather watch you.

FRANKIE. Do you ever watch the Channel 5 Movie Club on Saturday night? That's right, you got a VCR. They have this thing called the Movie Club. Talk about dumb gimmicks. You put your name and address on a postcard. If they draw it, you go on the

air and tell everybody what your favorite movie is and they show it, along with intermission breaks where they tell you certain little-known facts about the movie I just as soon wouldn't have known, such as "Susan Hayward was already stricken with a fatal cancer when she made this sparkling comedy." Kind of puts a pall on things, you know?

JOHNNY. I was on that program.

FRANKIE. You were not.

JOHNNY. Sure I was.

FRANKIE. What was your favorite movie?

JOHNNY. I forget.

FRANKIE. You probably don't even have one. *(JOHNNY has gotten up off the bed and comes over to where FRANKIE is working. He finds a place to sit very close to where she stands making the sandwiches.)*

JOHNNY. You know what I was thinking while I was looking at you over there?

FRANKIE. I should have guessed this was coming!

JOHNNY. I was thinking "There's got to be more to life than this" but at times like this I'll be goddamned if I know what it is.

FRANKIE. You don't give up, do you?

JOHNNY. I want to drown in this woman. I want to die here. So why is she talking about parakeets and meat loaf? The inequity of human relationships! I actually thought that word: "inequity." I didn't even know it was in my vocabulary. And what's that other one? Disparity! Yeah, that's it. The disparity between us at that moment. I mean, there I was, celebrating you, feasting on your loveliness, and you were talking about a fucking, pardon my French, parakeet!

FRANKIE. Maybe it's because I was ill at ease.

JOHNNY. Because of me?

FRANKIE. Maybe I don't like being looked at down there that way, how the hell should I know?

JOHNNY. Bullshit! You don't like being looked at, period.

FRANKIE. Ow!

JOHNNY. What happened?

FRANKIE. I cut myself.

JOHNNY. Let me see.

FRANKIE. It's all right.

JOHNNY. Let me see. *(He sucks the blood from her finger.)*

FRANKIE. Look, I don't think this is going to work out. It was very nice while it lasted but like I said. . . .

JOHNNY. You'll live. *(He releases her hand.)*

FRANKIE. . . . I'm a BLT down sort of person and I think you're looking for someone a little more pheasant under glass. Where are you going?

JOHNNY. I'll get a bandage.

FRANKIE. That's okay.

JOHNNY. No problem.

FRANKIE. Really. What are you doing? *(JOHNNY has gone into the bathroom. We hear him going through the medicine cabinet looking for a bandage as he continues to speak through the open door.)*

JOHNNY. I don't remember you saying you were a BLT down sort of person.

FRANKIE. I thought I implied it when I was talking about the meat loaf. *(JOHNNY comes out of the bathroom with a box of Band-Aids and a bottle of iodine.)*

JOHNNY. It's because I said you had a beautiful pussy, isn't it? Give me your finger. *(FRANKIE holds out her finger while JOHNNY disinfects and dresses it.)*

FRANKIE. It's because you said a lot of things. Ow!

JOHNNY. A man compliments a woman. All right, maybe he uses street talk but it's nice street talk, affectionate. It's not one of them ugly words, like the one I'm sure we're both familiar with, the one that begins with "c." I didn't say you had a beautiful "c." I was saying something loving and you took offense.

FRANKIE. I told you I wasn't very spontaneous!

JOHNNY. Boy, if you had said to me, "Johnny, you have the most terrific dick on you" I would be so happy. *(He finishes with the Band-Aids.)* There you go.

FRANKIE. Thank you.

JOHNNY. You want to see scarred fingers! *(He holds up his hands to FRANKIE)*

FRANKIE *(Wincing at the sight)*. Please!

JOHNNY. They don't hurt.

FRANKIE. I don't want to look.

JOHNNY *(Looking at them)*. It's hard to connect to them. I mean, I'm not the type who should have scarry hands.

FRANKIE. You're so good with knives. I've watched you.

JOHNNY. She admits it. The haughty waitress has cast a lustful gaze on the Knight of the Grill.

FRANKIE. "Can that new guy chop and dice," Dena tells me. "Look at him go."

JOHNNY. Now, sure! It's a breeze. I can dice

an onion blindfolded. These scars were then. On my way up the culinary ladder. I knew you were looking at me.

FRANKIE. It's human curiosity. A new face in the kitchen. Male. Look, I never said I was a nun.

JOHNNY. Hey, it's okay. It was mutual. I was looking at you.

FRANKIE. Besides, there aren't that many short order cooks who have a dictionary and a copy of Shakespeare in their locker.

JOHNNY. You'd be surprised. We're an inquiring breed. We have our own quiz show: COOKS WANT TO KNOW.

FRANKIE. The one before you, Pluto, I'm not kidding, he said his name was Pluto, I swear to God! you know what he would have done with your books? Cooked 'em!

JOHNNY. So you noticed what I was reading, too?

FRANKIE. Call me the Bionic Eye. I don't miss a trick.

JOHNNY. You know what I liked about you? The way you take the time to talk to that old guy who comes in every day about 3:30.

FRANKIE. Mr. Leon.

JOHNNY. With the cane and a copy of the Post and always has a flower in his lapel. You really are nice with him.

FRANKIE. He's really nice with me.

JOHNNY. You really talk to him. I also like the way you fluff up that thing you wear on your uniform. It looks like a big napkin.

FRANKIE. It's supposed to be a handkerchief.

JOHNNY. I like the way you're always fluffing at it.

FRANKIE. What are you? Spying on me from the kitchen?

JOHNNY. No spying. Watching.

FRANKIE. I'm going to be very self-conscious from now on.

JOHNNY. Watching and liking what I see.

FRANKIE. You in night school or something?

JOHNNY. This is my kind of night school.

FRANKIE. I meant the Shakespeare and the big words.

JOHNNY. I'm doing that on my own.

FRANKIE. Why?

JOHNNY. You don't want to be going out with a semi-illiterate, subcretinous, protomoronic asshole, do you?

FRANKIE. Listen, it's easy to use words I don't know.

JOHNNY. What? Asshole? God, I like you.

FRANKIE. You still want a sandwich before you go?

JOHNNY. I still want a sandwich.

FRANKIE. Then you're going. You're not staying over.

JOHNNY. We'll cross that bridge when we get to it.

FRANKIE. There's no bridge to cross.

JOHNNY. What are you scared of?

FRANKIE. I'm not scared. *(She has resumed making sandwiches.* JOHNNY *watches her intently.)* I'm not scared. I'm . . .

JOHNNY. Yes, you are.

FRANKIE. Well not like in a horror movie. I don't think you're going to pull out a knife and stab me, if that's what you mean. Could we change the subject?

JOHNNY. What do you mean?

FRANKIE. Oh come on! You're gonna stand there and tell me you're not weird?

JOHNNY. Of course I'm weird.

FRANKIE. There's a whole other side of you I never saw at work.

JOHNNY. You thought all I did was cook?

FRANKIE. There's a whole other side of you I never saw when we were doing it either.

JOHNNY. It was probably your first experience with a passionate, imaginative lover.

FRANKIE. My first experience with an animal is more like it.

JOHNNY. Did you ever see an animal do to another animal's toes what I did to yours?

FRANKIE. Will you keep your voice down?

JOHNNY. You got this place bugged?

FRANKIE. I'm sure the whole building heard you. Ooooo! Ooooo! Ooooo!

JOHNNY. What do you expect, the way you kept twirling your fingers around inside my ears?

FRANKIE. Nobody ever put their fingers in your ears before?

JOHNNY. Maybe for a second but not the way you did, like you were drilling for something. I thought to myself "Maybe she gets off on putting her fingers in guys' ears." But did I say anything? Did I call you weird?

FRANKIE. You should have said something.

JOHNNY. Why?

FRANKIE. I would have stopped.

JOHNNY. Are you crazy? I loved it. I'll try anything once, especially in that department. You got any new ideas? Keep 'em coming, keep 'em coming. I'll tell you when to stop.

FRANKIE. I can just hear you now at work: "Hey, guys, that Frankie put her fingers in your ears!"

JOHNNY. That is probably just about the last thing in the entire world I would ever do about tonight: talk about it to anyone, especially those animals at work. You really don't know me.

FRANKIE. It wouldn't be the first time one of the guys had yak-yak-yakked about it.

JOHNNY. Women yak, too. Hey, no catsup!

FRANKIE. Yeah, but about dumb things.

JOHNNY. All yakking is dumb. "I slept with Frankie." "Oh yeah, well I slept with Nancy Reagan." "Big effing pardon-my-French deal, the two of yous. I slept with Mother Teresa." So it goes. This wall of disparity between us, Frankie, we gotta break it down. So the only space left between us is just us.

FRANKIE. Here's your sandwich.

JOHNNY. Here's my guts.

FRANKIE. I'm sorry. I'm not good at small talk.

JOHNNY. This isn't small talk. This is enormous talk.

FRANKIE. Whatever you call it, I'm not good at it.

JOHNNY. Sure you are. You just have to want to be.

FRANKIE. Maybe that's it. I forgot the milk.

JOHNNY. Something's going on in this room, something important. You don't feel it?

FRANKIE. I told you what I felt.

JOHNNY. You don't want to feel it. Two people coming together: sure, it's a little scary but it's pardon-my-French-again fucking wonderful, too. My heart is so full right now. Put your hand here. I swear to God, you can feel the lump. Come on, touch it.

FRANKIE. You're too needy. You want too much. I can't.

JOHNNY. That's where you're wrong.

FRANKIE. You had the whole thing. There's no more where it came from. I'm empty.

JOHNNY. I know that feeling. It's terrible. The wonderful thing is, it doesn't have to last.

FRANKIE. Turn the light off! I want to show you something. *(*JOHNNY *turns off the light.)* Down one floor, over two buildings, the window with the kind of gauzy curtains. You see? *(*JOHNNY *has joined her at the window.)*

JOHNNY. Where?

FRANKIE. There!

JOHNNY. The old couple in the bathrobes? What about 'em?

FRANKIE. I've been watching them ever since I moved in. Almost eight years now. I have never seen them speak to one another, not once. He'll sit there reading the paper and she'll cook an entire meal without him looking up. They'll eat it in total silence. He'll help her wash up sometimes but they still won't say a word. After a while the lights go out and I guess they've gone to bed. (JOHNNY *has seen something else out the window.*)

JOHNNY. Jesus!

FRANKIE. Those two! The Raging Bull I call him. She's Mary the Masochist. They moved in about eighteen months ago.

JOHNNY. Hey!

FRANKIE. It's their thing.

JOHNNY. He's beating the shit out of her.

FRANKIE. She loves it.

JOHNNY. Nobody could love getting hit like that. We ought to do something.

FRANKIE. I saw her in the A&P. She was wearing a nurse's uniform. Living with him, that was a smart career choice. She had on sunglasses, you know, to hide the bruises. I went up to her, I figured it was now or never, and I said "I live in the building behind you. I've seen how he hits you. Is there anything I can do?" and she just looked at me and said, "I don't know what you're talking about."

JOHNNY. Jesus, Jesus, Jesus.

FRANKIE. Some nights when there's nothing on television I sit here in the dark and watch them. Once I ate a whole bunch of grapes watching them. One night she ended up on the floor and didn't move till the next morning. I hate being used to them.

JOHNNY. I would never hit you. I would never hit a woman.

FRANKIE. I think you had better finish that and go.

JOHNNY. You are missing one hell of an opportunity to feel with your own hand the human heart. It's right here.

FRANKIE. Maybe next time. (JOHNNY *looks at her and then downs the glass of milk in one long might gulp.*) Thank you.

JOHNNY. Your meat loaf is directly from Mount Olympus. Your father was a very lucky guy.

FRANKIE. It's his recipe. He taught me.

JOHNNY. Yeah? My old man was a great cook, too.

FRANKIE. Mine didn't have much choice.

JOHNNY. How do you mean?

FRANKIE. My mother left us when I was seven.

JOHNNY. I don't believe it! My mother left us when I was seven.

FRANKIE. Oh come on!

JOHNNY. Boy, you really, really, really and truly don't know me. Just about the last thing in the entire world I would joke about is a mother who wasn't there. I don't think mothers are sacred. I just don't think they're especially funny.

FRANKIE. Me and my big mouth! I don't think you realize how serious I am about wanting you to leave now.

JOHNNY. I don't think you realize how serious I am about us.

FRANKIE. What us? There is no us.

JOHNNY. I'm working on it. Frankie and Johnny! We're already a couple.

FRANKIE. Going out with someone just because his name is Johnny and yours is Frankie is not enough of a reason.

JOHNNY. I think it's an extraordinary one. It's fate. You also said you thought I had sexy wrists.

FRANKIE. One of the biggest mistakes in my entire life!

JOHNNY. It's gotta begin somewhere. A name, a wrist, a toe.

FRANKIE. Didn't they end up killing each other?

JOHNNY. She killed him. The odds are in your favor. Besides, we're not talking about ending up. I'm just trying to continue what's been begun.

FRANKIE. If he was anything like you, no wonder she shot him.

JOHNNY. It was a crime of passion. They were the last of the red hot lovers. We're the next.

FRANKIE. You're not from Brooklyn.

JOHNNY. Brooklyn Heights.

FRANKIE. I knew you were gonna say that! You're from outer space.

JOHNNY. Allentown, Pennsylvania, actually.

FRANKIE. Very funny, very funny.

JOHNNY. You've never been to Allentown.

FRANKIE. Who told you? Viv? Martin? I know, Molly the Mouth!

JOHNNY. Now who's from outer space? What the pardon-my-French fuck are you talking about?

FRANKIE. One of them told you I was from Allentown so now you're pretending you are so you can continue with this coincidence theory.

JOHNNY. You're from Allentown? I was born in Allentown.

FRANKIE. Very funny. Very funny.

JOHNNY. St. Stephen's Hospital. We lived on Martell St.

FRANKIE. I suppose you went to Moody High School, too.

JOHNNY. No, we moved when I was eight. I started out at Park Lane Elementary though. Did you go to Park Lane? This is incredible! This is better than anything in Shirley MacLaine.

FRANKIE. It's a small world and Allentown's a big city.

JOHNNY. Not that small and not that big.

FRANKIE. I still don't believe you.

JOHNNY. Of course you don't. It's one big pardon-my-French again fucking miracle and you don't believe in them.

FRANKIE. I'll tell you one thing: I could never, not in a million years, be seriously involved with a man who said "Pardon my French" all the time.

JOHNNY. Done. Finished. You got it.

FRANKIE. I mean, where do you pick up an expression like that?

JOHNNY. Out of respect for a person. A woman in this case.

FRANKIE. The first time you said it tonight I practically told you I had a headache and had to go home.

JOHNNY. That's so scary to me! That three little words, "Pardon my French," could separate two people from saying the three little words that make them connect!

FRANKIE. What three little words?

JOHNNY. I love you.

FRANKIE. Oh. Them. I should've guessed.

JOHNNY. Did you ever say them to anyone?

FRANKIE. Say them or mean them? My father, my first true love and a couple of thousand men since. That's about it.

JOHNNY. I'm not counting.

FRANKIE. You're really from Allentown? *(JOHNNY nods, takes a bite out of his sandwich and makes a "Cross My Heart" sign over his chest. Then he pushes his empty milk glass towards* FRANKIE *meaning he would like a refill, which she will get.)* How did you get so lucky to get out of there at eight?

JOHNNY *(Talking and eating).* My mother. She ran off with somebody she'd met at an A.A. meeting. My father took us to Baltimore. He had a sister. She couldn't cope with us. We ended up in foster homes. Could I have a little salt? I bounced all over the place. Washington, D.C., was the best. You go through that Smithsonian Institute they got there and there ain't nothing they're gonna teach you in college! That place is a gold mine. Portland, Maine, is nice, too. Cold though.

FRANKIE. You didn't miss much not staying in Allentown . . . My big highlight was . . .

JOHNNY. What?

FRANKIE. Nothing. It's stupid.

JOHNNY. I've told you stupid things.

FRANKIE. Not this stupid.

JOHNNY. No fair.

FRANKIE. All right! I played Fiona in our high school production of *Brigadoon.*

JOHNNY. What's stupid about that? I bet you were wonderful.

FRANKIE. It's hardly like winning a scholarship to Harvard or being the class valedictorian. It's an event; it shouldn't be a highlight.

JOHNNY. So you're an actress!

FRANKIE. You mean at this very moment in time?

JOHNNY. I said to myself "She's not just a waitress."

FRANKIE. Yeah, she's an unsuccessful actress! What are you really?

JOHNNY. I'm really a cook.

FRANKIE. Oh. When you put it like that, I'm really a waitress. I haven't tried to get an acting job since the day I decided I never was gonna get one. Somebody told me you gotta have balls to be a great actress. I got balls, I told 'em. No, Frankie, you got a big mouth!

JOHNNY. Would you . . . ? You know . . . ?

FRANKIE. What?

JOHNNY. Act something for me.

FRANKIE. What are you? Nuts? You think actors go around acting for people just like that? Like we do requests?

. JOHNNY. I'm sorry. I didn't know.

FRANKIE. Acting is an art. It's a responsibility. It's a privilege.

JOHNNY. And I bet you're good at it.

FRANKIE. And it looks like I'll die with my secret. Anyway, what happened to your mother?

JOHNNY. I tracked her down when I was eighteen. They were still together, living in Philadelphia and both drinking again. They say Philadelphia will do that to you.

FRANKIE. So you saw her again? You see, I never did.

JOHNNY. But how this potbellied, balding, gin-breathed stranger could have been the object of anyone's desire but especially my mother's! She was still so beautiful, even through the booze, but he was one hundred percent turkey.

FRANKIE. Mine was killed in a car wreck about three, no, four years ago. She was with her turkey. He got it, too. I didn't hear about it for almost a month.

JOHNNY. What people see in one another! It's a total mystery. Shakespeare said it best: "There are more things in heaven and on earth than are dreamt of in your philosophy, Horatio." Something like that. I'm pretty close. Did you ever read *Hamlet*?

FRANKIE. Probably.

JOHNNY. I like him. I've only read a couple of his things. They're not easy. Lots of old words. Archaic, you know? Then all of a sudden he puts it all together and comes up with something clear and simple and it's real nice and you feel you've learned something. This Horatio was Hamlet's best friend. He thought he had it all figured out, so Hamlet set him straight. Do you have a best friend?

FRANKIE. Not really.

JOHNNY. That's okay. I'll be your best friend.

FRANKIE. You think a lot of yourself, don't you?

JOHNNY. Look, I'm going all over the place with you. I might as well come right out with it: I love you. I'm in love with you. I personally think we should get married and I definitely want us to have kids, three or four. There! That wasn't so difficult. You don't have to say anything. I just wanted to get it out on the table. Talk about a load off!

FRANKIE. Talk about a load off? Talk about a crock of shit.

JOHNNY. Hey, come on, don't. One of the things I like about you, Frankie, is that you talk nice. Don't start that stuff now.

FRANKIE. Well fuck you how I talk! I'll talk any fucking way I fucking feel like it! It's my fucking apartment in the fucking first place and who the fuck are you to come in here and start telling me I talk nice. *(She has started to cry.)*

JOHNNY. I'm sorry.

FRANKIE. Out of the blue, just like that, you've decided we're going to get involved?

JOHNNY. If you want to understate it like that.

FRANKIE. Whatever happened to a second date?

JOHNNY. We were beyond that two hours ago.

FRANKIE. Maybe you were.

JOHNNY. I like your apartment. That's a nice robe. You're a very pretty woman but I guess all the guys tell you that. Is that what you want?

FRANKIE. I don't want this.

JOHNNY. That has occurred to me. Dumb, I am not. Nervy and persistent, those I plead guilty to. I'm also something else people aren't too accustomed to these days: courageous. I want you and I'm coming after you.

FRANKIE. Has it occurred to you that maybe I don't want you?

JOHNNY. Only a couple of hundred times. I got my work cut out for me.

FRANKIE. Just because you take me out to dinner—!

JOHNNY. That wasn't my fault!

FRANKIE. Then the movies—!

JOHNNY. It got four stars!

FRANKIE. And end up making love—!

JOHNNY. Great love.

FRANKIE. Okay love.

JOHNNY. Great love. The dinner and the movie were lousy. We were dynamite.

FRANKIE. Okay, good love. So why do you have to go spoil everything?

JOHNNY. I told you I loved you. That makes me unlovable?

FRANKIE. It makes you a creep!

JOHNNY. Oh.

FRANKIE. No, I take that back. You're not a creep. You're sincere. That's what's so awful. Well, I'm sincere, too. I sincerely do not want to continue this.

JOHNNY. Pretend that we're the only two people in the entire world, that's what I'm doing, and it all falls into place.

FRANKIE. And I was looking forward to seeing you again.

JOHNNY. I'm right here.

FRANKIE. "God," I was thinking, "make him want to see me again without him knowing that's what I want."

JOHNNY. I already did know. God had nothing to do with it.

FRANKIE. I said "see you again," not the stuff you're talking about. Kids for Christ's sake!

JOHNNY. What's wrong with kids?

FRANKIE. I hate kids.

JOHNNY. I don't believe that.

FRANKIE. I'm too old to have kids.

JOHNNY. No, you're not.

FRANKIE. I can't have any. Now are you happy?

JOHNNY. We'll adopt.

FRANKIE. You just don't decide to fall in love with people out of the blue.

JOHNNY. Why not?

FRANKIE. They don't like it. How would you like it if Helen came up to you and said, "I'm in love with you. I want to have your baby."

JOHNNY. Who's Helen?

FRANKIE. At work.

JOHNNY. That Helen?

FRANKIE. You'd run like hell.

JOHNNY. She's close to seventy.

FRANKIE. I thought love was blind.

JOHNNY. It's the exact opposite. Besides, I'd tell her I was in love with you.

FRANKIE. You don't know me.

JOHNNY. Is that what all this is about? Of course I don't know you. You don't know me either. We got off to a great start. Why do you want to stop?

FRANKIE. Does it have to be tonight?

JOHNNY. Yes!

FRANKIE. Who says?

JOHNNY. We may not make it to tomorrow. I might get knifed if you make me go home. You might choke on a chicken bone. Unknown poison gases could kill us both in our sleep. When it comes to love, life's cheap and it's short. So don't fuck with it and don't pardon my French.

FRANKIE. This is worse than *Looking for Mr. Goodbar.*

JOHNNY. Look, Frankie, I might see someone on the BMT tonight, get lucky and get laid, and think I was in love with her. This is the only chance we have to really come together, I'm convinced of it. People are given one moment to connect. Not two, not three, one! They don't take it, it's gone forever and they end up not only pardon-my-French-for-the-very-last-time screwing that person on the BMT but marrying her.

FRANKIE. Boy, are you barking up the wrong tree.

JOHNNY. I never thought I could be in love with a woman who said "barking up the wrong tree."

FRANKIE. You've driven me to it. I never used that expression in my entire life.

JOHNNY. You sure you don't want to feel this lump?

FRANKIE. Why won't you go?

JOHNNY. The only difference between us right now is I know how this is going to end—happily—and you don't. I need a best friend, too. Could I trouble you for another glass of milk?

FRANKIE. Okay, milk, but then I really want you to go. Promise?

JOHNNY. You drive a hard bargain. Milk for exile from the Magic Kingdom.

FRANKIE. Promise?

JOHNNY. Promise.

FRANKIE. Say it like you mean it.

JOHNNY. I promise.

FRANKIE. It's a good thing you're not an actor.

JOHNNY. All right, I don't promise.

FRANKIE. Now I believe you. (*She goes to refrigerator and pours a glass of milk.*)

JOHNNY. It's just words. It's all words. Words, words, words. He said that, too, I think. I read somewhere Shakespeare said just about everything. I'll tell you one thing he didn't say: I love you, Frankie. (FRANKIE *brings him a glass of milk.*)

FRANKIE. Drink your milk.

JOHNNY. I bet that's something else he never said: "Drink your milk," *The Merry Wives of Windsor,* Act III, scene ii. I don't think so. The Swan of Avon ain't got nothing on us.

FRANKIE. Did anybody ever tell you you talk too much?

JOHNNY. Yeah, I told you about half an hour ago. There's no virtue in being a mute.

FRANKIE. I'm not a mute.

JOHNNY. Did I say you were?

FRANKIE. I talk when I have something to say.

JOHNNY. Did I say she was a mute?

FRANKIE. You know, not everybody thinks life is a picnic. Some of us have problems. Some of us have sorrows. But people like you are so busy telling us what you want, how you feel you don't even notice the rest of us who aren't exactly jumping up and down for joy.

JOHNNY. I haven't done anything but notice you.

FRANKIE. Shut up!

JOHNNY. Who's jumping up and down!

FRANKIE. I said, shut up! Just drink your milk and go. I don't want to hear your voice again tonight.

JOHNNY. What do you want?

FRANKIE. I want to be alone. I want to watch television. I want to eat ice cream. I want to sleep. I want to stop worrying. I'm trapped in my own apartment with a fucking maniac.

JOHNNY. We all have problems, you know.

FRANKIE. Right now, mine begin and end with you. You said you'd go.

JOHNNY. I lied.

FRANKIE. All I have to do is open that window and start screaming.

JOHNNY. In this city? Lots of luck.

FRANKIE. I have neighbors upstairs, friends . . .

JOHNNY. No one's gonna want to get involved in us. They'll just tell you to call the police.

FRANKIE. Don't think it hasn't crossed my mind.

JOHNNY. They'll come, give or take an hour or two. They'll make me leave but I'll be right back. That's a very handy fire escape. If not tonight, then tomorrow or the day after that. Sooner or later, you're gonna have to deal with me. Why don't we just get it over with? Besides, tomorrow's Sunday. We can sleep in. *(At some point before this, the music on the radio has changed to Scriabin's Second Symphony. Neither* FRANKIE *nor* JOHNNY *heard the announcement. Ideally, the audience didn't either.)*

FRANKIE. I *am* trapped in my own apartment with a fucking maniac!

JOHNNY. You don't mean that. I'm trying to improve my life and I'm running out of time. I'm still going around in circles with you. There's gotta be that one thing I say that makes you listen. That makes us connect. What station are you on?

FRANKIE. What?

JOHNNY. It looks like it's around about ninety. You got a paper? *(He starts rummaging about for a newspaper.)*

FRANKIE. What do you think you're doing?

JOHNNY. I want to get the name of that piece of music you liked for you.

FRANKIE. I don't care anymore.

JOHNNY. Well, I do. When you come across something beautiful, you gotta go for it. It doesn't grow on trees, beautiful things. *(*JOHNNY *has found the radio station call letters in the newspaper.)* WKCC. *(As he dials information.)* I owe you a quarter.

FRANKIE. He's nuts. Out and out loco!

JOHNNY *(Into phone.)* Give me the number for WKCC. Thank you. *(To* FRANKIE.) Without the name, we'll lose that music and I'll never find it on my own. You let something like that slip through your fingers and you deserve rock and roll! *(He hangs up and immediately redials.)* I hate these recordings that give you the number now. One less human contact. *(To* FRANKIE) Where are you going?

FRANKIE. Out and you better not be here when I get back.

JOHNNY. You want to pick up some Haagen-Dazs Vanilla Swiss Almond while you're out?

FRANKIE. I said get out! *(She starts throwing things.)* You're a maniac! You're a creep! You're a. . . . Oh!

JOHNNY *(Into phone.)* May I speak to your disc jockey? . . . Well excuse me! *(He covers phone, to* FRANKIE.) They don't have a disc jockey. They have someone called Midnight With Marlon. *(Into phone.)* Hello, Marlon? My name is Johnny. My friend and I were making love and in the afterglow, which I sometimes think is the most beautiful part of making love, she noticed that you were playing some really beautiful music, piano. She was right. I don't know much about quality music, which I could gather that was, so I would like to know the name of that particular piece and the artist performing it so I can buy the record and present it to my lady love, whose name is Frankie and is that a beautiful coincidence or is it not? *(Short pause.)* Bach. Johann Sebastian, right? I heard of him. The Goldberg Variations. Glenn Gould. Columbia Records. *(To* FRANKIE.) You gonna remember this? *(*FRANKIE *smacks him hard across the cheek.* JOHNNY *takes the phone from his ear and holds it against his chest. He just looks at her. She smacks him again. This time he catches her hand while it is still against his cheek, holds it a beat, then brings it to his lips and kisses it. Then, into phone, he continues but what he says is really for* FRANKIE, *his eyes never leaving her.)* Do you take requests, Marlon? Then make an exception! There's a man and a woman. Not young, not old. No great beauties, either one. They meet where they work: a restaurant and it's not the Ritz. She's a waitress. He's a cook. They meet but they don't connect. "I got two medium burgers working" and "Pick up, side of fries" is pretty much the extent of it. But she's noticed him, he can feel it. And he's noticed her. Right off. They both knew tonight was going to happen. So why did it take him six weeks for him to ask her if she wanted to see a movie that neither one of them could tell you the name of right now? Why did they eat ice cream sundaes before she asked him if he wanted to come up since they were in the neighborhood? And then they were making love and for maybe an hour they forgot the ten million things that made them think "I don't love this person, I don't even like them" and instead all they knew was that they were together and it was perfect and they were perfect and that's all there was to know about it and as they lay there, they both began the million reasons not to love one another like a familiar rosary. Only this time he stopped himself. Maybe it was the music you were playing. They both heard it. Only now they're both beginning to forget they did. So would you play something for Frankie and Johnny on the eve of something that ought to last, not self-destruct. I guess I want you to play the most beautiful music ever written and dedicate it to us. *(He hangs up.)* Don't go.

FRANKIE. Why are you doing this?

JOHNNY. I'm tired of looking. Everything I want is in this room. *(He kisses her.* FRANKIE *responds. It quickly gets passionate.* FRANKIE *starts to undress.)*

JOHNNY. Let me.

FRANKIE. Hunh?

JOHNNY. Let me do it. *(He helps her out of her raincoat. Then he takes it and hangs it up.* FRANKIE *stands a little awkwardly in the center of the room waiting for him to come back to her.)* Make yourself at home. That was a little joke. No, that was a little bad joke. *(He turns off a lamp.)*

FRANKIE. What's the matter?

JOHNNY. Nothing.

FRANKIE. Leave the lights on.

JOHNNY. It's better off.

FRANKIE. I want to see you this time. *(*JOHNNY *has started unbuttoning her blouse.)*

JOHNNY. I don't like to make love with the lights on.

FRANKIE. Why not?

JOHNNY. I can't.

FRANKIE. That's a good reason. *(*JOHNNY *is having a little difficulty undressing her.)*

JOHNNY. It's because of Archie.

FRANKIE. Okay, I'll bite. Who's Archie?

JOHNNY. A huge Great Dane at one of my foster families. I mean, massive. Whenever I'd jack off, he'd just stare at me. At it. Talk about serious castration anxiety! So I got in the habit of doing it with the lights off.

FRANKIE. Sometimes I am so glad I'm a girl.

JOHNNY. I'm also a romantic. I think everything looks better in half-light and shadows.

FRANKIE. That's not romance, that's hiding something. Romance is seeing somebody for what they really are and still wanting them warts and all.

JOHNNY. I got plenty of them. *(He stops undressing her.)* I'm forty-five.

FRANKIE. You look younger. I'm thirty-seven.

JOHNNY. So do you. I'm forty-six.

FRANKIE. Honest?

JOHNNY. I'll be forty-eight the tenth of next month.

FRANKIE. What do you want for your birthday?

JOHNNY. To be able to stop bullshitting about things like my age.

FRANKIE. I'll be thirty-nine on the eleventh.

JOHNNY. We're both what-do-you-ma-call-its!

FRANKIE. Figures! Gimme a hand with the bed. I hate it when the sheets get like that. *(*FRANKIE *starts straightening up the bed.* JOHNNY *turns off another light in the room before helping her to smooth the sheets and blankets.)* I'm the one who ought to be hiding from the light. Me and my goddamn inverted nipples. I hate the way they look.

JOHNNY. Don't be silly.

FRANKIE. Yeah? You be a woman and have someone invert your nipples and see how you like it.

JOHNNY. I love your nipples.

FRANKIE. Well I hate 'em.

JOHNNY. What do you know? *(They stand on opposite sides of the bed shaking out the sheets.)* Listen, I wish I was circumcised.

FRANKIE. Sounds like you had your chance and blew it.

JOHNNY. Hunh?

FRANKIE. The dog. Skip it, skip it! I'll be forty-one on the eleventh.

JOHNNY. Big deal. So what do you want?

FRANKIE. The same thing you do and a new pair of tits.

JOHNNY. Hey, it means a lot to me you talk nice. *(*JOHNNY *crosses to window to close the shade.* FRANKIE *goes to bed and lies down on it.)* Jesus. *(He points to something outside the window and above it.)*

FRANKIE. Come away from there. It's not good for you.

JOHNNY. Come here. Quick. *(He stands at the window. Moonlight covers his body.)*

FRANKIE. I mean it. I've looked too long.

JOHNNY. There's a full moon! You can just see it between the buildings. Will you look at that! Now that's what I call beautiful!

FRANKIE. I ordered it just for you. Macy's. Twenty-five bucks an hour.

JOHNNY. Look at it!

FRANKIE. Later.

JOHNNY. It won't be there later. *(FRANKIE joins him at the window.)* You can almost see it move.

FRANKIE *(Lowering her gaze)*. All quiet on the Western front. For now. Come on. *(She moves to bed.)* Come on. I want you to make love to me. *(JOHNNY turns from the window)*

JOHNNY. I want to make love to you.

FRANKIE. Woof! Woof! *(Nothing.)* It was a joke, I'm sorry.

RADIO ANNOUNCER. This young man was very persuasive . . .

JOHNNY. Ssshh! Listen! *(He moves quickly to the bedside radio and turns up the volume.)*

RADIO ANNOUNCER. So although it's against my policy to play requests, there's an exception to every rule. I don't know if this is the most beautiful music ever written, Frankie and Johnny—and how I wish that really were your names but I know when my leg is being pulled—but whoever you are, wherever you are, whatever you're doing, I hope this is something like what you had in mind. *(Debussy's "Clair de Lune" is heard.* JOHNNY *switches off the bedside lamp and kisses* FRANKIE. *Then he gets up quickly and goes to window and reaches for the shade. He sees the two couples in the apartments across the courtyard. He looks up to the moon. There is moonlight spilling onto his face and body. He decides not to pull the shade, allowing the moonlight to spill into the room. He moves away from the window and disappears in the shadows of the bed. We hear a distant siren. We hear the Debussy. We hear the sounds of Frankie and Johnny starting to make love. Fifteen seconds of this. Abrupt silence. Total blackout.)*

End of Act One

ACT TWO

AT RISE: The only illumination in the room comes from the television set. In its grey light, we can see Frankie and Johnny in the bed, under the covers. They both stare at it. The only sound is coming from the radio: now it is playing "The Ride of the Valkyries." Thirty seconds of the Wagner.

JOHNNY. Is that Charles Bronson? *(JOHNNY turns down radio.)* Is that Charles Bronson?

FRANKIE. Or the other one. I always get people in those kinds of movies confused.

JOHNNY. James Coburn?

FRANKIE. I think that's his name.

JOHNNY. Whoever he is, I hate him. It's not Clint Eastwood?

FRANKIE. No. I know what Clint Eastwood looks like. Look, you don't have to make such a big deal about it.

JOHNNY. I'm not making a big deal about it.

FRANKIE. Then how come we stopped?

JOHNNY. I haven't stopped. We're taking a little break. Will you look at that! I am appalled at the violence in the world today.

FRANKIE. It's okay if we don't.

JOHNNY. I know.

FRANKIE. Really.

JOHNNY. I said I know. Jesus, he drove a fucking nail through his head!

FRANKIE. I had my eyes shut.

JOHNNY. And when did that asshole go from playing our song to those screaming meemies? I thought he liked us. That kind of music is bad enough during normal hours. But when you're trying to make love to someone . . . ! Talk about not knowing how to segue from one mood to the next! I ought to call that station and complain. *(We hear him trip over something.)* Goddamnit! *(FRANKIE turns on the bedside lamp.)*

FRANKIE. Are you all right?

JOHNNY. I wish you wouldn't leave—. Yeah. Since I'm up, you want something?

FRANKIE. Johnny.

JOHNNY. You're the one who's making a big deal about it. I'm fine. I'm not upset. Look, I'm dancing. Now yes or no? What do you want?

FRANKIE. A Western on white down and a glass of milk.

JOHNNY. Very funny. What do you want? A beer? *(We can see him in the light of the open refrigerator as he searches it for food and drink.)*

FRANKIE. I want a Western and a glass of milk.

JOHNNY. We're in the middle of something. This is a little rest, not a major food break. Besides, you just ate.

FRANKIE. I'm still hungry.

JOHNNY. I'm opening you a beer.

FRANKIE. I want a Western and a glass of milk.

JOHNNY. I never know when you're kidding me or not. I think that's one of the things I like about you but I'm not sure.

FRANKIE. I'm not kidding you. I'm starving and what I would like is one of your Westerns and a glass of milk. Everyone says you make a great Western.

JOHNNY. They do?

FRANKIE. So come on, Johnny, Johnny. . . . ravish me with your cooking.

JOHNNY. You mean, since I couldn't ravish you with my body?

FRANKIE. No, that's not what I mean.

JOHNNY. Look, this is a temporary hiatus. I would like to keep it that way.

FRANKIE. So would I. I'll eat fast.

JOHNNY. All I'm saying is that if we get into real food now and I start cooking you a Western and chopping onions and peppers, it's going to be very hard to get back into the mood for what we were doing and which, contrary to your impression perhaps, I was enjoying enormously. All I asked for was a little breather for Christ's sake!

FRANKIE. I only asked for a sandwich.

JOHNNY. You asked for a Western. Westerns mean chopping and dicing and sautéing and . . . you know what goes into a Western? Come on, Frankie, it's not like you asked for a peanut butter and jelly on a Ritz cracker. You want food food.

FRANKIE. I suppose I could call out.

JOHNNY. All right, all right! *(He starts getting ingredients out of the refrigerator and slamming onto work counter.)* I just wish somebody would tell me how we got from a mini-sex problem to a major pig out.

FRANKIE. I don't think there's a connection.

JOHNNY. I wasn't going to tell you this but since you're not sparing my feelings, I'm not going to go on sparing yours: this is the first time anything like this ever happened to me.

FRANKIE. So?

JOHNNY. Well if you can't make the connection . . . !

FRANKIE. Between what and what?

JOHNNY. It takes two to tango.

FRANKIE. You mean it's my fault you conked out?

JOHNNY. I didn't say it was anybody's fault. And I didn't conk out. I'm resting.

FRANKIE. Oh, the old And-On-The-Seventh-Day Syndrome!

JOHNNY. There's no need to be sarcastic.

FRANKIE. Then don't blame me your dancing dog didn't dance when you told it to. That sounds terrible. Don't blame me for your limp dick. Now what about my Western?

JOHNNY. You expect me to make you a sandwich after that?

FRANKIE. After what?

JOHNNY. Insulting my manhood.

FRANKIE. I didn't insult your manhood. I merely described a phase it was going through. Everything has phases. To talk about the new moon doesn't insult the old one. You have a lovely manhood. It's just in eclipse right now so you can make me one of your terrific Westerns.

JOHNNY. This is the first time this has ever happened to me. I swear to God.

FRANKIE. I believe you.

JOHNNY. I hate it. I hate it a lot.

FRANKIE. Just be glad you have someone as sympathetic as me to share it with.

JOHNNY. Don't make fun.

FRANKIE. I'm not. *(She goes to him and comforts him.)* It's okay.

JOHNNY. You're lucky women don't have problems like this.

FRANKIE. We've got enough of our own in that department.

JOHNNY. It's male menopause. I've been dreading this.

FRANKIE. You know what I think it was? The moonlight. You were standing in it. It was bathing your body. I've always been very suspicious of what moonlight does to people.

JOHNNY. It's supposed to make them romantic.

FRANKIE. Or turn you into a werewolf. That's what I was raised on. My grandmother was always coming into my bedroom to make sure the blinds were down. She was convinced sleeping in the moonlight would turn you into the wolfman. I thought if I slept in the moonlight I'd wake up a beautiful fairy princess, so I kept falling asleep with the blinds open and she kept coming in and closing them. She always denied it was her. "Wasn't me, precious. Must have been your guardian angel." Remember them?

JOHNNY. What do you mean, "remember"?

FRANKIE. One night I decided to stay awake and catch her in the act. It seemed like forever. When you're that age, you don't have anything to stay awake *about.* So you're failing geography, so what? Finally my grandmother came into the room. She had to lean across my bed to close the blinds. Her bosom was so close to my face. She smelled so nice. I pretended I was still sleeping and took the deepest breath of her I could. In that one moment, I think I knew what it was like to be loved. Really loved. I was so safe, so protected! That's better than being pretty. I'll never forget it. The next thing I knew it was morning and I still didn't look like Audrey Hepburn. Now when I lie in bed with the blinds up and the moonlight spilling in, I'm not thinking I want to be somebody else, I just want my Nana back.

JOHNNY. Nana? You called your grandmother Nana? That's what I called mine.

FRANKIE. It's not that unusual.

JOHNNY. It's incredible! I don't know anybody else who called their grandmother Nana. I always thought it was very unusual of me and more than anything else I wanted to be like everyone else.

FRANKIE. You, like everyone else?

JOHNNY. It was a disaster. "Why do we call her Nana?" I used to ask my mother—this was before Philadelphia—"Everyone else says grandma." "We just do," she told me. My mother was not one for great answers. Sort of a Sphinx in that department. Anyway, I for one am very glad you didn't wake up Audrey Hepburn. She's too thin. People should have meat on their bones. "Beware yon Cassius. He hath a lean and hungry look."

FRANKIE. Who's Cassius?

JOHNNY. I don't know. But obviously he was thin and Shakespeare thinks we should be wary of skinny people.

FRANKIE. Why?

JOHNNY. Well you know how they are. Grim. Kind of waiting and watching you all the time.

FRANKIE. Like Connie?

JOHNNY. Who?

FRANKIE. Connie Cantwell. She works weekends. Red hair, wears a hairnet?

JOHNNY. Exactly! Wouldn't you beware her?

FRANKIE. I've actually seen her steal tips.

JOHNNY. There you go! He's filled with little tips like that. "Neither a borrower nor a lender be."

FRANKIE. That's just common sense. You don't have to be a genius to figure that one out.

JOHNNY. Of course not. But he put it in poetry so that people would know up here what they already knew in here and so they would remember it. "To be or not to be."

FRANKIE. Everyone knows that. Do I want to kill myself?

JOHNNY. Well?

FRANKIE. Well what?

JOHNNY. Do you want to kill yourself?

FRANKIE. Of course not. Well not right now. Everybody wants to kill themself some of the time.

JOHNNY. They shouldn't.

FRANKIE. Well they do! That doesn't mean they're gonna do it. Could we get off this?

JOHNNY. The list just gets longer and longer.

FRANKIE. What list?

JOHNNY. The us list, things we got in common.

FRANKIE. What do you want to kill yourself about sometimes?

JOHNNY. Right now? My limp dick. I'm kidding, I'm kidding. I'm going to start warning you before I say something funny.

FRANKIE. You don't have to warn me. Just say something funny.

JOHNNY. I want to kill myself sometimes when I think I'm the only person in the world and the part of me that feels that way is trapped inside this body that only bumps into other bodies without ever connecting with the only other person in the world trapped inside of them. We gotta connect. We just have to. Or we die.

FRANKIE. We're connecting.

JOHNNY. Are we?

FRANKIE. I am. I feel very . . .

JOHNNY. Say it.

FRANKIE. I don't know what it is.

JOHNNY. Say it anyway.

FRANKIE. Protective, but that's crazy!

JOHNNY. It's nice.

FRANKIE. I'm looking for somebody to take care of me this time.

JOHNNY. We all are.

FRANKIE. Why do we keep going from one subject I don't like to another?

JOHNNY. We're like an FM station when you're out driving in a car. We keep drifting and we gotta tune ourselves back in.

FRANKIE. Who says?

JOHNNY. Hey, I'm being nice.

FRANKIE. May I say something without you biting my head off?

JOHNNY. Aw, c'mon!

FRANKIE. I mean it!

JOHNNY. You are the woman I've been looking for all my adult life. You can say anything you want. Speak, queen of my heart, speak!

FRANKIE. That's just what I was talking about.

JOHNNY. What? Queen of my heart?

FRANKIE. I'm not the queen of anybody's heart.

JOHNNY. Fine. So what is it?

FRANKIE. This is going to sound awfully small potatoes now.

JOHNNY. You couldn't speak in small potatoes if you wanted to.

FRANKIE. I still want a Western.

JOHNNY. You don't give up. You're like a rat terrier with a bone.

FRANKIE. I'm sorry.

JOHNNY. I didn't hear that.

FRANKIE. All right, I'm *not* sorry. I'm a very simple person. I get hungry and I want to eat.

JOHNNY. I'm also a very simple person.

FRANKIE. Sure you are!

JOHNNY. I see something I want, I don't take no. I used to but not anymore.

FRANKIE. What is that supposed to mean?

JOHNNY. My life was happening to me. Now I'm making it happen. Same as with you and this sandwich. You wanted it, went for it and won. *(He turns and opens the refrigerator.)* You can tell a lot about someone from what they keep in their icebox. That and their medicine chest. I would've made a terrific detective.

FRANKIE. Just stay out of my medicine chest. And I didn't appreciate you going through my purse either.

JOHNNY. Someone is clearly not prepared for the eruption into her what-she-thinks-is-humdrum life of an extraordinary man, chef and fellow worker. Why don't you try our friend on the radio again? *(FRANKIE will go to radio and turn it on.)* Personally, I think it was all his fault. When it comes to music, I'm a mellow sort of guy. That last thing he played was for people playing with themselves, not one another. "If music be the food of love, play on." You-Know-Who.

FRANKIE *(At the radio).* I would love a cigarette.

JOHNNY. Over my dead body.

FRANKIE. That doesn't mean I'm going to smoke one. *(She turns up volume. We hear the Cesar Franck Sonata for Piano and Violin.)* How's that?

JOHNNY. Comme ci, comme ça.

FRANKIE. It's pretty.

JOHNNY. Let's put it this way: he's no Bach. The first thing in the morning I'm going to buy you those Goldberg Variations.

FRANKIE. It's Sunday. Everything'll be closed.

JOHNNY. Monday then.

FRANKIE. I guess Bach was Jewish. The Goldberg Variations.

JOHNNY. I read somewhere a lot of great composers were.

FRANKIE. I thought you were Jewish.

JOHNNY. In New York, that's a good assumption.

FRANKIE. I just realized I don't know your last name.

JOHNNY. I don't know yours.

FRANKIE. Mine's right on the bell. It's all over this place.

JOHNNY. We don't need last names. We're Frankie and Johnny. *(Closing the refrigerator door.)* Boy, you just shot my icebox theory all to hell. You should be an Irish longshoreman from what you've got in there.

FRANKIE. I am. Had you fooled for a while there, didn't I? *(JOHNNY is getting ready to make the Western.)*

JOHNNY. Now watch how I do this. After this, you're on your own! *(JOHNNY begins to work with the food and the utensils. He works swiftly, precisely and with great élan. He is a virtuoso in the kitchen. FRANKIE will pull up a stool and watch him work.)*

FRANKIE. I know I'm going to regret saying this but I thought I was the only person I knew who referred to one of those things as an icebox.

JOHNNY. Now who's pulling whose leg?

FRANKIE. And I don't say things like phonograph or record player. Just "icebox" and I only dimly remember us having one when I was about that big.

JOHNNY. Do you know what the population of New York City is?

FRANKIE. Eight million?

JOHNNY. Nine million, six hundred eighty-four thousand, four hundred eleven. Exactly two of them refer to those things as iceboxes. Those two, after you-know-what-ing their brains out, are now engaged in making a Western sandwich somewhere in Hell's Kitchen.

FRANKIE. It's Clinton actually.

JOHNNY. You still gonna call that a coincidence? Boy, I bet the Swan of Avon would have had something to say about that!

FRANKIE. I believe there's a reason for everything and I like to know what it is. One and one are two.

JOHNNY. That's mathematics. We're talking people.

FRANKIE. One and one should be two with them, too. Too many people throw you a curve nowadays and you end up with a three.

JOHNNY. Do I hear the voice of bitter experience?

FRANKIE. I wasn't born yesterday, if that's what you're talking about. *(She has watched* JOHNNY *intently during this as he has continued to prepare the Western.)* That's something I've never seen anyone do.

JOHNNY. What?

FRANKIE. Chop the pepper that fine.

JOHNNY. 'Cause they're looking for shortcuts.

FRANKIE. You're incredible with that knife.

JOHNNY. Thank you.

FRANKIE. And don't say it's all in the wrists.

JOHNNY. It is.

FRANKIE. I hate that expression. It's such a "fuck you." What people really mean is "I know how to do it and you don't. Ha ha ha!"

JOHNNY. What brought that on? We're talking nice and Bingo! the armor goes up.

FRANKIE. What about your armor?

JOHNNY. I don't have any.

FRANKIE. Everybody has armor. They'd be dead if they didn't.

JOHNNY. Bloody but unbowed.

FRANKIE. Besides, I wasn't talking about you.

JOHNNY. Where's your cayenne?

FRANKIE. I don't have any. I don't even know what it is. What's that you just put in?

JOHNNY. Wouldn't you like to know? *(He does a good imitation of* FRANKIE.*)* "Ha ha ha!"

FRANKIE. C'mon!

JOHNNY. Salt, just salt!

FRANKIE. Is that all?

JOHNNY. Cooking's no big deal.

FRANKIE. It is if you can't.

JOHNNY. You just never had anyone to cook for. The way I feel about you I feel a Duck a l'Orange Flambé with a puree of water chestnuts coming on!

FRANKIE. I like food. I just never saw the joy in cooking it. My mother hated cooking. Her primary utensil was a can opener. I even think she resented serving us on plates. She used to eat right out of the pots and pans. "One less thing to clean. Who's to know? We ain't got company."

JOHNNY. This isn't the right kind of bread.

FRANKIE. Gee, I'll run right out!

JOHNNY. There you go again! You want a good Western down, you need the right bread.

FRANKIE. Did you always want to be a cook?

JOHNNY. About as much as you wanted to be a waitress.

FRANKIE. That bad, hunh?

JOHNNY. When I look at some of the choices I made with my life, it seems almost inevitable I would end up slinging hash.

FRANKIE. Same with me and waitressing. I was supposed to graduate high school and work for a second cousin who had a dental laboratory.

JOHNNY. That place down by the old train station?

FRANKIE. Yeah, that's the one.

JOHNNY. His son was in my class. Arnold, right?

FRANKIE. You knew my cousin Arnold?

JOHNNY. Enough to say hello. Finish your story.

FRANKIE. Anyway, they made bridges, plates, retainers, stuff like that there. A dentist would take a parafin impression of the patient's mouth and make plaster of paris molds for the technicians to work from.

JOHNNY. No wonder the acting bug bit.

FRANKIE. I never had what it takes. I hope I have what it takes to be something but I know it's not an actress. You know what I'm thinking about?

JOHNNY. What?

FRANKIE. You won't laugh?

JOHNNY. Of course not.

FRANKIE. I can't. It's too . . . I'll tell you later. I can't now.

JOHNNY. Okay. I'll tell you one thing. You didn't miss much not graduating high school. I had almost two years of college. We both ended up working for a couple of crazed Greeks. *(He imitates their boss.)* "Cheeseburger, cheeseburger" is right.

FRANKIE. That was very good.

JOHNNY. Thank you.

FRANKIE. A teacher.

JOHNNY. Hunh?

FRANKIE. What I'm thinking of becoming.

JOHNNY. Why would I laugh at that?

FRANKIE. I don't know. It just seems funny. Someone who can't spell "cat" teaching little kids to. I'll have to go back to school and learn before I can teach them but . . . I don't know, it sounds nice. *(She hasn't stopped watching* JOHNNY *work with the eggs.)* Aren't you going to scramble them?

JOHNNY. It's better if you just let them set.

FRANKIE. In the restaurant, I've seen you beat 'em. That's when I noticed you had sexy wrists.

JOHNNY. That's in the restaurant. I'm in a hurry. These are my special eggs for you. *(He starts cleaning up while the eggs set in a skillet on the stove top.)*

FRANKIE. You don't have to do that.

JOHNNY. I know.

FRANKIE. Suit yourself.

JOHNNY. I bet I know what you're thinking: "He's too good to be true."

FRANKIE. Is that what you want me to think?

JOHNNY. Face it, Frankie, men like me do not grow on trees. Hell, *people* like me don't. *(He holds his wet hands out to her.)* Towel? *(FRANKIE picks up a dish towel on the counter and begins to dry his hands for him.)* So you think I have sexy wrists?

FRANKIE. I don't think you're gonna break into movies with 'em.

JOHNNY. What do you think is sexy about them?

FRANKIE. I don't know. The shape. The hairs. That vein there. What's that?

JOHNNY. A mole.

FRANKIE. I could live without that.

JOHNNY. First thing Monday morning, it comes off. *(He is kissing her hands. FRANKIE lets him but keeps a certain distance, too.)*

FRANKIE. Are you keeping some big secret from me?

JOHNNY. It's more like I'm keeping several thousand little ones.

FRANKIE. I'd appreciate a straight answer.

JOHNNY. No, I'm not married.

FRANKIE. Men always think that's the only question women want to ask.

JOHNNY. So fire away.

FRANKIE. Well were you?

JOHNNY. I was.

FRANKIE. How many times?

JOHNNY. Once. Is that it?

FRANKIE. Men have other secrets than being married. You could be a mass murderer or an ex-convict.

JOHNNY. I am. I spent two years in the slammer. Forgery.

FRANKIE. That's okay.

JOHNNY. The state of New Jersey didn't seem to think so.

FRANKIE. It's no skin off my nose.

JOHNNY. Anything else?

FRANKIE. You could be gay.

JOHNNY. Get real, Frankie.

FRANKIE. Well you could!

JOHNNY. Does this look like a gay face?

FRANKIE. You could have a drug problem or a drinking one.

JOHNNY. All right, I did.

FRANKIE. Which one?

JOHNNY. Booze.

FRANKIE. There, you see?

JOHNNY. It's under control now.

FRANKIE. You could still be a real shit underneath all that.

JOHNNY. But I'm not.

FRANKIE. That's your opinion.

JOHNNY. You just want a guarantee we're going to live happily ever after.

FRANKIE. Jesus God knows, I want something. If I was put on this planet to haul hamburgers and french fries to pay the rent on an apartment I don't even like in the vague hope that some stranger will not find me wanting enough not to want to marry me then I think my being born is an experience that is going to be equaled in meaninglessness only by my being dead. I got a whole life ahead of me to feel like this? Excuse me, who do I thank for all this? I think the eggs are ready.

JOHNNY. Everything you said, anybody could say. I could give it back to you in spades. You didn't invent negativity.

FRANKIE. I didn't have to.

JOHNNY. And you didn't discover despair. I was there a long time before you ever heard of it.

FRANKIE. The eggs are burning.

JOHNNY. Fuck the eggs! This is more important!

FRANKIE. I'm hungry! *(FRANKIE has gone to the stove to take the eggs off. JOHNNY grabs her from behind and pulls her towards him.)*

JOHNNY. What's the matter with you?

FRANKIE. Let go of me!

JOHNNY. Look at me! *(They struggle briefly. FRANKIE shoves JOHNNY who backs into the hot skillet and burns his back.)* Aaaaaaaaaaaaaaa!

FRANKIE. What's the matter—?

JOHNNY. Ooooooooooooooo!

FRANKIE. What happened—?

JOHNNY. Ow! Ow! Ow! Ow! Ow! Ow! Ow!

FRANKIE. Oh my God!

JOHNNY. Oooo! Oooo! Oooo! Ooooo! Oooo! Oooooo!

FRANKIE. I'm sorry, I didn't mean to—!

JOHNNY. Jesus, Frankie, Jesus Christ!

FRANKIE. Tell me what to do!

JOHNNY. Get something!

FRANKIE. What?

JOHNNY. Ice.

FRANKIE. Ice for burns? Don't move. *(FRANKIE puts the entire tray of ice cubes on JOHNNY's back. The scream that ensues is greater than the first one.)*

JOHNNY. AAAAAAAAAAAAAA-AAAAAAAAAAAA!!!!!!!!!!

FRANKIE. You said to—! (JOHNNY *nods vigorously.*) Should I keep it on? (JOHNNY *nods again, only this time he bites his fingers to keep from crying out.*) We'd be a terrific couple. One of us would be dead by the end of the first week. One date practically did it. All I asked you to do was turn off the eggs but no! everything has to be a big deal with you. I would have made the world's worst nurse.

JOHNNY (*Between gasps of pain*). Butter.

FRANKIE. What?

JOHNNY. Put some butter on it.

FRANKIE. Butter's bad on burns.

JOHNNY. I don't care.

FRANKIE. I may have some . . . oh what-do-you-call-it-when-you-have-a-sunburn, it comes in a squat blue bottle?

JOHNNY. Noxzema!

FRANKIE. That's it!

JOHNNY. It breaks me out. Get the butter.

FRANKIE. It's margarine.

JOHNNY. I don't care. (FRANKIE *gets the margarine out of the refrigerator.*)

FRANKIE. It sounds like you got a lot of allergies.

JOHNNY. Just those three.

FRANKIE. Catsup, Noxzema and . . . what was the other one?

JOHNNY. Fresh peaches. Canned are okay. (FRANKIE *puts the margarine on* JOHNNY's *back.*) Ooooooooooooo!

FRANKIE. Does that feel good?

JOHNNY. You have no idea.

FRANKIE. More?

JOHNNY. Yes, more. Don't stop.

FRANKIE. You're gonna smell like a . . . whatever a person covered in margarine smells like.

JOHNNY. I don't care.

FRANKIE. To tell the truth, it doesn't look all that bad.

JOHNNY. You think I'm faking this?

FRANKIE. I didn't say that.

JOHNNY. What do you want? Permanent scars? (*Pause.* FRANKIE *puts more margarine on* JOHNNY's *back.*)

FRANKIE. Did your first wife do this for you?

JOHNNY. Only wife. I told you that.

FRANKIE. Okay, so I was fishing.

JOHNNY. No, checking. Were you married?

FRANKIE. No, never.

JOHNNY. Anyone serious?

FRANKIE. Try "terminal."

JOHNNY. What happened?

FRANKIE. He got more serious with who I thought was my best friend.

JOHNNY. The same thing happened to me.

FRANKIE. You know what the main thing I felt was? Dumb.

JOHNNY. I know, I know!

FRANKIE. I even introduced them. I lent them money. Money from my credit union. I gave her my old television. A perfectly good Zenith. They're probably watching Charles Bronson together at this very moment. I hope it explodes and blows their faces off. No, I don't. I hope it blows up and the fumes kill them. Aren't there supposed to be poison gases in a television set?

JOHNNY. I wouldn't be surprised.

FRANKIE. That or he's telling her she looks like shit, who told her she could change her hair or where's his car keys or shut the fuck up, he's had a rough day. I didn't know how exhausting unemployment could be. God, why do we get involved with people it turns out hate us?

JOHNNY. Because. . . .

FRANKIE. . . . we hate ourselves. I know. I read the same book.

JOHNNY. How long has it been?

FRANKIE. Seven years. (JOHNNY *lets out a long stream of air.*) What? You, too? (JOHNNY *nods.*) Any kids?

JOHNNY. Two.

FRANKIE. You see them?

JOHNNY. Not as much as I'd like. She's remarried. They live in Maine in a beautiful house overlooking the sea.

FRANKIE. I bet it's not so beautiful.

JOHNNY. It's beautiful. I could never have provided them with anything like that. The first time I saw it, I couldn't get out of the car. I felt so ashamed. So forgotten. The kids came running out of the house. They looked so happy to see me but I couldn't feel happy back. All of a sudden, they looked like somebody else's kids. I couldn't even roll down the window. "What's the matter, Daddy?" I started crying. I couldn't stop. Sheila and her husband had to come out of the house to get me to come in. You know what I wanted to do? Run that crewcut asshole insurance salesman over and drive off with the three of them. I don't know where we would've gone. We'd probably still be driving.

FRANKIE. That would've been a dumb thing to do.

JOHNNY. I never said I was smart.

FRANKIE. I'll tell you a secret: you are.

JOHNNY. I said I was passionate. I don't let go of old things easy and I grab new things hard.

FRANKIE. Too hard.

JOHNNY. There's no such thing as too hard when you want something.

FRANKIE. Yes, there is, Johnny. The other person. *(There is a pause.* FRANKIE *has stopped working on* JOHNNY'*s back. Instead she just stares at it.* JOHNNY *looks straight ahead. The music has changed to the Shostakovich Second String Quartet.)*

JOHNNY. What are you doing back there?

FRANKIE. Nothing. You want more butter or ice or something? *(*JOHNNY *shakes his head.)*

JOHNNY. It's funny how you can talk to people better sometimes when you're not looking at them. You're right there. *(He points straight ahead.)* Clear as day.

FRANKIE. I bet no one ever said this was the most beautiful music ever written.

JOHNNY. I don't mind.

FRANKIE. I don't know what the radio was doing on that station in the first place. That's not my kind of music. But I could tell you were enjoying it and I guess I wanted you to think I had higher taste than I really do.

JOHNNY. So did I.

FRANKIE. I liked what he played for us though, but he didn't say its name.

JOHNNY. Maybe it doesn't need one. You just walk into a fancy record shop and ask for the most beautiful music ever written and that's what they hand you.

FRANKIE. Not if I was the salesperson. You'd get "Michelle" or "Eleanor Rigby" or "Lucy In the Sky With Diamonds." Something by the Beatles. I sort of lost interest in pop music when they stopped singing.

JOHNNY. The last record I bought was the Simon and Garfunkel Reunion in Central Park. It wasn't the same. You could tell they'd been separated.

FRANKIE. Sometimes I feel like it's still the Sixties. Or that they were ten or fifteen years ago, not twenty or twenty-five. I lost ten years of my life somewhere. I went to Bruce Springsteen last year and I was the oldest one there.

JOHNNY. Put your arms around me. *(*FRANKIE *puts her arms over* JOHNNY'*s shoulders.)* Tighter. *(*FRANKIE'*s hands begin to stroke* JOHNNY'*s chest and stomach.)* Do you like doing that?

FRANKIE. I don't mind.

JOHNNY. We touch our own bodies there and nothing happens. Something to do with electrons. We short-circuit ourselves. Stroke my tits. There! *(He tilts his head back until he is looking up at her.)* Give me your mouth.

*(*FRANKIE *bends over and kisses him. It is a long one.)* That tongue. Those lips. *(He pulls her down towards him for another long kiss.)* I want to die like this. Drown.

FRANKIE. What do you want from me?

JOHNNY. Everything. Your heart. Your soul. Your tits. Your mouth. Your fucking guts. I want it all. I want to be inside you. Don't hold back.

FRANKIE. I'm not holding back.

JOHNNY. Let go. I'll catch you.

FRANKIE. I'm right here.

JOHNNY. I want more. I need more.

FRANKIE. If I'd known what playing with your tit was gonna turn into—.

JOHNNY. Quit screwing with me, Frankie.

FRANKIE. You got a pretty weird notion of who's screwing with who. I said I liked you. I told you that. I'm perfectly ready to make love to you. Why do you have to start a big discussion about it. It's not like I am saying "no."

JOHNNY. I want you to do something.

FRANKIE. What?

JOHNNY. I want you to go down on me.

FRANKIE. No.

JOHNNY. I went down on you.

FRANKIE. That was different.

JOHNNY. How?

FRANKIE. That was then.

JOHNNY. Please.

FRANKIE. I'm not good at it.

JOHNNY. Hey, this isn't a contest. We're talking about making love.

FRANKIE. I don't want to right now.

JOHNNY. You want me to go down on you again?

FRANKIE. If I do it will you shut up about all this other stuff?

JOHNNY. You know I won't.

FRANKIE. Then go down on yourself.

JOHNNY. What happened? You were gonna do it.

FRANKIE. Anything to get you to quit picking at me. Go on, get out of here. Get somebody else to go down on you.

JOHNNY. I don't want somebody else to go down on me.

FRANKIE. Jesus! I just had a vision of what it's going to be like at work Monday after this! I'm not quitting my job. I was there first.

JOHNNY. What are you talking about?

FRANKIE. I don't think we're looking for the same thing.

JOHNNY. We are. Only I've found it and you've given up.

FRANKIE. Yes! Long before the sun ever rose on your ugly face.

JOHNNY. What scares you more? Marriage or kids?

FRANKIE. I'm not scared. And I told you: I can't have any.

JOHNNY. I told you: we can adopt.

FRANKIE. I don't love you.

JOHNNY. That wasn't the question.

FRANKIE. You hear what *you* want to hear.

JOHNNY. Do you know anybody who doesn't?

FRANKIE. Not all the time.

JOHNNY. You're only telling me you don't love me so you don't have to find out if you could. Just because you've given up on the possibility, I'm not going to let you drag me down with you. You're coming up to my level if I have to pull you by the hair.

FRANKIE. I'm not going anywhere with a man who for all his bullshit about marriage and kids and Shakespeare. . . .

JOHNNY. It's not bullshit!

FRANKIE. . . . Just wants me to go down on him.

JOHNNY. Pretend it was a metaphor.

FRANKIE. Fuck you it was a metaphor! It was a blowjob. What's a metaphor?

JOHNNY. Something that stands for something else.

FRANKIE. I was right the first time. A blow-job.

JOHNNY. A sensual metaphor for mutual acceptance.

FRANKIE. Fuck you. Besides, what's mutual about a blowjob?

JOHNNY. I made that up. I'm sorry. It wasn't a metaphor. It was just something I wanted us to do.

FRANKIE. And I didn't.

JOHNNY. Let go, will you! One lousy little peccadillo and it's off with his head!

FRANKIE. Stop using words I don't know. What's a peccadillo?

JOHNNY. A blowjob! Notice I haven't died you didn't do it!

FRANKIE. I noticed.

JOHNNY. And let me notice something for you: you wouldn't have died if you had. Thanks for making me feel about this big. *(He gets up and starts gathering and putting on his clothes.)* I'm sorry, I mistook you for a kindred spirit. Kindred: two of a kind, sharing a great affinity.

FRANKIE. I know what kindred means!

JOHNNY. Shall we go for affinity!

FRANKIE. That's the first really rotten thing you've said all night. Somebody who would make fun of somebody else's intelligence, no worse, their education or lack of—that is somebody I would be very glad not to know. I thought you were weird, Johnny. I thought you were sad. I didn't think you were cruel.

JOHNNY. I'm sorry.

FRANKIE. It's a cruelty just waiting to happen again and I don't want to be there when it does.

JOHNNY. Please! *(Theres is an urgency in his voice that startles FRANKIE.)* I'm not good with people. But I want to be. I can get away with it for long stretches but I always hang myself in the end.

FRANKIE. Hey, c'mon, don't cry. Please, don't cry.

JOHNNY. It's not cruelty. It's a feeling I don't matter. That nobody hears me. I'm drowning. I'm trying to swim back to shore but there's this tremendous undertow and I'm not getting anywhere. My arms and legs are going a mile a minute but they aren't taking me any closer to where I want to be.

FRANKIE. Where's that?

JOHNNY. With you.

FRANKIE. You don't know me.

JOHNNY. Yes, I do. It scares people how much we really know one another, so we pretend we don't. You know me. You've known me all your life. Only now I'm here. Take me. Use me. Try me. There's a reason we're called Frankie and Johnny.

FRANKIE. There's a million other Frankies out there and a billion other Johnnys. The world is filled with Frankies and Johnnys and Jacks and Jills.

JOHNNY. But only one this Johnny, one this Frankie.

FRANKIE. We're too different.

JOHNNY. You say po-tah-toes? All right, I'll say po-tah-toes! I don't care. I love you. I want to marry you.

FRANKIE. I don't say po-tah-toes. Who the hell says po-tah-toes?

JOHNNY. Are you listening to me?

FRANKIE. I'm trying very hard not to!

JOHNNY. That's your trouble. You don't want to hear anything you don't think you already know. Well I'll tell you something, Cinderella: Your Prince Charming has come. Wake up before another thousand years go by! Don't throw me away like a gum wrapper because you think there's something about me you may not like. I have what it takes to

378 _____

give you anything and everything you want. Maybe not up here . . . *(He taps his head.)* . . . or here . . . *(He slaps his hip where he wears his wallet.)* . . . but here. And that would please me enormously. All I ask back is that you use your capacity to be everyone and everything for me. It's within you. If we could do that for each other we'd give our kids the universe. They'd be Shakespeare and the most beautiful music ever written and a saint maybe or a champion athlete or a president all rolled into one. Terrific kids! How could they not be? We have a chance to make everything turn out all right again. Turn our back on everything that went wrong. We can begin right now and all over again but only if we begin right now, this minute, this room and us. I know this thing, Frankie.

FRANKIE. I want to show you something, Johnny. *(She pushes her hair back.)* He did that. The man I told you about. With a belt buckle. *(JOHNNY kisses the scar.)*

JOHNNY. It's gone now.

FRANKIE. It'll never go.

JOHNNY. It's gone. I made it go.

FRANKIE. What are you? My guardian angel?

JOHNNY. It seems to me the right people are our guardian angels.

FRANKIE. I wanted things, too, you know.

JOHNNY. I know.

FRANKIE. A man, a family, kids . . . He's the reason I can't have any.

JOHNNY. He's gone. Choose me. Hurry up. It's getting light out. I turn into a pumpkin.

FRANKIE *(Looking towards the window)*. It is getting light out! *(FRANKIE goes to the window.)*

JOHNNY. You are so beautiful standing there.

FRANKIE. The only time I saw the sun come up with a guy was my senior prom. *(JOHNNY has joined her at the window. As they stand there looking out, we will be aware of the rising sun.)* His name was Johnny Di Corso but everyone called him Skunk. *(She takes JOHNNY's hand and clasps it to her but her eyes stay looking out the window at the dawn.)* He was a head shorter than me and wasn't much to look at but nobody else had asked me. It was him or else. I was dreading it. But guess what? That boy could dance! You should have seen us. We were the stars of the prom. We did Lindys, the mambo, the Twist. The Monkey, the Frug. All the fast dances. Everybody's mouth was down to here. Afterwards we went out to the lake to watch the sun come up. He told me he was going to be on American Bandstand one day. I wonder if he ever made it. *(JOHNNY puts his arm around her and begins to move her in a slow dance step.)*

JOHNNY. There must be something about you and sunrises and men called Johnny.

FRANKIE. You got a nickname?

JOHNNY. No. You got to be really popular or really unpopular to have a nickname.

FRANKIE. I'll give you a nickname. *(They dance in silence a while. Silence, that is, except for the Shostakovich which they pay no attention to.)* You're not going to like me saying this but you're a terrible dancer.

JOHNNY. Show me.

FRANKIE. Like that.

JOHNNY. There?

FRANKIE. That's better.

JOHNNY. You're going to make a wonderful teacher. *(He starts to hum.)*

FRANKIE. What's that supposed to be?

JOHNNY. Something from *Brigadoon.*

FRANKIE. That isn't from *Brigadoon.* That isn't even remotely from *Brigadoon.* That isn't even remotely something from anything. *(They dance. FRANKIE begins to hum.)* That's something from *Brigadoon.* You can't have kids in a place this size.

JOHNNY. Who says?

FRANKIE. How big is your place?

JOHNNY. Even smaller. We'll be a nice snug family. It'll be wonderful.

FRANKIE. Does it always get light so fast this time of year?

JOHNNY. Unh-unh. The sun's in a hurry to shine on us.

FRANKIE. Pardon my French but that's bullshit.

JOHNNY. You can sleep all day today.

FRANKIE. What are you planning to do?

JOHNNY. Watch you.

FRANKIE. You're just weird enough to do it, too. Well forget it. I can't sleep with people watching me.

JOHNNY. How do you know?

FRANKIE. I was in the hospital for my gall bladder and I had a roommate who just stared at me all the time. I made them move me. I got a private room for the price of a semi. Is this the sort of stuff you look forward to finding out about me?

JOHNNY. Unh-hunh!

FRANKIE. You're nuts.

JOHNNY. I'm happy!

FRANKIE. Where are you taking me?

JOHNNY. The moon.

FRANKIE. That old place again?

JOHNNY. The other side this time. *(JOHNNY has slow-danced FRANKIE to the bed. The room is being quickly flooded with sunlight.)*

FRANKIE. If you don't turn into a pumpkin, what do you turn into?

JOHNNY. You tell me. *(He kisses her very gently.)*

FRANKIE. Just a minute. *(She gets up and moves quickly to the bathroom. JOHNNY turns off all the room lights. He starts to close the blinds but instead raises them even higher. Sunlight pours across him. The Shostakovich ends. JOHNNY moves quickly to the radio and turns up the volume as the announcer's voice is heard.)*

RADIO ANNOUNCER. . . . that just about winds up my stint in the control room. This has been Music Till Dawn with Marlon. I'm still thinking about Frankie and Johnny. God, how I wish you two really existed. Maybe I'm crazy but I'd still like to believe in love. Why the hell do you think I work these hours? Anyway, you two moonbeams, whoever, wherever you are, here's an encore. *(Debussy's "Clair de Lune" is heard again. JOHNNY sits, listening. He starts to cry he is so happy. He turns as FRANKIE comes out of the bathroom. She is brushing her teeth.)*

JOHNNY. They're playing our song again.

FRANKIE. Did they say what it was this time?

JOHNNY. I told you! You just walk into a record shop and ask for the most beautiful music . . .

FRANKIE. Watch us end up with something from *The Sound of Music,* you'll see! You want to brush? *(She motions with her thumb to the bathroom. She steps aside as JOHNNY passes her to go in.)* Don't worry. It's never been used. *(Still brushing her teeth, she goes to the window and looks out.)* Did you see the robins? *(She listens to the music.)* This I can see why people call pretty. *(She sits on the bed, listens and continues to brush her teeth. A little gasp of pleasure escapes her.)* Mmmmm! *(JOHNNY comes out of the bathroom. He is brushing his teeth.)*

JOHNNY. I'm not going to ask whose robe that is.

FRANKIE. Sshh! *(She is really listening to the music.)*

JOHNNY. We should get something with fluoride.

FRANKIE. Sshh!

JOHNNY. Anti-tartar build-up, too.

FRANKIE. Johnny! *(JOHNNY sits next to her on the bed. They are both brushing their teeth and listening to the music. They continue to brush their teeth and listen to the Debussy. The lights are fading.)*

End of the Play

Joe Turner's Come and Gone

AUGUST WILSON

FOR MY DAUGHTER, SAKINA ANSARI, WITH LOVE AND GRATITUDE FOR HER UNDER-
STANDING

Initially presented as staged reading at the Eugene O'Neill Theater Center's 1984 National Playwrights Conference. It opened on April 29, 1986, at the Yale Repertory Theatre, Lloyd Richards, Artistic Director, Benjamin Mordecai, Managing Director, in New Haven, Connecticut, with the following cast:

SETH HOLLY	Mel Winkler
BERTHA HOLLY	L. Scott Caldwell
BYNUM WALKER	Ed Hall
RUTHERFORD SELIG	Raynor Scheine
JEREMY FURLOW	Bo Rucker
HERALD LOOMIS	Charles S. Dutton
ZONIA LOOMIS	Cristal Coleman and LaJara Henderson at alternate performances
MATTIE CAMPBELL	Kimberleigh Burroughs
REUBEN MERCER	Casey Lydell Badger and LaMar James Fedrick at alternate performances
MOLLY CUNNINGHAM	Kimberly Scott
MARTHA PENTECOST	Angela Bassett

Directed by Lloyd Richards
Sets by Scott Bradley
Costumes by Pamela Peterson
Lighting by Michael Gianitti
Musical Direction: Dwight Andrews
Sound Design: Matthew Wiener
Production Stage Manager: Margaret Adair
Stage Manager: Ethan Ruber
Casting: Meg Simon/Fran Kumin

"It is August in Pittsburgh, 1911.... From the deep and the near South the sons and daughters of the newly freed African slaves wander into the city. Isolated, cut off from memory ... they arrive dazed and stunned, their heart kicking in their chest with a song worth singing" (from August Wilson's introduction to *Joe Turner's Come and Gone*).

Joe Turner's Come and Gone was staged in 1986 at the Yale Repertory Theatre by Lloyd Richards, the theatre's artistic director. It then played at the Arena Stage, Washington, D.C., in 1987, and opened on Broadway at the Ethel Barrymore Theatre in March 1988. *Joe Turner* is the result of a close collaboration between Wilson and Richards, who have also worked together on Wilson's plays *Ma Rainey's Black Bottom, Fences, The Piano Lesson,* and *Two Trains Running.* Wilson and Richards admit that they work hand in hand on the extensive rewrites in the continuing revision process that has come to characterize their work together. Claude Purdy, who has also directed Wilson's plays, states, "These plays are dreams. They're so strong and the writing is so fresh that they're like Play-Doh: No matter who interprets them, they hold their shape."

Joe Turner is set in a Pittsburgh boardinghouse. Although the play centers on Herald Loomis and his search for his missing wife, it is really an ensemble piece in which all the inhabitants and frequenters of the boardinghouse reveal themselves in their search for self-identity and purpose in a mystical and poignant drama.

Originally written as a short story, Wilson turned *Joe Turner* into a play for the National Playwrights Conference at the Eugene O'Neill Center. The piece's inspiration was the Romare Bearden collage *The Mill Hand's Lunch Bucket*, depicting a boardinghouse scene in which a figure wearing a hat and coat is hunched over a table in a posture Wilson describes as "abject defeat." It is an image, he states, that haunted him. "I was intrigued. I began to wonder *why* he was sitting there like that. Ultimately, he became Herald Loomis. 'Herald' because he's a herald, 'Loomis' because he's luminous." Wilson gave his grandmother Zonia's name to Loomis's daughter, and his grandfather's name to the character Bynum. "I always have a sense that I'm standing in my grandfather's shoes.... I have some very valuable antecedents, which I think any playwright has to be aware of...."

A secondary inspiration came from a recording of W. C. Handy's (blues is the foundation from which, the playwright states, his plays spring). Wilson quotes: "Joe Turner had a chain with forty links to take forty men away each time. Then at evening, the women would come home and say to one another: 'Haven't you heard? Joe Turner's come and gone.'"

Wilson thinks of his plays as tools for his audience, as nourishment "to sustain a man once he has left his father's house," Wilson says, quoting a line from James Baldwin. He uses myth and ritual in his plays and thinks of himself as a storyteller. Lloyd Richards says, "Some of the oldest ... traditions in theatre exist in storytelling. What a playwright needs is wit and wisdom and a great respect for life.... August Wilson has that."

August Wilson was born in Pittsburgh in 1945, one of six children. His father, a baker born in North Carolina, was absent from home most of the time, leaving Wilson's mother to raise and support the family on her own. A reader since the age of four, Wilson recalls that he was always fascinated with words—how they were formed and what they meant. From the age of twelve, the public library became his classroom, and he discovered Richard Wright, Langston Hughes, James Walker, Lorraine Hansberry, and Ralph Ellison. As a youth, he also hung around the neighborhood places where men gathered to talk and play. "These men became a social father to me and I perceived that I could gain some kind of wisdom about life...." Preparing to become a writer, Wilson observed the behavior and speech of people around him while he worked as a stock clerk and cook. In 1978, he decided to relocate to St. Paul, where he wrote scripts for the Science

Museum of Minnesota and became involved with the Playwrights Center in Minneapolis. While he was away from Pittsburgh, Wilson began to hear in his mind the speech of his old neighborhood as if for the first time: "I began to listen for the poetry that was inherent in my characters' speech instead of trying to force poetry into their mouths."

Wilson's first major achievement as a playwright was *Ma Rainey's Black Bottom,* first produced by the Eugene O'Neill Center. Its Broadway production received the New York Drama Critics Circle Award and several Tony nominations in 1984. *Fences,* his next play, progressed to Broadway from the Eugene O'Neill Center in 1987, winning the Pulitzer Prize for drama, the New York Drama Critics Circle Award, and four Tony Awards. *Joe Turner* and *The Piano Lesson* (1986) followed, the latter winning the 1990 Pulitzer Prize and the New York Drama Critics Circle Award. *Jitney, Fullerton Street,* and *Two Trains Running* are Wilson's most recent plays. Wilson plans to write a play for each decade of the twentieth century about the issues that have confronted black people. The plays have concerned and will continue to concern the themes of responsibility and the search for identity.

Wilson states that he works from impressions—images, lines, or ideas that root themselves in his mind. "I know very little about my characters when I start the dialogue. . . . I hear them in my mind talking. . . . I'm writing this down but the characters are really in control. . . . I've always thought of playwriting as essentially a mystical process." Other works by Wilson include *Black Bart, Mr. Jelly Roll, Man Going Down, Seven Guitars,* and the as-yet-unproduced screenplay for *Fences.* Wilson's poems have been published in various magazines and anthologies.

Wilson is also the recipient of a Guggenheim Fellowship, a winner of the Whiting Writer's Award and the Governor's Award for Excellence in the Arts, and a member of New Dramatists.

CHARACTERS

SETH HOLLY, *owner of the boardinghouse*
BERTHA HOLLY, *his wife*
BYNUM WALKER, *a rootworker*
RUTHERFORD SELIG, *a peddler*
JEREMY FURLOW, *a resident*
HERALD LOOMIS, *a resident*
ZONIA LOOMIS, *his daughter*
MATTIE CAMPBELL, *a resident*
REUBEN SCOTT, *boy who lives next door*
MOLLY CUNNINGHAM, *a resident*
MARTHA LOOMIS, *Herald Loomis's wife*

SETTING

August, 1911. A boardinghouse in Pittsburgh. At right is a kitchen. Two doors open off the kitchen. One leads to the outhouse and SETH's workshop. The other to SETH's and BERTHA's bedroom. At left is a parlor. The front door opens into the parlor, which gives access to the stairs leading to the upstairs rooms.

There is a small outside playing area.

THE PLAY

It is August in Pittsburgh, 1911. The sun falls out of heaven like a stone. The fires of the steel mill rage with a combined sense of industry and progress. Barges loaded with coal and iron ore trudge up the river to the mill towns that dot the Monongahela and return with fresh, hard, gleaming steel. The city flexes its muscles. Men throw countless bridges across the rivers, lay roads and carve tunnels through the hills sprouting with houses.

From the deep and the near South the sons and daughters of newly freed African slaves wander into the city. Isolated, cut off from memory, having forgotten the names of the gods and only guessing at their faces, they arrive dazed and stunned, their heart kicking in their chest with a song worth singing. They arrive carrying Bibles and guitars, their pockets lined with dust and fresh hope, marked men and women seeking to scrape from the narrow, crooked cobbles and the fiery blasts of the coke furnace a way of bludgeoning and shaping the malleable parts of themselves into a new identity as free men of definite and sincere worth.

Foreigners in a strange land, they carry as part and parcel of their baggage a long line of separation and dispersement which informs their sensibilities and marks their conduct as they search for ways to reconnect, to reassemble, to give clear and luminous meaning to the song which is both a wail and a whelp of joy.

ACT ONE

SCENE ONE

The lights come up on the kitchen. BERTHA *busies herself with breakfast preparations.* SETH *stands looking out the window at* BYNUM *in the yard.* SETH *is in his early fifties. Born of Northern free parents, a skilled craftsman, and owner of the boardinghouse, he has a stability that none of the other characters have.* BERTHA *is five years his junior. Married for over twenty-five years, she has learned how to negotiate around* SETH'S *apparent orneriness.*

————

SETH *(at the window, laughing).* If that ain't the damndest thing I seen. Look here, Bertha.
BERTHA. I done seen Bynum out there with them pigeons before.
SETH. Naw . . . naw . . . look at this. That pigeon flopped out of Bynum's hand and he about to have a fit.
*(*BERTHA *crosses over to the window.)*
He down there on his hands and knees behind that bush looking all over for that pigeon and it on the other side of the yard. See it over there?
BERTHA. Come on and get your breakfast and leave that man alone.
SETH. Look at him . . . he still looking. He ain't seen it yet. All that old mumbo jumbo nonsense. I don't know why I put up with it.
BERTHA. You don't say nothing when he bless the house.
SETH. I just go along with that 'cause of you. You around here sprinkling salt all over the place . . . got pennies lined up across the threshold . . . all that heebie-jeebie stuff. I just put up with that 'cause of you. I don't pay that kind of stuff no mind. And you going down there to the church and wanna come home and sprinkle salt all over the place.
BERTHA. It don't hurt none. I can't say if it help . . . but it don't hurt none.
SETH. Look at him. He done found that pigeon and now he's talking to it.

BERTHA. These biscuits be ready in a minute.

SETH. He done drew a big circle with that stick and now he's dancing around. I know he'd better not . . .

(SETH *bolts from the window and rushes to the back door.*)

Hey, Bynum! Don't be hopping around stepping in my vegetables.

Hey, Bynum . . . Watch where you stepping!

BERTHA. Seth, leave that man alone.

SETH (*coming back into the house*). I don't care how much he be dancing around . . . just don't be stepping in my vegetables. Man got my garden all messed up now . . . planting them weeds out there . . . burying them pigeons and whatnot.

BERTHA. Bynum don't bother nobody. He ain't even thinking about your vegetables.

SETH. I know he ain't! That's why he out there stepping on them.

BERTHA. What Mr. Johnson say down there?

SETH. I told him if I had the tools I could go out here and find me four or five fellows and open up my own shop instead of working for Mr. Olowski. Get me four or five fellows and teach them how to make pots and pans. One man making ten pots is five men making fifty. He told me he'd think about it.

BERTHA. Well, maybe he'll come to see it your way.

SETH. He wanted me to sign over the house to him. You know what I thought of that idea.

BERTHA. He'll come to see you're right.

SETH. I'm going up and talk to Sam Green. There's more than one way to skin a cat. I'm going up and talk to him. See if he got more sense than Mr. Johnson. I can't get nowhere working for Mr. Olowski and selling Selig five or six pots on the side. I'm going up and see Sam Green. See if he loan me the money.

(SETH *crosses back to the window.*)

Now he got that cup. He done killed that pigeon and now he's putting its blood in that little cup. I believe he drink that blood.

BERTHA. Seth Holly, what is wrong with you this morning? Come on and get your breakfast so you can go to bed. You know Bynum don't be drinking no pigeon blood.

SETH. I don't know what he do.

BERTHA. Well, watch him, then. He's gonna dig a little hole and bury that pigeon. Then he's gonna pray over that blood . . . pour it on top . . . mark out his circle and come on into the house.

SETH. That's what he doing . . . he pouring that blood on top.

BERTHA. When they gonna put you back working daytime? Told me two months ago he was gonna put you back working daytime.

SETH. That's what Mr. Olowski told me. I got to wait till he say when. He tell me what to do. I don't tell him. Drive me crazy to speculate on the man's wishes when he don't know what he want to do himself.

BERTHA. Well, I wish he go ahead and put you back working daytime. This working all hours of the night don't make no sense.

SETH. It don't make no sense for that boy to run out of here and get drunk so they lock him up either.

BERTHA. Who? Who they got locked up for being drunk?

SETH. That boy that's staying upstairs . . . Jeremy. I stopped down there on Logan Street on my way home from work and one of the fellows told me about it. Say he seen it when they arrested him.

BERTHA. I was wondering why I ain't seen him this morning.

SETH. You know I don't put up with that. I told him when he came . . .

(BYNUM *enters from the yard carrying some plants. He is a short, round man in his early sixties. A conjure man, or rootworker, he gives the impression of always being in control of everything. Nothing ever bothers him. He seems to be lost in a world of his own making and to swallow any adversity or interference with his grand design.*)

What you doing bringing them weeds in my house? Out there stepping on my vegetables and now wanna carry them weeds in my house.

BYNUM. Morning, Seth. Morning, Sister Bertha.

SETH. Messing up my garden growing them things out there. I ought to go out there and pull up all them weeds.

BERTHA. Some gal was by here to see you this morning, Bynum. You was out there in the yard . . . I told her to come back later.

BYNUM (*To* SETH). You look sick. What's the matter, you ain't eating right?

SETH. What if I was sick? You ain't getting near me with none of that stuff.

(BERTHA *sets a plate of biscuits on the table.*)

BYNUM. My . . . my . . . Bertha, your biscuits getting fatter and fatter.

(BYNUM *takes a biscuit and begins to eat.*)

Where Jeremy? I don't see him around this morning. He usually be around riffing and raffing on Saturday morning.

SETH. I know where he at. I know just where he at. They got him down there in the jail. Getting drunk and acting a fool. He down there where he belong with all that foolishness.

BYNUM. Mr. Piney's boys got him, huh? They ain't gonna do nothing but hold on to him for a little while. He's gonna be back here hungrier than a mule directly.

SETH. I don't go for all that carrying on and such. This is a respectable house. I don't have no drunkards or fools around here.

BYNUM. That boy got a lot of country in him. He ain't been up here but two weeks. It's gonna take a while before he can work that country out of him.

SETH. These niggers coming up here with that old backward country style of living. It's hard enough now without all that ignorant kind of acting. Ever since slavery got over with there ain't been nothing but foolish-acting niggers. Word get out they need men to work in the mill and put in these roads . . . and niggers drop everything and head North looking for freedom. They don't know the white fellows looking too. White fellows coming from all over the world. White fellow come over and in six months got more than what I got. But these niggers keep on coming. Walking . . . riding . . . carrying their Bibles. That boy done carried a guitar all the way from North Carolina. What he gonna find out? What he gonna do with that guitar? This is the city.

(*There is a knock on the door.*)

Niggers coming up here from the back-woods . . . coming up here from the country carrying Bibles and guitars looking for freedom. They got a rude awakening.

(SETH *goes to answer the door.* RUTHERFORD SELIG *enters. About* SETH's *age, he is a thin white man with greasy hair. A peddler, he supplies* SETH *with the raw materials to make pots and pans which he then peddles door to door in the mill towns along the river. He keeps a list of his customers as they move about and is known in the various communities as the People Finder. He carries squares of sheet metal under his arm.*)

Ho! Forgot you was coming today. Come on in.

BYNUM. If it ain't Rutherford Selig . . . the People Finder himself.

SELIG. What say there, Bynum?

BYNUM. I say about my shiny man. You got to tell me something. I done give you my dollar . . . I'm looking to get a report.

SELIG. I got eight here, Seth.

SETH (*Taking the sheet metal*). What is this? What you giving me here? What I'm gonna do with this?

SELIG. I need some dustpans. Everybody asking me about dustpans.

SETH. Gonna cost you fifteen cents apiece. And ten cents to put a handle on them.

SELIG. I'll give you twenty cents apiece with the handles.

SETH. Alright. But I ain't gonna give you but fifteen cents for the sheet metal.

SELIG. It's twenty-five cents apiece for the metal. That's what we agreed on.

SETH. This low-grade sheet metal. They ain't worth but a dime. I'm doing you a favor giving you fifteen cents. You know this metal ain't worth no twenty-five cents. Don't come talking that twenty-five cent stuff to me over no low-grade sheet metal.

SELIG. Alright, fifteen cents apiece. Just make me some dustpans out of them.

(SETH *exits with the sheet metal out the back door.*)

BERTHA. Sit on down there, Selig. Get you a cup of coffee and a biscuit.

BYNUM. Where you coming from this time?

SELIG. I been upriver. All along the Monongahela. Past Rankin and all up around Little Washington.

BYNUM. did you find anybody?

SELIG. I found Sadie Jackson up in Brad-dock. Her mother's staying down there in Scotchbottom say she hadn't heard from her and she didn't know where she was at. I found her up in Braddock on Enoch Street. She bought a frying pan from me.

BYNUM. You around here finding every-body how come you ain't found my shiny man?

SELIG. The only shiny man I saw was the Nigras working on the road gang with the sweat glistening on them.

BYNUM. Naw, you'd be able to tell this fellow. He shine like new money.

SELIG. Well, I done told you I can't find nobody without a name.

BERTHA. Here go one of these hot biscuits, Selig.

BYNUM. This fellow don't have no name. I call him John 'cause it was up around Johns-town where I seen him. I ain't even so sure he's one special fellow. That shine could pass on to anybody. He could be anybody shining.

SELIG. Well, what's he look like besides being shiny? There's lots of shiny Nigras.

BYNUM. He's just a man I seen out on the road. He ain't had no special look. Just a man walking toward me on the road. He come up and asked me which way the road went. I told him everything I knew about the road, where it went and all, and he asked me did I have anything to eat 'cause he was hungry. Say he ain't had nothing to eat in three days. Well, I never be out there on the road without a piece of dried meat. Or an orange or an apple. So I give this fellow an orange. He take and eat that orange and told me to come and go along the road a little ways with him, that he had something he wanted to show me. He had a look about him made me wanna go with him, see what he gonna show me. We walked on a bit and it's getting kind of far from where I met him when it come up on me all of a sudden, we wasn't going the way he had come from, we was going back my way. Since he said he ain't knew nothing about the road, I asked him about this. He say he had a voice inside him telling him which way to go and if I come and go along with him he was gonna show me the Secret of Life. Quite naturally I followed him. A fellow that's gonna show you the Secret of Life ain't to be taken lightly. We get near this bend in the road . . .

(SETH enters with an assortment of pots.)

SETH. I got six here, Selig.

SELIG. Wait a minute, Seth. Bynum's telling me about the secret of life. Go ahead, Bynum. I wanna hear this.

(SETH sets the pots down and exits out the back.)

BYNUM. We get near this bend in the road and he told me to hold out my hands. Then he rubbed them together with his and I looked down and see they got blood on them. Told me to take and rub it all over me . . . say that was a way of cleaning myself. Then we went around the bend in that road. Got around that bend and it seem like all of a sudden we ain't in the same place. Turn around that bend and everything look like it was twice as big as it was. The trees and everything bigger than life! Sparrows big as eagles! I turned around to look at this fellow and he had this light coming out of him. I had to cover up my eyes to keep from being blinded. He shining like new money with that light. He shined until all the light

seemed like it seeped out of him and then he was gone and I was by myself in this strange place where everything was bigger than life. I wandered around there looking for that road, trying to find my way back from this big place . . . and I looked over and seen my daddy standing there. He was the same size he always was, except for his hands and his mouth. He had a great big old mouth that look like it took up his whole face and his hands were as big as hams. Look like they was too big to carry around. My daddy called me to him. Said he had been thinking about me and it grieved him to see me in the world carrying other people's songs and not having one of my own. Told me he was gonna show me how to find my song. Then he carried me further into this big place until we come to this ocean. Then he showed me something I ain't got words to tell you. But if you stand to witness it, you done seen something there. I stayed in that place awhile and my daddy taught me the meaning of this thing that I had seen and showed me how to find my song. I asked him about the shiny man and he told me he was the One Who Goes Before and Shows the Way. Said there was lots of shiny men and if I ever saw one again before I died then I would know that my song had been accepted and worked its full power in the world and I could lay down and die a happy man. A man who done left his mark on life. On the way people cling to each other out of the truth they find in themselves. Then he showed me how to get back to the road. I came out to where everything was its own size and I had my song. I had the Binding Song. I choose that song because that's what I seen most when I was traveling . . . people walking away and leaving one another. So I takes the power of my song and binds them together.

(SETH enters from the yard carrying cabbages and tomatoes.)

Been binding people ever since. That's why they call me Bynum. Just like glue I sticks people together.

SETH. Maybe they ain't supposed to be stuck sometimes. You ever think of that?

BYNUM. Oh, I don't do it lightly. It cost me a piece of myself every time I do. I'm a Binder of What Clings. You got to find out if they cling first. You can't bind what don't cling.

SELIG. Well, how is that the Secret of Life? I thought you said he was gonna show you the secret of life. That's what I'm waiting to find out.

BYNUM. Oh, he showed me alright. But you still got to figure it out. Can't nobody figure it out for you. You got to come to it on your own. That's why I'm looking for the shiny man.

SELIG. Well, I'll keep my eye out for him. What you got there, Seth?

SETH. Here go some cabbage and tomatoes. I got some green beans coming in real nice. I'm gonna take and start me a grapevine out there next year. Butera says he gonna give me a piece of his vine and I'm gonna start that out there.

SELIG. How many of them pots you got?

SETH. I got six. That's six dollars minus eight on top of fifteen for the sheet metal come to a dollar twenty out the six dollars leave me four dollars and eighty cents.

SELIG *(Counting out the money).* There's four dollars . . . and . . . eighty cents.

SETH. How many of them dustpans you want?

SELIG. As many as you can make out them sheets.

SETH. You can use that many? I get to cutting on them sheets figuring how to make them dustpans . . . ain't no telling how many I'm liable to come up with.

SELIG. I can use them and you can make me some more next time.

SETH. Alright, I'm gonna hold you to that, now.

SELIG. Thanks for the biscuit, Bertha.

BERTHA. You know you welcome anytime, Selig.

SETH. Which way you heading?

SELIG. Going down to Wheeling. All through West Virginia there. I'll be back Saturday. They putting in new roads down that way. Makes traveling easier.

SETH. That's what I hear. All up around here too. Got a fellow staying here working on that road by the Brady Street Bridge.

SELIG. Yeah, it's gonna make traveling real nice. Thanks for the cabbage, Seth. I'll see you on Saturday.

(SELIG exits.)

SETH *(To BYNUM).* Why you wanna start all that nonsense talk with that man? All that shiny man nonsense.

BYNUM. You know it ain't no nonsense. Bertha know it ain't no nonsense. I don't know if Selig know or not.

BERTHA. Seth, when you get to making them dustpans make me a coffeepot.

SETH. What's the matter with your coffee? Ain't nothing wrong with your coffee. Don't she make some good coffee, Bynum?

BYNUM. I ain't worried about the coffee. I know she makes some good biscuits.

SETH. I ain't studying no coffeepot, woman. You heard me tell the man I was gonna cut as many dustpans as them sheets will make . . . and all of a sudden you want a coffeepot.

BERTHA. Man, hush up and go on and make me that coffeepot.

(JEREMY enters the front door. About twenty-five, he gives the impression that he has the world in his hand, that he can meet life's challenges head on. He smiles a lot. He is a proficient guitar player, though his spirit has yet to be molded into song.)

BYNUM. I hear Mr. Piney's boys had you.

JEREMY. Fined me two dollars for nothing! Ain't done nothing.

SETH. I told you when you come on here everybody know my house. Know these is respectable quarters. I don't put up with no foolishness. Everybody know Seth Holly keep a good house. Was my daddy's house. This house been a decent house for a long time.

JEREMY. I ain't done nothing, Mr. Seth. I stopped by the Workmen's Club and got me a bottle. Me and Roper Lee from Alabama. Had us a half pint. We was fixing to cut that half in two when they came up on us. Asked us if we was working. We told them we was putting in the road over yonder and that it was our payday. They snatched hold of us to get that two dollars. Me and Roper Lee ain't even had a chance to take a drink when they grabbed us.

SETH. I don't go for all that kind of carrying on.

BERTHA. Leave the boy alone, Seth. You know the police do that. Figure there's too many people out on the street they take some of them off. You know that.

SETH. I ain't gonna have folks talking.

BERTHA. Ain't nobody talking nothing. That's all in your head. You want some grits and biscuits. Jeremy?

JEREMY. Thank you, Miss Bertha. They didn't give us a thing to eat last night. I'll take one of them big bowls if you don't mind.

(There is a knock at the door. SETH goes to answer it. Enter HERALD LOOMIS and his eleven-year-old daughter, ZONIA. HERALD LOOMIS is thirty-two years old. He is at times possessed. A man driven not by the hellhounds that seemingly bay at his heels, but by his search for a world that

speaks to something about himself. He is unable to harmonize the forces that swirl around him, and seeks to recreate the world into one that contains his image. He wears a hat and a long wool coat.)

LOOMIS. Me and my daughter looking for a place to stay, mister. You got a sign say you got rooms.

(SETH stares at LOOMIS, sizing him up.)

Mister, if you ain't got no rooms we can go somewhere else.

SETH. How long you plan on staying?

LOOMIS. Don't know. Two weeks or more maybe.

SETH. It's two dollars a week for the room. We serve meals twice a day. It's two dollars for room and board. Pay up in advance.

(LOOMIS reaches into his pocket.)

It's a dollar extra for the girl.

LOOMIS. The girl sleep in the same room.

SETH. Well, do she eat off the same plate? We serve meals twice a day. That's a dollar extra for food.

LOOMIS. Ain't got no extra dollar. I was planning on asking your missus if she could help out with the cooking and cleaning and whatnot.

SETH. Her helping out don't put no food on the table. I need that dollar to buy some food.

LOOMIS. I'll give you fifty cents extra. She don't eat much.

SETH. Okay . . . but fifty cents don't buy but half a portion.

BERTHA. Seth, she can help me out. Let her help me out. I can use some help.

SETH. Well, that's two dollars for the week. Pay up in advance. Saturday to Saturday. You wanna stay on then it's two more come Saturday.

(LOOMIS pays SETH the money.)

BERTHA. My name's Bertha. This my husband, Seth. You got Bynum and Jeremy over there.

LOOMIS. Ain't nobody else live here?

BERTHA. They the only ones live here now. People come and go. They the only ones here now. You want a cup of coffee and a biscuit?

LOOMIS. We done ate this morning.

BYNUM. Where you coming from, Mister . . . I didn't get your name.

LOOMIS. Name's Herald Loomis. This my daughter, Zonia.

BYNUM. Where you coming from?

LOOMIS. Come from all over. Whichever-way the road take us that's the way we go.

JEREMY. If you looking for a job, I'm work-ing putting in that road down there by the bridge. They can't get enough mens. Always looking to take somebody on.

LOOMIS. I'm looking for a woman named Martha Loomis. That's my wife. Got married legal with the papers and all.

SETH. I don't know nobody named Loomis. I know some Marthas but I don't know no Loomis.

BYNUM. You got to see Rutherford Selig if you wanna find somebody. Selig's the People Finder. Rutherford Selig's a first-class People Finder.

JEREMY. What she look like? Maybe I seen her.

LOOMIS. She a brownskin woman. Got long pretty hair. About five feet from the ground.

JEREMY. I don't know. I might have seen her.

BYNUM. You got to see Rutherford Selig. You give him one dollar to get her name on his list . . . and after she get her name on his list Rutherford Selig will go right on out there and find her. I got him looking for somebody for me.

LOOMIS. You say he find people. How you find him?

BYNUM. You just missed him. He's gone downriver now. You got to wait till Saturday. He's gone downriver with his pots and pans. He come to see Seth on Saturdays. You got to wait till then.

SETH. Come on, I'll show you to your room.

(SETH, LOOMIS, and ZONIA exit up the stairs.)

JEREMY. Miss Bertha, I'll take that biscuit you was gonna give that fellow, if you don't mind. Say, Mr. Bynum, they got somebody like that around here sure enough? Somebody that find people?

BYNUM. Rutherford Selig. He go around selling pots and pans and every house he come to he write down the name and address of whoever lives there. So if you looking for somebody, quite naturally you go and see him . . . 'cause he's the only one who know where everybody live at.

JEREMY. I ought to have him look for this old gal I used to know. It be nice to see her again.

BERTHA *(Giving JEREMY a biscuit)*. Jeremy, today's the day for you to pull them sheets off the bed and set them outside your door. I'll set you out some clean ones.

BYNUM. Mr. Piney's boys done ruined your

good time last night, Jeremy . . . what you planning for tonight?

JEREMY. They got me scared to go out, Mr. Bynum. They might grab me again.

BYNUM. You ought to take your guitar and go down to Seefus. Seefus got a gambling place down there on Wylie Avenue. You ought to take your guitar and go down there. They got guitar contest down there.

JEREMY. I don't play no contest, Mr. Bynum. Had one of them white fellows cure me of that. I ain't been nowhere near a contest since.

BYNUM. White fellow beat you playing guitar?

JEREMY. Naw, he ain't beat me. I was sitting at home just fixing to sit down and eat when somebody come up to my house and got me. Told me there's a white fellow say he was gonna give a prize to the best guitar player he could find. I take up my guitar and go down there and somebody had gone up and got Bobo Smith and brought him down there. Him and another fellow called Hooter. Old Hooter couldn't play no guitar, he do more hollering than playing, but Bobo could go at it awhile.

This fellow standing there say he the one that was gonna give the prize and me and Bobo started playing for him. Bobo play something and then I'd try to play something better than what he played. Old Hooter, he just holler and bang at the guitar. Man was the worst guitar player I ever seen. So me and Bobo played and after a while I seen where he was getting the attention of this white fellow. He'd play something and while he was playing it he be slapping on the side of the guitar, and that made it sound like he was playing more than he was. So I started doing it too. White fellow ain't knew no difference. He ain't knew as much about guitar playing as Hooter did. After we play awhile, the white fellow called us to him and said he couldn't make up his mind, say all three of us was the best guitar player and we'd have to split the prize between us. Then he give us twenty-five cents. That's eight cents apiece and a penny on the side. That cured me of playing contest to this day.

BYNUM. Seefus ain't like that. Seefus give a whole dollar and a drink of whiskey.

JEREMY. What night they be down there?

BYNUM. Be down there every night. Music don't know no certain night.

BERTHA. You go down to Seefus with them people and you liable to end up in a raid and go to jail sure enough. I don't know why Bynum tell you that.

BYNUM. That's where the music at. That's where the people at. The people down there making music and enjoying themselves. Some things is worth taking the chance going to jail about.

BERTHA. Jeremy ain't got no business going down there.

JEREMY. They got some women down there, Mr. Bynum?

BYNUM. Oh, they got women down there, sure. They got women everywhere. Women be where the men is so they can find each other.

JEREMY. Some of them old gals come out there where we be putting in that road. Hanging around there trying to snatch somebody.

BYNUM. How come some of them ain't snatched hold of you?

JEREMY. I don't want them kind. Them desperate kind. Ain't nothing worse than a desperate woman. Tell them you gonna leave them and they get to crying and carrying on. That just make you want to get away quicker. They get to cutting up your clothes and things trying to keep you staying. Desperate women ain't nothing but trouble for a man.

(SETH *enters from the stairs.*)

SETH. Something ain't setting right with that fellow.

BERTHA. What's wrong with him? What he say?

SETH. I take him up there and try to talk to him and he ain't for no talking. Say he been traveling . . . coming over from Ohio. Say he a deacon in the church. Say he looking for Martha Pentecost. Talking about that's his wife.

BERTHA. How you know it's the same Martha? Could be talking about anybody. Lots of people named Martha.

SETH. You see that little girl? I didn't hook it up till he said it, but that little girl look just like her. Ask Bynum. (*To* BYNUM.) Bynum. Don't that little girl look just like Martha Pentecost?

BERTHA. I still say he could be talking about anybody.

SETH. The way he described her wasn't no doubt about who he was talking about. Described her right down to her toes.

BERTHA. What did you tell him?

SETH. I ain't told him nothing. The way that fellow look I wasn't gonna tell him nothing. I don't know what he looking for her for.

BERTHA. What else he have to say?

SETH. I told you he wasn't for no talking. I told him where the outhouse was and to keep that gal off the front porch and out of my garden. He asked if you'd mind setting a hot tub for the gal and that was about the gist of it.

BERTHA. Well, I wouldn't let it worry me if I was you. Come on get your sleep.

BYNUM. He says he looking for Martha and he a deacon in the church.

SETH. That's what he say. Do he look like a deacon to you?

BERTHA. He might be, you don't know. Bynum ain't got no special say on whether he a deacon or not.

SETH. Well, if he the deacon I'd sure like to see the preacher.

BERTHA. Come on get your sleep. Jeremy, don't forget to set them sheets outside the door like I told you.

(BERTHA *exits into the bedroom.*)

SETH. Something ain't setting right with that fellow, Bynum. He's one of them mean-looking niggers look like he done killed somebody gambling over a quarter.

BYNUM. He ain't no gambler. Gamblers wear nice shoes. This fellow got on clodhoppers. He been out there walking up and down them roads.

(ZONIA *enters from the stairs and looks around.*)

BYNUM. You looking for the back door, sugar? There it is. You can go out there and play. It's alright.

SETH (*Showing her the door*). You can go out there and play. Just don't get in my garden. And don't go messing around in my workshed.

(SETH *exits into the bedroom. There is a knock on the door.*)

JEREMY. Somebody at the door.

(JEREMY *goes to answer the door. Enter* MATTIE CAMPBELL. *She is a young woman of twenty-six whose attractiveness is hidden under the weight and concerns of a dissatisfied life. She is a woman in an honest search for love and companionship. She had suffered many defeats in her search, and though not always uncompromising, still believes in the possibility of love.*)

MATTIE. I'm looking for a man named Bynum. Lady told me to come back later.

JEREMY. Sure, he here. Mr. Bynum, somebody here to see you.

BYNUM. Come to see me, huh?

MATTIE. Are you the man they call Bynum? The man folks say can fix things?

BYNUM. Depend on what need fixing. I can't make no promises. But I got a powerful song in some matters.

MATTIE. Can you fix it so my man come back to me?

BYNUM. Come on in . . . have a sit down.

MATTIE. You got to help me. I don't know what else to do.

BYNUM. Depend on how all the circumstances of the thing come together. How all the pieces fit.

MATTIE. I done everything I knowed how to do. You got to make him come back to me.

BYNUM. It ain't nothing to make somebody come back. I can fix it so he can't stand to be away from you. I got my roots and powders, I can fix it so wherever he's at this thing will come up on him and he won't be able to sleep for seeing your face. Won't be able to eat for thinking of you.

MATTIE. That's what I want. Make him come back.

BYNUM. The roots is a powerful thing. I can fix it so one day he'll walk out his front door . . . won't be thinking of nothing. He won't know what it is. All he knows is that a powerful dissatisfaction done set in his bones and can't nothing he do make him feel satisfied. He'll set his foot down on the road and the wind in the trees be talking to him and everywhere he step on the road, that road'll give back your name and something will pull him right up to your doorstep. Now, I can do that. I can take my roots and fix that easy. But maybe he ain't supposed to come back. And if he ain't supposed to come back . . . then he'll be in your bed one morning and it'll come up on him that he's in the wrong place. That he's lost outside of time from his place that he's supposed to be in. Then both of you be lost and trapped outside of life and ain't no way for you to get back into it. 'Cause you lost from yourselves and where the places come together, where you're supposed to be alive, your heart kicking in your chest with a song worth singing.

MATTIE. Make him come back to me. Make his feet say my name on the road. I don't care what happens. Make him come back.

BYNUM. What's your man's name?

MATTIE. He go by Jack Carper. He was born in Alabama then he come to West Texas and find me and we come here. Been here three years before he left. Say I had a curse prayer on me and he started walking down the road and ain't never come back. Somebody told me, say you can fix things like that.

BYNUM. He just got up one day, set his feet on the road, and walked away?

MATTIE. You got to make him come back, mister.

BYNUM. Did he say goodbye?

MATTIE. Ain't said nothing. Just started walking. I could see where he disappeared. Didn't look back. Just keep walking. Can't you fix it so he come back? I ain't got no curse prayer on me. I know I ain't.

BYNUM. What made him say you had a curse prayer on you?

MATTIE. 'Cause the babies died. Me and Jack had two babies. Two little babies that ain't lived two months before they died. He say it's because somebody cursed me not to have babies.

BYNUM. He ain't bound to you if the babies died. Look like somebody trying to keep you from being bound up and he's gone on back to whoever it is 'cause he's already bound up to her. Ain't nothing to be done. Somebody else done got a powerful hand in it and ain't nothing to be done to break it. You got to let him go find where he's supposed to be in the world.

MATTIE. Jack done gone off and you telling me to forget about him. All my life I been looking for somebody to stop and stay with me. I done already got too many things to forget about. I take Jack Carper's hand and it feel so rough and strong. Seem like he's the strongest man in the world the way he hold me. Like he's bigger than the whole world and can't nothing bad get to me. Even when he act mean sometimes he still make everything seem okay with the world. Like there's part of it that belongs just to you. Now you telling me to forget about him?

BYNUM. Jack Carper gone off to where he belong. There's somebody searching for your doorstep right now. Ain't no need you fretting over Jack Carper. Right now he's a strong thought in your mind. But every time you catch yourself fretting over Jack Carper you push that thought away. You push it out your mind and that thought will get weaker and weaker till you wake up one morning and you won't even be able to call him up on your mind.

(BYNUM gives her a small cloth packet.)

Take this and sleep with it under your pillow and it'll bring good luck to you. Draw it to you like a magnet. It won't be long before you forget all about Jack Carper.

MATTIE. How much . . . do I owe you?

BYNUM. Whatever you got there . . . that'll be alright.

(MATTIE hands BYNUM two quarters. She crosses to the door.)

You sleep with that under your pillow and you'll be alright.

(MATTIE opens the door to exit and JEREMY crosses over to her. BYNUM overhears the first part of their conversation, then exits out the back.)

JEREMY. I overheard what you told Mr. Bynum. Had me an old gal did that to me. Woke up one morning and she was gone. Just took off to parts unknown. I woke up that morning and the only thing I could do was look around for my shoes. I woke up and got out of there. Found my shoes and took off. That's the only thing I could think of to do.

MATTIE. She ain't said nothing?

JEREMY. I just looked around for my shoes and got out of there.

MATTIE. Jack ain't said nothing either. He just walked off.

JEREMY. Some mens do that. Womens too. I ain't gone off looking for her. I just let her go. Figure she had a time to come to herself. Wasn't no use of me standing in the way. Where you from?

MATTIE. Texas. I was born in Georgia but I went to Texas with my mama. She dead now. Was picking peaches and fell dead away. I come up here with Jack Carper.

JEREMY. I'm from North Carolina. Down around Raleigh where they got all that tobacco. Been up here about two weeks. I likes it fine except I still got to find me a woman. You got a nice look to you. Look like you have mens standing in your door. Is you got mens standing in your door to get a look at you?

MATTIE. I ain't got nobody since Jack left.

JEREMY. A woman like you need a man. Maybe you let me be your man. I got a nice way with the women. That's what they tell me.

MATTIE. I don't know. Maybe Jack's coming back.

JEREMY. I'll be your man till he come. A woman can't be by her lonesome. Let me be your man till he come.

MATTIE. I just can't go through life piecing myself out to different mens. I need a man who wants to stay with me.

JEREMY. I can't say what's gonna happen. Maybe I'll be the man. I don't know. You wanna go along the road a little ways with me?

MATTIE. I don't know. Seem like life say it's gonna be one thing and end up being another. I'm tired of going from man to man.

JEREMY. Life is like you got to take a chance. Everybody got to take a chance. Can't nobody say what's gonna be. Come on . . . take a chance with me and see what the year bring. Maybe you let me come and see you. Where you staying?

MATTIE. I got me a room up on Bedford. Me and Jack had a room together.

JEREMY. What's the address? I'll come by and get you tonight and we can go down to Seefus. I'm going down there and play my guitar.

MATTIE. You play guitar?

JEREMY. I play guitar like I'm born to it.

MATTIE. I live at 1727 Bedford Avenue. I'm gonna find out if you can play guitar like you say.

JEREMY. I plays it, sugar, and that ain't all I do. I got a ten-pound hammer and I knows how to drive it down. Good god . . . you ought to hear my hammer ring!

MATTIE. Go on with that kind of talk, now. If you gonna come by and get me I got to get home and straighten up for you.

JEREMY. I'll be by at eight o'clock. How's eight o'clock? I'm gonna make you forget all about Jack Carper.

MATTIE. Go on, now. I got to get home and fix up for you.

JEREMY. Eight o'clock, sugar.

(The lights go down in the parlor and come up on the yard outside. ZONIA *is singing and playing a game.)*

ZONIA. I went downtown
To get my grip
I came back home
Just a pullin' the skiff
I went upstairs
To make my bed
I made a mistake
And I bumped my head
Just a pullin' the skiff

I went downstairs
To milk the cow
I made a mistake
And I milked the sow
Just a pullin' the skiff

Tomorrow, tomorrow
Tomorrow never comes
The marrow the marrow
The marrow in the bone.

*(*REUBEN *enters.)*

REUBEN. Hi.

ZONIA. Hi.

REUBEN. What's your name?

ZONIA. Zonia.

REUBEN. What kind of name is that?

ZONIA. It's what my daddy named me.

REUBEN. My name's Reuben. You staying in Mr. Seth's house?

ZONIA. Yeah.

REUBEN. That your daddy I seen you with this morning?

ZONIA. I don't know. Who you see me with?

REUBEN. I saw you with some man had on a great big old coat. And you was walking up to Mr. Seth's house. Had on a hat too.

ZONIA. Yeah, that's my daddy.

REUBEN. You like Mr. Seth?

ZONIA. I ain't see him much.

REUBEN. My grandpap say he a great big old windbag. How come you living in Mr. Seth's house? Don't you have no house?

ZONIA. We going to find my mother.

REUBEN. Where she at?

ZONIA. I don't know. We got to find her. We just go all over.

REUBEN. Why you got to find her? What happened to her?

ZONIA. She ran away.

REUBEN. Why she run away?

ZONIA. I don't know. My daddy say some man named Joe Turner did something bad to him once and that made her run away.

REUBEN. Maybe she coming back and you don't have to go looking for her.

ZONIA. We ain't there no more.

REUBEN. She could have come back when you wasn't there.

ZONIA. My daddy said she ran off and left us so we going looking for her.

REUBEN. What he gonna do when he find her?

ZONIA. He didn't say. He just say he got to find her.

REUBEN. Your daddy say how long you staying in Mr. Seth's house?

ZONIA. He don't say much. But we never stay too long nowhere. He say we got to keep moving till we find her.

REUBEN. Ain't no kids hardly live around here. I had me a friend but he died. He was the best friend I ever had. Me and Eugene used to keep secrets. I still got his pigeons. He told me to let them go when he died. He say, "Reuben, promise me when I die you'll let my pigeons go." But I keep them to remember him by. I ain't never gonna let them go. Even when I get to be grown up. I'm just always gonna have Eugene's pigeons.

(Pause.)

Mr. Bynum a conjure man. My grandpap scared of him. He don't like me to come over here too much. I'm scared of him too. My grandpap told me not to let him get close enough to where he can reach out his hand and touch me.

ZONIA. He don't seem scary to me.

REUBEN. He buys pigeons from me . . . and if you get up early in the morning you can see him out in the yard doing something with them pigeons. My grandpap say he kill them. I sold him one yesterday. I don't know what he do with it. I just hope he don't spook me up.

ZONIA. Why you sell him pigeons if he's gonna spook you up?

REUBEN. I just do like Eugene do. He used to sell Mr. Bynum pigeons. That's how he got to collecting them to sell to Mr. Bynum. Sometime he give me a nickel and sometime he give me a whole dime.

*(*LOOMIS *enters from the house.)*

LOOMIS. Zonia!

ZONIA. Sir?

LOOMIS. What you doing?

ZONIA. Nothing.

LOOMIS. You stay around this house, you hear? I don't want you wandering off nowhere.

ZONIA. I ain't wandering off nowhere.

LOOMIS. Miss Bertha set that hot tub and you getting a good scrubbing. Get scrubbed up good. You ain't been scrubbing.

ZONIA. I been scrubbing.

LOOMIS. Look at you. You growing too fast. Your bones getting bigger everyday. I don't want you getting grown on me. Don't you get grown on me too soon. We gonna find your mamma. She around here somewhere. I can smell her. You stay on around this house now. Don't you go nowhere.

ZONIA. Yes, sir.

*(*LOOMIS *exits into the house.)*

REUBEN. Wow, your daddy's scary!

ZONIA. He is not! I don't know what you talking about.

REUBEN. He got them mean-looking eyes!

ZONIA. My daddy ain't got no mean-looking eyes!

REUBEN. Aw, girl, I was just messing with you. You wanna go see Eugene's pigeons? Got a great big coop out the back of my house. Come on, I'll show you.

*(*REUBEN *and* ZONIA *exit as the lights go down.)*

SCENE TWO

It is Saturday morning, one week later. The lights come up on the kitchen. BERTHA *is at the stove preparing breakfast while* SETH *sits at the table.*

———

SETH. Something ain't right about that fellow. I been watching him all week. Something ain't right, I'm telling you.

BERTHA. Seth Holly, why don't you hush up about that man this morning?

SETH. I don't like the way he stare at everybody. Don't look at you natural like. He just be staring at you. Like he trying to figure out something about you. Did you see him when he come back in here?

BERTHA. That man ain't thinking about you.

SETH. He don't work nowhere. Just go out and come back. Go out and come back.

BERTHA. As long as you get your boarding money it ain't your cause about what he do. He don't bother nobody.

SETH. Just go out and come back. Going around asking everybody about Martha. Like Henry Allen seen him down at the church last night.

BERTHA. The man's allowed to go to church if he want. He say he a deacon. Ain't nothing wrong about him going to church.

SETH. I ain't talking about him going to church. I'm talking about him hanging around *outside* the church.

BERTHA. Henry Allen say that?

SETH. Say he be standing around outside the church. Like he be watching it.

BERTHA. What on earth he wanna be watching the church for, I wonder?

SETH. That's what I'm trying to figure out. Looks like he be fixing to rob it.

BERTHA. Seth, now do he look like the kind that would rob the church?

SETH. I ain't saying that. I ain't saying how he look. It's how he do. Anybody liable to do anything as far as I'm concerned. I ain't never thought about how no church robbers look . . . but now that you mention it, I don't see where they look no different than how he look.

BERTHA. Herald Loomis ain't the kind of man who would rob no church.

SETH. I ain't even so sure that's his name.

BERTHA. Why the man got to lie about his name?

SETH. Anybody can tell anybody anything about what their name is. That's what you call him . . . Herald Loomis. His name is liable to be anything.

BERTHA. Well, until he tell me different that's what I'm gonna call him. You just getting yourself all worked up about the man for nothing.

SETH. Talking about Loomis: Martha's name wasn't no Loomis nothing. Martha's name is Pentecost.

BERTHA. How you so sure that's her right name? Maybe she changed it.

SETH. Martha's a good Christian woman. This fellow here look like he owe the devil a day's work and he's trying to figure out how he gonna pay him. Martha ain't had a speck of distrust about her the whole time she was living here. They moved the church out there to Rankin and I was sorry to see her go.

BERTHA. That's why he be hanging around the church. He looking for her.

SETH. If he looking for her, why don't he go inside and ask? What he doing hanging around outside the church acting sneaky like?

(BYNUM enters from the yard.)

BYNUM. Morning, Seth. Morning, Sister Bertha.

(BYNUM continues through the kitchen and exits up the stairs.)

BERTHA. That's who you should be asking the questions. He been out there in that yard all morning. He was out there before the sun come up. He didn't even come in for breakfast. I don't know what he's doing. He had three of them pigeons line up out there. He dance around till he get tired. He sit down awhile then get up and dance some more. He come through here a little while ago looking like he was mad at the world.

SETH. I don't pay Bynum no mind. He don't spook me up with all that stuff.

BERTHA. That's how Martha come to be living here. She come to see Bynum. She come to see him when she first left from down South.

SETH. Martha was living here before Bynum. She ain't come on here when she first left from down there. She come on here after she went back to get her little girl. That's when she come on here.

BERTHA. Well, where was Bynum? He was here when she came.

SETH. Bynum ain't come till after her. That boy Hiram was staying up there in Bynum's room.

BERTHA. Well, how long Bynum been here?

SETH. Bynum ain't been here no longer than three years. That's what I'm trying to tell you. Martha was staying up there and sewing and cleaning for Doc Goldblum when Bynum came. This the longest he ever been in one place.

BERTHA. How you know how long the man been in one place?

SETH. I know Bynum. Bynum ain't no mystery to me. I done seen a hundred niggers like him. He's one of them fellows never could stay in one place. He was wandering all around the country till he got old and settled here. The only thing different about Bynum is he bring all this heebie-geebie stuff with him.

BERTHA. I still say he was staying here when she came. That's why she came . . . to see him.

SETH. You can say what you want. I know the facts of it. She come on here four years ago all heartbroken 'cause she couldn't find her little girl. And Bynum wasn't nowhere around. She got mixed up in that old heebie-jeebie nonsense with him after he came.

BERTHA. Well, if she came on before Bynum I don't know where she stayed. 'Cause she stayed up there in Hiram's room. Hiram couldn't get along with Bynum and left out of here owing you two dollars. Now, I know you ain't forgot about that!

SETH. Sure did! You know Hiram ain't paid me that two dollars yet. So that's why he be ducking and hiding when he see me down on Logan Street. You right. Martha did come on after Bynum. I forgot that's why Hiram left.

BERTHA. Him and Bynum never could see eye to eye. They always rubbed each other the wrong way. Hiram got to thinking that Bynum was trying to put a fix on him and he moved out. Martha came to see Bynum and ended up taking Hiram's room. Now, I know what I'm talking about. She stayed on here three years till they moved the church.

SETH. She out there in Rankin now. I know where she at. I know where they moved the church to. She right out there in Rankin in that place used to be shoe store. Used to be Wolf's shoe store. They moved to a bigger place and they put that church in there. I know where she at. I know just where she at.

BERTHA. Why don't you tell the man? You see he looking for her.

SETH. I ain't gonna tell that man where that woman is! What I wanna do that for? I don't know nothing about that man. I don't know why he looking for her. He might wanna do her a harm. I ain't gonna carry that on my hands. He looking for her, he gonna have to find her for himself. I ain't gonna help him. Now, if he had come and presented himself as a gentleman—the way Martha Pentecost's husband would have done—then I would have told him. But I ain't gonna tell this old wild-eyed mean-looking nigger nothing!

BERTHA. Well, why don't you get a ride with Selig and go up there and tell her where he is? See if she wanna see him. If that's her little girl . . . you say Martha was looking for her.

SETH. You know me, Bertha. I don't get mixed up in nobody's business.

(BYNUM enters from the stairs.)

BYNUM. Morning, Seth. Morning, Bertha. Can I still get some breakfast? Mr. Loomis been down here this morning?

SETH. He done gone out and come back. He up there now. Left out of here early this morning wearing that coat. Hot as it is, the man wanna walk around wearing a big old heavy coat. He come back in here paid me for another week, sat down there waiting on Selig. Got tired of waiting and went on back upstairs.

BYNUM. Where's the little girl?

SETH. She out there in the front. Had to chase her and that Reuben off the front porch. She out there somewhere.

BYNUM. Look like if Martha was around here he would have found her by now. My guess is she ain't in the city.

SETH. She ain't! I know where she at. I know just where she at. But I ain't gonna tell him. Not the way he look.

BERTHA. Here go your coffee, Bynum.

BYNUM. He says he gonna get Selig to find her for him.

SETH. Selig can't find her. He talk all that . . . but unless he get lucky and knock on her door he can't find her. That's the only way he find anybody. He got to get lucky. But I know just where she at.

BERTHA. Here go some biscuits, Bynum.

BYNUM. What else you got over there, Sister Bertha? You got some grits and gravy over there? I could go for some of that this morning.

BERTHA (Sets a bowl on the table). Seth, come on and help me turn this mattress over. Come on.

SETH. Something ain't right with that fellow, Bynum. I don't like the way he stare at everybody.

BYNUM. Mr. Loomis alright, Seth. He just a man got something on his mind. He just got a straightforward mind, that's all.

SETH. What's that fellow that they had around here? Moses, that's Moses Houser. Man went crazy and jumped off the Brady Street Bridge. I told you when I seen him something wasn't right about him. And I'm telling you about this fellow now.

(There is a knock on the door. SETH goes to answer it. Enter RUTHERFORD SELIG.)

Ho! Come on in, Selig.

BYNUM. If it ain't the People Finder himself.

SELIG. Bynum, before you start . . . I ain't seen no shiny man now.

BYNUM. Who said anything about that? I ain't said nothing about that. I just called you a first-class People Finder.

SELIG. How many dustpans you get out of that sheet metal, Seth?

SETH. You walked by them on your way in. They sitting out there on the porch. Got twenty-eight. Got four out of each sheet and made Bertha a coffeepot out the other one. They a little small but they got nice handles.

SELIG. That was twenty cents apiece, right? That's what we agreed on.

SETH. That's five dollars and sixty cents. Twenty on top of twenty-eight. How many sheets you bring me?

SELIG. I got eight out there. That's a dollar twenty makes me owe you . . .

SETH. Four dollars and forty cents.

SELIG (Paying him). Go on and make me some dustpans. I can use all you can make.

(LOOMIS enters from the stairs.)

LOOMIS. I been watching for you. He say you find people.

BYNUM. Mr. Loomis here wants you to find his wife.

LOOMIS. He say you find people. Find her for me.

SELIG. Well, let see here . . . find somebody, is it?

(SELIG *rummages through his pockets. He has several notebooks and he is searching for the right one.*)

Alright now . . . what's the name?

LOOMIS. Martha Loomis. She my wife. Got married legal with the paper and all.

SELIG *(Writing)*. Martha . . . Loomis. How tall is she?

LOOMIS. She five feet from the ground.

SELIG. Five feet . . . tall. Young or old?

LOOMIS. She a young woman. Got long pretty hair.

SELIG. Young . . . long . . . pretty . . . hair. Where did you last see her?

LOOMIS. Tennessee. Nearby Memphis.

SELIG. When was that?

LOOMIS. Nineteen hundred and one.

SELIG. Nineteen . . . hundred and one. I'll tell you, mister . . . you better off without them. Now you take me . . . old Rutherford Selig could tell you a thing or two about these women. I ain't met one yet I could understand. Now, you take Sally out there. That's all a man needs is a good horse. I say giddup and she go. Say whoa and she stop. I feed her some oats and she carry me wherever I want to go. Ain't had a speck of trouble out of her since I had her. Now, I been married. A long time ago down in Kentucky. I got up one morning and I saw this look on my wife's face. Like way down deep inside her she was wishing I was dead. I walked around that morning and every time I looked at her she had that look on her face. It seem like she knew I could see it on her. Every time I looked at her I got smaller and smaller. Well, I wasn't gonna stay around there and just shrink away. I walked out on the porch and closed the door behind me. When I closed the door she locked it. I went out and bought me a horse. And I ain't been without one since! Martha Loomis, huh? Well, now I'll do the best I can do. That's one dollar.

LOOMIS *(Holding out dollar suspiciously)*. How you find her?

SELIG. Well now, it ain't no easy job like you think. You can't just go out there and find them like that. There's a lot of little tricks to it. It's not an easy job keeping up with you Nigras the way you move about so. Now you take this woman you looking for . . . this Martha Loomis. She could be anywhere. Time I find her, if you don't keep your eye on her, she'll be gone off someplace else. You'll be thinking she over here and she'll be over there. But like I say there's a lot of little tricks to it.

LOOMIS. You say you find her.

SELIG. I can't promise anything but we been finders in my family for a long time. Bringers and finders. My great-granddaddy used to bring Nigras across the ocean on ships. That's wasn't no easy job either. Sometimes the winds would blow so hard you'd think the hand of God was set against the sails. But it set him well in pay and he settled in this new land and found him a wife of good Christian charity with a mind for kids and the like and well . . . here I am, Rutherford Selig. You're in good hands, mister. Me and my daddy have found plenty Nigras. My daddy, rest his soul, used to find runaway slaves for the plantation bosses. He was the best there was at it. Jonas B. Selig. Had him a reputation stretched clean across the country. After Abraham Lincoln give you all Nigras your freedom papers and with you all looking all over for each other . . . we started finding Nigras for Nigras. Of course, it don't pay as much. But the People Finding business ain't so bad.

LOOMIS *(Hands him the dollar)*. Find her. Martha Loomis. Find her for me.

SELIG. Like I say, I can't promise you anything. I'm going back upriver, and if she's around in them parts I'll find her for you. But I can't promise you anything.

LOOMIS. When you coming back?

SELIG. I'll be back on Saturday. I come and see Seth to pick up my order on Saturday.

BYNUM. You going upriver, huh? You going up around my way. I used to go all up through there. Blawknox . . . Clairton. Used to go up to Rankin and take that first right-hand road. I wore many a pair of shoes out walking around that way. You'd have thought I was a missionary spreading the gospel the way I wandered all around them parts.

SELIG. Okay, Bynum. See you on Saturday.

SETH. Here, let me walk out with you. Help you with them dustpans.

(SETH *and* SELIG *exit out the back.* BERTHA *enters from the stairs carrying a bundle of sheets.*)

BYNUM. Herald Loomis got the People Finder looking for Martha.

BERTHA. You can call him a People Finder if you want to. I know Rutherford Selig carries people away too. He done carried a whole bunch of them away from here. Folks plan on leaving plan by Selig's timing. They wait till he get ready to go, then they hitch a ride on his wagon. Then he charge folks a dollar to tell them where he took them. Now, that's the truth of Rutherford Selig. This old People Finding business is for the birds. He ain't never found nobody he ain't took away. Herald Loomis, you just wasted your dollar.

(BERTHA *exits into the bedroom.*)

LOOMIS. He say he find her. He say he find her by Saturday. I'm gonna wait till Saturday.

(*The lights fade to black.*)

SCENE THREE

It is Sunday morning, the next day. The lights come up on the kitchen. SETH *sits talking to* BYNUM. *The breakfast dishes have been cleared away.*

———

SETH. They can't see that. Neither one of them can see that. Now, how much sense it take to see that? All you got to do is be able to count. One man making ten pots is five men making fifty pots. But they can't see that. Asked where I'm gonna get my five men. Hell, I can teach anybody how to make a pot. I can teach you. I can take you out there and get you started right now. Inside of two weeks you'd know how to make a pot. All you got to do is want to do it. I can get five men. I ain't worried about getting no five men.

BERTHA (*calls from the bedroom*). Seth. Come on and get ready now. Reverend Gates ain't gonna be holding up his sermon 'cause you sitting out there talking.

SETH. Now, you take the boy, Jeremy. What he gonna do after he put in that road? He can't do nothing but go put in another one somewhere. Now, if he let me show him how to make some pots and pans . . . then he'd have something can't nobody take away from him. After a while he could get his own tools and go off somewhere and make his own pots and pans. Find him somebody to sell them to. Now, Selig can't make no pots and pans. He can sell them but he can't make them. I get me five men with some tools and we'd make him so many pots and pans he'd have to open up a store somewhere. But they can't see that. Neither Mr. Cohen nor Sam Green.

BERTHA (*Calls from the bedroom*). Seth . . . time be wasting. Best be getting on.

SETH. I'm coming, woman! (*To* BYNUM.) Want me to sign over the house to borrow five hundred dollars. I ain't that big a fool. That's all I got. Sign it over to them and then I won't have nothing.

(JEREMY *enters waving a dollar and carrying his guitar.*)

JEREMY. Look here, Mr. Bynum . . . won me another dollar last night down at Seefus! Me and that Mattie Campbell went down there again and I played contest. Ain't no guitar players down there. Wasn't even no contest. Say, Mr. Seth, I asked Mattie Campbell if she wanna come by and have Sunday dinner with us. Get some fried chicken.

SETH. It's gonna cost you twenty-five cents.

JEREMY. That's alright. I got a whole dollar here. Say, Mr. Seth . . . me and Mattie Campbell talked it over last night and she gonna move in with me. If that's alright with you.

SETH. Your business is your business . . . but it's gonna cost her a dollar a week for her board. I can't be feeding nobody for free.

JEREMY. Oh, she know that, Mr. Seth. That's what I told her, say she'd have to pay for her meals.

SETH. You say you got a whole dollar there . . . turn loose that twenty-five cents.

JEREMY. Suppose she move in today, then that make seventy-five cents more, so I'll give you the whole dollar for her now till she gets here.

(SETH *pockets the money and exits into the bedroom.*)

BYNUM. So you and that Mattie Campbell gonna take up together?

JEREMY. I told her she don't need to be by her lonesome, Mr. Bynum. Don't make no sense for both of us to be by our lonesome. So she gonna move in with me.

BYNUM. Sometimes you got to be where you supposed to be. Sometimes you can get all mixed up in life and come to the wrong place.

JEREMY. That's just what I told her, Mr. Bynum. It don't make no sense for her to be all mixed up and lonesome. May as well come here and be with me. She a fine woman too. Got them long legs. Knows how to treat a fellow too. Treat you like you wanna be treated.

BYNUM. You just can't look at it like that. You got to look at the whole thing. Now, you take a fellow go out there, grab hold to a woman and think he got something 'cause she sweet and soft to the touch. Alright.

Touching's part of life. It's in the world like everything else. Touching's nice. It feels good. But you can lay your hand upside a horse or a cat, and that feels good too. What's the difference? When you grab hold to a woman, you got something there. You got a whole world there. You got a way of life kicking up under your hand. That woman can take and make you feel like something. I ain't just talking about in the way of jumping off into bed together and rolling around with each other. Anybody can do that. When you grab hold to that woman and look at the whole thing and see what you got ... why, she can take and make something out of you. Your mother was a woman. That's enough right there to show you what a woman is. Enough to show you what she can do. She made something out of you. Taught you converse, and all about how to take care of yourself, how to see where you at and where you going tomorrow, how to look out to see what's coming in the way of eating, and what to do with yourself when you get lonesome. That's a mighty thing she did. But you just can't look at a woman to jump off into bed with her. That's a foolish thing to ignore a woman like that.

JEREMY. Oh, I ain't ignoring her, Mr. Bynum. It's hard to ignore a woman got legs like she got.

BYNUM. Alright. Let's try it this way. Now, you take a ship. Be out there on the water traveling about. You out there on that ship sailing to and from. And then you see some land. Just like you see a woman walking down the street. You see that land and it don't look like nothing but a line out there on the horizon. That's all it is when you first see it. A line that cross your path out there on the horizon. Now, a smart man know when he see that land, it ain't just a line setting out there. He know that if you get off the water to go take a good look ... why, there's a whole world right there. A whole world with everything imaginable under the sun. Anything you can think of you can find on that land. Same with a woman. A woman is everything a man need. To a smart man she water and berries. And that's all a man need. That's all he need to live on. You give me some water and berries and if there ain't nothing else I can live a hundred years. See, you just like a man looking at the horizon from a ship. You just seeing a part of it. But it's a blessing when you learn to look at a woman and see

in maybe just a few strands of her hair, the way her cheek curves ... to see in that everything there is out of life to be gotten. It's a blessing to see that. You know you done right and proud by your mother to see that. But you got to learn it. My telling you ain't gonna mean nothing. You got to learn how to come to your own time and place with a woman.

JEREMY. What about your woman, Mr. Bynum? I know you done had some woman.

BYNUM. Oh, I got them in memory time. That lasts longer than any of them ever stayed with me.

JEREMY. I had me an old gal one time ...

(There is a knock on the door. JEREMY goes to answer it. Enter MOLLY CUNNINGHAM. She is about twenty-six, the kind of woman that "could break in on a dollar anywhere she goes." She carries a small cardboard suitcase, and wears a colorful dress of the fashion of the day. JEREMY's heart jumps out of his chest when he sees her.)

MOLLY. You got any rooms here? I'm looking for a room.

JEREMY. Yeah ... Mr. Seth got rooms. Sure ... wait till I get Mr. Seth. *(Calls.)* Mr. Seth! Somebody here to see you! *(To MOLLY.)* Yeah, Mr. Seth got some rooms. Got one right next to me. This a nice place to stay, too. My name's Jeremy. What's yours?

(SETH enters dressed in his Sunday clothes.)

SETH. Ho!

JEREMY. This here woman looking for a place to stay. She say you got any rooms.

MOLLY. Mister, you got any rooms? I seen your sign say you got rooms.

SETH. How long you plan to staying?

MOLLY. I ain't gonna be here long. I ain't looking for no home or nothing. I'd be in Cincinnati if I hadn't missed my train.

SETH. Rooms cost two dollars a week.

MOLLY. Two dollars!

SETH. That includes meals. We serve two meals a day. That's breakfast and dinner.

MOLLY. I hope it ain't on the third floor.

SETH. That's the only one I got. Third floor to the left. That's pay up in advance week to week.

MOLLY *(Going into her bosom)*. I'm gonna pay you for one week. My name's Molly. Molly Cunningham.

SETH. I'm Seth Holly. My wife's name is Bertha. She do the cooking and taking care of around here. She got sheets on the bed. Towels twenty-five cents a week extra if you ain't got none. You get breakfast and dinner. We got fried chicken on Sundays.

MOLLY. That sounds good. Here's two dollars and twenty-five cents. Look here, Mister . . . ?

SETH. Holly. Seth Holly.

MOLLY. Look here, Mr. Holly. I forgot to tell you. I likes me some company from time to time. I don't like being by myself.

SETH. Your business is your business. I don't meddle in nobody's business. But this is a respectable house. I don't have no riffraff around here. And I don't have no women hauling no men up to their rooms to be making their living. As long as we understand each other then we'll be alright with each other.

MOLLY. Where's the outhouse?

SETH. Straight through the door over yonder.

MOLLY. I get my own key to the front door?

SETH. Everybody get their own key. If you come in late just don't be making no whole lot of noise and carrying on. Don't allow no fussing and fighting around here.

MOLLY. You ain't got to worry about that, mister. Which way you say that outhouse was again?

SETH. Straight through that door over yonder.

(MOLLY exits out the back door. JEREMY crosses to watch her.)

JEREMY. Mr. Bynum, you know what? I think I know what you was talking about now.

(The lights go down on the scene.)

SCENE FOUR

The lights come up on the kitchen. It is later the same evening. MATTIE and all the residents of the house, except LOOMIS, sit around the table. They have finished eating and most of the dishes have been cleared.

_____

MOLLY. That sure was some good chicken.

JEREMY. That's what I'm talking about. Miss Bertha, you sure can fry some chicken. I thought my mamma could fry some chicken. But she can't do half as good as you.

SETH. I know it. That's why I married her. She don't know that, though. She think I married her for something else.

BERTHA. I ain't studying you, Seth. Did you get your things moved in alright, Mattie?

MATTIE. I ain't had that much. Jeremy helped me with what I did have.

BERTHA. You'll get to know your way around here. If you have any questions about anything just ask me. You and Molly both. I get along with everybody. You'll find I ain't no trouble to get along with.

MATTIE. You need some help with the dishes?

BERTHA. I got me a helper. Ain't I, Zonia? Got me a good helper.

ZONIA. Yes, ma'am.

SETH. Look at Bynum sitting over there with his belly all poked out. Ain't saying nothing. Sitting over there half asleep. Ho, Bynum!

BERTHA. If Bynum ain't saying nothing what you wanna start him up for?

SETH. Ho, Bynum!

BYNUM. What you hollering at me for? I ain't doing nothing.

SETH. Come on, we gonna Juba.

BYNUM. You know me, I'm always ready to Juba.

SETH. Well, come on, then.

(SETH pulls out a haromnica and blows a few notes.)

Come on there, Jeremy. Where's your guitar? Go get your guitar. Bynum say he's ready to Juba.

JEREMY. Don't need no guitar to Juba. Ain't you never Juba without a guitar?

(JEREMY begins to drum on the table.)

SETH. It ain't that. I ain't never Juba with one! Figured to try it and see how it worked.

BYNUM (Drumming on the table). You don't need no guitar. Look at Molly sitting over there. She don't know we Juba on Sunday. We gonna show you something tonight. You and Mattie Campbell both. Ain't that right, Seth?

SETH. You said it! Come on, Bertha, leave them dishes be for a while. We gonna Juba.

BYNUM. Alright. Let's Juba down!

(The Juba is reminiscent of the Ring Shouts of the African slaves. It is a call and response dance. BYNUM sits at the table and drums. He calls the dance as others clap hands, shuffle and stomp around the table. It should be as African as possible, with the performers working themselves up into a near frenzy. The words can be improvised, but should include some mention of the Holy Ghost. In the middle of the dance HERALD LOOMIS enters.)

LOOMIS (In a rage). Stop it! Stop!

(They stop and turn to look at him.)

You all sitting up here singing about the Holy Ghost. What's so holy about the Holy

Ghost? You singing and singing. You think the Holy Ghost coming? You singing for the Holy Ghost to come? What he gonna do, huh? He gonna come with tongues of fire to burn up your woolly heads? You gonna tie onto the Holy Ghost and get burned up? What you got then? Why God got to be so big? Why he got to be bigger than me? How much big is there? How much big do you want?

(LOOMIS *starts to unzip his pants.*)

SETH. Nigger, you crazy!

LOOMIS. How much big you want?

SETH. You done plumb lost your mind!

(LOOMIS *begins to speak in tongues and dance around the kitchen.* SETH *starts after him.*)

BERTHA. Leave him alone, Seth. He ain't in his right mind.

LOOMIS (*Stops suddenly*). You all don't know nothing about me. You don't know what I done seen. Herald Loomis done seen some things he ain't got words to tell you.

(LOOMIS *starts to walk out the front door and is thrown back and collapses, terror-stricken by his vision.* BYNUM *crawls to him.*)

BYNUM. What you done seen, Herald Loomis?

LOOMIS. I done seen bones rise up out the water. Rise up and walk across the water. Bones walking on top of the water.

BYNUM. Tell me about them bones, Herald Loomis. Tell me what you seen.

LOOMIS. I come to this place . . . to this water that was bigger than the whole world. And I looked out . . . and I seen these bones rise up out the water. Rise up and begin to walk on top of it.

BYNUM. Wasn't nothing but bones and they walking on top of the water.

LOOMIS. Walking without sinking down. Walking on top of the water.

BYNUM. Just marching in a line.

LOOMIS. A whole heap of them. They come up out the water and started marching.

BYNUM. Wasn't nothing but bones and they walking on top of the water.

LOOMIS. One after the other. They just come up out the water and start to walking.

BYNUM. They walking on the water without sinking down. They just walking and walking. And then . . . what happened, Herald Loomis?

LOOMIS. They just walking across the water.

BYNUM. What happened, Herald Loomis? What happened to the bones?

LOOMIS. They just walking across the water . . . and then . . . they sunk down.

BYNUM. The bones sunk into the water. They all sunk down.

LOOMIS. All at one time! They just all fell in the water at one time.

BYNUM. Sunk down like anybody else.

LOOMIS. When they sink down they made a big splash and this here wave come up . . .

BYNUM. A big wave, Herald Loomis. A big wave washed over the land.

LOOMIS. It washed them out of the water and up on the land. Only . . . only . . .

BYNUM. Only they ain't bones no more.

LOOMIS. They got flesh on them! Just like you and me!

BYNUM. Everywhere you look the waves is washing them up on the land right on top of one another.

LOOMIS. They black. Just like you and me. Ain't no difference.

BYNUM. Then what happened, Herald Loomis?

LOOMIS. They ain't moved or nothing. They just laying there.

BYNUM. You just laying there. What you waiting on, Herald Loomis?

LOOMIS. I'm laying there . . . waiting.

BYNUM. What you waiting on, Herald Loomis?

LOOMIS. I'm waiting on the breath to get into my body.

BYNUM. The breath coming into you, Herald Loomis. What you gonna do now?

LOOMIS. The wind's blowing the breath into my body. I can feel it. I'm starting to breathe again.

BYNUM. What you gonna do, Herald Loomis?

LOOMIS. I'm gonna stand up. I got to stand up. I can't lay here no more. All the breath coming into my body and I got to stand up.

BYNUM. Everybody's standing up at the same time.

LOOMIS. The ground's starting to shake. There's a great shaking. The world's busting half in two. The sky's splitting open. I got to stand up.

(LOOMIS *attempts to stand up.*)

My legs . . . my legs won't stand up!

BYNUM. Everybody's standing and walking toward the road. What you gonna do, Herald Loomis?

LOOMIS. My legs won't stand up.

BYNUM. They shaking hands and saying

goodbye to each other and walking every whichaway down the road.

LOOMIS. I got to stand up!

BYNUM. They walking around here now. Mens. Just like you and me. Come right up out the water.

LOOMIS. Got to stand up.

BYNUM. They walking, Herald Loomis. They walking around here now.

LOOMIS. I got to stand up. Get up on the road.

BYNUM. Come on, Herald Loomis.

(LOOMIS *tries to stand up.*)

LOOMIS. My legs won't stand up! My legs won't stand up!

(LOOMIS *collapses on the floor as the lights go down to black.*)

ACT TWO

SCENE ONE

The lights come up on the kitchen. BERTHA *busies herself with breakfast preparations.* SETH *sits at the table.*

────

SETH. I don't care what his problem is! He's leaving here!

BERTHA. You can't put the man out and he got that little girl. Where they gonna go then?

SETH. I don't care where he go. Let him go back where he was before he come here. I ain't asked him to come here. I knew when I first looked at him something wasn't right with him. Dragging that little girl around with him. Looking like he be sleeping in the woods somewhere. I knew all along he wasn't right.

BERTHA. A fellow get a little drunk he's liable to say or do anything. He ain't done no big harm.

SETH. I just don't have all that carrying on in my house. When he come down here I'm gonna tell him. He got to leave here. My daddy wouldn't stand for it and I ain't gonna stand for it either.

BERTHA. Well, if you put him out you have to put Bynum out too. Bynum right there with him.

SETH. If it wasn't for Bynum ain't no telling what would have happened. Bynum talked to that fellow just as nice and calmed him down. If he wasn't here ain't no telling what would have happened. Bynum ain't done nothing but talk to him and kept him calm. Man acting all crazy with that foolishness. Naw, he's leaving here.

BERTHA. What you gonna tell him? How you gonna tell him to leave?

SETH. I'm gonna tell him straight out. Keep it nice and simple. Mister, you got to leave here!

(MOLLY *enters from the stairs.*)

MOLLY. Morning.

BERTHA. Did you sleep alright in that bed?

MOLLY. Tired as I was I could have slept anywhere. It's a real nice room, though. This is a nice place.

SETH. I'm sorry you had to put up with all that carrying on last night.

MOLLY. It don't bother me none. I done seen that kind of stuff before.

SETH. You won't have to see it around here no more.

(BYNUM *is heard singing offstage.*)

I don't put up with all that stuff. When that fellow come down here I'm gonna tell him.

BYNUM *(singing).* Soon my work will all be done

Soon my work will all be done
Soon my work will all be done

I'm going to see the king.

BYNUM *(Enters).* Morning, Seth. Morning, Sister Bertha. I see we got Molly Cunningham down here at breakfast.

SETH. Bynum, I wanna thank you for talking to that fellow last night and calming him down. If you hadn't been here ain't no telling what might have happened.

BYNUM. Mr. Loomis alright, Seth. He just got a little excited.

SETH. Well, he can get excited somewhere else 'cause he leaving here.

(MATTIE *enters from the stairs.*)

BYNUM. Well, there's Mattie Campbell.

MATTIE. Good morning.

BERTHA. Sit on down there, Mattie. I got some biscuits be ready in a minute. The coffee's hot.

MATTIE. Jeremy gone already?

BYNUM. Yeah, he leave out of here early. He got to be there when the sun come up. Most working men got to be there when the sun come up. Everybody but Seth. Seth work at night. Mr. Olowski so busy in his shop he got fellows working at night.

(LOOMIS *enters from the stairs.*)

SETH. Mr. Loomis, now . . . I don't want no

trouble. I keeps me a respectable house here. I don't have no carrying on like what went on last night. This has been a respectable house for a long time. I'm gonna have to ask you to leave.

LOOMIS. You got my two dollars. That two dollars say we stay till Saturday.

(LOOMIS and SETH glare at each other.)

SETH. Alright. Fair enough. You stay till Saturday. But come Saturday you got to leave here.

LOOMIS *(Continues to glare at SETH. He goes to the door and calls.)* Zonia. You stay around this house, you hear? Don't you go anywhere.

(LOOMIS exits out the front door.)

SETH. I knew it when I first seen him. I knew something wasn't right with him.

BERTHA. Seth, leave the people alone to eat their breakfast. They don't want to hear that. Go on out there and make some pots and pans. That's the only time you satisfied is when you out there. Go on out there and make some pots and pans and leave them people alone.

SETH. I ain't bothering anybody. I'm just stating the facts. I told you, Bynum.

(BERTHA shoos SETH out the back door and exits into the bedroom.)

MOLLY *(To BYNUM).* You one of them voodoo people?

BYNUM. I got a power to bind folks if that what you talking about.

MOLLY. I thought so. The way you talked to that man when he started all that spooky stuff. What you say you had the power to do to people? You ain't the cause of him acting like that, is you?

BYNUM. I binds them together. Sometimes I help them find each other.

MOLLY. How do you do that?

BYNUM. With a song. My daddy taught me how to do it.

MOLLY. That's what they say. Most folks be what they daddy is. I wouldn't want to be like my daddy. Nothing ever set right with him. He tried to make the world over. Carry it around with him everywhere he go. I don't want to be like that. I just take life as it come. I don't be trying to make it over.

(Pause.)

Your daddy used to do that too, huh? Make people stay together?

BYNUM. My daddy used to heal people. He had the Healing Song. I got the Binding Song.

MOLLY. My mamma used to believe in all that stuff. If she got sick she would have gone and saw your daddy. As long as he didn't make her drink nothing. She wouldn't drink nothing nobody give her. She was always afraid somebody was gonna poison her. How your daddy heal people?

BYNUM. With a song. He healed people by singing over them. I seen him do it. He sung over this little white girl when she was sick. They made a big to-do about it. They carried the girl's bed out in the yard and had all her kinfolk standing around. The little girl laying up there in the bed. Doctors standing around can't do nothing to help her. And they had my daddy come up and sing his song. It didn't sound no different than any other song. It was just somebody singing. But the song was its own thing and it come out and took upon this little girl with its power and it healed her.

MOLLY. That's sure something else. I don't understand that kind of thing. I guess if the doctor couldn't make me well I'd try it. But otherwise I don't wanna be bothered with that kind of thing. It's too spooky.

BYNUM. Well, let me get on out here and get to work.

(BYNUM gets up and heads out the back door.)

MOLLY. I ain't meant to offend you or nothing. What's your name . . . Bynum? I ain't meant to say nothing to make you feel bad now.

(BYNUM exits out the back door.)

(to MATTIE.) I hope he don't feel bad. He's a nice man. I don't wanna hurt nobody's feelings or nothing.

MATTIE. I got to go on up to Doc Goldblum's and finish this ironing.

MOLLY. Now, that's something I don't never wanna do. Iron no clothes. Especially somebody else's. That's what I believe killed my mama. Always ironing and working, doing somebody's else's work. Not Molly Cunningham.

MATTIE. It's the only job I got. I got to make it someway to fend for myself.

MOLLY. I thought Jeremy was your man. Ain't he working?

MATTIE. We just be keeping company till maybe Jack come back.

MOLLY. I don't trust none of these men. Jack or nobody else. These men liable to do anything. They wait just until they get one woman tied and locked up with them . . . then they look around to see if they can get another one. Molly don't pay them no mind.

One's just as good as the other if you ask me. I ain't never met one that meant nobody no good. You got any babies?

MATTIE. I had two for my man, Jack Carper. But they both died.

MOLLY. That be the best. These men make all these babies, then run off and leave you to take care of them. Talking about they wanna see what's on the other side of the hill. I make sure I don't get no babies. My mama taught me how to do that.

MATTIE. Don't make me no mind. That be nice to be a mother.

MOLLY. Yeah? Well, you go on, then. Molly Cunningham ain't gonna be tied down with no babies. Had me a man one time who I thought had some love in him. Come home one day and he was packing his trunk. Told me the time come when even the best of friends must part. Say he was gonna send me a Special Delivery some old day. I watched him out the window when he carried that trunk out and down to the train station. Said if he was gonna send me a Special Delivery I wasn't gonna be there to get it. I done found out the harder you try to hold onto them, the easier it is for some gal to pull them away. Molly done learned that. That's why I don't trust nobody but the good Lord above, and I don't love nobody but my mama.

MATTIE. I got to get on. Doc Goldblum gonna be waiting.

(MATTIE *exits out the front door.* SETH *enters from his workshop with his apron, gloves, goggles, etc. He carries a bucket and crosses to the sink for water.*)

SETH. Everybody gone but you, huh?

MOLLY. That little shack out there by the outhouse . . . that's where you make them pots and pans and stuff?

SETH. Yeah, that's my workshed. I go out there . . . take these hands and make something out of nothing. Take that metal and bend and twist it whatever way I want. My daddy taught me that. He used to make pots and pans. That's how I learned it.

MOLLY. I never knew nobody made no pots and pans. My uncle used to shoe horses.

(JEREMY *enters at the front door.*)

SETH. I thought you was working? Ain't you working today?

JEREMY. Naw, they fired me. White fellow come by told me to give him fifty cents if I wanted to keep working. Going around to all the colored making them give him fifty cents to keep hold to their jobs. Them other fel-

lows, they was giving it to him. I kept hold to mine and they fired me.

SETH. Boy, what kind of sense that make? What kind of sense it make to get fired from a job where you making eight dollars a week and all it cost you is fifty cents. That's seven dollars and fifty cents profit! This way you ain't got nothing.

JEREMY. It didn't make no sense to me. I don't make but eight dollars. Why I got to give him fifty cents of it? He go around to all the colored and he got ten dollars extra. That's more than I make for a whole week.

SETH. I see you gonna learn the hard way. You just looking at the facts of it. See, right now, without the job, you ain't got nothing. What you gonna do when you can't keep a roof over your head? Right now, come Saturday, unless you come up with another two dollars, you gonna be out there in the streets. Down up under one of them bridges trying to put some food in your belly and wishing you had given that fellow that fifty cents.

JEREMY. Don't make me no difference. There's a big road out there. I can get my guitar and always find me another place to stay. I ain't planning on staying in one place for too long noway.

SETH. We gonna see if you feel like that come Saturday!

(SETH *exits out the back.* JEREMY *sees* MOLLY.)

JEREMY. Molly Cunningham. How you doing today, sugar?

MOLLY. You can go on back down there tomorrow and go back to work if you want. They won't even know who you is. Won't even know it's you. I had me a fellow did that one time. They just went ahead and signed him up like they never seen him before.

JEREMY. I'm tired of working anyway. I'm glad they fired me. You sure look pretty today.

MOLLY. Don't come telling me all that pretty stuff. Beauty wanna come in and sit down at your table asking to be fed. I ain't hardly got enough for me.

JEREMY. You know you pretty. Ain't no sense in you saying nothing about that. Why don't you come on and go away with me?

MOLLY. You tied up with that Mattie Campbell. Now you talking about running away with me.

JEREMY. I was just keeping her company 'cause she lonely. You ain't the lonely kind. You the kind that know what she want and how to get it. I need a woman like you to travel around with. Don't you wanna travel around and look at some places with Jeremy? With a woman like you beside him, a man can make it nice in the world.

MOLLY. Moll can make it nice by herself too. Molly don't need nobody leave her cold in hand. The world rough enough as it is.

JEREMY. We can make it better together. I got my guitar and I can play. Won me another dollar last night playing guitar. We can go around and I can play at the dances and we can just enjoy life. You can make it by yourself alright, I agrees with that. A woman like you can make it anywhere she go. But you can make it better if you got a man to protect you.

MOLLY. What places you wanna go around and look at?

JEREMY. All of them! I don't want to miss nothing. I wanna go everywhere and do everything there is to be got out of life. With a woman like you it's like having water and berries. A man got everything he need.

MOLLY. You got to be doing more than playing that guitar. A dollar a day ain't hardly what Molly got in mind.

JEREMY. I gambles real good. I got a hand for it.

MOLLY. Molly don't work. And Molly ain't up for sale.

JEREMY. Sure, baby. You ain't got to work with Jeremy.

MOLLY. There's one more thing.

JEREMY. What's that, sugar?

MOLLY. Molly ain't going South.

(The lights go down on the scene.)

SCENE TWO

The lights come up on the parlor. SETH *and* BYNUM *sit playing a game of dominoes.* BYNUM *sings to himself.*

_____

BYNUM *(Singing).* They tell me Joe Turner's come and gone
Ohhh Lordy
They tell me Joe Turner's come and gone
Ohhh Lordy
Got my man and gone

Come with forty links of chain
Ohhh Lordy
Come with forty links of chain
Ohhh Lordy
Got my man and gone

SETH. Come on and play if you gonna play.

BYNUM. I'm gonna play. Soon as I figure out what to do.

SETH. You can't figure out if you wanna play or you wanna sing.

BYNUM. Well, sir, I'm gonna do a little bit of both.

(Playing.)
There. What you gonna do now?
(Singing.)
They tell me Joe Turner's come and gone
Ohhh Lordy
They tell me Joe Turner's come and gone
Ohhh Lordy

SETH. Why don't you hush up that noise?

BYNUM. That's a song the women sing down around Memphis. The women down there made up that song. I picked it up down there about fifteen years ago.

(LOOMIS enters from the front door.)

BYNUM. Evening, Mr. Loomis.

SETH. Today's Monday, Mr. Loomis. Come Saturday your time is up. We done ate already. My wife roasted up some yams. She got your plate sitting in there on the table. *(To BYNUM.)* Whose play is it?

BYNUM. Ain't you keeping up with the game? I thought you was a domino player. I just played so it got to be your turn.

(LOOMIS goes into the kitchen, where a plate of yams is covered and set on the table. He sits down and begins to eat with his hands.)

SETH *(Plays).* Twenty! Give me twenty! You didn't know I had that ace five. You was trying to play around that. You didn't know I had that lying there for you.

BYNUM. You ain't done nothing. I let you have that to get mine.

SETH. Come on and play. You ain't doing nothing but talking. I got a hundred and forty points to your eighty. You ain't doing nothing but talking. Come on and play.

BYNUM *(Singing).* They tell me Joe Turner's come and gone
Ohhh Lordy
They tell me Joe Turner's come and gone
Ohhh Lordy
Got my man and gone

He come with forty links of chain
Ohhh Lordy

LOOMIS. Why you singing that song? Why you singing about Joe Turner?

BYNUM. I'm just singing to entertain myself.

SETH. You trying to distract me. That's what you trying to do.

BYNUM *(Singing)*. Come with forty links of chain
Ohhh Lordy
Come with forty links of chain
Ohhh Lordy

LOOMIS. I don't like you singing that song, mister!

SETH. Now, I ain't gonna have no more disturbance around here, Herald Loomis. You start any more disturbance and you leavin' here, Saturday or no Saturday.

BYNUM. The man ain't causing no disturbance, Seth. He just say he don't like the song.

SETH. Well, we all friendly folk. All neighborly like. Don't have no squabbling around here. Don't have no disturbance. You gonna have to take that someplace else.

BYNUM. He just say he don't like the song. I done sung a whole lot of songs people don't like. I respect everybody. He here in the house too. If he don't like the song, I'll sing something else. I know lots of songs. You got "I Belong to the Band," "Don't You Leave Me Here." You got "Praying on the Old Campground," "Keep Your Lamp Trimmed and Burning" . . . I know lots of songs.

(Sings.)

Boys, I'll be so glad when payday come
Captain, Captain, when payday comes
Gonna catch that Illinois Central
Going to Kankakee

SETH. Why don't you hush up that hollering and come on and play dominoes.

BYNUM. You ever been to Johnstown, Herald Loomis? You look like a fellow I seen around there.

LOOMIS. I don't know no place with that name.

BYNUM. That's around where I seen my shiny man. See, you looking for this woman. I'm looking for a shiny man. Seem like everybody looking for something.

SETH. I'm looking for you to come and play these dominoes. That's what I'm looking for.

BYNUM. You a farming man, Herald Loomis? You look like you done some farming.

LOOMIS. Same as everybody. I done farmed some, yeah.

BYNUM. I used to work at farming . . . picking cotton. I reckon everybody done picked some cotton.

SETH. I ain't! I ain't never picked no cotton. I was born up here in the North. My daddy was a freedman. I ain't never even seen no cotton!

BYNUM. Mr. Loomis done picked some cotton. Ain't you, Herald Loomis? You done picked a bunch of cotton.

LOOMIS. How you know so much about me? How you know what I done? How much cotton I picked?

BYNUM. I can tell from looking at you. My daddy taught me how to do that. Say when you look at a fellow, if you taught yourself to look for it, you can see his song written on him. Tell you what kind of man he is in the world. Now, I can look at you, Mr. Loomis, and see you a man who done forgot his song. Forgot how to sing it. A fellow forget that and he forget who he is. Forget how he's supposed to mark down life. Now, I used to travel all up and down this road and that . . . looking here and there. Searching. Just like you, Mr. Loomis. I didn't know what I was searching for. The only thing I knew was something was keeping me dissatisfied. Something wasn't making my heart smooth and easy. Then one day my daddy gave me a song. That song had a weight to it that was hard to handle. That song was hard to carry. I fought against it. Didn't want to accept that song. I tried to find my daddy to give him back the song. But I found out it wasn't his song. It was my song. It had come from way deep inside me. I looked long back in memory and gathered up pieces and snatches of things to make that song. I was making it up out of myself. And that song helped me on the road. Made it smooth to where my footsteps didn't bite back at me. All the time that song getting bigger and bigger. That song growing with each step of the road. It got so I used all of myself up in the making of that song. Then I was the song in search of itself. That song rattling in my throat and I'm looking for it. See, Mr. Loomis, when a man forgets his song he goes off in search of it . . . till he find out he's got it with him all the time. That's why I can tell you one of Joe Turner's niggers. 'Cause you forgot how to sing your song.

LOOMIS. You lie! How you see that? I got a mark on me? Joe Turner done marked me to where you can see it? You telling me I'm a marked man. What kind of mark you got on you?

(BYNUM begins singing.)

BYNUM. They tell me Joe Turner's come and gone

Ohhh Lordy
They tell me Joe Turner's come and gone
Ohhh Lordy
Got my man and gone

LOOMIS. Had a whole mess of men he catched. Just go out hunting regular like you go out hunting possum. He catch you and go home to his wife and family. Ain't thought about you going home to yours. Joe Turner catched me when my little girl was just born. Wasn't nothing but a little baby sucking on her mama's titty when he catched me. Joe Turner catched me in nineteen hundred and one. Kept me seven years until nineteen hundred and eight. Kept everybody seven years. He'd go out hunting and bring back forty men at a time. And keep them seven years.

I was walking down this road in this little town outside of Memphis. Come up on these fellows gambling. I was a deacon in the Abundant Life Church. I stopped to preach to these fellows to see if maybe I could turn some of them from their sinning when Joe Turner, brother of the Governor of the great sovereign state of Tennessee, swooped down on us and grabbed everybody there. Kept us all seven years.

My wife Martha gone from me after Joe Turner catched me. Got out from under Joe Turner on his birthday. Me and forty other men put in our seven years and he let us go on his birthday. I made it back to Henry Thompson's place where me and Martha was sharecropping and Martha's gone. She taken my little girl and left her with her mama and took off North. We been looking for her ever since. That's been going on four years now we been looking. That's the only thing I know to do. I just wanna see her face so I can get me a starting place in the world. The world got to start somewhere. That's what I been looking for. I been wandering a long time in somebody else's world. When I find my wife that be the making of my own.

BYNUM. Joe Turner tell why he caught you? You ever asked him that?

LOOMIS. I ain't never seen Joe Turner. Seen him to where I could touch him. I asked one of them fellows one time why he catch niggers. Asked him what I got he want? Why don't he keep on to himself? Why he got to catch me going down the road by my lonesome? He told me I was worthless. Worthless is something you throw away. Something you don't bother with. I ain't seen him throw

me away. Wouldn't even let me stay away when I was by my lonesome. I ain't tried to catch him when he going down the road. So I must got something he want. What I got?

SETH. He just want you to do his work for him. That's all.

LOOMIS. I can look at him and see where he big and strong enough to do his own work. So it can't be that. He must want something he ain't got.

BYNUM. That ain't hard to figure out. What he wanted was your song. He wanted to have that song to be his. He thought by catching you he could learn that song. Every nigger he catch he's looking for the one he can learn that song from. Now he's got you bound up to where you can't sing your own song. Couldn't sing it them seven years 'cause you was afraid he would snatch it from under you. But you still got it. You just forgot how to sing it.

LOOMIS (To BYNUM). I know who you are. You one of them bones people.

(The lights go down to black.)

SCENE THREE

The lights come up on the kitchen. It is the following morning. MATTIE, *and* BYNUM, *sit at the table.* BERTHA *busies herself at the stove.*

BYNUM. Good luck don't know no special time to come. You sleep with that up under your pillow and good luck can't help but come to you. Sometimes it come and go and you don't even know it's been there.

BERTHA. Bynum, why don't you leave that gal alone? She don't wanna be hearing all that. Why don't you go on and get out the way and leave her alone?

BYNUM *(Getting up).* Alright, alright. But you mark what I'm saying. It'll draw it to you just like a magnet.

(BYNUM exits up the stairs ad LOOMIS enters.)

BERTHA. I got some grits here, Mr. Loomis.
(BERTHA sets a bowl on the table.)
If I was you, Mattie, I wouldn't go getting all tied up with Bynum in that stuff. That kind of stuff, even if it do work for a while, it don't last. That just get people more mixed up than they is already. And I wouldn't waste my time fretting over Jeremy either. I seen it coming. I seen it when she first come here. She that kind of woman run off with the first man got a dollar to spend on her. Jeremy just

young. He don't know what he getting into. That gal don't mean him no good. She's just using him to keep from being by herself. That's the worst use of a man you can have. You ought to be glad to wash him out of your hair. I done seen all kind of men. I done seen them come and go through here. Jeremy ain't had enough to him for you. You need a man who's got some understanding and who willing to work with that understanding to come to the best he can. You got your time coming. You just tries too hard and can't understand why it don't work for you. Trying to figure it out don't do nothing but give you a troubled mind. Don't no man want a woman with a troubled mind.

You get all that trouble off your mind and just when it look like you ain't never gonna find what you want . . . you look up and it's standing right there. That's how I met my Seth. You gonna look up one day and find everything you want standing right in front of you. Been twenty-seven years now since that happened to me. But life ain't no happy-go-lucky time where everything be just like you want it. You got your time coming. You watch what Bertha's saying.

(SETH enters.)

SETH. Ho!

BERTHA. What you doing come in here so late?

SETH. I was standing down there on Logan Street talking with the fellows. Henry Allen tried to sell me that old piece of horse he got.

(He sees LOOMIS.)

Today's Tuesday, Mr. Loomis.

BERTHA (Pulling him toward the bedroom). Come on in here and leave that man alone to eat his breakfast.

SETH. I ain't bothering nobody. I'm just reminding him what day it is.

(SETH and BERTHA exit into the bedroom.)

LOOMIS. That dress got a color to it.

MATTIE. Did you really see them things like you said? Them people come up out the ocean?

LOOMIS. It happened just like that, yeah.

MATTIE. I hope you find your wife. It be good for your little girl for you to find her.

LOOMIS. Got to find her for myself. Find my starting place in the world. Find me a world I can fit in.

MATTIE. I ain't never found no place for me to fit. Seem like all I do is start over. It ain't nothing to find no starting place in the world. You just start from where you find yourself.

LOOMIS. Got to find my wife. That be my starting place.

MATTIE. What if you don't find her? What you gonna do then if you don't find her?

LOOMIS. She out there somewhere. Ain't no such thing as not finding her.

MATTIE. How she got lost from you? Jack just walked away from me.

LOOMIS. Joe Turner split us up. Joe Turner turned the world upside-down. He bound me on to him for seven years.

MATTIE. I hope you find her. It be good for you to find her.

LOOMIS. I been watching you. I been watching you watch me.

MATTIE. I was just trying to figure out if you seen things like you said.

LOOMIS (Getting up). Come here and let me touch you. I been watching you. You a full woman. A man needs a full woman. Come on and be with me.

MATTIE. I ain't got enough for you. You'd use me up too fast.

LOOMIS. Herald Loomis got a mind seem like you a part of it since I first seen you. It's been a long time since I seen a full woman. I can smell you from here. I know you got Herald Loomis on your mind, can't keep him apart from it. Come on and be with Herald Loomis.

(LOOMIS has crossed to MATTIE. He touches her awkwardly, gently, tenderly. Inside he howls like a lost wolf pup whose hunger is deep. He goes to touch her but finds he cannot.)

I done forgot how to touch.

(The lights fade to black.)

SCENE FOUR

It is early the next morning. The lights come up on ZONIA and REUBEN in the yard.

REUBEN. Something spookly going on around here. Last night Mr. Bynum was out in the yard singing and talking to the wind . . . and the wind it just be talking back to him. Did you hear it?

ZONIA. I heard it. I was scared to get up and look. I thought it was a storm.

REUBEN. That wasn't no storm. That was Mr. Bynum. First he say something . . . and the wind it say back to him.

ZONIA. I heard it. Was you scared? I was scared.

REUBEN. And then this morning . . . I seen Miss Mabel!

ZONIA. Who Miss Mabel?

REUBEN. Mr. Seth's mother. He got her picture hanging up in the house. She been dead.

ZONIA. How you seen her if she been dead?

REUBEN. Zonia . . . if I tell you something you promise you won't tell anybody?

ZONIA. I promise.

REUBEN. It was early this morning . . . I went out to the coop to feed the pigeons. I was down on the ground like this to open up the door to the coop . . . when all of a sudden I seen some feets in front of me. I looked up . . . and there was Miss Mabel standing there.

ZONIA. Reuben, you better stop telling that! You ain't seen nobody!

REUBEN. Naw, it's the truth. I swear! I seen her just like I see you. Look . . . you can see where she hit me with her cane.

ZONIA. Hit you? What she hit you for?

REUBEN. She says, "Didn't you promise Eugene something?" Then she hit me with her cane. She say, "Let them pigeons go." Then she hit me again. That's what made them marks.

ZONIA. Jeez, man . . . get away from me. You done see a haunt!

REUBEN. Shhhh. You promised, Zonia!

ZONIA. You sure it wasn't Miss Bertha come over there and hit you with her hoe?

REUBEN. It wasn't no Miss Bertha. I told you it was Miss Mabel. She was standing right there by the coop. She had this light coming out of her and then she just melted away.

ZONIA. What she had on?

REUBEN. A white dress. Ain't even had no shoes or nothing. Just had on that white dress and them big hands . . . and that cane she hit me with.

ZONIA. How you reckon she knew about the pigeons? You reckon Eugene told her?

REUBEN. I don't know. I sure ain't asked her none. She say Eugene was waiting on them pigeons. Say he couldn't go back home till I let them go. I couldn't get the door to the coop open fast enough.

ZONIA. Maybe she an angel? From the way you say she look with that white dress. Maybe she an angel.

REUBEN. Mean as she was . . . how she gonna be an angel? She used to chase us out her yard and frown up and look evil all the time.

ZONIA. That don't mean she can't be no angel 'cause of how she looked and 'cause she wouldn't let no kids play in her yard. It go by if you got any spots on your heart and if you pray and go to church.

REUBEN. What about she hit me with her cane? An angel wouldn't hit me with her cane.

ZONIA. I don't know. She might. I still say she was an angel.

REUBEN. You reckon Eugene the one who sent old Miss Mabel?

ZONIA. Why he send her? Why he don't come himself?

REUBEN. Figured if he send her maybe that'll make me listen. 'Cause she old.

ZONIA. What you think it feel like?

REUBEN. What?

ZONIA. Being dead.

REUBEN. Like being sleep only you don't know nothing and can't move no more.

ZONIA. If Miss Mabel can come back . . . then maybe Eugene can come back too.

REUBEN. We can go down to the hideout like we used to! He could come back every day! It be just like he ain't dead.

ZONIA. Maybe that ain't right for him to come back. Feel kinda funny to be playing games with a haunt.

REUBEN. Yeah . . . what if everybody came back? What if Miss Mabel came back just like she ain't dead? Where you and your daddy gonna sleep then?

ZONIA. Maybe they go back at night and don't need no place to sleep.

REUBEN. It still don't seem right. I'm sure gonna miss Eugene. He's the bestest friend anybody ever had.

ZONIA. My daddy say if you miss somebody too much it can kill you. Say he missed me till it liked to killed him.

REUBEN. What if your mama's already dead and all the time you looking for her?

ZONIA. Naw, she ain't dead. My daddy say he can smell her.

REUBEN. You can't smell nobody that ain't here. Maybe he smelling old Miss Bertha. Maybe Miss Bertha your mama?

ZONIA. Naw, she ain't. My mamma got long pretty hair and she five feet from the ground!

REUBEN. Your daddy say when you leaving?

(ZONIA *doesn't respond.*)

Maybe you gonna stay in Mr. Seth's house and don't go looking for your mama no more.

ZONIA. He say we got to leave on Saturday.

REUBEN. Dag! You just only been here for a little while. Don't seem like nothing ever stay the same.

ZONIA. He say he got to find her. Find him a place in the world.

REUBEN. He could find him a place in Mr. Seth's house.

ZONIA. It don't look like we never gonna find her.

REUBEN. Maybe he find her by Saturday then you don't have to go.

ZONIA. I don't know.

REUBEN. You look like a spider!

ZONIA. I ain't no spider!

REUBEN. Got them long skinny arms and legs. You look like one of them Black Widows.

ZONIA. I ain't no Black Widow nothing! My name is Zonia!

REUBEN. That's what I'm gonna call you ... Spider.

ZONIA. You can call me that, but I don't have to answer.

REUBEN. You know what? I think maybe I be your husband when I grow up.

ZONIA. How you know?

REUBEN. I ask my grandpap how you know and he say when the moon falls into a girl's eyes that how you know.

ZONIA. Did it fall into my eyes?

REUBEN. Not that I can tell. Maybe I ain't old enough. Maybe you ain't old enough.

ZONIA. So there! I don't know why you telling me that lie!

REUBEN. That don't mean nothing 'cause I can't see it. I know it's there. Just the way you look at me sometimes look like the moon might have been in your eyes.

ZONIA. That don't mean nothing if you can't see it. You supposed to see it.

REUBEN. Shucks, I see it good enough for me. You ever let anybody kiss you?

ZONIA. Just my daddy. He kiss me on the cheek.

REUBEN. It's better on the lips. Can I kiss you on the lips?

ZONIA. I don't know. You ever kiss anybody before?

REUBEN. I had a cousin let me kiss her on the lips one time. Can I kiss you?

ZONIA. Okay.

(REUBEN *kisses her and lays his head against her chest.*)

What you doing?

REUBEN. Listening. Your heart singing!

ZONIA. It is not.

REUBEN. Just beating like a drum. Let's kiss again.

(*They kiss again.*)

Now you mine, Spider. You my girl, okay?

ZONIA. Okay.

REUBEN. When I get grown, I come looking for you.

ZONIA. Okay.

(*The lights fade to black.*)

SCENE FIVE

The lights come up on the kitchen. It is Saturday. BYNUM, LOOMIS, *and* ZONIA *sit at the table.* BERTHA *prepares breakfast.* ZONIA *has on a white dress.*

———

BYNUM. With all this rain we been having he might have ran into some washed-out roads. If that wagon got stuck in the mud he's liable to be still upriver somewhere. If he's upriver then he ain't coming until tomorrow.

LOOMIS. Today's Saturday. He say he be here on Saturday.

BERTHA. Zonia, you gonna eat your breakfast this morning.

ZONIA. Yes, ma'am.

BERTHA. I don't know how you expect to get any bigger if you don't eat. I ain't never seen a child that didn't eat. You about as skinny as a bean pole.

(*Pause.*)

Mr. Loomis, there's a place down on Wylie. Zeke Mayweather got a house down there. You ought to see if he got any rooms.

(LOOMIS *doesn't respond.*)

Well, you're welcome to some breakfast before you move on.

(MATTIE *enters from the stairs.*)

MATTIE. Good morning.

BERTHA. Morning, Mattie. Sit on down there and get you some breakfast.

BYNUM. Well, Mattie Campbell, you been sleeping with that up under your pillow like I told you?

BERTHA. Bynum, I done told you to leave that gal alone with all that stuff. You around here meddling in other people's lives. She don't want to hear all that. You ain't doing nothing but confusing her with that stuff.

MATTIE (*To* LOOMIS). You all fixing to move on?

LOOMIS. Today's Saturday. I'm paid up till Saturday.

MATTIE. Where you going to?

LOOMIS. Gonna find my wife.

MATTIE. You going off to another city?

LOOMIS. We gonna see where the road take us. Ain't no telling where we wind up.

MATTIE. Eleven years is a long time. Your wife . . . she might have taken up with someone else. People do that when they get lost from each other.

LOOMIS. Zonia. Come on, we gonna find your mama.

(LOOMIS and ZONIA cross to the door.)

MATTIE *(To ZONIA)*. Zonia, Mattie got a ribbon here match your dress. Want Mattie to fix your hair with her ribbon?

(ZONIA nods. MATTIE ties the ribbon in her hair.)

There . . . it got a color just like your dress. *(To LOOMIS.)* I hope you find her. I hope you be happy.

LOOMIS. A man looking for a woman be lucky to find you. You a good woman, Mattie. Keep a good heart.

(LOOMIS and ZONIA exit.)

BERTHA. I been watching that man for two weeks . . . and that's the closest I come to seeing him act civilized. I don't know what's between you all, Mattie . . . but the only thing that man needs is somebody to make him laugh. That's all you need in the world is love and laughter. That's all anybody needs. To have love in one hand and laughter in the other.

(BERTHA moves about the kitchen as though blessing it and chasing away the huge sadness that seems to envelop it. It is a dance and demonstration of her own magic, her own remedy that is centuries old and to which she is connected by the muscles of her heart and the blood's memory.)

You hear me, Mattie? I'm talking about laughing. The kind of laugh that comes from way deep inside. To just stand and laugh and let life flow right through you. Just laugh to let yourself know you're alive.

(She begins to laugh. It is a near-hysterical laughter that is a celebration of life, both its pain and its blessing. MATTIE and BYNUM join in the laughter. SETH enters from the front door.)

SETH. Well, I see you all having fun.

(SETH begins to laugh with them.)

That Loomis fellow standing up there on the corner watching the house. He standing right up there on Manila Street.

BERTHA. Don't you get started on him. The man done left out of here and that's the last I wanna hear of it. You about to drive me crazy with that man.

SETH. I just say he standing up there on the corner. Acting sneaky like he always do. He can stand up there all he want. As long as he don't come back in here.

(There is a knock on the door. SETH goes to answer it. Enter MARTHA LOOMIS [PENTECOST]. She is a young woman about twenty-eight. She is dressed as befitting a member of an Evangelist church. RUTHERFORD SELIG follows.)

SETH. Look here, Bertha. It's Martha Pentecost. Come on in, Martha. Who that with you? Oh . . . that's Selig. Come on in, Selig.

BERTHA. Come on in, Martha. It's sure good to see you.

BYNUM. Rutherford Selig, you a sure enough first-class People Finder!

SELIG. She was right out there in Rankin. You take that first right-hand road . . . right there at that church on Wooster Street. I started to go right past and something told me to stop at the church and see if they needed any dustpans.

SETH. Don't she look good, Bertha.

BERTHA. Look all nice and healthy.

MARTHA. Mr. Bynum . . . Selig told me my little girl was here.

SETH. There's some fellow around here say he your husband. Say his name is Loomis. Say you his wife.

MARTHA. Is my little girl with him?

SETH. Yeah, he got a little girl with him. I wasn't gonna tell him where you was. Not the way this fellow look. So he got Selig to find you.

MARTHA. Where they at? They upstairs?

SETH. He was standing right up there on Manila Street. I had to ask him to leave 'cause of how he was carrying on. He come in here one night—

(The door opens and LOOMIS and ZONIA enter. MARTHA and LOOMIS stare at each other.)

LOOMIS. Hello, Martha.

MARTHA. Herald . . . Zonia?

LOOMIS. You ain't waited for me, Martha. I got out the place looking to see your face. Seven years I waited to see your face.

MARTHA. Herald, I been looking for you. I wasn't but two months behind you when you went to my mama's and got Zonia. I been looking for you ever since.

LOOMIS. Joe Turner let me loose and I felt all turned around inside. I just wanted to see your face to know that the world was still there. Make sure everything still in its place so I could reconnect myself together. I got there and you was gone, Martha.

MARTHA. Herald . . .

LOOMIS. Left my little girl motherless in the world.

MARTHA. I didn't leave her motherless,

Herald. Reverend Tolliver wanted to move the church up North 'cause of all the trouble the colored folks was having down there. Nobody knew what was gonna happen traveling them roads. We didn't even know if we was gonna make it up here or not. I left her with my mama so she be safe. That was better than dragging her out on the road having to duck and hide from people. Wasn't no telling what was gonna happen to us. I didn't leave her motherless in the world. I been looking for you.

LOOMIS. I come up on Henry Thompson's place after seven years of living in hell, and all I'm looking to do is see your face.

MARTHA. Herald, I didn't know if you was ever coming back. They told me Joe Turner had you and my whole world split half in two. My whole life shattered. It was like I had poured it in a cracked jar and it all leaked out the bottom. When it go like that there ain't nothing you can do put it back together. You talking about Henry Thompson's place like I'm still gonna be working the land by myself. How I'm gonna do that? You wasn't gone but two months and Henry Thompson kicked me off his land and I ain't had no place to go but to my mama's. I stayed and waited there for five years before I woke up one morning and decided that you was dead. Even if you weren't, you was dead to me. I wasn't gonna carry you with me no more. So I killed you in my heart. I buried you. I mourned you. And then I picked up what was left and went on to make life without you. I was a young woman with life at my beckon. I couldn't drag you behind me like a sack of cotton.

LOOMIS. I just been waiting to look on your face to say my goodbye. That goodbye got so big at times, seem like it was gonna swallow me up. Like Jonah in the whale's belly I sat up in that goodbye for three years. That goodbye kept me out on the road searching. Not looking on women in their houses. It kept me bound up to the road. All the time that goodbye swelling up in my chest till I'm about to bust. Now that I see your face I can say my goodbye and make my own world.

(LOOMIS takes ZONIA's hand and presents her to MARTHA.)

Martha . . . here go your daughter. I tried to take care of her. See that she had something to eat. See that she was out of the elements. Whatever I know I tried to teach her. Now she need to learn from her mother whatever

you got to teach her. That way she won't be no one-sided person.

(LOOMIS stoops to ZONIA.)

Zonia, you go live with your mama. She a good woman. You go on with her and listen to her good. You my daughter and I love you like a daughter. I hope to see you again in the world somewhere. I'll never forget you.

ZONIA (Throws her arms around LOOMIS in a panic). I won't get no bigger! My bones won't get no bigger! They won't! I promise! Take me with you till we keep searching and never finding. I won't get no bigger! I promise!

LOOMIS. Go on and do what I told you now.

MARTHA (Goes to ZONIA and comforts her). It's alright, baby. Mama's here. Mama's here. Don't worry. Don't cry.

(MARTHA turns to BYNUM.)

Mr. Bynum, I don't know how to thank you. God bless you.

LOOMIS. It was you! All the time it was you that bind me up! You bound me to the road!

BYNUM. I ain't bind you, Herald Loomis. You can't bind what don't cling.

LOOMIS. Everywhere I go people wanna bind me up. Joe Turner wanna bind me up! Reverend Toliver wanna bind me up. You wanna bind me up. Everybody wanna bind me up. Well, Joe Turner's come and gone and Herald Loomis ain't for no binding. I ain't gonna let nobody bind me up!

(LOOMIS pulls out a knife.)

BYNUM. It wasn't you, Herald Loomis. I ain't bound you. I bound the little girl to her mother. That's who I bound. You binding yourself. You bound onto your song. All you got to do is stand up and sing it, Herald Loomis. It's right there kicking at your throat. All you got to do is sing it. Then you be free.

MARTHA. Herald . . . look at yourself! Standing there with a knife in your hand. You done gone over to the devil. Come on . . . put down the knife. You got to look to Jesus. Even if you done fell away from the church you can be saved again. The Bible say, "The Lord is my shepherd I shall not want. He maketh me to lie down in green pastures. He leads me beside the still water. He restoreth my soul. He leads me in the path of righteousness for His name's sake. Even though I walk through the shadow of death—"

LOOMIS. That's just where I be walking!

MARTHA. "I shall fear no evil. For Thou art with me. Thy rod and Thy staff, they comfort me."

LOOMIS. You can't tell me nothing about no valleys. I done been all across the valleys and the hills and the mountains and the oceans.

MARTHA. "Thou preparest a table for me in the presence of my enemies."

LOOMIS. And all I seen was a bunch of niggers dazed out of their woolly heads. And Mr. Jesus Christ standing there in the middle of them, grinning.

MARTHA. "Thou annointest my head with oil, my cup runneth over."

LOOMIS. He grin that big old grin . . . and niggers wallowing at his feet.

MARTHA. "Surely goodness and mercy shall follow me all the days of my life, and I shall dwell in the house of the Lord forever."

LOOMIS. Great big old white man . . . your Mr. Jesus Christ. Standing there with a whip in one hand and tote board in another, and them niggers swimming in a sea of cotton. And he counting. He tallying up the cotton. "Well, Jeremiah . . . what's the matter, you ain't picked but two hundred pounds of cotton today? Got to put you on half rations." And Jeremiah go back and lay up there on his half rations and talk about what a nice man Mr. Jesus Christ is 'cause he give him salvation after he die. Something wrong here. Something don't fit right!

MARTHA. You got to open up your heart and have faith, Herald. This world is just a trial for the next. Jesus offers you salvation.

LOOMIS. I been wading in the water. I been walking all over the River Jordan. But what it get me, huh? I done been baptized with blood of the lamb and the fire of the Holy Ghost. But what I got, huh? I got salvation? My enemies all around me picking the flesh from my bones. I'm choking on my own blood and all you got to give me is salvation?

MARTHA. You got to be clean, Herald. You got to be washed with the blood of the lamb.

LOOMIS. Blood make you clean? You clean with blood?

MARTHA. Jesus bled for you. He's the Lamb of God who takes away the sins of the world.

LOOMIS. I don't need nobody to bleed for me! I can bleed for myself.

MARTHA. You got to be something, Herald. You just can't be alive. Life don't mean nothing unless it got a meaning.

LOOMIS. What kind of meaning you got? What kind of clean you got, woman? You want blood? Blood make you clean? You clean with blood?

(LOOMIS *slashes himself across the chest. He rubs the blood over his face and comes to a realization.*)

I'm standing! I'm standing. My legs stood up! I'm standing now!

(*Having found his song, the song of self-sufficiency, fully resurrected, cleansed and given breath, free from any encumbrance other than the workings of his own heart and the bonds of the flesh, having accepted the responsibility for his own presence in the world, he is free to soar above the environs that weighed and pushed his spirit into terrifying contractions.*)

Goodbye, Martha.

(LOOMIS *turns and exits, the knife still in his hands.* MATTIE *looks about the room and rushes out after him.*)

BYNUM. Herald Loomis, you shining! You shining like new money!

The lights go down to BLACK.

The Cocktail Hour

A. R. GURNEY

TO MY FAMILY

Premiered at the Old Globe Theatre, San Diego, California, in June 1988. It was first produced in New York City by Roger L. Stevens, Thomas Viertel, Steven Baruch and Richard Frankel at the Promenade Theatre, where it opened on October 20, 1988. The cast, in order of appearance, was as follows:

BRADLEY	Keene Curtis
JOHN	Bruce Davison
ANN	Nancy Marchand
NINA	Holland Taylor

Directed by Jack O'Brien
Settings and costumes by Steven Rubin
Lighting by Kent Dorsey
Managing Director: Thomas Hall
Production Stage Manager: Douglas Pagliotti

The Cocktail Hour takes place in upstate New York in the 1970s. In it, a playwright comes home to obtain the permission of his parents to produce a play, also called *The Cocktail Hour,* he has written about the family. At first, his parents are hostile to his request. His mother asks him, "What if you turned it into a book? . . . Books aren't quite so public. . . ."

The Cocktail Hour is based upon a true incident in A. R. Gurney's life: Upon viewing his 1971 play *Scenes from American Life,* which deals with a family of WASPs in Buffalo, New York (Gurney's hometown), the playwright's father found it difficult to speak to him for a full year afterward. Depicting an older couple whose adherence to tradition is unyielding in the face of a changing world, and whose reluctance to accept change in their children only finally begins to soften, *The Cocktail Hour* is a satiric and moving play that laughs not only at its subjects but at itself. A dissection of fading WASP culture as seen through the eyes of the black sheep of the family, the play makes subtle revelations about its characters with richly comic dialogue.

In *The Cocktail Hour,* we enter a world where "servants are the mainstay of civilization." Gurney grew up in Buffalo in a world "bounded by the Saturn Club, the Nichols School, the Friday-night dancing class . . . and the Trinity Episcopal Church, where my family had sat in the same pew for a hundred years. . . . From childhood, I was the guy who rebelled, not in action, but by what I said at the dinner table. I had a constant quarrel with that world, its prejudices, stuffiness, and closedness. Yet I found it congenial; it gave me a comforting sense of continuity. . . ."

For twenty-five years, Gurney has been teaching literature at MIT and writing during the summer months. Like Mamet and Foote, he records the characters and speech of a particular segment of society. "I feel some obligation to speak to, for, and about my people. . . . They have honor, decency, loyalty, a great sense of humor, a lot of charm, very good manners—they treat people courteously . . . are very hardworking and concerned about others. . . . Unfortunately, WASPs don't have a very good sense of self-worth . . . they have very little ability to deal with their feelings."

Gurney carries on the great tradition of drawing-room drama and fiction: Henry James, Noël Coward, Philip Barry, and S. N. Behrman. *The Cocktail Hour* revolves around that once-significant rite of the American manor: "It was the ritual of preparing the martini," states Gurney, "and after you had the glass in your hand, that was when you settled down and talked about those things that were really important to you. You confronted those issues that meant something and then you could enjoy your meal." "Everybody thinks that's their family," says Jack O'Brien, artistic director of San Diego's Old Globe Theatre and the director of the Los Angeles company of *The Cocktail Hour.* "That's my family as well as it is Pete's" (Gurney's nickname).

Albert Ramsdell Gurney, Jr., was born in 1930. His grandmother loved the theatre and took him to local matinées. As a youngster, he traveled to New York City to see *Death of a Salesman, A Streetcar Named Desire, Oklahoma!,* and *Kiss Me Kate.* While at St. Paul's Preparatory School, he won a prize for "Buffalo Meat," a story about his family; at Williams College, he came under the influence of Stephen Sondheim, an upperclassman who was already writing musicals.

Upon graduating from Williams College with a B.A. in 1952, Gurney entered the navy, and after a three-year hitch used his G.I. Bill scholarship to enroll in the Yale School of Drama. He wrote the first musical ever produced at Yale, *Love in Buffalo.* After his graduation in 1958, his first professional production, a musical version of *Tom Sawyer,* debuted in Missouri. Some of the one-act plays he wrote while at Yale were published in the late fifties in Margaret Mayorga's *Best Short Plays* books. One of them, *The Rape of Bunny Stuntz,* was produced Off Broadway in 1964. From 1962 to 1969, Gurney wrote

The Bridal Dinner, Around the World in Eighty Days, (a musical based on the Jules Verne novel), *The Comeback, The Golden Fleece, The David Show,* and *Tonight in Living Color.*

In 1971, the Lincoln Center Repertory Company presented Gurney's *Scenes from American Life,* for which the playwright received the Vernon Rice Drama Desk Award for 1971–72. *Children,* an adaptation of a John Cheever story, was presented in London in 1974, in the United States in 1979, and in Germany in 1980. Also in 1974, Gurney's first novel, *The Gospel According to Joe,* was published by Harper and Row. *Who Killed Richard Cory?* was staged in 1976, *The Wayside Motor Inn* in 1977, and *O Youth and Beauty,* another adaptation of a Cheever story, was presented on public television in 1980.

A second novel, *Entertaining Strangers,* was published by Doubleday in 1977. In 1981, Gurney took a sabbatical from teaching to write full time, and in 1982 and 1983, *The Middle Ages, What I Did Last Summer,* and *The Dining Room* were presented in New York City and in many regional theatres. Next came *The Golden Age* (1984) and *The Perfect Party* (1986), and a third novel, *The Snow Ball,* published by Arbor House. Also in 1986, Gurney's first Broadway production, *Sweet Sue,* opened. In 1988, *The Cocktail Hour* had its premiere in San Diego and then opened in New York, winning an Obie Award for actress Nancy Marchand, who played the mother. In 1990, Gurney's *Love Letters* was written and first produced. Sheridan Morley of the London *Times* has stated, "[Gurney] is the most elegant and accomplished writer to have come out of America since the war." Gurney is now at work on a musical that will focus on his own generation as parents instead of as children.

Gurney has also written *The Day the Pig Fell into the Well* (1956; an adaptation of the John Cheever story), *The Old One-Two* (1971), *The Open Meeting* (1983), and *Another Antigone* (1987). Gurney won a Rockefeller Award in 1977, an NEA Award in 1982, and an Award of Merit from the Academy of Arts and Letters in 1987. He is a member of the Dramatists Guild and became the president of the Dramatists Play Service in 1990.

CAST

BRADLEY
ANN, his wife
JOHN, their son
NINA, their daughter

The play takes place during early evening in early fall in the mid-seventies, in a city in upstate New York.

AUTHOR'S NOTE

The set is basically realistic, but should also be vaguely theatrical, reminding us subliminally of those photographs of sets of American drawing room comedies in the thirties or forties, designed by Donald Oenslager or Oliver Smith. In any case, it is a lovely step-down living room, with an arched entrance leading to a front hall, and perhaps the start of a staircase. There is an antique writing desk, a working fireplace with a mantelpiece, a fire bench, and a pretty good Impressionist painting hanging over it. The Upstage wall is full of good books, all hard-back, some leather-bound sets, some large art books, all neatly organized. The room also contains a baby grand piano on which are a number of black-and-white family photographs framed in silver or leather: portraits of children, snapshots of children at sports, pictures of dogs, large group shots of families, an occasional faded photograph of a 19th-century couple. Downstage, of course, is a large, comfortable couch with a coffee table in front of it, along with several comfortable chairs and a movable footstool. There might be a corner china cabinet displaying excellent china. All the furniture looks old and waxed and clean. There's a thick, warm Persian rug on the floor. Through the windows, a few barren branches are seen in the early evening light. The overall effect should not be opulent or grandiose or particularly trendy, but rather tasteful, comfortable, and civilized, an oasis of traditional warmth and solid good taste, a haven in a heartless world. On the coffee table, noticeably set apart from the china ashtrays and other objects, is a thick manuscript in a black cover.

ACT I

AT RISE: The stage is empty. The light from the windows indicates early evening, early fall. After a moment, Bradley enters, carrying a silver ice bucket. He is in his seventies and very well dressed. He is followed by his son, John, who is in his early forties and more informally dressed. John carries a silver tray with several liquor bottles and glasses on it.

───────

BRADLEY *(Turning on the light in the hall).* This is what's called bringing the mountain to Mohammed.

JOHN. Right.

BRADLEY. Otherwise we'd have to trek all the way back to the pantry whenever we needed to return to the well.

JOHN. Makes sense to me.

BRADLEY *(Setting down the ice bucket on the table behind the couch).* Of course when we had maids, it was different. You could just push the buzzer, and say bring this, bring that, and they'd bring it.

JOHN *(Setting down the tray).* I remember.

BRADLEY. Not that they could mix a drink. They couldn't make a martini to save their skin. But they could make ice, bring water, pass cheese. It was very pleasant.

JOHN. Before the war.

BRADLEY. That damn war. Those Germans have a lot to answer for. Well. Let's see … What are we missing? … Have we got the lemon for your mother's martini?

JOHN *(Taking it out of his pocket).* It's right here, Pop.

BRADLEY. Your mother likes a small twist of lemon in her martini.

JOHN. I know.

BRADLEY. And my Cutty Sark scotch.

JOHN. Oh yes.

BRADLEY *(Looking at the label).* It's a good scotch. Not a great scotch, but a good one. I always enjoy the picture on the label. The American clipper ships were the fastest in the world. Magnificent vessels. Beautifully built. Made our country great.

JOHN. The "Cutty Sark" was English, Pop.

BRADLEY. I know that. I'm speaking generally.

JOHN. Actually the clipper ships only lasted a few years.

BRADLEY. Not true.

JOHN. Only a few—before steam.

BRADLEY. Not true at all.

JOHN. I think so, Pop.

BRADLEY. I wish your brother were here. He'd know. He knows all there is to know about boats.

JOHN *(Going to the bookcase)*. I'll look it up.

BRADLEY. Never mind. I said, *never mind.* We are not going to waste the evening in pedantic arguments. *(JOHN returns from the bookcase.)* Now look what I did. I brought out a whole bottle of soda water. Automatically. Thinking your brother *would* be here. Won't drink anything else. Never did.

JOHN. Smart man.

BRADLEY. I telephoned him yesterday. Tried to get him to come up. "Come on, Jigger," I said. "Join us. John's coming. Your sister will be here. We'll all have cocktails and your mother will provide an excellent dinner. You can play the piano. We'll all gather around the piano and sing. Bring Sylvia, if you want. Bring the children. I'll pay for the whole thing." But no. Wouldn't do it. Jigger's a very positive person, once he's made up his mind.

JOHN. It's a tough trip for him, Pop.

BRADLEY. I know that.

JOHN. He's working weekends now. They've put him back in sales.

BRADLEY. We all have to sell. One way or another.

JOHN. He's looking for another job.

BRADLEY. I know all that. You don't need to tell me that. I'm in touch with him all the time. *(He returns to the bar.)* What'll you have, by the way?

JOHN. Some of that soda water, actually.

BRADLEY. You?

JOHN. That's what I'll have.

BRADLEY. You're the one who likes to tuck it away.

JOHN. Not tonight.

BRADLEY. And why not, may I ask?

JOHN. It makes me say and do things I'm sorry for later.

BRADLEY. That's the fun of it.

JOHN. Not for me.

BRADLEY. You're not in difficulty, are you?

JOHN. No.

BRADLEY. You're not in one of those organizations that make you give it up?

JOHN. I just like to keep a lid on myself, Pop.

BRADLEY. Suit yourself. *(Pours him a glass of soda water.)* Soda water it is. What is it Lord Byron tells us? "Let us have wine and women, mirth and laughter; sermons and soda water the day after" . . . Maybe you'll change your mind later on.

JOHN. Maybe I will.

BRADLEY *(Now pouring his own scotch and water very carefully)*. Of course, nobody drinks much these days. At least not with any relish. Marv Watson down at the club is now completely on the wagon. You sit down beside him at the big table, and what's he drinking? Orange juice. I said, "Am I confused about the time, Marv? Are we having breakfast?" Of course the poor thing can't hear, so it doesn't make any difference. But you go to parties these days and even the young people aren't drinking. I saw young Kathy Bickford at the Shoemaker wedding. Standing on the sidelines, looking very morose indeed. I went up to her and said, "What's that strange concoction you've got in your hand, Kathy?" She said, "Lemon Squirt." I said, "What?" She said, "Sugar-free, noncarbonated Lemon Squirt." So I said, "Now, Kathy, you listen to me. You're young and attractive, and you should be drinking champagne. You should be downing a good glass of French champagne, one, two, three, and then you should be out there on that dance floor, kicking up your heels with every usher in sight. And after you've done that, you should come right back here, and dance with me!" Of course, she walked away. *(He finishes making his drink.)* They all walk away these days. I suppose I'm becoming a tiresome old fool.

JOHN. Hardly, Pop.

BRADLEY. Yes, well, I can still keep the ball in the air, occasionally. I gave a toast at the Shoemakers' bridal dinner. It went over very well.

JOHN. Mother told me.

BRADLEY. Oh yes. I made a few amusing remarks. I complimented the bride. You know Sarah Shoemaker? She's terribly tall. She towers over the groom. So I began by saying she stoops to conquer.

JOHN. That's a good one, Pop.

BRADLEY. Yes, they liked that. I can still get on my feet if called upon. They still want me to be the Master of Ceremonies at the annual fund-raiser for the art gallery. They still ask me to do that.

JOHN. That's great, Pop.

BRADLEY. Of course, we all know what Emerson says, "The music that can deepest reach, and cure all ills, is cordial speech." Doesn't Emerson tell us that?

JOHN. I think he does, Pop.

BRADLEY. You're the publisher in the family. You should know.

JOHN *(Going to bookcase again).* Let me look it up.

BRADLEY. It doesn't matter.

JOHN. It'll be right here, in Bartlett's. *(Takes down a book.)*

BRADLEY. No! We are not going to destroy the rhythm of the conversation with a lot of disruptive excursions to the bookcase.

JOHN *(Putting the book back).* O.K.

BRADLEY. Besides, I know Emerson said it. I'm positive.

JOHN. O.K., Pop. *(BRADLEY sits in what is obviously his special chair.)*

BRADLEY *(After a pause).* Well. Your mother tells me you've written a play.

JOHN. That's right.

BRADLEY. Another play.

JOHN. Right.

BRADLEY *(Indicating manuscript on table).* Is that it?

JOHN. That's it.

BRADLEY. Do you think this one will get on?

JOHN. I think so.

BRADLEY. Some of them don't, you know.

JOHN. I know that, Pop.

BRADLEY. I don't mean just yours. Apparently it's a very difficult thing to get them done.

JOHN. That's for sure.

BRADLEY. Of course nobody goes to the theatre any more. Ted Moffatt just made a trip to New York to see his new grandson. I said, "Did you go to the theatre, Ted? Did you see any new plays?" He said he did not. He said all they do these days in the theatre is stand around and shout obscenities at each other. And then take off their clothes. Ted said he wouldn't be caught dead at the theatre. And Ted was once a big theatregoer.

JOHN. There's some good stuff down there, Pop.

BRADLEY. For you, maybe. Not for me. *(Pause.)* We liked that play of yours we saw in Boston.

JOHN. Thanks.

BRADLEY. Done at some college, wasn't it?

JOHN. Boston University.

BRADLEY. We liked that one. Your mother particularly liked it. She thought it was quite amusing.

JOHN. Tell the critics that.

BRADLEY. Oh well, the critics. They're not infallible.

JOHN. I'll keep that in mind, Pop. *(Pause.)*

BRADLEY. We liked that little play of yours we saw in New York a couple of years ago.

JOHN. I thought you *didn't* like it.

BRADLEY. No, we did. Miserable little theatre. Impossible seats. Impossible bathrooms. But the play had charm.

JOHN. Thanks, Pop.

BRADLEY. Or at least the actress did. What was her name again?

JOHN. Swoosie Kurtz.

BRADLEY. Yes. Swoosie Kurtz. Amusing name. Amusing actress. I hear she's gone on to do very well. Your mother saw her on television.

JOHN. She's great.

BRADLEY. Lovely profile. Lovely shoulders. She was very attractive in your play.

JOHN. I'll tell her.

BRADLEY. Yes, do. Tell her your father liked her very much. *(Pause. He eyes the manuscript on the coffee table.)* And now you've written another one.

JOHN. Tried to.

BRADLEY. Looks a little long.

JOHN. They'll make me cut it.

BRADLEY. I hope they make you cut it a good deal.

JOHN. They probably will.

BRADLEY. Nobody likes long plays.

JOHN. I know that, Pop.

BRADLEY. Everyone likes to get it over with promptly, and go home to bed.

JOHN. I know.

BRADLEY. Will Swoosie Kurtz be in this one?

JOHN. I doubt it.

BRADLEY. I hope you get someone who's just as much fun.

JOHN. This play's a little different, Pop.

BRADLEY. Different? How is it different?

JOHN. It's not as light as the others.

BRADLEY. Don't tell me you're getting gloomy in your middle years.

JOHN. Not gloomy, exactly, Pop.

BRADLEY. Are people going to scream and shout in this one?

JOHN. They might raise their voices occasionally.

BRADLEY. Are they going to take off their clothes?

JOHN. No, they won't do that, I promise.

BRADLEY. Put Swoosie Kurtz in it. She wouldn't shout. Though I suppose I wouldn't mind if she took off her clothes. *(Pause.)*

JOHN. This one's about us, Pop.

BRADLEY. Us?

JOHN. The family.

BRADLEY. Oh really?

JOHN. This one cuts pretty close to home.

BRADLEY. Oh well. I understand that. You have to deal with what you know. I do it when I'm toastmaster. I sometimes mention your mother. I refer occasionally to you children. At the Shoemakers' wedding, I told an amusing story about Jigger.

JOHN. This one's about you, Pop.

BRADLEY. Me?

JOHN. You.

BRADLEY. Just me?

JOHN. No, no. Mother's in it, of course. And Nina. And Jigger's referred to a lot. And I put myself in it. But I think it centers around you.

BRADLEY. Me.

JOHN. I thought I better tell you that, Pop.

BRADLEY. And it's going on?

JOHN. It's supposed to.

BRADLEY. In New York?

JOHN. That's the talk.

BRADLEY. When?

JOHN. Soon. Supposedly. *(Pause.)*

BRADLEY. Do you use our names?

JOHN. Of course not, Pop.

BRADLEY. But it's recognizably us.

JOHN. By people who know us.

BRADLEY. What about people who *don't* know us?

JOHN. They'll sense it's a personal play. *(Pause.)*

BRADLEY. I suppose you make cracks.

JOHN. Cracks?

BRADLEY. Wisecracks. Smart remarks.

JOHN. Not really.

BRADLEY. "Not really." What does that mean, "not really"?

JOHN. I just try to show who we are, Pop.

BRADLEY. Oh, I'm sure. I know what you write. I remember that crack you made about your grandmother in one of your plays.

JOHN. What crack?

BRADLEY. You know very well what crack. You poked fun at her. You ridiculed her. My dear sweet mother who never hurt a fly. That gracious lady who took you to the Erlanger

Theatre every Saturday afternoon. That saint of a woman without whom you wouldn't even know what a play *was!*

JOHN. I didn't ridicule her, Pop.

BRADLEY. People laughed. I was there. I heard them laugh at your grandmother. Complete strangers roaring their heads off at my poor dear mother—I can't discuss it.

JOHN. Come on, Pop.

BRADLEY. I don't think you've written anything in your life where you haven't sneaked in a lot of smart-guy wisecracks about our family and our way of life.

JOHN. Please, Pop . . .

BRADLEY. That story you wrote at boarding school, that show you did at college . . .

JOHN. You never came to that show.

BRADLEY. I didn't want to come. I knew, I *knew* what you'd say.

JOHN. It was just fun, Pop.

BRADLEY. Oh yes? Well, your idea of fun and my idea of fun are very different. My idea does not include making fools out of your family.

JOHN. Oh Jesus.

BRADLEY. And don't swear! It's demeaning to both of us.

JOHN. O.K., O.K. I'm sorry. *(Pause.)*

BRADLEY. And you've found producers for this thing?

JOHN. Yes.

BRADLEY. They'll lose their shirt.

JOHN. Maybe.

BRADLEY. They'll go completely bankrupt.

JOHN. Come on, Pop.

BRADLEY. What did that critic say about your last play? What was his remark?

JOHN. He said we weren't worth writing about.

BRADLEY. There you are. You see? Nobody cares about our way of life.

JOHN. I care, Pop.

BRADLEY. You? You've never cared in your life. You've gone out of your way *not* to care. Where were you for our fortieth anniversary? Where were you for my seventy-fifth birthday?

JOHN. You said not to come.

BRADLEY. I didn't want you snickering in the corner, making snide remarks. Oh God, I should have known. I should have known that's why you came up here this weekend. Not to visit your parents in their wanning years. Not to touch base with the city that nourished you half your life. Oh no. Nothing like that. Simply to announce that you plan to humilate us all in front of a lot of strangers in New York City.

JOHN. I came home to get your permission, Pop.

BRADLEY. My permission?

JOHN. I haven't signed any contract yet.

BRADLEY. Then don't.

JOHN *(After a moment)*. All right, I won't.

BRADLEY. How can I give my permission for a thing like that?

JOHN. All right, Pop.

BRADLEY. How can I approve of someone fouling his own nest?

JOHN. I don't foul—

BRADLEY. How can I possibly seal my own doom?

JOHN. Oh, come on, Pop.

BRADLEY. I suppose I have no legal recourse.

JOHN. The play's *off*, Pop.

BRADLEY. I mean, you don't need to write plays anyway. You have a perfectly good job in publishing.

JOHN. That just keeps me going, Pop.

BRADLEY. It's a fine job. It's a solid, dependable, respectable job.

JOHN. It's not what I really want to do.

BRADLEY. Well, do it anyway. Most men in this world spend a lifetime doing what they don't want to do. And they work harder at it than you do.

JOHN. Come on, Pop . . .

BRADLEY. After I'm dead, after your mother's dead, after everyone you can possibly hurt has long since gone, then you can write your plays. And you can put them on wherever you want—New York, Hollywood, right here in Memorial Auditorium, I don't care. But not now. Please.

JOHN. O.K.

BRADLEY. I'm tired.

JOHN. O.K., Pop.

BRADLEY. I'm not well.

JOHN. I know, Pop.

BRADLEY. I'm not well at all.

JOHN. Case closed, Pop. Really.

BRADLEY. Thank you very much. *(Pause. They are awkward alone.)* Sure you don't want a drink?

JOHN. No thanks. *(Pause.)*

BRADLEY. Where's your mother? . . . Suddenly I thoroughly miss your mother. *(Going to doorway, calling off.)* Darling, where are you?

ANN'S VOICE *(Offstage)*. I'm bringing cheese!

BRADLEY *(To* JOHN*)*. She's bringing cheese.

(Eyeing manuscript.) Did you tell her about this play?

JOHN. Yes.

BRADLEY. Did she read it?

JOHN. She said she didn't want to.

BRADLEY. Why not?

JOHN. I'm not sure.

BRADLEY. That's the trouble. We never are, with your mother. *(*ANN *enters, carrying a plate of crackers and cheese. She is a lovely woman, richly and fashionably dressed.)*

ANN. There. *(Both men immediately get to their feet.)* I think I may have established a modicum of order in the kitchen. *(She waits for* JOHN *to move his script out of the way, then puts the plate of hors d'oeuvres on the coffee table.)* And now I can at least pretend to relax.

BRADLEY. What would you like to drink, darling?

ANN *(Crossing to close the curtains)*. After almost fifty years of marriage, you know very well what I'd like.

BRADLEY. After almost fifty years of marriage, I know very well always to ask.

ANN. Then I'd like a very dry martini, with plenty of ice . . .

ANN AND BRADLEY. . . . and a small twist of lemon.

BRADLEY. Thy will be done. *(He goes to the bar, mixes the drink carefully for her.)*

ANN *(To* JOHN, *after she has partially pulled the curtains)*. Don't ask me when we'll eat. We are flying on a wing and a prayer in the dinner department.

JOHN. Who've you got out there, Mother? Mildred? Agnes? Who?

ANN. Neither one. Mildred has broken her hip, and Agnes has gone to meet her maker.

JOHN. Aw . . .

ANN. What I have, out there, is Agnes's cousin's niece, who arrived in a snappy red convertible, and whose name is Cheryl Marie, and who I suspect has never made gravy in her life.

JOHN. We should have just made dinner ourselves, Mother.

ANN. Oh, yes. "Ourselves." I've heard that one before. "Ourselves" . . . "Ourselves" means me. It means that yours truly is slaving away out there while the rest of you are enjoying the cocktail hour in here. No thank you, John. I believe in paying people to do things occasionally, even if the person paid happens to be named Cheryl Marie. *(She sits on the couch.)*

BRADLEY *(Handing her a drink).* Here you are, darling.

ANN. Thank you, dear. *(To* JOHN.*)* No, I'm sorry. The cocktail hour is sacred, in my humble opinion. Even when your father and I are home alone, we still have it. In the kitchen. While I'm cooking. *(She holds out her hand automatically for a cocktail napkin.)*

BRADLEY *(Handing her a stack of cocktail napkins).* That's why we did the kitchen over. So we could have it in there.

ANN. I know you children all think you're too busy to have it.

BRADLEY. You're missing something.

ANN. I think so, too.

BRADLEY *(Joining* ANN *on the couch).* We're never too busy for the cocktail hour.

ANN. It allows people to unwind.

BRADLEY. It allows people to sit down together at the end of the day . . .

ANN. To talk things over . . . Settle things down . . .

BRADLEY. The bishop used to say— remember this, darling?—Bishop Dow used to say when he came here for dinner that the cocktail hour took the place of evening prayers.

ANN. Well, I don't know about that.

BRADLEY. No, he did. That's what he said.

ANN. Well, all I know is I cherish it. And now I want to know what I've already missed.

JOHN. Nothing.

BRADLEY. We had a brief discussion of the contemporary theatre.

JOHN. Which terminated rather abruptly.

ANN *(Looking from one to the other).* Oh. *(Pause.)* Who'll have some brie? Bradley?

BRADLEY. No, thank you.

ANN. John?

JOHN *(Pulling up a footstool).* Thanks.

ANN. I must say I love the theatre.

BRADLEY. Used to love it.

ANN. It used to be very much a part of our lives.

BRADLEY. Years ago. Before the Erlanger Theatre was torn down.

ANN. All the plays would come here.

BRADLEY. All the good plays.

JOHN. I remember . . .

ANN. Such wonderful plays. With such wonderful plots. They were always about these attractive couples . . .

BRADLEY. And the husband would have committed some minor indiscretion . . .

ANN. Normally the wife did, darling.

BRADLEY. No, no. I think it was he . . .

ANN. She did it more, sweetie. The *wife* was normally the naughty one.

BRADLEY. Well, whoever it was, they were all very attractive about it. And they'd have these attractive leading ladies . . .

ANN. Gertrude Lawrence, Ina Claire, Katharine Hepburn . . .

BRADLEY. They'd all come here . . .

JOHN. I remember your talking about them . . .

BRADLEY. Your mother played tennis with Hepburn at the Tennis Club.

ANN. Oh, I think we hit a ball or two . . .

BRADLEY. Your mother beat her.

ANN. Oh, I don't think I *beat* her, Bradley.

BRADLEY. You beat Katharine Hepburn, my love.

ANN. I think we might have played a little doubles, darling.

BRADLEY. You beat Hepburn, six-three, six-four! *That* I remember!

ANN. Well, maybe I did.

BRADLEY. And we met the Lunts.

ANN. Oh, the Lunts, the Lunts . . .

BRADLEY. They were friends of Bill Hart's. So we all met at the Statler for a cocktail. After a matinee.

ANN. They were terribly amusing.

JOHN. I remember your telling me about the Lunts.

BRADLEY. They could both talk at exactly the same time . . .

(They do this, of course.)

ANN. Without interrupting each other . . .

BRADLEY. It was uncanny . . .

ANN. They'd say the wittiest things . . .

BRADLEY. Simultaneously . . .

ANN. And you'd understand both . . .

BRADLEY. It was absolutely uncanny.

ANN. Of course they'd been married so long . . .

BRADLEY. Knew each other so well . . .

ANN. They made you feel very sophisticated. *(They both unconsciously cross their legs at the same time.)*

BRADLEY *(Touching her hand).* They made you feel proud to be married.

ANN. Absolutely. I totally agree. *(Pause.)* I wish you'd write plays like that, John.

BRADLEY. Won't do it. Refuses to. Simply doesn't want to.

ANN. But I mean, there's a real *need.* Jane Babcock went to Connecticut last weekend to visit her old roommate from Westover, and they thought they'd go into New York to see a play. Well, they looked in the paper and there was absolutely nothing they wanted to see. Finally, they decided to take a chance on one of those noisy English musicals. But when they called for tickets, the man said he was going to charge them three dollars extra. Just for telephoning. When they were calling long distance anyway. Well, that did it, of course. They went to the movies instead. And apparently the movie was perfectly horrible. People were shooting each other—in the *face!* . . . and using the most repulsive language while they were doing it, and the audience was composed of noisy teen-agers who screamed and yelled and rattled candy wrappers all around them. Finally they walked out and drove back to New Canaan, thoroughly disappointed with each other and the world. Jane said they really didn't snap out of it until they had cocktails.

BRADLEY. It's all over. The life we led is completely gone.

ANN. Jane said if one of your plays had been on, John, they would have gone to that. And paid the extra three dollars, too.

JOHN *(Glancing at BRADLEY)*. My plays are a sore subject, Mother.

ANN. Oh dear.

BRADLEY. A very sore subject.

ANN. Yes, well, it seems that John at least makes some attempt to write about things we know.

BRADLEY. Oh yes. Undercutting, trivializing . . .

ANN. Oh now, darling . . .

BRADLEY *(Looking warily at manuscript)*. What's it called, this play?

JOHN. It's called *The Cocktail Hour*, actually.

BRADLEY. It's called the *what?*

JOHN. *The Cocktail Hour.*

BRADLEY. That's a terrible title.

ANN. Oh now, sweetheart . . .

BRADLEY. Terrible.

JOHN. Why is it terrible?

BRADLEY. To begin with, it's been used.

JOHN. That's *The Cocktail PARTY*, Pop. That's T.S. Eliot.

BRADLEY. Even worse. We walked out on that one.

ANN. This is *The Cocktail HOUR*, darling.

BRADLEY. Doesn't make any difference.

ANN. No, it does. A cocktail *party* is a public thing. You *invite* people to a cocktail party. A cocktail *hour* is family. It's private. It's personal. It's very different.

BRADLEY. Nobody will know that. It will confuse everyone. They'll come expecting T.S. Eliot, and they'll get John. Either way, they'll want their money back.

JOHN. They won't want anything back, Pop. I'm putting it on the shelf. Remember?

ANN. On the shelf?

BRADLEY. Where I hope it will remain for a very long time.

ANN. Is that the solution?

BRADLEY. That's the solution. We've agreed on that, that's what we've agreed on. *(He goes into the hall to check the barometer.)*

ANN. Oh dear. *(Pause.)* How's Ellen, by the way?

JOHN. Fine.

ANN. I wish she had come along.

JOHN. She had a conference today, Mother.

ANN. Oh, I think that's wonderful. I wish I'd had a job when I was young.

BRADLEY *(From the hall)*. All changing, all going . . .

ANN. And how are the children?

JOHN. Fine. Getting on. Growing up. Charlie already plans to go all the way out to the University of Colorado.

BRADLEY. All gone . . . Married couples leading totally different lives. Children scattered all over the map . . .

ANN. I wish you'd brought them all along.

BRADLEY *(Returning to the room)*. I wish Jigger had come.

ANN. I wish everyone had come. John's family, Jigger's . . .

BRADLEY. We could have made this a family reunion.

JOHN. Which is another play by T.S. Eliot.

BRADLEY *(Crossing to piano)*. I don't care about that. All I know is that if Jigger had come, we'd be gathered around that piano right now. We'd be singing all the old songs: *Kiss Me, Kate—Southern Pacific* . . .

JOHN. It's *"South" Pacific*, Pop.

BRADLEY. Whatever it is, Jigger could play it. I miss him. I miss him terribly.

ANN. We miss *all* the family, Bradley. Everyone.

BRADLEY. Yes. That's right. Of course. *(To* JOHN, *indicating the photographs on the piano.)* You have that lovely wife, you have those fine, strapping children, do you ever write about them? Do you ever write about how hard your wife has worked over those children? Do you ever tell how your son pitched a no-hitter in Little League? How your sweet

Elsie won the art prize? Do you ever write about your brother winning the Sailing Cup? Do we ever hear anything good in your plays? Oh no. Instead you attack your parents in their old age.

JOHN. It's not an *attack*, Pop.

ANN *(Quickly)*. What if you turned it into a book, John? Books aren't quite so public. Billy Leeming wrote some book about *his* parents, and our local bookstores didn't even bother to carry it. Is it all right if he puts us in a book, Bradley?

JOHN. I can't write it as a book.

ANN. You can certainly try. *(To* BRADLEY.*)* It seems a shame to waste all that work.

BRADLEY *(Looking out a window)*. Where's Nina? Where's our daughter? She's normally right on time.

ANN. I think she had to do something with Portia. She'll be here. Meanwhile, I'd like another drink, Bradley. A weak one—but nonetheless, another.

JOHN. I'll get it.

ANN. No, your father likes to get it.

BRADLEY. While I still can. *(He bends over to get her glass with some difficulty.)*

JOHN. Your back O.K., Pop?

ANN. He's got a pinched nerve.

BRADLEY. Your mother thinks it's a pinched nerve.

ANN. Dr. Randall thinks it's a pinched nerve.

BRADLEY. Well, I think it's something far more serious.

JOHN. What do you think it is, Pop?

BRADLEY. Never mind. We'll call it a pinched nerve because that makes people more comfortable. We'll settle for a pinched nerve. *(He goes to mix* ANN*'s drink.)*

ANN *(Silently mouthing the words to* JOHN*)*. It's a pinched nerve.

BRADLEY *(Mixing her drink)*. And when I was in the hospital with double pneumonia, it was just a cold. I was lying there half-dead with a temperature of one hundred and four, and people would telephone, very much concerned, and your mother would say, "Oh, he's fine, he's perfectly fine, it's just a cold." When they're lowering me into my grave, she'll tell all my friends that it's hay fever. *(He works on her drink.)*

ANN *(Eyeing the manuscript)*. I suppose I should at least read the thing.

JOHN. Don't if you don't want to.

ANN. Maybe if I read it, it wouldn't seem so frightening.

BRADLEY. Who's frightened? Nobody's frightened.

ANN. Trouble is, it's always so painful, John. Reading your things. And seeing them acted, it's even worse. With all those people *watching*.

BRADLEY. It won't be acted.

ANN. But it should be *done*, Bradley.

BRADLEY. Not this one, please.

ANN. But he's written it. It's his *career*.

BRADLEY *(As he stirs* ANN*'s drink)*. It's not his career. Publishing is his career. That's what's paid the bills and brought up those children. That, and considerable help from you and me. What we're talking about here is an amusing little hobby which probably costs more than it brings in. Which is fine. We all have hobbies. I like my golf. I like to travel. But I don't use my hobby to attack my parents or make them look foolish in the eyes of the world. *(ANN finally gets her drink out of his hands.)*

JOHN. It's not a hobby! And I don't attack!

BRADLEY. Well, I don't care. I don't want to be on some stage. I don't want to have some actor imitating me. I've got very little time left on this earth . . .

ANN. Oh, Bradley . . .

BRADLEY. Very little. Much less than anyone thinks.

ANN. Now stop that, Bradley.

BRADLEY. And I don't want people laughing at me, or critics commenting about me, or the few friends I have left commiserating with me in these final days. I don't want that, John. I'm sorry. No. *(He crosses to sit in his chair.)*

ANN. One thing, John. If you don't do it, you won't get your name in the paper. And that's a good thing, in my humble opinion. I've never liked the publicity which happens with plays. It always seemed slightly cheap to me.

BRADLEY. Of course it is.

ANN. And it's dangerous. People read your name, and think you're rich, and rob you. Peggy Fentriss had her name in the paper for her work with the Philharmonic, and when she went to Bermuda, these burglars backed up a whole truck. They even took a grapefruit she left in the refrigerator.

BRADLEY *(Suddenly)*. What do you stand to lose if you don't put this thing on?

JOHN *(Ironically)*. Just my life, that's all, Pop. Just my life.

BRADLEY. Money. I'm talking about money. How much money would you make on it?

JOHN. You can't tell, Pop.

BRADLEY. Give me an educated guess.

JOHN. Oh . . . A little. If we're lucky.

BRADLEY. "A little. If we're lucky." What kind of an answer is that? No wonder you never went into business.

JOHN. I don't *know*, Pop.

ANN. I don't see why we have to talk about money, Bradley.

BRADLEY. What's the average amount of money you've made on your other plays?

JOHN. Average?

BRADLEY. Give me an average amount . . . Five thousand? Ten? What?

JOHN. Pop . . .

BRADLEY *(Crossing to the desk)*. I will give you a check for twenty thousand dollars right now for not putting on that play.

ANN. Bradley!

BRADLEY. Twenty thousand dollars . . . *(He sits down at the desk, finds his checkbook, makes out a check.)*

JOHN. Oh, Pop . . .

ANN *(Putting down her drink)*. Twenty *thousand!*

BRADLEY. You can't cash it, of course, till Monday, till I've covered it from savings, but I am hereby giving you a check.

JOHN. I don't want a check.

BRADLEY. Well, you might as well take it, because if you don't, I'll simply leave you twenty thousand extra in my will.

ANN. Oh, Bradley, now stop it!

BRADLEY *(Holding out the check to JOHN)*. Here. It's a good deal. You'll be twenty thousand to the good, and you can still put the thing on after I'm dead.

JOHN *(Walking away from it)*. Pop, I can't . . .

BRADLEY *(Following him)*. And if you invest it, you'll have the interest besides, which you wouldn't have otherwise.

ANN. I can't stand this.

JOHN. I don't want that money, Pop!

BRADLEY. And I don't want that play! I want some peace and privacy in the few days I have left of my life. And I'm willing to pay for it. Now there it is. *(Puts the check on the table by his chair.)* If you have any business sense at all, you'll take it. And if you don't want it for yourself, then give it to your children, who I hope will show more respect for you in your old age than you've ever shown for me.

JOHN. Oh, Pop, oh, Pop, oh, Pop . . . *(NINA's voice is heard from the hall.)*

NINA'S VOICE. Hello!

ANN. Ah. There's Nina. *(Calling off.)* We're having cocktails, dear! *(To others.)* I think it might be time to change the subject. *(NINA enters, well-dressed, attractive, mid-forties, removing her raincoat.)*

NINA *(Kissing her mother)*. I'm terribly sorry I'm late. Portia's in trouble again.

ANN. Oh no.

JOHN. Who's Portia?

NINA *(Kissing her father)*. She was up all night, wandering from room to room, sighing and groaning.

ANN. Oh no.

BRADLEY. That sweet Portia.

JOHN. Who's Portia?

NINA. And we also think there's something radically wrong with her rear end. *(She tosses her raincoat on the banister.)*

ANN. Oh no.

BRADLEY. Poor thing.

JOHN. Who the hell is *Portia?*

NINA *(Kissing her brother)*. Portia is our new golden retriever, and we're very worried about her.

BRADLEY. Portia is a brilliant beast. You should write a play about Portia.

JOHN. I could call it *Practical Dogs*. As opposed to *Practical Cats*. By T. S. Eliot.

BRADLEY. What would you like to drink, Pookins?

NINA. Just white wine, please.

JOHN. I'll get it, Pop.

BRADLEY *(Crossing to bar)*. *I'll* get it. I'm still capable of officiating at my own bar.

NINA. Plenty of rocks, please. And plenty of soda water. My stomach is in absolute knots.

JOHN. Over Portia?

BRADLEY. Portia is superb. I adore Portia.

NINA. Over everything.

ANN. Poor Nina, and her nervous stomach.

NINA. Let's not talk abolut my stomach, Mother. Let's talk about John. I hear you've written another play, John. *(Sitting on the couch.)*

BRADLEY. We're not discussing it.

NINA. Why not?

ANN. It's a sore subject.

NINA. Why?

ANN. Apparently it's primarily about you-know-who.

NINA. Oh. *(Pause. She sees it on the coffee table.)* Is that it?

ANN. That's it. *(NINA gingerly lifts the cover and looks inside.)*

NINA *(Reading). The Cocktail Hour.* Hmmm.

BRADLEY. Stupid title.

NINA. They'll confuse it with Eliot.

BRADLEY. Exactly, Pookins.

NINA. Is it going on?

BRADLEY. No.

ANN. Maybe not.

JOHN. I came up to ask his permission.

BRADLEY. And I said no.

NINA. Hmmm.

BRADLEY *(Bringing her a glass of wine).* Here's your wine, darling.

NINA. Thank you. *(Pause.)* Is Mother in it?

ANN. Apparently I am.

NINA. Is Jigger?

BRADLEY. I hope not. *(He sits in his chair.)*

JOHN. Well, he is. In a way.

NINA. Are you in it, John?

JOHN. I'm afraid I am.

BRADLEY. I think we've said enough on the subject. I want to know where Ed is, Pookins. I thought Ed would be with you.

NINA. Ed's in New York. On business for the bank.

BRADLEY. I see. Well, we'll miss him.

ANN *(Now doing her needlepoint).* Oh yes. We'll miss Ed.

NINA *(To JOHN).* Am I in it?

JOHN. I think Pop wants us to change the subject.

BRADLEY. Thank you, John.

NINA. I just want to know if I'm *in* it.

JOHN. Yes, you are.

NINA. Oh God.

BRADLEY. Tell us about the children, Pookins. I want to hear about my grandchildren.

NINA. They're all fine, Pop. *(She picks up script, holds it to her ear.)*

ANN. What are you doing, dear?

NINA. I think I heard this thing ticking.

ANN *(Laughing).* That's funny.

NINA. Do you think we should drop it in a big bucket of water?

BRADLEY. I think we should change the subject. Tell me about Andy. Does he like his job?

NINA. He likes it fine, Pop. *(To JOHN, as she thumbs through the script.)* I hate to think what you do to me in this thing.

JOHN. You come out all right.

NINA. I'll bet. Am I the wicked older sister?

JOHN. No.

NINA. Am I the uptight, frustrated, bossy bitch?

JOHN. No, no.

NINA. Well, what am I, then?

JOHN. Actually, you play a relatively minor role.

ANN. Sounds like you're lucky, dear.

BRADLEY. Tell me about Wendy. Is Wendy doing well at Williams? Does she still want to be in business?

NINA. Do I get a *name*, at least? What's my name here?

JOHN. I call you Diana.

ANN. Diana?

JOHN *(To NINA).* Isn't that what you used to wish your name was? The Goddess Diana, Protectress of Wild Animals.

ANN. I knew a Diana Finch once. She used to climb down drainpipes and hang around drugstores. No, I don't like the name.

NINA. Well, it's better than *Nina*, Mother. Which means little Ann. Little you. Sweet little carbon copy.

BRADLEY. I asked you a question about Wendy, Pookins.

NINA *(Impatiently).* She's fine, Pop. *(She continues to thumb.)* I only see about ten pages of Diana here. *(More thumbing.)* and in the second act, less than that.

JOHN. It's what's known as a supporting role.

NINA. Supporting? What do I support?

ANN. I imagine all of us, dear. You give us all support. Which is true.

BRADLEY. May we talk about something else?

NINA. Do I get to bring in trays? Or do I just carry a spear?

JOHN. You come and go.

NINA. Come and go? Mostly go, I'd say, thank you very much. *(Reads.)* "Diana exits huffily." Oh boy, there it is. "Huffily." Jesus, John. *(She gets up huffily.)*

BRADLEY. All right, then. *(He goes to the bookcase, gets a large volume*—Life's Pictured History of World War II—*and takes it to a chair in the front hall where he begins to thumb through it determinedly.)* While all of you continue to concentrate on one very tiresome subject, I will try to exercise my mind. Let me know, please, if, as, and when you're willing to broaden the discussion. *(He turns his back on the group.)*

NINA. I just think it's interesting I always play a minor role in this family.

ANN. That's not true, darling.

JOHN. You were the one who always owned the dogs.

ANN. We gave you that lovely coming-out party.

JOHN. You got that trip to Europe.

ANN. You had the most beautiful wedding . . .

BRADLEY *(From the hall)*. You got my mother's tea set after she died, Pookins.

JOHN. Jigger and I used to call you the Gravy Train Girl.

NINA. Well, not any more, apparently.

ANN. Maybe you're lucky to get off the hook, dear.

NINA. Oh boy, John. I swear. It's the old story. Once again, you and Jigger, who never show up here, who come up once a year for a day or two, *if* we're lucky, when we have to drop everything we're doing and rush to be at your beck and call—once again, you two end up getting all the attention, whereas I, I, who have remained here since I was married, who have lived here all my *life* . . . who see Mother and Pop at least once a week, who have them for Christmas and Thanksgiving and even *Easter*, for God's sake . . . I, who got Pop to go to a younger doctor . . . I, me, who drove Mother all over town for *weeks* after her cataract operation . . . who found them a new cleaning woman when their old one just walked *out!* . . . once again I am told I play a goddamn minor ROLE!

ANN. Now, now . . . Now, now.

BRADLEY *(From the hall)*. You've been a wonderful daughter, Pookins.

NINA *(Crossing to the bar)*. Wonderful or not, I need another drink.

ANN. Be careful, darling. Your stomach.

NINA. Oh, what difference does that make? Who cares? I just play a minor role. If I get ulcers, they're minor ulcers. If I die, it's a minor death.

JOHN. Nina, hey, lookit. I kept trying to build up your part.

NINA. I'll bet.

JOHN. I did. But I never got anywhere.

NINA. Why not?

JOHN. I never could get your number.

BRADLEY *(From the hall)*. I don't know why anybody has to get anybody else's number.

JOHN. No, I mean, you always seem so content around here.

NINA. Con*tent?*

JOHN. Good husband. Good kids. Good life. You always came out seeming so comfortable and at home.

BRADLEY *(From the hall)*. I should damn well hope so.

NINA. *Me?* Is this *me* you're talking about? Comfortable and at home?

ANN. He's giving you a compliment, dear.

NINA. Is he? Is that a compliment? Comfortable and at home? Oh boy, that's a laugh. That's a good one, John. Boy, you've really painted me into a corner. Ask Dr. Randall how comfortable I am. Ask him to show you the X-rays of my insides. He'll show you what it's like to be at home.

BRADLEY *(Coming back in)*. Pookins, sweetheart . . .

NINA *(Revving up)*. Do you know anything about my *life*, John? Have you ever bothered to inquire what I *do* around here, all these years you've been away? Did you know that I am Vice-President of the S.P.C.A.?

ANN. *And* on the hospital board. *And* the School for the Blind. *And* the gift shop at the gallery . . .

NINA. Did you know that I am interested in seeing-eye *dogs*, John? Did you know that? I am profoundly interested in them. I'm good with dogs, I'm the best, everyone says that, and what I want to do more than anything else in the world is go to this two-year school in Cleveland where you do nothing but work with seeing-eye dogs.

ANN. You can't just commute to Cleveland, darling.

NINA. I *know* that, Mother.

JOHN. Why can't you?

NINA. Because I have a husband, John. Because I have a—*life!*

BRADLEY. And a very good life it is, Pookins.

NINA. I mean, what am I supposed to *do*, John? Start subsidizing Eastern Airlines every other *day?* Live in some *motel?* Rattle around some strange city where I don't know a *soul?* Just because I want to work with . . . because I happen to feel an attachment to . . . oh God. *(She starts to cry.)*

BRADLEY *(Going to her)*. Oh now, Pookins . . . Now stop, sweetie pie . . .

ANN. I didn't realize people could get quite so upset about dogs.

BRADLEY. It's not dogs, it's John. *(Wheeling on JOHN.)* You see what happens? You arrive here and within half-an-hour, you've thrown the whole family into disarray. It's happened all your life. Par for the course, my friend. Par for the course. *(Comforting NINA.)* Now calm down, sweetheart. He's not going to do the play anyway.

NINA *(Breaking away)*. Well, he should! He should do one about *me!* You've never written about me, John. Ever. Why don't you, some time? Why don't you write about a woman who went to the right schools, and married the right man, and lived on the right street all the days of her life, and ended up feeling perfectly terrible! *(She runs out of the room and upstairs.)*

BRADLEY. There you are, John. You satisfied? Will you put that in your play? Or do you still want to concentrate all your guns on your dying father? *(He goes out after* NINA, *calling.)* Wait. Nina. Pookins. Sweetheart . . . *(He follows her off and upstairs. Pause.)*

ANN *(Holding out her glass).* I might have just a splash more, John.

JOHN *(Taking her glass).* O.K., Mother.

ANN. Just a splash. I'm serious.

JOHN *(Mixing it).* Right.

ANN. You're not having anything?

JOHN. Can't seem to get away with it these days, Mother.

ANN. What does that mean?

JOHN. Very quickly, I turn into an angry drunk.

ANN. Good heavens. Why is that?

JOHN. I don't know . . . *(Looks where his father has gone.)* I guess I'm sore about something. *(Pause.)* Is he as sick as he says he is, Mother?

ANN. You know your father.

JOHN. He keeps saying he's dying.

ANN. He's been saying that for years. He announced it on his fortieth birthday. He reminds us of it whenever he gets a cold. Lately, when we go to bed, he doesn't say "goodnight" any more. He says, "goodbye," because he thinks he won't last till morning.

JOHN. But you think he's O.K.?

ANN. I think . . . No, I *know,* we all know, that he has a blood problem, a kind of leukemia, which seems to be in remission now. Somehow I don't think that will kill him. Something else will.

JOHN. You think my play will?

ANN. *He* seems to think it will.

JOHN. Oh God . . .

ANN. And *you* must think it might, John. Otherwise you never would have bothered to clear it with him.

JOHN. I almost wish I hadn't.

ANN. I'm glad you did. It shows you have strong family feelings.

JOHN. Family feelings, family feelings! The story of my life! The bane of my existence! Family feelings. Dear Mother, dear Pop. May I have permission to cross the street? May I have permission to buy a car? Would you mind very much if I screwed my girl?

ANN. Now that's enough of that, please.

JOHN. Well, it's true! Family feelings. May I have your approval to put on a play? Oh God, why did I come here? Why did I bother? Most playwrights dish out the most brutal diatribes against their parents, who sit proudly in the front row and applaud every insult that comes along. Me? Finally—after fifteen years of beating around the bush—I come up with something which is—all right, maybe a little on the nose, maybe a little frank, maybe a little satiric at times—but still clearly infused with warmth, respect, and an abiding affection, and what happens? I'm being censored, banned, bribed not to produce.

ANN. I still wish you'd make it a book.

JOHN. Oh, Mother . . .

ANN. No, I'm serious. Books are quieter.

JOHN. I can't write books.

ANN. You work on them all the time.

JOHN. But I can't write them.

ANN. Plays are so noisy.

JOHN. I know.

ANN. They cause such attention.

JOHN. I know.

ANN. I don't mean just for us. I mean for you, as well.

JOHN. I know, Mother.

ANN. Those reviews must hurt terribly. The bad ones.

JOHN. They do.

ANN. All coming out together. Wave after wave. Every little suburban newspaper putting in its two-cents worth. And they can all be so mean.

JOHN. Right.

ANN. Book reviewers seem kinder, somehow. You have the feeling that people who write books get their friends to review them.

JOHN. Yes . . .

ANN. But not with plays. I mean, who *are* those people who review plays? What do they do when they're not sitting around criticizing?

JOHN. I hear some of them are decent folks, Mother.

ANN. They well may be, but I don't think they have the faintest notion what you're writing about.

JOHN. Sometimes they don't seem to.

ANN. They don't like us, John. They resent us. They think we're all Republicans, and all superficial, and all alcoholics.

JOHN. I know.

ANN *(Taking a sip; with a twinkle).* Only the

latter is true. *(JOHN laughs, possibly hugs her.)* I also think . . .

JOHN. What?

ANN. Never mind.

JOHN. No, come on, Mother. What?

ANN. I also think he's scared you'll spill the beans.

JOHN. The beans?

ANN. The beans.

JOHN. What beans?

ANN. Oh, John, face it. Everyone's got beans to spill. And, knowing you, you'll find a way to spill ours.

JOHN. I'm simply trying to tell the truth, Mother.

ANN. Fine. Good. But tell the truth in a *book*. Books take their time. Books *explain* things. If you have to do this, do it quietly and carefully in a book.

JOHN. I can't, Mother.

ANN. You can try.

JOHN. I *can't*. Maybe I'm a masochist, but I can't seem to write anything but plays. I can't write movies or television. I'm caught, I'm trapped in this old medium. It's artificial, it's archaic, it's restrictive beyond belief. It doesn't seem to have anything to do with contemporary American life. I feel like some medieval stone cutter, hacking away in the dark corner of an abandoned monastery, while everyone else is outside, having fun in the Renaissance. And when I finish, a few brooding inquisitors shuffle gloomily in, take a quick look, and say, "That's not it. That's not what we want at all!" Oh, God, why do I do it? Why write plays? Why are they the one thing in the world I want to do? Why have I always done them?

ANN. Not always, John. You used to write the most marvelous letters, for example. From camp. From boarding school . . .

JOHN. But I wrote plays long before that. Long before I could even write, I put on plays.

ANN. Oh well. Those things you did down in the playroom.

JOHN. They were *plays*, Mother. I'd clear the electric trains off the Ping-Pong table so it could be a stage. And I'd use up all the crayons in the house doing the scenery. And use up all my allowance bribing Nina and Jigger to be in them.

ANN. And then you'd drag your father and me down and we'd have to sit through the damn things.

JOHN. But they were plays, Mother.

ANN. Yes. I suppose they were.

JOHN. What were they about, Mother? Do you remember?

ANN. I do not.

JOHN. My psychiatrist keeps asking me what they were about. He says they could open a few doors for me, but I've blocked them all.

ANN. I wish you'd block that psychiatrist.

JOHN. But if there was a pattern to the plots, if there was some common theme to what I was doing, it would . . .

ANN. It would what?

JOHN. Explain things . . . I wish you could remember. *(Pause.)*

ANN. You always gave yourself a leading part, I remember that.

JOHN. I'll bet.

ANN. And it seems to me you always played this foundling, this outsider, this adopted child . . .

JOHN. Is that true?

ANN. I think so. Your father and I would roll our eyes and think, what have we wrought. I mean, on you'd come, this poor prince who'd been adopted by beggars. Or else . . .

JOHN. What?

ANN. I remember one particularly silly one. You were the court jester. You put on a bathing suit and a red bathing cap and started dancing around, being very fresh.

JOHN. Hold it. Say that again. What did I wear?

ANN. You wore your little wool bathing trunks from Best and Company, and Nina's red bathing cap.

JOHN. *The Red-Headed Dummy.*

ANN. I suppose.

JOHN. No, I mean that was the title of my play: *The Red-Headed Dummy!* It's coming back!

ANN. Well, whatever it was, I remember it went on for*ever!* It made us late for dinner somewhere.

JOHN. Good God, Mother, I suddenly realize what I was doing in that play.

ANN. Well, *I* certainly don't.

JOHN. I think I know! And I think my shrink would agree!

ANN. I'm all ears.

JOHN. It's a little Freudian, Mother. It's a little raw.

ANN. Then I'm not terribly interested. *(Pause.)* What?

JOHN. What I was doing was parading my penis in front of my parents.

ANN. Oh, John, honestly.

JOHN. I was? The bathing suit, the red cap, *The Red-Headed Dummy!* Get it? I was doing a phallic dance.

ANN. John, don't be unattractive.

JOHN. No, no, really. I was playing my own penis. Smart kid, come to think of it. How many guys in the world get a chance to do that? Especially in front of their parents.

ANN. I think it's time to turn to another topic.

JOHN. No, but wait. Listen, Mother. I'll put it in a historical context. What I was doing was acting out a basic, primitive impulse which goes back to the Greeks. That's how comedy *originated*, Mother! The phallic dance! These peasants would do these gross dances in front of their overlords to see what they could get away with! And that's what I was doing, too, at three years old! Me! The Red-Headed Dummy! Dancing under the noses of my parents, before they went out to dinner! Saying, "Hey, you guys. Look. Look over here. I'm here, I'm alive, I'm wild, I have this penis with a mind of its own!" That's what I was doing then! That's what I've always done! That's what I'm doing right now, right in this room! And that's why I have to write plays, Mother. I have to keep doing it. *(Long pause.)*

ANN. Are you finished, John?

JOHN. For now, at least.

ANN. All right, then, I want to say this: I don't like all this psychological talk, John. I never have. I think it's cheap and self-indulgent. I've never liked the fact that you've consulted a psychiatrist, and your father agrees with me. It upsets us very much to think that the money we give you at Christmas goes for paying that person rather than for taking your children to Aspen or somewhere. I don't like psychiatrists in general. Celia Underwood went to one, and now she bursts into tears whenever she plays bridge. Psychiatrists make you think about yourself too much. And about the bedroom too much. There's no need!

JOHN. Mother—

ANN. No, please let me finish. Now I want you to write, John. I think sometimes you write quite well, and I think it's a healthy enterprise. But I think you should write *books*. In books, you can talk the way you've just talked and it's not embarrassing. In books, you can go into people's minds . . . Now we all have things in our lives which we've done,

or haven't done, which a book could make clear. I mean, I myself could tell you . . . I could tell you . . . I could tell you lots of things if I knew you would write them down quietly and carefully and sympathetically in a good, long book . . . *(BRADLEY enters.)*

BRADLEY. What book?

ANN. We were just talking about the value of a good book, dear.

BRADLEY *(Crossing to his chair)*. I agree with you. I'm reading the Bible now, John. I keep it right by my bed. It's surprisingly good reading. And excellent insurance.

ANN. How's Nina? And where's Nina?

BRADLEY. Nina is fine. Nina is dealing with a slight confusion in the kitchen.

ANN *(Jumping up)*. I knew it. I could feel it in my bones. Tell me what happened.

BRADLEY. There was a slight misunderstanding about the oven.

ANN. Explain that, please.

BRADLEY. The oven was inadvertently turned off.

ANN. You mean that beautiful roast of beef . . .

BRADLEY. Is at the moment somewhat underdone.

ANN. Oh, I could cry.

BRADLEY. Now don't *worry*, darling. The oven is now working overtime. And there's even talk of Yorkshire pudding.

ANN. How can that creature make Yorkshire pudding if she can't cook a simple roast?

BRADLEY. Because I asked her to, darling. And because I presented her with another package of peas from the deep freeze.

ANN. Why more peas? What happened to the peas she had?

BRADLEY. I'm afraid there was a lack of attention to the right rear burner, darling.

ANN. Oh, I can't *stand* this! We'll be lucky if we eat by nine! I should have known never to take a chance on someone named Cheryl Marie! *(She hurries out, adlibbing about the roast beef.)*

BRADLEY *(Calling after her)*. Her name is Sharon, dear. *Sharon* Marie. *(Pause; to JOHN.)* Do you have any servants in this play of yours?

JOHN. Not really.

BRADLEY. "Not really"? What does that mean, "Not really"? Does your producer have to pay for a maid or not?

JOHN. No, he doesn't, Pop.

BRADLEY. Probably just as well. Knowing you, you'd get them all wrong anyway.

JOHN. Thanks.

BRADLEY. Well, I mean, nobody understands how to treat servants today. Even your mother. She was born with them, they brought her breakfast in bed until she married me, and I'm afraid she takes them too much for granted. Your generation is worse. You don't even seem to know they're there. Now I went out just now and spoke personally to Sharon Marie. I inquired about her life. And because I took the time to converse with her, because I made her feel part of the family, you may be sure we will have a much more delicious dinner.

JOHN. And because you tipped her twenty bucks.

BRADLEY. Yes. All right. I did that, too. Because I firmly believe good service is important. You can't live without servants. At least you can't live well. Civilization depends on them. They are the mainstay of intelligent life. Without them, you and I would be out in the kitchen right now, slicing onions and shouting over the Dispose-All, and none of this would be taking place at all.

JOHN. You're probably right.

BRADLEY. Of course I'm right. (Pause.) I did something else while I was out there, besides buttering up Sharon Marie.

JOHN. What else did you do?

BRADLEY. I put in a call to your brother.

JOHN. Ah.

BRADLEY. Couldn't get him, of course. He's still with a client. Seven-thirty on a Saturday night. Yes, well, we all have to work. We all have to put our shoulder to the wheel. No substitute for good hard work. When the head of General Motors dies, they hire a new office boy.

JOHN. You think that's true, Pop?

BRADLEY. Of course it's true. Or was, until your friend Roosevelt came along and gave everyone a free ride.

JOHN. Hey, now wait a minute . . .

BRADLEY. I can't discuss it. Anyway, I spoke to Sylvia. She expects Jigger home any minute, and then he'll call.

JOHN. Good.

BRADLEY. So when he calls, we can all talk to Jigger. If we can't gather around a piano, we can still gather around a telephone.

JOHN. Fine. (BRADLEY goes to the bar to make himself another drink.)

BRADLEY. I wish you'd have a drink.

JOHN. No thanks, Pop.

BRADLEY. It will still be quite a while before we eat.

JOHN. I can last.

BRADLEY. (As he makes his drink). I hate to drink alone.

JOHN. That's O.K.

BRADLEY. As you know, I have very firm rules about alcohol. Never drink before six. Never drink after dinner. And never drink alone. You make me feel like an old souse.

JOHN. I'll have wine, then, Pop.

BRADLEY. Good. It's a convivial thing, drinking together. Even if it's just white wine.

JOHN. Have you got any red there, Pop?

BRADLEY. Red?

JOHN. I don't like white that much.

BRADLEY. You mean I have to go all the way out and open a whole new bottle of red wine?

JOHN. O.K., Pop. A drop of scotch, then.

BRADLEY. (Pours a glass). A little scotch. (Pours a strong one.)

JOHN. A little, Pop? That looks like a double.

BRADLEY. You can't fly on one wing.

JOHN. Fly? Should I fasten my seat-belt?

BRADLEY. Maybe I just want to have a good, healthy belt with my older son before the evening's over.

JOHN. O.K. (Raises his glass to his Father, takes a sip. It is obviously strong.) Ah.

BRADLEY. (Looking at the check). I notice my check is still there.

JOHN. I don't want it, Pop.

BRADLEY. Take it. I insist.

JOHN. I don't want it. (Pause.)

BRADLEY. (Settling into his chair). Tell me a little more about your play.

JOHN. (On the couch). It's not going on. I promise.

BRADLEY. I just want to know a little more about it.

JOHN. Pop, we'll just get into trouble . . .

BRADLEY. No, no. We're mature individuals. We're having a drink together at the end of the day . . . For example, does it have a plot?

JOHN. Not much of one, actually.

BRADLEY. I like a good plot.

JOHN. I can't seem to write them.

BRADLEY. I remember learning at Yale: there are three great plots in Western literature: Oedipus Rex, Tom Jones and I forget the third.

JOHN. Ben Jonson's Volpone.

BRADLEY. No, it wasn't that.

JOHN. According to Coleridge, those are the three great plots.

BRADLEY. No, no.

JOHN. I've just *edited* a textbook on Coleridge, Pop.

BRADLEY. Well, you're still wrong.

JOHN *(Starts getting up)*. I could look it—

BRADLEY. No!

JOHN. O.K. *(Pause. They drink.)*

BRADLEY. So you don't have a plot.

JOHN. Not much of one.

BRADLEY. You don't try to drag in that business about our family having Indian blood, do you?

JOHN. *Do* we?

BRADLEY. We do not. *(Pause.)* Though some people keep saying we do.

JOHN. What people?

BRADLEY. Your cousin Wilbur, particularly. He used to bandy it about. But it's an absolute lie. There is no Indian blood in our branch of the family. I want that absolutely understood before I die.

JOHN. O.K.

BRADLEY. Your Great-uncle Ralph may have had a relationship with an Indian woman, but that was it.

JOHN. Did he?

BRADLEY. *May* have. Besides, she was an Indian princess. She was very well born. According to your grandmother, she was quite beautiful. And she sewed very well.

JOHN. Sowed corn?

BRADLEY. Sewed moccasins. I don't know what she sewed. The point is that Indian blood never came down through our line. Harry Blackburn down at the club constantly brings it up. He says it accounts for our affinity for alcohol. It's not funny, and I told him so, and if he mentions it again, I'm going to punch him in the nose.

JOHN. Take it easy, Pop.

BRADLEY. Anyway, if you bring up that Indian blood stuff in your play, you are simply barking up the wrong tree.

JOHN. I never thought of it, Pop.

BRADLEY. Good. *(He crosses to sit next to JOHN on the couch.)* Did you bring up your grandfather's death? *(Pause.)*

JOHN. Yes.

BRADLEY. I knew you would.

JOHN. I don't make a big deal of it.

BRADLEY. I don't know why you have to make any deal of it at all.

JOHN. I think it helps say who we are.

BRADLEY. You're always harping on it. It seems to be an obsession with you.

JOHN. I just refer to it once, Pop.

BRADLEY. How? What do you say?

JOHN. Oh, well . . .

BRADLEY. I want to know what you say about my father.

JOHN. I say he was a good man, a kind man, one of the best lawyers in town . . .

BRADLEY. True enough . . .

JOHN. A leader in the community. A pillar of the church . . .

BRADLEY. True . . . All true . . .

JOHN. Who, one day, for no discernible reason, strolled down to the edge of the Niagara River, hung his hat, his coat, and his cane on a wooden piling, and then walked into the water and drowned himself. *(Pause.)*

BRADLEY. That's what you say in your play?

JOHN. That's what I say, Pop. *(Pause.)*

BRADLEY. He left a note.

JOHN. I didn't know that, Pop.

BRADLEY. Oh yes, there was a note in his breast pocket. Addressed to me and my mother. I have it in my safe deposit box.

JOHN. I didn't know he left a note.

BRADLEY. You can have it when I die. *(Pause.)* He says there will be enough money to support my mother and to send me through college. *(Pause.)* Which there was. *(Pause.)* Then he says he's terribly, terribly sorry, but he's come to the conclusion that life isn't worth living any more. *(Pause. BRADLEY turns away from JOHN, takes out a handkerchief and dries his eyes.)*

JOHN. Oh, Pop.

BRADLEY. Churchill had those dark moments.

JOHN. So does my son Jack.

BRADLEY. Jack too? That sweet Jack?

JOHN. He gets it in spades.

BRADLEY. Of course, it's just . . . life, isn't it? It's part of the equation. The point is, we don't complain, we deal with it. We divert ourselves. We play golf, we have a drink occasionally.

JOHN. We write plays.

BRADLEY. Well, we do *some*thing. What does that sweet Jack do?

JOHN. Builds model airplanes.

BRADLEY. Oh that poor boy. That poor, poor boy.

JOHN. Yeah, I know. *(Pause.)*

BRADLEY. And your play gets into all this?

JOHN. A little.

BRADLEY. Sounds like a very depressing play.

JOHN. It has its darker moments.

BRADLEY. But no plot.

JOHN. Not really. No.

BRADLEY *(Getting up).* Seems to me, you have to have some twist or something. I mean, it's your business, not mine, but it seems to me you need some secret or surprise or something. I thought all plays had to have that.

JOHN. Actually, there is. A little one. At the end of the first act.

BRADLEY. What is it?

JOHN. Oh well.

BRADLEY. Tell it to me.

JOHN. You don't want to hear, Pop.

BRADLEY. Tell it to me anyway.

JOHN. You'll just get angry, Pop.

BRADLEY. I want to hear it. Please. *(Pause.)*

JOHN. All right. At the end of the first act, I have this older man . . .

BRADLEY. Me. I'm sure it's me.

JOHN. It's you and it's not you, Pop.

BRADLEY. What does this fellow do?

JOHN. He tells his older son . . .

BRADLEY. You.

JOHN. *Partly* me, Pop. Just *partly.*

BRADLEY. Tells his son what?

JOHN. The father tells his son that he doesn't believe . . .

BRADLEY. Doesn't believe what?

JOHN. Doesn't believe his son is his true son.

BRADLEY. WHAT?

JOHN. He says he thinks his wife once had an affair, and the son is the result.

BRADLEY. That is the most ridiculous thing I ever heard in my life!

JOHN. I knew you'd get sore.

BRADLEY. Of course I'm sore. Who wouldn't get sore? Where in God's name did you get such a ridiculous idea?

JOHN. I don't know. It just happened. As I was writing.

BRADLEY. Thank God this play is not going on! It's demeaning to me, and insulting to your mother! Why in heaven's name would you ever want to write a thing like that?

JOHN. Because I don't think you ever loved me, Pop. *(A telephone rings Offstage.)*

BRADLEY. That's Jigger. *(The telephone rings again, as BRADLEY hurriedly exits Off and up the stairs. Then a half-ring. BRADLEY's voice is heard answering from Offstage.)*

BRADLEY's VOICE. Hello? . . . *(JOHN sits on the couch, looking after his father, then looking at his glass.)*

End of Act I

ACT II

Immediately after. JOHN *is sitting on the couch. His glass is now empty.* NINA *comes in with a plate of carrot sticks and celery.*

NINA. Here are more munchies. It might be a little while before we eat.

JOHN. What's new with Jigger?

NINA. I don't know. I just had a chance to say hello. But I know how these things work. Mother will get on the phone in their bedroom, and Pop will be on the extension in the guest room, and everyone will talk at once. *(She finds her glass.)* Don't you want to get in on the act?

JOHN. I'll wait till things settle down.

NINA. We're lucky that whoosie out there in the kitchen missed up on the meat. I told her we'll be a minimum of twenty minutes, during which time she can at least *think* about making gravy.

JOHN. You know. I just thought: isn't this familiar?

NINA. What?

JOHN. This. You and me. Sitting here. Stomach growling. Waiting to eat.

NINA. Because of the cocktail hour . . .

JOHN. Because of Jigger.

NINA. It wasn't always Jigger.

JOHN. Most of the time it was. I was the good little boy, remember? I'd dash home, do my homework, wash my hands, brush my hair, sit here all during cocktails, and then just as we were about to eat, Jigger would call to say that he was still at some game or something.

NINA. Sometimes.

JOHN. All the time. So you'd dig into another one of your Albert Payson Terhune dog books, and Mother and Pop would have another drink and talk about their day, and I'd just sit here stewing.

NINA. That's your problem.

JOHN. Well, it was the maid's problem, too, remember? All those maids, over the years, coming to the doorway in their rustly, starchy uniforms and saying, "Dinner is served, Missus," and Mother would say, "Give us five more minutes, Mabel, or Jean, or Agnes, or whatever your name is this month," but it would be five, it would be fifteen, it would be half an *hour*, before Jigger got home and our parents would rise from the couch and stagger into the dining room to eat.

NINA. They never staggered, John.

JOHN. No, you're right. They held it beautifully. The cook held dinner beautifully. And the maid kept the plates warm. The cocktail hour kept all of life in an amazing state of suspended animation.

NINA. But oh those meals! Remember those *meals?* Three courses. Soup, a roast, home-made rolls, a home-made dessert! Floating Island, Brown Betty, Pineapple Upside Down Cake . . .

JOHN. Stewed prunes . . .

NINA. Only occasionally. And even that was good!

JOHN. Maybe. But how did those poor souls put up with us night after night? Well, of course, they didn't. They lasted a month or two and then quit, one after the other. We were lucky that one of them didn't appear in the doorway some night with a machine gun and mow us all down!

NINA. Oh, honestly, John. We were good to everyone who worked for us. We'd always go out in the kitchen and make a huge fuss.

JOHN. Oh sure, and cadge an extra cookie while the poor things were trying frantically to clean up. Oh God, Nina, what shits we were about maids!

NINA. We drove them to church, we paid their medical bills . . .

(She takes her shoes off and sprawls on the couch.)

JOHN. We were shits! When Grandmother died, she left five hundred dollars to each of the three maids that had served her all her life, and the Packard to the chauffeur.

NINA. Mother made it up to them.

JOHN. Oh sure. She tried. And they tried to make it up to themselves all along the way. Remember the one who stole all that liquor? Or the one who started the fire, smoking in the cedar closet? Or the one who went stark raving mad at breakfast and chased Mother around with a butter knife? Oh they had their moments of revenge. But we still built our life on their backs. Has it ever occurred to you that every dinner party, every cocktail hour, good Lord, every civilized endeavor in this world is based on exploiting the labor of the poor Cheryl Maries toiling away offstage.

NINA. Her name is Shirley Marie. *(Pause.)* I think. *(Pause.)* And she's exploiting *us.* She's probably getting fifty bucks for three hours work, when Mother and I did most of it anyway.

JOHN. There you go. Now we're exploiting each other. Pop always carries on about the importance of civilized life, but think of what it costs to achieve it. Between what Freud tells us we do to ourselves, and what Marx tells us we do to each other, it's a wonder we don't crawl up our own assholes.

NINA. Nicely put, John. All I know is, according to your good wife, Ellen, whenever you and she give a party in New York, you're the first one to want to hire some poor out-of-work actor to serve the soup.

JOHN. Yeah, I know. It's a shitty system, but I can't think of a better one.

NINA *(Getting up, making another drink)*. I think *you're* a shit, John. I'll say that much.

JOHN. What else is new?

NINA. No, I mean now. Tonight. For this.

JOHN. For this?

NINA. Coming up here. Stirring things up. With your play.

JOHN. This is probably one of the most decent things I've ever done.

NINA. Badgering two old people? Threatening them with some ghastly kind of exposure in the last years of their lives?

JOHN. I came here to get their permission.

NINA. You came here to stir things *up,* John. You came here to cause trouble. That's what you've done since the day you were born, and that's what you'll do till you die. You cannot let people alone, can you? A rainy day, a Sunday afternoon, every evening when you finished your homework, off you'd go on your appointed rounds, wandering from room to room in this house, teasing, causing an argument, starting a fight, leaving a trail of upset and unhappy people behind you. And when you finished with all of us, you'd go down in the kitchen and start on the cook. And when the cook left, you'd tease your teachers at school. And now that you're writing plays, you tease the critics! Anyone in authority comes under your guns. Why don't you at least be constructive about it, and tease the Mafia or the C.I.A., for God's sake? *(She sits in a chair opposite him.)*

JOHN. Because I'm not a political person.

NINA. Then what kind of person *are* you, John? Why are you so passionately concerned with disturbing the peace? I mean, here we are, the family at least partially together for the first time in several years, and possibly the last time in our lives, and what happens: you torment us with this play, you accuse us of running a slave market in the kitchen, you make us all feel thoroughly uncomfortable. Have you ever thought about this, John? Has it ever come to mind that this is what you do?

JOHN. Yes.

NINA. Good. I'm so glad. Why do you suppose you do it?

JOHN *(Moving around the room)*. Because there's a hell of a lot of horseshit around, and I think I've known it from the beginning.

NINA. Would you care to cite chapter and verse?

JOHN. Sure. Horseshit begins at home.

NINA. He's a wonderful man.

JOHN. He's a hypocrite, kiddo! He's a fake!

NINA. Sssh!

JOHN. Talk about civilization. All that jazz about manners and class and social obligation. He's a poor boy who married a rich girl and doesn't want to be called on it.

NINA. That is a lie! He was only poor after his father died!

JOHN *(With increasing passion)*. Yes, well, all that crap about hard work and nose to the grindstone and burning the midnight oil. What is all that crap? Have you ever seen it in operation? Whenever I tried to call him at the office, he was out playing golf. Have you ever *seen* him *work?* Has he ever brought any work *home?* Have you ever heard him even talk on the *telephone* about work? Have you ever seen him spade the garden or rake a leaf or change a light bulb? I remember one time when I wrote that paper defending the New Deal, he gave me a long lecture about how nobody wants to work in this country, and all the while he was practicing his putting on the back lawn!

NINA. He's done extremely well in business. He sent us to private schools and first-rate colleges.

JOHN. Oh, I know he's done well—on charm, affability, and Mother's money—and a little help from his friends. His friends have carried him all his life. They're the ones who have thrown the deals this way. You ask him a financial question, he'll say, "Wait a minute, I'll call Bill or Bob or Ted."

NINA. Because that's *life,* John! That's what business *is!* The golf course, the backgammon table at the Mid-Day Club, the Saturn Club grille at six—that's where he *works,* you jerk!

JOHN. Well then that's where his family is, not here! Did he ever show you how to throw a ball or dive into a pool? Not him. Mother did all that, while he was off chumming it up with his pals. All he ever taught me was how to hold a fork or answer an invitation or cut in on a pretty girl. He's never been my father and I've never been his son, and he and I have known that for a long time. *(Pause. He sits exhaustedly on the piano bench.)*

NINA. Well, he's been a wonderful father to me.

JOHN. Maybe so. And maybe to Jigger. I guess that's why I've teased both of you all my life. And why I tease everybody else, for that matter. I'm jealous. I'm jealous of anyone who seems to have a leg up on life, anyone who seems to have a father in the background helping them out. Hell, I even tease my own children. I've bent over backwards to be to them what my father never was to me, and then out of some deep-grained jealousy that they have it too good, I tease the pants off them.

NINA. Jesus, John, you're a mess.

JOHN. I know. But I'd be more of one if I didn't write about it.

NINA. Well, write as much as you want, but don't go public on this one.

JOHN. I've already said I won't.

NINA. I'm not sure I believe you, John. You're too angry. You'll change a few words, a few names, and out it will come.

JOHN. Nina, I promise . . .

NINA. Then how come that check is still there? Mother told me about the check, and there it is. How come?

JOHN. I don't want it.

NINA *(Brings it to him)*. Take it, John. Take it, just so I'll be sure. I know you're gentleman enough not to do it if you take the dough.

JOHN. I'll never cash it. *(He takes the check.)*

NINA. I don't care, but it's yours now, and the play stays in your desk drawer now, until they're both dead. And until *I'm* dead, goddamnit.

JOHN *(Putting the check in his wallet)*. Or until he changes his mind.

NINA. Fair enough. *(She returns to the couch for more food.)*

JOHN *(Putting his wallet away)*. Actually I'm kind of glad it's not going on, Nina.

NINA. Why?

JOHN. Because, to tell you the truth, I haven't got the plot right yet.

NINA. What's wrong with it?

JOHN. I dunno. It's not right yet. It's not true yet. There's a secret in it somewhere, and I haven't quite nailed it down.

NINA. What secret?

JOHN. Oh, simply the secret of what went wrong between my father and me. Where, when, why did he turn his countenance from me? There must have been a point. Did I wake him too early in the morning with my infant wails before one of those constantly replaceable nurses jammed a bottle in my mouth? Or rather *refused* to jam a bottle in my mouth because I wasn't crying on schedule?

NINA. Here we go . . .

JOHN. Or when I was displayed to family and friend, did I embarrass him by playing with my pee-pee?

NINA. John, you have an absolute obsession with your own penis.

JOHN. Or—*I* know! Maybe this is what I did: I made the unpardonable mistake of contradicting him—of looking something *up* in the Book of Knowledge, and proving him wrong—no, not wrong, that makes no difference, right or wrong,—what I did was destroy the "rhythm of the conversation," maybe that's what I did wrong!

NINA. Oh good Lord . . .

JOHN. Yes well, I'd love to know what I did to have him say to himself—and to *me!*—"I don't know this boy. This is not my son." Because he's said it as long as I can remember.

NINA. And if he ever told you he loved you, you'd immediately do some totally irritating thing to make him deny it.

JOHN. You think so?

NINA. I know so. If he killed the fatted calf, you'd complain about the cholesterol.

JOHN. Jesus, Nina.

NINA. You would. I've got your number, John, even if you don't have mine. For instance, I know why you're writing this goddamn play.

JOHN. Why?

NINA *(Hurriedly, as she puts on her shoes).* You're writing it because he's dying. You're writing it because you love him. You're writing it to hold on to him after he's gone. *(*ANN *comes in.)*

ANN. John, don't you want to speak to your brother before your father hangs up.

JOHN. Sure. *(He angrily grabs some carrots and goes Off upstairs.)*

ANN *(Distractedly).* Well, that's that.

NINA. What?

ANN *(Vaguely).* I'd like a splash more, please, Nina.

NINA *(Getting* ANN*'s glass, going to the bar).* All right.

ANN. Just a splash. I'm serious.

NINA. All right.

ANN *(Sinking onto the couch).* I give up.

NINA. What's the *trouble*, Mother?

ANN. Jigger. Jigger's the trouble. He wants to move to California.

NINA. What?

ANN. He wants to pick up stakes and move. Wife, children, off they go.

NINA. What's in California?

ANN. A job. A new job. There's a man out there who builds wooden boats, who wants Jigger to work for him. For *half* of what he's making now.

NINA. But why?

ANN. Because he wants to. He says it's something he's always wanted to do.

NINA. He's always liked boats.

ANN. Don't I know it. That canoe he built in the basement. Those sailboats out on the lake . . .

NINA *(Joining her on the couch).* Which had to be *wood*, remember? No fiberglass allowed. All that labor every spring, because only wood sat naturally on the water . . .

ANN. Between his boats and your dogs we hardly had time to think around here.

NINA. He felt free on the water. I wish *I* felt free about something.

ANN. Well I hear they feel free about *every*thing in California.

NINA. And he's just . . . going?

ANN. Says he is. Says he plans to buy one of those grubby vans, and lug everyone out, like a bunch of Okies. Your father is frantically trying to talk him out of it.

NINA *(Musingly).* I should just go to Cleveland to that dog school.

ANN. Oh, Nina. Think of Ed.

NINA. I *have* thought of Ed. We've talked about it. He says, do it. Which makes it all the harder.

ANN. I should hope so.

NINA. Still. Maybe I should. I should just do it. What would you say if I did it, Mother?

ANN. Go to *Cleve*land?

NINA. Three days a week.

ANN. Just to be with *dogs*?

NINA. To *work* with them, Mother.

ANN. I've never understood your fascination with dogs.

NINA. I don't know. When I'm with them, I feel I'm in touch with something . . . basic.

ANN. Horses I can understand. The thrill

of riding. The excitement of the hunt. The men.

NINA. The men?

ANN. There used to be a lot of attractive men around stables.

NINA. Mother!

ANN. Just as there are around garages today.

NINA. Are you serious?

ANN. But I don't think they hang around kennels.

NINA. I'm interested in *dogs*, Mother.

ANN. I know you are, darling, and I don't think that's any reason to change your life. I mean if you had met some man . . .

NINA. Mother, have you ever watched any of those Nature things on TV?

ANN. I love them. Every Sunday night . . .

NINA. I mean, you see animals, birds, even insects operating under these incredibly complicated instincts. Courting, building their nests, rearing their young in the most amazing complex way . . .

ANN. Amazing behavior . . .

NINA. Well, I think people have these instincts, too.

ANN. Well, I'm sure we do, darling, but . . .

NINA. No, but I mean many more than we realize. I think they're built into our blood, and I think we're most alive when we feel them happening to us.

ANN. Oh well now, I don't know . . .

NINA. I feel most alive when I'm with animals, Mother. Really. I feel some instinctive connection. Put me with a dog, a cat, anything, and I feel I'm in touch with a whole different dimension . . . It's as if both of us . . . me and the animal . . . were reaching back across hundreds of thousands of years to a place where we both knew each other much better. There's something there, Mother. I know there's something there.

ANN. Oh Nina, you sound like one of those peculiar women who wander around Africa falling in love with gorillas.

NINA. Maybe I do. *(Pause.)* I hope I do. *(Pause.)* I'd rather sound like that than just an echo of you, Mother.

ANN. Well. I think we're all getting too wound up over boats and dogs. People, yes. Boats and dogs, no. The whole family seems to be suddenly going to pieces over boats and dogs.

NINA. And plays, Mother.

ANN. Yes. All right. And plays. *(BRADLEY comes in from upstairs.)*

BRADLEY. We've lost him.

ANN. Oh now, darling.

BRADLEY. We've lost him.

ANN. Oh no.

BRADLEY. I'll never see him again.

ANN. Oh, darling.

BRADLEY. I'll be lucky if he comes to my funeral.

ANN. Now, now. I'll tell you one thing. A good *meal* will make us all feel much better.

NINA. I'll tell Shirley.

BRADLEY. Her name is Sharon.

ANN. I still think it's Cheryl.

NINA. Well, whatever it is, I'll tell her we're ready to *eat!* *(She goes out. BRADLEY goes to the bar.)*

ANN. I wouldn't drink any more, sweetie. We're about to eat.

BRADLEY. I need this.

ANN. How about some wine with dinner? We'll have that.

BRADLEY. Wine won't do it.

ANN. Oh, Bradley . . .

BRADLEY *(Moving around the room).* I've lost my son. My son is moving three thousand miles away. I'm too old and sick and tired to go see him. And he'll be too tied up in his work to come see me.

ANN *(Following him).* Oh now, sweetheart . . .

BRADLEY. There are men, there are men in this world whose sons stay with them all the days of their lives. Fred Tillinghast's sons *work* with him every day at the office. He has lunch with them at noon, he has cocktails with them at night, he plays golf with them on weekends. They discuss everything together. Money, women, they're always completely at ease. When he went to Europe, those boys went with him and carried his bags. What did he do to deserve such luck? What did he do that I didn't? I've given my sons everything. I gave them an allowance every week of their lives. I gave them stock. I gave them the maximum deductible gift every Christmas. And now what happens? I reach my final years, my final moments, the nadir of my life, and one son attacks me while the other deserts me. Oh, it is not to be borne, my love. It is not to be borne. *(He sinks into his chair.)*

ANN. Oh, now just wait, Bradley. Maybe John is talking him out of it.

BRADLEY. John?

ANN. John always had a big influence on him.

BRADLEY. John? Jigger and John have fought all their lives. *I'm* the influence. I'm the father. What can John possibly say that I haven't said? *(JOHN enters quickly.)*

JOHN. I told him he should go.

BRADLEY. You didn't.

ANN. John!

JOHN. Sure. I said, go on. Make your move!! How many guys in the world get a chance to do what they really want?

BRADLEY. I should never have let you near the telephone.

ANN. I'm not sure that was entirely helpful, John.

BRADLEY. He has a fine job where he is.

JOHN. Pushing papers around a desk. Dealing with clients all weekend.

BRADLEY. That's an excellent job. He has a decent salary. He's made all sorts of friends. I got him that job through Phil Foster.

JOHN. You might as well know something else, Pop. I got him this new one.

BRADLEY. You?

JOHN. I put him on to it. The boatyard is owned by a college classmate of mine. I read about it in the *Alumni Review* and got an interview for Jigger.

BRADLEY. Why?

JOHN. Because he was miserable where he was.

BRADLEY. I should have known you were behind all this . . .

JOHN. He hated that job, Pop. Now he can work with boats, and join the Sierra Club, and do all that stuff he loves to do.

BRADLEY. It was none of your damn business.

JOHN. He's my brother!

BRADLEY. I'm his father! Me! *(NINA enters.)*

JOHN. Well, I'm glad he's going, Pop. And I think Nina should work in Cleveland, too . . . I think you should, Nina.

NINA. I think I will.

ANN. Oh Nina, no!

BRADLEY. That's ridiculous.

JOHN. So what if Ed has to cook his own spaghetti occasionally . . .

NINA. He'd do it gladly.

BRADLEY. Nonsense. Ed can't cook spaghetti . . .

NINA. No. I think I'll do it. I think I'll go. I'll stay there, and study there, and come home when I can. Put that in your play and write it, John.

JOHN. Maybe I will.

NINA. Sure. Have the goddess Diana come downstage and plant her feet, and give this marvelous speech about seeing-eye dogs, which will bring the audience rising to its feet, and cause your friends the critics to systematically pee in their pants!

ANN. That's not attractive, Nina.

JOHN. I don't know. I kind of liked it.

BRADLEY. You kind of like playing God around here, don't you?

ANN. Yes, John, I really think you should stop managing other people's lives.

BRADLEY. Yes. Do that in your plays if you have to, not in real life.

JOHN. Oh yeah? Well, I'm glad we're talking about real life now, Pop. Because that's something we could use a little more *of*, around here. Hey. Know what? The cocktail hour is over, Pop. It's dead. It's gone. I think Jigger sensed it thirty years ago, and now Nina knows it too, and they're both *trying* to put something back into the world after all these years of a free ride.

BRADLEY. And you? What are you putting back into the world?

JOHN. Me?

BRADLEY. You.

JOHN. I'm writing about it. At least I have the balls to do that.

BRADLEY. Leave this room!

ANN. Oh Bradley . . .

JOHN. Maybe I should leave altogether.

BRADLEY. Maybe you should.

NINA. Oh Pop . . .

JOHN *(Grabbing his bag in the hall)*. Lucky I didn't unpack . . .

ANN. John, now stop . . .

JOHN *(Throwing on his raincoat)*. Call Ellen, Nina. Tell her I'm coming home. Say I'm being banished because of my balls!

BRADLEY. I will not allow you to speak vulgarities in this house.

JOHN. Balls? Balls are vulgar?

ANN. Now that's enough.

JOHN *(Coming back into the room)*. Does that mean you don't have any, Pop? Does that mean we should all just sit on our ass and watch the world go by?

ANN *(Going to front hall)*. I think it's time to eat.

BRADLEY. I'll tell you what it means. It means that vulgar people always fall back on vulgar language.

ANN *(Beckoning to NINA)*. What's the food situation, Nina?

BRADLEY. It means that there are more im-

portant things in the world than bodily references.

ANN *(At the doorway)*. Food! Yoo-hoo, everybody! Food!

BRADLEY. It means that your mother and I,
and your grandparents on both sides, and
Aunt Jane and Uncle Roger and Cousin Es-
ther, and your forbears who came to this
country in the seventeenth *century* have all
spent their lives trying to establish something called civilization in this wilderness,
and as long as I am alive, I will not allow
foul-minded and resentful people to tear it
all down. *(He storms Off and upstairs. Long
pause.)*

ANN. Well. You were right about one
thing, John: the cocktail hour is definitely
over.

NINA. Um. Not quite, Mother.

ANN. What do you mean?

NINA. Come sit down, Mother.

ANN. Don't tell me there is more bad news
from the kitchen.

NINA *(Going to her)*. The roast beef is a little
the worse for wear.

ANN. What?

NINA. The roast is ruined.

ANN. No.

NINA. Sheila got confused.

ANN. Sheila?

NINA. It's *Sheila* Marie. I know, because
I just made out her check and said she
could go.

ANN. What did she do?

NINA. She thought that microwave thing
was a warming oven. It came out looking like
a shrunken head.

ANN. Oh, I can't *stand* it!

NINA. The peas are still good, and I found
some perfectly adequate lamb chops in the
freezer. They won't take too long.

ANN. Thank you, darling. Would you tell
your father? I imagine he's upstairs in the
television room, cooling off on the hockey
game.

NINA *(Taking one of the hors d'oeuvres plates)*.
I'll take him up some cheese, just to hold
him. *(She goes Off and upstairs.)*

ANN *(Calling after her)*. You're a peach,
Nina. You really are. Those dogs don't deserve you. *(Pause.)* That was an absolutely
lovely rib roast of beef.

JOHN. I'm sure.

ANN. Twenty-eight dollars. At the Ex-
Cell.

JOHN. I can believe it.

ANN. I suppose Portia might like it. Nina
can give it to Portia.

JOHN. Good idea. *(Pause.)*

ANN *(Beginning to clean up)*. I don't know
why I'm talking to you, John. I'm very angry.
You've caused nothing but trouble since the
minute you arrived.

JOHN. Story of my life.

ANN. I'm afraid it is.

JOHN. I wish I knew why.

ANN. Isn't that what your psychiatrist is
supposed to explain, at one hundred dollars
a throw?

JOHN. He never could.

ANN. Then I was right: They're a waste of
money. *(She starts out.)* I'd better check on
those lamb chops.

JOHN. Mother . . . *(She stops.)* Since I've
been here, I've discovered a big problem
with this play of mine.

ANN. I'd say it had lots of problems. In my
humble opinion.

JOHN. Well, I've discovered a big one. It's
missing an obligatory scene.

ANN. And what in heaven's name is that?

JOHN. It's a scene which sooner or later has
to happen. It's an essential scene. Without it,
everyone walks out feeling discontent and
frustrated.

ANN. I suppose you mean some ghastly
confrontation with your father.

JOHN. Hell no. I've got plenty of those.

ANN. You've got too many of those.

JOHN. I'm thinking of a scene with you,
Mother.

ANN. With me?

JOHN. That's what's been missing all my
life, Mother.

ANN. Oh, John, please don't get melo-
dramatic. *(She starts out again.)*

JOHN. I've also discovered why it's been
missing.

ANN. Why?

JOHN. Because you don't want it to happen.

ANN. I'll tell you what I want to have happen, John. I want us all to sit down together
and have a pleasant meal. That's all I want to
have happen at the moment, thank you very
much.

JOHN *(Leading her to the couch)*. Oh come on,
Mother. Please. This is the ideal moment.
Pop's sulking upstairs. Nina's busy in the
kitchen. And you and I are both a little
smashed, which will make it easier. Tell me
just one thing.

ANN. What thing?

JOHN. What went wrong when I was very young. Something went wrong. There was some short circuit . . . some problem . . . something . . . What was it?

ANN. I don't know what you're talking about.

JOHN. Come on, Mother. Please. Think back.

ANN *(Getting up).* John, I am not going to sit around and rake over a lot of old coals. Life's too short and I'm too old, and thank you very much. *(She goes out to the kitchen.)*

JOHN *(Calling after her).* And once again, there goes the obligatory scene, right out the door! *(A moment. Then* ANN *comes back in, putting on an apron.)*

ANN. You got lost in the shuffle, John. That's what went wrong. I mean, there you were, born in the heart of the Depression, your father frantic about money, nurses and maids leaving every other day—nobody paid much attention to you, I'm afraid. When Nina was born, we were all dancing around thinking we were the Great Gatsby, and when Jigger came along, we began to settle down. But you, poor soul, were caught in the middle. You lay in your crib screaming for attention, and I'm afraid you've been doing it ever since.

JOHN. That's it?

ANN. That's it. In a nutshell. Now I feel very badly about it, John. I always have. That's why I've found it hard to talk about. I've worked hard to make it up, I promise, but sometimes, no matter how hard you work, you just can't hammer out all the dents. *(She turns to leave again.)*

JOHN. Exit my mother, after a brief, unsatisfactory exchange . . .

ANN. That's right. Because your mother is now responsible for a meal.

JOHN *(Blocking her way).* I can see the scene going on just a tad longer, Mother.

ANN. How?

JOHN. I think there's more to be said.

ANN. About what?

JOHN. About you, Mother.

ANN. Me?

JOHN. You. I think there's much more to be said about you.

ANN. Such as?

JOHN. Such as, where were you, while the king was in the counting house and the kid was in his cradle?

ANN. I was . . . here, of course.

JOHN. Didn't you pick me up, if I was screaming in my crib?

ANN. Yes. Sometimes. Yes.

JOHN. But not enough?

ANN. No. Not enough.

JOHN. Why not? *(Pause.)*

ANN. Because . . . because at that point I was a little preoccupied.

JOHN. With what?

ANN. Oh, John.

JOHN. With what?

ANN. I don't have to say.

JOHN. With *what,* Mother? *(Pause.)*

ANN. I was writing a book.

JOHN. You were what?

ANN. I was sitting right at that desk, all day, every day, writing a big, long book. It took too much of my time, and too much of my thoughts, and I'm sorry if it made me neglect you . . . I've never told anyone about that book.

JOHN. Doesn't it feel good to tell me?

ANN. Not particularly. No. *(She sits at the desk.)*

JOHN. What happened to it?

ANN. I burned it.

JOHN. You burned it?

ANN. All six hundred and twenty-two pages of it. Right in that fireplace. One day, while your father was playing golf.

JOHN. Why?

ANN. Because I didn't like it. I couldn't get it right. It was wrong.

JOHN. Wow, Mother!

ANN. I know it. *(Pause.)* But then we had Jigger, and that took my mind off it.

JOHN. What was the book about, Mother?

ANN. I won't tell.

JOHN. Oh, come on.

ANN. I've never told a soul.

JOHN. One writer to another, Mother.

ANN. Never.

JOHN. You mean, the book you wrote instead of nursing me, the book that took my place at your breast . . .

ANN. Oh, John, really.

JOHN. The six hundred page book that preoccupied your mind during a crucial formative period of my own, I'll never get to know about. Boy. Talk about hammering out dents, Mother. You've just bashed in my entire front end. *(Pause.)*

ANN. I'll give you a brief summary of the plot.

JOHN. O.K.

ANN. Brief. You'll have to fill things in as best you can.

JOHN. O.K. *(He quickly gets a chair from the hall, and straddles it, next to her.)*

ANN *(Taken aback)*. First, though, I will have a splash more.

JOHN. Sure.

ANN. Just a splash. I'm serious.

JOHN. All right, Mother. *(He hurriedly mixes her martini.)*

ANN. I mean, it's no easy thing to tell one's own son one's innermost thoughts. Particularly when that son tends to be slightly critical.

JOHN. I won't criticize, Mother. I swear. *(He brings her her drink and again straddles the chair beside her.)*

ANN *(After taking a sip)*. All right, then. My book was about a woman.

JOHN. A woman.

ANN. A governess.

JOHN. A governess?

ANN. A well-born woman who goes to work for a distinguished man and supervises the upbringing of his children.

JOHN. Sounds like *Jane Eyre*.

ANN. If you make any cracks, I won't tell you any more.

JOHN. Sorry, Mother. It sounds good.

ANN. Now, this woman, this governess, does *not* fall in love with her employer. Unlike Jane Eyre.

JOHN. She does not?

ANN. No. She falls in love with someone else.

JOHN. Someone else.

ANN. She falls in love with a groom.

JOHN. A groom?

ANN. A very attractive groom. At the stable. Where she keeps her horse.

JOHN. I'm with you, Mother.

ANN. She has a brief, tempestuous affair with the man who saddles her horse.

JOHN. I see.

ANN. Well, it doesn't work out, so she terminates the affair. But the groom gets so upset, he sets fire to the stable.

JOHN. Sets fire.

ANN. The fire symbolizes his tempestuous passion.

JOHN. I see.

ANN. Naturally, she rushes into the flames to save the horses. And she gets thoroughly burned. All over her face. It's horrible.

JOHN. She is punished, in other words, for her indiscretion.

ANN. Yes. That's right. That's it exactly. But finally her wounds heal. The doctor ar-

rives to take off the bandages. Everyone stands around to see. And guess what? She is perfectly beautiful. She is even more beautiful than she was before. The children cluster around her, the master of the house embraces her, and so she marries this man who has loved her all along. You see? Her experience has helped her. In the long run. *(Pause.)* Anyway, that's the end. *(Pause.)* You can see why I burned it. *(Pause.)* You can see why I haven't told anyone about it, all these years. *(Pause.)* It's terribly corny, isn't it?

JOHN. No, Mother.

ANN. It's silly.

JOHN. No, it says a lot. *(He kisses her on the cheek.)*

ANN. John, you're embarrassing me.

JOHN. No, really. It's very touching.

ANN. Well, I never could get the *feelings* right. Especially with that groom. That passion. That tempestuous passion. Those . . . flames. I could never get that right in my book.

JOHN. I never could either, in a play.

ANN. Oh, it would be impossible in a play.

JOHN. Maybe.

ANN. That's why I wish you would write a good, long, wonderful book. *(She gets up.)* And now I really ought to give Nina a hand with supper.

JOHN. Mother, one more question . . .

ANN. You've asked too many.

JOHN. About the groom.

ANN. Ah, the groom.

JOHN. What happened to him?

ANN. Oh heavens. I can't remember. I think I sent him off to Venezuela or somewhere.

JOHN. In the book?

ANN. In the book.

JOHN. But what happened in life, Mother.

ANN. In *life?*

JOHN. Where did he go? Who was he?

ANN. I never said he *existed,* John. This . . . groom.

JOHN. But he did, didn't he? You met him before you had me. And he left after I was born. And you sat down and wrote about him. Now come on. Who was he?

ANN. John . . .

JOHN. Please, Mother. Tell me.

ANN. It was over forty years ago . . .

JOHN. Still, Mother. Come on. Whom did you base him on?

ANN. Oh, John, I don't know . . . Maybe I'm getting old . . . or maybe I've had too many cocktails . . . but I'm beginning to think I based him on your father. *(She starts out as* BRADLEY *comes in.)*

BRADLEY. Based what on me?

ANN. My life, darling. I've based my life on you. *(She kisses him and goes out. Pause.)*

BRADLEY. Your mother always knows when to walk out of a room.

JOHN. My mother is full of surprises.

BRADLEY. Well, she instinctively senses when a man needs to do business with another man. And out she goes.

JOHN. We're going to do business, Pop?

BRADLEY *(Going to his chair).* We're going to talk seriously. And I hope when you have to talk seriously with one of your sons, your sweet Ellen will bow out just as gracefully.

JOHN. What's on your mind, Pop?

BRADLEY. First, I'd like a glass of soda water, please.

JOHN. I'll have one, too.

BRADLEY. Good. Time for sermons and soda water, eh?

JOHN. It sure does feel like the day after. *(*JOHN *fixes the two drinks.)*

BRADLEY. John: you and I spoke angry words to each other a while back. It was most unfortunate. I blame you, I blame myself, and I blame alcohol. There's nothing more dangerous than a lengthy cocktail hour.

JOHN. I apologize, Pop. I got carried away.

BRADLEY. We both got carried away. We screamed and shouted, didn't we? Well, at least we didn't take off our clothes.

JOHN. Here's your soda water, Pop.

BRADLEY. Thank you, John. You know what I did upstairs instead of watching the hockey?

JOHN. What?

BRADLEY. I sat and thought. I thought about all of you. I thought about . . . my father. Do you suppose all families are doomed to disperse?

JOHN. Most of them do, Pop. Eventually. In this country.

BRADLEY. You don't think it's . . . me?

JOHN. No, Pop.

BRADLEY. People seem to want to leave me. There seems to be this centrifugal force.

JOHN. That's life, Pop.

BRADLEY. Well, whatever it is, I can't fight it any more . . . When I was upstairs, I telephoned Jigger. I called him back.

JOHN. Oh yes?

BRADLEY. What is it Horace Greeley tells us? "Go west, young man"? Well, he's young. It's there. I gave him my blessing.

JOHN *(Sitting near him).* That's good, Pop.

BRADLEY. "The old oak must bend with the wind . . . or break . . ." *(Looks at* JOHN.*)* Isn't that from Virgil?

JOHN. I think it's T. S. Eliot. *(Both laugh.)* But don't look it up. *(They laugh again.)*

BRADLEY. Maybe I've loved him too much. Maybe I've loved him at your expense. Do you think that's true? *(Pause.)*

JOHN *(Carefully).* I don't know . . .

BRADLEY. Maybe he's trying to get away from me. What do you think?

JOHN. I think . . . *(Pause.)* I think maybe he's trying to get away from all of us. I think maybe I got him to go because I was jealous. Hell, I think we all put our own spin on the ball—you, me, Nina, Mother—and guess what: it no longer matters. Jigger likes *boats,* Pop. He likes working with *wood.* Maybe he'll build a new clipper ship.

BRADLEY. Well, the point is, he'll be happy there. Sailing. He's a magnificent sailor. Remember right here on Lake Erie?

JOHN. I remember . . .

BRADLEY. I could sit in my office and look out on the lake, and sometimes I think I could actually see his sails . . .

JOHN. Yes . . .

BRADLEY. Of course, that friend of yours is hardly paying him a nickel out there. Hardly a plug nickel. And they'll have to buy a house. I mean, they all can't live in that stupid van. Even after he sells his house here, he'll need a considerable amount of additional cash. So I told him I'd send him a check. *(*BRADLEY *begins to look at, around, and under the table next to him for the check he gave to* JOHN.*)* And I told him the cupboard was a little bare, at the moment. A little bare. I'm no longer collecting a salary, as you know, and I do need to keep a little cash on hand these days. Doctors . . . Pills . . . If I should have to go into the hospital . . . *(*JOHN *takes the check out of his wallet, hands it to* BRADLEY.*)*

JOHN. Here you go, Pop.

BRADLEY *(Taking it).* Thank you, John. *(Pause.)* I mean, I refuse to sell stock. I can't do that. When I die, I want your mother to have . . . I want all of you to have . . . I've got to leave something.

JOHN. I know, Pop. *(*NINA *comes on.)*

NINA. I think we're almost ready to eat. Just so you'll know. *(She takes the hors d'oeuvre plate, starts out.)*

JOHN. We're discussing the National Debt.

NINA. Oh. *(Then she stops.)* Come to think of

it, Pop, you could do me one hell of a big favor.

BRADLEY. What, Pookins?

NINA *(Going to him).* I wonder if I might ask for a little money.

BRADLEY. Money?

NINA *(Sitting on the arm of his chair).* For Cleveland. Tuition. Travel. Living expenses. It costs money to change your life.

BRADLEY. I'm sure that Ed . . .

NINA. Ed would subsidize my commuting to the moon, if I asked him. Which is why I won't. I want to get back on the gravy train for a while, Pop. I'll borrow from you and pay you back, once I have a job. It's as simple as that.

BRADLEY. We'll work out something, Pookins. I promise.

NINA. Oh thanks, Pop. I knew you would. *(Kisses him, and starts to exit gloatingly.)* And as for you, John, I think you should get yourself a good dog. I'll tell you why but first I have to toss the salad. *(She goes Off.)*

BRADLEY. I suppose she'll want at least twenty as well.

JOHN. She might.

BRADLEY. And she should get it. It's only fair.

JOHN. Right.

BRADLEY. I am *not* going to cut into capital.

JOHN. I know . . .

BRADLEY. My father used to tell me every moment of his life . . .

JOHN. I know . . .

BRADLEY. Even as it is, I'm cutting close to the bone . . .

JOHN. You'll live, Pop.

BRADLEY. No, I won't. I'll die. But I'll die fair. I'll add twenty extra for you in my will. That's a promise. I'll call Bill Sawyer first thing.

JOHN. Thanks, Pop.

BRADLEY. So: You all get exactly the same amount of money.

JOHN. That's right.

BRADLEY. Jigger gets his boats . . . Nina gets her dogs . . .

JOHN. Right, Pop . . .

BRADLEY. And all I have to worry about is that damn play.

JOHN. It's not going on, Pop.

BRADLEY *(Getting up).* If only you'd put in some of the good things. The singing around the piano, for example. That was good. Or the skiing. That was very good. That's when we were at our best.

JOHN. It's hard to put skiing on the stage, Pop.

BRADLEY. You could talk about it. You could at least mention it.

JOHN. I do, actually. I bring it up.

BRADLEY. You do? You mention the skiing?

JOHN. The skiing and the piano both.

BRADLEY. Do you think you could mention anything else? *(ANN's voice is heard from Offstage.)*

ANN'S VOICE. I'm about to light the candles!

BRADLEY *(Calling Off).* Two more minutes, darling! Just two! *(To JOHN.)* I mean, if I were writing the darned thing, I'd want to prove to those critics we *are* worth writing about. I'd put our best foot forward, up and down the line.

JOHN. I have to call 'em as I see 'em, Pop.

BRADLEY. That's what I'm afraid of. *(ANN appears at the door.)*

ANN. Now Nina has just whipped together a perfectly spectacular meal. There's even mint sauce to go with the lamb chops. Now come on, or it will all get cold.

BRADLEY. Just a minute more, my love. We're discussing the future of American drama.

ANN. Couldn't you discuss it in the dining room?

BRADLEY. I'm not sure I can.

ANN. Well hurry, or Nina and I will sit down and dig in all by ourselves. *(She goes off.* JOHN *takes a necktie out of his jacket pocket, and begins to put it on, looking in a wall mirror.)*

BRADLEY. What happens at the end of this play? Do you have me die?

JOHN. No, Pop.

BRADLEY. Sure you don't kill me off?

JOHN. Promise.

BRADLEY. Then how do you leave me in the end?

JOHN. I'm not sure now.

BRADLEY. You could mention my charities, for example. You could say I've tried to be very generous.

JOHN. I could . . .

BRADLEY. Or you could refer to my feelings for your mother. You should say I've adored her for almost fifty years.

JOHN. I'll think about it, Pop . . . *(NINA enters.)*

NINA. Those lamb chops are just lying there, looking at us! *(NINA exits.* ANN's *laughter is heard Offstage.)*

BRADLEY. I suppose what you need is a kicker at the end of your play.

JOHN. A kicker?

BRADLEY. When I give a speech, I try to end with a kicker.

JOHN. A kicker.

BRADLEY. Some final point which pulls everything together.

JOHN. In the theatre, they call that a button.

BRADLEY. Well, whatever it is, it makes people applaud.

JOHN. You can't *make* people applaud, Pop . . .

BRADLEY. You can generate an appreciative mood. I mean, isn't that what we want, really? Both of us? In the end? Isn't that why I make speeches and you write plays? Isn't that why people go to the theatre? Don't we all want to celebrate something at the end of the day?

JOHN. I guess we do.

BRADLEY. Of course we do. In spite of all our difficulties, surely we can agree on that. So find a good kicker for the end.

JOHN. Kicker, kicker, who's got the kicker?

BRADLEY *(Picking up the script gingerly, like a dead fish, and handing it to him)*. Meanwhile, here. Put this away somewhere, so it doesn't dominate the rest of our lives.

JOHN *(Taking it)*. O.K., Pop.

BRADLEY *(Turning off various lights)*. Because there are other things in the world besides plays . . .

JOHN. Pop . . .

BRADLEY. Good food . . . congenial conversation . . . the company of lovely women . . .

JOHN. I've just thought of a kicker, Pop.

BRADLEY. Now *please* don't settle for some smart remark.

JOHN. Pop, listen. Remember the plot I was telling you about? Where the older son thinks he's illegitimate?

BRADLEY *(Starting out)*. I can't discuss it.

JOHN. No, no, Pop. Wait. Please. Here's the thing: suppose in the end, he discovers he's the true son of his father, after all. *(BRADLEY stops, turns, looks at him.)*

BRADLEY. That just might do it. *(ANN comes in again.)*

ANN. Now come ON. Nothing can be more important than a good meal. Bring the tray, please, John, so that we don't have to stare at a lot of old liquor bottles after dinner. *(To BRADLEY, taking his arm.)* Wait till you see what Nina has produced for dessert . . .

BRADLEY *(As he goes, over his shoulder, to JOHN)*. . . . I still don't like your title, John. Why don't you simply call it *The Good Father?* . . . *(JOHN stands, holding his play, watching his parents go Off, as the lights fade quickly.)*

The End

Spoils of War

MICHAEL WELLER

Original New York production by The Second Stage Theatre, artistic directors Carole Rothman and Robyn Goodman, opened May 17, 1988. It was produced on Broadway at the Music Box Theatre by Ed and David Marvish in association with The Second Stage Theatre. The Broadway cast, in order of appearance, was:

MARTIN	Christopher Collet
ANDREW	Jeffrey de Munn
ELISE	Kate Nelligan
PENNY	Marita Geraghty
EMMA	Alice Playten
LEW	Kevin O'Rourke

Directed by Austin Pendleton
Setting by Andrew Jackness
Costumes by Ruth Morley
Lighting by Paul Gallo

In the play's premiere production at The Second Stage, the role of Andrew was played by Larry Bryggman and that of Penny by Annette Benning.

Before its first public performance, three roles were cut entirely from the text. The playwright would like to thank the actors who were cast and rehearsed these characters:

CELIA (OLDER MARTIN'S WIFE): Cheryl Giannini
(OLDER MARTIN): JAMES REBHORN
MORTY (A PARTY GUEST): Anthony Picano

TIME: The 1950s

LOCATION: New York City

Spoils of War is based loosely on Michael Weller's own adolescence, and concerns the yearnings of a sixteen-year-old boy who tries desperately to orchestrate a reconciliation between his estranged parents, whom he sees not as they really are—two people whose needs are totally incompatible—but as he imagines they were in the 1930s: romantic leftists in love, rebelling against society.

The war of the title, Weller says, is "the silent war between the parents, felt through the child"; the spoils are Martin, the son whom both parents want. The title also refers to the legacy that the generation of the 1950s inherited: the lost ideals of the 1930s, the onset of the "Me" generation, and the rise of conservatism that climaxed in McCarthyism. Although the action of the play takes place during the course of one week, it touches on twenty years in the lives of Martin's parents.

The shallowness of her present life causes Elise, Martin's mother, to question the very nature of existence. "I want the passion, I want the closeness we all had once," she says. Martin asks the same questions: "Why can't things be different?" To which his mother replies: "Because we can't choose the way we love." By the end of the play, Martin learns to accept that which cannot be altered, to survive and mature in the midst of upheaval and change.

Michael Weller was born in New York City in 1943. His parents were artists who had worked for the WPA. His mother was "a beautiful woman named Rosa Rush, who died young and in tragic circumstances.... My background was artistic rather than commercial. I had it pretty easy; there was never any pressure on me.... My rebellion would have been to be a banker." Weller attended Brandeis University, where he studied musical composition and began to write plays. He thought of becoming a composer, and wrote several scores for student musicals, including one for an adaptation of Nathanael West's *A Cool Million*. He became a playwright almost by accident, when he was disappointed with the book that had been written for one of his scores. He bought a manual on playwrighting and copied the rules he learned from it onto cocktail napkins, which he would study while working as a bartender. He developed "a very cool attitude" toward his writing, he says. "I was never very romantic about it."

One of Weller's university instructors encouraged his developing interest in drama and urged him to go to England to study. Weller chose Manchester University, where the theatre course "consisted largely of a teacher bringing the aspiring writers, directors, and actors into a small theatre and telling them that he never, never wanted to see it empty. That gave me a dream of theatre I've never lost." Weller credits his Manchester Studies with instilling in him the "invaluable" English habit of close observation of character. In 1968, his play *How Ho Ho Rose and Fell in Seven Short Scenes* was produced by the *Sunday Times* Student Drama Festivals in England. Then Weller's *Cancer* was performed at the Royal Court Theatre in London in 1970. Retitled *Moonchildren*, it was subsequently produced in America and catapulted Weller to fame. (Even before *Moonchildren*, though, Weller had written more than a dozen plays, six of which had been produced in London in "lunchtime theatres," an opportunity he does not think he would have had here in the States.) In 1973, back in the United States, he became the first Playwright in Residence at the Mark Taper Forum of the Los Angeles Center Theatre Group, and was the recipient of a ten-thousand-dollar grant.

In 1975, Weller's *Fishing* (the second work of a trilogy that also includes *Moonchildren* and *Loose Ends*) was produced by Joseph Papp's Public Theater. His other works for the stage are *Fred, Happy Valley, The Body Builders, The Making of Theodore Thomas, Citizen, Tira Tells Everything There Is to Know About Herself, More than You Deserve, Now There's Just the Three of Us*, three sketches for the revue *Oh! Calcutta!, At Home, The Dwarfman, 23 Years Later, Master of a Million Shapes, The Ballad of Soapy Smith*, and *Ghost on Fire*. Weller's screenplays include *Hair* and *Ragtime* for Milos Forman, and an adaptation of *Loose Ends*.

Spoils of War represents a major shift away from Weller's typically detached style. "The rule I used in composing the play," he explains, "was that it was going to be an emotional autobiography . . . where the people are much more direct with each other. They live without the protection of wit; they don't defend themselves in the way my characters usually do, with a wisecrack right at the moment of great tension." Weller seems to be striving himself toward the commitment and communication that eludes many of his characters. "I saw certain patterns that I had followed as a writer that I decided I'm going to be conscious of . . . and not fall into them without a real calculating reason. You just feel a need to go in a new way. I don't know if it's just this one play or some direction I'm going to go off in. . . ."

CHARACTERS

MARTIN, the son, age 16
ELISE, his mother, late 30s
ANDREW, his father, early 40s
PENNY, father's girlfriend, 20s
EMMA, mother's friend, late 30s
LEW, a builder, 20s

ACT ONE

Elise's Place, a cramped apartment on the fifth floor of a dingy Greenwich Village walkup.

MARTIN *comes into the doorway, holding a valise. He surveys the room. Unmade pullout sofa bed with ashtray on it, heaped with cigarette butts. Half-read books on side table. The only visible storage is a crudely made wall-length affair; inside is a rod for hanging clothes and a bureau at one end. A curtain, now open, runs its length when closed, concealing the clutter within. Across the window, in matching material, is a curtain pulled shut. When it is open, we can see outside part of a neon sign that runs vertically, showing the letters H-A-R and the top of an M (for "Pharmacy").*

It is the mid-1950s.

MARTIN *enters, sets down the valise and begins straightening up, folding bed away, etc. He is just sixteen, his face still boyish and open, but with a veiled, secretive quality which shows itself from time to time. He rarely looks people in the eye. Noting the darkness of the room, he approaches the window to pull open the curtains. As he does so,* ELISE *enters and the room fills with light.* MARTIN *turns and sees her.*

MARTIN. Mom!

ELISE. Angel! (ELISE *breathless, sets down sketch case and shopping bag full of magazines.*) Sorry I'm late, they put us on double overtime again, have you been here long, god my feet are killing me, those stairs, let me look at you! Just as I thought, the handsomest man in the universe. Welcome home, angel! *(As they embrace, what sounds like Mexican bullfight music begins to play from next door, festive and bright.* ELISE *is in her late thirties, with a gypsylike beauty and a playful, seductive manner that is unconscious and natural. But there are also a poise and reserve about her that suggest a person who has learned to put a brave face on her loneliness. She is dressed for a wilting hot day in the early summer, something handmade that, like all her clothing, shows her own unique sense of flair and style. At*

their embrace, the music swells from next door.) Now then, first things first—how was the train ride down?

MARTIN. Just a train ride. Why is it so hot in here?

ELISE. It's nearly summer, that's why: cold in winter, hot in summer, any complaints see the man in the moon. *(Through the following.* ELISE *sits, removes shoes, massages feet, checks frayed hem, then pulls magazines from shopping bag and sorts them into piles on the table.)*

MARTIN. I'll open the window.

ELISE. The noise will drown out Mrs. Salvatore's music. She put her speakers right up against the wall especially for me, lovely neighbor, a gypsy, like your mother.

MARTIN. I'll turn on the fan . . .

ELISE. Stupid thing, two days after I had it repaired, *kaput*, a waste of money. Speaking of which, I'm the tiniest bit short till payday, so a major decision has to be made about this evening—dinner or a movie, you choose.

MARTIN. I'm seeing some friends from school.

ELISE. On your first night home?

MARTIN. It was kind of last minute, on the train ride.

ELISE. What am I running here, a halfway house for transient teens?

MARTIN. My summer job doesn't start till next Monday and there's an early train upstate, we have the whole week together . . . *(He exits with his suitcase.)*

ELISE. May I then expect the pleasure of his company on his last, if not his first night home?

MARTIN *(reenters)*. Absolutely.

ELISE. Sunday night, make a note.

MARTIN *(smiles)*. "Note."

ELISE. Now tell me all about Parents' Day. Did you read your essay out loud? In front of the entire school? Did they applaud, and anyone who didn't their name and address, I'll deal with them personally.

MARTIN. It went fine, Mom.

ELISE. "It went fine, Mom." Now doesn't that conjure a vivid picture, yes, I see it all . . .

MARTIN. I'll tell you while we eat, okay?

ELISE. Excellent! Raid the icebox, whatever you find, that's dinner. *(plops down some magazines conspicuously)*

MARTIN. Why the magazines?

ELISE *(reads titles)*. Construction Quarterly— Contractor's Annual—Perspectives in Extruded Plastic. These titles are sheer poetry.

MARTIN *(on the way out).* Changing careers again? *(exits)*

ELISE. Don't be such a Smart Smerdley, your mother has had the inspiration of a lifetime.

MARTIN *(off).* Not another one!

ELISE *(loud).* We are about to possess a home of our own. I mean a *real* home, what do you say to that?

MARTIN *(off).* The others weren't real?

ELISE *(loud).* They weren't *ours. (quieter)* The husband owns title, don't ask me why. Hus-*bands.* When love goes wrong, we don't stoop to payoffs—I don't, anyway. Pride. Tant pis pour moi.

MARTIN *(off).* I can't hear you. *(ELISE flips through magazines, circling an item, dog-earing a page, etc.)*

ELISE. Aren't you sick of all this moving around? Wouldn't it be lovely to live somewhere spacious and light and permanent where I could get back to my poetry and you had your own room for . . . well, whatever. What are you up to out there, plotting the Revolution?

MARTIN *(off).* Of course, what else?

ELISE *(smiles).* You see, it's all to do with these new materials they developed for the war. Now they're looking like mad for peacetime markets, like housebuilding—only contractors won't use anything new until it's proven, and how can you prove it till you use it. And *that,* my dear, is where we come in . . .

MARTIN *(reenters with milk bottle half-full).* This is all I could find.

ELISE. Milk! What luck, my absolutely favorite meal. You can live for years on nothing else, did you know that?

MARTIN. It's warm.

ELISE. As nature intended. Did you ever hear of a refrigerated cow?

MARTIN. Is the icebox broken, too?

ELISE. No, angel, there is nothing wrong with the icebox. Or the fan, for that matter. It's the electric company, I don't know what is the matter with those people . . .

MARTIN *(flipping wall switch).* The power's been disconnected?

ELISE. It was that or the phone. And since nothing exciting ever entered my life through the icebox, I paid the phone bill.

MARTIN. Mom, what do you live on?

ELISE *(snippy).* On the fact that I'm putting you through school and you'll have opportunities I never had. What a shame my Little

Lord Fauntleroy missed the Depression, or he wouldn't be so quick to judge his own flesh and blood . . .

MARTIN. Okay, take it easy, all I meant . . . never mind.

ELISE. What, angel? You're such a Moody Morris. I thought my little ambassador would come home glowing with triumph.

MARTIN. I guess I'm just tired. It's a long train ride down. Tell me your idea, I'll get the glasses for dinner. *(ELISE watches his exit to kitchen. Something is up.)*

ELISE. I'm approaching all the manufacturers with a proposition: they contribute their most controversial products from which I'll offer to design and build The Home of The Future. They get a free showcase, we get a free house, and free enterprise triumphs once again.

MARTIN *(Reenters, holding two mismatched glasses to the light to check for dirt).* What do we build this house on?

ELISE. On a piece of land, silly head, what else?

MARTIN. And where do we get this piece of land?

ELISE. In the fullness of time, all will be revealed: Sunday night.

MARTIN. What's the big deal about Sunday, just tell me.

ELISE *(teasing).* Curiosity killed the cat.

MARTIN. Mom, it's just another pipe dream.

ELISE. *Pipe dream?* Where on earth do you pick up these curious expressions?

MARTIN. You know what it means.

ELISE. Une rêve du pipe? Is that, for instance, when you send your son to one of the best progressive schools in the East and he's failing nearly every subject at mid-year? *(teasingly)* Plus caught drinking in the science lab? And taking the school jeep on a midnight joyride over very dangerous logging trails which nearly got him expelled, not to mention killed—and I hope you know how much I'd save having you at a public school here in the city—but no, the mother pesters and pleads till the headmaster gives him one last chance, all because she has this *pipe dream* he'll end up with an A-minus average, write a brilliant essay and be chosen as the school's first exchange student ever . . . is that what you mean by a pipe dream?

MARTIN. Why *did* you leave me up there? How come you didn't just bring me home?

ELISE. I feel innuendo peeking through the window. What are you trying to say, angel mine?

MARTIN. I'm not *trying* to say anything. I asked a question, you obviously don't want to answer, and that's the end of that.

ELISE. Mais quelle force! Quelle finalité. Je suis desolé. *(smiles)* Did you understand?

MARTIN. Why should I?

ELISE. Darling, you're not off to Switzerland as a tourist, you represent a school, an entire nation, you must be fluent in the language.

MARTIN. That was French, Mom. The Swiss speak German.

ELISE *(snaps)*. Don't lecture me about the Swiss. I knew a dwarf from Zurich once. He spoke French. To me, anyway.

MARTIN. Why do you say these stupid things when you don't know what you're talking about . . . !

ELISE *(grandly)*. Switzerland is a mountainous country full of very clean people who stayed neuter in the war. They eat lots of chocolate and always know what time it is. If they want to speak German, that's their problem.

MARTIN. Neutral, Mom. They were *neutral* in the war.

ELISE. That's what I said.

MARTIN. You said neuter.

ELISE. A pedant, no less. *(MARTIN starts out.)* Where do you think you're going?

MARTIN. I have to get ready.

ELISE. Darling, I only have you for one short week. Let's both try hard to make the most of our time together. Sit. *(MARTIN obeys. ELISE joins him and mimes that his head is a box with a lid she can unlock and open. An old game.)* Now then.

    Turn the key
    Open the lid
    Look where all
    The secrets are hid . . . !

MARTIN *(brushing her hand aside)*. Don't.

ELISE. Do you want me to say I'm sorry? Is that really necessary? You know I wanted to be at Parents' Day. Imagine how I felt missing my son's finest hour, but we were weeks behind on the autumn line and they asked us to volunteer for overtime—which does not mean *volunteer,* it means which of you is truly dedicated to Maison de Maurice Continental Fashions. If I'd taken time off . . . you know how hard I've worked all year for promotion . . .

MARTIN. Are we ever going to see Andrew?

ELISE. Ah. So *that's* what this is all about.

MARTIN. We've been back in the city for almost a year.

ELISE. Shouldn't you be getting ready for your friends?

MARTIN. You always do this.

ELISE. Do what?

MARTIN. I bring up his name and, bang, you change the subject.

ELISE. There's nothing to say. He's not interested in us, *finis.*

MARTIN. How do you know?

ELISE. After ten years out West we return to his city and nothing, not a peep—*(stops herself)* No, I swore I would never do this. I will not poison the well. I'm sure he has his reasons.

MARTIN. Was he the one who left?

ELISE. There was a war . . .

MARTIN. I mean after.

ELISE. Oh, who left who, what difference could it possibly make now? People change. He went away, he came back . . . different.

MARTIN. Why? What was he like before the war?

ELISE *(beat)*. Before the war . . . was a whole other world. Into the sunset, red flags waving, artists and workers of the world united.

MARTIN *(trying to get it straight)*. And I was . . . *after* that?

ELISE. You were never not there, my angel, my blessing.

MARTIN. Mom, I'm serious . . .

ELISE. Darling, I've had a long day. Tomorrow. We'll have a nice talk tomorrow, all right?

MARTIN. What if he did want to see us?

ELISE. What if the moon was green cheese. He could have seen you on his own at Parents' Day if it's me he's afraid of.

MARTIN. He didn't know you wouldn't be there.

ELISE. That's hardly the point . . . what do you mean "he didn't know."

MARTIN. How could he, we haven't been in touch.

ELISE. You said he *didn't* know . . .

MARTIN. I said . . .

ELISE. Martin, look at me, I heard you.

MARTIN. You heard wrong.

ELISE *(agitated)*. Have you been in touch with him, has he called you at school, was he at Parents' Day?

MARTIN. Of course not. How could you even think something like that?

ELISE. I'm sorry, darling. You'd have told me, wouldn't you.

MARTIN. Cross my heart and hope to die, okay?

ELISE. No secrets. Not between the two of us.

MARTIN. It's only 'cause you said we'd all be together when we got back East . . .

ELISE. Never . . .

MARTIN. You did, Mom, when we left New Mexico, that first night in the motel . . .

ELISE. I said no such thing. *(Tired of this, MARTIN goes off to wash. ELISE is puzzled by his behavior. As she explains herself, we can see an edginess in her manner. First, she glances around to make sure he is gone; then, talking, she removes a flask from her handbag, pours a slug of bourbon into her milk, sips, and replaces flask in bag.)* I may have touched on the possibility of an evening together—something along those lines. I don't consider it extravagant of me to assume, after ten years, he might be just the least bit curious about . . . us. *(quieter)* Who'd have thought he'd still be so terrified of contact.

MARTIN *(breezes in combing hair)*. Can I use your toothbrush? I left mine at school.

ELISE. What a handsome young man. You'll break some poor woman's heart one day. Not that one . . . !!!

(MARTIN has lifted the wrong glass of milk. Pause. He brings it to his nose and smells, then sets it down.)

ELISE. It's been a funny old year, darling. You see, I finally understand something, and it hasn't been easy. No one is going to help us. *(Brighter)* But when you return from Europe, we'll have our very own home, that's a promise. And we'll burn electricity till the wires hum hallelujah!

MARTIN. Mom.

ELISE *(distant)*. I thought I could leave this damn city behind.

MARTIN. *Mom.*

ELISE. What is it, angel?

MARTIN. I think the house is a great idea.

ELISE *(beams)*. In that case, I'm sure *some* people in Switzerland speak German. Prosit! *(raises glass)* Now then, a warm bath, then slide between the sheets with a nice, fat Russian novel while my little genius slips into the night, with his mysterious friends from school. Undo me. *(MARTIN hesitates, then unfastens his mother's dress down the back.)*

ELISE *(sings)*. I dreamed I saw Joe Hill last night

Alive as you or me

Says I, but Joe, you're ten years dead

ELISE *and* MARTIN. I never died, says he

I never died, says he . . .

(Elsewhere, Andrew's Place)

(ANDREW appears in a pool of light, watching something as he speaks.)

ANDREW *(like control tower)*. Zurich, Switzerland to inbound ST-107, do you read me . . .

ELISE *(to MARTIN)*. Thank you, angel . . .

ANDREW. Zurich, Switzerland to ST-107, come in . . .

ELISE *(hugging MARTIN)*. It's so nice to have company! *(ELISE exits. Alone at last, MARTIN breathes deeply, as if relieved of a great weight. His arms go out like an airplane and, as light dims on ELISE's Place, he begins to fly across the stage in a shaft of light.)*

MARTIN *(in flight)*. ST-107 to Zurich Control, ST-107 to Zurich Control . . .

ANDREW. You have clearance to land, Runway 2 is your active, exit Green-C, that's C for Charlie, do you read . . . ?

MARTIN *(in flight)*. Active runway is 2, exit Green-C, over and out . . .

(Lights up on ANDREW's Place, where MARTIN sits on packing box, ANDREW issuing commands. The room is bare, boxes around, a place being moved into. Among things being unpacked are books, a high-quality telescope, antique model square-rigger sailing ship, several crystal decanters, things of taste and elegance. ANDREW is an imposing man, forceful, energetic, used to giving orders and being listened to, but also capable of puzzling sudden delicacy of expression and manner, an almost pedantic fussiness.)

ANDREW. Good, now what?

MARTIN. Left flap down, right rudder . . .

ANDREW. No, no, no, you approach Zurich from the *south* flying *west*, bank to the left . . .

MARTIN. Sorry, Dad, west, *west*—left flap *up*, left rudder, *right* flap down . . .

PENNY *(breezes in)*. Hey, poops, can I borrow your shaving brush . . . *(sees MARTIN)* Whoops, sorry . . . *(PENNY is in a bathrobe, pinning her hair up behind. She is in her early twenties.)*

ANDREW. Ah . . . Martin, this is Penny, my . . . friend. Penny, Martin.

PENNY. I didn't hear the door.

MARTIN. How do you do.

PENNY. Fine, thanks. What's up?

ANDREW. We're landing in Zurich.

PENNY. Should I fasten my seat belt? *(starts out, stops)* Oh, is that okay, shaving brush?

ANDREW. Don't bang the water out, you loosen the hairs. Shake it dry. Shake it dry. *(illustrates)*

PENNY *(imitates, teasing)*. Shake it dry. *(She exits, wiggling her bottom playfully.)* Shake-it-dry, shake-it-dry . . . *(MARTIN watches her exit with interest. ANDREW notes this and acts.)*

ANDREW. Deet-deet-deet, red light, emergency . . .

MARTIN *(taken by surprise)*. You said a routine landing . . .

ANDREW. You've gone red in the air, what do you do—full throttle, get away from the ground as fast as you can, and why is that?

MARTIN. I forgot . . .

ANDREW. 'Cause we're soft and . . .

BOTH. . . . the ground is hard, it's no contest!

ANDREW. Okay, I threw you a little zinger there. You did well. Naaah, you did just great. Keep it up and we might get you into a real machine this summer . . .

MARTIN. A DC-7?

ANDREW. Whoa! That's a big bird you're talking about. Doubt I could fly one of those myself.

MARTIN. Why not, you're a pilot.

ANDREW *(amused)*. I'm a photographer, kiddo. I happen to be shooting a spread for the airline, bummed a few free lessons for the hell of it.

MARTIN. You're going to solo round the world, that's what you said.

ANDREW. I said *maybe,* and till maybe happens, what do we call it?

MARTIN. A pipe dream.

ANDREW. There you go, now back to work . . .

MARTIN. But say we're flying to, I don't know, Switzerland or something, and there's an emergency, the pilot has a heart attack, you could take over and land, right?

ANDREW. There's a copilot.

MARTIN. He's epileptic.

ANDREW. I'd change airline. How 'bout less with the mouth and more with the hands. *(Both return to unpacking boxes.)*

MARTIN. Great place. Kind of big for one person.

ANDREW *(beat)*. You don't mind that Penny joined us?

MARTIN. Why should I mind.

ANDREW. I'm glad you could make it over. Thought you'd have other plans, first night home from school.

MARTIN. Mom works late. It's a real hard job, lot of overtime.

ANDREW. She doesn't mind your dropping by?

MARTIN. I told you at Parents' Day, she's glad we're seeing each other. She appreciated your coming up to school when she's so busy. She wants us to spend time.

ANDREW. Sounds like she's changed.

MARTIN. She's pretty great. Talks about you all the time.

ANDREW *(abruptly)*. Open that box, I'll get us a Moxie, celebrate our first evening together, what do you say? *(Re box)* You'll find something inside—it's right on top. Had it framed.

MARTIN *(holds up framed photo)*. The cowboy? What for? Hey, this is *you!*

ANDREW. Lazy-Y Ranch.

MARTIN. You were a cowboy?

ANDREW. Well, I had a hat on my head and a horse under my butt, I guess so. And a fruit picker, sign painter, even deputy sheriff up in Idaho, you name it.

MARTIN. Mom never said.

ANDREW. Listen, kiddo. I quit school. I quit 'cause nothing made sense, what I saw going on around me—newspapers screaming prosperity, growth, record employment, while my dad and damn near everyone we knew could barely put meat on the table once a week, and still they believed the headlines. So, one day, bang, out the door, age fifteen, rode the rails west to see for myself, and you know what? After five years of knocking around, I knew the truth. The papers were lying. That's right. This country was a total god damn disaster. And they kept right on lying all the way to '29, when things got so bad they just couldn't anymore. You hold onto that *(the photo)* and remember—don't believe what they tell you. Go out and see for yourself. You know why I'm saying this?

MARTIN. Aren't we just talking?

ANDREW. I never "just talk." Think about it. I was in school; you're in school. I headed west; you're heading to Europe. Well?

MARTIN *(puzzled)*. Going away, is that what you mean?

ANDREW. I mean what's true and what's not true. I mean that essay of yours, the one you read at school.

MARTIN. The Cold War? What about it?

ANDREW. That's what I'd like to know. What about it?

MARTIN *(still puzzled)*. It won the contest. *(brighter)* They're gonna publish it in *Roots and Branches,* that's the yearbook, I can save you a copy. *(He is trying to slip out of this, lifting box to carry elsewhere.)*

ANDREW. Look at me, Marty. Tell me how it went.

MARTIN. I didn't memorize it, Dad. "The Cold War is both a war and not a war," something like that . . .

ANDREW. Keep going.

MARTIN. You heard it at Parents' Day.

ANDREW. Refresh my memory.

MARTIN. "It is two great powers, Russia and America, pitting their citizens against each other with propaganda, lies and silence—"

ANDREW. To me, Marty, to *me.*

MARTIN *(braving it).* But perhaps we have more in common than we know. Take our very initials, U.S., and U.S.S.R., both begin with *US,* and does this not suggest a greater unity . . .

ANDREW. Good, you're blushing . . .

MARTIN. I am not.

ANDREW. It's bullshit, and you know it. You're just parroting back what you know they want to hear up at that circus of a school, "International Brotherhood of Man" . . . christ alive . . .

MARTIN. Take it easy, that's just the motto . . .

ANDREW. It's a wet dream for radical has-beens. They hire a staff of academic rejects from around the world—at half price—and call it a *Global Environment.* How could she get suckered in, after everything we fought for back then.

MARTIN. Look, if you don't like the place, why don't you call Mom and we'll all get together and talk it over.

ANDREW *(beat).* Knowledge is everything, Marty. Everything. I don't want to see you open your mouth ever again to please another man. You say only what you truly believe, or you shut up.

MARTIN. Dad, what if. . . . Say I hadn't written that essay.

ANDREW. Did you?

MARTIN. Sort of. Not really. I cribbed it from this U.N. journal in the school library. I didn't mean for it to get all out of hand like this. *(beat)* Dad?

ANDREW. All right. Put it out of your head, I don't think you're that kind of kid. Are you?

MARTIN. I thought they'd catch me. I thought I'd be sent home. Someone has to be with her.

ANDREW. Who? Wait a minute. You tried to get yourself booted on her account?

MARTIN *(agitated).* She pretends everything's okay, but I know she doesn't mean it, not this time, or maybe it's just different now 'cause it was always, before, when we moved someplace she'd make it a big adventure and it was all going to be fine, but nothing's working out the way she planned and I don't know how to make it better—she doesn't eat right, she gives her money away, she forgets to pay her bills and now I'll be gone all year—

ANDREW. Stop right there. That woman is tough as old leather, and always has been. She doesn't want help. People have tried, believe me. You carry your own load, Martin. She'll be fine. Do you understand me.

MARTIN. Yes, sir.

ANDREW. Now let's have that Moxie.

PENNY *(reenters, still in robe).* Okay, last time, I promise. Toothbrush?

ANDREW. Sorry, kitten, you're out of luck.

MARTIN. I have one. *(takes it out)* Look, still sealed.

PENNY. You always carry that around, talk about ready for anything. I shouldn't, but since he won't let me keep one here . . .

ANDREW. Hey, mischief . . . !

MARTIN. Take it, I'll buy a whole new one tomorrow. The city's full of toothbrushes, I checked.

PENNY. You checked? Listen to the comedian.

MARTIN. It's extra-stiff bristle, is that okay?

PENNY. I wouldn't have it any other way.

ANDREW. Let's hop into something decent, dinner's on the way.

PENNY. Tell ya what, just for being such a sugarpie, I'm going to get you a little something of my own for Europe and give it to you at the party Sunday . . .

MARTIN. Party, what party?

ANDREW. Penny, some clothes . . .

PENNY. You haven't told . . . whoops.

ANDREW *(to MARTIN, offhand).* Just a little wingding to show off the new campsite here, maybe stir up a little wind about this new photo magazine I'm thinking of starting . . .

PENNY. Sure, poops, on Father's Day?!

ANDREW. Wasn't the invitation supposed to come *after* dinner?

PENNY. *That's* the part I forgot.

ANDREW. Miss Nervous here. *(to* MARTIN:*)* If you can make it. Pretty lively crowd shaping up. I know it's your last night in town. I don't want to cause any trouble at the other end.

MARTIN. Sunday?

PENNY. Seven o'clock on . . .

MARTIN. I'll have to let you know.

ANDREW. Either way, no big deal. Sort of last-minute thing . . . *(doorbell)* There's the Chinaman, rustle up some dishes, that box . . . *(Exits. MARTIN, left alone with PENNY, busies himself with a box.)*

PENNY. You're a real sweetheart helping with the move, it means a lot to Andrew. *(lifts a thick book)* Chinese dictionary. Typical, the old slyboots—one minute he's Mister Regular Guy, next thing he's jabbering away with a waiter in Chinese. "Oh, you know, I picked it up here and there." Are you like that, know tons of stuff and never let on? Like with this party—and don't let him fool you, the whole thing's for you, he's been acting like a ten-year-old ever since you got in touch. Hey, I have a terrific idea, let's make this a conversation.

MARTIN. Are you in love with my father?

PENNY. Oh, small talk, my favorite kind. You're a very intense young man. Nice, but intense. Andrew and I are having a very fun time together, yes.

MARTIN. That's not what I asked.

PENNY. And this isn't exactly the conversation I imagined having with my boyfriend's son.

MARTIN. Boy? He's old enough to be your father.

PENNY. Are we getting along or not?

MARTIN. Are we supposed to?

PENNY. Have it your way . . . *(moves to go)*

MARTIN. Do you love him?

PENNY. That's none of your business. *(gentler)* He keeps it simple, and simple is what I happen to want right now—clean, wholesome fun, and no strings. Like the animals I work with—grr-grrr, slither-slither, sniff-sniff, "Hello, beastie, I like you, let's play."

MARTIN *(laughs)*. You're nuts.

PENNY. You got a great smile, kid. You ought to use it more.

MARTIN. I'm not a kid.

PENNY. You know what I think? There's two kinds of Martin, they change by the hour, one of them's sweet, the other one's sour.

MARTIN. There's more than two of me. A lot more.

PENNY. Ooooow, mystery, chills-up-my-spine!

ANDREW *(reenters with Chinese food)*. Hey, chop-chop, a little movement in the clothing department.

PENNY. Now there's the big problem, sugar, nothing to wear.

ANDREW. Cut the games, Penny, not tonight.

PENNY. It's the god's honest truth, we've been cleaning the hippo compound, and when I went to shower and change the locker was jammed shut, and you wanted me here early to help with the move, so I had no time to go home and change . . .

ANDREW. All right, check the closet, take something of mine.

PENNY. See what I mean, if I just kept a few things here . . .

ANDREW. End of story . . .

PENNY. I'm not being devious, honeybun. No anchors are being dropped in your harbor.

ANDREW. Penelope . . .

PENNY. *Penny.* I hate that name.

ANDREW. *Clothes.*

PENNY *(to MARTIN)*. He's so cute when he's angry. *(exits)*

ANDREW *(beat)*. Loves to stir it up, that one. Every angle.

MARTIN. Are you going to marry her?

ANDREW. Penny? Marry her? *(chuckles)* Damn interesting gal, though. Saving up for fieldwork in Africa, Thompson's gazelle, migration, some such. Self-taught . . . why?

MARTIN *(sudden)*. I've made up my mind, Dad. I'm coming to the party.

ANDREW *(caught offguard, delighted)*. Yeah? You sure, now? Aw, Marty, that's dandy, that's just . . . hey, I'm tickled pink—this calls for a drink. Damn it, the Moxie, went clean out of my head. *(exits)*

MARTIN *(calls)*. Can I bring someone?

ANDREW *(off)*. It's your bash, kiddo. Yours and mine. School buddy? Girlfriend? *(reenters)* Hey, you got yourself a little steady up there . . . what's her name?

(Elsewhere, Elise's Place)

(Enter ELISE, dancing a sensuous, dramatic tango to music from next door. She wears a high-fashion gown, circa mid-1950s.)

MARTIN. I think you'll like her.

ANDREW. If she's your friend, she's mine.

ELISE *(to someone offstage)*. Dance, my dear, is ninety percent style, and style is ninety percent confidence. Just think: Tallulah!!!

MARTIN. What are you going to do with all this room, Dad?

ANDREW. Fill it full of whatever the hell I

want. *(enter* PENNY *in outsize clothes of* AN-DREW'*s)*

ANDREW. And here she is, let's dust off some dishes and tie on the feed bag . . .

(As lights fade on ANDREW'*s Place,* EMMA *enters to* ELISE, *dancing an awkward tango and wearing a pink gown that looks ludicrous on her petite, rotund body.)*

ELISE *(encouraging* EMMA'*s efforts).* Perfect, my dear, you'll be an absolute sensation tonight . . .

EMMA. I feel like a strawberry cupcake in a straitjacket, it's no use, Elise, I can't dance, I can't breathe, and my tush looks three sizes too big in this ridiculous contraption.

ELISE. Nonsense, you have a perfectly lovely Botticelli figure.

EMMA. Just my luck to be born four centuries late.

ELISE. A century early, like me, but until our time, we'll carry the flame by living as unspeakably as two men.

EMMA *(giggles).* You're *terrible.*

ELISE. . . . And don't you love it.

(Enter LEW *from the kitchen, holding a bottle of bourbon, half-gone. He is a powerful, gentle man in his mid-twenties.)*

LEW. Glasses?

ELISE. Try the sink. *(*LEW *exits)* What's his name again?

EMMA. Lewis-something, I think he said.

ELISE. Tsk-tsk-tsk, you naughty person. *(music has stopped)*

ELISE *(calling towards wall).* ONCE MORE, PRUDENCIA, POR FAVOR. *(to* EMMA:*)* She gets her records from South America, how I love that Latin yearning . . . *(vamping in the silence)*

EMMA. Are we really going out in these? What if someone recognizes the style?

ELISE. They'll have a sneak preview of the Maison de Maurice autumn formals.

EMMA. But if you're caught! It seems so reckless after how hard you've worked for promotion.

ELISE. They'll be back in the showroom long before they're missed, now stop worrying my darling Conscience, this is our night of the week, and damn the rules.

(Music has begun again.)

ELISE. Now there's a woman who understands! *(calls)* GRAZIA, SIGNORA, or whatever it is in South American—this time you lead. *(*ELISE *sweeps* EMMA *up in a dance,* EMMA *blushing.* MARTIN *enters and watches for a moment.)*

EMMA. Nooo . . . *(giggling)*

MARTIN. Hi, everyone, ladies' night out. Where'd you get those?

ELISE *(dances over).* Hello there, mysterious stranger, don't I know you from somewhere . . . ?

MARTIN *(gently changing the game).* Hi, Emma.

*(*EMMA, *busy adjusting the back of her gown, spins around startled.)*

EMMA. My god! *(recovering)* I'm sorry.

MARTIN. Did I say something?

EMMA. Your voice, it's exactly like. . . . It's gotten so husky since midyear . . .

MARTIN. Who is it like?

ELISE *(cutting in).* Join us, angel. Tell Emma she's thin in German.

EMMA. Isn't it exciting, a whole year in Switzerland! All that culture—and snow!

ELISE. And what has the mystery man been up to?

MARTIN. Nothing.

ELISE. Now doesn't that conjure a vivid picture, yes I see it all . . .

MARTIN. I have to change. By the way, Mom, you know on Sunday.

ELISE *(quick).* What about Sunday?

MARTIN. Nothing, I was just wondering—have you made any actual plan-plans?

ELISE. Every minute of the evening is accounted for, why?

MARTIN. Nothing. *(starts off)*

ELISE. "Nothing." Must be the new word of the fifties. And while we're at it, kindly remove your dirty laundry from the floor in there, I am not here to peel grapes for the Sultan of Bumbum. *(*LEW *has entered and stands in the doorway.)*

LEW. Don't let me interrupt . . .

ELISE. Say hello to Lewis, he's a friend of Emma's.

EMMA *(absurdly).* Lew is from Wichita . . . didn't you say?

LEW. Yes, ma'am. Sunshine State of Kansas.

MARTIN *(shakes hands with* LEW). Hi. See ya. *(exits.)*

LEW. Thing is, your fridge seems kind of warm, you keep the ice anywhere special?

ELISE. The day is far too hot for ice, Lew. Just pour and carry. *(*LEW *exits.)*

ELISE. Does Martin really sound like . . .

EMMA. I'm sorry, I couldn't help myself. The way he said "Hi, Emma" . . .

ELISE. He's certainly developing Andrew's manner. Imperious, full of disapproving looks. He blames me that his father hasn't been in touch, but what more can I do, I told him we were coming East . . .

EMMA. You spoke to Andrew?!

ELISE. Postcard, hello-goodbye. Emma, I need a favor, a very big one.

EMMA. How big is very?

ELISE. I bought some land. An entire acre.

EMMA. When? Where?

ELISE. Upstate, by a river somewhere.

EMMA. You haven't seen it?

ELISE. An inside deal, there wasn't time. I need a mortgage by the weekend, or the whole thing goes on public auction.

EMMA. How much?

ELISE. It won't be touched. Straight into my savings account, and when the upstate bank sees my collateral, I get the mortgage, and you get back every penny.

EMMA. You know I can't refuse you anything. So please don't ask unless you're sure you know what you're doing.

ELISE. Would you think me crazy if I told you that for the first time in years I feel *lucky*. Look how well Martin is doing—I'm reestablished in the city—I even started a new poem. And guess what? I didn't get the promotion.

EMMA. How can that be, they promised!

ELISE. Office intrigue, tushes unkissed. And not a word to Martin—nothing darkens this week of ours.

EMMA. All that overtime, the weekends, aren't you crushed?

ELISE. Not a bit, that's the whole point. I know what I really want now, and the rest is just weather, a few clouds, a light sprinkle, who cares. I've had my revenge, we're wearing it.

EMMA. Bring it to the union. File a complaint . . .

ELISE. . . . Sunday night I'm taking Martin to dinner, then *My Fair Lady*—yes, a special show for the union, I got front row center . . . balcony . . . and afterwards, by taxi to the Hawaiian Room where I've ordered champagne waiting, and as we raise our glasses to toast, I shall hand Martin the deed to an entire acre of land by a river in both our names—oh, Emma, I can't wait to see his face!

EMMA. You are crazy. Or the most resilent woman on earth.

ELISE. "Over a sea of endless sorrow/On we sail with reckless joy." That's the start of my new poem.

EMMA. The answer is yes—of course. If I have it. And it's what you really want.

ELISE (*sweeps* EMMA *into an impulsive dance of joy*). Darling Emma, sweet-wonderful-Emma, how did I manage for ten years away from you!?

EMMA. Stop! Elise! No, I can't!

LEW (*enters, two glasses in hand*). Rumba-dumba, lead me to the party.

EMMA. Lew! Oh, god, I forgot, you're here.

LEW. Two things: a) I like what I see and, b) you might have yourself an electric problem in the kitchen—flashlight and a screwdriver, I'll have a looksee.

ELISE. The condition is temporary and minor, thanks all the same.

LEW (*extends glasses*). Down the hatch.

EMMA. That's enough for ten people, Lew. We haven't even eaten yet. (LEW *gulps down most of one glassful and reextends glass to* EMMA.)

LEW. Try that.

ELISE. Who said chivalry was dead. (*takes other glass*)

LEW. This Greenwich Village is quite a proposition. How's about that place on the corner with the black toilet in the window. Kinda offbeat touch for a restaurant.

ELISE. Lew, may I ask you a direct question?

LEW. It's a free country.

ELISE. Who on earth *are* you, and why did you follow Emma here?

LEW. That's pretty direct.

EMMA. I don't normally attach myself to strange men in the street.

LEW. Am I that strange?

ELISE. To be found drifting in our bohemian latitudes, a little, yes. You strike me as a man with a more regular sort of wife—life, I mean; *life.*

LEW. If I'm a third wheel here, just say the word and I'll roll on down the road.

EMMA. Were you part of the demonstration or not?

LEW. I was following my nose, sightseeing is all. Heard women yelling out the windows, I look up and see bars, hell, couldn't believe it. Where I come from you don't put a woman's prison smack-dab in the middle of town. Then I see Emma and them down below with banners—I figure in the way of local color it's got the Circle Line beat all to hell.

ELISE (*amused*). We seem to have a slight misunderstanding.

LEW. No, ma'am, I understand when it feels real nice talking with someone.

EMMA. Lew was a frogman . . . isn't that what you said?

LEW *(shows tattoo on arm)*. Korea.

ELISE. And how many tadpoles did you leave behind, Lew?

LEW. Beg pardon? Oh, I get it. *(smiles)* Like if I had some kids out of wedlock. Pretty sneaky how you put that, sneaks up on you.

ELISE. Haven't you a glass?

LEW. In there. *(kitchen)* Refill anyone?

ELISE. Oh, bend my arm. *(extends her glass grandly)*

EMMA. I'm fine, thank you.

LEW. If you don't mind my saying so, you're a helluva lot better than fine, Emma. *(exits to kitchen)*

EMMA *(blushing at* ELISE's *amusement)*. Oh, god, how could I bring him here, what was I thinking?

ELISE. He's sweet, he's good-looking and he likes you. Perhaps my luck is rubbing off on a friend.

EMMA. No, no, it's too bizarre, what could he possibly want with a woman like me?

ELISE. Three guesses.

EMMA. Stop. Men never walk up to me like that—with a big smile, unless . . . *(realizes)* Oh my god, oh no . . . !

ELISE. What?

EMMA. That's exactly how they penetrate, find a demonstration . . .

ELISE. What on earth are you talking about?

EMMA. The FBI.

ELISE. *Emma!*

EMMA. Sure, sure, you think it all ended with Senator McCarthy, but you're wrong. Cedric's been getting mysterious phone calls upstairs. They listen and hang up. He's sure they're watching our building, and everyone knows I take his mail when he travels . . .

ELISE. . . . And they all know he was in our commune twenty years ago, oh yes, Cedric among the rustic revolutionaries, poison ivy from head to foot, *Das Kapital* in hand, sowing corn for the masses. Popping corn. I assure you, the FBI did not tremble at our labors.

EMMA. It's been so long since I was with a man—*that* way.

ELISE. Like riding a bicycle. Once you mount, the rest comes rushing back.

EMMA. You're *terrible.*

MARTIN *(enters)*. Anyone for the bathroom, I'm going to take a shower.

ELISE. Darling, guess what, due to a sudden change of plan, your mother is free as a bird tonight . . .

EMMA. You can't leave me alone with that man!

ELISE. Shush.

MARTIN. Sorry, Mom, tonight I'm booked.

ELISE. The mystery friends from school, no doubt.

MARTIN *(beat)*. Would you like to meet them?

ELISE. Me? You're asking your mother along to share your secret life?

MARTIN. There's a party Sunday.

ELISE. Sunday?

MARTIN. They planned this whole going-to-Europe thing for me. It was supposed to be a surprise.

ELISE. I'm sorry, dear, Sunday is out of the question.

MARTIN. Come on, Mom, it'll be great, they said I could bring someone. You always talk about meeting my friends, well now's your chance.

ELISE. Martin, there will be no discussion about this. We made a date, it's final.

MARTIN. How about if we just dropped in for a little while.

ELISE. I said no. If it's that important, tell them to have it in the afternoon.

MARTIN. How can they just change everything at the last minute?

ELISE. Oh, *they* can't but *I* can.

EMMA. Excuse me, I'll just help Lew in the kitchen . . . *(she doesn't move)*

MARTIN. The party's for me, Mom. You're not going to let me go to my own party?

ELISE. Honestly, you are the limit. You come breezing in and expect me to rearrange my life at your every whim.

MARTIN. No, Mom, if I said I was going to Parents' Day, I'd go.

ELISE. That was unworthy of you.

EMMA. Please excuse me . . . *(she stays put)*

MARTIN. Forget it, all right, let's just forget the whole thing . . . *(starts out)*

ELISE. You turn around and march yourself right back in here young man . . .

MARTIN. It's my party, and I'm going, with or without you.

ELISE. You do demand your pound of flesh.

MARTIN *(relenting)*. All I meant. . . . They never got a chance to meet you at school. You were busy, I understand, but you're free Sunday night, and I'd just be really proud if I could introduce you.

ELISE *(beat)*. Mister Tongue-of-Velvet. But afterwards, I demand a private hour alone with his majesty.

MARTIN. You'll get all dressed up, okay? Like you do sometimes?

ELISE. I shall not disappoint.

LEW *(enters with empty bottle)*. We got us a dead soldier here. I'll spring for a live one if you like.

EMMA. We've had more than enough, Lew.

MARTIN. Sorry I yelled. And thanks. Have a good old time . . . everyone. *(moves to go)*

LEW *(to MARTIN)*. I see you're looking at the critter.

MARTIN. The what?

LEW *(exposing tattoo)*. Bet you never seen one of these jobbies before.

MARTIN. A tattoo? I have, actually.

LEW. Not like this baby. See, the upper half's a man.

MARTIN. So it is.

LEW. How 'bout below the waist? I got me a watch right here says you can't guess what it is.

MARTIN. A frog.

LEW *(beat)*. I'll be darned. Smart hombre.

MARTIN. The web feet sort of give it away.

LEW *(removing watch)*. Whole outfit got 'em. Inchon Harbor, little Chinee fellow, two different-color eyes. *(holds out his watch)* There ya go.

ELISE. Lew, that's hardly appropriate.

LEW. A bet's a bet. Won it in a poker game to start with, easy come, easy go.

EMMA *(agitated)*. Lew, would you please put that back on and stop behaving this way.

MARTIN. Should I stick around, Mom?

ELISE. Take your shower. *(MARTIN exits. Pause.)*

LEW. He's your son? I thought it was more one of those brother-sister type things, you hardly look old enough . . .

ELISE. Lewis, are you in some kind of trouble?

LEW *(awkward)*. I'll just pop on downstairs for another bottle. You might want to give the electrical folks a call, I think you've been shut off. *(beat)* I didn't realize there was families involved here. *(exits)*

EMMA. This is not a stable man. Now what do we do, he knows where you live.

ELISE. He won't be back.

EMMA. How do you know?

ELISE. He left his wife recently. Or vice versa. I've made an informal study of men in his condition.

EMMA. So much for *my* luck. Shall we eat? I'm famished.

ELISE. Emma, I love you dearly. We'll al-

ways be together, won't we—eat, dance, grow old together, two leftover lefties in tennis shoes and sweat socks . . .

EMMA. I think I'll wear a cape—a black one!

ELISE. Yes, and we'll carry umbrellas, and if anyone is rude to us, we'll whack them on the ankles . . .

MARTIN *(off)*. LAST CALL FOR THE BATHROOM . . .

ELISE. I want the money. I'm asking you for it here and now. He'll see that I can carry through. That his strength comes from me. *(EMMA removes a checkbook from her handbag, signs and tears out a check, then holds open the ledger page for ELISE.)*

EMMA. That's my balance. Make it out for whatever you need.

ELISE. What do you really think, Emma?

EMMA. I think you have an extraordinary heart. I think you love better than you know.

ELISE. Dear Emma. Be close to me always . . . always.

(LEW stands in the doorway, sheepish. Both see him at the same time.)

LEW. I feel like a damn heel, slinking off like that. May I come in for a minute?

ELISE. I think Lew has something to tell us.

EMMA. Stop doing this, first you're inside, then you're outside, then you're back inside . . .

LEW. I know, I know . . .

EMMA. Stay put, just stay in one place until we're used to it . . . *(gulps down drink)*

LEW. My fault, I didn't mean to upset you . . . *(advances into room)* Fact is, I don't know what the hell I'm doing anymore. See, it looks a little like I might be leaving my wife. *(ELISE and EMMA exchange a look.)*

LEW. Came here for the expo, but that closed a few days back and I'm still here, floating around. We been gearing up to start on our own, me and my partner back home, Luigi, which happens to be Lew in Eyetalian. My card. *(LEW passes his business card to EMMA, who reads it out loud.)*

EMMA. "How can you lose when you use Two Lews . . ."

LEW. The slogan's more my idea. Needed something catchy.

ELISE *(takes card and reads out)*. "Contracting, renovation, modernizing, no job too big." *(beat)* You're a builder, Lew?

LEW. That's the plan. Bank's in. Made a ton of contacts at the housing show. Everyone seems to think we'll do real good. Only problem is, my heart's just not in it, and which how can you tell people when they're rooting for you all the way . . .

ELISE *(passes her drink to* LEW*).* Go on, Lewis, the natives are friendly.

LEW *(beat).* I been sleeping out in Central Park. Kind of an impulse-type thing. But I tell you, I haven't felt so damn happy since Korea. Like I was thinking, here I am, lying on my back in the middle of this great city on what's gotta be the most valuable piece of real estate going, but no one builds there. It's free for everyone to enjoy. Now doesn't that say something about people at their best. *(shy)* I say that kinda stuff back home and they look at me like I got a lump on my head the size of a grapefruit. Anyhow, that's my story. *(drains glass)* Thanks for hearing me out. *(moves to leave)*

ELISE. Lew, I think it's remarkable that you should happen along tonight. Please, allow us to buy you dinner, and ask you questions, and grow wise.

EMMA. Elise . . . !?

ELISE. The house.

EMMA. My goodness, yes. What luck!

ELISE. When it rains, it pours.

(Elsewhere, Central Park)

(Enter PENNY *in soiled zoo coveralls, looking for someone whom she spots in the distance.)*

PENNY *(calls).* Martin!

LEW. I hope you don't think this is all some kind of fancy line I'm handing you. I see how it must look, what I'm up to . . .

ELISE *(applying makeup).* We're big girls, Lew. Eyes open wide . . . et cetera.

PENNY *(calls, waving).* Yoo-hoo, over here!

LEW. I can't believe my luck running into the two of you.

ELISE. Yes, things seem to be looking up all around. *(calls)* DON'T BE TOO LATE, DARLING!

PENNY *(calls).* Over the footbridge!

ELISE *(grandly, from doorway).* Avanti!

*(*ELISE, EMMA *and* LEW *exit and lights go down on* ELISE'*s Place as* MARTIN, *with a shopping bag, enters to* PENNY *in Central Park)*

MARTIN. I got lost after the Sheep Meadow, sorry.

PENNY. They owe me a long lunch. You like my spot?

MARTIN. It's like being in the country.

PENNY. I sleep out here sometimes. The park's full of people at night. You can hear 'em in the bushes.

MARTIN *(removes food from bag).* Cheese and bread, is that okay?

PENNY. It was sweet of you to suggest this. After the other night, I wasn't sure where we stood.

MARTIN. I didn't expect someone so young. And pretty.

PENNY. If that's a compliment, I accept. *(She watches as* MARTIN *removes wine and a blanket.)*

PENNY. Wine! Aren't we French! But red? I believe for picnics in the park with your father's girlfriend, the wine of choice is white.

MARTIN *(puzzled).* There's no such thing.

PENNY. I'm joshing. I see we have the serious Martin today.

MARTIN *(takes wine).* I'll open it.

PENNY. You want to know a secret? Andrew has every single letter you ever wrote to him, all the way back to baby scrawl when he was overseas.

MARTIN. He told you that?

PENNY. I snooped. How else do I learn about Andrew. In the night table. I spend the night sometimes. Does that shock you?

MARTIN. I figured it went beyond Chinese food.

PENNY. Touché.

MARTIN. How come you're telling me this?

PENNY. An olive branch. You offer bread and wine, I offer a peek behind the Throne of Glory. *(Pause.* MARTIN *notices* PENNY *watching him.)*

MARTIN. What are you looking at?

PENNY *(beat).* You know—sometimes at the zoo, and no one's figured out why—this very peculiar thing happens. Bang, out of nowhere, the animals go berserk—bellow, screech, rattle the cages, throw themselves at each other. And then, just as suddenly, they go absolutely quiet. You can almost hear their hearts beating. It's as if they'd been in the grip of some wild, overwhelming passion, and now they're embarrassed by their own feelings. *(beat)* People are animals. *(beat)* Do you know what I'm saying?

MARTIN *(looks away).* Wine?

PENNY. So what's this all about?

MARTIN. All what?

PENNY. Some people just can't fake it with each other. It's cards on the table, or nothing.

MARTIN. It's about the party. I have a problem.

PENNY. That's better. See how easy it is?

MARTIN. I'm bringing someone.

PENNY. And . . . ?

MARTIN. Annnd . . . see, at school there's a lot of kids from the city. Which means stories get back sometimes, you know, like about our parents and everything. And that's real bad news, 'cause it's supposed to be you keep your home life kind of quiet.

PENNY. How come?

MARTIN. Oh, the old story, all of us sent away from home, sort of let's-not-talk-about-why.

PENNY. Ah, *that* old story.

MARTIN. Please don't take this the wrong way . . .

PENNY. I'm listening.

MARTIN. See, if word got back that my father dated real young girls . . . they can really make your life hell with gossip like that.

PENNY. You mean stop dating Andrew because it embarrasses you?

MARTIN. Don't be silly. It's just my date . . . she's from school, really nice girl, but she's got a big mouth and if she saw you with Andrew . . .

PENNY. What are you getting at?

MARTIN. Like if you couldn't make it Sunday night? There's a flu bug going around.

PENNY *(laughs)*. This is the first time I've ever been hustled by an adolescent.

MARTIN. It's no joke, Penny. One kid had a nervous breakdown when it got back his mom was a hooker . . .

PENNY. I know my overalls stink, but I can still smell bullshit when a truckload of it falls on my head. The answer is no, en-oh . . .

(Elsewhere, Elise's Place)

(ELISE bustles on in a morning rush, coffee mug, cigarette, hairbrush, calling towards bathroom.)

ELISE. Martin, hurry up in there, what are you doing, plotting the Revolution?!

MARTIN *(to PENNY, urgently)*. Just this once, it's the only favor I'll ever ask.

PENNY. I don't know what your game is, but count me out. You should study your father, Martin. God knows he has his faults, but he always plays straight . . . *(starts off)*

ELISE. Martin!

MARTIN *(to PENNY)*. Don't tell him we met . . . Penny! *(PENNY is gone. MARTIN circles to* ELISE'*s Place and enters.)*

ELISE. Martin . . . there you are, god what a dawdler, I'm centuries late for work . . .

MARTIN. On Sunday?

ELISE. Fashion waits for no man—keep an eye on the coffee pot— *(holds out mug)* here, take this, and do me up in back will you?

MARTIN. Mom, we have to talk . . .

ELISE *(bustling around)*. After work, meet me here at five and we'll grab a quick bite before the party, make it five-thirty . . . *(exits)*

MARTIN. There is no party. It's been called off.

ELISE *(beat; off)*. I'm sure I heard that wrong.

MARTIN. I made it all up. There is no party.

ELISE *(reenters, furious)*. Martin, you can't do this to me, I cancelled all our plans, I gave away tickets to a Broadway show.

MARTIN. I've been seeing Andrew.

ELISE *(pause)*. Oh. *(pause)* Since when?

MARTIN. Parents' Day.

ELISE. Of course. He's the one you wanted to be with tonight.

MARTIN. I'll be with you.

ELISE. Isn't it Father's Day?

MARTIN. Yes, Mom, we both know what day it is. You think I didn't know why you were making such a big deal about tonight . . .

ELISE. That was unworthy of you.

MARTIN. I wanted you to be at Parents' Day. Both of you. I thought maybe if I read the essay in front of everyone, and you'd be there all fixed up, maybe he'd see what he was missing . . .

ELISE. And have us back?

MARTIN. Why not?

ELISE. You dreamer.

MARTIN. 'Cause I'd be gone all year. You'd have all that time to see each other again. He could take you dancing on the roof of that hotel in Brooklyn, just like the old days.

ELISE. The St. George? He told you about that?

MARTIN. You did.

ELISE. Never.

MARTIN. In New Mexico. At that motel. The night we left Mr. Haverstock.

ELISE. *Sid?* Is that all he was to you—Mr. Haverstock?

MARTIN. What was he to you, Mom? What were any of them?

ELISE. I believe the word is "husbands," darling. And with any luck, fathers.

MARTIN. I only have one father.

ELISE. Is it so strange that I'd want to make a normal life for us? We came close with Sid. I almost learned to cook.

MARTIN. It's Andrew's party.

ELISE. Ah. The fog lifts.

MARTIN. I told him I was bringing a mystery date. A girl from school.

ELISE. Oh, Martin, stories and stories and stories.

MARTIN. I must be crazy. Are you real angry?

ELISE. I don't know what I am. I feel terribly betrayed.

MARTIN. Why do I have to give up on him just because you did? *(sees that he's gone too far)* I'll call him and cancel.

ELISE *(distant)*. I think that's the best idea.

MARTIN. Okay.

ELISE. Do me up.

MARTIN *(obeying)*. I'm sorry, Mom.

ELISE *(being fastened)*. Is he bald? He was always touching his hairline.

MARTIN. Women find him attractive.

ELISE. Do they now. He's seeing someone?

MARTIN. It's nothing, she's a kid.

ELISE. Bastard . . .

MARTIN. Mom!

ELISE. What do you do together, you and your father . . . and this kid?

MARTIN. He's teaching me to fly.

ELISE. He owns an airplane?

MARTIN. Just pretend. He gives commands, I carry 'em out.

ELISE. Yes, that sounds like Andrew.

MARTIN. He's trying to start his own magazine.

ELISE. I'm sure he'll succeed.

MARTIN. I showed him your picture.

ELISE. I have to run, angel . . . what picture?

MARTIN. The gypsy one. With the cigarette.

ELISE. How could you, I look hideous.

MARTIN. He didn't think so.

ELISE. He's being polite. He was always a gentleman. To give him a little more than his due.

MARTIN. He remembers dancing in Brooklyn. The picture reminded him.

ELISE. He said that? Martin, is this another story?

MARTIN. He got all quiet when he talked about you.

ELISE. What else did he say? This is silly, you really must watch that imagination of yours, it's contagious.

MARTIN. He wants us back, I know he does. He got this new apartment right after Parents' Day, it's enormous.

ELISE. Then why hasn't he been in touch?

MARTIN. He asked the same thing about you.

ELISE. Martin, look at me! Did he mention Brooklyn? You never showed him the picture, did you?! Honestly, darling, you must stop making up these stories.

MARTIN. If he saw you again, though. In the special dress, the silky one.

ELISE. Angel. You're so sure of yourself.

MARTIN. I know what he's thinking. He's my father.

ELISE. Is it a big party?

MARTIN. Pretty big.

ELISE *(beat)*. It would be quite a scene, wouldn't it. The two of us waltzing back into his life arm in arm. I wonder if any of the old gang . . .

MARTIN. Who's that?

ELISE. I used to make quite the impression when I entered a room. I stood perfectly still, and everything moved in my direction.

MARTIN. What's that smell?

ELISE. The coffee. *(MARTIN exits.)* Oh, Martin, I told you to keep an eye on it, honestly, you'd forget your head if it wasn't attached to your body. Never mind, I'll grab a cup on the way to work, I'm centuries late . . . *(MARTIN has reentered with charred, smoking coffeepot.)*

MARTIN. Right through the bottom.

ELISE. Oh well, no use crying over burnt metal. Give me a kiss, angel, we'll meet here at five-thirty on the nose, make it a quarter of . . . *(In a rush, ELISE collects handbag, sketch portfolio, whatever.)*

MARTIN. What's the big plan, dinner? Movies?

ELISE. On your last night in town? Doesn't that call for something more along the lines of a surprise party?

MARTIN. Really? You'll come?

ELISE. After all the pains taken, how could I disappoint? We should call and warn him, it's only fair. But on the other hand, in love and war. *(blows kiss)* Well? *(MARTIN catches it to his lips)* What a pair we are, you and I. *(ELISE exits. MARTIN stands with smoking coffeepot, a smile on his face. Lights fade.)*

ACT TWO

Emma's Place. Books, periodicals, newspapers, a cramped space, that of a woman who thinks little about her own needs and lives for others. Enter ELISE *and* EMMA *in semidarkness.*

EMMA. Come in, come in . . .

ELISE. Where were you?

EMMA. Up cleaning Cedric's place.

ELISE. What would that man do without you.

(EMMA turns on lights. ELISE is dressed and

made up stunningly. EMMA *is dressed for cleaning.* ELISE*'s manner is edgy, distracted, but she is attempting to master her nerves.)*

EMMA. My god, Elise, you look gorgeous! Why? I mean, what are you doing here, isn't this your night with Martin?

ELISE. He's with his father. They've been seeing each other in secret.

EMMA. Oh dear, that's terrible, that's . . . sit, sit.

ELISE *(not sitting)*. The surprise party—it's Andrew's. I'm the mystery date. Emma, I'm terrified.

EMMA. You're going to see him?

ELISE. Have you anything on hand of a liquid nature? I'm in need of courage tonight, Dutch or otherwise.

EMMA. I'll make coffee . . . *(starts off)*

ELISE. Stay.

EMMA *(beat)*. It was bound to happen sooner or later. The whole gang's been talking about it all year.

ELISE. What do they say? What do *you* say?

EMMA. I think you've been waiting to see who gives in first.

ELISE. So what's new.

EMMA. Martin, for one.

ELISE. Yes. He wants this so badly.

EMMA. And you don't?

ELISE. Who knows what I want anymore. I want the *passion.* I want that terrible closeness we all once had.

EMMA. Wasn't that mainly a housing problem?

ELISE. You know what I mean.

EMMA. We were young. No money, no jobs, what else did we have but each other?

ELISE. I ask too much, don't I. Why does everything feel so small and selfish and trivial now?

EMMA. I might have some wine. *(starts off)*

ELISE *(slips out flask)*. Oh, look what I found. Just a glass, my dear. Never mind. *(She pours shot into cap, pops it down, pours another quickly.)*

EMMA. It's the romance you miss, not the struggle. That goes on, with or without the dreamers.

ELISE. You still believe, don't you. My darling Red Emma, the last holdout.

EMMA. It's not a religion, for godsake—it's fact and process. You think the world will stand by forever while so few people grab so very much of it for themselves?

ELISE. They've certainly been slow to object.

EMMA. Enough, we'll only argue.

ELISE. Oh but let's, let's argue like the old days, late into the night over black coffee and cigarettes. Let's live for something bigger than rent and the price of hamburger, god, doesn't it make you sick.

EMMA. Not a bit.

ELISE. Why can't I be like you, given to an idea, to something that doesn't change.

EMMA. You mean someone who doesn't run off.

ELISE. He didn't run off.

EMMA. Fine.

ELISE. Why is it you so disliked him?

EMMA. Two reasons. Always, whatever the subject—Stalin, Hitler, architecture, the movement—always, always he had to be *right.*

ELISE. He always was.

EMMA. And that's the other reason. A man without innocence. And finally, a coward.

ELISE. No, no, never that.

EMMA. Why defend him? He took the easy way out, a uniform, a gun. Someone his age, almost thirty, and with a family. You think without the war you'd still be together? A loner is a loner.

ELISE. He might have changed.

EMMA. For you? Nonsense. You were the beauty, he was the leader—our glorious couple, in love with a moment in time— it was a house of cards, the first wind and, whhht!

ELISE. You're in a strange mood tonight.

EMMA *(pause)*. Cedric was arrested.

ELISE. What?!

EMMA. They grabbed him on the el this morning, took him off somewhere for deportation.

ELISE. But why? He wasn't even a party member.

EMMA. Why, why, as if they need a reason. He gets letters from China with Mao Tse Tung on the stamp. He hates the rich. He writes books full of long words—to them, that's a Communist.

ELISE. I'm so sorry. Do you want to be alone?

EMMA. Who *wants* to be alone?

ELISE. What'll you do?

EMMA. Carry on. He's gone, but there's still the work. They ransacked his apartment. His address book has our names. Careful on the phone. You see, it didn't end with McCarthy.

ELISE *(abstracted)*. Cedric proposed to me, that summer on the commune. His father was a duke. Imagine, here but for Andrew stands a duchess. Isn't it stupid to marry for love.

EMMA. Maybe you *should* go, Elise.

ELISE. I'm sorry. That was an awful thing to say.

EMMA. What are you doing here?

ELISE. Martin left without me. I was late getting home—with a few pit stops along the way, of course. I've been putting on my face, and taking it off, and putting it back on again ever since.

EMMA. You didn't answer my question.

ELISE. You're angry.

EMMA. Yes.

ELISE. What have I done?

EMMA. You came to see Lew.

ELISE. Lew? He's here?

EMMA. Don't. He told me you've met him at the Copper Pot for drinks. Twice.

ELISE. Advice about the house. Oh, Emma, you don't think I'd do anything so underhand.

EMMA. You don't mean to, I know.

ELISE. It's *you* I had to see. Please believe me, you're the only one who makes me feel the least bit forgiven.

EMMA. But you take advantage. And I let you, it's my fault—you just don't understand your power.

ELISE. Power? What power have I ever had over anything?

EMMA. Over Martin. Me. Your friends . . . even Lew. He talks about nothing else, day and night; what's she like, when did you meet her, has she mentioned me . . .

ELISE. He's such a baby . . .

EMMA. And you are wonderfully blind, Elise. It's your great strength. My god, the hours I have spent talking politics to some poor fool while he glances over my head at guess who across the room, surrounded by admirers. You never knew, you took it for granted. After all, who am I? The Friend. The Passport-to-an-Introduction.

ELISE. I wasn't even there when you met Lew. You brought him to my place.

EMMA. Who cares about that stupid man, take him, get him away from me, he talks nonsense, I can't stand having him underfoot all the time . . . *(stifles sob)*

ELISE. It's Cedric, isn't it.

EMMA. All we did was talk. I'd go up. He'd come down. It was enough. They'll never let him back.

ELISE *(approaches* EMMA*)*. I'll stay . . .

EMMA. Don't touch me. I'm fragile but coping.

ELISE *(beat)*. Cedric never proposed.

EMMA. I know.

ELISE. Why do I say these things?

EMMA. He slept with you once. You struck him as shallow.

ELISE *(surprise)*. Well, he's wrong. And a terrible lover. You missed nothing.

EMMA. Thank you for telling me.

ELISE *(offers flask)*. First aid?

EMMA *(tetchy)*. Can't you wait for a glass? *(Pause. They laugh.* EMMA *exits to the kitchen. Alone,* ELISE *is suddenly agitated again, checking her face in her compact mirror.* LEW, *having appeared quietly, watches her for a moment.)*

LEW. Like what you see?

ELISE. Lewis! Good evening.

LEW. I thought you were spoken for tonight.

ELISE. I was and I am. Emma had a little upset. I thought I should drop by.

LEW. What about later?

ELISE. Later hasn't happened yet.

LEW. Is that a yes or a no? *(*EMMA *reenters with mug and wineglass.* LEW *covers.)* I was just on my way out. Emma's been kind enough to let me use her couch . . .

EMMA. I think she already knows that, Lew.

LEW. Don't suppose either of you good ladies would care to join me?

EMMA. I'm afraid you can't stay here after tomorrow.

LEW. Getting too comfortable, huh? Time to face the music.

EMMA. I'm glad you understand.

LEW. I'll just head on down to the Copper Pot for a bite, maybe stick around till closing. *(beat)* Careful who you talk to about that house idea, Elise. I made some calls. It smells big. Real big. I'll run it down for you . . . anytime. *(beat)* Say, what's the deal with the blue laws around here? When do they stop serving Sunday?

EMMA. We wouldn't know, Lew. *(Getting the message,* LEW *starts out.)*

ELISE. Good night. *(exits)*

EMMA *(having poured, lifts mug)*. And here we are again. To us?

ELISE. You see—I begged Andrew to take us back. I know that's why he hasn't been in touch.

EMMA. Ah. The postcard.

ELISE. It was more than a postcard. Emma. It was my future, spilling onto paper, scribble, scribble, scribble—you know how I get

under the influence. New Mexico somewhere. Some hotel, some bar, the drive east.
Martin asleep down the hall. Always, till
then, I felt my life moving forward to a better
time. Then the ground slipped under my
feet. Just a little. And I felt completely alone.

EMMA. Aren't we being a little dramatic?

ELISE. No, I saw what I was that night, so
clearly—begging Andrew to rescue me. Or
Sid. Or the others. I've always been the same,
full of wonderful plans, but lacking some
vital gear to set me in motion and make me
sufficient, without a man. Oh God, Emma,
just to stand before him whole, that's all I
want. "There Andrew, I ask nothing, I need
nothing, only you." Then I have to go and
ruin the whole thing. *(beat)* Dear oh dear,
listen to her. You're right, I'm full of Russian
blood tonight, bring on the balalaikas.

EMMA. You know, Andrew called Cedric
your first month back. He wanted to know
was it true you were staying down here.

ELISE *(beat)*. You tell me this *now?!*

EMMA. Cedric hates meddling. He said two
things in this country were inevitable without our help—the Revolution, and your reunion with Andrew.

ELISE. Dear old Cedric.

(Elsewhere, Andrew's Place)
(Enter ANDREW *with a large cake.)*

EMMA. People don't get over you, Elise. Go
to your party. Just be yourself.

ELISE *(brighter)*. Incandescent? Ravishing?
Irresistible? Yes, I see what you mean. And
with a young man beside me anyone would
die to call their own. *(they hug)*

EMMA. Next week? Same time? Same
place?

*(*ELISE *exits, then* EMMA, *as* PENNY *enters quietly to* ANDREW *and watches him carefully place
candles in cake. The room is now furnished, but
there is still some junk and boxes in corners, plus
spare party supplies which define the space as a
utility area not to be used by guests. Party noises
from next door, and the sound of someone playing
the piano very well, perhaps a piece by Jelly Roll
Morton.)*

PENNY. You sweet old thing. *(*ANDREW *turns
suddenly.)* Don't worry, no one's coming in
here—he's got 'em all spellbound.

ANDREW *(animated)*. Can you believe that
little son of a gun? Where'd he learn to tell
stories like that, nonstop for hours, my own
kid . . . !

PENNY. You might want to watch him with
the liquor.

ANDREW. What the hell, let him make a
few mistakes of his own, he's had enough
mothering for one lifetime.

PENNY. He's overboard, sweetie. He wants
so much to make a good impression. Just let
him know he has nothing to prove—he's sixteen, for godsakes . . .

ANDREW. And he's twenty-five, and he's
ten. At his age it's all fever and hormones.
Just watch, the minute his girlfriend shows
up everything'll be fine.

PENNY. Is that what the big book said?

ANDREW. Book?

PENNY. The one you've been underlining
all week? *The Psychology of the Adolescent?*

ANDREW. A spy in my house, eh? What else
did you learn from all those clean-living upright Calvinists back on the farm?

PENNY. Very funny.

ANDREW. He's my son, kitten. I think I
know what he's going through, thank you.
Hey, you've been a great sport about fitting
in here, don't think I haven't noticed . . .

PENNY. Talk about unbelievable . . . !

ANDREW. *Now* what?

PENNY. You two seem to think, I don't
know, like you're this fabulous father-son
team, one of those portraits on the boardwalk, with a hole in it where every woman in
the city's just dying to stick her head and get
her picture taken.

ANDREW. Is someone getting a little complicated here?

PENNY. God forbid, we can't have that.

ANDREW. Penny, stop taking the damn
world on your shoulders. Your father is not
here drinking himself to death. Martin is not
in crisis. Everyone enjoyed meeting you.
Don't look for things to fix when everything's
okay.

PENNY *(finger gun)*. Pow! I'm right. Keep an
eye on him.

ANDREW. Come here you little snoop. You
gazelle. You sexy zoo creature, you. *(They
kiss warmly.* MARTIN *bursts in, flushed, as* AN-
DREW *and* PENNY *separate fast.)*

MARTIN. Hey, Dad, that bald guy out there
with the earring and the tee shirt . . .

ANDREW. Hey, out, out of here . . .

MARTIN. Isn't he on the television . . . ?

ANDREW. That's Mister Clean, now am-
scray . . .

MARTIN. And who's that Chinese guy that
keeps talking in a funny voice?

ANDREW. Oh, Jesus, Lee Chen must be
doing his Milton Berle imitation. Just tell

him "Uncle Milty, *how jee-la,*" he'll die a happy man.

MARTIN. *"How jee-la"?*

ANDREW. Having a good time?

MARTIN. Are you kidding? Wait'll they hear about this back at school—where's the vodka?

PENNY. Where's your date?

MARTIN *(stops)*. Date? *(smooth)* She had a few things to take care of. Don't worry, you'll meet her.

PENNY. I was thinking more of the condition she'll find you in.

MARTIN. I can hold my liquor, Penny. Thanks for your concern.

PENNY. Don't mention it.

ANDREW *(intervenes)*. How 'bout a Moxie? We'll split one.

MARTIN. Sure. *(PENNY exits.)*

ANDREW *(as she goes, to MARTIN)*. You're doing one helluva job out there. I'm starting to think this magazine thing might really take off, and no small thanks to the entertainment committee . . .

MARTIN *(spots cake)*. Hey, is that an airfield?

ANDREW *(shy)*. Zurich. The candles are landing lights. What do you think . . . I made it.

MARTIN. You? The whole thing?

ANDREW. Picked up a trick or two living solo.

MARTIN. I'll tell you my opinion, Dad. It's pretty corny.

ANDREW *(laughs)*. So it is, what the hell. Say, do you know this one? *(sings)*

Oh Mister Gallagher
Yes, Mister Sheen?

(explains) Vaudeville, this is, Gallagher and Sheen, the best . . . *(sings)*

Oh Mister Gallagher
Yes Mister Sheen?

Who was that lady that I saw you with last night?

Dum-dum-dum-de-dah-dah-dah . . . *(lost; explains)*

See, Gallagher takes her out in a rowboat and they're spooning away, when this wave comes and sploosh, into the water—they swim for their life, and in the end, this is Gallagher: *(sings)*

Pulled her up upon the shore
Now she's mine forever more
Who, the lady, Mister Gallagher?
No, the rowboat, Mister Sheen!

(laughs) What a team. Father took me . . . unforgettable. He knew every record by

heart. *(beat)* Well, I guess we'll leave the entertaining to you.

MARTIN. That was terrific, Dad.

ANDREW. Listen, kiddo, I had a thought. How'd you like a little company on the trip over.

MARTIN. You mean Europe?

ANDREW. Leave early, take a few weeks, Burma, Chinese border, show you some of the old army haunts, maybe shoot a travel piece, coffee-table stuff, then drop you off in Switzerland.

MARTIN. Just you and me?

ANDREW. Spend some time. Catch up.

MARTIN. Mom's never been abroad.

ANDREW. *Us,* Marty. Just the two of us.

MARTIN. You really hate her, don't you.

ANDREW. Hey, kiddo, how 'bout we stick to the subject here. I don't hate her, why should I hate her?

MARTIN. Aren't you even just a little curious to see what she's like?

ANDREW. Your mother is an all-or-nothing kind of person. Clean break, that's how she wants it, no calls, no letters—fine with me . . .

MARTIN. But if she had been in touch, just say—would you want to talk to her?

ANDREW. Sometimes things happen in your life that seem very very important at the time, but in the long run you realize they're just not the main event. It's no use living in the past.

MARTIN. Who wants to live there. I just want someone to talk about it.

ANDREW. Hey, tell ya what, and this is a promise. We travel together, and I'll jawbone you till my teeth fall out, okay? Till then, just remember, there's two sides to every story, and whatever you may have heard—I was always ready to listen to their side of things, even to help out where I could, and they know that. They always knew. Which is why, just by the way, a certain gentleman who's called me some pretty colorful names over the years—and in print—but a damn good man all the same, when he was arrested this morning, it wasn't the others he used his one phone call to ask for advice. What we might have done, if we'd all held together.

MARTIN *(abruptly)*. Dad, was I a mistake?

ANDREW. Okay, Marty, what's going on here?

MARTIN. I want to know.

ANDREW. Who the hell ever put an idea like that in your head?

MARTIN. It's just there.

ANDREW. Cut the games. All night I've been smelling the old routines, the hints, the innuendo, slippy-sliding around, I didn't like it then, I don't like it now. Something's on your mind, you look me in the eye and spit it out.

MARTIN. All right, my date is Mom.

ANDREW *(pause)*. Elise? She's coming here? Are you crazy?

MARTIN. No, Dad, I am not crazy.

ANDREW. She put you up to it. It's okay, you can tell me, I know the way she can back people into a corner.

MARTIN. It was me. I wanted you to see each other.

ANDREW. Why?!

MARTIN. Why do you think?

ANDREW. I think you're picking up some very bad ideas about what's acceptable behavior. You never pull this kind of stunt on me. That woman is a disruptive, unreliable and very treacherous individual—

MARTIN. Don't say that. She's generous. She's kind. Okay, maybe she's a little different, but there's no law against that. She cares, Dad. About everyone. I've seen her buy a whole meal for a total stranger just 'cause they were out on the street. People love her. Everyone does. You did, once. *(beat)* Didn't you?

ANDREW. This isn't for now.

MARTIN. Oh, *that* one.

ANDREW. Enough. Tonight's not the end of the world.

MARTIN. Good to know, Dad.

ANDREW *(sharp)*. Hey. I mean it. No more.

MARTIN. I'm sorry. Let's have a party.

ANDREW. When they're gone, maybe— we'll see. Now let's set fire to this damn airport and haul it outside.

MARTIN. You bet.

ANDREW. When she gets here, I want *you* to answer the door. I'll go out and talk to her in the hall.

MARTIN. Don't worry, Dad, she won't show up. It's Parents' Day. Another pipe dream.

(Elsewhere, ELISE's Place)
(Enter LEW, hopping like a frog, followed by ELISE, both giddy.)

LEW *(frog noise)*. Grrk-grrk, turn on the full moon, I can't see my darn lily pad.

ELISE *(laughing)*. Stop it, you goof, on your feet and behave.

ANDREW. How 'bout a hand with the candles?

LEW *(lighting candle in ELISE's place)*. And God said, "Let there be light."

ELISE. And Elise said, "No monkey business." I'll get the ground plans.

LEW *(brandishing bottle)*. And two straws.

ELISE. Lewis, I did not happen by the Copper Pot in search of hanky-panky. We have a house to discuss, is that understood?

LEW. You have my word as a gentleman, and a reptile.

(ELISE exits. ANDREW and MARTIN have lit all the candles on the cake.)

MARTIN. I'd like to travel with you, Dad. The two of us.

ANDREW. Everything's gonna work out fine, champ. Just go easy. *(re cake)* That's your end. *(ANDREW and MARTIN lift the cake and start out. ANDREW breaks into song.)*

Hail, hail, the gang's all here
What the heck do we care
What the heck do we care

ANDREW and MARTIN. Hail, hail, the gang's all here
What the heck do we care now . . .

(They exit. Meanwhile, LEW lights more of ELISE's candles, takes a drink from his bottle for courage, readies himself for action by smoothing his hair, etc. Just as we hear applause from ANDREW's party, ELISE reenters in robe, hair down, ground plans in hand.)

LEW. Oh, mama, the way you look.

ELISE. Beware, Lewis. There's danger in candlelight.

LEW. We'll see about that, lady. *(LEW scoots over on the couch to make room. ELISE notes this and moves pointedly to the table, where she spreads her plans.)*

ELISE. It's only a rough ground plan, I'm no architect.

(LEW, acknowledging the dodge, rises to join ELISE at the table.)

LEW. What's on the side here, you planning a gymnasium?

ELISE. Martin's room. My son.

LEW. Half the house? Kind of disproportionate, don't you think?

ELISE. A boy needs room to grow.

LEW. He can go outdoors every now and then, can't he?

ELISE. Other things we can discuss—not this.

LEW. You don't understand what we got here. Forget about one house, this idea is good for a whole damn development, Futureville, whatever, fifty, maybe a hundred units, but we gotta start with a basic layout that meets the needs of your average American family.

ELISE. The average American family does not interest me. I want a home for me and my son, finis.

LEW. You're quite a handful.

ELISE. Don't change the subject.

LEW. Elise, I gotta say this, I just do. See, I went AWOL in Korea—lived on a houseboat, Chinese family took me in, aunts, cousins, grandkids, I never did sort 'em all out. But they had something I never saw before, and being with them . . . I came home a stranger, 'cause I knew how little you need to be truly happy. Feeling close to someone is all. Peaceful close. Close in your heart—the way I feel with you right now.

ELISE. How young you are.

LEW. Sound crazy? My wife thought so the time I tried to tell her.

ELISE. What you saw was a gift. The truth. Hold onto it for all you're worth.

(Elsewhere, ANDREW's Place)
(Enter MARTIN, thoughtful. He looks around.)

LEW. Two people can hold onto something better than one. *(MARTIN lifts phone off sideboard, trying to decide if he should call.)*

LEW. Elise?

ELISE *(distant)*. What is it, angel?

LEW. You're a million miles away.

ELISE. Less than half a city, but never mind.

LEW. I'm very smitten with you.

ELISE *(suddenly delighted)*. Smitten?! Now there's a word worth bringing back, oh *yes!*

LEW. I guess I strike you as kind of basic.

ELISE *(gently)*. Go home, Lew. Stand in front of everything you love—children, wife, the what-is-it, Sunshine Sky over Wichita? Imagine losing it all, and without knowing what lies ahead, because who can know that? It may be desolation, regret, and a terrible aching loneliness. Do I frighten you, I hope so. Because until you can feel the loss, but still know a yearning greater than all you're letting go, you must never dare speak the magic word.

LEW. Being what?

ELISE *(pause)*. Good-bye.

LEW *(resolute)*. Where's your phone, I'll call her right now. *(MARTIN lifts the phone receiver to dial.)*

ELISE. Face to face, or not at all.

LEW. Shoot, Elise, why all this rigamarole, you can see as well as I can what's going on here. Will you marry me? *(MARTIN replaces receiver.)*

ELISE. Close your eyes.

LEW. How come?

ELISE. To please your bride-to-be.

LEW. All right, I'll play. *(closes eyes)*

ELISE. Tell me the color of my eyes.

LEW. Brown. Sort of hazel-to-brown.

ELISE. Gray-blue. And my wraparound?

LEW. That I can tell you. Green.

ELISE. And you'd have been right one night last week when it was, but tonight, alas, the accent is on rose. Pink I'd accept, but green? No, Lewis, a clear strike two.

LEW. This is silly.

ELISE. Haven't you noticed, I'm a silly woman, and I'll be your silly wife if you get this one right, which should be easy, after the intense scrutiny you've given it all evening. Am I or am I not wearing a brassiere?

LEW. Was I that obvious?

ELISE. It was sunshine to a flower, well?

LEW. No brassiere.

ELISE. Dear man. If only the laws of gravity were so kind. Strike three. You seem to have a different woman in mind. I'm jealous. *(LEW kisses ELISE suddenly. She allows it, and returns the kiss passionately.)*

LEW. I'll take you away from all this, as god is my witness.

ELISE. After so many frogs, a prince at last. *(They kiss passionately once again.)*

LEW. It's a damn crime someone like you living this way, electric off, no room to breathe, garbage on the stairs, I want to help you out of here.

ELISE *(Draws away, suddenly cold)*. I don't remember asking for your help.

LEW. Don't pull away. What's wrong with a little help? Like with the house.

ELISE. You're hardly in a position to be judging my life.

LEW. Take it easy. You deserve better is all. I'd like to give you what I think you're worth.

ELISE. All the right words from all the wrong men.

LEW. Look at me.

ELISE. You'll have to leave now. This was a mistake. Please forgive me, I'm expected elsewhere.

LEW *(outburst)*. Listen up, lady. I'm not letting anyone kick me out on my ass after I put in this kind of time. I had a sweet number working when you came into the Copper Pot and I dropped her *like that*, now you owe me.

ELISE *(folds away ground plan)*. From prince to beast in the blink of an eye—this fairy tale is going backwards.

LEW. Look, I didn't mean that—you got me all tied up in knots.

ELISE. Please don't be here when I return. Good night, Lew.

LEW. You're going out like that?

ELISE. But this is me, unadorned. Why do I feel so horribly sober.

(*Exits. As* LEW *collects himself and exits slowly, nonplussed,* PENNY *enters to* MARTIN.)

PENNY. So there you are.

MARTIN. Is it over?

PENNY. Some crowd, huh? As little on the ritzy side for us in the business of hippo turds. How 'bout a smile, I could use it . . .

MARTIN. I'm leaving now.

PENNY. Hey, I know what it's like being stood up. There's other girls, summer hotel, cute guy like you.

MARTIN. Through the service door. I'll catch an early train in the morning. I'm never going to see my parents again.

PENNY. Are you drunk?

MARTIN. No, Penny. My *mother* is drunk. She's at a bar somewhere. Or maybe at home. Maybe with a man, who knows? I started to call her, but what's the point, she'd just make up some story to protect me. And I'd pretend to believe it to protect her. It's a little game we play called No Secrets. You weren't supposed to be here tonight. And she was.

PENNY (*beat*). I see.

MARTIN. Do you? I was beginning to think no one saw anything, ever. Except Andrew. Because he never lets the little stuff get in the way. You look at what's in front of you and you call it by its name. I want to sleep with you.

PENNY (*beat*). Sure. Can you wait'll I get my purse?

MARTIN. Does that mean you think I'm joking?

PENNY. Martin, what's going on?

MARTIN. We've been flirting all night, that's what. No, no, let's get this exactly right—we've been flirting right from the start. Animals going wild. Stiff bristle?

PENNY. I was not flirting with you.

MARTIN. Will you come with me, yes or no?

PENNY. Of course not, are you crazy?

MARTIN. Very good. A clear, simple answer—no evasions, no mysteries. Thank you, Penny. Good night.

PENNY. Would you please stop being like this.

MARTIN. What, honest?

PENNY. Creepy. Just shut up and sit down for a minute.

MARTIN. You knew I was back here. You followed me. Why? To see how I was doing, okay, that's the excuse, that's the *game*, but the reason, Penny? The real reason. You see what I mean.

PENNY. You don't have to impress me, Martin.

MARTIN. I'm sick of the bullshit. I'm sick of pretending I don't see what's going on. Just say it, for godsake, why is that so difficult, you've been flirting with me, *say it, say it!*

PENNY. No, Martin. (*beat*) Yes. A little. Maybe. Look, I've noticed the glances. All right, I've *enjoyed* them. The smiles. Yes, the danger even—wondering if Andrew noticed. I've never been coveted by two generations of the same family.

MARTIN. You see? Underneath, everything's so simple. You want me. I want you. Sniff sniff.

PENNY. Would you cut it out, your father's right outside!

MARTIN (*loud, towards door*). I know where my father is! This has nothing to do with him.

PENNY. You are a naughty little boy.

MARTIN. And you are so damn beautiful.

PENNY. What an operator. I'm starting to see your technique, Mister Martin. A little mystery, a shock attack, I drop my guard and zip, in for the kill.

MARTIN (*puts hand on her breast*). This feels so right.

PENNY. Take your hand away.

MARTIN. Tonight is for us.

PENNY. The hand.

MARTIN. Are you afraid of my father?

PENNY (*removes hand*). That's enough. I won't breathe a word about this, but you have to behave now . . . talk about outrageous.

MARTIN (*suddenly defenseless*). Hold me. Please. I won't try anything. I need someone close to me.

PENNY. Oh, Martin, Martin, Martin, what are we going to do with you.

(PENNY *holds him comfortingly. Unseen by* PENNY, ANDREW *enters from party.* MARTIN *sees him and responds by taking* PENNY'*s hand, kissing it, then brushes his lips up her arm as she starts to yield.*)

ANDREW. Penny, go inside.

PENNY (*breaking away suddenly*). Poops. Thank god. You better find out what's going on here, I think your son's in big trouble.

ANDREW *(controlled fury)*. Inside. Now. *(PENNY exits)*

ANDREW *(as she goes)*. All right, Martin, let's have it, and this better the hell be damned good.

MARTIN. Want to split a Moxie? Or should we just look each other in the eye and spit it out.

ANDREW. What are you trying to prove?

MARTIN. I don't know. And I don't even care.

ANDREW *(beat)*. Her. This is all *her*.

MARTIN. It's me, Dad, I'm back. I'm back. *(Pause. Enter* PENNY, *hesitant, looking nervously over her shoulder.)*

PENNY. Andrew, someone just arrived, she asked for you, I don't know what to tell her . . . *(*ELISE *enters in her wraparound. All look at her.)*

ELISE. Hello, everyone. Sorry I'm late.

ANDREW. Elise!

MARTIN. Mom, what are you doing here?

ELISE. I believe I was invited.

MARTIN. But like that. You came here like that?

ANDREW. I'll handle this. Martin, Penny, wait outside.

ELISE. No need, Andrew, I come in peace.

ANDREW. I can imagine. A little earlier and you could have disrupted the entire evening, I hope you're not too disappointed.

ELISE. I'll get over it. And who might this be?

PENNY. My name is Penny.

ELISE. Penny! You didn't used to settle for such small change.

MARTIN. Mom . . .

ELISE. What, dear?

MARTIN. Just . . . behave, okay?

ELISE *(sweetly smiling)*. She's very attractive, and I admire her shoes. Hello, Penny, I'm the former Mrs. Andrew, and this is our son, oh, that's right, you've met. Welcome to our— what shall we call it—reunion?

PENNY. Excuse me. *(exits)*

ELISE. Not much fight in that one.

ANDREW. You've made your grand entrance, you've stirred up trouble, now what?

ELISE. Nothing. I've exhausted my repertoire.

ANDREW. That'll be the day.

MARTIN. Don't argue, please.

ELISE. Friendly banter, darling. No, no, when Andrew and I go for blood—what did they used to say?—after us the Revolution would be an anticlimax. Your father was not

amused. About himself he has, how much humor would you say, Andrew, on a scale of one to zero?

ANDREW. You haven't changed.

ELISE. Why thank you, you've held up pretty well yourself.

ANDREW. That's not what I meant . . . oh.

ELISE. Am I going too fast? You could keep up, once.

(Both ANDREW *and* ELISE *are trying desperately to master their feelings, but both are shaken by the sight of each other, and by the sudden total return of old emotional habits they had perhaps allowed themselves to believe long dead.)*

ANDREW. Still showing off? For who, Elise? Those days are gone, there's no one left to impress.

ELISE. Was it for them? Is that what we've decided? *(beat)* Oh, Andrew, let's bury the hatchet. Hasn't our little war of silence outlived whatever use it never served.

ANDREW. I'll say good-bye to my guests, then we can sit down together and have a quiet talk. Is that agreeable?

ELISE. The imperious command followed by the rhetorical question—vintage Andrew!

ANDREW. Fine. You tell me what *you'd* like to do.

ELISE. It's a profoundly sane and rational plan.

ANDREW. May we consider it settled?

MARTIN. She's just teasing. It doesn't mean anything.

ELISE. Thank you, dear.

ANDREW. I know what she's doing, I know exactly.

ELISE. Yes, you always know, don't you. Tell us how to make the perfect martini, and the correct way to say Carib*bean*, or is it Cari*bb*ean—and how to address the factory workers so they'll feel unity with us their creative comrades . . .

ANDREW. Are you trying to provoke me?

ELISE. Oh, phooey, Andrew, can't you take a little good-natured ribbing.

MARTIN. She just says stuff, Dad, ignore it. Talk to her.

ELISE. Wisdom from babes. Talk to me.

ANDREW *(measured)*. We should come to some formal arrangement about Martin—his schooling and so on. I'd like to contribute.

ELISE. To take charge, you mean. To send him where he'll learn dates and names and how to play the game, you certainly have changed sides.

ANDREW. Same old moves—one foot on

politics, the other on sentiment, and shift weight to keep us all off balance.

ELISE. Damn it, Andrew, you're the one that provokes, you and your Olympian calm. It's an act, look, look at your fists all clenched up in your pocket, take them out, show Martin the beast, god knows he's seen my faults.

ANDREW *(tense)*. *This will not work,* Elise.

ELISE. So it still hurts. Good. After all these years of silence, I wasn't sure.

ANDREW. Your silence, not mine. I kept in touch, only Martin wrote back.

ELISE. I wrote. I'm still waiting for an answer.

ANDREW. Don't do this, *please.* Always it starts with a small lie and ends in some bottomless fiction.

ELISE. You didn't get my letter? Andrew, is this cruelty, or extreme tact? *(Pause. Both* ANDREW *and* ELISE *are genuinely puzzled.)*

MARTIN *(blurts).* Shouldn't we say goodbye to the guests? Wasn't that the plan? Then we won't be disturbed, okay? I'll do it, I'll take care of everything . . .

ELISE. Let Andrew. A break might jog his memory.

MARTIN. Mom, would you get off the letter, forget about it, just talk, have a drink . . . I'll be back in a minute.

ELISE. What's going on?

MARTIN *(starting out).* Nothing.

ELISE. Martin, look at me.

MARTIN *(trying to shrug it off).* It got lost in the mail, you put the wrong address, who cares about a stupid letter, you're together now, that's what you wanted, that's what you wrote— *(stops suddenly, caught)*

ELISE. I see. And did you simply snoop, or did you snoop and destroy.

ANDREW. Martin, was there a letter?

MARTIN *(to* ELISE*).* You don't want him to see it.

ELISE. Did you keep my letter? Martin, answer me.

MARTIN *(confused).* You never show up. We make all these plans. I didn't know if you'd be here tonight . . .

ELISE. In which case, what? You'd show your father the damning evidence and I'd stand exposed . . . ?

MARTIN. But I didn't. You're here.

ELISE. This wasn't worthy of you, Martin. *(*MARTIN, *in frustration, takes the letter from his jacket pocket and throws it on the floor.)*

ANDREW. Put that away.

ELISE. No. What's done is done. Martin . . . ?

MARTIN *(urgent).* Mom . . . you don't remember what you wrote, you don't remember anything from that night.

ELISE *(steely).* My forgiveness has limits. *(*MARTIN *picks up and hands her the letter.)*

ELISE *(extending it to* ANDREW*).* For you.

ANDREW. Are you sure?

ELISE. Thank you. Yes.

ANDREW *(opens it and pulls out jumbled cocktail napkins).* What's all this?

ELISE. Cocktail napkins. The Campfire Lounge, if memory serves. Not my finest hour.

MARTIN. It was just that one night. She hardly ever drinks. Mom, take it back, please . . .

ELISE *(to* ANDREW*).* Shall I tell you what it says? I missed you. Not a day went by I didn't regret having left. But, you see, *you* left *me* once—true, with the war for an alibi and, true, you came back . . . that time. But what if you'd left me again one day, as it seemed all too clear you would—and so, very stupidly, I acted first . . .

MARTIN. Mom, that's not what you wrote . . .

ELISE. Let's say it was. And let's say you did not sneak it off the bureau that night knowing I was confused, because I taught you never to abuse anyone in their dark hour. And when the letter arrived, and your father learned how I felt, what was his reply? Tell me, Andrew?

ANDREW *(shaken).* Elise. A little restraint. A little balance. That's all I ever asked.

ELISE. Then why fall in love with me?

ANDREW. And if you wanted all this passionate excess . . .

ELISE. Yes, Mysteries.

ANDREW. Water under the bridge.

ELISE. Is it? *(*ELISE *takes out a cigarette, testing a memory.* ANDREW *understands. With a practiced gesture, he slips an expensive lighter from his pocket, lights her cigarette. She notes the lighter.)* It used to be wooden matches. You've come up in the world. And I'll bet you still don't smoke.

ANDREW *(softer).* I would like to help out in some way—financially, whatever.

ELISE. No doors are shut.

ANDREW. Maybe . . . at the end of the summer . . . before Martin leaves, we could plan a weekend.

MARTIN. You'll see us?

ELISE. Shhh, darling, you've meddled enough.

ANDREW. Do you still—ever dance?

ELISE. They closed the St. George.

ANDREW. Yes. Remember the Commune?

ELISE. Who could forget. Monday-night folk dancing . . .

ANDREW. God, yes, in the barn. Cedric, Emma, Phillip, all the true believers out there trying to learn, what was it?

ELISE. The Wedding Stomp . . .

BOTH *(shared joke)*. . . . of the Ukrainian Goatherd.

ELISE *(laughs)*. With whom we'd all, come the Revolution, be tending our flocks one day . . .

ANDREW. . . . in Central Park, no doubt. *(animated, to* MARTIN:*)* Lise and I . . . *(corrects himself)* Your mother and I had our own secret Victrola, no one knew. We'd sneak away from the barn with an armful of 78s . . .

ELISE. And that horrible cheap vodka . . .

ANDREW. You could drink any Russian we ever met straight under the table . . .

ELISE. You see, darling, a thing of legend, my capacity . . .

ANDREW. Take turns winding that infernal machine . . .

ELISE. . . . and dancing, dancing in the woods all alone to, oh god, Rudy Vallee . . .

ANDREW. Eddie Duchin . . .

ELISE. Horror, so bourgeois, Guy Lombardo, our dirty little vice . . .

ANDREW. Imagine if they'd caught us!

ELISE. The Goatherds!

ANDREW. The Holy Warriors!

ELISE *(to* MARTIN*)*. With me, your father could relax and be silly, oh so silly, and human, and adorable.

(sings)
I saw you last night and got
That old feeling
When you came in sight I got
That old feeling . . .

(ELISE moves towards ANDREW, humming as the old movements fill her body. For a moment, ANDREW resists what he's feeling, but finally begins to yield. PENNY enters, trying to control her fury.)

PENNY. You know, I think it would be a terrifically good idea to have at least one person saying good-bye out there who actually belongs to this family.

MARTIN *(pushing her out of room)*. Leave us alone. Close the door. No one comes in here.

ANDREW. He overdid the drink tonight, my fault, Elise, sorry.

MARTIN *(returns)*. You're getting along now, don't stop. Keep talking.

ANDREW. Hey, champ, a little cold water on the face, eh?

MARTIN. Dance with her. *(pulls ELISE by the hand towards ANDREW)* You two dance together, I'll go inside, I'll clean up, I'll take care of everything, you stay here alone and dance . . .

ANDREW. For christ sake, get ahold of yourself.

MARTIN. Forget about me, I'm not here.

ANDREW. That's enough, Martin, no more!

ELISE. Don't you dare talk to him that way.

MARTIN. He's right, Mom, I had too much to drink, it's my fault.

ELISE. No one here is at fault, angel.

MARTIN *(icy)*. I ruin everything. Don't look at me. Don't make me be here.

ANDREW. Will you stop this pathetic whining, wait in the living room.

ELISE. You have no right to order my son around. I want you to apologize.

ANDREW. He's getting away with murder, and you encourage it, all your weaknesses— the lies, the evasions, the self-pity—

ELISE. You bastard, I've tried to be fair, god knows I've said nothing against you in all these years, but he'll hear the truth now, all of it—

ANDREW. Truth? You don't know the meaning of the word. You told him I thought he was a mistake, isn't that what you said?

ELISE. Your behavior is all he needs to know that.

ANDREW. Listen to the way you bend and twist everything—

ELISE. Like the money?

ANDREW. Oh, yes, I can imagine what a meal you've made of *that* one—

MARTIN. What money?

ELISE. You see, I never even mentioned it, you have an unbiased ear, go on, Andrew, tell your son about the money—

ANDREW. Seeing you now, I don't regret it—

ELISE. Hundreds, was it? Thousands?

ANDREW. Is that the issue?

ELISE. He never said—winnings from a poker game on the troopship home, and how did he spend it—

ANDREW. After three-and-a-half years of my life—

ELISE. On his son, on his family; *no.* On

school to study architecture the way he'd talked about so passionately for years; *no!*

ANDREW. What was left when I returned?

ELISE. He spent it on *clothes!!!* That's right, this man of the people, who claimed to care nothing about dress in all his life went and ordered an entire wardrobe, tailor-made, just to walk among his former comrades and look as if he hadn't fallen behind.

ANDREW. That is a complete crock of shit and you know it—

ELISE. Ah, so we've hit a nerve at last—

ANDREW. I came home to nothing at all, *that's* what happened!

ELISE. You never came home, only half of you, and that half was all rage and judgment—

ANDREW. Was I supposed to forgive what happened while I was gone?

ELISE. Nothing *happened,* Andrew—

ANDREW. How damn right you are, worse than nothing—all we'd worked for, all we'd begun to build, they just walked away from it the same as they walked away from a filthy, thankless war we all agreed had to be fought, but no, once again, who did the dirty work? The same fool who organized meetings and settled disputes and trusted when he left they'd keep faith with the movement in some real way, not Cedric in his ivory tower of books and theory; in the streets, in the factory, anything, anything but abandon it to chase after their own precious careers. Well, I can play that game, too. I can out-abandon and out-career and out-dress that whole crowd till they see just how ugly their betrayal truly looks . . .

ELISE. You see every betrayal but your own.

ANDREW. I see what they let themselves forget.

ELISE. Have you forgotten the night you trembled in my arms and cried?

ANDREW. My god, now it's arms, crying . . . can't we please stick to the subject for five minutes?

ELISE. The night you showed me everything—

ANDREW. Fine, I was shipping out, you feel emotional, what are you trying to make it into—

ELISE. What you know it was—

ANDREW. A few tears—

ELISE. We touched that night. Say you don't remember it, you who can't lie, say you don't know it was a vow to live always by the moments that bind us, to measure ourselves against the power of our hearts, and with that strength everything we dreamed of making happen was possible. Say it.

ANDREW *(beat).* Then why did you abandon me? Why? Why, Elise?

ELISE. You're the one who went away.

ANDREW. But I returned, and you'd gone to them. I saw it the moment I stepped off the ship—you couldn't even bring yourself to look me in the eye.

ELISE. You fool, I was crying.

ANDREW. All year? Were you crying when they'd visit and the room fell stony silent when I'd dare remember that our gatherings used to have a real purpose, and you'd float off to the kitchen in, what, embarrassment at my naive persistence? And when you'd sleep alone on the couch, or stay out late with Martin—god knows where—keeping me away from all I had left to hold onto, were you crying then?

ELISE. I was afraid, Andrew—afraid of how I'd missed you—of needing you again as much as when you went away. It was pride, both of us, don't you see—stupid, foolish pride. We're human. We make mistakes. Can't we forgive now?

ANDREW. Wonderful, now we forgive. Does anything stay put with you? No wonder I had to get away. What do you want from me, what? Do you even know? Unity, Brotherhood, Power of Our Hearts, it's all talk . . . and I was dumb enough to believe it meant something, for five of the most wonderful fucking years of my life I trusted . . . no more. They're through with me, I'm through with them. I'll live my own way, I'll count on no one, and I'll wear any damn thing I please . . . *(stops, shaken)*

ELISE *(pause).* Come to me, sweet love. Tell me how you felt cheated of all that lonely, heroic time lost, and angry that things change, and we'll hold each other like we did that night until it all goes away.

ANDREW *(pause).* No more, Elise. Between us, the silence is a better idea.

ELISE. And that, dear Andrew, is what finally makes you small—

ANDREW. Don't do this—

ELISE. —and—sad

ANDREW. I'm warning you—

ELISE. —and so very, very alone.

ANDREW *(threatening gesture).* Shut up, shut up, damn it.

ELISE. Are you going to hit me?

ANDREW *(murderously)*. You are such a dangerous woman.

ELISE. And you're not worthy of me.

MARTIN. Mom, stop it.

ELISE. Go ahead, strike. Sooner or later you would have. Kill what comes too close.

ANDREW *(to MARTIN)*. Wait outside.

ELISE. We're going. You have what you always wanted, the goodies of the world. And the little changeling boy is mine. Come, angel, I think you've seen your father now.

MARTIN. I'm staying here.

ELISE. Get your jacket.

MARTIN. I've made up my mind. There will be no discussion.

ELISE *(pause)*. SAY SOMETHING TO HIM, FOR GODSAKE! ANDREW! *(Pause. ELISE exits. Pause.)*

MARTIN. Dad?

ANDREW *(shaken)*. Fine. I'm fine. Lost my bearings for a minute. Sorry you had to see that.

MARTIN. Everything's kind of screwy tonight. She makes you all tangled up. I know why you had to get away.

ANDREW. I could use a drink. *(beat)* No. Had enough.

MARTIN. It won't change our plans, will it? We'll still travel together . . .

PENNY *(enters)*. Everyone's gone now, and p.s., I'm real pissed off.

ANDREW. Put some coffee on, toots, we'll be right in.

PENNY. Good-bye, Andrew. Don't bother to call. *(exits)*

ANDREW *(beat)*. She turned heads, that woman. Everywhere she went . . .

MARTIN. Penny's leaving, shouldn't you talk to her . . .

ANDREW. Everyone wanted her. Thought I never stood a chance in hell. One night, knock-knock-knock; *her.* "We must visit Russia together and see what's really going on there." She never mentioned the subject again.

MARTIN. Can I help you straighten up?

ANDREW. Hmmmm? No need—cleaning lady. *(beat)* She had such promise.

MARTIN. Dad, are we still on for Europe?

ANDREW. Something about being tied down. It's not in me. Sorry, kiddo.

MARTIN. The hotel has to know if I'm going to quit early.

ANDREW. I know what you want. It's too late for all that to happen now. We can be

friends. Play it by ear. I'm glad as hell you're back.

MARTIN. I want to travel with you, Dad. I want to stay here. I don't want to see her again—ever.

ANDREW. She needs someone. Go home. Apologize. Try to work it out.

MARTIN. Why should I want to be with her when you didn't.

ANDREW. Not the point. You make a mess, you clean up.

MARTIN. Well guess what, Dad. Fuck you. Just go fuck yourself, because it's not my mess, and I'm not cleaning up after you anymore . . . *(exits)*

ANDREW. Martin . . . Martin, god damn it, you're a man now, stop asking for help . . .

(Elsewhere, ELISE's Place)

(ELISE lies sprawled on foldout bed, cover thrown aside, in a light restless sleep. MARTIN appears in doorway holding suitcase. He watches her for a moment, turns to go, then sets down valise, enters room and tries to pull covers gently over her. A flask falls on the floor with a clatter, waking ELISE. She props herself up, groggy with booze and sleep. They look at each other.)

ELISE. So the prodigal son returns.

MARTIN. I'm leaving.

ELISE. Yes, sneaking off into the night. Like father, like son.

MARTIN. I'm sure you'll find plenty of company at the Copper Pot.

ELISE. What did you say?

MARTIN. Isn't that how you work overtime? Isn't that what you were doing on Parents' Day?

ELISE. How dare you, after how you behaved tonight. Humiliate me in front of that man, steal my secrets, treat me like a foolish, irresponsible mother—you do not side against your own flesh and blood.

MARTIN. He's my flesh and blood, too . . .

ELISE. He is no part of my child—he ran away.

MARTIN. So did you.

ELISE. From a man who didn't want us!

MARTIN. Who'd ever want us, Mom. Look at how we are, I'm the same as you, full of the same crooked stuff inside, the same stupid pipe dreams that'll never happen . . .

ELISE. That is unworthy of you . . .

MARTIN *(withering sarcasm)*. Oh, I'm sorry, Mom, let's play I'm the Genius Boy, and next week you'll stop drinking and get back to your poetry and Andrew will call up

. . . no, let's play we don't even need him because we're going to have a home of our very own.

ELISE. But we are, I've promised you—

MARTIN. Cut it out, Mom, you know it's just a pipe dream!

ELISE. Is that so? Then suppose you tell me what you call this, Mr. Cynical, Mr. Ingratitude, Mr. Holier-Than-Thou . . . *(she rummages in bedclothes)*

MARTIN. What are you doing?

ELISE. Our land . . . ! *(searches desperately)* It was right under . . . two acres . . .

MARTIN. Put some clothes on, for godsake.

ELISE *(finds envelope)*. Voilà! Now what do you have to say for yourself?!

MARTIN *(seeing her)*. You're disgusting, Mom. You're sloppy, and careless, and drunk. This is why you don't want me at home, isn't it.

ELISE *(lowers envelope, defenseless)*. Yes. It's enough I have to see myself each day—why should you have to.

MARTIN. But I *know* all this. I've always known. We have no secrets—no real ones. *(ELISE is motionless.)*

MARTIN *(takes her robe)*. Put this on. *(ELISE is motionless.)*

MARTIN. I could stay for the summer. *(beat)* I'll find a job in the city. Sleep in the other room. I can make you happy, Mom, I know I can.

ELISE. No! It's time for you to go—to the summer, to Europe, to all the rest of it. Only promise me this: you'll never run from life, no matter how it hurts and burns . . . let it touch you everywhere, and *live!*

(Pause. MARTIN, impossibly drawn to comfort her, to make her happy, to move past the skin that separates them, embraces her. They hold each other and fall back on the bed together, faces inches apart, he above. A dangerous moment before an irrevocable act. ELISE suddenly pushes him aside, and he moves away to the table, not able to look at her. Pause.)

MARTIN. Why can't things be different?

ELISE *(beat)*. Because, my angel, none of us can choose the way we love. Any complaints, see the man in the moon.

MARTIN *(pause)*. I'd better get started.

ELISE. Oh, dear, yes, it's getting light. I used to love Monday. Shall I take a half-day off? We could grab a Sloppy Joe breakfast together and talk of cabbages and kings. We'll count the stairs going down, odd ones for me, even for you.

MARTIN. No, Mom. I can wait a minute if you want to come down with me.

ELISE. You run along. I have a few things to do before I'm ready to greet the day. Take a taxi, here . . . *(reaches for her handbag)*

MARTIN. We can't afford a taxi. I'll take the bus.

ELISE. You have his eyes, you know.

MARTIN. I have my own eyes. *(looks at bed)*

ELISE. I'll straighten all this later.

MARTIN. Sure, Mom. Sure you will. *(They hug awkwardly.)*

MARTIN. See you. *(MARTIN exits. ELISE listens to the door close.)*

ELISE. May you be loved one day even half as well as I've loved you. Good-bye, my angel. *(beat)* Good-bye *(ELISE sits alone. Lights fade.)*

End of Play

Other People's Money: The Ultimate Seduction

JERRY STERNER

Originally presented by The American Stage Company, Teaneck, New Jersey. The play was subsequently presented by Hartford Stage Company. The Hartford Stage Company production of the play was presented Off-Broadway by Jeffrey Ash and Susan Quint Gallin in association with Dennis Grimaldi at the Minetta Lane Theatre in New York City. The play opened February 16, 1989, with the following cast:

WILLIAM COLES	James Murtaugh
ANDREW JORGENSON	Arch Johnson
BEA SULLIVAN	Scotty Bloch
LAWRENCE GARFINKLE	Kevin Conway
KATE SULLIVAN	Mercedes Ruehl

SETTING: New York and Rhode Island

TIME: The present

Other People's Money was developed at the American Stage Company in New Jersey and at the Hartford Stage Company in Connecticut. Opening in New York at the Minetta Lane Theatre on February 16, 1989, it won three Outer Critics Circle Awards: Best Play, Best Playwright, and Best Actor (Kevin Conway). It was filmed by director Norman Jewison for Warner Bros. in 1990.

Playwright Jerry Sterner attended City College of New York, and later hired on as a token-booth clerk for the MTA. Working the graveyard shift so that he could write on the job, he completed seven plays in five years. He then began a career as a real estate broker. Twenty-five years later, at the age of forty-four, the president of a firm that owned four thousand apartments across the country, he left business to pursue his former love—playwriting. *Other People's Money* is Sterner's third post–real estate play. The first was never produced; the second, *Be Happy for Me,* played in 1986 at the Douglas Fairbanks Theatre in New York. Sterner says, "I'd rather be Neil Simon than Harry Helmsley any day. . . . One of the kinder reviews, [of *Be Happy for Me*] suggested I not give up my day job. . . . Then came *Other People's Money* . . . not simply a home run but a grand slam. I went from 'Mister, would you please read my script?' to 'Talk to my agent' in what seemed like a weekend. . . . Many other playwrights have written better, but no one has enjoyed having written more."

Other People's Money finds both the comedy and the drama in the hostile takeover of a small family-owned New England company by a ruthless Wall Street financier, Lawrence Garfinkle, known as "Larry the Liquidator." An urgent commentary on the recent Wall Street scandals, the play is a kind of Western, where the lines are unclearly drawn between the good guys and the bad guys.

KATE: You're playing Monopoly with other people's lives here.

GARFINKLE: I'm doing them a favor. I'm making them money. I thought that's what they were in business for.

BEA: How can you destroy a company . . . its people . . . for the sake of dollars you don't even need?

GARFINKLE: I do it for the money. . . . I love money more than the things it can buy. . . . Money is unconditional acceptance. It don't care whether I'm good or not, whether I snore or don't, which God I pray to . . .

Garfinkle pictures himself as a throwback to a more exciting era: "Didn't everybody want to be Butch Cassidy and the James boys? There's just a few of us modern-day gunslingers . . . but instead of galloping in with a six gun a-blazing in each hand, we're driven in, escorted by a herd of lawyers and investment bankers, waving our limited partnerships in one hand and our 13-D filings in the other. But they quake just as hard. And they wind up just as dead. And it's legal. And it's fun. And the money ain't bad either."

One of the play's "good" guys, the president of the targeted company, has several options to save his outmoded and failing business, but refuses them all, relying on his stockholders, whom he believes are completely loyal to him. With a single exception, the play's characters are selfish, although each has convinced himself that his motives are pure. The character Kate, for example, believes that she is trying to save the company; in reality, the twelve hundred jobs that will be lost if she fails mean little to her. What matters to her is the game: the pursuit, the competition, and the possibility of victory.

The play culminates in a confrontation between Garfinkle and Jorgenson, the company president, at a shareholder's meeting. In a scene reminiscent of the Act Three confrontation between Brutus and Mark Antony in *Julius Caesar,* the audience is at first clearly on Jorgenson's side:

JORGENSON: . . . At least the robber barons of old left something tangible in their wake . . . a coal mine. A railroad. Banks. This man leaves nothing. . . . If he said, "I could run this business better," well, that's worth talking about. He's not saying that. He's saying, "I'm going to kill you because at this particular moment in time you're worth more dead than alive." . . . A business is worth more than the price of its stock. It is the place where we make our living, meet our friends and dream our dreams. It is . . . the very fabric that binds our society together. . . .

GARFINKLE: Amen, amen . . . 'cause that's what you just heard—the prayer for the dead. . . . This company is dead. . . . It was dead when I got here. . . . Know why? Fiber optics. New technologies. Obsolescence. . . . Take that money. Invest it somewhere else. Maybe you'll get lucky and it will be used productively—and if it is—you'll create more jobs and provide a service for the economy and even make a few bucks for yourself.

Sterner based this play on his experience as a shareholder in a Michigan manufacturing company that received a hostile tender offer in 1985. At the raider's encouragement, he tendered his shares. Months later, Sterner drove through the town where the company's factory was located. "It was a devastated community. I began to question whether I had done the right thing by selling my stock to the raider who later dismantled the company." Sterner admits that his play has a strong anti-raider sentiment. "In corporate America now, we can't spend money on the necessary things like research and development. We're too busy meeting the interest payments on our leveraged deals." Yet he refuses to take sides. "There are no good guys or bad guys, just people with points of view that each believe to be absolutely true. And I don't give answers in this play—the answers don't matter as long as I have asked the right questions."

CAST

WILLIAM COLES, mid-forties. Attractive, polished, President of New England Wire and Cable.

ANDREW JORGENSON, chairman of New England Wire and Cable, 68 years of age.

BEA SULLIVAN, longtime assistant and friend of Jorgenson. An attractive woman in her early sixties.

LAWRENCE GARFINKLE, an obese, elegant, cunning New York "takeover artist." About forty.

KATE SULLIVAN, Bea's daughter. An attractive, sexy, Wall Street attorney, about thirty-five.

ACT ONE

Stage is dark. After a short pause, BILL COLES, *an attractive, well-groomed man in his mid-forties, emerges from the darkness and walks Downstage Center where a spotlight awaits him. He pauses a beat.*

─────

COLES. It's been said that you have to be a storyteller to tell a story. It's also been said that businessmen aren't good storytellers . . . not that we don't have a story to tell . . . we do. We tell it in numbers: you know, sales, earnings, dividends. We also express it in ratios: net worth to long term debt, long term debt to working capital. And we tell it every year. Have you ever read an Annual Report? . . . We're not good storytellers.

Which is too bad. For there's an important story that needs to be told. It goes way beyond numbers. It's about loyalty, tradition, friendship and of course, money. Lots of money. It's one heck of a story. And if it hasn't already affected your life, it will. *(Smiles.)* It affected mine. It only started a few years back. We were all naive, then. But you know something? I knew. I knew as soon as the Old Man told me about our expected visitor.

(Lights up on ANDREW JORGENSON'S *office. Throughout the play scene shifts occur with some rapidity. Rather than formal sets, locations are suggested by playing area, lights, platforms, etc., as the director, set designer and budget allow.* JORGENSON *sits behind a modest desk in his office. He's sixty-eight, a good looking man in good physical condition. He's a "hands on" type, more comfortable with his sleeves rolled up tinkering with a machine* than sitting in a boardroom. He speaks to an unseen COLES.)

JORGENSON. Why are you so nervous? Stop acting like an expectant father.

COLES *(Entering from Center Stage).* I heard that name before.

JORGENSON. So what?

COLES. Why would he come all the way from New York? We've never had anyone from New York before.

JORGENSON. Sure we have. Had someone directly from Wall Street a couple of years back.

COLES. I've been here twelve years. I've never seen anyone south of Connecticut.

JORGENSON. . . . Twelve years? Has it been that long? . . . The guy was sitting right there—all stiff and proper, taking notes on a clipboard. Some kind of analyst. Wouldn't get close to any of the walls. Scared of a little dust. Three piece suit, pointy shoes, tie up to here. He starts asking me all kinds of questions and I noticed he wasn't looking at me, looking at the wall back there. I turn around and wouldn't you know—meanest looking spider was halfway up the ceiling. You know what he says? Bill, you listening? He says, "Could you please get someone to dispose of it?" Not kill it, mind you—dispose of it. I told him since he was the one with the pointy shoes the job was his. *(Laughs at the memory.)* Didn't ask another question. Got up and left. Didn't even say goodbye.

COLES. Be careful what you say to him.

JORGENSON. Don't worry about me. Better check for spiders. *(Rises, put's an arm around* COLES' *shoulder.)* C'mon. C'mon. I was joking. I've never seen you this way.

COLES. Let me do the talking.

JORGENSON. You do the talking. I'll do the listening. "Nu Yawkas" are fun to listen to . . . Where the hell was that guy from? . . . Aha—Barney Smith.

COLES. Smith, Barney.

JORGENSON. Smith, Barney. Figures. Wall Street generally does things ass-backwards.

COLES. Have you looked at our stock lately?

JORGENSON. I already got a call from Ossie at the bank. Happier than a pig in shit. Told me it's up a couple of points. He owns fifteen thousand shares, you know. Has for years. I remember the day he bought. Same day I was made President. I was really scared. He called. Told me he was buying stock to show his confidence in me. Told me he wouldn't sell till I retired. The man kept his word for ... thirty-eight years now.

COLES. More shares traded in the last month than did all of last year.

JORGENSON. Bill, what's wrong with you? The stock is going up. Worry when the stock goes down.

(BEA enters hurriedly. She's excited.)

BEA. Come. Look. Look! *(She ushers them to the window.)* Is that something, Jorgy?

JORGENSON. That's a goddamned big car.

COLES. It's a stretch limo.

BEA *(To JORGENSON).* You see—manners. The chauffeur gets out first, walks all the way around ... opens the door. You could learn from that, Jorgy.

JORGENSON. Goddamned big car.

(Lights up on GARFINKLE, cross stage. He is an immense man of forty, though he looks older. He is always elegantly dressed, surprisingly graceful for his bulk. He is, in some way, larger than life. His deep, rich voice fills the stage. He looks about.)

GARFINKLE. Haven't seen a place this shitty since I left the Bronx.

BEA *(Moving to GARFINKLE, her hand extended).* Welcome. You must be Lawrence Garfinkle. I'm Bea Sullivan. Mr. Jorgenson's assistant. He's expecting you. *(She shakes his hand. They begin walking to JORGENSON's office.)* Would you like to invite your chauffeur in? We have a small reception area he could wait in—keep warm.

GARFINKLE. He's a "yard" chauffeur. Bring him inside and you'll spoil him.

BEA. ... Right this way, please. *(They enter office.)* This is Mr. Jorgenson, our Chairman. Mr. Coles, our President. Mr. Garfinkle.

JORGENSON. Call me Jorgy. Everybody else does. *(Moves from his desk. They shake.)* Welcome to New England Wire and Cable.

COLES. How do you do, Mr. Garfinkle?

GARFINKLE. I do good. Mind if I have a seat? I do even better when I sit.

JORGENSON *(Laughs).* I know what you mean.

(GARFINKLE dusts off chair with a handkerchief.)

Uh-oh, Bill ... better check for spiders. *(Moving to GARFINKLE.)* Wire and Cable is man's work. Gotta expect a little grime.

BEA. May I get you some coffee?

GARFINKLE. Is there a Dunkin' Donuts in this town?

BEA. Dunkin' Donuts? ...

JORGENSON. Never saw one.

GARFINKLE. Crispy Cremes? ... Something?

JORGENSON. There's Sam's on Beaver. Doesn't he make donuts?

BEA. I believe he does. He'd be your best bet. Just make a left when you leave the plant. Beaver is your second—

GARFINKLE *(Taking a large roll of cash from his pocket and handing BEA several bills).* Why don't you be a sweetheart and take a ride with Arthur and pick up a couple of dozen. Bring one here and leave one in the car for the trip back.

BEA. ... They might not have much of a selection. Which kind do you like?

GARFINKLE. I like them all. *(Smiling for the first time.)* Can't you tell?

(BEA exits.)

JORGENSON. Have a nice ride, Bea. You watch, she's going to take him the long way to Beaver. What'd you say your first name was?

GARFINKLE. Lawrence.

JORGENSON. Larry, you made her day. Last limo we saw up here was in '48 when Harry Truman was running for President. Came right here to the plant. *(Takes him to window.)* Stood right out there. Right there. Gave a speech. Just after the war. It was the golden age, rebuilding America and all. Had thirty-five hundred men working right here. Right at this plant. Going twenty-four hours a day, seven days a week. Truman gave a fine talk. Very impressive. Only Democrat I ever voted for.

COLES. What can we do for you, Mr. Garfinkle? What brings a busy man like you up this way?

GARFINKLE. Harry Truman stories don't grab you, huh?

COLES. We're all busy.

GARFINKLE. You're right. Let's do business. I got a computer back in New York. Call her Carmen. Every morning when I wake up—before I even brush my teeth, I punch out, "Carmen, computer on the wall, who's the fairest of them all?" You'll forgive me—my programmer isn't Shakespeare.

COLES. Go on.

GARFINKLE. Most mornings she spits out, "You are, Garfinkle, you're the fairest of them all." But once in a while, maybe two, three times a year she says something else. Six weeks ago she said: "Garfinkle, Garfinkle, scratch your balls, New England Wire and Cable is the fairest of them all." *(JORGENSON laughs.)* I thought it was funny, too. And I do it again. "Carmen computer on the wall, who's the fairest of them all?" She responds, "Don't be a schmuck, Garfinkle—do the numbers!"

COLES. I'm interested. Do the numbers.

GARFINKLE. Get a paper and pencil. Carmen will educate you.

(COLES takes a pad and pencil from JORGEN-SON's desk.)

The Wire and Cable business is a little soft. Has been for the last ten years. What's it worth?

JORGENSON. This would not be a good time to—

GARFINKLE. I know. I'm not blaming you. You've done a hell of a job. You've kept it alive. That's an accomplishment. Carmen agrees. I'll bet she thinks it's worth more than you do. She says you got equipment up here that cost 120 million. Worth, even at salvage, 30 to 35 million. Write down 30 million. How many acres you got here?

COLES. One hundred ten.

GARFINKLE. What's that worth?

JORGENSON. It would depend on what it's used for.

GARFINKLE. Worst case basis. Grazing land. Ten million fair? *(COLES nods.)* Good. Write down ten million. Put it underneath the thirty.

JORGENSON. We have other businesses, you know. Bill here has diversified us a good deal. He's done a hell of a job, despite my kicking and screaming.

COLES. What does Carmen think the rest of the company is worth, Mr. Garfinkle?

GARFINKLE. Let's see . . . what do you got? Plumbing supplies, electrical distribution, adhesives . . . boring. Nothing my friends on the street would get excited about. But dependable. Decent cash flow.

JORGENSON. With our cumulative losses at Wire and Cable we keep all the earnings from our other businesses. We haven't paid federal taxes in years.

GARFINKLE. You haven't made money in years.

JORGENSON. It'll turn. We got a good crew up here. Best in the business. When it does, we're gonna knock their socks off.

GARFINKLE. Everything is possible. Maybe a Dunkin' Donuts will open up next door.

COLES. What does your computer tell you the rest of our businesses are worth, Mr. Garfinkle?

GARFINKLE. Conservative . . . six times cash flow.

COLES. We had ten million in flow last year. This year we're projecting a fifteen per cent increase.

GARFINKLE. Carmen only knows what happened. She can't predict. Write down sixty . . . underneath the ten.

COLES. What else, Mr. Garfinkle?

GARFINKLE. Working capital. You got twenty-five million—ten million of it in cash—write down twenty-five.

COLES. Anything else?

GARFINKLE. Add it up. What do you got?

COLES. One hundred and twenty-five million.

GARFINKLE. Good. Now let's say Carmen was suffering from pre-menstrual syndrome. *(JORGENSON looks at him quizzically.)* A little crazed. Too optimistic. Forget twenty-five million. Take it off. What do you got?

COLES. One hundred million.

GARFINKLE. Nice round number. I like nice round numbers. Now make a line. Right down the middle of the page. Start a new column. Call it liabilities. Let's see what you got. Any debt?

JORGENSON. Not a penny. Don't believe in it.

GARFINKLE. Any lawsuits? Any environmental bullshit?

JORGENSON. None. We've complied with every law. That's a good part of our losses right there.

GARFINKLE. Pension liabilities?

COLES. Fully funded.

GARFINKLE. Ok. Add it up. What do you got?

JORGENSON. Didn't write anything.

GARFINKLE. That's exactly what I said to Carmen. Now here comes the fun part. How many shares you got outstanding?

COLES. Four million.

GARFINKLE. Divide four million into the hundred million. What do you got?

COLES. Twenty-five.

GARFINKLE. Good. Now that was all foreplay. Let's go for the real thing. What's your stock selling at?

COLES. You know very well what it's selling at, Mr. Garfinkle.

GARFINKLE. Aw, don't do that. I came all the way from New York. Don't break my rhythm. Let me do my thing. What's the stock at?

COLES. Ten—before you started buying.

GARFINKLE. That's ten for a twenty-five dollar number. Forty cents on the dollar. Carmen almost came. I had to change my underwear.

JORGENSON. This is a fine company, Larry. We've worked hard. We have a nice little story to tell but unless you make those little micro-chips or fry chicken it's hard to interest you money guys on Wall Street.

COLES. How many shares have you bought?

GARFINKLE. One hundred and ninety-six thousand. I recognize a good job when I see it. I'm happy to put my money here.

JORGENSON *(Laughing)*. I'll have to tell Ossie at the bank. He'll be mighty grateful to you. If you have time we'll have lunch together. Get him to spring for it. Tell him you're selling if he don't spring for it. Ossie's tighter than a duck's ass. How'd you figure out to buy such an odd amount? Why not two hundred thousand—nice even number. I thought you liked even numbers.

COLES. Two hundred thousand is five percent of our shares. At five percent he has to file a 13-D with the Securities and Exchange Commission. It then becomes public knowledge. *(To* GARFINKLE.*)* Plan on buying more?

GARFINKLE. Never can tell. Got to talk to Carmen.

JORGENSON. That's his business, Bill. He'll let us know when he wants to ... or when he has to. It's nice to know you have that confidence in us. Nice to have you as a stockholder.

GARFINKLE. Don't let me down. Get us to twenty-five. That's what we're worth.

JORGENSON. You know I can't control that. We do the best we can running the company. I can promise you one thing—we spend the stockholder's money with care. We don't squander it.

GARFINKLE. Not on paint at any rate.

JORGENSON. Not on anything. You watch the nickels and dimes and the dollars take care of themselves. My dad always said that. He founded this company. I guess I do too. As true today as when he said it.

(BEA enters with a bag of donuts.)

Bea, Larry here is our newest stockholder. Give the man a donut.

BEA. All they had was honey and whole wheat. I left six of each in the car.

(She holds out the bag. GARFINKLE *takes one out, grimaces, and puts it back.)*

JORGENSON. How was the ride?

BEA. Everyone stared. It's got a television, a bar, telephone, stock quote machine—

JORGENSON. And now donuts. If you have no objection, Larry, we're going to call you the "donut man."

GARFINKLE. Where's my change?

BEA *(Handing him the change)*. Oh—I'm sorry. Just a little flustered, I guess ... sorry.

GARFINKLE. I like to watch the nickels and dimes, too. *(*GARFINKLE *takes the bag and exits the playing area. They stare after him for a beat.)*

JORGENSON. So you really like being chauffeured around? I thought you'd be embarrassed.

BEA. Jorgy, riding in a limousine is not an acquired taste. One takes to it all at once.

(Lights out in JORGENSON*'s office. Lights up Center Stage.* GARFINKLE *is alone checking out the donuts.)*

GARFINKLE. Whole wheat and honey?! What—do I look sick? You eat this when you're sick—with tea. Step on it, Arthur. This whole goddamned place stinks. Make sure you get the car washed when we get home. *(*GARFINKLE *exits.)*

*(*COLES *moves to Center Stage. Lights up on* GARFINKLE*'s office as* COLES *enters.)*

COLES. That's an impressive office you have out there.

GARFINKLE. No big deal. Only lawyers. What can I do for you?

COLES. Thanks for seeing me on such short notice. I'm not really here on business. My wife and I came down to spend the evening with Bill, Jr. He's attending Columbia. Got two more after him. Both girls. Claire's out shopping now. It's always a treat to come to this city.

GARFINKLE. Great.

COLES. We're from small towns in Florida. Met at Florida State—

GARFINKLE. What'd you come here for—to give me your biography?

COLES. I didn't know I was boring you.

GARFINKLE. Now you know.

COLES *(Trying to control himself)*. .... I'll get to the point. I see by the latest 13-D you hold just over four hundred thousand shares. That's ten per cent.

GARFINKLE. Four hundred and twenty-five thousand. Bought some this morning.

COLES. The filing said they were purchased for "investment purposes only."

GARFINKLE. I never read filings.

COLES. What does "investment purposes only" mean?

GARFINKLE. Means I bought them to make money.

COLES. How much more do you intend on buying?

GARFINKLE. That's none of your business.

COLES. Can we speak frankly?

GARFINKLE. No. Lie to me. Tell me how thrilled you are to know me. Tell me how gorgeous I am.

COLES. You don't want to speak frankly?

GARFINKLE. I always speak frankly. I don't like people who say "Can we speak frankly?" Means they're bullshitting me the rest of the time.

COLES. I'm sorry. I won't use that phrase any more.

GARFINKLE. What do you want?

COLES. Two years. I want two years.

GARFINKLE. For what?

COLES. Jorgenson is sixty-eight. In two years he'll be seventy. He steps down at seventy.

GARFINKLE. Says who?

COLES. It's an agreement he has with the Board. His employment contract expires at seventy.

GARFINKLE. The Board are his cronies. He is the Board. What he wants done gets done.

COLES. He gave me his word. He's a man of his word.

GARFINKLE. Stop playing with yourself.

COLES. Twelve years ago he told me if I did the job it'd be my company to run when he steps down. That's why I came to that Godforsaken place. It's the same reason I'm here. I don't want the rug pulled out from under me so close to the finish line.

GARFINKLE. You're wasting your time. I don't have two years.

COLES. Listen, Mr. Garfinkle. I said we could grow our other businesses by fifteen per cent. I was being conservative. We'll grow them in excess of twenty. I can manage. I can manage the hell out of a company. In two years we'll be worth considerably more.

GARFINKLE. Billy boy, look at me. I weigh a ton. I smoke three packs a day. I walk from here to there, I'm out of breath. I can't even steal life insurance. Two years for me is forever. Do what you have to do now. I'm not a long term player.

COLES. I can't do it now. I can't do it till he leaves. If I try, I'm out on my ear.

GARFINKLE (Handing COLES his briefcase). That's the problem with working for a living.

COLES. Two years is not a long time. I have waited a lifetime for the opportunity.

GARFINKLE (Puts his arm around COLES' shoulder). You got stock, don't you?

COLES. Yes.

GARFINKLE. Fifty, seventy-five thousand, right?

COLES. Sixty.

GARFINKLE. Well, shit, look—want to feel better? (GARFINKLE taps out stock on his quote machine.) Before you heard my name your stock was ten. Now it's fourteen and a half. In two months I made you a quarter of a million dollars. Billy boy, the least you can do is smile. Ossie at the bank sends me flowers. All I'm asking from you is a smile.

(COLES rises, takes his briefcase and silently moves Center Stage. He is alone. All else is black.)

COLES. Several years ago my doctor told me my right arm is three-fourths of an inch longer than the left. "How do I correct that?" I asked. "Carry the briefcase with your left arm for the next twenty-five years." (Switches briefcase to the left arm.) Charged me a hundred fifty dollars and wished me a good day.

GARFINKLE (In the darkness). Smile, Billy boy, I just made you a quarter of a million dollars.

COLES. How come I like that doctor more than that pig? (He turns and faces JORGENSON's darkened office.) Jorgy, it's important.

(Lights up in office as JORGENSON rises to greet him.)

JORGENSON. Come on in. My door is always open. You know that.

(COLES enters.)

Welcome home. How was your trip to New York? How's Bill Jr.?

COLES. Fine.

JORGENSON. You must be exhausted. A day in New York is like a month anywhere else. Goddamned crazy city. Claire do any shopping?

COLES. Some.

JORGENSON. Only some? You got away lucky. Fay used to love to shop there—God rest her soul. Went to Bergdorf's Department Store, Lord and Taylor's Department Store, but she only bought at this Alexander's Department Store. She was a tight little so and so. Should've married Ossie.

COLES. She died the year before I got here. Jorgy—

JORGENSON. Last time we were in New York City was maybe . . . ten, fifteen years ago. We were in a taxicab on that highway coming in from the airport. Traffic? Nobody moved for maybe half an hour. Cars standing still as far as the eye can see. Suddenly some guy behind us went "beep!" Next guy went "beep beep" a little louder. Before you knew it there were these thousands of cars just parked blaring away. Like an orchestra gone mad—just one giant "beeeeep." Including my driver. You'd think he'd been thrilled just sitting there on his ass with his foot on the brake listening to that meter go tick, tick, tick.

COLES. I stopped by at Garfinkle's office.

JORGENSON. Let me just finish. You could hardly hear yourself think. I shouted to the driver, "If you ever reach the next exit turn around and take us back to the airport." And that's exactly what he did. Fay didn't say a word. Didn't have the nerve. That was the last time we were in New York City . . . and you know what was the most amazing thing? It wasn't even rush hour.

COLES. He intends to take over the company.

JORGENSON. Say that again?

COLES. He intends to take over the company.

JORGENSON. He said that?

COLES. He didn't have to. A man with a gun in his hand doesn't have to announce when he pulls the trigger. When you find out, you're dead.

JORGENSON. What are you talking about? What gun?

COLES. He now owns eleven per cent of the stock.

JORGENSON. I have a million shares. That's twenty-five per cent. If he has a gun—I have a cannon.

COLES. And he's still buying.

JORGENSON. So would you. This is an undervalued company. Give him credit for recognizing that and putting his money where his mouth is. As it is it's turned out to be a pretty good investment for him. The stock's a lot higher now than when he started buying in.

COLES. Because he's the one moving it up.

JORGENSON. Don't be ridiculous. I'm not saying that's not a factor, but it's not the only one. Ossie told me he bought five thousand shares himself last week. And there are others.

COLES. You don't understand. He's well known. What he does is not a secret. He's called "Larry the Liquidator." on Wall Street. He finds companies worth more dead than alive, gains control and kills them. Then he pockets the proceeds and goes on to the next one. He spelled it out for us right here in this office. It couldn't have been any clearer.

JORGENSON. Suppose you're right. What would you like me to do? Last time I looked it was a free country.

COLES. We could do things to protect ourselves.

JORGENSON. Like what?

COLES. We could change our by-laws to call for a two-thirds majority to effect control rather than fifty-one percent.

JORGENSON. Would that make you feel better?

COLES. Of course it would. At least we'd be fighting back. We wouldn't be rolling over and playing dead.

JORGENSON. Nobody's playing dead. What you propose . . . what would it entail?

COLES. Not much. We'd have to change our state of incorporation from Rhode Island to Delaware.

JORGENSON. Delaware? I've never even been to Delaware.

COLES. Neither have I. We needn't be there. We needn't even visit there. All we'd have to do is hire a local lawyer and get a post office box.

JORGENSON. What would it cost?

COLES. One hundred and seventy-five thousand dollars for the first year. Fifty thousand dollars a year thereafter, for local counsel.

JORGENSON. Reclaiming the old stock and issuing the new?

COLES. About two hundred and fifty thousand. But that would be a one shot deal.

JORGENSON. For lawyers?

COLES. Primarily.

JORGENSON. Why can't we keep it a Rhode Island company?

COLES. It's easier to get those changes done in Delaware. They're—geared to corporate needs. And we'll show Garfinkle we're not a sitting duck. We intend to fight.

JORGENSON. By running away?

COLES. Running away?

JORGENSON. From Rhode Island to Delaware.

COLES. Nobody's running anywhere. It's a paper transaction.

JORGENSON. I call it running away. This company was founded in Rhode Island. It thrived in Rhode Island. It will remain in Rhode Island.

COLES. It will remain in Rhode Island. All that's moving is the paper.

JORGENSON. And the paper will remain in Rhode Island. Don't talk to me about playing dead. You know me better than that. Our industry is littered with dead bodies. This country is infested with dead bodies. But we're still here. And the lights go on and the telephone rings and orders come in and product goes out and we have money in the bank. And we didn't get there by playing dead.

COLES. At least talk to a lawyer.

JORGENSON. I am not talking to a lawyer. Lawyers are like cab drivers stuck in traffic. They don't do anything—but their meter is always ticking.

COLES. Please . . . just think about it.

JORGENSON. I have thought about it. Maybe you ought to think about something. I own twenty-five per cent of this company. The Board owns another ten per cent. The employees' stock ownership plan five per cent. That's forty per cent. How is he going to get control?

COLES. From the sixty left.

JORGENSON. Please. They're long term holders. If they were looking to sell they would've sold when the stock was sixty. I'm sorry, I take your advice most of the time but in this instance you don't know what you're talking about.

COLES. I do know what—

JORGENSON. You are paid to manage this company. Manage it. It's my company. I'll see to it it stays that way, thank you.

(COLES *pauses a beat, turns and moves Center Stage. Lights out on* JORGENSON.)

COLES. "It's my company." Lord of the Manor with the House on the Hill . . . How long do you work for something till it's finally yours?

(*Lights up on* GARFINKLE *in his office.*)

GARFINKLE. How long do you deliver the mail before they give you the post office? Billy boy, they don't give pots of gold to errand boys. They give pensions.

COLES (*Whirling to* GARFINKLE). What?

GARFINKLE. Talk to me. What's happening? How come I don't hear from you? What am I—a creditor?

COLES. I'm busy running a company, Mr. Garfinkle. What can I do for you?

GARFINKLE. Talk to me. Have they broken ground on the Dunkin' Donuts next door?

COLES. I'm afraid not.

GARFINKLE. That's disappointing. Got any more disappointing news? (*Long silence.*) . . . Helloooo.

COLES. How many shares do you own now, Mr. Garfinkle?

GARFINKLE. You got a one-track mind. That's all you're ever interested in. Aren't you interested in me—my wife—my kids?

COLES. How are you, your wife, your kids?

GARFINKLE. I'm not married. Never was. Don't have any kids. Who would marry me? . . . Come to think of it, you might. Shit, with my five hundred thousand shares we're engaged already. Bought the last this morning at fifteen and one eighth . . . hellooooo . . . Ossie at the bank stopped sending me flowers. Now it's plants. Looks like a fucking greenhouse in here—smells up the place. Have you talked to him?

COLES. I don't talk to Ossie.

GARFINKLE. Not Ossie. Yorgy.

COLES. What about?

GARFINKLE. Don't act stupid with me, Billy boy. It does not become you—not to your fiancée. About restructuring.

COLES. Not yet.

GARFINKLE. You intend to?

COLES. Yes.

GARFINKLE. What are you waiting for?

COLES. The right opportunity.

GARFINKLE. You figure that could occur in my lifetime?

COLES. I don't know, Mr. Garfinkle. I'm not your doctor.

GARFINKLE. You got two weeks.

COLES. Two weeks?

GARFINKLE. Talk to him. Get back to me. Otherwise I'll have to take a ride up there again. Believe me, you don't want to see that happen. I'm much less charming the second time.

COLES. Two weeks is unrealistic. I need—

GARFINKLE. Two weeks. Say goodbye.

COLES. Mr. Garfinkle, two weeks—

GARFINKLE. Say goodbye!

(*Lights out on* COLES. GARFINKLE, *breathing hard, turns and yells Offstage.*)

Arthur—get the car ready. We're going back to the shitpit of the world. Bring donuts—and oxygen.

(*Lights out on* GARFINKLE. *Up on* JORGENSON'*s office.* COLES *and* BEA *are seated.* JORGENSON *rises from behind his desk cheerfully.*)

JORGENSON. Welcome, Larry, nice to see you again.

(GARFINKLE enters.)

GARFINKLE. Yumpin' yimminy, Yorgy, was that the sun I almost saw?

JORGENSON. It sure was. Come—look at it again. *(Leads him to the window. They stare out.)*

GARFINKLE. Living up here is like living in a limo. You're always looking out through tinted windows.

JORGENSON. Larry, spring is here.

GARFINKLE. Why not? It's been everywhere else.

JORGENSON. Come on. If a beautiful spring day doesn't bring out the sunshine in your soul, we'll have to—Bea, c'mon. Let's do it.

BEA. Now?

JORGENSON. Now. *(BEA exits, excited.)* Wait till you see this, Larry. I haven't even told Bill about it. *(Impatient, yells Offstage.)* C'mon, Bea. We're all waiting.

BEA *(Offstage)*. Hold your horses, Jorgy. I'll be right there.

JORGENSON. Been with me for thirty-seven years. Yelled at me the same way back then.

BEA *(Offstage)*. Ready?

JORGENSON. Ready. Ready.

(BEA enters pushing a stand-up rack on wheels filled with varying trays of donuts. Lots of them.) C'mere—I'll show you how it works. *(He turns the handle on top and donuts move up and down like an old-fashioned toaster. GARFINKLE quietly moves Center Stage, outside the office area, observing them.)*

BEA. Jorgy designed and built it this morning.

JORGENSON. Willard helped. He's our line foreman. And Kyle at the machine shop lent a hand. Larry, you're looking at a New England Wire and Cable product. Designed and built right here.

BEA. Keep turning.

JORGENSON *(Continuing to turn handle)*. This lady drove all the way down to Providence this morning, almost thirty miles—sixty, round trip—to get them.

BEA. Closest Dunkin' Donuts I could find. Will you keep turning, Jorgy?

GARFINKLE. With all the pricks in the world, I got to do business with a nice guy.

BEA. Look. Raspberry . . . toasted coconut.

JORGENSON. It comes apart. You could take it back to New York with you. A donut wheel for the donut man.

BEA. Chocolate sprinkles . . . chocolate icing . . . chocolate fudge . . . chocolate cream . . .

GARFINKLE *(Looking wistfully at the donuts)*. How unlucky can you get?

JORGENSON. Know the best part? Know who paid for the donuts? Ossie at the bank.

GARFINKLE. . . . Well, Ossie, . . . it's you and me, Babe . . . let's get to work.

(Stage goes black. Pause a beat. Lights go back up in JORGENSON's office. Everyone is there.)

JORGENSON. Larry, do me a favor. I'm a simple man. Restructuring, redeploying, maximizing—don't talk to me in Wall Street. Talk to me in English.

COLES. He wants you to sell the company.

JORGENSON. Is that what it's all about, Larry?

GARFINKLE *(To the tune of "Alfie.")*. What's it all about, Larry?

COLES. Tell him. He won't believe me. Tell him.

GARFINKLE. Not the company. Not the company. It's worth bupkus. You're lucky if you get the sixteen dollars a share it's selling at now.

JORGENSON. Then what, Larry? What do you want?

GARFINKLE. I want what every other stockholder wants. I want to make money.

JORGENSON. You are making money.

GARFINKLE. That's right. For all of us. I'm doing my part. Now you do yours.

JORGENSON. Do what? I don't have a printing press out there. I can't simply crank it out.

GARFINKLE. Get rid of the Wire and Cable division. It's a financial cancer. And it's starving out all the other boring things Billy boy runs. Nobody sees them. All they see is the cancer.

JORGENSON. So you want me to sell Wire and Cable.

GARFINKLE. Surgically remove it.

JORGENSON. To who, Mr. Garfinkle? Know anybody interested in buying a surgically removed cancer?

GARFINKLE. I'll find you a buyer.

JORGENSON. Who?

GARFINKLE. What's the difference?

JORGENSON. Who?

GARFINKLE. Some paper shuffling Wall Street types. They'll give you a buck for every four you give them in equipment. I told you that.

COLES. And they'll close this down, and deduct it from their taxes.

GARFINKLE. Easy. Just a paper transaction. Your hands won't even get dirty.

JORGENSON. And what happens to the plant?

GARFINKLE. Gets sold for scrap.

JORGENSON. And the men? And the town?

GARFINKLE. Not your problem. You're not the mayor. You're not a missionary.

JORGENSON. So that's what they mean when they talk about restructuring—maximizing shareholder values?

GARFINKLE. That's what they mean.

JORGENSON. Nice turn of phrase. We used to call it "going out of business."

GARFINKLE. Welcome to the wonderful world of Wall Street.

JORGENSON. Shouldn't surprise me. Those boys down there can't charge millions by going out of business. First they become lawyers and investment bankers—then they restructure.

GARFINKLE. On Wall Street, "Restructuring means never having to say you're sorry." Got it?

JORGENSON. I got it. Now you get it. I understand what you want. Thank you for coming.

GARFINKLE. Yorgy, are you dismissing me?

JORGENSON. I have no time for this. I have a company to run.

GARFINKLE (To BEA). Sweetheart, pass me a donut. (She looks at him, uncertain.) Come on, the chocolate cream.

BEA. Get it yourself.

COLES. Please leave before it becomes unpleasant.

GARFINKLE. Unpleasant? How quaint—how antiseptic—how "New England."

JORGENSON. Get out before I physically throw you out.

GARFINKLE. All right, forget the donut.

JORGENSON (Rising). Out!

GARFINKLE. Don't get your bowels in an uproar. We're just doing business.

JORGENSON. Do it somewhere else. You're not welcome here.

GARFINKLE. Now I'm going to tell you something. I don't like the way my company is being run. There is a goddamned fire raging out there and this whole industry is up in flames. And you call the Fire Department and who shows up? Nobody. Because they're all off in Japan and Singapore and Malaysia and Taiwan and every other shithole place where they're crazy about pollution. And they build factories over there and they stuff them full of little dedicated people who work for twelve cents an hour, ten hours a day, six days a week and then they go home at night and pray for their health so they can come back and do it again tomorrow. And while that goddamned inferno is raging you're out front tidying up, mowing the lawn, playing with your putz on my money.

JORGENSON. Now you listen to me. This plant was here before you were born and I promise you—it will be here long after you're gone. Its products helped build the roads, bridges and buildings throughout the face of New England. And I will not—do you understand me—will not have it commit suicide and kill these people and this town so you and your cronies can pocket the insurance money.

GARFINKLE. Don't think of it as suicide. Think of it as euthanasia.

JORGENSON. Go back to those other parasites on Wall Street. Tell them to restructure somewhere else.

(GARFINKLE moves out of the office towards Center Stage. BEA takes a donut from the bin and hurls it in his direction.)

BEA. Here's your lousy donut!

JORGENSON (Kicks over the bin. The donuts litter the floor). Here's all your lousy donuts! (They laugh. She comes over and they hug.) God damn it, Bea. It feels good to fight something other than imports for a change.

(Lights out in JORGENSON's office. GARFINKLE is alone Center Stage.)

GARFINKLE. Geez . . . You'd think I was asking them for a loan.

(Lights out on GARFINKLE. Stage is black.)

KATE (In darkness, laughing). Take over! (Lights up on KATE alone Onstage as she talks to her unseen MOTHER. KATE is an attractive, sexy woman, about thirty-five.) What's so funny? Taking over New England Wire and Cable is like taking over the psychiatric ward at Bellevue. It could be done, but who wants to . . . Mother, I'm sorry if it was in poor taste. That's who I am . . . well, why not take the money and run? You should have retired a long time ago. Now's your chance . . . Because I'm busy . . . Busy in like having no time.

(Lights up on BEA—Cross Stage.)

BEA. You can take one day off from Stanley Morgan and fly up here—

KATE. Morgan, Stanley.

BEA. Morgan, Stanley and fly up here and talk to us. Jorgy was always crazy about you.

KATE. I was never crazy about him.

BEA. I did not ask your opinion. I am stating that he would be more at ease speaking to you than some stranger. I expect you to give us a day.

KATE. . . . All right. I'm booked solid through the month. One day early next month.

BEA. I'll expect you here tomorrow.

KATE. Tomorrow?

BEA. Tomorrow. Catch the early flight. Come to the plant. We'll all be here.

KATE *(Sighs, resigned)*. . . . Coming, Mother. *(Lights out on* BEA.*)* Why is it that a grown woman, a lawyer, an executive with a staff of thirty and a budget of eight million plus, responsible for making hundreds of decisions every day, can revert to a spineless infant every time she talks to her mother? *(*KATE *picks up briefcase and moves to* JORGENSON's *office. Lights go up there.* BEA, COLES, *and* JORGENSON *await.)*

KATE. I understand what you said, but I don't understand what you want. Do you want me to help you negotiate a deal with him?

JORGENSON. There is no deal to be made with him.

KATE. Have you tried?

BEA. We want him to go away.

KATE. He's got half a million shares. No one walks away from half a million shares.

COLES. What do you suggest?

KATE. I'm a lawyer. Lawyers don't like to go to court. You never know what can happen. I suggest you settle.

JORGENSON. Meaning?

KATE. The man is motivated by dollars. Make it worth his while to leave.

COLES. Greenmail. Done all the time. Let's explore it.

JORGENSON *(Rising)*. Excuse me. If this discussion continues on this tack I am leaving. We are wasting our time. There is no deal to be made with predators. You kill them or they kill you.

KATE. I was asked what I suggested. It is not my company and it is not my decision. *(She begins to rise as well.)*

BEA *(To* KATE*)*. Please, Kate, we want to explore our options. Help us defend ourselves.

KATE *(Reluctantly sits)*. All right. Let's say, I'm not at this point recommending anything. Just going over what others in your position have done. "Exploring the options," Mother.

(Lights up on GARFINKLE *as he views, unseen by them, their meeting.)*

GARFINKLE. Wait till you hear this.

KATE. Traditionally, first thing, you hire some private investigators to see what dirt there is. We know some good ones. Hopefully, they'll find something that will make him go away.

GARFINKLE. Aw, Kate, you can do better than that.

BEA. Do you think there's a chance? Hasn't he been investigated before?

GARFINKLE. Investigated? I get sued or subpoenaed every week. I've become a professional witness.

KATE. It's unlikely we'll find anything. He's reasonably well known. I think the S.E.C. got him on a few technical violations.

GARFINKLE. That's right, girly. You mug somebody—you're walking the streets the same day. You don't file just one of fourteen hundred bullshit forms, they want to put you away for ten years.

COLES. We should do it. We have nothing to lose.

GARFINKLE. It's not his money. Us "stuckholders" will pay for it.

JORGENSON. Doesn't sound promising. We have better things to do with our money.

GARFINKLE. That man's got class . . . or he's cheaper than shit.

KATE. Get the Board to authorize a search for a white knight.

BEA. White knight?

KATE. A protector. A larger company that will buy you out and allow you to do business the way you want. You know, someone to rescue the damsel in distress . . . a white knight.

JORGENSON. I don't know anyone like that.

BEA *(To* KATE*)*. Do you?

GARFINKLE. Of course she doesn't *(Smiles, pats his middle.)* You got to have the stomach for it.

JORGENSON. Next.

KATE. We can formulate a "shark repellent."

BEA. Come again?

BEA. The purpose of a "shark repellent" is to make yourself undesirable to an unwanted suitor, i.e., shark.

BEA. How would that work?

GARFINKLE. Listen close. It's an education.

KATE. Take the most attractive part of the company—in this case I assume it's the non-wire and cable divisions—give someone, anyone—the option to buy that part of the business for a song. The option only gets triggered if and when anyone not presently on the Board acquires thirty per cent or more of the company's stock. Garfinkle buys more shares, the option gets triggered. He now owns a lot of shares that are worth considerably less than he paid for them.

JORGENSON. So do we. So do all the stockholders.

KATE. That's the risk. The hope is that the shark will go elsewhere to feed.

GARFINKLE. Ingenious, isn't it? Next.

JORGENSON. Next.

GARFINKLE. Mah *man!*

KATE. We could create a poison pill. It's a form of shark repellent, but one you might find more acceptable. Get the Board to authorize three million shares of preferred stock, one share for each share held by all but Garfinkle. If he gains control of thirty per cent or more, issue them for, say—a dollar a share.

JORGENSON. A dollar a share!

COLES. What a great idea. We'd make Garfinkle's shares worth less. We'd dilute them.

JORGENSON. We would be diluting ours as well. Book value and earnings per share would be halved.

KATE. Exactly. Once you swallow the poison pill you're no longer desirable. But you can still keep your business. To most everyone nothing has changed.

GARFINKLE. Except the stuckholder. People get paid big money—honored people—pillars of the community—to sit and dream this shit up. You know what I said when I first heard it?

JORGENSON. That's legal?

GARFINKLE. That's what I said.

KATE. So far.

GARFINKLE. Would you believe it?

KATE. It's not new. I can give you a list of companies—household names—that have it in their corporate by-laws.

GARFINKLE. If you or me tried it, they'd have us committed.

JORGENSON. How much would your firm charge for taking us on?

KATE. I don't know. That's not my department.

JORGENSON. Rough guess?

KATE. It would depend on how involved it got. If we were able to work it out peacefully and quickly—a million. Maybe two. If it turned out to be war, it could go to ten, twenty times that.

JORGENSON. Kate, your mother is the only

assistant I ever had. She is also the best friend I ever had. I remember clearly the day you were born. The whole plant shut down a full afternoon while we had birthday cake and celebrated. This whole plant . . .

BEA. Jorgy, please.

JORGENSON. And it is out of respect for that lady that I don't have you bodily thrown out of this office.

GARFINKLE. Bravo, Yorgy!

KATE. I'm sorry you feel that way. I'm only telling you how corporations under attack defend themselves. Don't blame the messenger for the message.

JORGENSON. The messenger, as I hear it, is saying pay him off or self-destruct. Either way, pay me my fee.

KATE. It is not my fee. Unfortunately, I'm only an employee. *(Picking up her briefcase to leave.)* I'm sorry we wasted each other's time.

JORGENSON. Have your firm send me a bill. That way only our time will have been wasted. I trust it'll be for something less than a million dollars.

KATE. It will. This one is on the house. And as long as it's my nickel, I want to tell you something. You, as they say on the street, are "in play." Garfinkle put you there. And now, right this second, all over the country there sit all kinds of boring, dull little men, hunched over their IBM PCs, buried under mountains of 13-D filings, looking for an edge to make a buck. And some of their little mini-computers have already noticed an obscure over-the-counter stock with a sixty per cent move in the last six months. "What's this? How come? What's going on?" they mutter. And then they notice Garfinkle's 13-D and his half-million shares. And they don't have to know diddly-doo about wire and cable. They know Garfinkle and they ride the coattails.

Congratulations. You're now "in play" in the big leagues where the game is called hardball and winner takes all. So if you want to play Mr. High and Mighty, Mr. Righteous, Mr. Robert's Rules of Order, better go to work for the Peace Corps where you'll be appreciated because you won't have any company left here to run.

(Begins to exit, turns.) And the shame of it is I would be perfect for this deal. Garfinkle is a blatant sexist. I love blatant sexists. They're my meat. But I wouldn't work for you if you begged me. I like being associated with winners.

(Lights out in JORGENSON's *office.)*

GARFINKLE *(Fanning himself).* Phew . . . some piece of work. *(Lights out on* GARFINKLE.*)*

BEA. How dare you talk to him that way.

KATE. Will you stop defending him? He is making the wrong decision. He will lose this company.

BEA. He is making the right decision. We will not lose this company.

KATE. We!? Since when is it "we"? He loses this company, he walks away with millions. You walk away with memories.

BEA. Don't you worry about me. I'm well provided for.

KATE. "Well provided for." You have running water and you think you're well provided for.

BEA. Why are we talking about my finances? What is this all about?

KATE. Anger. About thirty-five year's worth.

BEA. At whom?

KATE. At him. And you. And this God-awful company. It's your life. It always was. When he was happy, you were ecstatic. When he was depressed, you were distraught. When she died, you almost moved in. It was the talk of the town. With Dad keeping the dinner warm.

BEA. I loved him.

KATE. You were married, Mother.

BEA. Listen to me, Kate. In a life filled with rumors and gossip and sideways glances—I apologized to no one. Don't expect it of me now. You won't get it. You were asked here as our attorney, not our judge. If you can't handle the position—leave.

KATE. Why in God's name did you ever marry Dad?

BEA. I was nineteen. He asked. I thought I loved him. Until one day, thank God, I walked through that door. And there stood the most beautiful, scared young man I had ever seen. Had on blue jeans and a red flannel shirt with the sleeves rolled up. Said he just became President. I remember thinking, "How peculiar for a President. This company'll never last." And then the magic words: "How about it, Miss. I'm ready to take a chance with you. Ready to take one with me?" *(Turns to* KATE.*)* Sometimes life presents us with very limited choices.

KATE. I know.

BEA. Like now.

KATE. I don't believe you.

BEA. He trusts you. Don't make us deal with strangers in three piece suits. Maybe we can't play the game the way you want us to—help us play our game the best we can.

KATE. Oh Mother, don't you think I want to? Going up against Garfinkle, he's the best. And I'm as good as he is. It's the career opportunity of a lifetime.

BEA. So?

KATE. So, I said I wouldn't. Even if he begged me.

BEA. He's not. I am.

*(*KATE *pauses a beat, picks up her briefcase and crosses to her* MOTHER *on the way to* JORGENSON's *office. Looks back.)*

KATE. Well, c'mon. *(*BEA *moves to her and they begin their exit.)*

BEA. And you'll do something about those fees? They're horrendous.

KATE *(Laughing).* Mom, don't push it. *(They exit. Lights up on* GARFINKLE.*)*

GARFINKLE. You know what kills me? I've done maybe seven—eight deals like this. Know who I negotiate with? Skinny little joggers with contact lenses all stinking from the same aftershave. Don't believe me? Ever seen an arbitrageur? Ugliest people on the face of the earth. They won't use her. You'll see. I never luck out with a broad like that. Excuse me, woman like that. I've been accused of being a "womanizer." That's someone who likes broads. I remember when that used to be a good thing . . . although when you cut through the "Woman's Lib" bullshit all it really means is you can't call them "sweetheart" or "darling" unless you're schtupping them . . . . . . Then you can't call them anything else. *(Sits behind his desk, smiles.)* I can live with that. *(*KATE *enters his office. Hands him her business card.)*

KATE. That's me. We're the investment banker for New England Wire and Cable.

GARFINKLE *(Looking at card).* What are you—a fucking lawyer?

KATE *(Smiling).* Depends on who I'm with.

GARFINKLE *(Rises—opens arms—beams).* Welcome to my life!

KATE. All those cubby-holes have lawyers in them?

GARFINKLE. Mostly. *(She gives him a sad look.)* It's not as bad as you think. I don't have to talk to them. I just have to pay them.

KATE. You don't talk to them?

GARFINKLE. Talk to them? I'd rather talk to my mother. I write to them. *(Takes top sheet from pile on desk. Writes.)* "Fuck . . . them." *(Looks at* KATE.*)* Sue. *(Picks up next sheet.*

Writes.) "Trouble." *(Looks at* KATE.*)* Settle. *(Picks up the next sheet. Writes.)* "They're . . . morons." *(Looks at* KATE.*)* Let them sue. Don't give them a quarter. *(*KATE *laughs.)* See? Nothing to it. Sue. Settle. Defend. Which one are you?

KATE. I came to talk.

GARFINKLE. Now that's trouble. Lawyers want to talk, it's nothing but trouble. Who are you? How come I never heard of you?

KATE. They generally keep me locked away at bond closings, due diligence meetings, good stuff like that.

GARFINKLE. Life in the fast lane.

KATE. I'm not complaining. They pay well. I meet a lot of people. *(*GARFINKLE *yawns.)* Well . . . it's true. They don't have your . . . something.

GARFINKLE *(Opening desk drawer)*. Want a donut?

KATE. No, thanks.

GARFINKLE. Why not—you a health food freak?

KATE. No. Just not hungry.

GARFINKLE *(Incredulous)*. You have to be hungry to have a donut?

KATE. . . . You don't?

GARFINKLE. Are you shitting me? In all my life I never heard of such a thing. Have to be hungry? Why? It don't taste better that way.

KATE. How would you know?

GARFINKLE. My luck. A broad with a mouth.

KATE. Show me a broad worth knowing who doesn't have one.

GARFINKLE *(Laughs)*. I like you. Can you tell?

KATE. Not yet.

GARFINKLE. Hang in. You will.

KATE. That's what I came to see you about. I need a month to hang in.

GARFINKLE. Get lost.

KATE. I just got involved. I need time to get everybody's act together.

GARFINKLE. My act is together.

KATE. If you give me some time I think we can work something out.

GARFINKLE. Settle?

KATE. Work something out.

GARFINKLE. I only settle when I'm in trouble.

KATE. Or when it makes sense.

GARFINKLE. It only makes sense when I'm in trouble.

KATE. If you prefer, we'll go to court, get an injunction, have a fight, all kinds of allegations, cost them, cost you, and for what?

GARFINKLE. I live in court. You got to do better than that.

KATE. . . . I won't love you any more.

GARFINKLE. You got two weeks.

KATE. Standstill agreement.

GARFINKLE. Both sides.

KATE. No more buying.

GARFINKLE. Two weeks.

KATE. Thank you. *(*KATE *begins to exit.)*

GARFINKLE. Now let's talk about what I want to talk about.

KATE. What's that?

GARFINKLE. Your legs . . . your ass . . . your tits—

KATE. Sit. Sit!! *(He sits. She moves forward, her face close to his.)* Garfinkle, now listen close. I don't want to repeat this. You listening? Now take your right hand out of that donut drawer and put it between your legs. *(He looks at her, uncertain.)* Come on. They visit each other all the time.

GARFINKLE *(He laughs . . . a little nervously)*. . . . Can't.

KATE. Why?

GARFINKLE. I'm a lefty. *(Switches hands. Fumbles a bit.)*

KATE. Good. Now look directly down at the little guy and say—"You must behave yourself when you're in the presence of a lady."

*(*GARFINKLE *sits motionless, transfixed.)*

Garfinkle, if you don't say exactly that, right now, I'm resigning from this case. You'll deal with the Morgan Stanley "B" team. They think arbitrageurs are fun. *(He remains motionless. She rises, begins to exit.)*

GARFINKLE. All right. All right.

KATE. "You must behave yourself when you're in the presence of a lady."

GARFINKLE. . . . "You must—" *(*KATE *motions him to put his chin on his chest. He does.)* "You must behave yourself when you're in the presence of a lady."

KATE. See, not so hard. *(He does a doubletake. She rises to exit.)* Hey, Garfinkle, what kind of donuts you got in that drawer?

GARFINKLE. The good kind.

KATE. Toss one over. *(He reaches into drawer.)* With the right hand. See you in two weeks. *(He switches hands and tosses one over. She catches it and exits. He rises, takes a step or two Downstage, his voice filled with wonder.)*

GARFINKLE. . . . I think I'm falling in love

... *(Lights out on* GARFINKLE—*up on* KATE *as she munches donut.)*

KATE. The man does have . . . a certain undeniable . . . charm.

(Lights up in JORGENSON's *office.* JORGENSON, COLES, *and* BEA *await.)*

BEA. Charm? He has as much charm as a beached whale.

KATE *(Entering office).* Don't knock it. It bought us two weeks.

JORGENSON. For what?

KATE. For getting our act together.

JORGENSON. What did it cost?

KATE. A donut.

COLES. Where do we go from here?

KATE *(To* JORGENSON*).* Have you reconsidered the defenses we spoke about?

JORGENSON. We won't do that.

KATE. Can I threaten it?

JORGENSON. I don't make threats I won't fulfill.

KATE. It's probably too late in the game for that anyway. Here's what you can do. Get the Board together. Authorize the purchase of as many shares as you can afford. Do it right away.

JORGENSON. The dollars we have are our safety net. Most of it is earmarked for future expansion.

KATE. Then borrow the money.

COLES. We have excellent credit. There's a dozen banks happy to lend us the money. It would be no problem.

JORGENSON. It's never a problem borrowing money. It's only a problem paying it back. *(To* KATE.*)* What would that do?

KATE. Three things. One: For every share you acquire it's one less Garfinkle can get. Two: and more important, you'll drive the price of the stock up. Eighteen sounds terrific when the stock is ten. Twenty is not so terrific when the stock is eighteen. The more it costs, the more negotiable he becomes. Get the stock up.

JORGENSON. I understand what you're saying. I'm not sure I want to do that. We've been debt free since the Depression. It's what's permitted us to survive.

KATE. And it's that gorgeous balance sheet that also makes you so attractive—which is the third reason to buy the shares.

JORGENSON. What a strange new world. A strong, liquid balance sheet is no longer an asset. It's a liability.

KATE. Next, get a letter out to the shareholders. Tell them how great business is and how wonderful the future looks. Tell them how pleased you are that the investment community is finally beginning to recognize, in some small way, the real worth of the company. Thank them for their loyalty and support. Talk to as many of the larger shareholders as you can, personally. Under no circumstances mention any potential takeover.

BEA. I'll compile a list of everyone with more than five thousand shares.

JORGENSON. I don't need a list. I know who they are.

KATE. You have any political clout?

BEA. We're friendly with the Mayor and City Council.

KATE. Forget them. Too small. Do you have a relationship with the Governor?

BEA. Are you joking? He's a Democrat.

KATE. That's OK. I'll set it up from New York. We'll get some of our legislative people up there to talk to him. Prepare a statistical analysis of your dollar contribution to the local economy: jobs, payroll, taxes, etc. Make it as complete as possible.

COLES. You'll have it Monday.

KATE. Maybe we can get some anti-takeover legislation passed—quickly.

COLES. I don't mean to be crass . . . but . . . shouldn't we deal with something called . . . "golden parachutes"?

BEA. Golden parachutes?

KATE. You're premature. Don't muddy the water. We'll have time for that later.

JORGENSON. I think you've given us enough to tackle for the moment. We still have a business to run.

KATE. I agree. The important thing now is to get the stock up. I'll coordinate everything else. *(Begins to exit.)*

JORGENSON. Before you go, will you answer the question I asked you earlier?

KATE. What's that?

JORGENSON. Why did he give us two weeks? What did it cost?

KATE *(Smiling).* . . . I told you—a donut. Chocolate fudge with sprinkles. *(*KATE *exits.* JORGENSON *moves Center Stage. Lights go out in his office.)*

JORGENSON. Donut, my ass. Garfinkle would never give two weeks. He'd sell them.

BEA. Jorgy, what the hell is a "golden parachute"?

(Lights go out on JORGENSON *and* BEA. KATE *screams in the darkness.)*

KATE. You son-of-a-bitch! You goddamned son-of-a-bitch! *(Lights up in* GARFINKLE's *office.*

KATE *enters. Flings papers at him.)* Goddamned hypocrite liar!

GARFINKLE. But, sweetie-pie . . . but, honey-lamb—

KATE. We had an agreement. You gave me your word.

GARFINKLE. But, baby-poo—

KATE. Stop that. You lied to me.

GARFINKLE. Me?

KATE. We had a standstill. No more buying.

GARFINKLE. So?

KATE. So? What's this tender to buy New England Wire and Cable at twenty dollars a share all about?

GARFINKLE. Not me.

KATE. I bet. *(Picks up papers.)* OPM holdings—you know nothing about it?

GARFINKLE. OPM? Not a lot to know.

KATE. I'm sure. . . . Where's the money coming from—junk bonds?

GARFINKLE. Through Drexel. Give them fifteen per cent plus a fee and they'll get you the bucks to buy a slag heap in Mound City, Missouri.

KATE. Why did you have to lie to me? You embarrassed me with my firm. You embarrassed me with my clients.

GARFINKLE *(Slams his hand on desk. The ferocity of the blow startles* KATE*).* Enough! Who am I dealing with here—Mother Teresa? Don't come on so goddamned holy with me, girly. You think I'm a fool—I sit here and twiddle my thumbs while you drive the price of the stock up?

KATE. I did no such thing.

GARFINKLE. You're full of shit. All the buying was coming from some cock-a-mamie little brokerage firm in Rhode Island.

KATE. I know nothing about it.

GARFINKLE. Give me a break, will you? That cheapskate is so tight he won't even put paint on the walls. The only way he'd be paying seventeen for his stock is if someone stood behind him with a cattle prod. Now I got as good an imagination as most but I tell you it's tough picturing Mother Teresa with a cross in one hand and a cattle prod in the other. *(*KATE *begins to leave.)* Don't go, Katie. I'm not through. You want to play the game—let's play. Only I don't watch while you do "holier than thou." That's not the way this game is gonna get played.

KATE. Game, huh?

GARFINKLE. Goddamned right. The best game in the world.

KATE. You're playing Monopoly with people's lives here.

GARFINKLE. I'm doing them a favor. I'm making them money. I thought that's what they were in the business for.

KATE. I know this might be difficult for you to believe—for some people business means more than making money. They don't know how to play your game.

GARFINKLE. I'll teach them. It's easy. You make as much as you can for as long as you can.

KATE. And then what?

GARFINKLE. And then what? Whoever has the most when he dies—wins.

KATE. Goodbye, Garfinkle.

GARFINKLE. Aw, Katie, don't leave so soon. We haven't spoken about your thighs, your nipples, your—

KATE. See you in court.

GARFINKLE. At least have a donut.

KATE. Stuff it.

GARFINKLE *(Downstage Right).* You didn't have to leave. I'm not mad at you. Lying to protect your client is just doing your job good.

KATE. Round One to the fat man. It ain't over till it's over, fat man.

GARFINKLE. And you didn't even ask what OPM stands for. *(With a big smile.)* "Other People's Money."

Curtain

ACT TWO

KATE *with champagne bottle in hand in* JORGENSON'*s office.* JORGENSON, COLES, *and* BEA *are standing expectantly.*

KATE. To Judge Pollard.

BEA. Judge Jim Pollard? For what?

KATE. For granting us an injunction preventing Garfinkle from buying more shares. *(They cheer, delighted.)*

COLES. A permanent injunction?

KATE. No. Pending the results of a suit we filed in Washington with the S.E.C. But since our Annual Meeting is in five weeks, for the purposes of taking control at that time, you could consider it permanent.

COLES. No more buying?

KATE. No more buying. He'll look to overturn it but he doesn't have time.

JORGENSON. Not with Jim Pollard presiding. Used to play football together in high school. Slowest son of a bitch on the team.

KATE. Didn't move slowly here. Granted us the injunction in two hours.

GARFINKLE (Sings). "Territory folks should stick together."

KATE. Our legislative people met yesterday with the Governor and his Secretary of Commerce to discuss immediate anti-takeover legislation. They seem, I am told, very sympathetic.

GARFINKLE (Sings). "Territory folks should all be pals."

KATE. I want to organize bus trips to the state capitol. Get the workers, management, local politicians, everyone in town up there to see the legislators. And demonstrate, demonstrate, demonstrate.

GARFINKLE (Sings). "Cowboys dance with the farmer's daughters."

KATE. I want to see babies. I want to see balloons. I want to see "Save Our Town, Save Our Future" posters hung from every school, church, bank and whorehouse in this city. I want visibility. I want prayer meetings. I want pressure!

GARFINKLE (Sings). "Farmers dance with the rancher's gals!"

(Lights fade in JORGENSON's office. KATE moves Center Stage.)

KATE. God save me . . . I love this!

(Lights up in GARFINKLE's office as he screams at his unseen staff. KATE looks on in amusement.)

GARFINKLE. Seventeen lawyers on my payroll. Three goddamned law firms on retainer. And all of you together ain't worth some broad wet behind the ears. Some crew—you managed to work it out so in a free market in a free country I can't buy some shit-ass stock that every other asshole can buy. Congratulations. You know what? You—all of you— are destroying the capitalist system. And you know what happens when capitalism is destroyed? The Communists take over. And you know the one good thing that happens when the Commies take over? The first thing they do is kill all the lawyers!! And if they miss any of you—I'll do it myself.

(KATE, moving into his office, applauds.)

You liked it?

KATE. Loved it.

GARFINKLE. The Wall Street version of "Let's win one for the Gipper."

KATE. It was wonderful. It's a shame Judge Pollard couldn't hear you.

GARFINKLE. Stop gloating. It doesn't become you. What do you want?

KATE. A donut.

GARFINKLE (Mimicking her). It's too early to be hungry.

KATE (Mimicking him). You have to be hungry to have a donut?

GARFINKLE (Tossing her a donut). I see gloating is good for the appetite.

KATE. Who would know better than you?

GARFINKLE. My luck. I meet a broad . . . sweet, nice, Irish. In two weeks she turns into Don Rickles.

(KATE laughs.)

I like it when you laugh. You laugh nice.

KATE. You have the most incredible sense of humor. You make me laugh.

GARFINKLE. Uh-oh. Here it comes. I'm in trouble.

KATE (Flirtatious). Let's be friends. Let's work it out. Let's settle.

GARFINKLE. You've been eating too many donuts.

KATE. You only settle when you're in trouble. I thought I heard, "I'm in trouble."

GARFINKLE. Only with you. You're wet behind the ears. I want you wet between your legs.

(KATE chokes on her donut.)

Aha—gotcha.

(She nods, still choking.)

Nice to see a girl blush nowadays. (He moves behind her, gently and awkwardly patting her back as one would a child.)

KATE. . . . Not blushing . . . choking.

GARFINKLE. . . . Are you all right?

(She nods.)

Good. I don't want you to sue Dunkin' Donuts. The only thing better than their donuts is their stock.

KATE. Now that you almost killed me, can we talk?

GARFINKLE. Talk. I'm listening. Just don't die on me.

KATE. What do you want to go away?

GARFINKLE. . . . What do you mean?

KATE. What number do we buy you out at?

(GARFINKLE, feigning horror, pretends to draw drapes, check for bugs, etc.)

What are you doing?

GARFINKLE. Greenmail! Are you offering me greenmail?

KATE. Will you stop it?

GARFINKLE. Are you?

KATE. Stop acting like it's new to you. You've done it three times in the past.

GARFINKLE. I've done shit in the past. I don't play that way. It was never my idea. *(Talking into her briefcase.)* And I want the record to show it's not in this case either.

KATE. Why are you so uptight about it? It's not illegal.

GARFINKLE. No, it's not. It's immoral. That distinction has no relevance for you lawyers—but it matters to me.

KATE. For someone who has nothing nice to say about lawyers you certainly have enough of them around.

GARFINKLE. You have to. They're like nuclear warheads. They have theirs so you need yours—but once you use them they fuck everything up. They're only good in their silos.

KATE *(Laughs)*. I'll have to remember that.

GARFINKLE. Let me ask you something. You have authorization to offer me greenmail? . . . Bet your ass you don't. The others didn't either. It only comes from the lawyers. It's a lawyer's scheme. Everybody walks out happy. I get paid off. You get paid off. Yorgy keeps his company. Billy boy keeps his inheritance. The employees keep their jobs. Everybody comes out.

KATE. Sounds pretty good to me.

GARFINKLE. Except the stuckholders. Their stock falls out of bed. They won't know what hit them.

KATE. I don't believe this. We better stop hanging out together. I turn into Don Rickles and you turn into Albert Schweitzer.

GARFINKLE. Not Albert Schweitzer—Robin Hood. I'm a modern-day Robin Hood. I take from the rich and give to the middle class. Well . . . upper middle class.

KATE. Can we be serious now?

GARFINKLE. I am serious. I really believe that . . . So what's your number?

KATE. The stock is eighteen. We'll buy it back at eighteen.

GARFINKLE. First you laugh at me and then you insult me.

KATE. Why? Who else you know would buy a million shares of New England Wire and Cable at eighteen?

GARFINKLE. Me. I'll pay twenty for them.

KATE. You can't. You got trouble.

GARFINKLE. No trouble. Just delay.

KATE. I could maybe . . . get them to stretch to twenty.

GARFINKLE. Now, why would I sell you something at the same price I was willing to pay for it?

KATE. Your average cost was thirteen. Thirteen from twenty, times a million, isn't a bad day's pay on one little deal.

GARFINKLE. I'm not interested in seven million. I'm interested in value. The value here is no secret. I spelled it out for them. I was being conservative.

KATE. Spell it out for me. What's the number?

GARFINKLE. Twenty-five.

KATE. Impossible.

GARFINKLE. What's impossible—It's worth it or they'll pay it?

KATE. Both. That stock hasn't seen twenty-five in ten years.

GARFINKLE. You want history? That stock was once sixty. I was once skinny. . . . Well, skinnier.

KATE. Take twenty.

GARFINKLE. Take a walk. Twenty-five is my number. And that's a favor.

KATE. I can't deliver that.

GARFINKLE. I know. Let's talk about something nice. Let's talk about your eyes.

KATE *(Getting up to leave)*. I really thought we could work something out.

GARFINKLE. We can't. You're too far away.

KATE. You could lose it all.

GARFINKLE. I could. That's why so few of us have the balls to play the game.

KATE. Thanks for the donut.

GARFINKLE. Don't be depressed. You're in a tough place. Go fight your fight. It's not personal—it's principle. Hey, no matter what—it's better than working at the post office.

KATE *(Softly)*. Oh yeah . . . It's better than the post office.

(She smiles sadly and exits. He is alone.)

GARFINKLE. A lot better than working at the post office. It's the best there is. Like in the old westerns, didn't everyone want to be the gunslinger? Didn't everyone want to be Butch Cassidy and the James Boys? There's just a few of us—us modern-day gunslingers. There's T. Boone and the Bass Brothers out of Texas. Irwin Jacobs out of Minneapolis. Would you believe a gunslinger named Irwin Jacobs? The Belzberg Boys up north in Canada. And here in New York we got Saul Steinberg and Ronny Perlman and Carl Icahn.— *(Places his hand on his heart.)* Out of respect for the stupid, a moment of silence for our gunned-down colleague Ivan Boesky. *(With a big smile.)* It's assholes like him that give assholes like us a bad name. And last, but not least, Garfinkle from the wilds of the Bronx. But instead of galloping in with a six gun a-blazing in each hand, we're driven in, escorted by a herd of lawyers and investment bankers, waving our limited partnerships in one hand and our 13-D filings in the other. But they quake just as hard. And they wind up just as dead. And it's legal. And it's exciting. And it's fun. *(Moves to desk.)* And the money ain't bad either. *(Sits at desk.)* And every so often, every once in a while, we even wind up with the girl. *(Begins looking at papers on desk. Looks up.)* It's a nice business.

(As he works quietly for a beat, we hear KATE shouting Offstage.)

KATE. What? What are you so hysterical about—interrupting my meeting. *(She enters his office.)* What the hell is so important? You having a stroke—a nervous breakdown?

GARFINKLE. Just taking care of business.

KATE. You're worse than my mother.

GARFINKLE. Please. I know we're on different sides here—

KATE. I'm busy. What's so important? What do you want?

GARFINKLE. I feel bad about our last meeting. You left, you looked so depressed. I want us to be friends. I want us to end our dispute. I have two propositions. I'll give them to you in my order of preference.

(She sits.)

Sure. If I was having a stroke you'd tell me to dial 911—Now you're ready to spend the afternoon. How about the evening?

KATE. Proposition number one?

GARFINKLE. We leave here, right now, and go to my place where we make wild passionate love for the rest of the afternoon.

KATE. Number two?

GARFINKLE. Wait a minute. I'm not finished. The first one who comes, loses.

KATE. Loses what?

GARFINKLE. The deal. I come first I sell you back my shares at cost. I slink away never to be seen or heard from again. You come first, you tender all your shares to me at twenty.

KATE. You're serious?

GARFINKLE. Well, I don't slink. Big men don't slink. I . . . saunter away. Are you interested?

KATE. How do you suggest we write this up for the proxy statement?

GARFINKLE. Delicately. Under the heading easy come, easy go.

KATE. The garment center is too classy for you.

GARFINKLE. Come on, what do you got to lose—your virginity? I could lose millions.

KATE. You've thought of everything!

GARFINKLE. Not everything. What happens if we come together?

KATE. We call and make sure your life insurance premiums are paid. *(KATE moves out of office to Center Stage.)*

GARFINKLE. Hey, premiums are paid.

(Lights out on GARFINKLE. KATE is alone.)

KATE. You think he was serious? So help me, I don't know.

On the one hand, if he was serious . . . *(She laughs.)* We would have made Wall Street history . . . maybe. *(Moving to JORGENSON's office.)* And on the other hand, proposition number two is something to talk about.

(Lights up in JORGENSON's office. BEA, COLES and JORGENSON excitedly greet KATE as she enters.)

Don't get too excited. Don't break out the champagne. He gave me two propositions. Here's the one worth talking about. Inasmuch as Judge Pollard will not lift his injunction and inasmuch as his money is all tied up and inasmuch as your lawyer can be very persuasive, he's agreeable to swap you his shares for the Wire and Cable division.

BEA. . . . What?

KATE. He owns a million shares. He gives them to us. We give him the Wire and Cable division.

COLES. Makes sense. It costs him thirteen million for something he'll sell for thirty—thirty-five million.

JORGENSON *(Trying to control himself)*. What are the alternatives?

KATE. Don't dismiss it so quickly. On Wall Street it's know as "restructuring." Look what happens. The losses at Wire and Cable disappear. The earnings of the other divisions surface. Your stock skyrockets.

JORGENSON. What are the alternatives?

KATE. Better yet, when you get back his million shares you absolutely control this company. It's yours. No one can take it away.

JORGENSON. I'm asking you for the last—

KATE. I can't play with him in the courts forever. Ultimately he gets the injunction withdrawn, buys more shares . . . don't you understand?

BEA. We're not stupid—we understand. What are the alternatives!

KATE. Greenmail. Poison pills. Restructuring. You choose. I have given you the alternatives.

JORGENSON. You've given me nothing but different ways to kill myself.

COLES. Jorgy, this idea works. We're rid of the losses. We're in total control. And our stock doubles.

JORGENSON. To hell with the price of our stock. I will not do Garfinkle's dirty work for him.

KATE. I'm pleading with you. I'm imploring you.

JORGENSON. I will not do it. I will not kill these people and this town to enrich the man who is trying to destroy me.

KATE. You're a fool. You're a neanderthal. You deserve to lose this company!

BEA. Stop that. This is not a chess game. It's not simply a matter of tactics. What's the matter with you? This used to be your home. This is family.

KATE. Family!?

BEA. Yes. The kids you went to school with earn their livings at this plant. Family.

KATE. Oh, good God. Okay, let's talk about family. Let's start with Dad. Let's start with his dreams and his family.

BEA. Your father is dead. But we're not dead. And this plant is not dead. And our dreams aren't over and they'll never end with greenmail and poison pills.

KATE. Stop talking dreams. Look at the reality.

BEA. I am looking at the reality and I don't like what I see. It scares me. Who are you, Kate? What ever happened to that brave young girl who set out to do battle to heal all the world's ills? *(Distraught.)* What ever happened to my baby?

(JORGENSON *moves to* BEA. *With his arm around her shoulder, he begins ushering her off.)*

JORGENSON. Please.

BEA. What are you doing? She is my daughter. This is my fight.

JORGENSON. This is our company. This is my fight, too. I won't embarrass you. Promise.

(BEA *reluctantly exits.* KATE *begins to leave.)*

Hold on a minute . . . What do you want of me, Kate? Want me to say "I'm sorry"? For what? For loving your mother? I'm not. Look, we are fighting for our lives—here and now . . . Why are we even talking about this?

KATE. Because it still hurts.

JORGENSON. What do we do now, Kate? Go over it—resolve thirty-some odd years of hurt in the next fifteen minutes? Is that what you expect?

KATE. No, I don't. But I'll tell you what I do expect. I expect not to be lectured to about "family" by my mother and I expect not to be abused by you.

JORGENSON. Abused?

KATE. I turned my life upside down to come up here to help you out. I don't even get to take off my jacket and you're ready to have me "bodily thrown out of your office." Well, I'll make it easy for you. I'll leave. *(She turns to exit.)*

JORGENSON. Well, go ahead then and leave. You're a lousy lawyer anyway.

KATE. I am a lousy lawyer!? I want to tell you something. I'm a goddamned good lawyer. You are a lousy client. You say "No" to everything. You say "No" to what ninety-nine percent of other corporations say "Yes" to. If this was any other outfit they'd put a statue out there in the yard of the woman that saved this company.

JORGENSON. Saved this company? You're not looking to save this company. You're looking to save your own ass.

KATE. . . . What?

JORGENSON. Being beaten by Garfinkle wouldn't look so good on your resume, would it? Damn it, Kate—you want to win so badly, you don't even know what this fight is all about!

KATE. Oh, yes, I do. It's about your incredible—pigheadedness.

JORGENSON. Okay. Sure it is. But it's also about the twelve-hundred men who work here and their families—and their future. Let's ask them if you're trying to "save this company."

KATE. Why ask them? They're not stockholders.

JORGENSON. Does that mean they don't matter?

KATE. . . . Okay . . . Look. They matter. Nothing gets resolved but everything matters.

JORGENSON. What matters most is this is my nickel. So let's stop fighting about what I won't do and let's start fighting about what I will do.

KATE. Okay. Here's my problem. I'm a good lawyer. I'm a lousy mindreader. What will you do?

JORGENSON. I'll leave it up to the stockholders.

(KATE *laughs.)*

KATE. You will leave it up to the stockholders?

JORGENSON. They haven't let me down yet.

KATE. They haven't met Garfinkle yet.

JORGENSON. I don't have a choice. I do—not—have a choice I can live with.

KATE. Oh, why couldn't you be an asshole like everybody else?

JORGENSON. I'm sorry. I thought I was doing my best.

KATE. This 40% . . . This faithful 40% . . . Can you absolutely count on it?

JORGENSON. Absolutely. Come on, let's kick his ass all the way back to Wall Street.

KATE. Jorgy, if I play Garfinkle right. If I massage that ego just right, this could work!

(KATE and JORGENSON move into JORGEN-SON's office. COLES enters alone.)

COLES. It didn't seem the appropriate time to ask: "And what happens to me if we lose?" It never seemed the appropriate time to ask that. When you spend your life managing a business you're trained to think in contingencies. What happens if sales don't meet expectations? What happens if costs go up—the economy down? What happens if . . .

So . . . later that afternoon, with a lump in my throat, I asked, "What happens to me if we lose? I deserve," I said, "a golden parachute. Managements with far worse records than mine routinely give themselves at least five years' pay. It's done all the time. And it wouldn't cost you anything." . . . Know what he said?

JORGENSON *(In his darkened office).* Up here we don't plan the funeral until someone dies.

COLES. Isn't that something?

(COLES exits. Lights up in JORGENSON's office. KATE is preparing to leave.)

JORGENSON. So . . . You think he'll go for it?

KATE. . . . I don't know.

JORGENSON. You can do it. Use some of that home grown New England charm. Talk nice. Smile sweet. You'll get him.

KATE *(Exiting his office).* Don't go away. *(Moves Downstage Center. Lights out on JORGEN-SON's office. She turns to GARFINKLE's darkened office.)* Hey Garfinkle!

(Lights go up on GARFINKLE in his office.) Rumor has it you got balls.

GARFINKLE. I've been trying to show you for weeks.

KATE. Show me now. Let's leave it up to the stockholders. Run your own slate of directors at the Annual Meeting. You get 51% of the votes, it's your company. You buy everybody out at twenty. You don't get the votes, you sell us back your shares at thir-

teen. You slink away, never to be seen or heard from again . . . What do you say, Garfinkle? Hardball. Winner takes all.

GARFINKLE. Is that what you want?

KATE. A lot.

GARFINKLE. I don't know. It's a tough proposition. You control 40% of the votes going in.

KATE. What do you got to lose? On a worst case basis you come out even. It only cost you thirteen.

GARFINKLE. I don't know. It's gonna be close.

KATE. Robin Hood makes the deal.

GARFINKLE. . . . Yeah. Do it.

(Lights out on GARFINKLE's office. KATE turns to JORGENSON's office. Lights come up. BEA and JORGENSON are present.)

KATE. Done. *(She moves to exit.)*

JORGENSON. Hold on. Where are you going?

KATE. The airport.

JORGENSON. I'll give you a lift.

KATE. Don't bother.

JORGENSON. At least let me tell you how great you did.

KATE. We'll see at the Annual Meeting.

BEA. I know this wasn't your preference. Thanks for sticking your neck out. How does it feel?

KATE. Scary. It's going to be close.

JORGENSON. Close? We have forty percent. He has twenty-five. We would only need ten of the remaining thirty-five. That's less than one in three. If we can't get that—Christ, Richard Nixon could get that.

BEA *(To KATE).* Always wanted to be a politician.

JORGENSON. I did. Always wanted to be Harry Truman. Goddamned son of a bitch just went out and told the truth. *(To BEA.)* And that's what we're going to do. We're going out there and tell the truth. Send a letter to the stockholders? We'll visit them. Hell, we'll even have them over for dinner.

KATE. Harry and Bess hit the campaign trail. *(Begins to leave.)*

JORGENSON. Before you go. You said he gave you two propositions. What was the other?

KATE. Oh, just Garfinkle's idea of a tender offer. Come on. Drive me to the airport.

(Blackout. Lights up on GARFINKLE alone in his office. COLES enters, briefcase in hand.)

GARFINKLE. Aw, Christ—What do *you* want?

COLES. Good morning, Mr. Garfinkle.

GARFINKLE. Are you about to regale me with the latest saga of Bill Jr. at Columbia?

COLES. Strictly business, Mr. Garfinkle. As you know, I had sixty thousand shares of New England stock when we first met.

GARFINKLE. Excuse me—it'll be a history lesson instead.

COLES. Since becoming aware of your investment I have purchased an additional forty thousand shares. I now have a hundred thousand.

GARFINKLE. Congratulations.

COLES. I'm prepared to sell you the right to vote those shares at the Annual Meeting. Are you interested?

GARFINKLE. Sit down. I'm interested.

(COLES *sits.*)

How much?

COLES. A million.

GARFINKLE. Too much.

COLES. You need a million shares above what you own. I can get you ten percent of the way there in one transaction. Better yet, it's votes they're counting on for themselves. I think what I'm asking is fair.

GARFINKLE. If your shares make a difference—if I win by less than a hundred thousand—Otherwise I don't need them. I won't vote them.

COLES. I'm not selling you an option. I'm selling you the right to vote the shares. How you vote them, if you vote them, is your business. It's of no concern to me.

GARFINKLE. . . . If they make the difference, you got your million. If they don't, half a million.

COLES. Agreed. *(Reaching into his briefcase.)* I've prepared the papers. I just left the numbers blank. Have your lawyers review it. I'm staying over. I'll pick it up in the morning—along with a check. *(Places papers neatly on* GARFINKLE'S *desk.)* Good day, Mr. Garfinkle.

*(*COLES *exits* GARFINKLE'S *office. Moves Center Stage.* GARFINKLE *shouts after him, a beat after his exit.)*

GARFINKLE. And how is Bill Jr. doing with his studies?

*(*GARFINKLE *moves his clenched fist through the air in celebration. Lights out on* GARFINKLE. COLES *is alone.)*

COLES. Don't look at me like that. Everybody looks out after their own self-interest. "What's in it for me?" Isn't that, ultimately, what it's all about? Jorgenson looks out for his monument. Garfinkle for his money. Bea

for her man. Kate for her career. The employees for their paycheck. I kept this company alive. I helped make it all possible. Who looks out for me? *(*COLES *hurriedly exits. Lights up on* BEA *as she tries to get her bearings.)*

BEA. This way? . . . Through there . . .

(Lights up on GARFINKLE *in his office. She enters.)*

Good afternoon, Mr. Garfinkle.

GARFINKLE. Oh, no—the donut thrower. Wait—I got to get my catcher's mask.

BEA. I'm sorry. I didn't bring any.

GARFINKLE. Aw . . . And I was looking forward to some of your nutritious health donuts—you know—yogurt sprinkles—penicillin-filled.

BEA. . . . These offices are every bit as impressive as my daughter said they were.

GARFINKLE. . . . What do you know . . . I like your daughter. She's hot shit.

BEA. . . . I think so, too . . . assuming I know what you mean.

GARFINKLE. You know what I mean. She's terrific. And she didn't get that way working for those clowns at Morgan, Stanley. She must've got it from you.

BEA. That's kind of you.

GARFINKLE. Did she send you? I wouldn't put it past her.

BEA. She didn't send me. She would be upset with me if she knew. I expect this meeting will be held in confidence.

GARFINKLE. Have a seat.

(She sits.)

What can I do for you?

BEA. You can take the million dollars I'm about to offer you.

GARFINKLE *(Sitting).* . . . This is gonna be some day.

BEA. I thought that might interest you. There is a trust fund, in my name, with a million dollars, primarily in treasury notes, in it. I will turn it over to you if you call off your fight with us. We will buy back your shares at thirteen, which Kate informs me gets you even, plus you'll have a million dollars profit.

GARFINKLE. How come I never had a mother like you?

BEA. Is that acceptable?

GARFINKLE. My mother—I gotta send a check once a month. Would you like to meet her?

BEA. Is that acceptable?

GARFINKLE. How much money you make a year?

BEA. I don't see—

GARFINKLE. How much?

BEA. Forty thousand. Plus health insurance.

GARFINKLE. Why would you give up a million to save forty?

BEA. That's my affair. Is it agreeable to you?

GARFINKLE. Who are you doing it for?

BEA. Myself. I don't need the money.

GARFINKLE. I don't either.

BEA. Then why are you doing it?

GARFINKLE. That's what I do for a living. I make money.

BEA. You will have made money. If you accept my offer you will have made a million dollars. For a few weeks' effort you will have made more than most working a lifetime.

GARFINKLE. Go home. I don't want your money.

BEA. Why? Isn't it good enough for you?

GARFINKLE. It's good. It's just not enough.

BEA. I know a million dollars is not a great deal of money to you. It's all I have. If I had more I'd give you more. I had really hoped to appeal to whatever decent instincts you have left. I'm here to plead for my company.

GARFINKLE. Go home.

BEA. Please, Mr. Garfinkle.

GARFINKLE. I don't take money from widows and orphans. I make them money.

BEA. Before or after you put them out of business?

GARFINKLE. You're getting on my nerves. Go home.

BEA. I intend to. Before I go I'd like to know—I'd like you to tell me—how you can live with yourself?

GARFINKLE. I have no choice. No one else will.

BEA. How? How can you destroy a company . . . its people . . . for the sake of dollars you don't even need?

GARFINKLE. Because it's there.

BEA. . . . Because it's there?

GARFINKLE. What? People climb mountains—swim oceans—walk through fire—'cause it's there. This way is better. You don't get all sweated up.

BEA. There are people there. There are dreams there—

GARFINKLE. Do you want to give a speech or do you want an answer? 'Cause the answer is not complicated. It's simple. I do it for the money. I don't need the money. I want the money. Shouldn't surprise you. Since when

do needs and wants have anything to do with one another? If they did I'd be back in the Bronx and you'd be getting Yorgy his coffee up in Grimetown. You don't need the job. You need the million dollars. But you're prepared to give up what you need—a million dollars—for what you want—a stinking job. You're fucked up, lady. You're sick. Go see a psychiatrist.

BEA. You are the sick one. Don't you know that?

GARFINKLE. Why? 'Cause I know what I want and I know how to get it? Lady, I looooove money. I love money more than I love the things it can buy. And I love the things it can buy. You know why? Money is unconditional acceptance. It don't care whether I'm good or not, whether I snore or don't, which God I pray to—it still gets me as much interest in the bank as yours does. There's only three things in this world that give that kind of unconditional acceptance—dogs, donuts and money. Only money is better. It don't make you fat and it don't shit all over the living room floor.

BEA. I hope you choke on your money and die!

(She exits. GARFINKLE smiles sadly.)

GARFINKLE. How come I always bring out the best in people?

(Lights up on KATE Cross Stage.)

KATE. You bring out the best in me.

GARFINKLE. I know I do. Katie, me girl.

KATE. The Irish in me.

GARFINKLE. . . . Same thing.

KATE. What's the matter? Are you becoming melancholy on me?

GARFINKLE. Melancholy? Why would you say that? Just 'cause the Governor calls every hour . . . the unions are picketing my house . . . prayer meetings daily chant for my demise—

KATE *(Moving toward him)*. You're in the wrong profession. You should head the U.N. Nobody can bring people together like you . . . not even a chuckle? You must really be in bad shape. Feeling unloved?

GARFINKLE. Unappreciated. I'm doing the right thing. I'm taking unproductive assets and making them productive. Just following the law of free enterprise economics.

KATE. What law is that?

GARFINKLE. Survival of the fittest.

KATE. The Charles Darwin of Wall Street!

GARFINKLE *(Laughing)*. . . . I like that. The Charles Darwin of Wall Street.

KATE. Maybe they don't see it that way. Maybe they don't see it as survival of the fittest. Maybe they see it as survival of the fattest.

GARFINKLE. Aw, Katie, why are you so hard on me?

KATE. 'Cause you're not nice.

GARFINKLE. Since when do you have to be nice to be right?

KATE. You're not right. You're "What's happening." One day we'll smarten up and pass some laws and put you out of business. Ten years from now they'll be studying you at the Wharton School. They'll call it the "Garfinkle Era" and rinse out their mouths when they leave the room.

GARFINKLE. That's how you talk about family?

KATE. Family?

GARFINKLE. Immediate family. For every deal I find, you guys bring me ten. We happen to be in bed together, lady. Calling it family, that's being nice. Look at me, Kate.

KATE. I'm going to put you away, Garfinkle.

GARFINKLE. I'm not going away. They can pass all the laws they want—all they do is change the rules—they can't stop the game. I don't go away. I adapt. Look at me, Kate. Look at you. God damn it! We're the same!

KATE. We are not the same. We are not the same! We sit on opposite sides here. I like where I sit. You sit in shit.

GARFINKLE. You sit with me.

KATE. You sit alone.

GARFINKLE. Alone? Get off it, will you? We've come from "Ask not what your country can do for you" to "What's in it for me?" to "What's in it for me—today!" all in one short generation. That's why those stockholders all love me and that's why you guys all work for me. Nobody's putting a gun to anyone's head. Everybody's got their hand out.

KATE. Not everybody. Not me. Not them.

GARFINKLE. Forget them. It's about you and me, now, Kate. I'm the last thought you have when you fall asleep at night and the first when you wake in the morning. I make those juices flow and you know it.

KATE. Garfinkle, if you knew what you do to me you wouldn't brag about it.

GARFINKLE. Bullshit. And you know what makes the two of us so special? What sets us apart? We care more about the game than we do the players. That's not bad. That's smart.

KATE. That's grotesque. Garfinkle, you don't know me at all. You're not capable of knowing me. You can't see beyond your appetite.

GARFINKLE. Then what the fuck are you doing here!? You can't stay away. You don't want to stay away. Come—play with me. Be a player—not a technician. Feel the power. This is where you belong, Kate. With me. I know you. I know who you are. I like who you are. I want you, Kate.

(He reaches for her. She pulls away.)

KATE. I'm going to nail you, Garfinkle. I'm going to send you back to Wall Street with donuts up your ass and everyone's going to know how some broad wet behind the ears did you. And whatever happens from this day forward, whatever successes I achieve, none—none will be sweeter than this one!

(She exits. GARFINKLE, *a beat after the exit, yells to her.)*

GARFINKLE. You're so perfect for me! *(Turns, begins to exit.)* To be continued. In Grimetown.

(He exits. Lights up on JORGENSON *alone in his office.* BEA *enters.)*

BEA. Hey, good lookin', whatcha got cookin'. How's about cookin' something up with me?

(He smiles weakly.)

You okay?

JORGENSON. Just going over in my head what I want to say.

BEA. They're putting speakers out in the hallways. The auditorium won't fit everyone. I feel like we're Harry and Bess on election night.

JORGENSON. Harry was a better man than me. Went to sleep election night. I haven't slept good for days.

BEA. Talk to me.

JORGENSON. I'm scared, Bea. I'm scared time has passed us by. I'm scared I don't know this new environment. I'm scared what I do know doesn't count for anything any more.

BEA *(Moves behind him. Rubs his neck).* I'm not scared. I'm proud. I'm proud of the business we built. Most of all I'm proud of you. And if what we are counts for nothing anymore, that won't be our failing—it'll be theirs.

(He smiles. Squeezes her hand.)

It'll be all right. Just go out and tell the truth. Go out and give them hell, Harry.

(They remain frozen. GARFINKLE *enters. Looks at them.)*

GARFINKLE. The truth? Why don't you tell the truth, lady? The truth is Harry Truman is dead.

(Lights dim on BEA *and* JORGENSON *though they continue visible.* GARFINKLE *moves to his darkened office.* BEA *moves Downstage Center to a podium. We're at the Annual Meeting. Scene is played as if audience were the stockholders.)*

BEA. That concludes the formal aspect of our Annual Meeting. The one remaining item of business is the election of directors. Is there anyone entitled to vote who does not have a ballot? Please raise your hand. *(She looks about at the audience.)* Will the inspector of elections distribute the ballots? Please keep your hand raised so you can receive your ballot. Thank you.

(JORGENSON rises from his office and moves to lectern.)

JORGENSON. It's nice to see so many familiar faces . . . so many old friends . . . many of you I haven't seen for years. Thank you for coming and welcome to the 73rd Annual Meeting of New England Wire and Cable—the 38th of which I am addressing you as your Chief Executive.

Bill Coles, our able President, has told you about our year; what we accomplished—where we need to make further improvements—what our business goals are for next year and the years beyond.

I'd like to talk to you about something else. On this, our 73rd year, I'd like to share with you some of my thoughts concerning the vote you are about to make in the company you own.

We've had some very good years. We've had some difficult ones as well. Though the last decade has been troubling for us it's been devastating for our industry. Ten short years ago we were the twelfth largest manufacturer of wire and cable in the country, the fourth largest in New England. We're now the third largest in the country and the largest in New England.

We might not have flourished—but we survived. And we're stronger for it. I'm proud of what we accomplished.

So, we're at that point where this proud company, which has survived the death of its founder, numerous recessions, a major depression and two world wars, is in imminent danger of self-destructing this day in the town of its birth.

And there is the instrument of our destruction. I want you to see him in all his glory. Larry the Liquidator—the entrepreneur in post-industrial America—playing God with other people's money.

(GARFINKLE waves to stockholders. Sits once again.)

At least the robber barons of old left something tangible in their wake. A coal mine. A railroad. Banks. This man leaves nothing. He creates nothing. He builds nothing. He runs nothing. In his wake lies nothing but a blizzard of paper to cover the pain.

If he said, "I could run this business better." Well, that's something worth talking about. He's not saying that. He's saying, "I am going to kill you because at this particular moment in time you're worth more dead than alive."

Well, maybe that's true. But it is also true that one day this industry will turn. One day when the dollar is weaker or the yen stronger or when we finally begin to rebuild the roads, the bridges, the infrastructure of our country demand will skyrocket. And when those things happen we will be here—stronger for our ordeal— stronger for having survived. And the price of our stock will make his offer pale by comparison.

God save us if you vote to take his paltry few dollars and run. God save this country if *(Pointing to* GARFINKLE.*)* "that" is truly the wave of the future. We will then have become a nation that makes nothing but hamburgers, creates nothing but lawyers, and sells nothing but tax shelters.

And if we have come to the point in this country where we kill something because at the moment it's worth more dead than alive, then turn around and take a good look at your neighbor. You won't kill him because it's called "murder" and it's illegal. This, too, is murder, on a mass scale, only on Wall Street they call it "maximizing shareholder values" and they call it legal and they substitute dollar bills where a conscience should be.

Damn it. A business is more than the price of its stock. It is the place where we make our living, meet our friends and dream our dreams. It is, in every sense, the very fabric that binds our society together.

So let us, right now, at this meeting, say to every Garfinkle in this land, that here we build things—we don't destroy them.

Here, we care for more than the price of our stock.

Here . . . we care about people!

(JORGENSON moves from lectern back to table. BEA, COLES, and KATE stand and applaud. GARFINKLE follows JORGENSON back and as the applause dies, says to BEA, COLES and JORGENSON respectively:)

GARFINKLE. Amen . . . And Amen . . . And Amen. Say "Amen," someone, please! *(Moves to lectern in and says in a hushed tone.)* You'll excuse me. I'm not familiar with local custom . . . The way I was brought up you always said "Amen" after you heard a prayer. You hear someone praying, after he finishes, you say "Amen" and drink a little wine.

'Cause that's what you just heard—a prayer. The way I was brought up we called the particular prayer "the prayer for the dead." You just heard the prayer for the dead, and, fellow stuckholders, you didn't say "Amen" and you didn't even get to sip the wine.

What—You don't think this company is dead? Steel—you remember steel, don't you? Steel used to be an industry. Now heavy metal is a rock group.

This company is dead. Don't blame me. I didn't kill it. It was dead when I got here. It is too late for prayers, for even if the prayers were answered and a miracle occurred and the yen did this and the dollar did that and the infrastructure did the other thing, we would still be dead. Know why? Fiber-optics. New technologies. Obsolescence.

We're dead, all right. We're just not broke. And you know the surest way to go broke? Keep getting an increasing share of a shrinking market. Down the tubes. Slow but sure. You know, at one time there must have been dozens of companies making buggy whips. And I'll bet you anything the last one around was the one that made the best goddamned buggy whip you ever saw. How would you have liked to have been a stuckholder of that company?

You invested in a business. And that business is dead. Let's have the intelligence, let's have the decency, to sign the death certificate, collect the insurance and invest the money in something with a future.

Aha—But we can't, goes the prayer—we can't because we have a responsibility—a responsibility to our employees, our community . . . What will happen to them? I got two words for that—"Who cares?" Care about them? They didn't care about you. They sucked you dry. You have no responsibility to them.

For the last ten years this company has bled your money. Did this Community care? Did they ever say, "I know things are tough. We'll lower your taxes, reduce water and sewer?" Check it out. We're paying twice what we paid ten years ago. And the mayor is making twice what he made ten years ago. And our devoted employees, after taking no increases for three years, are still making twice what they made ten years ago. And our stock is one-sixth what it was ten years ago.

Who cares? I'll tell you—me! I'm not your best friend—I'm your only friend. I care about you in the only way that matters in business. I don't make anything? I'm making you money. And, lest we forget, that's the only reason any of you became stuckholders in the first place. To make money. You don't care if they manufacture wire and cable, fry chicken, or grow tangerines. You want to make money. I'm making you money. I'm the only friend you got.

Take that money. Invest it somewhere else. Maybe—maybe you'll get lucky and it will be used productively—and if it is—you'll create more jobs and provide a service for the economy and—God forbid—even make a few bucks for yourself. Let the Government and the Mayor and the unions worry about what you paid them to worry about. And if anyone asks, tell them you gave at the plant.

And it pleases me that I'm called "Larry the Liquidator." You know why, fellow stuckholders? Because at my funeral you'll leave with a smile on your face . . . and a few bucks in your pocket. Now, that's a funeral worth having. *(Breathing heavily, GARFINKLE pauses a beat and sits.)*

BEA. . . . Will the inspector of elections please collect the ballots.

(The lights dim. Players are now in shadows. COLES rises, moves slowly Center Stage.)

COLES. That's what happened. That's it. All of it.

BEA. Is there anyone entitled to vote who has not turned in a ballot?

COLES. It's happening everywhere. No one is immune.

BEA. To retain the present Board: 1,741,-416.

COLES. I think the old man gave the speech of his life. I can't think how he could have said it better.

BEA. For the opposition slate: 2,219,901.

COLES. What do we do? Pass another law. There's already a law against murder. All he did was supply the weapon.

BEA. Not voting: 176,111.

COLES. Garfinkle won in a landslide. Didn't even need my votes. Cost me the second half million, but I feel good about that. I feel better about getting the first half million. I feel best it cost him money he didn't have to spend. That's the only kind of lasting satisfaction you get when you deal with people like him.

BEA. Mr. Garfinkle, your slate is elected.

COLES. He had the nerve to ask me to stay on while he dismembered the company. Even offered me a raise. I said "no," of course. There's a point at which we all draw the line.

JORGENSON *(In his office)*. We can't leave now. I have to tell the men.

BEA. They know.

JORGENSON. . . . Already?

BEA. Let's go home. There'll be time tomorrow.

JORGENSON. Even . . . Ossie voted for him. *(He exits. She remains.)*

COLES. He didn't take it well. From me . . . I think he expected it. Ossie . . . kind of threw him. With all his money you'd think he would have left. Gone somewhere nice . . . somewhere warm. He didn't. Stayed right here. Died almost two years later. Left more than thirty million.

BEA. Jorgy, you only made one mistake in your life. You lived two years too long.

COLES. Bea became executor of his estate. Bought the land the plant used to sit on. Put up a kind of . . . Employee Retraining Center—Actually placed a few people . . . about a hundred of the twelve hundred or so that worked there when the plant closed. It wasn't easy retraining middle-aged men who are used to working with their hands. Some went to work for McDonald's . . . or as night watchmen.

Me? I didn't do too badly. I moved back to Florida. Run a mid-sized division for a nationally known food processor. I won't ever run the company . . . but I'm financially secure. And you can't beat the weather.

(Lights up on GARFINKLE.*)*

GARFINKLE. I'm sorry, Kate. I'm surprised myself. See, you do bring out the best in me . . . Come—Ride back to New York with me . . . You worried it wouldn't look right? Don't. It's the perfect ending . . . Come.

(She enters the playing area. Stops. Looks at him. He extends his arms to her, beckoning.)

Come.

(She doesn't move.)

I got donuts in the car.

COLES. Kate and Garfinkle? Well, three months later, which is as soon as she could work things out at Morgan, Stanley, she went to work for him.

*(*KATE *moves next to a seated* GARFINKLE *in his office.)*

She was very good. Three months after that she became his partner . . .

(Her arm moves to the back of GARFINKLE*'s chair.)*

. . . then his wife.

(Her arm is around his shoulder. GARFINKLE *beams.* BEA *exits.)*

They have two kids. Set of twins. Call them their "little bull and little bear." Friend of mine saw them the other day . . . *(Moves to exit.)* Said he never saw them happier. *(Exits.)*

Curtain

Driving Miss Daisy

ALFRED UHRY

FOR MAMA AND WILL—R.I.P.

Presented at Playwrights Horizons (Andre Bishop, Artistic Director; Paul S. Daniels, Executive Director) in New York City on April 15, 1987. The cast, in order of appearance, was as follows:

DAISY WERTHAN Dana Ivey
BOOLIE WERTHAN Ray Gill
HOKE COLEBURN Morgan Freeman

Directed by Ron Lagomarsino
Setting design by Thomas Lynch
Costumes by Michael Krass
Lighting by Ken Tabachnick
Incidental music by Robert Waldman
Press Representative: Bob Ullman
Production Manager: Carl Mulert
Production Stage Manager: Anne Marie Kuehling

Driving Miss Daisy has touched the hearts of almost everyone who has seen or read it. The play earned a Pulitizer Prize for drama in 1988 for playwright Alfred Uhry, and Obie Awards for Morgan Freemen and Dana Ivey, who created the roles of Hoke and Daisy. It also earned two Outer Critics Circle Awards. The film version received 1989 Golden Globe Awards for Best Comedy, Best Actor (Morgan Freeman), and Best Actress (Jessica Tandy), and was nominated for nine Academy Awards in 1990, winning Best Picture, Best Actress, and Best Screenplay Adaptation.

Driving Miss Daisy was originally presented by Playwrights Horizons, which transferred it to the John Houseman Theatre. It has since been produced all over the United States and in Europe, Brazil, South Africa, Israel, Canada, and Russia. No other contemporary play has been performed as extensively and by so many notable performers. In addition to Morgan Freeman, Hoke has been played by Earle Hyman, Bill Cobbs (who won Chicago's 1988 Joseph Jefferson Award for Best Actor in a Drama), and Brock Peters. Famous Daisys include Frances Sternhagen, Julie Harris, Dorothy Loudon, Charlotte Rae, and Wendy Hiller.

Driving Miss Daisy is a play of charm and humor, offering insightful glimpses into the life of a southern matriarch from 1948 to 1973. Capturing an intimate portrait of the South and of the assimilation of a Jewish family into WASP society, the play sketches an entire era in the American civil rights movement and depicts, on a universally understandable level, issues of growing old, dignity, prejudice, love, and humanity.

Daisy is a stubborn, crotchety, prejudiced elderly woman who can no longer drive by herself and is forced to allow herself to be driven by a black chauffeur, Hoke, who has some prejudices of his own. Over the years, a friendship develops in which each grows to respect and love the other. While the play is endearing, humorous, and poignant, it is never sentimental; its emphasis is on the strengths of its main characters.

That *Driving Miss Daisy* came to be written at all was fortunate, for Uhry was just about to abandon the theatre—to go back into teaching—when he began to write this play. For twenty-five years, he had worked in the theatre without financial success. "I had a family. Responsibilities. I realized I could have earned more in one week writing TV than I had made in four years in the theatre. But I decided to give it one last stab." Uhry was born in Atlanta and comes from a long line of German Jews who settled in the South before the Civil War. "I grew up in Atlanta and my mother had a black chauffeur. The character in my play is very much based on him."

The first musical Uhry saw as a child, *Carousel,* influenced him greatly. "When I was in the theatre, I was transformed. I had to find a way to do it too." After graduating from Brown University in 1958, he married and came to New York to become a lyricist. He worked with his friend and associate Robert Waldman for more than twenty-five years and attained a moderate success. "He was going to be Richard Rodgers and I was going to be Oscar Hammerstein III." From 1960 to 1962, the two worked in the song shop of Broadway composer Frank Loesser. "It was a marvelous experience," Uhry recalls, "because he taught you how to be succinct, to use the exact word." Uhry and Waldman eventually collaborated on *Here's Where I Belong,* a musical version of *East of Eden* that flopped on Broadway in 1968. An adaptation of Eudora Welty's *The Robber Bridegroom* proved more successful, earning both Tony Award and Drama Desk nominations in 1976. Other, less successful, musicals included adaptations of *An Italian Straw Hat, Little Johnny Jones,* and *Funny Face,* and an original, *Swing.* In 1984, Uhry spent two months at Northwestern University with director Gerald Freedman working on a musical called *America's Sweetheart,* about Al Capone. It was at this time that he decided to leave the theatre. Then came *Driving Miss Daisy* and "overnight" success.

Uhry's screenwriting, aside from his adaptation of *Driving Miss Daisy,* includes dialogue for the film *Mystic Pizza* and the screenplay for *Rich in Love,* based on a book by Josephine Humphries. He has recently written an original screenplay, *Charmed,* about a female teacher in a progressive New York private school, and is working on a remake of *The Bishop's Wife,* the 1947 film that starred Cary Grant, Loretta Young, and David Niven.

"A lot of things have been attributed to my play that I never consciously put there," Uhry says. "I just meant to write the truth about these two people and what happens to them. I didn't have any big messages. . . . All I did was to show the way it was. I think there's a lot to be learned from the past. . . . I do know that the story of Hoke and Miss Daisy pretty much parallels race relations in Atlanta during those years. I knew I was dealing with the truth."

This play takes place from 1948 to 1973, mostly in Atlanta, Georgia. There are many locales. The scenery is meant to be simple and evocative. The action shifts frequently and, I hope, fluidly.

CAST OF CHARACTERS

DAISY WERTHAN, a widow (age 72–97)
HOKE COLEBURN, her chauffeur (age 60–85)
BOOLIE WERTHAN, her son (age 40–65)

In the dark we hear a car ignition turn on, and then a horrible crash. Bangs and booms and wood splintering. When the noise is very loud, it stops suddenly and the lights come up on DAISY WER-THAN's *living room, or a portion thereof.* DAISY, *age 72, is wearing a summer dress and high heeled shoes. Her hair, her clothes, her walk, everything about her suggests bristle and feist and high energy. She appears to be in excellent health. Her son,* BOOLIE WERTHAN, *40, is a businessman, Junior Chamber of Commerce style. He has a strong, capable air. The Werthans are Jewish, but they have strong Atlanta accents.*

DAISY. No!
BOOLIE. Mama!
DAISY. No!
BOOLIE. Mama!
DAISY. I said no, Boolie, and that's the end of it.
BOOLIE. It's a miracle you're not laying in Emory Hospital—or decked out at the funeral home. Look at you! You didn't even break your glasses.
DAISY. It was the car's fault.
BOOLIE. Mama, the car didn't just back over the driveway and land on the Pollard's garage all by itself. You had it in the wrong gear.
DAISY. I did not!
BOOLIE. You put it in reverse instead of drive. The police report shows that.
DAISY. You should have let me keep my La Salle.
BOOLIE. Your La Salle was eight years old.
DAISY. I don't care. It never would have behaved this way. And you know it.
BOOLIE. Mama, cars, don't behave. They are behaved upon. The fact is you, all by yourself, demolished that Packard.
DAISY. Think what you want. I know the truth.
BOOLIE. The truth is you shouldn't be allowed to drive a car any more.

DAISY. No.
BOOLIE. Mama, we are just going to have to hire somebody to drive you.
DAISY. No *we* are not. This is my business.
BOOLIE. Your insurance policy is written so that they are going to have to give you a brand new car.
DAISY. Not another Packard, I hope.
BOOLIE. Lord Almighty! Don't you see what I'm saying?
DAISY. Quit talking so ugly to your mother.
BOOLIE. Mama, you are seventy-two years old and you just cost the insurance company twenty-seven hundred dollars. You are a terrible risk. Nobody is going to issue you a policy after this.
DAISY. You're just saying that to be hateful.
BOOLIE. O.K. Yes. Yes I am. I'm making it all up. Every insurance company in America is lined up in the driveway waving their fountain pens and falling all over themselves to get you to sign on. Everybody wants Daisy Werthan, the only woman in the history of driving to demolish a three week old Packard, a two car garage and a free standing tool shed in one fell swoop!
DAISY. You talk so foolish sometimes, Boolie.
BOOLIE. And even if you could get a policy somewhere, it wouldn't be safe. I'd worry all the time. Look at how many of your friends have men to drive them. Miss Ida Jacobs, Miss Ethel Hess, Aunt Nonie—
DAISY. They're all rich.
BOOLIE. Daddy left you plenty enough for this. I'll do the interviewing at the plant. Oscar in the freight elevator knows every colored man in Atlanta worth talking about. I'm sure in two weeks time I can find you somebody perfectly—
DAISY. No!
BOOLIE. You won't even have to do anything, Mama. I told you. I'll do all the interviewing, all the reference checking, all the—
DAISY. No. Now stop running your mouth! I am seventy-two years old as you so gallantly reminded me and I am a widow, but unless they rewrote the Constitution and didn't tell me, I still have rights. And one of my rights is the right to invite who I want—not who you want—into my house. You do accept the fact that this is my house? What I do not want—and absolutely will not have is some— *(She gropes for a bad enough word.)* some chauffeur sitting in my kitchen, gob-

bling my food, running up my phone bill. Oh, I hate all that in my house!

BOOLIE. You have Idella.

DAISY. Idella is different. She's been coming to me three times a week since you were in the eighth grade and we know how to stay out of each other's way. And even so there are nicks and chips in most of my wedding china and I've seen her throw silver forks in the garbage more than once.

BOOLIE. Do you think Idella has a vendetta against your silverware?

DAISY. Stop being sassy. You know what I mean. I was brought up to do for myself. On Forsyth Street we couldn't afford them and we did for ourselves. That's still the best way, if you ask me.

BOOLIE. Them! You sound like Governor Talmadge.

DAISY. Why, Boolie! What a thing to say! I'm not prejudiced! Aren't you ashamed?

BOOLIE. I've got to go home. Florine'll be having a fit.

DAISY. Y'all must have plans tonight.

BOOLIE. Going to the Ansleys for a dinner party.

DAISY. I see.

BOOLIE. You see what?

DAISY. The Ansleys. I'm sure Florine bought another new dress. This is her idea of heaven on earth, isn't it?

BOOLIE. What?

DAISY. Socializing with Episcopalians.

BOOLIE. You're a doodle, Mama. I guess Aunt Nonie can run you anywhere you need to go for the time being.

DAISY. I'll be fine.

BOOLIE. I'll stop by tomorrow evening.

DAISY. How do you know I'll be here? I'm certainly not dependent on you for company.

BOOLIE. Fine. I'll call first. And I still intend to interview colored men.

DAISY. No!

BOOLIE. Mama!

DAISY (Singing to end discussion). After the ball is over.
After the break of morn
After the dancers leaving
After the stars are gone
Many a heart is aching
If you could read them all—

(Lights fade on her as she sings and come up on BOOLIE at his desk at the Werthan Company. He sits at a desk piled with papers, and speaks into an intercom.)

BOOLIE. O.K., Miss McClatchey. Send him

on in. (He continues working at his desk. HOKE COLEBURN enters, a black man of about 60, dressed in a somewhat shiny suit and carrying a fedora, a man clearly down on his luck but anxious to keep up appearances.) Yes, Hoke, isn't it?

HOKE. Yassuh. Hoke Coleburn.

BOOLIE. Have a seat there. I've got to sign these letters. I don't want Miss McClatchey fussing at me.

HOKE. Keep right on with it. I got all the time in the worl'.

BOOLIE. I see. How long you been out of work?

HOKE. Since back befo' las' November.

BOOLIE. Long time.

HOKE. Well, Mist' Werthan, you try bein' me and looking for work. They hirin' young if they hirin' colored, an' they ain' even hirin' much young, seems like. (BOOLIE is involved with his paperwork.) Mist' Werthan? Y'all people Jewish, ain' you?

BOOLIE. Yes we are. Why do you ask?

HOKE. I'd druther drive for Jews. People always talkin' bout they stingy and they cheap, but don' say none of that 'roun' me.

BOOLIE. Good to know you feel that way. Now, tell me where you worked before.

HOKE. Yassuh. That what I'm gettin' at. One time I workin' for this woman over near Little Five Points. What was that woman's name? I forget. Anyway, she president of the Ladies Auxilliary over yonder to the Ponce De Leon Baptist Church and seem like she always bringing up God and Jesus and do unto others. You know what I'm talkin' bout?

BOOLIE. I'm not sure. Go on.

HOKE. Well, one day, Mist' Werthan, one day that woman say to me, she say "Hoke, come on back in the back wid me. I got something for you." And we go on back yonder and, Lawd have mercy, she have all these old shirts and collars be on the bed, yellow, you know, and nasty like they been stuck off in a chiffarobe and forgot about. Thass' right. And she say "Ain' they nice? They b'long to my daddy befo' he pass and we fixin' to sell 'em to you for twenty five cent apiece."

BOOLIE. What was her name?

HOKE. Thass' what I'm thinkin'. What WAS that woman's name? Anyway, as I was goin' on to say, any fool see the whole bunch of them collars and shirts together ain' worth a nickel! Them's the people das callin' Jews cheap! So I say "Yassum, I think about it" and I get me another job fas' as I can.

BOOLIE. Where was that?

HOKE. Mist' Harold Stone, Jewish gentleman jes' like you. Judge, live over yonder on Lullwater Road.

BOOLIE. I knew Judge Stone.

HOKE. You doan' say! He done give me this suit when he finish wid it. An' this necktie too.

BOOLIE. You drove for Judge Stone?

HOKE. Seven years to the day nearabout. An' I be there still if he din' die, and Miz Stone decide to close up the house and move to her people in Savannah. And she say "Come on down to Savannah wid' me, Hoke." Cause my wife dead by then and I say "No thank you." I didn' want to leave my grandbabies and I don' get along with that Geechee trash they got down there.

BOOLIE. Judge Stone was a friend of my father's.

HOKE. You doan' mean! Oscar say you need a driver for yo' family. What I be doin'? Runnin' yo' children to school and yo' wife to the beauty parlor and like dat?

BOOLIE. I don't have any children. But tell me—

HOKE. Thass' a shame! My daughter bes' thing ever happen to me. But you young yet. I wouldn't worry none.

BOOLIE. I won't. Thank you. Did you have a job after Judge Stone?

HOKE. I drove a milk truck for the Avondale Dairy thru the whole war—the one jes' was.

BOOLIE. Hoke, what I'm looking for is somebody to drive my mother around.

HOKE. Excuse me for askin', but how come she ain' hire fo' herseff?

BOOLIE. Well, it's a delicate situation.

HOKE. Mmmm Hmm. She done gone 'roun' the bend a little? That'll happen when they get on.

BOOLIE. Oh no. Nothing like that. She's all there. Too much there is the problem. It just isn't safe for her to drive any more. She knows it, but she won't admit it. I'll be frank with you. I'm a little desperate.

HOKE. I know what you mean 'bout dat. Once I was outta work my wife said to me "Oooooh, Hoke, you ain' gon get noun nother job." And I say "What you talkin' bout, woman?" And the very next week I go to work for that woman in Little Five Points. Cahill! Ms. Frances Cahill. And then I go to Judge Stone and they the reason I happy to hear you Jews.

BOOLIE. Hoke, I want you to understand, my mother is a little high-strung. She doesn't want anybody driving her. But the fact is you'd be working for me. She can say anything she likes but she can't fire you. You understand?

HOKE. Sho' I do. Don't worry none about it. I hold on no matter what way she run me. When I nothin' but a little boy down there on the farm above Macon, I use to wrastle hogs to the ground at killin' time, and ain' no hog get away from me yet.

BOOLIE. How does twenty dollars a week sound?

HOKE. Soun' like you got yo' Mama a chauffeur. *(Lights fade on them and come up on* DAISY *who enters her living room with the morning paper. She reads with interest.* HOKE *enters the living room. He carries a chauffeur's cap instead of his hat.* DAISY*'s concentration on the paper becomes fierce when she senses* HOKE*'s presence.)* Mornin', Miz Daisy.

DAISY. Good morning.

HOKE. Right cool in the night, wadn' it?

DAISY. I wouldn't know. I was asleep.

HOKE. Yassum. What yo plans today?

DAISY. That's my business.

HOKE. You right about dat. Idella say we runnin' outa coffee and Dutch Cleanser.

DAISY. We?

HOKE. She say we low on silver polish too.

DAISY. Thank you. I will go to the Piggly Wiggly on the trolley this afternoon.

HOKE. Now, Miz Daisy, how come you doan' let me carry you?

DAISY. No thank you.

HOKE. Aint that what Mist' Werthan hire me for?

DAISY. That's his problem.

HOKE. All right den. I find something to do. I tend yo zinnias.

DAISY. Leave my flower bed alone.

HOKE. Yassum. You got a nice place back beyond the garage ain' doin' nothin' but sittin' there. I could put you in some butterbeans and some tomatoes and even some Irish potatoes could we get some ones with good eyes.

DAISY. If I want a vegetable garden, I'll plant it for myself.

HOKE. Well, I go out and set in the kitchen, then, like I been doin' all week.

DAISY. Don't talk to Idella. She has work to do.

HOKE. Nome. I jes sit there till five o'clock.

DAISY. That's your affair.

HOKE. Seem a shame, do. That fine Oldsmobile settin out there in the garage. Ain't move a inch from when Mist' Werthan rode it over here from Mitchell Motors. Only got nineteen miles on it. Seem like that insurance company give you a whole new car for nothin'.

DAISY. That's your opinion.

HOKE. Yassum. And my other opinion is a fine rich Jewish lady like you doan b'long draggin' up the steps of no bus, luggin' no grocery store bags. I come alone and carry them fo' you.

DAISY. I don't need you. I don't want you. And I don't like you saying I'm rich.

HOKE. I won' say it, then.

DAISY. Is that what you and Idella talk about in the kitchen? Oh, I hate this! I hate being discussed behind my back in my own house! I was born on Forsyth Street and, believe you me, I knew the value of a penny. My brother Manny brought home a white cat one day and Papa said we couldn't keep it because we couldn't afford to feed it. My sisters saved up money so I could go to school and be a teacher. We didn't have anything!

HOKE. Yassum, but look like you doin' all right now.

DAISY. And I've ridden the trolley with groceries plenty of times!

HOKE. Yassum, but I feel bad takin' Mist' Werthan's money for doin' nothin'. You understand? *(She cut him off in the speech.)*

DAISY. How much does he pay you?

HOKE. That between me and him, Miz Daisy.

DAISY. Anything over seven dollars a week is robbery. Highway robbery!

HOKE. Specially when I doan do nothin' but set on a stool in the kitchen all day long. Tell you what, while you goin on the trolley to the Piggly Wiggly, I hose down yo' front steps. *(DAISY is putting on her hat.)*

DAISY. All right.

HOKE. All right I hose yo' steps?

DAISY. All right the Piggly Wiggly. And then home. Nowhere else.

HOKE. Yassum.

DAISY. Wait. You don't know how to run the Oldsmobile!

HOKE. Miz Daisy, a gear shift like a third arm to me. Anyway, thissun automatic. Any fool can run it.

DAISY. Any fool but me, apparently.

HOKE. Ain' no need to be so hard on yoseff now. You cain' drive but you probably do alota things I cain' do. It all work out.

DAISY *(Calling offstage)*. I'm gone to the market, Idella.

HOKE *(Also calling)*. And I right behind her! *(HOKE puts on his cap and helps DAISY into the car. He sits at the wheel and backs the car down the driveway. DAISY, in the rear, is in full bristle.)* I love a new car smell. Doan' you? *(DAISY slides over to the other side of the seat.)*

DAISY. I'm nobody's fool, Hoke.

HOKE. Nome.

DAISY. I can see the speedometer as well as you can.

HOKE. I see dat.

DAISY. My husband taught me how to run a car.

HOKE. Yassum.

DAISY. I still remember everything he said. So don't you even think for a second that you can—Wait! You're speeding! I see it!

HOKE. We ain' goin' but nineteen miles an hour.

DAISY. I like to go under the speed limit.

HOKE. Speed limit thirty-five here.

DAISY. The slower you go, the more you save on gas. My husband told me that.

HOKE. We barely movin'. Might as well walk to the Piggly Wiggly.

DAISY. Is this your car?

HOKE. Nome.

DAISY. Do you pay for the gas?

HOKE. Nome.

DAISY. All right then. My fine son may think I'm losing my abilities, but I am still in control of what goes on in my car. Where are you going?

HOKE. To the grocery store.

DAISY. Then why didn't you turn on Highland Avenue?

HOKE. Piggly Wiggly ain' on Highland Avenue. It on Euclid, down there near—

DAISY. I know where it is and I want to go to it the way I always go. On Highland Avenue.

HOKE. That three blocks out of the way, Miz Daisy.

DAISY. Go back! Go back this minute!

HOKE. We in the wrong lane! I cain' jes—

DAISY. Go back I said! If you don't, I'll get out of this car and walk!

HOKE. We movin'! You cain' open the do'!

DAISY. This is wrong! Where are you taking me?

HOKE. The sto'.

DAISY. This is wrong. You have to go back to Highland Avenue!

HOKE. Mmmm Hmmmm.

DAISY. I've been driving to the Piggly Wiggly since the day they put it up and opened it for business. This isn't the way! Go back! Go back this minute!

HOKE. Yonder the Piggly Wiggly.

DAISY. Get ready to turn now.

HOKE. Yassum.

DAISY. Look out! There's a little boy behind that shopping cart!

HOKE. I see dat.

DAISY. Pull in next to the blue car.

HOKE. We closer to the do' right here.

DAISY. Next to the blue car! I don't park in the sun! It fades the upholstery.

HOKE. Yassum. *(He pulls in, and gets out as* DAISY *springs out of the back seat.)*

DAISY. Wait a minute. Give me the car keys.

HOKE. Yassum.

DAISY. Stay right here by the car. And you don't have to tell everybody my business.

HOKE. Nome. Don' forget the Dutch Cleanser now. *(She fixes him with a look meant to kill and exits.* HOKE *waits by the car for a minute, then hurries to the phone booth at the corner.)* Hello? Miz McClatchey? Hoke Coleburn here. Can I speak to him? *(Pause.)* Mornin sir, Mist' Werthan. Guess where I'm at? I'm at dishere phone booth on Euclid Avenue right next to the Piggly Wiggly. I jes drove yo' Mama to the market. *(Pause.)* She flap a little on the way. But she all right. She in the store. Uh oh. Miz Daisy look out the store window and doan' see me, she liable to throw a fit right there by the checkout. *(Pause.)* Yassuh, only took six days. Same time it take the Lawd to make the worl'. *(Lights out on him. We hear a* CHOIR *singing.)*

CHOIR.

May the words of my mouth
  And the meditations of my heart
  Be acceptable in Thy sight, O Lord
  My strength and my redeemer. Amen.

(Light up on HOKE *waiting by the car, looking at a newspaper.* DAISY *enters in a different hat and a fur piece.)*

HOKE. How yo' Temple this mornin', Miz Daisy?

DAISY. Why are you here?

HOKE. I bring you to de Temple like you tell me. *(He is helping her into the car.)*

DAISY. I can get myself in. Just go. *(She makes a tight little social smile and a wave out the window.)* Hurry up out of here!

(HOKE starts up the car.)

HOKE. Yassum.

DAISY. I didn't say speed. I said get me away from here.

HOKE. Somethin' wrong back yonder?

DAISY. No.

HOKE. Somethin' I done?

DAISY. No. *(A beat.)* Yes.

HOKE. I ain' done nothin'!

DAISY. You had the car right in front of the front door of the Temple! Like I was Queen of Romania! Everybody saw you! Didn't I tell you to wait for me in the back?

HOKE. I jes tryin' to be nice. They two other chauffeurs right behind me.

DAISY. You made me look like a fool. A g.d. fool!

HOKE. Lawd knows you ain' no fool, Miz Daisy.

DAISY. Slow down. Miriam and Beulah and them, I could see what they were thinking when we came out of services.

HOKE. What that?

DAISY. That I'm trying to pretend I'm rich.

HOKE. You is rich, Miz Daisy!

DAISY. No I'm not! And nobody can ever say I put on airs. On Forsyth Street we only had meat once a week. We made a meal off of grits and gravy. I taught the fifth grade at the Crew Street School! I did without plenty of times, I can tell you.

HOKE. And now you doin' with. What so terrible in that?

DAISY. You! Why do I talk to you? You don't understand me.

HOKE. Nome, I don't. I truly don't. Cause if I ever was to get ahold of what you got I be shakin' it around for everybody in the world to see.

DAISY. That's vulgar. Don't talk to me! *(*HOKE *mutters something under his breath.)* What? What did you say? I heard that!

HOKE. Miz Daisy, you needs a chauffeur and Lawd know, I needs a job. Let's jes leave it at dat. *(Light out on them and up on* BOOLIE, *in his shirtsleeves. He has a phone to his ear.)*

BOOLIE. Good morning, Mama. What's the matter? *(Pause.)* What? Mama, you're talking so fast I . . . What? All right. All right. I'll come by on my way to work. I'll be there as soon as I can. *(Light out on him and up on* DAISY, *pacing around her house in a winter bathrobe.* BOOLIE *enters in a topcoat and scarf.)* I didn't expect to find you in one piece.

DAISY. I wanted you to be here when he comes. I wanted you to hear it for yourself.

BOOLIE. Hear what? What is going on?

DAISY. He's stealing from me!

BOOLIE. Hoke? Are you sure?

DAISY. I don't make empty accusations. I have proof!

BOOLIE. What proof?

DAISY. This! *(She triumphantly pulls an empty can of salmon out of her robe pocket.)* I caught him red handed! I found this hidden in the garbage pail under some coffee grounds.

BOOLIE. You mean he stole a can of salmon?

DAISY. Here it is! Oh I knew. I knew something was funny. They all take things, you know. So I counted.

BOOLIE. You counted?

DAISY. The silverware first and the linen dinner napkins and then I went into the pantry. I turned on the light and the first thing that caught my eye was a hole behind the corned beef. And I knew right away. There were only eight cans of salmon. I had nine. Three for a dollar on sale.

BOOLIE. Very clever, Mama. You made me miss my breakfast and be late for a meeting at the bank for a thirty-three cent can of salmon. *(He jams his hand in his pocket and pulls out some bills.)* Here! You want thirty-three cents? Here's a dollar! Here's ten dollars! Buy a pantry full of salmon!

DAISY. Why, Boolie! The idea! Waving money at me like I don't know what! I don't want the money. I want my things!

BOOLIE. One can of salmon?

DAISY. It was mine. I bought it and I put it there and he went into my pantry and took it and he never said a word. I leave him plenty of food every day and I always tell him exactly what it is. They are like having little children in the house. They want something so they just take it. Not a smidgin of manners. No conscience. He'll never admit this. "Nome," he'll say. "I doan know nothin' bout that." And I don't like it! I don't like living this way! I have no privacy.

BOOLIE. Mama!

DAISY. Go ahead. Defend him. You always do.

BOOLIE. All right. I give up. You want to drive yourself again, you just go ahead and arrange it with the insurance company. Take your blessed trolley. Buy yourself a taxicab. Anything you want. Just leave me out of it.

DAISY. Boolie ... *(HOKE enters in an overcoat.)*

HOKE. Mornin, Miz Daisy. I b'leve it fixin' to clear up. S'cuse me, I didn't know you was here, Mist' Werthan.

BOOLIE. Hoke, I think we have to have a talk.

HOKE. Jes' a minute. Lemme put my coat away. I be right back. *(He pulls a brown paper bag out of his overcoat.)* Oh, Miz Daisy. Yestiddy when you out with yo' sister I ate a can o' your salmon. I know you say eat the leff over pork chops, but they stiff. Here, I done buy you another can. You want me to put it in the pantry fo you?

DAISY. Yes. Thank you, Hoke.

HOKE. I'll be right wit you, Mist' Werthan. *(HOKE exits. DAISY looks at the empty can in her hand.)*

DAISY *(Trying for dignity)*. I've got to get dressed now. Goodbye, son. *(She pecks his cheek and exits. Lights out on him. We hear sounds of birds twittering. Lights come up brightly hot sun. DAISY, in light dress, is kneeling, a trowel in her hand, working by a gravestone. HOKE, jacket in hand, sleeves rolled up, stands nearby.)*

HOKE. I jess thinkin', Miz Daisy. We bin out heah to the cemetary three times dis mont already and ain' even the twentieth yet.

DAISY. It's good to come in nice weather.

HOKE. Yassum. Mist' Sig's grave mighty well tended. I b'leve you the best widow in the state of Georgia.

DAISY. Boolie's always pestering me to let the staff out here tend to this plot. Perpetual care they call it.

HOKE. Doan' you do it. It right to have somebody from the family lookin' after you.

DAISY. I'll certainly never have that. Boolie will have me in perpetual care before I'm cold.

HOKE. Come on now, Miz Daisy.

DAISY. Hoke, run back to the car and get that pot of azaleas for me and set it on Leo Bauer's grave.

HOKE. Miz Rose Bauer's husband?

DAISY. That's right. She asked me to bring it out here for her. She's not very good about coming. And I believe today would've been Leo's birthday.

HOKE. Yassum. Where the grave at?

DAISY. I'm not exactly sure. But I know it's over that way on the other side of the weeping cherry. You'll see the headstone. Bauer.

HOKE. Yassum.

DAISY. What's the matter?

HOKE. Nothin' the matter. *(He exits. She works with her trowel. In a moment HOKE returns with flowers.)* Miz Daisy ...

DAISY. I told you it's over on the other side of the weeping cherry. It says Bauer on the headstone.

HOKE. How'd that look?

DAISY. What are you talking about?

HOKE *(Deeply embarrassed)*. I'm talkin' bout I cain' read.

DAISY. What?

HOKE. I cain' read.

DAISY. That's ridiculous. Anybody can read.

HOKE. Nome. Not me.

DAISY. Then how come I see you looking at the paper all the time?

HOKE. That's it. Jes' lookin'. I dope out what's happening from the pictures.

DAISY. You know your letters, don't you?

HOKE. My ABC's? Yassum, pretty good. I jes' cain' read.

DAISY. Stop saying that. It's making me mad. If you know your letters then you can read. You just don't know you can read. I taught some of the stupidest children God ever put on the face of this earth and all of them could read enough to find a name on a tombstone. The name is Bauer. Buh buh buh buh Bauer. What does that buh letter sound like?

HOKE. Sound like a B.

DAISY. Of course. Buh Bauer. Er er er ere er. BauER. That's the last part. What letter sounds like er?

HOKE. R?

DAISY. So the first letter is a—

HOKE. B.

DAISY. And the last letter is an—

HOKE. R.

DAISY. B-R. B-R. B-R. Brr. Brr. Brr. It even sounds like Bauer, doesn't it?

HOKE. Sho' do, Miz Daisy. Thass it?

DAISY. That's it. Now go over there like I told you in the first place and look for a headstone with a B at the beginning and an R at the end and that will be Bauer.

HOKE. We ain' gon' worry 'bout what come 'n the middle?

DAISY. Not right now. This will be enough for you to find it. Go on now.

HOKE. Yassum.

DAISY. And don't come back here telling me you can't do it. You can.

HOKE. Miz Daisy . . .

DAISY. What now?

HOKE. I 'preciate this, Miz Daisy.

DAISY. Don't be ridiculous! I didn't do anything. Now would you please hurry up? I'm burning up out here. *(Light goes out on them and in the dark we hear Eartha Kitt singing "Santa Baby."* Light up on* BOOLIE. *He wears a tweed*

*See Special Note on copyright page.

jacket, red vest, holly in his lapel. He is on the phone.)

BOOLIE. Mama? Merry Christmas. Listen, do Florine a favor, all right? She's having a fit and the grocery store is closed today. You got a package of coconut in your pantry? Would you bring it when you come? *(He calls offstage.)* Hey, honey! Your ambrosia's saved! Mama's got the coconut! *(Back into the phone.)* Many thanks. See you anon, Mama. Ho ho ho. *(Light up on* DAISY *and* HOKE *in the car and out on* BOOLIE. DAISY *is not in a festive mood.)*

HOKE. Ooooooh at them lit-up decorations!

DAISY. Everybody's giving the Georgia Power Company a Merry Christmas.

HOKE. Miz Florine's got 'em all beat with the lights.

DAISY. She makes an ass out of herself every year.

HOKE *(Loving it)*. Yassum.

DAISY. She always has to go and put a wreath in every window she's got.

HOKE. Mmm Hmmm.

DAISY. And that silly Santa Claus winking on the front door!

HOKE. I bet she have the biggest tree in Atlanta. Where she get 'em so large?

DAISY. Absurd. If I had a nose like Florine I wouldn't go around saying Merry Christmas to anybody.

HOKE. I enjoy Christmas at they house.

DAISY. I don't wonder. You're the only Christian in the place!

HOKE. 'Cept they got that new cook.

DAISY. Florine never could keep help. Of course it's none of my affair.

HOKE. Nome.

DAISY. Too much running around. The Garden Club this and the Junior League that! As if any one of them would ever give her the time of day! But she'd die before she'd fix a glass of ice tea for the Temple Sisterhood!

HOKE. Yassum. You right.

DAISY. I just hope she doesn't take it in her head to sing this year. *(She imitates.)* Glo-o-o-o-o-o-o-o-o-o-o-o-o-o-oriaaaa! She sounds like she has a bone stuck in her throat.

HOKE. You done say a mouthful, Miz Daisy.

DAISY. You didn't have to come. Boolie would've run me out.

HOKE. I know that.

DAISY. Then why did you?

HOKE. That my business, Miz Daisy. *(He turns into a driveway and stops the car.)* Well,

looka' there! Miz Florine done put a Rudolph Reindeer in the dogwood tree.

DAISY. If her grandfather, old man Freitag,
could see this! What is it you say? I bet he'd
jump up out of his grave and snatch her
baldheaded! *(HOKE opens the door for DAISY.)*
Wait a minute. *(She takes a small package
wrapped in brown paper from her purse.)* This
isn't a Christmas present.

HOKE. Nome.

DAISY. You know I don't give Christmas
presents.

HOKE. I sho' do.

DAISY. I just happened to run across it this
morning. Open it up.

HOKE *(Unwrapping package).* Ain' nobody
ever give me a book. *(Laboriously reads the
cover.)* Hand Writing Copy Book—Grade
Five.

DAISY. I always taught out of these. I saved
a few.

HOKE. Yassum.

DAISY. It's faded but it works. If you practice, you'll write nicely.

HOKE *(Trying not to show emotion).* Yassum.

DAISY. But you have to practice. I taught
Mayor Hartsfield out of this same book.

HOKE. Thank you, Miz Daisy.

DAISY. It's not a Christmas present.

HOKE. Nome.

DAISY. Jews don't have any business giving
Christmas presents. And you don't need to
go yapping about this to Boolie and Florine.

HOKE. This strictly between you and me.
*(We hear a record of "Rudolph the Red-Nosed
Reindeer."*)* They seen us. Mist' Werthan
done turn up the hi fi.

DAISY. I hope I don't spit up. *(HOKE takes her
arm and they walk off together as the light fades on
them. Light picks up on BOOLIE wearing madras
bermuda shorts and La Coste shirt. He is in his late
forties, waiting by the car.)*

BOOLIE *(Calling).* Come on, Hoke! Get a
wiggle on! I'm supposed to tee off at the club
at eleven thirty. *(HOKE enters.)*

HOKE. Jes' emptyin' the trash. Sad'dy garbage day.

BOOLIE. Where's Mama?

HOKE. She back in her room and she say go
on widdout her. I think she takin' on 'bout
dis. *(They have gotten in the car, both in the front
seat. HOKE is driving.)*

BOOLIE. That's crazy. A car is a car.

HOKE. Yassuh, but she done watch over dis

*See Special Note on copyright page.

machine like a chicken hawk. One day we
park in front of de dry cleaner up yonder at
the Plaza and dis white man—look like some
kind of lawyer, banker, dress up real fine—he
done lay his satchel up on our hood while he
open up his trunk, you know, and Lawd what
he do that for, fore I could stop her, yo'
Mama jump out de back do' and run that
man every which way. She wicked 'bout her
paint job.

BOOLIE. Did she tell you this new car has
air conditioning?

HOKE. She say she doan' like no air cool.
Say it give her the neck ache.

BOOLIE. Well, you know how Mama fought
me, but it's time for a trade. She's losing
equity on this car. I bet both of you will miss
this old thing.

HOKE. Not me. Unh unh.

BOOLIE. Oh come on. You're the only one
that's driven it all this time. Aren't you just a
little sorry to see it go?

HOKE. It ain' goin' nowhere. I done
bought it.

BOOLIE. You didn't!

HOKE. I already made the deal with Mist'
Red Mitchell at the car place.

BOOLIE. For how much?

HOKE. Dat for him and me to know.

BOOLIE. For God's sake! Why didn't you
just buy it right from Mama? You'd have
saved money.

HOKE. Yo' Mama in my business enough as
it is. I ain' studyin' makin' no monthly car
payments to her. Dis mine the regular way.

BOOLIE. It's a good car, all right. I guess
nobody knows that better than you.

HOKE. Best ever come off the line. And dis
new one, Miz Daisy doan' take to it, I let her
ride in disheah now an' again.

BOOLIE. Mighty nice of you.

HOKE. Well, we all doin' what we can.
Keep them ashes off my 'polstry. *(Light out on
them and up on DAISY's driveway. DAISY wearing
traveling clothes and a hat, enters lugging a big
heavy suitcase. She looks around anxiously, checks
her watch and exits again. In a moment she returns
with a full dress bag and a picnic basket. She sets
them by the suitcase, looks around, becoming more
agitated, and exits again. Now she returns with a
large elaborately wrapped package. HOKE enters,
carrying a small suitcase.)*

DAISY. It's three after seven.

HOKE. Yassum. You say we leavin' at fifteen
to eight.

DAISY. At the latest, I said.

HOKE. Now what bizness you got draggin' disheah out de house by yoseff?

DAISY. Who was here to help me?

HOKE. Miz Daisy, it doan' take mo'n five minutes to load up de trunk. You fixin' to break both yo' arms and yo' legs too fo' we even get outta Atlanta. You takin' on too much.

DAISY. I hate doing things at the last minute.

HOKE. What you talkin' bout? You ready to go fo' the las' week and a half! *(He picks up the present.)*

DAISY. Don't touch that.

HOKE. Ain' it wrap pretty. Dat Mist' Walter's present?

DAISY. Yes. It's fragile. I'll hold it on the seat with me. *(BOOLIE enters carrying his briefcase and a small wrapped package.)* Well, you nearly missed us!

BOOLIE. I thought you were leaving at quarter of.

HOKE. She takin' on.

DAISY. Be still.

BOOLIE. Florine sent this for Uncle Walter. *(DAISY recoils from it.)* Well, it's not a snake, Mama. I think it's note paper.

DAISY. How appropriate. Uncle Walter can't see!

BOOLIE. Maybe it's soap.

DAISY. How nice that you show such an interest in your uncle's ninetieth birthday.

BOOLIE. Don't start up, Mama. I cannot go to Mobile with you. I have to go to New York tonight for the convention. You know that.

DAISY. The convention starts Monday. And I know what else I know.

BOOLIE. Just leave Florine out of it. She wrote away for those tickets eight months ago.

DAISY. I'm sure *My Fair Lady* is more important than your own flesh and blood.

BOOLIE. Mama!

DAISY. Those Christians will be mighty impressed!

BOOLIE. I can't talk to you when you're like this. *(DAISY has climbed into the car. BOOLIE draws HOKE aside.)* I've got to talk to Hoke.

DAISY. They expect us for a late supper in Mobile.

BOOLIE. You'll be there.

DAISY. I know they'll fix crab. All that trouble!

BOOLIE *(To HOKE)*. I don't know how you're going to stand all day in the car.

HOKE. She doan mean nothin'. She jes' worked up.

BOOLIE. Here's fifty dollars in case you run into trouble. Don't show it to Mama. You've got your map?

HOKE. She got it in wid her. Study every inch of the way.

BOOLIE. I'll be at the Ambassador Hotel in New York. On Park Avenue.

DAISY. It's seven sixteen.

BOOLIE. You should have a job on the radio announcing the time.

DAISY. I want to miss rush hour.

BOOLIE. Congratulate Uncle Walter for me. And kiss everybody in Mobile.

DAISY *(To HOKE)*. Did you have the air condition checked? I told you to have the air condition checked!

HOKE. Yassum. I done it. And what the difference? You doan' never 'low me to turn it on.

DAISY. Hush up.

BOOLIE. Good bye! Good luck! *(Light out on the car.)* Good God! *(Light out on BOOLIE and back up on the car. It's lunchtime. DAISY and HOKE are both eating. HOKE eats while he drives.)*

HOKE. Idella stuff eggs good.

DAISY. You stuff yourself good. I'm going to save the rest of this for later.

HOKE. Yassum.

DAISY. I was thinking about the first time I ever went to Mobile. It was Walter's wedding, 1888.

HOKE. 1888! You weren't nothin' but a little child.

DAISY. I was twelve. We went on the train. And I was so excited. I'd never been on a train, I'd never been in a wedding party and I'd never seen the ocean. Papa said it was the Gulf of Mexico and not the ocean, but it was all the same to me. I remember we were at a picnic somewhere—somebody must have taken us all bathing—and I asked Papa if it was all right to dip my hand in the water. He laughed because I was so timid. And then I tasted the salt water on my fingers. Isn't it silly to remember that?

HOKE. No sillier than most of what folks remember. You talkin' 'bout first time. I tell you 'bout the first time I ever leave the state of Georgia?

DAISY. When was that?

HOKE. 'Bout twenty-five minutes back.

DAISY. Go on!

HOKE. Thass right. First time. My daughter, she married to Pullman porter on the

N.C. & St. L., you know, and she all time goin'—Detroit, New York, St. Louis—talkin' 'bout snow up aroun' her waist and ridin' in de subway car and I say, "Well, that very nice, Tommie Lee, but I jes' doan' feel the need." So dis it, Miz Daisy, and I got to tell you, Alabama ain' lookin' like much so far.

DAISY. It's nicer the other side of Montgomery.

HOKE. If you say so. Pass me up one of them peaches, please, ma'am. *(She looks out the window. Suddenly she starts.)*

DAISY. Oh my God!

HOKE. What happen?

DAISY. That sign said Phenix City—thirty miles. We're not supposed to go to Phenix City. We're going the wrong way. Oh my God!

HOKE. Maybe you done read it wrong.

DAISY. I didn't. Stop the car! Stop the car! *(Very agitated, she wrestles with the map on her lap.)* Here! Here! You took the wrong turn at Opelika!

HOKE. You took it with me. And you readin' the map.

DAISY. I was getting the lunch. Go on back! Oh my God!

HOKE. It ain' been thirty minutes since we turn.

DAISY. I'm such a fool! I didn't have any business coming in the car by myself with just you. Boolie made me! I should have come on the train. I'd be safe there. I just should have come on the train.

HOKE. Yassum. You should have. *(Lights dim to suggest passage of time and come right back up again. It is night now. DAISY and HOKE are somewhat slumped on the seats, HOKE driving wearily.)*

DAISY. They fixed crab for me. Minnie always fixes crab. They go to so much trouble! It's all ruined by now! Oh Lord!

HOKE. We got to pull over, Miz Daisy.

DAISY. Is something wrong with the car?

HOKE. Nome. I got to bixcused.

DAISY. What?

HOKE. I got to make water.

DAISY. You should have thought of that back at the Standard Oil Station.

HOKE. Colored cain' use the toilet at no Standard Oil . . . You know dat.

DAISY. Well there's no time to stop. We'll be in Mobile soon. You can wait.

HOKE. Yassum. *(He drives a minute then stops the car.)* Nome.

DAISY. I told you to wait!

HOKE. Yassum. I hear you. How you think I feel havin' to ax you when can I make my water like I some damn dog?

DAISY. Why, Hoke! I'd be ashamed!

HOKE. I ain' no dog and I ain' no chile and I ain' jes' a back of the neck you look at while you goin' wherever you want to go. I a man nearly seventy-two years old and I know when my bladder full and I gettin' out dis car and goin' off down de road like I got to do. And I'm takin' de car key dis time. And that's de end of it. *(He leaves the car, slamming his door and exits.* DAISY *sits very still in the back seat. It's a dark country night. Crickets chirp, a dog barks.)*

DAISY *(Angry)*. Hoke! *(She waits. No sound. Then, less angry.)* Hoke! *(Silence. Darkness. Country sounds. Now she is frightened.)*

HOKE *(No answer. Light fades on her slowly and comes up on* BOOLIE, *in his office. He speaks into his phone in answer to intercom buzz.)*

BOOLIE. Well, hell yes! Send him right on in here! *(HOKE enters.)* Isn't it your day off? To what do I owe this honor?

HOKE. We got to talk.

BOOLIE. What is it?

HOKE. It Mist' Sinclair Harris.

BOOLIE. My cousin Sinclair?

HOKE. His wife.

BOOLIE. Jeanette?

HOKE. The one talk funny.

BOOLIE. She's from Canton, Ohio.

HOKE. Yassuh. She tryin' to hire me.

BOOLIE. What?

HOKE. She phone when she know Miz Daisy be out and she say "How are they treating you, Hoke?" You know how she soun' like her nose stuff up. And I say "fine" and she say "Well, if you looking for a change you know where to call."

BOOLIE. I'll be damned!

HOKE. I thought you want to know 'bout it.

BOOLIE. I'll be God damned!

HOKE. Ain't she a mess? *(A beat.)* She say name yo' sal'ry.

BOOLIE. I see. And did you?

HOKE. Did I what?

BOOLIE. Name your salary?

HOKE. Now what you think I am? I ain' studyin' workin' for no trashy somethin' like her.

BOOLIE. But she got you to thinking, didn't she?

HOKE. You might could say dat.

BOOLIE. Name your salary?

HOKE. Dat what she say.

BOOLIE. Well, how does sixty-five dollars a week sound?

HOKE. Sounds pretty good. Seventy-five sounds better.

BOOLIE. So it does. Beginning this week.

HOKE. Das mighty nice of you, Mist' Werthan. I 'preciate it. Mist' Werthan, you ever had people fightin' over you?

BOOLIE. No.

HOKE. Well, I tell you. It feel good. *(Light out on them. We hear a phone ringing. Light up on* DAISY's *house. It's a dark, winter morning and there is no light on in the house.* DAISY *enters, wearing her coat over her bathrobe and carrying a lit candle in a candlestick. She is up in her eighties now and walks more carefully, but she is by no means decrepit.)*

DAISY. Hello? *(Light up on* BOOLIE *at home, also dressed warmly.)*

BOOLIE. Mama, thank goodness! I was afraid your phone would be out.

DAISY. No, but I don't have any power.

BOOLIE. Nobody does. That's why I called.

DAISY. I found some candles. It reminds me of gaslight back on Forsyth Street. Seems like we had ice storms all the time back then.

BOOLIE. I can't come after you because my driveway is a sheet of ice. I'm sure yours is too.

DAISY. I'm all right, Boolie.

BOOLIE. I imagine they're working on the lines now. I'll go listen to my car radio and call you back. Don't go anywhere.

DAISY. Really? I thought I'd take a jog around the neighborhood.

BOOLIE. You're a doodle, Mama.

DAISY. Love to Florine.

BOOLIE. Uh huh. *(Light out on* BOOLIE. DAISY *talks to herself.)*

DAISY. Well, I guess that's the biggest lie I'll tell today. *(She tries to read by the candlelight without much success. She hears the door to outside open and close and then footsteps. She stands alarmed.)* Who is it? *(*HOKE *enters carrying a paper bag and wearing an overcoat and galoshes.)*

HOKE. Mornin', Miz Daisy.

DAISY. Hoke. What in the world?

HOKE. I learn to drive on ice when I deliver milk for Avondale Dairy. Ain' much to it. I slip around a little comin' down Briarcliff, but nothin' happen. Other folks bangin' into each other like they in the funny papers, though. Oh, I stop at the 7-11. I figure yo' stove out and Lawd knows you got to have yo' coffee in the mornin'.

DAISY *(Touched).* How sweet of you, Hoke. *(He sips his own coffee.)*

HOKE. We ain' had good coffee 'roun' heah since Idella pass.

DAISY. You're right. I can fix her biscuits and you can fry her chicken, but nobody can make Idella's coffee. I wonder how she did it.

HOKE. I doan' nome. Every time the *Hit Parade* come on TV, it put me in mind of Idella.

DAISY. Yes.

HOKE. Sittin' up in de chair, her daughter say, spry as de flowers in springtime, watchin' the *Hit Parade* like she done ev'ry Sad'dy the Lawd sent and then, durin' the Lucky Strike Extra all of sudden, she belch and she gone.

DAISY. Idella was lucky.

HOKE. Yassum. I 'spec she was. *(He starts to exit.)*

DAISY. Where are you going?

HOKE. Put deseheah things up. Take off my overshoes.

DAISY. I didn't think you'd come today.

HOKE. What you mean? It ain' my day off, is it?

DAISY. Well, I don't know what you can do around here except keep me company.

HOKE. I see can I light us a fire.

DAISY. Eat anything you want out of the ice box. It's all going to spoil anyway.

HOKE. Yassum.

DAISY. And wipe up what you tracked onto my kitchen floor.

HOKE. Now, Miz Daisy, what you think I am? A mess? *(This is an old routine between them and not without affection.)*

DAISY. Yes. That's exactly what I think you are.

HOKE. All right, then. All right. *(He exits. She sits contented in her chair. The phone rings.)*

DAISY. Hello? *(Light on* BOOLIE.)*

BOOLIE. It'll all be melted by this afternoon. They said so on the radio. I'll be out after you as soon as I can get down the driveway.

DAISY. Stay where you are, Boolie. Hoke is here with me.

BOOLIE. How in the hell did he manage that?

DAISY. He's very handy. I'm fine. I don't need a thing in the world.

BOOLIE. Hello? Have I got the right number? I never heard you say loving things about Hoke before.

DAISY. I didn't say I love him. I said he was handy.

BOOLIE. Uh huh.

DAISY. Honestly, Boolie. Are you trying to

irritate me in the middle of an ice storm? *(She hangs up the phone. Light out on her.* BOOLIE *stands a moment in wonder. Light out on him. In the dark we hear the sounds of horns blaring. A serious traffic jam. When the lights come up,* DAISY *is in the car, wearing a hat. She is anxious, twisting in her seat, looking out the window.* HOKE *enters.)* Well what is it? You took so long!

HOKE. Couldn't help it. Big mess up yonder.

DAISY. What's the matter? I might as well not go to Temple at all now!

HOKE. You cain' go to Temple today, Miz Daisy.

DAISY. Why not? What in the world is the matter with you?

HOKE. Somebody done bomb the Temple.

DAISY. What? Bomb the Temple!

HOKE. Yassum. Dat why we stuck here so long.

DAISY. I don't believe it.

HOKE. That what the policeman tell me up yonder. Say it happen about a half hour ago.

DAISY. Oh no. Oh my God! Well, was anybody there? Were people hurt?

HOKE. Din' say.

DAISY. Who would do that?

HOKE. You know as good as me. Always be the same ones.

DAISY. Well, it's a mistake. I'm sure they meant to bomb one of the conservative synagogues or the orthodox one. The Temple is reform. Everybody knows that.

HOKE. It doan' matter to them people. A Jew is a Jew to them folks. Jes like light or dark we all the same nigger.

DAISY. I can't believe it!

HOKE. I know jes' how you feel, Miz Daisy. Back down there above Macon on the farm—I 'bout ten or 'leven years old and one day my frien' Porter, his Daddy hangin' from a tree. And the day befo', he laughin' and pitchin' horseshoes wid us. Talkin' 'bout Porter and me gon' have strong good right arms like him and den he hangin' up yonder wid his hands tie behind his back an' the flies all over him. And I seed it with my own eyes and I throw up right where I standin'. You go on and cry.

DAISY. I'm not crying.

HOKE. Yassum.

DAISY. The idea! Why did you tell me that?

HOKE. I doan' know. Seem like disheah mess put me in mind of it.

DAISY. Ridiculous! The Temple has nothing to do with that!

HOKE. So you say.

DAISY. We don't even know what happened. How do you know that policeman was telling the truth?

HOKE. Now why would that policeman go and lie 'bout a thing like that?

DAISY. You never get things right anyway.

HOKE. Miz Daisy, somebody done bomb that place and you know it too.

DAISY. Go on. Just go on now. I don't want to hear any more about it.

HOKE. I see if I can get us outta here and take you home. You feel better at home.

DAISY. I don't feel bad.

HOKE. You de boss.

DAISY. Stop talking to me! *(Lights fade on them. We hear the sound of applause.* BOOLIE *enters in a fine three-piece suit, holding a large silver bowl. He is very distinguished, in his late fifties.)*

BOOLIE. Thank you, Red. And thank you all. I am deeply grateful to be chosen man of the year by the Atlanta Business Council, an honor I've seen bestowed on some mighty fine fellas and which I certainly never expected to come to me. I'm afraid the loss here, *(He touches his hair.)* and the gain here, *(He touches his belly.)* have given me an air of competence I don't possess. But I'll tell you, I sure wish my father and my grandfather could see this. Seventy-two years ago they opened a little hole-in-the-wall shop on Whitehall Street with one printing press. They managed to grow with Atlanta and to this day, the Werthan Company believes we want what Atlanta wants. This award proves we must be right. Thank you. *(Applause.)* One more thing. If the jackets whup the dawgs up in Athens Saturday afternoon, I'll be a completely happy man. *(Light out on him.* DAISY *enters her living room and dials the phone. She dials with some difficulty. Things have become harder for her to do.)*

DAISY. Hidey, Miss McClatchey. You always recognize my voice. What a shame a wonderful girl like you never married. Miss McClatchey? Is my son in? Oh no. Please don't call him out of a sales meeting. Just give him a message. Tell him I bought the tickets for the UJA Banquet. Yes, UJA banquet honoring Martin Luther King on the seventeenth. Well, you're a sweet thing to say so. And don't you worry. My cousin Tillie in Chattanooga married for the first time at fifty-seven. *(Light dims and comes right back.* BOOLIE *has joined* DAISY.*)*

BOOLIE. How do you feel, Mama?

DAISY. Not a good question to ask somebody nearly ninety.

BOOLIE. Well you look fine.

DAISY. It's my ageless appeal.

BOOLIE. Miss McClatchey gave me your message.

DAISY. Florine is invited too.

BOOLIE. Thank you very much.

DAISY. I guess Hoke should drive us. There'll be a crowd.

BOOLIE. Mama, we have to talk about this.

DAISY. Talk about what?

BOOLIE. The feasibility of all this.

DAISY. Fine. You drive. I thought I was being helpful.

BOOLIE. You know I believe Martin Luther King has done some mighty fine things.

DAISY. Boolie, if you don't want to go, why don't you just come right out and say so?

BOOLIE. I want to go. You know how I feel about him.

DAISY. Of course, but Florine—

BOOLIE. Florine has nothing to do with it. I still have to conduct business in this town.

DAISY. I see. The Werthan Company will go out of business if you attend the King dinner?

BOOLIE. Not exactly. But a lot of the men I do business with wouldn't like it. They wouldn't come right out and say so. They'd just snicker and call me Martin Luther Werthan behind my back—something like that. And I'd begin to notice that my banking business wasn't being handled by the top dogs. Maybe I'd start to miss out on a few special favors, a few tips. I wouldn't hear about certain lunch meetings at the Commerce Club. Little things you can't quite put your finger on. And Jack Raphael over at Ideal Press, he's a New York Jew instead of a Georgia Jew and as long as you got to deal with Jews, the really smart ones come from New York, don't they? So some of the boys might start throwing business to Jack instead of ole Martin Luther Werthan. I don't know. Maybe it wouldn't happen, but that's the way it works. If we don't use those seats, somebody else will and the good Doctor King will never know the difference, will he?

DAISY. If we don't use the seats? I'm not supposed to go either?

BOOLIE. Mama, you can do whatever you want.

DAISY. Thanks for your permission.

BOOLIE. Can I ask you something? When did you get so fired up about Martin Luther King? Time was, I'd have heard a different story.

DAISY. Why, Boolie! I've never been prejudiced and you know it!

BOOLIE. Okay. Why don't you ask Hoke to go to the dinner with you?

DAISY. Hoke? Don't be ridiculous. He wouldn't go.

BOOLIE. Ask him and see. *(BOOLIE exits. DAISY puts on an evening wrap and chiffon scarf over her hair. This is not done quickly. She moves slowly. When she is ready, HOKE enters and helps her into the car. They ride in silence for a moment.)*

DAISY. I don't know why you still drive. You can't see.

HOKE. Yassum I can.

DAISY. You didn't see that mailbox.

HOKE. How you know what I didn't see?

DAISY. It nearly poked through my window. This car is all scratched up.

HOKE. Ain' no sucha thing.

DAISY. How would you know? You can't see. What a shame. It's a bran' new car, too.

HOKE. You got this car two years come March.

DAISY. You forgot to turn.

HOKE. Ain' this dinner at the Biltmo'?

DAISY. You know it is.

HOKE. Biltmo' straight thissaway.

DAISY. You know so much.

HOKE. Yassum. I do.

DAISY. I've lived in Atlanta all my life.

HOKE. And ain' run a car in onto twenty years. *(A beat.)*

DAISY. Boolie said the silliest thing the other day.

HOKE. Tha' right?

DAISY. He's too old to be so foolish.

HOKE. Yassum. What did he say?

DAISY. Oh, he was talking about Martin Luther King. *(A beat.)* I guess you know him, don't you?

HOKE. Martin Luther King? Nome.

DAISY. I was sure you did. But you've heard him preach?

HOKE. Same way as you—over the TV.

DAISY. I think he's wonderful.

HOKE. Yassum.

DAISY. You know, you could go see him in person any time you wanted. *(No response.)* All you'd have to do is go over there to the—what is it?

HOKE. Ebeneezer.

DAISY. Ebeneezer Baptist Church some Sunday and there he'll be.

HOKE. What you gettin' at, Miz Daisy?

DAISY. Well, it's so silly. Boolie said you wanted to go to this dinner with me tonight. Did you tell him that?

HOKE. Nome.

DAISY. I didn't think so. What would be the point? You can hear him anytime—whenever you want.

HOKE. You want the front do' or the side do' to the Biltmore?

DAISY. I think the side. Isn't it wonderful the way things are changing?

HOKE. What you think I am, Miz Daisy?

DAISY. What do you mean?

HOKE. You think I some somethin' sittin' up here doan' know nothin' bout how to do?

DAISY. I don't know what you're talking about.

HOKE. Invitation to disheah dinner come in the mail a mont' ago. Did be you want me to go wid you, how come you wait till we in the car on the way to ask me?

DAISY. What? All I said was that Boolie said you wanted to go.

HOKE *(Sulking)*. Mmm Hmmm.

DAISY. You know you're welcome to come, Hoke.

HOKE. Mmmm Hmmm.

DAISY. Oh my stars. Well, aren't you a great big baby!

HOKE. Nevermind baby, next time you ask me someplace, ask me regular.

DAISY. You don't have to carry on so much!

HOKE. Das' all. Less drop it.

DAISY. Honestly!

HOKE. Things changin', but they ain't change all dat much. *(They are at the door.)* I hep you to the do'.

DAISY. Thank you, Hoke. I can help myself. *(DAISY get herself out of the car, which takes some effort. HOKE sits still in his seat. DAISY looks at him when she is out of the car, but thinks better of what she was going to say and walks slowly towards the door. Lights out on them and up on BOOLIE at his house.)*

BOOLIE *(On the phone)*. Hello, Hoke? How are you?

HOKE. I'm tolerable, Mist' Werthan.

BOOLIE. What can I do for you this morning?

HOKE. It yo' Mama.

BOOLIE. What's the matter?

HOKE. She worked up.

BOOLIE. Why should today be different from any other day?

HOKE. No, this ain' the same.

DAISY *(Offstage)*. Hoke?

HOKE. Yassum? *(Back to phone.)* She think she teachin' school. I'm real worried 'bout her. She ain' makin' sense.

BOOLIE. I'll be right there. *(Lights out on BOOLIE. He exits. DAISY enters. She is in disarray. Her hair is not combed and her housecoat is open, the slip showing underneath.)*

DAISY. Hoke? Hoke?

HOKE. Yassum?

DAISY. Where did you put my papers?

HOKE. Ain' no papers, Miz Daisy.

DAISY. My papers! I had them all corrected last night and I put them in the front so I wouldn't forget them on my way to school. What did you do with them?

HOKE. You talkin' outta yo' head.

DAISY. The children will be so disappointed if I don't give them their homework back. I always give it back the next day. That's why they like me. Why aren't you helping me?

HOKE. What you want me to do, Miz Daisy?

DAISY. Give me the papers. I told you. It's all right if you moved them. I won't be mad with you. But I've got to get to school now. I'll be late and who will take care of my class? They'll be all alone. Oh God! Oh Goddy! I do everything wrong.

HOKE. Set down. You about to fall and hurt yoseff'.

DAISY. It doesn't matter. I'm sorry. It's all my fault. I didn't do right. It's so awful! Oh God!

HOKE. Now you lissen heah. Ain' nothin' awful 'cep the way you carryin' on.

DAISY. I'm so sorry. It's all my fault. I can't find the papers and the children are waiting.

HOKE. No they ain'. You ain' no teacher no mo'.

DAISY. It doesn't make any difference.

HOKE. Miz Daisy, ain' nothin' the matter wit' you.

DAISY. You don't know. You don't know. What's the difference?

HOKE. Your mind done took a turn this mornin' thass all.

DAISY. Go on. Just go on now.

HOKE. You snap right back if you jes let yoseff.

DAISY. I can't! I can't!

HOKE. You a lucky ole woman, you know dat?

DAISY. No! No! It's all a mess now. And I can't do anything about it!

HOKE. You rich, you well for your time and you got people care about what happen to you.

DAISY. I'm being trouble. Oh God, I don't want to be trouble to anybody.

HOKE. You want something to cry about, I take you to the state home, show you what layin' out dere in de halls.

DAISY. Oh my God!

HOKE. An' I bet none of them take on bad as you doin'.

DAISY. I'm sorry. I'm so sorry. Those poor children in my class.

HOKE. You keep dis up, I promise, Mist' Werthan call the doctor on you and just as sho' as you born, that doctor gon' have you in de insane asylum fore you know what hit you. Dat de way you want it to be? *(DAISY looks at him. She speaks in her normal voice.)*

DAISY. Hoke, do you still have that Oldsmobile?

HOKE. From when I firs' come here? Go on, Miz Daisy, that thing been in the junkyard fifteen years or more. I drivin' yo' next to las' car now. '63 Cadillac, runnin' fine as wine.

DAISY. You ought not to be driving anything, the way you see.

HOKE. How you know the way I see, less you lookin' outta my eyes?

DAISY. Hoke?

HOKE. Yassum?

DAISY. You're my best friend.

HOKE. Come on, Miz Daisy. You jes—

DAISY. No. Really. You are. You are. *(She takes his hand. The light fades on them.* BOOLIE *enters. He is 65 now. He walks slowly around* DAISY's *living room, picking up a book here and there, examining an ashtray. He leafs through his mother's little leather phone book and puts it in his pocket.* HOKE *enters. He is 85. He shuffles a bit and his glasses are very thick.)*

HOKE. Mornin', Mist' Werthan.

BOOLIE. Well, Hoke, good to see you. You didn't drive yourself out here?

HOKE. Nawsuh. I doan' drive now. My granddaughter run me out.

BOOLIE. My Lord, is she old enough to drive?

HOKE. Michelle thirty-seven. Teach biology at Spelman College.

BOOLIE. I never knew that.

HOKE. Yassuh.

BOOLIE. I've taken most of what I want out of the house. Is there anything you'd like before the Goodwill comes?

HOKE. My place full to burstin' now.

BOOLIE. It feels funny to sell the house while Mama's still alive.

HOKE. I 'gree.

BOOLIE. But she hasn't even been inside the door for two years. I know I'm doing the right thing.

HOKE. Don' get me into it.

BOOLIE. I'm not going to say anything to her about it.

HOKE. You right there.

BOOLIE. By the way, Hoke, your check is going to keep coming every week—as long as you're there to get it.

HOKE. I 'preciate that, Mist' Werthan.

BOOLIE. You can rest easy about it. I suppose you don't get out to see Mama very much.

HOKE. It hard, not drivin'. Dat place ain' on no bus line. I goes in a taxicab sometime.

BOOLIE. I'm sure she appreciates it.

HOKE. Some days she better than others. Who ain't?

BOOLIE. Well, we'd better get on out there. I guess you have a turkey dinner to get to and so do I. Why don't we call your granddaughter and tell her I'll run you home? *(They exit and the light comes up on* DAISY, *97, slowly walking forward with a walker. She seems fragile and diminished, but still vital. A hospital chair and a table are nearby.* BOOLIE *and* HOKE *join her.)* Happy Thanksgiving, Mama. Look who I brought. *(*BOOLIE *helps* DAISY *from her walker into her chair.)*

HOKE. Mornin', Miz Daisy. *(She nods.)* You keepin' yoseff busy? *(Silence.)*

BOOLIE. She certainly is. She goes to jewelry making—how many times a week is it, Mama? She makes all kinds of things. Pins and bracelets. She's a regular Tiffany's.

HOKE. Ain't that something. *(*DAISY *seems faraway.)*

BOOLIE *(Keeping things going).* Hoke, you know I thought of you the other morning on the expressway. I saw an Avondale milk truck.

HOKE. You doan' say.

BOOLIE. A big monster of a thing, must've had sixteen wheels. I wonder how you'd have liked driving that around.

DAISY *(Suddenly).* Hoke came to see me, not you.

HOKE. This one of her good days.

BOOLIE. Florine says to wish you a Happy Thanksgiving. She's in Washington, you know. *(No response.)* You remember, Mama.

She's a Republican National Committee-woman now.

DAISY. Good God! *(HOKE laughs, BOOLIE grins.)* Boolie!

BOOLIE. What is it, Mama?

DAISY. Go charm the nurses.

BOOLIE *(To HOKE).* She wants you all to herself. *(To DAISY.)* You're a doodle, Mama. *(He exits. DAISY dozes for a minute in her chair. Then she looks at HOKE.)*

DAISY. Boolie payin' you still?

HOKE. Every week.

DAISY. How much?

HOKE. That between me an' him, Miz Daisy.

DAISY. Highway robbery. *(She closes her eyes again. Then opens them.)* How are you?

HOKE. Doin' the bes' I can.

DAISY. Me too.

HOKE. Well, thass all there is to it, then. *(She nods, smiles. Silence. He sees the piece of pie on the table.)* Looka here. You ain' eat yo' Thanksgiving pie. *(She tries to pick up her fork, HOKE takes the plate and fork from her.)* Lemme hep you wid this. *(He cuts a small piece of pie with the fork and gently feeds it to her. Then another as the lights fade slowly out.)*

The End